CORNELL STUDIES IN INDUSTRIAL AND LABOR RELATIONS

VOLUME XVII

Competition and Collective Bargaining in the Needle Trades, 1910–1967

CORNELL STUDIES IN INDUSTRIAL AND LABOR RELATIONS

Cornell Studies in Industrial and Labor Relations and International Reports are research monographs developed by faculty and staff at the New York State School of Industrial and Labor Relations.

CORNELL INTERNATIONAL INDUSTRIAL AND LABOR RELATIONS REPORTS

IN THIS SERIES

PUBLISHED AND DISTRIBUTED BY

THE NEW YORK STATE SCHOOL OF INDUSTRIAL AND LABOR RELATIONS

A Statutory College of the State University
Cornell University, Ithaca, New York

DR. PAUL ABELSON

September 27, 1878 — November 4, 1953

Competition and Collective Bargaining in the Needle Trades, 1910–1967

By Jesse Thomas Carpenter

Professor of Industrial and Labor Relations, Emeritus
Cornell University

New York State School of Industrial and Labor
Relations, Cornell University, Ithaca, New York
1972

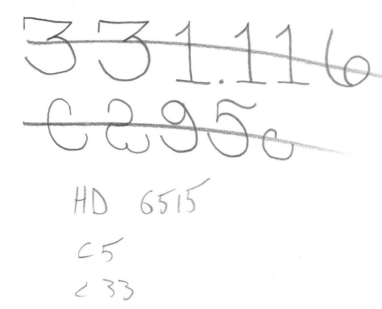
Price: $17.50

ORDER FROM
Publication Division, New York State School
of Industrial and Labor Relations,
Cornell University, Ithaca, New York

Library of Congress catalog card number: 79-630987
International standard book number: 87546-035-6

Composed by W. F. Humphrey Press and Vail-Ballou Press
Printed in the United States of America by
Vail-Ballou Press, Inc.

Contents

Contents

Introduction

THE teacher who devotes more than fifteen years of his available research time to a single project feels obliged to offer some defense for his conduct. If, for example, the twenty-two chapters of the two parts in this study could have been offered as separate projects (eight months to the chapter) — if the subject could have been divided into a dozen five-year chronological periods (fifteen months to each period) — if fifteen selected wearing apparel industries could have been treated separately (a year to each industry) — if the contributions of a single individual (Paul Abelson or Julius Henry Cohen, perhaps) could have produced a meaningful study short of integration into the complex background of collective bargaining — then the prolonged sense of futility that accompanied the early development of this project might have been averted. Yet no one who follows the inductive method of research can foresee the depth of his involvement nor predict the results of his efforts. For the inductive explorer must follow up every possible lead until, hopefully, he learns to distinguish the true from the false and sets his course accordingly. Too often, however, like the old mongrel hound that tracked every moving creature on a Carolina farm, baying vociferously from dawn to midnight — until he died, the inductive researcher who loves to hunt for whatever he might find may well spend his life in frustrated attempts to discover the true goals of his endeavors.

If the first few years of this project were lost in jumping the rabbit of "Competition and Collective Bargaining," the last few were spent in the unproductive task of proving its authenticity. For all those doubting Thomases who "don't believe a word of it," the manuscript has been heavily documented with 2,863 citations to sources of information: to trade journals, contemporary union newspapers, and the general daily press, 1,046 citations; to minutes of labor-management conferences, contract negotiations, union conventions, boards of grievances, and arbitration tribunals, 395 citations; to clauses from the texts of collective agreements negotiated over a span of fifty-five years, 383 citations; to official decisions of impartial chairmen, grievance boards, or boards of arbitration, 211 citations; to governmental publications of judicial decisions, of testimony before investigating commissions, of special studies, and of various activities under the NRA codes, 457 citations. These have been supplemented with 371 other citations to articles, leaflets, tracts, reports, books, correspondence, interviews, and statistical data, almost all of which are a product of those who in some capacity participated in the development of collective bargaining for the needle trades.

Indispensable for work on this project has been access to the documentary materials in the research department of the International Ladies' Garment Workers' Union, to the microfilm files of *Women's Wear* (1910–1926) and of *Women's Wear Daily* (1927-microfilmed through 1943), and to the correspondence and other materials filed in the Abelson papers deposited with the New York State School of Industrial and Labor Relations at Cornell University. Yet these storehouses of information have been far from exhausted, and many other sources remain unexplored. A few have been inaccessible. Over the years, the author's notebook labeled "Unsolved Problems" always seemed to grow in content more rapidly than it was depleted. For all this unfinished business, some consolation is derived from the thought that the essence of good scholarship may consist in presenting the known facts so skillfully as to divert attention from those that are unknown.

Certainly good scholarship demands more attention to detail and a higher measure of accuracy than characterizes the general level of industrial workshop reporting, where typographical errors abound, where words are frequently misspelled or misused, and where pertinent ideas are often lost in a confusion of sentence structure. Attempts to correct inconsistencies in the spelling of names — Pankin for Panken, as an example, — have been most exasperating. Even the wartime (1914–1917) mayor of New York City, J. P. Mitchel, could find his name often misspelled in reputable places. At least every person worthy of mention is entitled to a given name or to his identifying initials — a shortcoming particularly common in references to judges of the courts. These deficiencies have been tracked down and supplied wherever possible. Obvious typographical errors found in quotations have been corrected in lieu of killing off the reader with a scatter-load of *sics*.

More serious problems developed from attempts at a final verification of all references and quotations. Collective agreements were variously printed by labor unions, employers' associations, and trade papers. Copies of the same agreements were not always identical. The published proceedings of union conventions, including the reports of the union's general executive board, sometimes carried different titles and a different system of pagination from year to year — just as certain units of labor organizations, particularly the joint boards or joint councils, sometimes changed their composition and their names. Employer groups also realigned their forces and changed their titles in a succession of kaleidoscopic developments.

The processed minutes of joint conferences, grievance boards, and arbitration tribunals were variously compiled and bound, some containing more material than others, some bearing different titles than others. Not only did those who clipped the daily newspapers sometimes misdate their clippings, but the papers themselves changed their content from one edition to another on the same day. For all these reasons, footnotes cited in the body of the text to the specific sources of information, together with a detailed index at the end of the study, were deemed more useful and less confusing than a general bibliography. For clarity or convenience, the author has also taken certain liberties: (1) in omitting "Inc." from the titles of employers' associations; (2) in citing all union convention records as *Report and Proceedings;* (3) in referring to the names of ILGWU's two leading joint boards as *Cloakmakers'* and *Dressmakers';* and (4) in citing all proceedings of joint conferences, grievance boards, and arbitration tribunals as *Minutes.*

This project was first inspired by a lifetime arbitrator, Dr. Paul Abelson, who gave the School of Industrial and Labor Relations his extensive collection of papers gathered from almost half a century of personal contacts with collective bargaining in the needle trades. Unfortunately he died in 1953 before the School's new "Hound of Inductive Research" had yet jumped the "Hare of Competition and Collective Bargaining." But help did come over the years from perhaps a dozen or more graduate students who, working for short periods of time under research grants from the School, investigated specific ramifications of the subject. For example, Barry Blitstein and Edward Curtin searched the most pertinent files of the *Daily News Record* in the New York Public Library for contributions by the men's clothing trade to the growth of industry-wide bargaining; Miriam Mintz Freilicher searched the U.S. National Archives for contributions from collective bargaining in the needle trades to the evolution of the NRA code system; and Paul Zdrodowski searched the statutes of Canadian provinces for legal means of extending voluntary collective agreements to all competitors operating within a market area.

Help has also come from constructive interviews with those who still operated in the field particularly, in addition to interviews with Paul Abelson while he was alive, those with Morris Glushien, legal counsel, International Ladies' Garment Workers' Union; with Gerald Coleman, executive secretary, United Hatters, Cap and Millinery Workers' International Union; and with John W. Castles, 3rd, of New York law firm of Lord, Day, and Lord. Several other persons have offered helpful suggestions after reading all or parts of the manuscript at some stage of its development; in particular, Harry Uviller, impartial chairman, New York dress industry. Dr. Lazare Teper, research director of the International Ladies' Garment Workers' Union, and his staff have year after year generously shared their crowded library accommodations for a few days at a time to permit access to their documents. His able assistant research director, Walter Mankoff, has been the eyes of the author in locating materials. Finally, the School of Industrial and Labor Relations has made available the time and space, provided the materials, the library, the secretarial staff, and withal has borne the inordinate expense of seeing this project to a conclusion. Miss Frances Eagan, the School's editor and assistant director for academic publications, has graciously assumed the laborious task of editing the manuscript and otherwise preparing it for the printer. Yet, for all this help, the project from its very nature has had to be essentially a one-man operation, and for that reason one man alone must bear the responsibility for its shortcomings.

A Synopsis

SINCE 1910, collective bargaining in the needle trades has been the medium through which the substantial "legitimate" manufacturers, organized into employers' associations, have joined hands with their more "reputable" plant workers, organized into labor unions, for the purpose of protecting their mutual interests from the small-scale, irresponsible, unorganized fringe elements (workers and employers), who, with their reduced wage scales and lower price tags, create unbearable competition. In so far as this new alignment of industry's organized forces has prevented the undermining of "decent" labor standards and of "fair" trade practices, collective bargaining has produced more business and more profits for the organized manufacturers, while providing more jobs and higher standards of living for the organized workers. At the same time, by stabilizing their industries against the disruptive influences of the unorganized factions, the parties to collective agreements have promoted industry welfare and fostered industrial peace.

The objective of fostering "legitimate" business practices, as well as promoting "decent" labor standards, expanded the scope of collective bargaining until such subjects as controlling the jobber-contractor system of production received more attention at negotiating conferences than did the historic union goals of higher wages, shorter hours, or better working conditions. So broad a range of objectives readily united the parties in a joint determination to create the necessary machinery and develop the required procedures for implementing their programs. These concerted efforts to interpret and apply the terms of collective agreements have have produced joint agencies of visitation, inspection, and mediation at the shop level; joint grievance boards and conferences to supplement contract terms and to process charges of contract infractions at the intermediate level; and arbitration tribunals to render final and binding decisions at the top level. Outstanding have been the joint attempts to create a realm of "law and order" that would guarantee compliance with contract terms and with the decisions of arbitrators. These efforts have included, where necessary, the imposition of fines and penalties, the suspension or expulsion of culprits from the organized forces of industry, and, as a last resort, the use of strikes and lockouts as instruments of contract enforcement.

While the organized factions of each trade were putting their own houses in order (Part I), they were also seeking to extend their principles and to expand their institutions until all competitive centers of production would abide by the same basic labor standards and observe the same business practices (Part II). By increasing the memberships of labor unions and of employer groups within each trade, — by obligating labor unions to impose the terms of collective agreements negotiated with the organized manufacturers upon independent firms whose workers were organized, — by taking advantage of governmental freedoms to regulate production and distribution under the NRA code system, — by enlisting consumer support for decent labor standards and legitimate trade practices, the parties to collective agreements sought to establish the means for equalizing labor cost and stabilizing business conduct on an industry-wide scale.

Some of these self-imposed regulations implicated the parties in alleged violations of state and federal legislation to prevent restraint of trade. The final chapters of this study are, therefore, concerned with the combined efforts of employers' associations and labor unions to defend their objectives and to preserve their institutions against attack by governmental agencies assigned to enforce the Sherman Antitrust Act, the Federal Trade Commission Act, and the state antitrust laws, as well as state and federal labor legislation. In short, this is a study of *permissive* industrial self-government worked out on a major scale through labor-management collaboration to solve the complex human problems of the needle trades.

Part I

THE ENDS AND

THE MEANS

Into this industry came a union. Another nuisance to add to the plagues of the manufacturer: Is it any wonder that at first it was ignored, then fought, and only with reluctance accepted as a factor. Then, if, through the union, some order could be brought out of this chaos, hailed with hope! If all paid the same price for the same labor, as all paid for the merchandise, efficiency as manufacturers would count for something against unscrupulous competitors.

— Julius H. Cohen, counsel for manufacturers associations, *Law and Order in Industry* (1916), p. 91.

Chapter 1

The Arena of

Collective Bargaining

THE stage on which the prophets and seers of collective bargaining for the needle trades were to enact their drama of labor-management relations was officially set in New York City during the summer of 1910. But the foundations had already been laid by hordes of Jewish immigrants who streamed into the United States immediately before and after the turn of the present century. More than a million and a half arrived in America between 1881 and 1910. Most Jewish immigrants settled in New York City and turned to the needle trades for a source of livelihood. From the ghettos of eastern Europe, they had brought not only a capacity to become skilled craftsmen but also a heritage of community life that was to provide the human background for the development of industrial self-government. These European beginnings were to have a profound effect upon the ultimate course of the drama that was to unfold.

The Power of the "Bosses" and the Plight of the "People"

At the time the sponsors of collective bargaining first turned their attention to the human problems of industrial life, conditions in the needle trades were everywhere chaotic. During the early decades of the present century, the garment industries contained all the classic elements of the traditional conflict between capital and labor. The participants in this struggle were divided into the "bosses" who owned the shops and the "people" who worked in them. In New York City, as elsewhere, the power of the bosses and the plight of the people became the theme song of every social reformer.

In those years, the garment trades undoubtedly had more than their share of starvation wages, insufferable hours, and inhuman working conditions. They contributed heavily to the evils of sweat-shops, speed-ups, homework, and industrial diseases. They did more to exploit the immigrant and abuse the underprivileged than did the average American industry. Gertrude Barnum, the college-trained daughter of a municipal judge, who became an organizer for the International Ladies' Garment Workers' Union (ILGWU), has told the story of conditions as she found them in 1912, a story of mothers wheeling home baby carriages filled with bundles of materials to be sewed at night, of children bound to confining tasks over long weekends, of pieceworkers compelled to pay back a part of their meager wages for their needles, thread, oilcans, and whisk brooms, as well as for the rent of the machines they used.[1]

---

[1]Gertrude Barnum, *New York Herald Tribune,* April 27, 1912. "One could never rise so early in the morning nor go to bed so late at night that he could not hear the hum of some sewing machine." An observer of the Manhattan Jewish ghetto, as quoted in Melvyn Dubofsky, "New York City Labor in the Progressive Era: 1910–1918" (unpublished Ph.D. dissertation, University of Rochester, 1960), p. 129. Chapter 1 presents a striking account drawn from many sources of industrial life in New York City about 1910.

> Workers had to have their own sewing machines....You carried them on your back when you went out looking for a job....Well, I didn't own a machine. I had to rent one at $2 a month, hire a pushcart, trundle the load up to my new job, drag the machine up three or four flights of stairs, put it together, oil it, clean it and supply it with all sorts of gadgets and tools, including the needles....I might be told I wouldn't do for the job and had to reassemble my machine and return it to the store until I found another job.
> —Julius Hochman, "The Story of Labor: ILGWU—1900–1950," in *Women's Wear Daily,* May 23, 1950.

It was not until 1912, after a ten-year campaign by the cap makers' union, that the ownership of the sewing machine in the cap industry passed from the workers to the manufacturers. United Cloth Hat and Cap Makers of North America, *Report and Proceedings,* Thirteenth Biennial Convention (August 1921), p. 12.

Yet, for all this want and poverty, the "people" were far more outspoken about the prevalence of deliberate chiseling, rank favoritism, and unfair discrimination on the part of their "bosses." In the world of earning a living, the chains of slavery were often more sufferable than the millstones of injustice. The trifling wages offered men and women for their labor were insult enough, but to be repeatedly denied payment for work already done violated the basic principles of human honesty. To follow a pacemaker through successive stages of the speed-up was humiliating enough, but to see limited job opportunities go to friends of the foremen and members of his family was well-nigh intolerable.

Everywhere the tyrannies and prejudices of shop owners and their foremen created bitter resentment. Driven by the ruthless pressure of competition, many foremen in the men's clothing industry were described as "typical bullies and of low moral sensibilities" — petty autocrats who not only hired and fired to suit their unpredictable whims but who also imposed fines and wage deductions, ordered overtime work, cut piece rates, and locked out their workers with a free hand. Employers who could not be trusted to keep their word robbed their employees of all sense of security on the job — even for a day.[2]

Testifying before the grievance board of the New York dress and waist industry in 1915, a union member told how the foreman on his own authority would change rates for piecework. "We made a garment for $1.50 a dozen for the Standard Mail Order House," the worker stated, "and the foreman came down and said we have to make it cheaper and the foreman said we will have to reduce $.15 on a garment. Garment #129 we got paid $3.40 and he took us down to $3.00 a dozen."[3]

Union leaders attributed these evils to the prevalence of non-union shops and so justified their drives for new members. Reporting to the 1918 convention of the Amalgamated Clothing Workers, the union's general executive board noted that within shops where the workers were unorganized "the relations and conditions are

---

[2]Chicago Joint Board, Amalgamated Clothing Workers of America, *The Clothing Workers of Chicago, 1910–1922* (1922), p. 229.

[3]*Minutes*, Special Meeting of a Committee to Investigate All the Grievances of the Firm and the Workers of Joseph Rosenberg and Co. (Fcb. 8, 1915), p. 43. Copy filed in the Abelson papers.

determined in the simplest, most primitive and most ruthless manner: the employer commands without giving reasons and the workers obey without asking questions."[4]

Yet the presence of labor organizations in many of the shops did little to restrain employers before 1910. Unions could not prevent discrimination against their own men. Some shop owners compelled their workers to deposit cash security, augmented by regular deductions from their paychecks, as insurance against joining labor unions or participating in strikes. Other employers closed their shops long enough to rid themselves of union members and then reopened at other locations or under different names. Still others exchanged blacklists to prevent discharged union members from obtaining work elsewhere. In 1904, an association of twenty cap manufacturers in New York City posted notices that beginning on December 26 they would operate their shops on an "open shop" basis — a condition tantamount to the exclusion of all union men from employment.[5]

Employers everywhere insisted upon the full and free exercise of their power to govern as an evidence of what they believed to be their inherent right to govern. They harped upon the classic argument of a society organized to protect property rights against the ravages of the property-less classes. The "bosses" looked upon the "people" as tools to be utilized in the development of their property interests. In 1913, Louis D. Brandeis, soon to become a member of the United States Supreme Court, likened the employers of those years to medieval dukes, oppressive and arrogant, who "seemed to think it was their 'right' to do as they wanted with the men." And, in 1914, Samuel Gompers, founder and president of the American Federation of Labor, asserted that any attempt by the workers to request a change of conditions in a plant was looked upon as a "rebellion" against the employer — an insult to his position and to his dignity.[6]

---

[4]ACWA, *Report and Proceedings,* Third Biennial Convention (May 1918), p. 62.

[5]Joel Seidman, *The Needle Trades* (1942), p. 133.

[6]Louis D. Brandeis, as quoted in a newspaper article, "The New Spirit," by Hutchins Hapgood, clipping, n.d.n.p., filed in the Abelson papers; Samuel Gompers, testimony before the U.S. Commission on Industrial Relations, April 9, 1914, in the Commission's *Final Report and Testimony* (1916), vol. 1, p. 722.

Ideologically, the bosses and the people saw the industrial world through differently colored glasses. The minds of the bosses were given to economic considerations affecting costs and profits. With a dollar-and-cents approach to problems of production, the bosses weighed every labor policy on the scales of efficiency and economy of operations. "When the employer wants to diagnose a situation in his business," — runs an editorial in the *Annalist* for June 8, 1914 — "he investigates, reduces to percentages, boils down the result to a type-written page, and makes the alteration." But the minds of the people were not attuned to slide-rule tests or laboratory formulas for business success. They were stirred by new concepts of human rights and human dignities. They looked upon industry as a place where men lived — a place, noted the editor of the *Annalist,* where "politics, ethics, and economics have been royally mixed."[7]

The Power of the "People" and the Plight of their "Bosses"

There was another side to the sordid industrial scene upon which the advocates of collective bargaining were to play their assigned roles. For the employers themselves were subjected to many hazards of industry imposed upon them by their labor force. Throughout the needle trades, labor was the most unpredictable factor in production costs. Without a stable labor force there could be no stability in business enterprises. Many an employer shuddered at the thought of having his key men walk off the job without notice at some critical stage of production. Faced with the loss of indispensable men, employers in the needle trades suffered all the anguish experienced by workers whose jobs were suddenly terminated.

"You start up your factory at the beginning of the season," explained J. H. Cohen, a representative of the manufacturers in 1910. "You have there a group of men who are necessary — as neces-

---

[7]"We are dealing with tremendous social forces," once wrote J. H. Cohen, who, as a representative of the manufacturers, felt the pressure of those forces for more than forty years, "the inevitable movement for industrial discipline and efficiency coming up one avenue and the equally inevitable movement for industrial democracy coming up the other." J. H. Cohen, "The Revised Protocol in the Dress and Waist Industry," in *Annals,* American Academy of Political and Social Science, January 1917, vol. 69, pp. 186–187.

sary as your capital or your machinery . . . . At the height of the season you cannot go out and get more men for that particular job, just as you could get more stenographers or typewriters." That is why so many employers at the beginning of the busy season insisted upon having each of their workers — union or nonunion — deposit with them cash security of $200, more or less, to be forfeited should the workers leave their employment before the busy season ended. Certainly a walkout at critical periods of production could be as fatal to the business of employers as a lockout was fatal to the jobs of the workers.[8]

Yet at this time the mass of workers employed in the needle trades were by heritage, training, and temperament a very unstable lot. "The great majority of them came from Russia," explained J. A. Dyche, general secretary-treasurer of the ILGWU, to the U. S. Commission on Industrial Relations in 1914, "a large number of them have been engaged at home in fighting autocracy in fighting ukases of the Czar." Sidney Hillman, president of the Amalgamated Clothing Workers of America (ACWA) from its formation in 1914 until his death in 1946, was himself a refugee from the Russian Revolution — one of 100,000 Jewish immigrants to arrive in America in 1907, their heads "full of revolutionary stuff."[9]

In 1913, J. H. Cohen, counsel for the women's coat and suit manufacturers, characterized the Jewish worker as philosophically

---

[8]J. H. Cohen is quoted in Cloak, Suit and Skirt Manufacturers' Protective Association, *The Cloak Makers' Strike* (1910), p. 45. The use of cash security to keep workers on the job usually came to light in worker grievances over unsuccessful attempts to recover their deposits. Examples of such cases can be found in *Minutes,* Conference Committee, set up under the collective agreements of the fur manufacturing industry (Sept. 23, 1918), filed in the Abelson papers.

[9]*Final Report and Testimony* (1916), vol. 2, p. 1045; Matthew Josephson, *Sidney Hillman* (1952), p. 18; George M. Janes, "The Trend of Voluntary Conciliation and Arbitration in Labor Disputes," *Annals,* January 1917, vol. 69, p. 177. Here the secretary of the ILGWU is quoted as saying that, to the immigrants with their heads full of revolutionary stuff, the idea of adjusting disputes without strikes is gall and wormwood.

In his study, "New York City Labor in the Progressive Era, 1910–1918," p. 95, Dubofsky states that the presidents of the four leading needle trade unions during the period 1910–1918 "were of Russian-Jewish origin and the majority of their followers were similar in religion and origin."

a collectivist and temperamentally an individualist. "More discipline is necessary, and more oversight," he said, "if the collectivist is to prevail rather than the individualist." Many other employers believed with Cohen that the "individualist" in the Jewish worker had brought chaos to the needle trades. "And while we may have 900 people," observed Samuel Floersheimer, president of the Dress and Waist Manufacturers' Association in 1913, "75% may stick to the shop and 25% are of the drifting nature. They work here today and don't work tomorrow."[10]

This extreme individualism gave the Jewish workers a reputation for being good strikers but poor union men. Obeying orders — even the orders of their own unions — was repugnant to many of them. "They look upon the Union," runs an article in the *Jewish Daily Forward* for June 7, 1913, "as a despotic power which compels them to pay dues, to stop certain days, to work certain hours, etc. They want to be bosses over themselves. Their attitude towards the Union is the same as the anarchist's toward government."[11]

Many employers conceded that labor unions could become a powerful stabilizing influence in their trades. "The Company will be able to conduct its business more intelligently knowing in advance what its labor costs are to be," reads a 1917 labor contract in the men's clothing industry, "and that it will be able to ship its merchandize without the delays and disturbances inevitable

---

[10]J. H. Cohen in *Minutes,* Board of Arbitrators...[women's coat and suit trade] (Oct. 3, 1913), p. 132; Samuel Floersheimer in *Minutes,* Arbitration Proceedings between the Dress and Waist Manufacturers' Association and the ILGWU (Nov. 8, 1913), p. 147.

[11]These views, here taken from a translation in the Abelson papers, were supported by testimony on the women's coat and suit trade before the U.S. Commission on Industrial Relations, Jan. 16, 1914: "The people in this industry are good strikers but not good union men." J. H. Cohen, management spokesman, in the Commission's *Final Report and Testimony,* vol. 2, p. 1113. I. A. Hourwich, union spokesman, expressed similar views, *ibid.,* p. 1111.

> The great mass of the workers, never having been educated to union discipline or to consciousness of their democratic property in the union, did not feel that it was theirs, that they could make what they liked out of it. They regarded unions rather as outside agencies which could be paid to conduct strikes and negotiate settlements.
>
> —J. M. Budish and George Soule, *The New Unionism in the Clothing Industry* (1920), p. 72.

under the ever present threat of labor troubles. . . . The Company will also benefit by securing the willing co-operation of the Union in obtaining competent help, in maintaining discipline, in the production of satisfactory merchandize without stoppages and in the elimination of misunderstandings and disputes and the substitution of good will and co-operation in its business relations with its workers."[12]

Such hopes were often dashed upon the rocks of union disintegration. In the needle trades, composed almost entirely of small shops, labor organizations to be effective had to embrace the workers in many establishments. Unions that could not control their members at the shop level contributed little to the stability that employers sought in their labor force. "Our Union controls some 2,000 shops in New York," conceded Benjamin Schlesinger, president of the ILGWU, in 1915, "yet it was not the Union that controlled the [piece-rate] prices but 2,000 separate 'unions,' each shop

---

[12]Preamble to the individual contract between the firm of Schwartz, Jaffe and Jaffe and the ACWA (Jan. 1, 1917). Copy filed in the Abelson papers.

> On the part of the employer, it is the expectation and intention that this agreement will result in the establishment and maintenance of a high order of discipline and efficiency by the willing co-operation of union and workers; that by the exercise of this discipline, all stoppages and interruptions will cease; that good standards of workmanship and conduct will be maintained and a proper quantity, quality and cost of production will be assured; that co-operation and good will will be established between the parties thereto.
>
> On the part of the Union, it is the intention and expectation that this agreement will operate in such a way as to maintain and strengthen its organization so that it may be strong enough to co-operate, as contemplated in this agreement, and to command the respect of the employer; that they will have recourse to a tribunal in the creation of which their votes will have equal weight with that of the employer in which all of their grievances, including those concerning wages and working conditions, may be heard and all their claims adjudicated; that all changes during the term of this agreement shall be subject to the approval of an impartial tribunal.
>
> —From the preamble to an individual contract between E. V. Price & Co. and the ACWA, quoted in a printed collection of union affidavits submitted in the case of J. Friedman & Co. v. ACWA (1921) Supreme Court, New York County, p. 126.

Substantially the same terms were found in the Hart, Schaffner, and Marx agreement with the ACWA and in the agreement of the New York Clothing Trade Association with the ACWA, *ibid.*, pp. 127–128.

acting independently of the other." Many years were to elapse before most needle trade unions were able to suppress the demands of their members for local autonomy at the shop level.[13]

Despite such consideration of instability, employers were perhaps less concerned with the individualist temperament of the Jewish worker than with his collectivist philosophy. For had not the constitutions of the leading unions in the needle trades encouraged workers to organize themselves into class-conscious unions for the purpose of abolishing the capitalist system? The preamble to the first ACWA Constitution of 1914 asserted that "the industrial and inter-industrial organization built upon the solid rock of clear knowledge and class consciousness will put the organized working class in actual control of the system of production, and the working class will then be ready to take possession of it." And, as late as 1920, the general executive board of the ILGWU, noting a trend toward the time "when the workers will take over the entire management of industries into their own hands," urged the union's national convention meeting in Chicago to "step forth into the front ranks of this irresistible movement."[14]

---

[13]*Ladies' Garment Worker,* September 1915, vol. 6, p. 16.

[14]The preamble to the ACWA Constitution is from the union's *Report and Proceedings,* New York Convention (December 1914), recorded in *Documentary History of the ACWA, 1914–1916,* p. 75. The stand of the ILGWU's general executive board is printed in the union's *Report and Proceedings,* Fifteenth Convention (May 1920), p. 80.

> Resolved that the only way to secure our rights as producers and to bring about a system of society wherein the workers shall receive the full value of their product, is to organize industrially into a class conscious labor union, politically represented on the various legislative bodies by representatives of a political party whose aim is the abolition of the capitalist system so that we may be able to defend our common interests.
> —From the 1918 Constitution of the ILGWU as quoted in National Industrial Conference Board, *Trade Agreements in the Clothing Industry* (1918), p. 62.

As early as 1893, the American Federation of Labor — that bulwark of conservatism in the American labor movement — adopted a plank in its political platform favoring "the collective ownership by the people of all means of production and distribution." Neil Chamberlain, *Labor* (1958), p. 40. The fears of employers were forcefully presented in a printed collection of employer affidavits submitted in the case of J. Friedman & Co. v. ACWA (1921), Supreme Court, New York County. Copy filed in the Abelson papers. See also ACWA's newspaper, *Advance,* Jan. 28, 1921.

Radical unionism gained strength with every challenge to industrial warfare. A call to strike could usually be relied upon to
unite the working class, just as an appeal to arms brought national
unity to a nation torn by internal dissension. Even those who
persistently refused to join unions often rallied to the support of
their organized comrades during periods of industrial strife. The
cloakmakers' strike of 1910 that led to the first major labor agreement in the needle trades was characterized as a "gigantic up-
rising of a whole people against their oppressors" although fewer
than one in ten of the strikers were union members at the time
the strike began.[15]

Under radical leadership, grievances became "battles" to be
won at all costs, and strikes against the discharge of employees
were glorified as "acts of heroism," however just the cause for
dismissals. Here, noted J. A. Dyche, general secretary-treasurer of
the ILGWU, was "a primitive, instinctive form of unionism, the
unionism which knows only of 'fighting' and 'forcing.' " Everywhere employers denounced militant labor organizations more
given to sabotage and direct action than to law and order. Everywhere employers feared the day these unions would invade management's right to run the business.[16]

Unquestionably, the sudden power acquired from organization
went to the heads of the lowly immigrants who had found the
tyrants of American industry no less objectionable than the political tyrants of eastern Europe. "Workmen, who have been docile
all this time," explained Samuel Gompers, president of the Ameri-

---

[15]ILGWU, *Report and Proceedings,* Eleventh Convention (June 1912) at
p. 11 of the report by A. Rosenberg, president.

[16]*Jewish Daily Forward,* June 7, 1913, translation filed in the Abelson
papers; Dyche in ILGWU, *Report and Proceedings,* Twelfth Convention
(June 1914), p. 59.

> We have men who do not know what the American trades union means.
> We have a socialistic, communistic bunch of people who are trying to
> saddle upon us anarchistic, socialistic, communistic ideas and experiments.
> They have told us "You gentlemen can pay the rent and you can buy the
> materials, but we are going to run your shop...and you have got to do as
> we tell you to do."
>   —E. J. Wile, president, Cloak, Suit and Skirt Manufacturers' Protective
>   Association, as quoted in *Daily Trade Record,* June 2, 1916.

See also J. A. Dyche, *Bolshevism in American Labor Unions* (1926), p. 188.

can Federation of Labor, to the U. S. Commission on Industrial Relations, April 9, 1914, "who have regarded the employer as omnipotent and all powerful, when they finally revolt in desperation against that one-sided arrangement . . . , they imagine themselves all powerful and the employers as having no power at all."[17]

These evidences of economic and ideological differences between the "people" and their "bosses" might have produced a solid alignment of opposing forces on the industrial front, poised and ready for an all-out fight. Then the stage would have been set for the advocates of industrial peace to venture forth into the no-man's land of neutrality between labor and management to plant their banner of collective bargaining. How they would have fared or whether they would have survived in such a setting must remain in the realm of conjecture, for there never was a united front of the working class to oppose the tyrannies of the employing class. Nor was there ever a united front of employers to defend the rights of management against invasion by organized labor.

The War of Labor against Labor

The industrial conflicts that set the stage for the sponsors of collective bargaining were largely fratricidal in character. Employer was pitted against employer and labor was divided against itself. Civil war brought the needle trades to a state of chaos that left the participants helpless to defend themselves. Out of this chaos there emerged a new alignment of forces that gave rise to the institutions of industrial self-government.

Civil war within the ranks of labor took many forms. In the first place, the more experienced workers found themselves at war with the newly arrived immigrants. At the 1910 conference to end the cloakmakers' strike, A. Rosenberg, president of the ILGWU, told how capable pressers with twelve to fifteen years' experience could not get jobs for nine months each year. Instead of paying experienced pressers $16 or $18 or $20 a week, pressing contractors

---

[17]*Final Report and Testimony*, vol. 1, p. 722. "The difficulty is that the people, as soon as they join the union, expect that that act is going to bring the millennium for them. . . . And in some cases. . . it has given the impression that the employer feels sort of weak by recognizing the union and you can do with him everything you like." J. H. Cohen testifying Jan. 16, 1914, *ibid.*, vol. 2, p. 1120.

got their men from Ellis Island. "The minute he [the immigrant] comes from Ellis Island," observed Rosenberg, "the head presser goes out to Union Square, or somewhere else, and gets a green man and pays him $3.00 a week, in the beginning, to show him how to press, while the man who actually worked all his life lays [sic] around the streets for a month and has no means to live."[18]

In the second place, workers in New York City were at war with workers in out-of-town shops. Every successful attempt to raise labor standards in New York City gave workers in other localities a better opportunity to undercut the labor standards of their New York rivals. Work that otherwise would have been available locally was diverted to distant centers of cheap labor. Products that could have been made at home were "imported" from other towns and cities, or from foreign lands. While out-of-town labor was gaining employment, more and more local workers were left to walk the streets.[19]

In the third place, the organized workers were at war with the unorganized workers. The nature of this conflict was strikingly set forth in an account by a union representative from the fur dressing industry, as told in 1921:

About ten years ago I worked in a non-union shop. After we went around idle for weeks and months, the bosses came around to us and said "boys, you have to work cheaper." That time we worked rats for a cent and a half. Once he came around and said, "if you work the Scott rat for a cent and a quarter we will get you next week 25,000 rats." In a non-union shop you know how it is. We said, "go ahead."

---

[18]*The Cloak Makers' Strike,* p. 66. "The Union people in our business have been walking the streets, while green hands have been taken into a majority of these small shops." *Minutes,* Conference between Representatives of the Fur Manufacturers' Association and the Furriers' Union of New York City (Oct. 29, 1913), p. 15. The war between the new immigrant and the "Americanized" workers of the second generation is pointed up in Dubofsky, "New York City Labor in the Progressive Era, 1910–1918."

[19]In 1913, J. H. Cohen, counsel for the women's coat and suit manufacturers, observed how competition from Philadelphia and Cleveland was decreasing business in New York City and reducing the actual earnings of New York City workers. *Minutes,* Board of Arbitrators…[women's coat and suit trade] (Oct. 12, 1913), p. 6.

The next day he said "boys, you are working for six cents on foxes. Make it five cents and I can bring in a whole lot." "Go ahead," we said; we made it five cents. Then came a proposition for a cent on the rats....and we made it a cent for the rats and five cents for the foxes....

You must know there will always be competition. If we are getting five cents for foxes, if a man is out of town he will make it for four cents. If a union man makes four cents a non-union man will make it three cents.[20]

In the fourth place, the workers of the "inside" factories were at war with the workers of the "outside" shops. This warfare was founded upon differences in methods of production — a distinction which was to play a major role in the development of collective bargaining. The "inside" factories were owned by manufacturers who made their own garments from their own materials by employing their own labor force directly in their own establishments. The "outside" shops were those of contractors or submanufacturers who agreed to make up certain garments by contract for jobbers or inside manufacturers. "In other branches of industry and trade," explained the research director of the International Ladies' Garment Workers' Union, "the jobber is a middle man who buys ready-made articles for resale and has no connection with actual production. He purchases from manufacturers in large quantities (job lots) and then, in turn, sells to retailers in smaller quantities. In the women's clothing industry the jobber occupies a completely different position.... He purchases fabrics and other necessary materials, employs designers to create new styles, and then contracts for the manufacture of the desired garments according to set specifications and at a stipulated price."[21] (see diagram pg. 14)

After 1910, the distinction between inside and outside production corresponded closely with the distribution of union and non-union membership in the labor force. Inside factories became the strongholds of unionism, while outside shops remained the centers of nonunion production. This consideration further aggravated

---

[20]*Minutes,* Conference between Employers Representing Union Shops and Employees Representing Locals 2 and 3 of the International Fur Workers' Union (Jan. 10, 1921), pp. 19–20.

[21]Lazare Teper, *The Women's Garment Industry* (1937) p. 6.

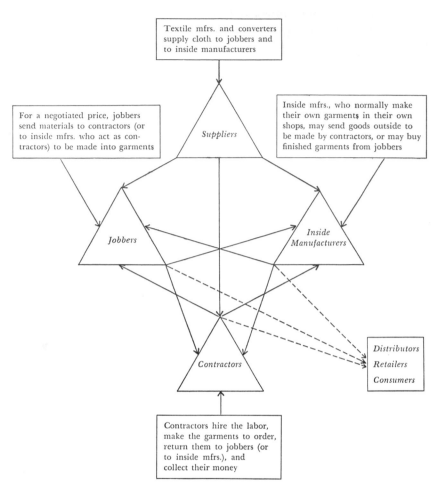

THE JOBBER-CONTRACTOR-INSIDE MANUFACTURER METHODS OF PRODUCTION. The normal flow of goods proceeded from suppliers to jobbers to contractors and back again to jobbers (or from suppliers to inside manufacturers who made their own garments) and thence through distributors and retailers to consumers. But there were many exceptions that confused the terminology and many short cuts that played havoc with the concept of regulated competition. To the extent that inside manufacturers had their goods made up outside, they became jobbers. To the extent that jobbers made garments in their own establishments, they became inside manufacturers. To the extent that inside manufacturers made goods for other manufacturers, or for jobbers, they became contractors. To the extent that contractors made garments directly for the trade, they became inside manufacturers. To the extent that contractors sublet goods to be made elsewhere, they became jobbers. This overlapping of functions tended to increase through the years.

the conflict over jobs between the inside workers and the outside workers. For the organized workers of the inside establishment who insisted on high labor standards were threatened with loss of employment to the unorganized workers of the outside shops.[22]

Naturally, the competition for jobs between the two groups of workers was very keen, particularly in the slack periods when there was not enough work to go around. Perez Cotler, recording secretary of Local 1, ILGWU, tells how the system operated: "It happened in one [inside] place that . . . they had work for 100 to 120 [sewing] machinists; and they asked them, 'how much do you want for a jacket?' And they said, '90 cents.' The manufacturers asked would they take 50 cents; and if they would not take 50 cents he would send outside." One year later, S. Polakoff, manager of the ILGWU protocol division, contended that a manufacturer had no right "to say to the people, if you are not going to have the [piece-rate] price cut in half, I am going to give the work out, and if not, I am going to close down the shop."[23]

Under such pressures, union leaders were faced with a dilemma: either they disregarded the wage clauses of their labor agreements in order to get work, in which case the contract provisions were useless; or they insisted upon maintaining union standards, in which case many union men lost their opportunity to work at all. Reporting to his cloakmakers' union in 1912, A. Bisno thus summed up the situation as he saw it:

Outside shops are working for a great deal less than the inside factories. The inside factories have little to do. Outside shops have not enough work, but they work for a great deal less money, so that

---

[22]In some cases, this alignment of union strength appeared to be at variance with the strongholds of unionism before the era of collective bargaining, for the antiunion inside manufacturers through their associations were in a more favored position to keep the union out than were the smaller outside producers. Selig Perlman, reporting on the state of unionism in the men's shirt industry, noted in 1914 that the union was weak in the big inside factories, mostly outside of New York City, and stronger in the contract shops of New York City. U.S. National Archives, microfilm, *Record Group no. 174.*

[23]Cotler, testimony, Jan. 15, 1914, *Final Report and Testimony,* vol. 2, p. 1048; Polakoff in *Minutes,* Special Investigation by the Committee on Immediate Action, Case of Charles S. Siemons Co. (March 5, 1915), p. 125.

the contractor system of manufacturing for jobbers, or for the trade, are the main questions in our industry today. . . . Unless we will have some stand. . . so established that we really and honestly enforce it, both in the contractors' shops and in the inside shops of the several associations and independent shops, our work is a pretense and a sham and is conducive to the injury instead of the benefit of our people, because. . . the more we defend our people, the less work they have to do to earn a living.[24]

Even among the organized workers within the same factory there were good union members employed by the week at war with equally good union members employed at piece rates. "We have it on the same floor," explained union spokesman S. Polakoff to the grievance board of the dress and waist industry, "let us say; in the front they are working, ten operators on week work, in the back another ten operators on piece work, or in the same line they are working, operators by week and operators by piece work. Now this is competition between the working men." Such a war was no less real because it was instigated by the "bosses" who ran the show. "If, for instance," continued Mr. Polakoff, "the piece workers ask a certain price for the work, and the firm does not like that price, and instead of conferring with them a price to name, and the dispute of price, they are taking the garments and giving them away to the week workers."[25]

Wherever a union was able to prevent an employer from installing competing methods of production within the same factory, there were other grounds on which the ties of union brotherhood did not always restrain some members from making war on their comrades, even to the extent of conniving with their employers to work for less than standard contract terms. On another occasion,

---

[24]As quoted in Louis Lorwin [Louis Levine], *The Women's Garment Workers* (1924), p. 246.

[25]*Minutes,* Joint Meeting of the Grievance Board and the Wage Scale Board of the Dress and Waist Industry (August 26, 1913), p. 58. At the time, Polokoff cited examples of week workers employed for $7 or $8.00 a week who for 25 cents could turn out a dress that would cost the employer twice as much if put together by pieceworkers making $12 to $15.00 a week under a minimum guarantee of 30 cents an hour, *ibid.,* pp. 51–52. The evils (or advantages) of having pieceworkers and week workers undercut each other when engaged in the same type of work in the same shop was also discussed in *Minutes,* Arbitration Proceedings between the Dress and Waist Manufacturers' Association and the ILGWU (Nov. 9, 1913), pp. 269–270.

S. Polakoff told of how a certain employer went about the business of fixing piece rates with the organized workers in his shop. "If the price could not be agreed upon on the fourth floor, it would be sent to the fifth floor and vice versa. There is a regular competition between worker and worker. . . . There is a system in the finishing department that when there is a dispute in prices, when the Jewish finishers do not agree, the Italians get the work, and vice versa."[26] In the struggle for employment, many union members had no scruples about depriving a fellow union member of the right to his job.

Within the ranks of organized labor, union locals sometimes fought against the positions taken by their joint boards, while joint boards went to war against their international unions. "The membership of the largest and strongest locals of the International divided into two warring groups," wrote Louis Lorwin of dissension within the ILGWU during 1913–1914, "which fought one another on the issues of industrial peace and industrial war, of leadership and democracy, of radicalism and compromise, of protocolism and anti-protocolism."[27]

Union members also differed violently among themselves in their fundamental philosophies and beliefs. Not all of those who officially subscribed to the overthrow of the capitalist system supported the doctrine in their hearts. Giving lip service to radical slogans was sometimes an organizing expedient. J. A. Dyche, who so vividly described the radicalism of the "progressive" Jewish unions, conceded that there were also conservative unions, like the clothing spongers' union, composed of American-born members who were at least one generation removed from their European background. These unions, he stated, were primarily con-

---

[26]*Minutes,* Special Meeting of a Committee to Investigate all the Grievances of the Firm and the Workers of Joseph Rosenberg and Co. (Feb. 8, 1915) pp. 3, 13.

"If the manufacturer has to pay $2 for a garment and the next man can turn them [*sic*] out for $1 or $1.25, the next man makes 50 cents profit, and he can do them that much cheaper; and our men are deprived of making a living in that way." A. Rosenberg, president of the ILGWU, testifying before the U.S. Commission on Industrial Relations, Jan. 15, 1914, in *Final Report and Testimony,* vol. 2, p. 1034.

[27]*The Women's Garment Workers,* p. 237.

cerned with the elimination of competition among workers of a particular trade in order to get a better price for their labor.[28]

The War of Employer against Employer

Every phase of the internal conflict within the ranks of labor had its counterpart within the ranks of management; for manufacturers, like workers, were divided among themselves. In the first place, producers of wearing apparel in New York City were at war with their out-of-town and foreign competitors. Not only were New York City manufacturers at war with producers in the outlying metropolitan districts but firms in New York, Philadelphia, Chicago, Boston, Baltimore, Rochester, Cleveland, Cincinnati, and St. Louis were at war with one another.

"New York will be stranded high and dry," predicted Morris Silberman, speaking for the New York women's coat and suit manufacturers' association in 1913. He foresaw a decline in the local cloak manufacturing industry rivaling that of the Maine shipbuilders — a decline in which "the question of making cloaks and suits would be simply reminiscent." And a year later, on January 17, 1914, J. H. Cohen, legal counsel for this association, told the U. S. Commission on Industrial Relations that New York City was "at the mercy of every other city in the country."[29]

But apparel manufacturers in other cities considered themselves under the heel of their New York competitors. The Philadelphia cloak merchants charged their New York rivals with instigating union organizing strikes in Philadelphia to drive business away from the city. Chicago fur manufacturers were infuriated at New York commission men who dumped their surplus furs at distress prices on the Chicago market. Midwestern manufacturers of

[28]*Bolshevism in American Labor Unions,* pp. 188–193.

[29]M. Silberman in *Minutes,* Joint Board of the Cloak and Skirt Makers' Unions of New York, and the Cloak, Suit and Skirt Manufacturers' Protective Association (July 8, 1913), p. 63; J. H. Cohen in *Final Report and Testimony,* vol. 2, p. 1130.

Fears of a declining market persistently haunted New York employers and workers over the decades and inspired such statistical studies as Elsie Gluck's "Is the Women's Garment Industry Leaving New York?" in ILGWU's *Justice,* Feb. 17, 1928; and D. J. Brown's "The Migration of Industry: the Shift of Twenty-four Needle Trades from New York State, 1926–1934," NRA Studies (March 1936), U.S. National Archives.

women's garments, so A. Rosenberg, president of the ILGWU, pointed out, "claim that on account of the cheapness of labor in the City of New York they cannot exist there, and every manufacturer with whom you talk will show you bills where goods are made in New York almost for nothing."[30]

The war with competitors from foreign lands was equally devastating. In 1913, the women's coat and suit industry was depicted as "particularly exposed to foreign competition, owing to popular preference for European styles, fabrics and makes." Labor costs were represented to be more than two and a half times higher in the United States than in Germany. At a joint board of grievances conference between employers and union representatives that year, L. E. Rosenfeld, chairman, thus summed up the case:

A garment over there, at the present time, costing twenty dollars [if made in the U.S.A.]...will be landed here for $13.50, and believe me, the merchants in this country will go to Europe and buy those garments, and the manufacturers will go there and buy those garments. ....In England...they are making today automobile coats, and street coats, walking coats, and they can sell them to the retailer in this country at such a price that he has got to turn down the manufacturers in this country and buy the English garments.[31]

In some trades, the paralyzing effects of foreign competition did not reach a peak until the Great Depression of the thirties. Testifying on a proposed NRA code of fair competition to control this traffic, spokesmen for the millinery industry in September 1933

---

[30]*Women's Wear,* Dec. 5, 1913; *Minutes,* Meeting of the Joint Board of the Cloak and Skirt Makers' Unions of New York, and the Cloak, Suit and Skirt Manufacturers' Protective Association (July 8, 1913), p. 82. See also *Women's Wear Daily,* Nov. 8, 1934, for charges and countercharges that David Dubinsky, president, ILGWU, and A. Silver, executive director, Philadelphia Waist and Dress Manufacturers' Association, hurled at each other. The Philadelphia manufacturers received judicial support for their position in the case of Alco-Zander Co. v. Amalgamated Clothing Workers, 35 F 2nd 203 (1929), p. 205. Discussed in Part II below.

[31]From a statement to Congress on revising the tariff on women's clothing, submitted by the Cloak, Suit and Skirt Manufacturers' Protective Association in May 1913, quoted in *Minutes,* Board of Arbitrators...[women's coat and suit industry] (August 3, 1913), pp. 249, 251–252. Rosenfeld in *Minutes,* Meeting of the Joint Board of the Cloak and Skirt Makers' Union of New York, and the Cloak, Suit and Skirt Manufacturers' Protective Association (July 8, 1913), pp. 71, 134, 142.

told how the importation of finished products from Japan, China, Sumatra, and elsewhere had "reduced the domestic industry to the point where it has sunk from a 30 million dollar industry to less than 2 million dollars, and now employs fewer than 700 persons as compared with around 10,000 a few years ago." Raw materials abroad were only one-fourth as expensive as in America, and, whereas domestic laborers in the millinery trade were paid $2.00 a day, similar labor in foreign countries worked for as little as 2 cents a day. In so far as this problem was beyond the scope of collective bargaining, advocates of controlled competition looked to the government for relief.[32]

In the second place, the *organized* manufacturers were at war with the *unorganized* manufacturers. Sooner or later, the more substantial manufacturers in each industry of the needle trades organized themselves into trade associations to consider many types of problems, including *problems of production,* how to handle and stabilize seasonal industries as fickle as changes in fashion or the weather; *problems of distribution,* the role of the middleman, retail selling, group buying, sales promotion, and chain-store operations; *problems of fair trade practices,* selling on consignment, discount rates, credit allowances, secret rebates, unfair advertising, selling below cost, defamation of competitors, commercial bribery, and the return of merchandise. In addition, the organized manufacturers frequently left to their association *problems of labor re-*

---

[32]*Women's Wear Daily,* Sept. 15, 1933. See also statement by Gerald R. Coleman, executive secretary, United Hatters, Cap and Millinery Workers' International Union, before the U.S. House Committee on Labor, July 21, 1961; and the statement of John M. Keating, counsel for the National Millinery Planning Board, before the U.S. Congress Subcommittee on the Impact of Imports and Exports on American Employment, John H. Dent, Pa. chairman, August 22, 1960. Copies of these statements are filed in the Abelson papers.

By 1967, the ogre of foreign competition had again assumed alarming proportions for the women's garment trades:

> Figures compiled by the union [ILGWU] on imports of apparel reveal that in the first 11 months of 1966, a total of 1 million wool coats were imported, or 44 percent more than in the corresponding period in 1965. Knitted dress imports rose by more than 69 percent, skirts by 110 percent, blouses by 150 percent and sweaters by 175 percent.
> —*New York Times,* Feb. 5, 1967, from a report by Lazare Teper, ILGWU research director, to the union.

lations, sometimes utilizing the machinery of their trade associations for this purpose, sometimes forming separate employer groups for collective bargaining.

Whatever the objectives of group action, employers found their own organizations an essential means of working together for their mutual advantage. "I solemnly pledge myself to abide by . . . all trade regulations and agreements adopted by the association on behalf of its members" — runs the oath to which all members of the Dress and Waist Manufacturers' Association subscribed in 1913 — "I will zealously endeavor to improve the general condition of the industry."[33]

Not all employers, however, could be persuaded to take such an oath. Many preferred to go their way alone. Mr. E. L. Lezinsky, a representative of the women's cloak and suit manufacturers, told of an interview with an applicant for association membership in 1912: "When I laid down the laws he would have to live up to, and what we would expect of him as a member, he told me he could do a great deal better, has done better, and would do better; and if we intended to enforce these rules he did not want to put in the application."[34]

Like their nonunion counterparts in the ranks of labor, the independent employers persistently refused to bear the burdens of organization, although they freely accepted the benefits. Over the years, they remained a thorn in the side of the organized employers, undermining their standards and frequently nullifying their programs of reform. In the first half of 1913, for example, not one independent manufacturer who approached the cloakmakers' association for membership had been observing the labor standards of association members. "The fact is," so Mr. Lezinsky speaking for the cloakmakers' association reported to a union official, "we are being driven out of business every day and other men you cannot watch, and cannot control are the men taking the place of our members."[35]

---

[33]Dress and Waist Manufacturers' Association, *Dress and Waist Bulletin,* no. 4, April 15, 1913, p. 3.

[34]*Minutes,* Meeting of the Cloak, Suit and Skirt Manufacturers' Protective Association (Dec. 3, 1912), p. 49.

[35]*Ibid.,* p. 51. "On one side of the street a cloak may be made for $5.00; on the other side it may be made for $4.00 by equally good union men. It is a

This alignment of the organized versus the unorganized manufacturers — like the conflict between union and nonunion labor —
corresponded closely with differences in methods of production.
The organized manufacturers for the most part represented the
larger "inside" firms that made their own garments from their own
materials by direct labor in their own factories. They were constantly at war with a host of small unorganized jobbers and "outside" contractors — fly-by-night operators, who resorted to every
means at their command for lowering production costs and undercutting their competitors. Variously known as "social" shops,
"loyalty" shops, "corporation" shops, "bubble" shops, "parasitic"
shops, these institutions were aptly described in an editorial of
the *Headgear Worker,* official organ of the United Cloth Hat and
Cap Makers of North America, for March 25, 1921:

In the needle industries the entry of the parasitic shop is comparatively easy. Little capital is necessary to establish a shop and during
dull times, when there is little work the temptation to do it is entirely
too great for the less experienced and less principled worker. It seems
to be so simple. A few workers put their little savings together, borrow
in addition whatever they can from their relations and friends, form
a so-called corporation and open a shop. . . .

What these parasitic shops do is to come to the legitimate manufacturers and offer to make for them the few orders they have at prices
which would not cover even the wages the members of the corporation
were getting as workers before they attempted to pose as "businessmen,"
not to speak of any overhead expenses or interest on the investment.
More than that. Quite frequently the prices such parasitic corporations
charge are not enough to cover even half the current rates of wages for
the work involved. To make ends meet the newly baked "bosses" have
to work all kinds of hours and are frequently compelled to draw no

---

system of 'scabbing' and of course the factories that make goods cheapest get
the lion's share of the business." J. E. Williams, impartial chairman, Hart,
Schaffner, and Marx, as quoted in Josephson, *Sidney Hillman,* p. 88, citing
Streator, Ill., *Independent Times,* May 29, 1915.

"I really believe," testified Abe Bisno, general manager of the Cloakmakers'
Union, before the U.S. Commission on Industrial Relations, "that the manufacturer ought to feel as strongly against the scab manufacturer as the union
men feel against scab workers, because this unlimited competition destroys the
manufacturers." Bisno believed that the presence of nonunion independent
shops competing against association shops caused the association shops to work
against the union. *Final Report and Testimony,* vol. 1, p. 584.

wages or salary at all. The hope, of course, is that they may in such a way build up a real business.

Small ruthless competitors were forever disrupting the ranks of the organized factors in the needle trades, setting association members at war with each other in an all-out struggle for existence. Faced with this competition, some association members did not hesitate to feather their own nests at the expense of other members of their own organizations. Forgetting their solemn oaths and declarations of allegiance to a common cause, the weak-hearted secretly connived with their workers to chisel on wage scales, permit homework, or violate overtime regulations. Other employers bought cheap goods from independent firms in outside shops. Altogether, concluded the editor of the *Headgear Worker,* the parasitic shop undermines all the recognized standards in the industry and by its cutthroat competition demoralizes the market.[36]

These forms of disloyalty and disunity among competing manufacturers were not wholly a by-product of issues arising out of unionism; nor were they confined to employers of the needle trades. A keen sense of individual competition, so characteristic of Jewish entrepreneurs, more or less pervaded the system of free enterprise in America. Industry was no place for sharing secrets or pooling resources. Men lived by beating their competitors to the draw. Survival of the fittest was the cornerstone of a competitive economy. Attempts to form industry-wide associations were destined "to suffer shipwreck on the shoals, either of anti-co-operative psychology, or of diversity of interest within the industry."[37]

Even when offered the inducement of the NRA code system for uniting to restrain trade under governmental sanction, employers

---

[36]*Headgear Worker,* March 25, 1921 and May 6, 1921.

Two large manufacturers of boy's clothing were discussing at lunch the "hold-up" of a pants contractor who was doing work for both of them. He refused to do their work unless they increased the price. Said manufacturer "H" to manufacturer "P", "Let's both refuse to send him any work and we'll bring him to our terms." "Good," replied "P" and they shook hands to pledge the agreement. As soon as "P" got to his office, he instructed his man to immediately send all the pants he had on hand to the hold-up contractor "because 'H' gave me his hand he would not send him any work, and we can get ours out so much quicker."
—Frank Chodorov in the *Daily News Record,* May 31, 1922.

[37]*Women's Wear Daily,* June 26, 1933.

of the early thirties were too divided among themselves to make the most of their opportunities. Writing on this division among manufacturers and on the maneuvering of rival employer groups during the early weeks of the NRA code system, one observer thus presented a case that was common to most needle trades:

These cleavages within specific industries are of several sorts. In some, the respective blocs are the small as opposed to the large producers, in others, open as against closed shop, in others still, manufacturers who make and distribute their own product as against those which contract their product for manufacture, or which distribute through selling representatives or jobbers.

Finally, and perhaps most complicatingly of all, there are the cleavages corollary to wide geographical scattering of an industry. Where the bulk of a given product is made in a fairly restricted section of the country, a greater uniformity of working conditions, wages, and merchandising policies tends to exist than where the aggregate production is divided among producers in every section of the land. Similarly, industries which are located partly in urban manufacturing centers, partly in isolated villages, will find it the hardest to coalesce for unitary activity. The fact of the matter is that the new law is going to make some strange bedfellows, and there is going to be considerable kicking and thrashing around before peace and quiet prevail in the dormitory.[38]

The Plight of the Needle Trades

The issues and alignments that divided employers against themselves were so strikingly analogous to those that divided the workers as to suggest that the "bosses" and the "people" were victims of a common plight inherent in the nature of their industries. Wherever out-of-town competitors deprived New York City manufacturers of business, those competitors to that extent deprived New York City employees of a chance to work. Wherever foreign manufacturers through lower production costs deprived American manufacturers of a market for their goods, European labor by the same token deprived American labor of so much employment. Wherever small-time contractors by undercutting the costs of larger "inside" firms took over a greater part of the trade, so small transient groups of nonunion workers in the "outside" shops

---

[38]*Ibid.* The extract is from one of a series of articles bearing on the general subject of dissension among manufacturers.

by undercutting the standards of union workers in the larger establishments took over a larger share of gainful employment.

Whenever an industry fell upon evil days, those who suffered most were as likely to be found within the ranks of management as within the ranks of labor. Adversity was no respecter of class groups. Clearly, the predicaments that overwhelmed workers and employers alike arose from general conditions in the needle trades. Those conditions, as they existed over a span of fifty years following 1910, constituted the arena in which the advocates of collective bargaining were to erect their institutions of industrial control.

The common hazards of occupation for all those who lived by the needle arose, in part, from the seasonal character of the apparel industries. Each year these trades experienced one or more busy seasons during which there were far too few hours to get out the work, and one or more slack seasons in which there were far too many hours for the amount of work to be done. These irregularities presented major problems of management for the shop owners and major problems of living for the workers. In October 1913, for example, the cloakmakers' union reported that all of its 52,000 members were fully employed. By Thanksgiving, however, they were employed on an average of four days a week and, within another month, one in eight had lost his job entirely. A year later, November 1914, following the end of the busy season, the same group of workers were employed only two days a week and during December of that year only 5,000 of the 52,000 — or fewer than one in ten — were employed at all.[39]

Corresponding conditions in the fur manufacturing industry were described a decade later in these words: "The industry is convulsed by short periods of brisk demand for labor; and before the workers have time to master the intricacies of style and warm up to the work before them, the laying-off process begins and many are forced to search for work. After weeks of idleness another apparent trade revival sets in. Work is begun, not always in the same shop, and after a while many workers are laid off again. So they keep going up to the shop and down again."[40]

---

[39]From a report by George Wishnat, manager of the Cloak and Skirt Makers' Union, summarized in the *New York Call*, Jan. 6, 1915.

[40]*Fur Worker*, December 1923.

The dress industry in the thirties, noted one observer, had to be capable of expanding to produce 2,730,000 dresses a week in mid-May and of contracting down to only 41,000 dresses a week by mid-June or shortly thereafter. For every 150 shops that were busy in May, only one shop needed to be in operation a few weeks later. Similarly, the millinery industry was subject to great fluctuations in employment and output. A report of the U. S. Department of Labor revealed that the industry in 1937 was busy only twenty-four weeks, slack fourteen weeks, and in transition fourteen weeks. That year more than half the employees in the industry worked less than half the year.[41]

Such drastic fluctuations in demands for labor frequently shifted the balance of control over wage policies and brought turbulent changes in wage rates. During the busy season, admitted the president of the International Ladies' Garment Workers' Union in 1910, the organized workers in certain shops get the employer "by the neck" and, regardless of previous standards, "demand five dollars for a garment that is actually worth only two dollars." But when business slackened, he added, the employer would "not pay more than $1.50 for a garment which is worth three or four dollars, because he is on the other side, in position to take advantage of the tailor."[42]

The Uncertainties of Production

Styles and the weather brought other hazards of uncertainty into the lives of all those who lived by the needle. Men shifted their preference in headwear from caps to hats, and as a result between 1919 and 1937 the number of cap manufacturers in the United States dropped from 709 to 258 or 63 percent, the value of their products fell from $44,539,861 to $11,752,013 or 62 percent, and the number of their workers dropped from 7,539 to 3,466

[41] On the dress industry, see Victor H. Bernstein's article in the *New York Times,* Feb. 9, 1936. On the millinery trade, see Bertha M. Nienburg, *Conditions in the Millinery Industry in the United States,* U.S. Department of Labor, Women's Bureau, Bulletin no. 169 (1939), pp. 1–2.

[42] A. Rosenberg at the Brandeis Conferences, as quoted in *The Cloak Makers' Strike,* pp. 87–88. "If you succeed in catching the employer by the throat in September, he is sure to return the compliment in the Month of May." Editorial, J. A. Dyche, ed. in the *Ladies' Garment Worker,* October 1911, vol. 2, p. 13.

or 54 percent. The corresponding decline in the number of cap workers in New York City alone was from 4,500 in 1919 to 1,200 in 1937, a decline of 73 percent. Industries also rose and fell with style shifts in women's headwear. At one time, about three-fourths of all ladies' hats were straw hats, but within a few years the straw hat had almost vanished from the market. And the fashion of bareheadedness made shambles of industries that were once thriving centers of production.[43]

A major change in women's fashions from suits to dresses in the mid-twenties forced 700 cloak and suit manufacturers to close their doors and threw 20,000 cloak and suit workers out of employment. In that decade, the manufacture of women's cloaks and suits was described as "an industry which deals in commodities which are little more stable than cut flowers." The coming of a new fashion in exposed knees led to an increase of 81 percent in the production of women's hosiery between 1925 and 1928. Style preferences also played havoc with the manufacturer of fur garments. The uncertainties of this trade were thus described in the *Fur Age Weekly* for May 16, 1932:

Should a pelt of any particular animal provide a colorful consonance with the prevailing mode, it means wealth for the trapper, the collector, the merchant, the manufacturer, the dresser, the dyer, and the retailer. Should the contrary be the case, the pelt merely is a dead number. The price of the garment may be slashed to a fraction of the actual cost of production; thousands of dollars may be spent in advertising its attractiveness and intrinsic value; yet it is to no avail.[44]

[43]On the cap trade, see United Hatters, Cap and Millinery Workers' International Union, *Report and Proceedings,* Third Convention (May 1939), pp. 137, 139, 143. See also, *ibid.,* Cap and Millinery Department, Second Convention (First Regular Convention), Oct. 4–7, 1936, pp. 15–17. Most of the decline came in the six or eight years between the middle twenties and the early thirties. Cloth Hat, Cap and Millinery Workers' International Union, *Report and Proceedings,* Eighteenth Biennial Convention (Oct. 16–23, 1933), p. 13. On women's straw hats, see *ibid.,* Seventeenth Biennial Convention (May 1929), p. 38.

[44]For changes in the women's coat and suit industry, see *Women's Wear,* July 10, 1922 and March 8, 1926. During the twenties, the value of the output of women's coats, suits, and skirts declined from $518,444,109 in 1923 to $371,503,323 in 1929, while the product value of dresses manufactured increased from $375,330,249 in 1921 to $823,271,414 in 1929. U.S. Department of Commerce, Bureau of the Census, "Special Study of the Women's Clothing

The dress industry was particularly bound by the ties of fashion. Styles that reaped profits one week brought losses the next. The industry thrived on the skills of its designers or floundered on its incapacity to judge consumer tastes. "It can create, at a profit, one hundred dresses of a brand-new style in one, two or three days, and then discard the fashion forever," wrote Victor H. Bernstein in the *New York Times,* February 9, 1936. "It is geared to provide a continuous flow of ever changing styles for a market that considers any style more than ten days old as superannuated." The inevitable impact of these figures brought continuing pressure on the manufacturer to raise piece rates and continued haggling with the workers to lower piece rates.

Summer rains brought smiles to the manufacturers of umbrellas and raincoats. Winter snows pleased the producers of cloaks, overshoes, gloves, mufflers, and fur garments. Cold wet springs brought sleepless nights to the manufacturers of spring dresses and their accessories. And, through all these unpredictable shiftings of wind and fashion, the "people" had cause to rejoice when their "bosses" rejoiced — had cause to weep when their bosses wept.

Wars and depressions left their marks on business stability. Fur manufacturers never foresaw that the First World War would more than treble the value of their products. Nor did the organized headwear workers predict a postwar depression that would throw half their members out of work within two months and cause 85 percent of the cap makers to lose their jobs between July and December of 1920. Again, the organized hosiery workers who shared the prosperity of the hosiery industry in the roaring twenties failed to anticipate that they would shortly accept repeated wage cuts, until their rates of pay in 1931 were less than half of what they were receiving in 1929.[45]

Even more drastic was the pressure of the depression on the price of the product. "Prior to the depression," reported the gen-

---

Industry for the Census Years 1923 to 1935," as cited in D. E. Robinson, *Collective Bargaining and Market Control in the New York Coat and Suit Industry* (1949), pp. 8–9. For the hosiery industry, see Dorothea de Schweinitz, "Saving a Prosperous Industry," *Survey,* Oct. 15, 1930, vol. 65, p. 71.

[45]*Fur Worker,* March 1923; United Cloth Hat and Cap Makers of North America, *Report and Proceedings,* Thirteenth Biennial Convention (August 1921), p. 19.

eral executive board of the United Hatters, Cap and Millinery Workers' International Union, "so-called 'popular hats' sold for about $24 a dozen. Hats selling at $16.50 per dozen were considered cheap. Today, as a result of the unchecked tendencies to cheapen the hat, about 60 per cent of all millinery produced is sold at $12 per dozen or less, and about 88 per cent at $24 per dozen or less. And continually the prices are driven downward, until millinery selling for $4 per dozen, or less, has gained a strong foothold in the industry." Meanwhile, the workers who held on to their jobs found their annual earnings had dropped from $1,405 a person in 1927 to $888.16 a person in 1932.[46]

Small-Scale Enterprise

To the fluctuations of seasons, styles, depressions, wars, and the weather must be added all the uncertainties of small-scale enterprise. The presumed advantages of mass-production techniques to the contrary, small-scale operators in the needle trades have always enjoyed some hope of competing successfully with larger manufacturing establishments. The larger firms held no monopoly on the art of designing attractive hats or creating successful new styles in women's garments. Nor could the large firms capitalize fully on the money they spent in creating new designs of their own. Although a large firm in the dress industry might introduce as many as 8,000 styles of women's dresses in a single year, the successful designs could always be copied as soon as the new garments were exposed to public view. Within a matter of days, if not hours, duplicates could be put on the market at much lower costs, without assuming any share of the designing and advertising charges borne by the originating firm.[47]

Yet the evil of instability arising from small-scale enterprise was everywhere acknowledged. In part, this lack of stability was at-

---

[46]*Women's Wear Daily,* Dec. 12, 1934; see also the union's *Report and Proceedings,* Second Convention (First Regular Convention), Oct. 4–7, 1936, p. 59.

[47]No sooner does the leader of fashion design a garment and it gets into the retailer's windows, than the cheaper manufacturer is outside the window with his sketchbook sketching it, and putting it into operation in his shop.

—J. H. Cohen in *Minutes,* Board of Arbitrators...[women's coat and suit trade] (August 5, 1913), p. B-351.

tributable to developments in the system of production. Reflecting on the historic evolution of production patterns, J. A. Dyche, general secretary-treasurer of the International Ladies' Garment Workers' Union from 1904 until 1914 and thereafter a manufacturer, wrote in 1930 as follows:

The truth of the matter is that the so-called "sweatshop" evil is as old as the industry itself. The cloak industry was born and cradled in it. Some 50 or 60 years ago when women's ready-to-wear garments made their appearance in the market, the "cloak man" was the owner of a "warehouse" where woolens were cut and trimmed and sent to the shop of the "bundle contractor" to be made up into garments.

Gradually the "cloak man" began to open workshops on his own premises and have his merchandise made up under his own supervision. The inside shop began to replace the contractor.

Since 1910 the wheel in the industry began to turn the other way. It began to decentralize. The manufacturers began to curtail the volume of merchandise that they made up on their premises and began to increase the amount of work which they sent to the outside contractor. Some of them gave up their inside factories and had all their work, including the cutting of materials, sent to the sub-manufacturer, and the former manufacturer became a jobber. The industry since then has been carried on by an ever increasing number of smaller productive units. Even the size of the contractors shop is now smaller than ever.[48]

The decline of inside manufacturing represented by large-scale firms reached astonishing proportions in the women's coat and suit trade after the First World War. Whereas, in 1921, some 85 percent of the shops and 85 percent of the workers engaged in manufacturing women's coats and suits throughout the United States were still classified as "inside," by 1925, in New York City, where most of the garments were produced, only 25 percent of the shops and 30 percent of the workers were so classified. These drastic changes were reflected in the declining membership of the inside manufacturers' association, which dropped from 440 firms employing 21,604 workers in 1916 to 188 firms employing 7,438 workers in 1924. Corresponding figures for the dress and waist industry revealed that whereas, in 1914, only 16 percent of

---

[48]*Women's Wear Daily,* Oct. 27, 1930. Two other articles by J. A. Dyche appear in *Women's Wear Daily* for Oct. 29 and 31, 1930.

all dresses were made in the shops of contractors, by 1919 contractors accounted for 25 percent of the total production, and by 1930 contractors were producing 40 percent of the total output of the trade. In 1936, nearly 75 percent, or 77,000 of 103,000 workers employed by the dress trade in the New York metropolitan area, worked in contractor shops.[49]

This drift to contracting accounts for the large number of competing firms to be found in each branch of the needle trades. In each of the major apparel industries, the number of business competitors ran into the hundreds or even the thousands. During the period of the mid-twenties, for example, there were approximately 3,000 separate establishments in New York City and its environs manufacturing women's coats and suits, approximately 4,000 separate "factories" contributing to the production of ladies' waists and dresses, over 4,000 separate firms devoted to the manufacture of men's clothing, and upward of 1,000 firms engaged in the manufacture of fur garments.[50]

---

[49]Morris Sigman in ILGWU's *Justice,* Nov. 4, 1927; Julius Hochman, *ibid.,* Jan. 15, 1936; John Dickinson and Morris Kolchin, *Report of an Investigation,* submitted to Governor Alfred E. Smith's Advisory Commission on the women's coat and suit trade, March 10, 1925, p. 11; W. A. Simon, "History of the Code of Fair Competition for the Dress Manufacturing Industry," NRA Studies (Sept. 23, 1935), U.S. National Archives, p. 73 ff. The growth of contracting in the millinery trade was thus described:

> In 1904, according to the United States Census reports, the amount paid out for contracting was negligible — $9,710. By 1909, it rose to $65,647. In 1925, it was close to $1,000,000. Faced by this type of competition the larger manufacturer found it advisable or necessary to give up manufacturing, and to job his goods from the small manufacturers or the contractors. The small manufacturer was in a position to produce his goods at a lower cost. He had no selling expense, very little overhead, and did part of the work himself.
>
> —United Hatters, Cap and Millinery Workers' International Union, Cap and Millinery Department, *Reports and Proceedings,* Second Convention (First Regular Convention), Oct. 4–7, 1936, p. 11.

[50]See the tables in B. M. Selekman, H. R. Walter, and W. J. Couper, *Regional Plan of New York and Its Environs, An Economic and Industrial Survey: The Clothing and Textile Industries* (1925), especially Table IV at p. 30, Table VI at p. 34, Table IX at p. 37, Table XVI at p. 50, and Table XXI at p. 67. See also two studies from the research department of the ILGWU: Abraham Tuvim in ILGWU's *Justice,* Feb. 16, 23, and March 2, 1923; Elsie Gluck, *ibid.,* Feb. 3, 17, and March 2, 1928. Later statistics on the

Not only was there a mere handful of employees to the shop, but the average number actually declined after 1910. In dress and waist making, the average number of workers to the factory fell from 34 in 1909 to 21 in 1929, while the number of firms employing not more than 5 workers rose from less than 10 percent of the total in 1909 to more than 27 percent of the total in 1929. By 1922, over one-half of the 4,077 firms manufacturing men's clothing in New York City employed fewer than 5 workers each, while less than 5 percent of the firms employed more than 50 workers. Between 1910 and 1924, the average number of workers in shops manufacturing women's coats and suits fell from 29 to 17. Even the inside manufacturers of the women's coat and suit trade — the aristocrats of the apparel industries — suffered a decline in the size of their inside establishments from an average of 49 employees in 1916 to an average of 40 in 1924.[51]

Nor did the Great Depression of the thirties that brought forth the National Industrial Recovery Act contribute materially to more substantial establishments in the needle trades. "We are small men," wrote the Apparel Industries Committee for the Renewal of NRA, near the end of the codes of fair competition. "In

---

number, size, and distribution of establishments in the dress industry and in the women's coat and suit trade can be found in the exhibits accompanying the testimony of Lazare Teper, research director, ILGWU, in *Study of Monopoly Power,* Hearings before the Subcommittee on Study of Monopoly Power, Committee on the Judiciary, House of Representatives, 81st Cong., 1st. sess. (July 22, 1949), Serial no. 14, Part 1, pp. 299–326.

Figures in this chapter and elsewhere throughout this study were largely taken from newspapers, trade journals, and union publications of the period. Much of the data not only vary with the source of publication but abound with inconsistencies and contradictions. Operating on the assumption that, for the purposes of this study, what was popularly published and widely disseminated was more important in determining policy than what was accurate by the standards of the U.S. *Census of Manufactures,* the author has made no attempt to reconcile these inconsistencies or to check them against original sources, even where sources were cited and are still available.

[51]See the footnote references for the preceding paragraph. Various classifications of data on the women's coat and suit industry for the period can be found in Dickinson and Kolchin, *Report of an Investigation.* A 1933 survey of 84 different manufacturing fields ranked women's clothing at the very bottom of the list in degree of business concentration. F. C. Pierson, *Collective Bargaining Systems* (1942), p. 141, citing R. S. Tucker and others, *Big Business — Its Growth and Its Place* (1937), pp. 42–43.

the 20,000 establishments of the various apparel industries throughout the country, the average number of workers totals 30." Certain branches of the headwear industry in the New York market suffered the greatest disintegration. "In the place of substantial shops which at one time employed as many as 200 and 300 workers in a single shop," stated the general executive board of the United Hatters, Cap and Millinery Workers' International Union, to the union's convention in May 1939, "the industry in New York has now reached a point where three-fourths of the shops employ four or five people."[52]

Mass competition among thousands of small shop owners in an already unstable industry was forever taking a heavy toll of business enterprises. More than one branch of the needle trades suffered a mortality rate of business establishments that at times ran as high as one-fifth, or even one-fourth, of all firms in the business each year. Contracting shops were the most vulnerable. In January 1936, Julius Hochman, general manager, Dressmakers' Joint Board, ILGWU, estimated that 33 percent of all dress contractors closed their doors each year, leaving 30,000 union members "thrust into the streets to look for jobs." Yet there were always new adventurers for those who fell by the wayside. For the 700 women's coat and suit manufacturers who closed their doors between September 1924 and March 1926 (the period when women turned to dresses), there were 724 new establishments that opened their doors for cloak and suit manufacturing over the same months.[53]

To offset the loss of 800 fur manufacturers who dropped out

[52]The letter, dated April 5, 1935, from the Apparel Industries Committee to Senator Pat Harrison is recorded in the *Investigation of the National Recovery Administration,* Hearings before the Committee on Finance, Senate, 74th Cong., 1st. sess., pursuant to Senate Resolution 79 (April 1935), Part VI, p. 2830. For the views of the millinery workers' union see United Hatters, Cap and Millinery Workers' International Union, *Report and Proceedings,* Third Convention (May 1939), p. 143. Many years earlier the general executive board of the United Cloth Hat and Cap Makers of North America had lamented the lack of substantial enterprises: "In other industries manufacturing requires some standing in the business community, some business training and capital. In our trade this is not the case. The door is open to every adventurer." See the union's *Report and Proceedings,* Fourteenth Convention (May 1923), p. 14.

[53]ILGWU's *Justice,* Jan. 15, 1936; *Women's Wear,* March 8, 1926.

of the industry during 1926–1927, there were 704 new fur manufacturers entering the business. Over the same period, the textile
industry lost 621 old firms, while gaining 620 new firms. For the
60 millinery shops that closed their doors in 1928, there were 59
new shops opening that year to take their places. Even in the depression of 1930, when 355 men's clothing manufacturers discontinued operations, in New York City there were 239 new firms
that started out in the same business for the first time. Over a span
of nine months, from October 1932 to June 1933, the jobbers
and inside manufacturers of the New York women's coat and suit
trade lost 178 of their 803 firms but picked up 138 new firms in
the same period. Five years later, the same group lost 176 of their
members but gained 133 others between mid-August 1937 and
mid-February 1939.[54]

Yet, despite the small size and short life of the average plant,
many branches of the needle trades were, in the aggregate, great
industries. As early as 1919, the annual value of women's and
children's apparel made in the United States had exceeded a billion dollars, and the value of men's and boy's clothing produced

[54]Metropolitan Life Insurance Co., *The Migration of Industry in the New
York Region for the Years 1926–1927,* Report of a Survey Made...in Cooperation with the Regional Plan of New York and Its Environs (1930); *Fur Age
Weekly,* Jan. 17, 1927; *Daily News Record,* August 10, 1931; *Women's Wear
Daily,* April 10, 1935 and March 1, 1939. In the first seven months of 1930, the
organized contractors of the women's coat and suit industry lost 242 members
but gained 104 others. *Women's Wear Daily,* August 6, 1930. Of 984 dress and
waist manufacturers operating in New York City in 1939, only 534 had been in
business before 1937. Julius Hochman, *Industry Planning through Collective
Bargaining* (1940, pamphlet), p. 107. Other evidence on the shifting sands of
industrial production in the needle trades can be found in D. J. Brown, "The
Migration of Industry: The Shift of Twenty-four Needle Trades from New
York State, 1926–1934," NRA Studies (March 1936), U.S. National Archives;
and in the exhibits accompanying the testimony of Lazare Teper, research
director, ILGWU, cited above at p. 32n.

Writing more recently of the turnover among employers and employees
in the needle trades, A. H. Raskin, labor reporter for the *New York
Times,* observed in 1959: "Seventeen percent of the companies in contractual relations with the union disappear each year. Often the same
parties will appear in two, three or four businesses in a single season.
Workers come and go with comparative rapidity. Fifteen percent are
replaced by other workers in a twelve month period."
—*New York Times,* April 26, 1959.

that year had also passed the billion dollar mark. Much of this value was added by manufacturing in New York City. In 1939 there were more than twenty separate branches of the needle trades, in each of which New York City manufacturers contributed over $5,000,000 to the value of the product. In nine of these branches, New York City's contribution represented over 60 percent of the total value added by manufacturing in the United States. Of the 1,100,000 workers employed during 1947 in the apparel industries, 353,475, or more than a third, were employed in New York City. Though the individual risks were great, the over-all stakes were high.[55]

Within this turbulent setting where the over-all stakes were high, competition was the key to success or failure. It unlocked the door of legitimate opportunity for the trained hand and the creative mind. But competition also opened the flood gates to unscrupulous operators who engaged honest producers and advocates of moderation in a bitter struggle for survival. Competition in the needle trades was a consuming fire that gutted the rotted timbers of complacency and incompetence. But in so doing, competition, when carried to an extreme, threatened to crumble the very foundations of the industrial structure. The evil effects of uncontrolled competition at its worst were once described by the general executive board of the United Hatters, Cap and Millinery Workers in terms that reflected conditions of the millinery trade during the thirties:

Competition is bitter and intense. The law of the jungle is the only law that has any chance of being observed. The price structure ceases to exist. Goods are offered for whatever price they will bring, irrespective as to whether it is sufficient to cover the costs of production and overhead, much less to allow for a profit. To obtain ready cash, higher and higher discounts are offered, sometimes amounting to as much as 15 percent, and all sorts of return privileges and other concessions are made to obtain a share of the dwindling business. Of course, workman-

---

[55]See tables based on the U.S. *Census of Manufactures* in appendix to Seidman, *The Needle Trades,* pp. 333–345; and tables prepared from U.S. Department of Commerce, Bureau of the Census figures, and from U.S. Bureau of Old-Age and Survivors Insurance figures appearing in the preface to J. T. Carpenter, *Employers' Associations and Collective Bargaining in New York City* (1950), pp. x-xii.

ship, values, materials — all are sacrificed in this desperate struggle for existence.[56]

Concluding Observations

These are but a few glimpses of the stage upon which the drama of collective bargaining in the needle trades was to be acted out. In 1915, Paul U. Kellogg, editor of the *Survey,* looked upon the stage — the women's coat and suit segment — and saw "an industry which in years past suffered more than anything else from extreme decentralization — cutthroat competition, mushroom firms, shop bargaining, the incoming of new immigration sucking down the standards gained by immigrant workmen of a longer residence, the guerilla tactics of irresponsible employers breaking down the standards of the older shops."[57]

In 1928, Benjamin Falk looked upon the stage — the rabbit fur segment — and concluded: "Lack of organization, ignorance of the market conditions, extravagance and waste, mutual distrust, petty jealousies, and underhand competition, these are the things that have nearly killed the rabbit industry." Similarly, James C. Worthy, reporting for the National Recovery Administration a few years later, looked upon another segment of the needle trades — the millinery industry — and found:

"Cut throat" is a mild term when applied to the competition existing in this industry. Possessed of little individual bargaining ability, manufacturers have no control over their own prices — let alone the price structure of the industry. They are forced to take what they can get from their distributors, and forced to pay for their materials what their supply houses dictate. The producer is fortunate if he can cover his costs of production. The rate of industrial mortality — about 20 percent per annum — indicates that in many cases he does not.[58]

---

[56]United Hatters, Cap and Millinery Workers' International Union, Cap and Millinery Department, *Report and Proceedings,* Second Convention (First Regular Convention), Oct. 4–7, 1936, p. 54.

[57]Paul U. Kellogg's editorial from the *Survey* is here taken from an unidentified newspaper clipping, dated Jan. 23, 1915, filed in the Abelson papers.

[58]For the rabbit fur industry, see Benjamin Falk, "The Rise and Fall of the Rabbit Skin Industry," in the *Fur Trade Review,* April 1928. For the millinery industry, see J. C. Worthy, "The Millinery Industry," NRA: Division of Review, Industry Studies Section (March 1936), p. ix.

Unemployment, low wages, illegitimate price cutting, devious and dubious business practices, have made it continuously more difficult for

For over half a century of collective bargaining in the needle trades, the casts of the show have changed as rapidly as have the stage settings. On the industrial scene, the "bosses" and the "people" were forever swapping characters. "The manufacturer and his worker," noted one observer of the fur trade in 1936, ". . . are not enemies but competitors; it is a counter not a barricade that divides them. They are both aware that tomorrow their roles may be reversed. If the skilled worker is not already competing with his boss by doing contract work for a jobber after hours in his home, he is making plans with the cutter at the next table to start a new firm as soon as the season is over."[59]

Writing in more general terms, Benjamin M. Selekman, later to become a distinguished professor at Harvard University, surveyed the scene — the men's clothing segment — and summed up the problems of the needle trades as he saw them in 1925:

New York is an immigrant city; the clothing trades use almost no other labor. Italians number about 400,000 in New York and Jews have come to be over 1,600,000. The idiosyncracies of these newly arrived people are expressed by the clothing trades at almost every point. Their untiring ambition, their intense individualism, their willingness to engage in cut-throat competition, their readiness to embark themselves among the risks of unstandardized and speculative enterprises, have all been thoroughly exploited. Slums and ghettos, obsolete and unsanitary working places, congested selling districts, have been among the materials with which the immense local structures of the clothing trades have been reared.[60]

---

the honest and high minded manufacturer and are more and more putting the trade at the mercy of the unscrupulous and the short sighted, with the consequent debasement of business standards and the growing deterioration of the industry as a whole.
    —E. R. A. Seligman, "The Millinery Industry: A Survey" n.d., pp. 5–6; copy filed in the Abelson papers.

[59]From a typewritten article in the Abelson papers, printed with slight modifications in *Fortune,* January 1936, vol. 13, p. 120.

[60]Selekman *et al., Regional Plan of New York and Its Environs, An Economic and Industrial Survey: The Clothing and Textile Industries,* p. 15.

Chapter 2

The Protocol of Peace

T HE pattern of collective bargaining for the needle trades evolved from the Brandeis Conferences of 1910 to settle the cloakmakers' strike and took its shape in the protocol movement that stemmed from those conferences. In the summer of 1910, the International Ladies' Garment Workers' Union represented by nine locals in the New York metropolitan area had undertaken for the first time to organize the entire women's coat and suit industry of New York City. A general strike had been called and the support for it was so overwhelming among both union and nonunion workers that production was brought to a standstill.

The manufacturers had countered the union move by forming the Cloak, Suit and Skirt Manufacturers' Protective Association. The members of this group had pledged themselves not to recognize the union nor to conclude agreements with it. The executive committee of the association notified the union that negotiations to end the strike would be futile so long as the workers demanded recognition of their union or insisted upon signing labor agreements. The manufacturers refused even to meet with union representatives so long as the issue of the closed shop (a shop that hires union members only) was on the agenda. From all appearances, the battle between the "bosses" and the "people" had come to a showdown.

Through the intercession of outside parties, however, the association and the union each agreed to send ten delegates and a legal adviser to a series of joint conferences beginning July 28, 1910, under the chairmanship of Louis D. Brandeis. Out of these negotiations came the essential principles of collective action later written into the original Protocol of Peace — the most far-reaching labor agreement ever to be adopted in the needle trades. What the records of the Constitutional Convention of 1787 disclosed concerning the aims of the framers of the U. S. Constitution, the minutes of the Brandeis Conferences revealed concerning the motives that impelled the participants to create the first major institutions of collective bargaining for their industry.

The official positions of the parties at the time of these conferences gave no evidence of the revolutionary concepts of union-management relations that were to be formulated behind closed doors. The union had submitted its usual complaints of low wages, night work, infringement of holidays and Sundays, discrimination against union men. It had proposed "to establish a living standard of wages, to regulate the hours of labor, to limit night work, to prevent work on holidays, to abolish all charges for electricity and appliances, to do away with tenement house work, to prevent discrimination...." In addition, the union, following the historic policy of organized labor in America, insisted upon official recognition and acceptance of the closed shop.[1]

With equal conformity to historic patterns, the manufacturers' association in a flourish of generosity had expressed concern for "the grievances of our employees" but had shown the usual contempt for "the demands of the union." Employers wanted no part of a union "led by agitators and demagogues instead of by sane men." They feared the consequences of union recognition and the closed shop. "To encourage an organization led by anarchists," cautioned the counsel for the employers' association, "is to produce anarchism; to encourage an organization that has fundamental principles that are inimical to the principles of American freedom, would be to tend to destroy American freedom." In a letter to the public, dated July 11, 1910, the manufacturers' associ-

---

[1]The minutes of these conferences together with other documentary materials of the period are recorded in a 158-page privately printed paper-bound volume, *The Cloak Makers' Strike,* issued by the Cloak, Suit and Skirt Manufacturers' Protective Association in 1910. All references in this chapter are to pages of this volume unless otherwise indicated. Quotation at p. 20.

ation solemnly announced that the employers were "quite prepared to go down in ruin" rather than accept the rule of their factories by the union.[2]

The New Approach to Collective Bargaining

Behind the scenes, however, devotions to ideologies were shaken by appeals to common sense. Once the parties had descended from their lofty citadels of class antagonism onto the plains of economic reality, they found a common cause in seeking to protect their joint interests from the unorganized segments of the trade. A new shuffling of industrial forces was in the making. Instead of pitting capital against labor, employers against employees, the "bosses" against the "people," the organized forces of both labor and management were about to combine against the unorganized forces of both labor and management. Through this new alignment, effective bargaining in the needle trades was born.

A foretaste of subsequent developments came on the eve of the first conference when the president of the employer group, A. E. Lefcourt, confided to J. A. Dyche, general secretary-treasurer of the ILGWU, the hope that the employers' association would agree to make the union strong enough "to protect the legitimate manufacturers from the small fry, who are cutting into their trade." Only a strong union, asserted the president, would be in a position "to make it impossible for the small manufacturers to cut out the large ones."[3] At that time, the Cloak, Suit and Skirt Manufacturers' Protective Association consisted of some seventy-five or more "inside" manufacturers who normally made their own products by direct labor in their own factories. In opposition to the host of small-scale contractors who lived from job to job, these employers maintained the largest establishments in the trade. They looked upon themselves as the "respectable" producers, the "legitimate" manufacturers, the "decent" business men of their industry — employers with a "social conscience."

But, in a local industry of many times their number, they were subjected to relentless pressure from unscrupulous competitors with no standards of business ethics and no sense of reponsibility

[2]*Ibid.,* pp. 1, 121, 122.
[3]*Ibid.,* pp. 106, 150.

for working conditions in their shops. Already this pressure — mostly from outside jobbers and contractors — had led some members of the newly formed association into methods of inside contracting, subcontracting, and submanufacturing. Small-time operators were engaged to finish garments by contract on the premises of the manufacturers. By working their men longer hours at a faster pace and with less pay, these petty bosses made their profits and still reduced costs to manufacturers who otherwise employed direct labor.

Under pressure from inside and outside contractors, the substantial firms of the industry were in danger of disintegrating into small contracting units lacking permanence or stability. Reckless competition threatened to demoralize the industry and had already driven many "honest" manufacturers into bankruptcy. A plan to standardize hours, wages, and working conditions throughout the industry would put a floor under competition and keep the "legitimate" manufacturers on their feet.

If the union could somehow be persuaded to strive for industry-wide standards of employment, and in particular to support the cause of inside manufacturing against the jobber-contracting system of production, then organized labor could become an ally of the manufacturers' association instead of its enemy. "You gentlemen feel that there is certain unfair competition existing among the manufacturers," observed J. H. Cohen, counsel for the association, addressing the union delegates. "We feel that there is certain unfair competition existing among the employees. Now we have got to protect one another."[4]

Union delegates at the conferences embraced the logic of this down-to-earth approach with outstretched arms. They saw the dangers that faced the legitimate manufacturers as well as themselves. "If our union fails in its present effort," warned Benjamin Schlesinger, a former president of the ILGWU, "then it would not take very long before a good many of the very small ones [manufacturers] will drive your people out of business." Even before the conferences began, J. A. Dyche, general secretary-treasurer of the ILGWU, had privately told the president of the newly formed manufacturers' association that the evils of unrestricted

---

[4]*Ibid.,* p. 38.

shop-to-shop bargaining had left the industry in a completely chaotic condition from which it could not hope to extricate itself without the help of the union and the organized employers.[5]

Other union delegates saw the necessity for putting a floor under competition. "I want to impress upon you gentlemen," announced Abraham Rosenberg, president of the ILGWU, "that we are here in this strike to eliminate competition to some extent — unfair competition." The organized workers were seeking the stability that came from uniform labor standards throughout the industry. "We realize," stated Meyer London, counsel for the union, "that if in one place the employee will get for a garment $5.00, while in the next place he will get for a garment which involved the same amount of work, $2.50, that the condition of the trade will remain just about as it is now."[6]

If the employers could somehow be convinced that the union was "merely organized for one purpose, that is, the equalization of conditions among the workers the same as the manufacturers are organized to equalize conditions among themselves," — as Alexander Bloch, chairman of the union delegation, put it — then the employers' association might become an ally of the union in helping to raise work standards, instead of an enemy. In so far as regulating hours of work, improving sanitary conditions, or establishing a living wage tended to eliminate fierce competition prevailing among manufacturers under the sweat-shop system, so Meyer London, counsel for the ILGWU, pointed out, "decent" employers represented at the conferences might cooperate to see that men and women were no longer "worked to death, without regard to life, without regard to safety, or without regard to health." For had not J. H. Cohen, counsel for the manufacturers, himself admitted that it made little difference to the employers

---

[5]*Ibid.*, Schlesinger at p. 139. J. A. Dyche recalling his conversation in July 1910 with A. E. Lefcourt, president of the Cloak, Suit and Skirt Manufacturers' Protective Association, as given in Dyche's *Bolshevism in American Labor Unions* (1926), p. 181, where he wrote: "The trade is unorganized. Until this strike was declared...there was no organization of employers. Everything was left to the will and whim of an individual employer, and the bargain he could strike with his working people. The result of this unbridled competition between employers and employees is that the industry is in a completely chaotic condition."

[6]*The Cloak Makers' Strike,* Rosenberg at p. 69; London at p. 75.

whether the wage standard of the workers was raised 50¢ an hour, or $1.00 an hour, so long as the same rule applied throughout the industry?[7]

A Realignment of Forces

Here, then, was the new approach to collective bargaining in the needle trades — namely, that the individual manufacturers of an industry, acting through their association, should join hands with the conservative leaders of organized labor, acting through their union, to wage war on the "small fry" (employers and workers) who were operating on the outer fringes of the trade. This possibility of accepting the union as an ally of the "legitimate" manufacturer accounted for the revolution in management attitudes toward organized labor. Soon after the close of the conferences, the very employers who had so bitterly attacked labor unions at the outset of negotiations declared "their belief in the Union and that all who desire its benefits should share its burdens."[8]

Nor did the employers stop with general platitudes of moral endorsement. "We seek in the organization of your union," boldly announced J. H. Cohen, counsel for the manufacturers, "one of the strongest means by which to prevent the inexorable law of competition." And on another occasion he declared: "We do not want to have any business dealings with you unless you are a strong organization, capable of effectively carrying out whatever you agree to." Still later in the sessions, Cohen again reiterated his association's change of policy: "We accept absolutely now the proposition that you should have a strong union." In the first Protocol of Peace, the very employers who had banned the "closed shop" as a topic of discussion at the Brandeis Conferences officially approved a union security clause

where, when hiring help union members are preferred, it being recognized that, since there are differences in degrees of skill among those employed in a trade, employers shall have freedom of selection as between one union man and another. . . .

---

[7]*Ibid.,* Bloch at p. 47; London at p. 51; Cohen at p. 76.

[8]Article XIV, Protocol of Peace for the women's coat and suit industry, effective Sept. 2, 1910. The text of this protocol may be conveniently found in Louis Lorwin [Louis Levine], *The Women's Garment Workers* (1924), Appendix III, pp. 542–545.

Then, as further proof of sincerity, the employers' association backed this official position with a provision agreeing to discipline any of its members who discriminated against union men.[9]

In some respects, this new approach to collective bargaining reflected a revolution in union thinking too. For years, unions had been occupied with drafting contract formulas for acceptance by individual employers. These employers, who had no part in creating such agreements, seldom read the documents or inquired of their terms. During the cloakmakers' strike of 1910, before the Brandeis joint conferences were ever convened, identical copies of a form contract drafted at union headquarters had already been signed by several hundred independent manufacturers who did not belong to the association. Such was the general pattern of bargaining in the needle trades at that time.

Under the formalities of one-way bargaining, shop owners blithely signed labor agreements with no intention of ever living up to their commitments. Contract clauses granting holidays with pay were nullified by closing up shop during the weeks in which the holidays occurred. Recognition of the union was little more than a pretext for identifying labor leaders to be discharged. Employers continued to haggle over wages that had already been fixed by the terms of these labor contracts. "We have been signing agreements with individual employers for twelve years," lamented Meyer London, counsel for the ILGWU, at the Brandeis Conferences, "...the signing of agreements became a farce." J. A. Dyche, general secretary-treasurer of the ILGWU, likewise admitted to A. E. Lefcourt, president of the employers' association, that "until this strike was declared, there was no union of the men strong enough to have any influence on the conditions of labor in this industry."[10]

Unlike previous experiences, the new approach called for emphasis upon contract enforcement. All concessions and arrangements made at the conferences, noted Meyer London, counsel for the union, would be worthless, unless "the proper methods of carrying the forms into execution will have been adopted." Most union leaders present at the conferences were convinced that the success of the new policy depended upon all-out cooperation with

---

[9]*The Cloak Makers' Strike,* Cohen at pp. 76, 79, 122.

[10]*Ibid.,* London at p. 104; Dyche in his *Bolshevism in American Labor Unions,* p. 182.

a strong employers' association. "Only by the cooperative efforts of a strong union, and a strong manufacturers' association," so J. A. Dyche, general secretary-treasurer of the ILGWU, confided to the president of the manufacturers' association, "can order be brought into the present chaotic condition existing in the industry, all of which is the result of unregulated competition."[11]

Casting aside any general aversion to dealing with employer groups, union delegates now encouraged manufacturers to organize to help control the industry. In a letter to the manufacturers' association shortly before the first conference, union leaders had written: "We believe in organization not restricted to the employees alone, but in organization of the employers as well." Obviously, the concept of collective bargaining that emerged from the Brandeis Conferences was one of group action on both sides — "collective" among employers, as well as "collective" among workers.[12]

Both parties to the new approach saw hope in the organized power of each group to take action against its own members. The counsel for the employers' association announced that he would urge his group to adopt trade regulations to "carry out the spirit of the agreement," and for violating these regulations he would propose "discipline, suspension in cases where the offense is of minor consequence, and ultimate expulsion if it is of serious or continuous flagrancy." In turn, the president of the international union stated that his organization would, as a last resort, expel its members for contract infractions, provided the association members would agree not to employ workers expelled from the union. Thus the new edifice of controlled competition was to be erected on the foundation of a strong labor union and a strong employers' association.[13]

The Scope of Competition

But, when the participants put their heads together to "give their best intellect" — as Cohen put it — to the erection of the new edifice, they encountered serious problems arising from their posi-

---

[11] *The Cloak Makers' Strike,* London at p. 104; Dyche in *Bolshevism in American Labor Unions,* p. 163.

[12] *The Cloak Makers' Strike,* p. 17.

[13] *Ibid.,* Cohen, counsel, at p. 122; Rosenberg, president, at p. 54.

tion in the trade. At that time, the different employer-worker groups within the women's coat and suit industry fell into four general categories represented by the diagram below:

Employer-Worker Groups in the Women's Cloak and Suit Industry

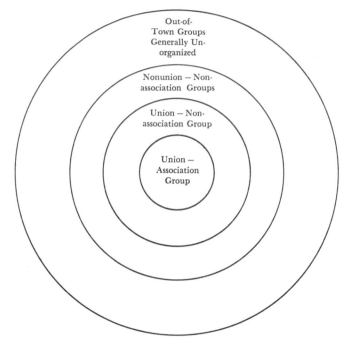

Not only were the parties to the proposed agreement faced with the problem of putting their own houses in order, but they were confronted with the dilemma of improving conditions outside their own establishments or of having their good work nullified by the shops over which they had no control. Plucking the motes from their own eyes was of far less concern than pulling the beams from the eyes of their competitors. Alexander Bloch, chairman of the union delegation, found less cause to complain against the "legitimate manufacturer who works on a nine or a nine and a half hour basis" than he found cause to attack the "unscrupulous employer" who works his men night and day to get out a ten-day order. In his own words, he conceded that "the fair employer is up against a hard game." Likewise, J. A. Dyche, general secretary-treasurer of the ILGWU, admitted to the president of the employers' association that conditions in the shops of association members were fairly satisfactory, but the trouble was that the association shops were in a minority.[14]

Every issue before the conference involved ramifications beyond the immediate control of the participants. Both parties to the negotiations wanted to abolish home work. The association offered to discipline its own members who gave out home work provided the union would discipline its members who accepted home work. But such a bargain would have no validity beyond shops represented by the association-union group. "We can only guarantee for those we do control," observed Abraham Rosenberg, president of the union. To this statement, J. H. Cohen replied for the manufacturers: "We cannot control people who are not members of our association." At this point, Mr. Brandeis, chairman of the conference, put the problem in its true perspective: "So far as it relates to persons outside of the Association it is a mere standard which they have created, and which they hope will be observed."[15]

So was it with the problems of health and safety. What was the object of establishing a board of sanitary control with a staff of competent inspectors unless the board had jurisdiction over shops of nonassociation employers as well as those of association members? "The gentlemen who are here," noted AFL special delegate, J. B. Lennon, "have shops that have reached probably the best level and the best standards that exist in the trade." By contrast, noted Abraham Bisno, a substitute union delegate, there are workshops in "very small bedrooms, packed with bed clothes and boarders, and clothes and skirts and bedbugs and germs of all kinds."[16] What was the use of a sanitary board if these holes of uncleanliness were beyond the pale of its authority?

Again, the employers listened sympathetically to charges against manufacturers who worked their employees "unlimited hours — day and night; Saturday and Sunday; seven days a week." Yet they hesitated to move toward a definite limitation on hours of work lest the regulation could not be enforced throughout the industry. "We will enforce our end of it," assured Alexander Bloch, on behalf of the union, "and the other side will enforce their end of it, and only by stipulating the number of hours that

---

[14]*Ibid.*, p. 53; Dyche, *Bolshevism in American Labor Unions*, p. 182.

[15]*The Cloak Makers' Strike*, p. 42.

[16]*Ibid.*, Lennon at p. 96; Bisno at p. 98.

people shall work and promising enforcement of the same by both sides can we actually equalize or try to equalize these conditions."[17]

Such a proposition was valid enough for the association-union shops, where two potentially powerful organizations stood ready to discipline their respective members for failure to observe established schedules. But who would see that such regulations were binding on the outer circles of the industry? "I venture the prediction, gentlemen," warned the counsel for the manufacturers, "that no matter what agreement we enter into as to the hours of labor in our shops, that we shall have more to contend with in the freedom on the part of those who do not belong to our organization or to yours, in working longer than those hours of labor."[18]

Thus, as one issue after another came up for discussion, fear of competition from the outer circles of the industry drove the two delegations into closer and closer collaboration against the unorganized segments of the trade. "You are concerned by the limitations of your side, and we are concerned by the limitations of ours," carefully noted J. H. Cohen, the association counsel, "and, unless we meet the law of competition by the law of co-operation, the competition will survive, and we will be hurt just as you will be hurt."[19]

Expanding Spheres of Competition

These fears were worse confounded because manufacturing centers were developing rapidly in other cities. "Cleveland is coming fast in the cloak making business," observed J. P. Lennon, special union delegate representing the AFL, "faster than any other city in the United States outside of New York." He thought Chicago, St. Louis, Cincinnati, Philadelphia, Baltimore, and Boston were also to be reckoned with. Another union delegate, former ILGWU President Benjamin Schlesinger, who had worked extensively in other cities, noted that the market for women's coats and suits had already become nationwide. "You are competing against every manufacturer in the country," he said.[20]

---

[17]*Ibid.,* pp. 51, 53.

[18]*Ibid.,* p. 53.

[19]*Ibid.,* p. 79.

[20]*Ibid.,* Lennon at p. 77; Schlesinger at p. 80.

Replying to a union proposal for a wage increase, J. H. Cohen stated that "nothing would contribute so much to Cleveland's taking the supremacy in the cloak trade from New York as for us to establish those rates of wages, while the rates of wages in Cleveland remain the same." So was it with piecework. "If we were to establish," he added, "the [minimum] rates per hour for piecework ...suggested here, while that rate should not prevail throughout the entire country, our business would be diverted to those other cities within a short while."[21]

Here, then, was the crux of the difficulty facing the two delegations at the Brandeis Conferences: how to improve the competitive position of association-union shops by establishing labor standards that could be enforced throughout the country. In the solution of that problem, both parties to the negotiations had everything to gain and nothing to lose.

As a means of resolving this issue, union leaders repeatedly harped on the potentialities of their own organization as a policing agency capable of enforcing labor standards throughout the industry. "Now, if we will have no opposition on the part of the bulk of the manufacturers in the City of New York against this instrument, which enables us to arrive at a standard of wages," argued J. A. Dyche, ILGWU general secretary-treasurer, "it will be a comparatively easy matter for us to raise wages throughout the city, and not only throughout the city but throughout the country.... If the manufacturers will in any way co-operate with us to have a strong Union, the stronger the Union the easier it will be for us to establish this standard."[22]

During the sessions, there was much conjecture and debate over the ability of the union to extend employment terms into plants beyond those of the organized manufacturers who would be bound by the proposed agreement. Some confidence was expressed in the power of the ILGWU to insist upon the same terms in the shops of independent firms bound by separate union contracts and obligated to employ union members only. The closed shop gave the union a strong lever with which to pry favorable terms of employment from these independent producers.

---

[21]*Ibid.,* p. 79.
[22]*Ibid.,* pp. 78–79.

Moreover, the ILGWU, unlike the employers' association, was organized on a national scale with many locals already established in other cities. Hence the union, unlike the association, was in a position to launch a nationwide program for standardizing terms of employment. In the long run, nothing short of industry-wide standards could adequately protect the organized manufacturers of New York City. Chairman Brandeis himself noted that the union "having a membership, presumably, that extends far beyond those who become members of the association," will be obligated to offer the organized employers "protection from unfair competition" at least "as far as they are able to give it."[23]

These attempts to inspire confidence among employer delegates were not altogether successful. At one stage of the discussions, J. H. Cohen expressed the fear that high labor standards might backfire against the organized factions by tending to "deunionize" the trade. "Your Union men will be bound by this agreement not to work for less than the amount which we agree upon in this conference," he submitted, "but if there is no work to be had, except among the poorer manufacturers who are bidding down the employees, won't the inducement be for the Union man to become a non-Union man, and to go to work in these shops at less than the standard wage, and compete with us?"[24]

In any case, the power of the union to control its own members in the shops of independent parties bound by labor agreements did not resolve the problem of competition from the great unorganized segments of the trade, particularly in other towns and cities. J. B. Lennon, special AFL delegate, insisted that the union could "eliminate what is the greatest danger to the cloak and suit manufacturers of New York City, and that is that the trade will be diverted to other cities." But the employers wanted more concrete evidence of how such promises could be fulfilled. Speaking for the manufacturers, J. H. Cohen expressed the hope "that what we

---

[23]*Ibid.*, pp. 42–43.

[24]*Ibid.*, p. 76.

Of course, if we are to insist upon ideal conditions among our own members, we will be increasing the cost of manufacturing in our establishments, and if you insist upon ideal conditions among your people in our shops it may result in driving the workers into shops where the ideal conditions do not exist.

—*Ibid.*, Cohen at p. 42.

do agree upon will be the standard of the industry." Still he was not willing to build foundations for the future upon hopes. "In addition to a hope," he added, "I want something practical."[25]

Prospects for Uniform Standards

From time to time, union delegates consoled the employers with gentle hints of possible sanctions their organization might use to enforce standards beyond the ranks of the association-union group represented at the conferences. The chairman of the union delegation, Alexander Bloch, who felt that his union was "in a position to do as a union a great deal to protect the manufacturers against unfair competition," suggested appropriate action that his union might take against the "unscrupulous" employer. "We could possibly curtail the output of his work unless he came up to the mark of you gentlemen here," he said.[26]

Likewise, J. B. Lennon, special delegate of the AFL, spoke of the power this union had over the manufacturer who does "an illegitimate business." Getting down to brass tacks, Lennon offered the employers this assurance: "We can put the fellow out of business — to talk plain — that won't deal on the square;" and, in similar fashion, J. A. Dyche sought to allay employer fears of competition from other cities with an inside observation. "I may tell you this in all confidence," assured Dyche, "that it requires but a telegram from me to stop [work in] most of the cities in a moment's notice."[27]

In addition to these potential sanctions, union delegates advanced the pattern theory of labor standards. Refuting J. H. Cohen's position on wage trends, J. B. Lennon argued for the union "that while in general, the tendency of wages is towards the lower pay, that where there is established an organization that fixes a minimum wage, that we absolutely overcome the general principle which applies generally in the industry, and that the

---

[25]*Ibid.,* Lennon at p. 77; Cohen at p. 43.

> It seems to me, gentlemen, that it is only fair to ask of you that in the event that we agree to a certain stand, you pledge yourself to enforce those standards throughout the country as well as throughout the city.
> —*Ibid.,* Cohen at p. 79.

[26]*Ibid.,* p. 38.

[27]*Ibid.,* Lennon at p. 125; Dyche at p. 78.

tendency is toward the Union wage." Alexander Bloch, chairman of the union delegation, extended the theory of pattern setting by the most reputable factions of an industry to control over home work. "I want to say this," so he told the conferees, "that whatever agreement may be reached at this conference will naturally become the ruling factor throughout the trade, whether they are members of the organization or not, and therefore we can well afford to say that we will insist on our members not taking any of their work home."[28]

When Mr. Cohen likened this theory to the proposition that water seeks its highest level, Mr. Lennon contended in reply:

> that where a standard of wages is fixed, and men naturally and of necessity live next door to each other, and the non-Union man or the Union man sees that his neighbor is getting the standard of wages, he does not seek to reduce the wages; he seeks to raise his own to the same level, and if the standards of wages can be agreed upon, which I believe it can, I will tell you that instead of the cut-throat policy which has been pursued, the Union, especially with the assistance of a considerable number of the manufacturers, will not only be able to hold that standard of wages in New York, but it will be able to hold it in some other cities.[29]

Thus the prospect of extending a pattern of wages into other cities depended upon creating a standard that would be approved by the leading manufacturers and their organized workers at the heart of the women's coat and suit industry.

---

[28]*Ibid.,* Lennon at pp. 76–77; Bloch at p. 43.

[29]*Ibid.,* p. 77. But the union's "leveling up" theory of wage determination was not to jibe with subsequent experiences under the first protocol. At least Morris Hillquit, legal counsel for the ILGWU, was later to advance the "leveling down" theory of shop-by-shop, piece-rate determination that led "to the survival of the unfittest, or to the survival of the meanest":

> In one shop we will find a certain garment is made, say at a dollar; in another shop the garment is made for a dollar and a half. That would not mean, most likely, that the employer who gets it for less will say, "Now, gentlemen, I see my neighbor makes it for a dollar fifty; I will add fifty cents." But it means that the man who makes it for a dollar, the other men will say, "He will take it for a dollar, and you, gentlemen, will have to take it for a dollar." In other words, it is the constant depressing of standards.
>
> —*Minutes,* Council of Conciliation...[women's coat and suit trade] (July 14, 1915), p. 35.

Both parties agreed that the most logical solution to the problem of variable work standards lay in a more thorough organization of the industry. To that end, Mr. Lennon pledged that the union would "immediately start with efforts to organize all the other cities of the country and put them on the same standard." Similarly, the manufacturers set their sights on a more complete coverage for their own organization. "We do not undertake to get into our association every cloak manufacturer in New York," stated Mr. Cohen, "but, Mr. Chairman, we propose to use every legitimate argument to convince every cloak and skirt and suit manufacturer in this town that it is his business to belong to our association."[30]

To further this objective, both parties agreed that each must support the other in building up its organization throughout the country. As far as possible, the union would steer every manufacturer into the association and the association would encourage all workers to join the union. "Unless there will be strenuous cooperation on the part of the Union and on the part of the Manufacturers' Association — one to make strong the other," warned J. A. Dyche, "all of these agreements, all of these details cannot hold; they cannot be carried out."[31]

With this understanding to support each other, the parties concluded their three days of intensive conferences and some weeks later, on September 2, 1910, signed the original Protocol of Peace. That agreement stood for something more than the minimum standards of employment it contained: the fifty-hour week, double time for overtime, the abolition of home work, more holidays with pay, and minimum wage scales. Nor did its provisions for a permanent board of arbitration, a committee on grievances, and a joint board of sanitary control in themselves reveal the motives that inspired this new approach to collective bargaining.

For here were the beginnings of a new type of labor-management structure, bearing the strange title, "Law and Order in Industry." Its foundations were laid on the solid rock of "legitimate" competition. Its builders were the organized forces of industry. And its chief architect was not a union man at all, but Julius Henry Cohen, counsel for the manufacturers' association —

[30] *The Cloak Makers' Strike,* Lennon at p. 78; Cohen at p. 112.

[31] *Ibid.,* p. 106.

the James Madison of the Brandeis Conferences. He it was who named the edifice that he helped to build, when, some years later, he entitled his own book on the subject, *Law and Order in Industry.*

Concluding Observations

And so began, some fifty-odd years ago, the first major episode of successful bargaining in the needle trades of New York City. The Protocol of Peace soon became a model for similar agreements in other segments of the apparel industries. After experiences somewhat similar to those in the women's coat and suit trade, the Dress and Waist Manufacturers' Association and the Dress Makers' Union of New York (Local 25, ILGWU) signed a protocol of peace on January 18, 1913, for the dress and waist industry. Then, in rapid succession, came the protocols for the house dress and kimono manufacturing industry (February 11, 1913); for the cotton garments (white goods and ladies' underwear) manufacturing industry (February 17, 1913); and for the children's dress manufacturing industry (March 8, 1913).[32] Other agreements followed the principles of the original protocol without the name.

In every case, the chief sponsors of the protocol movement, both among the "bosses" and among the "people," purported to represent the responsible "legitimate" elements of their trade. In every case, the organized factions of each industry — those labor unions and employers' associations that spoke for the constructive forces of the trade — were aligned against the unorganized workers and their unorganized employers who together constituted the disruptive elements within each trade. In every case, the movement was multiple-employer in its origin and industry-wide in its ramifications. And, in every case, the primary object of collective action was to establish a permanent system of controlled competition that would promote industrial stability against the ravages of unprincipled elements operating on the outer fringes of each industry.

---

[32]The texts of these protocols are printed in C. H. Winslow, *Conciliation, Arbitration, and Sanitation in the Dress and Waist Industry of New York City,* U.S. Dept. of Labor, BLS Bulletin no. 145 (April 10, 1914), pp. 128–131, 133–136, 138–140.

Chapter 3

The Scope and Purpose
of Collective Bargaining

H<small>AD</small> the new approach to collective bargaining been fully endorsed by the organized forces of industry, the control of competition would have been greatly simplified. But the idea that labor and management had common interests from which mutual benefits could be derived through collective action was a revolutionary concept at the time of the cloakmakers' strike. And it remained a revolutionary concept to plague the advocates of collective action for years to come. Indeed, the nature of the task that confronted the organized forces of industry cannot be fully understood apart from some knowledge of the general currents in the historic stream of collective bargaining that flowed from the early concepts developed in the Brandeis Conferences of 1910.

Eddies of Confusion

From the ranks of organized labor soon came ambitious individuals with radical philosophies to make political capital of the protocol movement. Men like Dr. I. A. Hourwich, ambitious supporter of the militant faction within the ILGWU, appealed to the rank and file to renounce all work of "collaborationists." He charged the conservative union leaders with becoming strikebreakers by signing the cloak protocol, and he declared that the association and the union had "coalesced into one." Under his leadership, the Protocol of Peace took on the aspects of a temporary truce between deadly enemies rather than a permanent treaty to abolish the sources of industrial conflict.[1]

The influence of the radicals was soon felt in the breakdown of enforcement machinery. "Appeals to the galleries are beginning to count much more than ability, experience, earnestness, or hard work," observed J. A. Dyche, general secretary-treasurer of the ILGWU. Reporting to his union, Dyche surveyed developments under the cloak protocol in these terms:

> Our Syndicalists, our so-called revolutionaries, the people who believe that we must apply the sacred principle of the "Class War" to our relations with the Manufacturers' Association have triumphed. The few men in the Organization who may believe in the possibility of co-operation and good will between the Employers' Association and the Union are afraid to open their mouths for fear of being accused of being agents of the Manufacturers' Association. The forces of primitive or "revolutionary" unionism are victorious.[2]

In the years ahead, advocates of the "class struggle" were to sponsor many more attempts at restricting output and disrupting production. Other industries succumbed to the force of revolutionary doctrines designed to confuse and discredit the existing economic system. Slowdowns and shop strikes became tools for uniting the working class against their employers. By 1916, the men's clothing industry had felt the weight of radical union leadership. Having overthrown the supporters of the protocol movement, noted a clothing manufacturer that year, the anticollaborationists had a clear field to carry out their policies: "No council,

---

[1]*The New Post,* June 27, 1913. Translation filed in the Abelson papers.

> The truth is, you understand me, that the Protocol has only abolished strife between officials of the Union and the officials of the Manufacturers' Association. The Union officers have ceased to struggle. The struggle goes on in the shops between the workers and the bosses and has never ceased, and when the Protocol was signed, nobody imagined that the class struggle in the shops ended.
> —Isaac Hourwich to Meyer London, as reported in the *Jewish Daily Forward,* Dec. 12, 1913. Translation filed in the Abelson papers.

[2]J. A. Dyche in ILGWU, *Report and Proceedings,* Twelfth Convention (June 1914), p. 58. This passage later appeared in the *New York Times* for Jan. 20, 1919, as a full-page advertisement of the dress manufacturers during a strike to end the dress protocol.

no board of arbitration, no Julius Henry Cohen, a big organization and free rein to war."[3]

These eddies of confusion were created, in part, by radicals in the labor movement who professed an allegiance to foreign ideologies. The Communists in the needle trades were to have their era during the twenties and thirties. Gaining control of the New York Joint Board of the cloakmakers' union in 1926, they inflicted upon the women's coat and suit industry the most disastrous strike in the history of the needle trades. What they failed to accomplish by force — the Communists lost the 1926 strike but wrecked the joint board — they sought to gain by indirection, sometimes boring from within existing unions and sometimes setting up rival unions to win their objectives. They were a constant menace to the advocates of law and order.[4]

Not all roadblocks to the protocol movement can be attributed to radical union leadership, however, for some of the obstacles thrown into the path of collective bargaining were clearly the work of rabid antiunion manufacturers. By tradition and association, these employers hated all forms of unionism. Solemn pledges written into the protocols did not change their attitudes overnight. Goaded by union radicals whose conduct belied all assurances that the workers would support the established order, these employers continued the antiunion tactics that had characterized their conduct in the preceding decades. They refused to meet with union representatives or to allow union agents in their shops. They reserved a preference in employment for nonunion workers, particularly for those who had been expelled from unions. They exchanged blacklists of union members and forced their employees to sign yellow-dog contracts not to join a union during employ-

---

[3]*Daily Trade Record,* March 9, 1916.

[4]The furriers unions are dominated by radicals, their officials are radicals, their philosophies of course of action are radical. The Socialists and other relatively conservative elements have been submerged. It is not only demonstrable but has also been most emphatically demonstrated in this trade, that a collective agreement between a radical group of workers activated by the inherent need for friction, and a conservative group of employers urgently needing certainty and continuity in their affairs is impractical and unworkable.

—D. C. Mills, labor manager of the Associated Fur Manufacturers, as quoted in the trade publication, *Furs,* February 1938.

ment. Their uncompromising attitudes permitted union radicals to found their slogans for the class struggle on the fundamental right to organize.

These rabid labor-haters were to have their biggest "day" in the nationwide open shop movement of the 1920's. For those employers who advocated a get-tough policy, this was the era of lockouts and broken agreements — the heyday of industrial violence, spies, strikebreakers, and detective agencies. For the less violently tempered manufacturers, this was the decade of welfare paternalism that saw the growth of company representation plans and the beginnings of personnel administration — ideas that were for the most part cleverly introduced as a substitute for unionism. Everywhere, conscious efforts were made to undermine labor organizations and to disparage their leaders, to the end that the "American Plan" of an industrial society devoid of labor unions should prevail.

Many of the organized manufacturers who had earlier supported the protocol movement joined in this antiunion crusade. After years of collective bargaining, the Associated Fur Manufacturers passed an open shop resolution in 1920. And in the following year, the Wholesale Hat and Cap Manufacturers began a campaign to collect from each of its members a cash bond that would be forfeited for failure to follow association policies in a drive against the union. Meanwhile, in the men's clothing industry, the New York Clothing Manufacturers' Association fell into the hands of a small antiunion group led by a labor-hating lawyer, Harry Gordon, the counterpart of Dr. Hourwich in the labor movement. Under the control of this employer group, noted Sidney Hillman, president of the Amalgamated Clothing Workers' Union, "the association insists on imposing its arbitrary will and holding the union to its wilful decision."[5]

---

[5]Instead of a joint determination of the facts you stand on a one-sided claim as to what the facts are and upon such one-sided, untested data you wish to impose upon the union a piece-rate system. The distinction is fundamental: the union says, "Let us together study and establish the facts and as a result determine together how production can best be furthered." The association says, "We know all the facts, and you have to take our facts, and also take our conclusions from these facts, namely that piece work is the only cure." Since production is the common concern, only by joint effort can we secure it.

Thus did the outcroppings of an age-old antagonism between labor and management move past the barriers of the protocols to block the highways of collective action. At such times, labor arbitrators were beset with a host of legalistic disputes over "union security" and "management prerogatives" — terms that stood for the rights of labor and the rights of management, respectively. Attempts to settle these disputes often took on the atmosphere of courtroom proceedings between opposing counsel, where no quarter was given and no holds barred. Victory for one side invariably spelled defeat for the other. Such were the eddies of confusion through which advocates of cooperation were compelled to pick their way.[6]

—Hillman in ACWA, *Report and Proceedings,* Fifth Biennial Convention (May 1922), p. 18. The passage is reprinted from a reply that President Hillman sent the clothing manufacturers' association on Dec. 3, 1920.

Harry Gordon was also counsel for the Dress and Waist Manufacturers' Association, and after the association had signed its 1919 collective agreement with the dressmakers' union, Local 25, ILGWU, Gordon announced that his organization had "taken up the gage of battle thrown down by the Union on the issue of whether the workers shall run the industry." From a copy of Gordon's announcement filed in the Abelson papers.

During a prolonged strike of millinery workers in 1919 against the open shop policies of the manufacturers, an official of the National Association of Ladies' Hatters asserted that "at no time during the strike has the association recognized the existence of a union; and therefore, it could not deal with anything that, so far as they are concerned does not exist." *Women's Wear,* Nov. 10, 1919.

[6]Even more extreme was the attempt by the New York men's clothing manufacturers in the winter and spring of 1920–1921 to have the Amalgamated Clothing Workers' Union dissolved by court order for its radical philosophies. Coming during a seven-month lockout of union members by the New York manufacturers' associations, the case of J. Friedman & Co. v. ACWA, Supreme Court, New York County, demonstrated the power of economics over law. Although Mr. Justice F. B. Delehanty had ruled that a union could be dissolved, the case never came to trial, for the employers were more concerned with getting their workers back on the job than with winning a legal decision. More important for the historian than the case itself were the voluminous affidavits covering the industry submitted on behalf of the plaintiffs and the defendants. Printed copies of these affidavits are filed in the Abelson papers. The background of the J. Friedman & Co. case is treated in ACWA, *Report and Proceedings,* Fifth Biennial Convention (May 1922), pp. 55 ff., especially pp. 70–73; and in the files of ACWA's newspaper, *Advance,* from November

In the over-all course of events, however, the warmongers of industrial society played a minor role. They often stirred the waters of labor-management relations but they could not change the course of the stream. I. A. Hourwich, whose militant leadership of the radical elements within the ILGWU threatened to split the union asunder, was ultimately characterized as a "revolutionary" and forced to resign from his position as union chief clerk under the original protocol. Likewise, Harry Gordon, labor-baiting lawyer of the manufacturers, who thrived on generating hostility toward the workers, was not only denounced by the ACWA in 1918 as a "professional mischief maker" and a "Judas to the working class" but he and his small group of "mischief makers" were condemned in 1921 by his own Clothing Manufacturers' Association of New York "for having deliberately planned and forced on the community a bitter labor war which neither the employers nor the wage earners wanted."[7]

The Doctrine of Mutual Interests

The great currents in the history of collective bargaining for the needle trades flow straight from the springs of the Brandeis Con-

---

1920 through June 1921, especially the issues of Jan. 28, Feb. 14 and 18, 1921. See also the issues of *Daily News Record* for February 1921, especially the issue of Feb. 10, 1921.

[7] On the influence of I. A. Hourwich, see Louis Lorwin [Louis Levine] *The Women's Garment Workers* (1924), pp. 253–275. On the influence of Harry Gordon, see ACWA, *Report and Proceedings,* Third Biennial Convention (May 1918), pp. 62–66; and W. M. Leiserson, "Report on the Clothing Trade Fight," in *Daily News Record,* Jan. 24, 1921, or Leiserson's "Report to the Public," in ACWA's *Advance,* Jan. 28 and Feb. 4, 1921. For these activities Leiserson, impartial chairman under the agreement, was dismissed by the New York manufacturers and left the city for Rochester for a similar position in the men's clothing industry there. *Ibid.*

The 1921 collective agreement of the Clothing Manufacturers' Association of New York with the ACWA, effective June 1, 1921, stated:

> The vast majority of the employers had no desire to give up the agreements. They were forced into a fight with the union by the small group on the market committee and their lawyer. A just public opinion will condemn these manufacturers for having deliberately planned and forced on the community a bitter labor war which neither the employers nor the wage earners wanted.
>
> —From the text of the agreement as printed in the *Daily News Record,* June 3, 1921.

ferences. One of these currents was the "doctrine of mutual interests." At those conferences, where the organized forces of labor and management were first aligned against the unorganized forces of labor and management, J. A. Dyche had denounced the "ridiculous and fallacious contention on the part of the manufacturers that the Unions are so idiotic that we want to destroy their business." Speaking for the collaborationists, Dyche had insisted that "only lunatics would want to try to break up a business from which they were making their living." Putting the case positively, Dyche later argued that "it is as much in the interest of the legitimate manufacturer to have the costs of labor standardized as it is in the interest of the union."[8]

Another outspoken champion of mutual interests was Sidney Hillman, first president of the Amalgamated Clothing Workers of America. During the post-World War I depression in the men's clothing trade, Hillman worked to restrain his union from demanding benefits beyond the capacity of the industry to pay. "The labor movement," so he told his union convention in May 1920, "has more to lose than any other element in our society from breaking the industry." And, in the following year, after his union had won a decisive strike-lockout victory over the manufacturers of the New York market, Hillman again observed: "We are not trying to determine how much indemnity we can force the manufacturers to agree to pay. It is conceivable that they might agree to anything; but agreements are one thing, the clothing industry is another. So long as the industry thrives we can all get along very nicely; but let the industry break down and we couldn't get a decent meal out of an agreement."[9]

[8]Cloak, Suit and Skirt Manufacturers' Protective Association, *The Cloak Makers' Strike* (1910), p. 106. Dyche's later statement is from an address to the representatives of organized labor, Dec. 27, 1913, copy filed in the Abelson papers.

Reporting to his union convention in 1914, Dyche stated: "Our union can only make progress in so far as it will succeed in creating and maintaining and extending union standards and in equalizing the price of labor. But to accomplish this, the union alone is powerless. It requires the cooperation and good will of a strong employers' association as well as a strong union." ILGWU, *Report and Proceedings*, Twelfth Convention (June 1914), p. 59.

[9]ACWA, *Report and Proceedings*, Fourth Biennial Convention (May 1920), p. 237. Hillman's 1921 observations are from the *New York World*, May 29,

The doctrine of mutual interests has been implicit in the language of collective agreements since the days of the protocols. "Both parties" — stated the 1916 collective agreement of the embroidery and lace manufacturing industry — believe in fair standards for the trade. "Both parties" — runs the 1924 contract of the pleating and stitching industry — desire to improve conditions in the industry. Similarly, the 1932 agreement for the millinery industry announced the intention of both parties to join collectively in stamping out the evils of the trade. And the 1936 belt industry agreement pledged both parties to cooperate in eliminating unfair methods of competition in the trade. Almost invariably, collective agreements pledged both parties to cooperate in seeing that the agreements were faithfully enforced and that conflicts were settled by pacific means.[10]

If the objectives of collective action were often stated in terms of mutual intentions, the results were often recorded in terms of mutual accomplishments. Typical were the reports of joint labor-management campaigns to promote industry products. Working on the assumption that any slack in consumer demands threatened both parties, labor unions instituted moves to cooperate with the employers in saving stricken industries from further loss of business. When the fashion of bareheadedness threatened the existence of the cap trade in the late twenties, the cloth hat, cap and millinery workers' union joined the textile producers, the leather sweatband makers, and the cap manufacturers in a general campaign "to educate the public as to the necessity of headwear as a protection to health and its importance for a well-groomed ap-

---

1921. Here from ACWA's Research Library, *Redbook of Clippings,* p. 301. "The evolution in the stabilization of the New York market is absolutely dependent upon the joint efforts of manufacturers and Union." J. S. Potofsky, assistant general secretary of the ACWA, Feb. 5, 1921, as recorded in a printed collection of union affidavits submitted in the case of J. Friedman & Co. v. ACWA, p. 72. Copy filed in the Abelson papers.

[10]"Both parties are desirous of bettering conditions in the cloth hat and cap industry, and of obtaining as far as possible equalization of standards of labor throughout the industry by methods of conciliation and arbitration." From the text of the 1922 collective agreement between the Cloth Hat and Cap Manufacturers' Association and the New York Joint Council of the United Cloth Hat and Cap Makers of North America, printed in *Monthly Labor Review,* September 1922, vol. 15, p. 615.

pearance." Likewise, the millinery industry had its trade protection committee set up by the Millinery Stabilization Commission — itself a labor-management creation of the mid-thirties.[11]

Since 1941, New York manufacturers and unions of the dress industry have jointly maintained a dress institute that has provided information to buyers, conducted publicity campaigns, and otherwise worked to promote New York fashions throughout the world. Collective agreements in this trade have repeatedly harped upon the mutual benefits of promotional campaigns to union members and employers alike. "Such a campaign," stated the 1941 master contract, "will result in increased business to the members of the organized dress industry and in material advantages to the members of the Union employed by them who will derive therefrom greater continuity of employment and increased annual earnings."[12]

---

[11]The Millinery Trade Protection Committee held two fashion shows a year, cooperated with other agencies in promoting style development, and campaigned continually to make the consumer more "hat conscious." See the reports and surveys of economic conditions in the millinery trade prepared and issued by the Millinery Stabilization Commission that had been set up in 1935 to carry on the trade activities of the NRA millinery code. The first report is entitled "Economic Conditions of the Millinery Manufacturing Industry in the New York Metropolitan Area, 1935–1936." Much of this material is filed in the Abelson papers.

[12]The 1941 collective agreements of the dress industry included a "promotion clause" directing the employers' association and the union to join in a cooperative promotional campaign "with the objective of increasing the volume of production of the New York market, improving further the quality of its product, and offering even better values to the consumer...by publicizing the outstanding position in the field of style, fine workmanship and sound values of the New York market, by stimulating consumer demand in the United States and elsewhere, and by establishing New York as the fashion center of the world."

This promotion clause and the means for its implementation received the sanction of the New York Supreme Court against the opposition of an employer who refused to help bear the expense of the program on grounds that the subject was beyond the scope of collective bargaining. Minkoff v. Jaunty Junior, Inc., New York Supreme Court, Special Term, New York County, 35 N.Y.S. 2nd, 507 Part I (1942).

For an account of the promotion campaign in the dress industry, see *Women's Wear Daily*, Feb. 14, 1941; ILGWU, *Report and Proceedings*, Twenty-fifth Convention (May-June 1944), p. 69.

More recently, employers' associations and labor unions of the needle trades have joined to meet growing competition from foreign countries. The historic emphasis on developing foreign markets for domestic products has been superseded by concerted efforts to protect local markets from an influx of foreign-made goods. The mutual interests of workers and employers have been reflected in heavy lobbying activities and in attempts to negotiate international trade agreements restricting imports. By the 1960's, the ILGWU, long a stronghold of free trade policy, had come out openly for protective tariffs.[13]

The Industry-wide Approach

A second discernible current in the historic stream of collective bargaining could be labeled, "the industry-wide approach." Protection to the industry had been the keynote of the Brandeis Conferences leading to the original Protocol of Peace. It was, indeed, the rallying point around which the doctrine of mutual interests had been built. Both parties to the conferences had traced the source of their troubles to the plight of their industry and both stood to gain from general improvements in the trade. In a letter to the manufacturers just before the conferences began, the union had expressed its desire to reach agreement on all matters "which would promote the best interests of the trade."

Those who understood the protocol movement best saw in it two major objectives: (1) promoting the welfare of the industry, and (2) providing for the settlement of individual grievances. The first of these objectives had largely monopolized the attention of the delegates to the Brandeis Conferences. Moreover, promoting the welfare of the industry continued to be the dominant note in the development of collective bargaining for the needle trades. Louis D. Brandeis who witnessed the birth of the protocol movement in 1910 and then served as first chairman of the board of arbitration under the original cloak protocol looked upon the first protocol not so much as a means of adjusting "a difference between man and man" in order to render "an individual piece of justice in view of past fact," but rather as "a means by which the parties would come together and recognize...a difficulty of

---

[13]See above pp. 19–20.

the garment trade which all of those interested should give their best thought and best endeavor to."[14]

But the parties to collective agreements were not content with proclaiming a mutual desire to assist in uplifting their trades. They were also determined to implement this policy by creating permanent agencies endowed with the power to promote industry welfare. Many of these agencies assumed the role of "watch-dog" committees with broad investigative and advisory functions of industry-wide appeal. Others had the power to recommend action for the welfare of their trades. And a few could proceed on their own authority to protect their industries from threatening evils of whatever source or nature. In the apparel trades, the first permanent institutions of collective bargaining were more concerned with industry-wide problems than with settling particular issues in local disputes.

Under some agreements, the function of promoting industry welfare fell upon special agencies created expressly for that purpose. Thus the first collective agreement (1912) in the fur manufacturing industry provided for a "permanent committee of three outside citizens" to which all the "larger questions affecting the entire industry" would be referred. The first collective agreement (1915) in the boy's clothing industry created a special committee on industry-wide problems to which "any abuses that may exist or arise in the industry" would be referred. In 1913, representatives of the United Garment Workers and of the United Manufacturers and Merchant's Association (men's clothing industry) agreed to name a joint committee of six association members and six union members to study comparative conditions in other cities and "to consider ways and means for the uplift of the industry as a whole."[15]

---

[14]*Minutes,* Board of Arbitrators...[women's coat and suit trade] (Oct. 4, 1913), p. 94.

[15]Text of the fur manufacturing agreement is found in C. H. Winslow, *Collective Agreements in the Men's Clothing Industry,* U.S. Department of Labor, BLS Bulletin no. 198 (1916), p. 131. The boys' clothing manufacturers' agreement, effective Dec. 4, 1915, is from the Abelson papers, as is the pamphlet, dated Jan. 17, 1913, containing the agreement between the United Garment Workers and the United Manufacturers' and Merchants' Association.

The parties to the agreement hereby constitute a council of moderators consisting of three members designated by the union, three members designated by the manufacturers, and three members chosen by both

From time to time, the parties to collective agreements have been encouraged to adopt the industry-wide approach. In 1915, Mayor J. P. Mitchel's council of conciliation, created to save the first protocol from disruption, was empowered not only to settle immediate issues but also to formulate a constructive policy on the fundamental problems of wage standards and their enforcement throughout the women's coat and suit trade. Dr. J. L. Magnes, member of the council and a leader of the Jewish community, suggested a general committee for industry problems, consisting of three manufacturers, three workers, and a member of the council "to meet regularly and frequently, to discuss in amicable fashion the problems of the industry as they arise from time to time."[16]

This early trend was no passing phase in the evolution of collective bargaining. Especially during the Great Depression of the thirties did employers' associations and labor unions hasten to create joint agencies that would help to formulate industry-wide policies and to eradicate the evils of their trades. One such agency was the joint council named to represent the ILGWU and the employers' associations of the dress industry in 1932. This agency was expected to rise above the factional strife that accompanied the periodic negotiation of contracts. The need for such a council was thus set forth by Adolph Feldblum, impartial chairman for the industry:

Heretofore the various groups have always waited until their collective agreement was about to expire; then they would attempt to solve their distracting and complicated problems in a period of stress and strain, in anticipation of a threatened strike. Their conferences were held, not for the express purpose of discussing, deliberating upon and deciding the questions as members of a great industry, but rather as partisans, each group attempting to gain as much as possible and to give as little as possible. It is perfectly obvious that this must bring about a spirit of contention rather than of judicious and friendly co-

---

sides from the public at large. The council of moderators shall act as a body of final appeal on all matters affecting the industry as a whole.
—From the collective agreement, effective July 20, 1915, between the American Clothing Manufacturers' Association and the ACWA.

[16]*Minutes,* informal meeting between representatives of the women's coat and suit manufacturers and representatives of the ILGWU, with J. L. Magnes representing the council of conciliation, Oct. 11, 1915. Copy filed in the Abelson papers.

operation. While temporary victories may be won by one group or the other, there remain latent antagonisms which preclude the solidarity necessary for permanent stabilization of the industry.[17]

Encouraged by the development of industry codes under the National Industrial Recovery Act of 1933, many more employer groups joined with labor unions to create special agencies that would carry on the work of the codes after the NIRA was invalidated in 1935. The most important, but by no means the only agencies of this type, were the National Coat and Suit Industry Recovery Board and the Millinery Stabilization Commission — both products of supplemental agreements negotiated between employers' associations and labor unions in the mid-thirties. Devoted to stabilizing their trades, these agencies, like their predecessors, operated under a wide range of specific powers, generally supplemented by such residual authority as that granted the Millinery Stabilization Commission "to do any or all things necessary for the good and welfare of the industry."[18]

But the industry-wide approach to collective bargaining was never confined to special agencies and supplemental agreements operating on the periphery of collective action. The ultimate end of collective bargaining was to equalize labor costs by creating uniform standards of employment to which all manufacturers and all workers in a trade would subscribe. "The time will come soon," predicted B. H. Gitchell, labor manager of the New York men's clothing market in 1919, "when the employees of a single factory

---

[17]*Women's Wear Daily,* July 19, 1932. Compare the views of Louis Gabbe, president of the Association of Dress Manufacturers, *ibid.,* Feb. 26, 1932. "It is the intention of this agreement that the Conference Committee [five members from each side together with the impartial chairman], shall devote its attention chiefly to the solution of problems and disputes affecting the entire industry." From the 1934 collective agreement of the Men's Neckwear Manufacturers' Association with the United Neckwear Cutters' Union, Local 6939 of the American Federation of Labor.

[18]From the bylaws of the Millinery Stabilization Commission, as quoted in the *Industrial and Labor Relations Review,* October 1948, vol. 2, p. 19. Under their 1944 collective agreement, the organized factions of the buttonhole industry created a "Special Committee" to determine "how and in what manner and by what means may a greater degree of stabilization in the industry be achieved." From the 1944 collective agreement of the Buttonhole Manufacturers' Association with the Buttonhole Workers' Union, ILGWU.

will not think of presenting to their employer a demand for increased wages. They will understand that this is a question to be taken up nationally for all the workers in the industry."[19]

While awaiting this utopia of industry-wide bargaining, the normal agencies of contract administration took over the function of promoting industry welfare. Operating in more limited spheres, these creatures of local agreements nevertheless assumed an industry outlook that transcended the scope of their authority and tempered all their decisions. Third parties in the role of mediators, permanent umpires, or boards of arbitration found an industry-wide approach for the solution of all labor-management problems. Disputes were resolved with an eye to the best interests of the trade. Following this leadership, the lesser lights of contract administration also assumed that the organized forces of industry should rise above their differences for the sake of their trade.[20]

Over the years, the industry-wide approach to collective bargaining has frequently been more a product of union initiative than of employer sponsorship. Chaotic conditions in industry have had a more immediate effect upon the workers' fight for survival than upon the employers' fight to remain solvent. Disparities in labor standards have impinged more directly upon the union's struggle against nonunion competition than disparities in labor

---

[19]At the time, Sidney Hillman, president of the Amalgamated Clothing Workers' Union, strongly endorsed Gitchell's view that wage bargaining by individual firms would soon be a thing of the past. *New York World,* July 27, 1919.

[20]Typical were the views of S. A. Rosenblatt, long-time arbitrator for the women's coat and suit trade. In rebuking a jobber for discriminating against three of his contractors, Rosenblatt decreed: "The interests of this firm must conform to the interests of this industry and the firm must conform to and abide by the provisions of the collective agreement, which conformity constitutes the sole guarantee of continued maintenance of high standards in the industry." S. A. Rosenblatt, *Decisions,* Case no. 1262 (Jan. 7, 1936).

When the jobbers of the cap industry formed an association and signed their first collective agreement with the cap makers' union in 1926, the two parties reached an understanding "that the representatives of the Union, the Jobbers' Association, and the contractors would meet in conference from time to time to consider ways and means to put the trade on a more sound foundation and check the chaotic conditions." Cloth Hat, Cap and Millinery Workers' International Union, *Report and Proceedings,* Seventeenth Biennial Convention (May 1929), p. 7.

costs have impinged upon the struggle of the organized manufacturers against the unorganized employer segments of their trades. That is why needle trade unions have appealed so fervently for employer support in solving trade abuses; and that is why these unions, in the absence of employer support, have nevertheless pursued the industry-wide approach to collective bargaining. The general executive board of the United Hatters, Cap and Millinery Workers' International Union once offered this explanation:

> While employers, after they have all but destroyed the industry in which they are engaged, may salvage enough of their assets to go elsewhere and enter into some new venture in another industry, working people cannot so readily transfer their attachment and their skills to other industries. The stake of the workers in their industry is therefore greater than that of the employer. It is the realization of this fact that enables labor to view the industry as a whole.[21]

By no means all collective agreements of the needle trades revealed a concern for the industry-wide approach. Many initial contracts of newly organized industries undertook to seal the scars of past grievances but offered no guidelines for future conduct. Doomed to failure were the efforts of outside mediators to unite the parties on long-term planning for the development of their trades. "Neither the working man's organization nor the manufacturer's organizations are interested in bettering the conditions of the trade," lamented Mayer Shoenfeld, a former union leader, reflecting on the existing status of the 1913 strike in the men's clothing trades. "Their object is simply to oppose the wishes of the opposing party."[22]

Expanding Spheres of Collective Action

Sooner or later, the "doctrine of mutual interests" merged with the "industry-wide approach" to form a new current in the historic stream of collective bargaining. This new current, common to each branch of the needle trades, might aptly be termed, the

---

[21]United Hatters, Cap and Millinery Workers' International Union, *Report and Proceedings,* Third Convention (May 1939), pp. 10–11.

"It seems to be clear," stated Morris Sigman, president of the ILGWU in 1924, "that the first and foremost duty of our union is to bring order into the industry." ILGWU, *Justice,* Feb. 29, 1924.

[22]*Daily Trade Record,* Jan. 15, 1913.

"expanding spheres of collective action." No problem of the industry from wage scales to price policies, from hours of work to methods of production, from labor standards to fair trade practices was beyond its scope. Delegates to the Brandeis Conferences assumed that the welfare of the industry had to be measured in terms of minimum labor standards, business stabilization, and legitimate competition. All of these terms were embraced by the subsequent growth of collective bargaining in the needle trades.

The original Protocol of Peace had attempted to put a floor under competition by establishing minimum labor standards for the industry: a "standard minimum weekly scale of wages" for each of seventeen crafts; standards of sanitary conditions to be imposed by a joint board of sanitary control; limitations on days of work to not more than six days a week; and prohibitions on time contracts, home work, and submanufacturing. In addition, the protocol required each manufacturer to maintain a "union shop" which was defined, first and foremost, as "a shop where union standards as to working conditions, hours of labor, and rates of pay as herein stipulated prevail."

Taking labor out of competition had been the foremost aim of all those who favored the new approach to collective bargaining. "Whether or not referred to in any of the provisions of this protocol," stated the first collective agreement for the dress and waist industry, January 18, 1913, "the parties agree that it is essential that competition in the industry, so far as labor is concerned, shall be placed upon a plane of equality (making due allowance for difference in skill), and that both parties to the full extent of their power shall establish such equality."[23]

J. A. Dyche, general secretary-treasurer of the ILGWU and a vigorous defender of the protocol movement from the days of the Brandeis Conferences, repeatedly insisted that his union had no other objective than to equalize the price of labor among competing manufacturers. "I know that in our industry at least," so

---

[23]This clause was repeated in the text of the house dress protocol (Feb. 11, 1913) and in the text of the children's dress protocol (March 8, 1913). Texts of the three protocols appear in C. H. Winslow, *Conciliation, Arbitration, and Sanitation in the Dress and Waist Industry of New York City,* U. S. Department of Labor, BLS Bulletin no. 145 (April 10, 1914), pp. 22–26, 128–131, 133–136.

Dyche reported to his union convention in 1914, "the interest of the legitimate manufacturer is to have prices standardized so that his competitors should be compelled to pay the same prices." This objective could not be attained, so Dyche contended, so long as some cutters working uptown received $24 a week, while other cutters doing similar work downtown were paid only $12 a week.[24]

But those who worked through collective bargaining for the welfare of the industry never confined their efforts to equalizing terms of employment or to standardizing labor costs. From the days of the Brandeis Conferences, the sphere of collective action has been as broad as the range of mutual interests. Parties to collective agreements have seldom been deterred by hard and fast concepts of management prerogatives or the exclusive rights of organized labor. On the whole, theories of respective rights and duties have given way to the practical advantages of collective action. Defense of management prerogatives in the realm of "business" problems

---

[24]ILGWU, *Report and Proceedings,* Twelfth Convention (June 1914), pp. 48, 59. See also J. A. Dyche on the objectives of unionism in *Minutes,* Meeting of the Cloak, Suit and Skirt Manufacturers' Protective Association (Dec. 3, 1912), pp. 3–4.

The "plane of equality" thesis, expressed in terms of equal labor costs or of uniform labor standards, was often affirmed and reaffirmed in the headwear industries. Soon after the negotiation of the first collective agreement between the Ladies' Hat Manufacturers' Protective Association and the millinery workers' union in 1915, the association announced to the officers of the union that "the main aim of our entire agreement is to eliminate competition in labor, and we cannot do this, unless a standard is adopted and maintained." Twelve years later, the general executive board of the Cloth Hat, Cap and Millinery Workers' International Union reported to the union convention that "the only way to keep up some standards of decency in the cap industry is by doing away with competition at the expense of labor; and that can only be brought about by the establishment of uniform working conditions throughout the industry." After still another decade, the Allied Hat Manufacturers and the United Hatters, Cap and Millinery Workers jointly expressed a desire to secure for their industry "such equalization of labor standards as will eliminate competition based solely on the maintenance of sub-standards of employment or the exercise of oppressive and unfair labor practices." See letter, dated Jan. 17, 1916, from the hat manufacturers' association to Locals 24 and 42 of the United Cloth Hat and Cap Makers of North America, filed in the Abelson papers; Cloth Hat, Cap and Millinery Workers' International Union, *Report and Proceedings,* Sixteenth Biennial Convention (May 1927), p. 175; collective agreement of the Allied Hat Manufacturers with the millinery workers' union, effective June 1, 1937.

never became a serious barrier to joint action that offered more effective control of "illegitimate" competition. Nor has union defense of "internal union affairs" prevented joint action with management on internal union problems where such action offered more attractive gains to organized labor.

Delegates to the Brandeis Conferences were as much concerned with methods of production as with wage scales or hours of work. Few topics received more attention than the control of subcontracting. When this matter came up for discussion, J. H. Cohen, counsel for the manufacturers' association, considered it "probably one of the largest subjects we have to deal with." Yet no one suggested that the use of contracting, subcontracting, or submanufacturing as a method of production was a management prerogative beyond the pale of collective action. "All the factors of industry," once observed Dr. Henry Moskowitz, an early arbitrator of the needle trades, "are so interrelated that you cannot discuss a minimum wage without discussing methods of manufacture and methods of arriving at efficiency."[25]

The right to run the business that some employers in 1910 would defend to the death against radical unionism was soon shared voluntarily with "conservative" unions through collective bargaining. The "cooperative commonwealth," so roundly denounced in principle at the Brandeis Conferences, soon appeared well on the way to reality under the banner of controlled competition. The first protocol was only two years old when a critic of the agreement noted with a touch of sarcasm that the parties had not only set up a joint grievance committee, a joint arbitration committee, and a joint sanitary board but also:

To carry on still further this inspiring scheme of capital and labor, to put an end to friction between them, and to enforce justice and equality, in all their relations, a committee of ten is empowered to decide upon all conditions of work and business competition, not only for themselves but very unselfishly for the entire industry. What is "desirable" and what is "undesirable" competition comes within its jurisdiction. The great cloak and suit trade is thus beneficially regulated. The Standard Oil Company never claimed to do more.[26]

[25] J. H. Cohen in *The Cloak Makers' Strike,* p. 61; Henry Moskowitz in the *Outlook,* May 10, 1916, vol. 113, p. 86.

[26] *Women's Wear,* Dec. 10, 1912. See also *ibid.,* Dec. 5, 1912 and *Daily Trade Record,* Dec. 6 and 11, 1912.

The organized segments of the women's coat and suit trade never lost sight of their original aims in collective bargaining. "You are not dealing here with an organization that represents the entire industry, like a Steel Trust or a railroad," explained J. H. Cohen to his industry's board of arbitration in 1913, "...you are dealing with a situation where there is competition all the time, and where you have got to meet it, as a homely fact, every minute of your manufacturing existence."[27] Jobbers, contractors, inside manufacturers, and union members continued to look upon their labor agreements as a medium for regulating this competition.

When negotiations for a new contract for the women's coat and suit trade broke down in the mid-twenties, Governor Alfred E. Smith named a special commission to study the industry and make recommendations to the parties. Like the parties themselves, the commission made no effort to limit the scope of collective bargaining. Its final report in 1926 was directed more at stabilizing the industry than at providing guides for the determination of wages, hours, and working conditions. "Whereas, among other things," noted the association of contractors in accepting this report, "the final recommendations include proposals to control unfair and destructive competition between jobbers and sub-manufacturers, to regularize production, to eliminate the non-union shop evil and to effect the equal enforcement of union standards throughout the industry..." be it resolved that the report be accepted.[28]

Union Views on Business Policies

Union supporters of the protocol movement were quite willing to encompass all aspects of production within the scope of the bargaining power. Most needle trade unions have always held the worker to be so tied up with the destiny of his industry that business problems logically fell within the sphere of collective action. "We know," stated the general executive board of the United Hatters, Cap and Millinery Workers' International Union in 1939, "...that an impoverished industry can not yield a substantial or adequate return to the workers employed in it. Im-

---

[27]*Minutes,* Board of Arbitrators...[women's coat and suit trade] (August 4, 1913), p. 421.

[28]Governor's Advisory Commission, *Final Recommendations* (May 20, 1926); *Women's Wear,* June 15, 1926.

poverished industries...easily become the prey for all sorts of parasites and adventurers, while the responsible and legitimate employers in it are driven from its midst."[29]

Unions in the headwear trades have been particularly active in demanding that manufacturers wake up to the need for working together to save their own industries. Since 1915, the general executive board of the United Cloth Hat, Cap and Millinery Workers' Union has periodically revealed to the union convention more information about the headwear industry than is available from any employer source. On the strength of this information, the union has from time to time proposed drastic measures to save headwear firms from bankruptcy. Their proposals have varied from forbidding employers to make hats they couldn't sell to striking against employers who didn't allow for a fair profit on the sale price of their products.[30]

"There has been no collective conscience in the industry on the part of the manufacturers," lamented Max Zaritsky, president of the Cloth Hat, Cap and Millinery Workers' International Union, addressing a joint conference representing the union and the Women's Headwear Group, October 20, 1931. "So much so that there is no control of the selling or of the merchandising or of

---

[29]United Hatters, Cap and Millinery Workers' International Union, *Report and Proceedings,* Third Convention (May 1939), pp. 10–11. In a typewritten statement, dated July 27, 1937, Nathaniel Spector, vice-president of the International and manager of the Millinery Workers' Joint Board in the New York area, had expressed similar views: "We know that whoever may be the immediate victim of cutthroat competition and chiseling practices, eventually labor must pay the price. An impoverished and stricken industry exacts a toll from all who depend upon it for a livelihood. None can escape the damage." Copy filed in the Abelson papers.

[30]"It is high time that our employers fully realize their obligations to the industry and give their wholehearted cooperation to the efforts by the Millinery Stabilization Commission to eliminate completely the production of non-profitable merchandise, unfair trade practices and contracting and sweatshops." Nathaniel Spector, an active union official for more than twenty years, to Paul Abelson, impartial chairman of the millinery industry, letter, dated Feb. 1, 1937, filed in the Abelson papers.

In May 1937 some 1400 millinery workers, members of Local 24, met and adopted a six-point program, one point of which stated that "firms will be prohibited from producing certain types of hats which they cannot sell." *Women's Wear Daily,* May 21, 1937.

the manufacturing end of the business. There is no coordination, no cooperation among the manufacturers themselves. As a result, every one participating in the industry pays the price — manufacturer and worker alike — whether it is in the form of losses or lack of profits or whether it is in the form of lack of earnings for the worker. . . ." As early as 1924, Zaritsky had pointed the way of things to come with this observation:

The all too free play of the blind economic forces of supply and demand work havoc under the special conditions of our trade. Far from benefiting the public they create instability and insecurity bordering on utter chaos, demoralization and degradation of the trade into a sweatshop menace. However great and essential our objections are against the trust controlled basic industries, such as steel, coal, oil, packing, etc. . . . the total lack of all such control and regularization is by far not an unmixed blessing.[31]

The institutions of collective bargaining were designed, in part, to offset this lack of cohesion among employers within each trade. Wherever the plight of an industry arose from cutthroat business practices, a floor under competition for business was as necessary to the welfare of the worker as a floor under competition for labor. "The employer and the employees have a mutual interest not only in labor problems," once stated David Dubinsky, president of the International Ladies' Garment Workers' Union, "but in employer problems such as returns, unfair competition, retailers' mistreatment and other abuses and unfair practices. We know that ultimately such practices affect us." When the women's coat and suit trade lost an estimated $7,100,000 in six months of 1937 from returned merchandise, Isidore Nagler, union manager of the Cloakmakers' Joint Board, was quick to point out that an unscrupulous practice between retailers and manufacturers was as much a menace to labor as to business competitors.[32]

---

[31]A typewritten copy of Zaritsky's 1931 address is filed in the Abelson papers. Zaritsky's 1924 statement is from a lecture on "What Ails the Cap Trade" as reported in the *Headgear Worker*, April 18, 1924.

[32]Dubinsky in *Consumers Protection Label* (pamphlet) [1940], p. 5. The estimated loss from returned merchandise was that of Samuel Klein, chairman of the Fair Trade Practice Committee of the National Coat and Suit Industry Recovery Board, set up in 1935 to carry on the work of the NRA codes. That estimate and Nagler's reaction appear in *Women's Wear Daily*, August 31, 1937.

In extending the scope of bargaining issues, the ILGWU has cut broad swathes through the exclusive domain of management prerogatives. Particularly where employers were suffering from business reverses has this union offered managerial guidance to keep alive firms on the brink of disaster. In the fall of 1923, the ILGWU and three associations of jobbers, contractors, and inside manufacturers in the women's coat and suit trade set up a joint commission which, among other things, proposed "to examine into the internal factors of the shops in question and see whether the fault lies in such things as inefficient management, lack of business acumen, ignorance of the principles of cost calculations, prohibitive overhead or any other internal factor." The Amalgamated Clothing Workers of America was equally concerned with the lack of competence among the manufacturers of men's clothing. "We have employers in the industry," observed one spokesman for the union, "who possess no more business ability than that of a peanut peddler; they do not know how to handle their own books and accounts."[33]

Contract Clauses on the Scope of Bargaining

Mutual support for a broad sphere of collective action was soon woven into the warp and woof of collective agreements. The original protocol of the dress and waist industry was amended in 1916 to provide for a board of protocol standards, which, among other things, was authorized to study methods of shop management and matters affecting efficiency of operations. Empowered to recommend new standards and regulations for the industry, this board, representing the union, the association, and the public, was first

---

[33]ILGWU, *Justice,* Nov. 16, 1923; for the ACWA, see J. A. Dyche, *Bolshevism in American Labor Unions* (1926), pp. 160–161.

This trade of cloakmaking is the only occupation they [the workers] know, and upon it they depend for a livelihood. It is to their interest, therefore, that this industry be strong, prosperous and progressive. To stand on the sideline and watch the industry go to perdition will not gain an ounce of bread for them or their dependents. They must take a hand in the control of its destiny; they must become industry-minded if they are to gain for themselves the power, influence and respect to which they are entitled as its most useful and productive force.

　　—ILGWU, general executive board, in the union's *Report and Proceedings,* Twentieth Convention (December 1929), p. 63.

assigned the task of making a thorough examination of competitive practices in the trade.[34]

Throughout the years, the organized forces of this industry have formally acknowledged the expanding range of their activities. Going beyond such general statements of purpose as "promoting the best interests of the clothing industry," the preamble to the major 1941 collective agreements for the dress industry contained this phrase: "Whereas the parties hereto recognize that employers and workers alike have much to gain through co-operative effort in stabilizing the industry, in providing for its efficient management, in planning for improvement therein, in encouraging and effecting the modernization of production units...." These agreements state further that the industry must be "strong, prosperous, and progressive" and that the workers must be "industry-minded."[35]

During the forties, collective agreements of the dress industry also contained "efficiency" clauses demanding efficiency in the use of plant equipment, efficiency in management supervision, and efficiency in the flow of work. An impartial chairman named in the contracts was empowered to "determine the procedure to be followed by the member of the Association in his shop to effectuate the above [efficiency] provision." Acting on the authority to promulgate rules and regulations to give effect to the efficiency clause, Impartial Chairman Harry Uviller in July 1941 established in his

---

[34]Lorwin, *The Women's Garment Workers,* pp. 300–317.

There shall be created a conference board under this agreement to consist of five representatives of the union and five representatives of the association for the purpose of from time to time considering and passing upon general trade problems, and to more effectually carry out the purpose and spirit of this agreement.
—From the 1925 collective agreement between the Association of Dress Manufacturers and the ILGWU. The text of this agreement is printed in *Women's Wear,* Jan. 19, 1925.

[35]The quotations are from the 1941 collective agreement between the United Better Dress Manufacturers' Association and the Dressmakers' Joint Board, ILGWU. Other dress agreements of this decade between the Dressmakers' Joint Board and each of the following associations — Affiliated Dress Manufacturers, National Dress Manufacturers' Association, United Popular Priced Dress Manufacturers' Association, and the Popular Priced Dress Manufacturers' Group — contain similar, if not identical, phrases.

office an efficiency engineering department staffed by three industrial engineers who were to visit the shops to advise and instruct employers on proper procedures for efficient operations. Upon complaint of the union, these engineers made investigations of alleged inefficiencies and issued appropriate instructions. The impartial chairman could impose appropriate penalties upon those who refused to comply. Within the first three years, he rendered eighteen formal decisions on the operation of the efficiency clause.[36]

Whole groups of employers signed away their managerial birthright to determine their methods of production or the character of their products. Jobbers who gave up their right to open inside shops with less than a full complement of workers (including fourteen machine operators), were on one occasion even denied the right to employ four or five samplemakers to help with designing women's coats and suits. Such a practice, observed Impartial Chairman R. V. Ingersoll in 1925, "would create a new type of business organization not contemplated when the agreements were signed and involving new and difficult problems." Even more drastic were contract provisions giving needle trade unions joint control with employers' associations over changes in the nature of the products to be manufactured. "It is agreed," stated the 1931 master contract between the New York Clothing Manufacturers' Exchange and the ACWA, "that a committee representing the parties hereto be appointed in the near future to devise suitable methods upon which a manufacturer may add, change, or discontinue any line of clothing heretofore or hereafter to be manufactured by him."[37]

---

[36]*Women's Wear Daily,* Feb. 14, 1941, contained the texts of the original efficiency clauses. See ILGWU, *Report and Proceedings,* Twenty-fifth Convention (May–June 1944), pp. 69–70. In 1941, the general office of the ILGWU announced the formation of a management engineering department which, among other things, was empowered "to assist in improving manufacturing techniques and operating methods of all branches of the ladies' garment industry with which the earnings of our workers are intimately bound," *ibid.,* pp. 50–54. Headed by a young production engineer, Dr. William Gomberg, this department in the early years of its existence helped the managements of some two hundred plants a year increase their productivity and get back on their feet.

[37]For Ingersoll's decision, see *Women's Wear,* Jan. 19, 1925.

Whenever an Employer shall desire to install a department for the manufacture of a line of millinery not heretofore manufactured by him

The expanding sphere of collective action likewise invaded the realm of "internal union affairs" — all in the name of promoting the welfare of the industry. In return for the closed shop, unions agreed to keep their doors open to receive new members, and on many occasions unions were directed to admit workers whom they did not want. "In the event that the question is raised as to the fairness and justice of the action of the Union in refusing a working card to a worker" — runs the 1932 collective agreement in the fur manufacturing industry — "the issue shall be determined by a special sub-committee of the Conference Committee consisting of two members of the Conference Committee representing the Employers (one from each Association) and two members of the Conference Committee representing the Union and the Chairman of the Conference Committee."[38]

From time to time, the joint machinery of contract administration has also exercised jurisdiction over such other normal subjects of internal union control as (1) the determination of dues and initiation fees, where collective agreements require them to be "reasonable"; (2) the status of union membership, where collective agreements dictate that the conditions of "good standing" must be "reasonable"; and (3) the allocation of union help to manufacturers. "Any claim of neglect or improper allocation of help to manufacturers in the supply of help by the Union," stated

---

in order to determine whether that line shall be profitable, he may do so provided that prior thereto, and upon notice to the Association and the Union, he shall apply to the Impartial Chairman and obtain the approval of the Impartial Chairman therefor, provided that the tenure of employment of the normal staff of workers employed by the Employer is not disturbed.
    —From the 1938 collective agreement of the Eastern Women's Headwear Association with the United Hatters, Cap and Millinery Workers' International Union and the Joint Board of Millinery Workers' Union, Locals 2, 24, and 42.

For a later collection of contract clauses, only a few of which are from the needle trades, dealing with various aspects of union-management cooperation, see *Management Rights and Union-Management Cooperation*, U.S. Department of Labor, BLS Bulletin no. 1425–5 (April 1966), pp. 25–68.

[38]From the 1932 collective agreement of the Associated Fur Coat and Trimming Manufacturers and the New York Fur Trimming Manufacturers with the American Federation of Labor and the International Fur Workers' Union and the Furriers' Joint Council of New York, Locals 101, 105, 110, and 115.

the 1922 collective agreement between the Cloth Hat and Cap Manufacturers' Association and the United Cloth Hat and Cap Makers' Union, "shall be considered and acted upon by the Board of Adjustment." Even the union label — that historic insignia of union standards of workmanship — passed from sole control of the union into the hands of the joint agencies of contract administration.

Collective Bargaining and Private Rights

To demonstrate that control over competition in labor costs was the primary motive behind collective bargaining for the needle trades is not to deny the existence of other motives that were a part of the movement to establish law and order in industry. In many instances, these other motives were the major considerations binding employers and workers alike to their joint agencies for industrial self-government. In many other cases, however, these additional motives were a disconcerting influence that diverted attention from the central theme of controlled competition and threatened to disrupt the unity of purpose essential for successful operations. Not everyone who participated in the processes of collective bargaining interpreted the work of his hands with a single mind.

Pre-eminent among these other motives was the use of collective bargaining as a means of preserving individual rights. At the Brandeis Conferences of 1910, J. H. Cohen, counsel for the manufacturers and a leading light in the protocol movement, conceded that the delegates were faced with "a very big human problem." In addition to business issues, he said, "there is the big problem of how to treat justly and fairly the 80,000 people who are in our industry, and still preserve our industry." Yet Cohen's half-hearted move to shift the focus of attention from the woods to the trees found little support. The original Protocol of Peace contained no industrial "bill of rights," not even a clause protecting workers from discharge without just cause.[39]

From a panoramic view of industry's toughest assignments, some would turn the spotlight of collective action upon specific grievances that beset the individual worker or the individual employer.

---

[39]*The Cloak Makers' Strike,* p. 25.

Here the crowning objective was that of protecting individuals from the forms of injustice that the "bosses" and the "people" heaped upon each other. A prominent Philadelphia dress manufacturer who had been approached to accept the principles of the protocol movement for his city put the two-pronged purpose of collective bargaining bluntly: If the object of the protocol "meant standardizing the trade and equalizing conditions," then he would "certainly welcome any standard which the market could stand, provided the Union would compel his competitors to come up to it." But he would have nothing to do with the movement if "it would mean that every time I discharged one of the 600 girls I employ, the clerks of the Union and the Association would cross-examine me to find out whether I was guilty of unfair discrimination."[40]

Whatever the views of the founding fathers, collective bargaining in the needle trades did at times become so involved with issues of private rights and industrial justice as to becloud the basic concept of controlled competition. This tendency became apparent from the administration of the very first collective agreement for the women's coat and suit trade. This original Protocol of Peace had provided administrative machinery adapted to the purposes for which the protocol movement was founded. The committee on grievances that became the legislative body for the industry naturally commanded the best brains of both parties to the collective agreement. The board of arbitration was composed of prominent leaders in business and the professions who sacrificed time from their other duties to render final decisions that set the pattern of conduct for the industry. Neither body was prepared for the type of work that soon fell into its hands.

Between April 15, 1911 and October 30, 1913, the agencies set up for administering the first Protocol of Peace adjusted 7,656

---

[40]ILGWU, *Report and Proceedings,* Twelfth Convention (June 1914), p. 58. "In the private executive sessions of the employers' association I have heard the president say repeatedly that the association stood for justice to the workers as well as to its own members, and that the efforts of its officers would be fruitless unless the industry were raised to a higher plane." J. H. Cohen, counsel for the Cloak, Suit and Skirt Manufacturers' Protective Association, party to the original Protocol of Peace in his *Law and Order in Industry* (1916), p. 16.

grievances. If the allotted time for handling these complaints had been evenly distributed over this period of two and one-half years, grievances would have been settled at the rate of sixty a week, twelve a day, or one every forty minutes. Obviously, this was no fitting assignment for the distinguished editor of the *Independent* (Hamilton Holt) and two brilliant lawyers (Morris Hillquit and Louis D. Brandeis), all three of whom had full-time responsibilities elsewhere than on the board of arbitration for the women's coat and suit trade. Nor could two trusted representatives of the workers and two respected delegates of the manufacturers serving as members of the committee on grievances be expected to neglect their other responsibilities to handle such a case load, not even after the committee's members were increased to five from each side and the committee became a board of grievances.[41]

Along with the devotees of industrial justice came the advocates of industrial democracy. Sensing that adequate protection to the individual must rest upon a joint determination of policies, these defenders of group participation would apply to their workshops a framework of government patterned after the political structure of civil society. Collective labor agreements would become fundamental constitutions of the industrial community defining and limiting the powers, rights, and duties of the parties, while joint agencies of the impartial machinery would be vested with legislative, administrative, and judicial powers comparable to those exercised by the legislatures, executives, and courts of civil society. While many who advocated worker participation in the government of industry were seeking a conservative escape from more radical schemes to overthrow the ownership of private property —

---

[41]See C. H. Winslow, *Industrial Court of the Cloak, Suit, and Skirt Industry of New York City*, U.S. Department of Labor, BLS Bulletin no. 144 (March 19, 1914), p. 19. In the early months of the dress protocol, the dress and waist industry encountered similar experiences. "The number of complaints on both sides," wrote the Dress and Waist Manufacturers' Association in a letter, dated Sept. 21, 1913, to Local 25, ILGWU, "is now more than 4000, representing at least one complaint for every half hour of every working day since the signing of the Protocol." As quoted in a printed complaint of the Dress and Waist Manufacturers' Association, dated Oct. 15, 1913, against the ILGWU, at p. 20; copy filed in the Abelson papers. Statistics on the 4,566 complaints filed in the first eleven months of the dress and waist protocol are given in Winslow, *Conciliation, Arbitration, and Sanitation in the Dress and Waist Industry of New York City.*

just as the advocates of industrial jurisprudence were seeking to avert a class war that would put the worker in control of industry — these new concepts nevertheless tended to create more eddies of confusion within the main stream of collective bargaining.

To assume that these were "distracting" diversions from the main stream of collective bargaining is not to imply that the delegates to the Brandeis Conferences of 1910, or that the signers of the first protocols, were devoid of human understanding for the rights of the individual or for the values of industrial democracy. Some inside manufacturers insisted all along that improving the lot of their employees — an impossible goal in the face of illegitimate competition — was a controlling motive behind their support for the protocol movement. "There can be no more question about the validity of the principle of collective bargaining in industry than there can be about the principle of constitutional government in a democracy," so J. H. Cohen, counsel for the manufacturers and father of the protocol movement, testified before the U. S. Commission on Industrial Relations, April 8, 1914. "The fact is, the working people have just as much right to have their grievances heard, and heard collectively, as the great mass of people have the right to vote at the polls upon the matters that affect them, and we are coming to recognize that fact in industry, just as we long ago recognized it in politics."

The entire history of collective bargaining abounds with evidences of respect for the rights of the individual. Many prominent manufacturers of the needle trades were members of the Society for Ethical Culture and would happily apply the humanitarian principles of their order to industrial relations. Also beyond reproach were the moral standards of Kehillah, the Jewish Community, whose matchless leader, J. L. Magnes, was to play an important role in the evolution of collective bargaining. Those who directed the institutions of industrial self-government never lost their souls. In scores of cases, the proceeds from fines collected for contract infractions went to the support of destitute groups or were contributed to the relief of suffering in foreign lands. Labor unions and employers' associations sanctioned these moves with equal enthusiasm.[42]

---

[42]See a summary of the principles of the Business Men's Group of the Society for Ethical Culture in the *Survey*, August 15, 1922, vol. 48, p. 619.

In a sense, the protocol movement owes its origin to the humanitarian reactions of satisfied workers who were "willing to starve for other people's sake." Associated with well-run factories where acceptable standards of employment already prevailed, these workers, nevertheless, assumed responsibility for wretched conditions in other shops and accepted leadership in precipitating strikes at the best-run plants to support revolt in the downtrodden segments of the trade. "All the 'welfare' work, all the decent treatment, all the consideration, all the effort to be fair and just to the people in our own shops," noted one observer in 1912, "is of no avail so long as there are conditions in the industry that make for protest."[43]

Humanitarian principles were likewise revealed by the expanding spheres of collective action. Protection from the hazards of old age, accidents, sickness, and unemployment were subjects of contract negotiations in the needle trades long before these issues had aroused sufficient public interest for effective political action. Then, when civil laws were finally enacted to help meet these hazards, the parties to needle trade agreements continued to build elaborate superstructures of protection upon the minimum foundations of state and federal legislation. Early in 1921 — to cite a single example — the organized cloak manufacturers of Cleveland and the ILGWU agreed that employers contribute 10 percent of their payrolls to an unemployment insurance fund that would provide each worker with one half his minimum wage for each week of idleness within a guaranteed employment period of forty weeks a year.[44]

Your fund procedure is noteworthy because it establishes as a matter of highly commendable routine the consistent giving to humanitarian causes, day after day, year after year, in good times and bad.

—Wendell L. Willkie, addressing a women's coat and suit industry banquet at which nearly half a million dollars raised in 1943 was given to twenty charitable and war relief agencies. *Women's Wear Daily*, Jan. 14, 1944.

[43]*Women's Wear*, Dec. 5, 1912; *Daily Trade Record*, Dec. 6, 1912.

[44]The "Cleveland Experiment" is reported in Sylvia Kopald and Ben Selekman, "The Epic of the Needle Trades," *Menorah Journal*, 1928–1929, vol. 15, p. 534. See also John R. Commons and others, *History of Labor in the United States, 1896–1932*, vol. III, pp. 262–266.

The humanitarian motive was outstanding in the contributions of third parties to the development of collective bargaining. Public-spirited citizens who offered their services were particularly disturbed by the lack of sanitary conditions in the workshops and by the interminable strikes and lockouts that entailed so much human suffering and sacrifice. Assuming the role of intercessors, these men found the termination of industrial strife as worthy a cause to support as was the termination of international warfare. They considered the goals of industrial peace as valid an objective as the goals of international peace. Since industrial warfare thrived on alleged mistreatment of the individual — just as international wars thrived on alleged mistreatment of the nation — the structure of industrial peace had to be erected on the solid foundation of industrial justice.[45]

Throughout the needle trades employers, too, were often the victims of injustice. Sudden strikes were as calamitous for the

---

"To those who look upon business as more than mere barter and money making, who consider it a form of social service, the spectacle of a board of directors of a business organization giving their valuable time and energy to safeguard the high standards of an industry, and at the same time to deal equitably with organized labor, is worthy of highest admiration." *Cloak and Suit Review,* organ of the women's coat and suit manufacturers, September 1911, as quoted by Gertrude Barnum, union organizer, in the *Independent,* Oct. 2, 1912, vol. 73, p. 778.

In his *Law and Order in Industry* at p. 16, J. H. Cohen, counsel for the women's coat and suit manufacturers, stated that his clients had shown "a definite determination to put the industry on a higher plane and to make of the business at least something which would not make the employer shamefaced when admitting to his neighbors and to his children than he was a cloak manufacturer."

[45]Hamilton Holt, editor of the *Independent* and an original member of the board of arbitration under the first Protocol of Peace, coupled the protocol with the peace treaties initiated by President Howard Taft, anticipating that "the time is not far distant when both industries and nations will be governed by law, rather than by brute force." See Gertrude Barnum's article in the *Independent,* Oct. 3, 1916, vol. 73, p. 777. Also prominent, since the turn of the century, in third party activities fostering good labor-management relations and promoting the peaceful settlement of industrial disputes was the work of the National Civic Federation. Several of its members were also active in the protocol movement during the formative years of collective bargaining. See Marguerite Green, *The National Civic Federation and the American Labor Movement, 1900–1925* (1956).

manufacturers as sudden discharges were disastrous for the workers; adequate production standards as indispensable to the employer's business as an adequate living wage was essential to the workers' employment. Business security was no less vital than security on the job. These considerations were universal in their application. They transcended questions of products or methods of production, questions of shop size or location of the plant or seasonal fluctuations or stages of the business cycle. Industrial justice was as basic to industrial society as justice in the courts was fundamental to civil society or as international justice was fundamental to the community of nations.[46]

Industry Problems and Individual Justice

Sponsors of the protocol movement acknowledged these impelling forces of industrial life. Nevertheless, their job was to put first things first. Reconciling concepts of personal justice with principles of controlled competition became a stark necessity if the protocol movement was to survive. At least some attention must be devoted to individual rights as well as to industry problems. Within months after the first protocol was signed, the board of arbitration set out "to formulate such effective methods of procedure and rules to govern all disputes that recourse to the Board of Arbitration would be unnecessary save in rare cases." The resulting extension of administrative machinery made possible the disposition of thousands of cases affecting individual workers and employers but tended further to divert attention from the central theme of collective bargaining.[47]

Those in the vanguard of the protocol movement were hard-pressed to keep the minds of the rank and file centered on the need

---

[46]After all, there are two leading principles underlying this contract: as far as the employer is concerned, it is the immunity against shop strikes, principally; as far as the workers are concerned, it is the peaceful redress of grievances, principally.
　　—Morris Hillquit, counsel for the ILGWU, in *Minutes,* Arbitration Proceedings between the Dress and Waist Manufactures' Association and the ILGWU (March 31, 1916), vol. 6, p. 1565.

[47]See "Rules and Plan of Procedure of the Board of Grievances" in C. H. Winslow, *Conciliation, Arbitration, and Sanitation in the Cloak, Suit, and Skirt Industry in New York City,* U.S. Department of Commerce and Labor, Bureau of Labor, Bulletin no. 98 (January 1912), pp. 220–224.

for controlling competition. Disputes over the structure and processes of collective bargaining were largely an outgrowth of differences over the purpose and function of collective bargaining. The worker's right to a job and the employer's right to discharge were far more appealing slogans on which to debate the principles of collective action. Referring to these conflicts over individual rights, J. H. Cohen once voiced the impatience of the employers at making their industry an "experiment station for society generally." But as spokesman for the cloak and suit manufacturers he was perfectly willing to have the labor union through collective agreements "welded into some sort of a police department for the industry."[48]

The highest official statement on the objectives of the protocol movement logically came from the supreme arbitrating authority for each trade. On January 21, 1915, such an opinion, couched in general terms, came from the board of arbitration for the women's coat and suit trade. Nathan Schuss, a coat and suit manufacturer, had "laid off" several operators for alleged reasons of incompetence or disloyalty, and he refused to take some of them back again. Charging a violation of protocol principles, the ILGWU carried the case through extended hearings and a deadlock by the board of grievances to the board of arbitration for final action. In the course of these developments (and subsequent elucidations following the case), the fundamental issues of private rights and industrial justice were thoroughly aired, if not thoroughly clarified. Fittingly, Louis D. Brandeis, chairman and public representative, spoke for the board in laying down the principles that were to prevail.

While conceding that the individual worker is entitled to "such fairness of general treatment and of conditions as may be possible and practicable," Brandeis made clear that the parties to the protocol should direct their efforts primarily toward "mitigating in large measure the present barbaric conditions which prevail in this industry." Speaking for the board of arbitration in this famous Nathan Schuss case, Brandeis proposed that procedures be adopted that would permit the brains of the industry to concentrate on the fundamental problems of the trade:

---

[48]Cohen, *Law and Order in Industry*, pp. 38, 159.

We believe that every case in which an employer or employee considers himself aggrieved, should receive careful and adequate consideration; because that is an essential part of the protocol, indeed the life of the protocol. Nevertheless that it ought to be possible now to devise methods and means so as to release the energies and the time of those who are best able to give attention to the larger problems of the industry. The individual grievances should be investigated and adjusted mainly through the efforts of the clerks or the Committee on Immediate Action. The time of the other officers in high stations among both employers and employees should be reserved for the consideration of the fundamental difficulties referred to, and the solution of which seems to us to be absolutely necessary to the satisfactory adjustment of the mutual relations and a satisfactory result to all concerned.[49]

On the particular issue of when and under what conditions employees may be discharged, the board would apply "the spirit of fairness and the rule of reason" — terms that were to be interpreted "in the light of the spirit and of the purpose of the protocol." Through Brandeis, the board directed that "the power of administration, discipline and discharge vested in the employer shall be exercised in a fair and reasonable manner, and if the propriety of the action is questioned, shall be subject to review." Going even further, Brandeis asserted that "the protocol was devised to enforce for the benefit of the employee a right to fair and just treatment or to put it another way, to secure through the instrumentality of the protocol, the reasonable certainty that the

---

[49]*Minutes,* Board of Arbitrators...[women's coat and suit trade] (Jan. 21, 1915), vol. 8, pp. 999, 1008–1009. Among other matters "even more far-reaching and of deeper significance" than questions of discharge or of other individual rights, noted Brandeis, was the necessity for standardizing piece rates, for regularizing employment, for controlling relations between protocol and nonprotocol shops, and for the adoption of a protocol label, *ibid.,* pp. 1003, 1007.

By insisting that the parties learn to put first things first, the board of arbitration won the hearty approval of J. H. Cohen, voice of the manufacturers and chief architect of the protocol movement. "I am very glad indeed," Cohen stated, "that the Board has impressed both sides with the importance of spending more time upon the root problems of this industry than the spending of time upon the smaller litigations.... The time of the executive officers should be released for the consideration of the big problems of the industry," *ibid.,* p. 1016. The pertinent passages may also be found in Cohen, *Law and Order in Industry,* Appendix C, p. 276.

employer would not exercise his legal rights oppressively or unfairly." Attempts to establish more meaningful criteria for the general application of these broad principles, however, were lost in a concerted focus on industry-oriented concepts of controlling competition by standardizing the terms and conditions of employment.[50]

Concluding Observations

After 1910, collective bargaining in the needle trades was something more than a means for determining wages, hours, and working conditions. Like the delta of a river fanning out into the sea, the subjects of negotiation were continually expanding to cover the growing needs for joint action among the organized factions of each trade. Controlling competition for the general welfare of an industry — the central theme of the protocol movement — took many forms and embraced many functions. Some features of this control fell within the normal orbits of bargaining over terms of employment; other features invaded the most sacred precincts of management prerogatives or trespassed upon the forbidden domains of internal union policy exclusively reserved for organized labor.

Through the door of collective bargaining passed all advocates of collaboration for the common good. Whether the issue be labor relations or trade relations, the organized jobbers, contractors, and inside manufacturers marched side by side with labor unions to wage war on the sources of illegitimate competition that plagued their trades. No clouding of the view by the intrusion of private rights, no diffusion of aims from the introduction of radical philosophies or from the appeals for individual justice ever concealed the lodestar of their united efforts. No conflicts over division of authority in the use of means to be employed ever deterred the organized forces of industry from their appointed goal.

---

[50]*Minutes,* Board of Arbitration...[women's coat and suit trade] (Jan. 21, 1915), vol. 8, pp. 994, 997, 998. Further discussions of discharge and other private rights issues appear in *Minutes* of the sessions for Feb. 5 and 6, dealing with the Schrank and Plonsky cases.

Chapter 4

Piece Rates and Contracting

Two spheres of activity best illustrate the scope and purpose of labor-management collaboration under the banner of collective bargaining. They involve the matter of determining piece rates and the subject of contracting out work. Both were directed toward creating standards of "legitimate" competition in the manufacture of wearing apparel — an objective that could be accomplished as readily through equalizing labor costs as through regulating sale prices. For more than half a century after 1910, the work of collective bargaining in the needle trades was largely concerned with these two spheres of activity.

Evils of Piece-Rate Bargaining

In developing standard labor costs for piecework, the organized forces of labor and management were undertaking to protect their own interests from "illegitimate" competitors who gained an advantage by abusing the piece-rate system of production. Strangely enough, this sphere of activity had its origin in the failures of the Brandeis Conferences. There the delegates had agreed upon minimum wage scales for week workers but had not agreed upon a centralized system for controlling piece rates. "As to piecework," stated Article 10 of the original Protocol of Peace, "the price to be paid is to be agreed upon by a committee of the employes in each shop, and their employer."

No provision could have been more fatal to the fundamental purposes of the new approach to collective bargaining. For the determination of piece rates at the shop level brought out the worst features of "excessive" competition. The procedure for "price-fixing," as it was called, was simple enough. When an employer meets with a price committee chosen from the workers in his shop, so Meyer London, counsel for the ILGWU, explained, "they bargain and bargain about each and every piece of each and every garment, or rather of each and every style." Every change of a button or a belt or a pocket or a pleat or a collar on a particular garment called for more negotiations. Every substitution of new material or new machinery, every shift in the flow of goods through the workshop, every change in shop organization or supervision affected earning power and called for still further negotiations.

While this highly democratic procedure may have charmed the advocates of industrial democracy, it opened the door to reckless competition between shops. For no shop could be a law unto itself. Both parties to shop-wide negotiations were driven by outside pressures quite beyond their control. "The moment the manufacturer finds out that his next-door neighbor can get a similar garment made cheaper," observed J. A. Dyche, testifying before the U. S. Commission on Industrial Relations, January 15, 1914, "he tries in every possible way to get it done cheaper." During slack seasons and periods of unemployment, the workers were at the mercy of the employer. "When I say $4.00," testified one member of a price committee, " the foreman says, 'What, are you joking? I will give you $1.50, and if you do not like it, take your hat and coat and get out. I do not need you.' "[1]

But when labor shortages prevented the dictation of piece rates, the unscrupulous employer found other means to attain his objectives. Not even the terms of his labor agreement prevented him from seeking the lowest level of piece rates available in the market. Where union contracts forbade manufacturers to offer outside workers an opportunity to bid on work that had previously been submitted to inside negotiations, the shyster operator of 1913 found a clever means of evading that restriction:

---

[1]J. A. Dyche in *Final Report and Testimony,* vol. 2, p. 1046; a price committeeman in *Minutes,* A Special Meeting of a Committee to Investigate All the Grievances of the Firm and the Workers of Joseph Rosenberg & Co. (Feb. 8, 1915), p. 28.

Today, a manufacturer, in the beginning of the season, takes garment No. 300. He calls in the inside price committee and tries to settle that garment with them. If the inside price committee should ask $3 for that garment, the manufacturer takes the same garment, sews on a white button instead of a black button, and calls it No. 305, and then he calls in the contractor's committee, and he asks them for their opinion as to what is the value of that garment. If they tell him $2.50 instead of $3, he settles it with them. If they should ask $3.50 for that garment, the white button goes off, the black button goes on, and it remains No. 300, and is settled for the $3 inside.[2]

Wherever labor agreements prohibited the changing of piece rates during a season, the ingenious employer of that era found a way of evading that restriction, too. At the beginning of each season, he handpicked a few workers with whom he negotiated favorable piece rates on garments to be manufactured. Only thereafter did he hire a full complement of workers who arrived on the job to find that piece rates had already been determined for the season. Even more brazen were those employers who followed the practice of juggling the style numbers assigned to particular garments (each number carried a price tag) "in such a manner that when it comes to the end of the week, they [the workers] do not really know whether they are being paid the proper prices or not."[3]

---

[2]George Wishnat, union representative, reported in *Minutes,* Board of Arbitrators...[women's coat and suit trade] (August 5, 1913), p. B-308; a similar case is cited at p. C-44. J. H. Cohen noted that the Cloak, Suit and Skirt Manufacturers' Protective Association, a party to the first protocol, enforced a rule prohibiting a manufacturer from playing off inside price committees against the outside price committees. An association could ask for bids from workers of his inside shop or from workers in his contractors' shops but not from both sources on the same garment. *Ibid.,* p. B-320.

[3]From a complaint, dated Sept. 27, 1915, against Joseph Rosenberg & Co., submitted by S. Polakoff, manager, union protocol division in Case no. 9929d, as recorded in *Minutes,* Committee on Immediate Action [dress industry] (Oct. 28, 1915), p. 487.

One employer hired five workers, fixed piece rates with them on the garments he intended to manufacture and then, while two of the five were leaving his employment, he hired 35 others who found that piece rates in the plant had already been fixed for the season. Case no. 11,198, involving the firms of Linde and Rubin, as reported in *Minutes,* Committee on Immediate Action [women's coat and suit trade] (Sept. 16, 1914).

After two years of such shenanigans under the cloak protocol, the president of the manufacturers' association, L. E. Rosenfeld, announced that he had never seen such differences in the piece rates paid for garments of exactly the same style — differences as high as five dollars in the manufacture of a single garment. It is small wonder that J. H. Cohen, counsel for the manufacturers and father of the protocol movement, should have declared that the "competitive problem is still unsolved in the cloak industry... 65 per cent of the workers work on piece work, and the protocol left the system of adjusting these prices where it was before the strike." He considered the existing system of piece-rate determination to be anarchy. "It is regulation per shop, not regulation per industry," Cohen said. "It is regulation per group, not regulation per union." Cohen was convinced that three-fourths of the garments made were the product of illegitimate competition arising from the lack of centralized control over piece rates.[4]

Some union leaders were equally disillusioned. "The great defect of the protocol to my mind," testified J. A. Dyche, general secretary-treasurer of the ILGWU, before the U. S. Commission on Industrial Relations, January 15, 1914, "is that 80 per cent of our people are pieceworkers, and the protocol makes no standards for pieceworkers.... At least 90 per cent of the trouble we have with the manufacturer is due to the fact that the protocol left no provision for any standards of piecework."[5]

The Movement to Control Piece Rates

That shop bargaining over piece rates would threaten the principle of law and order in industry was most certainly known to the delegates of the Brandeis Conferences. Indeed, standardizing piece rates had been one of the reforms that the employers wanted

---

[4]Rosenfeld in *Minutes,* Meeting of the Cloak, Suit and Skirt Manufacturers' Protective Association (Dec. 3, 1912), p. 16; Cohen in *Minutes,* Board of Arbitrators...[women's coat and suit trade] (August 3, 1913), pp. 78, 80. Three years later, Cohen wrote: "It is true that as to seventy-five percent of the prices for labor there is no standard, and each garment is separately estimated upon before it can be put into operation....So far as this fixing of piece rates is concerned, it is literally true that the employers deal with two thousand unions instead of with one." J. H. Cohen, *Law and Order in Industry* (1916), pp. 95, 96.

[5]Dyche in *Final Report and Testimony,* vol. 2, p. 1046.

most from those conferences. The original provision of the protocol leaving piece rates to each shop — a provision that scuttled all hopes for uniform piece-rate control — was attributed to union weakness. "The difficulty with the union," explained J. H. Cohen three years later, "has been right along that they realized the necessity for precisely the right kind of reform, but are unable to carry it through because of the psychological condition at the present time, and the prejudice on the part of the workers against trade union regulation of prices. . . . Because the Jewish worker in the Cloakmakers' Union is an individualist in temperament, and a Socialist in theory, they could not put this reform into effect at the present time. Both sides have to suffer during the evolutionary process."[6]

Louis D. Brandeis, first chairman of the board of arbitration for the women's coat and suit trade, was well aware of this shortcoming under the document that he had helped to create. "There ought not to be competition within the Union," he asserted in 1915, "but we have here in a sense 1,500 or 2,000 different competing units; for the piece prices are made independently in each shop." Likewise, A. C. Rosenberg, president of the ILGWU, acknowledged the folly of shop-to-shop competition among union members but conceded that he had been unable to establish the discipline necessary for united action. "I do not know whether the people in the shop will stand for price regulation by a Board," so he told the board of arbitration in 1913. "They want the firm to negotiate in their own shops, and I do not know how far we can go."[7]

---

[6]*Minutes,* Board of Arbitrators. . .[women's coat and suit trade] (August 3, 1913), p. 80. See also *Minutes* for August 6, 1913, p. C-18.

I do not believe any trade-unionism can exist for any length of time among people who are temperamentally individualists; it can not exist where people believe more in shop discipline among themselves than they do in their own union discipline, and my belief is that if it were not for the present union shop. . .we would have 2000 unions instead of 1. The real difficulty of this situation is that even under the protocol, while we have nominally 1 union, we are really dealing with 2000 unions.

—J. H. Cohen, testimony before the U.S. Commission on Industrial Relations, Jan. 16, 1914, *Final Report and Testimony,* vol. 2, p. 1120.

[7]Brandeis in *Minutes,* Board of Arbitrators. . .[women's coat and suit trade] (Jan. 21, 1915), vol. 8, p. 1004; Rosenberg in *ibid.* (August 4, 1913), p. 418. See

Although defeated in the early years of the protocol movement, the objective of uniform piece rates was ultimately won through persistent agitation and a program of education leading to gradual reform. In the protocol shops of the women's coat and suit trade, union leaders early adopted the practice of sending special delegates from shop to shop to advise local price committeemen during bargaining sessions. If possible, piece rates were to be adjusted in each shop so that the finisher of average ability would receive not less than 60¢ an hour and the operator of average ability would receive not less than 75¢ an hour. In time, the Cloakmakers' Joint Board, contrary to the protocol, authorized its local unions to put their stamp of approval on every shop-negotiated piece rate before it became effective. Although this move was directed to equality in earnings rather than equality in labor costs, it did impose some limitations on freedom to set piece rates at the shop level.[8]

Meanwhile, the dress and waist industry profited from the mistakes of the cloakmakers. In their protocol of January 18, 1913, the Dress and Waist Manufacturers' Association and the ILGWU gave their major attention to the determination of piece rates. Article VII provided:

The parties hereby establish a wage-scale board to consist of eight members — four to be nominated by the manufacturers and four by the union. Such board shall standardize the prices to be paid for piece and week work throughout the industry; it shall preserve data and statistics with a view to establishing as nearly practicably as possible a scientific basis for the fixing of piece and week work prices through-

---

also the testimony of J. H. Cohen, before the U.S. Commission on Industrial Relations, Jan. 16, 1914, *Final Report and Testimony,* vol. 2, p. 1120.

[8]The following notice was inserted in the *New Post,* official organ of the Cloakmakers' Joint Board, ILGWU, for Jan. 4, 11, and 18, 1913:

NOTICE TO SHOP CHAIRMEN AND PRICE COMMITTEES

In accordance with the order of the Executive, every shop chairman, price committee or member in general who will settle prices before they will report to the district office or in our office, will be considered a traitor to the Union and, as such, will be dealt with.

Members take notice! The whole power of the Union will be directed against the operators who will settle prices by themselves, betraying, in this way, the Union and the workingman.

—From a translation filed in the Abelson papers.

out the industry that will insure a minimum wage, and at the same time permit reward for increased efficiency. It shall have full power and authority to appoint clerks or representatives, expert in the art of fixing prices.... It shall have full power and authority to settle all disputes over prices, make special exemptions for week work where special exigencies arise, or a special scale is required.[9]

Through the activities of the wage-scale board, the old shop-by-shop procedure for determining piece rates on new garments was to be superseded by a centralized and highly scientific rate-setting process of general application throughout the trade. With jurisdiction over all controversies arising out of piece-rate setting, the wage-scale board was presumably in a position to enforce its standards in all the shops bound by the dress protocol. Instead of work stoppages to enforce union demands at the shop level — a procedure that played havoc with equality in labor costs — production on new garments could be continued, in case of disagreement over rates, until the new rates were centrally determined. The new rates then became retroactive to the beginning of production.[10]

To minimize the human element in rate fixing, a further refinement for determining piece rates was introduced. Known as the "schedule" or "log" system, this procedure, incorporated into the 1919 collective agreements for the dress and waist trade, required

---

[9]The protocol stated further that piece rates for operators shall in the first instance be settled by the employer and the piece price committee, but "in settling prices the price per garment shall be based upon the estimated number of solid hours it will take an experienced good worker to make the garment without interruption, multiplied by the standard price per hour." The standard price per hour for each craft was to be determined by the board of grievances on the basis of "a complete and exhaustive examination into the existing rates paid for labor, the earnings of the operatives, and the classification of garments in the industry." If the employer and the price committee were unable to agree upon the time required to complete a garment, workers were selected to make tests "for the purpose of determining the number of solid hours it will take an experienced good worker to make the garment in question." All controversies and misunderstandings were to be settled by the wage-scale board. The text of the protocol for the dress and waist industry is printed in C. H. Winslow, *Conciliation, Arbitration, and Sanitation in the Dress and Waist Industry of New York City*, U.S. Department of Labor, BLS Bulletin no. 145 (April 10, 1914), pp. 24, 25.

[10]N. I. Stone, *Wages and Regularity of Employment and Standardization of Piece Rates in the Dress and Waist Industry of New York City*, U.S. Department of Labor, BLS Bulletin no. 146 (April 28, 1914), pp. 189–298.

that garments be divided into working parts and that scheduled rates be fixed for each separate part. This greatly simplified the task of measurement. The piece rate was to be based on the number of solid hours a worker of average skill would need to make the part in question, multiplied by the standard base rate per hour, taking into account the quality of the work required, the variations in materials, the operating conditions of the factory, and the relations of each part to the other parts of the garment. The scientific method, centrally controlled and uniformly applied, was to supersede the unpredictable pressures of shop bargaining. Only to a very limited extent, however, was this system put into operation at that time.[11]

Week Work and Standards of Production

Meanwhile, a more radical movement to meet the evils of uncontrolled piece rates arose shortly after the First World War. At that time, three unions in the needle trades — the women's garment workers, the headwear workers, and the men's clothing workers — began an all-out effort to abolish the piecework system entirely. The organized manufacturers opposed this movement on two grounds. In the first place, workers varied so widely in their capacities, skills, and efforts that payment by the week offered no assurance of uniform labor costs for similar garments produced by competing manufacturers. In the second place, manufacturers who adopted the week-work system could not compete successfully against manufacturers who by remaining under the piecework system were able to estimate in advance the exact labor cost of each type and style of garment produced.

---

[11]In his short review of piece-rate controls in the dress and waist trade, J. H. Cohen reported that the log system had been introduced from experiences in the United Kingdom. J. H. Cohen, "The Revised Protocol in the Dress and Waist Industry," in *Annals,* American Academy of Political and Social Science, January 1917, vol. 69, pp. 194–195, citing *Report on Collective Agreements between Employers and the Work People in the United Kingdom* issued by the British Board of Trade in 1910. For a more extended discussion of issues in piece-rate controls, including the log system, use of test shops, and the section system of manufacturing, see *Minutes,* Arbitration Proceedings between the Dress and Waist Manufacturers' Association and the ILGWU (Feb. 5 and 7, 1916), vol. 4. A detailed index digest to this volume cites page references to various aspects of the subject.

During 1919–1920, all three unions gained their objective of abolishing piece rates in their major contracts, but not until they had accepted the principle that workers under a system of time payments must be responsible for standards of production. Thus the 1919 collective agreement between the Cloak, Suit and Skirt Manufacturers' Protective Association and the Cloakmakers' Joint Board, ILGWU, parties to the original Protocol of Peace, made clear that the union had assumed an obligation to protect the organized manufacturers from union members who might be guilty of soldiering on the job. "The union," stated this agreement, "believing in the principle of a 'fair day's work for a fair day's pay,' obligates itself in good faith for all its members, that they will perform their work conscientiously, faithfully, and efficiently."[12]

Could this principle have been implemented through some means for determining what to expect of employees doing similar work, the piece-rate principle of equalizing labor costs for similar garments produced by different manufacturers might still have been applied. Such, indeed, was the interpretation that the *Headgear Worker,* official organ of the Cloth Hat, Cap and Millinery Workers' International Union, placed upon "standards of production" under a time-payment system. "Standards of production," stated the issue of December 11, 1927, "make it possible for the manufacturer to know at all times what the labor cost of production is going to be on every article. The system of standards of production if properly arranged, would also introduce a uniform cost of production in every shop, thus doing away with the possibility of unfair competition at the expense of labor."[13]

Some employers had always operated on a time-payment plan, and most shops had always employed some week workers as well as piece-rate workers. To the extent that week work prevailed, standards of production had always been an issue in collective bargaining. The outside contractor whose time-payment workers produced ten garments a day maintained a 30 percent advantage in labor costs per garment over the inside manufacturer whose time-payment workers, employed at the same weekly wage rate, turned out only seven garments a day. These discrepancies were

---

[12]The text of this agreement was printed in the *Monthly Labor Review,* December 1919, vol. 9, pp. 1716–1719.

[13]See also the issue of August 12, 1937.

just as fatal to attempts at equalizing labor costs as was a piece-rate system in which the piece rate per garment for the contractor's shop was set at 30 percent below the piece rate per garment for the inside factory. Under either system of wage payment, the possibility of equalizing weekly income for the workers in the two shops might create an inequality in comparative labor costs per garment for the two manufacturers.[14]

Certain aspects of comparative labor costs under a system of time payments had been debated before the board of grievances for the women's coat and suit trade on March 16, 1916. There Morris Hillquit, counsel for the ILGWU, had proposed that the union establish for each type and grade of garment a maximum number of units that each week worker be allowed to produce each day. Hillquit would have production standards set in association shops, and he would then expect the union to see that association standards prevailed throughout the city. "If your [association] employee makes seven garments of a certain style [a day]," he explained, "the corresponding employee in the sub-manufacturer's shop shall not make more than seven a day of the same garment." Assuming that weekly wage rates in all types of shops were identical, controlled production standards would thus tend to equalize labor costs per garment among competing manufacturers.[15]

The most active leader in the movement to accompany week work with standards of production during the twenties was Sidney Hillman, president of the Amalgamated Clothing Workers' Union. "As a representative of this organization," so Hillman told his union convention meeting in Boston in May 1920, "I feel it my duty to say that we believe in production standards. . . . We have no quarrel with the industry. We are for production. The greatest enemy of our organization would be opposition to production." When the union delegates to this convention voted for time pay-

---

[14]"Nothing so undermines the security of the worker and renders so uncertain the cost forecast of the manufacturer or ignores the public interest as wage-fixing through consciousness of power regardless of production costs." Felix Frankfurter and S. F. Rosensohn, "Survey of the New York [men's] Clothing Industry" (May 28, 1920), in printed collection of union affidavits submitted in the case of J. Friedman & Co. v. ACWA (1921), p. 42. Copy filed in the Abelson papers.

[15]*Minutes,* Meeting of the Board of Conference. . .[women's coat and suit trade] (March 16, 1915), vol. 6, pp. 161–162.

ments over piece rates, they accepted week work only if accompanied by standards of production. "We must accept responsibility for production," Hillman insisted.[16]

Bold as was this position for a union leader, Hillman had good reasons for the stand he had taken. In the first place, Hillman feared the consequences to his union of a hastily conceived week-work system that recognized "the privilege of the individual to lay [sic] down on the job if he so desires." To sanction week work without standards, he argued, was to invite a struggle against the union. "We will not be able to make progress and organize those branches of the industry that are not organized today," so he stated in 1920. During the preceding year, Hillman had negotiated collective agreements for the men's clothing industry that included permanent arbitration machinery for the clothing markets of Rochester, Chicago, New York, Baltimore, Montreal, Toronto, and Cincinnati. Boston had been lost for over a year, so Hillman contended, for fear of a union resolution introducing week work without proper standards of production.[17]

In the second place, Hillman was industry-oriented to the extent of embracing scientific management, so long as more efficient methods of production were humanized and made subject to democratic controls. Whatever measures promoted the welfare of the trade, so he insisted, would operate to the best interests of the workers. Having terminated the system of piece-rate payments — a system that often substituted lower piece rates for managerial efficiency — Hillman was equally resolved to see that time pay-

---

[16]*Survey,* May 22, 1920, vol. 44, p. 274. "Whereas the piece work system carries with it overspeeding which is injurious to the health of the workers... Resolved that we recommend the week-work system with standards of production, and be it further resolved that the General Executive Board be empowered to inaugurate this system as soon as possible and determine standards as conditions may require." ACWA, *Report and Proceedings,* Fourth Biennial Convention (May 1920), pp. 343–344.

[17]*Ibid.,* pp. 350–352; see also *New York Times,* Oct. 5, 1919.

In one of his early decisions as arbitrator for the New York men's clothing industry after the First World War, W. M. Leiserson refused to permit an individual firm to cut wages to offset high unit-production costs. "If the labor cost is now too high, because any workers are not doing a fair day's work," so Leiserson ruled, "then the remedy is to get the proper production to bring down the costs." *Daily News Record,* Oct. 26, 1921.

ments did not lead to worker indifference toward production. Along with industry-wide wage scales, he fought continually for industry-wide standards of production that would equalize labor costs for all competing manufacturers.[18]

Frustrations in Week-Work Standards

With the endorsement of union leaders, production standards to accompany time payments were widely approved in collective agreements of the twenties. "Immediately upon the signing of this agreement," runs the 1922 master contract between the Cloth Hat and Cap Manufacturers' Association and the New York Joint Council, United Cloth Hat and Cap Makers of North America, "arrangements shall be made by the union and the association to continue the negotiations... for the establishment of a reasonable and uniform standard of production in the trade." Some agreements, like the 1922 master contract negotiated between the United Shirt Manufacturers' Association of New York and the Shirt Makers' Union, ACWA, provided for permanent joint committees to handle complaints regarding production standards. In the event of deadlocks, the appropriate clauses of collective agreements authorized appeals to an impartial chairman or board of arbitration for final and binding determinations.[19]

But accepting the principle of production standards left many questions still unanswered. What criteria would be used to implement a clause of the 1924 collective agreement between the New York Clothing Manufacturers' Exchange and the ACWA calling for a joint committee to establish minimum wages "dependent upon and commensurate with production"? Or by what standards would the Cleveland Garment Manufacturers' Association and the ILGWU apply the clause of their 1922 collective agreement directing that "wages paid thereunder shall have due regard to the productive value of the individual worker based on fair and

---

[18]For Sidney Hillman's views on scientific management, see the *New York World,* July 16, 1922, and ACWA, *Advance,* March 30, 1928; see also ACWA's research library, *Redbook of Clippings,* volume covering the years 1910–1920, especially pp. 315–330.

[19]Text of the hat and cap industry agreement appears in *Monthly Labor Review,* September 1922, vol. 15, pp. 615–618; text of the shirt industry agreement, *ibid.,* March 1922, vol. 14, p. 514.

accurate standards, which standards shall be under the joint control of the association and the union and subject to review by the referees"?[20]

For these and other reasons, the decade of the twenties brought continued frustrations in attempts at formulating standards of production to accompany the system of time payments. Despite exploratory investigations and extensive research, few such standards were ever established. Yet manufacturers repeatedly charged workers with creating inequalities in labor costs by underproducing on the job. Some employers refused to permit the union, or third parties, to participate in setting production standards. Some union members saw in production standards an official endorsement of the speed-up. Within eighteen months, the 1919–1922 collective agreement that introduced week work into the women's coat and suit trade was shipwrecked, partly because the guarantee that work would be performed "conscientiously, faithfully, and efficiently" could not be translated into a practical program for protecting employers against "soldiering on the job." The end came in the face of efforts by a special joint production commission created to find ways and means for bringing productivity up to reasonable levels of acceptability.[21]

More fundamental was the consideration that the "legitimate" forces of industry never dared to go all-out in support of the week-work system so long as many shops continued to operate under a piece-rate system. During the late twenties, a rise in the number

---

[20]The text of the Cleveland collective agreement for the women's coat and suit trade, printed in *Monthly Labor Review,* July 1922, vol. 15, pp. 103–109, also contains a "Supplementary Agreement Relative to Production Standards." Early progress toward the adoption of production standards in the women's coat and suit industry of the Cleveland market is reported in *Women's Wear,* Dec. 10, 1920.

[21]An account of these efforts and their consequences can be found in a decision of the New York Supreme Court, Schlesinger v. Quinto, 117 Misc. 735 (1920), 192 N. Y. Supp. 564; 201 App. Div. 487, 194 N. Y. Supp. 401. (See below pp. 323–324.)

As late as the 1932 negotiations for a new collective agreement in the women's coat and suit trade, the Industrial Council of Cloak, Suit and Skirt Manufacturers, unable to establish piece rates, was still holding out for "a measure of production" under the week-work system. But in the face of a prolonged strike, the association had to retract its stand. *Women's Wear Daily,* July 25, 1932.

of new shops using piece rates increased rather than diminished the number of piece-rate competitors. The great depression of the thirties further intensified the pressures of piece-rate competition, until many employers bound by the week-work system felt obliged to find ways of side-stepping their contractual obligations. Soon Samuel Klein, executive director of the inside manufacturers' association, was arguing vehemently for "legalized, controlled piece work, rather than the 'bootlegging' which is actually the way in which 60 percent of the industry now carries on production."[22]

Faced with the gradual disintegration of their time-payment plan, and under pressure to endorse piece work that had been authorized by the NRA codes of fair competition, needle trade unions once again joined the employers in an effort to evolve a procedure for determining piece rates that would equalize labor cost for similar garments produced by competing manufacturers. In the course of this development, the power to set piece rates largely passed from the hands of the individual producer and a committee of his workers. This evil that had plagued the advocates of controlled competition from the inception of the protocol movement was to be met by a centralized procedure for setting

---

[22]*Women's Wear Daily,* August 15, 1933. In a letter to employers in 1928, officials of the ILGWU stated that "hundreds of shops have sprung up in which piece work is the prevailing system of production and which operate in utter disregard of wages, hours, and other working standards supposedly established in the industry." The letter stated that "those shops work untold harm to the workers and fair employers alike," and it warned that conditions in the industry were "more precarious and intolerable than they have been in years." As quoted in a statement by Samuel Klein at hearings on the code of fair competition for the women's coat and suit industry, July 20, 1933. In so far as the dress industry condoned a piece-rate system in the twenties and early thirties, that trade allegedly created unbearable competition for the women's coat and suit trade. See the 1925 collective agreement between the Association of Dress Manufacturers (contractors) and the ILGWU, text in *Women's Wear Daily,* Jan. 19, 1925; and criticisms in *ibid.,* June 17, July 31, and Oct. 22, 1930.

The organized manufacturers of the headwear industry were in a similar plight. One manufacturer, writing to the Women's Headwear Group, May 28, 1934, stated: "In view of the fact that 99 percent of the manufacturers making my price hats are now working piece work and accordingly know exactly the cost of production for each hat, in the trimming department, our firm must be put on a par if we are to exist as a manufacturing concern." Letter filed in the Abelson papers.

piece-rate standards covering each basic operation in the production of different types and grades of garments.[23]

Control of Contracting

The second major sphere of activity in the history of collective bargaining consisted of attempts to restrict outside contracting. The Brandeis Conferences of 1910 had been sponsored by inside manufacturers and their organized employees. Both parties to the negotiations opposed the system of outside contracting. Henceforth, from the days of the original protocol, collective bargaining became in part a movement to defend a particular method of production. Those who initiated or subsequently supported the protocol movement continued to defend inside manufacturing by direct labor in preference to outside manufacturing under the jobber-contractor system.

"Whatever we have done," announced I. Grossman, in his 1929 presidential address before the Industrial Council of Cloak, Suit and Skirt Manufacturers (successor to the association of inside manufacturers that signed the original Protocol of Peace), "has been inspired by a determination to promote the stability of the legitimate inside shop manufacturers." And with equal frankness, Max Zaritsky, president of the Cloth Hat, Cap and Millinery Workers' International Union, admitted three years later that in the production of headwear "the union seeks to establish a highly centralized, highly stabilized industry based on inside manufacturing."[24]

---

[23] For subsequent developments toward a system for centralized piece-rate determination, see below, chap. 20 of this study.

[24] *Women's Wear Daily*, Grossman in issue of Feb. 19, 1929; Zaritsky in the issue of Jan. 5, 1932. See also the *New York Times*, March 14, 1932.

> One would expect the manufacturers to realize that the organization of the workers is indispensable for the [needle trade] industry;...and that the elimination of the Union would carry with it the elimination of the legitimate manufacturer—i.e. the manufacturer working for the trade directly. The elimination of the legitimate manufacturer would mean his substitution by the jobber who has always been the worst evil in the industry.
>
> —United Cloth Hat and Cap Makers of North America, *Report and Proceedings,* Fourteenth Biennial Convention (May 1923), p. 13 (report of the general executive board).

Those manufacturers who originally supported the protocol movement had been producers of better-class merchandise that was sold on the market for better-than-average prices. Neither party to the first Protocol of Peace knew much about the "lower end of the trade," nor was either party prepared to cope with the rising tide of competition from the producers of cheap goods soon to flood the market. Indeed, it was charged at the time the dress and waist protocol was negotiated in 1913 that the agreement was a frame-up to drive the lower-priced dress and waist manufacturers out of the industry.

The downfall of quality that accompanied the rise of mass production under the jobber-contracting system dealt a lethal blow to many inside manufacturers who profited from the good will of dependable management and reliable merchandise. Originality of style, pride of workmanship, uniformity of products, certainty of delivery — all these commendable features of large-scale inside manufacturing were soon to fall before the onslaught of the outside contractor with his lower price tag. Nor did the greater outlay of funds for developing new styles and types of garments guarantee the survival of the inside producer. "I have given my life to a study of design," observed an inside manufacturer of the early protocol period:

. . .I have gone abroad and purchased the Parisian products of the best fashion artists in the world. . . .My bills leap into the thousands of dollars both for expenses abroad and such models as I must purchase. . . .I have employed expensive artists here. . .as a result of their work and mine and the labors of my high priced sample-making department, I have created something which I believe will appeal to the American women. . . .Yet I know that within 48 hours after the first copy is exhibited in a retail department store, it will be purchased by one of my competitors and copied.[25]

The downfall of quality was no less a blow to the skilled craftsman of union allegiance. Every good unionist loathed the thought of carefully tailored garments reproduced so cheaply "that they should look like a regular rag." It is small wonder that the general executive board of the United Cloth Hat and Cap Makers, reporting to its union convention in 1923, should have longed for the

---

[25]As quoted in J. H. Cohen, *Law and Order in Industry*, p. 88.

good old days when "new styles, better workmanship, better grades of material, etc. became the factors for successful competition," a time when "New York was the leader, the creator of styles, the city . . .whose supremacy, above all, lay in the quality and workmanship of its products."[26]

Yet no one could deny that the jobber-contractor system of manufacturing was well adapted to meet the growing demands for low-priced merchandise. Admittedly, the system offered manufacturers a cheaper method of production through savings in overhead, closer supervision, greater specialization, and lower labor costs. More surprising were the economic and social advantages the system held out to the working man — advantages described in the *Jewish Daily Forward,* June 8, 1913:

The "inside" workingman receives a better price for his piece of work, but it is impossible to make as much work in the factory, as in the shop. The factory workingman loses a lot of time in his work. Every little thing that he needs, he has to go and get himself. There is what we term in English "a lot of red-tape" — a lot of unnecessary formalities. If an operator needs some cotton, he must stop his work, and go and find the girl who takes care of the cotton. If he needs a needle for his machine, he again must lose some of his time. First, he needs some trimming, then he needs one thing or another, and there is nobody who can give it to him. He must look himself, ask himself, and go himself; all this, costs him a lot of time.

It is quite different, in a contractor's shop. There, the boss is the workingman's messenger. There, the workingman gets everything on time. He is even saved the trouble of asking. When he works, he works; he does not have to stop every moment. Now there is a second important point. Throughout the season, there is usually made, hundreds and hundreds of different styles in the "inside" factory. There, the workingman does not get any "bundles," but small bundles or single

---

[26]United Cloth Hat and Cap Makers of North America, *Report and Proceedings,* Fourteenth Convention (May 1923), pp. 8, 10.

The garment of the inside shop can be standardized, uniformity of product can be made certain, quality can be assured. The trade mark and the label can be used to advantage on a standard product. The inside manufacturer will invest more in advertising. He will through advertising create a demand for his product, direct from the consumer. He can therefore effectively compete with the smaller firm that does not advertise to the consumer, and is not certain of a steady market.

—ACWA, *Advance,* April 2, 1926.

"garments," and every small bundle or single garment, is different than the other. Every garment is of a different style, with a different "stunt" and no matter how experienced or capable the workingman may be, he has to devote some of his time in examining and studying the new style, before he begins working on the garment. This "examining" takes time; and when he gets a few different styles a day, he loses a good deal of time. The workingman does not receive any extra pay for "examining" the garment. And then again, the work goes on much slower, when the kind of work changes very often. One who works on the same style, the same goods, the same color merchandise, the same trimming, and on the same cotton all day long, can make much more than the one who has to change the style, the merchandise, the trimming, etc. very often. Anybody can understand this, even if he never worked in a shop. . . .

The "outside" workingman does not know of "changing," very often. The manufacturer, often times sends out to a contractor, several garments of the same style. The contractor divides it among his workingmen, and they "work." It happens sometimes that the people of the "outside" shop, work on the same style and the same merchandise, for an entire week. Once in fifty (50) years such a thing can occur in an "inside" shop and perhaps not even that. We are not through yet.

Aside from these advantages of the "work proper," there are other reasons why many like to work "outside" rather than "inside." "Outside" (in an outside shop) the workingman feels more at liberty. He has more "privileges," more freedom than in the "inside" factory. In the "outside" shop, he may smoke, he may send out for a "pint" of beer; he may eat while working. In the factory, he cannot do this. Here, the discipline is much stronger. The "outside" shop is usually located near the tenement district, and the workingman can move near his shop. Living near the shop he can go home for dinner, every day; he does not have to eat in the restaurants; he does not have to shove and squeeze on the cars riding to and from work. In other words, it pays for the "outside" workingman to lower the prices. What he loses in prices he gains in comfort.[27]

---

[27]Translation filed in the Abelson papers. For a similar account of the advantages of contracting, see the testimony of A. Rosenberg, president of the ILGWU, before the U.S. Commission on Industrial Relations, Jan. 15, 1914, *Final Report and Testimony*, vol. 2, p. 1035.

The retailer also came to the defense of the jobber-contractor system:

Take away the jobber today and you'll drift back to old fashioned manufacturing conditions, where the retailer would come to the market months in advance, buy up enormous quantities of coats and suits and

The Abolition of Contracting

Through the medium of collective bargaining, the organized forces of industry conducted their campaign against contracting in three phases: (1) the abolition of contracting; (2) the suppression of the small-time operator; (3) regulation and limitation of large-scale contractors. The framers of the original women's coat and suit protocol had to be content with inserting a provision that "all sub-contracting within shops shall be abolished." Similar clauses against subcontracting, contracting, and submanufacturing in its various forms were written into other protocols and into various later agreements throughout the needle trades.

The case of the needle trade unions for suppressing this outside method of production was founded on the belief that no amount of control over jobber-contractor relations could ever salvage the potential values of contracting from the greater inherent evils of the system. "No matter how you call it, no matter how you label it, no matter where you conduct it, whether in the city, or in some suburb, as they do in a great many cases," so Morris Hillquit, counsel for the ILGWU, argued before the board of arbitration of the dress and waist industry in 1916, "you always find this proposition, that the employer who is at liberty to maintain contracting shops and to have work done there cheaper than in the inside shop, by underpaying and overworking his help, is in a position, first to make ruinous competition to the more decent manufacturers, and to force the more decent manufacturers either to establish the same system of contracting, or to depress standards in his own shop."[28]

The abolition of contracting was a union slogan from the inception of the protocol movement. At least those union factions supporting the protocols stressed the lack of security that accom-

---

hold them on his racks until the time comes when he could dispose of them. Naturally he would find himself with merchandise many months old paid for long before he has had a chance to market it and would find himself overburdened with the risks in buying at a time when he could not sell, with the hazards of meeting his bills long before he has ever had a chance to sell and above all with the probability of having a good deal of unseasonable merchandise on his hands.

—D. J. Brayer, a buyer, in *Women's Wear*, May 23, 1919.

[28]*Minutes,* Arbitration Proceedings between the Dress and Waist Manufacturers' Association and the ILGWU (Feb. 14, 1916), vol. 5, pp. 588–589.

panied the jobber-contracting system. Some workers opposed the system of outside production on ethical and social grounds as well. Their sense of dignity and moral values, noted the *Jewish Daily Forward,* June 8, 1913, kept them from dingy lofts and filthy basements in quest of the dollar. "To them the small shop in the old-fashioned building in the dark and narrow streets, is too close, too narrow for their spirit. They also hate the small boss, with his 'one-cent' soul. They despise the triflings, the half-cent bargainings. In a big factory they feel somewhat dignified, somewhat higher *spiritually.*"[29]

Leaders of the fur workers and of the headwear workers were particularly outspoken against the practice of contracting. During the twenties, A. Brownstein, manager of the Furriers' Joint Board, directed a vicious attack against the contractor who "produces without taking account of cost of production, and sells the product without regard to legitimate profit...and therefore makes it impossible for legitimate business to compete with him in the open market." This crusade to abolish contracting continued into the thirties. In March 1937, the Furriers' Joint Council reported that the union had "liquidated" nine contracting establishments during the preceding February and that it was still looking to the time when "the trade will finally be cured of a painful and destructive disease."[30]

In like manner, Nathaniel Spector, manager of the Joint Council of the Hat, Cap and Millinery Workers, for many years led

---

[29]From a translation in the Abelson papers.

> In the inside shops sanitary conditions are better. Abuses in the matter of hours and wages are infrequent, and grievances are more quickly reported and adjusted. Rates of pay average higher and, above all else in importance, the number of hours of work during the year averages 38 percent greater than in the outside shops. These facts are fully recognized by the Union, and every individual worker would prefer to be attached to an inside shop. Nothing would more directly benefit the workers than an increase in the number and size of the inside shops.
>
> —Governor [Alfred E. Smith]'s Advisory Commission for the [women's] Cloak, Suit and Skirt Industry, *Final Recommendations* (May 20, 1926), p. 8.

[30]A. Brownstein to S. N. Samuels, president, Associated Fur Manufacturers. Letters, dated March 20, 1921, April 27, 1923, and June 20, 1923, are filed in the Abelson papers. Furriers' Joint Council, *Furriers' Bulletin,* March 15, 1937.

the attack against contracting on behalf of his union. In 1935, he denounced the Women's Headwear Group of manufacturers for engaging in a practice "which for approximately 25 years, all legitimate elements in our industry have opposed as being destructive to the industry as a whole." After threatening to abrogate the collective agreement if the practice continued, Spector stated that "the union is determined, at all costs, to stamp out the evil of contracting."[31]

"Each employer," stated the most important collective agreement of the millinery trade in 1938, "shall manufacture all millinery dealt in by him upon his own premises. Employers shall not manufacture nor cause to be manufactured in places other than on the premises owned or leased by them any millinery sold, dealt in or otherwise handled by them. Employers shall not give out any millinery to be manufactured by other manufacturers or by contractors; nor shall any Employer, entirely or in part, manufacture or accept any basic material for manufacture of any millinery for and on account of any other employer, manufacturer, contractor, syndicate, jobber, retailer or any merchant purchasing, selling or otherwise dealing in millinery."[32]

Union support for such provisions arose from the unfair competition that outside contracting generated between inside and outside workers. Constantly in fear of losing their jobs through business failures of their employers, workers in contractors' shops were subject to greater pressures than were their counterparts of

---

[31]N. Spector to J. E. Helfer, executive director of the Women's Headwear Group. Letters, dated April 4, 1934 and March 6, 1935, are filed in the Abelson papers.

[32]From the 1938 collective agreement between the Eastern Women's Headwear Association and the United Hatters, Cap and Millinery Workers' International Union and the Joint Board of Millinery Workers' Union, Locals 2, 24, 42.

> The contracting system was the bane of our industry, just as it was the bane of other needle trade industries. We saw its dangerous potentialities in 1907, almost thirty years ago. It was then that the jobbers introduced the system of farming out to contractors their own materials and paying them only for labor.
> —United Hatters, Cap and Millinery Workers' International Union, Cap and Millinery Department, *Report and Proceedings,* Second Convention (First Regular Convention) Oct. 4–7, 1936, p. 11.

the larger inside establishments. When business was good and contractors were in great demand, workers could expect to receive at least the wage standards set for the trade. But when business turned bad — so Emil Schlesinger, attorney for the ILGWU, explained — workers in contractors' shops were "expected to act as a buffer between the survival and demise of each firm by taking a substantial cut in wages to a point far below subsistence level."[33]

Naturally, inside manufacturers joined in denouncing a system of outside production that flouted labor standards and undermined legitimate trade practices. Moreover, the inside manufacturer bound by collective agreements could not evade responsibility for meeting union labor costs, even if he chose to do so. "With a large investment and with an established position in the industry," noted a student of the problem in the early thirties, "he was a vulnerable target for the union to shoot at. He couldn't go out of business overnight and he couldn't go back into business overnight. When he made an agreement he had to live up to it."[34]

By contrast, jobbers and contractors, even if bound by union agreements, could effectively offset union pressures to meet labor standards by vanishing from the scene. Most of them lived from season to season or from job to job, with no permanent invest-

---

[33]Emil Schlesinger, *The Outside System of Production in the Women's Garment Industry in the New York Market* (1951), p. 8. This 106-page study printed for the ILGWU gives an illuminating analysis of the problems encountered by a system of outside production.

The Union, recognizing the inability of the contractor to prolong the season, to provide sanitary working places, and in general to obtain release from the driving pressure of competition, has officially declared itself in favor of the inside shop.
—Felix Frankfurter and S. J. Rosensohn, "Survey of the New York [men's] Clothing Industry," at pp. 17–43 of the union affidavits in the J. Friedman case. See above p. 59n.

[34]More than that, he wanted to live up to it. He wanted to give labor high wages, good working conditions, sanitary high-rent shops. He asked only one thing in return. Let his competitor also be controlled so that he, too, would have to pay the same high wages, provide the same good working conditions, maintain the same high grade plants. And this was the one thing he couldn't get. His competitor was a jobber....The jobber, through the contractor, evaded all responsibility for labor costs and conditions.
—Charles H. Green in *Women's Wear Daily*, August 15, 1933.

ments and no reputations at stake. Undercutting competitors and chiseling on agreements were the standards they lived by. "Contracting caused an epidemic of cut-throat competition which has driven the legitimate manufacturer to despair," lamented the director of the Rabbit Fur Manufacturers' Association in 1934. "Contracting is against every principle of fair competition."[35]

Union Expedients to Suppress Contracting

For reasons of law and public policy, labor unions rather than employers' associations assumed primary responsibility for implementing the program to abolish contracting. The machinery and procedures for this purpose were devised in the name of collective bargaining. Wherever unions dictated the terms of employment by drafting form contracts at union headquarters to be signed by individual employers, provisions against contracting, submanufacturing, or subcontracting could readily be incorporated. Hundreds of such contracts with individual employers of the men's clothing industry were signed during the general strike in 1913.

The jobber-contracting system that had dominated the production of men's clothing before the First World War came under double attack thereafter. Following this war, some of the more prominent producers turned to inside manufacturing as an escape from unreliable contractors, who, often in collusion with their organized workers, repeatedly insisted upon higher prices for themselves and higher wages for their men. At the same time, the Amalgamated Clothing Workers' Union, which had largely superseded the United Garment Workers in the men's clothing trade, began to devise expedients for promoting the inside factory at the expense of the contracting shop. With the help of local manufacturers' associations, this union conducted a campaign of peaceful propaganda that led to the opening of many more inside

---

[35]Joseph Zwerdling, managing director of the Rabbit Fur Manufacturers' Association, to the fur manufacturers. Letter, dated March 20, 1934, filed in the Abelson papers. This war upon contracting in the needle trades was continued under the National Industrial Recovery Act that introduced industry codes of fair competition, effective from June 15, 1933 to May 27, 1935. In 1934, for example, the code authority for the millinery industry recommended to the NRA administrator a provision to ban the use of hat contractors in the industry. *Code Authority News of the Millinery Industry.* Copy filed in the Abelson papers.

establishments. During 1919–1920, according to figures compiled by the assistant manager of the New York Joint Board, ACWA, the number of inside establishments manufacturing men's clothing in New York City rose from 35 to 225, while the number of contracting shops declined by about 10 percent.[36]

This union, like others in the needle trades, also contrived to force contractors out of business by prescribing the character of the lofts in which union members were allowed to work. Specifications required to meet union standards of health and sanitation were too high for most contractors who profited from substandard working conditions. In still another union effort to suppress contracting, the Amalgamated Clothing Workers moved in the late twenties to promote inside manufacturing by allowing large responsible coat shops to work by the piece, while denying this right to the small contracting shops. None of these efforts to eliminate contracting in the men's clothing trade during the twenties was successful, however.[37]

The fur workers' union was more aggressive in its attempt to drive contractors from the production of fur garments. Operating under a clause in its collective agreement with the Associated Fur Manufacturers that forbade "inside or outside contracting in any shape, form, or manner," the Furriers' Joint Council during the

---

[36]See a folder of documentary materials entitled "Collective Bargaining: Special Problems" in the ACWA Research Library; and an article by Frank Chodorov in *Daily News Record,* May 31, 1922. "Only the direct operation of their own shops by manufacturers will attain for New York the stability and dignity which the industry has attained elsewhere. We do not under-estimate the difficulties in the way of the inside shop movement. . . . Nothing, we believe, is more deserving of the thought and enterprise of the New York manufacturers and of the Union than the need for the inside shop." Felix Frankfurter and S. J. Rosensohn, "Survey of the New York [men's] Clothing Industry" at pp. 17–43 of the union affidavits. The quotation is cited from p. 42 of this collection, a copy of which is filed in the Abelson papers.

[37]On the scheme of the Amalgamated Clothing Workers, abetted by representatives of the men's clothing manufacturers, to drive out contractors under the ostensible banner of "sanitation," see Frank Chodorov in *Daily News Record,* May 31, 1922. On special concessions to inside shops, see *Women's Wear Daily,* June 5, 1928, quoting the *Jewish Daily Forward,* May 28, 1928. Under the 1927 collective agreements of the women's coat and suit trade, any association member having a work force of at least 35 employees was given additional reorganization rights denied to smaller firms.

thirties conducted open warfare on all contractors, often resorting to force where persuasion was ineffective. Union agents sought out contractor shops, closed their doors, and "liquidated" their businesses. The council conducted strikes against jobbers and forced them to open inside shops. Then its officials proudly reported to the membership:

Our first attack was on contracting, particularly finishing contracting. The result of this drive was that many contractors were obliged to give up their sweatshops. This made it possible for hundreds of Union finishers to obtain employment in the inside shops and generally resulted in higher wages and better conditions. Scores of shops which previously had not employed any finishers at all, were compelled to employ finishers, because of our drive.

Simultaneously with this, we carried through a systematic campaign of strikes against outstanding jobbers in the fur industry. We thus compelled these jobbers to open fur shops of their own which also gave employment to hundreds of workers and made more secure the union standards in all shops.[38]

When the harassed contractors organized to meet these attacks and called upon the courts to defend their right to exist, the organized fur workers soon found themselves in the clutches of the law. In 1936, the American Fur Liners' Contractors' Association and fifty-five independent contractors appealed to the New York Supreme Court for an injunction to restrain the International Fur Workers' Union and the Furriers' Joint Council from attempting to drive contractors out of business. The court granted the injunction with these observations:

In August 1935, the defendant union instituted a drive for the purpose of eliminating the contractor from the fur industry. Groups of eight to ten members entered the various places of business of the plaintiffs, demanded the inspection of their books for the purpose of ascertaining the names and addresses of the persons with whom they transacted business, ordered them to discontinue their business as contractors and directed their employees to report to the headquarters of the defendant union. The employees were with few exceptions intimidated and threatened by the acts of the defendant and induced to refrain from continuing in the employ of the plaintiff with the result that but a few of the employees ever returned to the plaintiff's places of business. . . .

[38]Furriers' Joint Council, *Furriers' Bulletin,* April 1, 1936.

The contractors' association is ready and anxious to enter into collective bargaining agreements with the union and conform to their requirements as to hours, wages, and working conditions. This is not the ordinary case of a conflict between the employer and the employee. The defendant is not seeking to compel the plaintiffs to conform to union standards but to force them out of the industry.[39]

Elimination of the Small Shop

Along with efforts to abolish the jobber-contracting system as a whole came a more general movement to eliminate the small-scale operator, who, almost invariably, was a small-time contractor. Concerted attacks on small-scale producers had marked the rise of collective bargaining for the needle trades. Charges that the larger manufacturers were conspiring to drive small businessmen out of existence were widespread. With large investments in equipment, supplies, and overhead, inside manufacturers of substantial means were seeking protection from the unlicensed competition of hand-to-mouth operators. "In our trade," observed J. A. Dyche, general secretary-treasurer of the ILGWU, addressing representatives of his union in 1913, "the manufacturer has much more to fear and is more injured by the unfair competition of the smaller employer than by the demands of the union."[40]

---

[39]Mr. Justice T. A. Leary in American Fur Liners' Contractors' Association v. Lucchi, New York Supreme Court, New York County, as reported in the *New York Law Journal*, Jan. 16, 1936, vol. 95, p. 282. The action was affirmed in 249 App. Div. 513 (1937); 293 N.Y. Supp. 1.

In spite of this decision, the struggle of the American Fur Liners' Contractors' Association to survive appears to have continued. Testifying before a congressional investigating committee on Sept. 8, 1948, J. J. Bernstein, counsel for the association, stated: "We have attempted to negotiate with the Furriers' Joint Council. We have said to them time and again, 'Look, we want to be in the business; we pay social security, we are American citizens. We pay the same wages, the same scale that exists. We are willing to take union help and pay the same wage. Regulate us, run us, boss us, do anything you want to do with any manufacturer, but recognize us.'" U.S. Congress, House Committee on Education and Labor, *Hearings on Investigations of Communist Infiltration into the Fur Industry*, 80th Cong. 2nd. sess. (pursuant to H. Res. 111, 80th Cong.), p. 7.

[40]J. A. Dyche, "Address for Representatives of Organized Labor on the Situation in the Women's Coat and Suit Trade," Dec. 27, 1913. Copy filed in the Abelson papers.

For charges of conspiracy by the large Fifth Avenue members of the

The organized workers, as well as the more substantial employers, had cause to make war on the small shop. Labor unions were seeking the security of permanent employment in large establishments that did not succumb to every shift in styles, seasons, or the business cycle. "The union does not want to see the legitimate man pushed out of the industry and his place taken by little irresponsible people," once declared Benjamin Schlesinger, president of the ILGWU. More than one union leader has expressed the sentiment that a major objective of collective bargaining is to drive out the "parasitic" element and "protect the industry from the adventurers therein."[41]

Merchants' Society of Ladies' Tailors and the ILGWU to drive the smaller operators out of business, see *Women's Wear,* Sept. 20, 1911; and for similar charges by the small-time manufacturers of women's waists against their larger "silk-stockinged" competitors, see *Women's Wear,* Feb. 14, 15, 16, 1916.

> There isn't any manufacturer that I know of that doesn't regard the selling side of the industry and the competition of the smaller man the two worst evils that we have to deal with. If we can make the "sweatshop" operator...toe the same mark as we do,...if we can make him go into sanitary shops and maintain the same rigid rules of fire protection for his people, pay the same wages and keep the same hours and holidays as we do, don't we get something more out of it than we give up, we decent employers?
> —"An Authority" [Paul Abelson] writing on "Union Recognition" in *Daily Trade Record,* Dec. 6, 1912.

[41]*Women's Wear,* May 25, 1922.

In 1913, A. W. Miller, representing the furriers' union, had warned the members of the fur manufacturers' association that "the ruination of their business" could be attributed to "these small people with three or four greenhorns" who time and again undersell the reputable producers. "Now it would be to your advantage," Miller added, "to help strengthen the Union and put these men out of business." The first minimum wage scales in collective agreements between fur manufacturers and the fur workers' union were introduced a year later as a means of suppressing small concerns that "get their work made up cheaper than the larger manufacturers" and thus bring "ruin and demoralization, both to the better class manufacturer and, even more so, probably, to the workers." Miller's views are found in *Minutes,* Conference between Representatives of the Fur Manufacturers' Association and the Furriers' Union of Greater New York (Oct. 29, 1913), p. 15. The purpose of the minimum wage is discussed in Joint Board, Furriers' Union, *Furriers' Bulletin,* December 1914.

The 1921 collective agreement between the Cleveland Garment Manufacturers' Association and the ILGWU stated that "the Association and the

Attacks upon the small shop that offered the brightest hope of success within the law came through cooperation between unions and employer groups to equalize labor costs among all competing producers. Only where such efforts were destined to fail did the parties to collective agreements move to exterminate their undersized competitors. But the conclusion that drastic action would be needed came early in the history of the protocol movement. In the very second case brought before the joint grievance board of the dress and waist industry, coming within a month of the signing of the dress and waist protocol, the Dress and Waist Manufacturers' Association, a party to the protocol, stated: "It is the belief of both Mr. Polakoff, as representing the Grievance Board for the Union, and Mr. Bartholomew, as representing the Association, that it will be impossible to enforce the standards named in the Protocol against these small shops manufacturing very cheap grades of goods, unless both sides are willing to take the responsibility of driving these manufacturers out of business and depriving their employees of work."[42]

Yet it was not until small-time contracting became the scourge of the garment trades after the First World War that the campaign against small shops began in earnest, and at that time the burden of leadership was shifted to the union. "Our association," declared Max D. Steuer, special counsel to the Cloak, Suit and Skirt Manufacturers' Protective Association, addressing the ILGWU in May 1922, "will do everything in its power to co-operate with you to do away with the evils resulting from the numerous small shops, conducted, as you say, by irresponsible contractors under conditions which make it almost impossible to subject them to reasonable regulations." While announcing that the members of his organization were already bound by association rules against doing business with small-scale contractors, Steuer informed the

---

Union commit themselves to the development of Cleveland, as a manufacturing community of large units, convinced that this policy is fair to the workers by keeping present forces intact and helpful to the manufacturers by reducing costs due to economy of large unit manufacturing." As quoted in *Women's Wear*, Dec. 24, 1921. Repeated in the 1922 agreement, text in *Monthly Labor Review*, July 1922, vol. 15, pp. 104–105.

[42]*Minutes*, Board of Grievances, Dress and Waist Industry (Feb. 6, 1913), Case no. 2, p. 2.

union that "the conditions under which the workers shall accept employment in all other shops are, and necessarily must be, regulated by your organization."[43]

The International Ladies' Garment Workers' Union sponsored many programs to suppress the small shop. But nowhere was this crusade more carefully planned than in the women's coat and suit trade during the spring and summer of 1922. This attack was centered on the "social shop" — a form of business organization usually consisting of a small group of intimate friends or close relatives, operating as a partnership or corporation, often in complete disregard of the standards set for the trade. The chief engineer of this particular drive was Benjamin Schlesinger, president of the ILGWU, who condemned the social shop as "a veritable cancer on the industry equally harmful to employers and workers." Before opening its attack, this union studied existing sources of production and compiled a list of small shops employing not more than eight or ten workers.

The major problem of the union was to put these shops out of commission without embarrassing the 25,000 union members who worked in them. On May 20, 1922, President Schlesinger outlined in some detail the union's proposal to accomplish this objective:

Of the 2,800 factories in New York there are about 1,000 legitimate places. The rest are either social shops or are legitimate places of such small size that industry would be better off without them. If the union could get the support of the legitimate manufacturers, it could start out to solve the situation gradually. Of the 1,800 small places in New York, there are about 500 places which are a real menace to the industry. They probably employ on an average about 10 workers each. This makes 5,000 workers which must be taken care of immediately if we are to take steps against the 500 worst social shops in this market.

The members of the Protective Association employ about 7,000 workers. The other large legitimate workers [manufacturers] in this

---

[43]*Women's Wear,* June 1, 1922. See also *Women's Wear,* Dec. 6, 1923.

In its *Final Recommendations* (May 20, 1926) at p. 8, the Governor's Advisory Commission on the women's coat and suit trade, after observing that the number of inside manufacturers who were members of the Cloak, Suit and Skirt Manufacturers' Protective Association had declined from 440 in 1916 to 188 in 1924, thus stated its position: "The Commission believes that there is urgent need that greater encouragement be given to the inside system of production and to larger production units throughout the industry."

market, including independents let us say, employ an additional 10,000 workers. This gives us a group of large legitimate manufacturers employing at present 17,000 workers. Now if these legitimate manufacturers should agree to increase their factories by 20 percent, if the union will take away the help from the 500 worst corporation shops in this market, the union will be in a position to issue an order to its members in these shops to leave their jobs.

The employers referred to above, by increasing their factories 20 percent would be in a position to give employment to about 4,000 of the 5,000 members of the union thrown out of employment by reason of the union's action against the 500 worst corporation shops in this market. The union would take care of the remaining 1,000 workers.

Now, if this experiment proves successful, the same thing can be repeated next season against an additional few hundred shops, employing, let us say, an average of 15 workers. In this manner, another 5,000 workers would be taken out from the corporation shops and placed in legitimate factories.

This procedure, followed up later on, would actually solve the problem in a comparatively short time. Furthermore, there would not be any new corporation shops coming into existence if those planning such shops will see that they are being put out of business.

Anyone acquainted with the situation in the industry today, anyone who saw 100 sub-manufacturers waiting at the office of a large jobber, and actually fighting for the chance to get an order at almost any price, must realize that the elimination of the worst 500 of the social shops in this market would have an immediate effect on the situation and would greatly relieve the legitimate manufacturers.[44]

---

[44]*Women's Wear,* May 25, 1922. For an account of the union's campaign against small shops, see ILGWU, *Report and Proceedings,* Seventeenth Convention (May 1924), pp. 19–20. In its drive to eliminate the small social shop, the ILGWU received enthusiastic support from the American Cloak and Suit Manufacturers' Association (contractors) whose members could refuse to work for jobbers who sent out materials to be finished by social shops. See *Women's Wear,* May 22 and July 10, 1922. ILGWU President Schlesinger's campaign against the small shops appears to have met with little lasting success, for in 1923 there were 585 more women's coat and suit establishments in the New York market area than in 1922 and most of these additional shops were among the smallest in size. *Women's Wear,* Dec. 6, 1923.

Early in the 1919 strike of this industry, the ILGWU had forced the closing of several hundred small social shops. "By the union's vigorous stand for centralization," commented M. Finkelstein, chief clerk for the union, "the

Simultaneous efforts to eliminate the small-scale producers came from other industries of the needle trades. Within two weeks after the president of the ILGWU had outlined his plan, the Amalgamated Clothing Workers' Union had threatened a general stoppage in the men's clothing trade to bring about registration of contractors and the elimination of small shops whose workers were not organized. At about the same time, the cloth hat and cap industry included the following paragraph in its collective agreement:

Both parties agree that the development of the social shop is bound to undermine the entire industry. For the cut-throat competition of the social shop is based on the lowering of all working conditions and trade standards, on a cheapening of the quality of the article, and on the gradual reduction of the trade to the position of a sweatshop trade. Both sides fully endorse the statement of the Board of Arbitration of May 1921, to the effect that the "illegitimate social shop is detrimental to the industry as a whole and therefore to the legitimate manufacturers and to the organized workers."[45]

---

cancer which has threatened the very life of the industry is about to be eradicated, both to the advantage of the legitimate employer and to the distinct gain of the worker." *Women's Wear,* May 20, 1919.

[45]For the ACWA, see *Daily News Record,* May 25, 1921, June 2, 1922. Text of the collective agreement, effective July 19, 1922, between the Cloth Hat and Cap Manufacturers' Association and the Joint Council of New York of the United Cloth Hat and Cap Makers of North America may be found in United Cloth Hat and Cap Makers of North America, *Report and Proceedings,* Fourteenth Biennial Convention (May 1923), Appendix I, pp. 64, 66. In the late thirties, small-scale millinery manufacturers still believed that the union was trying to drive them out of business: "Fear and discouragement keynoted a meeting of 350 millinery manufacturers called by the Greater New York Millinery Manufacturers' Association...to discuss plans for ending the current stoppage....Manufacturers muttered to one another that the union was planning to 'drive the little fellow out of business,' and that the union was in collusion with large manufacturers, who settled and resumed work early in the stoppage." *Millinery Research,* Oct. 12, 1937. When the organized factions of the dress and waist industry were invited to Albany in 1930 to consider ways and means of meeting the depression, L. L. Schwartz, president of the newly formed Affiliated Dress Manufacturers' Association (inside manufactures), sent a letter to Governor Franklin D. Roosevelt stressing the need for diverting a major part of dress production away from small shops to "large, wholesome and centrally located factories." *Women's Wear Daily,* Feb. 7, 1930.

But repeated failures to eliminate small-scale substandard producers never seemed to dampen the ardor of the parties to collective agreements. "The principal question before all in the cloak industry today," wrote Morris Sigman, who in 1923 had succeeded Benjamin Schlesinger to the presidency of the ILGWU, "is — How can we rid this trade of the small shops; how can we do away with the devastating competition between the shops?" In a series of articles on "A Survey and Forecast of Leading Events and Factors in the [women's] Coat and Suit Industry," printed in his union's newspaper, *Justice,* Sigman noted in 1927 that the ILGWU's general executive board had considered these questions at great length and, as a first step, had come up with the following suggestion:

Since the small sub-manufacturing shops manage to exist only because they produce cloaks cheaper than the "inside" shops by the dint of cheaper labor and production costs, we must first regulate labor costs in all shops and in this manner do away with the primary cause of the competition the sub-manufacturers keep up at the expense of the workers. . . . There is no doubt that such an adjustment of production costs would tend to give permanence and stability to the larger shops. . . . The regulations of the production costs would eventually drive the small shop out of the market.

Such an official restatement of a long-established policy did little to resolve the question of how production costs could be equalized in all shops. To implement such a program, President Sigman and his general executive board proposed "that the union, in conjunction with the associations, form a joint control and adjustment committee, which should visit every shop, the sub-manufacturing as well as the inside shops, to ascertain and regulate the wages and other labor costs in all the shops." Though such an investigation might disclose that a jobber paid each of twenty contractors a different price for identical work, at least the committee could "regulate at all times the wages to be paid the workers so that the labor would cost alike in each shop." For those in the industry who refused to go along with such a plan, Sigman proposed a system for limitation of contractors that would permit a weeding out of all nonconforming contractors.[46]

---

[46]ILGWU, *Justice,* Nov. 25, 1927. See also the issues of Nov. 4, 11, and 18, 1927. These ideas undoubtedly contributed to the establishment of the women's Coat and Suit Control Commission under the 1929 collective agreements. See below, chap. 17.

Size as a Criterion of Legitimacy

Establishing a minimum size below which no shop would be patronized by parties to collective agreements or allowed to participate in the program controlling competition was a widely used device for weeding out the small producers. As early as 1915, the American Clothing Manufacturers' Association agreed to a proposal of the ACWA that men's coat and vest shops consist of not fewer than eight sewing machines and that men's pant shops have not fewer than twelve machines each. It was estimated at the time that over two hundred contracting establishments employing four thousand operatives would be temporarily thrown out of employment if these provisions were put into effect.[47]

Likewise, the International Ladies' Garment Workers' Union won concessions that set a lower limit on the size of shops in the women's coat and suit trade. "The association and the union are in accord," stated the 1919 collective agreement between the Cloak, Suit and Skirt Manufacturers' Protective Association and the Cloakmakers' Joint Board, "that the interests of the industry will be best served by large factory units and to that end fix as a minimum fourteen (14) working machines to a factory organization." The fourteen machine rule was endorsed by Governor Smith's Advisory Commission in 1924; and in the collective agreements of that year the union shop was defined as "one that employs at least 14 machine operators and a corresponding number of employees in other branches of the work and is operated under a contract with the union."

In order to eliminate the chaotic condition that has been created by the multiplication of the sub-manufacturers and contractors who conduct shops in the industry, the union has requested, and all factors in the industry have approved, a reduction in the number of shops in the industry from 3,000 to nearer 1,500 by a process of consolidation

---

[47]*Daily Trade Record,* Dec. 30, 1915.

The cloak and suit industry in this city employs about 50,000 workers. Upon a rational organization there should be no more than a maximum of 500 producing units, i.e., at an average of one establishment for 100 workers. As a matter of fact, there are no less than 3000 cloak factories in New York, of which the vast majority are sub-manufacturers' or contractors' shops.

—ILGWU, *Report and Proceedings,* Seventeenth Convention (May 1924), p. 33.

that will permit no shop to be recognized under the agreement unless it employs at least fourteen machine operators and a corresponding number of employees in other branches of the work and is operated under a contract with the union.[48]

In 1924, the fur workers' union won its demand that fur contractors employ at least five workers to the shop. In 1926, the Cloth Hat, Cap and Millinery Workers' International Union sponsored a provision in its agreement with the Wholesale Hat and Cap Manufacturers' Association that would require each union shop to employ "not less than a cutter, a blocker, a packer, a lining maker, a trimmer, and a proportional number of operators." And, in 1938, the parties to the collective agreement of the belt industry recognized "that shops that employ less than six workers tend to undermine the standards of labor conditions established in this industry" and, therefore, agreed "that no less than six Union workers are to be employed in a shop of the employer, at least one of whom is to be an operator."[49]

---

[48]From the 1924 *Recommendations* of the Governor's Advisory Commission on the women's coat and suit trade, discussed in ILGWU, *Report and Proceedings,* Eighteenth Convention (November 1925), pp. 13–18. A full complement of workers in a women's coat and suit factory of fourteen machine operators would require a total of approximately fifty employees. *Women's Wear Daily,* Nov. 3, 1930. Texts of the 1919 collective agreements for the women's coat and suit trade were printed in *Monthly Labor Review,* December 1919, vol. 9, pp. 1716–1724.

[49]See the 1924 collective agreement between the Associated Fur Manufacturers and the Furriers' Joint Board and the International Fur Workers' Union; the 1926 collective agreement between the Wholesale Hat and Cap Association and the Joint Council of Hat, Cap and Millinery Workers; and the 1938 collective agreement between the Belt Association and Local 40, ILGWU. See also the *Fur Worker,* December 1923; the *Headgear Worker,* August 20, 1926; and the 1925 collective agreement between the Association of Dress Manufacturers and the ILGWU, the text of which is printed in *Women's Wear,* Jan. 19, 1925.

> It was understood between Mr. Pike [labor manager of the Associated Fur Manufacturers] and our office that no firm employing less than five workers would be admitted to membership in the Association in view of the fact that we decline to settle with independent firms who have less than five workers in their employ.
> —Ben Gold, manager, Joint Board, Furriers' Union, to Paul Abelson, acting chairman, Conference Committee. Letter dated August 26, 1925, filed in the Abelson papers.

Perhaps for legal reasons, the enforcement of "legitimate size" clauses was generally left to the needle trade unions. Eradicating "these elusive units run on a corporation or social basis" required an effective use of the union's power to strike. Even against association members, strike action was sometimes authorized where firms employed less than the minimum number of workers for an unreasonable length of time. Against independents the union was, of course, free to strike at any time and usually made its move at the height of the busy season. In September 1937, Locals 24 and 42 of the millinery workers' union ordered stoppages in hundreds of small shops to effect a "genuine housecleaning" that resulted in denying some fifty shops the right to make agreements with the union because of their size.[50]

Undoubtedly, in suppressing small shops, the needle trade unions were motivated by a desire to strengthen their own positions within their trades. At best, union membership and union conditions were difficult to control in small shops. One union official was convinced that effective policing of labor contracts was impossible in shops of fewer than one hundred workers. At the same time, the demands of these unions for shops of a minimum size played directly into the hands of the "legitimate" manufacturers who saw in these union objectives a chance to be rid of their most ruthless competitors. Here, then, was still another reason why the organized manufacturers who supported the protocol movement were so eager to play ball with the union at the bargaining table.

Regulation of Large-Scale Contractors

Attempts at eliminating the small-time operator, like the movement to abolish all contracting, were conducted in the face of growing demands for cheap goods. Although inside manufacturers undertook to meet this demand by producing three grades of garments — expensive, medium, and cheap — they could not equal the ability of contractors "to make cheap goods cheap." Furthermore, every change in style calling for less skill in production catered to the contractor whose operations were geared to quantity rather than quality. In the women's coat and suit trade, the phe-

---

[50]United Hatters, Cap and Millinery Workers' International Union, *Report and Proceedings,* Third Convention (May 1939), p. 79.

nomenal growth of contracting during the twenties was prompted in part by a fashion change from tight-fitting suits to loose-fitting coats, which could be made by less skilled labor.[51]

Nor did efforts to eliminate the contractor take care of growing needs for supplemental sources of production at the height of the busy seasons. These needs might arise from the nature of the product to be handled, or from the limitations of "inside" facilities, or from the pressures of time in which to get out the work. The more substantial manufacturers could not afford to prepare in advance for every possible change in volume of production or for every variation in materials and style that fashion might thrust upon them. All these vicissitudes of the business played directly into the hands of the contracting specialist whose tempo of change and economy of operations — like the destroyers of the navy — met the demands for flexibility that could not be matched by the inside establishments — the dreadnaughts of the fleet.

Most frequently, inside manufacturers were under pressure to meet production deadlines at a time when their facilities were already taxed to capacity. Such conditions appeared to justify a resort to outside contracting for emergency purposes, and for that reason many collective agreements that endorsed the principle of no-contracting still recognized the necessity for exceptions to the general rule. "We do not want at present to do away with the outside shops," declared a spokesman for the inside women's coat and suit manufacturers of the Cleveland market in the fall of 1922, "because we realize that at present a number of them are needed in the industry to help take care of the peak loads of the season; but we must take precautions that the outside shops should be properly controlled and put on a proper basis so as not to destroy the inside shops."[52]

---

[51]Comparative statistics on the distribution of production by inside establishments and contractor shops in the early twenties are given in ILGWU's *Justice*, August 6, 1926. President Sigman pointed out that whereas in 1921 some 86 percent of women's coats and suits were produced by inside manufacturers, four years later only 25 percent came from inside manufacturing. *Justice*, Nov. 4, 1927.

[52]*Women's Wear*, Oct. 30, 1922. See also the testimony of Max Friedman, president of the American Clothing Manufacturers' Association of the men's clothing industry, before the U.S. Commission on Industrial Relations, June 4, 1914, *Final Report and Testimony*, vol. 2, p. 1984.

These sentiments found expression in clauses of collective agreements forbidding a manufacturer to engage in outside contracting "so long as the workers of his inside shop are not fully supplied with work" or so long as "the workers of the inside shop are not fully employed." Some agreements forbade manufacturers to lay off or discharge inside workers while workers in the shops of their contractors were busy. Other agreements stated the issue positively: "Firms may give work to contractors, provided the entire force in the factory of the Firm is fully employed and the entire space therein is fully utilized." As a rule, these restrictive clauses also applied to buying finished products from outside sources. In some cases, outside buying was prohibited unless workers of both the inside shops and the contractors' shops were fully occupied.[53]

Where for lack of skill or equipment the inside factory could not make a particular garment, outside contractors were conceded an additional area in which to work. Some agreements permitted the inside manufacturer to send out work that he was "not adapted to make in his own shop" or that was "of a different nature or class than performed in his own shop." In the case of the leather goods industry, inside manufacturers were permitted to buy from outside contractors "such items as have never been made in the

---

[53]For typical clauses, see the 1925 collective agreement between the Greek Fur Manufacturers and the fur workers' union, the 1937 collective agreement between the National Skirt Manufacturers' Association and the Cloakmakers' Joint Board, ILGWU, and the 1938 collective agreement between the Industrial Association of Juvenile Apparel Manufacturers and Locals 91 and 10, ILGWU.

> It is agreed that all work will be given to the inside shops. If at any time during the life of this agreement, it is found that the workers are unable to meet the demands of output in any one season, or are unable to assume prompt delivery through any increase of business for that season, the firm shall have the right to place extra work in outside shops in order that undue injury through the cancellation of orders may be prevented. It is understood, however, that preference will be given to outside shops employing members of the Amalgamated Clothing workers.
> —From the 1921 collective agreement between the Clothing Manufacturers' Association of Montreal and the ACWA, quoted in *Daily News Record,* July 28, 1921.

inside shop because of considerations of quality, quantity or price."[54]

This movement to regulate the contracting system began with modest attempts at identifying contractors under the protocols and developed into elaborate schemes for limiting the number of contractors and controlling their assignments. The multiple objectives of the program guaranteed support both from labor unions and from employers' associations. Effective regulation could promote the growth of organized labor by weeding out the centers of nonunion production. At the same time, it could bring greater stability to business firms by controlling the major source of "illegitimate" competition. Collective bargaining was the medium through which the organized forces of industry sought to accomplish these objectives.

Most types of regulations had their origin in union pressures first directed against independent manufacturers and then extended wherever possible to association members. This was particularly true of the men's clothing industry, where manufacturing before the mid-twenties was so largely conducted by the contracting system. "Almost from the beginning," reported *Advance,* official organ of the Amalgamated Clothing Workers' Union, for June 11, 1926, "the Amalgamated was alive to the problem of control in a contract market. It very early in its history enforced the practice of registration of contractors. It made it difficult for the manufacturers to change from one contractor to another unless the Union was satisfied with the reasons for the change. It did not permit manufacturers suddenly to withdraw from one contractor, throw all of the employees of that contractor out of jobs and send the work to a new contractor. In substance, the union has constantly been enforcing the equal division of work rule between contractors within the market."[55]

---

[54] See the 1922 collective agreement of the Cloth Hat and Cap Manufacturers with the New York Joint Council of the United Cloth Hat and Cap Makers, the 1925 collective agreement of the Associated Leather Goods Manufacturers with the Fancy Leather Goods Workers' Union, and the 1936 collective agreement of the Infants' and Children's Wear Association with Local 91, ILGWU.

[55] "The early ILGWU position on contracting was presented in the union's demands for revision in 1913 of the original protocol of the women's coat and suit industry: (1) employers must register all contractors at the beginning of each season; (2) no new contractors may be taken on during the season unless

Recognition of Jobbers and Contractors

Tolerating the jobber-contracting system of production in any form conferred upon jobbers and contractors an element of legitimacy in their own right. Once the system had been condoned, many inside manufacturers turned to jobbing or contracting for their livelihood. The more substantial jobbers and contractors formed associations of their own and set themselves up as "respectable" producers, no longer to be associated with "the hundreds of small 'insects' of manufacturers" entering the needle trades each year. These new employer groups sought official recognition from other organized segments of their industries and wished to become partners in the new order of collective bargaining.[56]

Among the more active of these new groups was the American Cloak and Suit Manufacturers' Association, an organization of contractors formed at the close of the First World War. Its objec-

---

existing inside and outside shops owned or patronized by an employer are fully supplied with work; (3) no contractor may be discharged in the middle of the season except for very important reasons and only after an investigation; (4) all inside and outside shops owned or patronized by an employer are to be considered branches of the same factory." *Jewish Daily Forward,* July 13, 1913. Translation filed in the Abelson papers.

[56]On June 6, 1913, the *Jewish Daily Forward* had pointed out that the owners of most manufacturing establishments in the women's coat and suit trade had less than $50,000 invested in their businesses. "Such bosses must be afraid of the smallest competition. They must take into account every small boss, every small manufacturer, and hundreds of small 'insects' of manufacturers who take to the cloak trade every year." From a translation in the Abelson papers.

Supporting contractors' shops not only for meeting emergency needs but also for supplying small acorns from which the trees of big business grow, J. H. Cohen in 1916 defended the contractors of the dress and waist industry:

> They are not outlaws. They are legitimate manufacturers in many instances. They have learned the art of working, the art of controlling and producing efficient results. Now if the Union had seen...that those men must be met and met upon legitimate grounds...they would have succeeded in preserving and developing this industry....I have no patience with the argument that the contractor is an outlaw. He is not. There are men in the industry who are breaking down standards who are outlaws, but you must distinguish between the two.
>
> —J. H. Cohen in *Minutes,* Arbitration Proceedings between the Dress and Waist Manufacturers' Association and the ILGWU (Feb. 14, 1916), vol. 5, pp. 634–635.

tives were set forth in its own official publication, *American Garment News.* "Membership in the American Association is the stamp of responsibility," stated the issue dated January 26, 1922, ". . . we wish to put a line of demarcation between us, members of the Association and those irresponsible elements which undermine the industry by their illegitimate methods and alluring representations as to prices, workmanship and delivery; and by their complete disregard of the existing standards and obligations and by their unbusinesslike unscrupulousness and suicidal competitive practices." If groups of this type were to be given a place in the sun, however, their acceptance had to be reconciled with certain basic principles of the protocol movement favoring inside production.[57]

By recognizing contractors as potential employers of union members, labor unions had prepared the way for the entry of the organized contractors into the realm of law and order. While opposing the jobber-contractor system of production in principle, labor leaders for practical reasons were anxious to negotiate agreements with jobbers and contractors. Where industries were, in fact, operating on a jobber-contractor basis, no other policy would have been realistic. "There is no sense in having a protocol with a manufacturer who has no bundles to give," observed a writer for the *New Post,* organ of the ILGWU Cloakmakers' Joint Board, "and not have a protocal with the sub-manufacturer who has the bundles." Moreover, organizing the workers in contractors' shops offered the most effective means of controlling the kind of competition that had made the contractor the scourge of the needle trades.[58]

Such a realistic approach played directly into the hands of the substantial jobbers and contractors who believe their own cooperation to be essential for any effective regulation of industry. This belief was supported by the failure of labor unions and inside manufacturers to eliminate the evils of contracting, for none of

[57]ILGWU, *Justice,* Nov. 16, 1923, defined the legitimate contractor as "that contractor who has contractual relations with the union and preserves union standards."

[58]*New Post,* July 13, 1913. "If we do not succeed in this, we will eventually come to that state that, where the protocol is, there are no bundles; and where there are bundles, there is no protocol," *ibid.,* June 6, 1913. Translations filed in the Abelson papers.

the provisions that these two groups had devised to regulate contracting appeared to relieve the "driving pressure of competition"
generated among jobbers and manufacturers for available contractors, or among contractors for available work. In opening the
doors for cooperation from a new source, the proponents of the
protocol movement developed a broader concept of the "legitimate" forces in industry. They undertook to separate jobbers and
contractors — as well as workers and inside manufacturers — into
the sheep and the goats and to brand the sheep of each paddock
with the stamp of respectability.

The process of admitting "legitimate" contractors into the realm
of law and order began early in the men's clothing trade of New
York City. "We should be happy to see the contracting system
abolished," reported the general executive board of the Amalgamated Clothing Workers' Union to the union's Baltimore convention in 1918:

> But while it is not within our power to eradicate the evil, we have
> tried to regulate it and remove at least its most objectionable features,
> make it less brutalizing for the contractors, who are human beings
> like the rest of us, and less degrading for the workers. . . . Accordingly,
> we made our renewed agreement with the American Clothing Manu-
> facturers' Association in January, 1916, a tri-partite agreement, bring-
> ing in the contractors, through their organizations, in all such matters
> in which they might be concerned.[59]

Although this agreement became a dead letter, the movement to
accept the organized contractors into the established order gained
a new impetus after the First World War.

"The contractors are still with us and will undoubtedly continue
to remain in large numbers," concluded a special committee reporting on the men's clothing industry in 1920. "We believe it is
essential that they should be more intimately related to the impartial machinery since this means bringing them into effective
responsibility for the conduct of the industry." As a first step toward including certain contractors in the government of the industry, this committee proposed that a labor manager be appointed
for the contractor's association — a manager who would be "au-

---

[59]ACWA, *Report and Proceedings,* Third Biennial Convention (May 1918),
p. 65.

thorized to speak for all groups, competent to represent them and yet guided by the larger interests of the industry."[60]

These seed fell upon good ground. In 1921, the Clothing Manufacturers' Association of New York and the Amalgamated Clothing Workers provided through their men's clothing agreement for a special commission to lay down the rules under which contractors were to be included as parties to the agreement. The progress of those admitted to the established order was soon revealed through a report that three associations of contractors (one each for pants, vests, and coats) had combined with the ACWA to drive out of business all contractors who were not in favor with these groups.[61]

Meanwhile, the organized jobbers and the organized contractors of the women's garment trades were gaining admission into the realm of law and order established for their industries. Although the ILGWU had negotiated collective agreements with some contractor groups before 1920, it was not until the decade of the twenties that outside producers became full partners in the programs to control competition through collective bargaining. The entering wedge came through the help that outside producers offered the ILGWU in eliminating the "small fry" from the trades. At that time, the "legitimate" jobbers of the women's coat and suit trade — those who had previously been "forced by competition to resort to the corporation shop for a good amount of their production" — offered to help the union weed out these parasites. At the same time, the "responsible" contractors — members of the American Cloak and Suit Manufacturers' Association — agreed to get together with the ILGWU to take up "the matter of eliminating the small uncontrolled social shops of the cloak industry."[62]

The movement to recognize jobbers and contractors as "legitimate" factors in the women's coat and suit trade received a further boost from the 1924 recommendations of Governor Smith's Advisory Commission established to investigate the trade:

---

[60]Felix Frankfurter and S. J. Rosensohn, "Survey of the New York [men's] Clothing Industry" at p. 42 of the union affidavits. Copy filed in the Abelson papers. For later developments, see *Daily News Record,* June 3, 18, and 29, 1921.

[61]*Ibid.,* Sept. 13, 1922.

[62]*Women's Wear,* July 10, 1922.

The Commission believes that unless all of the different factors in the industry, unions, inside manufacturers, sub-manufacturers and jobbers, are brought together under a harmonious arrangement there can be no lasting peace in the industry.... The only hope for the future of the industry is to have the four elements mentioned assume mutual obligations that will bring about fair dealing that will not give one group an unfair advantage over the other and that will tend to restore stability and insure the maintenance of proper labor and sanitary standards in the industry.

Shortly thereafter, associations of jobbers, contractors, and inside manufacturers in the women's coat and suit trade entered into separate collective agreements with the ILGWU, but the agreements were essentially alike in their terms and employed the same impartial machinery for their administration. This procedure has characterized collective bargaining in several branches of the needle trades since the twenties.[63]

Limitation and Assignment of Contractors

Once admitted into the realm of law and order, the "legitimate" forces of outside production actively participated in developing plans both for limiting the number of contractors allowed to receive work and for assigning those contractors to particular jobbers or inside manufacturers. Having emerged from the role of "industrial termites," these organized jobbers and contractors now helped to eradicate other termites that worked beneath the floors of legitimate competition. By proposing to restrict the number and mobility of contractors, these newly accepted partners were merely joining a movement that had long been sponsored by the needle trade unions themselves.

From the early days of the protocol movement, labor unions at negotiating conferences repeatedly demanded that manufacturers and jobbers be forbidden to change or dismiss contractors

---

[63] The 1924 recommendations of the Governor's Advisory Commission may be found in ILGWU, *Justice*, July 18, 1924.

In 1923, the Dressmakers' Joint Board, ILGWU, signed collective agreements with an association of jobbers and an association of contractors in the dress and waist industry, thereby acknowledging a "change in the industry that had made the jobber rather than the manufacturer the dominating figure." But the organized forces of the dress industry lacked cohesion until the thirties when all factions of the industry were brought together to help solve the problems of the depression. *Women's Wear Daily*, Feb. 4, 1930.

during a busy season without justifiable cause. In May 1913, the Cloakmakers' Joint Board submitted to the organized women's coat and suit manufacturers the first comprehensive program for regulating the contracting system. Among the list of seventeen union proposals to amend the original Protocol of Peace was a provision that would prohibit a manufacturer from adding new contractors unless his inside and outside shops were busy. No contractor could be dropped without sufficient reason.[64]

"The demand for the limitation of contractors is a natural and necessary one," stated an editorial in *Justice,* official organ of the ILGWU, November 30, 1923. "The manufacturer should be allowed to employ contractors, limited in number to a quantity sufficient to produce his accustomed volume of business. Permission to employ new contractors should be granted grudgingly, and only on proof that the number previously agreed upon is insufficient for turning out his work. Discharge of contractors should be discouraged and fought. The net result would be a limitation on competition. . . ." Supporting this stand, the general executive board of the ILGWU recommended in 1924 "that each jobber employ only such number of contractors as he can provide with work to their full capacity."[65]

Union support for limitation of contractors was motivated by prospects of higher labor standards and brighter hopes of enforc-

---

[64]*Women's Wear,* May 24, 1913. A summary account of these various union demands to regulate the contracting system is given in Sherman Trowbridge, "Some Aspects of the Women's Apparel Industry," NRA: Division of Review, Industry Studies Section, Work Materials, no. 44 (March 1936), pp. 8–10. Trowbridge traces the development of this program into the post-World War I period.

For a penetrating analysis of the outside contracting problem in the dress industry with proposals for reform, see the views of Morris Hillquit, legal counsel for the ILGWU, in *Minutes,* Arbitration Proceedings between the Dress and Waist Manufacturers' Association and the ILGWU (Feb. 14, 1916), vol. 5, pp. 567–669.

[65]ILGWU, *Report and Proceedings,* Seventeenth Convention (May 1924), p. 34. Union views, as well as employer reactions, on the limitation of contractors can be found in the files of *Women's Wear* during the spring of 1924, particularly the issues of April 10 and 11, 1924. See also two lengthy articles in ILGWU's *Justice* by Morris Sigman, president of the union: "The Role of the Jobber in the Cloak and Dress Industry," in the issue of Feb. 29, 1924; and "Why We Must Limit the Number of Contractors for Jobbers," in the issue of March 7, 1924.

ing them. "It is thought," explained J. A. Dyche, who was for ten
years general secretary-treasurer of the ILGWU, "that if the jobber is limited to sending out work to only a limited number of
sub-manufacturers, then the sub-manufacturer will be in a position to get a better price per garment from the jobber in the
first instance, and the union will then be able to press a demand
for better wages from sub-manufacturers." Moreover, union leaders were convinced that labor standards could never be enforced
so long as the "auction block system" of letting out work to the
lowest bidding contractor prevailed. In the competition among
individual contractors for work, the pressure to undermine labor
standards would always be more than the machinery of contract
enforcement could effectively handle.[66]

But labor unions were not alone in favoring limitation of contractors as a method of regulating competition. Other advocates
of law and order were equally concerned with seeking relief from
the evils of the auction block system. In addition to the inside
manufacturers, who naturally supported any scheme that would
restrict outside competition, the "legitimate" contractors actively
favored proposals that would relieve them from being "made
miserable by the horde of open shop contractors who work for
anybody, for anything, anytime." In supporting limitation of contractors, Harry Uviller, executive director, American Cloak and
Suit Manufacturers' Association (contractors), welcomed attempts
by the union "to revamp the industrial fabric of the [women's]
coat and suit trade."[67]

---

[66]J. A. Dyche, *Bolshevism in American Labor Unions* (1926), p. 157.

Competition had pushed individual contractors and workers to the
wall, and squeezed out the fair earnings of the industry. The workers who
had suffered most now alone were organized to resist. But whereas they
had previously struck against the immediate "boss" [the contractor] with
whom they came in contact, they now recognized that the boss was caught
as they were in a system. Therefore their next move was to organize the
"bosses." It was a defensive alliance of workers and contractors. They
tried to make each manufacturer responsible for certain shops.
—Felix Frankfurter and S. J. Rosensohn, "Survey of the New York
[men's] Clothing Industry" at p. 24 of the union affidavits. Copy
filed in the Abelson papers.

[67]*Women's Wear*, April 10, 1924; *Journal of Commerce*, Oct. 3 and 4, 1928.
During the strike of 1930 over new terms of employment in the dress and waist

Like other organized factions of industry, the "legitimate" jobbers — those who assumed responsibility for the labor standards
of their contractors and wanted to maintain a floor under competition — found hope in a system of limiting the number of contractors available and assigning those contractors to the organized
jobbers and inside manufacturers of a trade. On one side, the
"legitimate" jobbers were harassed by the "illegitimate" jobbers
who "jump about in the market among an ever increasing number
of sub-manufacturers, preying upon the weaknesses of a system
that is at once ruinous to the sub-manufacturer and undesirable
and annoying to the workers." On the other side, these legitimate
jobbers were harassed by "illegitimate" contractors who disregarded labor agreements and observed no standards of business
conduct. Surveying the role of the jobber in the women's coat and
suit trade during the late twenties, one writer noted that "the
'legitimate' jobber has to fight hard against the 'bootleg' jobber,
who manages to get his merchandise from 'bootleg' contractors."[68]

Quite clearly, all the organized factions of an industry, including

industry, the contractors' association, more so than the union, insisted upon
"limitation" as a condition of settlement. *Women's Wear Daily,* Feb. 10, 1930.

> The contractor was being ground between two very heavy and very
> pitiless stones. One was the union, which imposed upon him definite
> pay and work standards, and bore down as hard as it could in enforce-
> ment of these standards.
> Bearing down on him from the other side was the jobber.
> "How much do you want to make this garment for me?" said the
> jobber.
> "Six dollars," said the contractor.
> "I will give you five."
> "But labor on this garment costs me $4.75, according to my agreement
> [with the union]. And I've got to pay my rent, and my overhead, and
> insurance out of the other $1.25 and then I'll get nothing at all for my
> own work."
> To which the jobber answered, and with truth: "There are contractors
> waiting here right now who'll take the work for $5.00 and gladly."
> The work was on the auction block.... The contractor took it for $5.00
> or maybe he got $5.25. In any event, to break even he had to make pri-
> vate deals with his workers, evade the contract in other ways, and even
> then, at the end of the season, he found himself with a deficit and was
> forced to go out of business.
> —C. H. Green in *Women's Wear Daily,* August 15, 1933.

[68] *Women's Wear,* April 10, 1924; *Journal of Commerce,* Oct. 4, 1928.

the labor union, stood to gain from a system of interlocking agreements, understandings, and exclusive tie-ins designed to help each
other at the expense of those outside the realm of law and order.
Any such arrangement called for binding agreements between
organizations of jobbers or inside manufacturers and organizations
of contractors. At the same time, each of these employer groups
had to maintain supporting agreements with the unions of the
workers in their plants. Bound by an interlocking chain of such
agreements, the participating groups would then show a proper
respect for the interests of all concerned. In the welfare of their
trade they found a common objective, and in collective bargaining
they found a common means to an end.

In 1926, the American Cloak and Suit Manufacturers' Association (contractors) presented a proposal for limiting and assigning contractors so that the organized factions of the women's coat
and suit industry — jobbers, inside manufacturers, contractors,
and the labor union — would be limited to dealing with each other.
That year the essentials of this proposal were incorporated into
the final recommendations of Governor Smith's Advisory Commission to investigate the industry: (1) a limited number of contractors should be designated by each manufacturer or jobber; (2)
no contractors should be changed except for cause shown; (3) the
flow of work to contractors should be regularized; (4) no work
should be given to other contractors unless those designated were
busy; and (5) equitable distribution of work should be made
among each producer's designated contractors.[69]

The unpredictable ways of the unscrupulous contractors were thus described
in 1921:

> Manufacturer "A" would call up the contractor to find out when he
> would get the lot which should have been delivered two weeks previous;
> an evasive answer brought him post-haste to the contractor's shop. There
> he would find his cut-up goods under benches or covered over with refuse
> in the middle of the shop, while in the machines was manufacturer "B's"
> work. There was no use pleading with the contractor; only money talked.
> Manufacturer "A's" goods went into the machines and "B's" were shoved
> aside. Or, perhaps, "C" came along with a tempting offer, and both "A"
> and "B" were writing their customers that they would get their suits
> soon, while, as a matter of fact, the suits were still only cut cloth.
> —Frank Chodorov in *Daily News Record*, May 31, 1922.

[69]*Final Recommendations,* p. 7.

Subsequently, the basic features of this program, with further restrictions and controls, were incorporated into collective agreements of the women's coat and suit trade and of the dress and waist industry. Typical of these controls were the following provisions in the 1929 collective agreement between the Merchants' Ladies' Garment Association (jobbers) and the American Cloak and Suit Manufacturers' Association (contractors):

The members of the American Association are recognized in this industry to be the efficient and standard shops, capable of assisting and stabilizing the industry and eliminating the so-called sweatshop evil and substandard shops and have this day executed an agreement with the Union, copy whereof is annexed to this agreement and marked Exhibit "B."

Accordingly, to assist the American Association to perform under its contract with the Union the parties hereto agree that the members of the Merchants' Association will confine the manufacture of merchandise made for them to members of the American Association exclusively and the members of the American Association undertake to give preference to the members of the Merchants' Association and the members of the Industrial Council of Cloak, Suit and Skirt Manufacturers [inside manufacturers] as against independents and the members of the American Association will do nothing in their business dealing that will adversely reflect upon the exclusive obligation here undertaken by the members of the Merchants' Association.[70]

---

[70]A copy of the agreement, effective July 16, 1929, is filed in the Abelson papers. See also *Women's Wear Daily,* Dec. 13, 1929, June 17 and August 1, 1930.

Commenting on similar clauses in collective agreements between the ILGWU and the jobbers' association, as well as between the ILGWU and the inside manufacturers' association, the general executive board of the ILGWU reported to the union's 1929 convention as follows:

This clause will limit the production of garments exclusively to those shops in contractual relations with the Union and which are members of the American Association.... This clause will enable the Union, through the Commission established in the new agreement, to limit the number of shops in the industry thereby eliminating those which cause the demoralization and evade control.

—ILGWU, *Report and Proceedings,* Twentieth Convention (December 1929), pp. 48–49.

For the analogous clause in the 1930 collective agreement between the Wholesale Dress Manufacturers (jobbers) and the Association of Dress Manufacturers (contractors), see *Women's Wear Daily,* Feb. 26, 1930.

Provisions for such interlocking relationships favorable to the organized forces of the women's garment trades received the official sanction of the NRA codes of fair competition and were continued in collective agreements of the thirties. Implementing a system for limiting and assigning contractors called for many supplementary regulations and administrative rules that could best be worked out by the impartial machinery of each industry. Inside manufacturers, jobbers, contractors, and labor unions were pledged to cooperate with the impartial machinery to see that the plans adopted were effectively enforced.

Concluding Observations

Methods of piece-rate determination and limitations on contracting out work were the key problems facing the parties to collective agreements. Neglected or sidetracked at the Brandeis Conferences of 1910, these critical issues received more and more attention at the bargaining table. Above all other factors, the solution of these two issues unlocked the secret to controlled competition on which the protocol movement had been founded. If attempts at resolving these problems carried the parties far afield from any direct concern for wages, hours, and working conditions, the organized forces of industry were merely accepting a fusion of trade and labor functions that had always characterized collective bargaining in the apparel trades.

Solving the problems of piece-rate determination and of the contracting system opened the gates to industrial stability. Issues of management prerogatives and of union security were forgotten in a concerted drive to clear the roadblocks that hampered the prosperity of the trade. Controlling methods of production not only brought profits to the "legitimate" manufacturer but paved the way to "giving the guy a raise." Under the direction of the organized factions within each trade, collective bargaining became a strange brew in which labor standards and trade practices were inextricably mixed. Goals were always stated in terms of industry-wide standards and the general welfare of the trade. It remains to be seen what institutions and what procedures could be devised for attaining these ultimate objectives.

Chapter 5

The Lawmaking Function

THE formulation of programs and policies with which to carry out the broad objectives of collective bargaining in the needle trades was a continuing process. No detailed plan for putting a floor under competition evolved from the joint conferences that gave rise to the first collective agreements. The framers of the original protocols harped upon certain problems of stabilizing their industries but made no attempt to foresee all eventualities. Although dedicated to the control of competition, the organized forces of labor and management did little more than initiate the procedures and set in motion the machinery through which this objective might ultimately be achieved.

Legislative Role of the Impartial Machinery

The original women's coat and suit protocol made provision for a board of arbitration of three members, one to represent the association, one the union, and one the public. To this board would be referred "any differences hereafter arising between the parties hereto, or between any of the members of the manufacturers and any of the members of the union." In addition, this agreement called for a committee on grievances composed of four members equally divided between the association and the union to handle "all minor grievances arising in connection with the business relations between the manufacturers and their employees." Together with a joint board of sanitary control representing the union, the association, and the public, these were the first permanent institutions of industrial self-government to be established under the protocol movement.

All subsequent protocols and major collective agreements in the needle trades provided for some form of "impartial machinery" to carry on the work of the "founding fathers." By accepted usage, the very term, impartial machinery, came to embrace all those individuals and agencies chosen to work in a continuing capacity during the life of an agreement for the common goals of collective action. With few exceptions, these agencies were pyramidal in their over-all structure. Forming the base of the pyramid were representatives of the employers' association and the labor union, operating at the shop level. At the apex of the pyramid sat the impartial chairman or the final arbitrating authority for the industry. Between these extremes were the intermediate agencies, like the committee on grievances, that attempted to resolve issues too important for the front-line operators, on the one hand, and too numerous for the final arbitrators, on the other.

Although these institutions were created primarily for administrative purposes, they soon began to exercise broad legislative powers as well. Indeed, some medium for the formulation of policies within the framework of the original protocols was indispensable, since the documents themselves had no termination dates and in some cases made no provision for their revision. In practice, policy making by the impartial machinery was carried on from the dates that the first protocols became effective. And, to varying degrees, policy making has been continued under all subsequent labor agreements regardless of their duration.

The need for continuous development of labor-management policies was everywhere recognized. "You have got to have an institution for legislation and you have got to have an institution for interpretation," observed J. H. Cohen, father of the protocol movement, testifying before the U. S. Commission on Industrial Relations, April 8, 1914. For legislative purposes, Cohen preferred the intermediate agencies of the impartial machinery on which both parties were equally represented. "In order to have those methods of legislation," Cohen continued, "the so-called conciliation method or conferential method is undoubtedly the best. In the cloak industry and in the dress and waist industry the grievance board, as you know, is the permanent legislative tribunal, and if the board deadlocks it goes to the board of arbitration."[1]

Louis D. Brandeis, who was the first chairman of the board of arbitration under both the dress and waist protocol and the women's coat and suit protocol, soon became convinced that "the functions of the Board of Grievances ought to be in the main legislative," and that these functions should be directed primarily toward "the consideration of the large questions affecting the welfare of the trade." For these reasons, Brandeis strongly supported the movement for committees on immediate action to handle minor disputes between the individual workers and their employers. "It is of course obvious that if such a committee is developed," so Brandeis argued in 1913, ". . . it would relieve the Board of Grievances of some of the rather trying and not very interesting questions which have come before it, and would give the Board of Grievances the opportunity to take up those larger constructive questions, which are of such vital importance in the development of the industry and for which the Board of Grievances was intended."[2]

Yet none of the original protocols or other early agreements defined the limits of this legislative power or described the procedures by which such power could be exercised. The first protocol

---

[1]U.S. Commission on Industrial Relations, *Final Report and Testimony* (1916), vol. 1, p. 577. See also the views of Earl Dean Howard, labor manager, Hart, Schaffner, and Marx, *ibid.,* p. 573.

In a paper, "The Protocol in the Coat, Suit and Skirt Industry and in the Dress Industry," J. H. Cohen stated that the grievance board was not only a trial court but a continuous conference body in which are initiated all legislative programs for the improvement of the economic side of the industry. Efficiency Society, *Transactions* (1913). Copy in the New York Public Library.

[2]*Minutes,* Arbitration Proceedings between the Dress and Waist Manufacturers' Association and the ILGWU (Nov. 9, 1913), p. 383; *Minutes,* Board of Arbitrators...[women's coat and suit trade] (Oct. 13, 1913), p. 384; (Jan. 24, 1914), p. 70. "The Board of Grievances, if it is allowed to work in the spirit in which it was created, has the opportunity of advancing the interest of all concerned through a manly, intelligent and calm consideration from all points of view of the problems which inhere in the trade....The very idea of the Board of Grievances was as a deliberative body, a body in which every man, each representative from each side, would come there with the best of his intelligence, fearlessly to talk out his view, to come and listen together." Louis D. Brandeis, *ibid.,* pp. 70, 72.

of the dress and waist industry, for example, provided that the board of grievances should be "the continuous conference body to which shall be brought all problems and all plans for improvement in the industry, which both parties are to consider." Did this clause imply that the board of grievances was to act as a clearing house, or permanent secretariat, for legislative proposals later to be submitted to a general conference between the parties? The rules adopted for the board of grievances of the cloak and suit industry in March 1911 suggested as much, for they specified that the board of grievances should call a conference of the parties whenever a revision of the protocol becomes necessary.[3]

Was the board of grievances itself to act as a negotiating conference, submitting whatever propositions it agreed upon to the contracting parties for ratification? Early in 1913, J. H. Cohen, spokesman for the manufacturers, assumed that when the board of grievances sat as a conference board it would become "a body for the purpose of initiating legislation to be submitted to both sides for referendum." Or did the board of grievances possess the final powers of a constitutional convention capable of revising the fundamental law without any further confirmation whatsoever? That procedure was clearly implied in the generally accepted proposition that legislative issues on which members of the board of grievances could not agree would be resolved by appeal to the board of arbitration whose decisions were final and binding on the parties.[4]

---

[3]See *Minutes,* Board of Arbitrators...[women's coat and suit trade] (August 3, 1913), pp. 47–48, 51–53. "Another feature of the protocol which afterwards assumed great importance was the institution of conferences between employers and employees. Whenever a suggestion would come from either side for a change or an amendment in the working rules, or for some supplementary arrangement, the parties would meet in conference, discuss it, dispose of it if possible, or sometimes if they reached a deadlock, refer it to the Board of Arbitration." Morris Hillquit, legal counsel, ILGWU, addressing the members of the Council of Conciliation in *Minutes,* Council of Conciliation... [women's coat and suit trade] (July 14, 1915), p. 16.

[4]J. H. Cohen in *Minutes,* Conference between the Cloak, Suit and Skirt Manufacturers' Protective Association and the ILGWU and the Cloakmakers' Joint Board (Feb. 3, 1913), p. 12. A few months later, Cohen appeared to support the second proposition:

> Under the rules, if the Grievance Board does not come to any understanding, you would have a right to go to the Board of Arbitration,

No one questioned the right of permanent administrative agencies to exercise quasi-legislative powers necessary to carry out the normal functions for which administrative bodies were created. The power of the impartial machinery to make rules and regulations for implementing the general provisions of the protocols was beyond dispute. There were, to be sure, many controversies over lines of demarcation between rules that constituted a "modus operandi" and rules that, in effect, revised the collective agreements themselves. Did a rule holding members of a manufacturers' association responsible for labor standards in their out-of-town shops change the character of the agreement or merely implement the objectives stated therein? Did a regulation providing back pay for pieceworkers who were wrongfully discharged involve the exercise of a primary lawmaking function or merely reflect the operation of a subordinate legislative power incidental to an administrative function?

Such questions of legislative competence as arose in the early years of the protocol movement were not directed so much to the impartial machinery as a whole as they were intended for particular administrative agencies that were attempting to exercise lawmaking powers. While grave doubts often arose over the power of *subordinate* agencies to legislate for the industry — at least beyond the accepted rule-making power — few held that general questions of legislative policy were beyond the competence of the highest authority sitting at the apex of the impartial machinery. All questions of policy affecting the welfare of an industry were presumed to fall within the jurisdiction of the impartial chairman, the permanent umpire, or the board of arbitration assigned to the trade. At least under the original protocols, appeal to arbitration

anyway, because the rules provide where the Grievance Board cannot agree on the subject matter of amendments to the protocol, the Board of Arbitration shall consider and decide.

—J. H. Cohen in *Minutes,* Meeting of the Joint Board of the Cloak and Skirt Makers' Union of New York and the Cloak, Suit and Skirt Manufactures' Protective Association (July 30, 1913), p. 726.

See also the views of Morris Hillquit, counsel for the ILGWU, supporting the power of the board of grievances for the dress industry to revise the dress protocol, in *Minutes,* Arbitration Proceedings between the Dress and Waist Manufacturers' Association and the ILGWU (Feb. 5, 1916), vol. 4, pp. 8 ff.

on questions of legislative policy was a generally accepted substitute for industrial strife.[5]

This complete lack of agreement on the proper agencies and procedures for creating legislative policy arose, in part, from more basic differences over the very nature and character of the protocols themselves. Did these early labor-management agreements take on the attributes of commercial contracts binding on the parties, or were they like political constitutions that carefully defined and limited the powers of the agencies they created, or were they modelled on treaties of peace that did no more than impose limited restrictions on the otherwise sovereign powers of the parties that negotiated them? Or, yet again, were these protocols no more than gentlemen's agreements held together solely by the faith of the contracting parties who were at liberty to mold their provisions into flexible guides for the welfare of their industries? If the protocols were gentlemen's agreements, they could be no more than symbols of a government of men rather than a government of laws — a concept once ably defended by Morris Hillquit, legal counsel for the ILGWU:

When the [first] protocol was adopted, it was adopted as a sort of general guide to prop up good practices, and time and time again the spiritual flower of the protocol, Mr. Brandeis and our Board of Arbitration, generally has [*sic*] emphasized this fact, that it is not a rigid document; . . . it is no more than the expression of certain general

---

[5]Paragraph 21 of the rules of the board of grievances adopted by the board of arbitration for the women's coat and suit industry in March 1911 provided that whenever revision of the protocol became necessary, the board of grievances should call a conference of the parties and deadlocks at the conference would be submitted to the board of arbitration for final determination. *Rules and Plan of Procedure* adopted by the Board of Grievances, March 11, 1911, and officially approved, as modified, by the Board of Arbitration in its decision of March 14, 1911 (printed pamphlet). Copy filed in the Abelson papers.

I think we regard this Board [of Arbitration] as a part of our legislative machinery, provided the procedure is instituted in accordance with Section 21. In other words, this Board could not legislate of its own motion previous to a conference, but after a conference has been made as an initial step, and after the conference has discussed the matter, and failed to agree, this Board of Arbitration has legislative power.
    —I. A. Hourwich, union official, *Minutes,* Board of Arbitrators. . .
    [women's coat and suit trade] (August 3, 1913), pp. 32–33 and ff.

social principles; no more than a general guide of conduct, an injunction to do the fair thing by each other under the circumstances,
and the method provided for the accomplishment of such results.[6]

While most arbitrators operating under the early agreements of
the needle trades appeared to follow the Morris Hillquit concept,
in that they accepted full responsibility for setting legislative policy, with or without the authority of their agreements, a few
questioned their power to legislate beyond such rule making as
was incidental to the judicial character of their functions. In the
spring of 1916, when a proposed amendment to the dress and
waist protocol, giving the board of arbitration jurisdiction over
every conceivable type of dispute between the contracting parties
or their respective members, came up for consideration, a colloquy
between dress arbitrator, Hamilton Holt, and counsel for the
manufacturers, J. H. Cohen, helped to dramatize the fundamental
issues:

Holt: Do you mean to say that on a judicial appeal any legislative
question can be brought up to us and we settle it as a legislature?

Cohen: Certainly and under this legislative provision that the Union
has proposed, every grievance of every kind that cannot be settled by
conference is left to you so long as the protocol exists....

Cohen: Now for the purpose of seeing to it that the machinery itself
is preserved, that the Union itself shall be preserved, that the Association shall be preserved, and that the treaty shall be preserved, I ask
this court to take up and consider some legislative proposals.

Holt: I can see how you can leave things to us which you can state in
what the nations call a preliminary protocol, which you have to draw
up and state, but to give us the power, which apparently you have
done if these words mean anything, by which we legislate and hear
both sides, and decide the thing, you are establishing something —

Cohen: But we have done that. There has never been any question
about it....May I call your attention to the fact that the entire rules
of procedure under which the Grievance Board operated in the cloak
industry was a piece of legislation passed by the Board of Arbitration.[7]

---

[6]*Minutes,* Council of Conciliation...[women's coat and suit trade] (July 14,
1915), vol. 2, p. 25.

[7]*Minutes,* Arbitration Proceedings between the Dress and Waist Manufacturers' Association and the ILGWU (March 31, 1916), vol. 6, pp. 1569–1578,
passim.

Who Makes the Laws?

Questions of competence aside, the power to change industry policies, procedures, or institutions during the life of a collective agreement was, in fact, initially exercised by the intermediate agencies of the impartial machinery — boards of grievances, conference committees, or boards of adjustment — representing equally both parties to the contract. Under the original women's coat and suit protocol, for example, the board of grievances, otherwise given to the settlement of particular disputes, soon voted to sit once a month as a joint conference committee to initiate general legislation for approval by the parties. With the development of subordinate machinery to handle individual disputes, this board became more and more preoccupied with legislative problems. Any proposition affecting the general standards of the trade fell within the province of the board acting as the "continuous conference body under the Protocol."[8]

In a very real sense, these intermediate agencies occupied the position of perpetual negotiating conferences, sometimes engaged in completing the unfinished business of contract negotiating committees and sometimes devoted to new issues never previously considered by the parties. The first collective agreement of the fur manufacturing industry, September 8, 1912, gave to a per-

---

[8]I got the officers of the Associations to agree that the [Grievance] Board should meet every first Tuesday of each month. Since we had no disagreements the clerks would report the results of their work and then the Board of Grievance would resolve itself into a Conference Board. At these conferences we began to discuss the creation of a standard rate for piece work for finishing.

—J. A. Dyche, general secretary-treasurer, ILGWU, in ILGWU, *Report and Proceedings,* Twelfth Convention (June 1914), p. 69.

The question of pay was quite another matter. Here both sides met in conference and together adopted an amendment to the [Dress] Protocol in conference, which stated that workers may not be paid in checks, that was distinctly adopted and recognized by both sides and is now a rule under which the Association must be governed.

—Mrs. Henry Moskowitz, chief clerk, Dress and Waist Manufacturers' Association, in *Minutes* of Investigation by the Committee on Immediate Action, in the matter of Union Complaint No. 8614 against the firm of Joel Isaacs and Sons (August 31, 1915), p. 3. Copy filed in the Abelson papers.

manent conference committee, representing equally the Associated Fur Manufacturers and the International Fur Workers' Union, the task of completing negotiations on all unsettled issues, including the subjects of contracting, subcontracting, overtime, and time contracts. From its inception, this joint conference committee has exercised the functions of a legislative body for the industry. Subsequently recognized as "the continuing conference body for collective action between the parties," the conference committee has, since the twenties, taken over responsibility for renewing, rejecting, or revising collective agreements as they expire.[9]

In practice, many intermediate agencies created under collective agreements of the 1910–1920 decade were permitted to exercise lawmaking powers without further confirmation by the parties themselves. Wherever such committees could reach agreement on matters of legislative policy, their decisions became the law of the industry without official ratification. Otherwise, all questions of legislative policy not resolved by the intermediate agencies were appealed for final determination to boards of arbitration, impartial chairmen, or permanent umpires assigned to the industry.[10]

---

[9]Some early agreements of the fur manufacturing industry and of the headwear industries gave each contracting party "the right to call upon the other side to designate, when occasion requires, a special committee to confer on matters of mutual concern." See the 1914 collective agreement of the Muff Bed Manufacturers' Association with Local 5 of the fur workers' union.

After providing for a permanent joint conference committee that would "devote its attention to the solution of problems and matters affecting the Industry," the 1919 collective agreement between the Fur Manufacturers' Association of Philadelphia and the International Fur Workers' Union stated: "Any agreement reached by the Conference Committee shall be duly executed by the respective organizations and become part of this agreement."

The 1932 collective agreement of the Associated Fur Coat and Trimming Manufacturers and the New York Fur Trimming Manufacturers with the International Fur Workers' Union and the Furriers' Joint Council of New York stated that "the Conference Committee is the continually functioning body dealing with the collective relations between the organized employers and the organized workers in the industry."

[10]"It shall be the duty of the Chairman of the Board of Adjustment to convene a conference upon the request of either party to the agreement, to take up matters of mutual concern. The Chairman of the Board of Adjustment shall preside at such conference, but shall have no vote. The agreements reached at such conferences by the accredited representatives of the Associa-

By specific provision of some agreements, certain issues of general interest were declared beyond the competence of the intermediate agencies and reserved exclusively for the highest arbitrating authority of the industry. The 1911 collective agreement between the Merchants' Society of Ladies' Tailors and Local 38, ILGWU, left the board of arbitration to decide "what rate of pay shall be made for overtime work" and "what remuneration, if any, shall be paid for legal holidays." But, on the fundamental issue of changing its provisions, the agreement stated that "any question regarding the modification of its terms shall be first submitted to the Board of Grievances, and in the event of its failure to agree, then to the Board of Arbitration appointed hereunder." However, no changes at all could be made in the agreement for the first year.

Since members of the intermediate agencies were often unable to agree on controversial issues, policy making fell upon the highest arbitrating authority created for each industry. Whatever doubts of legal competence may have restrained intermediate agencies, industry arbitrators acknowledged few, if any, limitations on their lawmaking powers. Whether exercising original jurisdiction or serving as tribunals of last resort — with or without official sanction of the collective agreements under which they worked — these arbitrators assumed blanket authority to determine policy for the mutual advantage of both parties. Some arbitrators, not content to wait for business, acted on their own initiative to forestall potential conflicts with appropriate legislation of their own making. Until well into the twenties, collective bargaining under the protocol movement revolved around the arbitrator, long before the idea of collective agreements negotiated solely by the parties on their own initiative had been generally accepted.[11]

---

tion and the Union, shall be recorded and have the force of amendments to the agreement." Collective agreement of the Pleaters' and Stitchers' Association with Local 41, ILGWU, effective March 25, 1924.

[11]C. H. Winslow, *Conciliation, Arbitration, and Sanitation in the Dress and Waist Industry of New York City*, U.S. Department of Labor, BLS Bulletin no. 145 (April 10, 1914), at p. 124, contains a chart summarizing terms in collective agreements for the ladies' garment trades in 1914. This chart lists three amendments to the women's coat and suit protocol, all of which were a product of action by the impartial machinery: (1) creation of a board of grievances with an elaborate set of procedures; (2) an increase in the wages of pressers; and (3) the creation of a committee on immediate action presided over by an impartial chairman.

The Participation of Third Parties

Effective bargaining in the needle trades owes its origin and development to third parties, who, in the role of mediators, first carved out the terms of collective agreements and then sat as permanent arbitrators to develop the work they had begun. The institutions of collective action did not arise from the grass-root demands of an oppressed working force united in a mass crusade to overcome injustice. Nor did they spring from a democratic upsurge of rank-and-file employers struggling for existence in overcrowded trades. Instead, the machinery and processes of collective bargaining were handed down by third parties to the "bosses" and the "people." The instrumentalities of law and order were scattered, like manna from heaven, by self-appointed saviors of industrial society.

The pattern was set at the very beginning of the protocol movement. During the general strike of 1910 in the women's coat and suit trade, outside parties, led by Lincoln Filene of Boston, induced Louis D. Brandeis to act as mediator in getting the participants to resolve their differences. As chairman of the conferences that bear his name, Brandeis maintained order and prevented disruption of the proceedings. By directing the discussions, he time and again steered the parties away from deadlocked issues until the basic principles of collaboration could be worked out. Then, following the conferences, he proposed one of the major compromises that found its way into the original protocol.

Having assisted in creating the first major collective agreement of the needle trades, Brandeis became chairman and public member of the first permanent board of arbitration named under the coat and suit protocol. In this capacity, with the help of the two other members, he was in a favored position to extend the aims

---

The board of arbitration established this institution of the clerks; in other words, the institution of the clerks was established to facilitate the enforcement of the protocol, and if the board of arbitration had authority to establish the institution of the clerks, to facilitate the enforcement of the protocol, certainly the board of arbitration has authority to modify its present institution, if it is defective in any particular respect.

—Henry Moskowitz, clerk of the board of arbitration for the women's coat and suit trade, testifying before the U.S. Commission on Industrial Relations, Jan. 17, 1914, *Final Report and Testimony*, vol. 2, p. 1147.

and purposes of collective action first set forth in the Brandeis Conferences. Under his leadership, the board of arbitration continued to develop the principles, perfect the institutions, and improve the techniques of collective bargaining. Undisturbed by legal questions of authority to act, the board did not hesitate to overhaul the impartial machinery from time to time or to change the conditions of employment as circumstances prescribed.

Other early arbitrators in the needle trades were men of firmer convictions and less restraint. Unlike Brandeis, many of them looked to the solution of industrial ills for the major objective of their life's work. They, too, were pioneers and crusaders who often cut the pattern of collective action to fit their own concepts of labor-management relations. From the negotiation of the first agreements, they became the hub of the collective bargaining wheel for their respective industries from whence all major developments radiated. Under their tutelage, collective bargaining had its origin in evolving forms of industrial self-government created for the people but not by the people.

The center of third party activity in New York City was Kehillah, the Jewish community — an organization of prominent Jewish citizens and businessmen devoted to protecting and promoting the welfare of the Jewish people. One of Kehillah's major functions was that of minimizing industrial conflicts that threatened to bring disaster upon the participants and disfavor upon the race. For this purpose, Kehillah maintained a bureau of industry with a committee on industrial relations available to help the "bosses" and the "people" resolve their differences. From 1910 until the mid-twenties — the formative years of collective bargaining — Kehillah intervened in many disputes and contributed many arbitrators to the impartial machinery it helped to create. Its distinguished leader, J. L. Magnes, devoted much of his own time to the settlement of industrial disputes, and for many years he served as the first impartial chairman of the fur manufacturing industry.[12]

Many other outside organizations and individuals offered their services to resolve industrial conflicts. The state chamber of commerce had its arbitration committee with headquarters in New

---

[12]See A. A. Goren, "The New York Kehillah: 1908–1922" (unpublished Ph.D. dissertation, Columbia University, 1966).

York City; the mayor of New York had his special agencies of conciliation; the State of New York its special commissions named by the governors, as well as its permanent board of mediation. There were social workers, philanthropists, ministers, judges, and other public spirited citizens who, individually or collectively, would alleviate the human ills of industrial society. Many of these voluntary peacemakers were assembled under the banner of the National Civic Federation. Whatever the source of outside help, the contributors had one attribute in common: those who came to resolve an immediate dispute usually remained to govern the industry.[13]

The pattern of outside interference was everywhere essentially the same. In 1914, for example, J. L. Magnes, on behalf of Kehillah and its committee on industrial relations, notified the parties to a dispute in fur manufacturing that the Jewish community stood ready to lend its moral and disinterested services so that the impartial machinery previously established for the industry might work for the welfare of all and the good of the community. Similarly, in the dress and waist industry a five-week strike during 1915 led the committee on industrial relations of Kehillah's bureau of industry to arrange a conference of the parties to work out the terms of a peaceful settlement. And, in 1916, Kehillah's bureau of industry was found imploring an association of ladies' tailors to submit its differences with the union to an unbiased person and to use Kehillah's services freely.[14]

The extraordinary respect conceded to outsiders who took on the role of industrial peacemakers and landed in permanent posi-

---

[13]When the original protocol was threatened with disruption in 1915, Mayor J. P. Mitchel of New York City named a council of conciliation, which although possessing advisory powers only, laid down the terms of settlement, modified the impartial machinery for the industry, and then named itself as the continuing agency of last resort to settle all unfinished business, as well as all other disputes that might subsequently arise. A summary account of the work of this council is given in Louis Lorwin [Louis Levine], *The Women's Garment Workers* (1924), pp. 289–291, 305–306, 309–310, 317.

On the work of the National Civic Federation for industrial peace, particularly the early contributions of John Mitchell and Marcus A. Hanna, see Marguerite Green, *The National Civic Federation and the American Labor Movement, 1900–1925* (1956).

[14]See the pertinent correspondence for the period, filed in the Abelson papers.

tions of authority arose, in part, from the heritage of voluntary self-government to which members of the Jewish communities had long been accustomed in the Old World. There, the necessity for a self-imposed system of law and order had led each Jewish community to accept the leadership of its most distinguished citizens. In turn, the intellectual and spiritual leaders of the community assumed a continuing responsibility for preserving law and order. Transferred to American industry, these concepts of voluntary self-government found expression in the role of third party arbitrators who fashioned the policies and created the institutions, as well as rendered the decisions, that would insure industrial peace.[15]

Arbitrators as Lawmakers

Against this background, outside arbitrators were able to establish a foothold from which they subsequently became virtual dictators of labor-management policy for their industries. As in the case of the first protocol, accepting the good offices of third parties usually led to joint conferences of the disputants presided over by an outsider who sooner or later was empowered to arbitrate all unresolved issues. Often left with the responsibility for

---

[15]"These immigrants came from parts of Europe where arbitration was an accepted method of settling disputes. The early successful development of arbitration boards in the needle trades can be traced directly to this experience. Moreover, every orthodox Jew had a thorough training in Jewish law—the Torah. His rabbi was for him always the final arbitrator." J. H. Cohen, *They Builded Better Than They Knew* (1946), p. 182.

Representing the concern of outstanding Jewish leaders toward industrial strife was the work of Jacob H. Schiff, New York philanthropist and social worker. In a letter to a Chicago banker seeking "a speedy determination of the deplorable industrial dispute between a large number of Jewish manufacturers and their workers," Schiff wrote: "Here in New York we have been able, through the instrumentality of the Jewish Community (Kehillah) and its Bureau of Industry, to avert and settle many serious industrial disputes. Surely the leaders of the Jewish people in Chicago ought to be able to do what we are doing with increasing success in New York....Mr. Julius Rosenwald, Judge Mack, Rabbi Hirsh and other prominent Jews in business and civic life, ought to take hold of this situation at once." From the letters of Jacob H. Schiff filed in the Abelson papers. For Schiff's contributions to peacemaking in the New York men's and boys' clothing industry during the winter of 1918–1919, see the correspondence quoted in ACWA, *Report and Proceedings,* Fourth Biennial Convention (May 1920), pp. 15–23.

writing much of the original agreement, these temporary arbitrators by design or mutual consent, then became the permanent impartial chairmen of their industries for the life of their agreements. From this post, they frequently continued for many years to exercise the broad range of legislative powers temporarily given to them.

Under the protocol movement, arbitrators differed among themselves in the procedures they followed for contract-making purposes. Some encouraged the parties to write their own terms. Others, holding the parties incapable of agreement, called upon them, not for the purpose of democratizing the process, but solely to obtain the necessary data on which to act. In fur manufacturing, the arbitrator himself became a separate party to the first collective agreement for the industry. Instead of direct negotiations, the Associated Fur Manufacturers and the Mutual Protective Fur Manufacturers' Association, representing the employers as parties of the first part, joined with J. L. Magnes, representing the public as party of the second part, and with the Furriers' Union of New York and vicinity and the Furriers' Union of Greater New York, Local No. 14263, American Federation of Labor, representing the workers, as parties of the third part, in negotiating and signing the agreement that became effective on September 8, 1912. Magnes, head of Kehillah, notified the associations that they were not dealing directly with the unions but indirectly with them through him.[16]

Indeed, the initiative assumed by third parties in the development of collective bargaining arose, in part, from the necessity for indirect negotiations to avoid semblance of equality that the unreconstructed manufacturers would perforce extend to union representatives by meeting with them face to face. Thus, to avoid

---

[16] J. L. Magnes, who became the first impartial chairman for the trade, saw more hope for industrial peace through direct relations between the employers' associations and the unions, but considered such action premature. The text of this agreement, except for the introductory paragraph, is printed in C. H. Winslow's, *Collective Agreements in the Men's Clothing Industry,* U.S. Department of Labor, BLS Bulletin no. 198 (September 1916), pp. 130–131. The second collective agreement for the industry, effective July 13, 1914, was entered into directly between the Associated Fur Manufacturers and the International Fur Workers' Union, together with the Joint Board of the Furriers' Union of Greater New York, comprising Locals 1, 5, 10, and 15.

direct dealings between the manufacturers' association and the Amalgamated Clothing Workers' Union during the 1913 strike in the men's clothing industry, a special third party commission of three members was created, first, to settle the strike and, then, to sit as a permanent board of arbitration under the resulting agreement. Efforts to extend the protocol principle into other segments of the men's clothing industry likewise had to be sponsored by outsiders.[17]

Third party control of lawmaking in the early development of collective bargaining for the needle trades was not peculiar to the New York area. The general strike of 1918 in Cleveland to organize the workers of the women's coat and suit trade was settled through the intervention of a board of referees of three public members who wrote the terms of the first collective agreement between the Cleveland Garment Manufacturers' Association and the ILGWU and then remained to govern the industry as the highest organ of the impartial machinery. "This board," stated the 1919 collective agreement, "shall have power to adjust matters that cannot be settled between the parties, to establish periodic wage scales for the industry, and to see that this Agreement is fairly lived up to by the parties." Only the board could authorize strikes or lockouts under the agreement.[18]

More pronounced was the legislative power exerted by third parties under the early collective agreements of the men's clothing industry. The 1910 strike of the United Garment Workers in Chicago against Hart, Schaffner, and Marx was settled through

---

[17]S. Perlman, "Present Industrial Relations in the Men's Clothing Industry," U.S. National Archives, Record Book 174, microfilm roll T 4–6–I: 456.

The 1919 collective agreement of the Clothing Manufacturers' Association of New York with the ACWA was largely the product of three reports by an outside advisory board consisting of Louis Marshall, W. Z. Ripley, and Felix Frankfurter — reports that led to the creation of the office of impartial chairman as a permanent institution. See Marshall, Ripley, and Frankfurter's "Report," dated Jan. 22, 1919, and Felix Frankfurter and S. J. Rosensohn's "Survey of the New York [men's] Clothing Industry," dated May 28, 1920, in printed collection of union affidavits submitted in the case of J. Friedman & Co. v. ACWA, at pp. 14–15 and 17–43, respectively. Copy filed in the Abelson papers.

[18]A copy of the 1919 collective agreement on the Cleveland women's coat and suit market may be found in the U.S. National Archives. See also an article on the Cleveland labor agreement in *Women's Wear*, May 14, 1925.

the intervention of Clarence Darrow and Carl Meyers, two outsiders who not only wrote the terms of the first labor agreement
but also named themselves the continuing arbitrators to resolve
future differences between the parties. The second (1913) and
third (1916) agreements between the United Garment Workers
and this firm were likewise largely a product of the arbitrators.
After other firms in the Chicago market were organized by the
Amalgamated Clothing Workers in 1918–1919, the first collective
agreement between the Chicago Clothing Manufacturers and the
ACWA, gave a board of arbitration the power to mold the agreement to meet future changes in the economic climate.[19]

At the close of the First World War, W. Z. Ripley and L. E.
Kirstein gave Rochester its institutions for settling disputes in the
manufacture of men's clothing, noting at the time that "the provision of this machinery for obviating strife in the industry is not
a temporary makeshift." Similarly, the dispute between the Baltimore Federation of Clothing Manufacturers and the Amalgamated
Clothing Workers of America, which led to the first multiple-
employer labor agreement in the men's clothing industry of Baltimore, was resolved by a special arbitration board of Messrs. J. M.
Moses, W. M. Leiserson, James Mullenbach, and H. A. Millis.
After settling the terms of employment, the board noted that if
changes in conditions subsequently warranted an increase in
wages, the board would take up the matter and grant an increase.
Writing in the early twenties, H. S. Gilbertson concluded that
arbitrators in the men's clothing trade of Chicago and Rochester
"were rapidly assuming the position of dictators and seriously

---

[19]See Chicago Joint Board, ACWA, *The Clothing Workers of Chicago,
1910–1922* (1922), chap. 3, "The Development of Arbitration"; chap. 8, "The
Great Wage Arbitrations."

> If there shall be a general change in wages or hours in the clothing
> industry, which shall be sufficiently permanent to warrant the belief that
> the change is not temporary, then the Board shall have the power to
> determine whether such change is of so extraordinary a nature as to
> justify a consideration of the question of making a change in the present
> agreement, and, if so, then the Board shall have power to make such
> change in wages or hours as in its judgment shall be proper.
> —From the emergency clause of the 1919 collective agreement for the
> Chicago market of the men's clothing industry, *ibid.,* p. 145.

invading what is usually regarded as the proper field of management."[20]

The pattern of third party control over labor-management policies was not a choice of the delegates to the Brandeis Conferences of 1910. Those responsible for the constructive ideas developed there would have preferred to rely upon the judgment of the contracting parties themselves. Brandeis himself later wrote of the first protocol that he was very loath to substitute the decision of an umpire for the resulting agreement between opposing parties. He considered the possibility of arriving at decisions by direct negotiations to be "one of the most valuable parts of the Protocol." Subsequently, labor unions and employers' associations of the needle trades were well-nigh universal in support of these views. Neither the Amalgamated Clothing Workers nor the Rochester Clothiers' Exchange could have felt at ease under an impartial chairman, who, in a single decision, transferred 7,000 men's clothing workers (55 percent of those employed in the Rochester market) from week work to piecework![21]

---

[20]H. S. Gilbertson, "Meeting the Labor Problem in the Clothing Industry," *Administration,* February 1923, vol. 5, p. 187.

> The administration of this agreement is vested in a Labor Adjustment Board consisting of representatives of the employers and of representatives of the workmen, together with an impartial chairman selected by both parties. . . .
>
> The Board shall have authority to make such rules, regulations and supplementary arrangements not inconsistent with this agreement as may be necessary to carry into effect the principles of this agreement, or to apply these principles to new questions whenever they arise. . . .
>
> Upon the petition of either party the Labor Adjustment Board shall have the power to determine whether important changes have taken place within the Clothing Industry, or in industrial conditions generally, which warrant changes in general wage levels or in hours of work; and if it is decided that such changes are warranted, negotiations shall begin between the parties hereto. In the event of a disagreement, the question shall be submitted to arbitration.
>
> —From the 1920 collective agreement between the Clothiers Exchange of Rochester and the ACWA.

On the origin of this agreement and, in general, see ACWA, *Report and Proceedings,* Fourth Biennial Convention (May 1920) and Fifth Biennial Convention (May 1922). Materials on the early Baltimore developments may be found in the ACWA Research Library collection of arbitration papers.

[21]The views of Brandeis were stated in a letter, dated May 10, 1912 to Henry Moskowitz, as quoted in Berman, "Era of the Protocols. . .1910–1916," at pp.

But the leaders at those early conferences never gained effective control over the rank and file of their respective organizations. They were compelled to endorse third party interference as the only available medium through which to gain acceptance for the new approach to collective action. Neither the organized manufacturers nor the organized workers who supported the protocol movement dared to oppose the policy-making role of permanent arbitrators so long as that procedure led to the goal of law and order in industry. Once the "enlightened" leaders of unions and employers' associations had grown strong enough to impose their own concepts of collective action directly upon an industry, they found reason enough for no longer favoring the principle of policy determination by outside authorities.

Restricting the Legislative Powers of Arbitrators

A substantial movement to restrict the legislative powers of arbitrators developed in the needle trades shortly after the First World War. The strength of this movement and the speed with which it came to light strongly suggest that embers of discontent with third party legislation had been smouldering throughout the war years, if not before. "With the growth and development of collective bargaining in the needle trades in New York City," wrote H. A. Gordon on behalf of the men's clothing manufacturers in 1921, "there were created many lucrative positions, as impartial chairman, managers of manufacturers' associations, and innumerable assistants, which were filled from among teachers, sociologists, professors, social welfare workers and uplifters of all kinds, instead of from among those who had practical knowledge and experience. . . . All classes of people, except the practical employer and worker, legislated for the clothing industry in New York during the past five years."[22]

276–277 from the Brandeis papers filed in the Law School of the University of Louisville, Louisville, Kentucky. The decision in the Rochester men's clothing market was by Impartial Chairman W. M. Leiserson; the text appears in the *Monthly Labor Review,* July 1921, vol. 13, pp. 153–154 and in the *Daily News Record,* May 4, 1921.

[22]H. A. Gordon, statement dated Feb. 9, 1921, in printed collection of employer affidavits submitted in the case of J. Friedman & Co. v. ACWA, pp. 66–67, and other observations at pp. 64–65. At the same time, W. A. Bandler, president of the Clothing Manufacturers' Association of New York City, lamented that the manufacturers of men's clothing "had for so long been

Five years earlier, Gordon had scathingly attacked "social uplifters" and "disinterested citizens" who undertook to legislate for
the dress and waist industry. "What does Mr. Brandeis, or Mr.
Mack, or Mr. Bruere [members of the board of arbitration] or any
of that clique know about making waists?" he asked. Previously,
Gordon had on another occasion condemned the "sophistry,
casuistry, and ethereal precepts" of certain "settlement workers,
social uplifters and reformers" who created industrial law that
confused both parties. Urging manufacturers and workers to extricate themselves from this labyrinth, Gordon advocated "complete
banishment of these alleged conciliators, legislators and industrial
Napoleons."[23]

Rumblings of discontent with third party legislation also came
from union sources early in the history of the protocol movement.
In 1913, one faction of the ILGWU charged the union leadership
with "putting the guidance of the cloakmakers' union into the
hands of doctors, professors, scientists and intellectuals who have
never in their lives been in the inside of a workshop." And, in
1916, the United Garment Workers opposed the intervention
of arbitrators to settle a strike over contract terms with the Shirt

---

accustomed to having outsiders legislate for the industry, that they came to
feel there was no other way of running their business," *ibid.,* p. 7.

[23]*Women's Wear,* March 1, 1916, May 4, 1915. E. J. Wile, president of the
Cloak, Suit and Skirt Manufacturers' Protective Association, had also attacked
the "uplifters" in his address before the National Association of Manufacturers in 1916. He even charged his own association's counsel, J. H. Cohen,
with becoming "a benevolent gentleman who belonged to the uplifting class."
And with equal derision, he characterized the mayor's council of conciliation,
composed of "a college professor, a preacher, an uplifter, a lawyer and what-
not but no business men," as just "another body of uplifters." *Daily Trade
Record,* June 7, 1916.

These earlier outbursts had undoubtedly been stimulated, in part, by developments under collective agreements that had materially extended the range
of third party control over the institutions of collective bargaining by re-
organizing the lower levels of grievance machinery to permit third party
representation on previously bipartisan committees and grievance boards.
Introduced to shortcircuit the delays in appealing deadlocked cases from
bipartisan boards, this move, in effect, substituted third party arbitration for
bipartisan conciliation in the processing of hundreds and thousands of
grievances. See Boris Emmet, "Trade Agreements in the Women's Clothing
Industries in New York City," *Monthly Labor Review,* December 1917, vol. 5,
pp. 1094–1095.

Manufacturers' Protective Association. "There has been a tendency of late to interest outside parties to arbitrate strike issues," observed A. Berkson, general organizer of the union, "but the workers in the shirt industry want no 'uplift workers' to attempt to settle its [*sic*] difficulties, as what do such people know about the needs of the trade."[24]

The fuse had already been lighted, therefore, when the Dress and Waist Manufacturers' Association of New York opened its negotiations in the winter of 1918–1919 with the ILGWU and its dressmaker locals for a new collective agreement. In a public statement to the press appearing in *Women's Wear* for December 30, 1918, the association made known its criticisms and thereby touched off an explosion that was presumably to revolutionize the processes of collective bargaining:

As constituted under the present agreement it [the board of arbitrators] is invested not merely with authority to determine disputes or misunderstandings between the parties, but with legislative functions. The result has been that lawyers, judges, settlement workers and reformers, all well meaning and estimable gentlemen, but having no practical knowledge of working conditions in the industry, have, to use the language of their spokesman "been guessing" and prescribing for the workers and employers what shall be the hours of labor, wages and other conditions in the industry. The result has been constant

---

[24]The position of the ILGWU faction is recorded in a translation by Paul Abelson of a 1913 article in the *New Post*. Berkson's observations are recorded in the *Daily Trade Record*, March 2, 1916.

In 1914, J. H. Cohen, spokesman for the manufacturers and a key figure in the evolution of the first protocol, had thus defended the role of third parties in developing the institutions of collective bargaining:

In the first place, although the man on the job knows more about the technique of the job, he does not always know as much about the general principles as a lawyer or an economist or a doctor who is called in from the outside. As a matter of fact, the protocol itself was made possible by an outsider. The invention of the preferential union shop by a lawyer in that situation resulted in the protocol. The very institutions that now make for peace in the industry are the inventions of lawyers — the board of sanitary control, the board of grievances, the clerks, the method of making precedents. This last thing, the committee on immediate action, is the joint invention of two lawyers.

—Testimony before the U.S. Commission on Industrial Relations, April 8, 1914, *Final Report and Testimony,* vol. 1, p. 578.

compromises as to vital principles and a mass of cumbersome and impossible rules and regulations.

Two weeks later, in a letter dated January 10, 1919, from Morris Weiss, president of the association, to the ILGWU, the manufacturers sought further to clarify their stand:

We are very anxious that our position with respect to arbitration, be clearly understood. There is no opposition on the part of this association to the submission of differences arising during the life of and under an agreement, to an outside tribunal for decision. In fact, it is specifically provided in the association's proposals to you that there be constituted for the life of the agreement a grievance board, consisting of an equal number of representatives from the association and the union who, if they are unable to agree, shall name an umpire, an impartial chairman, who shall sit with them and the decision of a majority of whom shall be binding upon the parties as to all disputes, complaints or grievances that may arise under the agreement. We are, however, unalterably opposed to what has been erroneously termed arbitration and which is nothing more than the delegation to outsiders, who necessarily are uninformed as to conditions in the industry, and are not interested parties, of legislative powers to fix wages, hours and other conditions of labor for workers and employers in our industry. ...No agreement affecting the relations of employer and employee can have permanency, unless made by the parties themselves.[25]

While other issues precipitated an eleven-week strike before the parties came to terms, there is little evidence that the union opposed the stand of the manufacturers on third party legislation. In any case, the dress manufacturers' proposals to the ILGWU to clip the wings of arbitrators were written into the final contract. "It is further understood and agreed," states one clause of this agreement, "that this contract shall be strictly construed, and that the rights and obligations of the parties hereto shall be deemed limited and defined by the express provisions hereof and not otherwise." The use of precedents and implied powers that had previously opened the door to legislative meanderings by permanent arbitrators was further restricted by providing that no right or obligation shall be deemed incorporated "by reason of any contract, matter or thing made or transpiring prior to the date hereof; and that none of the rights or obligations fixed by this

---

[25]*Women's Wear,* Jan. 11, 1919. This letter was reprinted in a full-page advertisement in the *New York Times* for Jan. 20, 1919.

contract shall be waived or modified save and except by an instrument in writing of equal formality."[26]

Opposition to third party legislation also contributed to major changes in collective agreements for the men's clothing trade during the early twenties. The 1922 three-year master contract for the Chicago market omitted the emergency clause that had previously allowed the board of arbitration to decide when, and whether, changes in conditions of the industry warranted changes in existing wage rates and, if so, to make such changes. In that year, too, the collective agreement negotiated for the Rochester market abolished the joint board of adjustment that had previously existed as a legislative body for the industry. Desire to terminate the legislative powers of the impartial machinery undoubtedly contributed to the substitution of permanent umpires for boards of arbitration. Lacking the bipartisan character of most multimember agencies, a single arbitrator, or impartial chairman, would presumably have less reason to usurp the legislative functions that rightfully belonged to the contracting parties.[27]

---

[26]As counsel to the Dress and Waist Manufacturers' Association, H. A. Gordon had insisted "that the agreement, instead of being vague and ambiguous, must be clear and definite in language, and unmistakably limit and define the obligations and rights of the parties, and not subject to interpretation, elaboration, modification, or revision by outsiders functioning as arbitrators and friends of industrial peace." From a typewritten statement, dated April 8, 1919, filed in the Abelson papers. See Gordon's views in *Women's Wear,* April 9, 1919.

[27]On the Chicago market, the *Daily News Record,* April 7, 1922, carried the text of the three-year, market-wide collective agreement, under which either party could request a change in wage scales ninety days prior to each anniversary date of the agreement. Should the parties fail to agree on proposed wage changes, either side could terminate the master agreement. For a report on the emergency clause, see ACWA, *Report and Proceedings,* Sixth Biennial Convention (May 1924), p. 78.

On the Rochester market, the *Daily News Record* of April 22, 1922 carried an article under the headline: "Rochester Pact Limits Powers of Arbitrator — Administration of Agreement Lies Directly in Hands of Parties." The issue of May 1, 1922 describes the collective agreement for the Rochester market as more administrative than constitutional — an agreement that discards the idea of having the organization of government in industry parallel the structure of political government, with legislative, judicial, and administrative agencies. In general, see H. S. Gilbertson, "Meeting the Labor Problem in the Clothing Industry," in *Administration,* February 1923, vol. 5, pp. 187–188.

One of the strongest advocates of direct negotiations between the contracting parties was the Amalgamated Clothing Workers' Union of the men's clothing industry. Reviewing events that led to control of lawmaking by arbitrators, the general executive board of the ACWA reported to the union convention in 1926 that the legislative powers of the impartial machinery had been carefully circumscribed after the First World War. The committee pointed out that by 1920 "the needs of both the manufacturers and the union were too serious to be settled lightly through judicial decision" and that, henceforth, "the major decisions involving wages and basic working decisions were reached through joint negotiations, whereas in the earlier and more prosperous period they might have been thrown with impunity to the arbitrator."[28]

In time, contract clauses forbidding impartial chairmen or permanent umpires to range beyond the terms of the agreements they administered became common. An increasing number of collective agreements expressly limited the power of arbitrators to resolving disputes arising from specific terms of their contracts and prohibited those arbitrators from modifying, deleting, or adding to the terms of those agreements. Finally, in 1945, this new philosophy was strongly endorsed by President Harry Truman's labor-management conference at which a committee of business executives and labor leaders unanimously recommended that "the impartial chairman, umpire, arbitrator, or board should have no power to add to, subtract from, change, or modify any provision of the agreement, but should be authorized only to interpret the existing provisions of the agreement and apply them to the specific facts of the grievance or dispute."[29]

---

[28] ACWA, *Report and Proceedings,* Seventh Biennial Convention (May 1926), p. 26.

Each time the union has to renew its agreement with the employers, the cloak industry goes into the hands of a receiver, to commissions, to philanthropists, politicians and all kinds of distinguished gentlemen, "disinterested outsiders," who investigate the cloak industry and hand out decisions. An industry which is being conducted with the aid of politicians, philanthropists and "friends of labor" of varying kinds, must sooner or later go to ruin.
—J. A. Dyche, *Bolshevism in American Labor Unions* (1926), pp. 93–94.

[29] *The President's National Labor-Management Conference, November 5–30, 1945: Summary and Committee Reports,* U.S. Department of Labor, Division

Lawmaking by Arbitrators after 1920

While this movement clipped the legislative wings of permanent arbitrators, in the needle trades it did not terminate their flights into the realm of lawmaking. In the first place, it did not change the usual procedure by which new branches of the needle trades were introduced to collective bargaining. Sooner or later, dozens of industries making specialized items and accessories of wearing apparel — belts, buckles, hat linings, artificial flowers, shoulder straps, pocketbooks, and the like — were brought within the fold of law and order first conceived at the Brandeis Conferences. With few exceptions, the original policies and machinery of collective action were still introduced to each trade by third parties who intervened to settle particular disputes and remained to govern the industry. Only gradually thereafter did the parties to an agreement take over the role of writing their own contract terms.

In the second place, industry arbitrators did not renounce their lawmaking powers after 1920 for the reason that collective bargaining in the needle trades permitted no clear-cut distinctions between legislative powers and administrative functions. The nature of manufacturing was such that policy determination could not be reserved for official negotiating conferences between the contracting parties at the renewal of each collective agreement. "It is recognized that no hard and fast agreement is possible," stated the preamble to the 1921 contract between the Clothing Manufacturers' Association of New York and the ACWA. "There must in reality be a new agreement every day to meet new situations as they arise."[30]

Particularly in the determination of piece rates were new rules likely to be a matter of day-to-day necessity. Since piece rates had to be adjusted with every change in material, style, type, and grade of garment, as well as with changes in the conditions of employment, these rates obviously could not be set for the life of an agreement. Under any piece-rate system, wage-fixing by its very nature becomes a continuing process. Unless these rates were to be left for determination by the individual shop, with no regard for uniform labor costs among competing manufacturers, they had

---

of Labor Standards, Bulletin no. 77 (1946), p. 46. The recommendation was adopted by the conference.

[30]Text of this agreement appears in *Daily News Record,* June 3, 1921.

to be reserved for some agency of the impartial machinery for each trade. Otherwise, the contracting parties would be forever assembling and reassembling to carry on the work of contract negotiations.

Regulating piece rates to limit variations in labor costs for manufacturing similar garments increasingly became a function of the impartial machinery. And to the extent that week work prevailed — especially during the twenties — attempts at setting standards of production to reduce variations in labor costs for garments manufactured by week workers was, likewise, left to the permanent agencies of administration. By the thirties, rate fixing — a legislative function — consumed most of the time of the impartial chairman for the dress industry. And, in the women's coat and suit trade, the procedure for piece-rate determination involved not only the owner of each shop and a committee of his employees but also association officials, union agents, and a deputy from the labor bureau in the office of the impartial chairman. Final authority to set piece rates was, if necessary, exercised by the impartial chairman or board of arbitration for the industry.[31]

There were other reasons why industry arbitrators continued to exercise broad policy-making functions after 1920. Both labor unions and employers' associations preferred the stability of long-time agreements that assured minimum standards of employment for the "people" and predictable labor costs for the "bosses." Both groups jointly demanded protection from the uncertainties of the hand-to-mouth operations that characterized the era before the protocols. Yet, at the same time, each side wanted a means of escape from existing standards, should unforeseen emergencies arise. No longer satisfied with collective agreements molded at will

---

[31]G. W. Alger, *Decisions,* Case no. 1029 (Jan. 1, 1934). For the extent to which the determination of piece rates had consumed the time of Impartial Chairman Harry Uviller and lower agencies of the impartial machinery under the 1935 collective agreements of the dress industry, see *Women's Wear Daily,* August 26, 1938, summarizing the disposition of disputes over piece rates for 359,343 individual styles between March 1936 and the end of June 1938. Of this number, 24,284 had reached the level of the joint Price Adjustment Bureau and 2,000 had been finally determined by the impartial chairman. In men's clothing, the number of piece-rate-fixing cases coming before the impartial machinery under the collective agreements of the Rochester market were estimated in 1930 to represent 99 percent of all cases handled. *Daily News Record,* Jan. 13, 1930.

by the arbitrators who administered them, nor yet willing to bind themselves to long-time commitments, the parties found a happy solution in directly negotiated contracts of substantial though limited duration, subject to some degree of flexibility introduced from time to time by the impartial machinery.[32]

The power to grant temporary exemptions from industry standards was a particularly effective device for preserving law and order from internal disruption threatened by the rise of new and unforeseen conditions. Meeting industry standards sometimes posed an insuperable problem for the marginal firm or the handicapped worker. Fulfilling industry requirements could embarrass sound firms that had fallen upon evil days — just as the adversity of old age could hound the workers no longer of gilt-edge competence. Visions of adversity became a nightmare that fostered collusion between workers and employers to undermine labor standards at the shop level, but stymied cooperation to support uniform work standards at the industry level. Whatever policy-making decisions could be made on the spot to save faltering firms and their employees from straying into the wilderness of the unorganized, operated in the long run to preserve the institutions of collective action.[33]

A new company joining the organized forces of industry could be granted a period of grace in which to meet the standards set for the trade. An established manufacturer, overcome by business reverses, might be permitted to forego payments into pension funds or unemployment reserves. Restrictions on overtime, on contracting, or on piecework might be temporarily lifted to help the

---

[32]At the end of two years of the operation of the [three-year] agreement, the Conference Committee shall take up for consideration the revision of the minimum scale of wages to conform with the economic conditions then prevailing and its decision shall become part of the collective agreement.

—From the 1929 collective agreement of the Associated Fur Manufacturers and Fur Trimming Manufacturers' Association with the Furriers' Joint Council and the International Fur Workers' Union.

[33]In the fall of 1930, Impartial Chairman R. V. Ingersoll modified the three-year collective agreement for the women's coat and suit trade, negotiated in 1929 between the Industrial Council of Cloak, Suit and Skirt Manufacturers and the ILGWU and its Cloakmakers' Joint Board, by reducing for a single manufacturer the minimum number of machines required to constitute a valid union shop. *Women's Wear Daily,* Oct. 31, 1930.

harassed employer back to his feet. At the same time, the aged, the handicapped, and the inexperienced workers who could not maintain production standards might have their work load lightened and their wages reduced below contract minimums to permit retention on the job. Through the power of exemption, whole industries whose firms were too varied in earning capacity to establish a satisfactory floor under competition could gradually be brought within the orbits of law and order conceived at the Brandeis Conferences.[34]

Most important of all, arbitrators continued to exercise broad policy-making functions after 1920 because the process of weeding out unscrupulous competitors, who sprang up like mushrooms overnight, could not be accomplished through comprehensive programs of action formulated in advance. Constructing a floor under competition by suppressing the nonunion shop, or eliminating the small-scale producer, or regulating the jobber-contracting system of production called for continual changes in legislation to meet the changing tactics of unscrupulous competitors. The need for new policies could not await the next negotiating conference. For practical reasons, therefore, the lawmaking or quasi-lawmaking power had to devolve upon the permanent institutions established for each trade.

Sources of Legislative Power after 1920

The continuing exercise of legislative powers by the impartial machinery after World War I had to be reconciled with the post-war concepts of formulating policy through direct negotiations between the contracting parties. Confining the permanent agencies of administration to the four walls of collective agreements put new emphasis on the phraseology of contract terms. Few collective agreements followed the lead of the dress and waist industry in limiting the powers of the impartial machinery to the "express

---

[34]Contract clauses permitting exceptions to the standards set for an industry were scattered throughout collective agreements of the needle trades. Often labeled "hardship clauses," these provisions gave administrative agencies, particularly the impartial chairman, the power to exempt firms from meeting the standard of certain clauses, usually for limited periods of time. For a summary treatment, see "Hardship Clauses and Escape Mechanisms" in J. T. Carpenter, *Employers' Associations and Collective Bargaining in New York City* (1950), pp. 284–291.

provisions" of the contract or in precluding any modification of contract terms "except by an instrument in writing of equal formality."

On the contrary, most parties to collective agreements negotiated after 1920 deliberately authorized a continuation of many legislative powers that permanent arbitrators had previously exercised on their own authority. Even where lawmaking functions were not expressly granted, the contracting parties conceded to their administrative agencies a broad range of "implied powers," arising either from specific contract clauses or from the general nature of collective agreements. Through the use of implied powers, arbitrators converted the great transition of the twenties into a case of old wine in new bottles. The sources of legislative authority had changed but the contents remained the same.

In the first place, the contracting parties continued to reserve for their industry arbitrators a prominent role in renewing and completing their successive agreements. The outside mediator who presided at the original conferences that produced the first contract for an industry, and who then often became the first permanent arbitrator under the collective agreement, was also generally empowered to take steps leading to the renewal of contracts as they expired. Not only was his experience under the agreement considered an indispensable asset in making revisions and modifications, but his aloofness and impartiality made him an acceptable medium for holding the parties together during the heat of negotiations.

By provision of some collective agreements, the impartial chairman was directed to call a conference of the parties several months before the old contract expired for the purpose of considering an extension of the agreement, with or without alterations, revisions, or amendments. The industry arbitrator named the time and place of meeting and invited the parties to send delegates and submit proposals. He also presided at the negotiating sessions. As moderator, he could be content to preserve order and decorum during debates, or he could endeavor "to harmonize discordant notes and induce the parties to direct their views to a point of common interest." Louis D. Brandeis himself set the pattern of action for chairmen of negotiating bodies by his method of conducting the Brandeis Conferences of 1910. So long as an arbitrator retained the respect of both parties, the longer he served an industry, the greater his potential influence at the bargaining table.

Some collective agreements continued to assign arbitrators the task of resolving all policy issues on which the negotiators were unable to reach agreement. Leaving unresolved issues to arbitration was a happy expedient for permitting a contract to become effective without further delay. This practice goes back to the first protocol of the dress and waist industry where a section entitled, "Immediate Problems for Arbitration," provided as follows: "The question of which legal holidays shall be observed in the industry shall be submitted to the Board of Arbitration created under this protocol." Often the first task of an industry arbitrator was to complete the unfinished business of contract negotiations referred to him by the two parties. The terms of his decision became a part of the collective agreement.[35]

Then, too, certain policy issues on the agenda of negotiating conferences were sometimes transferred, without prior consideration, to the impartial machinery for action. Perhaps the conferees were not adequately informed on the subject matter or some permanent agency of administration was deemed more competent to act. Such was often the case with rules governing sanitation, apprenticeship, unemployment insurance, or fines and penalties for contract violations. In some cases, further study and experimentation were considered necessary before final policy could be

---

[35]One example of this procedure occurred under the collective agreement, effective June 1, 1921, between the Clothing Manufacturers' Association of New York and the ACWA. Former arbitrator for the New York market, W. M. Leiserson, was recalled from Rochester to become temporary chairman of the board of arbitration that was empowered to complete the collective agreement by resolving the following key issues on which the parties could not agree: (1) the status of contractors in their relations to manufacturers and to workers, (2) the right of discharge and the procedures for discharges, (3) problems arising from the installation of new machinery affecting the earning power of the workers, (4) the discontinuance of unprofitable shops, and (5) the status of apprentices. *Daily News Record,* June 6, 1921. The text of this agreement is printed in the issue of June 3, 1921, and Leiserson's decision on the five questions appears in the issue of June 29, 1921. Another example from the hat and cap industry is given in the issue of Feb. 15, 1921. Under the 1922 collective agreement between the United Shirt Manufacturers' Association and the ACWA, five unresolved issues were left to the arbitrator. These issues and the text of the agreement appear in the *Monthly Labor Review,* March 1922, vol. 14, pp. 101–103.

adequately determined, as was frequently the case where new technological processes were introduced or where completely new products were submitted for manufacture.

Perhaps, too, the pertinent facts on which legislation depended would arise after the negotiators had concluded their work, as was invariably the case with recurring problems of unemployment, or the readjustment of piece rates to meet changes in style, materials, or conditions of employment. Leaving all such special issues to the impartial machinery permitted more deliberation where further study was needed and at the same time opened the door to more rapid policy determination where circumstances demanded speedy action. In all these areas of lawmaking, the contracting parties expressly permitted their permanent institutions to take action after 1920.

From these specific spheres of legislative activity assigned to permanent agencies of administration, the contracting parties in some instances took the further step of conferring upon their impartial machinery the power to resolve completely new issues, including the power to revise the collective agreement itself, should unforeseen exigencies arise for which the parties were unable to provide a solution. Where collective agreements permitted either party to call the other into conference at any time during the life of the contract to consider matters of mutual concern, the permanent arbitrator was still directed to preside at these conferences — even in some cases to convene conferences on his own authority. He was also empowered to settle any issue on which the parties could not agree. Presumably, this procedure would thwart attempts to disrupt production on grounds of unforeseen emergencies arising during the life of the agreement.[36]

---

[36]This agreement is not, however, all inclusive. In the nature of things it cannot cover everything. With relation to all matters not covered thereby, they shall be promptly submitted to conference, and if a satisfactory determination is not reached, then the matters are to be submitted to the board of arbitration, and the decision of that board shall be final upon the parties and shall immediately become part of this agreement as soon as rendered, the same as if they had been in this agreement fully set forth and incorporated.

    —From the 1921 collective agreement of the Clothing Manufacturers' Association of New York with the ACWA, text in *Daily News Record,* June 3, 1921.

Last, but not least, the contracting parties after 1920 tolerated a broad range of "rule-making" powers to supplement the specific grants of legislative authority conferred upon their impartial machinery. Collective agreements continued to state in general terms the major goals of the parties without prescribing the means through which those goals could be achieved. Supplementing these general statements of policy with rules and regulations to meet their objectives opened the door to a broad expanse of legislative activity. From time to time, agencies of the impartial machinery drafted "codes of procedure" on such subjects as the training of apprentices, standards of sanitation, the preferential shop, and control of contracting. Beyond approving such legislation in principle, the parties who negotiated the collective agreements renounced their lawmaking function with little concern for legal questions of delegating legislative power. Furthermore, administrative agencies in resolving disputes brought before them were allowed to impose general rules of future conduct upon employers and workers alike. Under the terms of some contracts, these rules were then carried over into subsequent agreements.[37]

The need for special rule-making powers to control jobber-contractor-inside manufacturer-union relationships accounted for the creation of a special administrative board under the 1936 collective agreements of the dress industry. Not only was this board, representing all factions of the trade, endowed with "full power and authority to effectuate the purposes" set forth in the paragraph on limitation of contractors, but it was also authorized "to formulate all necessary rules, regulations and methods of procedure not inconsistent with the covenants and principles set forth in applicable provisions of the collective agreements." Questions of

---

This clause also appears in the collective agreement of July 28, 1921, between the Clothing Manufacturers' Association of Montreal and the ACWA, text in *ibid.,* July 28, 1921.

[37]For example, the 1938 collective agreement between the Eastern Women's Headwear Association and the United Hatters, Cap and Millinery Workers' International Union permitted an employer to install an "experimental department" for the manufacture of new products, or the introduction of new techniques, only with the approval of the impartial chairman who must see that the tenure of the normal staff of workers not be disturbed. The first case involving this clause, which was new to the industry, led Impartial Chairman Isaac Siegmeister to spell out in detail how this contract provision was to be implemented. Isaac Siegmeister, *Decisions,* Case no. 84 (August 1, 1938).

assigning, transferring, substituting, and discharging contractors fell within its province. Neither inside shops nor outside shops could be enlarged without the knowledge and approval of the administrative board. Whenever participating board members were evenly divided on an issue, final action was reserved for the impartial chairman of the industry.[38]

Nor was the rule-making power always limited to implementing particular clauses and phrases of the written agreement. Confining the policy-determining functions of the impartial machinery to powers derived from the written word was of little consequence if, at the same time, the contract expressly conferred upon permanent arbitrators additional powers to make supplemental arrangements not inconsistent with the agreement. Nor was the care with which contract terms were so precisely phrased of any moment where arbitrators were given residual powers to do all things necessary for the successful operation of the agreement. For example, the 1921 collective agreement between the Clothing Manufacturers' Association of New York and the Amalgamated Clothing Workers authorized a board of arbitration to do all in its power to "insure the successful working of this agreement" having in mind "the necessity of making it workable and adaptable to the needs and conditions of the industry."[39]

---

[38]In addition to the 1936 dress industry agreements of the New York market, see Harry Uviller, impartial chairman for the industry, *Decisions,* Case no. D-31 (Jan. 21, 1937), vol. 2, pp. 10–11, and Case no. D-689 (May 19, 1937), vol. 3, p. 130. An early precedent for a similar administrative agency may be found in the 1916 collective agreement between the Boston Dress and Waist Manufacturers' Association and the ILGWU. The text was printed in *Women's Wear,* Feb. 10, 1916.

[39]This collective agreement stated further that the board of arbitration "has the absolute power to deal with any question that may arise, the disposition of which is essential to the successful working out of this agreement." Text of the agreement in *Daily News Record,* June 3, 1921.

The 1943 collective agreements of the women's coat and suit trade continued the board of stability and control created under the 1940 agreements with powers "additional to those contained in this collective agreement which may be found to be necessary to insure more faithful performance of the collective agreement by members of the ————— [association] and to provide a more uniform and more equal enforcement of the collective agreement." In addition, the board was directed to resolve differences between union contract proposals previously rejected by the employers and employer contract proposals previously rejected by the union. All such issues not re-

Concluding Observations

In seeking to implement the objectives of collective bargaining, the sponsors of the protocol movement created permanent legislative institutions capable of meeting the shifting pressures of competition generated from day to day by unpredictable changes in production. In determining the structure, defining the powers, and outlining the procedures of this lawmaking machinery, the "enlightened" leadership of the "bosses" and the "people" had to overcome constant hostility from the unreformed; particularly, from unreformed union members who demanded autonomous control at the shop level and from unreformed manufacturers who demanded independence in pursuing their own policies. Here the Jewish heritage of accepting community leadership permitted the creation of impartial machinery manned by the most honored and respected citizens of the industrial community. For reasons of expediency, if not on grounds of principle, the parties to collective agreements conceded to that type of leadership the responsibility for policy determination as well as for contract enforcement.

Even though the parties to collective agreements after the First World War rebelled against outside dictation of legislative policy and professed to assert direct control over their own lawmaking, they still left many types of legislative problems to be resolved by their impartial machinery. Reassembling the contracting parties for every unforeseen policy issue that arose was clearly out of the question. Equally unrealistic was the assumption that many of these issues could await the renegotiation of the next contract. The necessity for speed and authority to offset the shifting tactics of unscrupulous competitors precluded the usual deliberations that accompanied the renegotiations of contract terms. Moreover, reliance upon the seasoned judgment of those elected to the permanent institutions for the self-government of an industry offered the best opportunity of maintaining law and order among so many discordant elements. Hence, the lawmaking function of collective bargaining continued to revolve around the impartial chairmen or board of arbitration for each trade.

---

solved by the board were to be submitted to the impartial chairman for final determination.

Chapter 6

The Machinery and Methods
of Contract Enforcement

W HATEVER legislative powers fell to various agencies of the impartial machinery were over and above a primary responsibility originally assigned those agencies for administering and enforcing collective agreements. In formulating a new approach to collective bargaining, delegates to the Brandeis Conferences of 1910 had expressed grave concern over the prospects of adopting new policies that would never be enforced. Some assurance that contract terms would be observed was to differentiate the protocol movement from previous attempts at collective bargaining. Stressing the need for meeting their respective commitments, the two delegations had concluded their sessions in the high expectation of putting whatever standards they adopted into operation throughout their industry.[1]

The problem as they saw it was one of adequate jurisdiction, proper administration, and effective enforcement. The question

---

[1]Both parties to this protocol are desirous of raising conditions in the industry. . . . They recognize also the value of an understanding or agreement with adequate machinery and institutions to enforce and carry out the principles of the understanding.

—Protocol for the Children's Dress Industry (March 8, 1913). Text in C. H. Winslow, *Conciliation, Arbitration, and Sanitation in the Dress and Waist Industry of New York City*, U. S. Department of Labor, BLS Bulletin no. 145 (April 10, 1914), p. 133.

of jurisdiction was vital to the principle of industry-wide standards; for, not only were both parties to the first protocol expected to see that contract terms were faithfully executed within their own factories, but they also had to devise ways and means of extending and enforcing those terms upon the outer circles of their industry, namely, (1) the nonassociation, but "unionized" shops; (2) the nonassociation, nonunion shops; and (3) the out-of-town shops that were generally unorganized either by the employers or by the workers.[2]

Enforcement in Association-Union Shops

Within their own establishments, those who initiated the protocol movement never anticipated serious difficulties of enforcement. Sponsored by the "legitimate" elements of industrial society, the protocols had been constructed on an exalted plateau of business integrity. They were agreements among gentlemen whose word could be trusted. "We know we have the confidence of our members," assured J. H. Cohen, speaking for the women's coat and suit manufacturers, "so that our proposals and our acceptances of your proposals will be carried out by our association." If standards of business integrity did not suffice, the mutual interests of the parties would certainly prevail. Every contract infraction would bring down upon the culprit the censure of employers and workers alike. Finally, the pressure for noncompliance would gradually be lifted as uniform standards of employment were extended to all competitors within a trade.[3]

Unfortunately, a respect for the legitimate forces of industry that inspired the framers of the original protocols did not extend to all those subsequently bound by these agreements. At times, economic reverses or ideological beliefs undermined the best intentions of some who had officially accepted the principles of the protocol movement. Given the necessity of survival, the most loyal employer could forsake the ultimate goal of a fully organized, self-regulated industry for an immediate chance to stay in business. Faced with the realities of unemployment, the most ardent champion of union labor standards could desert his ultimate goal for

[2]See diagram above p. 46.

[3]Cloak, Suit and Skirt Manufacturers' Protective Association, *The Cloak Makers' Strike* (1910), p. 122.

the sake of an immediate job. "You can get members of the union to become nonunion," once observed Abe Bisno, an official of the cloakmakers' union, "if a man is starving and you offer him a job." Moral sanctions alone did not suffice to bind all subscribing members of either party to the terms of the protocols. Law and order in industry had to be sustained by an element of compulsion.[4]

Before the era of the protocols, unions were solely responsible for enforcing labor agreements with individual employers. Their chief agency of contract administration was the "walking delegate," whose methods were often high-handed and unpredictable. To ferret out infractions of an agreement, the walking delegate often appeared on the company's premises, unannounced and uninvited. As a policeman, he subjected some employers to rules and regulations far removed from the provisions of the contract. Yet he never bothered to see that other employers obeyed the most essential terms of their agreements. At the same time, he either condoned all contract infractions by the workers themselves or he reported these infractions to union headquarters for action. In all cases of alleged contract violations, final authority to determine guilt and inflict punishment resided in the executive board of the union itself.[5]

Employers resisted a system of contract administration that was neither fair nor impartial. They could not accept unwarranted intrusions by union agents upon their private property; and they saw no justice in the one-way administration of their agreements. However meritorious the idea of uniform labor standards, even when imposed upon individual employers by "identical" contracts drafted at union headquarters, no manufacturer could support a system of contract administration that was not only biased in favor of the worker but also led to wide differences in labor costs among business competitors.[6]

---

[4]A. Bisno, testimony before the U. S. Commission on Industrial Relations, April 8, 1914, in the Commission's *Final Report and Testimony* (1916), vol. 1, p. 584.

[5]Some labor contracts with individual firms provided for the possibility of an appeal to arbitration over the head of the union, if the firm was willing to pay the costs.

[6]"The signing of agreements without any intention of ever living up to them is an original gesture which has been worked out by the so-called 'progressive' unions of the East Side. In fact in the minds of these workers a

Delegates to the Brandeis Conferences of 1910 had contemplated a bipartisan system of administration based upon the activities of employers' associations and labor unions. They saw in collective bargaining between unions and associations the inherent advantage of a built-in mechanism for guaranteeing adherence to the contract. Each organization would hold its own wayward members to the terms of the collective agreement. Reflecting on the purposes of the original Protocol of Peace that he had helped to create, Louis D. Brandeis, chairman of the board of arbitration under that agreement, pointed out that one result of the protocol "was to create, through the strengthening of the employers' association on the one hand, and of the Union on the other, bodies which should be able to enforce compliance with the terms of the agreement which was made."[7]

Subsequent agreements have specifically obligated employers' associations and labor unions to discipline their respective members for undermining wage scales, dealing with nonunion shops, disregarding limitations on hours of work, or failing to observe restrictions on outside contracting. The nature and extent of these obligations have varied from subject to subject, agreement to agreement, and industry to industry, but the common intent of all such provisions has been to impose upon unions and associations the role of perpetual watchdogs over the conduct of their respective members during the life of collective agreements.[8]

---

union agreement...[is] one to be interpreted strictly in accordance with the ideas, wishes and desires of its walking delegate, shop chairman or any other member working in these shops." J. A. Dyche, *Bolshevism in American Labor Unions* (1926), p. 147.

[7]"It was recognized," Brandeis continued, "that without a strong Union of employees on the one side, and a strong employers' association on the other, the agreement could not attain the desired results." *Minutes*, Board of Arbitrators...[women's coat and suit trade], Nathan Schuss case (Jan. 21, 1915), vol. 8, p. 993. The protocol itself stated flatly that "the manufacturers will discipline any member thereof proven guilty of unfair discrimination among his employees."

[8]In addition to "pledging their good faith to co-operate" for the enforcement of their 1926 collective agreement, the Hat Frame Manufacturers' Association and the United Cloth Hat and Millinery Workers' International Union, together with the Ladies' Hat Frame Workers' Union, Local 50, also provided in their agreement as follows:

Opposition of the Rank and File

Beyond what was expected of labor unions and employers' associations, the need for special machinery of contract enforcement was never discussed at the Brandeis Conferences. The participants had relied wholly upon the power and loyalty of their respective organizations. What they had failed to reckon with, however, were the uncompromising temperaments of the rank and file, many of whom persisted in believing that all measures by associations or by unions to enforce collective agreements against their respective members were forms of treason — just as all attempts to bring pressures upon rebellious members in the opposite camp were forms of industrial warfare. Collaborating with the opposite party to an agreement — particularly to strengthen his position — was giving aid and comfort to an enemy. Partisan organizations were presumed to take biased stands in support of their own members. "The great mass of the people can not believe that it is possible for their organization to act in cooperation with an organization of employers," so J. A. Dyche, general secretary-treasurer of the ILGWU, told the U. S. Commission on Industrial Relations, January 15, 1914. "They think that every attempt in that direction is what I should call treachery."[9]

With sufficient backing from the rank and file, employers' associations and labor unions might have worked out orderly processes of effective contract administration; without this support, they stood in danger of disrupting their own organizations. The development of impartial machinery for contract administration

---

More specifically, the Association pledges itself for its members that they will live up in good faith to all the provisions of this agreement. The Union, on its part, likewise pledges for its members that they will in good faith live up to the provisions of this agreement.

—Text of this agreement, effective July 27, 1926, appears as Appendix no. 3 in Cloth Hat, Cap and Millinery Workers' International Union, *Report and Proceedings,* Sixteenth Biennial Convention (May 1927), pp. 233–237.

[9]*Final Report and Testimony,* vol. 2, p. 1041. Employers' associations apparently had their troubles, too. In his annual report of 1925 to the Associated Fur Manufacturers, William Pike, labor manager, warned that the association would not protect every member who "thinks that under the cloak of membership he is permitted to violate rules and that the association is supposed to protect him whether he is right or wrong." *Women's Wear,* Jan. 15, 1925.

stemmed, therefore, from the failure of unions and employers' associations to fulfill their assigned roles. Unable to accomplish their objectives through partisan organizations alone, the sponsors of the protocol movement turned more and more to impartial agencies that would have the confidence of both sides. Of necessity, they had to build their machinery of enforcement upon a non-partisan foundation. But impartiality, as they saw it, was not an exclusive virtue of third parties having no personal interest at stake, for whoever acted in the name of the impartial machinery thereby cast aside his cloak of partisanship and worked only for the good of the industry.[10]

"I would suggest that the union and the manufacturers' society establish a body of experts whose business it should be to settle the price for labor," stated Abe Bisno, union official, on the ever recurring problem of adjusting piece rates, ". . .and that these experts be paid by both the union and the manufacturers' association together, and that they be officers not only of the one side or of the other side but of both sides." J. H. Cohen, representing the manufacturers, expressed similar convictions: "Under the machinery developed through the machinery of the protocol the man who represents the union and the man who represents the employers' association is [sic] not only an advocate, but he is a judge

---

[10]For three years after the original Protocol of Peace was terminated in 1916, the Cloak, Suit and Skirt Manufacturers' Protective Association and the Cloak-makers' Joint Board, ILGWU, lived under a new agreement that clearly defined their respective roles as exclusive agencies of contract enforcement:

> The Association agrees to enforce the performance by its members of all the express provisions of this agreement on their part to be performed. If after investigation on the part of the Union, the Union shall establish by proper proof to the Association that there has been a violation of any such provisions, the Association will remedy any such violation, and, in a proper case, will discipline its members therefor.

> The Union agrees to enforce performance by its members of all express provisions of this agreement on their part to be performed. If, after investigation on the part of the Association, the Association shall establish by proper proof to the Union that there has been a violation of any of such provisions, the Union will remedy any such violation, and, in a proper case, will discipline its members therefor.

The failure of this experiment forever silenced those who would rely *wholly* upon employers' associations and labor unions to see that their respective members fulfilled their obligations under the collective agreement.

as well, and he has to be of that unique type, like the Howards and the Hillmans...that can be both advocate and judge at the same time."[11]

The need for some unbiased machinery of contract administration was conceded at the time the original protocols were finally drafted. Provision was made in these agreements for resolving differences between unions and associations through a board of arbitration, with minor disputes between employers and workers going first to a committee on grievances. The character and composition of these boards suggest, however, that they were intended to be appellate tribunals better adapted to resolving differences over the interpretation of agreements than designed to take over the job of policing an industry. Furthermore, as we have seen, these institutions — whatever the purpose for which they were conceived — soon became policy-determining organs, more in the nature of continuing legislative bodies than agencies of law enforcement for their industries.

Nature of the Enforcement Problem

During the life of an agreement, disputes over interpretations of rights and duties were far less important than the more numerous cases of contract infractions deliberately committed for the advantages to be gained. Here the problem was one of detection and punishment. Stealing and being caught, observed Meyer London, legal counsel of the ILGWU in 1913, was as much a problem of contract administration as settling disputes over differences of interpretation. A board of grievances, he conceded, might logically determine whether a foreman was particularly disagreeable or whether a workshop was adequately lighted, but such agencies were ill-suited to handle deliberate violations of contract terms where no difference of opinion was possible. "And no difference of opinion is possible," London argued, "where the scale says the

---

[11]U.S. Commission on Industrial Relations, *Final Report and Testimony,* Bisno at p. 584; Cohen at p. 578. Earl Dean Howard, a professor at Northwestern University, was also manager of the labor department at Hart, Schaffner, and Marx; Sidney Hillman was president of the Amalgamated Clothing Workers of America.

rate is $27 and you pay $17." Such cases, so he insisted, called for the exercise of "police powers" only.[12]

Morris Silberman, president of the Cloak, Suit and Skirt Manufacturers' Protective Association, had spoken on this subject a few months earlier. He, too, would distinguish between procedures for handling alleged infractions of contract clauses that were subject to varying interpretations and procedures for handling deliberate contract infractions that were clear on their face. Whereas resort to a quasi-judicial tribunal, like the board of arbitration, might be logical in the first case, only an enforcing agency was required in the second.

The occasion for Silberman's observations on the nature of the enforcement problem arose from the introduction of a union rule that had further limited the use of overtime beyond restrictions found in the protocol. Whereas the women's coat and suit protocol had expressly forbidden the use of overtime for only four months of the year, the cloakmakers' union wanted to prohibit union members from working overtime in any month that machines were idle during the normal working hours. Dr. I. A. Hourwich, speaking for the union, suggested that such a rule be applied to association shops, as it had unilaterally been applied to inde-

---

[12]*Minutes,* Board of Arbitrators...[women's coat and suit trade] (Oct. 13, 1913), pp. 282–283.

> If you will examine the official reports of Mr. Winslow, in the Bulletin of the Bureau of Labor for January, 1912, you will find that over 25 percent of the grievances of the Union against the Manufacturers involved personal dishonesty....Paying under the scale, What is that if not dishonest? In compelling people to work longer hours and paying less than the protocol provides for overtime. What is that, if not dishonesty? Forced reduction of settled prices. What is that if not dishonesty? Non-payment for holidays. What is that if not dishonesty?
> —Meyer London in *Minutes,* Conference between the Representatives of the Cloak, Suit and Skirt Manufacturers' Protective Association and the ILGWU and the Cloakmakers' Joint Board (Feb. 4, 1913), p. 165.

Many years later, Julius Hochman, general manager, Dressmakers' Joint Board, ILGWU, reviewing some 1,200 cases brought in the mid-thirties before the impartial chairman of the dress industry by the dress contractors' association against members of the dress jobbers' association, observed: "Most of these cases were not honest differences of opinion between the various parties of the agreement. They were cases against jobbers who had committed outright crimes." ILGWU's *Justice,* Jan. 15, 1936.

pendent shops. He conceded that the enforcement might be suspended while the validity of the new rule was submitted to the industry's board of arbitration for a decision. On the contrary, M. Silberman, speaking for the employers, believed the provisions of the protocol to be so clear on overtime that any attempt to "interpret" the new union rule as falling within the scope of the protocol's overtime regulations would insult the intelligence of the board. He insisted that the one-way adoption of such a rule did not call for an official "interpretation" of the agreement but for the exercise of "police powers" to suppress an obvious violation of the contract.[13]

Presumably, employers' associations and labor unions were the proper agencies to exercise such police powers as were necessary to enforce collective agreements. But when experience proved that partisan organizations, left to their own devices, could not resist pressure to take partisan stands, the "police functions," originally reserved for the contracting parties, were gradually transferred to impartial agencies of administration. That is why the impartial machinery had to be expanded downward from the top-level boards created by the protocols until they embraced operators on the front lines of labor-management relations. That is why the permanent institutions for contract administration had to take on the form of a pyramid with the highest arbitrating authority sitting at the top and with subordinate bodies fanning outward and downward through intermediate agencies into a broad base of representatives operating at the plant level.

Within months after the first protocol became effective, the task of visiting and inspecting plants for evidences of contract infractions was conferred upon "clerks" and "deputy clerks" — offices created by the board of arbitration to supplement the agencies of administration named in the protocol. Although the parties to the protocol each selected and paid for its clerks and deputy clerks,

---

[13]*Minutes,* Conference between Representatives of the Cloak, Suit and Skirt Manufacturers' Protective Association and the Joint Board of Cloak and Skirt Makers' Unions (Feb. 28, 1913), vol. 1, pp. 2 ff., especially pp. 37–39. Silberman held similar views about other union attempts to stretch the protocol: "By the wildest stretch of imagination," so he argued, "you cannot interpret any part of the protocol to say or tell an employer how many men he shall employ, or how many men he shall not employ, and when he must employ them and when he must lay them off," *ibid.,* p. 17.

these officials were, in fact, a part of the impartial machinery and operated in its name. Unfortunately for the success of the protocol movement, the acquisition of a new title bearing the stamp of the impartial machinery did not always guarantee a change of approach. Particularly where newly selected officials of the impartial machinery retained positions they previously held in their own organizations did the glow of partisanship tend to penetrate the robes of impartiality. Yet the success of this magic transformation in the personnel of the impartial machinery was essential to the maintenance of law and order in industry.

Above the front-line clerks and deputy clerks, who were later called "representatives" or "managers," and below the conference committees or boards of grievances, the machinery of contract administration sometimes provided for other intermediate agencies most often entitled, "committees on immediate action." These committees further relieved superior agencies of administrative detail by handling cases of minor importance. In addition, special committees were constituted from time to time to cope with unusually difficult problems of contract enforcement. Finally, above the conference committees or boards of grievances sat the highest arbitrating authority for the industry — a permanent umpire, an impartial chairman, or a board of arbitration.

Once official responsibility for contract administration had been shifted to the "impartial machinery," labor unions and employers' associations were in a position to become agents of a higher authority. In so far as these organizations were directed to carry out the decisions of clerks, joint committees, or arbitrators, they formed a part of the impartial machinery responsible for enforcing the agreement. When functioning in this capacity they, too, officially doffed their cloaks of partisanship and put on the robes of impartiality. At least this device of acting on behalf of the permanent institutions dedicated to the welfare of the industry permitted both organizations to execute their assignments with less criticism from their own rank-and-file members.

The presumed effects of this transformation were exemplified in the case of Limelight Hat Co. brought before Impartial Chairman Isaac Siegmeister of the millinery industry. In this dispute, both the employer and his workers had resorted to direct action in contravention of advice from their respective organizations. Appearing before the highest arbitrating authority of their industry, each party to the dispute stood condemned by a representative of his own organization. "I certainly hold no brief for a manufacturer . . . who is not big enough to take orders from his [association's] representative, be they [*sic*] right or wrong," testified the spokesman for the Eastern Women's Headwear Association. "He can still investigate further, but as a good soldier he should always take orders."

The spokesman for the United Hatters, Cap and Millinery Workers' International Union was no less emphatic in condemning direct action by the workers of the shop: "In accordance with the provision of this agreement, there can't be and should not be a stoppage or cessation of work, or strike or lockout in any shop of a member under this Collective Agreement, but everything in dispute of a controversial nature shall and must be taken up in the proper form of procedure and there is ample provision for redress for the Association and the Union as well." Endorsing both these statements, the impartial chairman subordinated the immediate issues of the dispute to the fundamental concepts that had been established. "The principle that is more important in this controversy," he stated, "is that each side fully realizes the full impact of the obligations imposed upon each under the Collective Agreement."[14]

Maintaining a Floor under Competition

Within the association-union group of factories, success in applying the principles of the protocol movement hinged largely upon finding a solution to three major problems: (1) how to prevent such chiseling upon the minimum standards of the collective agreement as would demolish the floor under competition; (2) how to forestall shop-to-shop "improvements" upon established work standards — improvements that threatened to destroy the essential uniformity of labor costs among competing firms during the life of an agreement; (3) how to prevent such dealings with outside shops between periods of contract negotiations as would undermine the stability of the industry. Resolving these issues was rendered the more difficult because individual employers and the

---

[14]Isaac Siegmeister, *Decisions,* Case no. 131 (Sept. 28, 1938).

particular workers in their shops both stood to gain from engaging in many of these prohibited activities.

Maintaining a floor under competition was clearly the most important task facing the impartial machinery during the life of an agreement. The protocol movement had originated in 1910 as an attempt by the organized forces of industry to put a floor under competition for the mutual advantage of "legitimate" employers and "respectable" members of the labor force. Ever since that date, collective bargaining in the needle trades has been directed primarily toward creating and maintaining minimum standards of employment, below which no association member would be allowed to operate and no union member would be allowed to work. All collective agreements have been negotiated, interpreted, administered, and enforced largely in the light of this fundamental concept.

Shortly after the first protocol was signed on September 2, 1910, it became apparent that many employers had subscribed to the agreement in name only. By their conduct, if not by their words, scores of shop owners renounced their solemn commitments with complete indifference to the protocol. Such an employer pattern of lawless conduct was, like a similar union pattern, inherited from experience with single shop bargaining in the years before the protocols. At that time, flouting the terms of union-drafted "form" agreements accepted under duress carried no moral stigma and aroused no adverse criticism from the business community. On the contrary, whatever contract provisions an employer could transgress with impunity were all to his credit. Just as single shop contracts were continually expanding at the hands of dictatorial union agents, so were they also continually disintegrating at the hands of individual employers who held them in contempt.

The protocol movement had presumably ended all this. Here an abiding respect for contractual obligations was acknowledged to be the *sine qua non* of all successful attempts at regulating industry. Rigid adherence to the terms of collective agreements had been the closing note at the Brandeis Conferences. Nonetheless, employer attitudes and practices that had made shambles of labor agreements under single shop bargaining before 1910 filtered through the transition period to influence employer conduct under the original protocols and under the collective agreements that followed them.

The Loophole of Interpretations

There were, to be sure, legitimate questions of interpretation about which honest differences of opinion prevailed. Under all the protocols — and subsequent agreements as well — scores of debatable issues invariably arose over the application of wage clauses, sanitary standards, overtime provisions, methods of production, vacations, holidays, outside contracting, and grievance procedures. May union members refuse to accept overtime work? Must employers pay for holidays that fall on Saturdays? May employers reduce wages so long as the rates do not fall below the contract minimums? In all such questions of reasonable doubt, manufacturers could scarcely be condemned for initially adopting interpretations favorable to themselves — at least until their presumptions were challenged by interested parties through the grievance procedure.[15]

Nor could manufacturers bound by the protocols be strongly condemned for taking advantage of nice distinctions between the spirit and the letter of the law. Certain employers religiously followed the letter of their contracts but had no scruples about violating the spirit of their agreements. Other association members, who found the spirit more to their liking, never hesitated to violate the letter of their agreements in the name of the higher law that was intended to prevail. "While the wording of the Agreement undoubtedly permits firms to buy outside," once noted the impartial chairman of the fancy leather goods industry, "it is just as true that the spirit of the Agreement also means that the inside workers shall be given an opportunity to do all the work which can be done inside." All such differences of interpretation fell within the range of reasonable conflict that the machinery of contract administration had been devised to resolve.[16]

---

[15]Perhaps no provision of the original protocol aroused more legitimate questions of interpretation than the preferential union shop clause — a clause that inspired endless debates over numerous issues at all levels of contract administration. On the recurring issue of whether this clause obligated an employer to discharge a worker deficient in paying his union dues, see *Women's Wear*, Feb. 19, 21, 23, 26, and 28, 1916.

[16]C. B. Barnes, *Decisions,* case of R. I. Shank & Co. (May 24, 1922), filed in the Abelson papers. See also discussion in *Women's Wear,* March 9, 1926. "If a manufacturer does not violate the letter of the Protocol, but continues violating the spirit of it, while he is careful to keep, so to say, within the letter of the law, our people will naturally act the same way." J. A. Dyche, general

Frequently, however, so-called "interpretations" were too far-fetched to provide more than a thin veil of defense for employer conduct. Thus, some manufacturers seeking to evade payments for holidays closed their shops one day before the holidays began, then opened them again after the holidays were over. Those employers having to meet the "fourteen machine" rule that set the minimum number of operators to a plant, simply bought the required number of machines but left them unattended. Those manufacturers seeking to avoid contract prohibitions on lockouts still permitted the workers to take their seats but sent out all their goods to be made up elsewhere. At least one employer, hoping to avoid compensation for overtime, withheld all overtime payments until the end of the season. The contract requirement that wages must be paid each Monday in cash applied only to "regular" wages for a "normal" week's work, he said.[17]

Most employer transgressions were clearly outside the pale of logical or tenable differences over the meaning of contract terms. Admittedly, they were acts beyond the province of those interpretations that did not border on the absurd. During the hearings before the U. S. Commission on Industrial Relations, June 5, 1914, Jacob Panken [Pankin], attorney for the United Brotherhood of Tailors, was asked whether a contract could be drafted that was not subject to different interpretations on vital points. "Yes. Of course you can set down a question of hours," Panken replied. "You can set down the question of the employment of union men, without a question of interpretation. He is either a

---

secretary-treasurer, ILGWU, in a letter, dated Dec. 7, 1911, to the president of the manufacturers' association. Letter filed in the Abelson papers.

[17]*Minutes,* Committee on Immediate Action [fur manufacturing industry], case of Kresel and Young (Nov. 9, 1917), copy filed in the Abelson papers. On the evasion of the fourteen machine rule, see *Women's Wear,* April 10, 1924.

If a strike must not necessarily be that the workingmen leave the shop and are on guard picketing it, but is also such when the workingmen remain in the shop and refuse to work, then a lockout should be considered in the same way. It is not only a lockout when the manufacturer throws out the workingmen and takes on others in their places, but it is also a lockout when he lets them sit in the shop, but takes away from them the work and gives it to others.

—Editorial in the *New Post,* June 6, 1913. Translation filed in the Abelson papers.

union man or is not a union man. The employees are either working 50 hours or they are not working 50 hours. The employer is
either giving the minimum scale or is not observing the minimum
scale."[18]

No union member would concede the possibility of an interpretation that would cover manufacturers who, in deliberate violation
of clearly specified contract provisions, refused to pay their workers
on designated paydays, or insisted that piecework be done before
piece rates were set, or surreptitiously sent materials to be finished
in outside shops. Above all, the prescribed hours of work and the
wage scales in collective agreements were beyond the range of
flexible interpretations. "If hours and wages are set," queried A.
Bisno, agent for the cloakmakers' union in 1914, "why haggle over
65 percent or 75 percent or 85 percent of the wages stated in the
agreement?" Similarly, piece rates, once fixed for particular garments, were beyond the range of variable interpretations. "We
settled this waist for 94¢ and one 75¢," testified Miss Fannie Yaeger
before the committee on immediate action of the dress industry
in 1915, "and Thursday we got pay and I saw that the waist that
was settled for 94¢ was paid 65¢."[19]

Employers' Associations as Enforcing Agencies

These cases of unquestioned contract infractions were particularly suited for disposition by the organized employers themselves.
Here no impartial machinery was needed to determine guilt.
Moreover, employers' associations had the motive and the means
to detect and punish their own offenders. By making violations
of their labor agreements an infraction of their own bylaws, these
employer groups could use the machinery of their own organizations to determine guilt and inflict punishment. Within months
after the first protocol was adopted, the Cloak, Suit and Skirt
Manufacturers' Protective Association on May 11, 1911 named a
special committee to recommend suitable penalties against its
members for contract infractions; and on December 27, 1911 this

---

[18]*Final Report and Testimony,* vol. 2, p. 2020.

[19]Bisno also discusses this issue in his testimony before the U. S. Commission
on Industrial Relations, June 5, 1914, *ibid.,* vol. 2, p. 1135. Miss Yeager's
testimony is in *Minutes,* Committee on Immediate Action [dress industry],
case of Joseph Rosenberg & Co. (Oct. 30, 1915), p. 549.

association adopted a resolution on discipline setting forth standards of punishment for the first, second, and third offenses against the labor agreement.[20]

During the first few years under the women's coat and suit protocol, scores of noncomplying employers were penalized by reprimand, fine, suspension, or expulsion from their association for such varied offenses as failing to pay minimum wages, permitting work on Sunday, falsifying work records, bribing union business agents, giving work to nonregistered contractors, or having goods made up in out-of-town shops. Under their constitutions and bylaws, other employers' groups bound by collective agreements took similar steps to penalize their members for violating the terms of their contracts.[21]

Not content with punitive measures, many associations openly encouraged their members to stand by their commitments. During a hearing before the board of arbitration for the dress and waist industry in November 1913, a member of the board inquired of Walter Bartholomew, labor manager for the dress and waist manufacturers, "whether, quite apart from questions of discipline, the Association had adopted any constructive policy of educating its own members in the terms of the Protocol and methods of meeting those terms." Although the dress protocol had been in effect only nine months, Mr. Bartholomew could point to a number of "constructive" steps that his association had taken:

We issued four bulletins which commented upon those things which, from our clerks, we learned members were most in the dark about. We also advised them through these bulletins, of the matters which the Union was particularly desirous that we should put em-

---

[20]For the first offense, the firm would be reprimanded by the executive committee of the association; for the second offense, the firm would be fined $100 to $250; for the third offense, the firm would be expelled from the association, unless extenuating circumstances existed, and it would not again be eligible for membership. See "Disciplinary Action by the Association," typewritten copy filed in the Abelson papers.

[21]Records of disciplinary action reported by employers' associations to the impartial machinery of their respective industries may be found in the Abelson papers. See, for example, "Chronological Order of Disciplinary Action Taken by the Executive Board" listing the firm, the charge, and the disciplinary action in forty-seven cases during 1911–1912 initiated by the Cloak, Suit and Skirt Manufacturers' Protective Association of the women's coat and suit trade. Copy filed in the Abelson papers.

phasis upon. We have had two general meetings at which the whole situation was gone over with our members, very much in the nature of lectures to them, as to their duties. The clerks of the Grievance Board are instructed at meetings which we hold about every two weeks on points which seem to be not clear to the minds of the members, and they are instructed, in going about on cases, always to tell the manufacturer what he should do under the Protocol. My office is visited by dozens of them day after day who come in for nothing but advice. They come in to ask me about things. I try to do all I possibly can to instruct them in the true meaning of the Protocol and particularly in its spirit.

This employers' association had also appointed an investigator to go from shop to shop without regard to complaints and to report on the personal traits of each employer, as well as on the general conditions of his factory. "Where we found upon the report of our own investigator that things were not as they ought to be," so Mr. Bartholomew explained, "we always sent for that member and had a heart-to-heart talk with him in the office."[22]

In fur manufacturing — to cite a later instance — association members were repeatedly reminded of their contractual obligations toward overtime pay. "Failure to enforce the terms, which provide for time and a half payment for overtime," warned William Pike, labor manager of the Associated Fur Manufacturers at the annual meeting of the association, in January 1925, "would result in complete demoralization in the wholesale trade.... If the association does not enforce the agreement with the union in this regard, no one will suffer more through it than yourselves. The offending member will have obtained his labor at a lower cost. He competes with you, under-sells you as he can readily do, and in no time there will be a complete demoralization of the industry."[23]

---

[22]*Minutes,* Arbitration Proceedings between the Dress and Waist Manufacturers' Association and the ILGWU (Nov. 8, 1913), pp. 85–86.

[23]As quoted in *Women's Wear,* Jan. 15, 1925.

The member authorizes the association to prepare and agrees to use the standard agreements to be so prepared to cover contractual relations with employes or others and to cover other conditions common to substantially all members; and failure to use and enforce any such agreement may be deemed a violation of this agreement in the discretion of the association.

Despite such official statements, many leading association members failed to set a pattern of conduct that matched the announced policies of their own organizations. While the difficulties of controlling marginal members who had joined the ranks to avoid shop strikes was generally conceded, employer groups were at least expected to see that their more important members lived up to their collective agreements. Certainly it was essential to have association officials practice the philosophy that they preached. Yet, at the very time the Dress and Waist Manufacturers' Association was urging its members to support the collective agreement, the dressmakers' union was able to cite 29 of the largest firms in this association as constituting the "most flagrant cases" of failure to observe the preferential union shop clause. At that time, union officials claimed that none of the 5,000 workers employed by those 29 firms belonged to the union! Altogether, noted Meyer London, attorney of the union, some 35 or 40 of the 290 firms in the association had never employed a single union member![24]

Even more astounding than failure to give preference to union members were union charges, based on an investigation by the

---

—From the text of an agreement between and among the members of the Associated Fur Manufacturers, party since 1912 to the major collective labor agreements negotiated with the fur workers' union in the fur manufacturing industry, as printed in *Women's Wear Daily*, Feb. 24, 1928.

[24]*Minutes,* Arbitration Proceedings between the Dress and Waist Manufacturers' Association and the ILGWU (Nov. 8, 1913), p. 15; C. H. Winslow, *Conciliation, Arbitration, and Sanitation in the Dress and Waist Industry of New York City,* p. 45.

The number of manufacturers who employ almost exclusively non-union workers is growing instead of diminishing, and there are still members of your governing committees who do not employ any members of the union....For 12 months we left it to the association to get its members to cooperate with us. Twelve months is a pretty long time to show good faith....And it is almost a rule without any exception that wherever the provisions relating to preference are violated, every other vital provision of the protocol is being violated. We must either be released from the obligation not to strike against such manufacturers or your association must find some other effective way of getting your members to carry out the provisions of the protocol relating to preference.

—Letter, dated Feb. 25, 1914, from the general manager of the Dress and Waist Makers' Union, Local 25, ILGWU, to the Dress and Waist Manufacturers' Association, *ibid.,* pp. 44–45.

dress industry's wage-scale board, that 93 out of every 100 association members violated every other important provision of the protocol, including wage scales, hours of work, and subcontracting. Forming an overwhelming majority of the association's membership, these violators of the protocol, stated the union, were evidently shaping the policy of the association. "But to make the situation more tragical and more desperate," observed Meyer London, counsel for the ILGWU, "almost every member of the Executive Committee violates the agreement." London bitterly denounced the "bosses" for failure to support their own organization. "As soon as they believe that a strike no longer threatens them," he said, "they have no use for an association."[25]

Labor Unions as Enforcing Agencies

With such prevalence of widespread violations in high places, the evidences were overwhelming that employers' associations either could not or would not keep their members from undermining minimum contract standards. Correspondingly, there was even less evidence that labor unions could or would control the activities of their union members who willfully violated the terms of their contracts. "The Union," so charged the dress and waist manufacturers before their industry board of arbitration in 1913, "has disciplined very few, if any, of its members for violating the provisions of the Protocol or for conduct violating the spirit of the Protocol and tending to promote friction and hostility between employers and workers."[26]

Behind the efforts of labor unions to discipline their own members was a long history of shop-to-shop bargaining under which the workers in each plant insisted upon taking the law into their own hands. Before 1910, a labor union had been more like a springboard for direct action by small groups of rebellious workers at the shop level than like a disciplined army for united action

---

[25]*Minutes,* Arbitration Proceedings between the Dress and Waist Manufacturers' Association and the ILGWU (Nov. 8, 1913), pp. 14, 18, 72. "That is the problem here, 270 out of a total of 290 have violated this agreement. Their bond is as good as their word, and their word is as worthless as their bond. They violate a law of the State of New York, not only the Protocol. What is a Protocol between friends, and what is the law between friends?" Meyer London, *ibid.,* p. 18.

[26]*Ibid.,* p. 67.

through centralized control at the industry level. Steeped in a heritage of revolution, rank-and-file workers could not be converted overnight into law-abiding union members through the efforts of their own institutions. For every failure by employers' associations to control affiliated business firms, similar examples could be cited of failure by labor unions to control their own organized members. Lack of discipline was especially evident in repeated outbreaks of unauthorized shop strikes.[27]

From such experiences arose the conviction that neither labor unions nor employers' assocations could be assigned sole responsibility for compelling their respective members to abide by their commitments. Where employers' associations failed to control their rebellious firms, labor unions must be permitted to step in with sanctions of their own. Conversely, where labor unions failed to restrain their noncomplying members, employers' associations must be permitted to meet these deficiencies with appropriate action. If moving directly against members of the opposite camp took on the attributes of industrial warfare, at least the practice was well established before 1910. At the time of the first protocol, employers were well versed in the use of lockouts, wholesale discharges, and sudden business transfers as forms of direct action against their organized workers. And labor unions had long followed the practice of striking against employers who violated their agreements. Perhaps a resort to direct action could be condoned under the protocol movement if the weapons of industrial warfare were used solely for the preservation of law and order in industry.

So far from opposing union pressures against association firms that violated their contracts, employer groups were more likely to rely upon unions for corrective action. Despite the well-con-

---

[27]Each of the parties undertakes to insure rigid compliance by their respective members of the terms of this contract, and covenants that noncompliance thereof will result in the expulsion of such members of the Association or the Union who shall fail to comply with this contract, and further undertakes to provide and enforce such suitable and reasonable penalties as the Association and the Union may lawfully make and enforce.
—From the 1934 collective agreement between the Men's Neckwear Manufacturers' Association of New York and the United Neckwear Makers' Union, Local 11016, AFL.

ceived principle that each organization should keep its own members in line, a great many manufacturers obviously expected labor unions to take over a primary — if not the sole — responsibility for seeing that employers as well as workers lived up to their contracts. Vast numbers of rank-and-file employers never expected to be punished by their own organizations for violating labor agreements, nor would they have joined an association so readily had they foreseen such consequences.[28]

That union business agents would police the enforcement of the collective agreement for both parties appears to have been a widespread assumption, based on experiences before 1910. Union leaders obviously anticipated such a role, for they repeatedly assured association officials that the union would take care of enforcement, provided the organized employers would only "squeal" upon their noncomplying members. "If you know of a manufacturer that pays under the scale, give us the name of the manufacturer, and we will do the work," so union leader S. Polakoff assured the organized employers of the dress and waist industry in 1913. "If you know that manufacturer B works sixty hours a week, please tell it to us and we will go on the job."[29]

---

[28]The assumption that labor unions would take over a major responsibility for disclosing contract infractions was borne out by the following clause from the 1919 collective agreement of the American Cloak, Suit and Skirt Manufacturers' Association with the Cloakmakers' Joint Board and the ILGWU:

A duly authorized officer or representative of the union shall have access to the factory of the members of the association at all hours for the purpose of investigating the conditions of the shop, and for the purpose of ascertaining which provisions of this agreement are fully complied with. Such investigation will be conducted so as not to cause unnecessary interference with the work. He shall also have access to the firm's books for the purpose of ascertaining the correct earnings of the workers employed in the shop and for the purpose of ascertaining the names of manufacturers and jobbers for whom the firm is doing work, or the names of the manufacturers and contractors to whom the firm is sending work. Whenever an investigation involves the examination of the firm's books a member may call in a representative of the association to partake in such investigation, provided the investigation is not thereby delayed.

—Text in *Monthly Labor Review,* December 1919, vol. 9, pp. 1719–1724 at p. 1720.

[29]*Minutes,* Joint Meeting of the Grievance Board and the Wage-Scale Board of the Dress and Waist Industry (August 26, 1913), p. 39. "The Union has taken it upon themselves to take away the contractor from our control. . . .

In any case, unions that became parties to the original protocols embarked upon their own programs of preserving minimum contract standards against all attempts by employers to undermine them. Nor did these unions subsequently relinquish the right to act on their own behalf, despite the rising opposition of the organized employers or the growing use of impartial machinery for contract administration. Not only was the institution of the "walking delegate" brought over from pre-protocol days until superseded by the "clerks" of the impartial machinery, but unions continued on particular occasions and for special purposes to use their own patrol system for detecting infractions of collective agreements.[30]

Unions found their own patrols particularly useful in detecting excessive hours of work. In the dress industry, for example, the dressmakers' union from time to time dispatched roving squads of union members to visit the dress manufacturing district both before and after normal working hours, as well as on Saturdays, Sundays, and holidays. Likewise, the millinery workers at times sent out special patrol squads to cover the hat manufacturing shops day and night seven days a week. On one occasion, a special squad of 165 union members was selected for this work. And in fur manufacturing, the fur workers' union was most vigilant in patrolling the many small shops of the industry to enforce restrictions upon hours of work.[31]

Officials of employers' associations often contended that union-

---

The Union simply came along and said 'Here, you have nothing to do any more with your contractors; they are under our control.' The contractors were stopped from work. They had to go to the Union and put up money as bond." E. J. Wile, manufacturer, in *Minutes,* Council of Conciliation...[women's coat and suit trade] (Oct. 22, 1915), vol. 7, pp. 54–55.

[30]Typical was the creation by the Dressmakers' Joint Board of a "Violation Prevention Bureau" to check widespread infractions of wage clauses under the collective agreements of the dress and waist industry in the late thirties. Through the initiative of the union, one firm alone had been forced to pay $54,100 to meet underpayments in wage rates and other violations of the agreement over a three-year period. *Women's Wear Daily,* March 4, 1937. The cutters' local of the ILGWU employed a number of enforcement committees and controllers to inspect the shops in the outlying metropolitan area for evidences of wage-scale violations. ILGWU's *Justice,* Sept. 1, 1935, p. 15.

[31]For the millinery union's special police force, see *Women's Wear Daily,* June 11, 1935.

named agencies of detection violated the letter and spirit of collective agreements in that the function of contract administration had been conferred upon joint agencies of the impartial machinery. These objections were most likely to arise where special union committees were created at the shop level to disclose contract infractions — a function that would otherwise have fallen to the clerks and deputy clerks representing both the association and the union. Such association complaints of unilateral action by the union were usually made at the instigation of association members who were more concerned with maintaining loopholes for contract evasion than with observing the terms of their labor agreements.

Union-directed Strikes to Enforce Contracts

Not only have union agents acted on their own authority to uncover contract infractions, they have also taken steps of their own to correct these evils. Quite apart from any joint agencies of contract administration, labor unions of the needle trades proceeded in the tradition of their earlier experiences to rely upon their own weapon of contract enforcement: they simply refused to work for employers violating the agreement. The very first protocol was still in its infancy when the Cloakmakers' Joint Board devised a scheme requiring all association firms bound by the agreement to obtain and display in their shop windows "Certificates of Union Conditions." Every three months the union issued new certificates to all employers found to be observing the terms of the protocol. Shops not displaying valid certificates were deprived of their usual employees.

Subsequently, the union practice of refusing to work for manufacturers who did not conform to the terms of their collective agreements was further developed. Not only was the strike-bound firm compelled to meet the standards of the contract before the workers would return to their jobs, but the employer was also forced to pay the workers for time lost during the strike. In the absence of such a penalty, so the union contended, unscrupulous employers had everything to gain and nothing to lose by disregarding their contractual obligations until detected and forced to obey. Where a noncomplying employer was willing to cease and desist from paying wages below scale or working abnormal hours without the necessity of a strike, the union still insisted that he compensate the workers for their losses and, in addition, pay the union a suitable fine to offset the advantage he had gained.

Shop strikes sponsored by the union on its own authority to preserve the minimum standards of collective agreements were at times widespread, particularly among the smaller firms of employers' associations. In 1925, for example, Ben Gold, manager of the Furriers' Joint Board, boasted that he had collected $5,095.49 over a four-month period from the employers for time lost by union workers in strikes to enforce compliance with the agreement. At the same time, Gold also reported that the union over a five-month period had collected $26,624.00 in "cash security" from smaller employers who would otherwise have been more likely to disregard their contractual obligations.[32]

Similarly, Nathaniel Spector, manager of the Millinery Workers' Union, Local 24, announced in January 1934 that forty-one strikes had broken out against forty-one firms of the Women's Headwear Group for wholesale evasion of minimum wage scales fixed in the collective labor agreement. These attempts at chiseling, Spector charged, had been made with the tacit acquiescence of the association, leaving the union to take care of its own interests through strike action. Such attempts by needle trade unions to become their own enforcement agency were openly conducted throughout the apparel industries, quite apart from joint agencies of contract administration, and without regard to whether the impartial machinery of an industry had undertaken to resolve the issues involved.[33]

---

[32]Report on union activities, May 23 to Oct. 1, 1925, in *Furriers' Bulletin,* November 1925. Clipping filed in the Abelson papers.

[33]*Women's Wear Daily,* clipping dated 1934, filed in the Abelson papers. Strikes of this character were much more common against independent firms violating their labor agreements. In August 1935, N. Spector announced that thirty such strikes had been called within a span of twenty-four hours against thirty manufacturers employing three hundred workers. *Women's Wear Daily,* August 22, 1935.

In his *Collective Bargaining Systems* (1942), chap. 7, "Enforcement in the [women's] Coat and Suit Industry," pp. 133–169, Frank C. Pierson deals at length with the union's role in contract enforcement through the use of strikes, which, for the most part, were apparently called by locals of the ILGWU acting on their own authority.

Unions defended this procedure as the most practical means of protecting minimum labor standards during the life of an agreement. Their point of view was ably set forth by Jacob Panken [Pankin], counsel for the United Brotherhood of Tailors, in his testimony before the U. S. Commission on Industrial Relations on June 5, 1914. Panken doubted the wisdom of waiting for the impartial machinery to act where the existence of a contract infraction was beyond question and where delayed action would thwart the ends of justice. In the course of a prolonged discussion over methods of contract enforcement, Panken stated:

We have had the experience in some of the trades connected with the needle industry, where there are sometimes breaches of a contract by an employer who is a member of the association; and by the time we are ready with the decision made by the board of arbitration, the people who have been aggrieved are no longer in the shop, or the season is over, and nothing can be done. . . .

Now, here is another experience under this protocol: the employers were to pay for legal holidays. There was no question about that. But they did not pay for the legal holidays and we had to submit that to arbitration and it was two months before we got a decision from the board saying as to whether the money should be paid or not. Many of the people had left the shop. Some of the people had left New York. Some of them had got disgusted.[34]

By contrast, permitting the union to make use of the strike guaranteed that every defaulting employer would suffer the consequences of contract evasion immediately and inescapably. Where the terms of the collective agreement were fixed beyond the range of variable interpretations — as was the case with the clauses on minimum wages, maximum hours, holidays with pay, or the employment of union men — the employer who violated these fixed provisions, so Panken contended, automatically terminated his membership in his association and cast himself beyond the pale of his collective agreement. Thereafter, he could no longer look to the impartial machinery of his collective agreement for protection. The no-strike, no-lockout clause of his contract no longer applied. Like other independent employers who signed individual

---

[34]*Final Report and Testimony,* vol. 2, pp. 2019–2020.

agreements with the union, the former association member was now at the mercy of the union itself.[35]

On principle, all manufacturers who supported the protocol movement might have endorsed this direct and effective means of preventing unscrupulous competitors from undermining the labor standards of collective agreements. The strike provided the union with a potent weapon for preserving a floor under competition without involving the association members in activities that might create dissension within their own ranks. The success of this plan did not necessarily depend upon the cooperation of employer groups in "squealing" on their own members. Association officials who, in their own terms, "don't want to squeal," were not compelled to do so for, sooner or later, the workers would find occasion to report contract infractions to their union, even where the workers themselves were implicated in contract violations.[36]

Whatever may have been the original intention of the employer delegates at the Brandeis Conferences of 1910, more and more association members subsequently took the position that labor unions should not be conceded the power to strike on their own authority against noncomplying firms. Experiences under the protocols soon revealed that the organized workers, if left to their own devices, would not limit strike action to employers charged with obvious infractions of the collective agreement. Strikes invoked against *deliberate* and *unquestionable* violations could readily be extended into the realm of union control over *dubious* or *unintentional* violations. Such questionable strikes were actually encouraged by contract clauses exempting from misconduct those

---

[35]"For instance, [in] the ladies' waist and dress industry, the minimum scale was $6 a week. . . . Now, then, Mr. Stone showed that there were a great number, — I don't remember exactly the figures, but somewhere up in 30 or more percent — getting less than $6, less than $5 a week, contrary to that provision. I say that is a breach of the agreement on the part of the employers. There can be no dispute that $6 is the minimum wage and that if he pays less than $6 he reads himself out of that agreement. That is the way I feel about it." Jacob Panken [Pankin], *ibid.,* p. 2020.

[36]See statement of S. Polakoff, union representative, in *Minutes,* Joint Meeting of the Grievance Board and the Wage Scale Board of the Dress and Waist Industry (August 26, 1913), p. 39.

workers who refused to obey employer orders *made in violation of the collective agreement.* For the associations that represented the "bosses" and the unions that represented the "people" seldom saw eye to eye on whether an employer order did, in fact, violate the terms of the labor agreement.[37]

From the use of strikes to suppress questionable infractions, direct action might then become a tool through which union officials imposed new rules of their own making upon the organized employers bound by collective agreements. Roving bands of union business agents, travelling from shop to shop, could always back up their own self-imposed regulations with threats of immediate strike action. Such a procedure appeared all the more likely where similar rules had already been imposed by union decree upon independent employers. Union agents might logically assume that the extension of these rules to association members would be consistent with the principle of uniformity throughout an industry. That, at least, was the premise on which unions had always operated.

For yet another reason, the organized employers would deny labor unions the privilege of striking on their own authority to enforce minimum labor standards of collective agreements. Soon after 1910, the leadership of employers' associations realized that the ideals of the protocol movement as originally conceived could not be immediately applied in the face of rank-and-file opposition from within the organized forces of industry. Still less likely were the prospects of extending protocol standards to the unorganized segments of each trade. Lacking assurances that collective agreements would be universally applied, the most faithful supporters of the protocol movement had to keep open a door of escape from too rigid an enforcement of their contracts. Since the original protocol was a permanent document with no termination date and no designated means of revision, the organized manufacturers dared not entrust the union with an enforcement weapon capable of driving employers into bankruptcy.

---

[37]A typical exemption from a misconduct clause can be found in the 1911 collective agreement of the Merchants' Society of Ladies' Tailors and Dressmakers with the Ladies' Tailors and Dressmakers' Union, Local 38, ILGWU. See the text of this agreement in the *Ladies' Garment Worker,* October 1911, vol. 2, pp. 2–4.

The Impartial Machinery as an Enforcing Agency

In so far as the business of detecting and punishing contract chiselers could not successfully be left solely to labor unions or to employers' associations acting in their own names, these functions had to be assumed by the impartial machinery of each trade. For that reason clerks and deputy clerks, representatives and special agents, committees on immediate action, and boards of grievances representing both parties came to play a more and more prominent role in maintaining a floor under competition. Working below the level of the highest arbitrating authority but within the orbits of the impartial machinery, these joint agencies took over more and more responsibility for policing the contract. Having the welfare of the industry at heart, they could operate successfully where the angels of partisanship feared to tread.

Over the years, the task of ferreting out contract chiselers and bringing them to justice grew in complexity, for an ever increasing number of association members — and union members as well — became masters at devising clever schemes for undermining the labor standards of their collective agreements. Kickbacks and false bookkeeping covered up evasion of wage scales. Rush orders and lack of time were offered as excuses for failing to adjust piece rates. Doors were locked and entrances barred to avoid detection of work after hours. Secret hideouts were provided for nonunion workers during attempts to check union membership cards.

The number and variety of these devices to evade contract standards multiplied during the Great Depression of the thirties. "The record shows," noted Sol A. Rosenblatt, impartial chairman for the women's coat and suit industry, April 13, 1936, "that particularly since examination made on or about October 3, 1933 and thereafter, every device of concealment and subterfuge was employed by the firm. Not only is the record replete with instances of use of different names, different bank accounts, different books and different records for purposes of concealment, but testimony was adduced by the firm on each occasion which thereafter was proved inaccurate and untrue. . . . It was necessary to use a magnifying lens in order to decipher the original entries which had either been crossed out or erased, and in any event all of the pertinent books and records were not forthcoming."[38]

---

[38] S. A. Rosenblatt, impartial chairman, women's coat and suit trade, *Decisions,* Case no. 1306 (April 13, 1936).

Shenanigans that were the product of collusion between the "bosses" and the "people" were always the most troublesome to detect. By consent of the workers, chiseling employers were permitted to disregard overtime regulations and forego payments for holidays or vacations. To facilitate evasion of wage scales, shop owners were allowed to shift from week work to piecework, or vice versa; and to downgrade their employees into classifications drawing less pay. At times, the workers in certain shops voluntarily requested reductions in pay to increase their opportunities for more employment. "In almost every case of the 42 shops so far handled by the Union," reported the *Furriers' Bulletin* for December 1922, "employers laid the blame [for overtime violations] on the workers whom they charged as pleading for overtime at any price." Some employers with the consent of their workers even escaped payment of awards for wage deficits levied against them by the impartial machinery.[39]

Shop loyalties intensified the pressure for collusive deals. "One of the things that we all will have to recognize sooner or later," observed J. H. Cohen, counsel for the cloak manufacturers, addressing the board of arbitration for his industry, August 4, 1913, "is this peculiar shop esprit de corps which is characteristic of the Jewish shop in New York City, the hanging together of the people, of their loyalty to each other, and their loyalty to the boss." Cohen then went on to explain how the aspiring immigrant rose from presser to head presser to contractor and to manufacturer. "And

---

[39]When work is scarce, as it usually is except for a few weeks in each season, the workers are told that in order to meet the exigencies of price competition and bring some work into the shop, they must enter into secret arrangements contrary to the minimum labor standards which have been agreed upon, and which are pretty successfully enforced in the larger shops of the inside manufacturers.

These concessions by the workers take various forms. They chiefly involve wages, hours, rates of pay for overtime, work on holidays, and the substitution of piece work for pay by the hour. All this is done without the knowledge of the Union officials and is frequently concealed in the books of the firm. Incidentally, it subjects the inside manufacturers to such unfair competition as tends to drive out of legitimate manufacturing into jobbing all except those producing garments of the most exclusive and expensive styles.

—Governor[Alfred E. Smith]'s Advisory Commission for the [women's] Cloak, Suit and Skirt Industry, *Final Recommendations* (May 20, 1926), p. 5.

as soon as he becomes a manufacturer," Cohen continued, "he gathers together the people who are persona grata to him, and when he gets that shop, we can fulminate about the Protocol, we can fix standards of wages, but he will always have a private agreement." These shop allegiances were often stronger than the ties that bound the parties to their collective agreements. "The tendency to regard the contract with the Union as being of no value at all," concluded Cohen, "is so great in this industry that, throughout the entire industry, you have to search with a searchlight to find out the rate of wages that are really paid."[40]

At times, these problems of detection were further complicated by the connivance of union officials in schemes to undermine the fixed terms of employment. For a sufficient price, too many employers could buy exemptions from the enforcement of their collective agreements. Too many union officials could be induced to accept bribes for winking at employer violations of labor standards. Perhaps these concessions were sometimes justified to tide handicapped workers or marginal firms over temporary emergencies, but once this spillway to special privilege was opened, a flood of unwarranted concessions was sure to pour through.

Visitation and Inspection

The impartial machinery had to be expanded to meet the burden of an ever increasing work load. Clerks and deputy clerks in sufficient numbers had to be constantly available for investigating alleged violations of contract clauses or for acting on their own initiative to disclose evidences of collusion that undermined con-

---

[40]*Minutes,* Board of Arbitrators...[women's coat and suit trade] (August 4, 1913), pp. 405–406.

What's a union regulation between friends? — and between contractor and his few employees a condition of friendship can spring up. The contractor is a neighbor to some of his workers; he belongs to the same lodge; a few of them are his relatives; with one or two he spent his boyhood in the old country; he made the acquaintance of another in the steerage coming over; none of his 30 or 40 employees are strangers to him. Under these conditions you can always "pull off" a confidential arrangement. You can always get a few key men in the shop to accept a little bonus on the side for speeding up. That is all you need, for the key operators determine the production of the others.
    —Frank Chodorov in *Daily News Record,* May 31, 1922.

tract standards. Committees on immediate action had to be capable of meeting a growing demand for the preservation of employment standards from disintegration at the shop level. To meet particularly difficult enforcement problems, more and more special agencies had to be created from time to time — joint committees on nonunion production, joint violation prevention bureaus on the underpayment of wages, joint boards of sanitary control to enforce standards of health and safety, and numerous subcommittees of the boards of grievances. Last but not least, the impartial chairman, or highest arbitrating authority under each agreement, was empowered to name his own staff of accountants, investigators, auditors, and price experts to uncover substandard practices.

All of these agencies required access to the workshops in order to conduct investigations on the spot. So essential was the power to investigate at the most opportune time and place that some collective agreements directed manufacturers to keep their doors unlocked so that agents of the impartial machinery might at any time enter the premises undetected and undisturbed. The officials of one union insisted that the manufacturers had agreed to declare employers working behind locked doors guilty of violating the collective agreement and subject to penalties.[41]

From the early days of the protocol movement, the right of visitation and inspection, so vehemently denied to the union's walking delegate, was expressly granted to agents of the impartial machinery. "Upon the written request of any member of the Board of Grievances," stated the "Rules and Plan of Procedure" as finally adopted in the spring of 1911 to govern the conduct of the board of grievances under the original Protocol of Peace, "a committee of two, consisting of members of the board or of clerks or of deputy clerks, one representing each side, shall visit any shop for the purpose of ascertaining whether the provisions of the Protocol are being observed, and report on the conditions of such shop to the board."[42]

---

[41]Board of Arbitration, Cloak, Suit and Skirt Industry, *Intensive Study of the Records of the Board of Grievances, April 15, 1911 — October 31, 1913,* pp. 15, 22; *Women's Wear Daily,* Jan. 2, 1939.

[42]C. H. Winslow, *Conciliation, Arbitration, and Sanitation in the Cloak, Suit, and Skirt Industry in New York City,* U.S. Department of Commerce and Labor, Bureau of Labor, Bulletin no. 98 (January 1912), p. 220. The purpose of this particular rule was explained in a decision of the board of arbitration

The right to inspect company pay records and accounts came more slowly. Authority to look at the books was at first granted only on complaint supported by tangible evidence of contract infractions. But agitation for granting the impartial machinery broader powers of inspection continued with increasing success into the twenties. In 1926, Governor Smith's Advisory Commission for the women's coat and suit trade recommended that all books and records of employers be subject at all times to inspection by a permanent committee representing both sides and under the supervision of the impartial chairman for the industry. Not until the thirties, however, did clauses in collective agreements granting the impartial machinery such extensive controls become common. At that time, the power to examine was accompanied by the power to prescribe books and records.[43]

"A uniform set of books and records relating to pay rolls, labor cost, and outside production shall be adopted by all members of the Council and by the entire industry," runs the pertinent clause in the 1933–35 collective agreement between the Industrial Coun-

---

for the women's coat and suit trade, March 14, 1911. This decision and the "Rules and Plan of Procedure" for the board of grievances were printed in a pamphlet issued by the Cloak, Suit and Skirt Manufacturers' Protective Association. A copy is filed in the Abelson papers.

In a letter, dated March 8, 1917, to J. L. Magnes, head of Kehillah, an organization of the Jewish community, A. W. Miller, president of the International Fur Workers' Union, consented to the rule of joint visitation that would protect manufacturers against dictatorial union agents accustomed to giving orders during their visits to nonassociation shops. "Confirming our understanding," Miller wrote, "I wish to state in writing that we regard it as an essential principle of this collective agreement that no representatives of our organization shall at any time enter the premises of the manufacturers for any purpose whatever, unless accompanied by the Manager or Assistant Manager of the Association." Letter filed in the Abelson papers.

[43]See *Minutes*, Special Meeting of the Conference Committee of the Fur Manufacturing Industry, Nov. 24, 1914. See also Louis Lorwin [Louis Levine] *The Women's Garment Workers* (1924) at p. 305 for a summary of the broad powers given the short-lived board of protocol standards created under the revised dress and waist protocol of 1916. See further, *Final Recommendations* of Governor Smith's Advisory Commission, copy filed in the Abelson papers. "The Council on its own motion will investigate any or all of the books and records of its members to ascertain whether they are giving work to or dealing with non-union shops." From the 1926 collective agreement between the Industrial Council of Cloak, Suit and Skirt Manufacturers and the ILGWU.

cil of Cloak, Suit and Skirt Manufacturers and the Cloakmakers' Joint Board, ILGWU. "The form of such records and books shall be prescribed by the Impartial Chairman. Such records and books shall be open to the examination of the Impartial Chairman or his accountants at all reasonable times." By acquiring permission to install a uniform set of books for all firms and by obtaining the right to visit and inspect on its own authority, the impartial machinery took a long step beyond the more limited power to investigate upon complaint of an interested party.[44]

Under association-wide agreements, the impartial machinery adopted many techniques of contract enforcement developed by unions having separate contracts with individual firms. Just as union business agents or special union patrol squads visited the shops of independent employers to check overtime work, so representatives of the association and the union, acting in the name of the impartial machinery, jointly covered association shops to enforce restrictions on overtime. Just as unions issued their own "certificates of union conditions" to independent employers found to be observing their contracts, so joint conference committees or boards of grievances issued "certificates of protocol compliance" to the owners of association shops that successfully passed inspection. And, in the same manner that unions required independent employers to register their contractors, so the parties to multi-employer agreements required association members to register their contractors as a prerequisite for enforcing clauses regulating outside production.

Punitive Measures against Chiselers

Agencies of the impartial machinery with power to inspect the premises and examine the books also had authority to take action against those found to be violating the collective agreement. Under the protocol system for contract administration, the power to

---

[44]Typical of the NRA codes of fair competition for industries of the needle trades in the 1930's was the clause giving the code authority of the men's clothing industry "authority and power to examine all books of accounts and records of employers in the Clothing Industry so far as practicable for the purpose of ascertaining their respective observance or nonobservance of the provisions of this Code and the standards of operation set forth therein." From the text of the men's clothing code, approved August 26, 1933.

detect contract violations was sooner or later accompanied by the power to apprehend the culprits and bring them to justice. Clerks and deputy clerks, committees on immediate action and boards of grievance, as well as permanent arbitrators, followed up their investigative powers with the judicial functions of determining guilt and imposing punishment.

As a rule, the power to take corrective action by apprehending the offenders and bringing them to justice evolved through a succession of stages. In the early years of the protocol movement, agencies of the impartial machinery merely established the existence of contract infractions and then relied upon the contracting parties for appropriate action. At most, these impartial agencies compiled the evidence, named the transgressors and directed them to cease their lawless conduct, leaving the enforcement of these orders and the imposition of penalties to the culprits' own organizations. It was presumed sufficient to declare that decisions of the impartial chairman or the board of arbitration "shall be final and binding on the parties."

Under such procedures, labor unions and employers' associations, now acting in the name of the impartial machinery, assumed the dual obligation of seeing that their rebellious members corrected their ways and of taking whatever punitive action was appropriate for the particular type of misconduct. Both organizations were required to report to the board of grievances whatever measures they had taken against their respective members. Failure of the association or the union to discipline a member for violating the agreement or for refusing to abide by a decision of the impartial machinery created a new complaint that could be submitted to the highest arbitrating authority for the industry.

Exemplifying this procedure were the provisions of the first collective agreement between the United Shirt Manufacturers' Association and the Amalgamated Clothing Workers in the mid-twenties. Under Paragraph 18 of this contract, the association and the union "agree to assume responsibility for the carrying out of these provisions for the individual members of the respective bodies in the following manner, to wit:

In each instance where individual members do not comply with the decisions under this agreement, both bodies agree, where demanded upon conviction, to properly penalize such members and to fine and expel them from the respective bodies. The Manufacturers' Association shall determine the amount of the penalty of its members, and the Union shall determine the amount of the penalty of its members. Both bodies agree to enforce to the fullest extent this entire paragraph.[45]

Such a procedure for disposing of contract infractions had much to commend it. Neither employers nor workers wished to be condemned and punished by their respective organizations. The prospects of public censure by fellow members in the "lodge" operated as a strong deterrent against wrongdoing. At the same time, neither employers' associations nor labor unions could any longer be branded as traitors for penalizing their respective members, since each organization was now acting as an agent of the impartial machinery. In some cases, the employer representatives on the board of grievances appeared before the employers' association to prefer charges against wayward employers, while union representatives on the board of grievances appeared before the union to prefer charges against rebellious workers.[46]

Moreover, this procedure of calling upon each organization to discipline its own members stimulated a sense of collective responsibility toward observance of the labor agreement. Through his own separate organization, each employer and each worker became a part of the machinery to see that the contract was obeyed. Furthermore, those who knew the culprits best were in a favored position to see that the punishment fit the crime. Finally, the requirement that periodic reports be made to the impartial machinery on the disposition of all cases forestalled attempts to evade responsibility while operating behind closed doors.[47]

---

[45]"Each of the parties...undertakes to provide and enforce suitable and reasonable penalties as the Association and the Union may lawfully make and enforce." From the enforcement clause of the 1934 collective agreement between the Men's Neckwear Manufacturers' Association and the United Neckwear Workers' Union, ACWA.

[46]"Resolved, that it is the sense of the Grievance Board that without giving Mr. Marguiles any further time, he be brought up for trial before the Executive Committee of the Association, and that the members of the Grievance Board representing the Manufacturers' Association prefer charges against him for disobeying a decision of the Board." *Minutes,* Meeting of the Board of Grievances...[Dress and Waist Industry] (Feb. 13, 1913), p. 1.

[47]The thirty-five-hour, five-day week clause of the 1935 collective agreement between the American Cloak and Suit Manufacturers' Association (contractors) and the Cloakmakers' Joint Board, ILGWU, stated: "Should a

Minutes of the boards of grievance established under the original protocols bear evidence that this system of contract administration was for a while operating with some measure of success. Reports by employers' associations and labor unions on the disposition of contract infraction cases brought to their attention were regular items of business on the agenda of board meetings. The records show that employers' associations repeatedly imposed disciplinary measures upon their members who had been adjudged by the impartial machinery to be guilty of giving out home work, maintaining black lists, violating price scales, falsifying records, bribing union officials, and the like.

Testifying before the U. S. Commission on Industrial Relations, January 16, 1914, Morris Silberman, cloak manufacturer, had occasion to review his association's policy on discipline. "From the manufacturer's side," he explained, "we have certainly been very severe. Where a complaint has been filed and the board of grievances found that the manufacturer was guilty of violating any part of that protocol, our system has been that if it was a mild violation, a reprimand should be given; if it was a little more violent in its violation, a fine was imposed, and we have fined our members in numerous cases as high as $500 for a breach of the protocol; and our records are open to this commission, where we have an accurate record of those cases, and we have always meted out the various punishments to every offending member."[48]

Labor unions had a less impressive record of action taken against their members adjudged guilty of undermining contract standards. Some evidence exists of punishments imposed upon organized workers for offenses against the collective agreement, particularly for collusion with employers to disregard minimum wage-and-hour standards. Like employers' associations, unions maintained their own grievance boards for handling these cases. "More than 500 workers were fined by the [union] Grievance Board," reported Ben Gold, manager of the Furriers' Joint Board, in the *Furriers' Bulletin* for November 1925. "These were fined for various offenses:

---

member of the Association violate the provision of this clause, the Association will proceed to impose a fine for the first offense, under the authority contained in its by-laws and its agreement with its members....A repeated offense shall subject the member to suspension or expulsion."

[48]*Final Report and Testimony,* vol. 2, p. 1090.

working overtime, working on someone else's book, etc. The fines amount to $4000. We want to assure the reader that we derive no pleasure whatever from fining workers. . . . But let those who need it be warned that we intend to use all organization methods to retain the discipline and our union standards."[49]

Despite such examples of union responsibility for disciplining workers who violated their contracts, the rising complaint of the organized employers was that unions seldom, if ever, lived up to their obligations as agents of the impartial machinery. From the earliest days of the protocol movement, employers insisted that union reports to the board of grievances of the women's coat and suit industry on action taken in disciplinary cases were generally unsatisfactory. Ninety-nine times out of one hundred, stated Morris Silberman, in his testimony before the U. S. Commission on Industrial Relations, January 16, 1914, the records show that union officials "can not find the man, or they can't find the place, or he has been punished enough because he lost his job."[50]

Unions were most often charged with failure to punish their members for participating in unauthorized strikes. Frequently, workers who were the victims of employer misconduct would not await the orderly processes of the impartial machinery to enforce the provisions of their collective agreements. They chose, instead, to defend their contractual rights by direct action. In all such cases, the impartial machinery would first officially condemn the strike, then it would direct the union to return the striking workers to their jobs and to impose suitable penalties upon them for their lawless conduct. Employers were most vehement in denouncing unions for failure to carry out these mandates.[51]

---

[49]The Cutters' local, ILGWU, was a leader in punishing its members for violating the terms of the collective labor agreement. Within a little more than a week early in September 1924, this local collected fines of over $2000 for such violations. ILGWU's *Justice,* Sept. 12, 1924. Other examples are cited in Pierson, *Collective Bargaining Systems,* pp. 147–148, 161.

[50]*Final Report and Testimony,* vol. 2, p. 1090.

[51]Members of our Association have been severely disciplined by expulsion and by fine for failure to observe protocol conditions. We have, however, failed to receive on your part any information concerning the expulsion or fining of any of your members who have violated the protocol by inciting and encouraging stoppages of work, and actually themselves stopping work. Moreover, these stoppages are increasing in-

Records of employers' associations as disciplinary agencies did not remain unchallenged either. A year before Morris Silberman had defended the manufacturers, Abe Bisno, a former general manager of the Cloakmakers' Joint Board, was insisting that the power to punish offenders be transferred to the board of grievances, precisely because the cloak manufacturers' association could not be trusted to impose adequate penalties. Not only had the association failed to take any action whatever in many cases, but it had also repeatedly failed to inflict punishment commensurate with the offense. Reprimands were issued where stronger action was demanded as an effective deterrent against future offenses.[52]

Not even in the thirties, when the regulation of competition in trade practices as well as in labor costs was considered a prerequisite for meeting the depression, did the organized manufacturers always pull their part of the load. Soon after the millinery manufacturers organized a new association — the Women's Headwear Group — in 1932 and signed an agreement with the millinery workers' union to effect a "general stabilization of the industry," the union was forced to complain that the employers had fallen short of their obligations. "The millinery manufacturers are carrying on a more wild cut-throat competition than ever before," stated a letter from the union to the association. "The whole burden of this unscrupulous competition is being placed on the shoulders of the millinery workers."[53]

Impartial Agencies Recommend Punishment

These criticisms led to further developments of the power to punish. Agencies of the impartial machinery gradually acquired

---

stead of diminishing. During August there were eighteen stoppages of work, taking up the time of our officers, and entailing a serious loss to the employer in each instance, without redress to him.
   —Cloak, Suit and Skirt Manufacturers' Protective Association to A. Bisno, general manager, Cloak and Skirtmakers' Union. Letter, dated Oct. 4, 1912, filed in the Abelson papers.

[52]Lorwin, *The Women's Garment Workers,* p. 248.

[53]Letter, dated Dec. 22, 1932, to J. Helfer, executive secretary, Women's Headwear Group. The letter and a copy of the first agreement, effective March 1, 1932, between the association and the union are filed in the Abelson papers. Text of this agreement also appears in *Women's Wear Daily,* March 4, 1932.

or assumed the authority to *recommend* punishment. No longer were employers' associations or labor unions free to use their own discretion. Whether these recommendations defined the nature of the penalty to be inflicted, or prescribed the extent of the punishment, or merely directed a penalty "commensurate with the degree of the offense," they carried the weight of the impartial machinery behind them and increased the pressure upon the contracting parties for positive action. "The Conference Committee," stated the 1915 collective agreement between the National Association of Men's Neckwear Manufacturers and the United Neckwear Cutters' Union, Local 6939, AFL, "shall have power to recommend the disciplining of any Union Employer or of any member of the Union for a violation of the terms of this agreement after due trial, and both parties agree to enforce any recommendations made by the Conference Committee."[54]

Operating under similar clauses, the Associated Fur Manufacturers and the International Fur Workers' Union during the twenties identified the consequences that might follow a refusal of either party to carry out the recommendations of the impartial machinery. After giving their joint conference committee the usual power "to recommend the disciplining of any member of the Union or a member of the Association for violations of the terms of this agreement after due trial," the contracting parties in their 1924 collective agreement stated that "failure by either party to the agreement to enforce a decision of the Conference Committee upon notification in writing by the Chairman of the Conference

---

[54]In the event the Clerks or their Deputies agree upon a finding that either an employer or a worker has been guilty of an evasion or violation of a provision of this agreement, and it is certified by either of the Clerks of the respective parties hereto or their Deputies, that in his judgment a penalty should be imposed upon the offending party, or in the event such finding is made by the Grievance Board, or such finding and certificate are made by the Impartial Chairman, as hereinafter provided, said finding shall be considered by the Grievance Board, and the Grievance Board shall have the power to recommend to the respective organization of which such offending party is a member, the fine or penalty to be imposed upon such offending party, and such fine or penalty may include expulsion from membership.

—From the collective agreement, effective April 7, 1919, of the Dress and Waist Manufacturers' Association with the ILGWU and Its Locals 10, 25, and 58; text in *Women's Wear*, April 9, 1919.

Committee, may in the discretion of the Chairman be declared as equivalent to a repudiation of the agreement."[55]

Earlier in the twenties, the joint conference committee of the fur manufacturing industry had adopted a standard procedure for disposing of cases involving association firms that were found guilty of such offenses as working excessive overtime, keeping false books, destroying records, or giving false testimony. In a number of such cases, the conference committee unanimously

RESOLVED, that the Conference Committee goes on record that it regards the conduct of the firm...as shown by established charges, as reprehensible in the extreme, and as deserving the severest condemnation and discipline.

RESOLVED, that a copy of the record of the case be forwarded to the Association with this resolution for disciplinary action, and that a report of the Association's action be submitted to the Conference Committee.

Similarly, whenever union members were implicated in collusive deals to undermine work standards, the conference committee voted "that the union discipline the workers affected for being parties to a violation of the agreement."[56]

---

[55]When Henry Moskowitz, impartial chairman for the fancy leather goods industry, found certain union members guilty of collusion with an employer to work for less than the established wage scales, he not only directed the company to make up the wage deficit but ordered the union to punish its members for their misconduct. Henry Moskowitz, *Decisions*, Case no. 34a (May 23, 1932).

[56]See *Minutes* of the Conference Committee of the fur manufacturing industry for Dec. 7 and 9, 1922, March 26, 1923, and Dec. 9, 1924, under the collective agreements between the Associated Fur Manufacturers and the International Fur Workers' Union. Copy filed in the Abelson papers.

In the event that an employer or worker fail to carry out the agreement of the clerks or the decision of the Committee on Adjustment, the Committee on Adjustment can take any action it sees fit and recommend to the side concerned appropriate discipline, and the Union and the Association pledge themselves to carry out such recommendations and to report in writing to the Board of Adjustment the action taken, pursuant to the recommendation of the Board of Adjustment.

—From the 1921 collective agreement between the Ladies' Hat Manufacturers' Protective Association and the United Cloth Hat and Cap Makers of North America, and the Joint Board of Millinery and Ladies' Straw Hat Workers' Union, comprising Locals 24, 42, and 43, and Millinery Branch Local 2.

The Impartial Machinery Imposes Punishment

From the power of recommending punishment to the contracting parties, the impartial machinery next acquired or assumed the authority to impose its own penalties directly upon the offenders. Parties to collective agreements no longer exercised an official role in determining guilt or in assessing penalties. Instead, the impartial machinery not only issued corrective orders to those it adjudged guilty of contract infractions — orders to forfeit kickbacks, make up wage deficits, cease overtime violations, discharge nonunion men, abandon outside shops, terminate collusive deals, or end wild-cat strikes — but it also accompanied those orders with the imposition of definite fines and penalties designed to offset the advantages gained from a contract infraction and to act as an effective deterrent against future transgressions.[57]

This power of the impartial machinery to impose penalties was not always assumed without a challenge. In 1918, for example, the executive board of the Associated Fur Manufacturers, party to a collective agreement with the fur workers' union, resolved "that this Board go on record that the Conference Committee has no right to levy a fine upon any member of the Association, that being solely within the jurisdiction of the Association itself." And, in

---

[57]In the event the Board of Adjustment shall adjudge any member of the Association guilty of any violations of any of the terms, conditions and provisions of this agreement, it may, in addition to any further directions or orders which it may make in the premises, impose a fine in money which shall be paid by such member of the Association within three days after the imposition of such fine. The amount of such fine shall be discretionary with the Board of Adjustment and shall be determined with reference to the nature and extent of the violation; it shall be sufficiently adequate to offset any advantage gained by the employer by reason of such violation and in addition thereto to appropriately and fairly penalize him therefor.

—From the 1936 collective agreement of the Eastern Women's Headwear Association with the Cap and Millinery Department, United Hatters, Cap and Millinery Workers' International Union and the Joint Board of Millinery Workers.

One of the earliest examples of such powers was found in the 1920 collective agreement between the Clothiers' Exchange of Rochester and the ACWA, wherein a bipartisan board of adjustment was empowered to "define, describe and limit the penalties to be imposed for the violation of any of the provisions of this agreement."

1925, the president of this association again contended that "the form of punishment of members violating the collective agreement can only be determined by the [association's] Board of Directors and it is not within the power of the Conference Committee to fix the punishment or penalty."[58]

In most industries, disputes over who should punish offenders were sooner or later resolved by expressly authorizing the impartial machinery to follow up its assessment of guilt with such penalties as it chose to inflict. Even the clerks and intermediate committees of the impartial machinery were authorized to impose penalties, always with the possibility of appealing disagreements over the nature and extent of the punishment to the impartial chairman of the trade. Other agreements authorized the creation of a comprehensive code of penalties for different types of offenses. In some industries, the power of punishment was assigned exclusively to the highest arbitrating authority. "In the event of the violation of any of the terms of this agreement," runs the 1926 collective agreement between the New York Clothing Manufacturers' Exchange and the Amalgamated Clothing Workers' Union, "the parties to it shall be subject to penalty to be determined by the impartial chairman."[59]

The final stage in the development of the power to punish came with the adoption of contract provisions that, in effect, circum-

---

[58]The association's resolution of Jan. 3, 1918, and the letter, dated August 5, 1925, from S. N. Samuels, president of the association, to Paul Abelson, acting chairman of the conference committee, are filed in the Abelson papers.

[59]"The Conference Committee shall formulate a system of uniform and adequate penalties for violations of all provisions of the agreement." From the 1934 collective agreement between the United Fur Manufacturers and the Greek Fur Workers.

> In the event of a violation of the provisions of this agreement by a member of the Association, the managers of the Association and the Union, by a joint decision, are hereby given the power to decide the amount of damages to be paid by the employer for such violations....
> Should the managers disagree upon the amount of damages, the matter shall be submitted to the Impartial Chairman, who is likewise vested with the power to make such decisions, and his decision shall be final and binding upon all the parties and their respective members.
> —From the 1938 collective agreement between the Children's Dress, Cotton Dress and Sportswear Contractors' Association and Local 91, ILGWU.

scribed the freedom of administrative agencies to impose penalties of their own choosing. Some of these restrictions set minimum penalties for all offenses against the contract. Thus, the amount of damages assessed against an offending member of the Industrial Association of Juvenile Apparel Manufacturers under the 1938 collective agreement with Locals 91 and 10, ILGWU, had to be "sufficient to offset any advantages intended to be accrued to the employer by such violation and to discourage him from similar further violations."[60]

Other collective agreements defined the type and extent of punishment that could be imposed for violation of particular clauses. The leading 1929 fur manufacturing agreement fixed the penalty for violation of overtime regulations at a sum equal to the wages due the workers; for the second offense, the penalty was doubled. The same standards were applied to violations of minimum wage clauses. In later agreements, these fines were fixed at $75 for the first offense, $150 for the second offense, with suspension from the association for the third offense. The more serious offenses of kickbacks and falsifying books drew down the penalty of a three-month suspension from the association for the first infraction and a year's suspension for the second infraction. The impartial chairman for the industry retained discretionary power to fix the penalty for offenses not separately listed.[61]

Not all stages in the evolution of the power to punish can be

---

[60]After authorizing the association of inside manufacturers for the women's coat and suit trade to impose fines for contract violations upon its members under the association's bylaws, the 1935 collective agreement for the inside manufacturers of the trade stated that "the amount of the fine shall be determined with reference to the nature of the violation and shall be sufficiently high to offset the advantages gained by the members from such violation together with an appropriate penalty." From the 1935 collective agreement of the Industrial Council of Cloak, Suit and Skirt Manufacturers with the ILGWU, text in *Women's Wear Daily,* July 11, 1935.

[61]See the collective agreements of the Associated Fur Coat and Trimming Manufacturers with the Furriers' Joint Council and the International Fur Workers' Union during the thirties, copies filed in the Abelson papers. The 1937 collective agreement between the Allied Hat Manufacturers and the United Hatters, Cap and Millinery Workers' International Union directed the joint board of trade to prescribe damages for kickbacks and underpayment of wages at "no less than double the amount of such violation of the agreement."

traced through every industry of the needle trades, nor did these stages always follow a fixed order of sequence. In some industries, a change of policy toward methods of imposing punishment reflected by successive agreements was more closely associated with the maturity of collective bargaining than with any chronological period of time. Certain industries never got beyond the original practice of leaving penalties entirely up to the contracting parties. Others began collective bargaining with an advanced concept of permitting the impartial machinery to fix the punishment as well as determine the guilt. On the whole, the terms of collective agreements were more likely to reflect practices already initiated by administrative agencies than to introduce new processes or initiate new techniques. Influential members of the impartial machinery, particularly the impartial chairmen, were a creative force in gaining compliance with agreements as well as in the negotiation of those agreements.

Watchdogs and Executioners

Permitting the impartial machinery to determine the punishment against offenders whom it had convicted did not relieve employers' associations and labor unions of all further responsibilities. Having officially lost or transferred to the impartial machinery the successive tasks of detecting contract chiselers, determining their guilt, and defining their punishment, the contracting parties still retained the important roles of watchdogs and executioners. The impartial machinery had no funds of its own to support its operations, no sheriffs to carry out its orders, no jails in which to confine those guilty of noncompliance with its decisions.

If the system of law and order was to prevail, both employers' associations and labor unions still had to assume responsibility for (1) naming suitable representatives — clerks, committeemen, or arbitrators — to the impartial machinery and seeing that they performed their duties; (2) requiring both workers and employers to follow administrative procedures for resolving disputes in preference to forms of direct action; and (3) compelling both workers and employers to accept the penalties and carry out the orders imposed upon them by their permanent administrators.

Supplying the impartial machinery with suitable personnel in adequate numbers, although indispensable to the work of contract

administration, occasioned the least disturbance in the development of collective bargaining. Both employers' associations and
labor unions had an interest in naming their own appointees to
permanent agencies at each level of the administrative structure.
As a rule, the more members each party contributed, the more
likely it was to be satisfied with the results. While those selected
for a niche in the structure of contract administration presumably
cast off their cloaks of partisanship, each party found consolation
in contributing personnel of its own choosing to the permanent
institutions established for the government of the industry.

Yet neither the selection process nor the conduct of the personnel assigned to the impartial machinery was without its shortcomings. Officials of employers' associations repeatedly complained
that union-chosen agents of their joint institutions never grew in
statesmanship to match their new roles in industry. The leopards
of partisanship changed their titles but never changed their spots.
"The Union," so stated the official charges of the Dress and Waist
Manufacturers' Association in 1913, "has failed to require that
those deputy clerks of the Board of Grievances who are appointed
by the Union should work with the Association deputy clerks to
the end that substantial justice should be done; and the Union
deputy clerks have shown generally a disposition to be arbitrary
and unfair and an unwillingness to consider complaints upon their
merits. The general attitude of the Union deputy clerks indicated
that they desire to win for their side, rather than to promote substantial justice, and that they proceed upon the assumption that
the interests of the workers are essentially opposed to the interests
of the employer."[62]

Walter Bartholomew, chief clerk for the Dress and Waist Manufacturers' Association, specifically charged the union-appointed
clerks with insulting the manufacturers and impugning their
motives in the presence of workers in the shops. Moreover, he
could find only one case on the records of the board of grievances

---

[62]*Minutes,* Arbitration Proceedings between the Dress and Waist Manufacturers' Association and the ILGWU (Nov. 8, 1913), pp. 69–70. The association's charges were also separately printed under date of Oct. 15, 1913. The
debates on the charges, together with the answers set out by the union, are
recorded in the *Minutes* for Nov. 8, 1913, and they are summarized in C. H.
Winslow, *Conciliation, Arbitration, and Sanitation in the Dress and Waist
Industry of New York City,* pp. 62–63.

in which union-appointed representatives on the board had cast the deciding votes favoring the association in a dispute over contract infractions; whereas the association-named representatives on the board had voted with the union on numerous occasions. By supporting the position of the union, willy-nilly, the union-selected clerks and representatives often deadlocked proceedings and prevented affirmative action.[63]

In denying these charges, the Dressmakers' Joint Board insisted that every deputy clerk of the union was instructed to use his own judgment in reaching a decision. So far from being partisan in their own outlook, the union clerks had been "continually complaining that they found the minds of the representatives of the Association closed to argument." Perhaps no member of the impartial machinery could ever forget the origin of his tenure or the source of his income. Those who acted too independently of their organizations always stood in danger of losing their jobs. But union-selected representatives on the impartial machinery were particularly bedeviled by the pressures of internal union politics. Union-appointed clerks, more so than clerks named by employer groups, suffered from exposure to overdoses of democracy within their own organizations.[64]

---

[63]*Minutes,* Arbitration Proceedings between the Dress and Waist Manufacturers' Association and the ILGWU (Nov. 8, 1913), pp. 30–32. "There is a constant tendency for Union members to wink at violations that are profitable to them," *ibid.,* p. 73.

After becoming a manufacturer, J. A. Dyche, for ten years general secretary-treasurer of the ILGWU, explained differences in approach between employer representatives and union representatives on various agencies of the impartial machinery in these terms:

> They [representatives of the employers' associations] sit in a judicial capacity. They show their liberality and independence by invariably giving the union representatives the benefit of the doubt. They are the first to make a motion in favor of the union, whenever in their judgment a representative of the union succeeds in establishing his case. And they do so unhesitatingly because of their independence....
>
> The officers of the union are paid officials. They cannot address their members in the same way. Neither are they free to act in a judicial capacity as the employers are. They cannot act judicially because they are paid by the plaintiff.
>
> —Dyche, *Bolshevism in American Labor Unions,* pp. 195, 196.

[64]*Minutes,* Arbitration Proceedings between the Dress and Waist Manufacturers' Association and the ILGWU (Nov. 8, 1913), p. 70.

Union complaints against associations for their attitudes toward the selection of personnel for the impartial machinery were most often directed to a lack of adequate help in carrying out the front-line work of contract enforcement. Union officials repeatedly attributed the rising backlog of cases requiring investigation to employer sabotage of the impartial machinery. By refusing to assign more than one representative to the work of the clerks or to the committees on immediate action, employers' associations could materially slow down the handling of grievances. "It is imperative," wrote the Joint Board of Millinery Workers to the Ladies' Hat Manufacturers' Association on January 11, 1917, "that some arrangement is made by which Mr. Seideman [association representative] get some assistance in the performance of his duties."[65]

Even where a sufficient number of clerks or committeemen was named, the organized employers were still charged with failure to see that these appointees fulfilled their obligations with diligence and dispatch. On more than one occasion, employer appointees insisted that they were too busy at other things to be bothered with the time-consuming task of visiting shops and processing grievances. Sometimes, employer groups deliberately restrained their appointees from participating in grievance procedures. The prevalence of such tactics led unions to insist that employers' associations be expressly obligated to furnish a sufficient number of clerks to handle the case load. Some collective agreements so provided and stated, in addition, that the failure of association representatives to accompany union representatives to the shops would, after a lapse of twenty-four hours, permit the union representatives to proceed alone.[66]

---

[65]Letter filed in the Abelson papers. "We had hoped that during the months of November and December these accumulated claims could be investigated and adjusted; unfortunately, however, the number of Association representatives has been reduced, and Mr. Greenberg remains the only one to devote his attention to the numerous complaints on hand." Letter, dated Nov. 22, 1926, from the joint board of the fur workers' union to the Associated Fur Manufacturers, filed in the Abelson papers.

[66]The Association will endeavor to provide sufficient representatives who shall accompany the Union representatives in the adjustment of all complaints or investigations to be made in the shops. Should the association fail to provide sufficient representatives, then the representatives of the Union shall have free access to the shop of the Employer during its

Measures to Insure Compliance with Awards

Problems of personnel were overshadowed by the all-important tasks of enforcing compliance with grievance procedures and with the binding decisions of the impartial machinery. Some workers and employers who violated their contracts willingly accepted the jurisdiction of the impartial machinery but failed to abide by the verdicts. Others, foreseeing the outcome, refused at the outset to subscribe to established procedures. In either case, the impartial machinery, lacking an adequate enforcing arm of its own, had to call upon the contracting parties to preserve the procedures and execute the judgments of their joint agencies for contract administration. Whatever else labor unions and employers' associations might have shifted to the shoulders of their permanent institutions, they could not escape the responsibility for keeping workers and employers upon the well-defined tracks of administrative procedures and for compelling all contract offenders to accept the decrees that awaited them at the end of the line.

Happily for the cause of industrial peace, the impartial machinery of each industry was capable of generating its own pressures for compliance with its orders and decisions. As previously shown, it could direct employers' associations and labor unions to discipline their respective members for noncompliance with awards. Such was the normal course of procedure following the refusal of a convicted offender to obey orders or accept the penalties imposed upon him. "The union and the association," stated the 1921 collective agreement between the Clothing Manufacturers' Association of New York and the Amalgamated Clothing Workers, "are each pledged to uphold the decisions of the Board of Arbitration, or of the deputies when they agree without the intervention of the Board of Arbitration, and each will use upon their respective members every disciplinary power by it possessed in order to enforce the said decisions."[67]

---

operation for the purpose of investigating whether all the terms and conditions of this agreement are lived up to by the Employer in good faith.

—From the 1938 collective agreement of the United Knitwear Manufacturers' League with the Knitgoods Workers' Union, Local 155, ILGWU.

[67]*Daily News Record,* June 3, 1921.

Moreover, from the very first year of the protocol movement, failure to obey an award constituted a new offense for which a separate action could be brought. "Noncompliance with awards" became an established category for classifying grievances. At times, this classification contained the most important group of cases coming before the impartial machinery. Workers and employers alike were haled before the appropriate agency and asked to defend themselves against charges of refusing to obey orders. Those found guilty of failing to carry out decisions were subject to additional penalties for noncompliance. Only the most hardened offenders could withstand the increasing pressures of public opinion generated by these procedures.

Still there were some offenders who cast aside the verdicts of noncompliance with the same disdain shown for original decisions. Nor would they submit to the disciplinary action imposed by their own organizations. These chiselers had to be restrained by more drastic action, lest their examples destroy all respect for collective agreements. "It shall be the duty of the contractors' association to discipline such members as are found guilty of violation of the terms of the agreement," states the revised rules adopted for the children's dress industry. "Should the contractor thus disciplined fail to submit to the order of his organization, the matter shall be reported to the Board of Grievances. The Board shall then direct such action as is necessary to maintain the integrity of the agreement and of the organizations which are parties to the agreement."[68]

One possible procedure against the evil of noncompliance with awards, or with the terms of collective agreements, would reduce forms of disciplinary action, beyond official warnings and reprimands, to a common basis of monetary damages that could be collected through a system of cash deposits made in advance. Financial losses could then be inflicted upon noncomplying firms over the opposition of the offender. Some employers' associations, through their own bylaws, or by mutual agreement with the union, accepted a responsibility for maintaining cash security funds on

---

[68]From a draft of an agreement of the Children's Dress Manufacturers' Association and of the Misses' and Children's Dress Contractors' Association of Greater New York with the ILGWU and Locals 10 and 50, ILGWU. Copy filed in the Abelson papers.

behalf of their members. "For the faithful performance of this agreement on the part of the individual members of the Association," stated the 1929 collective agreement between the Associated Employers of Fur Workers and Locals 2 and 3 of the International Fur Workers' Union, "it is hereby agreed that the Association will collect from each member of the Association the sum of $1,000. This sum shall be deposited with a Bank or Trust Company in the name of Fur Dressing Security Trust Fund of the City of New York." Money could be withdrawn from this fund only under the following conditions:

In the event a complaint by the Union before the Joint Board of Arbitration and Conciliation against any member of the Association shall, after a trial, result in a decision awarding to the Union, or to any workers of the said member, a sum or sums of money, the member of the Association affected by said decision shall pay the said sum or sums so awarded within seventy-two hours after rendering of the decision. If the member fails to pay such sum or sums within the time specified, the said amount shall be drawn from this Security Trust Fund up to the sum deposited by the said member. A member of the Association affected by such proceeding shall be required to deposit into the Trust Fund the equivalent of the sum drawn out within seventy-two hours of the drawing of such amount from the Security Trust Fund. If he shall fail to do so he shall forfeit the protection of the agreement.

Cash security funds were particularly useful in forcing association members to meet their wage deficits. For this purpose, unions demanded that employers' associations assume responsibility for the payment of back wages regardless of whether or not defaulting members kept up their contributions to cash security funds. Under some collective agreements, payments from a cash security fund were a direct contribution from the association to the union and, with each withdrawal from the fund to meet wage deficiencies, the association itself had to replenish the fund on penalty of giving the union opportunity to abrogate the collective agreement. But, in such cases, liability for wage deficits was usually limited to payments for periods of not more than a week or two.[69]

---

[69]The association hereby agrees that as security for the faithful performance of this agreement on its part and on the part of all the manufacturers constituting its membership, the said association shall deposit

Specific Performance of the Contract

Levying fines against offenders did not guarantee adherence to the principles of the protocol movement. Not all forms of contract infractions could be readily translated into "monetary damages" nor were financial penalties an adequate form of relief for all types of contract evasion. In practice, the payment of fines was often a welcomed substitute for observing the contract. Although these fines sometimes ran into the thousands of dollars and were increased with each repetition of an offense, they seldom acted as an effective deterrent against undermining contract standards. Many employers, once detected and convicted, willingly paid their fines and continued along their lawless ways. Just as the union contract itself became the employer's license to operate legally, so payment of a fine became his license to operate illegally.[70]

---

the sum of $50,000 (fifty thousand dollars) with the Union Exchange National Bank as trustee hereunder. If any manufacturers shall violate any of the terms of this agreement, the union shall serve notice thereof upon the association and such complaint shall be referred to an adjustment committee....The adjustment committee shall decide on the amount of the damage to be paid to the union by reason of the breach of this agreement....The damages so to be sustained by the union shall be paid to it out of the deposit by the trustees immediately upon the receipt of notice of the committee's award and the association shall restore the amount of such withdrawal to such deposit within seventy-two (72) hours thereafter.

—1919 collective agreement of the American Cloak and Suit Manufacturers' Association with the Cloakmakers' Joint Board and the ILGWU, text in *Monthly Labor Review,* December 1919, vol. 9, p. 1724.

For other examples of cash security clauses in multiemployer labor contracts, see the 1924 collective agreement between the Cloth Hat and Cap Manufacturers' Association and the Joint Council of the United Cloth Hat and Cap Makers' Union in the *Headgear Worker,* July 12, 1924; and the 1925 collective agreement between the Association of Dress Manufacturers and the ILGWU in *Women's Wear,* Jan. 19, 1925. For the most part, the use of cash security as an enforcement weapon was reserved for separate union contracts with independent firms that were not otherwise restrained by membership in employers' associations. See below, chap. 12.

[70]When employers, testifying before the U. S. Commission on Industrial Relations in 1914, contended that unions suffered no penalties for breach of contract and could not be sued — a status of irresponsibility that could be partially alleviated by the use of cash security bonds to be required of all unions signing collective agreements — the unions replied (as summarized by

There were no adequate substitutes for specific performance of the contract. Only by getting unauthorized strikers to return to their jobs, only by inducing manufacturers to give up bootleg piece rates for legitimate time payments, only by preventing underpayment of wages or excessive overtime work could the principles of controlled competition within an industry be maintained. "Since from the industrial standpoint," once observed Impartial Chairman Sol. A. Rosenblatt in an award for the women's coat and suit trade, "the entire machinery of the Impartial Chairman's Office is primarily intended to secure compliance with the provisions of the collective agreements, the fact that compliance has been secured from the three contractors involved is far more important than the assessment of liquidated damages."[71]

In so far as specific performance of the contract offered the most effective stabilizer of work standards against waves of uncontrolled competition, the state courts were in a favored position to render valuable assistance. Some collective agreements expressly acknowledged that the contracting parties were entitled to equitable relief from the courts against violations of the contract. Moreover, the arbitration laws of New York State soon came to the aid of impartial chairmen or industry arbitrators who issued prohibitions against breaches of collective agreements. If their awards, directions, or prohibitions were not obeyed, the aggrieved party could apply to the courts for confirmation of the award and enforcement of the mandatory decree. While the organized employers had long resorted to equity courts against labor unions charged with illegal conduct, the reverse procedure was slower to develop.[72]

---

the Commission) that "putting up a forfeitable bond would lower the entire plane upon which the observance of contracts now stands, and would simply mean a financial calculation on the part of the union to see whether a breach of contract would leave a balance in favor of the members after the bond was forfeited." U. S. Commission on Industrial Relations, *First Annual Report* (Oct. 23, 1914), p. 25.

[71]S. A. Rosenblatt, *Decisions,* supplementary decision to Cases 1591, 1592, and 1593 (June 7, 1938). Forgiving fines in return for a promise of future contract observance was a common procedure with needle trade arbitrators. See, particularly, Isaac Siegmeister, *Decisions* for the year 1938 and following in the millinery industry.

[72]The decision reached by the managers of the parties hereto or their deputies, or rendered by the Impartial Chairman, shall have the effect of a judgment entered upon an award made, as provided by the Arbitration

Yet, if employers ignored prohibitions on runaway shops, or selected contractors not permitted by their agreements, or hired nonunion workers where closed shop agreements prevailed, or deliberately breached awards handed down by industry arbitrators, the union involved could request the courts to grant injunctions against further infractions of the collective agreements. "To deny to the plaintiff union the right to invoke the aid of a court of equity to prevent an unlawful violation of its contract," stated New York Supreme Court Judge Edward Riegelmann in 1929, "it must necessarily follow that the right of collective bargaining will be impaired, leaving the labor union to resort solely to strikes and picketing, which would entail not only serious financial loss, but protracted and needless friction and possible breaches of the public peace and security."[73]

Laws of the State of New York, entitling the entry of judgment in a court of competent jurisdiction against the defaulting party who fails to carry out or abide by the decisions.

—From the 1947 collective agreement of the Affiliated Dress Manufacturers' Association with the ILGWU and the Dressmakers' Joint Board.

[73]Ribner v. Racso Butter and Egg Co., 135 Misc. 616 (1929) at p. 621; 238 N.Y. Supp. 132. The precedent-setting case came in the early twenties, when the ILGWU sought the help of the courts in restraining the employers' association that had signed the original Protocol of Peace from alleged violations of its 1919 collective agreement with the union. "It is elementary and yet sometimes requires emphasis," stated New York Supreme Court Justice Robert F. Wagner in Schlesinger v. Quinto, 117 Misc. 735 (1922) at p. 735; 192 N.Y. Supp. 564, "that the door of a court of equity is open to employer and employee alike. It is no respecter of persons — it is keen to protect the legal rights of all." This position was affirmed by Mr. Justice A. R. Page (201 App. Div. 487 at 498; 194 N.Y. Supp. 401): "The cases thus far decided have been at the suit of the employer against combinations of labor for the simple reason that this is the first time that labor has appealed to the courts. . . . The remedies are mutual; the law does not have one rule for the employer and another for the employee. In a court of justice they stand on an exact equality; each case to be decided upon the same principles of law impartially applied to the facts of the case, irrespective of the personality of the litigants." Other aspects of this case are discussed below, pp. 323–324.

For a review of cases upholding the enforceability of collective agreements in equity courts, see a 48-page printed pamphlet entitled *David Dubinsky and Joint Dress Board v. Blue Dale Dress Company,* consisting of the brief of Emil Schlesinger, attorney for the ILGWU, in the case of that title, 162 Misc. 177 (1936); 292 N.Y. Supp. 898. See also, E. E. Witte, "Labor's Resort to

Expulsion as a Penalty

Those who persistently refused to follow directions or carry out awards, even in the face of conviction for noncompliance with decisions of the impartial machinery, were subject to expulsion from the realm of law and order. Ejected from their respective organizations, the culprits would then be at the mercy of their historic enemies: employers kicked out of their association would again become victims of union dictation; workers kicked out of their union would again be subject to the arbitrary power of their employers. Expelling the nonconformists would at least preserve the institutions of self-government for the use of those remaining loyal to the principles of the protocol movement.

Casting offenders into outer darkness was an extreme form of punishment widely authorized in collective agreement throughout the needle trades. "Each of the parties," runs the 1934 contract between the Men's Neckwear Manufacturers' Association of New York and the United Neckwear Workers' Union, ACWA, "undertakes to insure rigid compliance by their respective members of the terms of this contract, and covenants that non-compliance thereof will result in the expulsion of such members of the Association or the Union who shall fail to comply with this contract."

Where the penalty of expulsion was not expressly provided by the terms of the contract, it was often imposed by order of the impartial machinery for the industry. In one case of a fur manufacturer who was found guilty of hiring nonunion men, working them overtime at straight pay, employing inside contractors, violating minimum wage scales, and attempting withal to conceal or destroy all evidences of misconduct, the conference committee of the fur manufacturing industry resolved, pursuant to Article 23 of the 1925 collective agreement, "that the firm of Weiss and Sons is unfit and unworthy of enjoying the benefits afforded by the Collective Agreement, and that it recommends disciplining of this firm by expulsion from the Association for gross and willful violation of the terms of the Agreement."[74]

---

the Injunction," *Yale Law Review,* 1930, vol. 39, p. 375; and P. F. Brissenden and C. O. Swayzee, "The Use of the Labor Injunction in the New York Needle Trades," *Political Science Quarterly,* December 1929, vol. 44, pp. 548–568; March 1930, vol. 45, pp. 87–111.

[74]*Minutes,* Special Meeting of the Conference Committee of the Fur Manufacturing Industry (July 29, 1925). Copy filed in the Abelson papers.

Banishing obstinate employers and rebellious workers into the wilderness of the unorganized was, however, more often like restoring their freedoms than feeding them to the wolves. Too many of the culprits, like Br'er Rabbit of tar baby fame, had been born and bred in the briar patch. The punishment designed for the renegades turned out to be a blessing in disguise. In February 1916, J. H. Cohen, father of the protocol movement, offered to submit evidence before the board of arbitration of the dress and waist industry showing that "the unscrupulous and illegitimate manufacturer can do better outside of our Association than he can in our Association." Many an association member, expelled from his organization for violating the collective agreement with the union, had been able to continue in business free of union control and of enforceable labor standards. Many a union member expelled from the ranks of organized labor had found freedom to work for what he pleased but, above all else, to find employment even though he worked in a nonunion shop.[75]

What had an employer who was thrown into the ranks of the unorganized contractors for the dress and waist industry to fear in 1916, so long as only 275 of the 600 contractors of the trade belonged to an employers' association? What had a worker banished to the nonunion ranks of the headwear industry in the early thirties to fear, so long as 46 percent of the trade was still unorganized? Or what had an employee banished from the union of the children's wear industry to fear in 1930, so long as 60 percent of the industry's products were still made in nonunion shops? Released from the confining restrictions of their former organizations, these outcasts sometimes preyed upon the business of their former masters until they had brought down the very institutions they once helped to erect.

Instead of expelling these stubborn offenders, the advocates of law and order had to devise ways of preserving their institutions against disintegration from loss of membership. No one could be

---

[75]*Minutes,* Arbitration Proceedings between the Dress and Waist Manufacturers' Association and the ILGWU (Feb. 5, 1916), vol. 4, p. 30. Earlier, J. H. Cohen had pointed out the difference between debarring a lawyer from his profession and kicking a manufacturer out of his association. Unlike the case of the lawyer, there was no way to keep an expelled manufacturer out of his trade. *Minutes,* Council of Conciliation...[women's coat and suit trade] (July 14, 1915), vol. 2, p. 43.

permitted to escape the obligations of a collective agreement by the simple expedient of resigning or getting kicked out of his organization. If expulsion became necessary, then the long arm of law enforcement had to follow the outcast into the wilderness.

Concluding Observations

Joint labor-management efforts at controlling competition through collective bargaining were frequently upset by opposition to the enforcement of contract terms. Although dedicated to a common purpose, employers' associations and labor unions often found themselves at war with each other over the methods and procedures for carrying out their objectives. So widespread and ingenious were the schemes to undermine contract standards during the life of collective agreements that unity of purpose among the organized forces of industry was sometimes lost in a flurry of distractions that violated all concepts of law and order. At times, neither organization showed much interest in controlling its own members or in following the leadership of the impartial machinery on which the contracting parties so heavily relied for the achievement of their goals.

From time to time, those who first led the "bosses" and the "people" into the Canaan's Land of Controlled Competition were overthrown, but the ideas they had conceived lived after them. So long as employers' associations denounced labor unions more for failing to abide by their contracts than for insisting on the right to bargain — so long as labor unions condemned employer groups more for failure to meet their commitments than for hostility toward unions — so long as both contracting parties measured the shortcomings of collective bargaining more in terms of current imperfections than in terms of basic purposes, the presumption was strong that those who supported the protocol movement would sooner or later learn to work together for a rigid enforcement of contract terms. How far they were willing to go in this direction was further exemplified by their attitude toward "legalizing" the use of strikes and lockouts as weapons of contract enforcement.

Chapter 7

Authorized Strikes

THE pressures to devise workable means of enforcing collective agreements led the contracting parties to fall back upon instruments of force and coercion. Impelled by the grim necessity of eliminating cutthroat competition at all costs, the sponsors of the protocol movement reluctantly sanctioned the use of strikes and lockouts. This development, however, was not a reversion to the earlier practice of conceding to each party an unrestricted use of force against those impinging upon the rights of its members. Such a practice smacked too much of unsuccessful attempts to create a stable society of nations by leaving the enforcement of international law to the member states. Much like the development of international law that would convert wars from instruments of national policy to instruments of international policy under control of the United Nations, the organized forces of industrial society would harness the powerful but dangerous weapons of industrial warfare to enforce the principles of industrial law and order. Strikes and lockouts that the "bosses" and the "people" so vehemently denied to each other when acting in their separate capacities, they ultimately bestowed upon each other when acting in their joint capacities.

The possibility of permitting unions to call strikes or employers to declare lockouts had by implication been written into the original Protocol of Peace. This first collective agreement for the women's coat and suit trade did not expressly outlaw all strikes and lockouts; it merely prohibited their use until all other methods of enforcing contract terms had been exhausted. "In the event of any dispute arising between the manufacturers and the unions, or between any members of the manufacturers and any members of the unions," stated the original Protocol of Peace, September 2, 1910, "the parties to this Protocol agree that there shall be no strike or lockout concerning such matters in controversy until full opportunity shall have been given for the submission of such matters to said Board of Arbitration, and in the event of a determination of said controversies by said Board of Arbitration, only in the event of a failure to accede to the determination of said board."[1]

Within a matter of months after this first protocol became effective, at least one form of direct action had been officially sanctioned and put into operation. The joint board of sanitary control created by the women's coat and suit protocol was empowered "to establish standards of sanitary conditions to which the manufacturers and the unions shall be committed." Accordingly, the board devised a series of steps for gaining compliance with its regulations — steps that began with attempts at peaceful persuasion and led as a last resort to approval of a "sanitary strike." Where no other means would suffice, the board openly conceded that union members might refuse to work for employers who failed to comply with the board's directions. During the first two years of the protocol, this "unique, practical, militant striking machine" — as it was called — swung into action on twenty-seven different occasions.[2]

From these modest beginnings, strikes and lockouts, although denounced in principle as the outlaw twins of industrial society, gradually wormed their way into the framework of the protocol movement. From inferences of limited toleration in the first protocol, authorized strikes and lockouts gained wide acceptance under

---

[1]Text of the original protocol is given in Louis Lorwin [Louis Levine] *The Women's Garment Workers* (1924), Appendix, pp. 542–545.

[2]C. H. Winslow, *Conciliation, Arbitration, and Sanitation in the Cloak, Suit, and Skirt Industry in New York City,* U.S. Department of Commerce and Labor, Bureau of Labor, Bulletin no. 98 (January 1912), pp. 253–255, 264. Henry Moskowitz, "The Joint Board of Sanitary Control in the Cloak, Suit and Skirt Industry," in *Annals,* American Academy of Political and Social Science, November 1912, vol. 44, p. 46. See also, chap. 12 below.

later agreements. Either they were expressly sanctioned in needle trade contracts or they were condoned, if not openly supported, by industry arbitrators and permanent umpires. Wherever the contracting parties could not, or would not, otherwise enforce their agreements or carry out the judgments of their impartial machinery, then the weapons of industrial warfare were brought into play. Within the established order, enforcing collective agreements by strikes and lockouts was considered preferable to dissolving the bonds of allegiance, thereby plunging whole industries into the chaos of unregulated competition.

Legalizing the use of strikes and lockouts raised a thousand perplexing issues and opened a veritable Pandora's box of potential evils. Who was to sanction the use of strikes and lockouts or limit the time and conditions under which these powers were to be exercised? How were such drastic weapons, once unleashed, to be kept within the bounds of "police functions" assigned to them? Could the rank and file among the "bosses" or the "people" ever learn to distinguish between strikes and lockouts that were "legal" and those that were "illegal"? While, for the most part, other alternatives open to employers removed the lockout from practical consideration, the use and control of strikes as a legitimate weapon of contract enforcement remained the most controversial problem in the whole range of collective bargaining. No other issue aroused such violent diversities of opinion or led to such widespread discrepancies in theory and practice.

Strikes as a Last Resort

Within the organized forces of industry the role of officially authorized strikes and lockouts varied from that of a "gun behind the door" to be used only in case of extreme emergency to that of a "policeman on the beat" presenting an ever present danger to would-be transgressors of the law. At one extreme, these strange instruments of law and order were reserved for final use in carrying out the judgments of industrial tribunals; at the other extreme, they constituted an omnipresent hand of warning more to restrain potential wrongdoers than to bring culprits to justice. Between these extreme positions there were countless variations in policy and practice.

At the conservative extreme, strikes and lockouts became acceptable instruments of contract enforcement only after the following procedures had previously been followed:

1– charges of contract infractions had been filed with the association or the union whose member was involved and also at the office of the impartial chairman;

2– after failure to settle the controversy directly through representatives of the association and the union, the impartial machinery had conducted hearings, established guilt, issued directions, and set the penalties;

3– the transgressor had then refused to obey orders or to accept the penalties imposed upon him;

4– the impartial machinery had then charged and convicted the offender for noncompliance with its decisions and had imposed additional penalties for this new offense;

5– the obstinate wrongdoer had still refused to correct his lawless conduct or to accept the additional penalties imposed upon him for noncompliance;

6– the employers' association (or labor union) to which the transgressor belonged had repeatedly demonstrated its indifference toward the offense or its inability to enforce compliance with the collective agreement and with the decisions of the impartial machinery.[3]

Even then, the rebellious offender sometimes had to be officially ejected from the coverage of his collective agreement or else temporarily expelled from his own organization before the drastic weapons of industrial warfare could be sanctioned for use against

---

[3]Especially to be noted in this procedure is the extra precaution of a trial for noncompliance with a decision of the impartial machinery.

On Thursday, July 30, 1936 the Impartial Chairman ruled that stoppages occurring any time before, during or after the adjustment of a complaint in the absence of a formal non-compliance decision are contrary to the collective agreement and relations set by them. Neither the union nor the association had filed a claim of non-compliance with a decision of the trial board or the clerks here. A party has no right by itself to determine facts of non-compliance.

—*David Dubinsky and the Joint Dress Board v. Blue Dale Dress Co.,* printed pamphlet consisting of the brief of Emil Schlesinger, attorney for the ILGWU, p. 48. Copy in the New York Public Library. See also A. Feldblum, impartial chairman, dress industry, *Decisions,* Case no. A-1081 (Dec. 17, 1934), and Case no. A-1177 (Dec. 24, 1934).

him. Whether this exclusion followed automatically from preceding events (as was prescribed under some collective agreements) or required some positive action by the highest arbitrating authority within each industry (as was dictated under other agreements), the general effect of these long-drawn-out procedures was to withhold the use of strikes and lockouts until every other available resource had been exhausted.

With all these precautions, many sponsors of the protocol movement still refused to sanction the use of strikes and lockouts as weapons of contract enforcement. Resorting to the instrumentalities of warfare, they insisted, could never be reconciled with the concept of an industrial society governed by law and order. Every stoppage, once asserted Louis D. Brandeis, is taking the law into one's own hands. He contended that there could not be a legal strike so long as the protocol existed. To allow acts of warfare in the form of strikes, whenever in the union's opinion the other side had done something wrong, would, he said, be "absolutely anarchical."[4]

In these views, Brandeis set the standard that many succeeding arbitrators were to follow. W. M. Leiserson, one of the first arbitrators in the men's clothing industry of New York City, repeatedly held that any stoppage was a violation of the collective agreement. Henry Moskowitz, in his first award as impartial chairman of the fancy leather goods industry, denounced strikes and lockouts as "cardinal sins of the collective agreement." He would tolerate no exceptions to the rule against striking. "There are no degrees of guilt or innocence in the violation of this fundamental obligation," he stated. Others were more outspoken in branding strikes of whatever nature during the life of an agreement as forms of insurrection, lynch law, or revolt against established authority. Time and again, tribunals of the impartial machinery throughout the needle trades refused to draw a line between justifiable and unjustifiable strikes.[5]

---

[4]*Minutes,* Board of Arbitrators...[women's coat and suit trade] (Oct. 3, 1913), pp. 73–75, 83.

[5]Henry Moskowitz, *Decisions,* Case no. 1a (Dec. 16, 1929). See also the early decisions of W. M. Leiserson. "If a line is to be drawn between stoppages that are justified and those that are not justified it is to say that the Agreement is good in some cases but that direct action is permissible and proper in other

Certainly most arbitrators could find support in the language of their collective agreements for their uncompromising stand against strikes. Over the years, many no-strike clauses have expressly barred stoppages of every form, extent, and purpose during the life of an agreement. "No conditions shall warrant a stoppage of work in any shop or shops," stated the 1921 collective agreement between the Clothing Manufacturers' Association of New York and the Amalgamated Clothing Workers' Union. "Any stoppage of work is a violation of this agreement." Strikes were often defined to embrace all conceivable forms of deliberately interrupting work: sit-downs, lie-downs, slow-downs, and other novel devices of whatsoever nature that had the intent or effect of retarding or disrupting production.[6]

Strikes for Dodging Judicial Procedures

Yet, from this highly restrictive official position, policies and practices descended by various gradations toward the opposite extreme of utilizing strikes and lockouts as the first line of defense against contract infractions. Over the years, the trend was toward prescribing or condoning wider and wider use of strikes and lockouts as weapons of law enforcement. This transition was, in part, the result of a general breakdown in the exalted level of business integrity upon which the protocol movement had been founded. Amid the reckless competition generated by hordes of immigrants seeking employment and by thousands of small-time contractors seeking work, business ethics gave way to the cold facts of industrial life. Every decrease in the size and stability of the workshop brought a corresponding increase in the number of reckless competitors. The resulting degeneration in the moral fibre of industrial society was reflected in lack of respect for contractual obli-

---

cases," announced the joint trade board set up under the collective agreement of the men's clothing industry in the Chicago market following the First World War. "The Board does not subscribe to this view although holding that the arbitrary action of one side may be balanced against the arbitrary action of the other side in assessing the measure of blame for purposes of discipline." Quoted from Case nos. 712 and 713 of Trade Board Decisions in "Digest of Trade Board Decisions (Nos. 1 to 1000) and Board of Arbitration Decisions to October 1921," at p. 52. Copy filed in the Abelson papers.

[6]Text of this agreement is given in *Daily News Record,* June 3, 1921.

gations, and increased the pressure for more drastic action to save the institutions of collective bargaining.

One important factor in transforming the strike from a "gun behind the door" to a "policeman on the beat" was the refusal of contract offenders to follow grievance procedures prescribed by collective agreements. Under the protocol movement, the difficulties of obtaining submission to administrative procedures increased with prospects of success in executing the judgments of the impartial machinery. Neither employers nor workers objected to the established mode of grievance procedure so long as they were not compelled to abide by the results. Only where contract offenders could not escape the "verdict" did they refuse to submit to the "court." While efforts to obtain compliance with decisions of the impartial machinery could be drawn out through many channels short of force, a blanket refusal to follow prescribed procedures stymied the possibility of orderly settlement at the outset and increased the futility of delaying strike action.

Failure to cooperate with the permanent institutions for maintaining contract standards began with denying the right of entry to official representatives of the impartial machinery and ended with refusal to appear before the established agencies for determining guilt and imposing penalties. The rights accorded clerks and deputy clerks to visit the premises and inspect the books were sometimes thwarted by employers who repeatedly turned back the inspectors until a more favorable time. Often clerks found themselves barred at the door, where persistent knocking or ringing of doorbells brought no response. In these hideouts, the secret peephole was an essential attribute of wanton contract evasion.[7]

Where clerks or committeemen by one means or another gained admittance, they were often denied access to the books or permission to examine the records. At times, agents of the impartial machinery suffered the indignities of abusive language and even physical violence. More than one industry agent was physically ejected from the premises. Then, when these hostile employers were summoned before the board of grievances to give an ac-

---

[7]See, for example, the union's view on the Joseph Rosenberg case in *Minutes,* Arbitration Proceedings between the Dress and Waist Manufacturers' Association and the ILGWU (Nov. 9, 1913), pp. 243–244.

count of their conduct, they ignored the summons and defied the authority of their own institutions.

Still other employers refused to follow the adopted procedures for setting piece rates on thousands of new items continually being introduced to meet changes in style, materials, or market demands. Not only did they fail to meet with the price committee of the organized workers in their shops before putting the new items into production, as required by the contract, but they also refused to permit interference in price-fixing by higher authorities of the impartial machinery. The advantage was always with the employer who successfully delayed the negotiation of piece rates until after the items in question had been produced. In all such cases, business competitors as well as the workers became the scapegoats.

Against these practices, the impartial machinery could hope to accomplish little by ordering the defiant employers to cease and desist from their resistance to established procedures. Even less were the fines and penalties assessed against absent offenders likely to be accepted. Nor could employers' associations, with troubles enough from their members who accepted jurisdiction of the impartial machinery but failed to carry out the awards, always hope to win compliance from those of their members who refused to be shackled by grievance procedures. Member firms that defied the procedures of their impartial machinery reacted with equal disdain toward the disciplinary processes of their own associations. Attempts to hale the nonconformist before the board of directors or the disciplinary committee of his own association were stubbornly resisted.

Both contracting parties soon became aware that these outlaws among the organized manufacturers could best be restrained, if at all, by timely use of the strike. Hence, more and more collective agreements directly or indirectly authorized strikes against employers refusing to accept the jurisdiction of the impartial machinery. Unions were permitted to call strikes as soon as employers jumped the established procedures. Where piece rates were involved, workers were authorized to strike until piece rates were set. If this right to strike did not exist in the written agreement, it was sometimes authorized or at least condoned by action of the impartial machinery itself.

Strikes against "The Law's Delays"

In time, greater freedom to strike was also authorized against employers who accepted the jurisdiction of the impartial machinery but refused to carry out the awards. Here, the demand for more direct action arose principally from the evils of delayed enforcement. In seasonal industries of small-scale producers, the employer who could for a few months take advantage of his workers (as well as of his competitors) seldom ever paid the full penalty for his action. Once the busy season had ended, the "people" whom he had victimized were likely to be scattered or else the "boss" himself might vanish from the scene. At worst, the unscrupulous producer who made his profits for a season could always go out of business in anticipation of turning up later as a partner in a different firm. Within the needle trades, only a speedy enforcement of labor agreements could preserve the principles of collective action.

Yet the normal operation of the impartial machinery permitted delays at every turn. The original work of detection was often held up by employers who refused to cooperate. Assigning cases to the calendar, preparing briefs, and conducting hearings created more delays, particularly where either party to a dispute could obtain repeated postponements to suit his convenience. Cases before grievance boards were frequently sent back to the clerks or referred to special subcommittees for further investigation or additional evidence. Hearings on charges of noncompliance with decisions of the impartial machinery, consumed still more time. Appeals were always necessary where the lower echelons of the administration could not reach agreement on the disposition of a case, and appeals were often tolerated even where agreement at lower levels could be reached. Although decisions of the lower agencies were immediately binding upon the parties until set aside by higher authorities, these awards were, in fact, seldom put into operation while appeals were pending, provisions of the contract to the contrary notwithstanding.

Delays in gaining compliance with decisions of the impartial machinery were largely attributable to the lack of an effective enforcing arm. Certainly in the early years of the protocol movement, agencies of the impartial machinery had to operate with gloved hands; they could invite, cajole, and implore — even threaten or demand — but they could not execute their decisions. The case of the Triangle Waist Company illustrates the typical procedure. On February 1, 1915, the chief clerks of the dress and waist industry found that this company had underpaid its workers, and awarded $808.02 in back wages to be paid immediately. Failure to obey this decision led the union to bring a new complaint of noncompliance before the board of grievance on March 10. At this meeting, the board moved that the chief clerks be authorized to expedite matters pertaining to the company and report at the next meeting.

Five days later, the union representative again complained to the board of grievances that the decision had not been carried out. This time, the board granted a request of the chief clerk of the employers' association, Mrs. Henry Moskowitz, that she be given time to visit the plant to see that the award was carried out. Two weeks later, March 31, the charge of noncompliance was brought before the board of grievances for the third time. Thereupon, the board "resolved that this Board instruct the Triangle Waist Company to send a check for the money due under the decision in question, by Monday, April 5, 1915, and that this decision be carried out in full." On April 16, the firm sent a check for $396.02, leaving an unpaid balance of $412 which became a subject for further consideration at the meeting of the board of grievances on April 23. Almost three months had elapsed since the initial decision of the clerks, yet the case was still not closed.[8]

No issue created a more persistent cause of complaint among organized workers than the evils of the law's delays. Seeing the enforcement of their agreements vanish in a mirage of stalling tactics, union leaders were forever hounding officials of employers' associations and representatives of the impartial machinery for relief. No "cool and common reason" of peaceful settlement, wrote Nathaniel Spector, manager of the Hatters' Joint Board in 1919, can bring satisfaction or prevent excitement in the shops "where the carrying out of the slightest matters is postponed for months." Manufacturers who conscientiously supported the principles of collective action were equally concerned over the breakdown of

---

[8]*Minutes,* Grievance Board Meeting...[dress and waist industry] (April 23, 1915), Case no. 8854 (the Triangle Waist Company), bound with *Minutes,* Wage-Scale Board, Conferences and Special Investigations (1915), pp. 285–287.

labor standards attributable to the law's delays. Here, again, nothing short of the right to strike would apparently provide the required stimulant for speedy action.[9]

Waiting several months for the right to strike often defeated the purpose of striking. "You see," testified Jacob Panken [Pankin], attorney for the United Brotherhood of Tailors, before the U. S. Commission on Industrial Relations, June 5, 1914, "it [the grievance board] is a cumbersome way to arrive at the right to have a strike. It may take three months. Mr. Lennon says it is a question of machinery, but if you have any grievance brought up and you have your clerks make your investigations and then going to the grievance board, and then you are going to the arbitration board, and the arbitration board meets sometimes no more than once in three months, and by the time the board of arbitration hands down the decision the point gained is no longer a gain."[10]

After 1910, the major trend in the use of direct action to help enforce collective agreements consisted in reducing the time interval between the commission of an offense and official permission to strike against the offender. In the needle trades, the tempo of this development varied from industry to industry and reached its peak during the depression decade of the thirties. This movement for greater freedom to strike in support of the contract was reflected both in the terms of collective agreements and in the decisions of the impartial machinery. Progress toward a more liberal use of authorized strike action can be traced through its various stages of evolution.

In the first phase of this transition, authority to strike for failure to obey decisions of the impartial machinery was granted without awaiting supplemental trials for noncompliance with awards. Under certain collective agreements, strike action following a decision of the impartial machinery was postponed until the employers' association to which the firm belonged was given ample opportunity to obtain compliance from its offending member. A waiting period was then granted during which the offender might reconsider his position. Only thereafter was strike action officially

---

[9]N. Spector to S. D. Seidman, letter, dated April 9, 1919, filed in the Abelson papers.

[10]U. S. Commission on Industrial Relations, *Final Report and Testimony* (1916), vol. 2, p. 2021.

recognized. But, at least, the contracting parties had eliminated the additional delays that accompanied grievance procedures in trials for noncompliance with arbitration awards.

A second phase of this transition further shortened the days of grace allowed for complying with awards. Collective agreements in this group provided no waiting period for supporting action by employers' associations beyond a definite time limit in which decisions of the impartial machinery had to be obeyed. These limitations were generally expressed in hours rather than days. As a rule, compliance within twenty-four or forty-eight hours was necessary to avoid the consequences of authorized strike action. "No worker," stated the 1938 collective agreement between the United Knitwear Manufacturers' League and the Knitgoods Workers' Union, Local 155, ILGWU, "shall be required to work for any member of the Association who has failed for more than forty-eight (48) hours to comply with the decision of the representative of the parties or of the Impartial Chairman until such decision has been fully complied with."[11]

Some collective agreements prescribed no specific time limits for compliance with the decisions of the impartial machinery,

---

[11]Although the 1914–1917 collective agreement between the Associated Fur Manufacturers and the Furriers' Unions prohibited strikes and lockouts "during the continuance of this agreement, for any reason whatsoever," the joint Conference Committee created by this agreement outlined the following steps leading to strikes against association members failing to carry out decisions of the impartial machinery:

(1) When the Committee on Immediate Action finds a decision of the impartial machinery is not carried out, it notifies the secretary of the Conference Committee who sends a statement of such failure to the Impartial Chairman of the Conference Committee.

(2) The Chairman of the Conference Committee then notifies the president of the Association who must see that the firm carries out the decision within 48 hours or else the firm cannot claim the protection of the agreement.

(3) Forty-eight hours after the notice is sent to the president of the Association, the secretary of the Conference Committee notifies the chairman whether the decision has been obeyed.

(4) If the decision has not been carried out, the Chairman notifies the Union and the Association that the firm in question cannot claim the protection of the agreement against strikes.

—*Minutes,* Conference Committee of the Fur Manufacturing Industry (Dec. 21, 1917), filed in the Abelson papers.

and in such cases unions generally assumed that strikes were permissible against every employer who did not carry out the terms of an award immediately. Once the fact of noncompliance had been determined, the members of a union were at liberty to act. This was the inference to be drawn from the no-strike clause of the original Protocol of Peace. Following a decision of the board of arbitration established under the protocol, the cloakmakers' union was free to strike "only in the event of a failure to accede to the determination of said board." Whether specific days of grace for compliance with industrial awards were named in collective agreements or whether some reasonable time for compliance was merely implied, unions that declared strikes against noncomplying employers were presumed to be at liberty to continue the strike until the offender had fully complied with the decisions of the impartial machinery.[12]

Authorized Strikes Preceding Awards

All these attempts to speed up compliance with decisions of the impartial machinery had no effect, of course, upon the delays that preceded the rendering of awards. Yet dilatory tactics in bringing a complaint to a hearing or in arriving at a final verdict could be as formidable a barrier to effective contract enforcement as delays in carrying out awards. Here, the dangers in defeating the purposes of collective action were all the more likely because agencies of contract administration often employed delaying tactics in an effort to "cool off" the participants and reveal the true nature of their dispute. Whatever the causes of delay, no adequate form of pressure was ever derived to speed up remedial procedures against contract offenders, short of authority to strike.

Except for strikes against employers who refused to submit to established grievance procedures, the right to strike before the

---

[12]"If the member of the Association fails to comply with the decision of a dispute made in a pending case," stated a provision in the 1935 collective agreement between the National Association of Blouse Manufacturers and Local 25, ILGWU, "then there shall be no obligation on the part of the Union to return the workers to work until all pending disputes have been fully adjusted." Contrast this right of a union to continue *authorized* strikes until pending disputes are adjusted, with the prohibition on this practice in the case of *unauthorized* strikes, discussed below at pp. 270–274.

impartial machinery had rendered its decisions was a radical departure from other uses of strike action to enforce awards. Yet this development had its origins in the early history of the protocol movement and became widespread during the great depression of the thirties. Here, too, the primary objective of tolerating strikes was to forestall the administrative delays that so effectively nullified the purposes of collective action. Under this group of collective agreements, strikes were authorized where the impartial machinery failed to conduct its investigations and render its decisions within given time limits. In most cases, this time interval was cut to a matter of hours following notice of a complaint.

Striking against firms that failed to settle complaints within prescribed time limits was a normal procedure under union-drafted form contracts signed by independent employers. "All complaints of an individual worker, group of workers, or of the Union," stated the 1936–1938 form contract of the fur manufacturing industry, "shall be adjusted within forty-eight hours from the time the complaint arises, unless the time is extended by mutual consent. Should the Firm fail to adjust a complaint or carry out an adjustment in time, the Union is at liberty to enforce the agreement."

Evidences that the parties to collective agreements were willing to accept this standard began to crop up in the first decade of the protocol movement. As early as 1913, the conference committee under the collective agreement of the fur manufacturing industry resolved that there should be no strikes over pending disputes, provided representatives of the association and the union, or the conference committee itself, settled the dispute within forty-eight hours. Such provisions soon became common in collective agreements of the fur manufacturing trade. Likewise in the millinery trade, beginning with the first collective agreement of the Ladies' Hat Manufacturers' Association with the Millinery Workers' Joint Board, December 20, 1915, collective agreements have generally required all disputes to be adjusted within forty-eight hours of their submission to the impartial machinery, unless the time limit be extended by mutual consent. Otherwise, unions were presumed to have the right to strike for the enforcement of the contract.[13]

---

[13]The failure of any of the parties to attend any hearing shall not delay any proceedings before the Board of Arbitration or the Impartial Chairman and the matter shall be determined and decided without delay. The

The 1916 collective agreement between the Cloak, Suit and Skirt Manufacturers' Protective Association and the ILGWU, Article 22, provided that "the Union shall neither call nor sanction any shop strike until at least twenty-four (24) hours shall have elapsed after it shall have given notice of the grievance to the Association; nor shall the Association order or sanction any shop lockout until at least twenty-four (24) hours shall have elapsed after it shall have given notice of the grievance to the Union." Commenting on the operation of this clause, Benjamin Schlesinger, president of the ILGWU, stated: "During these 24 hours the grievances shall have been straightened out either by the chief clerks or by the grievance board, or, if it becomes necessary, by an impartial person. If no adjustment within the stipulated 24 hours is reached, the union shall have the right to call a strike in that shop, or the employer to order a 'lockout.' "[14]

Strikes as a First Line of Defense

The final step in transforming the authorized strike from a "gun behind the door" to a "policeman on the beat" came with official recognition of the right to strike immediately against those found to be violating their collective agreements. Strikes of this character, called before the impartial machinery was given a chance to act, became the first line of defense against contract infractions. Had such permission to strike been extended to all alleged infractions of contract clauses, the status of enforcement procedures would have reverted to union practices under single-shop bargaining with independent employers. At least the sponsors of the protocol movement undertook to distinguish between contract infractions

---

Board of Arbitration shall decide any controversy or disputes submitted to it within forty-eight hours from the time of submission unless such time be extended by mutual consent. All determinations and decisions made by the Board of Arbitration shall be carried out within forty-eight hours.

—From the 1938 collective agreement of the Eastern Women's Head-wear Association with the Millinery Workers' Union.

The children's dress protocol (March 8, 1913) gave the board of grievances five days in which to resolve a dispute submitted to it.

[14]Benjamin Schlesinger, address before the Dress and Waist Manufacturers' Association. Newspaper clipping, n.d.n.p., filed in the Abelson papers.

that were patent on their face and alleged violations about which there was some doubt.

Here, the parties to collective agreements adopted the logic advanced by unions for meeting contract infractions that were so clear and deliberate as to preclude the possibility of falling within the orbits of permissible conduct. In all such cases, so the union had contended, the basic objectives of collective action could be defeated if known offenders escaped the consequences of their action under the cloak of grievance deliberations. Between the danger of hasty and unwarranted strike action and the hazards of self-defeating delays in grievance procedure, the advocates of law and order finally pursued a middle course. They permitted immediate strike action where contract infractions were beyond question and they prohibited strike action in all other cases — at least until their impartial machinery had thoroughly explored the issues and rendered a final judgment.

If, for example, employers refused to grant the additional wage increases automatically required of them at the end of the first six months under the contract — if jobbers neglected to remove cutting facilities from their shops before a certain date specified in their contract — if contractors failed to pay their workers on the payday designated by their labor agreement — if business firms hired nonunion men, extended the maximum hours of work, reduced the minimum rates of pay, or denied compensation for designated holidays — all in direct contravention of their clearly stated contractual obligations — then in all such cases immediate strike action was a commonly recognized remedy, often condoned by the impartial machinery if not expressly permitted by the collective agreements.[15]

Some collective agreements endorsed immediate strike action in general terms that were susceptible of varying interpretations. A

---

[15]During the term of this agreement, there shall be no general lockout, general strike, individual shop lockout, or individual shop strike or shop stoppage for any reason or cause, but work shall proceed in operation, subject to the determination of any dispute or grievance as hereinafter provided, except in cases where garments are not settled in the manner provided for in this agreement or wages are not paid on their due date as provided for herein.

—From the 1936 collective agreement of the Affiliated Dress Manufacturers with the Dressmakers' Joint Board and the ILGWU.

number of contracts directly or indirectly sanctioned strikes for any "substantial violation" of the agreement, or for any infraction of a "major clause" in the agreement, or for violations of "clearly specified provisions," or for failure to maintain "safe" or "sanitary" conditions in a plant. "Refusal to work where sanitary conditions do not prevail shall not be considered a breach of this contract," states the 1919 collective agreement of the fur dressing industry. A few contracts went so far as to declare that workers were "not responsible for a strike," or else "reserved the right to strike" against a company violating the agreement. Under these clauses, any strike immediately following an alleged infraction of the contract would be condoned at least until the union's charge of an infraction was repudiated by the impartial machinery.

Provisions authorizing strikes against employers who violated their contracts were, in some cases, accompanied by the requirement that strikers and their union be paid for losses sustained in upholding the collective agreement. If strikes were to be recognized as legitimate instruments of contract enforcement, then there was logic in paying the piper that played the tune. In 1922, when the fur workers' union ceased to work for an employer who was charged with deliberately refusing to obey a decision of the committee on immediate action, the conference committee under the collective agreement between the union and the Associated Fur Manufacturers recommended "that the association impose a fine upon the firm equal in amount to the loss of wages sustained by the workers who stopped work in protest of the conduct of the firm." Under similar circumstances a decade later, the impartial chairman for the dress and waist industry directed a noncomplying firm to pay the dressmakers' union $50 as a "reasonable reimbursement for expenses incurred by it [the union] on calling a strike under the circumstances."[16]

The Strike Power in Disguise

So drastic a reversal of the no-strike, no-lockout policy to which the founders of the protocol movement had subscribed could not

---

[16]*Minutes,* Conference Committee of the Fur Manufacturing Industry (Dec. 9, 1922), filed in the Abelson papers; A. Feldblum, impartial chairman of the dress industry, *Decisions,* Case no. A-139 (Dec. 18, 1933).

have been achieved save on the basis of experience and under the disguise of a clouded terminology. Even where the average association member could be sold on the necessity for drastic action to preserve protocol standards, he could not easily reconcile certain provisions of a collective agreement that prohibited all strikes and lockouts with other provisions of the same agreement that expressly sanctioned strikes and lockouts. For that reason, few collective agreements expressly authorized strikes and lockouts as instruments of law enforcement.

Instead, the typical collective agreement opened the door for direct action under the disguised terminology of having the contract offender "forfeit the benefits of the agreement" or "lose all the rights and privileges under the agreement." Sometimes a rebellious employer was declared to have repudiated his agreement or to have placed himself outside his contract, or to have suspended himself from his association. In the women's coat and suit trade, industry arbitrators were often content to declare association members who violated their contracts and defied decisions of their industry tribunals to be in "noncompliance" with their collective agreement. Regardless of terminology, the general effect was to give the union power to proceed as if the culprit were an independent firm. Once offenders were "eliminated" from the coverage of their collective agreements, unions were at liberty to "use other methods" to see that exiled firms became worthy of reinstatement.

"In the event of the failure on the part of any member of the Association or the Union to comply with any decision of the Chief Clerks, Grievance Board, or Impartial Chairman within seventy-two hours," stated the 1919 collective agreement of the Dress and Waist Manufacturers' Association with the ILGWU and its Locals 10, 25, and 58, "said member, shall in addition to other penalties herein provided for, forfeit all the rights and benefits of this agreement, so long as said party remains in default." Later agreements of this industry strengthened the implied right to strike against defaulting employers by specifying that "the Union shall be free to take action to enforce the rights of the workers against such members." Thus was the door to direct action that had been so carefully guarded by the explicit language of collective agreements forced ajar by the implied power to strike against noncomplying firms.[17]

The formulation of policies and techniques for "legalizing" strikes did not arise from any conscious consideration of theoretical principles. There were no formal conferences between the contracting parties to weigh the pros and cons of direct action as a method of contract enforcement. While an analysis of a thousand separate incidents might have revealed an evolving pattern of "legitimate" strike action, no participant in the collective bargaining process ever detached himself from his involvement with day-to-day problems long enough to take stock of whence "authorized" strikes had come or whither they were bound. Here, as in other spheres of collective action, abstract principles gave way to the practical solution of immediate problems in the workshop. Sufficient unto the day were the evils thereof.

Control of Authorized Strikes

That strikes as weapons of law enforcement would be extremely difficult to control appeared inevitable. A single case will suffice

---

[17]All decisions reached by the managers of the parties hereto or their deputies or rendered by the Impartial Chairman shall be complied with within twenty-four hours. Should any member of the Affiliated fail to comply with such decision within such time, he shall automatically lose all rights and privileges under this agreement and the Union shall be free to take action to enforce the rights of the workers against such member.
—From the 1936 collective agreement of the Affiliated Dress Manufacturers with the Dressmakers' Joint Board and the ILGWU.

Under another dress industry agreement of the mid-thirties, the ILGWU ordered a strike against an association firm charged with falsifying its records. After Impartial Chairman A. Feldblum had investigated the case and found the charges to be true, he concluded "that the member has lost all rights and privileges under the Collective Agreement and that the Union was in consequence entitled to stop the workers in its shop." A. Feldblum, *Decisions,* Case no. B-901 (August 30, 1935).

In the event it is established before the Impartial Chairman that the employer has failed to abide by the decision of the Board of Adjustment and the Impartial Chairman, the firm shall forfeit the right to the protection of the collective agreement, and the Union shall have all legal and equitable remedies as it may find necessary and desirable.
—From the 1936 collective agreement between the Eastern Women's Headwear Association and the Cap and Millinery Department of the United Hatters, Cap and Millinery Workers' International Union and the Millinery Workers' Joint Board.

to illustrate the complex nature of the problem. The 1929 collective agreement of the Association of Dress Manufacturers with the Dressmakers' Joint Board and the ILGWU had declared that members of either contracting party who failed to obey a decision of the impartial machinery within forty-eight hours lost the protection of the agreement. Although the trial board of the impartial machinery had sustained a union complaint against a member of the association for unjustifiable discharges, neither the employers' association nor the trial board could induce the firm to reinstate the workers. After waiting for several days, the union ordered a strike in the shop to enforce compliance with the decision.

Once the strike had been called, the union refused to return the workers until the company had compensated it for the expense of enforcing the arbitrator's award. The legality of the union's action came before the impartial chairman whose opinion merits extensive quotation:

It appears from the evidence that the decision of the Trial Board reached the office of the association by special messenger from the impartial chairman's office between 1 and 2 p.m. on Friday, October 24, 1930. The decision was communicated by telephone to the firm by the manager of the labor department of the association, and the firm refused to comply with it. In a number of communications over the telephone between the officers of the association and of the union on Friday afternoon and Saturday morning, it was made clear by the officers of the association that the firm still refused to comply with the decision.

The union thereupon gave notice that it would have to take its own steps to enforce the decision, and on Monday morning, that is, at the expiration of more than 48 hours, the union notified the association that it had called a strike in the shop to enforce the decision. On Tuesday afternoon, after the workers had been out on strike for a day and a half, the firm indicated to the association its readiness to comply with the decision of the Trial Board, whereupon the association asked for the immediate cessation of the strike.

The union took the position that the firm, having refused to comply with the decision of the Trial Board, it placed itself outside the pale of protection of the agreement, and the union having been within its rights in calling the strike, it would not return the workers until a proper settlement was made by the firm which would provide not only for the compliance with the decision of the Trial Board, but also for compensation for time lost by the workers and a penalty for the trouble and expense caused the union by the necessity to call a strike....

The union is undoubtedly in the right in demanding prompt and unconditional compliance with a decision of the Trial Board. To permit members of the association or of the union to refuse or to delay compliance with a decision would tend to weaken the entire structure of the impartial machinery provided in the agreements. It would cause losses to employers and to workers and might lead to many other abuses. On the other hand, it would be dangerous to permit either side to declare when the other side has failed to comply, and to take punitive action on its own initiative, since it is conceivable that a decision might be rendered which it wasn't practical to carry out immediately in whole or in part, and that either side, in a moment of excitement, might take hasty action in declaring the other side outside the protection of the agreement.

The contention of the association that the announcement that a firm is outside the protection of the agreement should come from the impartial chairman and not from the other side, therefore, seems well taken. The procedure should be as follows: Upon the failure of a firm to comply with a decision of the Trial Board, it shall be the duty of the association to suspend such firm from membership, whereupon the union will be free to take such action against the firm as it may see fit. In the case of failure to suspend such a member, the union may bring charges before the impartial chairman, who thereupon may order the suspension of the firm by the association and declare it outside the protection of the agreement.

So much for the future. As regards the present case, it cannot be denied that the firm had ample time to comply with the decision of the chairman both Friday afternoon, when the discharged pressers reported for reinstatement, after the decision had been announced, and on Monday morning, by which time two and one-half days had elapsed from the time the decision was announced and several efforts had been made by the officers of the association to induce the firm to comply with the decision. There having been no rule in the past which calls for further action by the chairman, and the association clearly having indicated its inability to induce its members to comply with the decision, the union cannot be charged with having been unduly hasty in calling a strike in order to enforce the decision....

Bearing in mind the foregoing considerations, the chairman is of the opinion that the union, having been unnecessarily put to the trouble of calling a strike to enforce the decision of the Trial Board through the willful and obstinate refusal on the part of the firm to comply with the decision for four days after the decision had been communicated to it, the union is entitled to some compensation in the settlement of the strike. The matter is hereby referred to the union and the association for settlement by mutual agreement failing in which, the case may be brought before the Trial Board for final adjudication.[18]

Concluding Observations

Only an unswerving devotion to a common objective of overwhelming concern to their welfare could have persuaded the organized manufacturers and the organized workers of an industry to sanction the use of strikes and lockouts as weapons of law enforcement. Nowhere else did the sponsors of the protocol movement more clearly reveal their dedication to the cause of controlling competition or acknowledge their faith in the machinery of collective bargaining. To give one faction of the industrial community the power to use force against another faction, in the name of law and order, was to invite a reign of lawlessness; yet no less drastic solution appeared adequate to maintain contract standards in the face of rising pressures to evade obligations jointly assumed by the organized forces of industry.

Fear of authorized strikes undoubtedly restrained many would-be transgressors and brought many a backsliding employer to his knees. It stimulated some employers' associations to encourage contract observance and prodded the impartial machinery to minimize the evils of "the law's delays." Opposed in principle, but endorsed in practice, the authorized strike became an enforcing arm of widespread application. Time and again, it kept wayward employers within the confines of the established order. Just as the community of nations would employ armies as instruments of international policy to help maintain international peace, so here the organized forces of industry would employ strikes as instruments of industrial policy to promote the general welfare of the trade.

---

[18]From the decision of Impartial Chairman N. I. Stone as reported in *Women's Wear Daily,* Nov. 17, 1930.

The 1946 collective agreement of the National Association of Ladies' Hatters with the United Hatters, Cap and Millinery Workers' International Union and the Joint Board of Millinery Workers' Unions expressly directed union members not to work on millinery products that did not bear the Consumers' Protection Label of the Millinery Stabilization Commission. The agreement also directed that employers be forced to pay for time the workers lost by refusing to work on nonlabeled goods.

At the same time, this key weapon for enforcing collective agreements became the greatest source of weakness in the protocol system. It tended to shift responsibility for contract observance from employers' associations to labor unions where this responsibility had resided before 1910. As authorized strikes became more and more prevalent, the organized manufacturers were less and less inclined to take the initiative in punishing their own members for failure to meet their commitments. They tended to shift blame upon the union for every breakdown in contract standards. They were content to reap the benefits of law and order without sharing the obligations. Each instance of passing the buck to the union increased the need for more strike action than might otherwise have been required.

More far-reaching was the influence of authorized strikes upon unauthorized strikes. Whereas outlawing all forms of direct action during the life of an agreement permitted the contracting parties to draw reasonably definable lines of distinction between legal and illegal conduct in the area of self-help, corresponding attempts to differentiate between "legal" and "illegal" strikes opened the door to a broad range of interpretations that tended to substitute force for the orderly processes of peaceful settlement. Moreover, the very act of striking to enforce collective agreements encouraged the organized workers to rely upon direct action for additional advantages not yet encompassed by existing agreements. Just as unlicensed wars have continued to be instruments of national policy, so unauthorized strikes have continued to be instruments of union policy.

Chapter 8

Unauthorized Strikes

O FFICIALLY endorsing the strike as a legitimate weapon of contract enforcement inevitably tended to undermine respect for law and order. Particularly in so far as the validity of strike action turned on fine distinctions between "clear" violations and "questionable" infractions of a contract did labor unions find an open door for blanket use of the strike power. In their zeal to protect contract standards, union agents often employed farfetched interpretations of their collective agreements to support charges of chiseling that appeared to them self-evident. Acting on premonitions and assumptions not borne out by the evidence, they sometimes called strikes that were in direct contravention of the no-strike clauses of their contracts. Or the organized workers at the shop level erroneously concluded that the terms of their contract had been broken and concertedly walked off the job.

Furthermore, union members steeped in the ways of direct action to preserve the legitimate objectives named in their contracts were often led to employ strikes for illegitimate objectives not named in their contracts. Multiple-employer bargaining, which subjected all association members to the same minimum labor standards, stimulated the workers in the more prosperous firms to seek further gains during the life of their agreements. Where companies were able to pay, additional gains could often be had for the asking. Once this procedure was begun, there was no logical point of termination. Few employers would endanger their immediate success by holding out for uniform standards in the face of strike action. Even the daily exercise of normal managerial prerogatives fell within the shadow of strike threats. If, as so often happened, threats alone were sufficient to bring the desired results, the workers were thereby encouraged to make still further use of direct action.

From these ventures in lawless conduct came the perennial cry of employers that unions through ignorance or neglect failed to enforce contract restrictions upon the right to strike. Herein lay the chief task that the impartial machinery undertook to perform on behalf of the organized manufacturers. In the absence of effective action by the union itself, how could the impartial machinery force union members to confine their strikes to the legitimate purposes set forth in collective agreements? This challenge brought sleepless nights to contract administrators from front-line clerks to permanent umpires. Too often the impartial machinery could not save the good ship, *Collective Bargaining*, from breaking up on the rocks of direct action.

Piercing the Ceiling over Competition

In its most aggravated form, the "illegal" strike became a weapon for improving conditions of employment during the life of an agreement. Generally initiated by small groups of organized workers, with or without the backing of their union, strikes to raise work standards threatened to break down the essential uniformity of labor costs among competing manufacturers. To be sure, where direct action was applied simultaneously in all plants embraced by a collective agreement, no serious harm could be inflicted upon the principle of uniform work standards. Although employers who looked to their contracts for estimating labor costs were quick to condemn the practice, they at least found some consolation in knowing that all competitors were subject to the same uncertainties. Moreover, if changes of general application were introduced only at specified time intervals, the employers might still retain a limited ability to predict labor costs in advance of production.

Far more often, however, the drive for better terms was confined to particular plants. Here the organized workers, building upon the foundations of the master agreement, created their own superstructure of employment standards, limited only by their ability to win further concessions from each employer. In presenting new demands, these worker groups respected no time intervals and held no scruples against coming back for more. To what end did the organized forces of labor and management establish a floor under competition if the ceiling over competition could be pierced by supplementary wage increases and better working conditions? Yet union pressure at the shop level often transformed association-wide plateaus of uniform labor standards into mountain ranges of towering peaks and deep ravines.[1]

Organized attempts at the plant level to raise the work standards of those already bound by a collective agreement were an evil inherited from union procedures developed before 1910. In the era of single shop bargaining, form contracts drafted at union headquarters were sent out to be signed by individual employers who had previously operated nonunion shops. In accepting these terms, the employers unwillingly opened their doors to further "rules and regulations" subsequently imposed by direction of union agents or by decree of the organized workers in the shops. Employers who failed to conform to these changing standards were threatened with strikes and picket lines that effectively closed their plants. More important than the original contracts were the conditions imposed under them.[2]

---

[1]No one condemned the use of direct action at the shop level to raise wages above contract standards more strongly than did J. A. Dyche who, as general secretary-treasurer of the ILGWU, participated in the protocol movement from its inception and then, after becoming a manufacturer, continued to support the theme that equality in labor costs must be the first objective of collective bargaining. "Just as the union must watch that the employer in a particular shop does not reduce the labor standards," Dyche wrote in 1926, "so must the [labor] organization be equally on the alert that the workers in a particular shop do not abuse the power of the organization, to raise wages above those agreed upon by the union and the employers in the industry." J. A. Dyche, *Bolshevism in American Labor Unions* (1926), p. 132.

[2]In a letter, dated June 11, 1914, to a New York arbitrator, the secretary of the Leopold Morse Company (Morse was a Boston manufacturer of men's clothing who had signed a labor agreement with the clothing workers' union) complained bitterly that his company was "subject to Union made rules that govern every phase of employment, division of labor, shop conditions, discharge of operatives and adjustment of disputes." Contrary to the terms of the labor agreement, the firm was compelled to recruit its labor from the union hiring hall and had lost the right to discharge altogether. "Last August," so the letter continued, "a vote by the Union Coat makers abolished piece work....this spring another Union vote abolished the so-called outside finish-

Although these practices violated every principle of law and order identified with the protocol movement, they were nevertheless carried over into many plants of association members bound by collective agreements after 1910. The protocol of the dress and waist industry, for example, was less than a year old when Walter H. Bartholomew, labor manager of the Dress and Waist Manufacturers' Association, charged the union with claiming rights in matters on which the protocol has nothing to say. "On this basis," Bartholomew stated, "the Union has repeatedly interfered with the internal administration of the shops of the manufacturers; has issued orders prohibiting the doing of certain things and has frequently required the manufacturer to grant concessions as to matters over which the union positively has no jurisdiction." Specifically, the union was charged with going beyond the collective agreement in:

1– forbidding piece workers to ring time clocks;

2– keeping employees from work on certain days;

3– prohibiting the introduction of a particular accounting system;

4– decreeing how work shall be divided among employees;

5– insisting upon the reinstatement of workers discharged for disobedience and impertinence;

6– preventing the transfer of employees within the shops;

7– substituting its own rules for the jointly accepted plan of adjusting piece rates;

8– nullifying decisions of the board of arbitration relating to legal holidays;

9– placing its own interpretations on the preferential union shop clause;

10– deciding what workers could be laid off during slack seasons;

11– denying an employer permission to change his work force when he changed the character of the products he was manufacturing.[3]

Meanwhile, the organized manufacturers in the women's coat and suit trade were likewise assailing the union practice of introducing new rules and putting them into effect during the life of a

---

ing of pants, a process identified with pants making in every city." Leon Strauss to Leo Mannheimer, letter, dated June 11, 1914, filed in the Abelson papers.

[3]*Minutes,* Arbitration Proceedings between the Dress and Waist Manufacturers' Association and the ILGWU (Nov. 8, 1913), pp. 38–39.

collective agreement. On one occasion, during conferences between the women's garment manufacturers and the garment workers' union to arrive at minimum hourly earnings for piece-rate workers, Abe Bisno, general manager of the Cloakmakers' Joint Board, overnight prepared and had published in the joint board's *New Post* a "manifesto" unilaterally decreeing the minimum hourly earnings for tailors, operators, and finishers working on piece rates. When the joint conference was reassembled, the manufacturers were up in arms. "Now how can we keep on discussing a situation when you have officially settled the matter for us," queried M. Silberman, president of the Cloak, Suit and Skirt Manufacturers' Protective Association, "...the Joint Board cannot pass rules and stuff it [*sic*] down our throats. If you want to enlarge the protocol, it cannot be done by you. It must be done by mutual consent."[4]

A month later, President Silberman renewed his attack on union practices. "This thing has been going on for six months," he announced indignantly. "The entire trouble is that the Board of Grievances issues rules but the executive board of the Union issues their rules. Now, if the executive board issues rules contrary to the rules of the Board, you can readily see where we get to." He continued:

We have been harassed almost daily by this set of rules. It is just the same as if New York or Massachusetts were to pass a law against the federal laws. Now, as we will know, that cannot be done. The same thing holds good here. Neither the Association nor the Unions can pass a law, or the rulings on a law against the law or rules laid down by the Board of Grievances. When the Board in executive session has decided certain cases, and in similar cases your clerks try to overthrow such rulings, it cannot be done.[5]

---

[4]*Minutes,* Meeting between Members of the Cloak, Suit and Skirt Manufacturers' Protective Association and Members of the Garment Workers' Union (Dec. 11, 1912), pp. 63, 69.

[5]*Minutes,* Board of Grievances, Cloak, Suit and Skirt Industry (Jan. 27, 1913), p. 9. See also, *Minutes,* Conference between the Cloak, Suit and Skirt Manufacturers' Protective Association and the Cloakmakers' Joint Board, ILGWU (Feb. 3, 1913), p. 42. At this session J. H. Cohen, counsel for the association, expressed similar views: "The Joint Board cannot pass rules and press them down our throats. If you want to enlarge the protocol you must do it in Conference. You cannot say that you have decided. You cannot decide anything." *Ibid.,* p. 18.

The employers were even more irritated when union agents attempted to enforce their one-way rules through the impartial machinery established by the protocols. When subjected to these regulations, the employers would ask: "Now, what has this case that has been decided against me got to do with the provisions of the Protocol?" Nor were they satisfied to be told that the enforcement of these rules was in the interest of the general welfare. "There came a time," noted W. H. Bartholomew, speaking for the manufacturers, "when there was a general impression in the minds of our people that this business had gone too far, that the Protocol and the Board of Grievances was [sic] being used as a shelf for the Union to stand on from which to reach another shelf a little higher up, and get something more than it had any right to."[6]

Strikes for New Concessions

Many union members never understood that collective bargaining on a multiple-employer scale had invalidated one-way union dictation in the shops. Or, if they understood, they obstinately refused to accept the new principle. The protocols, they insisted, were not havens of refuge from the storms of uncertainty, but points of departure along the road to higher ground. Nor would they, in seeking further improvements during the life of an agreement, be limited to changes introduced by mutual consent or authorized by the impartial machinery. Forms of direct action were often more effective than established procedures for raising employment standards at the shop level. Most workers would not

[6]*Minutes,* Arbitration Proceedings between the Dress and Waist Manufacturers' Association and the ILGWU (Nov. 9, 1913), pp. 355–356.

At times, union leaders complained of one-way company rules that supplemented the collective agreement affecting employer-employee relationships. The one-way rule that factory doors must be kept locked to prevent theft had led to the disastrous Triangle fire. "If a rule is objected to because it is unreasonable," contended Meyer London, counsel for the ILGWU, "there should be a discussion as to whether the rule is a reasonable one or not, and no employer should be permitted to adopt a rule which changes the relation between employer and employee, without discussing it with the Union. That is the very essence, the very substance of collective bargaining." *Minutes,* Arbitration Proceedings between the Dress and Waist Manufacturers' Association and the ILGWU (May 17, 1914), p. 20.

concede that the protocol movement had destroyed their sacred right to strike at any time for better terms of employment.

Yet the organized manufacturers ranked strike control at the very summit of all attempts to stabilize industry through collective action. Effective restraint upon the right to strike during the life of a contract was considered the key to any workable system of law and order in industry. In 1915, J. H. Cohen, father of the protocol movement, likened shop strikes to a cancer "eating its way into the very roots of collective bargaining." Year after year, a no-strike clause was among the top demands of the organized manufacturers at bargaining sessions. On a much later occasion, during the negotiation of a new agreement in fur manufacturing, the Associated Fur Coat and Trimming Manufacturers declared a no-strike clause to be "the only provision in the Agreement which gives any semblance of protection to the members of the Association."[7]

Moreover, no-strike clauses were the chief drawing cards for attracting outside firms into association membership. Independent employers came seeking refuge from direct action. For no jobber, contractor, or inside manufacturer could survive the perils of unlimited strikes so long as his organized competitors were shielded from all forms of direct action that undermined business stability and increased labor costs. During the life of a collective agreement, a ceiling over competition was as essential to the concept of law and order as was a floor under competition.

The task of preserving a ceiling over competition by keeping wages down offered many contrasts to the task of maintaining a floor under competition by keeping wages up. Whereas employer attempts to scuttle the floor under competition occurred most often in slack seasons and during periods of business depression, worker attempts to penetrate the ceiling over competition were more prevalent during rush seasons and in periods of business prosperity. While employers' associations were hardpressed to keep their members from lowering standards during the dark thirties, labor unions were equally pressed to keep their members from raising standards

---

[7]*Daily Trade Record,* Dec. 31, 1915; *Women's Wear,* Dec. 30, 1915; Associated Fur Coat and Trimming Manufacturers, "In the Matter of the Union's Proposals of Additions and Modifications of the Present Existing Collective Labor Agreement," a typewritten submission of the association, dated Jan. 5, 1938. Copy filed in the Abelson papers.

during the roaring twenties. Just as union members in times of depression were sometimes guilty of collusion with employers to lower wages (a method of stealing jobs from fellow workers) so employers in prosperous times were often guilty of collusion with union members to raise wages (a method of stealing workers from fellow competitors).

In periods of business prosperity, shop strikes to raise wages shattered all attempts at stabilizing labor costs during the life of an agreement. Even if unsuccessful, these strikes interrupted production and so raised the costs of manufacturing. Shortly after the First World War, for example, there were so many shop strikes for wage increases in the men's clothing industry of New York City that manufacturing costs for the New York market went up and and up, until they were estimated to exceed those of other principal markets by 50 percent.[8]

In the fur manufacturing trade, shop strikes to raise wages were so numerous during the twenties as to endanger the very principle of collective action. Year after year, employers bombarded their association and the impartial machinery of their industry with complaints of work stoppages in their plants. A report of the Associated Fur Manufacturers for 1925 attributed most of the fifty-eight strikes occurring in the industry that year to group action at the shop level for wage increases. And, in 1929, all of the six strikes in the industry were attributed to that cause. Even worse was the plight of the New York dress manufacturers. "It is an outstanding fact," proclaimed the Dress and Waist Manufacturers'

---

[8]The adverse effects of shop strikes on uniform labor costs were discussed by William Bandler, president of the New York Clothing Manufacturers' Association, in a letter appearing in the *New Republic,* Jan. 12, 1921, vol. 25, p. 201. The letter was in reply to an editorial, "War in the Clothing Industry," that had appeared in *ibid.,* Dec. 15, 1920, vol. 25, p. 59. The issue of Jan. 12, 1921 also contained a lengthy comment on Bandler's letter by Felix Frankfurter, who attributed the outburst of shop strikes and individual "laydowns" to economic prosperity which had led manufacturers into competitive bidding for labor, with the result that the workers were offered voluntary wage increases even in the face of official union resistance to wage increases above the negotiated contract levels.

See also, *Minutes* of the Board of Grievances of the women's coat and suit trade (March 4, 1915), for 144 pages of discussion on the Gershel Co. case involving a strike for more pay by the firm's employees during the life of a labor agreement.

Association in a public statement on wildcat strikes, "that within the last six months there have been over 200 stoppages of work in the factories of the members of the association."[9]

Within several different branches of the needle trades, shop strikes for higher wages often accompanied the fixing of piece rates for new styles and variations in garments. Problems of this character were continually arising wherever payment by results prevailed. Union members sometimes refused to work on settled numbers because they felt the price was too low; or else they participated in production slowdowns until they had won their demands. On many occasions, workers resorted to direct action without waiting for the impartial machinery to determine piece rates. "It has come to be a matter of dread," declared the dress and waist manufacturers in January 1916, "to go through the beginning of a season, when in the course of the settlement of prices, the stoppage of work is resorted to as freely as though the protocol did not exist, and as though there were no agreement to continue working on garments, although prices were disputed."[10]

To what avail would the Dress and Waist Manufacturers' Association of Philadelphia seek to guarantee its member firms an element of stability in labor costs through collective bargaining with the dressmakers' union on piece rates, if subsequent demands of the workers, backed by unpredictable strike action, nullified the concerted efforts of individual employers, shop price committees, union business agents, and association officials? Yet, noted Samuel Schlein, adjuster and manager of this association, not only had the workers jumped at every pretense of an excuse to demand higher rates, including buyers' reorders for more dresses of a particular style, but piece-rate settlements made over the preceding months, he said, "have frequently been repudiated within 24 hours, necessitating two or three resettlements before a satisfactory adjustment could be made."[11]

---

[9]*Women's Wear*, Dec. 20, 1920. On the fur industry, see "Report of the Labor Department," Associated Fur Manufacturers, in a letter, dated Jan. 12, 1926, to S. N. Samuels, chairman of the board of directors of this association; and a similar report, dated March 26, 1930, covering the year 1929. Copies are filed in the Abelson papers.

[10]*Women's Wear*, Jan. 19, 1916.

[11]*Ibid.*, Dec. 31, 1919.

Many of these strikes had the sanction of local unions, and some of them were clearly instigated by union officials. "As a general rule," explained Boris Maruchess, labor manager of the Dress and Waist Manufacturers' Association, in February 1920, "what happens in these cases is that workers in individual shops are advised 'on a quiet' to take the law into their own hands." At such times, he pointed out, union clerks never "put in their appearance at the offices of the association for the purpose of going out with our clerks to adjust disputes." Yet, he noted that these union clerks had recently approached at least fifteen members of the employers' association demanding wage increases for the workers. "When, as in the great majority of cases, members of our association refused to discuss matters with the union representatives and pointed out to them that the agreement was being violated," added Mr. Maruchess, ". . . the usual reply was a threat to call out the workers, unless the matter was taken up immediately."[12]

Presumably, any local union officials found to be instigating shop strikes for better terms of employment would be strongly denounced by their parent international unions, if not removed from their positions of authority and forever banned from union membership. Certainly, if the orderly processes of industrial self-government were to survive, the organized manufacturers had a right to expect as much. Yet there were cases in which the frayed bonds that held together a tottering realm of law and order were subject to even greater strains. For, on occasion, the officials of

---

[12]*Ibid.*, Feb. 26, 1920. Similar complaints of union connivance in shop strikes for wage increases came from the fur manufacturing trade. One such complaint turned up in a letter dated Jan. 21, 1920 from D. C. Mills, labor manager of the Associated Fur Manufacturers, to J. L. Magnes, head of Kehillah, and impartial chairman under the industry's collective agreement:

> I regret very much that Mr. Kaufman and his associates in the [Fur Workers'] Union are doing absolutely nothing to return the people, inform us that they cannot get hold of the workers, and otherwise evade the issue entirely. In some instances we understand that the workers have refused to return informing the employers that their orders to strike are direct from the Union. In one case in particular three shop meetings were held in succession, the first being attended by one union official and two "strangers," the second being attended only by the two "strangers," at the third the two "strangers" order the people to go on strike.
> —*Minutes,* Conference Committee of the Fur Manufacturing Industry, Jan. 23, 1920.

union joint boards and the leadership of international unions themselves defended on principle the right of union members at the local shop level to strike for higher wages during the life of collective agreements.

Such an instance arose immediately after the First World War, when the employers' association and the labor union that had been parties to the original Protocol of Peace came face to face on this issue. "Notwithstanding the fact that our [1919] agreement is barely six months old and that it expressly prohibits stoppages of work and strikes," wrote the Cloak, Suit and Skirt Manufacturers' Protective Association to the Cloakmakers' Joint Board, ILGWU, "yet there are at the present time 28 strikes in the shops of members of the association (some of which are more than two weeks old), and you have failed to respond to our repeated demands to return the men to work in accordance with the terms of our agreement." The reaction of the Cloakmakers' Joint Board and of an international vice-president to this charge (as reported in *Women's Wear*, December 31, 1919) must have confounded the most ardent supporters of collective bargaining as a means for controlling unlicensed competition:

The Joint Board, it was learned, will again attempt to justify its position of failing to recognize the present shop strikes as violations of the agreement on the ground that the terms and stipulation of the pact does [sic] not prohibit any worker or set of workers from demanding more pay. Then, again, the Protective Association will be told, it was said, that the union is willing to comply with the specific term of the agreement provided that it does not interfere with the union's right to demand more than the minimum set forth.

Morris Sigman, manager of the Joint Board [and vice-president of the ILGWU], when asked this morning what the union intends to do next said: "...The Joint Board does not know of any strikes. The workers, in the cases where they may have left their shops, have done so not because they were ordered by the union to strike, but because they were dissatisfied with the pay they were receiving and unless the manufacturer is willing to meet the workers' demands, the union is powerless to act."

Against this background, the task of containing shop groups of organized employees within the four walls of the collective agreement sometimes overwhelmed the supporters of the protocol movement and sorely taxed the power of the impartial machinery to maintain law and order. Unless expressly authorized, shop bargaining for higher wages was outlawed by the very nature and function of collective action. Leaving nothing to implication, however, many agreements specifically prohibited group bargaining at the shop level for better terms of employment. "There shall be no collective bargaining over and above the minimum scale," runs the pertinent clause in collective agreements of the fur manufacturing industry. While an individual worker might approach his employer for a raise in pay above the contract scale, group negotiations through a committee of the workers was strictly forbidden. Directly or indirectly, all strikes to raise wages or otherwise to improve conditions of employment during the life of an agreement were clearly outlawed.

Union Efforts to Control Shop Strikes

As responsible parties to collective agreements, the unions themselves should have solved the problem of shop strikes by their own members. This, indeed, was a basic assumption upon which the protocol movement had been founded. No impartial machinery was required to determine guilt or inflict punishment for unauthorized use of direct action so long as organized labor was able to maintain discipline within its own ranks. Admittedly, the task of the union leadership was complicated by the heritage and temperament of the Jewish people. The basic concepts of discipline had to be instilled into hordes of immigrants nurtured in political revolution and imbued with hatred for political authority. The mental approach of the worker toward organized society somehow had to be altered. This was primarily a responsibility of the union.

But the gap between the enlightened union leadership and the rank and file of union members was too vast to be closed overnight. For years, the impotence of unions to control shop strikes was evident in strike statistics and the outcries of strike victims. During 1915, for example, J. H. Cohen, counsel for the Dress and Waist Manufacturers, noted that exactly 141 strikes had been called against the 211 members of his association. And, in the following year, *Women's Wear* reported the near death of the dress and waist protocol from strike disease: "There are very few plants in which some workers do not take it upon themselves to run things as they see fit. To refuse to work is a common occurrence, the people laughing when the employer threatens to discharge them."[13]

Labor unions in the needle trades did assume a measure of responsibility for instilling their workers with a respect for law and order. From the inception of the protocol movement, the International Ladies' Garment Workers' Union undertook to train and educate its members against lawless conduct. "In the agreement, the Union is in duty bound not to make any stoppages," runs an official union notice to the membership, signed by ILGWU officials and appearing in the *New Post,* organ of the Cloakmakers' Joint Board, October 19, 1912. "No member has a right to use the might of a strike without asking the Union whether the power of might shall be used. . . . The workingmen who belong to the Union and who enjoy its privileges and its protection, must once and for all be imbued with the idea that, to belong to a Union, means that one must obey the rules of the Union."[14]

These admonitions were backed by threats directed to the disobedient. "Against those members who break the discipline of the Union," continued this notice to the members, "the Union will have to take severe measures. . . . It must, therefore, be clear to every member of the Union that, in such cases where there is a question of the breaking of discipline, and in cases of unjustified stoppages of work, the Union will have to act with the greatest possible strictness." Further to stress the importance of respect for law and order, the ILGWU wrote into its constitution the penalties that might be anticipated from lawless conduct by its members. In 1914, J. A. Dyche, general secretary-treasurer of the Union, told of how he would take a copy of the union constitution out to the shops and read to the workers from bold letters printed on the first page that "no member is allowed to stop from work, or come out on strike, without the order of the union, for such illegal strike is a violation of the union rules, and such member will be fined or expelled."[15]

[13]*Daily Trade Record,* Dec. 31, 1915; *Women's Wear,* May 22, 1916.

[14]Translation filed in the Abelson papers.

[15]J. A. Dyche, testimony on Jan. 17, 1914, before the U.S. Commission on Industrial Relations, in the Commission's *Final Report and Testimony* (1916), vol. 2, p. 1123. An example of Dyche's method is reported in Hyman Berman, "The Era of the Protocols . . . 1910–1916" (unpublished Ph.D. dissertation, Columbia University, 1956), p. 287.

The constructive leaders of other needle trade unions also worked to develop a rank-and-file loyalty to the principles of the protocol movement. They, too, vigorously opposed illegal shop bargaining that disrupted uniform labor standards at the industry level by fostering strike action at the plant level. "For the sake of uniformity, for the sake of eliminating competition of one worker against the other, we deal collectively with the manufacturers," explained Max Zaritsky, president of the United Cloth Hat and Cap Makers, at the 1919 union convention. ". . . For if you deal individually, separately, you must have chaos, you must have anarchy." Zaritsky further stressed the consequences of dealing with employers individually: "Shall we have guerilla warfare?" he asked. "Shall we have an individual system by which every individual worker, or every individual group, or every individual shop, shall deal with his, or its own employer, and leave it to the survival of the fittest?"[16]

Union Participation in Shop Strikes

Attempts to maintain discipline within the ranks were sometimes directed against local union officials and on occasion against local unions themselves. "We demand of our loyal, honest members not to obey the command of your shop chairmen, who tell you to get up from your work and go down on strike (for a short or long period) without an order of an official of the Joint Board," stated

---

Some success must have followed union efforts to maintain discipline in the first years of the protocol movement, for a union spokesman stated in 1913 that the 250 association members under the collective agreement of the women's coat and suit trade had suffered only nine strikes in two seasons, whereas independent shops had been subject to many more strikes. *Jewish Daily Forward,* June 21, 1913. Translation filed in the Abelson papers.

In 1916, Morris Hillquit, counsel for the ILGWU, agreed to publicize in the union newspaper that union members striking in violation of their labor agreement or in contravention of arbitration awards would be subject to expulsion from the union, if the Dress and Waist Manufacturers' Association would take similar action against member firms declaring lockouts. Samuel Floersheimer, president of the association, gladly accepted: "Our association has always stood ready to expel members who failed to live up to their obligations." *Women's Wear,* April 3, 1916.

[16]United Cloth Hat and Cap Makers of North America, *Report and Proceedings,* Twelfth Biennial Convention (May 1919), pp. 157–158 (printed in the June 1919 issue of the *Headgear Worker*).

the message of October 19, 1912, from officers of the Cloakmakers' Joint Board and the ILGWU to the union membership. "The prime duty that a member of our Union must fulfill is, not to *his shop,* but to the *Union.*"[17]

During the first years of the protocol movement, when Local 38, ILGWU, persisted in striking to gain its objectives — despite official condemnation of its action by the impartial machinery for the womens' coat and suit industry — the international union revoked the local's charter and then reported to the union convention of 1912, as follows: "Not until the rank and file of the former Local No. 38 will become convinced that no organization can be under the jurisdiction of the International Union that is not willing, or that cannot maintain discipline in its ranks and make its members live up to the fundamental principles of unionism, can a change for the better take place. . . . The present dispute of former Local No. 38 is practically a fight between the General Executive Board [of the international union] and its conception of unionism and that of the Executive Board of Local No. 38, and its ideas of conducting a Union on a system of 'direct action.' "[18]

No one within the union movement fought the shop strike for higher wages more vigorously than did Sidney Hillman, president of the Amalgamated Clothing Workers. But, when economic conditions favored the prospects of higher pay, the task of unions in controlling these strikes was often aggravated by employers who deliberately bid up wages in a competitive orgy of labor-pirating among themselves. Moreover, union leaders found all attempts at suppressing shop strikes for higher wages so unpopular in prosperous times that the initiative toward effective control had to be taken by the impartial machinery itself. Whatever part the union was to play in strike control had to be done largely by direction

---

[17]*New Post,* Oct. 19, 1912. The article was signed by J. Halprin, president of the Cloakmakers' Joint Board; M. Perlstein, secretary of the joint board; A. Rosenberg, president of the ILGWU, and J. A. Dyche, general secretary-treasurer of the ILGWU. Translation filed in the Abelson papers.

[18]ILGWU, *Report and Proceedings,* Eleventh Convention (June 1912), pp. 31–32. The quotation was later repeated by J. H. Cohen, counsel for the manufacturers' association, in his attack on the breakdown of union discipline. *Minutes,* Board of Arbitrators. . . [women's coat and suit industry] (Oct. 4, 1913), p. 97. An extended account of this conflict is given in Berman, "The Era of the Protocols. . . 1910–1916," pp. 223–267.

of the permanent institutions established for the general welfare of the industry.

When acting on behalf of the impartial machinery, however, a labor union was no less in need of effective control over its membership. A union that was too weak to maintain discipline on its own initiative never became a reliable agency of the impartial machinery for contract enforcement. There was no magic in having a joint conference committee rather than the union itself declare that "in case workers in a shop should, contrary to the terms of the Agreement and this Memorandum, undertake collectively to secure raises in wages over the minimum by concerted action through stoppages of work, they shall be deemed to have violated the terms of the Agreement and are subject to discipline." Nor was the problem of internal union control solved by adding that "in case of necessity, the Union undertakes to announce in the press that a strike or stoppage of work of the kind described is not authorized by the Union and the union men may work in such place."

Getting people to participate in the business of self-government through the union, observed J. E. Williams, first chairman for the committee on immediate action established under the original Protocol of Peace, is the most important step in educating union members on the virtues of self-discipline. In his testimony before the U. S. Commission on Industrial Relations, April 9, 1914, Williams asserted that union leaders were often confronted with a membership possessed of "too much individualism, and perhaps too much ignorance and lack of training and lack of knowledge." He insisted that a union leader must be something more than a man at the head of a lot of undisciplined guerrillas. As an agent of the impartial machinery, a union leader must be able to act through channels of centralized control. "If you give him a strong union," added Williams, "he can always bring the small group to terms."[19]

---

[19]U.S. Commission on Industrial Relations, *Final Report and Testimony* (1916), vol. 1, p. 700.

I recall very distinctly that the first thing that happened in the cloak industry in 1911 was this matter of the stoppages of work. At that time, Mr. Hillquit was on the Board of Arbitration, and we sought to meet that situation by providing severe penalties for those who went out on strikes

Accepting the virtues of centralized control, industry arbitrators invariably looked to the international unions and their joint boards for supervising the conduct of local union officials and their members. During the early years of the protocol movement, many disputes arose over the division of responsibility within unions for the enforcement of contracts. In some cases, grave doubts existed as to whether the local union, the union joint board, the international union, or some combination of the three had, in fact, become the responsible party to a collective agreement. The original dress and waist protocol was only months old when the Dress and Waist Manufacturers' Association charged the ILGWU with repudiating its obligations by treating the agreement as one between the association and Local 25 (the Ladies' Dress and Waist Makers' Local).[20]

In all such controversies, the impartial machinery assumed that international unions and their joint boards would guarantee the enforcement of contracts. As chairman of the board of arbitration under the original women's coat and suit protocol, Brandeis himself took the position that the international union and the Cloakmakers' Joint Board were both responsible for enforcing the pro-

---

without the orders of their Union. Naturally it is the most difficult thing in the world for a Union to enforce a penalty against any of its members. It requires a tremendous amount of education to convince working people that they have surrendered the right to strike or call a shop strike in order that they may get in place of it the rational method.

　—J. H. Cohen in *Minutes,* Arbitration Proceedings between the Dress and Waist Manufacturers' Association and the ILGWU (March 31, 1916), vol. 6, pp. 1488–1489.

[20]When we got the signatures of the International's officers, we were content, and we relied upon it, and we have done business. We have known the difficulties of signing agreements with locals, and we have avoided them by signing with the International.

　—J. H. Cohen, counsel for several manufacturers' associations, in *Minutes,* Arbitration Proceedings between the Dress and Waist Manufacturers' Association and the ILGWU (May 17, 1914), p. 177.

On the responsibility of the ILGWU and its joint boards for the sanctity of contracts, see J. H. Cohen's testimony before the U.S. Commission on Industrial Relations, Jan. 17, 1914, *Final Report and Testimony,* vol. 2, pp. 1124–1126; Berman, "The Era of the Protocols...1910–1916," pp. 223–267, 295–300, 330–333.

tocol. "They stand, for all practical purposes, exactly in the same relation as if they had been partners in entering into this agreement," he said. Brandeis rejected the contention of ILGWU President A. Rosenberg that the international union fulfilled its mission by advising its locals on problems of contract enforcement. "The International cannot discharge itself of [its] obligation in the matter," concluded Brandeis, "by simply saying 'we give advice and the advice is not taken.' "[21]

The Impartial Machinery and Shop Strikes

Where appeals for restraint by the union leadership failed to suppress shop strikes, the impartial machinery was left to devise measures of its own for limiting strike action to its officially assigned role. These devices ran the gamut of possibilities from peaceful persuasion, on the one hand, to discharge from the job and expulsion from the union, on the other. By whatever means at their command, industry arbitrators repeatedly sought to convince union members that unauthorized strikes would break down their own organizations as well as the institutions of collective bargaining.

---

[21]*Minutes,* Board of Arbitrators...[women's coat and suit trade] (Oct. 4, 1913), pp. 102–103. This was the second rebuke in 1913 that the board of arbitration had given the ILGWU for failure to see that the Cloakmakers' Joint Board and its union locals observed the no-strike clauses of their collective agreements with the Cloak, Suit and Skirt Manufacturers' Protective Association. J. H. Cohen, *Law and Order in Industry* (1916), pp. 108–109.

Most of the major collective agreements in the needle trades of New York City have been signed on behalf of the workers by representatives of international unions and by representatives of the appropriate joint boards comprising a number of local unions covered by the agreement. Samuel Gompers, president of the American Federation of Labor, himself signed the second protocol — that of the dress and waist industry — stating over his signature that "the American Federation of Labor will stand back of the International Ladies' Garment Workers' Union in the faithful performance of the foregoing protocol."

There were strong historical precedents from labor unions outside the needle trades for the position that international unions should undertake to control forms of radicalism and direct action within their rebellious locals. For a study of the means by which these centralized controls were exercised, see George M. Janes, "The Trend of Voluntary Conciliation and Arbitration in Labor Disputes," in *Annals,* American Academy of Political and Social Science, January 1917, vol. 69, pp. 173–182.

"I am immeasurably mortified to learn that the operators have not returned to work so far," wrote J. L. Magnes, impartial chairman of the fur manufacturing industry, during a strike in May 1919 for higher wages at the shop of A. Weckstein & Sons. "Words cannot express my disappointment at this lawless notion of some workers in the Union who want to be a law unto themselves contrary to the rights of the other workers in the shop, to the orders of the Union officials and to the sacred pledges of a collective agreement. . . . A Union cannot expect to have the support of public opinion and of those who sympathize with the cause of labor if fair agreements made are not solemnly lived up with."[22]

"A stoppage is an illegal strike and undermines the authority and prestige of the union," wrote Henry Moskowitz in his first award as impartial chairman for the fancy leather goods industry. ". . . The chairman calls upon the Union to take steps to impress its members with the seriousness of stoppages, showing that a stoppage has all the weakness of mob rule and lacks all the strength of organized and disciplined Union activity. The Union should stress the futility of direct action by a group of workers, because it defeats its own ends and the importance of respecting the orderly processes provided in the agreement by the impartial machinery for the redress of workers' grievances."[23]

Far more important than such exhortations to the wayward, however, was the elementary rule, widely adopted by arbitrators and boards of grievances in the needle trades, that the merits of particular disputes behind unauthorized shop walkouts would in no case be discussed until the strikers had returned to their jobs. This rule appears to have been inspired by the practice of fixing piece rates at the shop level where shop workers soon learned that an ounce of force was worth a pound of logic. Why argue over every revision of piece rates to compensate for every change of design, fabric, or method of production when walking off the job was sure to win the point? "There is a veritable hell in the factory every time a price is to be set for a garment," lamented J. H. Cohen, chief disciple of law and order in industry. To meet these interminable insurrections, the board of grievances for the women's

---

[22]J. L. Magnes to M. Kaufman, manager, Furriers' Joint Board. Letter, dated May 23, 1919, filed in the Abelson papers.

[23]Henry Moskowitz, *Decisions,* Case no. 1A (Dec. 16, 1929).

coat and suit trade ruled that piece rates could not be settled until the workers returned to their jobs.[24]

As an additional incentive for returning to work immediately, the strikers were granted the concession of having the complaints that triggered their strike receive top priority on the complaint calendar setting forth the order of business to be transacted by the appropriate agency of the impartial machinery. Union members returning to work were thus assured of a hearing without delay on the fundamental issues underlying their strike. Thus, by the simple expedient of walking off the job and back on again, workers could bring up for immediate action all grievances that were considered critical enough to justify a temporary walkout. Whatever the opportunities for misuse of this procedure, restoring the status quo as a condition of obtaining justice was still considered preferable to having fundamental issues determined under a sword of Damocles held aloft by striking employees.

So generally accepted was this rule of the impartial machinery, requiring strikers to get back to work before the resolution of their grievances, that several years apparently were to elapse before the merits of this procedure were seriously questioned in hearings of any board of arbitration representing the highest authority of industrial self-government. When the pros and cons of this issue did come up for extensive debate in arbitration proceedings for the dress and waist industry during the spring of 1916, J. H. Cohen, legal counsel, stated the case for his client, the Dress and Waist Manufacturers' Association:

The principle as it was originally established in the rules of the Board of Grievances under the cloak protocol provided that there could be no discussion, no consideration by the clerks, of a grievance, until the law was obeyed. And the union representatives in the case of a shop strike were charged with the duty of saying to the workers, "We can do nothing for you until you have returned to your places. No grievance under the rules can be taken up until you have returned to work."...What we do object to is that the representative of the Union shall come to us and say "Before we get the people to work you must promise so and so." And so our experience teaches us that the

---

[24]*Minutes,* Conference between the Cloak, Suit and Skirt Manufacturers' Protective Association and the ILGWU and the Cloakmakers' Joint Board (Feb. 3, 1913), pp. 20–21.

moment we endure that practice, even for an instant, it creates this impression in the minds of the workers: "We can get what we want a great deal easier if we go on strike than if we do not."...We want to put the Union representative clearly in the position of being obliged to say to the people, "I can't even get the justice to which you are entitled until I come into court with clean hands. I have first got to see you go back to your places."[25]

Cohen received vigorous support from management's chosen operatives in the front-line trenches of industrial conflict. Mrs. Henry Moskowitz, chief clerk for the manufacturers, could see no other course than that which Cohen had outlined. Entertaining any discussion of the issues while the workers were on strike would defeat the purpose of keeping the peace during the life of collective agreements. "We find that this process of listening to grievances may last two or three days," she said. "I want it distinctly understood that when stoppages occur I am not compelled to give the Union something in order to get them to tell the people to go back to work."[26]

The occasion for these extended debates was a consideration of two dress protocol amendments covering procedures to be followed in getting unauthorized strikers back to work. The Dress and Waist Manufacturers' Association had proposed that "no grievance of any kind or character shall be taken up, either by the clerks or the Committee on Immediate Action, until the people have been returned to work;" while the ILGWU had offered an alternative amendment stating that "no grievance of any kind shall be adjusted by the clerks until the work has been resumed." The fine distinction between these two very similar propositions immediately

---

[25]*Minutes,* Arbitration Proceedings between the Dress and Waist Manufacturers' Association and the ILGWU (March 31, 1916), vol. 6, pp. 1506–1507. He also objected to the "priority of complaint settlement" rule:

> Now you are a worker. You are in Shop "X". You come into contact with workers in shop "Y". You find that the workers in shop Y went on strike, and that by the shop strike their grievances were taken up and adjusted before the workers who were peaceably in their shop could get their grievances adjusted. You are putting a premium upon the lawless and disorderly way of doing business.
> —J. H. Cohen in *ibid.,* p. 1510.

[26]*Ibid.,* p. 1505.

caught the eye of Judge J. W. Mack, chairman of the board of arbitration:

> Their [the union's] wording says it shall not be adjusted. Yours [the association's] says it shall not be "taken up." In other words, if I catch any distinction between "taken up" and "adjusted" it would mean that "taken up" means that you should not listen to any grievance and that they shall be immediately ordered back to work and go back to work, and not another word shall be said. That it "shall [not] be adjusted" means that you may listen to their grievances but that you shall not attempt to settle their grievances until they have come back to work.[27]

The difference between "taking up" the issues leading to a strike and, officially, "adjusting" the disputes while the workers were still out was held to be fundamental. Although spokesmen for the ILGWU accepted the general principle that no grievance of any kind shall be "adjusted" during a strike, union leaders insisted upon the right to explore informally the causes of a walkout as a means of getting the strikers back on the job. Thus, union clerks proceeding to the scene of a shop strike, so Morris Hillquit, counsel for the ILGWU, contended, should have an opportunity "to discuss the proposition itself, to mollify the parties, and then to return them to work." To deny all opportunity for discussion with the strikers might accentuate, rather than allay, friction:

> No matter how high the feelings run, a shop strike may be caused by something trivial. The Union representative takes up the question with the workers. "Why are you out on strike? You know that it is contrary to the protocol provisions." Well, they will tell him their story with indignation. It will perhaps appear that it is based on misunderstanding, or something or other. Our clerk turns to the clerk of the Association and says "These people believe so and so." Well, they have no case. They consult with the employer and clear out the misunderstanding, and they go back to work. Under this provision as worded here all that would be precluded. What we used to call in the olden times the good offices of the clerks which means the mediative services and functions, and which goes to the very soul of the agreement, would be absolutely discarded.[28]

---

[27] *Loc. cit.*

[28] *Ibid.*, pp. 1503–1504, 1508–1509. "To say to the people who are in a highly excitable condition...'Shut up and go back to work, and don't tell us any of

Not only did the union win its procedural point of "discussing" issues with the strikers, but it ultimately rescinded its more basic concession that work must be resumed before disputes could be "adjusted." Unhappily for the cause of orderly self-government, the sound principle established under the first protocols that grievances could not be resolved while workers were on strike sooner or later gave way to the practical necessity of getting out production for highly seasonal markets at any price. Faced with immediate disaster, employers bowed to worker demands for a satisfactory settlement of their grievances as a condition of returning to work. Efforts to maintain law and order had to be redirected toward punishing wildcat strikers who remained off the job and defied the authority of their industry tribunals. The rules of the protocols provided that manufacturers could file separate complaints of illegal strikes and that hearings on those charges would take precedence over all other types of complaints. The presence of the striking workers or of their spokesman at the hearings was not essential to the determination of guilt or to the infliction of punishment.

Formalized Controls over Shop Strikes

The more formalized procedures for handling unauthorized shop strikes — procedures that were outlined in collective agreements and amplified by the rules of administrative agencies — were likely to embrace most, if not all, of the following steps:

1– Immediately after the outbreak of the strike, the victimized employer reported the walkout to his association and insisted that the workers be returned to their jobs.

2– The employers' association informally conveyed this information

---

your troubles at all' seems to me to be based on a very false psychology." Judge J. W. Mack, chairman, board of arbitration, *ibid.*, pp. 1505–1506.

Mr. Polakoff [union representative] tells me of an occurrence in one of the shops where, when he came in in an effort to find out the situation and to adjust it, the employer pulled out his watch and said, "You have five minutes to return the workers to work." Sometimes it may happen that within the five minutes they may be returned. Sometimes it may happen, if our time is limited to five minutes, and the employer stands with his watch in his hand, it will result in an absolute break, although if we had fifteen minutes perhaps we could induce the workers to return.
—Hillquit in *ibid.*, pp. 1514–1515.

to the union (usually the manager of the union joint board) with a request for immediate action; and at the same time formally reported the contract infraction to the headquarters of the impartial machinery.

3— The permanent umpire or impartial chairman for the industry informally urged the union to restore the status quo so that the dispute causing the strike could be settled on its merits; and at the same time formally called upon his clerks to see that the workers returned to their jobs.

4— A continuation of the strike, despite the efforts of the clerks, led to a trial of the workers before the board of grievances or the impartial chairman on charges of failing to observe the no-strike clause and of refusing to obey orders of the clerks to resume work.

5— Upon conviction, the strikers who still remained off the job were subject to appropriate penalties.[29]

Neither the elaborate machinery for settling disputes nor the initial emphasis on informal settlement prevented strike cases from running the gamut of grievance procedure without reaching a satisfactory solution. The disrespect for established authority inherent in direct action made it highly unlikely that strike cases would be resolved informally during the course of formal deliberations. More likely than not, the cessation of unauthorized strikes had to await the imposition of sanctions or, at least, the threat of sanctions. After agencies of the impartial machinery had found the participants guilty of lawless conduct and had directed the strikers to return to their jobs, little more could be done in the face of continued disobedience, short of punitive action against the strikers or against the union that failed to control them.

Imposing effective sanctions upon groups of striking workers was no easy task. Yet policies and practices directed to this end gradually evolved through a number of experimental stages. Just as industry arbitrators preferred that employers' associations force their rebellious firms to comply with contracts and with arbitration

---

[29] The 1921 collective agreement of the Clothing Manufacturers' Association of New York with the New York Joint Board of the Amalgamated Clothing Workers' Union — a contract that prohibited all forms of strikes during the life of the agreement — stated: "If any stoppage should occur, a deputy from each side shall attend at the shop or shops in question. It shall be the duty of the deputy, if it be found that the employees stopped work, to order them to immediately return to their work." Text of the agreement is printed in *Daily News Record,* June 3, 1921.

awards, so the impartial machinery likewise preferred that labor unions take whatever punitive action became necessary to coerce their striking members into resuming their duties. Turning obstinate strikers over to their union for disciplinary action was the procedure outlined by the founders of the protocol movement. The official rules and plan of procedure adopted in the spring of 1911 by the impartial machinery of the women's coat and suit trade under the original Protocol of Peace stated that a violation of the no-strike clause would "constitute a grievance to be presented to the Board of Grievances." Then, if the board after a hearing found the defendants guilty as charged, the order of the board was to be "made the basis of prompt discipline" by the union. The rules stated further that "the action so taken shall forthwith be reported in writing to the Board of Grievance."[30]

Thirty-five years later, this industry was still wrestling with the problem of how to induce a union to carry out such a mandate under collective agreements. In the summer of 1946, Impartial Chairman Charles Poletti was presented with several cases involving strikes against certain association firms to improve the terms of employment during the life of the 1943–1948 collective agreement between the Industrial Council of Cloak, Suit and Skirt Manufacturers and the Cloakmakers' Joint Board, ILGWU. The association asked the impartial chairman to direct the union to impose specific penalties to end the walkouts. Poletti refused to dictate the means but insisted upon the principle of union responsibility:

Under the collective agreements, the union has obligated itself in good faith that all of its members will live up to their provisions. If the workers do not return to work as ordered, the union must undertake to find the means by which it will compel them to comply with the collective agreements and the award. The union has a real responsibility in securing compliance. The chairman refrains from prescribing the particular method which the union shall use to meet its responsibility. By taking adequate disciplinary action against its

---

[30]This rule, no. 18, applied to employers charged with lockouts, as well as to unions charged with strikes. These rules may be conveniently found in C. H. Winslow, *Conciliation, Arbitration, and Sanitation in the Cloak, Suit, and Skirt Industry in New York City,* U.S. Department of Commerce and Labor, Bureau of Labor, Bulletin no. 98 (January 1912), p. 222.

members who have in concert with others caused stoppages of work in violation of the award or who may do so in other similar cases or by refusing to grant them working cards directed to other union shops or by adopting some other effective measures, the union would show the kind of good faith to which it obligated itself under the collective agreements.[31]

The impartial machinery was more likely to receive support from the international unions and union joint boards, where local strikers walked off their jobs in direct opposition to the local union leadership. Whenever union discipline within the shop was clearly at stake, the entire union organization usually stood behind the orders of the impartial machinery. And respect for local union authority was clearly at stake when, as so often happened, striking employees returned to work upon the arrival of a union official, only to walk off the job again as soon as the union official left the shop. If official union efforts at returning the men were not always successful in such cases, the union had at least met the initial step toward ending the walkout.

A good example of cooperation from the higher union leadership occurred in fur manufacturing shortly after the First World War. In the spring of 1919, the clerks of the impartial machinery for the fur manufacturing industry failed to suppress a wildcat strike for higher wages by certain operators of A. Weckstein & Sons. Thereupon, Impartial Chairman J. L. Magnes wrote M. Kaufman, manager of the Furriers' Joint Board, in part as follows:

But whatever may be the reason for the stoppage of work I must insist as Chairman of the Conference Committee and by virtue of the authority vested in me under Article 23 of the agreement that the people return to work immediately, that you use the authority and the discipline of the Union to the limit with the full backing of the Joint Board and the International Union to the end that the operators in the shop of Messrs. A. Weckstein and Son shall return to work and that the law of the agreement and not the law of violence and force on the part of a group of workers shall prevail.[32]

---

[31]Charles Poletti, *Decisions,* Case nos. 4760–4764 (June 27, 1946). Here cited from Bureau of National Affairs, *Labor Arbitration Reports,* vol. 5, pp. 372–374.

[32]Magnes to Kaufman, letter, dated May 23, 1919, filed in the Abelson papers.

In response to this mandate, Union Manager Kaufman undertook to assemble the strikers in his office for a conference, and when they failed to appear, he sent out to each of them a copy of the following letter:

I learn that you together with the other operators of Weckstein & Son stopped work Wednesday noon, May 21st and have not come back since.

I made every attempt to communicate with all of you, but you failed to show up to this office up to the present time.

You must know that your strike or stoppage is *illegal* contrary to the terms of the Union agreement with the Association, and against the rules of the Union, and I therefore urge and *command* you to return to work at once.

Should you fail to report to work between now and tomorrow, Saturday May 24th by 10 o'clock in the morning the following will be the results:

First: you will be fined $10 each for refusing to take the Union order.

Second: the firm will be permitted to engage new operators and you will be unable to return there under any terms.

Third: the Union will be obliged for the sake of not endangering the peaceful relations and conditions in the trade to assist the firm in securing new operators.

Fourth: the unfortunate development may result in a condition that you will be hindered in getting jobs elsewhere.

I regret the fact that I am forced to take these rigid measures, but it is yourself and your unorganization-like ways that is responsible for the affair.[33]

Such vigilant support for the institutions of collective action was seldom forthcoming where local union officials were themselves implicated in wildcat strikes against established authority. Wherever shop loyalties were stronger than union ties, local union representatives — whether shop stewards, price committeemen, or business agents — often turned their backs upon the forces of discipline within their international union to cast their lot with the forces of revolution within their shop groups. They acquiesced

---

[33]Kaufman to the strikers, letter, dated May 29, 1919, filed in the Abelson papers.

and condoned where they did not connive or instigate. Least of all would some local union representatives take positive action to prevent wildcat strikes in their shops. On more than one occasion, local officials even promised to see that workers got paid for loss of time for striking in violation of their agreement. This defection of union officials at the local level divided the union against itself and struck at the very heart of the union's power to maintain discipline within its ranks.[34]

Further to aggravate the problem of enforcing no-strike clauses, union-chosen agents of the impartial machinery were themselves sometimes contaminated by dissension within their unions. Some union clerks who worked with association clerks on the front lines of labor-management relations forsook the highways of statesmanship for the byways of union politics. Although clothed in the robes of impartiality, they refused to instruct rebel union members that direct action violated the collective agreement as well as union rules and the union constitution. Prejudiced by personal ambitions or swayed by political feuds, certain union-chosen clerks of the impartial machinery have at times boycotted the work of the board of grievances even while the board was engaged in suppressing shop strikes for higher wages.[35]

---

[34]Paying workers for time lost by striking for higher wages in violation of the collective agreement was a bitter pill for the organized manufacturers:

> At a meeting of the executive board of the Cloak, Suit and Skirt Manufacturers' Protective Association charges were preferred against the firm of Samuel Samuels for having committed acts which were opposed to the policies and principles of the association. In order to compromise a shop strike which had lasted about 10 days in defiance of the orders of the [association's] ways and means committee, he agreed with his workers to pay them all the wages lost by them during the time they were out on strike....The executive board could do nothing else but expel him from membership, because under no circumstances could the board tolerate an action of this kind, which might have most far-reaching consequences.... Should it come to the attention of the executive board that any other members pay for time lost by workers out on strike similar action will be taken.
> —Statement of the Cloak, Suit and Skirt Manufacturers' Protective Association in *Women's Wear,* Dec. 31, 1919.

[35]See J. H. Cohen, counsel for several manufacturers' associations, testimony before the U.S. Commission on Industrial Relations, Jan. 16, 1914, *Final Report and Testimony,* vol. 2, p. 1118.

Assuming the right to differentiate between authorized and unauthorized strikes, union clerks on occasion have initiated their own illegal forms of direct action to enforce their own interpretations of existing contract clauses. In February 1931, during a shop inspection by agents of the impartial machinery for the fur manufacturing industry, the labor adjuster (clerk) of the fur manufacturers' association criticized the labor adjuster (clerk) of the fur workers' union for insisting that a nonunion worker leave the shop at once. Thereupon, noted the association's clerk, the union representative "got into a terrible rage," demanded the return of his complaint book and threatened direct action regardless of established procedures. "We will send our own committees to investigate the rest of these shops," the union clerk shouted, "and on Monday morning there will be several stoppages because you don't allow me to stop off this man."[36]

Penalties for Shop Strikes

Disaffection among local union officials, and especially among union-chosen agents of the impartial machinery, pointed up the weaknesses of permitting labor unions complete freedom to control strikes by their rebellious members. "Throughout the last two years," charged the Associated Fur Coat and Trimming Manufacturers in 1938, "the union has repeatedly countenanced, encouraged and called strikes in reckless and utter disregard of its contractual obligations, despite the emphatic protest by the Association and the Impartial Machinery, which wholly failed to curb the Union in its wilful and direct violations of the contract." Against such possibilities there appeared to be two logical courses of action: either the impartial machinery would directly punish workers for striking in violation of their collective agreements or it would hold the union responsible for the acts of its members and impose sanctions upon the union itself.[37]

---

[36]J. G. Greenberg, labor manager of the Associated Fur Manufacturers to Paul Abelson, impartial chairman of the fur manufacturing industry, letter, dated Feb. 14, 1931, filed in the Abelson papers.

[37]Associated Fur Coat and Trimming Manufacturers, "In the Matter of the Union's Proposals of Additions and Modifications of the Present Existing Collective Labor Agreement," a typewritten submission, dated Jan. 5, 1938. Copy filed in the Abelson papers.

Pursuing the first alternative, the impartial machinery began by defining the disciplinary action that unions must take against their striking members and ended by establishing penalties that could be enforced without the assistance of the union. In its first official rules for the women's coat and suit trade, the board of grievances under the original Protocol of Peace specified that the discipline to be imposed by the union upon all illegal strikers "shall consist of a suitable fine or expulsion." Wherever subsequent collective agreements failed to name the penalties for unauthorized strikes, the impartial chairman generally set the penalty to fit the crime. "Stoppages under this agreement are prohibited," stated the 1931 collective agreement between the New York Clothing Manufacturers' Exchange and the Amalgamated Clothing Workers' Union. "If such occur, the Arbitrator shall have the power to impose appropriate discipline."[38]

The most severe penalty assessed against striking employees who refused to resume their work was termination of employment. Strikers rejecting the pleas of their union or the orders of their impartial machinery to get back on the job were either subject to discharge at the discretion of their employer or else they were deemed to have discharged themselves automatically by the act of striking. "It is very apparent from the evidence that on the Friday when the workers did not come back to work at the request of the firm, a stoppage was caused," announced Impartial Chairman C. B. Barnes of the fancy leather goods industry, in an award dated September 22, 1921. "And it is further apparent that, by the refusal of the workers to return on Monday, after being instructed to do so by their manager, they discharged themselves from the employ of this firm and lost all rights to which they had previously held to their positions with the Progressive Leather Goods Company."[39]

---

[38]For the "Rules and Plan of Procedure" on shop strikes, lockouts, or general refusal to work adopted by the board of grievances and the board of arbitration under the original Protocol of Peace in the New York women's coat and suit trade, see C. H. Winslow, *Conciliation, Arbitration, and Sanitation in the Cloak, Suit, and Skirt Industry in New York City*, p. 222.

[39]C. B. Barnes, *Decisions*, Case no. 28 (Sept. 22, 1921), copy filed in the Abelson papers. Barnes did not think that termination of employment was in itself an adequate remedy. After announcing that the strikers had discharged themselves by their conduct, Barnes added: "For this direct action on the part

Striking employees, who weighed the consequences of continuing a strike at the price of discharge, did not always evade punishment by returning to work as directed. In the first place, strikers might lose their pay during walkouts of even a few hours' duration. Following a three-hour strike in a shop of the fancy leather goods industry in 1930, Impartial Chairman Henry Moskowitz during the course of his award settling the controversy had this to say: "Such direct action by shop workers in disregard of the orders of the union and in violation of the agreement is industrial anarchy, especially, as the agreement provides prompt means for the redress of worker's grievances under the procedure of the impartial machinery. . . . For this offense there shall be deducted from the workers involved in this stoppage the amount which could have been earned by them during the three hours of the stoppage on May 29."[40]

In addition to loss of pay during a walkout, shop strikers might also be forced to compensate their employer for disrupting his production schedule. Some impartial chairmen required workers who had participated in unauthorized strikes to reimburse their employer for his losses by working overtime at regular rates of pay. Others imposed direct fines upon the strikers. In the 1925 case of Charles Burnstein and Sons, twenty operators refused to show

---

of the workers some form of discipline must be imposed, to the end that those coming under the Agreement may learn that when they have any grievance whatsoever, either fancied or real, it must be taken up and settled through the machinery provided for in the Agreement."

When 37 workers in a Philadelphia full-fashioned hosiery mill walked out in protest against the arbitrary firing of two employees, George Taylor, impartial chairman under the collective agreement for the industry, ordered the reinstatement of the two unjustly dismissed employees but confirmed the discharge of the 37 workers who walked out in violation of the no-strike clause. As reported in *Knickerbocker News,* Feb. 15, 1935. Clipping filed in the Abelson papers.

[40]Henry Moskowitz, *Decisions,* Case no. 16-A (June 10, 1930). Fines of $10 a day imposed upon individual workers for striking an employer's shop prior to an investigation of a dispute, or fines of $1,000 a day imposed upon individual employers for locking out his workers prior to such an investigation, had been a feature of the Canadian Industrial Disputes Investigation Act of 1907. See the testimony of W. L. Mackenzie King, who drafted the act and directed its early administration, before the U.S. Commission on Industrial Relations, April 9, 1914, *Final Report and Testimony,* vol. 1, pp. 713–718, 732–738.

up for work because their employer refused to raise their wages. Although the union officials succeeded in returning the workers to their jobs by three o'clock of the same day, the employer, nevertheless, insisted that the strikers be disciplined. Rejecting the union plea that a warning against further direct action would be adequate penalty under the circumstances, Impartial Chairman C. B. Barnes wrote as follows:

The Chairman believes that a violation such as this stoppage cannot be passed over lightly. On account of the stoppage, the workers did not go to work until three o'clock in the afternoon, which meant a loss of six hours production in this shop. It is therefore ruled that the employer is to pay the operators causing the stoppage straight pay for six hours of their overtime work. As additional discipline for their action in this matter, it is ruled that the pay for one hour's work of each individual operator is to be collected by the Union and remitted to the Joint Grievance Board Fund.[41]

To control the flood of unauthorized strikes that plagued the men's clothing industry of Chicago after the First World War, the joint trade board established under the collective labor agreement of the Chicago men's clothing market worked out, case by case, a series of restrictive measures that can be summarized from a digest of the board's decisions under two separate headings:

I. *Responsibilities of the Shop Chairman*
   (1) He must not threaten or even intimate to the firm a possibility of strike action, but must give orders to prevent a pending strike.

---

[41]C. B. Barnes, impartial chairman, fancy leather goods industry, *Decisions,* Case no. 123 (Oct. 26, 1925), filed in the Abelson papers. In a similar case eight years later, Henry Moskowitz, who had become impartial chairman of the fancy leather goods industry, wrote:

The attitude of the Impartial Chairman towards stoppage is well known. He regards it as a flagrant violation of the agreement. Those who indulge in it are guilty of a cardinal sin, since the agreement is based upon continuity of employment for the manufacturer and quick and speedy solution of the workers' grievances. Resort to stoppage is mob rule and denies the employer continuity of production. It undermines Union discipline. The workers are ordered to make up the four hours lost through the stoppage by working Saturday morning, October 21st., on single time.
   —Henry Moskowitz, *Decisions,* Case no. 45 (Oct. 17, 1933).

(2) Shop chairmen may be suspended and denied employment elsewhere for failing to take positive action to prevent or stop a strike.

(3) Shop chairmen who order work stoppages may not only be compelled to vacate their positions but may become personally responsible for loss of wages to workers during a stoppage; and even for loss of time by workers who appear as witnesses at complaint hearings.

II. *Forms of Discipline against the Strikers*

(1) Conditions under which the Trade Board will confine discipline to reprimand and warnings.

(2) Conditions under which fines of varying amounts will be imposed on the striking workers.

(3) Conditions under which the Trade Board will not render favorable awards to workers who have engaged in stoppages to win their case.

(4) Conditions under which overtime will be imposed at regular pay.

(5) Conditions calling for the automatic forfeiture of the strikers' jobs.[42]

Union Liability for Shop Strikes

Some employers' associations demanded that the punishment imposed on striking employees be supplemented by penalties against labor unions for failure to control strikes. In November 1913, W. H. Bartholomew, labor manager for the dress and waist manufacturers, stated his association's position before the industry's board of arbitration. At that time, the dress manufacturers

---

[42]"Digest of Trade Board Decisions (Nos. 1–1000) and Board of Arbitration Decisions to October 1921." See, especially, cases cited under "Stoppages," pp. 52–55. Copy filed in the Abelson papers.

If any worker shall willfully violate the spirit of the agreement by intentional opposition to its fundamental purposes and especially if he carry such willful violation into action by striking or inciting others to strike or stop work during working hours, he shall, if charge is proven, be subject to suspension, discharge or fine. Provided, that if a fine is imposed its amount shall be determined by the chairman of the Trade Board, and shall not be less than $1 or more than $5 for each offense.

—From the rules laid down by the board of arbitration under the 1913–1916 labor agreement of the Hart, Schaffner, and Marx men's clothing company in *The Hart, Schaffner, and Marx Labor Agreements* (pamphlet) filed in the Abelson papers.

contended that the union itself should pay the employer for losses sustained from illegal strikes. They charged the dressmakers' union with instigating stoppages and with preventing the strikers from returning to work. To assess the union with the cost of such strikes, so the association argued, was as logical as assessing employers for losses that the workers sustained during illegal lockouts.[43]

Certainly the failure of union officials to see that striking employees resumed work within hours following an illegal stoppage violated an express contractual mandate common to most collective agreements of the needle trades. But the punishment, if any, to be inflicted upon unions for violating this mandate was seldom, if ever, specified. Perhaps in the absence of such clauses, agents of the impartial machinery might direct labor unions to contribute from their coffers whatever financial compensation was necessary to offset the losses that employers sustained from wildcat strikes — a policy that could have been facilitated by having unions deposit in advance with the impartial machinery a sum of money from which damages might later be collected for violations of the no-strike clause. Or the impartial chairman, with or without express authorization, might oust local union officials from their positions for failure to take positive steps toward suppressing shop strikes.

The issue of union liability for damages to employers from shop strikes was debated before the board of arbitration for the dress and waist industry in the spring of 1916, at the time of hearings on the procedural question of whether striking workers should first return to their jobs before their grievances could be settled on their merits. Union leaders, who later renounced their support for the proposition that grievances of striking workers should not be "adjusted" while the workers were still on strike, could hardly be expected to accept the manufacturers' additional proposition that failure of union officials or union clerks to return the strikers would require the union to "make good all pecuniary damages suffered by the employer in consequence thereof." The union rejected this proposition, even where there was evidence of connivance by union officials in authorizing the strike.[44]

---

[43]*Minutes,* Arbitration Proceedings between the Dress and Waist Manufacturers' Association and the ILGWU (Nov. 8, 1913), pp. 61–67.

[44]These debates are recorded in *Minutes,* Arbitration Proceedings between the Dress and Waist Manufacturers' Association and the ILGWU (March 31,

A few months previously, in the Monroe Froehlich case, involving an attempt by the Dress and Waist Manufacturers' Association to collect $1,018 in damages from the union for loss to an employer arising out of a strike during a fire drill, the board of arbitration had found union officials responsible for not terminating the strike, but the board had held that it had no jurisdiction to award damages to the manufacturer. The extent of union liability for shop strikes was, therefore, a burning question when Judge J. W. Mack, chairman of the board, reopened the issue for debate at the session of March 31, 1916.[45]

Speaking for the dress and waist manufacturers, J. H. Cohen pressed the board to hold that wherever union officers failed to perform their duty in ordering striking employees back to work, the union should pay for damages suffered by the employers. "The Association has made good," Cohen declared, "gone down into its own treasury, paid hundreds and hundreds of dollars to the Union for default of its own members. . . . then certainly this organization [the ILGWU] should be willing to make good the damages which are caused by reason of its officers' conduct, and by reason of their failure to perform their contracts." The law of group responsibility for contract infractions should work both ways. "Now it is fallacious," so Cohen argued, "to say here that you can go on imposing financial burdens upon this association and upon its members, but you must not impose any financial burdens upon the Union because you destroy the union."[46]

During these discussions, Chairman J. W. Mack wanted to know of Mr. Cohen whether exceptions should ever be made to the rule

---

1916), vol. 6, pp. 1484–1681. A partial summary appears in *Women's Wear,* April 1, 1916.

[45]A discussion of the Monroe Froehlich case is reported in *Women's Wear,* Dec. 30, 1915 and Feb. 7, 1916; and in *Daily Trade Record,* Dec. 31, 1915.

[46]*Minutes,* Arbitration Proceedings between the Dress and Waist Manufacturers' Association and the ILGWU (March 31, 1916), vol. 6, pp. 1492, 1532–1542. Cohen had proposed the following amendment to the no-strike clause of the revised protocol in the dress and waist industry: "If the chief clerk or any deputy shall fail to perform his duty under this article, or if any officer of the union shall authorize a shop strike, the union will make good all pecuniary damage suffered by the employer in consequence thereof." J. H. Cohen, "The Revised Protocol in the Dress and Waist Industry" in *Annals,* American Academy of Political and Social Science, January 1917, vol. 69, p. 192.

that unions should pay for the losses sustained from strikes in violation of the agreement:

Mack: Suppose the employer deliberately violates a substantial term of the agreement, — perfectly deliberately; compels overwork, refuses to pay the proper wages, knowing that he is doing it; deliberately saying, "well you can not strike anyway. You have no business to strike. You can adjust it, we will have a hearing on it." But it is clearly shown that he is deliberately abusing it. Suppose one employer permits his foreman, unrebuked, to insult the girls in his shop — indecent proposals — these things have happened, of course — and they go out on strike because of it, stop work because of it, would you suggest any limitations of that?

Cohen: Within two weeks after the protocol was signed — the first protocol, the one that we are living under, and before any machinery had been established at all — John Dyche [general secretary-treasurer, ILGWU] — or it was within four days after the protocol was signed — John Dyche came to the representative of the Association, Mr. Bartholomew, and said, "An indecent proposal has been made by a foreman to the girls in one of the shops." A hearing was held immediately. The girls were called in and gave their testimony. Immediately that employer was ordered to discharge that superintendent, who had been there nine years, and he was discharged.

Mack: Now suppose he hadn't been?

Cohen: Then the employer should have been expelled from the association.[47]

Speaking for the union members, Morris Hillquit, ILGWU counsel, asserted that nothing like a damage clause had ever before

---

[47]*Minutes,* Arbitration Proceedings between the Dress and Waist Manufacturers' Association and the ILGWU (March 31, 1916), vol. 6, pp. 1497–1498.

Most likely it was just such exigencies as Chairman Mack suggested that accounted for the insertion of the 24-hour "cooling off" clause, so common to needle trade agreements beginning with the twenties. Under this provision, a stoppage in violation of the no-strike clause obligated the union, upon notice by the association, "to return the striking workers and those who have stopped work, to their work in the shop within twenty-four hours after the receipt by the Union of such notice, and until the expiration of such time, it shall not be deemed that the striking workers have abandoned their employment." From the 1919 collective agreement between the Cloak, Suit and Skirt Manufacturers' Protective Association and the ILGWU and Its Cloakmakers' Joint Board. Text in *Monthly Labor Review,* December 1919, vol. 9, pp. 1716–1719.

been put into a trade agreement, and he insisted that trade unions could not assume financial responsibility for unauthorized strikes. Referring to the effects of the Taff Vale decision establishing union responsibility in England, Hillquit predicted that insistence upon a damage clause in the revised dress protocol would probably destroy the agreement. In his stand Hillquit was merely restating the position that his union had taken three years earlier. A letter, dated July 12, 1913, from the ILGWU to the Dress and Waist Manufacturers' Association had stated:

The Union has undertaken and is ready to use its best efforts to prevent stoppages of work. Stoppages occur even under prison discipline. Human beings cannot and should not be handled as inanimate things. It is utterly absurd to hold the Union responsible for pecuniary damages caused by a stoppage of work.[48]

Presented with these forceful arguments, the board of arbitration wavered but finally turned down the proposal to make unions financially responsible for damages arising from shop strikes. "Whatever our sympathies may be as to the question of pecuniary compensation," concluded chairman J. W. Mack, "we deem it inexpedient at this time to incorporate in the protocol any provision for the redress of damages due to the act of the clerks of the Union not ordering a return to work. There are too many possibilities of exceptions and of investigations into the prior underlying causes that would seriously involve the question of damages." However, the board promised to draft appropriate disciplinary measures for breaches of the protocol that could be applied to the association and the union, as well as to individual employers or individual members of the union.[49]

------

[48]The letter is quoted in "Answer by the Union to Complaint of the Dress and Waist Manufacturers' Association" (Oct. 25, 1913), printed copy in the ILGWU research library. Hillquit's position before the board of arbitration is found in *Minutes,* Arbitration Proceedings between the Dress and Waist Manufacturers' Association and the ILGWU (March 31, 1916), vol. 6, pp. 1517, 1521. The debates are summarized in *Women's Wear,* April 1 and 3, 1916.

[49]*Minutes,* Arbitration Proceedings between the Dress and Waist Manufacturers' Association and the ILGWU (March 31, 1916), vol. 6, pp. 1580–1581. Here the board of arbitration for the dress and waist industry of New York was following the conclusions reached by the Industrial Council of the British Board of Trade from an investigation of industrial agreements in Great

Soon thereafter, the board of arbitration announced its official position on union liability for unauthorized strikes in an award that became a part of the revised protocol for the dress and waist industry. Still refusing to saddle the union with pecuniary damages suffered by an employer for the failure of union clerks, deputy clerks, or union officials to suppress wildcat strikes, the board of arbitration, nevertheless, reached new heights of support for the principle of union responsibility. J. H. Cohen, spokesman for the organized manufacturers, considered this decision "the most forward step ever taken in any collective agreement either in this country or abroad." It was, alas for the manufacturers, to become the highwater mark in the movement to hold labor unions accountable for wildcat strikes by their members. The provisions of the revised protocol called for the following steps to be taken in sequence against wildcat strikes:

1. Immediately following a wildcat strike, the union shall order the strikers to return to work at once;

2. For refusing to obey these orders, the striking workers shall forfeit all their rights under the protocol and be subject to punishment by their union, and the form of punishment shall be reported promptly to the employers' association.

3. Union deputies or officials who condone or connive in shop strikes or fail to perform their duties in respect thereto, shall, on request of the employers' association, be punished by the union.

4. Failure of the union to act promptly and fairly shall constitute an association grievance to be presented to the board of arbitration, which shall have the power to direct the union to take disciplinary measures against their deputies or officials — such measures to include fines, suspension or removal from office as the board may deem proper.

5. On failure of the union to carry out the decision of the board of arbitration, the employers' association may present a new complaint to the board which "shall have power to impose such fine, as in the judgment of the board shall seem just or necessary in the premises."[50]

Britain in 1913. See the *Report of the Industrial Council of the British Board of Trade on Its Inquiry into Industrial Agreements,* reprinted in U.S. Department of Labor, BLS Bulletin no. 133 (August 18, 1913), especially the sections on "Monetary Penalties" and "Monetary Guarantees" at pp. 18–23.

[50]The pertinent terms of the revised protocol were quoted in J. H. Cohen, "The Revised Protocol in the Dress and Waist Industry," *Annals,* January 1917, vol. 69, p. 191. These terms were also made applicable to employer lockouts, with corresponding procedures to be followed.

Sporadic Steps toward Union Responsibility

In the decades that followed this highwater mark of collective action, no generally accepted principles of union responsibility for unauthorized strikes were ever evolved for the dress industry, although a few later agreements in various branches of the needle trades did authorize penalties against unions or their officers for failure to control unauthorized strikes. As a rule, however, union leaders appeared more amenable to the assessment of fines against their unions for violating other contract terms than for violating the no-strike clause. Morris Hillquit, who was uncompromising in his opposition to union liability for wildcat strikes, once conceded to the board of arbitration for the dress and waist industry that his union should be subject to a fine if it were found conniving in the practice of permitting its members to work at nonunion scales below the standards of the collective agreement.[51]

In addition, some permanent umpires took action on their own initiative against union officials for failure to meet their obligations. Union shop chairmen were a special target for attack. Those who instigated walkouts, or who failed to exert any positive effort to prevent walkouts, were ordered removed from their positions. One of the earlier cases of this character arose during 1921 follow-

---

[51]See *Minutes,* Arbitration Proceedings between the Dress and Waist Manufacturers' Association and the ILGWU (Feb. 5, 1916), vol. 4, pp. 263–264.

> The Union agrees to provide and continuously maintain a blanket surety company bond in the sum of Ten Thousand ($10,000.00) dollars to protect the Association and/or its Members, to cover any assessment or penalty which may be imposed by the Impartial Chairman for any breach under this agreement.
> —From the 1930 collective agreement between the Full Fashioned Hosiery Manufacturers of America and the American Federation of Full Fashioned Hosiery Workers.

This type of clause, repeated in later agreements of the 1930's, exacted a corresponding obligation from the employers' association, and was rare among association-wide contracts that have come to light, in that it required a labor union, as well as an employers' association, to put up funds in advance as a source of protection against future violations of the contract. In fact, the first national labor agreement for this industry, negotiated in 1929 between the union and a committee of thirty manufacturers and drafted for individual signatures, had also required a $10,000 union bond but had left fines against individual employers for contract violations to be imposed and enforced by the impartial chairman without the protection of previously deposited bonds.

ing a strike at the Progressive Leather Goods Company over a division of work. The management requested the impartial machinery to depose the shop chairman, I. Kleinbaum, from his office for having "exceeded his authority and in effect caused a stoppage of several workers of the firm." After the joint grievance board had tried in vain to reach agreement on the issue, the case was referred for decision to C. B. Barnes, impartial chairman for the fancy leather goods industry, who wrote as follows:

The shop chairman holds a very difficult and responsible position and must be regarded as the representative of the Union in his particular shop. For this reason he is not to be considered as an ordinary worker. The privileges that he had as shop chairman entails on him accompanying responsibilities. When the management directed the workers to come to work at a certain time it was not proper for the shop chairman or the workers to disobey the direction of the management in that regard. If the shop chairman or the workers felt that there might be some question about the validity of this particular order, it should have been carried out and if any wrong was done the group or any particular individuals, this wrong should have been taken up in the regular way. Mr. Kleinbaum in attempting to escape from the consequences of his action says that he only told the workers that they did not have to go to work if they did not want to. It was his duty when he failed to get in touch with the foreman on the Wednesday evening in question to have told the workers to follow out the order given them and then later to take up the matter if he found that the firm was making any wrongful division of work among the operators....

He could not take a passive stand in this matter. It was his duty when he found that the workers were inclined to disobey the orders of the management to use his power as shop chairman to see that they did follow out the orders given them and return to work the next day. His action was, in effect, the cause of the stoppage, one of the things which a shop chairman is expressly expected to guard against.

For this reason the Chairman directs that the Fancy Leather Goods Workers' Union immediately suspend Mr. Kleinbaum from his office of shop chairman in the factory of this firm.[52]

---

[52]C. B. Barnes, *Decisions,* Case no. 20 (June 17, 1921). For a number of similar cases in the Chicago market of the men's clothing industry, see "Digest of Trade Board Decisions (Nos. 1–1000) and Board of Arbitration Decisions to October 1921," pp. 53–54. Copy filed in the Abelson papers.

Other obligations, more positive in character, were sometimes imposed upon labor unions to help control unauthorized strikes. Unions were not only forbidden to interfere with plants attempting to continue operations in the face of "illegal" strikes, but they were directed to help the victimized employers find other workers for their shops. When the cutters for a certain firm in the women's coat and suit industry called a wildcat strike for better terms during the life of the 1924 collective agreement for the trade, Impartial Chairman R. V. Ingersoll condemned the workers for taking the law into their own hands in defiance of their union and their contract, and threatened them with automatic loss of employment if they failed to return to their jobs within a designated time. He also directed the union (1) to publish a notice disavowing the strike, (2) to punish the workers for their misconduct, and (3), if called upon, to cooperate with the firm in securing a new set of cutters.[53]

In other cases, impartial chairmen instructed unions to grant working cards to substitute employees taking jobs vacated by wildcat strikers and also encouraged those unions to deny working cards to wildcat strikers seeking employment elsewhere. Some impartial chairmen would grant the strike-bound firm the privilege of having its goods made up in outside shops, even though the contract provided that a preference be given to the inside workers. Others would punish striking union members by subsequently denying them the privilege of extra work, even though this extra work might henceforth be given to nonunion shops. Perhaps the most drastic of all steps ever devised to suppress illegal walkouts came from a rule that workers striking to gain their objectives in contravention of established procedures thereby foreclosed all subse-

---

[53]R. V. Ingersoll, *Decisions,* Case no. 66 (1925). Not only did the 1924 collective agreement between the Industrial Council of Cloak, Suit and Skirt Manufacturers and the ILGWU obligate the union to return striking workers to their shops within 24 hours, but the terms of the contract also stated that "the Union agrees that if the striking workers fail to return to work within the stipulated time it will forthwith state in writing and in the appropriate press or otherwise that there is not a strike in or against such shop in which the work has been stopped and that the shop is in good standing with the Union and entitled to all the rights, benefits and privileges provided for by the terms of this contract."

quent possibility of a favorable decision from the impartial machinery on the substance of their complaint.[54]

Many of these diverse and persistent efforts on the part of the impartial machinery to control unauthorized strikes were hampered by the reaction of the organized manufacturers who derived more profit from giving in to union demands than from attempting to enforce the no-strike clause of their collective labor agreements. Why should an employer exercise his right to discharge the strikers whose labor offered the only hope of getting his production out on time? Even the right to terminate the collective agreement for reason of illegal strikes sometimes offered the employer no more than the option of jumping from the frying pan into the fire! Yet, on at least a few occasions, those employers who kowtowed to the demands of wildcat strikers were expelled from their own associations, lest such precedents "have most far reaching consequences."[55]

---

[54]"The Trade Board [Chicago market — men's clothing industry] takes this occasion to state it as a general rule that it will not make favorable awards after workers have violated the Agreement by repeated stoppages." "Digest of Trade Board Decisions (Nos. 1–1000) and Board of Arbitration Decisions to October 1921," Case no. 159 at p. 55. The Trade Board "serves notice that ordinarily it will permit no increase in prices when a stoppage occurs," *ibid.,* Case no. 236. In Case no. 707, the Trade Board refused to remove a nonunion man from a shop because the union members, who had a legitimate employment grievance, chose to enforce their protest by an illegitimate strike, *ibid.*

[55]A typical example of such action by an association is reported in *Women's Wear,* Dec. 31, 1919. Some impartial chairmen, who encouraged employers to hold out against strike-supported demands for wage increases at the shop level, later denied all employers kowtowing to such demands any relief from the additional burdens they suffered. See, for example, A. Feldblum, impartial chairman of the dress industry, *Decisions,* Case no. B-2131 (Dec. 30, 1935).

It is undisputed that the coat and suit industry is presently confronted with a tight labor market. There is a great demand for cloakmakers, and practically none is available. To hold that the workers in the [wildcat strike] cases before me have abandoned their employment will not accord relief to their employers, who are unable to obtain any other workers to take their places.

—Charles Poletti, impartial chairman, women's coat and suit trade, *Decisions,* Case nos. 4760–4764 (June 27, 1946), as recorded in Bureau of National Affairs, *Labor Arbitration Reports,* vol. 5, p. 374.

Here groups of workers were walking out of their shops and obtaining higher wages elsewhere:

What an employer policy of giving in to wildcat strikers did for compliance with collective agreements was most forceably expressed by an impartial chairman for the men's clothing industry in the Chicago market. When a foreman in a Chicago clothing factory sought out the wildcat strikers and offered them a wage increase in direct contravention of the labor agreement which limited piece-rate changes to prescribed bargaining procedures, Impartial Chairman Harry Millis wrote in disgust: "What respect the workers must have for orderly procedure; what confidence in their deputy, under such circumstances! If one were to attempt deliberately to destroy the agreement and break down effective control by the organization it would be difficult to find a more effective way than that followed by the foreman in this case!"[56]

Some employers in the industry have been giving their workers additional increases in wages in order to dissuade them from going to work elsewhere, and other employers have been inducing workers employed elsewhere to come to work for them at increased wages. . . . A continuation of these practices will impair the stability of the industry in which the union as well as the manufacturers have such a deep and genuine interest.

[56]*Decisions* of the Trade Board under the Chicago market collective agreement. Case nos. 854 (July 23, 1921) and 963, 964 (Oct. 1, 1921), as quoted in Chicago Joint Board, ACWA, *The Clothing Workers of Chicago, 1910–1922*, pp. 208–209.

The average producer was not willing to risk the money loss of a "lay down" and yielded to pressure from his own workers. Moreover, the unrest was encouraged by deliberate bidding for labor. Foremen stood at the doors of other factories as the men came out. . . .

Through the height of the season shop and section demands were made, and refusals were often met by stoppages or by the more effective and elusive method of "laying down." Workers constantly moved about, often giving up a position on the gamble of being able to make better terms elsewhere. These "wage speculators," as they were called, in going to new places, asked for a higher wage than was being paid to the former workers, which if given to one or two often resulted in a levelling up of the shop. . . .

The situation resulted in widespread concessions in individual shops. After these obtained headway they bred a restlessness over the market which forced a general increase. Three such mid-season wage awards were finally granted. Collective bargaining put its sanction on a condition established by individual action.

—Felix Frankfurter and S. J. Rosensohn, "Survey of the New York [men's] Clothing Industry" (May 28, 1920) in printed collection of

Concluding Observations

All efforts to maintain uniform standards of employment were as readily dissipated by raising wages at the shop level above industry standards as they were disrupted by reducing wages at the shop level below industry standards. In either case, attempts to control competition in labor costs were thwarted by lack of discipline within the ranks of the organized forces supporting the protocol movement. The greatest hazard that the organized manufacturers faced during the life of collective agreements came from unpredictable labor costs produced by unauthorized shop strikes to raise wages and other conditions of employment above accepted industry standards. Only a rigid enforcement of the no-strike clause in collective agreements could preserve the principles of controlled competition on which the protocol movement was founded.

Yet no other clause of collective agreements was so difficult to enforce. At its best, the unauthorized strike was an exercise of the inherent right of revolution — a right that justified the "people" in overthrowing established authority that had become oppressive. At its worst, the unauthorized strike was an example of lynch law in operation — a method of substituting blind force and coercion for the orderly processes of industrial self-government. To the lowly immigrants escaping the tyrannies of eastern Europe, the right to strike was another expression of that heritage of freedom acquired in the new world. And all the machinery for law enforcement that the protocol system could devise was incapable of blotting out that heritage overnight.

In practice, the enforcement of "no-strike" clauses on which the organized manufacturers so heavily relied for the preservation of law and order seldom got beyond pleas and supplications to the striking workers and their union. Wherever employees at the shop level supported their demands for higher wages and better working conditions with strike action, the impartial machinery was hard-pressed to maintain the uniformity of labor standards that was the first goal of collective action. During the life of collective agree-

union affidavits submitted in the case of J. Friedman & Co. v. ACWA, pp. 32–33, copy filed in the Abelson papers.

For further information on pirating in the men's clothing trade, see W. M. Leiserson, "Report to the Public," in ACWA's *Advance,* Jan. 28, 1921.

ments, labor unions were less vigilant in containing their wildcat strikers who would pierce the ceiling over competition than were employers' associations in restraining their rebellious members who would scuttle the floor under competition. At the same time, the impartial chairman could devise no practical means of penalizing wildcat strikers sufficiently to act as an effective deterrent against repeated use of direct action.

Unfortunately, the threat of discharge was least effective at the very time that workers were most likely to strike for better terms of employment. During the busy season, striking workers who lost their jobs could readily find employment elsewhere. Moreover, the manufacturers were less willing to discharge their workers at critical stages of production. In highly seasonal industries, where production schedules had to be met within prescribed time limits, bowing to the demands of the strikers might be less disastrous than failure to find other competent workers. For the employer who could not afford the additional costs of averting a strike, nor yet withstand the delay in hiring and training new workers, the horns of the dilemma offered no means of escape.

Chapter 9

The Life of
Collective Agreements

T HE original Protocol of Peace for the women's coat and suit trade had sought to replace the chaos and confusion of unregulated competition with a system of law and order that was intended to be perpetual. This 1910 agreement between the Cloak, Suit and Skirt Manufacturers' Protective Association and the International Ladies' Garment Workers' Union was a symbol of perpetuity: it not only lacked provisions to meet drastic changes in economic conditions with appropriate amendments, but, having no expiration date, it offered no exit to individual victims or unforeseen adversities, or of insufferable hardships arising from possible inequities of contract administration. These shortcomings, common to other agreements of indefinite duration, created a growing demand for an official means of escape from the protocol. Whether this demand was ever intended to seek more than an emergency exit, it at least threatened to introduce still more flexibility into collective bargaining systems. Not content with flexible interpretations of existing contracts, these advocates of change now came up with new concepts governing the duration, revision, and termination of collective agreements.

Stability versus Flexibility

Creating a lawful means of escape from the obligations of collective agreements was in a sense beating a retreat from the high ideals that had inspired the original sponsors of the protocol movement.

Taking their cues from the movement to banish wars among nations, men like Hamilton Holt, member of the first board of arbitration under the women's coat and suit protocol, and Morris Silberman, president of the Cloak, Suit and Skirt Manufacturers' Protective Association, had worked for the introduction of "peace treaties" in labor-management relations that would forever put an end to industrial strife. It was from this idea that the term, Protocol of Peace, had been derived. "As you know," observed Mr. Silberman in May 1911, "the protocol is a permanent treaty of peace. Treaties of peace do not have to be renewed. They are not broken or abrogated except when the conditions that made the peace advisable no longer exist. Such is not the status of affairs as regards the protocol. The agencies created by that instrument are sufficient to meet all misunderstandings that arise."[1]

But the very permanence of the first protocol turned out to be its undoing. The perpetuity of this agreement forbade a thorough reassessment of its merits or a complete overhauling of the institutions it created. Lacking provision for the periodic renegotiation of its terms, the first protocol offered no formal outlet for the release of suppressed emotions — no safety valve of strike action to keep the smoldering steam of incipient revolution within the bounds of reason. No one conceived that periodic release from the bonds of collective agreements might actually contribute to the stability of labor-management relations. Least of all did the sponsors of the protocol movement suspect that their proposed realm of law and order would need to be watered by the blood of revolution every few years.

For practical reasons, the concept of a perpetual peace under the provision of a permanent protocol soon gave way to more realistic objectives. Henceforth, collective agreements usually ran for a definite period of time. "I think one of the weaknesses of the protocol is that it is indefinite," testified J. A. Dyche, general secretary-treasurer of the ILGWU, before the U. S. Commission on Industrial Relations, January 15, 1914. "I believe the union should enter into an agreement with the manufacturers for a specified date — two or three years." Dyche told of how radical union leaders had won support from the rank and file by proposing new demands

---

[1] *Daily Trade Record,* May 9, 1911.

that were impossible of attainment under the first protocol. Harping on the slavery imposed by the permanence of this agreement, union politicians were able to keep the workers in a continual state of turmoil constantly agitating for reforms.

Whereas, Dyche continued, an agreement of definite duration might at least provide a period of peace during which business could be conducted with a measure of stability, the women's coat and suit protocol by its very permanence defeated its own purposes. "There is no stability to the protocol," Dyche argued. "If we had an agreement which has a specified time, say three years, then we would know there could be no agitation for a general strike. That is to say, during three years we would have a rest, and the trade would not go to other cities. . . ." Even if the parties agreed to reopen negotiations under a three-year contract upon a three-month notice of discontent with certain of its provisions, so Dyche contended, "at least we would be free from this constant agitation among our people by certain disgruntled parties."[2]

This concept of war for a while and peace for a while helped to solve the problem of strikes during the life of collective agreements. For it presented the possibility of herding most outbreaks of direct action into the comparatively brief periods between the termination of one agreement and the beginning of another. Given a chance of re-exploring the very mudsills of industrial relationships at periodic intervals, the most violently tempered members of labor and management might be persuaded to forego drastic action between negotiating periods. Whatever was sacrificed in loss of opportunity for long-term planning was regained in the prospects of greater short-term stability.

At least this was the hypothesis on which collective agreements of limited duration were founded. When strikes threatened to disrupt the "treaty of peace" signed on September 19, 1911 between the Merchants' Society of Ladies' Tailors and the Ladies'

---

[2]U.S. Commission on Industrial Relations, *Final Report and Testimony* (1916), vol. 2, pp. 1042–1043. "We do not desire to revive the Protocol with its intricate machinery and perpetual duration, but propose instead a simple working agreement limited in time to one or two years." ILGWU to Cloak, Suit and Skirt Manufacturers' Protective Association, letter, dated Jan. 18, 1915, filed in the Abelson papers. See also editorial comment on "The End of the Protocol," in the *New Republic*, May 29, 1915, vol. 3, pp. 84–85.

Tailors and Dressmakers' Union (Local 38, ILGWU), the board of arbitration chosen for the industry insisted that the main object of the treaty was to prevent conflicts and cessation of work during the life of the agreement. "Unless," they said, "this most essential part of the treaty is obeyed, the usefulness of the Board is at an end."[3]

This idea of a time for war and a time for peace also brought into focus the more basic conflict between stability and flexibility that characterized the history of collective bargaining for the needle trades. As a rule, the organized forces of labor and management — at least those who supported the protocol movement — held out for binding commitments of substantial duration which would insure business stability even at the price of sacrificing freedom. On the other hand, the unorganized forces of industry — those who lived from hand to mouth — generally cried out for freedom to grasp every passing advantage, even at the price of sacrificing stability. Every switch in personnel from one group to the other invariably brought a corresponding shift in viewpoints. Collective bargaining thus became the flywheel of industrial socity ever seeking to maintain stability against change.

Accepting this general proposition, however, did not imply that a judicious mixture of flexibility with stability would weaken the brew. Still to be resolved, therefore, was the issue of how much flexibility ought to be permitted in labor standards and to what extent should this flexibility be reflected in the duration, revision, and termination of collective agreements. Between the extremes of signing agreements that were revokable at the whim of either party and signing agreements that offered no formal means of escape, the road was open for a wide range of possibilities. Contracts of two or three years duration — the Dyche standard — offered a substantial element of stability and at the same time provided an opportunity for completely rebuilding the institutions of collective action at periodic intervals.

This issue of flexibility versus stability in labor-management relations permeated every aspect of the conflict over wages, hours, and working conditions. In 1916, for example, Morris Hillquit,

---

[3]As quoted in *Ladies' Garment Worker,* May 1912, vol. 3, p. 19. Text of the 1911 agreement is reproduced in *Women's Wear,* Sept. 20, 1911.

counsel for the ILGWU, pointed out the evils that arose from having price committees at the shop level set piece rates with their employers for an entire season. Some price committees may be "exceedingly short-sighted and weak," Hillquit argued. They may depart for other shops leaving the workers to suffer for a season. Should we not have a right to resettle prices where prices are intolerable, he asked, as we did before 1910?

But William Klein, speaking for the Cloak, Suit and Skirt Manufacturers' Protective Association, foresaw complete chaos if piece rates, once fixed, could be changed during a season: "It would put the manufacturer at a loss. He would not know at what time somebody might come in and make a claim that the price was not right. He would not know at what time during the season somebody might come in and make a readjustment. His profit, based on the figures that he made, would be entirely gone. He would have to go either to his customers and ask, if the price were changed, a higher rate, or he would have to take the loss himself, and in that way he would never know just where he was at."

Klein was ably supported in his position by Max Meyer, another representative of the association. The sanctity of piece rates must be safeguarded, Meyer argued. Experts may be called upon to help determine the original price, but once the price is fixed, no change should be tolerated. If some mistakes are made, the boss may voluntarily change them, so Meyer contended, but the workers must have no right to order a change. Otherwise, the chaos that existed before 1910 would prevail. "We have enough anarchy in the situation today," so Meyer concluded. ". . . If you reopen one case, even as a question of principle, you rip the industry wide open."[4]

Protection against Changed Conditions

Differences over the stability-flexibility issue revealed in fixing piece rates at the shop level were also reflected in more fundamental considerations on the duration, revision, and termination

---

[4]*Minutes,* Council of Conciliation. . .[women's coat and suit trade] (Feb. 16, 1916), vol. 9, Hillquit at p. 302, Klein at p. 291, Meyer at p. 300. Earlier that month a parallel discussion had arisen in the dress and waist industry between Morris Hillquit and J. H. Cohen. See *Minutes,* Arbitration Proceedings between the Dress and Waist Manufacturers' Association and the ILGWU (Feb. 6, 1916), vol. 4, pp. 383–386.

of collective agreements. Strangely enough, both the advocates of stability and the advocates of flexibility thought they had found their ideal in the original Protocol of Peace. Those who wanted flexibility held that the protocol, like an international treaty of peace, could under a change of conditions be terminated at will by acts of renunciation, if not by words to that effect. Each party was its own judge of whether changing conditions justified termination of the protocol.[5]

On the other hand, those who insisted upon rigidity were equally convinced that the protocol, like the constitution of a state, was not affected by factional strife among the warring elements of industrial society. Brandeis himself believed there was no way to suspend the protocol except by joint action of both parties. When the board of arbitration for the women's coat and suit industry in February 1913 officially cast its lot with the constitutional theorists, the stage was set for introducing some formal means of escape from the obligations of collective agreements.[6]

The pressures for an official exit from the realm of law and order were not confined to demands for short-lived agreements that opened the gates every two or three years for all to escape. The advocates of flexibility insisted upon some official means of terminating agreements between negotiating periods, whatever the life of the contract. Not only did individuals seek an opportunity for

---

[5]There was much confusion of thought between the concept of a protocol that grew through revision or amendment and the concept of a protocol that could be terminated on account of changed conditions. At hearings before the mayor's council of conciliation, J. H. Cohen, counsel for the manufacturers, challenged Morris Hillquit, counsel for the ILGWU, on the view that the protocol was perpetual. Hillquit saw room for growth in the power of the conference committee to amend the protocol. *Minutes,* Council of Conciliation...[women's coat and suit trade] (July 13, 1915), vol. 2, p. 16.

> The old Protocol was called "perpetual" because it had no definite time limit. It was less perpetual than the newer document, for it could be terminated at any time. Every two years the new document is subject to revision, and it may be expected that controversy will be left to accumulate for such occasions and possibly make for serious friction again. On the other hand, under the old agreement there might be controversy at any time.

—J. H. Cohen, *Law and Order in Industry* (1916), p. 189.

[6]*Minutes,* Board of Arbitrators...[women's coat and suit trade] (Oct. 3, 1913), p. 69.

release from their binding commitments — a procedure that would not otherwise disturb the operation of the collective agreement — but the contracting parties themselves saw benefits in being able to abrogate any agreements that operated to their detriment. Obviously, in this confusion of positions, none of the factions could have its cake and eat it too.[7]

Demands for release from binding commitments between negotiating periods were likely to be founded on one of two considerations: either drastic changes in economic conditions imposed undue hardship upon those bound by collective agreements or else inability to enforce contract terms uniformly throughout an industry created inequities for which relief was held to be mandatory. The first consideration could be met by opening the door to frequent revisions of the contract or to special concessions under the contract, without destroying the collective agreement itself. Herein lies the origin of the annual wage reopening clause and of other provisions to reconsider contract terms that had become oppressive. Herein, too, lies the origin of special exemptions and concessions granted individual employers or employees to offset the peculiar circumstances under which they operated.

Still, there were times when one or the other of the contracting parties refused to await the normal procedures of reopening clauses to offset drastic changes in conditions arising during the life of an agreement. Either the party seeking relief feared the delays involved, or doubted the adequacy of the remedy, or wanted an excuse for deliberately terminating its obligations. Breaking the shackles of collective agreements on the pretext of unforeseen circumstances that rendered observance intolerable was a common

---

[7]The first national collective agreement of the full fashioned hosiery industry negotiated in 1929 between the Full Fashioned Hosiery Manufacturers of America and the American Federation of Full Fashioned Hosiery Workers was designated as "a continuing agreement automatically renewing itself from year to year until terminated as hereinafter provided." In addition, the agreement contained the following termination clause: "Either party shall, however, have the right to terminate this agreement at any time during the first year or any subsequent year by giving to the other party 60 days' written notice, by registered mail, of its election to terminate the agreement at the end of said 60-day period; upon the giving of such notice, the agreement shall come to an end at the expiration of the notice period." Text of the agreement appears in *Women's Wear Daily,* Sept. 6, 1929.

practice during the open shop movement of the twenties and in the Great Depression of the thirties. Caught up in the movement to drive organized labor from the citadels of American industry, employers' associations of the needle trades found "unforeseen circumstances" of the post-World War I depression a good pretext for terminating their agreements. A decade later they found more solid grounds for their claims of "unforeseen conditions" in the stark reality of having to survive the Great Depression.

Whatever may have induced the organized manufacturers to take action, the wholesale abrogation of collective agreements during the twenties played havoc with the concept of stability on which the protocol movement had been founded. On December 6, 1920, the New York Clothing Manufacturers' Association passed a resolution abrogating its collective agreement with the Amalgamated Clothing Workers in the New York market of the men's clothing industry. That very day the men's Clothing Manufacturers' Association of Boston also abrogated its agreement with the Amalgamated Clothing Workers. Shortly afterward, certain smaller clothing firms in Baltimore announced that they, too, would no longer observe their agreements with the union. Sooner or later, employers' associations in women's garments, fur manufacturing, and the headwear industries had their turns at deliberately abrogating their agreements. Even in the vacillating realm of international relations, few treaties of peace were so brazenly abandoned.[8]

---

[8]The abrogation of collective agreements in men's clothing was reported in a statement, dated Feb. 5, 1921, of J. S. Potofsky, assistant general secretary, Amalgamated Clothing Workers found at p. 60 ff. in a printed collection of union affidavits submitted in the case of J. Friedman & Co. v. ACWA. Copy filed in the Abelson papers. The wholesale abrogation of collective agreements in the women's garment trades was thus reported by Louis Lorwin [Louis Levine] in *The Women's Garment Workers* (1924), at p. 343:

On Oct. 6, 1920, the New York Cloak and Suit Manufacturers' Protective Association stopped the machinery for the adjustment of grievances under the agreement of May, 1919. A few days later, the New York Children's Dress Manufacturers' Association broke its agreement with the Children's Dress Makers' Union, Local 50. In November, the Boston Cloak Manufacturers' Association abrogated its agreement with the union .... The cloak manufacturers of Toronto and Toledo also abrogated their agreements with their workers and reintroduced piece-work into their shops.

Termination through Contract Violations

The second contention — namely, that the failure to enforce contract provisions uniformly on all parties justified the termination of collective agreements because of the inequities created — was fraught with still more drastic consequences for the principles of the protocol movement. For, if the contracting parties, or any of their members, acquired the right to terminate their collective agreements or to suspend the operation of the impartial machinery wherever the weight of contract enforcement fell unevenly upon them, then the régime of law and order could be no more stable than the judgment of those empowered to pass on contract infractions. Once a charge of unequal enforcement was established, the entire bargaining system would be subject to immediate dissolution.

Of course, there were some who saw no danger in this method of operation, for they believed that no collective bargaining system could long endure without voluntary cooperation from all contracting parties. The very threat of terminating collective agreements would act as an effective deterrent against contract infractions. The very possibility of dissolving the protocol system overnight would cause the organized forces of industry to work more diligently toward solving their own problems, lest they be faced with the alternative of utter destruction through a return to unregulated competition. Fear of the consequences would restrain potential transgressors from touching off a general holocaust of cut-throat competition which could wipe out all "legitimate" elements of industrial society.

Obviously, any right to abrogate collective agreements because of persistent contract infractions that created inequities among competitors had to be carefully circumscribed if, indeed, the right were to be conceded under any conditions. Only the highest arbitrating authority of an industry should authorize so drastic a step.

When the Consolidated Rabbit Dressers' Association abrogated its collective agreement with Local 58, International Fur Workers' Union, in 1928, the association not only reduced the price its workers received for dressing 100 skins from $2.00 to $1.50 but it also announced that the association members would henceforth refuse to recognize the union. H. Begoon, secretary-treasurer, International Fur Workers' Union, to Paul Abelson, impartial chairman of the fur industry, letter, dated Jan. 27, 1928, filed in the Abelson papers.

In the early days of the protocol movement, permanent umpires, impartial chairmen, or boards of arbitration did on occasion exercise the same power to terminate collective agreements that they exerted over the negotiation and revision of those agreements. They not only released employers' associations or labor unions from further responsibilities toward their commitments but even threatened to walk off the job in the face of wanton contract infractions. During the spring of 1916, all members of the council of conciliation for the women's coat and suit trade and of the board of moderators for the men's clothing industry resigned their posts because of failures by the parties to carry out their contractual obligations.[9]

Contrary to expectations, this outlet to freedom from the obligations of collective agreements failed to warm the cockles of employers' hearts. Prospects of deserting the protocol ship for a rowboat life on the seas of unregulated competition failed to bring a sense of security or relief. "It will not do, gentlemen of the Board," fervently argued J. H. Cohen, manufacturers' spokesman, before the dress industry's board of arbitration "to continue to denounce stoppages of work. It will not do for you to say that you will retire from the situation unless they do stop, because the only alternative then is chaos." Aware that his employers were

---

[9]*Daily Trade Record,* May 27, 1916; *New York Times,* May 26, 1916. On May 17, 1916, the council of moderators (three public citizens named under the collective agreement between the American Clothing Manufacturers' Association and the Amalgamated Clothing Workers of America) wrote the president of the association, after unsuccessful attempts to terminate a shop strike, as follows: "Since your association feels that it has reached the limit of patience waiting for this shop to return to work, the undersigned, who negotiated this understanding, hereby declare that your Association is absolved from any responsibility which it has undertaken by the terms of this Agreement."

One week later, the moderators (J. L. Magnes, Henry Moskowitz, and C. L. Bernheimer) wrote: "At the present writing, 4 P.M., May 25th, 1916, there is no resumption of work in the Kevitz shop. We regret to say that inasmuch as the Union has failed to return the workers to the Kevitz shop, which despite the agreement has been on strike, the Amalgamated Clothing Workers of America has not lived up to this stipulation of the agreement of May 5th. Under these circumstances, we feel much to our regret that our usefulness as Moderators representing the public is at an end." From correspondence filed in the Abelson papers.

still unable to shift for themselves, Cohen thus continued to plead his case:

Chaos should not be the only course for rational men. Tear up your protocol — of course you are tempted to do it when such situations come. But what comes after? You must not let the situation go with mere admonition. The process of education and discipline of the workers must be done, and it cannot be done until there is a penalty for failure to obey the law. The law in unenforcible [*sic*]. Any law is unenforcible [*sic*] unless there is a penalty.[10]

Years later, after the organized forces of industry had become less dependent upon the guidance of outside arbitrators, the contracting parties worked out their own terms of abrogating collective agreements for reasons of nonenforcement. By the thirties, a definite pattern of procedure for terminating agreements on these grounds had evolved, and the conditions justifying abrogation had in principle been established. Major agreements negotiated in that decade could be terminated whenever a "substantial violation" persisted in defiance of all efforts to gain compliance with contract terms. Upon the impartial machinery of each industry was bestowed the power of defining when such a substantial violation existed. "In the event of either party claiming for itself the right to terminate this agreement because of a claim of substantial violation of the agreement by the other side," stated the 1936 master contract between the Eastern Women's Headwear Association and the Millinery Workers' Joint Board, "the Impartial Chairman and the Board of Adjustment shall determine on all the facts and circumstances involved the existence or non-existence of a substantial violation of this agreement."

There were many variations in the terminology and intent of these substantial violation clauses. Some gave individual employers, as well as their associations, the right to "terminate" the collective agreement should the highest arbitrating authority find that the union had substantially violated its terms or failed to comply with the decisions of the impartial machinery. Upon employers' associations fell the initial responsibility of deciding whether to support their members in such moves or whether to demand the total abrogation of the collective agreement. Likewise, the union

---

[10]*Minutes,* Arbitration Proceedings between the Dress and Waist Manufacturers' Association and the ILGWU (March 31, 1916), vol. 6, p. 1493.

faced an initial responsibility in demanding a termination of the collective agreement whenever an employers' association or any of its members substantially violated the agreement. While the right of individual firms to absolve themselves of further responsibilities toward the collective agreement was not intended to destroy the operation of the collective agreement itself, permitting employers or workers to renounce their obligations to the organized forces of their industry for any cause tended to undermine the basic purposes of the protocol movement.

Contract Termination for Illegal Strikes

Undoubtedly, the chief purpose of the substantial violation clause was to control illegal strikes and lockouts. During the twenties, at which time this provision appears to have originated, collective agreements of the women's coat and suit trade clearly restricted the option of terminating collective agreements to violations of the no-strike, no-lockout clauses. The right to terminate an agreement following a strike or lockout became operative only after the contracting party charged with an illegal strike or lockout had failed for at least twenty-four hours to restore the status quo. Only a substantial failure to maintain the peace gave the aggrieved party an option to terminate the agreement. Even then, the impartial machinery had to pass upon the existence or nonexistence of a "substantial" violation.[11]

Terminating collective agreements for failure to keep the peace invited open warfare. Once the bonds of organized society had been dissolved, retaliatory lockouts could be instituted to suppress illegal strikes, just as retaliatory strikes could be used to suppress illegal lockouts. Mass picketing and wholesale dismissals were, of course, legitimate weapons of industrial warfare. It was the fear of these consequences that created the demand for every precaution that could be taken to preserve collective agreements and maintain the orderly processes of peaceful settlement. For both parties were aware that exercising the power to terminate agreements in order

---

[11]See the 1922 amendments to the 1919 collective agreement between the Cloak, Suit and Skirt Manufacturers' Protective Association and the ILGWU. *Women's Wear,* July 16, 1922. See also the detailed no-strike, no-lockout clause of the 1926 collective agreement of the Industrial Council of Cloak, Suit and Skirt Manufacturers with the Cloakmakers' Joint Board and the ILGWU.

to meet force with force could leave no victors on the battlefield of industrial relations.

As a last resort, short of terminating collective agreements, some employers' associations claimed the right of retaliatory action *within the bounds of collective bargaining systems*. Such a proposition could, of course, be applied to any type of contract infraction. On one occasion, a cloak manufacturer had assigned certain work to his contractor only to discover later that the contractor had finished 818 garments of the manufacturer's design and sold them directly to the retail trade. Instead of presenting his grievance to be processed under the established procedures of the impartial machinery, this manufacturer retaliated by refusing to send this contractor any more work. For his resort to direct action, the manufacturer was strongly rebuked by the impartial chairman. "I must, therefore, deplore the action of any party who attempts to circumvent the methods of adjudication prescribed in the contract and takes the law into his own hands," asserted Impartial Chairman J. J. Walker. "If this practice is winked at, it will become progressive, resulting in the undermining of the contract, and its ultimate destruction."[12]

For the most part, however, the doctrine of retaliation was given a more limited context. Drawing an analogy from the international law of peace that permitted reprisals between nations as a last means of averting international warfare, employer groups of the needle trades assumed that limited forms of retaliation against unauthorized strikes might also help to preserve industrial peace. Their method was to bottle up the operation of the impartial machinery by withdrawing their clerks, deputy clerks, labor managers, and assistants from the work of contract administration. Adopting the premise that a resort to direct action by union members had in itself suspended the work of the impartial machinery, employers' associations refused to participate in further administrative deliberations until the strikers returned to their

---

[12]J. J. Walker, impartial chairman for the women's coat and suit trade, *Decisions,* Case nos. 3551 and 3664 (Dec. 3, 1942). See also A. Feldblum, impartial chairman of the dress industry, *Decisions,* Case nos. B-116 (Feb. 20, 1935) and B-1031 (Oct. 1, 1935). In these cases, contractors took it upon themselves to withhold deliveries of dresses being manufactured until their jobbers complied with the decisions of the impartial machinery.

jobs. Hopefully, the added pressures on union officials from irate union members, whose grievances could no longer be processed, would restore normal procedures for grievance settlement without the need for dissolving the bonds of collective agreements.[13]

Meeting lawless attacks with lawless reprisals did little to preserve a system of law and order in industry. Refusing to provide personnel for the agencies of contract administration while workers were on strike may have increased pressures on union officials, but this form of retaliation, as often practiced, could scarcely be judged a fair example of an eye for an eye and a tooth for a tooth. More than one employers' association attempted to interrupt the work of the entire impartial machinery throughout all the shops bound by a collective agreement on the mere pretext of a wildcat strike by a handful of workers in a single shop. "You have no right to take the law into your own hands," bitterly protested I. A. Hourwich, union chief clerk, seeking an extraordinary session of the board of grievances for the women's coat and suit trade. "You have no right to go on strike. You have no right to stop the machinery of the protocol in 499 shops, which are in no way involved and whose employees are in no way responsible for the transgression of the people of that one shop."[14]

Retaliation versus Termination

The case for and against retaliation within the framework of collective bargaining systems had presumably been thrashed out in the early years of the protocol movement. J. H. Cohen, counsel for the manufacturers, had once contended before the board of arbitration for the dress and waist industry that there ought to be

---

[13]Needle trade unions often defended their own strike action against arbitrary employer conduct as a form of retaliation that was justifiable quite apart from the use of authorized strikes to help enforce collective agreements. A strike against an employer charged with deliberately reducing wages below contract standards once drew the following defense: "The workers see that the firm takes the law into their [*sic*] own hands and cuts down the price, and believe that it is right for them to take the law into their own hands too." S. Polakoff, union chief clerk, in *Minutes,* Special Meeting of a Committee to Investigate All the Grievances of the Firm and the Workers of Joseph Rosenberg & Co. (Feb. 8, 1915), p. 4.

[14]*Jewish Daily Forward,* Jan. 24, 1913, translation as quoted in Hyman Berman, "The Era of the Protocols...1910–1916" (unpublished Ph.D. dissertation, Columbia University, 1956), p. 295.

a form of limited war against uncontrollable strikers — an authorized use of force short of a general conflagration endangering the collective agreements themselves. Assuming that the protocols were more like treaties of peace than political constitutions, Cohen argued that the bonds of allegiance ought not to be broken by the conduct of one employer or a small group of workers. "It is not right," Cohen stated, "that a whole industry should be plunged into war because of some one officer in the union."[15]

In 1913, the board of arbitration for the women's coat and suit trade was squarely presented with the issue of determining whether unauthorized strikes permitted the organized manufacturers to withdraw from the machinery of contract administration and still remain within the framework of the collective agreement. The first occasion for a full-fledged debate on the pros and cons of this fundamental issue (although not the first time that the employers had resorted to such a practice) was a strike called by the employees of Goldfield and Lachman to force a renegotiation of piece rates through a special union price committee not constituted according to the rules laid down by the board of grievances for the industry.

The position of the striking workers, apparently supported by their local union officials, was clearly in violation of the original Protocol of Peace. Yet neither the combined efforts of the clerks nor direct negotiations between the employers' association and the union succeeded in terminating the strike. Finally, the employers' association directed the clerks it had chosen as agents of the im-

---

[15]*Women's Wear,* April 1, 1916.

Seeking remedies within the structure of collective bargaining, Cohen shied away from the prospect of having manufacturing groups terminate collective agreements on the pretext of wildcat strikes. Such a doctrine, he said, put into the hands of single individuals, who are lawless for the time being, who ignore the binding obligations of the treaty, "the power to turn an industry upside down and send it back for ten or fifteen years to chaos."

"Are we to be left remediless except to terminate the treaty?" Cohen queried. "In other words, you are negotiating today a treaty as between two nations, and you say that an ordinary disturbance caused through the loss of life of a single individual by the unauthorized act of one of the representatives of a country shall not be redressed except by tearing up the treaty and by war." *Minutes,* Arbitration Proceedings between the Ladies' Dress and Waist Manufacturers' Association and the ILGWU (March 31, 1916), vol. 6, pp. 1537, 1538. See also p. 1493.

partial machinery to cease all further activities on other cases arising under the collective agreement. Since the union clerks could not act alone on behalf of a bipartisan agency, this strategic retaliatory move by the organized manufacturers effectively tied up the machinery of contract administration.[16]

During this long-drawn-out controversy, the union and the employers' association each charged the other with declaring war on the protocol system. In a letter to the employers' association, dated January 25, 1913, the union chief clerk, I. A. Hourwich, wrote:

Mr. J. Zimmerman, one of our deputy clerks, reports that on the 24th inst., when he called at the offices of your Association in order to confer with your clerk and deputy clerk under the terms of the Protocol, he was informed that the deputy clerks of your Association had been ordered to suspend all negotiations with our deputy clerks in regard to specific grievances in factories other than that of Messrs. Goldfield & Lachman, until our union would accede to the views of your side on the Goldfield & Lachman controversy.

A reference to the terms of the Protocol will readily convince you that such a stand is absolutely unjustifiable. It is tantamount to a declaration of war on the part of your Association. We are ready and willing to meet every controversy that may arise, in the manner provided by the Protocol, and are willing to abide by the decisions of the bodies created under the terms thereof. We cannot, however, concede to your Association the right to be the final arbitrator in any particular controversy.[17]

On the same day the association answered as follows:

Replying to your communication of January 25th, we call your attention to the fact that, underlying the protocol and the decisions of the Board of Arbitration, are certain fundamental principles forming the basis of the protocol, without which the existence of harmonious relations between the Union and the Association is impossible.

---

[16]For a discussion of the Goldfield and Lachman case, see *Minutes,* Board of Grievances...[women's coat and suit trade] (Jan. 12 and 27, 1913); *Minutes,* Conference between the Cloak, Suit and Skirt Manufacturers' Protective Association and the ILGWU and the Cloakmakers' Joint Board, Feb. 3 and 4, 1913; *Minutes,* Board of Arbitrators...[women's coat and suit trade] (Oct. 3, 1913).

[17]*Minutes,* Conference between Representatives of the Cloak, Suit and Skirt Manufacturers' Protective Association, the ILGWU, and the Cloakmakers' Joint Board (Feb. 4, 1913), p. 32.

The first of these is, that the rules of the Board of Grievances and the decisions of the Board of Grievances are binding upon both sides, and it is the duty of the responsible officials of both sides to carry these out in good faith. The failure of the [union] officers to carry out these rules automatically stops the machinery. The second of these is, that, whenever either side deliberately fails to carry out in good faith, a decision made by the Board of Grievances or a fundamental principle of the protocol, the machinery stops automatically.

When the Union, contrary to the rules and understandings, prevents a manufacturer from working *for two weeks,* by ordering the people of the shop not to settle prices according to the established rules and practices, such action is, in every sense of the term, a deliberate breach of the protocol on the part of the Union. Under such circumstances, the officers of the Association have no other recourse than to refuse to attend to other cases until the Union, in good faith, carries out the rules. . . .

The machinery for carrying out the terms of the protocol in adjustment of difficulties is, as you know, the machinery of the Board of Grievances and the Clerks. By the rules of the Board, *all business is subordinated to the business of returning people to work who have either stopped themselves or have been ordered to stop.* . . . Consequently, whenever your representatives refuse to order people back to work pending the adjustment of grievances, the machinery is stopped. . . .

In the particular case of Goldfield & Lachman, the Union, by refusing to carry out the rules, is the aggressor, and its action is "tantamount to the declaration of war" to use your own phrase. The Association is on the other hand only defending a right which cannot be abrogated, and which has been accepted in practice.[18]

This exchange of views, couched in the context of a dispute between nations, was shortly continued in debates before the board of arbitration for the industry. There I. A. Hourwich restated the position of the union as follows:

This automatic stoppage of the machinery is, in my judgment, a somewhat one-sided adjudication. If the Protocol can be suspended whenever one side is dissatisfied, is that not an automatic attitude? This is a case where your Association has taken the law into its own hands. Suppose the Sheriff does not carry out the mandates of the Court, now what will happen? If the Sheriff does not want to execute a judgment

---

[18]*Ibid.,* pp. 33–34.

of the Court, we will have to declare a strike against the Court, and will now take the law into our own hands? No! We shall go and ask a remedy against the Sheriff, but we shall not stop the administration of justice, unless we declare war.

Of course, every sovereign nation has always the power to declare war. If it be war, we shall consider whether we shall go to war or accede to the demands of the Balkan Allies.[19]

In reply, J. H. Cohen, counsel for the manufacturers, restated the position of the organized employers:

There is no remedy for the treasonable conduct of a representative on either side — conduct in violation of the rules of the Grievance Board — except refusal to do further business with him. The Association does not refuse to do further business with the Union; it does not refuse to go into conference with you. But it must refuse to deal with your accredited representatives, who are lawless, and who refuse to follow the rules that your organization and this organization have adopted. As soon as you send representatives who will observe order — proceed with business in orderly fashion — business will be resumed....

We didn't raise this issue; but when your stoppages of work get to such a point that our members cannot do business, when our peace treaty becomes a joke, and a state of warfare exists,...and we have got a stoppage of work in one shop which has lasted four weeks, what are we going to do? Haven't we the right to insist that the rules of the Board of Grievances will be carried out? This isn't a question of argument. We didn't declare war. When the enemy sends in its battleships to my coast and begins firing, the notice to the other country isn't the act of war. The act of war is something that comes before the notice is sent. The act of war is the refusal on their side to settle the differences in the Goldfield & Lachman shop.[20]

---

[19]*Ibid.,* p. 67.

[20]*Ibid.,* pp. 45–46, 87, quoting from *Minutes,* Board of Grievances, Cloak, Suit and Skirt Industry (Jan. 27, 1913), p. 12.

As an aftermath of the Monroe Froehlich case (see above p. 286) Cohen sought a hearing before the board of arbitration of the dress and waist industry on the failure of union officials to do their duty in returning strikers to their jobs. Such a procedure within the framework of the collective bargaining system was held preferable to a termination of the agreement:

In other words, it is as if the United States of America and Germany, having a treaty of peace, the treaty shall not be terminated simply because some diplomatic agent or some admiralty officer has violated the good

Whatever the justification, if any, for the strike at the Goldfield & Lachman shop, the board of arbitration refused to condone acts of the employers' association in stopping operation of the impartial machinery. "It seems to us entirely clear," noted Chairman Louis D. Brandeis following the long debate, "that the action of the stopping of the machinery was an action which was in violation of the protocol...and the failure of individual [union] officers to assert their authority such as they had, to compel men to go back to work, failure of the policemen, as it were, to do their duty, did not amount to an automatic suspension of the agreement." The contention that work stoppages "automatically put an end [to] or suspended the operation of the machinery which had been devised," stated Mr. Brandeis on behalf of the board, "is unsound as a proposition of law, and if we were called upon to act as arbitrators in passing upon it, we should so declare unhesitatingly and emphatically."[21]

A similar incident arose a year later (1914) in a dispute at the plant of R. Berg, fur manufacturer, following the discharge of an employee who was a union shop chairman. Without consulting the impartial machinery or awaiting an official investigation of the grievance, the fur workers deliberately called a shop strike. In addition to publicly advertising the strike in the labor press, the union placed pickets at the entrance to the shop to prevent the substitution of other workers in the plant. Thereupon, the Mutual Protective Fur Manufacturers' Association, on behalf of its member firm, contended that the persistent refusal of the union to send the workers back to the shop constituted an indirect violation of the protocol that justified a refusal to participate in further deliberations about the case.

---

faith of the principle of good spirit that should exist, but that there should be opportunity for the disposition of the matter.
—J. H. Cohen in *Minutes,* Arbitration Proceedings between the Dress and Waist Manufacturers' Association and the ILGWU (March 31, 1916), vol. 6, pp. 1557–1558.

[21]*Minutes,* Conference between Representatives of the Cloak, Suit and Skirt Manufacturers' Protective Association, the ILGWU, and the Cloakmakers' Joint Board (Feb. 4, 1913), pp. 213–214. Later, Brandeis held that there could be no setting aside of the protocol on the claim of one party that the other party had violated the agreement. *Minutes,* Board of Arbitrators...[women's coat and suit trade] (Oct. 3, 1913), pp. 68–69.

"Under the circumstances," wrote an association representative to J. L. Magnes, impartial chairman of the industry, "the Board of Directors considers the protocol inoperative, and even suspended, until the Union sees their way to abide by what they agreed to, 'not to call strikes.'" In his decision, J. L. Magnes conceded that the union's action in the case was "censurable in the highest degree"; nevertheless, he took an uncompromising stand on the power of either party to suspend the agreement. "I beg to inform you that it is entirely beyond the power of your Association to consider the 'protocol', as you call it, 'inoperative and even suspended'. . . . Whatever be the merits of the Berg case, the agreement of September 8, 1912, is to continue in operation until September 8, 1914, as agreed upon in Paragraph 10."[22]

Employers' Associations and Direct Action

Denying employers' associations the right to initiate retaliatory measures by suspending the work of the impartial machinery within the framework of the protocol movement did not stop the organized manufacturers from continuing to seek whatever type of remedy would hasten the return of striking employees to their jobs. Waiting for the orderly processes of the impartial machinery to run their appointed course against strikers and their union could never be an adequate substitute for an immediate return to work. No penalties, however drastic, that the impartial machinery might impose upon the strikers or upon their union could ever fully compensate the employers for an interruption of production at the critical stages in highly seasonal industries.

Wherever orders had to be filled within definite time limits or else be cancelled, specific performance of the contract was indispensable to the life of the trade. If strikes could not lawfully be prevented during this critical period, then they must be cut short by whatever means was available. "Shop strikes and departmental

[22]Louis Dorfman, counsel for the manufacturers, to J. L. Magnes, impartial chairman (March 10, 1914); D. M. Rappaport, association committeeman to J. L. Magnes (March 11, 1914); J. L. Magnes to D. M. Rappaport (March 12, 1914); Frederick Spicer, chairman, board of directors, Mutual Protective Fur Manufacturers' Association to J. L. Magnes (March 18, 1914); and J. L. Magnes, *Decision*, "In the Matter of the Difficulties between the Firm of R. Berg and his Employees" (April 2, 1914). Correspondence filed in the Abelson papers.

strikes have no reason or justification under our system of joint control and adjustment," wrote Adolph Engels, president of the Associated Fur Manufacturers. "They can and must be prevented. It is not sufficient that they be adjusted after they occur; they must be prevented from occurrence."[23]

The evil of shop strikes at critical periods was compounded by the sectional method of manufacture. With eighty to a hundred separate operations required in the manufacture of a man's coat and with forty to fifty separate operations required to produce a pair of men's pants, noted one observer of union tactics in the early twenties, a strike or slowdown on one operation could stop all other operations. The manufacturer who had to ship his merchandise for the fall season or lose his only opportunity to realize a profit on his investment would quickly capitulate. Then, as soon as one section gained its objective, another section would curtail production until its members had received more pay. The repetition of this procedure was known as the "pyramiding of wage scales."[24]

The organized manufacturers soon found that the certainty of immediate punishment was the most effective deterrent against unauthorized strikes. Even though strike cases were given priority in grievance procedures, waiting for the normal operations of the impartial machinery did not provide a certainty of punishment immediate enough to be effective. Locking the door after the horse was stolen did not help the manufacturer who had but one horse. Bankruptcy generally arrived before retribution. The employers contended that this was a case for preventive justice which could only be achieved by the use of direct action. The possibility of a general lockout, not only in the troubled plant, but throughout all the plants of association members, would subject hit-and-run strikers to great pressure from their fellow workers.

Used in this sense, the lockout became a weapon of contract enforcement that was the exact counterpart of union-sponsored strikes. Whether used as a last resort to enforce awards of arbitrators or imposed immediately upon alleged infractions of contract terms, the lockout stood on exactly the same "legal" or "illegal" foundation as the strike. When Jacob Panken, counsel for the

---

[23]Adolph Engels to J. L. Magnes, impartial chairman, letter, dated Feb. 25, 1919, filed in the Abelson papers.
[24]*Daily News Record,* May 17, 1921.

United Brotherhood of Tailors, was arguing before the U. S. Commission on Industrial Relations, June 5, 1914, for the right of a union to strike on its own authority against employers violating their contracts, he was asked whether he would concede to the employers who claimed that the union had broken the agreement "a right to lock everybody out." Panken readily accepted the two-way character of his proposition. "Where both sides know they have got to live up to their provisions of the contract — they have to take the consequences — they live up to them," he said.[25]

In the evolution of enforcement machinery, lockouts, like strikes, were ultimately given a legitimate status and summoned to the aid of law and order. Collective agreements that conceded the organized workers a right to strike against firms violating their agreements also gave the organized manufacturers a similar right to lock out workers refusing to meet their contractual obligations. These rights were similarly circumscribed in both cases. Authorized lockouts, like authorized strikes, were most often confined to use as a last resort short of terminating the collective agreements themselves. "The employer reserves the right to lock out any department or dismiss the entire personnel of such department and/or the entire mill," stated the 1933 national collective agreement of the full fashioned hosiery industry, "where members of the Union in any department refuse to carry out the decisions of the Impartial Chairman, duly rendered, within twenty days after service upon the Union of such decision."[26]

---

[25]*Final Report and Testimony,* vol. 2, p. 2020. A few years later, Panken could have cited experiences in the women's coat and suit trade to support his views on the unrestricted use of strikes and lockouts to enforce collective agreements. After the violent death of the original Protocol of Peace in the spring of 1916, the Cloak, Suit and Skirt Manufacturers' Protective Association and the ILGWU, on August 1, 1916, entered into a new three-year agreement that substituted for the impartial machinery an absolute right of the union to strike and an absolute right of the employers to discharge or lockout. The results were less disturbing to the reign of law and order in industry than might have been anticipated. See Boris Emmet, "Trade Agreements in the Women's Clothing Industries in New York City," *Monthly Labor Review,* December 1917, vol. 5, pp. 1093–1102.

[26]Not all union leaders would concede to employers' associations the right of direct action that labor unions themselves had found so effective. When the Eastern Women's Headwear Association in the mid-thirties threatened a "strike" to enforce union compliance with the collective agreement for the

In so far as the use of authorized lockouts only as a last resort came too late to meet the immediate crisis of shop strikes at critical periods, employers' associations continued to seek out more drastic remedies for an evil that destroyed the basic purposes of the protocol movement. The early opinions of Brandeis and Magnes to the contrary, some employer groups continued to withdraw from the operations of the impartial machinery as a means of terminating shop strikes. Early in 1935, for example, the Women's Head-wear Group of millinery manufacturers not only "abrogated" the impartial machinery of its collective agreement with the millinery workers' union, without terminating the agreement itself, but also voted unanimously to raise a security fund of $100,000 "as a means of aiding those employers who have been subjected to unjust stoppages by the millinery union." Where such actions did not prevail, the organized manufacturers could still go to the extreme of declaring the collective agreement itself abrogated.[27]

In every case, employer threats preceded employer action. On some occasions, threats at least toned down the pace of lawless

---

millinery industry, Max Zaritsky, union president, was up in arms. Under the caption, "Zaritsky Hails Employers' Move as Revolutionary," *Women's Wear Daily,* Nov. 6, 1935, carried some of Zaritsky's views that had the ring of so many appeals from organized manufacturers to labor unions on the subject of direct action. "In the past," stated Zaritsky, "the practice has been to conduct industrial relations on the theory that conciliation and arbitration are methods far more effective and beneficial to the industry than turmoil and strife, such as the Association now seeks to provide."

[27]*Women's Wear Daily,* Jan. 17, 1935. As in the early years of the protocols, employer refusal to participate in the work of the impartial machinery remained a potent weapon where this action left the union with scores of pending grievance cases that it could otherwise easily have won — cases of unfair discharges, of overtime infractions, of nonpayment for legal holidays, and the like. The point is illustrated in the following correspondence:

> There are pending before the Board of Grievances 15 cases concerning the non-payment by the manufacturers for a legal holiday (Decoration Day), and these cases could not be taken up because of the failure of the representatives of the Association on the Grievance Board to function. There is a case of discharge which is now pending before the Grievance Board for several months and which was not acted upon for the same reason.
>
> —M. Goldman, organizer, Ladies' Hat Frame Workers' Union, to J. E. Helfer, secretary, National Hat Frame Manufacturers' Association, letter, dated June 18, 1927, filed in the Abelson papers.

conduct by wildcat strikers. In 1926, for example, the Associated Fur Manufacturers threatened "to adopt such measures as will be advisable under the circumstances," unless the furriers' union returned the workers to their respective shops immediately. After repeated charges of persistent and willful violations of the no-strike clauses that year, the association threatened to take the matter of strike control out of the hands of the impartial machinery and put it up to the association's membership for "emergency treatment." At a special meeting of the association on July 19, 1926, at which shop strikes for higher wages were roundly denounced, strong sentiment was expressed for a lockout of workers to end "the pyramiding of wage scales in the market."[28]

Meanwhile, industry arbitrators continued to condemn employer attempts at suspending the operation of the impartial machinery. One important case arose in 1930 out of a shop strike over piece rates in the plant of an employer who belonged to an association of dress manufacturers. Charging that piece rates had not been settled (the agreement prohibited work on garments until the rates were fixed), the dressmakers' union refused to return the striking workers to their jobs. Equally convinced that the prices had already been settled, the employers' association, after denouncing the union for refusing to return the strikers, called off all association clerks from their duties with the impartial machinery. Recalling the clerks, so the employers alleged, suspended the operation of the machinery for the adjustment of disputes between the association and the union and rendered the agreement inoperative.

Bypassing all issues concerning the validity of the strike itself, N. I. Stone, impartial chairman for the dress and waist industry, hit directly at the association's move to suspend the agreement:

Nothing is said in the agreement which by any construction warrants either party to take the law into its own hands and suspend the operation of the agreement because it thinks that the other party has violated the agreement. If this were permitted, there would be nothing to prevent the manager of either organization from stopping the opera-

---

[28]See S. N. Samuels, president, Associated Fur Manufacturers, to Paul Abelson, impartial chairman, fur manufacturing industry, letter, dated July 15, 1926; "Resolutions Adopted Unanimously by the Board of Directors of the Associated Fur Manufacturers," August 31, 1926, and accompanying letter, dated Sept. 1, 1926, to the Furriers' Joint Board. These materials are filed in the Abelson papers. See also *Women's Wear Daily,* July 20, 1926.

tion of the agreement whenever he considered the other party wrong. The whole spirit of the agreement is to do away with one-sided action, calling for reprisals from the other party, and to substitute arbitration through a continuously operating machinery for the adjustment of every conceivable dispute.[29]

Employer Approach to Contract Termination

Repeatedly thwarted in attempts to employ direct action within the framework of the protocol system, the organized manufacturers were forced to fall back on the possibility of total escape from the realm of law and order. Taking the position that labor unions by failing to control strikes had renounced their "treaties of peace" with employers' associations, the organized manufacturers insisted that these "treaties" had been abrogated and were null, void, and of no force and effect whatsoever. Following this unconditional termination of collective agreements, each employer, with or without the assistance of his association, was at liberty to pursue such policies against his striking employees as he might devise.

In the early years of the protocol movement, a number of collective agreements met a violent death that employers attributed to the outbreak of unauthorized and uncontrolled shop strikes. "Shop strikes terminated the protocol in the cloak and suit trade," declared J. H. Cohen, founder of the protocol movement. "The crisis in 1913 was the result of a shop strike. The same in 1911. The ladies' tailors' protocol went smash on account of shop strikes, and if we look into the records we find that the Industrial Relations Commission reported that employers refused to enter into collective bargaining agreements because of the failure of the union to suppress shop strikes."[30]

The first collective agreement in men's clothing between the American Clothing Manufacturers' Association and the Amalga-

---

[29]N. I. Stone, impartial chairman for the dress industry, *Decision* (1930). Text in *Women's Wear Daily,* Oct. 14, 1930.

[30]*Women's Wear,* Dec. 30, 1915; April 1, 1916. Charging that the union had violated the no-strike clause of the collective agreement by ordering strikes before grievances were heard by the impartial machinery, the North West Cloak and Suit Manufacturers' Association of Chicago sent a letter to the union "abrogating the agreement" and announcing that the association members would reopen their shops on Dec. 15, 1915 as "open shops" only. *Women's Wear,* Dec. 6, 1915.

mated Clothing Workers' Union likewise met a sudden death. Employers attributed the catastrophe to shop strikes — just as they attributed the death of the first women's coat and suit protocol to shop strikes. "The union's action in conducting shop strikes despite the fact that under the agreement strikes are prohibited, terminated both agreements," noted a reporter for the *Daily Trade Record* on May 29, 1916. "The contention of the employers in the two industries are virtually the same and embody the fact that the unions are unable to control their own members and that flagrant violations of the provisions of the agreements are not discouraged by the union leaders to their followers."

Officially terminating or abandoning collective agreements on the treaty of peace theory held out certain advantages over weakening the régime of law and order by tolerating forms of direct action within collective bargaining systems. Authorized lockouts or wholesale discharges to enforce decisions of the impartial machinery might induce unauthorized lockouts and unjustifiable discharges to support the employers' own interpretations of the contract. Such "illegal" lockouts or discharges could, in turn, lead to the use of these devices to counteract those decisions of the impartial machinery that employers did not wish to accept. Thus, by imperceptible stages, a useful weapon to prevent strikes and enforce awards might come to defeat the very purposes for which it was intended.

In 1915, a dress manufacturer bound by the dress and waist protocol refused to accept a decision of the clerks calling for extra compensation on piece rates. His immediate reaction was to lock out the cutters *who insisted upon compliance with the award!* A year later, the manufacturers' association of the women's coat and suit trade responded to an award by the council of conciliation, requiring employers to see that their workers were "union members in good standing," by locking out all 25,000 of the workers in the shops of the association's 409 members. Perhaps the institutions of collective bargaining had better be dissolved than allowed to disintegrate through the use of internal force and violence which threatened to destroy all respect for established authority.[31]

---

[31]*Minutes,* Meeting of the Board of Grievances of the Dress and Waist Industry (April 23, 1915), pp. 39–40; Lorwin, *The Women's Garment Workers,* p. 310.

The most publicized of all attempts by employers to abrogate collective agreements came from the Cloak, Suit and Skirt Manufacturers' Protective Association that had been a party to the original Protocol of Peace. In 1919, this association and the Cloakmakers' Joint Board, ILGWU, signed a three-year agreement that among other things substituted week work for piecework. During the post-World War I depression, the manufacturers charged their employees with maintaining inadequate standards of production for the pay they were receiving. By the terms of a "supplemental agreement" of June 3, 1921, the contracting parties established a joint production commission to investigate the possibilities of "working out measures which would... bring up the productivity of the workers to a point fair and proper to both sides." The committee was to study "shop and production records" and to bring in a final report of its findings on November 1, 1921, several months before the original three-year contract expired.

A month before the report was due, however, the employers' association, on the pretext that the union had previously abrogated the 1919 agreement by failing to suppress individual shop strikes, refused to participate further in the activities of the joint production commission. Then, on October 25, 1921, the association adopted a resolution looking to a "radical readjustment of industrial standards" including a change from week work to piece rates, with new wage scales and hours of work to be established by the executive committee of the association. The introduction of these unilateral changes was an outright violation of the 1919 agreement and signalled the outbreak of a general strike in the industry. Thereupon, the employers' association met and formally declared the collective agreement abrogated.

For the first time in the history of collective bargaining, the ILGWU then called upon the courts to restrain an employers' association from breaking a collective agreement. A preliminary injunction issued by New York Supreme Court Justice Charles L. Guy on November 29, 1921 was followed by a permanent injunction from New York Supreme Court Justice Robert F. Wagner on January 11, 1922. Rejecting the argument that the three-year collective agreement had at any time been terminated by action of the union, Mr. Justice Wagner permanently restrained the employers' association from "combining and conspiring in any way to order, direct, instigate, counsel, advise, or encourage the members of the Cloak, Suit and Skirt Manufacturers' Protective Association, or any of them, to cease performing, or to violate the agreements of May 29, 1919 and June 3, 1921."[32]

Concluding Observations

A consideration of the fundamental issues bearing on the character, duration, and abrogation of collective agreements provides a fitting climax to the development of instrumentalities for attaining the objectives of collective action. Only a common determination to achieve goals of mutual benefit to both parties could have led the sponsors of the protocol movement into exhaustive efforts at perfecting their institutions of industrial self-government. Despite theoretical discussions drawn from analogies to civil government and to the international community of nations, the parties to collective agreements fashioned their tools of operation more from trial and error than from the application of abstract principles. Theirs was the task of reconciling industrial democracy with the necessity for law and order, of compromising direct action with orderly procedures for settling disputes, of permitting flexibility within the limits of stability required for business operations, and of defending the continuity of logical development against the sudden upheavals of a changing world.

So long as their eyes were fixed on the ultimate objective of fair competition, the organized forces of each industry survived the turmoil of wars, depressions, and seasonal industries and held their ranks against rising pressures from the unorganized elements among workers, suppliers, manufacturers, distributors, and retailers. Fears of starvation or threats of bankruptcy may have warped the logic and cooled the zeal of the staunchest advocates for joint action, but neither evil could break the ranks of the "enlightened"

---

[32]Chronologies of this episode appear in *Women's Wear,* Jan. 17, 1922, and in the *New York Call,* Jan. 19, 1922. Mr. Justice A. R. Page thoroughly rehashed the history of the case in his opinion for the Appellate Division of the New York Supreme Court sustaining the injunction. Schlesinger v. Quinto, 201 App. Div. 487 (1922); 194 N.Y. Supp. 401. Mr. Justice Wagner's decision from which an appeal was taken is reported at 117 Misc. 735 (1922); 192 N.Y. Supp. 564. A general treatment of this case and of similar cases in other cities may be found in Lorwin, *The Women's Garment Workers,* pp. 343–349.

leadership who understood the consequences of defeat. The protocol movement suffered many deaths but was always born again, usually with the help of new machinery and new procedures constructed to offset the shortcomings disclosed by experience. How this evolving system contributed to the cause of fair competition can best be seen in the administration of restrictions on outside contracting.

Chapter 10

Enforcing Controls
over Contracting

A LL the weapons of contract enforcement from peaceful persuasion to threats of violence and the use of force were sooner
or later brought to bear upon the evils of outside production. The
war to prevent inside manufacturers from burrowing beneath the
floors of minimum work standards in their own shops could not
preserve the principles of the protocol movement so long as chiselers could resort to outside contracting for an escape from their
obligations. Maintaining protocol standards over inside establishments was wholly ineffective against those who found in the
jobber-contracting system an alternative means of gaining their
objectives. If the principles of controlled competition were to
prevail, then the agencies of law enforcement had to move from
the highways of inside establishments to the byways and hedges
of outside production.

Equal Standards for Outside Shops

Maintaining controls over outside contracting was essentially a
problem of seeing that wages and working conditions in the outside shops — patronized by the organized jobbers — and inside
manufacturers did not fall below the minimum labor standards
prescribed for the inside establishments. The pressure to move
outside for the advantages of lower production costs would cease

to exist if conditions of employment were equalized between the inside factories and the outside shops. "The same conditions as prevail in the shops of the members of the Association," stated the 1914 collective agreement of the Associated Fur Manufacturers with the Furriers' Joint Board of Greater New York, "shall be maintained in the shops of contractors working for members of the Association."

By far the most important of these conditions was the equalizing of hourly or weekly wage rates for time-payment workers and the application of a single piece-rate standard to all those paid according to output. "All [piece-rate] prices for garments designed, originated or directly or indirectly made by a member of the association," stated the 1916 collective agreement between the Boston Dress and Waist Manufacturers' Association and the ILGWU, "shall be settled in his own shop, and the prices so settled shall be paid in the outside shops as well as in the inside shops." This agreement also provided for a joint board of control representing the union, the association, and the public to see that no work was sent to outside contractors whose labor standards were lower than those of the inside shops.[1]

In the early years of the protocol movement, however, efforts to achieve these ends were for the most part directed toward the compulsory registration of all contractors. Information on the names, character, type of work, and location of contractors was a prerequisite for effective regulation. Under the original protocol for the women's coat and suit trade, registration of contractors was first imposed by a resolution of the board of grievances in 1912. Soon the requirement for registration became a part of the collective agreements themselves. The Children's Dress Protocol, effective March 8, 1913, for example, expressly stated that "the manufacturer may employ outside contractors, provided, however,

---

[1]The text of this agreement is printed in *Women's Wear*, Feb. 10, 1916. For early ideas on the development of methods and procedures for controlling outside production in the women's coat and suit trade, see John Dickinson and Morris Kolchin, *Report of an Investigation,* submitted to Governor Alfred E. Smith's Advisory Commission for the industry on March 10, 1925. For similar proposals by the union and the manufacturers in the dress and waist industry, see *Minutes,* Arbitration Proceedings...[dress industry] (Feb. 14, 1916), vol. 5, p. 586; and a decision of Judge J. W. Mack, chairman of the industry's board of arbitration, reported in *Women's Wear,* Feb. 28, 1916.

that the manufacturer shall disclose to Local No. 50 the names and addresses of such contractors."

Whatever the controls to be established over the system of contracting, administrative agencies had to be designated to enforce the rules of the game. Unions, and sometimes associations, not only became depositories for contractor registration lists but they were also given responsibility for keeping those lists up to date to reflect all the changes in contractor assignments. Few jobbers or inside manufacturers cared to disclose the sources of their outside production. Still less could the contractors themselves be relied upon to reveal the sources of their income. In the first two decades of the protocol movement, the Amalgamated Clothing Workers of America conducted a continuing nationwide campaign to expose all contractor operations in the manufacture of men's clothing. More and more, however, responsibility for regulating and restricting the use of contractors fell upon some agency of the impartial machinery.[2]

Jobbers' Responsibility for Contractors' Labor Standards

Along with the requirement for registration of all contractors came a second expedient for insuring uniformity in labor standards between inside and outside shops. This device called for making jobbers directly responsible for the terms of employment in the shops of their contractors. The belief was widely entertained that uniformity in labor costs between inside and outside shops could be enforced only if jobbers and inside manufacturers were held accountable for keeping wage scales and working conditions in the contractor shops they patronized up to the level of inside establishments. The enforcement of such measures would obligate jobbers and inside manufacturers to reimburse the employees of

---

[2]Under their 1921 collective agreement, the Clothing Manufacturers Association of New York and the Amalgamated Clothing Workers provided for a clothing commission representing jobbers, contractors, and inside manufacturers, as well as the workers, to administer clauses on contracting, the chief of which prohibited contractors from changing their manufacturers and manufacturers or jobbers from changing their contractors, except on approval of the parties or with the consent of the board of arbitration created by the 1921 agreement. *Daily News Record,* June 18, 1921. The text of this agreement is printed in the issue of June 3, 1921.

contractors for whatever losses those workers suffered from infractions of the labor standards by these contractors.

Inside responsibility for outside labor standards had always been a union slogan based on the premise that outside contractors who turned bundles of cut cloth into finished products were little more than foremen of jobbers or inside producers receiving pay for supervisory functions. On the other hand, jobbers and inside manufacturers argued that contractors supplied their own capital and controlled their own movements; nor could they be prevented from dealing directly with the retail trade. The contractor, so jobbers and manufacturers concluded, was the real employer of labor and should therefore assume sole responsibility for labor standards in outside shops.[3]

So long as the organized jobbers and inside producers rejected all responsibility for the labor standards of their contractors, the ILGWU could enforce its objective only against independent firms through unlimited strikes that compelled jobbers to meet all contractor wage shortages. In the last three months of 1922, for ex-

---

[3]They [contractors] did not perform a single function which was different in any way from those performed by the production man or foreman in the inside shop. They had nothing to do with the designing of the garment, the making of the original pattern or selecting the styles. They had nothing to do with the purchase of any materials or trimmings, or with the selection of fabrics or their colors. They maintained no showrooms and employed no salesmen; they had no garments to sell and no customers to whom to sell. Their only profit was the difference between what they got from the jobber and what they paid out to themselves for their own services, to others for overhead, and to their workers in wages.

—Emil Schlesinger, *The Outside System of Production in the Women's Garment Industry in the New York Market* (1951), pp. 14–15, 63–72.

In reality the jobber is the manufacturer. The sub-manufacturer is the foreman who works for the jobber, under a piece system. The goods belong to the jobber, the style belongs to the jobber and, therefore, everything of importance pertaining to the production of the garment belongs to the jobber.

—Morris Sigman, president of the ILGWU, as quoted in *Women's Wear*, March 4, 1924.

See also Morris Sigman in ILGWU, *Justice,* Feb. 29, 1924. For an opposing viewpoint, see the text of a statement by Samuel Blumberg, counsel for the Merchants' Ladies' Garment Association (jobbers), in *Women's Wear*, April 11, 1924.

ample, the Amalgamated Clothing Workers' Union collected from independent men's clothing jobbers and inside manufacturers some $80,000 for wage deficiencies that their contractors failed to meet. But the extension of this principle to the organized segments of the trade had to await the acceptance of the principle by the organized groups themselves.[4]

Actually, employer groups accepted the basic principle of jobber responsibility for the labor standards of outside contractors long before this principle could be implemented or enforced. Beginning with the 1926 collective agreement, all contracts negotiated between the Industrial Council of Cloak, Suit and Skirt Manufacturers (inside producers) and the ILGWU held association members responsible for wage payments on work done for them by outside contractors. By the mid-thirties, clauses of this character were common throughout the needle trades. "Should a contractor fail to meet the payroll due the workers," stated the 1935 collective agreement between the National Association of Blouse Manufacturers (jobbers) and Local 25, ILGWU, "then notice of said failure to pay shall be given to the member of the Association for whom the contractor worked, within three days after the payroll became due, and the payroll is then to be paid by the member of the Association to the workers."[5]

---

[4]*Daily News Record*, Dec. 26, 1922. The organized contractors naturally supported the union stand. Their plight in the absence of jobber responsibility for wage scales was described by Isaac Fleisher, manager of the United Coat Contractors' Association, representing 438 organized contractors of the men's clothing trade:

> We might just as well shut up shop as continue under the present conditions. The manufacturers [jobbers] have given the workers increases in pay, but they have made the gift in name only. We have to pay the money and get no extra from the manufacturer [jobber] for doing so. If all the burden is falling on the shoulders of the contractors then we are entitled to some consideration.
>
> —*Daily Trade Record*, July 28, 1916.

[5]Reporting on the introduction of the elaborate system of controls over outside contracting under the 1936 dress industry agreements, *Women's Wear Daily*, March 30, 1936, noted that "part of the big idea is to drive home to the jobbers particularly that they are just as surely responsible for the workers as if they could hear the machines whizzing in their back room." The 1936 collective agreement between the Belt Association and Local 40, ILGWU, stated that the manufacturer who sends work to outside shops "assumes full

The difficulty of enforcing these provisions arose from the inability of the various factions to devise a scheme through which all interested parties could participate in determining the extent of their liabilities. To assume responsibility for underwriting the labor standards of their contractors, the organized jobbers and inside manufacturers demanded the right to participate in setting those standards. Naturally, the organized contractors who paid the bills in the first place also expected to help determine the extent of their obligations to their workers. Only by having interested jobbers, contractors, and inside manufacturers negotiate jointly with the union could the proper incentive be found for implementing this principle.

Formal negotiations of this magnitude, however, were unsuited to the determination of piece rates which required continual adjustment in each shop for variations in materials, styles, types, and sizes of garments, as well as for changes in methods of production. The evil of shop bargaining, so widely condemned but not resolved by the original sponsors of the protocol movement, had to give way to more centralized procedures for price-fixing by the permanent impartial machinery of each trade. Not until help came from the federal government through codes of fair competition were the interested parties able to work out procedures that would permit acceptance of jobber responsibility for contractor wage scales.[6]

---

responsibility for the conditions of such outside shops and for the payment of the wages of workers employed by such outside shop, with the same force and effect as if that shop would be owned directly by the said member of the Association."

The Amalgamated Clothing Workers of America early took the position that in the absence of responsibility by jobbers and inside manufacturers of the men's clothing industry for the labor standards of their contractors, these jobbers could "enjoy the full benefits of the ruthless exploitation and bear none of the responsibilities for it." Accordingly, the union subsequently insisted upon such contract clauses as that found in the 1935 collective agreement with the New York Clothing Manufacturers' Exchange making manufacturers "responsible for carrying out the terms of this agreement, whether the work is performed in an inside shop or in a contract shop." See ACWA, *Report and Proceedings*, Third Biennial Convention (May 1918), p. 64.

[6]See article by C. H. Green in *Women's Wear Daily*, August 15, 1933.

Minimum Costs of Production

A third measure to facilitate the enforcement of uniform labor standards in outside shops would establish minimum production costs that contractors be guaranteed for their work. The necessity for such a move arose from the inability to control wage chiseling in contractor shops where "the capacity for competition is determined by the power to exploit the workers." Contractors could not be prevented from recouping their losses by helping themselves to their workers' wages. "In some cases," observed ACWA's general executive board in 1918, "reductions in wages are forced on the workers, in others the contractor absconds with the entire payroll, reduced or otherwise."[7]

Some unions of the needle trades had long contended that jobbers must guarantee their contractors payments beyond what was necessary to meet union labor standards in order to relieve contractor pressures for chiseling on wage scales and working conditions. As far back as 1912, the ILGWU won a ruling from the board of grievances for the women's coat and suit trade that a definite amount be paid contractors for overhead, in order to forestall chiseling on accepted work standards. In the mid-twenties, the principle of minimum production costs received intensive study from the Governor's Advisory Commission for the women's coat and suit trade as a method of raising competition to a higher level. The organized factions of the dress industry — jobbers, contractors, and the ILGWU — were among the first officially to accept the principle of minimum production costs, along with the principle of jobber responsibility for contractors' wage payments, as a means of insuring uniform labor costs among competing firms.[8]

---

[7]ACWA, *Report and Proceedings,* Third Biennial Convention (May 1918), p. 64.

[8]The 1912 ruling is cited at p. 61 of the Union Brief in support of the Initial Decision of the Hearing Examiner in the Matter of the California Sportswear and Dress Association, Inc., *et al.,* Federal Trade Commission, Docket 6325. For the work of Governor Smith's Advisory Commission, see Dickinson and Kolchin, *Report of an Investigation,* pp. 138–142.

The 1925 collective agreement between the Wholesale Dress Manufacturers' Association (jobbers) and the Association of Dress Manufacturers (contractors) guaranteed contractors "a minimum of 7 percent for overhead and expense, as a part of the cost of manufacture of the garments, which shall be based upon the total costs of materials, labor and all incidentals that enter into

By the mid-thirties, the principle of minimum production costs was widely accepted throughout the women's garment trades. Some collective agreements set a figure for overhead at 30 percent to 35 percent of the total labor costs; others would allow the contractor a fee for "administration" equal to a certain percentage of all the costs of production. Some industries forbid contractors to submit bids for work at a price below that required to meet labor standards and to make a reasonable profit. All these measures for maintaining a floor under total costs of production were a further extension of the original protocol idea for establishing minimum standards of wages and working conditions covering all competing firms within a trade. Guaranteeing that contractors could meet standard labor costs would obviously facilitate the enforcement of uniform work standards in the shops of contractors.[9]

Limitation and Assignment of Contractors

Further progress toward extending the work standards of inside establishments over outside shops came through assigning all qualified contractors to specific jobbers or inside producers, through raising the qualifications of all contractors eligible for assignments, and through restricting the opportunities of all "legitimate" contractors to compete for work. Barring such controls, contractor could be set against contractor and worker group against worker group. Given a wild scramble to get orders, contractors who re-

---

the manufacture of the garment." The text of this agreement is printed in *Women's Wear,* Jan. 30, 1925; the text of the jobber-union agreement in the issue of Jan. 31, 1925; and the text of the contractor-union agreement in the issue of Jan. 19, 1925.

[9]"The minimum amount allowed the contractor or sub-manufacturer for his overhead shall be not less than $33\frac{1}{3}$ percent of the direct labor cost in the production of garments, except where such labor cost is $2.50 or less, the percentage shall be 30 percent instead of $33\frac{1}{3}$ percent." From the 1935 collective agreement between the Merchants' Ladies' Garment Association (jobbers) and the American Cloak and Suit Manufacturers' Association (contractors).

"A member of the Affiliated whose garments are made in contracting shops shall pay to such contractors at least an amount sufficient to enable the contractor to pay the workers the wages and earnings provided for in this agreement, and in addition a reasonable payment to the contractor to cover his overhead and profit." From the 1936 collective agreement of the Affiliated Dress Manufacturers with the ILGWU and the Dressmakers' Joint Board.

ceived samples from jobbers on which to bid for work would huddle with their own shop price committees to pare estimates of costs to the bone. The more nearly unrestricted the competition, the greater the pressure upon contractors and their workers to submit the lowest bid.

By excluding nonunion contractors and eliminating small-scale producers — by requiring inside workers to be fully employed before goods could be sent to outside shops — by restricting outside production for each jobber or inside manufacturer to a limited number of designated contractors who were members of a particular contractors' association — by requiring designated contractors to give a preference in work to their designated jobbers — by prohibiting contractors from working for other firms than those to which they were assigned — by all these means, the organized forces of industry attempted to confine their realm of law and order to areas over which they could presumably exercise effective control. Only the "legitimate" sources of outside production fell beneath the canopy of the collective agreement, and the very essence of legitimacy was obedience to the regulations established for the trade.[10]

Role of the Impartial Chairman

The sheer task of putting into operation these controls over outside production was a major undertaking in itself. Increasingly complex clauses of collective agreements limiting and regulating the jobber-contracting system had to be interpreted and applied. Detailed rules of procedure had to be drafted for supplementing each measure of control. If jobbers and inside manufacturers were to be responsible for labor standards in outside shops, then some plan for distributing responsibility among several firms using the the same contractor had to be worked out. If contractors were to be guaranteed minimum costs of production, then some means satisfactory to all parties would have to be devised for determining minimum costs of production, and a workable system for enforcing such regulations would need to be developed. If concessions to outside contracting were ever to be tolerated, then the circumstances justifying exceptions to the general rule of inside manufacturing had to be defined for every exigency that might arise.

---

[10]See above pp. 104–138.

The impartial chairman, or board of arbitration, for each industry became the final authority for giving form and substance to measures adopted for control of contracting. Where not directly empowered to permit or deny outside production, the highest arbitrating authority could, by formulating general statements of policy from particular cases and controversies, define the rights and duties of all interested parties and set the future standards of conduct for each trade. Thus, in one of his 1930 awards for the women's coat and suit trade, Impartial Chairman Raymond V. Ingersoll outlined the following steps to be taken in fixing minimum prices that contractors must receive for their work:

1– the jobber formulates an order to manufacture certain garments and sends it to his contractor for consideration;

2– the contractor takes the offer back to his shop for study in terms of the labor and yardage involved;

3– if, in the opinion of the contractor, the jobber's figure for the work is not adequate, the contractor returns to the jobber for further negotiations;

4– should the contractor finally accept a figure that turns out to be inadequate to meet wage scales and overhead, he may later file a complaint of alleged violations of minimum price requirements.

All unresolved differences over prices that jobbers or inside manufacturers should pay their contractors were, as a last resort, settled by the industry's impartial chairman, who, if necessary, fixed the minimum scales himself.[11]

Sometimes, these price-fixing decisions of the impartial chairman were unpopular with one faction or another. "If we are forced to accept this scale," asserted Harry Uviller, manager of the organized contractors in criticism of an Ingersoll decision, "we shall be unable to give any guarantees that the union standards of the past year can be maintained by our members because the new minimum scale is entirely too low to permit this and show a reasonable mar-

---

[11] R. V. Ingersoll, *Decisions*, Case no. 526 (1930). See also G. W. Alger, impartial chairman for the women's coat and suit trade, *Decisions*, setting minimum prices to be paid contractors for the fall season of 1931 (Case no. 596), and for the spring term of 1932 (Case no. 677, parts I and II). For further treatment of this issue, see *Women's Wear Daily*, Dec. 29, 1931 and Dec. 28, 1932. The role of the Joint Control Commission of the women's coat and suit trade (see below Part II) in fixing minimum prices is discussed in *Women's Wear Daily*, Sept. 5, 1929.

gin to the shop owners. As a matter of fact, our members are entitled to figure their overhead and reasonable return before any sum in remainder can be allotted to the workers, and this is exactly what will happen. If these prices are insufficient, the workers will suffer, and union conditions may not be able to be enforced in our shops." Such criticisms were a forecast of troubles that were sure to arise on the enforcement front.[12]

Administering provisions for minimum production costs invariably raised perplexing issues. In one case, a dress contractor who had agreed to manufacture a certain number of dresses for a jobber at a designated price per garment later found that the price he had agreed upon was not sufficient to pay the wage scales fixed in the collective agreement with the union and to leave a reasonable amount for overhead. The impartial machinery was thereupon presented with these questions:

(a) Is the jobber liable to the workers for the deficiency in wages?

(b) If the contractor makes up the deficiency to the workers, can he recover the amount of the deficiency from the jobber?

(c) If the price agreed upon between the jobber and the contractor does not, after meeting the wage scale, leave 35 percent of labor costs for overhead, may the contractor recover the difference from the jobber?

The arbitration tribunal gave an affirmative answer to all three questions. "Taking the agreement as a whole," stated Impartial Chairman A. Feldblum, "it must be held that a jobber, agreeing on a price with a contractor, takes the risk that this price will not later, in actual experience, turn out insufficient, and that he may have to pay an additional sum."[13]

---

[12]*Women's Wear Daily,* Dec. 9, 1930.

[13]"Of course," continued Feldblum, "if it can be shown that the minimum was not earned because of some factor other than the nature of the work itself, or if some other valid grounds appear, the jobber can show this in defense of the claim." A. Feldblum, *Decisions,* Case no. A-76 (Nov. 22, 1933); see also Case no. A-96 (Dec. 13, 1933). For a similar case in the women's coat and suit trade, see R. V. Ingersoll, impartial chairman, decision reported in *Women's Wear Daily,* April 10, 1931.

Most of the collected decisions of impartial chairmen cited in this study are available at the School of Industrial and Labor Relations; many of these and others are available at union headquarters in New York City, particularly in the research library of the ILGWU.

There were many other issues in disputes over contracting that impartial chairmen or boards of arbitration were called upon to resolve. In deciding these issues, the highest arbitrating authority for each trade often became a virtual dictator of production policies. Here, the powers of arbitrators flowed out beyond the normal concepts of control over labor policies into the broad realm of trade relations. Typical of these extended powers was the right to decide the following issues:

(1) May an inside manufacturer resign from his association, liquidate his inside business, and join an association of jobbers?

(2) May a jobber pressed to remain solvent drop some of his designated contractors?

(3) May a member of a jobbers' association who establishes an inside shop on his premises thereby deprive his designated contractors of business and their employees of work?

(4) May the employees of a designated contractor collect damages from a jobber who buys British goods in preference to having his garments made up by the contractors assigned to him?

(5) May a contractor acquire an interest in a jobbing concern without giving up his business as a contractor?

(6) May a jobber, given an additional contractor "for mannish garments only," thereafter send all his work to the new contractor, while his other assigned contractors remain idle?[14]

Even more important were the contributions of permanent arbitrators to implementing the general provisions of collective agree-

---

[14]The following citations are to decisions of impartial chairmen bearing on each of the six questions raised: (1) R. V. Ingersoll, Case nos. 91 (1926) and 521 (1930); G. W. Alger, Case nos. 664 (1931) and 1109 (1934–1935). (2) S. A. Rosenblatt, Case nos. 2771 and 2775 (both on June 19, 1940); A. Feldblum, Case no. B-2 (Jan. 12, 1935). (3) G. W. Alger, Case no. 958 (Jan. 3, 1934) discussed in *Women's Wear Daily*, Jan. 4, 1934; A. Feldblum, Case nos. A-460 (May 22, 1934) and B-2094 (Jan. 13, 1936). (4) S. A. Rosenblatt, Case no. 1532 (Nov. 29, 1937). (5) S. A. Rosenblatt, Case no. 5773 (May 17, 1948). (6) S. A. Rosenblatt, Case nos. 1719-A and 1719-B (June 13, 1938).

On the general subject of whether employees of designated contractors should receive pay for the work they lose when the contractor's assigned jobbers turn to nondesignated contractors or to nonunion shops, see S. A. Rosenblatt, *Decisions*, Case no. 1189a (Dec. 12, 1935). The issues in this case were discussed in *Women's Wear Daily*, Oct. 24, 1935. For an earlier decision bearing on this issue, see G. W. Alger, *Decisions*, Case no. 665, reported in *Women's Wear Daily*, Dec. 19, 1931.

ments for limitation and assignment of contractors. If a contractor were restricted to a single jobber or inside manufacturer, how could he escape the same disaster that befell his jobber or inside manufacturer who set out to produce a "bad line" of garments? If a jobber or inside manufacturer were confined to one or two designated contractors who were qualified to produce only certain types and styles of garments, how could he escape the disaster of a change in fashions that called for new types of garments beyond the skills of the contracting shops assigned to him? Above all else, how could the provisions for exclusive dealings between jobbers and their assigned contractors be enforced against the pressures for more profitable business elsewhere?[15]

Certainly the system of limiting and assigning contractors required more flexibility than could be appropriately introduced at negotiating conferences. This flexibility had to be provided by impartial chairmen as occasion arose. Even the general rule against outside contracting was sometimes accompanied by clauses bestowing upon the impartial chairman full authority to make exceptions to the rule.[16]

---

[15]See, for example, the case of a contractor, member of the United Association of Dress Manufacturers, who complained that a jobber, member of the National Dress Manufacturers' Association, had let out work to New Jersey and Connecticut contractors contrary to the restrictive clause of the collective agreement between the jobbers' association and the contractors' association, in A. Feldblum, impartial chairman, *Decisions*, Case no. B-19 (March 1, 1935), also reported in *Women's Wear Daily*, March 4, 1935.

During the mid-thirties, the collective agreement for the popular-priced dress industry forbade an inside manufacturer, who also dealt with contractors, from enlarging his inside shop without the approval of the impartial machinery set up to administer the contract. On behalf of one of its members, the Popular-Priced Dress Group applied to the impartial chairman for permission of its member to expand his inside shop from 22 to 40 machines. Although this manufacturer had employed only two contractors both of whom had worked on a temporary basis to take care of surplus production at the peak of the season, the petition was denied. Harry Uviller, impartial chairman, dress industry, *Decisions*, Case no. D-46 (Jan. 29, 1937), vol. 2, pp. 19–20.

[16]The 1933 collective agreement between the Merchants' Ladies' Garment Association (jobbers) and the American Cloak and Suit Manufacturers' Association (contractors) provided that if a jobber, after designating his contractors, "shall at any time change the character of his product and the

Impartial chairmen have, likewise, had to interpret and apply provisions regulating the minimum size of shops, an issue that for the most part involved the shops of contractors. On one occasion, R. V. Ingersoll, impartial chairman for the women's coat and suit trade, was called upon to decide whether a manufacturer could divide his factory into two separate components, putting his cutters and sample makers into one building and his other workers into a separate building. "The Board believes that the division of workers here contemplated might cause unfortunate complications in the industry," announced Mr. Ingersoll for the board of arbitration. "It runs contrary to the effort to maintain satisfactory production units, as represented by the fourteen machine standard. In fact, sub-division of this character, if approved, might have a tendency even more demoralizing than the straight out existence of small shops."[17]

Maintaining the fourteen machine rule to eliminate the small shops was a perpetual headache for contract administrators. Small-time employers charged with violating this clause often promised reforms but failed to build up the size of their shops to meet minimum requirements. After repeated procrastinations one such employer was expressly directed by Impartial Chairman Ingersoll to employ six additional men in order to bring the number of his operators up to 14. At the same time, the employer was ordered to keep a full complement of workers in other crafts. The firm was also prohibited from working overtime or from sending any work outside so long as it failed to meet the requirements of size set forth in the collective agreement. If the authority of the impartial machinery to resolve such issues appeared to be more an invasion of management prerogatives than a regulation of wages and hours, the exercise of this power was nevertheless in keeping

---

contractors or sub-manufacturers designated by him or any of them shall be incapable of meeting his changed requirements, the member may substitute and/or add such other contractors or sub-manufacturers in place of those incapable of meeting his changed requirements. Such substitution and/or addition shall not be made until after the decision of the Impartial Chairman on notice and hearing within forty-eight (48) hours."

[17]R. V. Ingersoll, *Decisions*, Case no. 34 (December 1924–February 1925). See also Harry Uviller, impartial chairman, dress industry, *Decisions*, Case no. E-1402 (May 24, 1938), vol. 4, p. 290.

with the central theme of controlled competition on which the protocol movement had been founded.[18]

Evasion of Controls over Outside Production

The original Protocol of Peace had scarcely become effective before certain manufacturers bound by the agreement established subsidiary plants outside of New York City. These plants, so the manufacturers contended, were beyond the range of the protocol. When this position became untenable, the manufacturers turned to outside contracting on the ground that the protocol had abolished "sub-contracting within shops" but had not prohibited all outside contracting. Once outside contracting, wherever conducted, had been brought within the realm of law and order, those still seeking escape from restrictions on outside production turned to submanufacturing — a process that differed from contracting only in that the submanufacturer cut the materials given him as well as sewed them into garments. Finally, when submanufacturing was brought under the rules that governed contracting, many inside producers, pressed to meet competition, gave up their inside establishments altogether in favor of free-lance jobbing or contracting.[19]

Everywhere unscrupulous jobbers, contractors, and inside manu-

---

[18]R. V. Ingersoll, *Decisions,* Case no. 537 (Jan.–May 1931). In March 1926, Harry Uviller, general manager of the American Cloak and Suit Manufacturers' Association (contractors), asserted that between 30 and 40 percent of the women's coat and suit manufacturers employed fewer than 14 operators. *Women's Wear,* March 9, 1926. Two lengthy articles in *Women's Wear Daily* for Nov. 3, 1930 shed considerable light on the history and application of the 14 machine rule in the women's coat and suit trade. At the time, Impartial Chairman R. V. Ingersoll had just handed down the first arbitration award involving the clause. The text of this decision was printed in *Women's Wear Daily,* Oct. 31, 1930.

[19]Dr. Abelson [labor representative of the manufacturers' association] has created the term of "sub-manufacturer".... What is a sub-manufacturer? A sub-manufacturer is a contractor. They do not register a sub-manufacturer; of course not. They register the contractor; so they have created a new term. They have invented a new word; "sub-manufacturer." They do not register the sub-manufacturer.

—Meyer London, counsel of the ILGWU, in *Minutes,* Board of Arbitrators...[women's coat and suit trade] (August 5, 1913), p. B-3.

facturers were active in devising "interpretations" of their labor agreements that would justify an escape from limitations on outside production. The rule that acceptable contractors must employ union members only was evaded by sending goods to union shop contractors who sublet the materials to be made in nonunion shops. Bans on outside contracting while inside workers were idle were evaded by stockpiling materials until the manufacturer could supply all his inside workers and still send the bulk of his "surplus" orders to outside contractors.[20]

If a jobber or inside manufacturer wished to bypass the contractors assigned to him, he could always claim the right to establish additional inside shops. Or if he wished to change the number of his contractors, or to substitute others for those assigned him, he invariably found some justification in the clauses of the collective agreement for his action. Officially, he discharged his contractors "for cause" — poor workmanship or late deliveries. Officially, he substituted other contractors because he required new skills to produce new products. Officially, he demanded additional contractors to fill rush orders or meet deadlines set by his customers. But all these official explanations were sometimes little more than over-the-table excuses for under-the-table deals to evade the restrictions on contracting and so take advantage of lower production costs.

There were still more subtle means of evading the restrictive clauses of collective agreements on outside production. With the help of talented lawyers whose far-fetched "interpretations" provided a cloak of legality for questionable conduct, many association members manipulated their forms of business organization to justify evasion of the limitations on contracting. Some took refuge in the reorganization of their firms to rely upon the "protective coloration of a new name;" others created dummy corporations that were contracting shops in disguise; while still others formed

---

[20]On subletting materials to nonunion firms, see S. A. Rosenblatt, impartial chairman, women's coat and suit trade, *Decisions,* Case nos. 1591, 1592, 1593 (Dec. 22, 1937) and no. 1714 (May 5, 1938). On stockpiling materials for outside contractors, see Board of Arbitration, Chicago market, men's clothing industry, Case no. 14-A (July 25, 1922), summarized in ACWA, *Advance,* Jan. 5, 1923. A later case involving the Chicago women's coat and suit jobbers under the NRA codes is reported in *Women's Wear Daily,* June 5, 1934.

partnerships whose members held a controlling interest in outside shops. To meet these subtle devices, some collective agreements expressly authorized the impartial chairman "to determine whether an alleged subsidiary, auxiliary or affiliate of a member is such subsidiary, auxiliary or affiliate" and to decide whether the presence of an affiliate in fact tends "to establish a plan, scheme or device, on the part of such member to avoid or evade the provisions of this agreement by or through such subsidiary, auxiliary or affiliate, manufacturing, directly or indirectly, garments covered by this agreement."[21]

Often association members bent upon outside production made no pretense at justifying their conduct, but relied instead upon concealing the true character of their operations. Some kept a separate set of books for their illegal transactions. Others found collusion with contractors to evade minimum production costs the only safe medium for hiding their activites. Kickbacks were a favorite device of illicit jobber-contractor relationships. "The evidence produced by the Union," stated the impartial chairman of the women's coat and suit industry in a typical case, "showed that a joint investigation had been made by the representatives of the Union, the American Association [contractors] and the Merchants Association [jobbers] and that upon such joint investigation on the premises of the jobber it was disclosed that a constant practice on the part of the jobber was to deliver checks apparently in full payment in accordance with settled prices to the contractor, that

---

[21]From the 1943 collective agreement of the Merchants' Ladies' Garment Association with the Cloakmakers' Joint Board and the ILGWU. During the thirties, a certain jobbing firm of the women's coat and suit trade created a subsidiary through which it operated until its action was barred by the impartial machinery for the industry. When this case reached the board of arbitration, Impartial Chairman G. W. Alger, speaking for the board, concluded "that the concern must be considered as a unit, that it has no right to terminate its inside shop, lock out its workers and continue the operation of its subsidiary as though such subsidiary were an entirely different, distinct, and separate concern, particularly since the subsidiary itself, so-called, is not even a member of the Merchants' Association and has no industrial existence under the collective agreements except as an adjunct of the member in question." G. W. Alger, *Decisions,* Case no. 1109 (1934–1935). For other cases bearing on different types of evasions, see S. A. Rosenblatt, *Decisions,* Case nos. 1398 (Dec. 7, 1936) and 5773 (May 17, 1948). See also *Women's Wear Daily,* Dec. 22, 1936.

thereupon the contractor endorsed such checks and returned the same to the jobber, and the jobber thereupon cashed the same and paid the contractor a stipulated sum per garment which was below the settled prices."[22]

Some members of contractors' associations refused to limit their work to assigned jobbers, particularly where their jobbers failed to supply sufficient work. Other contractors refused to give preferences to the organized jobbers or inside manufacturers so long as greater profits could be derived from dealing with independent firms. Nor did unscrupulous contractors hesitate to enter into collusive deals with their workers to evade the established standards of their trade. Contractor-worker collusion to undermine labor standards was very easy to introduce and extremely difficult to detect. The law of self-interest, reinforced by the personal ties of the workshop, closed the mouths of both workers and employers against squealing on contract evasions.

Extent of Evasion

Charges of violating rules on outside production were widespread throughout the needle trades. A buttonhole manufacturer was found deliberately bypassing both his inside shop and his outside shop. "He doesn't give the manufacture of these buttonholes to his outside shop," observed the industry arbitrator, S. A. Rosenblatt, "nor provide for their making in his inside shop, but permits them to be made completely away from his inside or outside premises, so that their making is, in effect, away from the control and regulation of the collective agreement." Again, during a special campaign to abolish contracting in the headwear industry, a millinery manufacturer was discovered sending work to thirty different contractors while his own inside labor force of fifty workers were largely unemployed. And in the women's coat and suit trade, a "legitimate" contractor was charged with deliberately violating five different provisions of his collective agreement on the subject of contracting.[23]

---

[22]S. A. Rosenblatt, *Decisions,* Case no. 1321 (June 11, 1936).

[23]*Ibid.,* Case no. 1305 (March 31, 1936). The millinery case is reported in *Women's Wear Daily,* Feb. 6, 1933.

The respondent in charged by the Union, in three separate complaints, with violating the collective agreement under which it is bound in the

From the inception of the protocol movement, outside contracting threatened to become the graveyard of controlled competition. These threats became more and more alarming with the widespread growth of the jobber-contracting system after the First World War. Preventing inside producers from undermining labor standards in their own establishments was a simple matter compared to the monumental task of keeping up labor standards in contracting shops. Settling disputes over alleged infractions of rules governing outside production became a major source of administrative determinations. More than any other subject, the interrelations among jobbers, contractors, and inside manufacturers affecting work standards commanded the attention of the impartial chairman.[24]

Reporting in 1927 on the activities of the impartial machinery under the collective agreement between the New York Clothing Manufacturers' Exchange and the Amalgamated Clothing Workers' Union, Boris Maruchess, labor manager of the men's clothing

---

following five respects: (1) members of the respondent firm perform the work of cutters, in violation of Paragraph "Sixteenth" of the collective agreement; (2) the respondent employs non-union workers, in violation of Paragraph "Third" of the collective agreement; (3) the respondent manufactures garments for non-union jobbers and for jobbers who have not been duly designated by the respondent, in violation of Paragraph "Twentieth" of the collective agreement; (4) the respondent refused to permit an examination of its records by Retirement Fund accountants, deputized by the Impartial Chairman, in violation of the Rules and Regulations of the Retirement Fund which are incorporated in and are part of the collective agreement; (5) the respondent refuses to produce books and records for examination by the Impartial Chairman's accountants, in violation of Paragraphs "Fourth" and "Fifth" of the collective agreement.
    —S. A. Rosenblatt, *Decisions,* Case nos. 5328, 5359 (April 29, 1948).

[24]Within months after the first dress and waist protocol became effective in 1913, Meyer London, counsel for the ILGWU, reported to the board of arbitration for the industry that subcontracting was carried on extensively in direct violation of the protocol. "We have sub-contracting in 93 shops," he stated, "sub-contracting in which the employer divests himself of all responsibility to the individual employees and in which an ignorant and oppressive sub-contractor is made the direct employer of the workers." *Minutes,* Arbitration Proceedings between the Dress and Waist Manufacturers' Association and the ILGWU (Nov. 8, 1913), p. 17.

association, presented the following summary of complaints handled over the first three years of the agreement:[25]

Complaints Involving Inside Shops

Stoppages	48
Establishment of production standards	26
Noncompliance with decisions	21
Wage readjustments	19
Requests to reorganize shops	21
Lockouts	5
Complaints of underproduction	71
Other classifications	10
Total Cases	**221**

Complaints Involving Contractors

Stoppages	458
Contractors' demands for reduction	173
Not sending work to registered contractor	555
Requests for additional contractors	704
Work to nonregistered contractors	493
Sending work to nonunion shops	349
Unsatisfactory workmanship	130
Nonpayment of wages by contractor	58
Lockouts by contractors	8
Contractor demands for price increases	58
Money due contractors	97
Refusals to finish work	93
Adjustment of wage increases	236
General lockout by pant contractors	24
General organization stoppages	52
Use of nonunion canvas	17
Total Cases	**3505**

---

[25]Boris Maruchess also had a classification of 347 additional complaints under the heading "Cutters' Cases." Miscellaneous groupings brought the total number of cases in dispute to 4,569, only 8 percent of which were submitted to Impartial Chairman Jacob Billikopf for final solution. ACWA, *Advance,* August 5, 1927. See also Billikopf's, *Decisions* (approximately 500 cases, 1925–1929).

Similarly, in the dress and waist industry, a tabulation by subject matter of 682 awards signed by Impartial Chairman A. Feldblum during the period from July 3, 1934 to March 8, 1935 showed that 300 or 44 percent of the total awards were directly concerned with the contracting system in cases classified as follows:[26]

Dress Industry Awards on Contracting
July 1934 — March 1936

Amount of money due contractor	148	awards
Amount of money due jobber	2	"
Contractor withholding garment from jobber ...	7	"
Discrimination against contractor	45	"
Sending out work cut in the shop	1	"
Jobber registering unnecessary contractor	7	"
Nonunion, nondesignated dealings	12	"
Removal of contractor	70	"
Right of contractor to instigate court action	1	"
Sending out work while inside shop is not fully supplied	7	"
Total......	300	"

These compilations of decisions by industry arbitrators throw a revealing light upon the work of collective bargaining in the

---

[26]Compiled from the decisions of A. Feldblum on file in the Abelson papers. The 300 cases do not include those arising in contracting shops from among the 180 discharge cases, the 42 work-stoppage cases, the 35 reorganization cases, the 27 failure-to-comply cases, the 18 cases of union refusals to approve a firm for membership in the association, the 20 improper-pay-to-workers' cases, or the 13 lockout cases.

For other tabulations showing similar results, see D. E. Robinson, *Collective Bargaining and Market Control in the New York Coat and Suit Industry* (1949), pp. 88–90; and Frank Pierson, *Collective Bargaining Systems* (1942), pp. 163–164. During 1936–1937, about 50 percent of several hundred dress industry arbitration awards by Impartial Chairman Harry Uviller involved controversies between employer groups, and in none of these cases was the ILGWU or the Dressmakers' Joint Board a party. See Harry Uviller, *Decisions* (March 1936 to Dec. 31, 1937), 3 vols. (mimeo.). In an earlier two-year period, the impartial chairman for the dress industry received 2,584 cases of which 1,220, or approximately 50 percent, were brought by the dress contractors' association against members of the dress jobbers' association. Julius Hochman, general manager, Dressmakers' Joint Board, in ILGWU's *Justice*, Jan. 15, 1936.

needle trades. Individual disputes between the "bosses" and the "people" over alleged mistreatment, as well as the more general issues of wage levels and working conditions, had given way to joint regulation of productive processes for the mutual benefit of all organized factions within each trade. Whether designed to regulate business conduct or introduced to gain compliance with labor standards by indirection, these forms of control over methods of production had been the chief concern of arbitrators and umpires sitting at the helm of the impartial machinery for their respective trades.

Unions as Enforcing Agencies

From the early years of the protocol movement labor unions played an important role in governing jobber-contractor-inside manufacturer relationships. Not content to arouse employer groups to the need for controlling outside production, they assumed direct responsibility on their own authority for making and enforcing their own policies on contracting. Not only did labor unions assume leadership in more radical schemes to abolish all contracting and to eliminate the small producer, but they set up the machinery and procedures to enforce controls over "legitimate" contracting. Given the full backing of employers' associations and immunity from the clutches of the law, these unions might have suppressed all employers who turned their backs on controlled competition in their own shops to enjoy the forbidden fruits of outside production.

Under the original protocol, the ILGWU and its New York City locals set out to standardize piece rates between inside and outside shops. The union tried to introduce the practice of having joint inside-outside price committees negotiate a standard price for each garment, regardless of where it was to be manufactured. Failing to establish this rule, the union next sought to accomplish the same ends by sending out business agents to approve all price-fixing at the shop level, whether in the shops of contractors or in the shops of inside manufacturers. In some cases, the union was able to establish the rule that goods submitted for consideration of the inside price committee could not also be submitted to outside contractors for lower bids.

Early in the history of the first protocol, the Cloakmakers' Joint

Board, as a part of its own program to enforce protocol standards under its original agreement with the Cloak, Suit and Skirt Manufacturers' Protective Association, extended to contractors, subcontractors, and submanufacturers its practice of awarding "certificates of union conditions" to association firms observing the labor standards established for the trade. Union agents inspected all outside shops patronized by association members every three months. Those failing to maintain work standards of the inside establishments lost their certificates and the right to their employees. Once the contractor or submanufacturer had been deprived of his workers, he was forced to apply at the office of the union for a new certificate and he had to meet union terms before receiving further help.[27]

In the fur manufacturing trade, the limited use of finishing contractors permitted under collective agreements after the First World War set the fur workers to devising enforcement controls over contractors beyond those assigned the impartial machinery. Although the power to grant or withhold "certificates of compliance" based on periodic inspection of contractor shops had passed to the joint agencies of administration, the union sought more drastic means of insuring compliance with industry standards. On one occasion, the Furriers' Joint Board even renounced its right to appropriate cash securities deposited in advance by contractors to insure the enforcement of their agreements. Refunding the cash to its owners, the manager of the Furriers' Joint Board informed the manager of the Associated Fur Manufacturers that the noncomplying contractors had abrogated their agreement and were no

---

[27]*Minutes,* Informal Conference between Representatives of the Cloak, Suit and Skirt Manufacturers' Protective Association and the ILGWU and the Cloakmakers' Joint Board (Feb. 4, 1913), p. 118.

Among the 15 proposed amendments to the original protocol offered in 1913 by the ILGWU were the proposals (1) that inside and outside shops be considered as branches of the same factory; (2) that all new contractors must be registered at the beginning of each season; (3) that no new contractors could be acquired until all the inside and outside shops of a firm were supplied with work; and (4) that no old contractors could be discharged in the middle of the season except for important reasons and then only after an investigation into the facts. *Jewish Daily Forward,* July 13, 1913. Translation filed in the Abelson papers. See also, *Minutes,* Board of Arbitrators... [women's coat and suit trade] (August 6, 1913), p. C-31.

longer eligible to receive work. This drastic procedure hastened an amendment to the collective agreement requiring that "the entire garment shall be made on the same premises and no section of the garment shall be given out to contractors."[28]

By the mid-thirties, the ILGWU had discovered a new approach to gaining compliance with restrictions on outside production. The operation of the contractor system of necessity called for transporting unfinished goods from jobbers to contractors and for returning the finished products from contractors back to jobbers again. Controlling this two-way flow of traffic, like controlling commerce on a river that connects two lakes, was far easier than inspecting all the hideouts along the vast lake fronts of garment manufacturing. Short of such controls, the throughways of carting and trucking could become clogged with illicit traffic to and from nonunion, nondesignated contractors. Indeed, running the blockade for illegitimate producers might well be more profitable for the carting and trucking business than conforming to the rules of the legitimate elements within a trade.

The first step in controlling this traffic was to bring the employees of the carting and trucking firms into the fold of the ILGWU. Local 102 of this union was set up in 1933, not only to improve the working conditions of drivers and helpers, but also "for the additional purpose of strengthening enforcement regulations covering the production of jobber merchandise in union contractor shops only." But the ultimate objective of this movement was to negotiate written agreements with the associations of carting and trucking firms that would lead to cooperation among all the organized segments of the trade. While awaiting this development, the Cloakmakers' Joint Board in February 1938 created a special control department to check all trucking deliveries to and from the premises of jobbers and contractors. "In April 1939," reported ILGWU's general executive board, "the [Cloakmakers']

---

[28]A. Brownstein, manager, Furriers' Joint Board to William Pike, manager, Associated Fur Manufacturers, letter, dated April 14, 1925, filed in the Abelson papers. The 1919 collective agreement had provided that no contractors could receive finishing work "who have either failed to secure Conference Committee certificates, or whose certificates have been revoked by the Conference Committee." The use of cash securities is discussed above at pp. 221–222 and in chap. 12 below.

Joint Board signed the first written agreement with the truck associations handling coat and suit deliveries in the metropolitan district by which these associations agreed to become a part of the organized structure of the trade." Similar steps were taken for the dress industry.[29]

Under these agreements, the primary purpose of which was to halt the unauthorized flow of goods to and from outside shops, no trucking firms could deliver goods to nondesignated contractors, or to strike-bound firms, or to firms that had been suspended from their associations. Union agents were empowered to examine the books of truck owners, to check all trucks en route, and, if necessary, to accompany the truck drivers on all their trips. Union inspectors often discovered that false papers or the physical transfer of goods to other trucks during transit concealed the ultimate destination of the product. Truck owners caught deliberately violating the provisions of these agreements were subject to a variety of penalties including strikes and liquidated damages. Trucking firms that lost money by complying with the agreement received compensation from the manufacturing industry at a rate fixed by the impartial chairman, if not otherwise determined between the union and the association.[30]

When the four-way trucking contract for the dress industry was signed in 1939 by the United Association of Dress Manufacturers

---

[29]ILGWU, *Report and Proceedings,* Twenty-third Convention (May 1937), pp. 149–150; Twenty-fourth Convention (May-June 1940), pp. 46, 57, 59–60.

The Association undertakes to commence immediate negotiations for and agrees to enter into a collective agreement with the association or associations of truck owners in the dress industry for the inclusion of delivery of all garments manufactured in Manhattan...and for responsibility on the part of the association of truck owners and the members thereof in the enforcement of the collective agreements in the dress industry.

—From a new clause in the 1939 collective agreement between the United Association of Dress Manufacturers (contractors) and the ILGWU and its Dressmakers' Joint Board.

[30]The text of a typical trucking agreement for the women's coat and suit industry may be found in *Women's Wear Daily,* April 21, 1939. Similar terms for a trucking agreement covering the dress industry are summarized in *Women's Wear Daily,* March 7, 1939. For a case in which a jobber was fined $5,500 for violating the contractor clause by collusion with truckmen, see S. A. Rosenblatt, *Decisions,* Case no. 2375 (Jan. 15, 1940).

(contractors), the Affiliated Ladies' Apparel Carriers' Association (trucking firms), the New York Dressmakers' Joint Board (ILGWU), and the Dress Drivers' and Helpers' Union (Local 102, ILGWU), Mayor LaGuardia's fact-finding commission that had helped to reach an agreement issued the following report: "The agreement reached between the truckowners, the union and the dress producers brings the truckowners for the first time into the frame of industrial self-government so characteristic of collective bargaining in the dress industry. We are confident that the writing of the contract will lead to the elimination of certain abuses which were a constant cause of irritation and disturbance." At the same time Julius Hochman, manager of the Dressmakers' Joint Board, hailed the new agreement as "a most constructive instrument which carries the stabilization of the dress industry an important step forward."[31]

Over the years, more and more collective agreements of the needle trades expressly conferred upon union agents authority to apprehend and punish all infractions of the established rules on contracting. Manufacturers who had earlier held out for joint administrative agencies to the exclusion of the union's "walking delegate" seldom raised objections to union-inspired programs for disclosing and suppressing illegitimate sources of outside production. Some union shop stewards and roving business agents were expressly granted the power to inspect the employers' premises and examine the employers' books for evidences of noncompliance with accepted terms. In a few cases, by mutual agreement, contracting was permitted only with the consent of the union!

The chief instrument of union control over outside production was, of course, the strike. Whether called with the sanction of collective agreements and the support of inside manufacturers, or called solely on authority of the union, sudden strikes were a sword of Damocles over the heads of all contractors and jobbers seeking to evade the restrictions of collective agreements. Given the resources of an international union, strikes were particularly effective against small contracting shops otherwise difficult to control. If a contractor persistently refused to comply with the labor standards

---

[31]*Women's Wear Daily*, March 7, 1939. For the effect of these trucking contracts on the growth of membership in the ILGWU, see below, chap. 20.

for his industry, a sudden strike in his shop backed by a picket line would normally put him out of business. The troubles thus created for the jobber or inside manufacturer whose work was left unfinished would presumably be reflected in additional pressures upon the contractor to keep the straight and narrow path.

The Role of Employers' Associations

Meanwhile, employers' associations were displaying far more enthusiasm for maintaining controls over outside production than they had shown for the enforcement of most other provisions in their collective agreements. Like most labor unions, the organized employer groups also devised measures of their own against contracting and endeavored to win the support of their members for the restrictions named in their collective agreements. Because the organized employers were more willing to cooperate in this sphere, they were given a more prominent assignment in the joint machinery to control the jobber-contracting system. Under many contracts employers' associations were expressly authorized to participate extensively on their own authority in the detection and punishment of offenses that threatened to undermine industry standards in outside shops.

As early as 1912, the Cloak, Suit and Skirt Manufacturers' Protective Association enacted bylaws holding all its members responsible for protocol conditions in the shops of their contractors. Registration of contractors was made compulsory and registration lists had to be kept up to date. Penalties were assessed against members failing to register their contractors: $100 for the first offense, $250 for the second offense, and expulsion from the association for the third offense. Through a series of letters to the membership in 1913, the association again indicated its intention of enforcing these bylaws. Finally, it issued an ultimatum directing members to submit revised registration lists of contractors within forty-eight hours on penalty of possible fine or expulsion from the association.[32]

Years later, by the terms of the 1926 collective agreements of the women's coat and suit trade, employers' associations (jobbers, con-

---

[32]See letters dated May 15, 1912, July 15, 1913, and July 21, 1913 from the Cloak, Suit and Skirt Manufacturers' Protective Association to the members of the association. Correspondence filed in the Abelson papers.

tractors, and inside manufacturers) were expressly directed to investigate the books and records of their members for evidences of doing illicit business with outside nonunion firms. Subsequently, the impartial chairman for the industry promulgated special rules of procedure that gave associations a prominent role in processing charges of dealing with nonunion and nondesignated contractors. Whether complaints were filed by the union or arose from reports by officials of the impartial machinery, they were referred to special grievance boards of the appropriate association. These regulations of the impartial chairman provided, in part, that. . . .

2. Grievance boards of the several Associations are to meet weekly. Complaints theretofore made and sustained, and as to which action by the Board is required, are to be acted upon by the Grievance Board during the week in which such complaints have been sustained. . . . The Association shall report immediately to the Union and to the Impartial Chairman the results reached by the Board.

3. If such a complaint, as described in paragraph 2, is not brought before the Grievance Board within the specified time, the complaint may be brought and heard before the Impartial Chairman, unless the Chairman finds that sufficient reason exists in the particular case for the delay in proceeding under paragraph 2 above.

4. Decisions or adjustments reached by the Grievance Boards under the collective agreements are to be enforced by the Associations and complied with as decisions or adjustments reached under the collective agreements.[33]

The Impartial Machinery and Outside Contracting

Although the parties to collective agreements were deeply concerned with the evasion of industry-wide standards through the medium of outside contracting, neither employers' associations nor labor unions could be counted upon to provide the self-enforcing machinery to keep wayward employers and rebellious

---

[33]S. A. Rosenblatt, "Rules and Regulations Promulgated September 19, 1935: Non-Designated and Non-Union Dealings" filed in S. A. Rosenblatt, *Decisions,* Case no. 1186 (Sept. 18, 1935). The rules are also quoted in *Women's Wear Daily,* Sept. 25, 1935. See further the instructions relating to the limitation of contractor clause issued by Mortimer Lanzit, executive director of the National Dress Manufacturers' Association (jobbers) to the association members operating under the 1936 dress industry agreements of the New York market. These instructions are printed in *Women's Wear Daily,* March 3, 1936.

workers in line. Not everyone could resist the opportunity for collusion between representatives of two or more industry factions to overthrow the standards of competition set for the trade. Generally labor unions and inside manufacturers joined hands to suppress outside contracting. But at times unions and contractors combined to take advantage of jobbers and inside producers. Or else jobbers and contractors united to keep down the demands of organized workers.

If the relationships among jobbers, contractors, inside manufacturers, and workers established by collective agreements were to be preserved, then the enforcement machinery had to guard against collusion among the parts to defeat the interests of the whole. Only those institutions that rose above the separate desires of the different factions gave promise of keeping the conflicting interests on an even keel. Policing an industry to disclose unauthorized contracting, therefore, fell more and more upon clerks and deputy clerks, upon joint intermediate committees and subcommittees, and upon the staff technicians attached to the office of impartial chairman.[34]

Most valuable of the staff agencies were the accountants widely introduced after the mid-twenties. "An accountant," stated the 1927 collective agreement of the Merchants' Ladies' Garment Association (jobbers) with the Cloakmakers' Joint Board and the ILGWU "shall be permanently attached to the staff of said im-

---

[34]An example of this shift to the impartial machinery was found in the garment trucking agreements of the women's coat and suit trade. Whereas the first garment trucking agreements were enforced largely through the control department of the ILGWU, later agreements authorized the impartial machinery to detect and punish offenses of carting goods to nonunion shops. Early in the forties, inspectors representing the impartial chairman began checking trucks in the streets to determine the destination of their goods, while accountants from the office of the impartial chairman examined books and records that truck drivers and truck owners were required to keep. Thereupon the union abandoned its control department and subordinated its activities to the work of the impartial machinery. In 1941, Impartial Chairman J. J. Walker levied the first fine to be imposed by the impartial machinery upon a trucking firm for carting goods to nonunion shops. J. J. Walker, *Decisions,* Case no. 2986 (Feb. 13, 1941). See also the report of Samuel Klein, executive director of the Industrial Council of Cloak, Suit and Skirt Manufacturers, commending Impartial Chairman J. J. Walker for putting teeth into the trucking agreements, printed in *Women's Wear Daily,* Feb. 25, 1941.

partial chairman for the purpose of making, with or without formal notice of complaint, investigations under his direction in any establishment in the industry in order to ascertain whether the contracts entered into between the parties are carried out." From an inspection of the books, accountants were often able to detect false fronts in business organizations, and to disclose cases of collusion between jobbers and contractors or between contractors and workers to violate the terms of their agreements. On one occasion, a thorough examination of the work assigned to three contractors revealed a common practice of subletting out the fabrication of materials they received from jobbers.[35]

Many of these cases were ultimately dumped into the lap of the impartial chairman for final decision. Under the four-way collective agreements of the dress industry — agreements reached in February 1930 between and among jobbers, contractors, inside manufacturers, and the ILGWU — Impartial Chairman N. I. Stone was soon hard pressed to maintain peaceful relations between jobbers and contractors. Each group charged the other with violating terms of their collective agreements. "One probe," reported *Women's Wear Daily* for October 30, 1930, "brought to light that the members of the wholesalers' association [Wholesale Dress Manufacturers' Association] give work to 692 [693?] contractors, of which 463 belong to the Association of Dress Manufacturers [to whose members all work should be assigned], and 230 operate non-union shops." During the fall of 1930, the jobbers' association refused to entertain complaints of the contractors or to carry out decisions of the impartial chairman, who was faced with the task of restoring an open break in relations between the two groups.[36]

Correction and Punishment

In handling cases of infractions against the rules on outside production, the impartial machinery sought first and foremost to restore law and order by inducing the offenders to "cease and de-

---

[35]S. A. Rosenblatt, *Decisions,* Case nos. 1591, 1592, 1593 (Dec. 22, 1937 and June 7, 1938). For a history of these cases see ILGWU, *Justice,* Jan. 1, 1938. Text of the 1927 collective agreement is printed in *Women's Wear Daily,* Jan. 14, 1927.

[36]See also *New York Times,* Nov. 13, 1930; *Women's Wear Daily,* Oct. 17, 1930.

sist" from their wayward conduct. Jobbers sending materials to nondesignated contractors were ordered to withdraw their unfinished garments. Contractors subletting their work to nonunion shops were instructed to terminate their nonunion connections. Manufacturers keeping false or inadequate records were ordered to set up full, accurate, and complete accounts as prescribed for the trade. Employers paying below established wage scales or jobbers receiving kickbacks from contractors were ordered to make up the deficits. Workers participating in collusive deals with contractors were directed to stop undermining the standards of the trade.

Industry arbitrators used all their powers of persuasion to help the culprits mend their ways. They suspended fines, delayed punishment, and otherwise forgave past transgressions in return for the promise of a change of heart. First offenders were reported to their respective organizations with words of censure and pleas for reform. "It is the sort of conduct which leads to strikes and stoppages, brings the impartial machinery into disrepute and ultimately disrupts the industry," wrote Impartial Chairman Jacob Billikopf to the labor manager of the New York Clothing Manufacturers' Exchange in May 1925. He was rebuking an employer who had sent out his materials to be made up by a nonunion contractor. "Although I feel that the union is justified in seeking to protect itself against offenses of this kind, I shall not this time grant the request to penalize the firm," Billikopf concluded. "Should there be a repetition of the offense, however, I shall be obliged to appeal to the executive committee of the Exchange to take vigorous disciplinary measures."[37]

On one occasion, a jobber of the women's coat and suit trade, who had rejected the pleas of his impartial chairman, was turned over to his employer group, the Merchants' Ladies' Garment Association, for disciplinary action. After an investigation of the case, the association imposed upon the jobber a fine equal to three times the savings of fifty cents a garment that the firm had derived from having 1,000 garments made up by nonunion contractors in violation of the collective labor agreement. Generally, however, the profits derived from illicit outside contracting were so great, and

[37]ACWA, *Advance,* May 22, 1925.

the chances of apprehension so slight, that the penalties imposed by any agency — employers' associations, labor unions, or the impartial machinery — seldom convinced the culprits that jumping the barriers of their collective agreements did not pay.[38]

The punishment was likely to be more effective where the impartial machinery exercised some control over the nature and extent of the penalties imposed, or else where the collective agreements themselves prescribed minimum scales of penalties for outside contracting in violation of the collective agreement. At one stage, the impartial chairman for the women's coat and suit trade thus interpreted the pertinent clauses of the 1935 collective agreement and defined the role that he was to play in the procedure:

This paragraph, in dealing with fines and penalties upon a jobber giving work to or dealing with a non-union shop or a non-designated shop, says: (a) the Association shall impose a fine, and (b) the amount of such fine is to be determined with reference to the sum involved and shall be sufficiently high to offset the advantage gained by the member through such transactions, together with an appropriate penalty.

In other words, the determination of the amount of the fine rests in the first instance with the Association, whose discretion in the matter is unimpaired (subject to review by the Impartial Chairman upon filed complaint) but with certain factors which may not be overlooked in the fixing of the fine. . . .

In other words, while the fine upon the non-complying member of the Association *may not be less than* a determination with reference to the sum involved and the offsetting of any advantage gained, nevertheless these considerations provide only the minimum base for the fine and do not impair the right of the Association to make the fine any amount higher than that which might strictly be required by these considerations.[39]

---

[38]*Women's Wear Daily,* Oct. 24, 1935.

[39]S. A. Rosenblatt, *Decisions,* Case no. 1189-A (Dec. 12, 1935). "No work shall be sent out by any member of the ASSOCIATION to be made outside of his own shop unless the workers in his New York factory are fully supplied with work. . . . If a member of the ASSOCIATION shall violate . . . [this rule], the Impartial Chairman may, after [a] hearing in the manner in this agreement provided, direct the member to reimburse the workers employed in his New York factory for the loss of wages sustained by them by reason of such violation." From the 1938 collective agreement of the Associated Corset and Brassière Manufacturers with the ILGWU and Local 32.

As a rule, the evolution of disciplinary procedures for infraction of clauses on outside production followed the procedures that evolved for punishing other types of contract infractions. Exemplifying this development was the movement to enforce restrictions on contracting in the manufacture of fur garments. In the late twenties, collective agreements of the fur manufacturing industry contained the usual clauses on contracting: registration of contractors, minimum size of shops, preferences to inside workers, prohibitions on inside contracting, and permission to deal only with contractors holding union labor agreements that met the standards set for the trade — standards negotiated between Associated Fur Manufacturers and the International Fur Workers' Union.

To enforce these elaborate provisions the 1929 collective agreement provided that "the conference committee shall have authority to recommend to the Associations penalties for violations of the provisions of this agreement in regard to contracting." Later, however, specific penalties for offenses against the contracting clauses were incorporated into collective agreements of the fur manufacturing industry. Definite fines were indicated for the first two offenses against contracting, while the third offense generally carried the penalty of suspension or expulsion from the employers' association. Workers as well as employers were to be penalized for violating the restrictions on contracting.

Whether penalties for unauthorized contracting were fixed in collective agreements, left to the discretion of the contracting parties, or directly imposed by agencies of the impartial machinery, drastic measures were sometimes necessary to collect the fines that were levied and to carry out the punishment imposed. Here, the parties to collective agreements were more willing to permit the use of direct action, particularly where outside contracting was carried on in non-union shops. Sometimes, the official uses of strikes to enforce restrictions on outside production were disguised in phrases denying offenders the "rights and privileges" of the agreement; in other cases, the collective agreement expressly authorized strikes to enforce established limitations on contracting. Following the enforcement pattern applied to other provisions, some collective agreements confined official strikes to the last resort in a series of measures supporting the awards of industry arbitrators; others sanctioned strikes for repeated cases of outside dealings without awaiting action of the impartial machinery.[40]

Some Cases and Examples

Whatever the forms of punishment inflicted upon those who managed to circumvent restrictions on outside production, the impartial chairman or highest arbitrating authority for each industry at least undertook to convince offenders that crime does not pay. For having 9,791 garments made up in 1925 by 37 nonunion contractors, a women's coat and suit manufacturer was fined $1,958.20 to offset a cost advantage of 20 cents a garment favoring nonunion production. Impartial Chairman R. V. Ingersoll assessed the firm an additional $500 to act as a deterrent against repeating the offense. Except for $300 to meet the cost of investigation, all the money was turned over to the union to help compensate the workers for their loss of employment.[41]

Similarly, Impartial Chairman C. B. Barnes in 1928 levied a fine of $150 on a leather goods manufacturer for having 35 dozen pocketbooks made up outside after he had agreed to let his inside workers do the job at a higher price. Again, in 1931, Impartial Chairman G. W. Alger assessed damages of $750 on a women's coat and suit manufacturer for sending materials to outside shops while his inside workers were idle. In 1935, Impartial Chairman Henry Moskowitz fined a manufacturer of children's garments $500 for bypassing his registered contractor to favor a nonunion contractor in Fall River, Massachusetts. And, in 1937, Impartial Chairman Harry Uviller ordered a jobber to return to his dress contractor $1,861.80 that the jobber had received in kickbacks.[42]

---

[40]A number of collective agreements offered more than one form of penalty to insure compliance with restrictions on outside contracting. See, for examples, the pertinent provisions in the 1937 collective agreement of the Infants' and Children's Coat Association with the ILGWU and the Cloakmakers' Joint Board; and similar clauses in the 1937 collective agreement of the National Skirt Manufacturers' Association with the Cloakmakers' Joint Board and the Skirt Makers' Union, Local 23, ILGWU.

[41]R. V. Ingersoll, *Decisions,* Case no. 184 (Sept.-Dec., 1925).

[42]C. B. Barnes, *Decisions,* Case no. 201 (Dec. 19, 1928); G. W. Alger, *Decisions,* Case no. 655 (Nov. 18, 1931), discussed in *Women's Wear Daily,* Nov. 19, 1931; Henry Moskowitz, *Decisions* (Sept. 6, 1935); Harry Uviller, *Decisions,* Case no. D-1651 (Sept. 28, 1937), vol. 3, p. 63.

Where offenders refused to open their books or permit inspection of their premises, industry arbitrators were hard pressed to arrive at a figure that offset the advantages accrued from violating the provisions on outside production. The profits derived from unauthorized dealings with outside contractors were often subjects of separate investigations. During the thirties, a contractor assigned to work exclusively for a particular jobber surreptitiously accepted orders from a Chicago firm and managed to conceal his operations until he had completed a considerable number of garments in violation of the collective agreements of the women's coat and suit trade. Later, he was apprehended by the impartial machinery and charged with violating the limitation of contractors clause in the 1934–1935 agreements.

"The clause referred to is an essential part of the means adopted by the contracting parties for the stabilization and regulation of the industry," announced Impartial Chairman G. W. Alger in his award. After citing the contract provision that penalties for non-union and nondesignated dealings must be sufficiently high to offset the advantages gained, Alger continued:

The procedure required would normally call for disciplinary action by the American Association, which has not been taken in this case. The Trial Board has not before it information sufficient to ascertain what, if any, pecuniary advantage has been gained by the violation. A further investigation will be ordered in order that this may be ascertained and the parties will be given an opportunity to consider the report before final disposition of the matter and an appropriate penalty will then by imposed.[43]

Fines were imposed for all types of contract violations bearing on jobber-contractor relationships. In 1943, Impartial Chairman J. J. Walker of the women's coat and suit industry imposed upon a firm

> liquidated damages in the sum of Three Thousand ($3000) Dollars for its non-union dealings; Three Thousand ($3000) for its continual refusal to produce all of its books and records, and Five Hundred ($500) Dollars to cover the cost of voluminous investigations made necessary by the complete lack of co-operation by the firm, making a total of Six Thousand Five Hundred ($6500) Dollars to be paid forthwith to the office of the Impartial Chairman.
>
> —J. J. Walker, *Decisions,* Case no. 3939 (August 18, 1943).

See also S. A. Rosenblatt, *Decisions,* Case no. 1997 (Oct. 11, 1939).

[43] G. W. Alger, *Decisions,* Case no. 1092 (June 1, 1933-May 31, 1935).

In their efforts to control outside production, the parties to collective agreements were not averse to calling upon the state courts for help. Injunctive relief against threatened infractions of established jobber-contractor relationships was sometimes considered to be the only adequate means of preserving justice between the parties to collective agreements. In 1934, for example, the contractors' association of the women's coat and suit trade sought and obtained from New York State Supreme Court Justice J. E. McGeehan an injunction against the jobbers' association restraining the jobbers from violating the exclusive contracting clause in the agreement of September 20, 1933 between the two associations, by:

1– manufacturing or producing women's coats, suits, and any and all other garments on their own premises;

2– causing women's coats, suits, and any and all other garments to be made on their behalf at any plant, factory, or premises other than the plant, factory or premises of the plaintiffs, members of the American Cloak and Suit Manufacturers' Association, Inc., designated by them as their contractors or sub-manufacturers;

3– purchasing in whole or in part women's coats, suits, and any and all other garments from jobbers, factories, persons, firms or corporations other than the plaintiffs, members of the American Cloak and Suit Manufacturers' Association, Inc., designated as their contractors, or sub-manufacturers;

4– inequitably distributing their production among the plantiffs, members of the American Cloak and Suit Manufacturers' Association, Inc., designated as their contractors.[44]

In another case, injunction relief was sought and obtained against a single jobber who had defied all the organized forces of his industry. During the fall of 1929, Joseph Stein, a cloak jobber and member of the Merchants' Ladies' Garment Association, was charged upon affidavits filed by accountants of the impartial machinery for the women's coat and suit trade with sending out work to seven nonunion contractors and with buying garments outright from 28 nonunion shops — all in violation of the 1929 collective

---

[44]As reported in *Women's Wear Daily*, Feb. 13, 1934. The agreement at issue was that between the Merchants' Ladies' Garment Association (jobbers) and the American Cloak and Suit Manufacturers' Association (contractors), dated Sept. 20, 1933, *ibid.*, Jan. 17, 1934.

agreement between the jobbers' association and the Cloakmakers' Joint Board, ILGWU. As soon as this information was transmitted from the office of impartial chairman to the association, the grievance committee of the association met on October 26, 1929 and voted to impose a fine of $250 on the jobber. This decision was approved by the association's board of directors. But Mr. Stein refused to pay the fine or to cease his nonunion contractor dealings.

Three months later, on February 17, 1930, Mr. Stein was suspended from membership in his jobbers' association, but he still continued manufacturing through nonunion contractors "thus threatening the stability of the industry which the collective agreements of July 1929 were intended to maintain." After the jobbers' association and the ILGWU had devoted several additional months of fruitless effort trying to win compliance with industry standards from this suspended jobber, the two organizations combined to seek relief from the courts on the ground that the conduct of the firm was causing irreparable damage to the association and the union. Acting on the combined pleas of three groups of employers — the Merchants' Ladies' Garment Association (jobbers), the American Cloak and Suit Manufacturers' Association (contractors), and the Industrial Council of Cloak, Suit and Skirt Manufacturers (inside manufacturers) — together with the plea of the International Ladies' Garment Workers' Union — Supreme Court Justice Alfred Frankenthaler enjoined Joseph Stein from continuing to have his garments made up by nonunion contractors or from purchasing finished garments produced in nonunion shops.[45]

Not only did the state courts at times enjoin those who threatened to violate, or continued to violate, provisions of collective agreements regulating the jobber-contractor system, not only did these courts, if requested, come to the aid of industrial arbitrators who could not enforce their awards, but they also had authority to compel participation in the established procedures through

[45]*Women's Wear Daily,* April 8 and 9, May 15, and June 12, 1930. *New York Times,* May 15, 1930. Subsequently, Stein was readmitted to his association after paying a fine of $250, a special assessment of $150 to cover a debt that had accrued during his suspension, and the costs of the counsel fees of the plaintiffs. Before being permitted to meet these financial requirements, however, he had to promise "to do his utmost to assist the various factors in the cloak industry to bring about a more perfect stabilization of it." *Women's Wear Daily,* June 13, 1930.

which arbitration decisions were rendered. During 1938, Jesse Lyons and Samuel Goldfarb of Lyons and Goldfarb, jobbers in the women's coat and suit trade, were charged with nonunion and non-designated contractor dealings. To avoid pressure for an investigation, these men resigned from the Merchants' Ladies' Garment Association and, in effect, declared their independence of the industry's organized structure. Thereafter, the partners persistently refused to appear before the industry arbitrator or to permit examination of their records by representatives of the impartial machinery.

Finally, upon application by the legal counsel for the Cloakmakers' Joint Board, ILGWU, Mr. Justice Ferdinand Pecora of the New York State Supreme Court, issued a "body attachment" directing the sheriff to bring the men before the arbitrator. A newspaper reporter's account of the case follows:

With the sheriff seated between the arbitrator and the two respondents, Mr. Schlesinger [union spokesman] began his case after the witnesses were sworn in. He showed how an examination of the firm's records was sought without success by the accountants of the impartial machinery. A complaint was filed with the impartial chairman, asking the firm to appear. Failing to get an appearance from the firm members, letters by registered mail were issued and telegrams sent, but to no avail.

On July 14, accountants visited the firm to examine their records and on the same day the Merchants' Ladies' Garment Association received a letter advising of the resignation of their member, Lyons & Goldfarb. From then on a series of attempts to have the firm appear before Mr. Rosenblatt [impartial chairman] were made without results. On July 25 the firm was served with a subpoena to appear two days later, and again they failed to show up. The union then went to Justice Pecora and obtained a court order permitting a deputy sheriff to bring the parties before the arbitrator.

On questioning by union counsel Mr. Goldfarb at the adjourned hearing quickly admitted that he had dealt with non-union and non-designated contractors. One shop was in Huntington, L. I., another in New Jersey and one in Brooklyn. He said, after pleading for more time, that he was ready to show all his books and records and agreed for an examination to begin this morning.

Somewhat stunned at the rapidity of events, the witness said he was ready to mend his ways. Together with his partner he was ready to do as ordered and agreed to appear next Tuesday, when a report of his books and records would be presented at a hearing before the impartial chairman.

"I admit I made a mistake and am ready to start over again under your terms," Mr. Goldfarb told the crowded room.[46]

Concluding Observations

The number and character of cases and controversies that arose from attempts to enforce controls over outside contracting gave the administration of collective agreements for the needle trades a direction markedly at odds with the usual course of contract enforcement. Issues affecting jobber-contractor-inside-manufacturer relationships were a strange substitute for disputes over hours, wages, and working conditions. Equally at odds with the normal course of collective bargaining was the strange alignment of the parties. Instead of management against labor, employers against the workers, or the "bosses" against the "people," this new alignment, most strikingly revealed in attempts to control outside production, saw the organized forces of both labor and management pitted against the unorganized employers and their nonunion labor force. Those who would control competition either by extending the labor standards of inside establishments into the shops of outside contractors, or else by limiting the operations of those contractors, were aligned against those who bowed only to the law of the lowest bidder.

The battle to preserve the principles of the protocol movement was waged on many fronts and with many weapons. Calling upon the judicial power of New York State to preserve the institutions of collective action pointed up the futility of trying to maintain islands of law and order in a sea of unregulated competition. So long as the organized forces of industry were surrounded by a vast expanse of unorganized elements, the headlands of legitimate business would continue to be pounded by the tides of illegitimate competition. "I thought I could try something and get away with it," confessed Samuel Goldfarb in the case cited above. "Others have done it and are still running wild."

At one stage in the early history of the protocol movement, unsuccessful attempts to prevent contamination of inside standards from outside sources were alleged to have magnified the evils of

---

[46] *Women's Wear Daily*, August 17, 1938.

uncontrolled competition. At least such was the conclusion of the leading student of union history during the period. Summarizing the failures of the original Protocol of Peace in the women's coat and suit trade, Louis Lorwin wrote:

> The hope that the protocol would rapidly lead to the standardization of wages and of other conditions in the industry and thereby weed out the backward non-standard shops did not materialize. The number of shops was too large, the seasonal character of the industry too marked, the competitive habits of the workers in the industry too strong to allow the unions to cope with this task successfully in a short time and single-handed. But failure in this respect merely made conditions worse. The employers, driven by the fear of competition of the small outside shops, tried to make these shops serve their interests. It was thus that they themselves stimulated the growth of the small and non-standardized outside shops by helping to set up sub-manufacturers and other subsidiary shops. In other words, the fear of competition made competition in the industry worse.[47]

Yet the early contributions of those who sponsored and founded the protocol movement are not to be minimized. The early leaders of employer groups and labor unions, aided, if not directed, by third parties, conceived the ideas, evolved the principles, created the machinery, outlined the procedures, and profited from experiences that together made possible a framework of industrial self-government on which to hang their objective of controlling competition for the welfare of the "legitimate" elements within each trade. Theirs was a problem not only of generating support for mutual cooperation but also of translating that initiative into action, even though faced with overwhelming odds. The permanence of their contributions reflects the success of their efforts. Most of the creative work in building the institutions and procedures through which to achieve the goals of collective action took shape within the first two decades of the protocol movement. Few constructive ideas have been added within the last forty years. J. H. Cohen, a leader in this evolving drama, once sized up the situation in terms as applicable to 1967 as to 1914 when he testified before the U.S. Commission on Industrial Relations:

---

[47]Louis Lorwin [Louis Levine], *The Women's Garment Workers* (1924), p. 314.

It does not mean that where you have mutual confidence the thing works perfectly; we have some strikes in the cloak industry today, and we have officials of the union who violate the law, subordinate officials; we have employers who violate the law, just as in political societies you have lawbreakers, but you have the machinery for bringing those people to book and correct any mistakes that they make, and that is the value in the system of collective bargaining. It substitutes a constitution for chaos, it substitutes law for disorder, and it substitutes reason for force.[48]

---

[48]*Final Report and Testimony* (1916), vol. 1, p. 579. See also J. H. Cohen, *Law and Order in Industry* (1916).

Chapter 11

Principles Restated:

the Work of Paul Abelson

THE principles of competition and collective bargaining which evolved in the needle trades after 1910 can no longer be restated with the detachment from contemporary events that accompanied the production of the preceding chapters. For this study had been virtually completed before the sudden upsurge of insurrection in the sixties had challenged so many of our industrial, political, social, educational, and religious institutions. Once the current "age of revolution" had begun to threaten other segments of the established order, not even the author could reread his own manuscript without attributing to the sponsors of the protocol movement a prophetic insight into the continuing need for protecting industrial society from the unpredictable outbreaks of force and violence. Moreover, in the light of recent developments, it would now appear that the volumes, so far from being a product of inductive research, had been fashioned from highly selected materials to support a general thesis appropriate to the times.

A New Era of Revolution

It is true that the current champions of revolution find their most cherished precedents in the action of organized workers who from time to time in the earlier years of industrial growth defied the shackles of the law by impinging upon the rights of others, even to the extent of threatening the public safety. Where else in the history of our country can better support be found for tolerating force and violence as a means to an end? But the precedents to be gathered from the history of collective bargaining in the needle trades all point in the opposite direction. There, the founders and advocates of the protocol movement measured their success in terms of their ability to control the excesses of revolt. "But above all," wrote Gertrude Barnum, the early union organizer, assessing developments of the first two years under the original Protocol of Peace, "it is awe inspiring to watch a hetero-geneous multitude of 50,000 men and women, an immigrant population of diverse creeds and nationalities, slowly and pain-fully learning the lesson of subordinating the individual's self for the common good; curbing passion, submitting to reason, learning to value organization, practicing scrutinizing the actions of their leaders and endeavoring to choose wisely its [sic] spokes-men."[1]

Conversely, the specter of failure to harness industrial society to the self-imposed restraints of orderly procedures hung like a cloud over all those who sought to accomplish the objectives of the protocol movement. "Sabotage and direct action and force," lamented the editor of the *American Cloak and Suit Review,* official magazine of the American Cloak and Suit Manufacturers' Association, in the issue of January 1915, "meant more than mediation or arbitration, save when mediation and arbitration meant decisions in their [the workers'] favor." Along with the need for clarifying their goals — a virtue seldom stressed by the current apostles of revolt — the leaders of the protocol move-ment clearly understood the necessity for building their hopes upon a solid foundation of law and order. Whatever the ends of group action, the means must be tempered by imposing re-straints on the right to revolt. Not even the Communists, after their short-lived attempt to take over the New York Cloak-makers' Joint Board in the mid-twenties, cared to operate on less than a solid foundation of economic stability and security. For many years, the professed Communist leaders of the Inter-national Fur Workers' Union defended the orderly procedures

---

[1] Gertrude Barnum, "How Industrial Peace Has Been Brought About in the Clothing Trade," in the *Independent,* Oct. 3, 1912, vol. 73, p. 778.

of collective bargaining in the fur trade with a zeal that defied their long-range objectives.[2]

But leaders of the current revolts have obviously taken a different approach. As long as the use of physical force to deprive others of their personal and property rights has brought a measure of success, the new advocates of revolution have shown little desire to fall back upon less aggressive means of accomplishing their ends. Not even the law of the land has restrained those who demonstrate to their own satisfaction that violence has been more fruitful than submission to established procedures. This current assessment of the means to be employed — whether in the realm of education, religion, politics, or civil rights — has backfired to put a new blight on the emerging history of industrial relations. In the new "age of revolution," militant labor groups are achieving unexpected successes through flouting all legal restraints — legislative, judicial, or administrative — imposed on the exercise of what they choose to include in their "right to strike." Recently, an official of a union of public employees in New York State publicly announced that his union would not give up its right to strike, no matter what laws against striking the legislature might enact!

The sponsors of collective bargaining in the needle trades foresaw the danger of revolt against those in authority and sought to meet it — not so much with pious appeals to the "rule of reason" as with constructive proposals and concrete programs that would offer workable substitutes for the evils of force and violence. At times, their efforts to contain the urge for revolt encountered obstacles beyond those presented to other segments of organized

---

[2]J. A. Dyche, a union leader of the protocol movement from its inception, found a similar vein of economic conservatism beneath the radical philosophies of other immigrant Jews: "High sounding phrases were to the Yiddish worker what beer is to the German, whiskey to the Irishman and opium to the Chinaman. They feel relieved when they find an opportunity either to indulge in or listen to them. And the radicals in the Yiddish labor movement are the extremest of the extreme — when it affects someone else's interest. Scratch this radical, touch him in the spot that affects his personal interest, and you will find him an ultra-conservative." Dyche, *Bolshevism in the American Labor Movement* (1926), preface, p. xiii. This underlying respect for law and order in industry had much to do with the success of collective bargaining in the needle trades.

society. The Brandeis Conference of 1910, for example, offered no basic principles on which to erect industrial self-government comparable to the political principles offered civil society by the Constitutional Convention of 1787. Nor did the Protocol of Peace in 1910 hand down a framework of industrial self-government through which to implement those principles, comparable to the political framework of government outlined for the "state" in the federal Constitution of 1789. Only by trial and error over years of experimentation did the institutions of collective bargaining succeed in bringing industrial order out of chaos.

Moreover, this progress toward industrial self-government had to be achieved without the overpowering weapon of compulsion available to the state during periods of incipient revolt. The back-wash from the right of revolution so ably set forth in Thomas Jefferson's Declaration of Independence did not for many years return to haunt the agencies of political government, once British authority had been overturned. Contributing to this immunity of the state from revolt was the dominant political theory of the time — that the best government was the least government — and the knowledge that an open frontier always beckoned the politically discontented. By contrast, the growth of industrial empires in America was accompanied by the dominant theory of an all-pervading, omnipotent management — a concept so incompatible with the growth of political democracy that it was sure, sooner or later, to stimulate revolt. Nor could the discontented industrial worker in an age of giant factories and specialization of labor so easily escape the limitations of his job by heading westward for other means of employment.

Once the concept of political sovereignty residing in the state and exercised through the instrumentalities of civil government had lost some of its preeminence over other forms of authority, and once disrespect for civil law had seemingly become as prevalent as disrespect for other rules of conduct, the ugly specter of complete anarchy began to raise its bloody head. Even when used to suppress the most blatant evidences of injustice, revolt against any form of authority is by its very nature a disintegrating force in organized society. In the best of circumstances, its salvaging influence may, like the pesticide DDT, set off a chain reaction that ultimately does more harm than good. The logic of Thomas

Jefferson's Declaration of Independence advanced to justify separation from England was later propounded by Alexander H. Stephens, United States Senator from Georgia, to justify separation of the South from the union; and Stephens foresaw that Georgia might with equal logic rely upon the right of revolution to separate from the southern confederacy. In like manner, the Georgia uplands might break away from the Georgia tidewater, and so on until, alas, the road to revolution became the road to anarchy.

If, as the evidence so far suggests, the trend of current revolts is along the road to anarchy in which each individual becomes a law unto himself, such was clearly not the case with those who directed the growth of collective bargaining in the needle trades. There, workers and employers alike were not only urged, but voluntarily agreed, to join their respective organizations and to abide by the rules of the game. These employers' associations and labor unions were in turn not only urged, but they voluntarily agreed, to work together for their mutual interests. The use of machinery to negotiate, mediate, and arbitrate industrial disputes of one community was then extended to other competing communities in the hope that all competitors could be united into a pyramid of industry-wide scope, where industry-wide standards of employment and industry-wide standards of business conduct could prevail. In achieving these objectives, the rights of the individual, though not ignored, were often subordinated to the common welfare of the trade.

But the integrating influence of collective bargaining extended far beyond the boundaries of each trade. Unlike the new "robber barons" in labor unions and among other militants in society, who show little concern for the impact of their actions upon others beyond their own group, the organized forces of the needle trades never presumed that economic stability could survive in a hostile atmosphere of general disruption. Even those who would feather their own nests saw the logic of cultivating the support of the consumer, the government, and the general public. The principle of interlocking directorates that bound all factions of the apparel trades to the worlds of politics, education, religion, and social relationships precluded the shortsighted view of grabbing whatever was within reach. This principle not only contributed to the movement for industry-wide standards but it also explains why the voice of the outside world was so often represented on the councils of those who were named to create, interpret, and apply the terms of collective agreements. Like Holmes' chambered nautilus, the cells of industrial life were forever combining into more stately mansions. Such was the philosophy of Brandeis and of Holt, of Cohen and of Dyche, of Hillman and of Hillquit, and of scores of others who contributed to the ideals of the protocol movement.

The Work of Paul Abelson

While the principles of the protocol movement were generated in high places, the success of the program hinged upon unselfish support from devoted men who were capable of applying those principles to conditions in the workshop. Throughout the needle trades, propagating the gospel of the protocols was scarcely less important than creating it. In terms of actual accomplishments, Paul Abelson (1878–1953) led the parade of those who helped to translate the doctrine of competition and collective bargaining into a way of industrial life. While he contributed many refinements to the evolving concepts of law and order in industry, his primary function, like that of his biblical namesake, was to spread the gospel into the far-flung corners of his own professional experience and to see that it was accepted by the many industries he served. Operating as adviser, negotiator, mediator, arbitrator, impartial chairman, or special umpire, he held at one time or another continuing positions of responsibility in more than a score of different industries within the needle trades, and in several other industries as well. More often than not, he helped to introduce collective bargaining into each of the industries he served, and in many cases he remained to direct the course of its development. In a profession where assignments were generally as short-lived as those of labor arbitrators, Paul Abelson stood alone in the tenure of his offices, which, in some cases, ran for as many as five, ten, fifteen, twenty or more years, or until he resigned or died.[3]

---

[3] This sketch highlighting some of the contributions that Paul Abelson made to the subject of competition and collective bargaining in the needle trades is in no sense a comprehensive account of his life's work. Unless otherwise identified, the source of all quotations or paraphrased materials in the following sections on Paul Abelson is found in the Abelson papers, which, among

Soon after the original Protocol of Peace set in motion the new program for collective bargaining, Paul Abelson left the schoolroom and a potential life of social work to join forces with those dedicated to solving the human ills of industrial society. Although never trained for industrial relations (his graduate dissertation was written on "The Seven Liberal Arts, A Study in Medieval Culture"), Abelson nevertheless brought to his new profession the tools of success. He was, in the jargon of the workshop, a man "with a handle to his name." Abelson had earned the title of "Doctor" (Ph.D. in political science at Columbia University, 1906), and he lived among a people who, at the time, still presumed to find some discernible connection between intellectuality and morality, as well as between intellectuality and public service. Most other leaders who contributed so heavily to the institutions of collective bargaining were likewise men with handles to their names – Ph.D.'s, M.D.'s, LL.B's, rabbis, judges, mayors, governors, or United States senators. The prestige that Dr. Abelson and others like him carried to their positions of trust and responsibility was insured in advance by the mark of distinction that was the "handle" to their names.

A second tool of success that helped Abelson to win the confidence of opposing parties to industrial conflicts was an approach that could – like George Washington's declaration of neutrality in time of war – be defined as a policy "friendly and impartial" to both sides. After three years of introductory contacts with collective bargaining as labor representative (clerk) of the Cloak, Suit and Skirt Manufacturers' Protective Association under the original Protocol of Peace, Dr. Abelson resigned his position and moved in 1914 to the headquarters of Kehillah, the Jewish community – an organization once described by the president of the

---

other documents, correspondence, newspaper clippings, etc., also include disc-recorded personal interviews and tape-recorded public lectures at Cornell University. The Abelson papers are filed by chronological dates within each industry in the Labor-Management Documentation Center of the New York State School of Industrial and Labor Relations, Cornell University.

Among his many assignments, Paul Abelson was impartial chairman for the fur manufacturing industry, the millinery industry, the men's hat and cap industries, infants' and children's wear, juvenile apparel, cotton goods, full fashioned hosiery, ladies' pocketbooks, the pleaters and stitchers, luggage and leather, dolls, novelty toys, bakers, and movies.

Associated Fur Manufacturers, as "a symbol of public opinion assuring fair play and calm judgment in all matters that are vital to the interest of workers and employers alike." Operating thereafter through Kehillah's bureau of industry, of which he became chairman, and through its nonpartisan committee on industrial relations, Dr. Abelson was soon involved in numerous third party assignments in various branches of the needle trades.

He approached every assignment with meticulous care to cultivate and preserve his friendly and impartial status. He never allowed himself to be associated with Protestant, Catholic, or Jewish church groups (he met his religious needs through the Society for Ethical Culture); he never joined a political party and he never ran for public office. He never accepted an invitation to help resolve an industrial dispute or to serve as impartial chairman for an industry unless both parties voluntarily sought his assistance. On one occasion, during a critical stage of contract negotiations for the millinery trade, where third party counsel and advice was sorely needed to break a deadlock, neither party dared ask for Dr. Abelson, lest a call for outside help be construed as a sign of weakness. Thereupon, a representative from each side secretly arranged to have Dr. Abelson "by mistake" crash the negotiating sessions in progress at a local hotel. At the appointed time, Dr. Abelson dutifully opened the door to the conference room, but his profuse apologies were drowned by pleas from all sides of the table to join the discussions.

Dr. Ableson's approach to impartiality, however, ran much deeper than external evidences of neutrality; least of all did it embrace the concept that an arbitrator's duty was to halve the distance between the opposing parties. Though cutting the baby in twain would often have been the easiest way out, he, like King Solomon, first sought to discover the truth and then rendered his decision accordingly. More than any other arbitrator of his time, he spent his life in acquiring a thorough knowledge of the industries that employed him and in seeking to understand the people whom he served. "Of course, as soon as I got into a situation [industry]," he explained, while chatting informally in a disc-recorded interview,

I made it my business to know and know and know what it was all about — reading the papers and reading the literature and the trade papers and finding out everything about it. And from one industry to the other there is much similarity between them and I made it a point to find out what it was all about so as to understand them. Clipping all the time — here you see a clipping I cut out today from the paper about the toy industry — what the resident buyers say about the toy situation. That's part of the things I cut out and I have it. I'm sure the union hasn't got that clipping nor the employers, probably, but it is my business to know it.

Dr. Abelson was equally concerned about the facts in each individual dispute. "It was more important to me to find out the truth than to render a decision," he remarked at a dinner given in his honor after his twenty-five years of service to the fur trade. "Others say it is better to get a decision than to wrangle over it. No, it is better to build up the habit of truth-finding." Earlier, he had written of his methods in the millinery trade: "the impartial chairman in formulating his conclusion has sought to reach to the very bottom of the problem, and not to judge by the surface indications; to find the underlying causes of the industrial sickness, the better to be able to offer the prescription that would cure the disease."[4]

Unlike ivory-tower arbitrators, Dr. Abelson wished to begin each investigation at the source of the trouble. He likened himself to circuit judges who moved from county to county, holding court near the scene of the crime. His urge to operate in the front-line trenches of every industrial dispute was one of his strongest professional virtues, but, for reasons of physical limitations, it became one of his professional shortcomings. Early in his career as arbitrator, Dr. Abelson was sometimes able to satisfy his passion for first-hand knowledge of facts and personalities by receiving assignments to more than one official position in the hierarchy of grievance procedure. Both in the men's clothing trade of East Side Manhattan and in the local millinery trade, he became a public member of the committee on immediate action that conducted field investigations of disputes and rendered initial decisions on the issues. In both cases, he was also chairman of the conference committee that entertained appeals from the committee on immediate action and exercised original jurisdiction over matters of general concern. In addition, he was secretary in both industries to the board of arbitration which rendered final and binding decisions on all unresolved issues. As secretary to the board, he became a

---

[4]Abelson, *Decisions,* Lish Co. case (June 29, 1935).

last-ditch mediator helping the parties to reach agreement among themselves before a final decision was imposed upon them.[5]

Abelson on the Ends of the Protocol Movement

The third and most important aid to success that Dr. Paul Abelson brought to his new profession was the banner of the protocol movement embodying the concept of competition and collective bargaining. Labor-management conflicts over wages, hours, and working conditions could be more readily terminated, given the prospects of a settlement that would be mutually advantageous to both contestants. The disintegrating influence of glorifying individual rights at the expense of industrial society could be submerged if a united drive to promote the welfare of the trade brought more freedom and prosperity to all those who depended upon the industry for a livelihood. Even the sacred "right to strike" might soon wither from disuse should an industrial system of law and order succeed in dispensing more justice to more people than a system of turbulence and disorder could ever guarantee. And if there be any warlike instincts among the members of industrial society, would it not make sense for the more reputable elements of labor and of management, organized into labor unions and into employers' associations, respectively, to unite against their common enemies, the disreputable elements who undermine established labor standards and threaten the legitimate profits of business?

Declaring himself to be a disciple of Louis D. Brandeis, Dr. Abelson readily endorsed the principles of the protocol movement and wholeheartedly supported collective bargaining as an appropriate means of implementing those principles. Like other leaders of the movement, he insisted upon working through the "legitimate" elements of industrial society. On one occasion, shortly after receiving an LL.B. degree from the New York Law School in 1918 and after being admitted to the bar, Dr. Abelson refused

---

[5]"The impartial chairman becomes the friend of the industry, the friend of both sides," so Dr. Abelson wrote in one of his early decisions as impartial chairman for the full fashioned hosiery industry. "He brings to the solution of problems a knowledge of the business, an understanding of the minds of employers and of the workers, a trained mind in economics. . . . That function he cannot perform if he is aloof from the industry and its problems."

an offer to become legal counsel for an association of contractors (the American Cloak and Suit Manufacturers' Association) until he was assured that the members represented the more substantial and reputable contracting firms that possessed the capacity and moral strength to exert a constructive influence upon the problems of their industry. Later he was not only caught up in the post-World War I movement to limit contracting and outlaw the small irresponsible shops but he became a leader in the movement. His statement in a decision early in May 1921, on behalf of the board of arbitration for the cloth hat and cap industry denouncing the illegitimate social shop as "detrimental to the industry as a whole and therefore to the legitimate manufacturer and to the organized workers" was bodily incorporated into the industry's collective agreement effective May 23, 1921.[6]

Excluding the disreputable elements which operated on the fringes of each trade, Dr. Abelson was a builder who consistently supported the "good of the whole" above the conflicted interests of its component parts. Every labor-management dispute that he helped to resolve — particularly those involving temporary differences over wage scales or other conditions of employment — became a cause for seeking to establish more stable human relations through an integration of industrial forces. When called into a local millinery dispute in 1915 — an experience which was to mark the beginnings of more than twenty-five years of continuous service in this or related branches of the headwear trades — he sold the disputing parties on the need for adopting permanent institutions and procedures of collective bargaining to meet the future problems of their industry. Soon after the First World War, Impartial Chairman Paul Abelson commended his board of arbitration for the cloth hat and cap industry, not so much for its "formal determination of specific issues raised by the manufacturers or the

---

[6]The matter of abolishing contracting work as the Agreement requires is a basic problem facing the industry and to the abolishing of which the Collective Agreement and the Association and the Union are whole-heartedly committed to as perhaps the most constructive effort to re-habilitate the Millinery Industry in the City of New York.... The Impartial Chairman decides that within ten days from the writing of this decision, the firm must do the operating work under its own management and not by contract system.
     —Abelson, *Decisions,* case of Ander Hats (Jan. 29, 1937).

workers" (the purpose for which the board was called into action), but for its "attempted solution of a vexed problem in industrial engineering and relations" — a subject which he explained as follows: "It has laid a reasonable foundation for a system of industrial relationships, in harmony with the spirit of the times. It has created a system of collective dealings through organized manufacturers and organized workers, and has established an administrative machinery, presided over by an impartial specialist, which shall continuously function for the life of the agreeement."[7]

Under his direction, other employer groups and worker groups through their respective organizations in other trades were induced to sign multiple-employer collective labor agreements. Such action was likely to be taken at some sacrifice of individual — or minority group — rights and privileges, but always in anticipation of greater economic stability and security within a competitive industry-market area. Once the protocol form of collective bargaining among the organized factions of each local trade had established a solid core of industrial strength, Dr. Abelson worked with equal zeal to extend or combine these local centers of collective action into larger and larger bargaining units until the goal of a single collective agreement for each industry, negotiated and administered between a national employers' association and a national labor union, could be achieved. Only then could wages and working conditions be so standardized that differences in the costs of labor would be virtually eliminated from the competitive forces affecting production.[8]

---

[7]*Daily News Record,* May 5, 1921; *Headgear Worker,* May 20, 1921. Many years later in one of his few business excursions beyond the New York metropolitan district, Special Umpire Abelson made short shrift of his assignment to settle numerous piece-rate problems for the millinery shops in the Danbury, Conn., area and, instead, devoted the bulk of his time to introducing permanent machinery for the negotiation and administration of collective agreements. This new form of self-government created for the area was to be maintained through the joint efforts of an employer group and the union locals with the help of a permanent umpire to render final and binding decisions in all disputes or controversies not otherwise resolved. See *Danbury News-Times,* July 26, 1937.

[8]The economic justification of recognition of the Union from the point of view of an employer is that wages are taken out of the competitive process, in other words, that the Union tends to standardize hours and wages, so that labor conditions throughout the market are

The pressure for industry-wide uniformity in labor costs was perhaps nowhere more urgent than among the producers of needle trade products in New York City; and no one was more conscious of disparities in labor costs detrimental to local manufacturers and to their labor force than Dr. Abelson himself. His attacks upon these disparities expanded with the growth of competition, first into the outer metropolitan district, then into the neighboring states, and finally into more far-flung production markets of the industry. Once the competition of these outer markets had been intensified by the Great Depression, the national government moved to the rescue with the National Industrial Recovery Act of 1933 and its industry codes of fair competition.

During the two years of this act, Dr. Abelson was appointed to serve as government representative for the National Recovery Administration on no less than seven of these industry codes. Even more important, he was chairman of the special fur commission assigned to make exhaustive studies of comparative labor costs in leading centers of fur production throughout the country and to recommend changes in wage differentials to promote fair competition among different regional areas. He was also a member of the special millinery board created by the millinery code to undertake the prodigious task of entertaining and passing upon appeals from hundreds of firms, regional areas, and local markets for concessions and exemptions from industry standards. After the collapse of the codes had brought a return to lower wage standards in out-of-town markets, Dr. Abelson worked to save New York industries, even at the price of reducing local wages, until another movement for industry-wide standards could be successfully launched.[9]

---

equalized and that the same quantity of work, in general, tends to cost every employer the same amount of money. Competition is thus raised to a higher and more humane plane. Employers compete in regard to skill in management, capital available, reputation in the trade for fair dealing, salesmanship ability and foresight in purchase of raw material and ability to secure credit and many other legitimate forms of competition, excluding the competition of wages.

—Abelson, *Decisions*, Fuchs Bros. case (Nov. 30, 1926), text also printed in *Women's Wear*, Dec. 1, 1926.

[9]The industry codes of fair competition and their relation to the protocol movement are discussed in Part II below.

Along with his support for expanding the *area coverage* of collective agreements within each trade until every production unit was subject to the same labor standards (or preferably the same labor costs for comparable work), Dr. Abelson also would expand the *substantive contents* of collective agreements until every conceivable issue of direct or indirect concern to the manufacturers and their labor force fell within the scope of the bargaining power. In this one respect, Dr. Abelson may have outdistanced the protocols themselves. For, whereas the founders and early sponsors of the protocol movement acknowledged the necessity of protecting business standards as well as labor standards, early excursions into the realm of trade relations under the banner of collective bargaining were less frequent and more closely tied to labor relations than was the case with collective agreements negotiated and administered under his watchful eye.[10]

Indeed, by the time Dr. Abelson had reached the "take charge" stage of introducing collective bargaining to different industries, as he had done for the millinery trade in 1915, the range of subject matter falling within the sphere of collective action was for all practical purposes unlimited. Certainly for each trade in which the original collective agreement bears the Abelson stamp, the reasons for entering into group negotiations, usually set forth in the preamble to the contract, pointed up problems that primarily concerned the employers just as prominently as they pointed up problems that primarily concerned the workers. During a crisis threatening the children's dress protocol, Dr. Abelson sponsored a pledge to save the protocol "for the welfare of the industry and the welfare of all concerned in it." When he drafted the first collective agreement between the Ladies' Hat Manufacturers' Protective Association and the millinery workers' union in 1915,

---

[10]"The conferees have shown a remarkably realistic approach to the problems confronting the industry.... The conferees have, moreover, not confined themselves to an analysis of the situation as it affects directly labor relations, but have explored the indirect influences on these relations and the role that other factors in the Industry play in the problems for which solutions are sought. The contracting problem has been fully studied...." Statement of Paul Abelson, impartial chairman, on progress of negotiations for a new collective agreement between the Cloth Hat and Cap Manufacturers' Association and the New York Joint Council of the United Cloth Hat and Cap Makers of North America, *Daily News Record,* May 5, 1921.

the purpose of bargaining was revealed in the opening clause: "Whereas, illegitimate competition by employers at the sacrifice of workers' wages, brought chaos and destruction to the entire millinery industry. . . ." Many years later while introducing collective bargaining to the women's belt industry, of which he also became impartial chairman, he helped the parties to negotiate an agreement designed, among other stated objectives, "to eliminate unfair methods of competition and effect a general stabilization of the industry."

Likewise in providing machinery for contract administration, the parties to collective agreements that Dr. Abelson helped to introduce often created joint union-association agencies that by their very titles indicated the broad range of their powers and responsibilities. Such was clearly the case with the "Board of Trade," the chief administrative agency under the 1937 collective agreement between the Allied Hat Manufacturers and the headwear workers, or with the "Trade Board of Control and Arbitration" in the 1934 bakery industry agreement, or with the "Trade Problems Committee" created by the 1936 collective agreement of the luggage and leather goods industry "to consider general problems of trade affecting labor relations." The jurisdiction of such administrative agencies over differences or controversies arising between individual employers and their workers or between the employers' association and the labor union that were parties to the contract was seldom confined to the interpretation and application of specific contract clauses.[11]

Dr. Abelson would have no part of fine distinctions between "labor" issues subject to collective bargaining and "trade" issues beyond the sphere of the bargaining power. Nor would he distinguish managerial prerogatives (matters solely within the competence of management) or union prerogatives (matters solely within the competence of unions) from matters of labor-management concern clearly subject to negotiations at the bargaining table.

---

[11]The 1938 collective agreement between the Association of New York Handbag Manufacturers and the Pocketbook Workers' Union gave to the administrative agencies it created the authority to investigate and settle "any and all complaints, disputes, differences of opinion or misunderstandings arising between the Association and the Union and/or between members of the Association and members of the Union affecting directly or indirectly their relations as employer or employee during the term of this agreement."

Inability to compete with lower labor costs elsewhere, observed Dr. Abelson in one of his decisions, may be as much a matter of obsolete machinery or antiquated production methods as it is a matter of high wage rates or restricted hours of work; and he insisted that the proper relief may as logically call for the installation of new machinery or the introduction of improved production methods as for a general lowering of wage rates. For a business undergoing technological change, so he stated on another occasion, an engineering study (a managerial prerogative) may be more vital to the success of collective bargaining on labor issues than a wage study. And if peace is to be maintained in the industry, the door must be kept open to the possibility of negotiating every conceivable issue affecting the interests of both parties, as well as to the possibility of settling every conceivable type of dispute during the life of an agreement through the established grievance machinery of contract administration.

Abelson on the Means to the Ends

No one doubted the value of Abelson's contributions to the protocol objectives of eliminating competition in labor standards (or in labor costs), and of controlling the excesses of competition in standards of business conduct. Nevertheless, most of Abelson's work was directed to developing the means through which those ends could be accomplished. Certainly, Dr. Abelson will best be remembered for supporting the organized efforts of the "legitimate" factions within each trade to establish a foundation of law and order in industry. So great was his passion to relieve the human ills of industrial society that he seldom looked beyond the immediate need for instrumentalities and procedures — doctors and hospitals, as it were — to attend the victims of injustice and discontent. Concentrating on preventive measures, he worked to develop collective bargaining into a permanent institution which would strike at the sources of the disease. In so doing, he reversed the means-to-ends direction of the protocols by using the movement to gain the cooperation of workers and employers for a system of industrial self-government that would insure justice and peace. Happily, the ends of stability and security that the sponsors of the protocol movement most sought could not have been achieved on any less worthy a foundation.

The system of collective bargaining that Dr. Abelson helped to establish was, like political systems of government, founded on high principles and broad purposes. "I regard the methods and systems of industrial arbitration in the evolution of which in the needle trades I have played no small part," Dr. Abelson once stated, "as the civilized method of meeting the serious problem of preserving our democratic civilization in which logic, reason, decency, and humanity are supposed to play at least a predominant part as against force and brutality by whatever party used or exercised." The structure of collective bargaining, like its functions, also bore some resemblance to certain features of civil government but lacked a fixed distribution of powers or precise methods of procedure. Invariably, the heart of the bargaining system under Abelson-sponsored agreements was the conference committee whose members were equally divided between representatives of the employers' association and representatives of the labor union that were parties to the contract. From his personal experiences over more than twenty-five years, Dr. Abelson once described the conference committee of the fur trade as "a parliament of the manufacturing industry in which labor and employers meet on equal terms to solve their problems, specific and general, with the aid of an impartial chairman" — a definition that left few functions beyond its sphere of control.[12]

This "parliament" of the fur trade possessed certain attributes common to most other collective agreements of Abelson's sponsorship, whether in the needle trades or otherwise. It was, as its name implied, a legislative body for the lawmaking functions assigned to it by the collective agreement. During the 1926 fur industry contract negotiations, marked by a six-month strike, one of the issues in dispute was the question of how many foremen a fur manufacturer should be allowed: whether one for each separate activity of nailing, operating, cutting, and finishing would be adequate, or too many, or too few. Though the new agreement permitted a separate foreman for each function, future problems were resolved by specifying in the agreement that the conference committee shall have the authority to legislate on the subject as the needs of the situation may demand. This "parliament" also

---

[12]The definition is from Abelson, *Decisions* on issues pending before the conference committee of the fur trade (Jan. 14, 1939).

exercised the hybrid function, common to most conference committees of needle trade agreements, of handling "specific" problems arising from individual disputes falling within the compass of the contract's grievance machinery.

A particularly Abelsonian characteristic of this "parliament of the manufacturing industry" was its function as a safety valve against bulging pressures of discontent for which no other outlets were provided during the life of collective agreements. By meeting at any time on request of either party for any purpose that was a matter of mutual concern — or on the initiative of the impartial chairman — the conference committee provided an unlimited opportunity for free discussion, not unlike that once offered the participating members of the General Assembly of the League of Nations or, more recently, the United Nations. Sometimes these safety-valve conferences led to reviewing past actions, modifying general policies, authorizing further studies, overriding administrative decisions, or even turning the "parliament" into a constitutional convention for exercising whatever powers were conferred upon it to amend the collective agreement itself. Where these sessions did no more than air the grievances of the discontented or expose the fallacies of their positions, as was often the case, this outlet to suppressed emotions at least helped to delay potential explosions that might otherwise have wrecked the orderly processes of collective bargaining before the contract expired.[13]

---

[13]When Dr. Paul Abelson in 1936 succeeded the deceased Dr. Henry Moskowitz, as impartial chairman of the children's dress industry for the remaining life of the contract, Dr. Abelson wrote the United Infants' and Children's Wear Association as follows:

> Regrettably, I find that at the very outset of my service a situation that has developed arising out of the dispute in connection with the firm of G. H. & D. Frayberg, a member of your association, which whatever the outcome threatens the peace of the industry. As the peace officer of the industry I feel it is my duty to suggest that before issues are joined that a conference be held between the proper persons of the association and the union with me so that the problem can be canvassed in a spirit looking towards a reasonable solution and the maintenance of peace. Your collective agreement does not provide for a system of conferences. I hold, however, that the right and duty to confer on matters of common interest is of the essence of the relationship under a collective agreement.

After a long history in the fur trade of unrestricted conferences on matters of mutual concern, the fur workers' union in 1939 failed to respond to a

This safety-valve function of conference committees became a part of the mechanism to achieve a workable compromise between the forces of stability and the forces of flexibility within a collective bargaining system. Dr. Abelson was a staunch supporter of contracts of limited duration but, within the life of the agreement itself, he insisted upon the finality of all determinations, subject only to unpredictable emergencies. It was utterly foolish, so he contended, to hold, as some did, that the entire contract should be subject to revision or termination during a reopening of the contract normally confined to wage revisions based on unforeseen changes of circumstances. It was equally foolish, he argued, to contend, as some did, that a violation, however flagrant, of a single contract clause, however important, would justify the claim that the entire agreement had been terminated or that it was subject to termination by the aggrieved party. Security of tenure for personnel assigned to the agencies of contract administration was also essential to the finality of determinations. Subjecting the clerks at the lowest level of the impartial machinery to recall during the life of an agreement, Abelson contended, would be intolerable, since they could be ejected for enforcing the agreement. Permitting the permanent umpire to be fired during the life of an agreement would be equally absurd, since the practice would destroy all sense of finality in the institution he represented.

Abelson extended the finality-of-determinations doctrine – a vital stabilizing influence covering the life of collective agreements – to all supplemental agreements, understandings, or decisions reached by mutual consent of the contracting parties. Of no less importance was respect for the finality of arbitration awards. The worker will never be convinced that arbitration and reason can replace strife, Abelson observed in 1917 during a millinery industry dispute over piece rates, if the machinery of settlement is discredited by the refusal of either party to obey the decisions of the impartial chairman. By holding that his own arbitration

---

request of the organized manufacturers for a conference to "explore the possibilities" of relief from a contract clause forbidding more than one partner in a firm to work. Astounded at this turn of events, Dr. Abelson, impartial chairman, announced that for the first time in twenty-seven years a party to the fur industry agreements had refused a request to meet, whatever the purpose of meeting.

awards were necessarily binding only for the life of the collective agreement, with no compulsory validity or precedent-setting value thereafter, Abelson may have been compromising the future for greater assurance of immediate stability. From experience he had learned that his decisions were more likely to be accepted if they were inviolable only for the life of the agreement.

On many occasions, Abelson managed to work himself out of unwanted predicaments of having to resolve critical issues, like the recurring problem of setting piece rates, by imposing upon the parties a decision that, under the worst of circumstances, he thought they should be willing to accept for the remaining months of a two- or three-year contract, especially if the most likely alternative were a threat of revolt that might wreck the collective bargaining system. Abelson's decisions, therefore, like the collective agreement itself, did no more than offer the parties an enforced period of experimentation, after which every particular detail of past agreements, past practices, or past decisions would be subject to reversal at the next negotiating conference. Dr. Abelson was always careful to point out that his own authority as impartial chairman ended abruptly with the expiration of the collective agreement, unless, of course, the contract had previously been renewed or revised.[14]

In so far as the "parliament" of the fur trade participated in amending, revising, renewing, or renegotiating collective agreements, it pointed up another attribute of collective bargaining that Dr. Abelson, like other leaders of the protocol movement, often

---

[14]When the parties to the 1938 collective agreement between the Association of Juvenile Apparel Manufacturers and Local 91, ILGWU, working with their impartial chairman, Dr. Abelson, failed to agree on how to implement a vacation plan their agreement had authorized, Abelson wrote a series of decisions temporarily settling the issues. "Since the parties are required to confer within 60 days prior to the end of the agreement," he stated, "they will be free to negotiate an agreement on this matter instead of relying on the plan of operation devised by the arbitrator for this experimental period ending December 31, 1939 [the expiration date of the contract]." In the renewal terms of the 1940 agreement, the clauses in the old contract giving Abelson authority to work out vacation provisions were eliminated, and substituted for them in the new agreement was a provision that the decisions of Dr. Abelson of June 6, July 7, and Oct. 15, 1938, and of June 28, 1939, with respect to a week's vacation with pay "be made a part of this agreement as if it [*sic*] were incorporated herein."

recognized and fully accepted. Under collective agreements of the needle trades, conference committees were in theory creatures of the powers that created them. "Sovereignty," or supreme authority in the protocol system of bargaining, resided not in the conference committee nor in the mass of the workers and the mass of the employers *bound by* the agreements but in the labor unions and in the employers' associations that were *parties to* the agreements. The practical effect of this concept was to attune the procedures as well as the ends of collective bargaining to meet the demands of the organized factions within each trade. The case of Fuchs Brothers, fur manufacturers, under the 1926 fur industry agreement between the Associated Fur Manufacturers and the International Fur Workers' Union, exemplified the principle. Here, ten or twelve workers of the firm had voluntarily accepted wage reductions in return for protection against layoffs during the dull season. The union's charge that wage reductions violated the collective agreement was refuted by the employers' contention that the reduced wages were still above the minimum base pay stipulated in the contract wage scales for the jobs involved. Dr. Abelson's decision as impartial chairman was clearly geared to supporting the goals of the organized factions that were parties to the collective agreement:

It is a truism that one of the objects of a collective agreement between a Union and Association is to stabilize labor conditions and not to make them more chaotic than they are in the absence of a collective agreement. . . . The desire to reduce wages when the dull season sets in is for the purpose of enabling the firm to underbid other manufacturers in the sale of merchandise and the desire of the particular worker is to underbid other workers whom the firm would feel under obligation to retain in its employment during the period of division of work. Both of these motives are, from the point of view of the individual worker and the employer, contrary to the general interests of the industry, of the Association, and of the Union. And it goes without saying, that in a conflict between the needs of the organization and the desires of the individual members or workers, the rights of the bodies are superior to the rights of the individuals and must prevail.[15]

---

[15]Abelson, *Decisions,* Fuchs Bros. case (Nov. 30, 1926). Text also printed in *Women's Wear,* Dec. 1, 1926.

Abelson's faith in collective action through the organized forces of industry found expression in his determination to support the types of organizations that would possess the strength and courage, as well as the ethical fortitude, to play a constructive role in promoting the growth of industrial self-government. Among numerous small-time but highly competitive enterprises typical of the needle trades, Abelson saw no hope for separate shop unions bargaining independently with each and every shop owner at the shop level. In one of his rare references to communism in the needle trades, he attacked the procedure of letting each shop decide every type of issue before it, "as the Commies suggest," because such a practice would be contrary to the very idea of collective agreements. Like other leaders in the protocol movement, he believed that the presence of two thousand unions would in no way help to develop a strong labor organization. The more nearly a single labor union controlled the entire labor force of an industry, the more weight it could exert in negotiating, administering, and enforcing labor agreements.[16]

Dr. Abelson was equally convinced of the need for strong and responsible employer organizations devoted to the ends of the protocol movement. He found that rival employer groups operating in the same trade area were as disconcerting as rival unions. While serving in the mid-thirties as impartial chairman under two separate collective agreements between two different employers' associations and two separate groups of the millinery workers' union covering the same field of the millinery industry, Dr. Abelson, when presented with certain technological issues arising, as they frequently did, over intercontract disputes, was provoked to remark: "It is self-evident that industrial relations cannot function properly without a strong association and a strong union working together; two rival unions and two rival associations destroy the smooth working of the machinery." In this case he resolved the conflict by assigning to one association and its organized labor force exclusive control over hat shops manufacturing hats to sell at or above a certain price, while reserving to the other

---

[16]See Abelson's testimony before the U.S. Commission on Industrial Relations, Jan. 16, 1914, in the Commission's *Final Report and Testimony* (1916), vol. 2, p. 1073–1079.

association and its organized labor force exclusive control over shops manufacturing hats to sell below that price range.[17]

In at least one industry, Dr. Abelson helped the participating manufacturers and workers to establish precisely the types of organizations that came nearest to meeting the qualifications of those who sought through industry-wide bargaining to eliminate variations in labor costs from among the competitive factors of production. In the summer of 1929, Dr. Abelson was invited to become impartial chairman of the full fashioned hosiery industry with headquarters in Philadelphia. At his first interview, he asked to see the labor agreement then in effect, whereupon the hosiery workers' union pointed with pride to the fact that the union had already established uniform standards through identical contracts signed individually by most employers of the industry. But Abelson was not impressed by these inadequate steps to progress. Propounding the doctrine that collective bargaining must be collective on both sides, Abelson insisted that identical contracts could not operate successfully unless all the employers signing the agreements constituted themselves into an association for the purpose of representing their interest as a whole in hearings before him, and unless that association became nationwide in scope to balance the national organization which represented the interests of the worker group. Before he resigned his position two years later, Dr. Abelson had firmly established the principle of national agreements of industry-wide coverage between a national organization of employers (Full Fashioned Hosiery Manufacturers of America, Inc.) and a national organization of workers (American Federation of Hosiery Workers).[18]

Abelson on Negotiation, Mediation, and Arbitration

When Dr. Abelson glorified the conference committee of the fur trade as a "parliament of the manufacturing industry" empowered to solve general and specific problems *with the aid of an impartial chairman,* he added a feature highly uncommon to the usual work of labor arbitrators. Yet this unusual feature was a characteristic manifestation of Dr. Abelson's broad range of legislative activities that included a variety of lawmaking functions

---

[17]See below pp. 532–542.
[18]Abelson, *Decisions,* hosiery industry, Series D, no. 1 (1931).

far beyond the commonly accepted role of an impartial chairman. In fact, it is not unlikely that Paul Abelson, more than anyone else, created the office of impartial chairman and made it into a profession quite different from that of a labor arbitrator. From the inception of his work under the original Protocol of Peace, he had introduced collective bargaining to the people of many trades amid such complete indifference, sheer ignorance, and utter misunderstanding of its purposes, methods, and virtues that he was, perforce, compelled to assume responsibility for educating the parties, framing the issues, directing the negotiations, reconciling the differences, and drafting any contract provisions that reflected a meeting of the minds. For the contracting parties, the resulting agreement invariably ushered in a new era of progress toward industrial self-government, à la Abelson.

Undoubtedly, Dr. Abelson's initial success in assuming control over negotiations prior to the first agreement often won for him the respect and confidence that led to his designation as the first impartial chairman for the industry. Having set this initial precedent, he could logically be expected to attend future negotiating conferences called before the expiration of the old agreement to consider the possibilities of termination, renewal, or revision. Lest the exercise of this indispensable function be unduly delayed or overlooked entirely, Abelson, in the early years, assumed responsibility for notifying the parties of the need for action, and often suggested a place and time for meeting. For similar reasons of foresight and experience, he often became moderator of the negotiating conferences where his dignity and the respect for his work helped to maintain order. Although the parties themselves, with each experience in renegotiating their agreements under Abelson's direction, became more capable of hammering out their own contract terms, there were usually some issues on which differences of opinion were so tenacious that the resolution of these differences was conveniently left to the impartial chairman for action after the new agreement became effective.

Once named the first impartial chairman of an industry under its first collective agreement, Paul Abelson became the best informed man, if not the only one, with experience in setting up a framework of government or in laying down rules of conduct for supplementing, interpreting, and applying the terms of the contract. Of necessity, he outlined the structure of the impartial machinery and devised the steps in grievance procedure. He instructed the agencies of contract administration on their duties and apprised the parties to the collective agreement of their obligations for contract enforcement. He became a key member of the conference committee in the exercise of its policy-making determinations and guided the committee in the use of its delegated or implied powers to amend, or to assist in amending, the fundamental law of the agreement itself. Such were the lessons of Abelson's experience that gave the impartial chairman credit for becoming the hub of the collective bargaining process.

But neither Abelson nor the parties for whom he worked would rest his case for participation in the lawmaking function on historical grounds alone. Time and again, either Abelson himself, or those who benefitted from his participation, defended his presence at lawmaking conferences of whatever character by pointing to the potential advantages of his guidance. "What did Abelson contribute?" was an oft-repeated question that brought forth a variety of favorable and sometimes convincing replies. "The virtue of inexhaustible patience; he never stopped anyone who had something to say" was a typical response. Throughout his career, Abelson met all deadlocks between the parties or between their respective members over the terms of new contracts or over policy-determining issues arising under existing agreements with a singularly stubborn one-track mind: bargain and bargain and bargain and bargain. He attributed failure of the protocols to the fact that they were handed down from above. Critical issues like use of the discharge power or the meaning of "union preference" in employment could never be settled by decree, he said; they must be fought out between the parties themselves. Once, during an extended strike in 1936 over new contract terms in the fur trade, Dr. Abelson, the impartial chairman, so exhausted the parties with fruitless bargaining sessions that he declared an intermission that was unexpectedly extended for six months. But when he finally recalled the parties to the bargaining table, they continued where they had left off, with more bargaining until, with Abelson's help, the parties worked out a solution to all their problems.

Abelson defended his own participation in the negotiation of collective agreements and in other policy-making conferences both for the substantive contributions he could make beyond the role of moderator and for the inside knowledge on the intent of the parties he could acquire for future use. The latter was particularly helpful in applying contract clauses on general statements of policy often drawn in vague terms that called for frequent interpretations. With rare exception, no one at policy-determining conferences of whatever nature could speak with authority to match that of Dr. Abelson, nor could anyone else match his remarkable memory for recalling detailed facts and pertinent incidents from the past.

On the one hand, Dr. Abelson's knowledge extended beyond the horizons of the particular agreement into the broader fields of industry standards and trade practices. By his own announced standard, an impartial chairman, partly through reading trade papers, must know more of the industry than the parties know. On the other hand, his insights into the shortcomings of existing contracts and into troubles with administrative policies enacted thereunder sprang from his broad personal experiences with the grievance machinery, from the office of impartial chairman down to and including the work of the clerks at the shop level. Altogether, so he told a Milwaukee audience, "the impartial chairman must not only be a friend and student of the industry, capable and willing to act as consultant to either side, but he also becomes the interpreter who interprets the needs and problems of one side to the other." Obviously, this function was most effectively exercised through his presence at negotiating conferences for a new agreement. In so far as he helped the parties to avoid that dreaded no man's land of "no contract, no work," his constructive participation in negotiating sessions contributed to industrial peace.

Along with his varied negotiating functions, Abelson worked in the realms of mediation and arbitration. In his own lexicon, definitions of *mediation* and *arbitration* could scarcely have embraced more than the concept of adjuncts to the legislative process. Agreement, he contended, is always better than a decision — even an agreement with which the arbitrator does not agree. "A hearing before an arbitrator," he once explained, "is a joint investigation in his presence." Arbitration itself he once defined as "mediation with the power to decide." His own compilation of awards attests to his dislike for arbitration. With rare exceptions, particularly a few processed decisions in the full fashioned hosiery industry,

Abelson's awards were never reproduced, nor were they ever numbered or systematically filed by industry and date. For a half-century-long operator in the field of industrial relations — especially one who, with a sense of history, collected materials of all kinds, ranging from scrap worksheets and Yiddish newspaper clippings to collective agreements — Abelson produced astonishingly few written decisions. A union leader stated the case tersely: "He'd sooner lose his right arm than write a decision."[19]

In his position as impartial chairman of an industry, Dr. Abelson never attempted to differentiate the functions of negotiation, mediation, and arbitration as a means of categorizing the work that fell within the broad range of his activities. Whenever he participated in contract negotiating conferences or in the work of other policy-determining bodies, sometimes even serving on their special committees to study particular problems, he knew that any changes in contract provisions, or in supplemental regulations to implement those changes, could as well have been influenced either by reactions to the administrative methods he employed or by the formal and informal decisions that he rendered. Certainly the practice of suggesting that his awards were in the nature of temporary experiments subject to revision at the next policy-determining sessions to renew the contract could have stimulated legislation as readily as did his presence at the conferences.[20]

[19]Dr. Abelson was responsible for introducing the term, *board of adjustment,* for the usual term, *board of arbitration,* to constitute the highest authority of the impartial machinery in some of the headwear trades. The board of adjustment consisted of two representatives from each of the contracting parties with a fifth (Dr. Abelson) to be added in case of a deadlock. Since he insisted on being present while the bipartisan board was in session (to prevent rehearings before him in case of deadlocks), he undoubtedly supported this expedient further to strengthen the likelihood that, with his help, the two parties would arrive at an agreement. The same thinking undoubtedly applied to the term, *board of arbitration and conciliation,* used to identify the highest level of grievance machinery in several of the Abelson-sponsored collective agreements. Here, conciliation gains a toe hold on the top round of the ladder, a position that Abelson would surely endorse and support in practice, whatever the title of the board.

[20]Like other arbitrators who had taken liberties with amending or modifying collective agreements in the early years of the protocol movement, Dr. Abelson became more conservative after the twenties. In a decision, dated July 7, 1939, as impartial chairman of the belt industry he wrote: "The authority of the Impartial Chairman, as described in Article '30' cannot be interpreted to

Though he collected tangible evidences of the past, Abelson preferred to be an architect of the future. He wanted to work in a field more in need of creative reforms than of arbitration awards, which, like judicial decisions, were generally based on past practice and existing laws. That is why Abelson sought out the potentially creative facets of his profession, from harmony in the workshop to industry-wide controls, from the lawmaking process to the machinery for contract enforcement. With so many fingers in the pie of industrial relations, Abelson was not surprised to be charged with "hogging the show" to the long-time detriment of those he served. Among the over-all criticisms directed to his work — and there were very few — this was the most unjustifiable. Abelson was a teacher, not a dictator. And the virtue of humility that helped to make him a great teacher also contributed to his success as an impartial chairman. He acted only where necessity or expediency dictated; otherwise he was primarily a coach, counselor, and friend. "There were lots of times," so he told his Cornell audience, "when I have had to fight with both sides not to [make me] decide." He abhorred the rising practice among the post-World War II arbitrators of charging excessive fees for their services, and he attended the first meeting of the National Academy of Arbitrators to work for limiting those fees.[21]

As he grew older, so members of the impartial machinery for the bakery industry explained, Abelson would hurry to a 2 o'clock session of the conference committee (board of adjustment, board of grievances), half an hour late, take a seat at the head of the table, remove from his brief case a papier-mâché sandwich and chew on it vigorously while apologizing for arriving late without lunch. Then he would carefully restore the sandwich to its niche in his brief case, and soon thereafter fall asleep, while the parties

mean that he has authority to modify the agreement on the facts before him. Only in the case of a supplementary agreement, duly signed and executed with the same formality as the main agreement can a collateral understanding specifically contrary to the terms of the main agreement be recognized by the Impartial Chairman and authorize him to modify the terms of the contract."

[21]At a joint conference of the women's coat and suit trade on Feb. 28, 1917, J. H. Cohen, counsel for the manufacturers' association, remarked that if Abelson showed strength in meeting a critical dispute, "it was because he has sweat blood in the situation, and studied it, and has not written philippics from the throne."

across the table from each other attended to matters of business. "But don't try to put anything over on him," one official warned, "the old fox knows what is going on." Nevertheless, when he died leaving a number of industries, including the bakers, stranded for lack of direction — as he had previously done by retiring from similar positions in other trades — the quality of his instruction soon became apparent: they mourned his loss but followed his teaching.

Abelson on Peace in the Workshop

Paul Abelson played yet another role that was unique among the sponsors of the protocol movement. He worked toward the same goals as did the organized forces of industry operating under the banner of competition and collective bargaining, but he moved in the opposite direction. While many leaders of employers' associations and labor unions, often with the support of private counselors and public officials, kept their eyes upon the soaring eagles of economic security and industry stabilization, Abelson's eye was on the sparrow of the workshop where opposing forces of war and peace, reason and prejudice, justice and injustice, authority and revolt were continually struggling for supremacy. Some thought it undignified that an impartial chairman should go into the workshops; others would relegate the settlement of petty shop grievances to the less competent, while major issues of industry-wide concern drew the talents of the best brains in the trade. Yet, even among the most ardent devotees of industrial self-government, no other man ever spent so much of his life so near the center of his prime concern. Not until half a century later had students of industrial relations, if not advocates of the protocol movement, come to acknowledge the full impact of peace in the workshop upon the ultimate success of major collective bargaining systems.

Operating on the principle that a fireman should follow the smoke, and that no amount of water will suffice if the cause of the blaze remains undetermined, Abelson went about the business of resolving local disputes as if peace in the workshop were the sine-qua-non of successful bargaining on a market-wide or industry-wide scale. Abelson was a good fireman who never hesitated to abandon a burning building if necessary to confine the flame or prevent a later outbreak. He was less concerned with the spark that lit the blaze than with the background conditions which contributed to the origin, spread, and intensity of the conflagration. As fire chief of the workshop, Abelson's first objective, therefore, was to look behind the immediate causes of industrial strife to the underlying sources of the trouble. On many occasions, he found that "human frailties" figured more prominently than "economic necessities" in the fundamental causes of industrial conflict.[22]

Early in the life of the dress protocol, Abelson received a typical grievance case that grew out of a work stoppage called against a dress manufacturer for alleged contract violations arising from the employer's use of the discharge power and his interpretation of clauses limiting outside production. Setting aside the technical issues of immediate concern, Abelson plunged into a search for the underlying facts bearing on the case. "The main source of trouble," he concluded, as he did on many other occasions, "is the temperament of the factory manager and the shop chairman." For that type of dispute, the pertinent clause of the collective agreement was one stating that "the firm shall not use abusive or vile language on the workers." In another decision, dated July 31, 1914, involving a series of strike-lockouts generated by several months of continual discord and ill will between the firm and the workers, Dr. Abelson wrote:

While the difficulties apparently are due to disputes in price [piece rate] making, the lamentable state of affairs is no less due to the utter inability of the people and the employer to realize the respective rights of the parties. Under these circumstances it would be futile to render a decision on one or two specific issues presented to the arbitrator. In a situation where minor mistakes lead to the inevitable climax [of strikes and lockouts], no group of facts can be singled out as the cause of the trouble, and no single finding can save the situation. The arbitrator

---

[22]"You have to get down to the proposition as a human problem. Very often it is a question of relations, and ignorance and spite and suspicion and all those human frailties which people of a certain type of mind and certain training and certain environment and certain industries, say the tailoring industry, and things of that kind have. You have to approach the situation from the realities of the situation." Abelson testimony before the U.S. Commission on Industrial Relations, Jan. 16, 1914, on the duties of the clerks, in the Commission's *Final Report and Testimony*, (1916) vol. 2, p. 1076.

therefore approaches the problem before him from the point of view of a constructive solution looking to the future, instead of passing judgment on acts in the past.[23]

As a second objective, Paul Abelson, fire chief of the workshop, undertook to choose the most appropriate types of equipment for extinguishing all types of fires. First to be rejected as ill-adapted to the "realities of the situation" were the normal facilities and processes of the civil and criminal courts. Although Abelson studied law to qualify for handling certain legal technicalities of his trade, no evidence has come to light that he ever once referred to his status as a member of the bar; the "affiants" and the "appellants" he buried with his legal diploma. Courts and lawyers, he once remarked, ruin collective bargaining by legal interpretations of contract provisions they know nothing about. More than his dislike for legal terminology or for labor lawyers ignorant of industrial relations was his conviction that the legal approach to resolving conflicts in the workshop was inherently wrong. Whenever Abelson turned to his own "judicial system speaking through the impartial chairmanship," so he explained, "the approach was not legalistic, not in the nature of a contest to result in a victory to the one or a defeat to the other but rather in the nature of a problem requiring solution by analysis of all the facts, only then was a solution found through the amalgam of reason and fair dealing to management and worker alike."[24]

If the legal approach to industrial conflicts was inadequate, the consequences of that approach could be devastating. After a typical court case, in which justice is rendered, so Abelson explained many times over, the parties go their separate ways, perhaps forever, while the opposing lawyers go out and have lunch together; but after a similar case involving a dispute between the workers and their boss, "the parties go next day to the shop and make clothes." Abelson compared this distinction to one between a special domestic relations court, which undertakes to save the institution of marriage, and the adjudication of disputes between husband and wife in the usual courts where the law is satisfied but the winner thumbs his (or her) nose at the loser, while the fight

---

[23]Abelson's *Decisions*, case of Kraus v. Petofsky (July 31, 1914).

[24]From Abelson's article prepared in 1948 for a book to commemorate thirty years of collective bargaining in the ladies' handbag industry.

between them, now intensified, begins all over again. "The impartial chairman," Abelson reminded his Milwaukee audience, in a lecture on April 14, 1930, "must so settle differences that the parties can live and work together. There can be no divorce in industry between employers and employees."

In his search for machinery and processes to quench the fires of industrial conflict, Abelson preferred to find help within each industry where those who contributed their services would at least have a personal interest at stake. Should the additional help of external forces become necessary they, too, should preferably come from the local community and be familiar with local problems. Abelson pointed out that Kehillah's bureau of industry through its familiarity with the parties and with the products had long provided a superior alternative to the work of the state mediation board. Above all else, Abelson liked the prospects of voluntary fire brigades, especially since the parties were already organized into employers' associations and labor unions that met the basic tenets of his requirements for peace. For Abelson had concluded from his years of experience that what an industry most needed at times of crisis in the workshop was someone "above the situation" who had the confidence of the parties and could act from a detached viewpoint without delay and, if necessary, with authority.

The structure of Abelson's fire-fighting force for peace was, therefore, founded on the potentialities of control through labor unions and employers' associations, both of which were represented in the workshop. Only with reluctance did Abelson consent to build from representatives of both parties a jointly sponsored superstructure of "impartial machinery" that would operate more or less independently of either organization but would, nevertheless, be heavily dependent upon both organizations for support. For without labor unions and employers' associations there was no possibility, short of help from the state, that the policies and decisions of the impartial machinery could ever be enforced. So, when it came to compelling noncomplying workers or noncomplying employers to observe the standards of conduct set forth in collective agreements or in decisions of the impartial machinery, Abelson himself, sitting at the apex, preferred to call directly for help from one or both organizations representing, separately, the organized workers and the organized employers of the industry.

A *labor union*, Dr. Abelson once explained, is a policeman for controlling the worker who rebels against the government of the industry. For the purpose he had in mind, Dr. Abelson might, with equal validity, have added another term to his glossary (Abelson was editor-in-chief of an encyclopedic English-Yiddish dictionary): an *employers' association* is a policeman for controlling the employer who rebels against the government of the industry. To the functions of detection, apprehension, and detention, Dr. Abelson might also have accredited each organization with the additional roles of prosecutor, judge, jury, and executioner. Sometimes the proceedings before either organization were summary, the verdict arbitrary. In one case, when a shop owner was informed that, to prevent further reductions in pay, all existing payrolls had by mutual consent of the contracting parties become a part of the collective agreement, he immediately tore up his payroll. Without further ado, Impartial Chairman Abelson asked his employers' association to expel him, which it summarily did, leaving him at the mercy of direct action by the union. Usually, however, the impartial machinery identified the offenses, and after trying the suspects, turned those adjudged guilty over to their respective organizations for the imposition of appropriate penalties. In one of his own early decisions involving the Finkelstein Shirt Company, Dr. Abelson wrote:

> Mr. Finkelstein's conduct and manner is such as to provoke the men in the shop by his overpowering conduct and abuse. In order that in the future such unseemly clashes as have occurred between him and the shop chairman shall not again occur, the arbitrator directs that the Association be hereafter directly charged with the responsibility for Finkelstein's conduct in reference to abusing the people in the shop. As to what method the Association shall adopt to carry [out] the responsibility imposed by the arbitrator, the arbitrator leaves to the discretion of the Executive Board of the Association; whether it be by fine to be imposed, or by a warning threatening to withdraw the protection of the Association against a stoppage of work in case of unprovoked abuses and insults to the workers, or whether it be by any other effective measure.[25]

From the positions he held in many trades, Abelson gained wide experience with different types of administrative agencies falling

---

[25]Abelson's *Decisions*, case of Finkelstein Shirt Co. (June 7, 1915).

within the over-all structure of the impartial machinery. In the early years of the protocol movement, for example, a much debated issue was directed to the question of whether the committee on immediate action (or the clerks), representing equally the employers' association and the labor union and constituting the first round in the ladder of grievance procedure, with original powers of investigation and decision, should remain bipartisan or whether a third party should be added to insure a decision on every issue. At one time or another, Abelson served in the capacity of an association representative (clerk) on a bipartisan committee and also in the capacity of third party for a different committee on immediate action. He knew the practical advantages of immediate decisions (deadlocks on bipartisan committees had overloaded the upper rounds in the ladder of grievance procedure), but on principle he opposed any institution that turned the search for mutual agreement between the parties by processes of investigation, negotiation, and reconciliation into a court on which a third party would hold a balance of power.

Abelson had similar experiences at the top round in the ladder of grievance machinery. In some industries, he was a member of a board of arbitration, always its chairman and its only third party member (other members were equally divided between representatives of the employers' association and representatives of the labor union). He often acted alone on behalf of the board and invariably wrote its decisions; nevertheless, his role was that of one among the many. In other trades, he occupied the office of impartial chairman, the highest position within the impartial machinery, and, like the board of arbitration, a tribunal of last resort in rendering decisions within the competence of the office. Where other means existed to gather the views of the opposing parties, as was usually the case with Abelson through his contacts with the conference committee or other boards of adjustment, the distinction between a board of arbitration and the office of impartial chairman was of little practical importance. Perhaps he saw reasons to recommend one type of agency over the other in particular circumstances, but it appears likely that his own personal reactions to the alternatives never got beyond following the preferences of the parties themselves.[26]

---

[26]In still another capacity, Paul Abelson, throughout his professional career, served with great distinction as secretary to numerous boards and commissions.

Directing the employers' association in the Finkelstein case to punish any *future* improprieties of the shop owner toward his workers suggested a third means through which Paul Abelson hoped to establish peace in the workshop. In addition to exposing the fundamental causes of industrial conflict, and in addition to providing the means for punishing those who engage in such conflicts, Paul Abelson, fire chief of the workshop, proposed to sponsor a "fire-prevention" service to forestall the development of conditions leading to industrial conflagrations. Responsibility for directing a program that would thwart shop strikes and lockouts could logically have been expected to fall upon employers' associations and labor unions, which, as guardians for their respective members, might well have found an ounce of prevention to be worth a pound of cure. Yet it was Paul Abelson who exercised the most ingenuity on behalf of strike-lockout prevention by diverting his judicial function of resolving disputes from the usual pattern of meting out justice to the new concept of sacrificing immediate issues to a future program of prevention — a concept that might lead to offering an ounce of cure for the immediate victims of injustice while dispensing a pound of prevention against future strife in the workshop.

Beyond the early years of the protocol movement, neither employers' associations nor the labor unions in the trades with which Paul Abelson was associated ever initiated of their own accord a general safety-first program that would help to prevent local differences in their workshops from degenerating into hotbeds of hatred and distrust capable of exploding momentarily into violent outbreaks of direct action. Only when the impartial chairman himself charged one or both of these organizations with specific duties toward their respective members in particular shops did either of these organizations appear willing to participate in strike-lockout prevention programs. In a millinery industry decision, dated November 6, 1936, Impartial Chairman Abelson denied the

---

Usually consisting of prominent citizens voluntarily rendering a temporary service, with little knowledge of the background to the issues they faced, these special agencies were fortunate to obtain a secretary of Abelson's knowledge, devotion, and experience. Those who considered Abelson an empire builder should have looked to the services he rendered and the satisfactions he derived from filling the modest position of secretary.

right of a firm to discharge an ignorant chairlady who had no idea of her duties and "does silly things." At the same time, Abelson discovered that the firm needed the help of the industry's impartial machinery to "get established as a going concern." Looking to the future, he directed that a representative of the employers' association and a representative of the union spend some time with the management and some time with the workers in an effort to "establish a common sense relationship" between the two. He further directed that a good chairlady capable of cooperating with the management be found. His additional contributions to future developments were to be inferred from his parting remark: "I will look back again soon."

Abelson often found his disputes-settlement function to be a convenient excuse for promoting his look-to-the-future prevention program. In the Kraus and Petofsky case, cited above, in which a variety of strikes and lockouts had left the shop in a "deplorable state of ill will and disorganization," Impartial Chairman Abelson, turning from the evils of past acts to the prospects of future reforms, directed a representative of the employers' association and a representative of the labor union to be present whenever the shop owners and the price committee of their workers met to determine piece rates. If necessary to prevent further strife, these two individuals, who sat above the situation, were to take over the determination of piece rates themselves. In addition, Abelson named a special committee of three, one to come from the association, one from the union, together with himself as chairman, "to look into the reestablishment of peace and order and harmonious relations" in the shop. Another case in the millinery trade featured charges and countercharges against the chairlady that produced a state of chaos and ill will. Again looking to the future, Abelson engineered a New Year's party for the firm and the workers and thereafter named a committee of two (one each from the association and the union) to study the situation in the shop and report to him. Again Abelson's parting word was a promise to "follow the doings of the shop."

Even where he failed to call for help from the employer and worker organizations, Abelson continued to apply his new prevention technique of promoting future peace in the workshop through the disposition of cases and controversies brought before him. Following this policy, he never offered an alleged victim of injustice more than an ounce of cure if his case could be used to distribute a pound of prevention against future strife in the workshop. In the holeproof hosiery industry case arising at the depth of the Great Depression, the owner of the firm desired "to inaugurate a change in working hours in the Center Street plant affecting somewhat the customary hours of work of the day shift and very substantially the hours of work of the night shift...in order to escape payment for the use of electricity during hours for which the electric company makes an extra charge." Presumably, the increased profits of the firm would redound to the benefit of the workers through the prospects of higher wages. But the workers objected. Abelson's decision was brief and to the point: the savings to the firm that could possibly be effected by the new schedule of hours could not offset "the imponderable elements of ill will that will result from the change in the fixed habits of hours of work and the home life of the workers."

Most of Abelson's decisions balancing the immediate rights of individuals against the future peace of the workshop revolved around the use of the discharge power. In a 1918 millinery industry case, for example, a worker was discharged for insulting the owner of the shop. Whatever the nature of the insult, be it questionable or aggravated, whatever the justification for the outburst, so Abelson concluded, to reinstate the worker would be detrimental to everyone connected with the shop. Wherever personal relations between an individual worker and his boss threatened to ignite an explosion at any time, the impartial chairman, stated Abelson, must look to the peace of the shop. To avoid the dilemma of supporting the individual or protecting the peace of the shop, Abelson introduced one of his original contributions to the foundations of law and order in industry. In addition to the historic alternatives of unqualified discharge or unrestricted reinstatement with back pay and no loss of status, Abelson offered two other alternative solutions: (1) the worker might be restored to his job without back pay, or (2) he might be forced to forfeit his job subject to compensating action, usually the offer of another position or separation pay in cash. In a 1936 luggage and leather goods case, for example, Abelson refused to sustain the discharge of a shop chairman but liquidated his right to the job, subject to (1) offering him minimum separation pay that was to be increased according to his difficulty in finding work elsewhere, (2) directing the association and the union to help find the ex-shop chairman another job, and (3) directing the union to replace its lost representative with a suitable substitute. Four days later, after the victim of the liquidation process had found a better job elsewhere, Dr. Abelson presented him with $100 in cash.

Such relentless devotion to the human problems of the workshop, especially to the omnipresent task of eliminating conflict and keeping the peace, endeared Paul Abelson to all those leaders of the protocol movement who operated so closely to his work that they could appreciate his contributions. Dr. Abelson in turn became devoted to his faithful followers who adhered to his principles and adopted his teachings. Looking back over thirty years of progress through collective bargaining in the ladies' handbag industry, Abelson wrote of the leaders who, with his help, had primarily been responsible for this development:

They were intelligent, devoted persons whom the necessities of the situation developed into industrial statesmen. What were these necessities? In the first place, they were all functioning in a highly competitive industry consisting of small business establishments. The higher labor standards in New York City created an ever present menace of dispersal to the Ladies Handbag Industry. Only by consistent care and cooperation on the part of labor and industry can the industry be safe to function in the City of New York. Labor and management, employer and employee, union and association thirty years ago learned that if "they didn't hang together they would hang separately...."

The executive staff of the association and the union from the very beginning of this 30 years Odyssey approached...each and every problem, whether it affected the industry, or individual firms, or individual workers in a spirit of fairness and human decency...nor were the legitimate necessities of the business ignored. Unlike other conventional arbitration proceedings, the decisions and awards of the Impartial Chairman were results in which labor and management jointly with the Impartial Chairman contributed to a clarification of the situation and its needs.[27]

Some years later, after the death of Dr. Abelson, several of these leaders were interviewed collectively for information about the

---

[27]From Abelson's article prepared in 1948 for a book to commemorate thirty years of collective bargaining in the ladies' handbag industry.

man. One of them, who surmised what was in the offing, submitted a plea that was heartily endorsed by all: "Don't call him 'labor arbitrator,'" he urged, "call him 'industrial statesman.'"

Participants in the current revolution may be hardpressed to understand why a man of Abelson's stature should deal in the "elusive psychology of the shop," while other leaders of the protocol movement kept their sights on the economic advantages of national organizations for industry-wide bargaining. Nor could those now in the forefront of revolt against authority see the need for glorifying the intangible mores of ethical conduct, or the elemental standards of human decency, or the common-sense rules of reason and fair play, so long as the simple but effective weapon of revolt invariably brings home the bacon. Long ago, members of labor unions discovered that officers of the law could not handle mass picketing that blocked the highways, destroyed property, deprived individuals of their personal rights, and at times superseded local governments. To be sure, union members were not the only faction of society advocating the use of force and violence, as the La Follette committee report on free speech and the rights of labor in the thirties will attest, but they were the most numerous. They knew that politicians would not shut their eyes to the number of votes involved, nor could a jury system handle so many cases, nor the jails hold all the culprits.

With what disdain would the current advocates of direct action harp on the naiveté of the official trappings used in the summer of 1912 in attempting to obstruct a wildcat strike in the shop of a member of the Cloak, Suit and Skirt Manufacturers' Protective Association, party to the original Protocol of Peace! "The circumstances of this stoppage of work and the evidence which we have at hand," wrote Eugene Lezinsky, general manager of the employers' association, to the Cloakmakers' Joint Board, ILGWU, in a letter dated June 19, 1912,

are such that, much to our regret, we are compelled to charge either a deliberate breach of faith on the part of some representative of the Union or a lawless attempt on the part of the people in the inside and the outside shop to take matters into their own hands, in order, in some way, to force an adjustment of the dispute in factory No. 2.

At 8:30 this morning we received a letter by messenger from the firm that, at a meeting last night, the people were instructed to quit work at 9 o'clock this morning. I then and there notified your office and spoke to Mr. Kaplowitz. I stated to him the information which reached us from the firm and warned him that, unless he prevented a stoppage of work at 9 o'clock, a case of deliberate and premeditated violation of the protocol in ordering a strike in a factory would be made out against the Union. Nothing was done by the Union, and the stoppage did occur at 9 o'clock.

From the beginnings of his career in industry (he was labor manager of the employers' association at the time of the Lezinsky letter), Abelson faced the dangers of a house built on the sand. He knew that his realm of law and order could not withstand the floods of revolution fed by wildcat strikes and illegal lockouts in the workshops. Like the floods from summer rains, the effects of local contributions to revolt were cumulative. If building dikes of human understanding and good will was unrealistic, experience had at least demonstrated that there were no short cuts to protection from mass lawlessness. Certainly, as evidenced by the collective agreements he sponsored or worked under, Abelson denounced strikes and lockouts with a zeal that left nothing to be desired. The no-strike, no-lockout clauses of the 1914 fur industry agreement (under which Abelson won his spurs as mediator-arbitrator), the similar provisions of the 1915 millinery industry agreement (on which Abelson built his reputation as a lawmaker, having written the terms himself), and the pertinent clauses of the 1936 luggage and leather goods agreement (revealing that Abelson's intense aversion to strikes and lockouts had not changed in twenty years) are but three examples of Abelson's resolute determination to condemn direct action during the life of collective agreements in every form, shape, or fashion.

Perhaps Abelson never squarely faced the issue of whether, as a last resort to enforce the terms of a contract or the decisions of an impartial chairman, "authorized" strikes and lockouts should ever be condoned during the life of a collective agreement. To Abelson, the dangers of such a concession would have been obvious, and he undoubtedly would have preferred to cast the culprits into outer darkness before feeding them to the wolves of direct action.[28] Certainly, he did not tolerate the use of authorized

---

[28]It is agreed that during the life of the Agreement, if the firm is proven to have violated the terms of the Agreement in regard to contracting in any form, such finding shall operate as a resignation from the Association.

strikes as a first line of defense against alleged contract infractions. On one occasion, Dr. Abelson not only condemned the practice under a special labor agreement covering a single firm but he also directed these clauses permitting the union to strike against alleged infractions of the contract to be stricken from the agreement as an essential prerequisite to maintaining peace in the plant. Compelling obedience through the use of strikes, like keeping the peace through war, had long been an accepted mode of procedure under individual contracts between the union and independent firms. But, for the organized segments of industrial society, Abelson insisted upon more civilized procedures.

More than anyone else, Paul Abelson foresaw the possibility that every outbreak of revolution in the workshop under the banner of direct action might inflict a mortal blow to the cause of law and order in industry. Although his carefully nurtured plans for peace had been defeated once "war" was declared, Abelson nevertheless followed the army of revolters into the field, still seeking to induce a change of course. His last hope lay in a rule of procedure, written into some agreements of his sponsorship, that was intended to demonstrate the folly of revolting. Directed primarily to wildcat strikers, but applicable to others taking the law of the contract into their own hands, this rule forbade the impartial machinery of contract administration to process grievances leading to the revolt until the rebels had returned to their jobs.

Requiring strikers to go back to work before their grievances could be heard encountered stubborn resistance in the women's coat and suit trade in 1916, although prior to that time, even from the inception of the original Protocol of Peace, the rule had been almost universally applied throughout the needle trades. From bitter experiences, more and more employers argued that in time of emergency production to meet deadlines during the busy season, the option of surrendering immediately to the demands of the strikers to get them back to work was often the least of all evils.

The refusal to supply information called for by the Committee on Immediate Action in connection with any grievance about contracting shall operate as a finding that there has been a violation and shall operate as a resignation from the Association.
—Decision of the Conference Committee of the Fur Industry (Abelson participating) in the Oldman Bros. case (August 12, 1937).

Yet Abelson had held out tenaciously for the principle of "no work — no help," and somehow managed to enforce this rule in every industry and under every collective agreement for which he served as impartial chairman. However logical this course of action, Abelson's achievement in forcing its adoption, while other arbitrators were bowing to union pressures and employer disloyalties, must stand as the most surprising, if not the most distinctive, success of his long career. Exemplifying the operation of this rule in the fur industry, which Dr. Abelson served for twenty-five years, were the following three communications, each dated July 9, 1929:

Dr. Paul Abelson,
Chairman of the Conference Committee

Dear Sir:

We are informed by our member, H. Berger & Company that a committee of several workers in the shop appeared before Mr. Berger this noon demanding collectively a raise in wages, with the alternative that if same was not granted they will go down on strike in order to force the firm to raise their pay. The workers told Mr. Berger that these instructions were given them at a shop meeting held last night at the office of the Union.

Mr. Berger states that he explained to the committee that no collective bargaining is permitted under the Collective Agreement, but that he would take up any grievances or adjustments in pay with each individual worker according to his or her merit. Whereupon the entire shop went down, and at this writing at 2:30 P.M. have not returned to work.

This matter is now called to your attention in order that the workers be returned forthwith, as this action of the workers and the Union is contrary to the provisions of our Agreement, and at the same time we desire to have you impress on the Union that actions of this nature will not be tolerated by our Association.

Very truly yours,
Associated Fur Manufacturers, Inc.,
S. W. Eckstein, Labor Department

Mr. Charles Stetsky
Manager, Joint Council, Furriers' Union

Dear Sir:

I am in receipt of a communication from the Associated Fur Manufacturers, Inc., to the effect that the workers of H. Berger and Company have stopped work.

Whatsoever be the nature of the grievance, if any, on the part of the workers against the firm, a stoppage of work under the Collective Agreement is not and cannot be the remedy. Indeed, their grievances cannot be taken up by the Committee on Immediate Action or by the Conference Committee until after the workers have returned to work.

By the terms of the Collective Agreement, I hereby direct you to see to it that the workers return to work at once. Upon their resumption of work, I shall immediately set the machinery of the Agreement in motion, to adjust any and every dispute or difficulty or grievance.

Very truly yours,
Paul Abelson,
Chairman of the
Conference Committee

Dr. Paul Abelson, Chairman,
Conference Committee, Fur Industry

Dear Sir:

In reply to your letter of this date, I wish to state that I have instructed my secretary to send out special delivery letters to all the workers of H. Berger to report to the office tomorrow morning at 10 A.M. so that I may direct them to return to work.

In connection with this matter, however, there is something very aggravating which resulted in a stoppage of work, for which the firm of H. Berger is responsible because of the brutal and insulting attack upon two of the workers of the shop by Mr. H. Berger. From the information which was given to me by some of the workers, he called them vile names which are not fit to print, threw a telephone book at the chairman of the shop, and kicked another worker with his foot, threatening that he would kill them. Immediately upon the action taken by Mr. Berger, the workers of the shop walked out in protest.

You will realize the difficulty we will have in convincing the workers of the shop to return to work. However, I promise you that I will do everything I possibly can in order to comply with your request.

Very truly yours,

Charles Stetsky,
Manager, Joint Council
Furriers' Union

Ten years later, just before Dr. Abelson retired from the fur industry, the rule was stoutly supported by an official of the International Fur Workers' Union who applied it to mass violations of certain contract clauses by members of the Associated Fur Coat and Trimming Manufacturers. The facts of the case and the importance that the union official attached to the enforcement of the rule against hearing grievances during mass violations of the contract are revealed in the following letter addressed to Dr. Abelson, impartial chairman. Coming from a member of the Communist party, the letter is a particularly strong tribute to Abelson's success in building institutions of law and order that could withstand the onslaught of revolution and mass lawlessness.

January 11, 1939

Dr. Paul Abelson,
Impartial Chairman of
the Fur Industry

Dear Sir:

We wish to call to your attention that since January 1, 1939 two important and fundamental provisions of the collective contract in the fur industry are being violated by the Association and its members. These two provisions are that only one member of the firm is permitted to do productive work, and that firms that employed less than five workers in 1938 are no longer entitled to the protection of the collective agreement. We regret to state that these provisions are being violated by the Association and its members with your knowledge. To our sorrow you have condoned these violations which the Association has practiced under the pretext that conferences are in progress between Union and Association representatives on the matters involved.

Permit me to call to your attention that such action on your part is contrary to the letter and spirit of the collective agreement and definitely contrary to your own rulings, decisions and practices which you established in the course of many years. In this connection we wish to recall to you that on numerous occasions in the past when workers of any Association shop stopped work for one reason or another, you lost no time in addressing written or oral instructions to the Union directing the immediate return of such workers to their shops in order to comply with the provisions of the contract. It was always your firm position that the Union must first carry out the contract and then negotiate any complaints or grievances it may have. Moreover, on numerous occasions you emphasized that no conferences between the Union and the Association are possible under your chairmanship while any provision of the contract was not being fully observed. The Union never took issue with you on your rulings in such matters and because of their fundamental correctness, we readily carried them out. Such rulings were recognized by all concerned and were thus accepted as the cornerstone of the collective agreement and the collective relationship between the Union and the Association in the fur industry....

We wish to impress upon you that the provisions of the contract we are alluding to are not matters of dispute or matters that require any interpretation. These provisions are clearly specified and become an organic part of our collective contract as a result of a fifteen weeks lockout and general strike in the industry and as a result of a number of painstaking conferences lasting days, nights and weeks where the matters in question were exhaustively discussed and analyzed and finally agreed upon in good faith. Moreover these provisions of our collective contract as well as all others were approved and ratified by the membership of the Association and the Union and became public knowledge and property....

The Union has no objection whatsoever to any negotiations with the representatives of the Association for any proposals they wish to advance in the interest of the industry, as long as such negotiations are not carried on while the Association is violating fundamental provisions of the collective contract, and thus deprive the workers of their jobs and union conditions. The Union responded to your call for conferences to negotiate proposals of the Association. However, we made it clear from the very outset that while such conferences are in progress you as the Impartial Chairman should direct the Association to carry out the letter and the spirit of the collective contract. This request on our part was and is made in accordance with your rulings, decisions and practices continuously in effect for the many years that you have acted as the Impartial Chairman in the fur industry.

You surely must be aware of the danger involved in the present tactics employed by the Association and particularly in your failure to act in the matter. Such a practice might indeed encourage and enable the Association to employ the same methods whenever it sees fit to violate fundamental provisions of the contract.

In view of the above, we wish to register our protest against your present position which is unprecedented, contrary to your own rulings and practices, contrary to the letter and spirit of the collective agreement, definitely detrimental to the interests of the workers and the Union and contrary to the very conception of the collective contract and its application. . . .

We strongly urge you again to direct the employers immediately to carry out the letter and spirit of the contract. We would appreciate a copy of your written instructions to the Association to this effect.[29]

Very truly yours,
Irving Potash
Manager, Furriers' Joint Council

Concluding Observations

Like so many other leaders of the protocol movement, Paul Abelson clothed the bare framework of industrial self-government with warmth and vitality. Through the sheer force of hard work, native intelligence, and adaptability to circumstances, Abelson managed to imbue the "bosses" and the "people" of the workshop with the virtues of reason and common sense ("it doesn't seem to make good sense" was Abelson's classic comment at the bargaining table). By reason of the respect, bordering on worship, that he generated through his knowledge of the facts, his understanding of the parties, and his personal traits of character, Abelson repeatedly welded the discordant elements of industrial societies into communities of law and order. Above all, his passion for industrial peace channelled his efforts into seeking the underlying causes of industrial strife, and into taking steps to eradicate those causes. While the policies and procedures which he introduced and applied seemed well adapted to meet the problems of a simple and

---

[29]For all the respect that he commanded, Paul Abelson was never immune from adverse criticism. Particularly at critical stages of contract negotiations, or of disputes settlement, did Abelson's suggestions often fall in line of fire from both sides. But at the farewell dinner given in his honor by the fur industry, Dr. Abelson heard only words of praise from representatives of both parties. Given an opportunity to respond to these glowing eulogies, he arose meekly and came out thoughtfully with what was on his mind: "It's all kind of new to me." Then, after stating his lifetime philosophy of searching for the truth, he at least hinted that life behind the scenes had not always been a bed of roses: "I have approached the problem of human relations in a spirit of humility. That is why I have stood for so much; for a man who is sensitive to abuse becomes a tyrant." *Fur Age Weekly*, 1939, vol. 35, no. 26.

unsophisticated, although highly competitive, industrial society of small businessmen and their widely dispersed labor force, Abelson's contributions to self-government in the workshop were invaluable to the larger objectives of the protocol movement. A study of his methods may still yield handsome returns for other trailblazers facing the unanswered human problems of more complex industrial societies.

Part II

INDUSTRY STANDARDS
AND TRADE CONTROLS

We are dealing specifically with the problem of only a part of the garment trade but your problems are in large measure the problems of all industries.

— Louis D. Brandeis, chairman, board of arbitration, women's coat and suit trade, Nathan Schuss case (Jan. 21, 1915).

Chapter 12

Competition from
Independent Unionized Shops

THE protocol movement was originally sponsored by groups of organized manufacturers who preferred to make their own products in their own factories and by groups of organized workers who preferred the security of large inside establishments. Both labor unions and employers' associations wanted to avoid the small-time competition of the jobber-contracting system that undermined all hope of security for themselves or stability for their trades. But when demands for mass production of cheap goods forced the jobber-contracting system upon their industries, the sponsors of the protocol movement undertook to admit the "legitimate" jobbers and contractors into the realm of law and order. These new additions were brought under collective agreements governing the trade.

So long as collective agreements fell short of industry-wide coverage, however, not even the inclusion of the more responsible groups of organized jobbers and contractors could solve the problem of ruthless competition. For beyond the realm of law and order ruled by the legitimate elements of industrial society were substantial areas of production in which competition was still uncontrolled. The influence of these areas necessarily affected the pattern of conduct for all firms operating within the boundaries of collective agreements. Above all else, the marked differences in wage rates, hours of work, and conditions of employment, which had always been the scourge of legitimate competition for the needle trades, demanded some form of regulation that would become applicable throughout an industry. To protect their own institutions, therefore, the organized jobbers, contractors, and inside manufacturers had to team up with labor unions to devise ways and means for controlling the outer circles of each trade.[1]

Distribution of Shops by Extent of Organization

The shops and factories still operating beyond the canopy of collective agreements generally fell into one of two categories: those plants in which the workers were organized while the employers were not or those shops in which neither the workers nor the employers were organized. (In a few plants, the employers were bound by the ties of association membership, while the workers were still not organized into unions.) The world of industrial relations was thus divided into segments. Beyond the fully organized core of industrial society were the half-organized plants in which only the workers or the employers, but not both, were organized. And beyond these half-organized plants were those that were wholly unorganized: neither labor unions nor employers' associations had yet gained a foothold. (See diagram, p. 46 above.)

At the time of the Brandeis Conferences in the summer of 1910, the Cloak, Suit and Skirt Manufacturers' Protective Association, a party to the negotiations, had enlisted only 75 members, although this number was increased to 122 by the time the first Protocol of Peace was signed on September 2, 1910. By August 1913, the inside shops of association members numbered 258, while the outside shops of association members stood at 275, making a total of 533 shops operating under the protocol out of an estimated 1,885 shops in the city. Two years later, there were 450 inside producers organized into associations, while an additional 1,350 inside producers were classified as "independents." By 1926, after the organized jobbers and the organized contractors had

[1]Writing in *Women's Wear*, June 27, 1913, on "The Future of the Protocol," J. Fuchs illustrated the point by reference to standards of sanitation: "As for sanitary precautions and appliances, the signatories to the Protocol were forced, in maintenance of competition on equal terms, not only to abolish glaring abuses within their own ranks, but to insist upon the enforcement of existing laws outside of the reach of their corporate jurisdiction and to promote new legislation safeguarding the health and security of all operatives within the trade." See Fuchs' three articles in the issues of June 20, 27, July 11, 1913.

been admitted to the realm of law and order, not more than half the 400 inside manufacturers or more than half the 225 jobbers belonged to their respective associations in the women's coat and suit trade. Although numerically in the minority, association shops probably accounted for at least half the total output of the local trade.[2]

Distribution of shops by extent of organization in the dress and waist industry followed a similar pattern. In November 1913, some months after the original dress and waist protocol became effective on January 18, 1913, the local dress and waist industry was divided into 284 fully organized "protocol" shops belonging to members of the Dress and Waist Manufacturers' Association, into 242 half-organized shops whose independent owners were bound by separate labor contracts with the union, and into 135 wholly unorganized shops that were both nonunion and nonassociation. Approximately 25,000 workers were employed in the association shops, 7,000 workers were employed in the nonassociation shops with union contracts, and 3,000 workers were employed by independent firms operating nonunion shops. By the later part of April 1914, there were 709 dressmaking shops, of which 310 were in the association, 259 were independent with separate union contracts, and 140 were not subject to the jurisdiction of the association or of the union.[3]

The division of independent employers into those holding separate contracts with the union and those operating strictly non-

---

[2]*The Cloak Makers' Strike* (1910), p. 150; *Minutes,* Board of Arbitrators... [women's coat and suit trade] (August 3 and 4, 1913), pp. 111–112, 412; *Minutes,* Council of Conciliation . . . [women's coat and suit trade] (July 14, 1915), vol. 2, p. 13; *Women's Wear,* July 1, 1926.

[3]*Minutes,* Arbitration Proceedings between the Dress and Waist Manufacturers' Association and the ILGWU (Nov. 8, 1913), p. 137; N. I. Stone, *Wages and Regularity of Employment and Standardization of Piece Rates in the Dress and Waist Industry of New York City,* U.S. Dept. of Labor, BLS Bulletin no. 146 (April 28, 1914), p. 20. A still later compilation showed that, on Feb. 5, 1916, the Dress and Waist Manufacturers' Association had 200 members, controlled one-half the trade, and employed one-half the workers. The other half of the business was about equally divided between independent shops operating under separate union contracts and independent shops employing nonunion labor. *Minutes,* Arbitration Proceedings between the Dress and Waist Manufacturers' Association and the ILGWU (Feb. 5, 1916), vol. 4, p. 6. See also *Women's Wear Daily,* Feb. 4, 1930. For comparable figures in 1923, see *Monthly Labor Review,* June 1923, vol. 16, p. 142.

union shops was of primary concern to the union, which often listed its individual contracts with nonassociation firms but seldom publicized the number of nonunion shops. In 1915, for example, the Furriers' Joint Board reported that the fur workers' union held contracts with 210 independent fur manufacturers in addition to its collective agreement with the Associated Fur Manufacturers covering 150 association firms. The number of nonunion shops was not estimated. Twenty-two years later, the relative sizes of the groups in fur manufacturing had not materially changed. Figures for 1937 show 600 association employers bound by the collective agreement for the industry and 1,400 nonassociation employers, divided into one group of 635 independents with separate union contracts and into another group of 765 independents operating nonunion shops.[4]

Roughly, and with some marked variations, these illustrations reflect the general pattern of distribution that prevailed over the years throughout the needle trades. In each industry, the organized manufacturers were generally the less numerous but the more productive. Most inside manufacturers, as well as the jobbers and contractors of substantial means, were found within the ranks of their respective associations, and perhaps half of the workers in each trade were employed by these organized groups. The independent employers, however, still constituted a substantial proportion, if not a numerical majority, of the local manufacturers. Barring drastic measures of control, the independents were always strong enough to constitute a threat to the cause of regulated competition.

The hazards of external competition which plagued the organized manufacturers also beset the unions representing the workers in their shops. For union strength could be sapped by the growth of nonunion shops that offered destructive competition to the organized workers of a trade. Failure to enforce association-wide labor standards in nonassociation shops holding separate union contracts could also undermine the strength of a union as well as

---

[4]The 1915 figures are from Furriers' Joint Board, the *Furriers' Bulletin,* April 1915, and the later figures are from a "Report of the Members of the Associated Fur Coat and Trimming Manufacturers on the Joint Commission to Make an Industry-wide Study" (April 19, 1937), filed in the Abelson papers. Similar figures were compiled for the men's clothing industry and the women's headwear trades.

that of an employers' association. Wherever cheaper production costs tended to draw business away from the "legitimate" association-union shops, these conditions likewise induced workers to follow new sources of employment. The difficulty of controlling small, unstable shops, where collusion between the "people" and their "bosses" was most likely to prevail, further retarded the growth of union membership. The threat of "illegitimate" competition for jobs was the nightmare of every labor union — just as the threat of "illegitimate" competition for business was the nightmare of every employers' association.

Union Control of Independent Firms

Aside from those independents who worked as contractors for association firms and so were already bound by collective agreements, other unorganized employers operated in direct competition with the organized manufactures of each trade. The initial steps in extending the employment standards of collective agreements over this group rested with the needle trade unions. By organizing the workers of independent firms, a union could at least get its foot in the door. Once the unions gained control of the labor force, they could exert pressure to see that independent firms did not prosper by undercutting the standards of association firms.

Turning independent firms over to the union had been a basic tenet of the Brandeis Conferences in 1910. The ILGWU was expected to bind independent manufacturers to labor standards at least as high as those negotiated with employers' associations — an obligation which applied to out-of-town shops as well as to those in New York City. Within two years after the Brandeis Conferences, spokesmen for the association and the union that were parties to the first protocol restated this principle of their agreement. "The Association will assume responsibility for the maintenance of protocol conditions in out-of-town shops of members," wrote M. Silberman, chairman of the executive board of the Cloak, Suit and Skirt Manufacturers' Protective Association to Abe Bisno, chairman of the board of directors of the union, "and the Union assumes responsibility for the maintenance of the same conditions in all shops in the locality (i.e., the same town or city), including non-Association shops." To this Bisno replied: "It is in our interest to raise the standard of the industry everywhere. Within the limits of our ability we intend to treat non-Association employers out-of-town the same as Association employers."[5]

To gain this objective, needle trade unions used more than one method of approach. The most obvious course of action was to bind independent employers to association standards through the use of superior bargaining power. Backed by the resources of joint boards and strong national organizations, local unions could exact their demands of single employers by threats of economic coercion. Indeed, the most common procedure for "negotiating" individual agreements consisted in having the union draft at its

---

[5]M. Silberman to A. Bisno (April 6, 1912), A. Bisno to M. Silberman (April 12, 1912); letters filed in the Abelson papers.

> We realize that if we come before the Association and ask for certain wage increases or reduction of hours, we can only do that upon the assumption that their competitors would do likewise. As far as the Association is concerned, we can regulate our relations by agreement. . . . As far as outside employers are concerned, we will have to deal with them as an organized labor union, by the usual methods, in order to bring about the same standards.
> —Morris Hillquit, counsel for the ILGWU, in *Minutes,* Arbitration, Proceedings between the Dress and Waist Manufacturers' Association and the ILGWU (Feb. 5, 1916), vol. 4, p. 12.

> In the program made in Philadelphia, addressed to the manufacturers, one of the things that the Union assures the manufacturers that it can give them, give the manufacturers, in return for what they are asked to give, is the limitation of illegitimate competition, the fixing of standards for the entire industry. . . . Whatever is agreed to for the members of the association, the Union will undertake to enforce for the rest of the industry.
> —J. H. Cohen, counsel for the organized women's coat and suit manufacturers, in *Minutes,* Joint Board of Cloak and Skirt Makers' Unions of New York and the Cloak, Suit and Skirt Manufacturers' Protective Association (July 15, 1913), pp. 386–387.

In the collective agreement, effective Dec. 15, 1921, of the Ladies' Hat Manufacturers' Protective Association with the United Cloth Hat and Cap Makers and the Joint Board of Millinery and Ladies' Straw Hat Workers' Unions, provision was made for a joint committee on adjustment, which, among other duties, was to establish sanitary conditions for all factories in the trade. "In the event that such standards are established," stated this agreement, "the Union shall assume the obligation of enforcing such standards on manufacturers who are not members of the Association." Text in the Abelson papers.

headquarters a "form" contract, a copy of which was offered to each independent employer as his "license to operate." Here the union was free to dictate terms identical with those negotiated through employers' associations.[6]

The unorganized employers seldom did more than accept the document as submitted. "Kindly notify this office within the next five days," stated a communication from the millinery workers' union to the independent millinery manufacturers in 1932 "[of] your readiness to sign the new agreement which will be presented to you upon application, so that proper arrangements may be made by us to put the terms contained in the agreement into effect." So great was the power to dictate that unions often used independent contracts as a means of prying more favorable terms from employer groups. By settling with the independents first, a union could proclaim to the organized manufacturers that the labor standards for their industry had already been established![7]

Since this bargaining strategy was seldom successful against strong employers' associations, the more common practice, where unions first settled with independent firms, was to condition the final terms of individual contracts upon the final terms of the master agreement subsequently to be negotiated with the organized manufacturers of the trade. "The life and terms of this agreement," stated a 1931 form contract drafted by the Furriers' Joint Council for the use of independent employers, "is subject to the general agreement to be concluded in the fur trade by this union." On the other hand, when individual settlements with the unorganized employers followed the signing of a collective agreement, the terms of the separate contracts were not only modeled on the terms of the collective agreement but they were sometimes so

---

[6]See a section on "Collective Agreements in Non-Association Shops," in C. H. Winslow, *Conciliation, Arbitration, and Sanitation in the Dress and Waist Industry of New York City,* U.S. Department of Labor, BLS Bulletin no. 145 (April 10, 1914), pp. 45–47, 152–154. For comparable information on the men's clothing trade, see C. H. Winslow, *Collective Agreements in the Men's Clothing Industry,* U.S. Department of Labor, BLS Bulletin no. 198 (September 1916), pp. 122–123.

[7]*Women's Wear Daily,* March 11, 1932. "It is the aim and desire of our union to bring about stability and order in the entire industry in New York and to introduce in the shops an equitable and uniform standard of labor conditions for all workers in the trade," *ibid.*

worded as to embrace any changes subsequently introduced into the master contract.[8]

Union Concessions to Independent Shops

In practice, unions did not always exercise their power to equalize conditions of employment between the nonassociation shops and the association shops. Not only were the terms of independent contracts sometimes more favorable to the unorganized employers and less favorable to the union, but additional concessions were likely to be granted independent firms during the life of their agreements. To be sure, union officials generally found causes satisfactory to themselves for these discrepancies. With some justification, unions permitted some individual manufacturers entering contract negotiations for the first time to sign agreements that fell short of the standards set for the trade. Here a period of transition was deemed essential to bring the nonunion firm up to the accepted standards of the unionized plants. Otherwise, sudden changes from nonunion status to union

---

[8]In May 1913, the vice-president of the ILGWU, reporting to the union's general executive board, submitted evidence showing that independent contracts for the dress industry did not differ in their terms from association contracts, and that any changes in wage rates introduced into association contracts had also been introduced into separate contracts with independent employers. As cited in Winslow, *Conciliation, Arbitration, and Sanitation in the Dress and Waist Industry of New York City*, p. 46 note.

Two years later, when the struggles to preserve the original Protocol of Peace were brought before Mayor J. P. Mitchel's council of conciliation, Morris Hillquit, counsel for the ILGWU, thus surveyed past developments:

The Protective Association now before you, while thus representing comparatively speaking a small percentage of the men engaged in the industry, between 20 to 25 per cent — is nevertheless a very important factor for this reason, that it is composed of the leading manufacturers in the industry, and by custom in the industry, the standards set in the shops of this Association are generally recognized and made binding upon all manufacturing establishments in the industry. This is done partly by force of moral supremacy or business supremacy, but in a larger part by the action on the part of the Union, which takes the agreement with the Protective Association as a standard, and then enforces compliance upon manufacturers outside of the Association.
—*Minutes,* Council of Conciliation ... [women's coat and suit trade] (July 14, 1915), p. 13.

wage scales and working conditions might force the employer into closing his business.[9]

With some justification independent firms, more often than others, were granted exemptions or deviations from industry standards during the life of their separate union contracts. Generally constituting the smaller, less stable members of an industry, these independents were often in need of temporary relief from the standards set for the organized manufacturers. When threatened with adversity, independent firms were on occasion excused from contributing to unemployment funds or from paying time and a half for overtime. Or else they were allowed to forego the usual payments for holidays or for vacation time — at least until they could regain their feet.

There was also some defense for the action of labor unions in permitting a few very large independent manufacturers who had successfully defied the organized forces of collective action to sign their first labor agreements at substandard terms. This was a recognized expedient through which a union slipped its foot into the door to await more aggressive action at a later date. In all such exigencies, the independent competitor with a weak union contract might still be preferred to an independent competitor with no union contract at all.[10]

---

[9]Mr. Polakoff, as Chairman of the Settlement Committee of the Union, admits that the Union has made certain settlements with independent manufacturers . . . at less than the standards specified in the Protocol. Mr. Polakoff explains that it was necessary to do this, because the only alternatives were either to discharge incompetent employees not able to earn the wages specified in the Protocol, or, in case these standards were enforced, to put the manufacturer out of business.

—*Minutes,* Grievance Board, Dress and Waist Industry (Feb. 6, 1913), Case no. 2, p. 3.

The dress and waist protocol of Jan. 18, 1913, expressly gave individual employers signing separate contracts with the ILGWU a period of time in which to conform to sanitary standards fixed by the joint board of sanitary control established under the first protocol. For union refusal to extend association-wide standards to independent shops where those standards would hamper union organization in the early thirties, see *Women's Wear Daily,* Feb. 24, 1930.

[10]The general subject of individual deviations below the floor of labor standards in collective agreements is treated in J. T. Carpenter's *Employers' Associations and Collective Bargaining in New York City* (1950), pp. 279–291.

But the employers' associations bound to collective agreements with these unions seldom conceded the wisdom of such discrepancies. Experience soon taught that any differentials in contract terms or in the standards of contract enforcement, however justified at the moment, became an opening wedge for the breakdown of industry standards. Still less willing were the organized employers to accept other defenses for differences in wage rates and working conditions. Most other reasons advanced to grant independent producers better contract terms, or less rigid enforcement of contract standards, were held to be shallow attempts at disguising conduct that deliberately undermined the principles of the protocol movement.

Occasionally, there were flagrant cases of labor unions openly conceding to independent employers more favorable terms than those accorded association shops. More than likely, the objective was deliberately to sap the strength of the organized manufacturers. Despairing of protocol principles, some unions would cast off association bargaining for the freedom of individual bargaining. They feared the power of the organized employers and longed for the omnipotence of one-way dictation. Not every association member could resist the inducement to desert his organization for the lure of better contract terms through direct negotiations with the union. Still more devious was union support for rival associations that would divide the organized employers among themselves and thus decrease their power at the bargaining table.

Last but not least, flagrant discrepancies in contract standards between independent shops and association shops were sometimes attributed to the greater ease with which independent employers could evade their contracts or else buy exemptions from their obligations. No guiding arm of an employers' association hovered over the heads of the independent producers. Presumably, no pangs of conscience restrained their conduct. At the same time, union agents when policing independent shops unaccompanied by representatives of an employers' association were subject to greater temptations. It was so easy to accept a bribe for neglecting to police a small shop hidden away in a loft or a cellar. Especially where workers and employers jointly collaborated to evade the standards set for their trade were union business agents who knew of these discrepancies tempted to pass by on the other side.

Why should a union agent disturb a happy state of shop collusion when he could get paid for keeping quiet?

Most Favored Employer Clauses

For all these reasons, the organized manufacturers who supported the principles of the protocol movement refused to leave unions to their own devices in controlling independent firms. Although the needle trade unions had repeatedly pledged themselves to take care of the rest of their industries if the employers' associations would keep their own manufacturers in line, the organized producers preferred to translate these solemn pledges into definite contractual obligations. Nor would they be satisfied to leave unions with the option of writing into their form contracts specific obligations that the unions themselves could revoke with impunity. The responsibility for carrying association-union standards into the shops of independent firms had to become an enforceable part of the collective agreements themselves.

This responsibility began with the early protocols, only the first of which failed to impose upon unions an obligation toward the content of agreements they signed with individual employers. "If any employer in the industry shall fail to join the association," stated the first protocol of the dress and waist industry, January 18, 1913, "and shall enter into an individual contract with the union, there shall be no difference in maximum standards of hours, or minimum standards of wages, or sanitary conditions." By the time the protocol of the house dress industry was signed a month later, the corresponding provision had already assumed the essential terminology of "most favored employer" clauses which were to characterize subsequent collective agreements of the needle trades. The clause in this agreement provided that individual contracts between the union and nonassociation employers "shall in no respect be more favorable to the employer than the provisions of this protocol."[11]

---

[11] Texts of these protocols may be found in Winslow, *Conciliation, Arbitration, and Sanitation in the Dress and Waist Industry of New York City*, pp. 22–26 and 128–131. The white goods protocol, dated Feb. 17, 1913, between the Cotton Garment Manufactures of New York and the ILGWU and its Local 62 provided that "any contract with shops or firms not members of the association will specify conditions at least equal to the terms of this agreement." *Ibid.*, p. 139.

Subsequently, "most favored employer" clauses were carefully drafted to thwart every potential avenue of evasion. "The Union," — runs a typical clause in the collective agreements of the women's coat and suit trade after the mid-twenties — "obligates itself to enter into no contract, oral or in writing, expressed or implied, directly or indirectly, by reason whereof any person, firm or corporation engaged in the cloak, suit or skirt industry in the Metropolitan District, shall receive any benefit or aid not accorded the members of the Council, pursuant to the terms of this agreement."[12]

A number of "most favored employer" clauses, modeled more closely after the "most favored nation" provisions of international trade agreements, were so worded that any more favorable concessions the union might subsequently grant to nonassociation firms would automatically apply to association members. Clauses of this type reduced the general level of labor agreements for an industry to the lowest common denominator of wages, hours, and working conditions that the union would tolerate in any shop. Every organized manufacturer bound by a collective agreement could renounce his own obligations to the extent that the union at any time or for any reason made more favorable concessions elsewhere. The union thus set a new floor under competition for an industry each time it offered any one employer more liberal terms than it offered others.[13]

---

[12]From the 1929 collective agreement between the Industrial Council of Cloak, Suit and Skirt Manufacturers (inside producers) and the International Ladies' Garment Workers' Union and the Cloakmakers' Joint Board.

[13]Should the Union at any time make an agreement with any other Association of clothing manufacturers or any individual clothing manufacturer in the same branch of the trade more favorable in its terms to such Association or individual than this agreement, then this agreement shall be modified accordingly so that in no event shall this agreement be more onerous in its terms to the Association or any of its members than any other agreement that may hereafter be made by the Union as aforesaid.

—From the 1913 collective agreement for the men's clothing industry negotiated between the East Side Retail Clothing and Manufacturers' Association and the United Garment Workers of America. Copy filed in the Abelson papers.

In referring to contract clauses in agreements between the union and individual firms, the 1938 collective agreement between the Associated Corset and Brassière Manufacturers and Local 32, ILGWU, stated:

Wherever "most favored employer" clauses in collective agreements obligated unions to see that no less onerous terms were imposed upon independent firms, the organized manufacturers first wanted some assurance that separate contracts with individual employers measured up to these requirements. Disclosing the terms of individual agreements was an obvious prerequisite to keeping those terms on a parity with association contracts. Employers' associations sought and were sometimes given the power to inspect independent contracts. More often, collective agreements required the filing of all labor contracts within an industry with some permanent agency of contract administration. "The Union agrees," runs a provision of the house dress protocol of February 11, 1913, "to lay before the board of grievances every original contract entered into between it and each and every individual employer." There the contracts were open to inspection.[14]

In the second place, the life of individual contracts was not to

---

It is agreed that if upon inspection it is found that any of such agreements contain any provisions more beneficial to the employer than those herein contained then such more favorable clauses shall immediately be regarded as having been incorporated in this agreement and the members of the Association shall be entitled to the benefits thereof.
—Copy filed in the Abelson papers.

[14]The Union agrees that all individual contracts entered into between such Union and manufacturers not members of the Association, shall contain terms and conditions at least equal to those in this agreement specified.

The Union agrees at all times and upon the written request of the Association, to permit the Association to inspect all individual contracts entered into between the Union and manufacturers of dresses or waists who are not members of the Association.
—From the 1919 collective agreement between the Dress and Waist Manufacturers' Association and the ILGWU and its Locals 10, 25, 28. Text filed in the Abelson papers and printed in *Women's Wear*, April 9, 1919.

In the mid-twenties, Governor Alfred E. Smith's Advisory Commission on the women's coat and suit trade recommended that the ILGWU make no more favorable terms with independent firms than with employers' associations; and to insure the enforcement of this provision, the commission recommended that all independent agreements between the ILGWU and individual employers be open for inspection by a representative of the association or by the impartial chairman. See the Governor's Advisory Commission for the [women's] Cloak, Suit and Skirt Industry, *Supplementary Recommendations* (July 10, 1925), printed in *Women's Wear*, July 11, 1925.

extend beyond the life of the collective agreement. Preferably all contracts for an industry — both collective agreements and individual agreements — would expire simultaneously and the master agreement with the employers' association would be renegotiated first. Provisions to this effect would insure that the terms of the master contract would be known to the union at the time separate contracts were signed with independent firms. Such clauses precluded the possibility of having the union exert pressure upon the organized manufacturers to meet the standards already forced upon individual employers.

In a number of cases, either the employers' association or the impartial machinery for an industry acquired the power to approve in advance all separate union contracts negotiated with independent firms. To that end, a memorandum accompanying the 1915 collective agreement between the Associated Boys' Clothing Manufacturers of Greater New York and the Amalgamated Clothing Workers' Union provided "that [for] every settlement to be made with any manufacturer not a member of this Association, full information will be given to this Association and the approval obtained before final settlement." Again, when the dress manufacturers and the ILGWU were concluding their 1916 labor agreements, provision was made for a representative of the board of arbitration under the master contract between the Dress and Waist Manufacturers' Association and the ILGWU to be present at the signing of every independent contract "with a view to checking up the terms of the agreement made so that all standards in the industry will be equal."[15]

"Before making a new contract with any individual jobber," runs the pertinent terms of the 1927 collective agreement between the Merchants' Ladies' Garment Association (jobbers) and the Cloakmakers' Joint Board, ILGWU, "the union shall submit to the association a copy of the proposed contract. If the association shall have a grievance against the jobber or objections to the terms of the proposed contract, it shall give to the union within five days a written statement containing full particulars of the grievance or objections. The union may undertake to adjust the grievence or rectify the provisions objected to; or it may submit

---

[15]Text of the 1915 boys' clothing agreement is filed in the Abelson papers. The dress industry quotation is from *Women's Wear*, Feb. 17, 1916.

the question or questions to the impartial chairman of the industry for adjudication."[16]

Supplemental Legislation and Independent Contracts

If independent employers were to operate under labor standards equal to those of association members, then all changes introduced during the life of collective agreements between unions and employers' associations must likewise extend to independent employers operating under separate union contracts. Conversely, no amendments or interpretations of individual contracts must be allowed to undermine the standards of collective agreements. So long as agencies of the impartial machinery established under collective agreements exercised broad legislative as well as administrative powers, contract terms identical for both association and nonassociation shops at the time the agreements became effective might later come to vary widely through informal growth. Even more subject to change were the individual contracts that could be shaped and reshaped at the whim of union officials.

For the most part, unions of the needle trades accepted the proposition that all understandings reached with employers' associations during the life of collective agreements, and all changes introduced by action of the impartial machinery under those agreements, should be automatically extended to union contracts with independent firms. After the dress and waist protocol was

---

[16]The text of this agreement is printed in *Women's Wear Daily,* Jan. 14, 1927.

In the 1930–1931 national collective agreement of the full fashioned hosiery industry, the hosiery workers' union agreed that "it will not enter into any agreements with other manufacturers of hosiery without first submitting such proposed agreements with said other manufacturers to the Impartial Chairman for his opinion and approval as to whether such proposed agreement or agreements are equitable and fair and in keeping with the spirit of this agreement."

Perhaps the ultimate solution toward which such provisions were pointing was that proposed by the organized dress contractors to the ILGWU during negotiations for their 1936 collective agreement. The contractors sought to have the union terminate all separate contracts with individual firms and thereafter force all individual firms not members of the association to accept the master collective agreement negotiated between the association and the union. See *Women's Wear Daily,* Dec. 27, 1935. The first (1929) collective agreement of the full fashioned hosiery industry appears to have met this standard. The text of this agreement is found in *ibid.,* Sept. 6, 1929.

adopted in 1913, for example, Locals 10 and 25, ILGWU, drafted a form contract (copies of which were signed by more than 250 independent dress manufacturers) that required each employer to comply with the rule-making decisions of the board of arbitration established under the protocol. In addition, each employer was compelled to maintain such sanitary standards "as the joint board of sanitary control established under the protocol of peace now existing between the International Ladies' Garment Workers' Union and the Waist and Dress Manufacturers' Association may determine."[17]

Even though the original protocol for the women's coat and suit industry contained no most favored employer clause, J. H. Cohen, counsel for the cloak manufacturers and father of the protocol movement, insisted in 1913 that the rulings of the board of arbitration under the women's coat and suit protocol were automatically applicable to independent shops. "It does not lie in the mouth of the Union to say that because an independent manufacturer did not like this tribunal, he shall not accept its determinations," Cohen argued. "It is the Union's business to see that the tribunal's determinations are accepted by the rest of the industry, precisely the same as they do in the case of sanitary conditions." At the time, Meyer London, counsel for the ILGWU, endorsed Cohen's position.[18]

---

[17]Winslow, *Conciliation, Arbitration, and Sanitation in the Dress and Waist Industry of New York City,* pp. 46, 153.

A form contract for independent firms drafted by the ILGWU during the 1919 contract negotiations between the Cloak, Suit and Skirt Manufacturers' Protective Association and the ILGWU contained the following clause: "If a board or council shall be established by such collective agreement with power to modify standards or provide rules to guide the relations between employer and workers in the industry, the Employer will comply with its decisions and regulations." *Women's Wear,* June 9, 1919.

Independent agreements of the dress and waist industry during the early twenties contained a clause stating that "if any understanding between the union and any of the associations with which the union has at present or may in the future have collective agreements, shall be reached, which understanding may involve an increase in wages, reduction in hours, or a general elevation of the standards in the industry, such understanding shall become part" of the agreement between the union and the independent firm. *Ibid.,* Feb. 14, 1921.

[18]*Minutes,* Meeting of the Joint Board of the Cloak and Skirt Makers' Unions of New York and the Cloak, Suit and Skirt Manufacturers' Protective

By the mid-twenties, individual contract clauses extending changes in collective agreements to independent firms were common. "It is agreed," stated the form contract of the fur workers' union for the use of independent firms in 1924, "that any decision or resolution which may be adopted during the life of this agreement by the Conference Committee which functions under the collective agreement between the Associated Fur Manufacturers, Inc. and the Joint Board Furriers' Union, and relating to conditions to be maintained, reforms to be introduced and abuses to be corrected in the fur industry shall be binding upon the parties to this agreement."[19]

Union Enforcement of Independent Contracts

Having imposed upon labor unions the obligation to see that the terms and conditions of employment for association members were extended to the shops of independent firms, the organized forces of industry might then have left the enforcement of these individual contracts solely to the union. Wherever the law of self-interest prompted unions of their own accord to establish for independent firms the same work standards negotiated with the organized manufacturers, this law should also have encouraged unions to enforce work standards in nonassociation shops at least to the extent those standards were observed in as-

---

Association (July 15, 1913), pp. 387–388. Meyer London's views are given at pp. 683–684.

[19]Another paragraph of this form contract provided that any unemployment insurance fund plan subsequently adopted by the conference committee under the master contract would be carried into effect by the parties to the individual contract. When such a plan was formulated in 1925, the conference committee under the master contract resolved that "the Union obligated itself to require all firms with which it has contractual relations in Greater New York but which are not members of the Associated Fur Manufacturers to execute an identical unemployment agreement and to observe its provisions." A copy of the resolution, dated Feb. 18, 1925, is filed in the Abelson papers.

From the millinery industry comes this clause found in the 1924 independent contract of Moss Manufacturing Company with the Straw Hat Workers' Union: "In the event that during the continuance of this agreement the Union shall either as a result of a general strike or, through negotiations generally, establish changes in conditions in the trade in the City of New York, the firm agrees that such changes shall become a part of this agreement."

sociation shops. Certainly, a union with power to drive contract terms down the throats of independent employers also had the power to compel those employers to live by the terms of their agreements.

Some unions freely made use of their potential powers to enforce contract observance by independent shops. Roving bands of union business agents visited nonassociation firms bound by separate labor agreements to seek out contract infractions. Under their own interpretations of the contract, these union agents acted as investigators, prosecutors, judges, juries, and executioners. Appeals, if any, were generally heard by the executive board of the union, whose decisions were seldom, if ever, subject to review. Fines levied and penalties imposed by judgment of the union were executed under threat of strike action. "From September 1912 to July 1st, 1913," so Meyer London, counsel for the ILGWU, reported to the board of arbitration for the organized factions of the women's coat and suit trade, "we have had 900 cases of non-association shops in which men were dragged before the Grievance Committee of the Union, and were severely fined."[20]

Not only did unions employ "negotiation" strikes to extend association-union standards into nonassociation shops where unions were represented, but most unions freely relied upon "enforcement" strikes to maintain those standards during the life of an agreement. "All complaints of an individual worker, group of workers or of the Union," runs a typical provision in a form contract for independent firms of the fur manufacturing industry, "shall be adjusted within 48 hours from the time the dispute arose, unless the time is extended by mutual consent. Should a firm fail to adjust a complaint or carry out the adjustment in time, the Union is at liberty to declare the shop on strike as a last resort to enforce the agreement."[21]

Some unions forced independent firms to pay for losses sustained from strikes called to gain compliance with labor agreements. This practice was of dubious validity when applied to association members under collective agreements that were subject

---

[20]*Minutes,* Board of Arbitrators . . . [women's coat and suit trade] (August 5, 1913), p. B-14.

[21]From a 1919 form contract for individual firms with Local 53, International Fur Workers' Union. Copy filed in the Abelson papers.

to joint administration; but it was undoubtedly legitimate when applied to independent firms operating under separate union contracts that were subject to union administration. No one questioned the right of the fur workers' union to charge an independent fur manufacturer exactly $158 for the costs of the first strike that the union had to call against the firm to enforce a provision of the labor agreement. As manager of the Furriers' Joint Board, Ben Gold, who subsequently became president of the International Fur Workers' Union, collected thousands of dollars during the twenties from independent employers to meet the costs of union "enforcement" strikes, yet no one questioned his authority.[22]

Cash Security and Independent Contracts

Aside from the use of enforcement strikes, the most valuable weapon in the union's arsenal for making war on independent employers who violated their contracts was the imposition of cash security. Requiring individual employers to deposit cash in advance against subsequent failure to meet their contractual obligations was a well-known union device employed under single shop bargaining since the turn of the century. Sometimes used as an additional weapon against the organized manufacturers (see above, p. 221), cash security found its greatest value when directed against independent firms in lieu of the pressures for contract observance that employers' associations exerted against their members. Where the union became the depository of employer cash security funds, no disappearing act or other form of employer shenanigans to evade the contract could forestall the imposition of a financial penalty for misconduct.[23]

---

[22]The charge of $158 was set in the case of Latterman and Sobelman (May 1, 1931). Document filed in the Abelson papers. The report of Ben Gold is from the *Furriers' Bulletin*, November 1925.

[23]For the early use of bonds to insure the faithful performance of labor contracts, see the *Reports of the [U.S.] Industrial Commission on Labor Organizations, Labor Disputes and Arbitration and on Railway Labor* (1901), vol. 17, p. 414.

In its supplementary recommendations of July 10, 1925, Governor Smith's Advisory Commission on the women's coat and suit trade proposed that all contracts between the union and independent jobbers, contractors, or inside manufacturers "shall provide for the deposit in cash or its equivalent, with the Union, of a sum sufficient to cover any damage by reason of any violation committed" by these employers. *Women's Wear*, July 11, 1925.

The ease with which unions could manipulate cash security funds on behalf of contract enforcement was further enhanced by the concept of "liquidated damages." Under this principle, the aggrieved party need not await a judicial determination of the damages he had sustained or an impartial assessment of the compensation he should receive. Liquidated damages called for paying out a flat amount for every infraction of the contract, whatever the character or extent of the violation. "The said firm agrees," runs the 1931 contract of the fur workers' union with the firm of Latterman and Sobelman, "that for each and every violation or failure to perform any of the conditions or covenants of this agreement, on its part, it shall pay to the said Union the sum of Two Hundred (200) Dollars as ascertained and liquidated damages."[24]

Exacting cash security from independent employers was part of the normal procedure for negotiating individual contracts. A striking example occurred in 1916 when the Amalgamated Clothing Workers' Union undertook to force independent firms of the men's clothing industry into accepting separate contracts modeled after the collective agreement previously signed with the American Clothing Manufacturers' Association. To accomplish this objective, the union called a strike against all independent firms refusing to sign the prepared contract. Employers were then directed to the Union Square Hotel where, according to a reporter for the *Daily Trade Record,* January 19, 1916, they were subjected to the following procedure:

---

[24]On one occasion the union listed the following infractions of which the firm was adjudged to be guilty: (1) Violations for paying below the minimum scale to seven workers. Liquidated damages — $200. (2) Employment of nonunion finisher by the name of Rosengart. Liquidated damages — $200. (3) Employing workers overtime when overtime is prohibited during the year 1931. Liquidated damages — $200. Informed that the firm had applied for membership in the Associated Fur Coat and Trimming Manufacturers, the union noted that "after all claims are liquidated, the firm is at liberty, if it so desires, to join the association." A typewritten copy of the claims against the firm of Latterman and Sobelman and a copy of the firm's labor agreement are filed in the Abelson papers.

Over three years just prior to May 1937, the Dressmakers' Joint Board collected more than $745,000 in liquidated damages from employers, mostly for underpayment of the workers. ILGWU, *Report and Proceedings,* Twenty-third Convention (May 1937), p. 38.

After the employer has registered with a committee in one room all the names of the contractors he employs, he is ushered into a room where the leading lights of the labor organization are in session with their attorney. The people of the shop operated by the manufacturer, or a committee, are with him and the work commences.

"You wish to settle peacefully with the union?" inquired the lawyer. The manufacturer replies in the affirmative. That is what he is there for. "Then you will arrange all the prices for your people," he is informed. This done, the agreement covering four pages is filled in with his name and other particulars and given the manufacturer to sign. . . .

"Then you will please sign this note for $300, as per clause 21 of the agreement," adds the lawyer. He reads the clause to the Manufacturer. Here it is:

"The firm hereby agrees and does deposit with the union as security for the faithful performance of the conditions, convenants and promises herein contained, a promissory note in the sum of three hundred dollars. Said sum of three hundred dollars is to be considered as liquidated damage to the union for a violation of any of the provisions of the contract on the part of the firm. The reason why the sum is herein fixed as liquidated damage, is because it will be impossible with any degree of certainty or accuracy to fix and assess the damage that the union may suffer by reason of such breach of contract on the part of the firm. The firm hereby authorizes the union to fill in the blank space in said note as far as the duration of said note is concerned."

The note, which is a regular promissory note, is made payable to "ourselves" for "three hundred dollars" and is signed and endorsed by the manufacturer. The date is left open, subject to the time "when the contract is broken," when, according to the labor organization lawyer, the union will fill in the date, transfer the note and collect.

Cash security funds forfeited for breach of contract became the property of the union with no strings attached. "This provision for liquidated damages accrues only to the benefit of the Union and is not to be construed as preventing any individual employee under this agreement from enforcing any legal remedy that he may have by reason of a breach of this agreement," runs the 1919 form contract drafted by the ILGWU for independent firms of the women's coat and suit trade. "Title to the moneys deposited with the union as aforesaid, is to pass to the Union upon the signing of this agreement, and such sum shall be returned by the Union to the firm after ———— and then only upon proof satisfactory to the Union that the employer has performed all terms of this agreement on his part to be performed.''[25]

Association Controls over Enforcement of Independent Contracts

Despite the many evidences of good faith in obtaining compliance from independent employers, unions did not always measure up to the standards of enforcement that the organized manufacturers expected of them. There were too many contrary evidences of union members working for independent employers on substandard terms; of "partners" in small establishments doing the work of union members but immune from the labor agreement; of workers in unionized shops kicking back a part of their wages to their employers; of union agents privately winking at collusion between the "people" and their "bosses" to violate labor standards; and of union members paying for the privilege of working in nonunion shops.

Above all else, there was indisputable evidence that scores of small-time independent contractors with hole-in-the-wall shops employing unionized labor, seldom, if ever, saw a union agent from one year to another. "When our establishments are scattered to such an extent that even to locate them physically becomes an almost impossible task," admitted the ILGWU in its testimony before Governor Smith's Advisory Commission on the women's

---

[25]From the text of the agreement printed in *Women's Wear,* June 9, 1919. The power of union leaders to manipulate cash security funds led some employers to write off their contributions as a cost of maintaining peace with the union. Many employers assumed that, irrespective of guilt, they would never see their funds again. For the organized manufacturers, pointing to industry standards, however, the injustices of the system were of less concern than the brighter prospects of holding independent firms to their contractual obligations.

Another early example of a cash security clause appears in the 1913 form contract drafted by the ILGWU for independent firms of the dress and waist industry. The text of this contract is printed in Winslow, *Conciliation, Arbitration, and Sanitation in the Dress and Waist Industry of New York City,* pp. 52–54. Surprisingly, some form contracts in the fur manfacturing trade also required the fur workers' union to deposit cash security that would be forfeited to the employer in case of contract infractions by the workers. Copies of such contracts are filed in the Abelson papers. For other specimen clauses, see the section on "Liquidated Damages" in Elias Lieberman, *The Collective Labor Agreement* (1939), pp. 141–144.

coat and suit trade in the mid-twenties, "they elude the efficient control of the union." If labor standards were overenforced in some independent shops, they were widely underenforced in others.[26]

The degree of underenforcement was likely to vary directly with the distance from the Manhattan center of the major collective agreement for each trade. Never was this distinction more obvious than in the late thirties, following the death of the NRA codes. Even where the post-code terms of individual contracts were identical with the terms of collective agreements, the supplemental rules to implement these terms and the type of supervision provided to interpret and enforce those terms varied substantially between New York City and other markets. "One set of union regulations prevails in town, and a wholly different set of regulations governs operations out of town," noted Mortimer Lanzit, executive director of the National Dress Manufacturers' Association in 1938. He had prepared a message for distribution to civic officials, real-estate owners, bankers, and others who were interested in saving the New York dress market:

> A contributing factor to this disastrous situation is the "out-of-town [union] officer." He is king in his little kingdom, unconcerned, uninfluenced, and uncontrolled by the forces so necessary to the stabilization of the dress industry. So-called supplemental union agreements are to him scraps of paper; provisions for graduated increased earnings of workers are completely ignored and unenforced. Under the justification of unskilled workers, he condones a violation of the collective agreement providing for one uniform system of work....
>
> The New York dress market, which has ample evidence of the supervisory power of the union through the New York Joint Board and the Joint Board's alertness in constant investigations, examina-

---

[26]The quotation is here cited from M. P. Glushien, legal counsel, ILGWU, Brief in support of Initial Decision of Hearing Examiner in the Matter of the California Sportswear and Dress Association, Inc., *et al.*, p. 13, Federal Trade Commission Docket no. 6325.

The larger the number of shops in the trade and the smaller their size, the more officials and help the union needs to control them. The irresponsible small contractor is more brazen and "nervy." He is not afraid of trouble with the union as the large shop is, because he has nothing to lose.

—Morris Sigman, president, ILGWU, in ILGWU's *Justice,* Nov. 11, 1927.

tions, and enforcement of labor standards in New York City, is amazed by the contrast of inaptitude and indifference in control, supervision and enforcement by the union's out-of-town division, in which the New York Joint Board regrettably does not participate.[27]

Drawing upon such evidences as these, the organized manufacturers were no more disposed to grant unions complete control over the enforcement of independent agreements than they were willing to concede unions complete freedom to write the terms of those agreements in the first place. Whatever these independent contracts might provide, unions could not be left with the discretionary power to inspect or not to inspect, to punish or not to punish, to strike or not to strike independent shops violating the labor standards set for the trade. Employer groups must have the right to complain against union indifference. Like the original determination of work standards in nonassociation shops, the enforcement of those standards had to become an obligation imposed on the union under collective agreements negotiated between the organized factions of each trade. Otherwise, an employers' association would have no grounds for action against a union that failed to guarantee compliance with contract standards in nonassociation shops.

For example, a clause in a union-drafted form contract obligating each independent dress manufacturer to deposit $5,000.00 cash security for the faithful observance of his contract gave the employers' association, party to a collective agreement, no lever of control over the union that failed to enforce such a provision. But a similar clause in a collective agreement with an employers' association under which "the union agrees that it will not enter into any contract with any dressers not a member of the Association unless such firm not a member of the Association deposit $5,000 security" opened the door for association charges of noncompliance against the union that failed to require cash security of its independent employers.[28]

Joint Administrative Controls over Independent Contracts

But the organized manufacturers were not satisfied to bring

[27] M. Lanzit in *Women's Wear Daily*, Sept. 10, 1938.

[28] See the 1929 collective agreement of the Associated Employers of Fur Workers with Locals 2, 3, 4, and 54, International Fur Workers' Union.

grievances against needle trade unions for enforcement discrepancies that might come to light. Further to insure that association standards would be observed by independent firms, the organized employers would either drive independents into the ranks of employers' associations or subject those independents to forms of joint administrative control. Since driving independents into associations raised grave problems of legality, the second alternative appeared the more practical. Giving the organized manufacturers a hand in the administration of outside contracts could be accomplished either by permitting the normal impartial machinery of collective agreements to extend its jurisdiction over contracts negotiated between the union and independent firms or else by creating special union-association agencies that would jointly supervise the enforcement of independent contracts. Some preferred one alternative; some, the other; and, as it turned out, the organized employers were not to be satisfied with less than both.[29]

The merits of having the normal machinery of collective agreements, or special joint agencies of administration, or both, exercise controls over independent contracts had been debated at length before the boad of arbitration of the women's coat and suit trade as early as the summer of 1913. At that time J. H. Cohen, counsel for the organized manufacturers, had argued that the machinery to enforce the master contract could readily be utilized to enforce separate union contracts with independent firms. He proposed that the board of grievances under the original protocol be given jurisdiction, not only to equalize piece rates between association and nonassociation shops, but also to enforce its rulings by exercising the power "to appoint committees

---

[29]The ultimate objective of those sponsoring joint administrative agencies with control over independent contracts was embodied in the following concise clause from the 1929 collective agreement between the Industrial Council of Cloak, Suit and Skirt Manufacturers and the ILGWU and its Joint Board of Cloak, Skirt, Dress and Reefer Makers' Union: "the Union agrees to insert a clause in all its agreements with the independent employers to the effect that such employers will submit to the supervision of the Impartial Chairman and of the [Special Control] Commission herein provided for." See ILGWU, *Report and Proceedings,* Twentieth Convention (December 1929), p. 53.

of investigation, to make inquiry into such shops, where they will be admitted for such inquiry."[30]

Even at that time, a precedent for this proposal had already been set by the joint board of sanitary control, one of three permanent institutions created in the original Protocol of Peace. Representing equally the employers' association and the ILGWU, with additional members drawn from the public, the joint board of sanitary control was empowered to formulate its own rules of health and safety for all shops covered by the collective agreement. Moreover, the board became its own enforcing agency. It conducted inspections to see that its standards were observed and issued "sanitary certificates" to those shops found to be in compliance with its regulations. As a final measure of enforcement, the board endorsed the use of sanitary strikes against noncomplying firms. No union member would work in shops that were unable to obtain sanitary certificates. (See above, p. 230.)

Through action of the union, jurisdiction of the joint board of sanitary control was extended over nonassociation shops in which the workers were organized. All rules governing health and safety issued by the board were made applicable to independent shops as well as association shops. The board's inspectors visited independent shops as well as association shops. The same type of "sanitary certificate" received by association members found to be in compliance with the board's regulations were issued to independent firms obeying the rules. And the same type of "sanitary strike" that threatened association members found to be guilty of noncompliance also threatened independent firms for similar offenses.[31]

What the joint board of sanitary control was empowered to do for the rules of health and safety, the organized manufacturers would have other agencies of the impartial machinery do in their respective areas of competence. If a joint price commission were

---

[30]*Minutes*, Meeting of the Joint Board of the Cloak and Skirt Makers' Unions of New York and the Cloak, Suit and Skirt Manufacturers' Protective Association (July 30, 1913), p. 703.

[31] Beginning in 1919, all independent employers bound by separate union contracts either in the women's coat and suit industry or in the dress and waist industry were officially brought under the jurisdiction of the sanitary boards and taxed $10 a year for their support. Louis Lorwin [Louis Levine], *The Women's Garment Workers* (1924), p. 470.

authorized to administer uniform piece rates in association shops, then such an agency should have the right to enforce its standards in nonassociation shops. "What I mean by standardizing the industry," stated manufacturer M. Silberman at a joint labor-management conference in 1913, "I do not mean the Association houses; I mean the entire industry. I mean that we shall have the right to go to any shop, just the same as the Joint Board of Sanitary Control today has the right to go into any shop and hang up its certificate. I mean that this Board shall have the absolute right to go into any shop."[32]

Manufacturer A. E. Lefcourt supported Silberman's position. "If you want to standardize the whole industry, I am perfectly agreeable, if you will only standardize the entire industry," he stated. ". . . If we pay $1.00 an hour, or 75 cents an hour, I should like to see that every shop in the industry, no matter where he is, and no matter who he is, shall do the same thing." But Lefcourt would not concede that the union should be left alone to enforce these standards in nonassociation shops, although every worker in these shops were a union man. "I do not question that you have a thorough Union shop in every cloak shop at all, and I am glad to see it, but I do object to this, Mr. Chairman, and gentlemen, that where two parties are really sincere in standardizing the industry, why one of the parties should say to us, 'you have only a right to inspect your own shops, and never mind about the shops that are not in your Association.' "[33]

A further step toward extending the control of joint agencies created by collective agreements over the enforcement of separate union contracts with independent firms occurred in the dress and waist industry under the revised protocol of 1916. This agreement between the Dress and Waist Manufacturers' Association and the ILGWU created a board of protocol standards composed of three members to represent the union, three, the association, and three, the public — a board that was endowed with "comprehensive power to investigate regularly throughout the entire industry and to enforce standards to the full extent of the power of both organizations." Its chief function, therefore, was

---

[32]*Minutes,* Meeting of the Joint Board of the Cloak and Skirt Makers' Unions of New York and the Cloak, Suit and Skirt Manufacturers' Protective Association (July 30, 1913), pp. 679–680, 702–703.

[33]*Ibid.,* pp. 690–691, 701.

to see that standards set by collective agreements (excluding sanitary standards) and carried over into independent contracts were enforced with equal vigor in association shops and in the shops of independent firms. Beset by the complexity of its tasks and plagued by disssension within its ranks, the board soon expired along with the death of the revised dress protocol and was never reconstituted.[34]

The Pros and Cons of Impartial Supervision

Most employers' associations of the needle trades were aware of certain drawbacks in subjecting independent firms to the control of joint administrative agencies under collective agreements. For one thing, extending the jurisdiction of the impartial machinery over independent firms carried privileges as well as imposed obligations. If submission to the permanent institutions of collective agreements reduced the opportunities of independent firms to evade their contracts, access to these institutions also provided independents with greater protection against strike action by their workers. This protection weakened the movement

---

[34] J. H. Cohen, "The Revised Protocol in the Dress and Waist Industry," in *Annals*, American Academy of Political and Social Science, January 1917, vol. 69, pp. 192–193. A brief account of the board of protocol standards may be found in Lorwin, *The Women's Garment Workers*, pp. 305–309. More information may be gleaned from the files of *Women's Wear*, especially for February 1916.

During the 1919 negotiations for a new collective agreement between the Cloak, Suit and Skirt Manufacturers' Protective Association (party to the first protocol) and the ILGWU, the union signed more than 125 independent firms to separate but identical contracts that contained the following clause:

If a board or other instrumentality shall be established by a collective agreement for the regulation and enforcement of uniform standards throughout the industry in reference to wages, hours of labor, overtime, legal holidays or similar purposes, the Employer hereby agrees that he will submit to the jurisdiction of such board in the same way and with the same force as if he had been a party to such collective agreement; that he will allow inspectors and representatives of such board free access to his establishment at all times and will furnish them with information in connection with his pay roll, wages, accounts and similar subjects as may be required of him; that he will comply with all requirements, rules and regulations of such board and that he will bear his share of the expense in maintaining such board.

—From the text of the independent form contract as printed in *Women's Wear*, June 9, 1919.

to expand association membership. Why should an independent employer ever join his association if he received the benefits of the impartial machinery without contributing to its support?

Even where collective agreements required independents to help meet the costs of the impartial machinery, as some agreements did, access to these permanent agencies of law and order was still available without the financial outlay and the loss of time that accompanied association membership. Moreover, extending the controls of the impartial machinery over independent firms with separate union contracts carried inferences that the advocates of law and order had endorsed a permanent status of industrial society in which some manufacturers were organized while others were not. At least some leaders of the protocol movement continued to prefer shooting for the goal of all-inclusive associations, with no temporizing concessions to independent firms along the way.[35]

Among those who in the mid-twenties favored the more radical solution of driving independents into associations or else out of the industry were certain officials of the Industrial Council of Cloak, Suit and Skirt Manufacturers, successor to the original association that had signed the first Protocol of Peace. In a brief submitted to Governor Smith's Advisory Commission appointed to help mediate a dispute in the women's coat and suit trade, this association of inside manufacturers would deny the facilities of the impartial machinery to independent firms operating under separate union contracts. Largely the work of the association's executive director, Samuel Klein, this brief stated in part:

The Industrial Council desires at this time to enter a most emphatic and unqualified protest against any provision that will provide for an adjudication, by the impartial machinery, of differences arising between the independent manufacturers and the union. . . .

The union, in the past, has freely signed up independent manufacturers and placed stumbling blocks in the way of such manu-

---

[35]The parties to the first collective agreement between the Merchants' Society for Ladies' Tailors and Local 38, ILGWU, in 1911, did not wish to allow independent firms access to their impartial machinery. None of the 300 independent firms whose individual contracts had to be modified to conform with the terms of the association agreement was permitted to receive the benefits of the grievance machinery established by the master contract. *Ibid.*, Sept. 20, 1911.

facturers becoming members of an association. It is our suggestion that anything that appeals to the minds of the commission as being helpful to make uniform and standardized conditions can only be accomplished by way of an association. An association acts as the proper medium to enforce a contract upon its members, and the union obtains a proper sponsor for the enforcement of its collective agreement.

It is our contention that only members of an association shall be privileged to enjoy whatever benefit may be derived through a collective agreement and those who do not want to become members of an association be barred from such privileges and should be catered to by an independent union contract. If this suggestion is adopted, it will readily be seen that an independent, to enjoy the benefits accruing through a collective agreement, would become a member of an association.

It must be clear to all that if the entire industry were controlled by one union and one or more associations, it would be the easiest and most effective way of correcting the evils which tend to undermine union conditions.[36]

In its supplementary recommendations of July 10, 1925, the Governor's Advisory Commission proposed that "the Impartial Chairman and his machinery should be reserved for the adjustment of disputes between the members of associations and the Union, who are parties to the collective agreement in the industry, except in so far as controversies involving independents may, by the consent of the parties to the collective agreements, be submitted to the Impartial Chairman." The commission did not favor having independents contribute to the expenses of the office of impartial chairman but did favor contributions by independent firms to the industry's bureau of research established under the collective agreement.[37]

---

[36]*Ibid.*, June 11, 1925. "In my opinion the independents ought to sign an agreement through the associations. That would help cure the ills of the industry." Lieutenant Governor Herbert H. Lehman, as quoted in the *New York Times,* Jan. 11, 1929, at the time the organized factions of the women's coat and suit industry of New York City were undertaking to organize a joint control commission to supervise the maintenance of uniform standards for the trade.

[37] The Governor's Advisory Commission for the [women's] Cloak, Suit and Skirt Industry, *Supplementary Recommendations* (July 10, 1925), p. 5. The text is also printed in *Women's Wear,* July 11, 1925.

The greater the number and variety of restrictions that needle trade un-

The commission also recommended that the books of independent firms against whom the union or the employers' association had filed a complaint should be open for inspection "at such times and under such circumstances as the impartial chairman for the industry shall prescribe." And in its final report of May 20, 1926, the commission further recommended "that an accountant be permanently attached to the staff of the Impartial Chairman for the purpose of making, with or without notice or formal complaint, investigations under his direction in any establishment in the industry, in order to see whether the contracts entered into between the parties are being carried out." Most of these recommendations, along with the provision that the impartial chairman have the power to prescribe the same form of books and accounts for independent firms that he prescribed for association members, subsequently found their way into collective agreements of the women's coat and suit trade.[38]

Elsewhere in the needle trades, the application of most favored employer clauses led employers' associations to insist upon the right to inspect nonassociation firms and to take a look at the books. "The Union," stated the 1926 collective agreement of the Wholesale Hat and Cap Manufacturers' Association with the Joint Council of the Cloth Hat, Cap and Millinery Workers'

---

ions imposed on independent firms, the brighter the prospects of preventing those firms from hitting below the belt. In the 1932 contract negotiations for the organized factions of the women's coat and suit trade, the Merchants' Ladies' Garment Association (jobbers) recommended "inclusion of a provision that the union will not enter into any contract with any [independent] firm without first receiving the written approval of the other contracting parties and the Impartial Chairman, and then only (1) upon payment of a minimum of $2,500 annually, this sum to be added to a fund to be used for the support of the impartial machinery in the industry; (2) that such independent may not be permitted to enjoy the privileges of the machinery used by the members of the respective organizations, and (3) that such independent shall be required to deposit a substantial cash security as a guaranty for his faithful observance and performance of the terms and conditions of such independent contract, such amount to be fixed by the Impartial Chairman, but after conference with all contracting parties." *Women's Wear Daily,* May 25, 1932.

[38] Governor's Advisory Commission for the [women's] Cloak, Suit and Skirt Industry, *Supplementary Recommendations* (July 10, 1925), p. 5; *Final Recommendations* (May 20, 1926), p. 9. The text of these recommendations were printed in *Women's Wear,* July 11, 1925; May 20 and 21, 1926.

International Union, "shall supply the Board of Adjustment with certified copies of all agreements entered into with employers in Greater New York, not members of the Association, upon complaint by the Association that the Union is not in fact enforcing the terms of its agreement with any employer not a member of the Association. The Chairman of the Board of Adjustment will be afforded all facilities to convince himself whether the letter and the spirit of such agreement is carried out."[39]

Formal charges were occasionally preferred against unions of the needle trades for failure to enforce most favored employer clauses. A typical case came before George W. Alger, impartial chairman for the women's coat and suit trade in the early thirties. The case involved the question of whether certain manufacturers of women's and children's wear, who operated in competition with some forty members of the Industrial Council of Cloak, Suit and Skirt Manufacturers, were receiving more favorable terms from the union than had been accorded the members of the Industrial Council. After the parties to the case had presented their evidence and concluded their arguments, the impartial chairman, on behalf of the board of arbitration, wrote an opinion which stated, in part:

This is a complaint by the Industrial Council against the Union that the Union has violated the terms and spirit of the collective agreement between it and the Industrial Council by permitting a large number of firms, engaged in the manufacture of infants' and children's coats, to operate in the industry under more favorable conditions than the members of the Industrial Council and without requiring from them either membership in one of the established associations of the industry or the execution of independent contracts

---

[39]From the text of the 1926 agreement as found in ILGWU, *Report and Proceedings,* Sixteenth Biennial Convention (May 1927), p. 229.

Any and all agreements with employers other than members of the Association shall, in addition, contain a provision by which employers signatories thereunder shall be obligated to produce their books and records of account for examination by the Impartial Chairman at his request, for the purpose of determining whether or not such employers are conforming to the standards herein.
—From the 1938 collective agreement between the Eastern Women's Headwear Association and the United Hatters, Cap and Millinery Workers' International Union.

containing terms at least equivalent to the terms under which the Industrial Council is obliged to conduct its relations with the Union under the collective agreement between it and the Union.

Paragraph "Fifteenth" of the agreement between the Union and the Industrial Council provides that the Union may not enter into any contract, orally or in writing, expressed or implied, directly or indirectly, by reason whereof any firm engaged in the industry shall receive any benefit or aid not accorded to the members of the Industrial Council. The contract also provides specific limitations upon agreements with reference to independent employers requiring them to submit to the supervision of the Impartial Chairman of the Industry and that they be required to contribute to the maintenance of the collective machinery in the industry and to deposit cash security for the performance of the agreement on their part, based upon a schedule which takes into account the size of the shop and volume of business and requires that such contract shall not run longer than the period of the Union's agreement with the Council. The whole spirit of the contract and its history . . . unite in supporting the proposition that so far as the Union is concerned, it is to create, so far as possible, equitable conditions of competition under agreed terms between concerns engaged in this industry in which its members are employed. . . .

The Industrial Council complains that the Union has violated the terms of its agreement with them, as indicated above, by permitting its workers to be employed in shops of a number of manufacturers of children's clothes without any written contract and under very shadowy arrangements for the maintenance of Union standards. These concerns, as they stand today, are under no obligation to contribute to the expense of the organized industry. They are not amenable to industrial controls through the Impartial Chairman's office on complaints made against them. They are in substantial competition in a highly competitive branch of the industry, with some forty members of the Industrial Council. . . .

After due consideration the Board has concluded and decides that the complaint of the Industrial Council is justified and that if the Union permits its members to be employed by concerns in the coat and suit industry in the Metropolitan area, not now members of any association, under definite contractual relations with the Union in this industry, it should require an independent contract with each such concern, which contract should contain at least the substance of the terms now applicable to the Industrial Council with the usual provisions for security for the observance of their agreements to the

Union and subjecting them to the ordinary machinery of the industry, centering in the Impartial Chairman's office.[40]

Enforcement Failures in Nonassociation Shops

None of these devices guaranteed that separate contracts between unions and independent employers would be enforced as effectively as collective agreements were enforced against the organized manufacturers of an industry. In the first place, labor unions were not likely to be as vigilant in holding independent employers to their obligations. With inadequate assistance and limited financial backing, union officials could ill afford to exhaust their resources seeking out contract evasions in small isolated independent shops. The same expenditure of time and effort would produce more substantial results when applied to the larger shops of association members.

In the second place, union agents appointed to supervise the enforcement of contract standards in nonassociation shops were by the very nature of their jobs subject to less effective supervision. Assigned to jobs of less prestige, if not less pay, and operating alone beyond the light of publicity, these union business agents were more exposed to lucrative inducements for conniving at shop infractions of contract standards. Nor was the enforcement problem always solved by authorizing agents of the impartial machinery to visit and inspect the independent shops. Something more than good intentions was needed to enforce labor standards in small nonassociation shops that were repeatedly undergoing changes in character, production, personnel, and location. These slippery competitors required constant surveillance that was seldom forthcoming.

From the days of the first protocol, the organized manufacturers of the women's coat and suit trade have repeatedly charged the

---

[40]G. W. Alger, *Decisions,* Case no. 922 (no date). Copy filed in the Abelson papers.

Previously, the manufacturers of infants' and children's wear had organized the Infants' and Children's Wear Association but had been denied separate recognition by the union on the ground "that it would be for its best interests and [that] of the industry if they became a branch of the Industrial Council, at least so far as infants' clothing were concerned." Forced to negotiate with the union individually, these manufacturers had allegedly been given more favorable terms than those provided in the collective agreement for members of the Industrial Council. *Ibid.*

ILGWU with failing to prevent marked discrepancies in labor standards between association and nonassociation shops. Speaking for the organized manufacturers in 1913, J. H. Cohen asserted that "in Philadelphia and Cleveland and Toronto and in Boston, the Union has not yet succeeded in bringing the market up to our present level here." And what is more important, he added, "They have not succeeded in bringing the market level up in our own city." Two years later, these organized manufacturers who had been a party to the original Protocol of Peace alleged that union officials "either closed their eyes or their policemen slept on the beats while walking in the neighborhood of the shops outside the association."[41]

With no less vehemence, the dress and waist manufacturers in the early months of 1916 condemned the discrepancies that had developed between association shops and independent shops of their industry. "We are assailed on all sides by statements of discriminative inequality and proofs of more favorable adjustments in non-association shops," asserted officials of the Dress and Waist Manufacturers' Association through a letter to the ILGWU in January 1916. "The whole trend of adjustment in the association shops had been increasingly aggressive on the part of the union," so this letter continued. "Everything taking place in association shops is subject to the light of day. We work with the public opinion of an association daily enforcing standards."[42]

A month later, Mrs. Henry Moskowitz, chief clerk for the Dress and Waist Manufacturers' Association, descended to particulars. At a hearing before the industry's board of arbitration, she testified that she had examined about 450 independent contracts and had found 368 variations in 279 of them. Many of these differences, she stated, were in the vital area of wage scales that were below those set in the association contract. J. H.

---

[41]Cohen in *Minutes*, Board of Arbitrators... [women's coat and suit trade] (August 4, 1913), p. 494. Views of the cloak manufacturers in 1915 are from the *American Cloak and Suit Review*, Feb. 15, 1915, which also stated: "All the ingenuity and all the constructive work done by the association was in vain as long as it had to meet the competition of shops that neither maintained the Protocol hours nor worked under the Protocol scale," p. 297.

[42]*Women's Wear*, Jan. 19, 1916. "We have evidence of agreements made with manufacturers who have been granted to them the very concessions which this association has time and again argued with the union to secure and failed," *ibid*.

Cohen, counsel for the association, came to her support with numerous citations of union concessions granted independent firms but denied association members. Going still further, Cohen proposed to the board of arbitration a specific remedy for this infringement of protocol standards. He would have the board reverse some of its prior decisions favorable to the union.[43]

Deeply stirred by these charges that the union had failed to maintain a parity of labor standards between association and non-association shops, the board of arbitration rescinded its former decision awarding union members in association shops higher minimum wages, shorter maximum hours and improved overtime standards, and guaranteeing those members a continuation of piecework that at the time was more profitable than week work. "Stripping the situation of its technical features," observed J. H. Cohen, "this means, broadly, that the board of arbitration, when presented with the facts, accepts as a guiding principle that greater burdens are not to be imposed upon members of the association than the union can enforce against non-association competitors." The organized manufacturers were elated. "Probably never before," noted *Women's Wear*, February 26, 1916, "has a labor organization received a rebuke from the hands of a Board of Arbitration to equal that which was passed to the Ladies' Waist and Dressmakers' Union by Judge Julian W. Mack, Robert Bruere and Hamilton Holt, the members of the local board last night."[44]

Charges of growing discrepancies in labor standards between association and nonassociation shops received more official sanction when news began to leak out that the board of protocol standards — a joint agency representing the union, the association, and the public set up under the revised dress protocol of 1916 to insure uniform enforcement of standards — had found widespread differences in labor costs between association houses

---

[43] *Minutes,* Arbitration Proceedings between the Dress and Waist Manufacturers' Association and the ILGWU (Feb. 25, 1916), vol. 5, pp. 993–994 ff. "We want standards, not favors," Cohen asserted. "If we have no standards, then the whole game is not worth the candle." *Women's Wear,* Feb. 26, 1916.

[44] See *Minutes,* Arbitration Proceedings between the Dress and Waist Manufacturers' Association and the ILGWU (Feb. 25, 1916), vol. 5, pp. 1163–1281; and J. H. Cohen, "The Revised Protocol in the Dress and Waist Industry," in *Annals,* American Academy of Political and Social Science, January 1917, vol. 69, p. 193.

and independent firms. Partial results from the investigation, noted *Women's Wear,* July 13, 1916, "show that in many instances standards are an unknown quality in the non-association shops and that the supposed protocol conditions are a farce."

Wherever unions failed to keep up the enforcement of labor standards in nonassociation shops, demands were sure to arise for less rigid enforcement of labor standards in the plants of the organized manufacturers themselves. Faced with union concessions to independent shops, disgruntled association members directed complaints against their own organizations for insisting upon a rigorous enforcement of contract standards. In the mid-twenties, these complaints by members of the Industrial Council of Cloak, Suit and Skirt Manufacturers were summarized as follows:

Those who belong to the association feel, it is pointed out, that they are subjected to a two-way policing system that forces them to live up to every detail of the collective agreement while those in other organizations and outside of organization are able to "get away" with all manner of infractions of union rules. By this is meant that not only is the union able to keep a close check on conditions within manufacturing shops, but that the Industrial Council itself, through its agents, continually forces the members to observe the agreement with the union in full.[45]

Some manufacturers sought relief by proposing that the association negotiate a new collective agreement with the union. Others would give up their inside factories and enter the jobbing field. Still others preferred to sign individual contracts with the union on the assumption "that the enforcement of the contract would be in the hands of the union entirely rather than in the hands of the union and the Industrial Council." Whatever the official action taken on these proposals, the evidence shows that the enforcement of labor standards in association shops tended to fall

---

[45]*Women's Wear,* April 28, 1926. See also, statement of Samuel Blumberg, counsel for the Merchants' Ladies' Garment Association, in the March 8, 1926 issue.

It was pointed out time and again that the association has formed a sort of policeman for the union, and that whereas the association members have been forced to live up to union rules, others outside the association have been able "to get away" with all kinds of violations.
—*Ibid.,* May 25, 1924.

to the level of enforcement in the nonassociation shops. In the dress industry, the final tentative report of the board of protocol standards issued in early September 1916 showed that both association shops and nonassociation shops fell about equally short of protocol standards.[46]

One thing was certain: association members obviously could not withstand competition from independent shops that worked overtime when they could not, that resorted to piecework when they could not, that reduced established pay scales while they could not, that engaged in subcontracting while they could not, that reduced the size of their shops while the organized manufacturers could not. If, as the dress manufacturers' association contended in 1916, association firms were in fact "paying anywhere from 35 to 50% more to produce their merchandise than many others"; or if, as the fur manufacturers' association contended some twenty years later, the union "has utterly failed to suppress, unionize or impose the same labor conditions as are imposed upon our members, upon the direct competitors of members of our Association," — then the competitive disadvantage facing the organized manufacturers would appear to be overwhelming.[47]

Futility of Employer Attempts to Seek Relief

Yet an effective solution to the double standard of enforcement between independent shops and association shops was not easy to devise. The organized manufacturers could brandish the mailed

---

[46]The quotation is from *ibid.*, April 28, 1916. Information on the report of the board of protocol standards is from Lorwin, *The Women's Garment Workers,* pp. 105–109.

Under the terms of the 1937 collective agreement between the Full Fashioned Hosiery Manufacturers of America and the American Federation of Hosiery Workers — terms that were to apply "uniformly with full force and effect to each and every branch, body, or local of the union" — the failure of any union local to force independent firms to live up to the standards of the collective agreement for the industry would open the door to association members to get their goods from nonunion mills. For similar provisions in the 1938 agreement, see *Women's Wear Daily,* July 18, 1938.

[47]On the dress manufacturers, see *Women's Wear,* July 13, 1916. On the fur manufacturers, see Associated Fur Coat and Trimming Manufacturers' answer, dated Jan. 5, 1938, to union proposals for a new contract. A copy of this answer is filed in the Abelson papers.

fist by demanding their rights under the collective agreements, or they could extend the gloved hand by imploring the unions to observe their commitments toward independent shops. In the first case, the employer groups could hale labor unions before the highest tribunals of their industries, charge them with violating their contractual obligations, and perhaps gain the official right to abrogate the collective agreements. But to what end would all parties then re-embark upon the wild seas of unregulated competition? Or, in keeping with the mailed-fist policy, employers' associations might resort to direct action against unions and independent producers who undercut the standards for the trades. But here they would face the danger of falling into the clutches of the civil and criminal law, particularly state and federal statutes on restraint of trade.

An episode that involved the employers' mailed-fist policy to insure uniform standards of enforcement occurred in the women's coat and suit trade during the summer of 1930. By the terms of the 1929 collective agreements, members of the American Cloak and Suit Manufacturers' Association (contractors) were given exclusive rights to all the outside work of the organized jobbers (Merchants' Ladies' Garment Association) and the organized inside manufacturers (Industrial Council of Cloak, Suit and Skirt Manufacturers). When certain Brooklyn contractors formed the Brooklyn Ladies' Garment Manufacturers' Association and sought to obtain a share of this outside work, they were admitted into the orbits of the collective bargaining system only as an affiliated branch of the American association. For a time, all contracting work within the organized segment of the New York trade was divided equitably between the Manhattan association and the Brooklyn association.[48]

Then the Brooklyn association was charged with permiting

---

[48]On July 22, 1929, the American Cloak and Suit Manufacturers' Association and the Brooklyn Ladies' Garment Manufacturers' Association signed a three-year agreement whereby the Brooklyn group was bound to observe the same terms of employment and abide by the decisions of the same impartial machinery as did the Manhattan group. The Brooklynites yielded "unrestricted authority" to the Manhattanites in return for the "full advantage and benefit" of the Manhattan labor agreements. The American association could impose the same rules and take the same disciplinary action against Brooklyn members as it did against its own members. *Women's Wear Daily,* July 23, 1929.

substandard conditions to flourish in the shops of its members. Investigations by the Alger Cloak Control Commission (a special joint association-union agency set up under the 1929 collective agreements to enforce industry standards and stabilize the trade) had disclosed that 90 percent of the members of the Brooklyn association were operating below the standards of the collective agreements. Raymond Ingersoll, impartial chairman for the industry, was apprized of developments. "Although failure to keep proper books and records in those shops seems to amount to almost a system," so he wrote Harry Uviller, manager of the American association, "enough information was secured to show that piecework and other irregularities have been almost universal." The impartial chairman suggested that the American association reorganize the Brooklyn contractors or else admit them individually into the American association.[49]

When the American association chose, instead, to expel the Brooklyn group, it thereby denied these Brooklyn firms access to further work from the organized jobbers, contractors, and inside manufacturers of the trade. But the exiled Brooklyn contractors refused to accept their fate. Charging the ILGWU, the Alger Commission, and the three associations of jobbers, contractors, and inside manufacturers with operating under collective agreements that unreasonably restrained trade, the Brooklyn contractors sought and obtained from the courts a temporary injunction preventing interference with their right to bid for work. "The decision was a great surprise to all who guide the destinies of labor control in the coat and suit trade," reported *Women's Wear Daily* for July 29, 1930:

> Men high in association and impartial machinery circles regarded the granting of the injunction as a hard blow to all efforts to maintain wage and working standards, even if it is eventually vacated, because meanwhile the Brooklyn contract shops, already declared non-union and substandard, will continue to operate without union interference, under the court order, and influence a lowering of standards in Manhattan, according to authorities in the trade.
>
> At the same time, it is asserted, the stabilizing work of the Alger Commission, Impartial Chairman Raymond V. Ingersoll, the three coat associations and the union will be seriously hampered under the cloud and handicap of the injunction. . . .

---

[49]*Ibid.,* June 11, July 3, 1930. *New York Times,* July 29, 1930.

That the responsibility of maintaining union standards in Manhattan shops as well as those in Brooklyn, following the injunction decision of Justice Strong in Brooklyn, rests with the union is the statement of several leaders in coat manufacturing circles. These factors, who are strong in their criticism of the union's alleged failure properly to organize Brooklyn contract shops heretofore, claim that the union is the only element in the industry which has the power to prevent a complete breakdown of all labor standards in the stabilizing machinery that has been attempted the past year.[50]

While an appeal to extend the temporary injunction was still pending in the courts, the Manhattan contractors met with the Brooklyn contractors and signed a new agreement on January 20, 1931, reinstating the Brooklyn Ladies' Garment Manufacturers' Association as a branch of the American Cloak and Suit Manufacturers' Association, with all the obligations that had been imposed on the Brooklyn group by the original agreement. Almost immediately, the parent association complained that the Brooklyn contractors were again undermining labor standards. Again, the Brooklyn group refused to permit inspection of its plants. Nor would the Brooklyn association concede the right of the Manhattan group to impose disciplinary measures. Finally, in the fall of 1931 the American Cloak and Suit Manufacturers' Association sought and obtained from New York Supreme Court Justice S. A. Cotillo an injunction restraining the Brooklyn group from violating its agreement with the Manhattan association.[51]

If brandishing the mailed fist could be illegal, extending the gloved hand could be impotent. Experiences under the first collective agreement of the muff bed fur industry revealed the im-

---

[50]No injunction can compel a decent manufacturer or a decent jobber to give work to substandard shops or to racketeering shops. As for manufacturers and jobbers who are not decent and would like to see a return of the sweat shop system, the union has always fought them and will continue to fight them now.

—Benjamin Schlesinger, president of the ILGWU, as quoted in *Women's Wear Daily*, July 29, 1930.

[51]American Cloak and Suit Manufacturers' Association v. Brooklyn Ladies' Garment Manufacturers' Association, 143 Misc. 319 (1931), 255 N.Y. Supp. 614; *Women's Wear Daily*, Jan. 20–21, Oct. 15, and Nov. 25, 1931. "The decision means that there will be uniform control in the industry, which will greatly benefit the submanufacturers, the contractors, the jobbers and the inside manufacturers." Harry Uviller, general manager, American Cloak and Suit Manufacturers' Association, as quoted in *ibid.*, Nov. 24, 1931.

potence of the gloved-hand policy. Here the organized manufacturers who produced linings for fur muffs could not by sup-
plication or cajolery induce the fur workers' union to maintain
employer-group standards in the shops of independent firms. A
"most favored employer" clause in the three-year master contract,
effective September 12, 1914, between the Muff Bed Manufacturers' Association and Local 51, International Fur Workers'
Union, had pledged the Muff Bed Workers' Union to see that
in all other agreements with employers in Greater New York, "the
stipulated conditions of work and wages shall be in no way less
than the terms of this agreement." The union further obligated
itself "to the utmost of its ability and financial resources, with
due regard to local conditions, to endeavor to obtain these conditions in the entire industry in the country."[52]

Then followed a chain of events designed to induce union
compliance with these obligations. After the joint conference
committee of the impartial machinery created by the collective
agreement had adopted rules to implement the most favored
employer provisions of the master contract, the labor manager
for the employers, A. School, sent copies of the regulations to the
impartial chairman, to members of the employers' association,
and to A. W. Miller, president of the International Fur Workers'
Union. The association requested the union "to circulate a
similar letter among the Independent manufacturers, so that the
members of this Association shall feel that rules of such nature are
actually for the entire trade, and not as a result of their connection with this Association."[53]

Apparently the union did not comply with this request, for in
the course of a conference committee session some months later,
Mr. Miller conceded that the union's plan "for fully co-operating
in good faith with the Association" had been neglected. Under
pressure from the manufacturers, he solemnly promised the
conference committee "that from now on the union would fully
co-operate with the association," in holding independent shops to
association standards. At that session, Miller supported a motion
that the committee on immediate action operating under the
master contract "at once hold a meeting in order to work out

---

[52]A copy of this agreement is filed in the Abelson papers.

[53]A. School to Leo Mannheimer, letter dated Jan. 29, 1915, filed in the
Abelson papers.

a practical plan for establishing conditions in the Muff Bed Industry in accordance with the terms and spirit of the Agreement of 1914."[54]

Following these instructions, the committee on immediate action conducted an investigation and reported back to a special meeting of the conference committee held on August 2, 1915. Almost a year had passed since the master agreement became effective, yet the union had made little progress in fulfilling its obligations toward the independent shops over which it had control. But there was still hope, for the committee on immediate action reported that "the representatives of the Union agree to bring about a higher degree of co-operation" and that the union "promises to make an immediate investigation of the Muff Bed Shops which are not members of the Association in order to bring their standards up to those in the Association." The committee further reported that the union had again guaranteed "to take such action as will insure the full performance of the terms of the Agreement."[55]

Meanwhile, the organized manufacturers were despairing of hope from reliance on its gloved-hand policy. On July 21, 1915, the manager of the employers' association dispatched a letter of a different tone to the chairman of the conference committee:

We can cite many instances where neither the time nor wage conditions are even approximated by shops outside of this organization. There is such complete lack of control among those who have signed up direct with the Union, as well as those who have not signed with any, that our members find themselves in the exceedingly embarrassing position of being tied up by an Agreement which makes it impossible for them to compete successfully in this field. It is not only impossible to compete while living up to the present standards, but conditions outside of the organization have become so demoralized that it would be difficult to compete successfully even if this organization were to be working on conditions prevailing before the new conditions were established.

All of this we respectfully submit to the Conference Committee, being ready to establish our charges by positive proof. Inasmuch as we believe that the uniformity and standardization that can be made

---

[54]*Minutes,* Meeting of the Conference Committee of the Muff Bed Industry July 27, 1915, p. 66, filed in the Abelson papers.

[55]*Ibid.,* August 2, 1915, p. 69.

possible by properly conducted methods on the part of the Union, and in fact by their mere observance of the spirit of their oral agreement, would be of the utmost benefit to the Muff Bed Industry, we call upon the Conference Committee to proceed without further delay whatever to bring about these conditions.[56]

Concluding Observations

Controlling competition by means of uniform work standards to equalize labor costs was difficult enough when limited to inside establishments under the watchful eyes of employers' associations and labor unions operating through the impartial machinery of their trade. But the task became infinitely more complicated with the rise of the jobber-contracting system. Yet in so far as jobbers and contractors were organized and brought within the realm of law and order, collective agreements and their permanent institutions of administration could embrace the "legitimate" jobbers and contractors, as well as the inside manufacturers. Presumably, mutual self-interest among these organized groups would operate to enforce labor standards within their ranks.

Beyond these organized forces, however, were numerous independent producers who roamed at large preying upon the advantages of unregulated competition. Here the lines of group responsibility for maintaining uniform work standards became more tenuous. Only the union could act directly against independents with whom it negotiated contracts. Only through the union could the organized jobbers, contractors, and inside manufacturers get a foot in the door of the independent shop. Nevertheless, these employer groups took full advantage of their limited opportunities. Through "most favored employer" clauses in collective agreements, they virtually dictated to the union the terms and conditions of employment for nonassociation shops. Through other appropriate clauses, the organized employers directed the union to see that independents were brought, willy-nilly, under the impartial machinery of the collective agreement. If the organized employers could not force independents into associations by subjecting them to the obligations of collective agreements while denying them the benefits, then at least inde-

---

[56]A. School to S. J. Rosensohn, chairman of the conference committee, letter, dated July 21, 1915, filed in the Abelson papers.

pendent producers with separate union contracts should be denied the alleged advantages of remaining outside the fold.

On the whole, unions of the needle trades were more willing than able to play ball with the manufacturers. Unfortunately, the responsibilities that unions assumed toward independents were not matched by a corresponding power to keep independents in line. The small-time contractor hidden away in a loft or basement with his loyal, though unionized, labor force was the graveyard of union discipline. Nor did unions always live up to their capabilities. A chance to sacrifice uniform labor standards for personal profit was too much for some union agents assigned to police independent shops. The tides of contract enforcement varied widely among independent firms bound by separate labor agreements. Some independents suffered more severely from strict enforcement of their contracts than did their organized competitors under collective agreements. But, for the most part, unions could not prevent independents with separate labor agreements from burrowing beneath the floors of legitimate competition.

Chapter 13

Competition from

Nonunion Sources

FAILURE to extend the work standards of collective agreements into nonassociation shops bound by separate union contracts was attributed, in part, to competition from other sources still further removed from the highly organized centers of each trade. Beyond the unionized shops of the independent producers were other shops in which neither the employers nor the workers were organized. These wholly unorganized shops undercut the standards of independent employers operating under separate union contracts — just as these independent shop owners undercut the standards of the association shops in which both employers and workers were fully organized. Trapped between pressures to meet the higher standards of the association-union shops, on the one hand, and the necessity of competing with the lower standards of wholly unorganized shops, on the other, these half-organized shops — those with unions but no employers' associations — were threatened with extinction. Unable to meet the objectives of the one or to fight off the competition of the other, they played the role of smaller fleas having lesser fleas to bite them.

Like successive waves from a pebble dropped into a pool, groups of "illegitimate" competitors radiated out from the organized core of each industry centered in the heart of New York City. The association-union shops of Manhattan Island were surrounded by the independent but "unionized" shops of the New York Metropolitan District; and these shops, in turn, were surrounded by independent, nonunion shops of other towns and cities. As a rule, the farther shops were removed from the needle trade centers of Manhattan the more ruthless the competition they offered the "legitimate" manufacturers and their organized labor force.

It soon became apparent that employers' associations and labor unions bent on preserving the protocol system of controlled competition would need to focus their sights upon the totally unorganized segments of their trades. "More important than enforcing agreements," stated J. H. Cohen, counsel for the manufacturers and guiding spirit of the protocol movement, in his 1914 brief to the U. S. Commision on Industrial Relations, "is the problem of extending agreements to end competition between employers within the association and those without." He argued that the sole remedy for controlling nonassociation firms employing nonunion workers lay with the union and its power to strike. He cited the experiences of Great Britain and quoted as follows from a report by the British Industrial Council: "Where a considerable minority is outside the association and the union is not sufficiently strong to control them, real danger exists that the agreement cannot be maintained."[1]

Yet the evils of which Cohen warned were to multiply rather than diminish. Ten years later, the organized manufacturers were railing with more fury than ever against competition from the unorganized firms that the union had failed to control. "Within a few blocks in this busy metropolis," heatedly announced William Klein, counsel for the Cloak, Suit and Skirt Manufacturers' Protective Association, in 1924, "are countless numbers of sub-manufacturers and shops working . . . all hours of the day and night, Sundays and holidays, under no restraint, and under a piece-work or any other kind of a system, and are turning out, on an overburdened industry, a far greater quantity of cloaks and suits than the industry really requires." Lambasting the union for not organizing and controlling these shops, while association firms were held to strict accountability, this voice of the manufacturers continued: "Why compel our association, with its 178 members, employing, as you say, 10,000 men, to compete with 3000 shops

---

[1] J. H. Cohen, "A Constructive Program" (pamphlet) in New York City Public Library.

employing, as you say, 30,000 workers, under such conditions? Why give us conditions so terribly more onerous than other shops not in our association, and permit these other shops to compete with us on the question of labor against labor?"[2]

Participants in the Brandeis Conferences of 1910 had solemnly resolved to expand the number of organized manufacturers and to extend the ranks of organized labor until collective agreements negotiated between unions and employers' associations would automatically cover every shop of the women's coat and suit trade. The framers of the first protocols clearly anticipated that the terms of their collective agreements would ultimately embrace every manufacturing establishment in their respective industries. They firmly believed that the impartial machinery created for each trade would soon spell out the conditions of employment governing the daily conduct of all direct competitors in the manufacturing process.

Union Security Clauses

Attempts to achieve complete organization of employers and workers for each industry formed an important chapter in the history of collective bargaining for the needle trades. In this long-drawn-out struggle, the decisive battle should have been won at the Brandeis Conferences of 1910 where the protocol idea was born, for the first protocols were founded on the premise that employers' associations and labor unions would be strong enough to maintain law and order in their respective trades. To thwart the growth or impair the strength of either organization was to defeat the purposes of the protocol movement. To encourage the growth and promote the strength of either organization was to open a highway to the goals of collective action. Perhaps the greatest victory of this campaign was won at the outset when the principle of complete organization was initially accepted by both sides as a prerequisite for effective action.

The most difficult phase of the campaign to organize all industry consisted in winning the support of employers and employers' associations for the growth and expansion of labor unions. The new approach to collaboration with unions initiated at the Brandeis Conferences had constituted a virtual revolution in

---

[2]*Women's Wear,* April 1, 1924.

management thinking. Not all loyal association members, who considered themselves the "legitimate" manufacturers of their trade, saw eye to eye on the policy of strengthening labor unions for the good of the industry. Brought up in the antiunion tradition, even the "respectable" employers hesitated to accept a new bedfellow they had previously spurned. Although the idea of hiring union men only was consistent with the principles introduced at the Brandeis Conferences, this fundamental tenet of union security had to be compromised in the first Protocol of Peace.

The Brandeis invention of a "preferential union shop" sweetened the pill of union security for the hesitant employers, without substantially changing their attitudes toward the union. Brandeis himself explained that his idea was based on the assumption that "unions should be so strengthened that in the course of time they might have practically all, if not all, of the operatives in the shops as their members." This ultimate objective was thinly veiled in the final wording of the first preferential union shop clause. For the term *union shop* was there defined as "a shop where union standards as to working conditions, hours of labor, and rates of wages as herein stipulated prevail," while the phrase *union men are preferred* was elaborated to grant employers "freedom of selection as between one union man and another." In addition, this first protocol stated that the manufacturers "declare their belief in the union, and that all who desire its benefits should share in its burdens."[3]

Adopted in a number of other agreements, the preferential union shop clause was soon strengthened by interpretation or amendment. A literal construction of the original clause would appear to limit preferences to union members at the time of hiring only. But those who supported the objectives of the protocol movement insisted that the intent of the clause was to

---

[3] J. H. Cohen, counsel for the manufacturers, in his *Law and Order in Industry* (1916) at p. 147 pointed out that the issue of applying the preferential union shop clause was not over the substitution of a nonunion man for a union man but over the substitution of one union man for another. On the development and analysis of the preferential union shop clause, with frequent references to the views of Brandeis, see the extended discussions in *Minutes,* Council of Conciliation . . . [women's coat and suit trade] (Feb. 16 and 18, 1916), vol. 9, pp. 210–274, 316–365.

give union men preferences so long as they were employed, including preferences in retention at the time of layoffs. Such interpretations appreciably strengthened the position of the union in the shop and soon led to corresponding changes in the collective agreements themselves.[4]

Once the protocol movement had survived its early critics, the preferential union shop clause was supplanted by "closed shop" provisions that required the employment of union members only. This development was less a product of growing union strength than evidence of changing employer attitudes toward the needle trade unions. "The Association that fought so bitterly against the 'closed shop,'" so J. A. Dyche, general secretary-treasurer of the ILGWU, stated before his 1914 union convention, "in the end practically helped the Union to completely unionize their [*sic*] factories. The preferential shop turned into a complete Union shop."[5]

Union Members in Good Standing

Some of the early union security clauses were substantially nullified by disloyal workers who became union members in

----

[4]A "Preferential Union Shop" is hereby defined to be a shop in which standards of safety, sanitation, working conditions, hours of labor and rates of wages herein specified, prevail, and in which members of the Union in good standing shall be preferred in the hiring, employment and retention of help, and in the distribution of work.

—From the 1919 collective agreement of the Dress and Waist Manufacturers' Association with the ILGWU and its Locals 10, 25, and 58. Text of the agreement is printed in *Women's Wear*, April 9, 1919.

[5]ILGWU, *Report and Proceedings, Twelfth Convention* (June 1914), p. 49. The first collective agreement of the Associated Fur Manufacturers with the fur workers' union, effective September 8, 1912, contained no clause giving a preference to union members. The second agreement, effective July 1, 1914, prohibited discrimination against union members, while the third agreement for the industry, effective April 2, 1917, incorporated the closed shop provision limiting employees to union members only. Other early closed shop provisions may be found in the 1913 collective agreement of the West Side Retail Clothing Manufacturers' Association with the United Garment Workers, in the 1913 collective agreement of the Textile Union Finishers' Association with the Cloth Examiners and Spongers' Union, and in the 1915 collective agreement between the National Association of Men's Neckwear Manufacturers and the United Neckwear Cutters' Union, Local 6939 of the American Federation of Labor.

name only, paying no union dues, attending no union meetings, and observing no union laws. To meet these subterfuges, contract clauses on union security were strengthened by requiring all workers to keep up their "good standing" in the union. No person could be employed unless he was a union member in good standing, nor could he hold his job unless he remained a union member in good standing. Under collective agreements, a union member in good standing was variously defined as one who not only carried a union membership card but who "has complied with all the rules and regulations of the Union" or who "has fully paid up his dues or assessments, or who is in arrears for not more than two months in the payment of dues or assessments." Ex-unionists were sometimes expressly barred from employment until they had regained their good standing in the union.[6]

Additional contract clauses were sometimes incorporated to facilitate the enforcement of union security provisions. To insure that only union members would be hired, some collective agreements directed manufacturers to apply to their association for new workers. The employers' association then made arrange-

---

[6]A member in good standing is one who has fully paid up his dues or assessments, or who is in arrears for not more than two months in the payment of dues or assessments, to the International Ladies' Garment Workers' Union, and who carries a Union membership card.
—From the 1924 collective agreement between the Pleaters' and Stitchers' Association and Local 41, ILGWU.

No fancy leather goods worker shall be employed who was previously a member of the Fancy Leather Goods Workers' Union and subject to discipline under its rules, until he has been reinstated in good standing, and by good standing is meant a member of the Union who has complied with all the rules and regulations of the union.
—From the 1921 collective agreement between the Associated Leather Goods Manufacturers and Local 5, Fancy Leather Goods' Workers.

The members of the Association requiring help shall apply to the Association, which in turn, shall arrange with the Union for the adequate supply of such help.
—From the 1926 collective agreement of the Wholesale Hat and Cap Manufacturers' Association with the Joint Council of New York of the Cloth Hat, Cap and Millinery Workers' International Union. Text is printed in the union's *Report and Proceedings*, Sixteenth Biennial Convention (May 1927), Appendix no. 1, pp. 224–225.

ments with the union for the help requested. Other agreements required association members to apply directly to the union employment office for additional help. Short of requiring employers to hire through the union office, many contracts obligated manufacturers to see that their newly chosen workers held valid union cards showing their good standing in the union at the time of their employment. Those without proper cards were to obtain such cards within a matter of hours. Some agreements directed employers to send their prospective workers to the union for "working cards" made out to the individual firm. In fur manufacturing during the thirties, all union members were required every three months to obtain new working cards giving their names and signature, as well as the name of the firm for which they were working.

A number of collective agreements further outlined the procedures for checking union membership to determine the good standing of workers in the shops. A typical clause authorized joint inspection under arrangements worked out by some agency of the impartial machinery. "The Conference Committee," stated the 1919 collective agreement of the fur manufacturing industry, "may arrange for periodic inspection by a representative of the Association and a representative of the Union of such shops of the Association as are subjects of complaint to determine whether all workers are in good standing in the union." Under some agreements, the union alone was authorized to examine the status of union membership. In either case, those found to have lost their good standing had to be discharged by their employers at the request of the union.[7]

Failure to enforce these provisions in association shops brought

[7]See the 1919 collective agreement of the Associated Fur Manufacturers with the Fur Workers' International Union and the Joint Board of Furriers' Unions of Greater New York.

> The members of the Association shall cease to employ any and all employees who are not members of the said Union in good standing, and who do not conform to and comply with the Constitution or other laws or regulations of said Union whenever the employer is notified to that effect by the representatives of the Union.
> —From the 1934 collective agreement between the Fur Manufacturers' Protective Association of Philadelphia and the Fur Workers' International Union.

In the 1929 collective agreement between the Industrial Council of Cloak, Suit and Skirt Manufacturers and the ILGWU, the union for the first time

perennial complaints from union leaders who supported the movement to regulate competition. Morris Hillquit, spokesman for the ILGWU, who often reiterated his belief that strong unions, as well as strong associations, were the foundation of the protocol movement, could see no hope for strong unions so long as the organized manufacturers refused to discharge workers for failure to meet their union obligations. Presenting his complaint to Mayor J. P. Mitchel's council of conciliation for the women's coat and suit industry in February 1916, Hillquit explained that the union could strike against the presence of delinquent union members in nonassociation shops.

But in association shops, where unions were denied the right to strike, union action against delinquent union members was largely limited to the imposition of fines, with no effective recourse against those failing to accept this penalty. Even though unions held that delinquent members refusing to pay their union fines within a specified time automatically ceased to be union members, they were still helpless to enforce discipline unless delinquent workers were thrown out of employment. Not even union members violating the protocol could be adequately punished, Hillquit contended, if the organized employers refused to discharge those workers failing to accept union penalties for contract infractions.[8]

Hiring Outside Help

Other clauses undertook to minimize the inevitable confusion which resulted from permitting employers to hire nonunion workers where unions could not meet the demands for help. Few

was officially accorded the right to visit the shops of the association members once a year expressly to examine the union standing of the workers.

[8]The Association promises to give preference in employment to members of the Union and to only members of the Union who are certified by the Union to be in good standing, and on a notification from the Union that an employee is not in good standing or no longer a member of the Union to discharge said employee or have said employee discharged at the end of the day or week as the case may be when the term of such employment shall end.

—From the 1913 collective agreement between the Textile Union Finishers' Association and the Cloth Examiners' and Spongers' Union of Greater New York.

See also, *Minutes,* Council of Conciliation . . . [women's coat and suit trade] (Feb. 16, 1916), vol. 9, pp. 232–294; and *Women's Wear,* Feb. 17–19, 23–24, 1916.

closed shop provisions failed to acknowledge the necessity of permitting manufacturers to hire nonunion workers in the open market where competent union members were not available. Yet this exception to the rule of employing only union members created a hole in the dike of union security that at times threatened to engulf all organized labor. For the question of what amounted to "competent" help, or of what constituted a "reasonable opportunity" in which to provide competent help, opened the door to endless evasions of employer responsibility toward the employment of union members.

Several types of provisions were introduced to limit the potential evils of having to employ outside help. The most obvious, as well as the most common, type of clause required outside workers to join the union within a limited period of time after employment or lose their jobs. Other clauses gave the union a certain number of hours — 24, 48, or 72 — in which to find the help requested; only thereafter was the employer permitted to look elsewhere. Some clauses reduced the incentive to look elsewhere for help either by compelling employers to pay outside workers the same wages that union members would have received or by requiring that outside help be discharged as soon as regular union members became available. Many clauses omitted the word "competent" from the help that unions were called upon to supply, and in at least one case the collective agreement prohibited the manufacturers from hiring outside help "as long as the 'Union' shall have on hand ready to be furnished to the 'Firm' any help irrespective as to what class such help may belong."[9]

---

[9]From the 1929 collective agreement between the Associated Employers of Fur Workers and the International Fur Workers' Union and its Locals 2 and 3.

> In the event that the Union cannot supply competent workers within forty-eight (48) hours after formal request is made, the employer may secure such workers from other sources, it being understood, however, that the employer shall pay to such workers the same scale of wages as hereinafter set forth and that such workers, when such workers so request, shall become members of the Union within fifteen (15) days after their employment; should, however, such workers fail or refuse to make such request, then and in that event if the Union can within fifteen (15) days after their employment replace them by competent help from the Union, such outside workers shall be discharged by the employer immediately upon such replacement.

Extra Protection for Union Officials

Many collective agreements also gave special consideration to union officials and shop representatives. In fur manufacturing, for example, the position of shop chairman was first recognized by resolution of the conference committee under the original collective agreement of 1912. After a provision on the shop chairman had been incorporated into the collective agreement of 1914, the conference committee resolved "that members of the Associated Fur Manufacturers, Inc., be instructed that inasmuch as a shop chairman is provided for each shop by the agreement, it is incumbent upon members of the Association to facilitate the election of such chairman." Contracts that required the presence of a shop chairman in each shop by inference precluded the employer from laying off the person elected to that position.[10]

Most early collective agreements limited the functions of shop chairmen to the collection of dues, doubtless because other union officials shared with employer representatives a joint responsibility for visiting the shops and investigating alleged contract infractions. But the 1918 collective agreement of the Associated Mirabeau Manufacturers with Local 74, International Fur Workers, authorized the shop chairman not only to collect dues

---

—From the 1929 collective agreement of the full fashioned hosiery industry. Text is printed in *Women's Wear Daily,* Sept. 6, 1929.

Other interesting clauses on the employment of outside help can be found in the 1929 collective agreement of the United Shirt Manufacturers' Association with the ACWA, the 1931 collective agreement of the New York Clothing Manufacturers' Exchange with the ACWA, and the 1925 collective agreement of the Association of Dress Manufacturers with the ILGWU.

[10]*Minutes,* Conference Committee of the fur manufacturing industry (Sept. 21, 1913 and Sept. 1, 1914), filed in the Abelson papers.

The Associated Fur Manufacturers issued instruction to its members outlining the procedures to be followed in facilitating the election of union shop chairmen. See letter, dated Sept. 2, 1914, from D. C. Mills, association manager, to the member firms, filed in the Abelson papers.

> There shall be at all times in the shop of the employer a shop chairman elected by the union members of the shop at a shop meeting called for the purpose, in the presence of a representative of the union. The shop chairman is to act as a representative of the employees in all their dealings with the employer.
> —From the 1925 collective agreement of the Association of Dress Manufacturers with the ILGWU. Text is printed in *Women's Wear,* Jan. 19, 1925.

from union members but also "to see that the provisions of the agreement were lived up to by both parties," and "to peacefully enlist these non-union workers in the shops of the manufacturers to join the Union." As a representative of the union and of the workers in the shop, the shop chairman had to maintain lines of communication with union headquarters and to perform the duties the union imposed upon him.

The types of union security clauses that prohibited employers from discriminating against union members in general were most likely to benefit officially chosen union representatives who played a more active role in the shops. Particularly were contract clauses forbidding discrimination for "union activities" or for "insisting upon a strict enforcement of the contract" more likely to offer protection to aggressive union agents than to other workers. General prohibitions forbidding antiunion discrimination in the employment, transfer, or retention of personnel also were used most frequently on behalf of union agents in the shops.[11]

The better to free union agents from the fear of reprisals that might arise from their work in the shops, some unions insisted upon extra concessions offering protection to union officers beyond that accorded union members in general. Such was the request that union officials, unlike union members in general, should be given a hearing in discharge cases to determine "just cause" before they were discharged. While denying this request in 1916, Judge J. W. Mack on behalf of the board of arbitration for the dress and waist industry nevertheless acknowledged a peculiar status to be accorded union representatives in the shops:

However, it must be recognized that the shop chairman, assistant shop chairman, and members of the price committee are in a different position from the other employees. In performing such duties they act in a representative capacity. The very performance of those duties

---

[11]It is agreed, however, that in the employment or discharge of workers, there shall be no discrimination against Union workers, nor against any Union worker because of his peaceful and orderly conduct of Union propaganda outside of working hours, nor against any employee because of his orderly insistence upon the strict observance of the terms of the agreement.

—From the 1914 collective agreement of the Associated Fur Manufacturers' Association with the International Fur Workers' Union and the Joint Board of the Furriers' Union of Greater New York.

may, at times, compel them to take positions that might tend to cause their discharge. Complaints by them of wrongful discharge should, for this reason, be given an immediate hearing in priority to other grievances that may be pending.

We therefore award that complaints of the wrongful discharge of a shop chairman, assistant shop chairman, or a member of the price committee shall be taken up for immediate hearing and adjustment in priority to other complaints pending in the shop.[12]

Association Support for Union Expansion

If labor unions were to enjoy the prestige necessary for expansion, however, their leaders had to be openly encouraged and their organizations actively supported. Historically, union security clauses had been little more than a defense mechanism wrung, like the Great Charter at Runnymede, from a reluctant tyrant. Provisions for hiring union members only and for protecting union members from discrimination had been forced upon employers by their organized workers long before the era of the protocols. Brought over from union-drafted individual contracts, these stock clauses were incorporated into collective agreements of the protocol era more from custom than from hope.

Regardless of the closed shop or other formal union security provisions, the workers wanted assurances that their employers openly accepted labor unions. "We must have the full and honest co-operation of the employers more than in any other industry," asserted Meyer London, counsel for the fur workers' international union in 1913. Where men work for only four months a year, so London observed, the worker is afraid to belong to the union if he has the slightest suspicion that his employer is against the union. "If his employer opposes the Union, he [the worker] will have nothing to do with the Union; he will not hear of it; he will not be seen near the Union so as not to get in bad favor with his employer."[13]

The manufacturers were well aware of their power over the

---

[12]This award was printed in *Women's Wear,* Feb. 28, 1916. Some collective agreements did provide that union agents should be given a hearing by the impartial machinery for the administration of the contract before they were discharged.

[13]*Minutes,* Conference between Representatives of the Fur Manufacturers' Association and the Furriers' Union of Greater New York and Vicinity (Sept. 29, 1913), p. 52.

workers. They knew that no collection of union security clauses would offset open hostility toward the union as an institution. "You cannot make a union man out of a non-union man," admitted J. H. Cohen, counsel for several employers' associations, "without the co-operation of the employer — unless you get the co-operation spiritually with the employers." The chief problem of union growth, therefore, was to create this spirit of cooperation and to convince the workers that it existed.

The laws of self-interest provided an incentive for employer cooperation in union membership drives. Failure to eliminate the nonunion worker was as fatal to the cause of "legitimate" competition as was failure to control the independent employer who refused to join his association. Fear of competition from the unorganized workers hampered every move of the enlightened leadership on both sides to solidify the organized forces of industry. Only an all-inclusive participation by workers as well as by employers could insure an all-inclusive victory for the advocates of law and order. "We but express the consensus of opinion of all groups in the market," stated Felix Frankfurter and S. J. Rosensohn, summarizing their study, *Survey of the New York [men's] Clothing Industry,* dated May 28, 1920, "in saying that without the exercise of joint control a chaos of unbridled, abnormal competition would have existed in the market."[14]

With more and more evidence of the need for an all-inclusive union to standardize the terms of employment and check unfair trade practices, leadership in the battle to win employer support for a thoroughly organized labor force shifted from union headquarters to the headquarters of employers' associations. "Every reasonable effort should be made by members to induce their employees to join the union," runs an editorial in the *Dress and Waist Bulletin,* official organ of the dress manufacturers in 1913. "A strong union will be a benefit to the manufacturers, and members of the association should make every effort to increase the membership in the union so that its officers may have complete control of the workers and be enabled to discipline them when necessary. With half the shop union and the other half non-

---

[14]The quotation is from the text of this survey as given at pp. 39–40 in a printed collection of union affidavits submitted in the case of J. Friedman & Co. v. ACWA, New York Supreme Court, New York County (1921). A copy of this collection is filed in the Abelson papers.

union, it is easy to be seen that this is impossible and that friction is bound to result."[15]

"We need a strong union in this industry," observed Walter Drew, legal counsel for the New York Clothing Manufacturers' Association of the men's clothing industry in 1919, "and we hope to help to make it strong and keep it strong." His association was seeking protection "against the unfair and unscrupulous employer who won't maintain proper standards," and it favored a strong union to ward off illegitimate competitors. "I think in last analysis," continued Drew, testifying before an advisory board of distinguished citizens, "the manufacturers are just as much interested as the union in keeping a strong, effective union in this market, because there are manufacturers who need to be disciplined and held in line and the progressive manufacturers need a strong union to help them discipline those in their own ranks who perhaps would not observe proper standards otherwise."[16]

---

[15]As quoted in C. H. Winslow, *Conciliation, Arbitration, and Sanitation in the Dress and Waist Industry of New York City*, U.S. Department of Labor, BLS Bulletin no. 145 (April 10, 1914), p. 37.

> The manufacturers' association has no quarrel with trade unions. It believes that the trade union has done much for the industry. It believes that it can do more through the wage-scale boards, through boards of sanitary control, and through the apprenticeship agreements with the cutters.... The association of cloak manufacturers believes in trade-unionism; it believes in collective bargaining; it believes in voluntary arbitration as a means of settling controversies between employers and employees.
>
> —J. H. Cohen, testimony before the U.S. Commission on Industrial Relations, Jan. 16, 1914, in the Commission's *Final Report and Testimony* (1916), vol. 2, pp. 1116, 1129.

[16]From the testimony of Walter Drew before an advisory board of W. Z. Ripley, Felix Frankfurter, and Louis Marshall, as reported in a statement, dated Feb. 5, 1921, of J. S. Potofsky, assistant general secretary, ACWA, given in a printed collection of union affidavits submitted in the case of J. Friedman & Co. v. ACWA, New York Supreme Court, New York County (1921), pp. 64–65. Copy filed in the Abelson papers.

> In order to bring this [law and order] about, the manufacturers recognize the fact that the Union must be preserved and maintained upon a strong and efficient basis, so that it can control its own people and carry out its side of any plan entered into. Instead of harboring any purpose to weaken or destroy the Union, our Association is willing to assist in any proper measures to maintain and strengthen it.
>
> The manufacturers . . . are equally interested with the workers in main-

Several years later, when the Communists in the needle trades gained control of the Cloakmakers' Joint Board in New York City and virtually wrecked the ILGWU, the organized employers of the women's coat and suit industry had the chance of a lifetime to escape the entanglements of their labor unions. Some would take advantage of this opportunity. But Samuel Klein, executive director of the Industrial Council of Cloak, Suit and Skirt Manufacturers (successor to the association that had signed the original Protocol of Peace) was quick to point out the evil effects of union disintegration upon the women's coat and suit trade. Addressing the annual meeting of his association in February 1928, Klein, on whom the cloak of J. H. Cohen, leading proponent of the protocol movement, had fallen, spoke as follows:

It is a known fact and admitted by everyone in private conversations that never since 1910 has there been such reckless and criminal cutthroat competition as now exists in the industry, which is attributable solely to the caving in of the union's strength. Were this chaos to be completed by the union eliminating itself, simply because of our protests that we cannot live under the agreement because of prevailing conditions, the result would be beyond imagination and would reflect itself throughout the entire industry and retailing of ready to wear.

I have noticed that whenever a firm charges that the Industrial Council is the sole source of strengthening the union, the charge is uttered by one who temporarily, because of the union's weakness from internal dissension, is enabled to enter into collusive bargains with his workers and thereby profits at the expense of his fellow manufacturers.[17]

When the three-year agreement of this industry came up for renewal in 1929, the organized manufacturers, far from renouncing support for labor organizations, insisted upon doing business with

---

taining proper conditions of work and in eliminating the vicious and disastrous competition which develops when the observance of proper standards is not secured by some central control. They are willing to join with the Union in maintaining such control as to make such competition and a subsequent lowering of work standards impossible.
—Max Friedman, president of the American Men's and Boys' Manufacturers' Association, to Jacob Schiff, letter, dated Dec. 27, 1918, quoted in ACWA, *Report and Proceedings,* Fourth Biennial Convention (May 1920), p. 21.
[17]*Women's Wear Daily,* Feb. 23, 1928.

a "real union" — one that would have sufficient strength to enforce standards upon the industry. "We were, indeed, fully aware of the weakened condition of the union," later explained Samuel Klein. "Rather than take advantage of that helplessness and create further disorganization, we sat down with its leaders and conferred with them in behalf of a new agreement and vouchsafed our support to the strengthening of the demoralized union. We did that because we believed that a powerful union and a correspondingly powerful association would be the most effectual means of reestablishing high standards in our industry."[18]

Contract Clauses Promoting Union Growth

Wherever such statements of prounion policy were translated into appropriate clauses of collective agreements, the objective was not to concede minimum union privileges but to promote maximum union growth. Such clauses were not introduced to preserve the bare life of the union but to help it flower into maturity. Why else would a collective agreement declare it to be the "duty" of a union, as well as the "right" of a union, to represent all the workers of an industry? Or why else would an employers' association be granted the power *on its own motion* to "investigate any or all of the books and records of its members to ascertain whether they are giving work [to] or dealing with nonunion shops?" Why else would an employer group seek approval of a union before admitting another employer to association

---

[18]*Ibid.*, June 29, 1929 and August 6, 1930. "Are we to complete annihilation of the industry fostered by internal dissensions in the labor ranks, or are we to go on with the union as a partner?" so Klein had argued in support of the proposed 1929 master contract for the organized factions of the industry. "... The new agreement will aid in stabilizing the trade. It is an instrument ... which solves the ever-present problem of the independent in relation to the association member.... It takes care of the members who leave the association.... It safeguards the investment of manufacturers and jobbers." *Ibid.*, July 16, 1929.

Strong support for labor unions in the dress industry came from Louis Schwartz, a director of the Association of Dress Manufacturers (see *ibid.*, July 22, 1929), and from Mortimer Lanzit, executive director of the National Dress Manufacturers' Association, who, several years later, wrote to the industry's impartial chairman, Harry Uviller, in part as follows: "One of the essentials for a prosperous dress industry is one STRONG UNION. Another essential is one STRONG EMPLOYER ASSOCIATION." *Ibid.*, Sept. 29, 1936.

membership? Or why else should the contracting parties agree that the fines collected for violations of their commitments must go into a fund to be administered jointly by the association and the union for the purpose of organizing the industry?

Wherever both parties mutually pledged themselves to "co-operate in good faith to strengthen each other," wherever the organized employers recognized "the moral obligation of every worker in the industry to belong to the union," wherever a manufacturers' association agreed "that every member of the association will do everything in his power to induce the workers to belong to the union," in all such cases the inferences were strong that the organized employers were not only tolerating labor unions but accepting them with open arms. Clauses of this general tenor, widely scattered throughout collective agreements of the needle trades, date back to the original protocols. The dress and waist protocol, effective January 18, 1913, recognized the value "of an organization representing the workers in the industry," while the protocol for the white goods (ladies' under-wear) industry, effective February 17, 1913, officially acknowl-edged the necessity for a "strong union."[19]

Further to promote the growth of unions, certain labor agree-ments specifically exempted organizing strikes from the coverage of nonstrike clauses. These exceptions to the general rule against striking could be initiated by the union itself or by the union with the sanction of the impartial chairman for an industry. In either case, the belief that a general strike might succeed in or-ganizing the workers of an industry released the union from the no-strike pledge, and permitted it to proceed with an organizing drive without incurring a breach of contract. Permission to shut down an entire industry, including the shops already organized, gave the union an opportunity to show its strength. The organized shops soon returned to work, while the nonunion shops remained closed until their workers joined the union.

---

[19]Under the first collective agreement of the fur manufacturing industry, the joint conference committee, representing the contracting parties, resolved on Sept. 22, 1913 "that every member of the Association do everything in its power to induce the workers to join the union." *Minutes,* Conference Com-mittee, Fur Manufacturing Industry, Sept. 22, 1913. Copy filed in the Abelson papers.

Dealing with Strike-Bound Firms

Many collective agreements contained other specific clauses so regulating employer conduct as to encourage the growth of labor unions. Among the most important provisions of this type were clauses prohibiting employers from doing business with strike-bound firms. In the movement to establish industry-wide standards, nothing was more demoralizing for the union than employer attempts to undermine the effective use of organizing strikes in nonunion shops. So long as strike-bound firms could obtain help from outside sources conducting business as usual, unions were hampered in their drives for new members. Barring successful drives for new members, the organized workers could hardly be expected to guarantee uniform conditions of employment beyond the membership of employers' associations.

In 1915, Morris Hillquit, counsel of the ILGWU, told of how generously the cloakmakers' union had contributed its funds to strikes supporting the extension of inside standards into outside shops. These efforts, however, had been largely nullified by inside manufacturers who asked their own employees to work overtime on garments that would otherwise have been made in the strike-bound shops of contractors. The same self-defeating policies applied to competition between cities. Cleveland, so Hillquit pointed out, was the chief competitor of New York City in the manufacture of women's coats and suits. Yet, when the ILGWU spent half a million dollars to organize the Cleveland workers and to enforce the New York standards upon Cleveland manufacturers, the New York employers helped to defeat the organizing drive by making garments for their Cleveland competitors. During the long unsuccessful organizing strike of 1911, Cleveland manufacturers were able to supply the demands of their customers by having orders filled in New York.[20]

---

[20]*Minutes,* Council of Conciliation ... [women's coat and suit trade] (July 14, 1915), vol. 2, pp. 79–83. See also, Louis Lorwin [Louis Levine], *The Women's Garment Workers* (1924), pp. 205–206.

In our experience we find that whenever we start to organize shops, ... the manufacturers start to buy goods somewhere else and in this way discourage organization by openly threatening the workers that unless they remain non-union they will stop manufacturing or reduce manufacturing to a minimum. When the organization of such shops results in

Through their collective agreements, the organized manufacturers accepted an official responsibility to deny strike-bound firms the assistance that would permit them to resist union pressure. This pattern of conduct was openly accepted by the employers' associations that had originally signed the protocols for the dress and waist industry and for the women's coat and suit trade. "No member of the Association," stated the 1919 collective agreement between the Dress and Waist Manufacturers' Association and the International Ladies' Garment Workers' Union and its Locals 10, 25, and 58, "shall do work for any other employer of labor whose workers are on strike, nor shall any work be supplied by any member of the Association to any firm during the pendence of a strike." Associations were expected to enforce such restrictions upon their members.[21]

Lest employers disregard these restraints, other contract clauses gave union members the privilege of refusing to work on goods coming from strike-bound plants or on goods destined for delivery to strike-bound plants. After the First World War, collective agreements in the headwear and fur dressing industries contained particularly strong provisions authorizing union members to cease handling goods destined for or coming from manufacturing firms whose workers were on strike. "The workers shall not be required to work for any firm, although a member of the Association," stated the 1921 collective agreement between the Cloth Hat and Cap Manufacturers' Association and the Joint Council of New York of the United Cloth Hat and Cap Makers of North

---

strikes, the manufacturers are able to hold out, on account of the supply of manufactured goods that has been ordered in other cities in the name of other non-union manufacturers or jobbers. The only way we could put a stop to that is if we, the organized workers, should work only on goods that are made for union manufacturers and refuse to work on any goods that are sold to non-union manufacturers.

—Max Zuckerman, secretary-treasurer, United Cloth Hat and Cap Makers of North America, in the union's *Report and Proceedings*, Twelfth Biennial Convention (May 1919), p. 50.

[21]See also the 1920 collective agreement of the Women's Garment Manufacturers' Association of Philadelphia with the ILGWU. Text in *Women's Wear*, August 4, 1920. The house dress protocol of Feb. 11, 1913 prohibited, on request of the union, association members from sending work to strike-bound firms outside the 25-mile limit, provided at least half of the employees responded to the strike. Winslow, *Conciliation, Arbitration, and Sanitation in in the Dress and Waist Industry of New York City*, p. 130.

America, "which will work for or supply work to any firm during the pendency of strikes called or conducted by the Union against the latter firm." Obviously, the substandard producer could not long survive a strike if he were cut off from his usual orders for work, deprived of the opportunity to shift his production elsewhere, and denied access to the usual markets for his products.[22]

Nor could strike-bound firms escape union pressure by taking refuge in associations where they would be protected by no-strike clauses. Early in the history of the first protocol, the board of arbitration for the women's coat and suit trade ruled that the names of all candidates for association membership be submitted to the union before these firms were accepted as association members. This procedure gave the union an opportunity to acquaint the association with conditions in the factory of the candidate, lest unrevealed hostility to unions and to protocol standards threaten the institutions of collective action from within. No firm under dispute with the union was admitted to association membership until the dispute was settled.[23]

This rule, subsequently written into many collective agreements of the needle trades, was particularly applicable to strike-bound employers seeking association membership. Thus, by the terms of the 1919 collective agreement for the dress and waist industry, a firm applying for membership in the association was

---

[22]An almost identical clause is found in the 1919 collective agreement between the Cotton Garment Manufacturers of New York and Locals 10 and 62, ILGWU. Typical also was the following clause from a later contract:

> Should an effective strike occur in the shop of a contractor, then the member of the Association shall immediately cease sending any work to such contractor. Should the member of the Association fail so to do, a cessation of work by the Union or the workers in his Union shops in the Metropolitan area, shall not be deemed a breach of this agreement.
> —From the 1938 collective agreement between the Industrial Association of Juvenile Apparel Manufacturers and Locals 91 and 10, ILGWU.

For typical arbitration decisions enforcing a similar clause in the dress industry, see Impartial Chairman Harry Uviller, *Decisions,* vol. 2, Case nos. D-288, D-289, D-290 (March 11, 1937), p. 53.

[23]A discussion of this rule, first adopted by the board of arbitration in March 1911, occurred at a special meeting of the board on Oct. 3, 1913. *Minutes,* Board of Arbitrators . . . [women's coat and suit trade], (Oct. 3, 1913), pp. 80–81.

denied admittance "during the pendence of a strike" in the plant. In such case, the union was given three weeks during which to check on the status of union membership. The agreement provided further that "it shall be a condition of membership that at least seventy-five (75%) per cent of the workers of said applicant shall become members of the Union, and that the applicant shall endeavor to have the remainder of said employees join the Union."[24]

Dealing with Nonunion Shops

More substantial help for the growth of labor unions came from contract clauses obligating the organized manufacturers to cease dealing with nonunion shops. Production by nonunion shops had been at the heart of the movement to abolish outside contracting. Prohibiting manufacturers from dealing with nonunion shops of whatever character would obviously promote the

---

[24]The 1919 collective agreement was that between the Dress and Waist Manufacturers' Association and the ILGWU for itself and its Locals 10, 25, and 58.

> Before admitting a new member, the association shall inform the union in writing of the application for membership. If a strike or dispute shall be pending between the applicant and the union at the time, the union shall give to the association within five days a written statement containing full particulars of the matter in dispute and the association will not admit such applicant until the dispute has been adjusted.
>
> The association may undertake to adjust the dispute and (or) may submit such adjustment to the impartial chairman of the industry. Such adjustment shall be made on the basis of the agreement existing between the union and the applicant and the rights of the union and its members under such agreement shall be preserved up to the date of such adjustment.
>
> —From the 1927 collective agreement of the Merchants' Ladies' Garment Association with the ILGWU and the Cloakmakers' Joint Board. Text in *Women's Wear Daily*, Jan. 14, 1927.

Refusal of a union to recognize an employer as a member of an association or union refusal to permit an employer to change his association has at times led to heated discussions and criticisms. See *Minutes,* Arbitration Proceedings between the Dress and Waist Manufacturers' Association of New York and the ILGWU (May 17, 1914), vol. 2, pp. 75–187. Unresolved disputes over the application or interpretation of such clauses were submitted to the impartial chairman. See, for example, Harry Uviller, impartial chairman, dress industry, *Decisions,* vol. 2, Case no. D-73 (Jan. 25, 1937).

extension of union membership into the shops where the workers were unorganized. The protocol movement was still in its infancy when the principle was generally conceded that workers would gravitate to the sources of employment. Doing business with non-union shops or with shops maintaining substandard conditions was an open invitation to unemployed union members to re-nounce their union allegiance and forsake their union standards. By rejoining the ranks of the nonunion workers they could at least find employment. Conversely, to the extent that nonunion shops were shut off from sources of supply or from markets for their products, their unemployed workers would tend to join unions in order to obtain work.

Some contract provisions for controlling relations with non-union shops forbade association members from having an in-terest, financial or otherwise, in any shop not under written con-tract with the particular union that was a party to the collective agreement. Manufacturers were not only forbidden to "open, manage, operate, finance, or become directly or indirectly inter-ested in" nonunion shops but they were also prohibited from doing business of any kind with nonunion shops: sending out materials to be fabricated in nonunion shops; receiving from nonunion shops unfinished goods to be completed; buying the finished products of nonunion shops, or selling union-made goods outright to nonunion shops. What was it worth to the dressmakers' union to have the organized dress contractors and the organized dress jobbers agree among themselves "to work only with union firms who are in contractual relations with the ILGWU?"[25]

---

[25]See the text of the 1925 collective agreement between the Wholesale Dress Manufacturers' Association (jobbers) and the Association of Dress Man-ufacturers (contractors) in *Women's Wear,* Jan. 30, 1925. The 1926 collective agreement between the Wholesale Hat and Cap Manufacturers' Association and the Joint Council of New York of the Cloth Hat, Cap and Millinery Workers' International Union stated: "None of the merchandise manufac-tured by any member of the Association shall be directly or indirectly manu-factured for or sold to or for the account of any manufacturer or jobber of the greater metropolitan area of New York City, who is not under contract with the Union to observe and maintain Union standards." The text of this agreement can be found in the union's *Report and Proceedings,* Sixteenth Biennial Convention (May 1927), p. 227. The 1927 collective agreement of the United Shirt Manufacturers' Association with the Amalgamated Clothing

The most important application of these restrictions came in acquiring or supplying accessories for the major products of the women's garment trades: laces and embroideries, buttons and belts, shoulder pads, artificial flowers, fur trimmings, and the like. To meet competition from other centers of production, New York manufacturers who maintained union standards in their own plants insisted that they be able to buy accessories from whatever source at the lowest possible price. Yet support for nonunion production of accessories indirectly tended to undermine union strength in plants producing the major items of wearing apparel. Hence clauses were incorporated into collective agreements limiting manufacturers and contractors to the purchase and use of union-made accessories produced under the labor standards established for the trade.[26]

In order to enforce restrictions on nonunion dealings, some collective agreements required unions and employers' associations

---

Workers' Union and the Shirtmakers' Joint Board permitted exceptions to the rule against dealing with nonunion shops, with the consent of the executive director of the association and the manager of the union's joint board, or by decision of the impartial chairman. A copy of this agreement is filed in the Abelson papers. An example of restrictions on having an interest in nonunion shops is found in the 1934 collective agreement of the Luggage and Leather Goods Manufacturers with the Suitcase, Bag and Portfolio Union, filed in the Abelson papers.

[26]Whenever the Union notifies the Association that any of its members cause to be manufactured belts, covered buttons, buckles, neckwear, artificial flowers, bonnaz embroideries, hemstitching, pleating and tucking on garments by or purchase such articles from firms which are not in contractual relations with the International Ladies' Garment Workers' Union, or against whom the said International has declared a strike, the Association will immediately order its members to cease further dealings until such strike is settled and/or until such firm enters into a collective agreement with the International Ladies' Garment Workers' Union, and the member of the Association shall cease further dealings after receiving such notice.

—From the 1937 collective agreement of the National Skirt Manufacturers' Association with the Cloakmakers' Joint Board and the Skirt Makers' Union, Local 23, ILGWU.

When trucking firms that carted goods between jobbers or inside manufacturers and contractors were brought within the established order of the women's coat and suit trade, they, too, were forbidden to handle goods of nonunion origin or nonunion destination. See above, pp. 349–351, and below, pp. 799–800, and references there cited.

frequently to exchange lists of shops through which they operated. More important, these agreements also set forth in some detail the penalties to be inflicted upon the organized manufacturers for dealing with nonunion shops. Thus, after requiring association members to withdraw work in the hands of nonunion producers, the 1927 collective agreement between the Merchants' Ladies' Garment Association (jobbers) and the ILGWU continued:

Should a member of the association be found giving work to or dealing with a non-union manufacturer, the association will proceed to impose a fine for the first offense under the authority contained in its by-laws and its agreement with its members. The amount of such fine shall be determined with reference to the sum involved and shall be sufficiently high to offset the advantage gained by the members through such transactions, together with an appropriate penalty.

A second offense shall mean expulsion, and in this connection the association shall adopt such other measures as in its judgment are necessary and expedient to prevent members from giving work to nonunion shops. The proceeds of fines collected shall be deposited in a fund to be jointly administered by the union and the association and to be used towards defraying the expenses incurred in investigations respecting the existence and operation of non-union shops.

The association on its own motion will investigate any or all of the books and records of its members, to ascertain whether they are giving work or dealing with non-union shops. Upon complaint filed by the union, the privilege will also be accorded to a representative of the union to accompany a representative of the association to examine the books and records of the member against whom a complaint has been filed, for the purpose only of determining whether such member is giving work to non-union shops. Such examination shall be undertaken within 48 hours from receipt of the request, and shall be conducted under such conditions and limitations as the impartial chairman hereinafter mentioned, upon the request of either party, may prescribe.[27]

Just as unions were permitted to use direct action against employers dealing with strike-bound firms, so were they also authorized to rely upon strike action as a means of enforcing prohibitions against dealing with nonunion firms. Union members

---

[27]From the 1927 collective agreement of the Merchants' Ladies' Garment Association with the ILGWU and the Cloakmakers' Joint Board. Text in *Women's Wear Daily*, Jan. 14, 1927.

were expressly given the privilege of boycotting all sources of nonunion production. Either they could cease work on goods and materials coming from nonunion shops or they could refuse to work on products destined for nonunion outlets. Thus, after directing the employers' association to impose a fine for the first offense of dealing with nonunion firms, the 1925 collective agreement between the Wholesale Dress Manufacturers' Association (jobbers) and the Dressmakers' Joint Board, ILGWU, provided that repeated violations of this restriction would give the union "the right to order a stoppage-of-work of such association member until the matter has been fully adjusted."[28]

By expressly authorizing strikes and boycotts to enforce restrictions on nonunion dealings, the parties to collective agreements paid their highest respects to the role of unions in controlling competition. Only an implicit faith in union organization as a means of eliminating the worst features of excessive competition could have induced the organized manufacturers to permit cessation of work on commodities of nonunion origin or nonunion destination. Here the dedication to the cause of union growth was more far reaching than could be expressed by the usual clauses on union security. Perhaps nothing short of outright prohibitions on nonunion dealings, together with extreme measures for the enforcement of those restrictions, could have guaranteed unions of the needle trades sufficient strength to become an effective force in suppressing cutthroat competition within their industries.

Blocking out the unorganized factions of an industry from their normal sources of supply or from the normal outlets for their products raised questions of legality that offered the possibility of judicial relief for the unorganized manufacturers and their nonunion labor force. Cut off from the normal stream of production

---

[28]Whenever it shall appear that a member of the association gives work to a non-union manufacturer, the association shall immediately direct him to withdraw his work from such non-union manufacturer, whether such work be in process of operation or otherwise. If a member of the association shall refuse to comply with such directions, or fail to withdraw his work within 36 hours from the receipt of notice, he shall automatically forfeit all rights and privileges under this agreement.
—From the 1925 collective agreement between the Wholesale Dress Manufacturers' Association and the ILGWU. Text in *Women's Wear*, Jan. 31, 1925.

through the operation of collective agreements between the organized employers and their organized workers, these outcasts appealed to the courts in defense of their right to a livelihood. By the time this issue had assumed major importance in the mid-twenties, the organized forces of the needle trades could find good legal precedents for their positions. In the leading case on the refusal of union members to work with nonunion men or to handle nonunion products, members of the Brotherhood of Carpenters and Joiners had refused to work with materials coming from a nonunion mill. "It is not illegal, therefore," concluded Mr. Justice E. A. Chase for the New York Court of Appeals, "for the defendants to refuse to allow members of the Brotherhood to work in the plaintiff's mill with nonunion men. The same reasoning results in holding that the Brotherhood may, by voluntary act, refuse to allow its members to work in the erection of materials furnished by a nonunion shop."[29]

Nevertheless, this general issue was kept alive over the years by repeated appeals to the courts. In the summer of 1949, for example, nine manufacturers of fur garments petitioned the New York Supreme Court for a temporary injunction to prevent the Furriers' Joint Council and the Fur Wholesalers of America from conspiring to destroy the business of the unorganized producers. "From early 1947 until the present time," stated one of the plaintiffs in his affidavit, "members of the Fur Wholesalers of America, Inc. . . . have refused to purchase fur garments from me because I am a non-union manufacturer and have threatened to continue to so refuse. Their conduct has been in strict compliance with the requirements of the various collective bargaining agreements entered into by Furriers' Joint Council and Fur Wholesalers' Association since early 1947. Because of the conspiracy between Furriers' Joint Council and Fur Wholesalers' Association to drive me out of business, I have in fact suffered a severe economic setback which jeopardizes my capital investment and have been on many occasions since early 1947 prevented from entering into profitable relations with various members of the Fur Wholesalers' Association."[30]

---

[29]Bossert v. Dhuy, 221 N.Y. 342 (1917); 178 N.Y. Supp. 344, reaffirmed in Maisel v. Sigman 123 Misc. 714 (1924); 205 N.Y. Supp. 807.

[30]The complaint further stated that the Furriers' Joint Council "refused to bargain collectively with any of the plaintiffs, except in bad faith and

Union Obligations to Expand

Many collective agreements did not stop at imposing certain rules of conduct upon the organized manufacturers to encourage the growth of union membership. They also imposed upon labor unions specific obligations to organize the unorganized segments of the labor force. Employers' associations repeatedly insisted that something more than the law of self-interest should impel labor unions to expand their memberships. Under collective agreements, the "right" of the union to organize became a solemn "duty" of the union to bring into the fold all the unorganized workers of an industry. Beginning in 1915, several successive contracts between the Cotton Garment Manufacturers of New York and the ILGWU and its Locals 10 and 62, expressly directed the union to make "every effort" to organize all workers of the industry, barring certain workers who were expressly exempted by the collective agreement.[31]

By the mid-twenties, collective agreements of the women's coat and suit trade had recognized the objective of organizing all workers in the metropolitan district — a district defined as "the City of New York and all such cities and towns in the State of New York, New Jersey, Connecticut and Pennsylvania in which garments are being manufactured by or for members of the Industrial Branch or for any other jobbers or manufacturers do-

---

under terms and conditions so arbitrary and unreasonable as to render plaintiffs' continuance in business impossible." *Women's Wear Daily,* July 12, 1949.

By this time, the legal issues in refusing to manufacture or handle goods of nonunion origin or nonunion destination were assuming national importance in provisions of the national labor laws. See particularly, the secondary boycott provisions of the Labor-Management Relations (Taft-Hartley) Act of 1947, as amended.

[31] "The party of the first part in entering upon this agreement recognizes the right and duty of the parties of the second part to represent the workers in the industry.... Every effort shall be made by the Union to organize all those workers who do not come within the category described above, and the members of the party of the first part agree, in good faith, to co-operate with the parties of the second part to that end.

——From the 1925 collective agreement of the Cotton Garment Manufacturers of New York with the ILGWU and its Locals 10 and 62.

ing business in the City of New York." Clearly, the purpose was to organize thoroughly the area of greatest competition within the trade. "The parties hereto recognize the necessity of unionizing the entire industry in the Metropolitan District," stated the 1924 collective agreement of the Industrial Council of Cloak, Suit and Skirt Manufacturers with the ILGWU and the Cloakmakers' Joint Board, ILGWU. "In order to bring about such unionization the Union will make every effort to organize all employees and shops in the industry, and the Industrial Branch will co-operate with it in such efforts."[32]

Conversely, labor unions were inhibited from adopting union policies that would have the effect of impairing the growth of union membership. In addition to the contractual obligation to keep their doors open to new members, some unions were restrained by their collective agreements from permitting their members to work in nonunion shops. Seeking supplemental employment wherever it could be found, sometimes over weekends and after normal working hours, many union members contributed to the success of nonunion shops by openly or surreptitiously working for nonunion employers at substandard rates. Denying nonunion shops this access to a competent labor force could be as vital to the suppression of nonunion competition as cutting off markets or sources of raw material.[33]

Enforcing Contract Clauses to Strengthen Unions

Enforcing contract provisions designed to strengthen and promote the growth of labor unions required more faith in the protocol movement than a great many of the organized manufacturers could muster. Giving lip service to contract terms favoring strong unions was for them a permissible concession only so long as no pressure was exerted to enforce those terms. Scores of employers otherwise loyal to their associations never believed

---

[32]See also the 1927 collective agreement of the Merchants' Ladies' Garment Association with the ILGWU and the Cloakmakers' Joint Board. Text printed in *Women's Wear Daily*, Jan. 14, 1927.

[33]Normally, working with nonunion men was contrary to the official position of labor unions as stated by Morris Hillquit, legal counsel, ILGWU: "A man has a right to determine with whom he will work and with whom he will not work, and Unions as a rule determine that they will not work with non-union men." *Minutes,* Council of Conciliation . . . [women's coat and suit trade] (Feb. 16, 1916), vol. 9, p. 236.

that such clauses were to be taken seriously. Although union leaders cried out for "complete control over the workers," lest discipline within the ranks be rendered "absolutely nugatory," many organized manufacturers never raised a hand to maintain union membership among the workers of their own shops. Yet the annals of the needle trades abound with evidences that employers' associations openly attempted to help unions build up their organizations and extend their coverage, even at the risk of dissension within ranks of the organized manufacturers themselves.

During the first few years under the original Protocol of Peace the Cloak, Suit and Skirt Manufacturers' Protective Association sought to strengthen the union's position by directing its member firms (1) to prod their workers into joining the ILGWU; (2) to insist that union members pay their dues; (3) to act as channels of communication between workers and union officials; and (4) to discharge workers for failing to keep up their good standing in the union. The operation of these provisions largely accounted for the report of the *Jewish Daily Forward,* June 15, 1913, that it was "practically impossible for a cloakmaker to get a job in a good shop without a union card."[34]

Other employers' associations during the early years of the protocol movement were equally cooperative. Under the 1914 collective agreement of the fur manufacturing industry, the Associated Fur Manufacturers called a series of membership meetings to explain the meaning of contract clauses on union security and to suggest ways and means of implementing those provisions. When member firms showed no interest in discussing the pledge that both parties "shall co-operate in good faith to strengthen each other" or in clarifying the principle that "those who share the benefits of this Agreement should bear the burdens," the association announced that henceforth members would not be protected against strikes unless they saw that all workers in their establishments held union cards indicating their good standing in the fur workers' union.[35]

Because many of the newly organized dress and waist manu-

---

[34]From a translation in the Abelson papers.

[35]Adolph Engel, president of the Associated Fur Manufacturers, to the association members, letter, dated August 19, 1915. Copy filed in the Abelson papers.

facturers knew nothing of their obligations under union security clauses, most of the initial gains in union membership that accompanied the adoption of the first dress and waist protocol in January 1913 were wiped out within a year. Membership in the dressmakers' union fell from 25,000 in 1913 to 16,000 in 1914. To turn the tide that was running against unionism, the organized dress and waist manufacturers whose ranks had grown from 62 members in 1913 to 292 members in 1914 were expressly instructed to see that all union members met their financial obligations to the union. Those workers failing to pay their dues were to be discharged. Unable to afford the loss of good workers during the busy season, some manufacturers even paid the dues and initiation fees of their employees who had failed to keep up their membership or their good standing in the union. Since the chief source of misunderstanding was the preferential union shop clause, the Dress and Waist Manufacturers' Association directed a clarifying letter, dated February 2, 1914, to each of its members:

GENTLEMEN: There seems to be a lack of understanding on the part of our members as to the precise meaning of the "Preferential union shop" provisions of the protocol. I have had written out the extracts from Bulletin No. 98, which are made a part of the protocol of peace, and enclose them herewith. I also enclose extracts from a recent decision of the board of arbitration in the dress and waist industry, in reference to the matter. Please file these for ready reference.

The protocol has come to stay. So has the association, and so has the union. We are gradually building up institutions like the joint board of sanitary control, the wage-scale board, and the board of grievances, which will ultimately solve the very difficult problems that exist in our industry. We are today considering standardizing piece prices, plans for industrial education, and the protocol white label. . . .

None of these institutions can possibly exist without the hearty cooperation of the union and the association. They are for the benefit of the manufacturer and the worker alike. The principle underlying the preferential union shop is that since the workers get benefits from these institutions, they should belong to their organization, just as the manufacturer who gets the benefits should belong to our organization. Some of our members have failed to appreciate that the work of cooperation between the association and the union would fail if the union did not have the moral support and cooperation of the manufacturers, as guaranteed by the protocol. The first place at which this moral support and cooperation is established tangibly on the part of the manufacturers is in the observance of the principle of the "Preferential union shop."[36]

Employer Support for Union Organizing Drives

While employers' associations were thus supporting unionism in the plants of their member firms, they were also helping to extend the span of union control into the outer circles of their industries. From the very inception of the protocol movement, the organized manufacturers have continued to cry out for a more thorough organization of the workers in their trades. More than once they have initiated conferences with unions to discuss problems of eliminating the nonunion shop, and from time to time they have devised means of their own to accomplish this objective. Since organizing the workers of an independent shop was a prerequisite for admitting the shop owner into an association, the manufacturers could strengthen their own ties by helping to extend union membership.

The major contribution that the organized manufacturers could make to the growth of unions came at the time of union organizing drives. These carefully prepared union campaigns to conquer new fields normally involved the use of organizing strikes. Although officially exempt from the no-strike clauses of collective agreements, organizing strikes owed more of their success to the active cooperation of supporting employer groups. Assistance from the organized manufacturers varied from moral support to open participation. For the most part, employers' associations did not publicize their contributions nor did they admit the full extent of their participation. But the evidence of their support appears throughout the history of the needle trades.

At the time the first dress and waist protocol was under negotiation early in 1913, the organized manufacturers of the dress and waist industry helped to put the dressmakers' union on its feet. Unlike their fellow cloakmakers, whose strike call in 1910

---

[36]As quoted in Winslow, *Conciliation, Arbitration, and Sanitation in the Dress and Waist Industry of New York City*, p. 39. See also *Minutes,* Arbitration Proceedings between the Dress and Waist Manufacturers' Association and the ILGWU (Nov. 9, 1913), pp. 145, 175, 178–179; and Hyman Berman, "Era of the Protocols . . . 1910–1916" (unpublished Ph.D. dissertation, Columbia University, 1956), p. 351.

had won general support from the unorganized workers of the women's coat and suit trade, the members of the dressmakers' union failed to win general support from among the 10,000 workers in the 50 association plants, or from among the 30,000 workers, most of whom were nonunion, employed elsewhere in the local trade. But the Dress and Waist Manufacturers' Association, observing the benefits that the coat and suit protocol had brought to the coat and suit trade, came to the support of the struggling dressmakers by nurturing their union along until the dress and waist protocol was signed.

To organize the workers of the local dress market, the employers' association joined with the union in cooking up a general strike that would involve the employees of association firms for two days only. Thereafter, these employees would return to their jobs on terms previously reached between the association and the union. This exemplary pattern of conduct by the workers in association shops would presumably be followed by nonunion workers in the strike-bound shops of independent employers. "When this strike broke out," testified S. Floersheimer, president of the Dress and Waist Manufacturers' Association, appearing before the industry's board of arbitration, "we persuaded 28,000 women to join the Union."[37]

Three years later, after the Dress and Waist Manufacturers' Association and the union had accepted a revision of the dress protocol, the contracting parties again arranged for a general strike to effect a "thorough organization" of the industry. For the association shops, this was also to be a two-day "demonstration strike" to help organize the rest of the trade. But the strike in association shops actually lasted several more days because the workers, unhappy at participating in a strike that had been

---

[37]*Minutes,* Arbitration Proceedings between the Dress and Waist Manufacturers' Association and the ILGWU (Nov. 8, 1913), p. 115. At the time of the signing of the dress and waist protocol, S. Floersheimer is reported to have added: "Gentlemen, we are giving to you on a silver plate 10,000 Union members. We are going to be responsible for those 10,000 workers that they will belong to your Union, but we will not sign your contract, unless you will show us that the majority of the trade enrolls in its membership." As quoted by S. Polakoff, chief clerk and vice-president of Local 25, ILGWU, in *ibid.* (Nov. 9, 1913), p. 321. On this episode, see also Lorwin, *The Women's Garment Workers,* pp. 224–226.

arranged through collusion with an employers' association, refused to return to their jobs when ordered back by the union.[38]

Other industries apparently followed the pattern of the dressmakers. In 1929, three associations of the women's coat and suit
trade (jobbers, contractors, and inside manufacturers) supported
the union in a general walkout that was alleged to have been a
"manufactured strike" engineered by the ILGWU and the Industrial Council of Cloak, Suit and Skirt Manufacturers to help
organize the trade. And, in 1932, the Women's Headwear Group
at the time of its first collective agreement with the millinery
workers allegedly helped the union to cook up a fake strike that
would strengthen union membership throughout the trade. In
this last case, the workers of 109 selected association firms were
to go back to work the day after the union called the strike, while
the workers of all other association firms were to return on
Monday of the following week.[39]

Union Initiative in Membership Drives

With or without help from the organized manufacturers,
unions of the needle trades embarked upon their own programs

---

[38]*Women's Wear*, March 1, 1916. A similar episode is reported in the
Feb. 1, 1921 issue. See also the history of the dress industry's five major
strikes in *Women's Wear Daily*, Feb. 4, 1930.

> The union has asked us to permit the workers in our shops to have
> a "demonstration holiday" at their own expense, during which they may
> show their sympathy with those on strike, and may be properly reg-
> istered. The association has agreed to this, and all our members have
> consented.
> —Statement of Mrs. Henry Moskowitz, labor manager, Dress and
> Waist Manufacturers' Association, in *Women's Wear*, Feb. 9, 1916.

See also *ibid.*, Feb. 10, 14–16, 1916, and, in general, Lorwin, *The Women's
Garment Workers*, pp. 303–304. At that time, Harry Gordon, representing
an insurgent group within the membership of the Dress and Waist Manufacturers' Association, struck a sour note by attacking the association's policy
toward helping the dressmakers' union:

> You dress and waist manufacturers were sold into slavery. It was a
> crime against law, a crime against industry for you people to have made
> a conspiracy in 1913 and to have agreed to collect dues for the union.
> It was a crime for you to have sent the workers out on strike recently.
> —As quoted in *Women's Wear*, March 1, 1916.

[39]*Women's Wear Daily*, July 2, 1929, March 17–18, 1932. For an earlier
alleged case of support from the manufacturers of the millinery trade for
the millinery workers' union, see *Women's Wear*, August 1, 1916.

for organizing the nonunion workers. Most unions took seriously their obligation to gain such control over the labor force of each industry as would enable them to dictate work standards beyond the realm of employers' associations. In the absence of employer collaboration, the usual pattern of procedure was to call out the workers of the nonassociation shops at the time collective agreements were negotiated with the organized employers. This procedure was exemplified in 1916 when the Amalgamated Clothing Workers, having signed a collective agreement with the American Clothing Manufacturers' Association, ordered a strike in the shops of independent manufacturers, except for those shops producing for members of the association.[40]

Between general whoop-it-up organizing drives, labor unions resorted to less publicized means of strengthening their institutions and extending their membership. Some encouraged union membership by penalizing union members caught working with nonunion men. Others employed forceful tactics to win new members in the shops. Fur workers' unions were noted for sending union agents from shop to shop to check union membership cards. Any worker found without a valid union card was dispatched forthwith to union headquarters with instructions not to return until he had squared his accounts with the union. In their enthusiasm to wipe out the nonunion worker, union agents did not always exempt the shops of association members from high-handed organizing procedures. Time and again the organized manufacturers spoke out against the union practice of breaking into their plants in search of nonunion workers and disrupting production in violation of collective agreements. But such procedures were more readily condoned when applied to independent competitors operating nonunion shops.[41]

---

[40] *Daily Trade Record,* Jan. 14, 1916. Other examples of union organizing strategy occurred in the 1921 and 1929 strikes against the nonassociation shops of the dress and waist industry. The second of these strikes resulted in the addition of more than 12,000 members to the ILGWU membership. Two years later, the millinery workers conducted a similar drive to organize 4,000 trimmers in the women's headwear industry. *New York Times,* Feb. 14, 1930. See also *Women's Wear Daily,* Jan. 12, Feb. 29, March 11, 17–18, 1932.

[41] "We regret exceedingly that the members of the Conference Committee representing the manufacturers are obliged to report that the workers as they were about to enter the factory of one of our members were forced by threats and actual violence to go to the Union in a

Once a needle trade union had succeeded in organizing a substantial majority of the workers in the New York market of an industry, that union invariably turned its attention to other towns and cities. For years, the general executive board of the ILGWU reported to its successive biennial conventions on progress that the union had made in organizing out-of-town centers. To the convention of 1918, the board measured union success in Chicago by reporting that the Chicago cloakmakers had "succeeded in signing a collective agreement with the two cloak and suit manufacturers' associations in that city, and in introducing uniform standards." At the same time, the board acknowledged that the union had not succeeded in organizing the Cleveland market although the problem was "one which we have tried our utmost to solve, having in view the interests of the cloak industry of the entire country as a whole."[42]

At the ILGWU convention of 1920, the union's general executive board reported on union organizing drives in small towns — drives that had been undertaken as a means of halting the movement of plants from larger centers of production. And, in 1924, the board reported that the union was considering an extensive organizing campaign in Toledo, Ohio, "in view of the fact that Toledo is developing quite a large cloak trade at the expense of the markets in the organized cities." Also considered

---

body, as we are informed, where they were told that no one could return to work until he had paid his dues, if he were a member, or had joined the Union and paid the initiation fees, etc., if he were not a member.

—S. N. Samuels, representing the Associated Fur Manufacturers, to Impartial Chairman J. L. Magnes, letter dated Oct. 15, 1913, filed in the Abelson papers.

See also the *New Post,* Nov. 23, 30, and Dec. 28, 1912; Feb. 1, 1913. Seventeen years later, Samuels directed a letter of the same tenor to Impartial Chairman Paul Abelson, letter, dated Oct. 29, 1930, filed in the Abelson papers.

In the early thirties, the Cloakmakers' Joint Board created an emergency volunteer committee to check each building in the garment area of New York City, not only for evidences of overtime violations, but also to see that all workers of the trade in these buildings were union members in good standing. The efforts of this committee led to organizing the workers in 42 shops, the owners of which thereupon joined their appropriate employers' association. *Women's Wear Daily,* March 10, 1931.

[42]ILGWU, *Report and Proceedings,* Fourteenth Convention (May 1918), pp. 11, 14.

were the problems faced by the newly created Out-of-Town Organization Department through which subsequent drives were to be funneled. The work of this new department was doubled with the mass exodus of small contracting shops from the New York area during the early thirties.[43]

These out-of-town organizing drives pleased the New York manufacturers whose fear of nonunion competition grew with the rise of manufacturing in other markets. Once the production of men's clothing had spread to neighboring communities, the Amalgamated Clothing Workers of the New York market conducted a special organizing drive in 1927 to bring the workers of these areas into the union fold. As an initial step, the union established offices in New Haven, Conn., Perth Amboy, N.J., Allentown, Penn., and Philadelphia to introduce the "union idea" to places where workers had scarcely ever heard of unions.[44]

The death of the NRA codes in 1935 stimulated the movement of New York manufacturers to out-of-town districts and intensified the efforts of needle trade unions to organize the out-of-town shops. Early in 1936, the United Hatters, Cap and Millinery Workers won the acclaim of the New York headwear manufacturers by calling a general strike to clean out the "chiseling elements" of the trade. Max Zaritsky, president of the union's cap and millinery department, boasted at that time that his union had tripled its membership within the preceding four years by gaining control over outside markets. Powerful local unions, he said, had been firmly established in Chicago, St. Louis, Milwaukee, and Cleveland, as well as in areas of New Jersey, Georgia, and California. Each local or joint board found its appropriate niche in the over-all structure of the union's national organization.[45]

With the moral support of New York employers' associations, David Dubinsky, president of the ILGWU, initiated a movement

---

[43]ILGWU, *Report and Proceedings,* Fifteenth Convention (May 1920), pp. 49–50, 53–54. See also ILGWU, *Report and Proceedings,* Seventeenth Convention (May 1924), pp. 60, 101–102. For a discussion of the work of the Eastern Out-of-Town Department of the ILGWU, see ILGWU, *Report and Proceedings,* Twenty-second Convention (May–June 1934), pp. 120–124.

[44]*Daily News Record,* June 27, 1927. For a summary account of union organizing drives in the various markets of the men's clothing trade, see C. E. Zaretz, *The Amalgamated Clothing Workers of America* (1934), especially chaps. 7 and 8, pp. 105–159, "Unionization of the Clothing Markets."

[45]*Women's Wear Daily,* Feb. 5, 1936.

that led to the formation of a Needle Trades Alliance representing all the needle trade unions. Joint union offices were soon opened in Connecticut, New Jersey, and Pennsylvania from which union organizers succeeded in winning over the workers in many nonunion shops. After personally investigating union organizing efforts in these areas, one observer concluded that "the main reason for stopping city manufacturers from moving to out-of-town districts is the result of the combined forces of various unions and other associations in helping to organize labor in these out-of-town districts."[46]

The Impartial Machinery and the Growth of Unions

In the movement to strengthen labor unions, the impartial machinery for each trade has played an important role. Neither specific contract provisions guaranteeing a minimum of union security nor more general clauses promoting a maximum of union growth could have been enforced without the strong hand of the impartial machinery on which both parties could rely. Joint agencies of contract administration frequently stepped in to fortify the position of labor unions where employers' associations hesitated to act and where union representatives feared to tread. During the early years of the protocol movement, the front-line operators of the impartial machinery — clerks, deputy clerks, managers, committees on immediate action, and subcommittees of grievance boards — generally adopted a construction of the preferential union shop clause that would give the greatest encouragement to the growth of union membership. Time and again these joint agencies came to the defense of workers who were penalized for their vigilance in promoting union solidarity or for their insistence upon a rigid enforcement of the collective agreement.[47]

Over the years, agencies of the impartial machinery have enter-

---

[46]Harry Shuster in *ibid.,* Oct. 21, 1936.

[47]Even after employer criticism of the first women's coat and suit protocol had forced the reorganization of the Cloak, Suit and Skirt Manufacturers' Protective Association and had put reactionaries in control, the chief clerks for the association and the union, Eugene Lezinsky and Sidney Hillman, entered into secret deals that prompted employers to support unionism at a time when the announced policies to that end were unpopular among the organized employers. — *Minutes,* Council of Conciliation . . . [women's coat and suit trade] (Feb. 16, 1916), vol. 9, p. 241. These minutes deal extensively with the problem of increasing and maintaining union membership; see, especially, pp. 212–294.

tained thousands of complaints that disclosed a wide variety of employer techniques for hampering union activities. Among the more common employer practices contrary to protocol principles and to the purposes of collective action were the following: (1) urging workers not to pay their dues; (2) convincing employees their union officials were agents of the firm; (3) bypassing the shop chairman to deal directly with employees; (4) refusing to deliver notices of union meetings; (5) exploiting the use of nonunion "learners" who could be hired for less pay; (6) withholding work from the shop until the shop chairman was removed from office; and (7) granting wage increases to all employees before the agreement expired, *except the union officials.* All these activities in contravention of protocol principles fell within the province of the impartial agencies responsible for administering union security clauses in collective agreements.[48]

At one time or another, some agency of the impartial machinery for one or more industries of the needle trades ruled: (1) that unions may appoint dues collectors with access to the shops for the collection of union dues; (2) that union agents hold a favored position (superseniority) over other workers for retention in service during a reduction of force; (3) that the door of the union must be kept open for the reception of new members on reasonable terms; (4) that employers' associations must encourage their member firms to see that workers join unions and maintain their "good standing"; (5) that unions must discipline their members who work in nonunion shops; (6) that companies cannot employ strikebreakers without the consent of the union; (7) that manufacturers may be penalized for undermining the union; (8) that unions may strike to enforce decisions ordering a company to cease employing nonunion men.[49]

Still more important to union growth has been the attitude of

---

[48]Examples of these practices can be found in the Abelson papers, particularly those of the fur manufacturing industry. Of the 8,029 complaints raised by the fur workers' union against members of the Associated Fur Manufacturers during the years 1929, 1930, and 1931, approximately 80% (6,054) fell under the general category of workers operating without union books, workers employed who were not in good standing, and workers who failed to attend shop meetings. — From an analysis of the work of the association's labor department, submitted by J. G. Greenberg, executive manager, to Paul Abelson, formerly impartial chairman, in a letter, dated Oct. 6, 1950, filed in the Abelson papers.

[49]Examples of these types of decisions can be found in the Abelson papers.

permanent umpires sitting at the apex of the administrative structures. Whether engaged in penalizing employers for violating union security clauses or in sponsoring general labor-management conferences on the broader aspects of nonunion competition, impartial chairmen have from the inception of the protocol movement become key figures in the movement to organize the workers of each industry. In substantial measure, labor organizations throughout the needle trades owed their strength to the work of impartial chairmen who have been outstanding advocates of strong unions. Dedicated to the principle of regulated competition for the good of their industries, these "labor statesmen" have consistently adhered to the principle of complete organization for workers and employers alike.[50]

Shortly after the First World War, Impartial Chairman W. M. Leiserson in one of his most publicized decisions directed employers of the Rochester men's clothing market to suspend delinquent clothing workers from their employment until they paid their union dues. Denied the right to enforce union discipline by refusing to work with delinquent members — a procedure that would violate the no-strike clause of the collective agreement — the Amalgamated Clothing Workers, so the impartial chairman concluded, must be given a "place in court" to enforce union discipline. "Until such a legal method of enforcing disciplinary rules is provided," Leiserson stated, "the agreement would have the effect of weakening the union, members could defy the organization with impunity, and the attempts of the Labor Adjustment Board to hold the union responsible for compelling its members to live up to the provisions of the agreement and to the decisions of the impartial chairman would be futile."[51]

---

[50]In 1929, the ILGWU suggested, and the organized contractors of the women's coat and suit trade accepted, a proposition to establish a permanent joint committee under the immediate direction of the impartial chairman to "supervise the enforcement of standards, unionization of shops and all other activities conducive to complete organization of the industry." *Women's Wear Daily,* May 17, 1929.

[51]The dues are the taxes required to maintain the governmental agencies for the industry set up by the agreement and any individual in whose behalf the agreement was signed who avoids the payment of the tax is violating an obligation assumed by him when the membership of the union voted to accept the agreement.

—W. M. Leiserson, *Decisions,* Case no. 451 (May 25, 1921). The

However important the interpretation and enforcement of union security clauses, industry arbitrators made their greatest contributions to the growth of labor unions by helping to enforce prohibitions against doing business with strike-bound plants and with nonunion shops. In the women's coat and suit trade, "non-union dealings" became the most important subject under which arbitration awards were classified. Often the impartial chairman of this industry set the penalties to be inflicted upon manufacturers for dealing with nonunion shops. On one occasion, the impartial chairman imposed a heavy fine on a first offender although the culprit had admitted his guilt, regretted his action, and promised complete cooperation in the future. Neither his change of attitude nor the fact that his workers had joined a union saved this employer from paying for his misconduct. "The offense itself is a serious one," stated Impartial Chairman G. W. Alger in an award fixing the penalty at $2,000.00, "and due regard for the rights of the industry requires the imposition of a substantial penalty."[52]

Under collective agreements of the women's coat and suit trade, employers' associations assumed the initiative in detecting and punishing member firms for nonunion dealings, just as they did for outside contracting. For a time, at least, the role of the impartial chairman was largely confined to supplementing deficiencies and alleviating injustices that crept into the administration of these clauses. He could take over complaints that employers' associations refused to process or he could increase the punishment associations sought to inflict. During the early thirties, the impartial chairmen for this industry entertained numerous appeals which unions had instigated to review and revise disciplinary action taken by employers' associations. Inadequate fines that associations had imposed upon their members

---

text of this decision is reported in *Daily News Record*, June 20, 1921, and in ACWA's *Advance*, June 24, 1921.

[52]G. W. Alger, *Decisions*, Case no. 1114 (no date) on "Non-Union Dealings." In so far as industry arbitrators required those jobbers who sidestepped their designated contractors for nonunion shops to pay the union employees of their designated contractors for the loss of earnings "they rightfully should have received," the enforcement of the nonunion dealings clause of collective agreements hastened the organization of workers in the shops of nonunion contractors. See *Women's Wear Daily*, Oct. 24 and Dec. 17, 1935.

for nonunion dealings were frequently doubled and, on one occasion, increased fivefold. On behalf of the fivefold award, Impartial Chairman George W. Alger stated:

> In view of the great extent of non-union dealings disclosed and the concealment of non-union dealings, the fine of $500 imposed by the [Association's] Grievance Board seems wholly insufficient. Other members of the Merchants' Association, as well as the Union, are entitled to adequate protection against practices of this kind which are unfair to the industry as a whole. Having given due consideration to the disastrous character of the past season and with every desire to extend leniency under these conditions, where possible, this concern which has been a major offender during the season should not be permitted to avoid proper penalty for its infractions of its obligations under the contract. The fine is increased from $500 to $2,500.[53]

Employers Denounce Inadequate Union Growth

For all the concerted efforts of employers' associations, labor unions, and the impartial machinery, the growth of union membership did not keep pace with the expanding centers of production. Union representatives were never able to speak with industry-wide authority on behalf of the workers at the bargaining table; nor did they ever command industry-wide support from a united labor force in the administration of collective agreements. And to make matters worse, the "enlightened" union leadership faltered when organizing drives were most needed to meet intensified competition from nonunion workers in the Great Depression. The ebbtide of union growth ran lowest in the thirties when union strength was most needed to weed out nonunion competition.

The needle trade unions were not altogether to blame for this flaw in the armament of the protocol movement. Neither union threats nor drastic action of the impartial machinery could prevent employer defections to the ranks of the open shop movement during the twenties nor could these measures stop employer

---

[53]G. W. Alger, *Decisions*, Case no. 825 (no date). See also Case nos. 821, 824, and 1092; and a similar collection of earlier decisions of R. V. Ingersoll, Case nos. 576 to 584, classified under the heading "Inadequate Disciplinary Action for Non-Union Dealings." A copy of these decisions can be found in the Abelson papers.

desertions to the ranks of nonunion producers during the depression of the thirties. Just at the time when the "legitimate" manufacturers should have been most aggressive in supporting their philosophies and institutions, they withered under intensive competition from independent firms, small-time contractors, and nonunion shops. Time and again they bolted decisions of their own impartial chairman who had stood out so forthrightly in defense of strong labor organizations. For all the high principles that inspired the protocol movement, efforts to win employer support for union expansion continued to be an uphill battle.

Whatever the causes of stagnation in the growth of union membership, every needle trade union that fell short of industry-wide coverage brought down upon its head the wrath of the organized employers who had remained faithful to the principles of the protocol movement. For in each trade these manufacturers attributed their plight to the presence of unorganized shops which the unions had allowed to thrive. Every standard of wages, hours, or working conditions that led to variations in labor cost between the organized shops and the unorganized shops raised anew the cry that unions had failed to organize the workers. Charges and countercharges on this familiar theme further strengthened the premise that collective bargaining was essentially a medium for controlling competition.

Employer charges of union indifference toward competition from nonunion sources were most likely to be touched off by evidences of failure to organize the trade. One such occasion arose in the dress and waist industry three years after the Dress and Waist Manufacturers' Association and the International Ladies' Garment Workers' Union had signed the dress protocol in January 1913. Charging the ILGWU with failure to enforce the "plane of equality" clause in the dress protocol, the organized manufacturers thus continued their complaint:

> At the time that the agreement was entered into, it was clearly recognized by both parties that it could not be made effective unless the union was in control over the rank and file of its membership, and substantially covered the entire industry. The protocol was conditioned upon the establishment of this fact. It was the union's business to bring into its membership the majority of the workers in the trade. This the union has completely failed to accomplish....

The evidence is indisputable that the union has not retained a majority of the workers in the trade in its membership, and that instead of strengthening the association the opposite has taken place. Because of the failure of the union to organize the remainder of the industry and to maintain, in the shops over which the union has control, standards which equal those prevailing in the association shops, there is at the present time a condition of chaos in the industry which the associations find unendurable.[54]

Union failures to protect the organized manufacturers from the competition of nonunion shops led to more specific contract clauses defining the obligations of these unions to organize all the workers in their respective trades. Beyond the general obligation to "make all reasonable efforts" or to "use all available means" to expand union membership — an obligation common to many collective agreements of the twenties — some needle trade unions were pledged to organize their trades within definite time limits. The union's success or failure in this endeavor could affect the status of jobber-contractor, or contractor-inside manufacturer, agreements. "If the union will make intensive efforts during the next three months to organize the dress jobbers," stated a spokesman for the Association of Dress Manufacturers (contractors) at the time of concluding an agreement with the Wholesale Dress Manufacturers' Association (jobbers), "and if it succeeds in this effort, then the provisions of the agreement which would make for industrial stabilization will be in force for the full two years. If the union falls down on the job, and fails to organize the nonunion jobbers, then the situation will be different."[55]

[54]*Women's Wear,* Jan. 19, 1916. Union leaders refuted such charges. An example came from Morris Hillquit, counsel for the ILGWU in 1915:

> Last year ... we succeeded in organizing practically every man and woman in the trade, we forced an agreement upon the employers, and we raised standards very considerably.... The point I'm making is that the efforts made to standardise conditions in the industry, to make it a fair and reasonable competition, and not a cut-throat competition, came from the Union and not the employers.
> —*Minutes,* Council of Conciliation ... [women's coat and suit trade]
>   (July 14, 1915), vol. 2, p. 83.

[55]*Women's Wear Daily,* Feb. 24, 1930. In return for having the Pleaters' and Stitchers' Association submit to the union a list of all shops "engaged in tucking, stitching, pleating, and novelty work," Local 41, ILGWU, solemnly pledged in its 1932 collective agreement with this association that by February 1, 1933, "it will have organized at least 80 per cent of such shops in

Once the Great Depression of the thirties had reduced competition to a bare struggle for survival, most employers' associations in the women's garment trades were ready to concede that labor unions alone could save the institutions of law and order built up over two decades of collective bargaining. Yet, at this critical period between 1930 and 1932, ILGWU membership fell from around 39,000 to less than 24,000 — a drop of more than 38 percent. "The number of union members is at present a negligible proportion of the total," charged the Affiliated Dress Manufacturers (inside producers) in 1932, "and of course places the union firms at a demoralizing disadvantage in competition with the non-union, substandard resources."[56]

Such an unexpected turn of events was contrary to the purposes of the 1930 collective agreements negotiated in the dress trade. "We entered into the aforementioned collective agreement," stated the Association of Dress Manufacturers in a letter to the ILGWU, "with high hopes and great expectations that the union would be able to effect and extend the unionization of the trade so that the standards and conditions adopted in the agreement would be made uniform for the entire dress industry. But our hopes were frustrated and our expectations doomed to disappointment. The 30 per cent or 35 per cent unionization obtained through the strike of February 1930 has since dwindled to less than 20 per cent. The result has been that a small minority has had to bear the burdens of union conditions and union control, while the vast majority of dress contractors, manufacturers and jobbers were 'free lancing.' "[57]

---

order that such shops may maintain conditions and standards equal to those herein enumerated." *Ibid.*, April 1, 1932.

[56]*Ibid.*, Jan. 25, 1932. A chart showing changes in the membership of the the ILGWU from 1901 to 1944 appears in the addenda to the report of the general executive board to the twenty-fifth convention of the ILGWU. See the union's *Report and Proceedings* (May–June 1944), between pp. 193 and 219.

[57]*Women's Wear Daily*, Sept. 21, 1931. "It has never been our desire to give up union shops," stated Jed Sylbert, president of the Association of Dress Manufacturers (contractors) in 1931, "but we have always hoped that the union would stage a real organization program and bring into line those firms which have continually flouted all union obligations." *Ibid.*, June 19, 1931.

When the 1932 collective agreement in the dress industry was signed, Philip Salkin, president of the Affiliated Dress Manufacturers' Association

Loss of union membership in the early depression years was still more pronounced in out-of-town markets where collective bargaining systems for controlling competition had never been so well established. In men's clothing, for example, the Philadelphia market was finally organized in the late twenties after years of intensive effort by the Amalgamated Clothing Workers' Union. But in the early thirties men's clothing manufacturers of Philadelphia reverted almost completely to nonunion shops, whereupon they again became a serious threat to the organized markets of the industry.[58]

This decline in union strength was particularly demoralizing to the inside manufacturers of the women's coat and suit trade. Samuel Klein, executive director of the Industrial Council of Cloak, Suit and Skirt Manufacturers, railed out against the marked increase of jobbers and contractors operating nonunion shops at a time when the cloakmakers' union had been given a mandate to contain the growth of the jobber-contracting system. In February 1931, this vigilant champion of controlled competition supplied the impartial chairman of his industry with the names of three hundred nonunion jobbers and manufacturers located on Seventh Avenue in the heart of New York City. "The union's powerlessness to curb the growth of nonunion production," Klein asserted, "is responsible for the swift multiplication of the substandard units and these no longer make an effort to obscure their identity." He insisted upon more effective clauses in the new collective agreement obligating the union to suppress "the overwhelming number of nonunion factories operating in the industry."[59]

(inside producers) issued a statement contending that the agreements "would be inconsequential unless the union made a determined attempt to bring about greater unionization in the dress industry." *Ibid.,* Feb. 29, 1932; also, issue of Jan. 25, 1932.

[58]R. G. Brown, "The Influence of Profitability, Unionism and Government Policy on Wages in the Men's Clothing Industry" (unpublished M.S. thesis, Cornell University, 1961), pp. 81–82.

[59]*Women's Wear Daily,* Feb. 17, 1931. See also the issues of Nov. 18 and Dec. 22, 1931.

"We therefore demand that the union give definite assurances to carry on a vigorous and unceasing campaign throughout the life of any new agreement to unionize the unorganized factors operating in the industry." From the demands of the Industrial Council upon the ILGWU for contract changes, in *ibid.,* May 25, 1932.

Formal Charges of Failure to Organize

On at least two occasions, the women's coat and suit industry witnessed the spectacle of an employers' association hailing a labor union before the industry's highest tribunal on charges of failing to organize the trade. In June 1930, Samuel Klein, speaking for the inside manufacturers, formally charged the ILGWU and the Cloakmakers' Joint Board with failing to make adequate efforts to extend union control throughout the women's coat and suit industry. He cited the provisions of the 1929 collective agreements wherein the union undertook "to organize all employees and shops in the industry," against a local background of 342 nonunion firms operating in direct competition with the members of his association. His complaint, filed with the impartial chairman for the industry, continued:

This competition is especially acute and disastrous in certain sections of the industry. Conservative estimates indicate that at least 60 per cent of the production of children's and infant's wear takes place under sub-standard conditions. Nor is this production confined to cheap merchandise. There are non-union stylists of children's wear, whose lower labor costs make competition by our members difficult if not impossible.

If the union had the will to correct these conditions, it could have obtained the information presented to you by us from the same source that we have employed. The union has been negligent in failing to do so. If the union were alive to the situation and were making every possible endeavor to unionize the industry, and yet found itself unable to accomplish its purpose, our grounds for complaint would not be so serious. The fact of the matter, however, is that the union is indifferent to the existence of these non-union firms. It makes sporadic attempts to live up to its obligations, but it does so only because of prodding by the impartial machinery or by manufacturers. The duty of organizing the industry is the union's, and this duty cannot be shifted to any other agency or group.

It is of the essence of the collective agreement that the union shall control substantially the entire industry in the metropolitan district. We charge that it has failed to make any effective efforts in this direction and we ask for relief.[60]

---

[60]Full text of the charges of the Industrial Council of Cloak, Suit and Skirt Manufacturers against the ILGWU appears in *ibid.*, June 17, 1930.

Ten days later, Morris Hillquit, counsel for the ILGWU, submitted a formal reply to the complaint filed by the manufacturers' association. This reply on behalf of the union pointed out that the number of unionized shops had more than doubled (669 to 1,386) following the general organizing strikes of 1929; that the union had spent $350,000 in organizing campaigns for the women's coat and dress industries; and that the union had at times maintained in the field no less than 150 paid organizers who, with help from the union, had succeeded in organizing 90 percent of the workers in the women's coat and suit trade. Moreover, so the reply continued, the union was under no contractual obligation to organize the industry within any prescribed time limits. "Its duties," Hillquit contended, "are limited to steady, energetic, and bona fide efforts to increase its members."[61]

On August 5, 1930, Samuel Klein returned to the wars with a rebuttal to the union's reply. He contested the validity of figures submitted by the union. Only 177, instead of 717, shops were unionized as a result of the 1929 strike, so he contended, and only one-fifteenth of 1 percent of manufacturers' products were purchased from outside sources. Klein strengthened his case with new figures from the records of the industry's National Credit Office showing that, as of August 1, 1930, there were 336 non-union jobbers and manufacturers in the city as against 651 jobbers

---

[61]The clause in question from the 1929 collective agreement of the Industrial Council of Cloak, Suit and Skirt Manufacturers with the ILGWU and the Cloakmakers' Joint Board reads as follows:

The parties hereto recognize the necessity of unionizing the entire industry in the Metropolitan District. In order to bring about such unionization, the Union will make every effort to organize all employees and shops in the industry and the Council will co-operate with it in such efforts.

Hillquit contended that the object of the clause "was not primarily to encourage the union to organize the workers" but rather "to assure to the union the cooperation of the members of the Council in the efforts to organize the workers." In his counterclaim, Hillquit charged the association with a gross violation of this agreement in that 41 of the council's members, according to a report, dated May 21, 1930, by the industry's Cloak and Suit Control Commission, had purchased 46 percent of their total output from nonunion shops.

Full text of the union's reply to the council's charges appears in *Women's Wear Daily*, July 31, 1930.

and manufacturers bound by union contracts. Klein estimated that the nonunion firms did at least 19 percent of the business and surmised that if 90 percent of the workers were organized, many union members must have been working in nonunion shops. "It is a matter of common knowledge," contended Klein, "that cloak-makers with union cards in their pockets and constituting part of that group of 90 per cent of all the workers which the union says it has organized, are resisting the unionization of the non-union shops in which they are employed because they do not want to substitute the week-work system in their shops for the piecework system under which they are thriving."

Summarizing his charges of union neglect in organizing and controlling the workers of the coat and suit trade, Klein did not seek to have the agreement nullified nor the union disbanded. Instead, he asked for the following relief: "That the impartial chairman shall hold that the union has failed to live up to the terms of the collective agreement in so far as it has disbanded its organization machinery many months ago, and that he will direct the union to re-establish it for the purpose of organizing the many non-union units whose competition imposes great hardships on the members of the Industrial Council."[62]

After hearing and compiling all the evidence, Impartial Chairman R. V. Ingersoll reviewed the contentions of both sides and came to the following conclusion:

The Union by its very nature wishes to increase its own member-ship and to bring unorganized shops within its jurisdiction. There is no doubt that the present officers of the union are actuated by this desire and purpose. The office of the impartial chairman is made con-stantly aware of this through union efforts to hold jobbers and manu-facturers to their agreement not to supply work to unorganized sub-manufacturers. It is also a fact that the regular officers and staff of the union devote a part of their time from week to week in the effort to extend the field of organization. How much more they can do may depend upon industrial conditions and upon the state of union finances. Neither workers nor firms can be compelled to organize and some will always remain outside the union fold ... If there is more that the union can reasonably do, it should be undertaken. Some of the information presented by the council in these proceedings will be of value in such efforts and should not be overlooked.

---

[62]The text of Klein's rebuttal appears in *ibid.*, August 6, 1930.

The conclusion on this point is that, although the organizing results of the past year are by no means wholly satisfactory, it can not be held that the union "has violated the agreement in that it has made no adequate effort."[63]

Three years later, the Merchants' Ladies' Garment Association (jobbers) initiated another formal complaint against the union for failing to organize the women's coat and suit trade. This association requested the impartial chairman to declare a provision of the collective agreement on the limitation of contractors to be inoperative because the union had not fulfilled the conditions prescribed in paragraph 19 of the collective agreement. The clause in question read as follows: "The above provisions for the limitation of submanufacturers are accepted by the Association upon the express undertaking on the part of the Union that it will make diligent efforts to increase its control of the workers in the industry, that it will exert its efforts to more effectively unionize the industry, and that it will obtain substantial results in that direction." Complaints or disputes arising from the operation of this clause, if not adjusted between the parties, were to be submitted to the impartial chairman who was authorized to grant appropriate relief.[64]

When this complaint, accompanied by the usual charges and replies, claims and counterclaims, came before Impartial Chairman G. W. Alger, who had succeeded R. V. Ingersoll, he likewise reviewed the contentions of the two parties and, on behalf of the board of arbitration, rendered an award favorable to the union. His opinion throws considerable light on the purposes and processes of collective action.

The Merchants' Association contends that the Union has failed to meet the requirements of the first paragraph quoted above and the relief which it asks is the abrogation by the Impartial Chairman of the provisions of the contract providing for limitation of contractors. The case therefore involves a consideration of the operation of the Union with respect to unionization and the results obtained. The obligation assumed by the Union has obviously two aspects — first, that

---

[63]R. V. Ingersoll, *Decisions,* Case no. 470, as quoted in ILGWU's *Justice,* Sept. 12, 1930.

[64]The quotation is here taken from G. W. Alger, *Decisions* (1932–1933), Case no. 819-B. For the complaints of the jobbers, see *Women's Wear Daily,* Nov. 16, 1932.

it will make diligent efforts to increase its control of the workers in the industry and to more effectively unionize the industry, and second, that it will obtain substantial results in that direction. As to the first of these matters there is no substantial dispute between the parties. The counsel for the Merchants' Association frankly concedes that diligent efforts have been made by the Union to increase its control and to effectively unionize the industry but it is contended that the Union has, notwithstanding these efforts, failed to obtain substantial results in that direction.

The proof shows that the union has made diligent unionization efforts, the details of the work done and expenditures made both of time and money in connection with that campaign being fully shown in the record, showing unionization work done under the direction of the Joint Board, maintaining organization committees and separate offices for their operation in various sections and in conducting strikes against some two hundred and forty-nine non-union cloak manufacturers and contractors. So far as concerns results obtained from these efforts, the Union states without contradiction that eleven firms previously non-union have been induced to join the Merchants' Association, twenty to join the Industrial Council and ninety-six to join the American Association. The foregoing does not include two large non-union jobbing firms which, it states, have been induced to join the Merchants' Association since the close of the hearing.

The testimony as to the number of non-union workers who have become unionized through these efforts is not entirely satisfactory, the membership of the Union somewhat fluctuating, and exact figures on fixed dates not being readily ascertainable. The estimate of the Union is that there has been an increase in membership of about ten percent since the date of the new agreement, August 2, 1932. The Union has, it says, no record sufficiently definite in character to make exact figures possible as to the number of non-union workers or the proportion of such non-union workers to the entire industry. . . .

The union also contends that it has produced results of great importance in industrial control by resisting and arresting the threatened process of disintegration of the unionized institutions in the industry, by helping materially to eliminate the association of Brooklyn contractors as a factor in the industry as well as by increasing the membership of the three employers' associations operating under collective agreements with it as stated above.

The question of whether or not the Union has obtained substantial results as required by its contract should be determined in the light of the conditions under which such results are to be obtained. What might be insubstantial results under favorable conditions might be substantial results under adverse conditions. The Union points out the fact that the past season has been one of extraordinary difficulty for all factors in the industry — extreme loss in volume of business, low prices, intense competition particularly on the low-cost merchandise, extraordinary strains upon the depleted income of the Union itself.

The Union contends that the results which it has obtained under conditions briefly outlined above are substantial and more particularly as it contends in view of the failure of the Merchants' Association itself to render the cooperation which it agreed to furnish and which, on the contrary, added to the unionization difficulties of the Union itself. In this regard it contends that there has been a failure on the part of the Merchants' Association to co-operate in the elimination of non-union dealings by its own members and the failure of its Grievance Committee to discipline its members for non-union dealings on its own initiative, or when complaint is made by the Union and sustained by the representatives of the Merchants' Association to impose adequate fines against its members found guilty of offenses against the industry.

There is no substantial evidence introduced to contradict the claim made by the Union as to its efforts or as to the extent of their success in unionization. The proof with reference to the extent of unionization as had been stated is not complete nor in all respects satisfactory. Adverse conditions, moreover, have doubtless played their parts in the results obtained. The proof, however, does not justify a finding by the Board that these results have not been substantial under the circumstances shown. The Union will be expected to continue without abatement its efforts for the further unionization of the industry and in which it is entitled to receive and should receive from all factors such cooperation and assistance as is possible to accomplish an end highly desirable for all factors in the industry.

After careful consideration of all testimony and of the conditions under which the work of unionization has been attempted and the proof of the results obtained, the Board is constrained to conclude that the complaint of the Merchants' Association as made has not been sustained.[65]

Concluding Observations

Beyond the barricades of controlled competition manned since 1910 by the organized forces of industry lay the outposts of independent shops with separate union contracts. And beyond

---

[65]G. W. Alger, *Decisions* (1932–1933), Case no. 819-B. See *Women's Wear Daily,* Dec. 19, 1933.

these outposts sprawled the dense jungles of unrestrained competition where roamed the unorganized workers and the unorganized employers preying upon the decent labor standards of their trades. No one contended that this setting could long endure. Nor did anyone believe a compromise with the unorganized elements of industry could provide a lasting settlement. Either the forces of law and order would conquer the unorganized and bring them into the fold or else the realm of law and order would fall before the barbaric attacks of uninhibited competitors. In this war of attrition, the needle trade unions were called upon to bear the brunt of the fighting.

The campaigns in this battle of the wilderness were a patchwork of misguided intentions, cross purposes, and utter confusion. From the very beginning, the needle trade unions were beset by indifference within their own membership and by treachery from the organized employers. Lack of funds handicapped their operations and desertions to the enemy depleted their ranks. Leading manufacturers goaded union officials into greater efforts with one hand, while knifing them in the back with the other. And, at the end, the ILGWU was twice hailed before the highest tribunal of the established order to account for its conduct. Surely if the battle against the unorganized was to be won, then employers' associations as well as labor unions had to participate in the attack.

Chapter 14

The Growth of

Employers' Associations

S TRIVING for a completely organized and well-disciplined labor force was only half the battle of preparing for industry-wide standards of production. Equally important was the struggle for a more thorough organization of the manufacturers in each trade. From the beginnings of the protocol movement, the concept of all-inclusive employers' associations went hand in hand with the concept of all-inclusive labor unions. Not only were strong employer organizations a central theme of the Brandeis Conferences in 1910 but this objective remained in the forefront of all plans to regulate competition in the needle trades. "Both parties agree," runs a clause in the white goods protocol of February 17, 1913, "that in order to maintain fair competition in the industry the conditions of work shall be equalized and the cost of labor standardized ... [and] to this end a strong organization of the employers and a strong union are necessary, each working to strengthen the other."

Organizing the Manufacturers

The movement for a more thorough organization of the manufacturers was supported from many sources. Some employers were compelled to seek the protection of an association by union pressures at the bargaining table. Others, in later years, were encouraged to organize employer groups because of governmental legislation, particularly the National Industrial Recovery Act of

1933 and the National Labor Relations Act of 1935. Still others were led to create or join employers' associations through the influence of the impartial machinery established under collective agreements for each trade. In the vanguard of the movement to organize the employers, however, were the "enlightened" labor leaders and the "legitimate" manufacturers — those standard-bearers of the protocol movement, who, by one means or another, jointly or severally, exerted the necessary pressure that brought independent employers to see the need for cooperating with the organized factions of their trades.[1]

Inspired by self-interest or prodded by unions, employers' associations from time to time initiated membership drives of their own. "Every effort shall be made by the Association to enlist as its members all manufacturers who are not now members of the Association," runs a clause in the 1917 collective agreement of the Cotton Garment Manufacturers' Association with Locals 10 and 62 of the ILGWU. Taking a leaf from union membership drives, employer groups prepared and distributed to independent employers letters and circulars listing the advantages of united efforts to combat the evils of their trades. Or they set up organizing committees and sent out representatives to interview the independent producers in the hope of winning their cooperation for the struggle against illegitimate competition. Or they offered special inducements to new members by suspending initiation fees or otherwise reducing the usual costs of membership.[2]

---

[1]The right of employers to organize in associations or groups and to bargain collectively, through chosen representatives, is recognized and affirmed. This right shall not be denied, abridged, or interfered with by the workers in any manner whatsoever.

> —"Principles and Policies to Govern Relations between Workers and Employers in War Industries for the Duration of the War," report of the War Labor Conference Board, March 29, 1918, in U.S. Department of Labor, *National War Labor Board*, BLS Bulletin no. 287 (December 1921), p. 32. An analogous provision guaranteed the right of the workers to organize.

[2]For examples of special inducements to join employers' associations, see *Women's Wear*, Jan. 16, 1919. Early employer successes in creating a sense of group responsibility toward their common problems were reflected in the following extract from the *Jewish Daily Forward*, June 3, 1915: "The condition is such that a prominent manufacturer is ashamed not to belong to the Association. He is looked upon just as a scab is among workingmen. If a member leaves the Association, he is damned by all the members — he is

As a rule, the organized groups of "legitimate" manufacturers appealed only to the independent employers with separate labor union contracts — those firms that could contribute to the stability of their industries. No invitations to membership were issued to "corporation" shops or to other fly-by-night operators who represented the outcasts of their trades. "Between these two extremes — legitimate and illegitimate shops — " stated the *American Garment News,* organ of the American Cloak and Suit Manufacturers' Association (contractors) in the issue of January 26, 1922, "there are a number of independent concerns which though not organized and not subject to uniform methods adopted by one single organization, are in many instances, 'on the level.' These shops must be tackled in our crusade against the rapacity and destructiveness of the corporation shops. These firms must be induced by our members to become their comrades under the banner of the American Association."[3]

Strong support for building up the membership of employers' associations also came from third parties. Brandeis himself in 1912 expressed the desire that the employers' association for the women's coat and suit trade expand until its membership include

practically considered an outcast." From a translation filed in the Abelson papers.

For a report on a campaign to get 75 independent inside manufacturers into the Industrial Council of Cloak, Suit and Skirt Manufacturers, see *Women's Wear,* July 9, 1926. See also, "A Call to Action," explaining why all eligible employers should join the Association of Dress Manufacturers. This call, appearing in *Women's Wear Daily,* August 10, 1931, officially opened a campaign by the association to increase its membership.

[3]See above, pp. 128–129.

In the 1913 collective agreement between the United Manufacturers' and Merchants' Association and the United Garment Workers, the association agreed to take into its membership all men's, young men's, and children's clothing manufacturers "of such character and financial standing as will justify the Association in assuming responsibility for the faithful performance of the agreement with the union." *United Garment Workers' Conference* (pamphlet, dated Jan. 8, 1913), Appendix A, pp. 5–6.

"It was unanimously decided that the Manager of the Muff Bed Association shall call upon the Manufacturers who have independent agreements with the Union, for the purpose of winning their support for the Association, for the reason that the Association is planning to improve conditions not only for the association shops, but for the entire Muff Bed Industry." From a report of the Committee on Immediate Action of the Muff Bed Industry, dated Feb. 8, 1915, filed in the Abelson papers.

at least 75 percent of the manufacturers in the trade. Further support came from the U. S. Commission on Industrial Relations in 1916. After completing its extensive inquiries into labor-management relations of the needle trades and other industries, this Commission submitted a report strongly favoring a system of collective bargaining between employers' associations and labor unions, with each organization so constituted as to match the power and strength of the other. In its final analysis, the Commission advanced the following set of conditions most likely to produce successful bargaining.

Where the association of employers and the union participating in the joint agreement cover the entire competitive district, it becomes possible to regulate the trade or the industry, not merely with reference to wages and hours, but with reference to unemployment, the recruiting of the trade, and the introduction of machinery and new processes. . . .

The essential element in a system of joint agreements is that all action shall be preceded by discussion and deliberation. If either party through lack of organization is unable to participate effectively in the discussion and deliberation, to that extent the system falls short of the ideal. . . .

The thorough and effective organization of the employers is lacking in many trades in which the workmen are well organized. It is highly desirable that such organization should be brought about.[4]

Provisions Favoring Employers' Associations

The success of the movement to strengthen employers' associations for collective bargaining depended to a substantial degree upon the reaction of labor unions. Whereas support from the organized workers could become an effective means for bringing independent producers into the ranks of employers' associations, hostility from labor unions was likely to stall all efforts at developing strong employer organizations of industry-wide

---

[4]U.S. Commission on Industrial Relations, *Final Report and Testimony* (1916), vol. 1, p. 119. A study by the British Board of Trade had arrived at similar conclusions: "The value of efficient organization on the part of employers and work-people as a means of securing the due fulfillment of industrial agreements is very clearly demonstrated by the experience of the different trades of the country." *Report of the Industrial Council of the British Board of Trade on Its Inquiry into Industrial Agreements,* reprinted in U.S. Department of Labor, BLS Bulletin no. 133 (August 18, 1913), p. 17.

coverage. Union leaders approached the issue of all-inclusive associations with mixed feelings. On the one hand, they feared the power of all-inclusive associations at the bargaining table; on the other hand, they feared even more the evil effects of illegitimate competition from independent producers who remained outside the fold. Not every union leader preferred the stabilizing effect of association-wide bargaining to one-way dictation through separate agreements with each employer.[5]

From the beginning of the protocol movement in 1910, collective bargaining in the needle trades was as much concerned with protecting employer groups from the hostility of labor unions as it was directed toward protecting labor unions from the hostility of employers. Needle trade unions have acknowledged the value of an employers' association in maintaining standards throughout an industry, just as the organized employers have acknowledged the value of a labor union for that purpose. Contract provisions on union security were generally matched by contract provisions on the security of employers' associations. Decisions of the impartial machinery to protect labor organizations were paralleled by decisions of the impartial machinery to protect employer organizations.[6]

---

[5]The outstanding example of union opposition to dealing with employers' associations of the needle trades came in the millinery industry during the open shop decade of the twenties. Charging that too many manufacturers were hostile to unions and tended to abuse their powers through associations, the millinery workers in New York City between 1922 and 1932 successfully insisted upon dealing with individual employers. Cloth Hat, Cap and Millinery Workers' International Union, *Report and Proceedings,* Eighteenth Biennial Convention (October 1933), p. 17.

But this attitude was abruptly changed in the 1932 collective agreement between the Women's Headwear Group and the Cloth Hat, Cap and Millinery Workers' International Union. The text, printed in *Women's Wear Daily,* March 4, 1932, stated that both parties find it "necessary to have an organization representing the workers in the industry and an organization representing the employers and a collective agreement between the two organizations both pledging their good faith to cooperate for the enforcement of such an agreement."

[6]See the protocol of peace of the New York Association of House Dress and Kimono Manufacturers with the ILGWU and its Locals 10 and 41, effective Feb. 11, 1913. Text in C. H. Winslow, *Conciliation, Arbitration, and Sanitation in the Dress and Waist Industry of New York City,* U.S. Department of Labor, BLS Bulletin no. 145 (April 10, 1914), Appendix B, pp. 128–131.

In the original dress and waist protocol of January 18, 1913, for example, the International Ladies' Garment Workers' Union recognized "the moral obligation of every employer in the industry to belong to the manufacturers' association and to contribute to the expense of the institutions created by the two parties for the uplift of the industry." Furthermore, the union assumed a definite obligation to help achieve this goal. "Accordingly," continued this section of the protocol, "all employers desiring to settle with the union in the pending strike will be referred first to the association and requested to apply for membership." Those employers refusing to join their association were to receive no superior benefits from negotiating individual contracts with the union.[7]

Later, collective agreements placed other responsibilities upon labor unions to help strengthen employers' associations. Beyond the general union obligation to "co-operate with the association in its effort to increase its membership," labor unions were directed to take specific steps that would tend to drive independent manufacturers into associations and help to keep them there. One common device was to require unions to exact of independent producers a cash security for contract performance which would be high enough to offset all the costs of association membership: initiation fees, annual dues, special assessments, and contributions for the support of the impartial machinery. If this cash security were forfeited each year for some contract infraction, as appeared likely, then the financial outlay for signing a separate labor contract would be at least as heavy as the total costs of association membership.[8]

Other contract provisions were designed to promote association membership by denying independent firms more advan-

---

[7]*Ibid.*, p. 25. Subsequently, clauses of this nature were widely adopted in contracts of the needle trades.

[8]After consenting to "co-operate with the association in its effort to increase its membership," the Dressmakers' Joint Board and the ILGWU in their collective agreement, dated Feb. 12, 1930, with the Association of Dress Manufacturers (contractors) guaranteed to exact from nonassociation contractors: "a cash deposit as security for the performance of their agreements in amount at least as large as the amounts of initiation fees, membership dues and other charges which members of the association may be required to deposit or pay to the association during the term of this agreement." The text of this agreement is printed in *Women's Wear Daily*, Feb. 18, 1930.

tageous terms under separate contracts with the union. Some collective agreements required labor unions to see that independent manufacturers with separate union contracts not only maintained the same wage scales but also met the same sanitary standards, kept the same uniform set of books and records, submitted the interpretation of their contracts to the same impartial machinery, and fell under the same specialized institutions of market-wide control. Unions that were aggressively vigilant could subject independents to even more rigid enforcement controls, for they had the power to settle all disputes on their own authority under the threat to strike independent firms without awaiting the operation of the grievance procedure.[9]

A stronger inducement for association membership came with the encouragement given unions to impose on independent firms more onerous conditions than the terms of contract settlement covering the organized manufacturers. Sometimes, this encouragement was merely suggested in the requirements of master agreements that unions make the terms of individual contracts *at least* as onerous as those of the collective agreement. At other times, this policy of imposing heavier burdens on independents was more clearly stated. "The purpose and effect of collective bargaining is to place association firms at an advantage over independent jobbers and manufacturers," frankly conceded Samuel Blumberg, legal counsel of the Wholesale Dress Manufacturers' Association, in 1930. "It must be apparent that collective bargaining fails if individual manufacturers or jobbers, who have made independent contracts with the union, secure by the making of such agreements advantages over association competitors."[10]

---

[9] "The union, recognizing the value of the association for the maintenance of standards throughout the industry, hereby agrees that it will refer all employers desiring to enter into agreement with the union, to the association. Should such employers fail to join the association and enter into individual contracts with the union, such contracts shall provide for the observance and enforcement of all standards herein set forth." From the 1916 collective agreement between the Boston Dress and Waist Manufacturers' Association and the ILGWU. The text is printed in *Women's Wear*, Feb. 10, 1916.

[10] *Women's Wear Daily*, Feb. 19, 1930. For examples of more onerous terms imposed on independent shops of the house dress industry in 1913, see Winslow, *Conciliation, Arbitration, and Sanitation in the Dress and*

For the most part, however, labor leaders required no urging to raise the labor standards of independent firms. The goals that unions fought to obtain from employers' associations they first won from individual employers who could not help themselves. Unorganized firms became the campground for union experimentation with piecework, limitations on contracting, and controls over the hazards of unemployment, accidents, sickness, and old age. Like the pattern of higher wages and shorter hours, these new "fringe" clauses — as well as other union-made rules introduced during the life of a contract — could be forced upon independent firms through use of the strike. Each new concession won from the independents then became a lever with which to pry similar gains from employers' associations.

Generally, the unorganized employers flocked to their associations as a refuge from union controls over the terms of employment. The would-be independent clung to his association because he could not escape without falling prey to union dictation. "He knows very well," observed the *Jewish Daily Forward* for July 6, 1913, "that the moment he leaves the Association the Union will compel him to sign a contract with it, and then he will be entirely under its control." Some labor leaders were more disturbed at losing their power over independents than they were concerned with any lack of industry-wide coverage by employers' associations. Only because so many union members preferred to keep some, if not all, employers outside their associations was it necessary for the organized manufacturers to insist upon "association security" clauses in collective agreements.[11]

Protection against Loss of Association Membership

Association security was not only aimed at acquiring new members for the ranks of the organized manufacturers, it was equally

Waist Industry of New York City, pp. 131–132. A typical "at least" clause appears in the 1919 collective agreement of the Dress and Waist Manufacturers' Association with the ILGWU and its Locals 10, 25, and 58. "The union pledges itself that in order to carry out the spirit of this agreement it will not enter into any agreement with any employer not a signatory hereto or a counterpart hereof which will provide terms as favorable as those herein contained." From the text of the 1929 Full Fashioned Hosiery Industry Agreement as reproduced in *Women's Wear Daily,* Sept. 6, 1929.

[11]From a translation filed in the Abelson papers. See also *Women's Wear,* Feb. 26, 1920.

concerned with retaining those employers who had already joined. Keeping the organized manufacturers in "good standing" with their associations was no less difficult than keeping the organized workers in "good standing" with their unions. In either case, where the requirements of good standing called for strict adherence to the terms collective agreements, many who had cast their lot with the organized forces of their industries later decided to renounce their allegiance in the hope of dodging the obligations of their labor contracts. The inevitable result in both cases was a turnover in membership that at times rocked the foundations of industrial stability.

After 1910, the membership of employers' associations, like the membership of labor unions, tended to fluctuate with changes in the business climate. During periods of depression, inability to control competition in labor standards brought wholesale desertions from the ranks of the organized manufacturers. Following the First World War, membership in the association that signed the original Protocol of Peace fell from 409 firms in 1918 to 187 in 1924; and a decade later membership in the successor organization, the Industrial Council of Cloak, Suit and Skirt Manufacturers, fell from 289 firms on January 1, 1930 to 165 firms on January 1, 1933. Even in prosperous times, membership turnover in this organization, the bellwether of the protocol movement, was disturbing. Between July 1, 1926 and the middle of June 1929, this association lost 98 members: 37 were dropped for conducting nonunion shops; 11 left the association to sign separate contracts with the union; 27 firms went out of business; 19 went bankrupt; three joined other associations; and one became a nonunion jobber.[12]

Some associations sought to hold their membership by imposing restrictions on the right to resign. "No member of the Association," stated the bylaws of the Cloth Hat and Cap Manufacturers'

[12]*Women's Wear*, April 1, 1924; *Women's Wear Daily*, June 19, 1929 and Jan. 23, 1933. On Jan. 20, 1932, *Women's Wear Daily* reported that 45 firms had left the Industrial Council within the preceding six weeks. Vigilant recruitment became an indispensable policy. Thus, between August 24, 1925 and Feb. 20, 1926, the American Cloak and Suit Manufacturers' Association (contractors in the women's coat and suit trade) lost 119 members through resignations; but in the same period 118 new firms joined the association. *Women's Wear*, March 8, 1926. See above, pp. 33–34.

Association of New York, "shall be permitted to resign on less than sixty days' notice in advance of his intention to resign, nor during pendency of any strike or lockout, nor shall any resignation be accepted from any member in arrears of any dues or payments or assessments, or while charges are pending against him." Of course a member could always evade these restrictions by taking action that would lead to his suspension or expulsion.

The most logical restraint against loss of association membership was the inability of the deserter to obtain release from the obligations of the collective agreement. "Notwithstanding the resignation, suspension or expulsion of any member of the Association from membership thereof," stated the 1930 collective agreement between the Associated Employers of Fur Workers and several locals of the fur workers' union, "the member so resigning, suspended or expelled shall continue to be bound by the terms of this agreement for the full fixed term thereof and all obligations of such member to the Union and to the Association hereunder shall remain unimpaired during such term."[13]

This type of provision hit directly at the practice of resigning from an association to dodge an adverse decision of the impartial chairman. Employers who were caught violating their obligations would never await certain conviction if they could remove themselves from the jurisdiction of the court by resigning from their association. "The union would spend several hours, sometimes several days, arguing cases before the impartial board," explained Alex Cohen, manager, shirt department, ACWA, in 1927, "then, after all this time had been spent, it would be informed that the manufacturer had resigned from the manufacturers' as-

---

[13]The duty of former members to observe their collective agreements was likewise continued where entire associations were dissolved before the expiration of their labor agreements. Under some agreements, this obligation of association members to observe the contract prevailed even though the union itself should terminate the master agreement for reasons of noncompliance. A clause of the 1935 collective agreement of the Children's Dress and Sportswear Contractors' Association with the ILGWU stated that in case of such termination "the individual members of the association shall continue to be liable under this agreement with the same force and effect as if they individually entered into this agreement." See other specimen clauses with notes in Elias Lieberman, *The Collective Labor Agreement* (1939), pp. 139–141.

sociation and was no longer subject to the rulings of the arbitrator.''[14]

Perhaps a more effective measure to restrain members from resigning would be to authorize union control of grievance procedure for the exiled firm — a policy applied by W. M. Leiserson, as impartial chairman of the men's clothing industry in New York City just after the First World War. Fears of union control over grievances could more readily be aroused if the consequences were written into collective agreements themselves. Such was precisely the purpose of the following clause from the first collective agreement of the Belt Association with Local 40, ILGWU, in 1936:

Should a member of the Association resign or be suspended or expelled or have his membership terminated for any other reason whatsoever, then it is expressly agreed that such member's liability under this agreement shall continue until the 15th day of August, 1938, but that such member shall not be entitled to the arbitration of disputes as provided for in this agreement; neither shall it be entitled to have a representative of the Association accompany a Union representative at the time a Union representative visits the shop of such member for purposes of investigation, as provided for in paragraph "18" of this agreement; and that the decision of the representative of the Union in cases of disputes shall be binding upon such member; and, in cases of dispute, the workers shall not be obligated to continue with their work in the shop until the dispute has been fully settled, anything in this agreement to the contrary notwithstanding.[15]

---

[14]*Daily News Record,* June 27, 1927. Writing for the *New York Times,* July 21, 1929, Louis Stark pointed out that an independent who left his association to dodge a three-year labor contract could not only be sued in the courts for the fulfillment of his contractual obligations, but he also suffered a heavier burden by having to deposit cash security with the union in addition to continuing his usual contributions toward maintaining the office of the impartial chairman established under the collective agreement between the association and the union. See also *Women's Wear Daily,* July 12, 1929. In 1920 W. M. Leiserson, impartial chairman for the men's clothing industry of New York City, ruled that a firm could not resign from an association to avoid a decision by the impartial chairman. ACWA, *Report and Proceedings,* Fifth Biennial Convention (May 1922), p. 8.

[15]A similar clause appears in the 1938 collective agreement between the United Knitwear Manufacturers' League and Local 155, ILGWU. The 1938 collective agreement of the Eastern Women's Headwear Association with the United Hatters, Cap and Millinery Workers' International Union and the

Operating on the assumption that the right to strike was the most effective weapon of union domination over exiled firms, organized employers have at times encouraged union strikes against deserters from association ranks. An example occurred in 1916 when Local 24 of the Millinery and Straw Hat Workers' Union declared strikes against two former members of the Ladies' Hat Manufacturers' Protective Association. One union member was told that the strikes had been instigated by the employer group. "When I made a protest and questioned our leaders how we could support so many strikers with such a meager treasury as we have," so he later recalled, "I was told that I should not worry as these two strikes were being supported by the protective association and that the treasury of the union would not suffer by the transaction."[16]

There was no reason, of course, why union domination of the exiled firm should be limited to one-way control over grievance procedures. The plea of the organized manufacturers was that the *substantive* terms of independent contracts, as well as the

---

Joint Board of Millinery Workers, Locals 2, 24, and 42, expressly stated that "the Union shall not permit such former member of the Association to employ the machinery of arbitration and adjustment provided for in this agreement." See also a brief prepared by Morris Hillquit, general counsel, ILGWU, for the Governor's Advisory Commission on the women's coat and suit trade, suggesting various restraints that his union might exert over expelled association members. *Women's Wear*, April 19, 1925.

[16]*Ibid.*, August 1, 1916. "A member suspended shall not be entitled to the protection of the strike clause or any other provision of the collective agreement." From the 1936 collective agreement between the Associated Fur Coat and Trimming Manufacturers and the New York Furriers' Joint Council, International Fur Workers' Union.

Several months prior to the expiration of the 1936 pact, a considerable number of dress firms, members of the Popular, National, and Affiliated associations, resigned from their respective groups with the apparent aim of engaging in non-union production. Though this attempted exodus was surrounded by a great deal of secrecy, the Union was soon in possession of the names of the firms which were planning this coup. In January 1939, the Joint Board served notice on these firms that unless they rejoined their associations, steps would be taken against them. The plot soon fizzled out as most of these firms returned to their old affiliations — after some pressure had been exerted by the Union.

— Report of the union's general executive board, ILGWU, *Report and Proceedings*, Twenty-fourth Convention (May–June 1940), p. 57.

procedural terms, be more onerous; and this plan was doubly stressed for those firms that had resigned or had been expelled from their associations. A case in point arose in 1924 when a firm of women's coat and suit manufacturers whose owners were formerly affiliated with the Cloak, Suit and Skirt Manufacturers' Protective Association had to accept a union-drafted contract. The terms of this agreement were far more onerous than the terms of the association agreement in designating a higher number of workers to be employed and in determining the conditions for contracting out work.[17]

More important was the restriction that none of the firm's contractors could be discharged or changed during the life of the agreement "except for good cause and upon the written consent of the union." The firm was forbidden to lay off workers during the dull season but had to divide the work among all those on the payroll. Moreover, the firm was compelled to open its premises to union inspection at any time and to submit "all books, business correspondence, and memoranda" that union agents might wish to see for possible violations of the agreement. For each contract infraction, the union automatically collected $3,000 in liquidated damages that the firm was compelled to keep on deposit at all times. The owners of the firm publicly denounced the agreement as "vicious, tyrannical, one-sided, and un-American" and they eventually appealed to the courts for an injunction against the ILGWU, but their action was to no avail.[18]

The possibility of isolating deserters and renegades from all dealings with the organized forces of an industry provided the ultimate pressure for keeping employers in good standing with their associations. In some cases, unions assumed an obligation not to negotiate separate contracts with ex-members until those firms had settled all their accounts with their association. In other cases, separate union contracts were forbidden without the

---

[17]By the terms of the new contract, the firm was obligated to employ at all times "not less than 25 operators, 10 pressers, seven cutters, 10 finishers, six examiners and four finishers' helpers;" and each of the firm's six assigned contractors had to employ "not less than 14 operators and cutters at each establishment and workers of all other crafts in proportion." *Women's Wear*, Jan. 15, 1924.

[18]*Ibid.* See also the lengthy opinion of Mr. Justice W. P. Burr in Maisel v. Sigman, New York Supreme Court, 123 Misc. 714 (1924), 205 N.Y. Supp. 807.

consent of the impartial chairman or the board of arbitration for the industry. Occasionally, deserting employers were barred from separate union contracts altogether. Wherever an industry was highly organized, union refusal to furnish workers was more effective than employer boycotts in driving renegades and deserters completely from the trade. The women's garment industry trucking agreements of the late thirties forbade deliveries of goods to companies that had been suspended from their associations.[19]

Labor Unions and "Closed Shop" Associations

Refusal to work for ex-association members was but a step short of refusal to work for any employer who did not belong to an employers' association. From the days of the Brandeis Conferences, many supporters of the protocol movement advocated that all independent firms be denied access to the organized workers of their trade. Employer membership in an association was to be a prerequisite for obtaining competent help, just as worker membership in a labor union became a qualifying condition for obtaining employment. Under the union "closed shop" rule,

---

[19]In its *Supplementary Recommendations* of July 10, 1925, Governor Alfred E. Smith's Advisory Commission for the women's coat and suit trade recommended that no manufacturer, jobber, or contractor suspended from membership in his association be allowed a separate contract with the union until he had paid all his debts to his association and had settled all outstanding claims against him under the collective agreement. The essence of this recommendation was later incorporated into a number of collective agreements in the needle trades. See, for example, the pertinent clause in the 1938 collective agreement of the Eastern Women's Headwear Association with the Joint Board of Millinery Workers and the United Hatters, Cap and Millinery Workers' International Union.

Addressing the Merchants' Ladies' Garment Association in March 1926, Samuel Blumberg, association counsel, roundly denounced the ILGWU for permitting a firm expelled from the association to continue in business without a union contract and with no responsibility for maintaining union standards. He also lambasted the union for granting an ex-association firm an independent agreement on deposit of only $500 cash security — a sum that represented only about one-half the dues and assessments that association members paid into their organization. Mr. Blumberg urged the adoption of appropriate regulations "that would not make it quite so easy for the jobber, manufacturer, or sub-manufacturer who has violated the agreements to make independent contracts." He suggested that independent ex-members be permitted to sign separate union contracts only with the consent of the impartial chairman. *Women's Wear,* March 8, 1926.

manufacturers were required to hire union members only. Under the employer "closed association" rule, union members would be permitted to work for association firms only. Presumably, the operation of this rule would drive all employers into associations or else force them out of the industry.

Refusing to work for independent firms as a means of driving employers into associations became a subject of discussion at the hearings of the U. S. Commission on Industrial Relations, April 8, 1914. There, Abe Bisno, chairman of the ILGWU educational committee and former general manager of the Cloakmakers' Union, testified that the objectives of the women's coat and suit protocol could not be attained "until the manufacturers' association themselves will increase their membership by taking in almost everybody in the industry." Under questioning he conceded that the union might contribute substantially to this end by refusing to work for employers who did not join the association. "The union can help a manufacturer to get out of business if he is not a member of the manufacturers' association," acknowledged the union leader. But J. H. Cohen, counsel for the manufacturers, felt at the time that any action taken by the union that would force employers into associations or else drive them out of business would be un-American and illegal.[20]

If unions of the needle trades did not resort to such extremes to

---

[20]*Final Report and Testimony* (1916), vol. 1, Bisno at pp. 584–585, Cohen at pp. 588–589.

Refusal of a printing trades union to permit its members to work for a commercial printer who refused to join the San Francisco Printers' Board of Trade was later sustained by the District Court of Appeals of California in Overland Publishing Co. v. Union Lithograph Co., 207 Pac. 412 (1922). This case was discussed in an article, "Exclusive Collective Agreements to Establish Labor Monopoly," in *Monthly Labor Review,* December 1922, vol. 15, pp. 1389–1391. In 1939, however, Elias Lieberman, legal counsel for several unions, cited cases to support the view that union members could not refuse to work for employers who would not join a particular employers' association. "An agreement between a union and an association," so Lieberman concluded, "providing that union members will work only for employers who are members of the association has been held illegal, against public policy as tending to create a monopoly," citing Brescia Construction Co. v. Stone Masons' Contractors' Association, New York Supreme Court, 195 App. Div. 647 (1921), 187 N.Y. Supp. 77, and Falciglia v. Gallagher, New York Supreme Court, 164 Misc. 838 (1937), 299 N.Y. Supp. 890. Lieberman, *The Collective Labor Agreement,* p. 80.

encourage association membership, the evidence suggests that they at least exerted more pressure on independent employers than was often sanctioned in collective agreements. Especially during the settlement of disputes over the terms of new contracts was the union able to exert effective pressure on independent firms to join their association. The negotiation of the 1929 collective agreements for the women's coat and suit trade provides a good example. In return for employer acceptance of a new contract, the ILGWU resolved to strengthen the position of the associations in the trade. "The campaign to organize the coat and suit industry that is being carried on actively by the International Ladies' Garment Workers' Union is showing results every day," announced Isidore Nagler, general manager of the Cloak and Dressmakers' Joint Board. Progress was reported in *Women's Wear Daily* under such revealing front-page captions as, "Drive Nets Eight for Jobbers' Group — Stops 50 Submanufacturers Causing Jobbers to Apply to Merchants' Association for Membership, Says Dubinsky" (August 29, 1929); and "Union Cloak Trade Drive Progressing — Nagler Reports Nine Firms Joining Council and Four Wholesalers Affiliating with Merchants' Ladies' Garment Association" (August 30, 1929).

In support of this campaign, the ILGWU not only continued to strike independent firms but it also refused to enter into separate agreements with them. This policy, noted the union's general executive board in its subsequent report to the 1929 ILGWU convention, had a salutary effect upon the size of the memberships of the three associations (jobbers, contractors, and inside manufacturers). Within a period of four months, according to this report, the Industrial Council (inside manufacturers) grew from 140 to 320 members; the American Cloak and Suit Manufacturers' Association (contractors) expanded from about 400 to nearly 1,100 members; and the Merchants' Ladies' Garment Association (jobbers) increased its membership from 40 to 115. On the basis of these statistics, the union's general executive board concluded that the most important achievement of the strike that year was the permanent check placed on the "dismemberment of the industry into small irresponsible production units."[21]

---

[21]ILGWU, *Report and Proceedings,* Twentieth Convention (December 1929), p. 62. A different set of figures reflecting the growth of these three associations appears at p. 77. For still another compilation of statistics cover-

After contributing so heavily in 1929 toward increasing the membership of employers' associations for the women's coat and suit trade, the ILGWU leadership made an equally outstanding move in 1930 to promote the better organization of employers in the dress and waist industry. Having extended the expiring dress contracts for twelve months in order to concentrate on the coat and suit trade, the union now turned its attention to the formation of a new association for the inside dress manufacturers. This new employer group — the Affiliated Dress Manufacturers' Association — was to become the counterpart of the powerful Industrial Council of the women's coat and suit trade. During a general strike of all dress and waist manufacturers that year, the ILGWU actively supported the new association by favoring a return to work of all strikers employed in association shops while delaying the return of strikers in nonassociation shops. Within a period of two months, membership in the "Affiliated" increased from 22 to 130 firms.[22]

At the same time, the organized jobbers (Wholesale Dress Manufacturers' Association) and the organized contractors (Association of Dress Manufacturers) signed collective agreements with the ILGWU on an understanding that the union would attempt to drive independent jobbers and contractors, as well as inside manufacturers, into their respective organizations. In so far as union efforts in this direction were limited by the number of unionized shops, the hope of expanding association memberships gave the organized employers an additional incentive — along with the need for uniform labor standards and equal labor costs — for demanding a more thorough organization of the work-

---

ing the growth of membership in these three associations, see *Monthly Labor Review*, September 1929, vol. 29, p. 528.

During the union's campaign to organize the manufacturers, Samuel Blumberg, legal counsel, Merchants' Ladies' Garment Association, helped the cause by announcing that "the union has undertaken to keep away from the independents altogether"; as did Harry Uviller, general manager of the American Cloak and Suit Manufacturers' Association (contractors) in his public remarks on the new agreements awaiting signature: "We shall have a provision in the contract which states that the union cannot settle with independent contractors. The clauses pertaining to this are absolute and unqualified." *Women's Wear Daily*, July 15, 1929.

[22]*Ibid.*, Feb. 4, 1930; *New York Times*, Feb. 2, 14, 1930.

ers in the trade. Reflecting the boost in association memberships which accompanied the negotiation of these agreements, Jed Sylbert, president of the Association of Dress Manufacturers, observed that "contractors have been waiting in line from 8:30 in the morning til 9 o'clock at night to join the association." Stubborn isolationists who had always preferred to go it alone, so Sylbert observed, were now flocking into the association.[23]

These early gains were soon dissipated, however, by the growing economic strains of the Great Depression. Long before the dress industry contracts were scheduled to expire on December 31, 1931, the organized manufacturers had charged the union with losing its grip on the workers of the trade and hence with failure to build up the membership of the three employer groups. During the late summer and fall of 1931, the dressmakers' union and the employer groups carried on a running verbal battle in defense of their positions. The organized manufacturers complained that the union had not only failed to organize the workers in more shops but had failed to exert pressure upon the owners of the newly organized shops to join an association. When Julius Hochman, general manager of the Dressmakers' Joint Board, noted that his union had recently organized the workers in 100 additional contractor shops, the organized contractors replied that only 55 new contracting firms had been brought into the membership of the Association of Dress Manufacturers. Moreover, so the association's general manager, Jed Sylbert, pointed out, had all 100 firms joined the association, the goal of a thoroughly organized industry would still be far from realized; for his association included only 500 to 600 members compared to a much larger group of some 2,000 independent contractors operating nonunion dress shops in the local New York market.[24]

---

[23]*Ibid.*, Feb. 15, 1930. Among the demands of the United Dress Manufacturers' Association (contractors) submitted to the ILGWU at the 1935 dress industry negotiations was one forbidding the union to enter into any more agreements with firms not members of the association. *Women's Wear Daily*, Dec. 7, 1935.

[24]*Ibid.*, Sept. 18, 21–23, 1931. During the March 1932 negotiations of the first collective agreement between the manufacturers' newly organized Women's Headwear Group and the Cloth Hat, Cap and Millinery Workers' International Union, a one-day work stoppage resulted in 153 additional firms joining the ranks of the new association. *Ibid.*, March 21, 1932.

One Association — One Union — One Collective Agreement

From promoting association membership by refusing to work for independent firms, some needle trade unions took the further step of agreeing to work only for members of a particular association to the exclusion of other organized employers who were members of rival groups. The idea of *one* association, *one* union, and *one* collective agreement for each industry or competitive market area had always directed the thinking of those who supported the protocol movement. "The implicit, if not the explicit understanding of the protocol," once reflected J. H. Cohen, counsel for manufacturers' associations and chief architect of the protocol system, "was that there should be one large employers' association and one large Union, and that the experiment should be made of organizing and enforcing standards throughout the industry by a Union and an employers' association."[25]

This concept was clearly written into the 1913 collective agreement between the Textile Union Finishers' Association and the Cloth Examiners' and Spongers' Union of Greater New York. Here, the 364 union members who were engaged in sponging and examining cloth for men's clothing represented 99 percent of all workers in the local trade. In return for better conditions of employment, the union agreed to furnish union workers and to supply union labels only to employers who were members of the Textile Union Finishers' Association, thereby depriving all other producers of the wherewithal to enter or remain in the trade.[26]

---

[25]*Minutes,* Council of Conciliation . . . [women's coat and suit trade] (July 14, 1915), vol. 2, p. 72.

[26]"Members of the union are not to work for any cloth-sponging concern, whether incorporated or not, who are not members of the association, excepting that such members of the union who can not secure employment with members of the association may obtain other employment." From the text of the 1913 cloth-sponging agreement as printed in C. H. Winslow, *Collective Agreements in the Men's Clothing Industry,* U.S. Department of Labor, BLS Bulletin no. 198 (September 1916), at p. 125.

The 1929 collective agreements for the women's coat and suit trade limited acceptable contractors to those maintaining union shops, but specified that "no sub-manufacturer or contracting firm shall be considered a union shop unless such firm is a member of the American Association." This provision followed up an earlier decision of the industry's impartial chairman, who had ruled that "under all the agreements prevailing in the New York market no firm of sub-manufacturers or contractors is to be recognized for

Unlike the fight for the one-association concept, the fight for the one-union principle was largely resolved by the unions themselves. Interunion rivalry between different unions representing the women's garment workers, the men's clothing workers, the headwear workers, and the fur workers were generally fought out within the ranks of organized labor. Jurisdictional disputes between locals of the same international union were usually resolved by the international union itself. Only the rise of Communist-led unions in the twenties and early thirties created the type of rival unionism that seriously threatened the concept of union monopoly control over the workers of each industry. And here the employers' associations generally supported the more responsible union groups.

Preference for a united labor force which could exert more effective controls over "illegitimate" competition had always been a slogan of the organized manufacturers in the needle trades. The employers could see no good to be derived from a union organization torn by internal dissension that invited a disparity in labor standards and hampered the uniform enforcement of identical contract terms among competing manufacturers. Even a Communist-led union with monopoly control over the workers of a trade could support the reign of law and order through the power of its leadership to make and carry out decisions. For years, the greatest stabilizing influence in the fur manufacturing trade was generally conceded to be Benjamin Gold, a professed Communist, who was president and guiding spirit of the International Fur Workers' Union.[27]

---

transacting business in this market unless it holds membership in the American Association." R. V. Ingersoll, *Decisions,* Case no. 416 (1926–1927). For later examples of a union's obligation to limit its negotiations to a single association within each industry, see the 1938 collective agreement of the Children's Dress, Cotton Dress and Sportswear Contractors' Association with Local 91, ILGWU, the 1938 collective agreement of the women's belt industry in New York City, and the 1944 collective agreement between the United Knitwear Manufacturers' League and Local 155, ILGWU.

[27]You ask me who the power is bigger than Gold. There never was a bigger man in the fur trade than Gold. He ran the fur trade, and he could put the babies [of his own union] in line. He could put Potash, Winogradsky, Schneider — when Gold talked, everything stopped, and he could talk, and he was persuasive, and I do not deny the fact that he could outargue us all, and he knew what the hell he was talking about,

In the needle trades, rivalry among employers' associations was more pronounced than rivalry among unions. Competing employer groups usually sprang up from among independent producers who had originally remained aloof from the established association of their trade. Some firms because of their inadequate size were denied permission to join the established association. Harassed by labor unions and forced to accept the terms of multiemployer contracts, these unorganized manufacturers pooled their strength by forming "independent" associations for the purpose of bargaining. In 1938, for example, some four hundred small-scale fur manufacturers, who were depicted as being ground beneath the heels of their oppressors (the Associated Fur Coat and Trimming Manufacturers and the Furriers' Joint Board), were invited to join the American Fur Manufacturers and so become a power in the trade.[28]

Some rival employer groups were sponsored by labor unions expressly to weaken or disperse the power of established associations. Under the original Protocol of Peace, the Cloak, Suit and Skirt Manufacturers' Protective Association soon charged the Cloakmakers' Joint Board with sponsoring a rival employers' organization, the United Association of Cloak and Suit Manufacturers. The presence of two associations, so it was contended, had destroyed the uniformity of labor standards essential to the principle of controlled competition. For, wherever the union exacted higher standards from the members of one association than of the other or granted more concessions to the members of one group than to the other during the life of an agreement, these discrepancies invariably created discontent both among the employers and among the workers.[29]

---

and he knew what it was all about . . . and we had a hard time to keep up with him. . . .

 —Testimony of Harry Bloom, 2nd vice-president, Associated Fur Coat and Trimming Manufacturers (Sept. 10, 1948). U.S. Congress, House, Committee on Labor and Education, *Hearings on Investigation of Communist Infiltration into the Fur Industry*, 80th Cong., 2nd sess. (pursuant to H. Res. 111), p. 118.

[28] *Women's Wear Daily*, Jan. 13, 1938.

[29] Reviewing one aspect of this development, J. H. Cohen, counsel for the older association, pointed out that when the cloakmakers' unions wanted a favorable interpretation of the holiday clause, they went first to the United Association and then tried to enforce the ruling of the United upon the

The employers vehemently condemned such tactics and repeatedly sought for themselves the same type of monopoly control they would confer upon their unions. At a joint conference on December 11, 1912, between representatives of the Protective Association and the cloakmakers' unions, President Morris Silberman of the "Protective" insisted that the members of "United" join his organization. Drawing analogies to the need for unity in the labor movement, Silberman pleaded with the union for the principle of one association for each trade.

Suppose we took three or four men in the Union and said to them, "now gentlemen, we will furnish you with the necessary financial aid and backing. You get ten thousand men. You form a new union. We will back you." And in the meantime we were sitting across the table from you holding conferences. What would you say to us? Would you think that was playing fair?

That is just what you are doing; the same identical thing. You are holding conferences here. We are holding Grievance Board meetings disciplining our members; you are disciplining your members — you are supposed to — and in the meantime there is another organization that you are hobnobbing with, treating with and working with. If we expel a member from our organization he leaves and goes and joins the United for less money....

If you would not foster this other organization, let them come into our ranks. You must deal with one body. There is no necessity for two boards of grievances, a double set of officers and agents and a double set of offices....[30]

Union Support for Monopoly Associations

While the subsequent role of the cloakmakers' unions in helping to consolidate these two employer groups remains clouded, the dressmakers' unions left no doubt of their position

---

Protective Association. *Minutes,* Council of Conciliation... [women's coat and suit trade] (July 14, 1915), vol. 2, p. 100.

[30]*Minutes,* Meeting between Members of the Cloak, Suit and Skirt Manufacturers' Protective Association and Members of the Garment Makers' Union (Dec. 11, 1912), pp. 102, 111. Morris Hillquit, counsel for the ILGWU, saw no logic behind the association demand that the ILGWU be responsible for consolidating the employer groups. If the "Protective" doesn't like a rival in the "United," observed Hillquit, then it is up to the "Protective" to combine the two organizations. *Minutes,* Council of Conciliation... [women's coat and suit trade] (July 14, 1915), vol. 2, pp. 90–91. The two associations were consolidated in 1916. *Women's Wear,* Feb. 21, 1916.

when a similar situation arose in the dress and waist industry. Shortly after the Dress and Waist Manufacturers' Association and the Dressmakers' Joint Board, ILGWU, had revised their original protocol in 1916, the two parties engineered a drive to force independents into the association or else to drive them out of business because of their small size. In self-defense, the independents organized the "Independent Dress and Waist Manufacturers' Protective Association" and asked to be recognized by the union. This new employer group offered to negotiate with the union a collective agreement which would provide the same wage scales as those prevailing under the revised protocol. But the union, loyal to the principle of one association for each trade, insisted upon negotiating a separate contract with each individual employer who did not join the older association.

This procedure, so the counsel for the new association contended, had placed the members of his organization at a competitive disadvantage. That year the union and the older association had signed an agreement for a 10 percent wage increase, whereas the members of the new association, negotiating separately, had been forced to concede a 20 percent increase in wages. "It is clear," stated Joseph Nemerov, counsel for the new association, "that the independent employers, those who do not care to join the older organization of manufacturers, cannot exist if they have to pay such an advance in wages, and this situation would seem to lend credence to the charge which was made when our workers were on strike, that the demonstration was in reality an attempt to force the smaller independent shops into the Dress and Waist Association." Thereupon, the new association announced "that unless the labor body would enter into a collective agreement with it on exactly the same basis as with the older employers' body, that court proceedings will be resorted [*sic*] to ascertain if any particular group of manufacturers can exercise a monopoly of the protocol."[31]

---

[31]*Ibid.*, Feb. 21, 1916. For earlier background information, including resort to a strike to support a monopoly association, see *ibid.*, Feb. 14–16, 1916.

A later example of this union's power to control association membership occurred in 1937 when a manufacturer of covered buttons resigned from his association — the Covered Button and Buckles Creators — and joined the more recently organized National Covered Button and Buckle Manufacturers' Association, whose other members, like himself, had previously belonged to the older association. Thereupon, the ILGWU refused to negotiate with

Among the inside manufacturers of men's clothing in New York City, the goal of monopoly organization was sought through the assistance of the Amalgamated Clothing Workers of America. Instead of opposing new employer groups that were potential rivals of the established association, however, this union in the mid-twenties helped a new group of men's clothing manufacturers to supplant the older one. Shortly after the New York Clothing Manufacturers' Exchange was organized, allegedly with the knowledge and eager encouragement of the union, the old Associated Clothing Manufacturers that had previously negotiated contracts with the union asked for a new collective agreement but was promptly refused. Instead, the ACWA offered members of the older employer group the option of joining the Exchange, signing individual agreements, or facing a strike. The result of this move was to retain the principle of one association, one union, and one collective agreement in this branch of the local men's clothing trade.[32]

In defense of such actions, needle trade unions have often alleged that rival employers' associations seeking union recognition and the right to bargain for their member firms have been wolves in sheep's clothing. Many of these rival groups, so the unions have contended, were originally formed from the anti-union elements within their trades. Though they pretended to seek the cooperation of the organized factions, the past records of their members belied the sincerity of their approach. Where associations of manufacturers, as in the men's clothing industry, were historically formed for trade, credit, or commercial purposes, the first foray into labor relations was likely to be anti-union. This was clearly the case with the National Clothiers'

---

this manufacturer until he returned to "Creators." Allegedly, the union brought additional pressure upon him by forbidding his customers, the garment manufacturers who were in contractual relations with the union, to use his buttons until he returned to Creators. Defending its right to exist, the more recently organized association sought an injunction against the ILGWU to halt union attempts to drive National's members back into Creators, or else to drive National itself into becoming an affiliate of Creators. Facts from Weitzberg v. Dubinsky, New York Supreme Court, 173 Misc. 350 (1940), 18 N.Y.S. 2nd 97. The motion for a temporary injunction was denied. The background of the case is reviewed in *Women's Wear Daily*, Nov. 30, 1939.

[32] *Women's Wear*, July 10, 1924.

Association of the United States, founded in 1897, that in 1903–1904 established a separate National Labor Bureau of Clothing Manufacturers to make war on organized labor through its affiliated local market labor bureaus. A similar group of nonunion women's coat and suit manufacturers formed the Affliated Coat and Suit Association in the early thirties with the intention of having its materials made into garments by out-of-town, nonunion shops. Although the attorney for the group insisted that the members wanted to do business with the union, the ILGWU persistently refused to recognize an "outlaw organization."[33]

About the same time, a similar incident had arisen in the dress and waist industry. The newly formed Metropolitan Dress Contractors' Association claiming to represent over a thousand members with control over 85 percent of production in the dress market sought affiliation with the organized factions of the industry. Refusing to recognize this association for bargaining purposes, the ILGWU announced that the Wholesale Dress Manufacturers' Association (jobbers), the Association of Dress Manufacturers (contractors), and the Affiliated Dress Manufacturers (inside producers) were the only employer groups that would be recognized in the trade. This union policy was, of course, backed by the privileged employer groups, none of which would concede the new association a place in the established order.[34]

---

[33]The ILGWU consistently held that the women's coat and suit industry had room for only one association of jobbers (Merchants' Ladies' Garment Association), one association of contractors (American Cloak and Suit Manufacturers' Association), and one association of inside manufacturers (Industrial Council of Cloak, Suit and Skirt Manufacturers). *Women's Wear Daily*, July 10, 1933.

The story of the National Labor Bureau is told in Harry A. Cobrin's *The Men's Clothing Industry: Colonial through Modern Times* (1970), pp. 88–91.

[34]*Women's Wear Daily*, Jan. 17, 1933. See also the issues of Jan. 23–25, 30–31, Feb. 1–2, 8, 13, 1933.

A more recent example of union support for monopoly associations occurred during the summer of 1952 when eight locals of the Cloakmakers' Joint Board conducted a strike against 55 key jobbers, some 40 of whom were organized into the Independent Association of Women's Apparel Manufacturers. These organized jobbers sought to have the union recognize their association for bargaining purposes, and to support their demands they proceeded to picket the headquarters of Local 117, ILGWU. At that time, ILGWU President David Dubinsky again reiterated his union's stand that manufacturing groups within the women's coat and suit trade were already

As a rule, the principle of one association, one union, and one collective agreement was limited to spheres of direct competition within rather narrowly drawn divisions of the needle trades. Sometimes, as in the women's dress industry and the ladies' hat industry, attempts at exclusive control were confined to products falling within a given price range. There were associations for popular priced products, associations for medium priced products, and associations for the more expensive products, with corresponding labor agreements for each group. In other cases, membership in an association was restricted to employers making similar contributions to the manufacturing process. There were separate but exclusive employer groups for suppliers, jobbers, contractors, and inside manufacturers. Whenever rival groups sprang up within any of these limited spheres, one association was likely to absorb the other, usually with the secret connivance, if not the open support, of the labor union involved.[35]

---

organized along lines of their interests into associations of jobbers, inside manufacturers, contractors, and children's wear manufacturers. Insisting that no more associations were needed, Dubinsky gave these jobbers the option of joining existing associations or of negotiating independent contracts with the union. *New York Herald Tribune*, August 20, 1952.

[35]In 1932 Max Zaritsky, president of the Cloth Hat, Cap and Millinery Workers' International Union, announced that his union would resist efforts to form another manufacturers' association in competition with the Women's Headwear Group with which the union already had a collective agreement. His opposition, however, did not prevent the National Association of Ladies' Hatters from signing a collective agreement with another headwear union, the United Hatters of North America. After the two unions were consolidated, the controversy over the associations was resolved by the inclusion of the following clause in the National's labor agreement.

To meet the special problems arising from the existence of two associations having the same collective agreement and to prevent unfair competition and rivalry for membership by the respective associations which would be highly detrimental to the effective operation of the machinery of the collective agreement, it is agreed that the principles of demarcation of jurisdiction on membership shall govern, namely: the National Association of Ladies' Hatters, Inc., shall have jurisdiction over what is known as the $4-line and over and the Women's Headwear Group, Inc., shall have jurisdiction below that line.

—From the 1934 collective agreement between the National Association of Ladies' Hatters and the Cap and Millinery Department of the United Hatters, Cap and Millinery Workers' International Union. For Paul Abelson's part in this episode, see above, p. 388.

The Fur Workers' Union and Monopoly Associations

The most sustained struggle to maintain the principle of one association, one union, and one collective agreement for each industry came in the fur manufacturing trade. Early in the history of group bargaining relationships dating back to 1912, the Associated Fur Manufacturers and the International Fur Workers' Union had accepted the rule that there should be but one collective agreement in the New York fur manufacturing area. By the mid-twenties, the collective agreements between the parties expressly forbade the fur workers' union to deal with other associations. When the United Fur Manufacturers' Association (employers of Greek workers) and the Fur Trimming Manufacturers' Association were formed in the twenties, these associations were forced to accept the agreement negotiated between the Associated Fur Manufacturers and the union. Later, the fur trimmers consolidated with the original employer group into the Associated Fur Coat and Fur Trimming Manufacturers.[36]

During the thirties, another rival group, the New York Fur Trimming Manufacturers' Association, sprang up to threaten again the principle of one association, one union, and one collective agreement for the fur manufacturing trade. When this group of 240 to 300 firms that claimed to employ 40 percent of the labor in the industry was denied participation in the 1935 negotiations for a new collective agreement, its president, J. B. Gross, sent the following message to the Furriers' Joint Council.

We understand that the Associated Fur Coat and Trimming Manufacturers, Inc., have demanded that we be excluded from participa-

---

On Zaritsky's opposition to rival associations, see *Women's Wear Daily*, March 22, April 4, 27, 1932. The text of the first agreement of the millinery workers' union with the Women's Headwear Group appears in *ibid.*, March 4, 1932; the text of the first agreement between the National Association of Ladies' Hatters and the United Hatters of North America appears in *ibid.*, April 19, 1932.

[36]In 1927 T. V. Miller, president of the United Fur Manufacturers' Association, accused Ben Gold, manager of the Furriers' Joint Board of conspiring with S. N. Samuels, president of the Associated Fur Manufacturers to force "United" under the control of "Associated" on the assumption that only one association and one agreement should exist in the industry. But the strength of national origins, whatever the measures of control, helped the "United" to survive until the 1960's. *Ibid.*, March 10, 1927.

tion in the agreement now to be negotiated and have demanded that but one collective agreement be made covering labor in the industry with their association as the only employer signatory thereto. . . .

To enter into an agreement with the Associated which excludes all possible participation therein by our association and the members thereof is a virtual restraint of trade. Concededly, you have exclusive control of all labor in the industry and our members can receive no competent workers through any other sources than your own. . . .

If the demand of the Associated Fur Coat and Trimming Manufacturers, Inc., for our exclusion from the contract is carried out with your assistance and consent, it will be a virtual ultimatum to the members of our Association that they must join the Associated Fur Coat and Trimming Manufacturers, Inc., in order to receive labor protection under the collective agreement. . . .

If the demand of the Associated for our exclusion from the collective agreement is carried out, we shall have no course but to vigorously pursue such proceedings as may be justified under our civil and criminal laws for the prevention of such restraint of trade.[37]

A year later, the fur workers' union used similar tactics against the American Fur Manufacturers' Association, even though this employer group offered to accept terms identical with those of the collective agreement between the union and the Associated Fur Coat and Trimming Manufacturers. By refusing to sign a separate contract with American, the union, which controlled 99 percent of the workers in the local trade, forced the members of this association to abandon their own organization and join the Associated or else sign separate union agreements that denied them the advantages of arbitration as well as the protection of

---

[37]*Fur Age Weekly*, Dec. 16, 1935. During the 1936 negotiations for new contracts, the fur workers' union again insisted that the only agreement it would recognize was the agreement with the Associated Fur Coat and Trimming Manufacturers — a policy that left the New York Fur Trimming Manufacturers to select one of three courses of action: join the Associated, sign individual contracts with the union, or be subjected to a strike. Reflecting the employers' position, a prominent fur manufacturer observed that the key to successful negotiations "is the strong belief existing among some leaders, that a highly centralized condition in the fur industry in the form of one manufacturer association and one union is a necessary prerequisite for the solution of other vital problems." Letter of T. V. Miller to the editor of *Women's Wear Daily* printed in the issue of Jan. 15, 1936. See the views of the union in the issue of May 11, 1936.

a no-strike clause. Their only other recourse was to leave the industry.

Alleging a violation of the New York State antitrust laws (Donnelly Act), the American Fur Manufacturers' Association and its nineteen member companies petitioned the New York Supreme Court for an injunction to restrain the Associated Fur Coat and Trimming Manufacturers and the International Fur Workers' Union of the United States and Canada and the Furriers' Joint Council of New York from conspiring by means of their agreement to give the defendant association a monopoly in the trade association business of the industry. The chief point at issue was the legality of the contract provision stating that "there shall be but one collective labor agreement in the fur manufacturing industry in the Greater City of New York."

In denying the petition for relief, Mr. Justice S. I. Rosenman traced the history of statutory and common law restraints on monopolies in New York State and of labor union exemptions from those restraints — exemptions which were expressly written into the 1933 amendments to state antitrust legislation excluding "*bona fide* labor unions" from the operation of such laws. "Obviously," he stated, "the intention was to remove from labor unions all prohibitions which have their basis in restraint of trade." These exemptions covered not only the formation and activities of labor unions but their contracts and agreements as well. "I have concluded," he wrote, "that the collective agreement, attacked by this complaint, is cloaked with immunity by virtue of subdivision 2 of section 340 [General Business Law] which exempts labor unions."[38]

Impediments to the Growth of Monopoly Associations

The road to the goal of monopoly associations was not always so easily paved. Sometimes, union leaders were no more successful at winning support from their rank-and-file members for all-inclu-

---

[38]American Fur Manufacturers' Association v. Associated Fur Coat and Trimming Manufacturers, New York Supreme Court, 161 Misc. 246 (1936), 291 N.Y. Supp. 610 at 617, 614. Various accounts of the case, which set a precedent in defining the legal sphere of collective bargaining, can be found in the *New York Times,* Nov. 25, 1936; *Women's Wear Daily,* Nov. 25, 1936; and in the *Furriers' Bulletin,* organ of the joint council of the fur workers' union, Jan. 15, 1937.

sive associations than association leaders were able to win support from rank-and-file employers for all-inclusive labor unions. Those who followed their respective leaders seldom lost sight of the potential hazards in building up monopoly organizations on the other side of the fence. In both camps, support for monopoly bargaining groups created internal dissension that sometimes cost officials their positions of leadership.

Dissension within union ranks was soon reflected in alleged failures of needle trade unions to meet their contractural obligations of encouraging the growth of employers' associations. Instead of inflicting more stringent contract terms and more rigid standards of contract enforcement on independent firms — or, better yet, refusing to deal with those firms at all — unions were charged with granting independents more favorable overtime provisions or more extensive contracting privileges. Even where agreement terms were identical with those of association contracts, unions were sometimes charged with letting independents off the enforcement hook by tolerating lower wages, longer hours, and less rigid standards of sanitation.

Failure of the union to bring independents into the association fold, or to control those who remained outside, ultimately prompted the manufacturers' association that had signed the original Protocol of Peace to terminate collective bargaining on behalf of its members. On May 24, 1924, after fourteen years of dealing with the ILGWU and the cloakmakers' unions, the Cloak, Suit and Skirt Manufacturers' Protective Association adopted a resolution that sounded the death knell of its labor activities:

Whereas there are 3,000 manufacturers of cloaks and suits in the City of New York, non-members of this association employing 25,000 workers, none of whom are bound by the same sanitary conditions and the same high standards as the members of the association and the workers in our association are bound by, and who work in sweatshops, tenements and unsanitary conditions and, therefore, turn out work cheaper than the labor employed by us. . . .

Resolved . . . that the labor department of this association be given up and cease functioning on June 1, 1924, and be it further. . . .

Resolved that the members of this association be free, from and after June 1, 1924, to enter into any agreement with labor employed by such members and are released from any pledges made to this association, with respect to individually contracting with their workers from and after such date, namely, June 1, 1924, so that each may determine for himself whatever agreement he may wish to make with his workers and the union.[39]

Throughout the needle trades, the organized manufacturers themselves were partly to blame for their lack of effective organization. From the time Meyer London, counsel for the ILGWU, cautioned the employer representatives at the Brandeis Conferences of 1910 that they must persuade a much larger number of manufacturers to organize, union leaders backing the protocol movement have lambasted employers for not keeping faith with their promises to strengthen their own bonds. The charges and countercharges that the parties to collective agreements hurled at each other for failure to support and strengthen labor unions were no more vehement than those the parties hurled at each other for failure to expand and strengthen the ranks of employers' associations.

The Impartial Machinery and Growth of Associations

Wherever manufacturers violated their contractural responsibilities to expand their own organizations, and wherever unions neglected their contractural obligations to promote the growth of employers' associations, the impartial machinery of each industry was empowered to meet these shortcomings with appropriate action. Sometimes, this action took the form of unofficial suggestions, reminders, or recommendations from some joint agency of contract administration, usually the impartial chairman. On other occasions, action of the permanent institutions set up for control of the industry was reflected in official decisions and formal decrees. Where the right to take such action was not derived from specific clauses of collective agreements, the impartial machinery often assumed the power to act from the very nature of his obligations toward the contracting parties.[40]

As a rule, the impartial machinery assumed an obligation to

---

[39]*Women's Wear,* May 25, 1924.

[40] "Ingersoll Asks 'Independents' to Join Groups — Impartial Chairman Urges Firms Outside Cloak Associations to Become Members Without Delay — Cites New Pact Clauses on Non-members," such were the front-page headlines of *Women's Wear Daily* for July 15, 1929. In the accompanying article, Impartial Chairman R. V. Ingersoll noted that each union contract with an independent firm would henceforth contain a clause requiring the firm to submit to investigation and supervision by the newly created Control Commission, as well as to the supervision of the impartial chairman, and in addi-

keep employers' associations open for new members. Indeed, some of the original protocols expressly authorized an appeal to the impartial machinery from the refusal of an employers' association to admit new members. "If for any reason the association rejects their application," stated the first protocol for the dress and waist industry, January 18, 1913," the grounds for such rejection shall be stated to a committee on review, consisting of six members — three nominated by the union and three by the manufacturers." Some impartial chairmen fought to maintain an open door to association membership with the same zeal they displayed for open unions. In one of his earliest decisions during the mid-twenties, R. V. Ingersoll, impartial chairman for the women's coat and suit trade, gave two firms that would otherwise have been forced to sign individual agreements with the union the right to join the Industrial Council of Cloak, Suit and Skirt Manufacturers.[41]

Nor were unions permitted without good cause to close the doors upon new firms seeking admittance to employers' associations. Early in the life of the original Protocol of Peace the board of arbitration for the women's coat and suit industry had ruled that the cloakmakers' union must permit the manufacturers' association to take in new members. No fear of a strong association would justify attempts to restrict employers from joining their associations. Even where unions expressly retained the right to veto applicants for association membership on grounds that candidates were seeking to evade some previously acquired responsibility toward their workers, impartial chairmen in the course of applying such provisions could override union objections to association membership.[42]

In applying other contract clauses which affected the security

---

tion independent firms would be compelled to make substantial contributions to the support of these institutions.

[41]R. V. Ingersoll, *Decisions,* Case no. 5–6 (1924 ff.). A clause in the 1913 collective agreement of the United Manufacturers' and Merchants' Association with the United Garment Workers required the association to submit to a joint conference representing the employers and the workers a statement of the grounds on which the association rejected an applicant for membership. *The United Garment Workers' Conference* (pamphlet, Jan. 8, 1913), Appendix A, pp. 5–6.

[42]*Decision of the Board of Arbitration, March 14, 1911, and Rules and Plan of Procedure Adopted by the Board of Grievances* (pamphlet, n.d.), filed in the Abelson papers.

of employer organizations, the impartial machinery showed the same zeal for strong associations that it demonstrated for strong labor unions. Whether a given association had made an honest effort to take in all the manufacturers of a trade or whether the union had fulfilled its mandate to cooperate heartily in promoting association membership were general issues that in the last analysis could be brought before the impartial chairman for final determination. Under the first collective agreement for the muff bed fur manufacturing industry, the Joint Conference Committee expressly charged the Committee on Immediate Action, an agency of the impartial machinery, with the enforcement of that clause in the collective agreement calling for mutual cooperations between the contracting parties to support and strengthen each other.[43]

The impartial machinery also exerted its power to check the disintegration of employer groups through loss of membership. Under the 1929 collective agreement between the organized employers of fur dressers and the fur dressers' union, the board of arbitration could, for example, determine whether the cash security of $1,000 that each association member was forced to deposit with the board of arbitration for faithful performance of the contract should be returned to an employer resigning from the association. To permit a return of the deposit, the board had to be satisfied that the resigning member had settled all his accounts with the association and with the union, and that his departure would not lead to opening a nonunion shop! Under other collective agreements, the impartial chairman exercised a restraining hand on the would-be deserter through power to determine how much cash security a resigning or expelled employer, seeking a separate contract with the union, must put up before the union would be permitted to provide him with workers.

Last, but not least, the impartial machinery representing the manufacturers and the workers could and sometimes did use its influence to effect a vertical integration of the trade, so that suppliers and processors of raw material, as well as the distributors and retailers of the finished products, could work hand-in-

---

[43]See "Report of the Committee on Immediate Action and Cooperation in the Muff Bed Industry to the Conference Committee" (Jan. 14, 1915), filed in the Abelson papers.

hand with the manufacturing interests to maintain uniform standards for the trade. Outstanding in these efforts at cooperation was the work of the Joint Control Commission set up under the 1929 collective agreements of the women's coat and suit trade. This agency not only encouraged independent manufacturers to join their respective employer associations but it repeatedly sought to gain the support of suppliers and retailers necessary for the enforcement of uniform standards.[44]

Regional Associations and Runaway Shops

All these measures to give the organized factions of industry effective control over their trades gradually lost strength with the dispersion of manufacturing to other areas. There was a time when monopoly control over competing firms in the Borough of Manhattan permitted dictation of industry policies, but such control ended with the growth of competitive firms in other boroughs of the city. Likewise, city-wide organizations were no longer able to dictate industry standards once manufacturing had spread to the larger environs of the New York metropolitan district. Not even monopoly control over manufacturing in Metropolitan New York would permit dictation of industry standards where competing firms were springing up like mushrooms in the hinterlands of New Jersey, Pennsylvania, New England, and upstate New York.

This trend toward dispersion of manufacturing was intensified by the movement of firms from the heart of New York City out to the suburbs and beyond. Seeking an escape from the controls

---

[44] *New York Times,* July 11, 1929; *Women's Wear Daily,* July 17, 1929. The work of the Control Commission is discussed below at pp. 695–699.

On April 7, 1932, the joint conference committee operating under the major collective agreement of the fur manufacturing trade passed a resolution to create a special committee consisting of two representatives from each of the following associations: Associated Fur Coat and Trimming Manufacturers, New York Fur Trimming Manufacturers, Associated Employers of Fur Workers, Dressers' and Dyers' Association, American Rabbit Dealers' Association, United Fur Manufacturers' Association, American Fur Merchants' Association, the International Fur Workers' Union, and the American Federation of Labor. It was felt that only through the organization of some such vertically integrated, all-inclusive agency could effective measures be taken to regulate competition in the trade. A copy of the resolution is filed in the Abelson papers.

imposed by the organized segments of a trade, more and more firms closed their doors and fled to the hinterlands. This subterfuge to evade the responsibilities of association membership and the obligations of collective agreements led to the introduction of "runaway shop" clauses that forbade employers from closing down their New York plants and reopening at different locations. Prohibitions against this practice were usually stated in terms of forbidding employers to move their plants beyond the range of the local subway fares.

Labor unions generally took the initiative in apprehending runaway shops and in seeing that they were brought before the impartial chairman of the industry for violating their contracts. Escaping employers were followed to their secret destinations where they were detected operating under new names and with nonunion labor. Those firms refusing to return to their old establishments were at least expected to accept their old workers and observe their old contract standards. Or else they were obligated to pay the workers they left behind for whatever losses those workers had sustained from this maneuver. In any event, union organizers were determined to see that all nonunion workers employed at the new plants became union members.

Typical of the action arising from runaway shop clauses was the case of the Nassau Coat Co. and/or Nassau Sportswear that belonged to the American Cloak and Suit Manufacturers' Association through which it was bound by the collective agreement between the association and the ILGWU. Without notice to the workers, to the union, or to the association, the owners of this firm closed down their business at Valley Stream, Long Island, and moved to Glen Cove, Long Island, where they organized the Glen Cove Coat Corporation and began operations as a nonunion enterprise. Insisting that the old firm had been dissolved and that the new firm was not bound by the collective agreement, the owners, now happily suspended from their association, refused to allow union representatives to enter the plant or to permit accountants from the office of the impartial chairman to examine their books. On complaint from the union, the owners were haled before S. A. Rosenblatt, impartial chairman of the women's coat and suit trade, and charged with violating the collective agreement. After hearing the evidence, the impartial chairman rendered a decision against the firm.

I find as a fact that Glen Cove Coat Corporation is the alter ego of the firm of Nathan Slutzky doing business as Nassau Coat Co., and/or Nassau Sportswear. A firm cannot absolve itself from liability under its collective agreement with the Union by merely changing its name and creating a different corporate structure. This presents a clear case for piercing the corporate veil. It is my clear duty to do so. The testimony of David Slutzky that the Union "can't beat us. We will skip there [in Glen Cove] and open up again" gives a clear picture, not only of what the firm intends to do in the future, but what it actually did in Valley Stream, Long Island, to avoid its Union contract.

Mr. Rosenblatt awarded the union $10,540.00 damages for a breach of contract and directed the firm to offer immediate employment at its Glen Cove plant to all the workers previously employed in the Valley Stream shop.[45]

Occasionally the state courts were called upon to supplement the work of the impartial machinery in controlling runaway shops. In his opinion on the Nassau case, Impartial Chairman Rosenblatt stated flatly that "if the firm continues to be in non-compliance with this decision or if the firm continues to violate the collective agreement subsisting between the Union and the American Association, under which the firm is bound, the Union is not to be deemed precluded from applying to a court of competent jurisdiction for the purpose of obtaining injunctive relief to restrain the firm from violating the collective agreement in the respects noted and to compel compliance with my decision and award."[46]

Just such a procedure arose in the dress and waist manufacturing industry during the mid-thirties. Acting on the assumption that a strike had terminated the collective agreement between the Popular Priced Dress Manufacturers' Group and the ILGWU, two employers resigned from their association and on the same night secretly removed their machines from New York City to Archbold, Pennsylvania, where they planned to open a new shop with nonunion labor. Immediately the manufacturers' association alerted the dressmakers' union and together they joined the workers of the New York plants in appealing to the courts for relief.

---

[45]S. A. Rosenblatt, *Decisions,* Case no. 5519 (May 18, 1948).
[46]*Ibid.*

In his opinion on the case, Mr. Justice P. J. McCook considered the departure to be a lockout as well as a direct violation of the contract clause forbidding a firm to move beyond the 5¢ subway fare. He ordered the company to return the machines, reemploy the workers, and pay them appropriate damages to be assessed by a referee. McCook pointed out that the association and the union had combined for protection against unfair competition and that strong measures were necessary to prevent unscrupulous employers of labor from playing one community off against another, thereby "unlawfully depriving New York City of her business and her inhabitants of their livelihood."[47]

To the extent that dispersion of manufacturing did not come from runaway shops, the organized forces of the New York market had to seek other means for maintaining controls over industry standards. The most logical solution was to extend the membership of local employers' associations over all competing firms in outlying areas. Then all competitors would be bound by the standards of a common labor agreement. This approach had been used in 1930 to bring Brooklyn contractors within the orbit of the Manhattan collective bargaining system for the women's coat and suit trade (see above, pp. 455–457). And it was to be used many times over in a concerted effort to control such a proportion of competing firms as to permit dictation of industry policies.

Another example of attempting to expand association membership over outlying areas came in the dress industry during the fall of 1939. A group of competing firms, mostly contractors, had sprung up in Pennsylvania where lower labor costs permitted

---

[47]Dubinsky v. Blue Dale Dress Co., New York Supreme Court, 162 Misc. 177 (1936), 292 N.Y. Supp. 898. An extended account of this case with copious extracts from the judge's opinion appeared in the *New York Herald Tribune* for Dec. 31, 1936. See also ILGWU, *Report and Proceedings,* Twenty-third Convention (May 1937), pp. 46–47.

The largest number of cases involving runaway shops to reach the courts or the impartial machinery of an industry appears to have arisen in the millinery trade. Several of these cases are summarized in the reports of the general executive board to the conventions of the millinery workers' union during the thirties; other cases may be found in the *Decisions* of Paul Abelson, impartial chairman for the industry. Some of these cases were resolved by the National Labor Relations Board, which ruled that runaway shops were guilty of discriminating against the union or else of refusal to bargain. See United Hatters, Cap and Millinery Workers' International Union, *Report and Proceedings,* Third Convention (May 20, 1939), pp. 83–86.

garments to be produced more cheaply than in New York City. These firms sought to take business away from New York contractors who belonged to the United Association of Dress Manufacturers by offering to reduce the price of making dresses for the New York jobbers who were members of the National Dress Manufacturers' Association.

Now the New York collective agreements for the dress industry had since 1933 restricted outside contracting to members of the United Association of Dress Manufacturers. Only by joining this association and thereby subscribing to the New York collective agreements could Pennsylvania contractors become eligible to receive work. But the Pennsylvania contractors refused to join United on the ground that meeting New York labor standards would put them out of business. Thereupon, the National Association of Dress Manufacturers (New York jobbers), acting in accordance with the New York collective agreements, directed its members to "discontinue shipment of any work to dress contractors in the Commonwealth of Pennsylvania."

Not until Governor A. H. James of Pennsylvania had written Governor H. H. Lehman of New York requesting an investigation of the "sort of boycott" that New York dress manufacturers had imposed on Pennsylvania dress manufacturers was a compromise worked out. By the terms of this settlement, the Pennsylvania dress manufacturers through their own association were to operate as an affiliate of the New Jersey Dress Manufacturers' Association, which, in turn, was an affiliate of the United Association of Dress Manufacturers. Under this arrangement, the Pennsylvania contractors would be permitted to negotiate separate agreements with the ILGWU. Price differentials, if any, between New York and Pennsylvania contractors for producing the same type of garments would be fixed by the impartial chairman for the industry.[48]

The Growth of National Employers' Associations

The fight for area-wide employer groups to match the spread of manufacturing soon gave way to the demand for national em-

[48]*Women's Wear Daily,* Sept. 15, 1939; Wilkes-Barre, Pa., *Leader,* Oct. 3, 1939. For an account of earlier relationships between the United Association of Dress Manufacturers and its out-of-town affiliates, the New Jersey Contractors' Association and the Connecticut Contractors' Association, see A. Feldblum, impartial chairman of the dress industry, *Decisions,* Case no.

ployers' associations to meet the extension of manufacturing throughout the country. Unlike labor unions, the employer groups that became parties to the first protocols, and to subsequent collective agreements of the needle trades, were not organized on a national scale. With few exceptions, the employers' associations that engaged in collective bargaining spanned no more than a single market area.

Wherever the "enlightened" manufacturers in a new center of production saw the need for establishing a floor under competition which would stabilize their trade, they organized their own local associations and proceeded to deal with unions of their workers quite independently of what employers in other markets had done. In time, the organized factions of one or more needle trades in Baltimore, Philadelphia, Boston, Chicago, Rochester, Cleveland, Cincinnati, and St. Louis attempted something akin to the protocol movement of New York City. But rarely did the organized employers of the various markets undertake to consolidate their forces into a national organization or even to form a national federation of local employers' associations operating in the same trade.

This weakness sorely affected the success of the movement to establish and maintain industry-wide standards of employment. Without the help of national associations of employers, as well as national unions of workers, industry-wide standards of employment were difficult to establish and still more difficult to enforce. The lack of an employer superstructure at the national level particularly hampered the formation of impartial machinery with industry-wide jurisdiction over problems of contract administration. In the absence of such machinery, whatever uniformity in contract terms could be established piecemeal through bargaining at the local levels would likely be dissipated by a wide variety of local interpretations and by wide differences in standards of local enforcement.

This lack of national employers' associations was a matter of growing concern to needle trade unions whose leaders saw more clearly than did their employers the need for national organizations to participate in programs of industry-wide control. Early in the history of the protocol movement, the ILGWU began

B-19 (March 1, 1935) under the title of Jay Day Frocks, Inc. Text of the decision is given in *Women's Wear Daily,* March 4, 1935.

campaigning for industry-wide employers' associations to help maintain industry-wide standards of employment. In 1916 Morris Hillquit, counsel for the ILGWU, charged the organized manufacturers of the dress and waist industry with complacency toward extending uniform labor standards beyond the shops of their own members. At that time, he took the position that the Dress and Waist Manufacturers' Association should have called a "general strike" of employers all over the country to "associationize" the whole industry.[49]

A year earlier, Hillquit had roundly denounced the women's coat and suit manufacturers of New York City for lack of any coordinated effort to extend the terms of their collective agreements to other competing markets. "The International Ladies' Garment Workers' Union," observed Hillquit, "'within the last five years expended no less than a million dollars, money contributed in the last instance by these workers in the industry, for the sole purpose of raising the standards all through the country." Meanwhile, so Hillquit contended, the New York coat and suit manufacturers, faced with ruinous out-of-town competition, had not "undertaken a single step to bring together the representatives of this industry in the various cities and to agree with them upon some sort of a common standard."[50]

As a first step toward concerted action on a national scale, Hillquit had earlier proposed that the union and the manufacturers' association select a group of outsiders to consider the evils of nationwide competition and to make a report on which to base further action. Even more direct was the proposal in 1915 of the Cloakmakers' Joint Board, ILGWU, to the New York coat and suit manufacturers that "steps shall be immediately taken to bring about a national conference of employers and employees in the cloakmaking industry of the United States with a view to establishing approximately uniform wages and labor conditions throughout the country."[51]

---

[49]*Minutes,* Arbitration Proceedings between the Dress and Waist Manufacturers' Association and the ILGWU (Feb. 5, 1916), vol. 4, pp. 52–61.

[50]*Minutes,* Council of Conciliation . . . [women's coat and suit trade] (July 14, 1915), vol. 2, pp. 82–83.

[51]*Minutes,* Meeting of the Board of Conference . . . [women's coat and suit trade] (March 16, 1915), vol. 6, pp. 150, 166–167; *Women's Wear,* March 19, 1915.

The continuing lack of support among New York employers for organization on a national scale undoubtedly stemmed from the key position of the New York market in the manufacture of needle trade products. So long as the New York metropolitan area largely monopolized the output of an industry's products, employer groups lacked the foresight of unions in preparing for the spread of manufacturing to other areas. In 1932, for example, an official of the local Pleaters' and Stitchers' Association, upon signing a collective agreement with the ILGWU, boasted that his association already controlled 95 percent of his industry's total output. Only in the men's clothing trade, where production was widely scattered among several competing markets, was a substantial effort made to form a national employers' association prior to the thirties.[52]

Shortly after the First World War, men's clothing manufacturers who had previously formed local associations to bargain with the Amalgamated Clothing Workers in the different markets undertook to form a national association for industry-wide bargaining. Their professed objective was to accomplish on a national scale what they had succeeded in accomplishing on a local scale. By standardizing the terms of employment, local agreements had ruled out killing competition among organized employers of the same market area. So by standardizing terms of employment between markets, national bargaining would rule out killing competition that had developed from playing off one market against another. It now behooved the employer groups of the various organized markets to create an institution through which this objective could be accomplished.

In July 1919, representatives from four leading markets for the manufacture of men's clothing — New York, Baltimore, Rochester, and Chicago — met in New York City and formed the National Industrial Federation of Clothing Manufacturers. Through its board of governors, composed of one representative from each market, the new organization was authorized "to bind the participating manufacturers to an agreement with the Amalgamated Clothing Workers of America, and to make rules and regulations governing the industrial relations between management and workers." The board of governors was to be responsible

---

[52]*Women's Wear Daily*, April 1, 1932.

"for establishing an industrial government with all necessary organization of administrative, judicial and legislative functions to stabilize wages, hours, standards of efficiency and all conditions of employment."[53]

Below this national superstructure, each market in turn was to have its own market-wide committee representing local manufacturers or employers' associations in the area. Chicago, for example, had its own Chicago Market Industrial Federation of Clothing Manufacturers, with its own Chicago Market Committee (representing two associations and Hart, Schaffner, and Marx) and its own Chicago Board of Labor Managers, whose chairman served on a National Board of Labor Managers. With this elaborate and centralized hierarchy of employer organizations for collective bargaining and contract enforcement, prospects for industry-wide standards in the men's clothing trade were never brighter. George Bell, impartial chairman under the New York men's clothing agreement, called this machinery for national bargaining the first achievement in the United States looking toward standardization of an industry on a national basis with the right of the workers to help set the standards.[54]

---

[53] ACWA, *Report and Proceedings,* Fourth Biennial Convention (May 1920), p. 227. See also the statement, dated Feb. 5, 1921, of J. S. Potofsky, assistant general secretary, ACWA, outlining the steps in the development of this movement, found in the printed collection of union affidavits submitted in the case of J. Friedman and Co. v. ACWA, copy filed in the Abelson papers. The pertinent material is found at pp. 53–55 of this collection.

Early in 1920, this national board of governors created the office of National Director of Industrial Relations, the chief function of which was to keep the manufacturers of the various markets apprised of labor developments and to seek united action against the demands of the ACWA. W. E. Hotchkiss was the first appointee to the office. H. S. Gilbertson, "Meeting the Labor Problem in the Clothing Industry," *Administration,* February 1923, vol. 5, p. 185. H. A. Cobrin has an account of the National Industrial Federation in his *The Men's Clothing Industry: Colonial through Modern Times,* pp. 127–131.

[54] See the text of the Articles of Federation, Chicago clothing market, in a pamphlet filed in the Abelson papers. See also articles by W. L. Chenery, G. L. Bell, and E. D. Howard in the *Survey,* Sept. 13, 1919, vol. 42, pp. 843–846.

Plans for labor managers and a market committee for the New York market with a delegate to represent the New York market on the National Board of Labor Managers of the Industrial Federation of Clothing Manu-

Unfortunately, before this scheme was given a chance to prove its worth, it vanished in the post-World War I depression and the open shop movement of the early twenties. Nevertheless, it represented the high-water mark of serious efforts before the 1930's to create strong national employers' associations on which to hang the institutions of collective bargaining. Unhappily for the cause of controlled competition, most attempts to form national employer organizations in the needle trades during the twenties were designed to defeat the purposes of collective action. Such clearly were the objectives of those sponsoring the "United Waist League of America" and the "National Headwear Manufacturers' Association." A number of such organizations were particularly interested in thwarting the introduction of the 40-hour week.[55]

Concluding Observations

Organization was the foundation stone of the movement to control competition through collective bargaining. The growth of employers' associations was as indispensable to the success of this movement as was the growth of labor unions. Lacking the publicity and fanfare that accompanied union organization drives, competing employers of similar position in the needle trades nevertheless united to form bargaining associations of ever expanding coverage. In these efforts they were aided and abetted by the "enlightened" segments of the needle trade unions and by the guiding hand of the impartial machinery established under collective agreements.

Like labor unions seeking to establish the closed shop, the organized manufacturers set their sights on monopoly control over the labor policies for their industries. One all-inclusive association for each trade, like one all-inclusive union, was the ideal foundation on which to erect industry-wide standards of

---

facturers were reported in *Daily News Record,* Oct. 3, 1919. The impact of this development on industry-wide bargaining is discussed below at pp. 565–569.

[55]During 1926–1927, Percy Ginsburg, manager of the Cap Manufacturers' Association of Chicago, visited every other local center of the cap trade in an effort to organize a national cap manufacturers' association "to standardize and stabilize the trade." His appeal to the cap makers' union for help in this move was regarded with suspicion because his association had opposed the 40-hour week. See the *Headgear Worker,* July 15, 1927, and Cloth Hat, Cap and Millinery Workers' International Union, *Report and Proceedings,* Seventeenth Biennial Convention (May 1929), p. 9.

employment. Just as employers held the key to union success in organizing the workers, so labor unions held the key to employer success in organizing the manufacturers. But union support failed to arouse the "legitimate" manufacturers to the need for organizing on a national scale in preparation for the day when expanding markets would minimize the importance of bargaining at the local level. Because this day of reckoning arrived late in the needle trades — New York City remained the outstanding producer of needle trade products — too many local employers closed their eyes to a growing menace of intermarket competition that had been foreseen from the inception of the protocol movement.

Chapter 15

Industry-wide Standards
before the NRA

For many years after the signing of the first protocols, collective bargaining in the needle trades was chiefly concerned with equalizing labor costs among competing producers within a single market area. Since New York City was the cradle of the apparel industries in America and has long remained the major source of production for most of these trades, those who advocated "industry-wide" standards of employment thought largely in terms of "market-wide" standards covering New York City and its immediate environs. So long as the overwhelming majority of an industry's products came from this single market area, relatively little concern was expressed for competition from other market sources. Only with the rise of seriously competitive markets in other towns and cities did the term *industry-wide* come to embrace all producing areas throughout the United States.[1]

---

[1] For figures based on the U.S. Bureau of the Census showing the total dollar value added by manufacturing in each of twenty needle trade industries of New York City in 1939, compared with similar figures for those industries throughout the United States, see the table in J. T. Carpenter, *Employers' Associations and Collective Bargaining in New York City* (1950), preface, p. x. As late as 1937, according to figures compiled by the National Coat and Suit Industry Recovery Board, the New York area produced 82 percent in total dollar sales value of the women's coats and suits made in the United States. *Women's Wear Daily,* August 24, 1937. "Of the country's

But this confusion of terms never blinded the sponsors of the protocol movement to the evils that would ultimately accompany the growth of competition between markets. Delegates to the Brandeis Conferences of 1910 foresaw the possibility that out-of-town competition might some day deprive New York City of its business and her inhabitants of their livelihood unless New York standards became uniform throughout the country. They were aware that New York manufacturers and their organized labor force could never shake loose from the rising spectre of "foreign" competition. When J. A. Dyche, a key union delegate to these conferences, was later asked to testify before the U. S. Industrial Commission on January 15, 1914, concerning the effects of protocol standards on intermarket competition, he set out his views in the following colloquy.

Coms. O'Connell: You talk of taking the trade out of the city. Has the [dress] protocol resulted in having that effect?

Dyche: Not yet; but I have seen it go on for this last five or six weeks, and it certainly will have.

O'Connell: Are the New York rates under your agreement or protocol higher than the rates outside of New York?

Dyche: Most decidedly.

O'Connell: The employer who ordinarily worked under open-shop conditions a year or years ago, does he now, under the protocol, send his goods over to New Jersey?

Dyche: Yes.

O'Connell: Supposing you and I are employers, we enter into a contract to pay so much. We would pay on the same basis, but I would slip out quietly and go to Philadelphia and have them made quietly.

Dyche: If you did it quietly, the protocol does not provide for Philadelphia.

O'Connell: Does it prohibit a manufacturer who is under the protocol and paying a price in New York from taking his goods to Jersey and having them made for a dollar or fifty cents?

Dyche: Through an opinion expressed by the board of arbitration, an employer can not do it.

---

half billion dollar annual output of dresses nearly 90 per cent is produced by 105,000 workers within a fifty mile circle surrounding its heart and center, the garment district in Manhattan." *New York Times,* Feb. 8, 1936.

O'Connell: And what do they do with him if he does?

Dyche: They fine or expel him from the association.[2]

Out-of-Town Competition

With each passing year the trend throughout the needle trades was toward more and more competition from out-of-town markets. Every new source of production magnified the importance of industry-wide standards and minimized the importance of local conditions. Not until market-wide agreements with all their highly developed instrumentalities for lawmaking and law enforcement were superseded by industry-wide agreements of equal effectiveness could the ultimate ends of the protocol movement be achieved. The first protocol for the women's coat and suit trade was only a few months old when the board of arbitration for the industry ruled that the association and the union must for their own protection extend the scope of their protocol beyond the confines of New York City.[3]

Advocates of protocol principles were less concerned with the growing number of competitors from other regions than they were alarmed at the increasing margin of comparative advantage in labor costs that accrued to out-of-town producers. The organized forces of the New York market never rejected the idea of competition from whatever source derived so long as the effect was to stimulate management and labor into greater productive efforts. "As a labor organization, we are not interested in destroying or stifling competition," the general executive board of the United Hatters, Cap and Millinery Workers' International Union once declared. "We believe that if conducted legitimately, competition has its advantages. It creates an incentive and a rivalry for new and better methods of production, it produces a desire to make available style merchandise which is attractive to the consumer, and it introduces, or could introduce, improvements that in the long run should stimulate the industry and benefit the community."[4]

Sooner or later competition from the outer circles of each

---

[2] U.S. Commission on Industrial Relations, *Final Report and Testimony* (1916), vol. 2, p. 1043.

[3] See the decision of the board of arbitration for March 14, 1911 in a printed pamphlet in the Abelson papers.

[4] But the type of competition which we have described as prevalent in the millinery industry does none of these things. It is harmful to the manufacturer, for it drives him to resort to illegitimate practices in

trade threatened the very existence of local manufacturing. By preying upon decent labor standards for their workers, by lowering the quality of the product, by destroying the integrity of reliable firms, and by shattering the confidence of the consumer, unscrupulous out-of-town producers defeated every principle of fair competition that could preserve the stability of their trades. No amount of managerial skill by New York manufacturers and no display of inspired cooperation from New York unions could offset the overwhelming advantages in production costs that fell to the unorganized employer from the hinterlands of nonunion labor. Some types of competition clearly defeated the very purposes of a competitive economy.

In 1913, a member of the Dress and Waist Manufacturers' Association offered his better dresses for sale at $5.50 each, only to have his customer reply that he could buy identical reproductions out of town at $2.25 each, less than half the price! Bound to wage scales of the dress and waist protocol, another manufacturer lost 40 percent of his business to Philadelphia competitors. More than twenty-five years later, the dress and waist industry was still wrestling with the problem of comparative labor costs. From the report of a two-year study on apparel trends in New York City, the following differentials in average hourly earnings of the "unit-priced" dress industry during the spring of 1939 were found to exist between New York City and the rest of the country.[5]

---

a desperate attempt to survive, or it crushes him, with the result that others, less scrupulous and less legitimate, become the dominant force in the industry.

—United Hatters, Cap and Millinery Workers' International Union, *Report and Proceedings,* Third Convention (May 1939), p. 67.

[5]*Minutes,* Arbitration Proceedings between the Dress and Waist Manufacturers' Association and the ILGWU (Nov. 9, 1913), pp. 118–119, 202, 279–280. For an example of alleged "gross inequalities" in the weekly wages of cutters under the New York agreements and under the Boston agreements, see *Women's Wear,* Feb. 10, 1916.

The 170-page report on apparel trends, released by the Institute of Public Administration, was prepared by L. A. Drake and Carrie Glasser for Mayor LaGuardia's business advisory committee. The study found that comparative labor costs favorable to out-of-town firms had been largely responsible for the retarded growth of New York City as a center for the manufacture of women's garments, and that reductions in labor cost differentials would be essential to thwart still further resort to out-of-town dress production at the expense of the New York market. At the time, the ILGWU attacked the validity of these conclusions. *Women's Wear Daily,* April 21, 1942.

Average Hourly Earnings

Occupation	(Cents)		Differential % under N. Y. City
	N. Y. City	Rest of U. S.	
All factory employees	90.0	62.3	30.8
Machine operators ...	91.6	61.4	33.0
Cutters	127.4	91.2	28.4
Pressers	150.6	94.5	37.3

No organized group of workers or employers in the New York market was more concerned with alleged discrepancies in labor standards than the millinery workers. During the thirties, the United Hatters, Cap and Millinery Workers attacked the "vicious circle" of intermarket competition that defeated all efforts to maintain decent labor standards. Strikes for better terms of employment in the New York market, noted the union's general executive board, only encouraged the growth of the industry in other parts of the country. The rise of out-of-town shops to fill local needs in other cities reduced the demand for New York goods and further increased the pressure upon the union to lower New York standards. Even a lockout by the New York manufacturers to protest union demands "would divert business to other markets, thus intensifying the problems of the New York market, and creating additional hardships for the workers, who depend upon the New York market for a livelihood."[6]

Max Zaritsky, president of the union, had earlier presented tables citing recent shifts in the location of the millinery industry. He pointed out the case of New Jersey where only 13 millinery plants were operating in 1929. But with the coming of the Great Depression, manufacturers tended to move from the metropolitan area into smaller communities that offered cheap labor. By 1933, the number of establishments in New Jersey had increased to 41. "With the business conducted on the basis of labor costs," so Zaritsky concluded, "each market in turn loses to another with a lowered wage scale . . . a vicious circle results with all losing in the end."[7]

---

[6]United Hatters, Cap and Millinery Workers' International Union, Cap and Millinery Department, *Report and Proceedings*, Second Convention (First Regular Convention), Oct. 4–7, 1936, pp. 10, 73.

[7]Max Zaritsky's testimony before the National Recovery Administration on a proposed millinery code, as summarized in *Women's Wear Daily*, August

Other local branches of the needle trades faced a similar pre-
dicament. As early as 1913, the New York women's coat and suit
manufacturers claimed to be operating at a 20 percent disadvantage in wage rates over the rest of the country. Likewise in 1919,
the local manufacturers of men's clothing were alleged to be
paying wage scales which were $16 a week higher than those of
their competitors in Rochester and $14 a week higher than those
of their competitors in Chicago. And — to cite another example —
a New York leather goods manufacturer contended in the early
thirties that he was paying $48 a gross for getting handbags sewed,
while his Pennsylvania competitors paid out only $36 a gross for
sewing and finishing the bags. Such charges of substantial differences in wage rates were commonplace.[8]

The Plight of the Organized Manufacturers

Of all variations in labor standards this intermarket type of dis-
crepancy was most likely to drive the organized manufacturers of
the New York City area to despair. The theory advanced at the
Brandeis Conferences in 1910 that the pattern of labor standards
set by the organized forces of labor and management would draw
all wages and working conditions upward to the levels established
at the heart of each industry had failed to materialize. On the
contrary, cheap labor and cheap goods, like Gresham's law of
cheap money, had tended to drive dearer labor and more expensive goods out of the market place. Threatened with extinction,
some employer groups were reduced to the option of falling upon
the union's neck and pleading for permission to stay in business

2, 1933. Between 1919 and 1933, New York City's share of the cap manufacturing business declined from 50 percent of the nation's output to about
28 percent, while the proportion of workers New York furnished to the industry as a whole fell from 75 percent to about 40 percent. United Hatters,
Cap and Millinery Workers' International Union, Cap and Millinery Department, *Report and Proceedings*, Second Convention (First Regular Convention), Oct. 4–7, 1936, p. 25.

[8]For women's coat and suit manufacturers, see *Minutes*, Meeting of the
Joint Board of the Cloak and Skirt Makers' Unions of New York and the
Cloak, Suit and Skirt Manufacturers' Protective Association (July 8, 1913),
p. 63; for men's clothing manufacturers, see *Daily News Record*, May 31, 1922;
for leather manufacturers, see Henry Moskowitz, impartial chairman, *Decisions*, Case no. 34A (May 23, 1932). Copy filed in the Abelson papers.

or else of throwing off the yoke of collective bargaining for the jungles of unregulated competition.

Attempts to throw off the yoke were more publicized, if less numerous, than pleas to stay in business. Threats of extinction, so it was alleged, had driven the [women's] Cloak, Suit and Skirt Manufacturers' Protective Association to abrogate its labor agreement in 1921 and to abandon its labor department in 1924. Again, threats of extinction had allegedly driven the Eastern Women's Headwear Association in 1935 to announce through its executive secretary, J. E. Helfer, that "not a wheel will turn or any factory [be] permitted to reopen until the union alters its policies and brings about an adjustment of wages both in New York and out of town that will enable everyone to compete on an equal basis."[9]

These more drastic measures weakened but never killed support for the protocol movement. Within a matter of months after the inside manufacturers of the women's coat and suit trade had abolished their labor department in 1924, leaving each employer to shift for himself, the inside manufacturers were organized under a new name (the Industrial Council of Cloak, Suit and Skirt Manufacturers) and the bonds of collective action were re-established with the union. In the tradition of the protocol movement, the collective agreement of the new association with the ILGWU, effective July 16, 1924, expressed the mutual desire of both parties to "eliminate such of the manufacturing establishments as operate under unfair conditions of labor and sanitation." Similarly, the determined movement for a "protest strike" by the millinery manufacturers in 1935 collapsed before the general lockout ever became effective.[10]

---

[9]Leading the six hundred members of his association into direct action, Helfer planned to conduct a stoppage of production "in the same manner as a strike," with committees of manufacturers set up to picket the shops and buildings of the millinery district wherever evidences existed of inequality in wage rates "brought about by the union's policy of making special deals." As an alternative to bankruptcy, this procedure, so Helfer believed, would "give the association an opportunity to get a clear picture of those manufacturers who may find nourishment at the expense of others." *Women's Wear Daily*, Nov. 1, 5, 1935. The two actions of the [women's] Cloak, Suit and Skirt Manufacturers' Protective Association are reported at pp. 323 and 543. See references there cited.

[10]Technically, the Industrial Council was an autonomous group taking over the work of the labor department within the old protective association.

Such episodes did, however, point up the futility of seeking to protect the "legitimate" forces of an industry so long as the terms of collective agreements were confined to a single market. Time and again the rise of intermarket competition brought new demands that standards of employment become nationwide in their coverage. No effort to control competition in New York City could prevail unless similar efforts were extended to the outer circles of each trade — circles that included out-of-town independent shops operating under separate union contracts as well as the out-of-town shops of independent producers generally employing nonunion labor.

The Institutional Framework for Industry-wide Standards

Logically, industry-wide standards of employment should be derived from a system of industry-wide bargaining between national employers' associations and national labor unions. Only those organizations that embraced all the competing markets of an industry were qualified to determine uniform labor standards for that industry. Only national unions and national associations could properly devise the machinery and adopt the procedures for the administration of industry-wide agreements. Otherwise, workers and employers in unrepresented markets would have no voice in formulating the rules or establishing the institutions by which they were governed. Having no voice in these deliberations, the unrepresented groups would be less disposed to abide by the standards set for the trade.[11]

The text of the original constitution of the Industrial Council appeared in *Women's Wear*, July 17, 1924. The text of the labor agreement, as given in *ibid.*, July 18, 1924, carries the name of the old protective association, but the text of the same agreement, separately printed, names the Industrial Council as the employer party to the contract.

[11]The concept of industry-wide agreements jointly negotiated between national associations and international unions had been firmly established in other industries long before the protocol movement of the needle trades was ever conceived. Near the turn of the century, the Stove Founders' National Defense Association, the National Founders' Association, the National Metal Trades Association, and the National Erectors' Association were parties to national agreements with their respective unions. About the same time, several national arbitration agreements were negotiated between the American Newspaper Publishers' Association and unions in the printing trades. Encouraged by these and other industry-wide agreements, the New York State Bureau of Labor Statistics in its annual report for 1906 stated that

Short of national employers' associations, the manufacturers of competing markets might still have contributed something to a framework for industry-wide bargaining had they been willing to organize a federation of local employer bargaining groups. Although the balance of power under a loose federation remained in the separate market groups, this superstructure might have provided a means for adopting common policies or advancing common programs to be followed in local negotiations on all issues of industry-wide concern. Some progress would thus have been registered toward certain nationwide standards, even though the final adoption, application, and enforcement of those standards were left to the different market organizations. If nothing more, the competing manufacturers of various markets might at least have arranged for occasional conferences to exchange views on how best to channel the processes of collective bargaining into controlling the excesses of competition.[12]

But failure of the employers to form national associations or to create any substitute comparable to national unions of workers destroyed the potential symmetry of the structure for industry-wide bargaining and put additional pressure upon labor unions to provide the necessary framework through which industry-wide standards could be established and enforced. By 1916 Julius Henry Cohen, counsel for the manufacturers and father of the protocol movement, despaired of ever organizing the manufacturers on a national scale for collective bargaining. Whether from sheer indifference or for fear of legal restraint, employers shied away from industry-wide associations for purposes of collective bargaining. Six years after launching the first protocol as a joint labor-management enterprise, Cohen placed the responsibility for extending New York standards into other markets squarely on the shoulders of the union. "The efforts of the Union," he said,

---

collective bargaining had found "its consummate flower in the trade agreement between national organizations of employers and workers." See C. E. Bonnett, *Employers' Associations and Collective Bargaining* (1922), pp. 50, 68, 104, 139, 209, 251; U.S. Commission on Industrial Relations, *Final Report and Testimony* (1916), vol. 1, p. 756; Carpenter, *Employers' Associations and Collective Bargaining in New York City*, p. 156 n., and references there cited.

[12]The early movement toward national employers' associations in the needle trades, particularly in the men's clothing industry, is discussed above, pp. 551–556.

"are, as we must all concede, the only way outside of legislation by which standards are raised, and we have not yet devised the legislative method."[13]

Unlike the employers whose local associations lacked a national framework, unions of the needle trades boasted of national organizations long before their locals and joint boards had penetrated many growing centers of outside production. Union weakness at the grass roots of competing markets had given rise to the perennial cry of the manufacturers to organize the out-of-town workers. If unions were to provide the institutional superstructure for negotiating and enforcing industry-wide standards of employment, then they must cover at least a majority of all the workers in each of the competing markets. Encouraged by the New York manufacturers, needle trade unions with national headquarters in New York City, where most of their members were employed, willingly accepted the challenge to increase their out-of-town strength.[14]

Before the era of the NRA codes, the outstanding contribution of needle trade unions to industry-wide labor standards undoubtedly came from the men's clothing industry. Through the initiative of Sidney Hillman, president of the Amalgamated Clothing Workers' Union, men's clothing manufacturers were not only urged to organize on a national scale — a movement that had led in 1919 to the formation of the National Industrial Federation of Clothing Manufacturers (see above, p. 554) — but, in the absence of a national employers' association, they were induced to make the most of assistance from local employer groups in the various markets.

Hillman's first objective was to create market-wide labor standards through multiple-employer bargaining in each of the major

---

[13]*Minutes*, Arbitration Proceedings between the Dress and Waist Manufacturers' Association and the ILGWU (Feb. 5, 1916), vol. 4, p. 61.

[14]Our Union is a national organization; it has branches of cloakmakers, say, in the City of New York, in Philadelphia, in Cleveland, in St. Louis, and everywhere, and it is the only factor which unites the industry all through the country. It is the only factor which at least potentially has the power of developing uniform standards all through the country.

    —Morris Hillquit, counsel for the ILGWU, in *Minutes*, Council of Conciliation ... [women's coat and suit trade] (July 14, 1915), vol. 2, p. 82.

cities manufacturing men's clothing. Contrary to the association-wide origins of the protocol movement in the women's coat and suit trade of New York City, collective bargaining in the men's clothing industry of Chicago, where Hillman began work in the labor movement, was at first confined to single firms, with Hart, Schaffner, and Marx providing the outstanding example in 1910–1911. Several years were to elapse before Hillman and his Amalgamated Clothing Workers — a union that had largely succeeded the United Garment Workers after 1914 — established the principle of market-wide standards through multiple-employer bargaining in Hillman's own home town.[15]

In other cities, however, Hillman and his union worked from the outset to establish collective bargaining on a multiple-employer scale. Aside from New York City where manufacturers required no encouragement for group action, serious union efforts were made during 1919 to organize the workers and negotiate market-wide agreements with associations of men's clothing manufacturers in Rochester, Cleveland, Cincinnati, Baltimore, Boston, Montreal, and Toronto. Hillman could attribute his phenomenal success in these areas partly to the support the federal government had offered unions and collective bargaining during the war years and partly to the idea of joint labor-management councils or market boards that were organized to consider problems of production affecting the local area, if not the entire trade. Employers could be sold on the virtues of collective bargaining wherever there were prospects of eliminating competition in labor costs through cooperation with the union.

From market-wide agreements Hillman moved toward his ultimate goal of industry-wide standards. After the manufacturers of four leading markets — New York, Baltimore, Rochester, and Chicago — had formed the National Industrial Federation of Clothing Manufacturers, representatives of this federation met with representatives of the Amalgamated Clothing Workers in Rochester to form a National Industrial Council through which

---

[15]During May 1919, most of the substantial manufacturers of men's clothing in Chicago signed a multiemployer contract with the Amalgamated Clothing Workers of America. The text of this agreement appears in the *Daily News Record,* May 16, 1919. See also, J. M. Moses, "Labor Agreements with a Powerful Union," in *Annals,* American Academy of Political and Social Science, September 1919, vol. 85, pp. 166–179.

nationwide standards of employment were to be negotiated. But friction between employer representatives of the various markets prevented the consummation of a national agreement, whereupon the determination of wages, hours, and working conditions, as well as of other issues of industry concern, was again left to the various markets.[16]

Pattern Setting for Industry-wide Standards

The institutional framework of national union organizations made possible certain other approaches to industry-wide standards short of industry-wide bargaining. Needle trade unions might take the initiative in seeing that market-wide agreements conformed to an industry-wide pattern. When Sidney Hillman and the Amalgamated Clothing Workers were thwarted in their efforts to introduce industry-wide negotiations for the men's clothing industry after the First World War, they fell back upon the nearest substitute: concurrent bargaining in the various markets. Plans were made to have Hillman and a representative of the National Federation of Clothing Manufacturers go from market to market during the concurrent negotiations where their influence would help to establish industry-wide standards of employment.[17]

---

[16]Various accounts of this episode looking to industry-wide standards in the men's clothing industry after the First World War appeared in the contemporary newspapers and magazines. For representative selections, see the "Red Book of Clippings" maintained by the Research Library of the ACWA. See also the *New York World*, July 27, 1919; the *Survey*, Sept. 18, 1919, vol. 42, pp. 843–846; H. S. Gilbertson, "Meeting the Labor Problem in the Clothing Industry," in *Administration*, February 1923, vol. 5, pp. 181–187; and *Daily News Record*, May 15, 1919. In the fall of 1919, Secretary of Labor W. B. Wilson had proposed that the federal government through the Department of Labor promote the formation of national conference boards representing unions and employers' associations of each industry. These boards were apparently to be modeled after the National Industrial Council of the men's clothing industry. They would have for their objective: "the consideration of all subjects affecting the progress and well being of trade." *Daily News Record*, Oct. 10, 1919.

[17]*Ibid.*, Feb. 10, 15, 1922. The extent to which Hillman and his union achieved their goal of uniform labor standards in their 1922 renewed labor agreements for the Chicago, Cleveland, Rochester, and Baltimore markets is shown in a four-page chart comparing in parallel columns the chief features of these four contracts in Margaret Gadsby, "Development of Collective

Other needle trade industries in which the employers were not organized on a national scale expected the union of their workers to overcome this handicap by applying the terms of New York agreements to all competing markets. "Any agreement negotiated, concluded, and ratified," reported the officials of New York's Associated Fur Coat and Trimming Manufacturers to the association's 27th annual meeting in 1939, "is made on the premise and theory that it applies to the entire industry." Such a theory was in keeping with the obligations that needle trade unions had voluntarily accepted since the Brandeis Conferences of 1910. "When negotiating new agreements in the out of town markets in the cloak industry," runs the pertinent clause of the 1929 collective agreement between the Industrial Council of Cloak, Suit and Skirt Manufacturers (inside producers) and the ILGWU, "the International Ladies' Garment Workers' Union will endeavor in good faith and to the utmost of its ability to introduce the same standards in such out of town markets as are contained in this agreement with respect to hours of work, provisions for overtime, and methods of production."[18]

Whatever successes accompanied the efforts of needle trade unions in this direction invariably brought forth words of encouragement and songs of praise from New York producers of needle trade products. Thus, the New York dress and waist manufacturers were overjoyed at hearing Morris Hillquit, counsel for the ILGWU, report in 1916 that the union had "made Herculean efforts, within the last couple of years particularly, to raise the industry in other centers in the country to the level of the City of New York." Likewise, the cloak and suit manufacturers viewed with pride the account of how the union had just obtained its first collective agreement with manufacturers in Philadelphia by routing out "a nest of the worst competitors, the most unconscionable competitors in the industry." These were competitors "of a different type than the manufacturers in New York — a much smaller, pettier type." These firms that had been uprooted, so Hillquit explained, were companies that "underbid and under-

---

Bargaining in the Men's Clothing Industry in the United States," *Monthly Labor Review*, June 1922, vol. 14, pp. 1102–1105.

[18]A copy of the fur manufacturers' report is filed in the Abelson papers.

sell New York manufacturers because the labor is cheap" and because "absolutely no standards of any kind" prevail.[19]

Even though the ILGWU sometimes made exceptions to uniform standards for the benefit of marginal firms in remote markets, the principle of industry-wide uniformity through pattern setting would at least have been acknowledged. New York manufacturers had always conceded the necessity for temporary concessions to offset adverse conditions affecting labor costs of some firms. But they expected the union to get its foot into the door of every competing market that threatened the security of New York producers. Once the union was established in a new market, more substantial progress could be made toward the ultimate goal of industry-wide standards. A sagging floor beneath competition in the hinterlands of substandard production was still better than no floor at all.

Naturally, New York manufacturers viewed with alarm every failure of the needle trade unions to extend local standards into all other competing markets. The issue of the 40-hour week raised just such a furor during the twenties. New York manufacturers had no quarrel with the principle of the 40-hour week so long as all other competitors followed the same standard. In more than one industry they accepted the principle on the assumption that the unions would extend the 40-hour week throughout the trade. But soon after this standard had been written into the 1926 collective agreement between the Wholesale Hat and Cap Manufacturers and the headwear workers' union, the employers' association, party to this agreement, announced that "tremendous competition" had aggravated the disparity in labor costs between local association-union shops and the wholly unorganized shops. The manufacturers demanded a conference with the union to work out some form of relief lest the burden of the 40-hour week force the association to take other steps "to protect its own interests."[20]

The women's coat and suit trade also accepted the 40-hour

[19]*Minutes,* Arbitration Proceedings between the Dress and Waist Manufacturers' Association and the ILGWU (Feb. 5, 1916), vol. 4, p. 53; *Minutes,* Council of Conciliation ... [women's coat and suit trade] (July 14, 1915), vol. 2, p. 83.

[20]*Daily News Record,* June 21, 1927.

week strictly on the assumption that the union would be able to impose the same standard throughout the industry. But the ILGWU, torn by internal dissension from Communist domination of the Cloakmakers' Joint Board in the mid-twenties, was unable to meet this obligation. This failure threatened to disrupt the employers' association. Disgruntled manufacturers called upon their association to justify its conduct at the bargaining table. Addressing a membership meeting in 1929 on the terms of a previous agreement with the union, Samuel Klein, executive director of the Industrial Council of Cloak, Suit and Skirt Manufacturers, stated frankly: "We wish to assure you as emphatically as we can that had we the slightest inkling of the union's inability to control other shops, we would never have been parties to an agreement calling for the introduction of the 40-hour week and other high standards contained therein."[21]

The Great Depression of the thirties brought on the final debacle of the pattern-setting theory for establishing industry-wide standards of employment through action of the union. While the need for a common floor under labor standards was never so urgent, the union's institutional framework through which this objective would be accomplished was falling apart at the seams. That "supposedly powerful structure of unionism in the cloak and suit industry," lamented Samuel Klein, outspoken employer advocate of controlled competition, "is merely a house of cards in imminent danger of complete collapse."[22]

The prospects of "confiscatory competition" during the depression likewise appalled representatives of the dress and waist industry. "It is no fun for our members to be locked in a vise of strict union rules and to see their competitors working under all manner of non-union conditions," announced Jed Sylbert, general manager of the Association of Dress Manufacturers (contractors) in 1931. And with equal conviction, Louis L. Schwartz, president of the newly formed Affiliated Dress Manufacturers

[21]*Women's Wear Daily*, Feb. 19, 1929. For charges made by Samuel Klein that the ILGWU had granted special concessions to Chicago cloak manufacturers, see *ibid.*, July 20, 1931.

[22]*Ibid.*, June 16, 1930. "We see union leaders forgetting their responsibility of organizing non-union shops.... The non-union rat-holes multiply and undermine the stability of the trade; the union is either unable or unwilling to cope with these slimy elements which threaten to tear down the industry." Samuel Klein, *ibid.*, Jan. 28, 1931.

(inside producers) asserted that "if the union does not take hold of the situation existing in the trade and meet the employers half way, it will only be a matter of time until a large portion of the industry is driven out of New York."[23]

Pattern Setting by Third Parties

The possibility also existed that pattern setting might become a tool of third parties who in one capacity or another settled disputes over the terms of employment and then remained to apply and interpret the agreements they had helped to create. Some of these highly respected neutrals operated in more than one market and thus were in a key position to contribute to the formation of intermarket standards. Others holding similar positions in different markets could exchange views on the proper standards to be established for the trade. In any case, outside advisers, citizens' committees, mediators, arbitrators, permanent umpires, and impartial chairmen — all those who acted as a coagulating agent to mold a common policy for the good of an industry — could look to the standards accepted at the heart of each trade for criteria on which to base their decisions. Although they be limited in jurisdiction to a single group of manufacturers and workers in a single market, their desire to promote industry welfare should lead them to support industry-wide standards of employment.[24]

Third parties who contributed most to the solution of needle trade problems have been notoriously industry-minded. They would have the participants in local disputes rise above their

---

[23]Jed Sylbert, *ibid.,* June 25, 1931; L. L. Schwartz, *ibid.,* Feb. 18, 1930. "Confiscatory competition" is discussed in the Oct. 8, 1931 issue.

[24]When W. Z. Ripley and L. E. Kirstein were chosen as arbitrators to settle a wage dispute which involved only one or two men's clothing manufacturers in Rochester, they announced that the award would apply to the entire market:

> Our investigations of wage conditions will not be confined to the adjustment in those two cases and our decision, when made, will according to the understanding, apply to the houses of practically the entire market. And finally it is hoped that the standardization of wages in Rochester, thus attained, will operate to promote national industrial standardization in this regard.
>
> —From a statement of W. Z. Ripley quoted in ACWA, *Report and Proceedings,* Fourth Biennial Convention (May 1920), p. 40.

petty jealousies in a common cause of promoting industry welfare for their mutual advantage. Outside contributors have approached this goal by insisting upon a thorough knowledge of industry conditions. The history of collective bargaining in the needle trades abounds with examples of special research agencies, joint labor-management committees, and neutral investigators expressly chosen to provide the factual background for an industry-oriented solution to current disputes. Decisions were often based upon a storehouse of information concerning wage scales, hours of work, fringe benefits, comparative labor costs, and the status of competition among different factions and between different markets of a given trade.[25]

On the other hand, third parties, whether in the role of mediators, advisers, or arbitrators, borrowed little from one another in the formative years of collective bargaining. They maintained no common organization and sought to develop no common principles. Those operating in the same industry or in the same market area seldom communicated with one another, nor were their decisions readily available for inspection. There was no pool of common knowledge from which precedents might contribute to the development of uniform standards. Some third parties were not even consistent in their own decisions from one case to an-

[25]In 1916 Henry Moskowitz, president of the Municipal Civil Service Commission of New York City, who for five years had served as secretary to the board of arbitration under the original Protocol of Peace, and was to become a distinguished arbitrator in the needle trades, attributed the shortcomings of arbitration as a means for settling disputes over the terms of collective agreements to ignorance of industry-wide conditions. In the absence of such information, he said, arbitrators, compelled to balance opposing pressures in local markets, might render decisions that, in the light of competitive conditions elsewhere, would do the parties more harm than good. To what end would an arbitrator meet a local union demand for an operator's minimum wage of 75¢ an hour if the decision led to closing down local plants and boosting production elsewhere?

Dr. Moskowitz would create for each industry a national fact-finding board which would be "continually at work collecting and recording facts about the ever changing conditions" of a trade. Then in the absence of industry-wide agreements negotiated between national employers' associations and national labor unions, arbitrators in local markets, presented with unresolved disputes over the terms of local contracts, would at least have the factual information on which to base intelligent decisions that could be expected to work out for the best interests of both parties. See "The Garment Trade and the Minimum Wage: An interview with Dr. Henry Moskowitz," in the *Outlook,* May 10, 1916, vol. 113, pp. 66, 83–87.

other or from one time to another. Each was inclined to hoe his own row in keeping with his own interpretation of the facts and according to the dictates of his own conscience.

Nevertheless, expediency and common sense called for industry-wide standards of employment that in the long run would provide maximum security and stability to all parties bound by collective agreements. That is why the board of arbitration under the 1919 collective agreement of the men's clothing industry in Chicago voted a wage increase that would raise the level of wages to the wage levels existing in the Rochester, Baltimore, and New York markets. And that is why a special arbitration board chosen to resolve differences between the Baltimore Federation of Clothing Manufacturers and the Amalgamated Clothing Workers held sessions in Chicago and Rochester to study comparative labor standards before deciding what terms to write into the Baltimore agreement.

During the first decade of the protocols, New York arbitrators, who were often empowered to write the terms of collective agreements, acknowledged on more than one occasion their role as pattern setters for their industries. In referring their 1913 dispute over hours of work to arbitration, the Merchants' Tailors' Association of Greater New York and the United Garment Workers of America gave specific instructions that the arbitrators' findings "shall be on the basis of establishing a standard of working hours per week that will maintain the industry in New York on a competitive basis with other markets for the present and for the future." By investigating hours of work in the men's clothing industry of Chicago, Baltimore, Rochester, and Philadelphia, this board of arbitration found 54 hours a week to be the standard for men's clothing; nevertheless the board held that New York City as the leading market should set the pace toward shorter hours. Leaving the door open for future changes, the arbitrators announced that "from time to time we hope to be able to make a further study of conditions in this industry and bring such recommendations as in our judgment are warranted by competitive conditions."[26]

Several years later, the hours-of-work issue, along with the demand for higher wages, was again raised — this time in a dispute

---

[26]The decision called for a gradual reduction in hours of work from 54 hours a week to 48 hours a week. Correspondence dealing with this case during February and March 1913 may be found in the Abelson papers.

between the American Men and Boys' Clothing Manufacturers' Association and the Amalgamated Clothing Workers of America. After an extended lockout over these issues in the winter of 1918–1919, the association and the union agreed to submit their dispute to a public advisory board for settlement. The members of this board, W. Z. Ripley, Louis Marshall, and Felix Frankfurter, set another precedent for the clothing industry by endorsing a 44-hour week. "The hope is earnestly expressed that this precedent be recognized throughout the industry, in view of the desirability of bringing about its proper standardization," noted the board. "It would be regarded as unfortunate if the hours of labor should vary in this industry in the several important centers where it is extensively conducted."[27]

For seven years, the Chicago cap manufacturers and cap makers' union had a provision in their collective agreement obligating the employers to abide by whatever changes in working conditions might be accepted in the New York market. This rule was applied to the 44-hour week, the unemployment insurance fund, and then to the 40-hour week when these standards were first introduced into the New York agreements for the cap industry. When a dispute over an increase in wages and over the 40-hour week in Chicago went to the board of adjustment for a decision under the collective cap agreement for that market, the Chicago board simply based its decision on the terms of the corresponding agreement negotiated in the New York market. Moreover, adjustments were made in standards of production for the Chicago market so that labor costs for the two markets would become more nearly equal.[28]

---

[27] Text of the board's report, dated Jan. 22, 1919, may be found in ACWA, *Report and Proceedings,* Fourth Biennial Convention (May 1920), pp. 25–26. On the nationwide application of the 44-hour week, see *ibid.,* pp. 34–35.

In another report on a "Survey of the New York Clothing Industry," dated May 28, 1920, Felix Frankfurter and S. J. Rosensohn noted that the problem of the 44-hour week standard adopted by the New York market "was greatly eased by the speedy adoption of the same schedule of hours in all other markets." The text of this report may be found at pp. 17–43 in a printed collection of union affidavits submitted in the case of J. Friedman & Co. v. ACWA, filed in the Abelson papers.

[28] Cloth Hat, Cap and Millinery Workers' International Union, *Report and Proceedings,* Seventeenth Biennial Convention (May 1929), p. 18; the *Headgear Worker,* August 20, 1926, July 15, 1927.

Third parties found good cause to accept the leadership of the New York market where the overwhelming bulk of needle trade products was made. The organized forces of New York City could boast of the longest and most successful experiences in negotiating terms of employment. Most new concepts in the development of collective bargaining originated there. Nowhere else had the impartial machinery of collective agreements contributed so much to the solution of industry problems not resolved at the bargaining table. Nowhere else had umpires and arbitrators gained so much experience in adapting labor standards to conform with conditions arising during the life of a collective agreement. Refined in the caldron of trial and error, New York labor standards were most likely to withstand the pressures inevitably thrust upon them.

Yet arbitrators assigned the task of setting labor standards in other markets were bombarded with good reasons for refusing to accept New York standards as a guide. New York manufacturers, so it was contended, could afford higher labor costs because their other costs of production were lower. The great size and strategic location of New York City, together with the city's long history as a leading garment center, gave New York manufacturers a decided advantage in sales and distribution over manufacturers in other centers scattered throughout the United States. Moreover, New York manufacturers could afford higher labor standards because their workers were more productive. The whole tempo of industrial life was geared to a faster pace. Other markets had no comparable reservoir of skilled workers seeking employment. Elsewhere, apprentice training was expensive if not impossible.

Appeals to Consumers and the General Public

In any case, the road to industry-wide standards could never be completely paved by third parties who worked only at resolving differences that arose within the organized segments of an industry. The greatest barrier to uniformity in labor standards came from the unorganized segments of competing markets. Where unions failed to organize the workers in out-of-town centers, the sponsors of the protocol movement had to find other means of penetrating the unorganized shops.

From the beginning of the protocol movement, the parties to

collective agreements had relied upon the weight of public opinion for relief from the evils of nonunion competition. Public opinion had always been a factor in determining the outcome of industrial wars between the "bosses" and the "people" of the needle trades. Social reformers knew how to play upon the heartstrings of humanitarianism to halt a conflict. Led by ministers, teachers, editors, philanthropists, and social workers, public opinion could be fired to arouse the conscience and rekindle the souls of those responsible for industrial strife. By attacking the evils of nonunion competition, public opinion could be directed to wiping out the underlying causes of industrial warfare.

Still more promising was the thought of having those who ultimately used the products of industry take part in the war upon nonunion competition. As early as 1912, the parties to the first collective agreement of the women's coat and suit trade proposed a nationwide campaign "to enlist and educate consumers to meet their responsibilities by casting the industrial ballot of their purchasing power for garments made in protocol factories." Gertrude Barnum, a union organizer, was in the forefront of this movement. "The consumer," she said, "casts an industrial ballot every time he buys a manufactured article. He can peacefully revolutionize industry and abolish sweatshops and most industrial accidents." If properly directed, the consumer might determine the outcome of protocol battles between the "legitimate" forces of an industry and the "illegitimate" forces. Here the lines of distinction between right and wrong could be more easily drawn.[29]

Given a statement of the issues and a knowledge of the facts, consumers of needle trade products might distribute their patronage to support the cause of "legitimate" competition everywhere. They could be taught to respect a label that stood for decent conditions of employment. Whereas the typical union label had long been used to focus attention on the sanitary conditions under which garments were manufactured, a different type of label jointly sponsored by labor unions and employers' associations might become a useful tool for constructing a floor under competition in places otherwise beyond the reach of the parties to collective agreements. Garments not manufactured according to indus-

[29]*New York Herald Tribune,* April 27, 1912; *Daily Trade Record,* Dec. 6, 1912; *Independent,* Oct. 3, 1912, vol. 73, pp. 777–781.

try standards would be denied such a label; and, under the threat of a consumer boycott, garments without labels could not be sold in the market place.

No one was more aware of this possibility than J. H. Cohen who had led the manufacturers into the protocol movement. Cohen repeatedly argued for a label that would be a symbol of production under protocol standards. The cure for the nonunion shop, so he told the board of arbitration for the women's coat and suit trade on August 4, 1913, "was to get the co-operation of the consumer, by regulating the industry in a perfectly legitimate way, by indicating by a label that a garment has gone through the provision of the Protocol." Two months later, Cohen again spoke up for a label which would "certify compliance by the shop with standard sanitary and wage conditions." Cohen argued that the withdrawal of a protocol label "for cause determined by an impartial tribunal" would become "a greater weapon than the strike" for the enforcement of protocol standards.[30]

Cohen would change the union label into an instrument of all organized factions within a trade, and in addition he would assure the public a voice in its administration. "Instead of a union label under the control and disposition of the union," so Cohen wrote in 1916, "it seemed to me that a joint label under the supervision of a triangular board, the representatives of the public, the workers and the employers, could be transformed into a commercial as well as a social asset." Earlier, in his testimony before the U. S. Commission on Industrial Relations, January 17, 1914, Cohen had stated his views on how to reach the shops the union had failed to organize:

Now, for that there is a remedy. I have suggested it, and it is now being considered in the dress and waist industry, and that is this, that as soon as the public is interested in knowing whether the garments that are being made are made under sanitary conditions, and whether a fair wage is paid to the worker, the consuming public should be brought into the game; and the National Consumers' League is today ready to join with the union, with the manufacturers, and with the workers to secure a label which shall be attached to every garment that is made under fair conditions — a label that shall secure to the

---

[30]*Minutes,* Meeting of the Board of Arbitrators . . . [women's coat and suit trade] (August 4, 1913), p. 411; (Oct. 14, 1913), pp. 14–15.

person who is wearing the garment that it has been made under proper sanitary conditions and made with proper pay to the workers and under proper hours, and is educated up to the immorality of wearing clothes where the laborer is not properly paid. The manufacturer will then be placed somewhere near a proper plane of competition with the rest of the community.[31]

The International Ladies' Garment Workers' Union was more than willing to follow Cohen's leadership in transforming the label into a more effective weapon of attack upon the shops that the union could not control. Early in the life of the first protocol, Abe Bisno, educational director of the union, set about winning the support of rank-and-file union members to Cohen's suggestion of a label jointly administered by the union and the association. In March 1915, the ILGWU proposed to the manufacturers that "immediate arrangements shall be made for the adoption and use of a suitable protocol label which shall be the property of both parties and shall be administered under joint control." Morris Hillquit, counsel for the ILGWU, was among others who considered such a program indispensable to the control of small contractor shops in the dress trade.[32]

---

[31]J. H. Cohen, *Law and Order in Industry* (1916), pp. 216–217; U.S. Commission on Industrial Relations, *Final Report and Testimony*, vol. 2, p. 1130.

[32]For Abe Bisno's contributions, see Louis Lorwin [Louis Levine], *The Women's Garment Workers* (1924), p. 247. The union's 1915 proposal is reported in *Women's Wear*, March 19, 1915. Hillquit's views are indicated in the following observations of J. H. Cohen:

> As Mr. Hillquit says, there is no conceivable way today, and there hasn't been found any way in the three years under the Protocol by which the Union, with the best of faith, can control that [small] shop and make standards in that shop observable.... That shop is going to exist. This Board can write on paper it shall not exist. This Board cannot stop it. That shop will exist. If it doesn't sell to members of our Association it will sell direct to the mail order houses and retailers, and those goods will be sold, and will be worn by the consuming public. That fact cannot be disputed, and Mr. Hillquit admits that the Union can't stop it. The Board of Enforcement can't stop it, because the Board of Enforcement may go there and find that the conditions exist, tell the Union to call the people out on strike, the Union calls them out on strike, and within forty-eight hours another group of people will be in that shop working under the same standards. It is simply impossible until the industry is controlled by some power of the consumer to control the small shop.
>
> —*Minutes,* Arbitration Proceedings between the Dress and Waist

Further to strengthen this movement, the board of arbitration for the women's coat and suit trade in 1915 officially endorsed an appeal to the public for aid in suppressing the evils of outside competition under the original Protocol of Peace. Operating on the assumption that the community wished to have protocol conditions established generally, Louis Brandeis, speaking for the board, recommended that the contracting parties give careful consideration to the use of a protocol label as a means of enlisting consumer support. Certainly, concluded the chairman of the board, the contracting parties "are entitled not only to the sympathetic consideration, but to the help of the rest of the community."[33]

Perhaps the type of label that carried the most popular appeal was one that stood for minimum standards of health and safety under which garments were manufactured. The question of a "prosanis label" — one based on standards of sanitation — was a continuing issue during the twenties. Responsibility for supervising the use of such a label would logically fall within the province of the "Joint Board of Sanitary Control" — an institution created by the terms of the original women's coat and suit protocol in 1910 and later extended to cover several other apparel trades. No institution of collective bargaining was more widely acclaimed than the joint board of sanitary control.[34]

The activities of this institution representing the employers,

---

Manufacturers' Association and the ILGWU (Feb. 14, 1916), vol. 5, pp. 590–591. See also J. H. Cohen in *Minutes,* Council of Conciliation ... [women's coat and suit trade] (July 14, 1915), vol. 2, p. 60.

[33]Protocol conditions are conditions which the community desires to have established generally. There are scarcely any, whether employers or employees or consumers, who do not wish to accomplish exactly what those who are in the industry are seeking to accomplish by way of bettering the relations of employers and employees. Some method ought to be devised of enlisting the co-operation of the community in the great and difficult task of working out these problems.

— Brandeis in the Nathan Schuss case, *Minutes,* Meeting of the Board of Arbitrators ... [women's coat and suit trade] (Jan. 21, 1915), pp. 1006–1007.

[34]To make more effective the maintenance of sanitary conditions throughout the industry, to insure equality of minimum standards throughout the industry, and to guarantee to the public garments made in the shops certified by the board of sanitary control, the parties agree

the workers, and the public are duly recorded in the board's annual reports, particularly those for the first, fifth, tenth, and fifteenth years. In its first year of operation, the board found that 236 of the women's coat and suit shops inspected had no drop ladders, 94 percent of the shops inspected had outside doors that opened inward, 87 percent of the shops had no protection against eye strain, and 79 percent of the shops had no dressing rooms. From these disclosures of the more obvious deficiencies in the workshop, this remarkable agency plugged away year after year under the inspired leadership of Dr. George M. Price to establish adequate standards of fire protection, light, heat, ventilation, first aid, sanitation, and medical and dental care.[35]

Through frequent shop inspections (12,891 of them in 1919) and through the power to issue or withdraw "sanitary certificates," the joint board of sanitary control could enforce its standards in the shops of association members bound by collective agreements and in the shops of independent firms operating under separate union contracts. Only employers displaying valid "sanitary certificates" could retain association membership or enjoy the privileges of the protocol system. But the board had no power to enter wholly unorganized shops which were beyond the control of the union or the employers' associations. Pressure upon these shops to observe minimum sanitary standards had to come from other sources.

To exert pressure upon nonunion shops, Governor Alfred E. Smith's Advisory Commission on the women's coat and suit trade in the mid-twenties strongly recommended support for a sanitary

---

that there shall be instituted in the industry a system of certifying garments by a label to be affixed to the garment.
—From the protocol in the dress and waist industry, Jan. 18, 1913.
J. H. Cohen, counsel for the manufacturers, claimed credit for the inclusion of this provision.

[35]"It is the first attempt in the history of this or other countries to control its [the industry's] own sanitary destiny." Gertrude Barnum, "How Industrial Peace Has Been Brought about in the Clothing Trade," the *Independent*, Oct. 3, 1912, vol. 73, p. 779. For other references to the work of the board of sanitary control, aside from the annual reports, see the *Survey*, Feb. 1, 1913, vol. 29, pp. 557–559, 631–632; *Annals* of the American Academy of Political and Social Science, November 1912, vol. 44, pp. 39–58; and J. H. Cohen, "The Protocol in the Cloak and Dress and Waist Industries," in *Transactions* of the efficiency society for 1913. Copy in the New York Public Library.

label that would enlist "the potent force of public opinion" against substandard production. "It will operate as a very powerful influence in maintaining proper labor standards and in preventing their undermining by unwholesome competition," so the commission concluded in 1924. A year later, it restated its convictions — "We strongly urge the fullest possible development of the use of the label" — and in its final report of May 20, 1926 again stressed its belief that "the best weapon against non-union manufacture is in the proper enforcement of the provisions of the contracts relating to the use of the sanitary label."

By recommending the "fullest possible development" of the label, this commission had in mind something more than informing customers that labeled garments were made under sanitary conditions. With the support of labor unions, employers' associations, and the public, a sanitary label, so the commission believed, could be used to establish production boycotts as well as consumer boycotts against nonlabeled goods. The label would be particularly effective if nonlabeled goods could not find their way into the market place. In its first report the Advisory Commission favored the idea of having each association member obligate himself not to handle or deal in garments that do not bear the label. And to carry out label provisions, the commission recommended more elaborate inspection by a "Label Division" together with a list of penalties to be imposed against those violating the label requirements.[36]

Following these recommendations, the women's coat and suit manufacturers and the ILGWU made provision for a "prosanis label" in their collective agreements. Likewise, the collective agreements of the dress industry provided for a label, and for the supporting use of a production boycott to help make the label an effective instrument of control. "No member of the association," stated the 1925 collective agreement between the Wholesale Dress Manufacturers' Association and the ILGWU, "shall handle

---

[36]The texts of the Advisory Commission's original recommendations, dated July 8, 1924, together with supplements through Feb. 8, 1925, are printed at pp. 157–164 in the appendix to John Dickinson and Morris Kolchin, *Report of an Investigation,* prepared for the commission and transmitted on March 10, 1925. A copy of this report and of the commission's separately printed *Supplementary Recommendations* dated July 10, 1925, as well as its *Final Recommendations,* dated May 20, 1926, are filed in the Abelson papers.

or deal in garments that do not bear the label adopted by the Joint Board of Sanitary Control."[37]

Unfortunately, there is no evidence that the absence of a label ever became more than a harmless reminder to observing customers that certain garments lacked positive proof of production under sanitary conditions. Beyond New York City the absence of a label was seldom used to justify the imposition of production boycotts as a means of eliminating substandard production. At best, the prosanis label, like the joint board of sanitary control itself, was a product of the New York manufacturing interests; its requirements did not apply to retailers or to out-of-town centers of production. Effective use of a label to block the production, distribution, and sale of unlabeled products had to await the codes of fair competition drafted under the National Industrial Recovery Act of 1933.

Industry-wide Standards by Government Compulsion

There was yet another road to industry-wide standards of employment — one that would bring the unorganized forces of an industry into the realm of controlled competition by means of governmental compulsion. Minimum standards set by employers' associations and labor unions at the heart of an industry could by law be extended to the unorganized manufacturers and their non-union labor force operating on the outer fringes of a trade. Then, no employer or worker of whatever rank, business, or location could undermine the standards set for his trade without violating the law of the land and bringing down upon his head the stern hand of civil authority.

Calling upon the forces of civil authority to invade the realm of industrial self-government was contrary to the heritage and temperaments of the Jewish migrants who had brought over from the Old World a capacity for resolving their own problems of community life. Relying upon political power to set the standards of industrial society was the antithesis of what most migrants entering the needle trades had hoped to find in America. Yet this time-honored concept of freedom from governmental

---

[37]Text of this dress agreement appears in *Women's Wear*, Jan. 31, 1925. A similar clause appeared in the 1926 collective agreement between the Industrial Council of Cloak, Suit and Skirt Manufacturers and the ILGWU.

interference was to fall before the onslaught of unbridled competition that threatened to topple the needle trades in ruin.[38]

The proposal for resorting to governmental compulsion as a means of establishing industry-wide standards of employment — like the proposal for a label to enlist the support of consumers — was a favored thesis of Julius Henry Cohen, counsel for the manufacturers and key figure in the development of protocol principles. Cohen had no love for employment standards set by government decree. But in the presence of employer obstinacy toward cooperation on a national scale, and in the absence of union power to organize all the workers of an industry, Cohen believed that the "legitimate" forces of the needle trades had no other means of withstanding pressure from their "illegitimate" competitors.

Cohen would support governmental intervention to create industry-wide standards of employment only as a means for reinforcing the existing institutions of collective bargaining. So far from having the government fix wages, hours, and working conditions by direct legislation, Cohen would leave the initiative in setting labor standards to employers' associations and labor unions through the negotiation of collective agreements. Wherever such agreements covered substantial bodies of employers and workers in their respective trades, or wherever the terms of such agreements were widely accepted by the bulk of an industry, Cohen would "utilize Federal power in making such agreements 'voluntarily come to' binding upon the unscrupulous and illegitimate employer."[39]

---

[38]When the law sets up its tribunals to settle disputes between workers and their employers, it deprives them of the incentive to consult with each other, in the attempt to make agreements. They become litigants before a court; their purposes are utterly at variance.
—Samuel Gompers, president of the American Federation of Labor, in opposing a proposal for labor courts after the First World War, as quoted in *Daily News Record*, Feb. 15, 1921.

[39]*Law and Order in Industry*, p. 226. See also Cohen's views in *Minutes*, Arbitration Proceedings between the Dress and Waist Manufacturers Association and the ILGWU (Feb. 5, 1916), vol. 4, pp. 60–64.

In February 1921, Matthew Woll, vice-president of the AFL, addressing the American Civic Federation, spoke up for the legalization of joint agreements between employers and workers "leaving employers and workers free to determine voluntarily wages, hours and conditions of employment." *Daily News Record*, Feb. 15, 1921.

Cohen had made a study of corresponding efforts in Great Britain to standardize terms of employment throughout each trade. In 1912, J. Ramsay MacDonald had introduced into the British Parliament a bill to provide for uniformity of work standards in the Port of London. The bill required that standards of wages, hours, and working conditions reached through voluntary agreement between a sufficient number of employers and workers in the area should become "the implied terms of every contract for employment of a workman in the Port of London." Thus, without setting wages, Parliament would sanction industry-wide observance of collective agreements.

"Study of the proceedings and report of the Industrial Council of Great Britain," Cohen wrote in 1915, "led me to the conviction that at the root of the difficulty in both the making and observance of joint agreements lay the problem of equal enforcement of standards throughout the industry. I found that the Council had considered various methods proposed, and that, on the whole, the best opinion seemed to be in favor of extending the standards by law to cover the entire industry." Drawing heavily on the recommendations of the Industrial Council to the British Parliament, Cohen in January 1914 had submitted to the U. S. Commission on Industrial Relations an extended brief giving points and arguments supporting a proposed outline of legislation which would extend the major collective agreement of a trade to all manufacturers and workers of that trade.[40]

Cohen's plan called for the creation of a permanent National Industrial Board on which the organized employers, the organized workers, and the public would be equally represented. Among its many duties directed toward peace and stability in

[40]Cohen, "A Constructive Program" (pamphlet, 1914); "A League to Enforce Industrial Peace" (pamphlet, 1916). Both pamphlets are in the New York Public Library. Cohen refers to a *Report on Collective Agreements between Employers and the Work People in the United Kingdom* issued by the British Board of Trade, Labor Department, in 1910; and to a *Report of the Industrial Council of the British Board of Trade on Its Inquiry into Industrial Agreements* (July 24, 1913), reprinted in the U.S. Department of Labor, BLS Bulletin no. 133 (August 18, 1913). See especially the section on "Extension of Agreements" at pp. 25–33. See also *Conciliation and Arbitration in Great Britain* in U.S. Department of Commerce and Labor, Bureau of Labor, Bulletin no. 98 (January 1912), pp. 123–160.

industry, the board would have the power to extend sanitary standards, hours of work, and minimum wages set forth in collective agreements to all employers and workers in a trade. "Whenever it shall appear that the agreement covers a substantial portion of the industry," stated one of Cohen's proposals, "the parties to the agreement may apply for its *extension* to the entire industry." This proposal then provided that "upon proper hearings, to those not yet affected, the Industrial Board may make an order *extending* the agreement to cover the entire industry."[41]

In advocating an extension of the major collective agreement negotiated within each trade to all plants of that trade, J. H. Cohen did not ignore the potential dangers of monopoly power that would reside in the parties to such an agreement. But the opportunity to be heard that was guaranteed those not yet covered, together with the necessity of having the agreement approved by a government agency, presumably offered adequate protection for the public interest. He at least found consolation in the thought that representatives of the general public on the government board should be men "whose standards and influence in their respective communities shall be beyond question."

Under Cohen's proposal, no collective agreement would be approved until the federal board had held an inquiry to determine whether that agreement "is a proper agreement and one that might suitably be extended." If the public interest demanded some modification of its terms, the parties were encouraged to make the necessary changes. During the hearings, all minority groups were entitled to have their day in court. Only when completely satisfied with the product would the federal board certify "that the trade agreement is entered into in good faith

---

[41]*Law and Order in Industry*, p. 291. In this volume, Cohen discusses his general thesis, especially at pp. 225–228 and 291–292. Appendix E of this volume, entitled "Industrial Agreements," consists of the bill introduced into the British Parliament in 1912 by J. Ramsay MacDonald to "make agreements come to voluntarily between employers and workmen in the Port of London legally enforceable in the whole trade." Appendix F consists of a "Skeleton Outline of Provisions of a Bill," proposed for congressional enactment. The bill would create a National Industrial Board with powers analogous to those of the British Industrial Council under the English "Trades Dispute Act."

and for the best interest of the community." After all these precautions, the board's certification would then "raise an irrebutable presumption that the agreement is in fact made in good faith and not in restraint of trade."[42]

This distinctive feature of Cohen's "Constructive Program" was favorably received by members of the U. S. Commission on Industrial Relations, who expressed their views as follows:

> It appears to us that the progress of joint agreement systems might be appreciably advanced by legislation which would under certain conditions enforce the terms reached under a joint agreement upon all the employers in the trade. The possibility of maintaining a joint agreement is seriously affected by the refusal of some employers to enter the system. . . . The Commission therefore proposes that Congress invest a Trade Commission with power to extend terms of joint agreements to all employers and employees upon joint application by the parties to the agreement.

Members of the Commission then proposed a special means for gaining compliance with negotiated contract standards that were extended throughout a trade. "The extension should be made effective," they held, "by excluding from interstate commerce any goods made under other conditions of employment than those stipulated in the agreement."[43]

In its own recommendations, the U. S. Commission on Industrial Relations accepted the general pattern of procedure Cohen had outlined. No agreement would be approved for extension to an industry until the federal agency was satisfied that the terms were reasonable and not against the public interest. All outside parties not already bound by the agreement must have an opportunity to state their objections. The original parties to the agreement must voluntarily remove all unreasonable clauses, as well as those held to be against the public interest. Yet, in spite of the care with which these plans had been thought out, they remained in the realm of ideas until the arrival of the NRA codes.[44]

---

[42]*Ibid.*, pp. 291–292.

[43]U.S. National Archives, (microfilm) Wisconsin I: 4584, p. 197.

[44]*Ibid.*, p. 194. Compare the views of Henry Moskowitz, well-known needle trade arbitrator, who in 1916 foresaw the need for government compulsion on a national scale to establish an effective floor under competition for wages. He favored special government commissions that would utilize facts

Concluding Observations

Failure of the manufacturers in the various markets of each trade to create an institutional framework for negotiating and administering industry-wide standards of employment accounts for the defeat of all efforts at controlling competition on a national scale before the thirties. Short of national employers' associations capable of dealing with national labor unions at the bargaining table, responsibility for establishing and maintaining uniform work standards fell squarely upon the unions of each trade. Failure of the unions to organize the workers of competing markets forced an appeal to public opinion and to consumers for help in establishing a floor under hours, wages, and working conditions. When this move failed to materialize, J. H. Cohen, chief architect of the protocol movement, was ready to enlist the help of civil government in extending labor standards set by collective agreements to the far-flung corners of each trade.[45]

---

assembled by national fact-finding boards (see above, p. 574) to reach decisions on wage controversies of national import. "When the decision is reached," so he contended, "it will have the authority of neutrally gathered facts and be backed by the sovereignty of civilized law." "The Garment Trade and the Minimum Wage: An Interview with Dr. Henry Moskowitz," in the *Outlook,* May 10, 1916, vol. 113, pp. 66, 83–87.

[45]The influence of Cohen's proposals to enlist governmental support for industry-wide application of collective agreements voluntarily negotiated between the organized factions of a trade can be seen in the early procedures envisioned by the sponsors of industry "codes of fair competition" under Title I of the National Industrial Recovery Act, June 15, 1933. (See the following chapter.) And experiences in the United States with NRA codes of fair competition may in turn have helped to account for some Canadian adaptations of Cohen's principles which are still in operation. Beginning with the Quebec Collective Labor Agreements Extension Act, 1934, the Canadian Province of Quebec has permitted voluntary collective agreements negotiated between employer groups and labor unions representing a substantial proportion of an industry to be extended by law throughout a designated locality or area of competition.

All employers and their employees in the lines affected are subject to the terms of the collective agreement whether or not they are parties to it. For instance, an employer who has increased wage rates under a collective agreement cannot be subject to competition from employers who have not entered into collective agreements and pay lower wages. Also, under generalization by law the collective agreement is generalized by an Order-in-Council. It, therefore, takes the force of law and becomes enforceable by the joint committees of employers and employees.

 —A. C. Crysler, *Labor Relations and Precedents in Canada* (1949),
  p. 47.

In Quebec, these agreements take on the aspects of codes of fair competition and are so designated. See Gerard Picard, *Labor Code, Province of Quebec* (1957), pp. 63–93. A less comprehensive system for extending certain terms of voluntary labor agreements exists in other Canadian provinces.

Chapter 16

Labor Standards
and the NRA

TITLE I, "Industrial Recovery," of the National Industrial Recovery Act of June 16, 1933, embodied objectives that had long dominated collective bargaining in the needle trades. The announced policy of Congress

to provide for the general welfare by promoting the organization of industry for the purpose of cooperative action among trade groups;

to induce and maintain united action of labor and management under adequate governmental sanctions and supervision;

to eliminate unfair competitive practices;

to improve standards of labor;

and otherwise to rehabilitate industry

might well have been taken from any one of scores of collective agreements between employers' associations and labor unions of the needle trades. Under this broad sweep of authority, the federal government sponsored industry codes of fair competition that undertook to accomplish by law what the sponsors of the protocol movement had previously sought to achieve through collective bargaining.[1]

---

[1]Other declared purposes of Title I of the act were (1) to promote the fullest possible utilization of the present productive capacity of industries; (2) to avoid undue restriction of production; (3) to increase the consumption of industrial and agricultural products by increasing purchasing power; and (4) to reduce and relieve unemployment.

The Codes and Collective Agreements

All needle trade codes of fair competition drafted under this statute bore a striking resemblance to collective agreements. Like the announced purpose of the statute itself, the declared objectives of the codes, stated in such phrases as "improving standards of labor and eliminating unfair trade practices with the aim of rehabilitating" the industry, could have served equally well for the preambles to collective agreements. Both the codes and collective agreements were designed to control competition by regulating trade practices as well as labor standards. Both were initially intended to be a product of voluntary cooperation among the organized forces of each industry. Both were founded on the assumption that standards set by the organized factions of each trade would ultimately be extended to cover all competing firms of whatever size, character, or location.

For all essential purposes, the first code of fair competition was conceived at the Brandeis Conferences of 1910 and embodied in the original Protocol of Peace for the women's coat and suit trade. Failure of the protocol system to differentiate officially between trade functions and labor functions was only a superficial distinction. Those who participated in collective bargaining looked upon competition in labor costs as the one unfair "trade" practice that most plagued their industries. The need for restricting this type of competition had produced excursions into the realm of controlling jobber–contractor–inside manufacturer relationships. "An industry demoralized by destructive trade practices," advertised the National Association of Dress Manufacturers, in urging support for the dress industry's new code of fair competition, "is at a serious disadvantage in its efforts to provide long periods of employment at decent wages."[2]

---

[2]*Women's Wear Daily*, Nov. 13, 1933. The text of the dress industry code appears in the issue of Nov. 1, 1933.

If the code system were a continuation of the protocol system, then the provisions for industrial recovery through codes of fair competition embodied in Title I of the National Industrial Recovery Act could be traced to experiences with collective bargaining in the needle trades. Little has been published on the origin of the code system, but such evidence as has come to light tends to support this thesis. See the following: (1) William H. Davis, "The Philosophy and the Spirit of N.I.R.A. — Disclosing Enough of Its Background to Identify Its Author" (Oct. 6, 1933, pamphlet). Davis points to

Moreover, the power to establish uniform labor costs through industry codes of fair competition might well have been more useful to the needle trades than the power to fix prices, allocate markets, or limit output. Even after the National Industrial Recovery Act opened the door to restrictive trade practices that would otherwise have been illegal, the needle trades did not forsake the basic issue of equal labor costs for the more tempting fields of regulating sales, limiting production, or fixing prices. "In our view," concluded a special millinery board operating under the code of fair competition for the millinery industry, "the keenest and most disastrous form of unfair competition is the competition arising from unfair and unequal costs of direct labor per unit of product. This code has endeavored to find a solution for this."[3]

Herein lies the great paradox of the NRA code system for the needle trades. Whereas those who had previously participated in collective bargaining had devoted much of their time to regulating methods of production — a subject clearly within the purview of trade practices — those who helped to draft and administer codes of fair competition directed their attention chiefly to devising and maintaining industry-wide standards of employment, a subject clearly within the scope of collective bargaining. Thus, in the first few weeks of the NIRA, the New York manufacturers

President Franklin D. Roosevelt: (2) ——, "Legislative History of the NIRA" (processed, no date). This history points chiefly to the Senator Robert F. Wagner group which included several persons familiar with needle trade bargaining experiences. (3) Two lengthy articles by Hy Kravif in the *Daily Worker*, June 17, 20, 1933. The captions for these articles disclose the nature of their contents: "New Bill Modeled on War Labor Board and Protocol of 1910" and "Recovery Act, like 1910 Garment Protocol, Will Work to the Employers' Advantage." (4) John T. Flynn, "Whose Child Is the NRA," *Harpers' Magazine*, September 1934, vol. 169, pp. 385–394. (5) Hugh Johnson, *The Blue Eagle from Egg to Earth* (1935). In addition to the limited congressional debates — the bill was rushed through Congress within a month — see *National Industrial Recovery*, Hearings before the Committee on Ways and Means, U.S. House of Representatives, 73rd Cong., 1st sess. (May 18–20, 1933), and before the Committee on Finance, U.S. Senate, 73rd Cong., 1st sess. (May 22–June 1, 1933).

[3]*Women's Wear Daily*, Jan. 19, 1934. "The welfare of the dress industry," stated the Association of Dress Manufacturers in its proposed code of fair competition for the dress industry, "makes it imperative that the labor costs of garments be made uniform," *ibid.*, July 20, 1933.

of women's coats and suits who had engineered the protocol movement in 1910 hastened to submit to Washington a proposed code of fair competition devoted almost wholly to labor standards. No provisions for restraints on business conduct were incorporated. Only a covering letter referred to a "Code of Ethical Trade and Business Practices to be hereafter submitted."[4]

Under the NRA codes, as under collective bargaining, uniform labor costs for the needle trades were to be achieved by eliminating the nonconformist from the ranks of industrial competitors. Hitherto, all attempts at industrial stabilization had been wrecked by unscrupulous minorities operating on the outer fringes of each industry. Henceforth, with the help of the law, all minority groups plying the highways of legitimate competition would be forced to live by the rules of the road. "The belief is," reported *Women's Wear Daily*, May 9, 1933, in summarizing the views of the women's coat and suit industry toward pending legislation for industrial recovery, "that if by some Federal legislation the unorganized forces in the coat trade could be brought into line with legitimate trade much of the chaos and price competition could be eliminated."[5]

Whatever the views from other industries, the producers of wearing apparel were clearly out to impose their concept of

---

[4]The text of this proposed code submitted by three New York employers' associations appears in *ibid.*, July 14, 1933. The usual fair trade practice provisions common to most codes were not incorporated into the women's coat and suit code until this code was revised a year later. The text of fourteen trade practices suggested for the women's coat and suit trade to become a part of the code when adopted is given in *ibid.*, Feb. 19, 1934. Similarly, the National Association of Blouse Manufacturers had drafted a "code of fair trade practices" to be incorporated as Part II of its code of fair competition for the blouse industry. Part I of the association's proposed code had regulated hours, wages, and working conditions. *Ibid.*, July 21, 1933.

"In spite of the fact that standards of 'fair' commercial practices were a prominent feature of the [women's coat and suit] Code, nine-tenths, so to speak, of the attention of the NRA's Code Authority ... was directed toward the achievement of the greatest practicable measure of wage uniformity throughout the United States." D. E. Robinson, *Collective Bargaining and Market Control in the New York Coat and Suit Industry* (1949), p. 210.

[5]"The Industrial Council [of Cloak, Suit and Skirt Manufacturers] has communicated with Senator Wagner relative to the proposed Federal control of industry," continued this news report. "Senator Wagner has arranged to provide the Council with an opportunity [to be heard] on the industrial stabilization bill." *Women's Wear Daily*, May 9, 1933.

majority rule upon all straggling minorities within their trades. So vigorously had these spokesmen pursued their objective that other advocates of legislation for industrial recovery were soon extolling the virtues of conformity-to-majority rule. Even the President of the United States in seeking appropriate legislation to combat the Great Depression, repeatedly expressed approval of the industry-by-industry, conformity-to-majority principle. "I can assure you," so President Roosevelt told the U. S. Chamber of Commerce during the hectic weeks of formulating recovery legislation, "that you will have the co-operation of your Government in bringing these minorities to understand that their unfair practices are contrary to sound public policy."[6]

Except for new titles, most of the provisions in the first code of fair competition approved for the women's coat and suit industry could not be distinguished from the terms of a collective agreement. Even the cost of maintaining the code authority like the cost of upkeep for the impartial machinery was to be shared by the union and the employers of the trade. Moreover, the code expressly provided that "wherever in this industry agreements between employers and employees arrived at by collective bargaining shall exist or shall come into existence hereafter, all the provisions of such agreements with reference to labor standards not prohibited by law and not inconsistent with NIRA shall be administered as though a part of this Code."[7]

---

[6] *Ibid.*, May 5, 1933. In signing the National Industrial Recovery Act, President Roosevelt stated: "Its goal is the assurance of reasonable profits to industry and living wages for labor with the elimination of piratical methods and practices which have not only harassed honest business but also contributed to the ills of labor." Brookings Institution, *The National Recovery Administration: An Analysis and Appraisal* (1935), p. 3.

Donald Richberg, who helped to draft the NIRA and later became NRA general counsel, argued for remedial legislation in terms long familiar to the needle trades: "The manufacturer who desired to put out a decent product at a decent price, and at the same time pay decent wages, found that he was simply up against a competition that he could not meet, and willy nilly, he had to cut wages and he had to work long hours and he simply had to oppress his employees, although he might have desired to do the square thing and the right thing." *National Industrial Recovery*, Hearings before the Committee on Ways and Means, U.S. House of Representatives, 73rd Cong., 1st sess., on H.R. 5664 (May 18–20, 1933), p. 66.

[7] The U.S. Congress itself appears to have preferred the negotiation of collective agreements to the code-making process for arriving at the labor standards of each trade. Title I, sec. 7 (b) of the NIRA provided as follows:

The interlocking of code provisions with contract terms was also evident in other needle trades. While the lingerie and underwear industries were deadlocked in disputes over the terms of their new labor contracts in September 1933, the chairman of the New York branch of the NRA wired the national recovery administrator to delay action on pending codes for these trades until the parties had concluded their collective agreements so that the terms could be incorporated into the codes. Similarly, the original code of the fur dressing and fur dyeing industry, approved December 18, 1933, provided that when collective labor agreements had been filed with the code authority "full recognition of the contractual obligations under said agreements shall be accorded in the administration of this code, subject to the approval of the Administrator."[8]

Conversely, the parties to negotiated labor agreements generally endorsed, accepted, or incorporated the NRA codes of fair competition as an integral part of their collective bargaining systems. Five days after President Roosevelt had approved the first code of fair competition for the women's coat and suit trade on August 4, 1933, the cloakmakers' union of New York City voted to accept the code as the basis of a new collective agreement for the industry. A month later, the Merchants' Ladies' Garment Association (jobbers) and the American Cloak and Suit Manufacturers' Association (contractors) adopted the code of fair competition as part of their agreement, so that jobbers were required to pay contractors enough to meet the wages "provided for in the Code for the Coat and Suit Industry and [in] the agreement between the American Association and the Union."[9]

The President shall, so far as practicable, afford every opportunity to employers and employees in any trade or industry . . . to establish by mutual agreement, the standards as to the maximum hours of labor, minimum rates of pay, and such other conditions of employment as may be necessary in such trade or industry or subdivision thereof to effectuate the policy of this title; and the standards established in such agreements, when approved by the President, shall have the same effect as a code of fair competition, approved by the President under subsection (a) of Section 3.

[8]*New York Times,* Sept. 16, 1933.

[9]This agreement of September 20, 1933 between the jobbers and the contractors stated that the code of fair competition approved on August 4, 1933, for the women's coat and suit trade, "is hereby made a part of this agree-

Manufacturers of the dress and waist industry also looked upon the codes as a continuation of the principles already endorsed through collective bargaining. "In order to induce and maintain the united action of labor, contractors, manufacturers and jobbers in the dress industry under adequate governmental or private sanctions and supervision, to eliminate unfair competitive practices in all branches of the dress industry . . . to improve standards of labor and living and otherwise rehabilitate the dress industry . . ." — runs the proposed code drafted by the Affiliated Dress Manufacturers' Association — "this code of fair competition governing the dress industry is adopted." Most of the code ultimately approved for the trade was taken bodily from the collective labor agreement of the New York market. "As far as the dress trade is concerned," later explained Mortimer Lanzit, executive director of the National Dress Manufacturers' Association, "the collective labor agreement and the code are virtually one and the same."[10]

---

ment with the same force and effect as though each of the provisions therein contained were here set out at length." But, in case of conflicts between the code and the collective agreement, the code was to have precedence: "If any of the provisions of this agreement conflict with, alter or change any of the provisions of the Code, it is understood that the provisions of the Code shall prevail and that this agreement shall amplify but not change or modify the provisions of the Code."

The 1933 collective agreement between the Industrial Council of Cloak, Suit and Skirt Manufacturers and the Cloakmakers' Joint Board, ILGWU, made collusion between a member of the council and a contractor to underpay wages "subject to the penalties provided by and under the National Industrial Recovery Act."

"The Code for the cloak and suit industry recently approved by you has been adopted by the workers as a basis for collective agreement with employers." Telegram from ILGWU's President David Dubinsky to President Franklin D. Roosevelt. This message and a similar one to General Hugh Johnson, NRA administrator, are quoted in ILGWU, *Report and Proceedings,* Twenty-second Convention (May 1934), pp. 28–29. See also, Harry Haskel, *A Leader of the Garment Workers: The Biography of Isidore Nagler* (1950), p. 176. It is not surprising that the editor of the *New York Times,* for August 12, 1934, observed: "The code fitted this particular trade like one of its own cloaks."

[10]The text of the proposed dress code submitted by the Affiliated Dress Manufacturers appears in *Women's Wear Daily,* July 24, 1933. Mortimer Lanzit's statement is from a memorandum to the NRA, reported in *ibid.,* Jan. 30, 1935.

Throughout the needle trades, codes of fair competition were more a codification of existing practices than a series of sweeping innovations in labor standards or trade relations. The hours of work and rates of pay, the provisions for health and safety, the methods of regulating production and controlling trade practices that were written into the codes followed an industry pattern previously established through collective bargaining. "The new process [of working with codes] which had thrown most industries into such a flutter of bewilderment," wrote G. J. Hexter, correspondent for the *Women's Wear Daily*, July 5, 1933, "represents merely an extension of the collective bargaining principle and method, and as such can be adopted with a minimum of re-education by the comparative rare industries which, like men's clothing, are already familiar with collective bargaining."[11]

The fusion of industry codes and collective agreements extended into the realm of administration. The impartial machinery created under collective agreements was empowered to apply the terms of industry codes — just as the machinery of code enforcement was authorized to carry out the terms of collective agreements. Impartial chairmen under labor contracts also became official code administrators. Both G. W. Alger, impartial chairman under collective agreements for the women's coat and suit trade, and A. Feldblum, impartial chairman under collective agreements for the dress and waist industry, held key positions on code authorities for their trades. Arbitrators in men's clothing, headwear, fur manufacturing, and numerous apparel accessories occupied important posts on code agencies. Neither the regalia of dress nor the official trappings of prescribed procedures served to differentiate the role of contract administrator from the role

---

[11]*Ibid.*, July 5, 1933. Writing for its first NRA anniversary issue, June 15, 1934, C. W. Call stated:

> Sensing a fine opportunity, the International Ladies' Garment Workers' Union, long before a code could be written for the trade, moved into the driver's seat, took the reins, cracked the whip, and organization was a living thing. So thorough was the union control that the hours and wages of the code simply echoed what had been written into collective agreements a short time before.

See further, the text of the proposed code for the fur dressing industry submitted by the Associated Employers of Fur Workers and printed in *ibid.*, August 11, 1933. The text of the code which was finally approved for this industry appears in the Dec. 18, 1933 issue.

of code administrator. Many officials found their interlocking functions hopelessly confusing.[12]

Potential Values of the NRA Code System

For those who had long supported the protocol movement, the system of industry codes operating under governmental sanction and supervision offered potential advantages over collective bargaining as a means of controlling competition in labor costs. Perhaps the greatest of these assets was the prospect of creating for each industry certain standards of employment that would be applied uniformly to every shop of the trade. "The difficulty for years," observed M. W. Amberg, director of the millinery code authority, "was that the legitimate manufacturers who sought to improve working conditions were forced to compete with those who disregarded every rule of fair competition and who thrived on the oppression of labor."[13]

---

[12]G. L. Bell, first impartial chairman under collective agreements in the men's clothing industry, was also a member of the first code authority for that industry. Paul Abelson, who served as impartial chairman for more needle trade industries than anyone else, also held numerous official positions under several needle trade codes. Where workers were represented on code authorities — a common practice in the needle trades — their representatives came from among outstanding union leaders in collective bargaining.

In dress manufacturing, a special commission consisting of A. Feldblum, impartial chairman under the collective labor agreements, and B. H. Gitchell, chairman of the dress industry code authority, worked jointly to resolve many problems that fell within the jurisdiction of both the dress industry code and the collective labor agreements. In the spring of 1934, for example, they not only held hearings that brought out a wide range of suggestions for putting teeth into the enforcement of the code and of the collective agreements, but they also acted jointly to help settle a major dispute between the organized contractors and the organized jobbers of the industry. On this episode, see the files of *Women's Wear Daily* from the middle of April through the middle of May 1934.

And when the Industrial Council of Cloak, Suit and Skirt Manufacturers expelled nine of its members for failing to pay fines imposed by the association for violating both the women's coat and suit code and the collective labor agreements by sending out work to nondesignated contractors, the association made clear that it must do everything in its power to see that its members uphold the code as well as the collective agreements. *Ibid.*, April 20, 1934.

[13]*Ibid.*, April 18, 1934, quoting Amberg's affidavit submitted to the federal court in support of the legality of the millinery code.

The objective of bringing all competitors within the bounds of effective controls was clearly in the minds of the organized women's coat and suit manufacturers whose efforts were responsible for the first approved code in the needle trades. In submitting their proposed code, so Samuel Klein, executive director of the inside manufacturers, announced, these associations of the coat and suit trade were acting on the assumption that the code would bind the entire industry. "If accepted," Klein stated, "there will cease to be in the market a 'free lance fringe' of firms that have succeeded in remaining aloof from any and all organized control." Samuel Blumberg, counsel for the Merchants' Ladies' Garment Association (jobbers), likewise looked to the code to overcome the difficulties of controlling independents. "These firms have found it profitable," so Blumberg stated at a public hearing on the women's coat and suit code, "to remain independent and never was an opportunity afforded this industry to exercise a complete domination and control over this group which has done much to demoralize the industry."[14]

Where the protocol system had failed, the code system gave promise of success. "The organized industry is looking hopefully to Washington to help with this problem of uneconomic, ruthless and insane competition . . ." wrote G. W. Alger, impartial chairman for the women's coat and suit trade, to Secretary of Labor Frances Perkins, more than a month before the National Industrial Recovery Act was passed. "We believe that we are on the verge of a new era if the law will permit the decent to live industrially by giving them some reasonable protection against these destructive forces, consistent with fair protection to the consuming public." In urging Congress to act, President F. D. Roosevelt called for a "great cooperative effort throughout all industry" supported by legislation that would prevent "cut-throat underselling by selfish competitors unwilling to join in such public spirited endeavor," and he expressed the conviction — notwithstanding the need for antitrust laws — that "the public interest will be served if, with the authority and under the guidance of government, private industries are permitted to make agreements and codes insuring fair competition."[15]

[14]*Ibid.,* July 14, 20, 1933.

[15]President Roosevelt's special message to Congress, May 17, 1933, proposing a recovery act, text in the *New York Times,* May 18, 1933. G. W. Alger is quoted from an article by R. L. Duffus in *ibid.,* August 12, 1934.

The terms of the National Industrial Recovery Act, which became law on June 16, 1933, embodied the President's convictions. By inducing united action of labor and management "under adequate governmental sanctions and supervision," Congress sought to insure that uniform, industry-wide trade and labor standards would minimize the excesses of competition that hampered the rehabilitation of industry. Unless these standards covered all segments of a trade — large and small, union and non-union, organized and unorganized, jobbers, contractors and inside manufacturers, north, east, south, and west — the remedy might defeat its own purposes for it would tend to intensify competition between covered establishments and those beyond the pale of the law. Above all else, the new law through its industry codes would support the principles of regulated competition by introducing an element of compulsion that would guarantee the application of industry standards to all segments of each trade.[16]

The law expressly stated that an approved industry code would contain the "standards of fair competition" for a designated trade, and that all violations of these standards would constitute an "unfair method of competition" within the meaning of the Federal Trade Commission Act. Accordingly, the NIRA directed the Federal Trade Commission on request of the President to "make such investigations as may be necessary to enable the President to carry out the provisions of this title," and it imposed upon U. S. district attorneys the duty to seek injunctions from the U. S. district courts against real or threatened code infractions. These courts were expressly granted jurisdiction "to prevent or restrain violations of any code of fair competition approved under this title."

The law also provided criminal sanctions for those who failed to observe the codes. "When a code of fair competition has been approved or prescribed by the President under this title," stated the National Industrial Recovery Act, "any violation of any provision thereof in any transaction in or affecting interstate or foreign commerce shall be a misdemeanor and upon conviction

---

[16]In December 1933 Max Jasper, president of the Fur Dyers' Trade Council, praised the fur dressing and fur dyeing code as "the first step in a process of stabilization," not so much because the code set wage rates and fixed prices to be charged for dressing or dyeing furs as because "the standards established have the force of the United States Government behind it [*sic*] and take the force of law." *Women's Wear Daily,* Dec. 20, 1933.

thereof an offender shall be fined not more than $500 for each offense, and each day such violation continues shall be deemed a separate offense." As a further means of compliance, the President of the United States could require a license of all business enterprises of a given trade whenever he found that "destructive wage or price cutting or other activities contrary to the policy of this title are being practiced in any trade or industry or any subdivision thereof."

After such a finding, no person in the trade affected was permitted to carry on business "unless he shall have first obtained a license issued pursuant to such regulations as the President shall prescribe." The President was empowered to suspend or revoke these licenses for violations of the terms under which they were issued. Furthermore, "any person who, without such a license or in violation of any condition thereof, carries on any such business for which a license is so required, shall, upon conviction thereof, be fined not more than $500, or imprisoned not more than six months, or both, and each day such violation continues shall be deemed a separate offense." Through these various clauses, the law was made severe enough to stem the tide of nonenforcement that had swept so many collective bargaining systems into obscurity. "The day of the chiseler will now pass into limbo," happily observed one of the code framers in 1933. "You will either play the game rightly and fairly or not play it at all."[17]

Aside from this distinctive feature of governmental compulsion, so indispensable to driving all chiselers, backsliders, and nonconformists from the citadels of legitimate competition, the potential values of the NRA code system appeared to arise from the encouragement given each industry to work out its own salvation. Herein

---

[17]*Ibid.,* August 15, 1933. The virtues of governmental power were also evident in helping industries to meet the dangers of competition from foreign sources. Upon a complaint by a labor organization or an employer group that imported articles were seriously endangering the maintenance of codes of fair competition — or upon his own authority — the President could regulate the entry of goods into the United States on "such terms and conditions and subject to the payment of such fees and to such limitations in the total quantity which may be imported (in the course of any specific period or periods) as he shall find it necessary to prescribe in order that the entry thereof shall not render or tend to render ineffective any code or agreement made under this title." The President's power to license was extended to cover imports.

the rules and procedures for creating and administering code systems followed the long established practices of collective bargaining in the needle trades. Under the NIRA, as under the protocol system, both employers and workers were encouraged to organize for effective self-government. The whole structure of a code system was based on voluntary group action. Independent firms played no part in the original formation of needle trade codes and such recognition as they later received by law came long after most needle trade codes had been drafted. Initially, employers' associations, so long as they were representative of their trades and kept their doors open to new members, were recognized as the source of all action and the center of all movement toward industry codes of fair competition.[18]

Likewise, the NIRA left to each industry a responsibility, subject to governmental "sanctions and supervision," for designing and controlling administrative agencies to implement the NRA codes. At the apex of the administrative system were code authorities, who, like permanent umpires, boards of arbitration, or impartial chairmen under collective agreements, were surrounded with hordes of inspectors, accountants, investigators, and other agents of lesser stature to seek out evidences of code infractions. The code authorities themselves, like their counterparts under collective bargaining, operated not only under specific powers but also under general grants to act for the welfare of their trades. Each authority might appropriately have been designated "the continuing conference body to which shall be brought all problems and all plans for the improvement of the industry."[19]

---

[18]Workers were encouraged to organize through the famous NIRA declaration:

Every code of fair competition, agreement, and license approved, prescribed, or issued under this title shall contain the following conditions: (1) that employees shall have the right to organize and bargain collectively through representatives of their own choosing, and shall be free from the interference, restraint, or coercion of employers of labor, or their agents, in the designation of such representatives or in self-organization or in other concerted activities for the purpose of collective bargaining or other mutual aid or protection; (2) that no employee and no one seeking employment shall be required as a condition of employment to join any company union or to refrain from joining, organizing, or assisting a labor organization of his own choosing.

[19]Writing on the origin of the code authority, Travis Brown observed:

The National Recovery Administration in its early months relied

While these features of the codes extolled the virtues of self-help, the National Industrial Recovery Act also recognized the need for certain restraints upon the freedom of organized groups empowered to act for their trades. Protection of minorities, consumers, and the public interest was not forgotten. Aside from the general requirement of governmental "sanctions and supervision" and specific limitations on creating monopolies (see below, p. 723), the law permitted the President, as a condition of approving a code, to "impose such conditions ... for the protection of consumers, competitors, and others, and in furtherance of the public interest," as he deems necessary to effectuate the purposes of the act. Under the President's power to prescribe rules and regulations, not only were NRA officials charged with the responsibility of seeing that the codes fairly represented the sentiments of the industries they covered but public hearings at which employer groups, labor groups, and consumer groups, as well as individuals, could air their grievances and express their views were required before any pending code was approved.[20]

Minimum Wage Rates

But the favorable features of government-sponsored code systems did not bring to collective bargaining the millennium of controlled competition that had been so long in the making. The potential utopia of standardized labor costs created by translating the terms and conditions of collective agreements into legal codes of industry-wide application never fully materialized. All the evils that had beset the sponsors of the protocol movement in apply-

---

upon these associations not only to draft and present codes but also to administer them. Thus in NRA Bulletin #7 (page 4) issued on January 22, 1934, appeared a statement by Hugh S. Johnson, Administrator: "It is the policy of NRA to build up and strengthen trade associations throughout commerce and industry so that they may perform all code administration functions. A Trade Association Division has been established in NRA to carry out this policy and to advise and assist industry in the performance of these functions.

—Travis Brown, "Code Authorities and Their Part in the Administration of the NIRA" (processed), NRA Studies (1936), p. 55.

[20] The NIRA also provided "that where such code or codes affect the services and welfare of persons engaged in other steps of the economic process, nothing in this section shall deprive such persons of the right to be heard prior to the approval by the President of such code or codes."

ing their principles of controlled competition now remained to plague those who would accomplish the same ends through codes of fair competition. Not even the arm of the law could overcome the obstacles which had always hampered the introduction of industry-wide labor standards.

Drafting codes of fair competition aroused all the internal bickerings, factional jealousies, and smoldering hostilities that had characterized collective bargaining since 1910. Needle trade industries were faced with the dilemma of resolving old issues in a new context: namely, how to eliminate or overcome by law certain disparities in labor costs already existing between metropolitan centers and outlying districts, between inside manufacturing and outside contracting, between large firms and small shops, between the organized elements and the unorganized elements, between New York City and the rest of the country. By authorizing codes of fair competition, the government did not resolve the disturbing issues of how the codes should be drafted, whose codes should govern, or what such codes should contain.

Three key issues dominated conflicts over the terms and the operation of needle trade codes: (1) the character and content of wage provisions; (2) the control of code authorities; and (3) special concessions and exceptions to established code standards. On all three issues the code makers, like their counterparts in the protocol movement, sought to overcome a basic cleavage of opinion between the organized factions of New York City and the unorganized factions of other competing markets. In as much as wages were the key to comparative labor costs, wage rates and wage differences created the most trying problem for needle trade code makers. More than twenty years of exhaustive efforts at creating a standard wage structure that would avoid the shoals of "illegitimate" competition had done little to guide the skippers of the code systems.[21]

In the race to win approval for their own concepts of wage standards, the employers' associations and labor unions of New

---

[21]These were not the only issues on which the organized factions of labor and of management representing the New York market differed from the position taken by the manufacturers and workers in other markets. See H. A. Brickley, "History of the Code of Fair Competition for the Fur Manufacturing Industry" (processed), NRA: Division of Review (March 1936), p. 25, U.S. National Archives.

York City won a head start. With separate minimum wages for various crafts and occupations already pegged by collective bargaining, these organized groups had to fight for extending their accepted standards throughout their trades. New York manufacturers could hardly expect their workers to tolerate a reduction in wage rates, nor would New York unions permit regional differences in wage rates to threaten the survival of New York industry. Having the benefit of long established organizations devoted to the problem of controlling competition, New York producers of women's garments, men's clothing, headwear, furs, and other items of wearing apparel lost no time submitting their own preferences for wage standards. In this move, they were aided and abetted by needle trade unions whose representatives directly or indirectly participated in drafting the code proposals.

In drafting the wage terms of proposed codes, the organized New York manufacturers set their sights on two objectives. Their first aim was to create minimum wage scales for each separate craft or occupation in contradistinction to a single flat minimum rate applicable to all jobs within each trade. Their second aim was to prevent such geographic disparities in classified wage minima as would endanger the continued success of New York manufacturing. Both issues aroused long and bitter struggles in which organized labor and organized management of the New York market were aligned against the unorganized forces of labor and management in other towns and cities.

Classified Wage Minimums versus *Flat Minimum Rates*

In several of the needle trades, the issue of a single minimum wage for each industry, as against a separate minimum wage rate for each job classification within the industry, rekindled old controversies between the organized forces of the New York market and the unorganized elements of the hinterlands. Instead of a single minimum wage for women's headwear, the New York millinery manufacturers insisted upon separate minimum wage rates for blockers, operators, cutters, and milliners. Similarly, the men's clothing manufacturers demanded separate minimum rates for tailors, pressers, operators, and cutters. The fur dressing industry held out for separate minimums for cutters, operators, nailers, and finishers. Building a wage floor under each craft or occupation not only protected the New York manufacturers, who were already bound by the classified wage minimums, but it also protected the skilled and semiskilled workers who, like their employers, were subject to destructive competition from out-of-town sources.

By contrast, the unorganized manufacturers of other towns and cities set their sights on keeping down the wage minimum to a level that would permit local manufacturers to meet New York competition. Since flat minimum rates for each industry would affect only the lowest paid workers at the very bottom of the wage structure, unscrupulous employers could still thrive on discrepancies for comparable work in skilled and semiskilled job classifications. They might even offset a wage floor for unskilled workers by lowering the rates on skilled and semiskilled jobs. Nonunion workers reluctantly fell into line with this policy only because these low-paying jobs in their local community were more enticing than other available job openings and certainly they were preferable to no jobs at all.

In this clash of opinions over the flat minimum wage vs. classified wage minimums, differences in points of view based on geographic location were less important than distinctions between firms bound by collective labor agreements and those that were not. In the millinery industry, for example, firms in the unorganized markets of other towns and cities changed their positions as soon as they were brought under collective labor agreements.

Unionization not only removed the objections of these markets to occupational minima but made them vigorous proponents thereof. Representatives of the Chicago [millinery] market, for instance, had been during the summer [of 1933] among the leaders of the anti-classification faction. Immediately, upon the settlement of the Chicago strike in favor of the union, however, these same representatives unblushingly swung to the other side and became outstanding advocates of classification. The Chicago group should not, however, be accused of unwarranted perfidy. Their position merely changed with changing circumstances. The union agreements to which they became bound called for the payment of minimum wages graded according to occupation. They were naturally anxious that similar burdens be borne by all their competitors. It was impossible, for the moment at least, to hope that this result could be accomplished by the activities of the union. The only instrument available was the Code.[22]

------

[22]From a report of the National Recovery Administration as quoted in United Hatters, Cap and Millinery Workers' International Union, *Report*

After the initial drafting of proposed codes by competitive groups within each industry, the battle of the codes shifted to Washington where the National Recovery Administration conducted public hearings on all codes submitted for each trade. Here, the fight between the warring factions for favorable code terms sometimes raged for weeks and months before decisions could be reached on whose code should govern and what terms the code should contain. No subject was more bitterly contested than the issue of wage rates and no industry contributed more vociferous antagonists on this issue than the millinery trade.

When the rival codes of the millinery trade came up for consideration in the summer of 1933, the Women's Headwear Group, speaking for the New York manufacturers bound by collective agreements, clashed head-on with the National Millinery Council representing the nonunion shops of other towns and cities. The usual heated arguments punctuated the proceedings. New York manufacturers contended that existing wage discrepancies had already permitted out-of-town producers "to manufacture and sell merchandise at absurdly ridiculous low prices," and that these disparities had forced manufacturers in the New York metropolitan area "to sell their merchandise below cost." The New York group insisted that a flat minimum wage would not prevent "unfair and cut-throat competition." Fear was expressed lest the industry be driven out of New York City to smaller centers where "coolie wages" would prevail.[23]

---

and Proceedings, Second Convention (First Regular Convention) Oct. 4–7, 1936, pp. 63–64.

> We are about to conclude our hearings and negotiations both on the millinery code and on the cap code. Whatever code you will get, you will find it to be a compromise between the employers of organized workers and the employers of non-union workers. That compromise will be the code that will be written for the millinery industry and for the cap industry.... The workers in New York, for example, have nothing whatsoever to expect from the code. The code will not give them shorter hours, not one minute less per week or per day, unless they fight for it.
> —I. H. Goldberg, chairman, Committee on Officers' Report, in Cloth
> Hat, Cap and Millinery Workers' International Union, *Report
> and Proceedings,* Eighteenth Convention (October 1933), p. 83.

[23]*Women's Wear Daily,* August 1, 2, 3, 1933. See also, J. C. Worthy, "The Millinery Industry" (processed), NRA: Division of Review, Industry Studies Section (March 1936); and United Hatters, Cap and Millinery Workers' International Union, Cap and Millinery Department, *Report and Proceedings,* Second Convention (First Regular Convention), Oct. 4–7, 1936, pp. 57–65.

In this position, the New York manufacturers were strongly supported by the organized millinery workers. During the hearings, Max Zaritsky, president of the Cloth Hat, Cap and Millinery Workers — a union that claimed to represent over 90 percent of the 14,000 millinery workers in New York City as well as a small percent of the 12,000 millinery workers in out-of-town markets — demanded wage classifications to provide minima for the skilled and semiskilled workers as well as for the unskilled workers. He held that the plan of the National Millinery Council for a flat wage minimum was nothing more than a scheme to pay all labor, including skilled workers, a flat minimum wage.[24]

On the other hand, representatives of the National Millinery Council with equal conviction attacked the labor standards proposed by the New York Headwear Group. They contended that the minimum rates of $1.00 an hour for cutters, blockers, and machine operators, of 60¢ an hour for trimmers, and of $14 a week for all other workers set out in the proposed code of the New York manufacturers would overwhelm the rest of the industry. "My God," exclaimed the president of the Knox Hat Company on behalf of the out-of-towners, "give these fellows a chance to see what they can pay without driving them out of

---

Text of the proposed code of the National Millinery Council appears in *Women's Wear Daily*, July 20, 1933; text of the proposed code submitted by the Women's Headwear Group in the July 25, 1933 issue.

[24]*New York Times*, August 2, 1933; *Women's Wear Daily*, August 3, 1933. Key statements for and against classification of wage scales in the millinery code are quoted with references to original sources, in Worthy, "The Millinery Industry."

> The year which intervened between the enactment of the law [NIRA] and the signing of the Code for the cap industry was one of endless bickering, in which the non-union manufacturers resorted to dilatory tactics to delay, and, if possible, to prevent, the adoption of the Code for the industry.
>
> —United Hatters, Cap and Millinery Workers' International Union, Cap and Millinery Department, *Report and Proceedings*, Second Convention (First Regular Convention), Oct. 4–7, 1936, p. 17.

New York needle trade unions did not always see eye to eye with New York maufacturers on other code issues — week work or limitation of contractors, for example — to be incorporated into their industry codes of fair competition. See Haskel, *A Leader of the Garment Workers: The Biography of Isidore Nagler*, p. 175; ILGWU, *Report and Proceedings*, Twenty-second Convention (May–June 1934), pp. 26–29; Morris Hillquit, "Objections of the ILGWU," a typewritten manuscript filed in the ILGWU research library.

business.... If we go into the red again, then the government will have to employ the workers, and all that you will have left is sovietism." In such vein, the conflict raged for five months before the first code of the millinery trade was finally approved.

Similar battles were fought on other needle trade fronts. In men's clothing, the New York Clothing Manufacturers' Exchange led the fight of the organized markets for separate craft wage minimums that would retain existing wage differentials between the skilled and unskilled categories. Consolidating their forces into the newly formed Clothing Manufacturers' Association of the United States, these organized markets waged a bitter war on the position taken by nonunion producers who had formed the Industrial Recovery Association of Clothing Manufacturers in part to oppose the principle of classified wage minimums.[25]

In pointing out the difficulties of applying separate minimum wage scales to different crafts or occupations, advocates of a flat minimum wage for each industry argued that (1) the content of jobs and the use of machinery varied from shop to shop and were constantly changing; (2) the substitution of the sectional system of manufacturing for the tailoring system upset job content and threw wage scales out of kilter; (3) freezing minimum wage scales for each job title hampered the freedom of management to re-organize for more efficient production. Above all else was the vital consideration that creating separate wage standards for each job classification would substantially increase the costs of out-of-town production without affecting costs to New York manufacturers who were already bound by craft differentials in collective agreements. Such a major disturbance of existing relationships between markets, so the nonunion producers contended, would tend to drive manufacturers of other centers out of business.[26]

---

[25]See the New York Clothing Manufacturers' Exchange, *The New York Story: A History of the New York Clothing Industry, 1924–1949.*

[26]A special fur commission assigned to study comparative costs for fur manufacturing in different markets doubted the wisdom of classified wage schedules on the ground that (1) complexity of the industry would make the determination of uniform wage structures for each job classification arbitrary and unscientific; (2) classified wage schedules would be subject to manipulation by interested groups and would drag the government into the industry's quarrels; (3) classified wage schedules could not be enforced. As summarized by Brickley, "History of the Code of Fair Competition for the Fur Manufac-

But the New York advocates of separate wage minima for each craft or occupation insisted that their position was more in keeping with the objectives of governmental policy. The NIRA expressly empowered the President to differentiate minimum rates of pay "according to the experience and skill of the employees affected." The President's Re-employment Agreement confirmed and established the principle of regulating wages above a flat minimum for each trade. The Black-Connery 30-hour-week bill, though defeated on other grounds, provided that whenever trade associations and labor unions negotiate collective agreements embracing 50 percent of their trade, the wage minima adopted for each craft would be automatically extended throughout the industry. Above all was the practical consideration that rising competition from out-of-town centers of production would otherwise soon drive New York City manufacturers out of business and defeat the purposes of collective bargaining.[27]

When the smoke of battle had lifted, the major needle trade codes, like previous collective agreements for those industries, had imposed upon manufacturers separate minimum wage rates for different crafts or occupations. But the initial settlement of these disputes, unlike the resolution of similar issues at the bargaining table, did not for a moment suppress the losing factions. The concept of war for a while and peace for a while that actuated organized groups bound by collective agreements was never applicable to codes of fair competition. Out-of-town groups immediately began clamoring for code revision which would

---

turing Industry," p. 81. For details, see Paul Abelson, W. E. Adkins, and F. La Rue Frain, "Report of the Special Commission on Wages and Hours in the Fur Manufacturing Industry" (processed), NRA: "Work Materials," no. 6 (March 1936).

[27]Text of the President's Re-employment Agreement, sometimes called the "blanket code," may be conveniently found in Lewis Mayers, ed., *A Handbook of NRA*, 2nd ed. (1934), pp. 335–342. See also, Herbert Hoover, "The President's Re-employment Agreement" (processed), NRA: Division of Review, Organization Studies Section (March 1936); and Harry Mulkey, "The So-called Model Code, Its Development and Modification" (processed), NRA: Division of Review, Organization Studies Section (March 1936). More than 80 such special studies, bearing the additional label "Work Materials" and dealing with various aspects of code activities are available in the U.S. National Archives and in a few other libraries. Many deal with the needle trades.

supplant occupational wage minima written into codes with a flat minimum wage for each industry.[28]

Geographical Wage Differentials

With this initial victory for the advocates of classified wage minimums, the center of the wage controversy shifted to the issue of whether the wage rates to be included in each industry's code of fair competition should be uniform throughout the industry. Whatever the nature of the wage structure, both the needle trade manufacturers and the needle trade unions of the New York market stoutly opposed the concept of geographical wage differentials. Already bound by collective agreements with relatively high wage scales, the organized forces of the New York market feared that any deviations from uniformity based on the location of the firm would create more havoc with the principle of controlled competition than the good that could be done. At a hearing in Washington on the proposed millinery code, the general executive board of the millinery workers' union insisted that the disparity between the wage standards of the organized markets, principally in New York, and the unorganized markets scattered elsewhere throughout the country "must be eliminated if the industry is to overcome the deadly competition caused by sub-standard markets."[29]

The idea of governmental sanctions for regional wage differentials ran contrary to all concepts of industry-wide standards that had motivated the sponsors of the protocol movement. Since 1910, the organized forces of labor and management had worked to extend the terms of their collective agreements over all competitors within each trade. Lack of national organizations among manufacturers had forced needle trade unions into roles of mis-

---

[28]The first official proposal for revision of the National Industrial Recovery Act came from NRA's Labor Advisory Board and called for an amendment that would "specifically provide for including different minima for common, semi-skilled and skilled labor in codes of fair competition." *Women's Wear Daily*, Dec. 17, 1934.

[29]"This can best be done," continued the general executive board, "by raising the minima in the unorganized areas, since the minima would not apply to New York, where the prevailing rates are far in excess of even the code minima proposed by the union." United Hatters, Cap and Millinery Workers' International Union, *Report and Proceedings*, Second Convention (First Regular Convention), October 1936, p. 59.

sionaries to the heathens of the hinterlands. Spurred on by the duty of applying "most favored employer" clauses to their independent agreements, and bound by contractual obligation to conduct out-of-town organizing drives, these unions had sought to convert the unorganized elements to the principle of uniform wage rates throughout their trades. Nothing was farther from the minds of those who had supported collective bargaining than the thought of freezing geographical wage differentials to the permanent embarrassment of New York industry.

Parties to collective agreements in New York City fully expected codes of fair competition to become instruments for carrying out their long-sought objectives of creating for each trade uniform standards of employment. Accordingly, they drafted code proposals that made no allowances for geographic differentials in labor standards. Conversely, code proposals submitted to the NRA administrator from out-of-town centers stressed geographic differentials in labor standards which more or less reflected current practices. Here again, the clash of interests between New York City and the rest of the country was pointed up at the public hearing on code proposals.

From the outset, however, the New York manufacturers faced the prospect of having to modify their stand. The law itself authorized the President in prescribing limited codes of fair competition to differentiate the terms of such codes "according to the locality of employment." Moreover, the administration in Washington repeatedly voiced its opposition to excessive dislocation of industry. Such a dislocation might result from disturbing established wage relationships between different regions, markets, or areas within the same industry. On one occasion, the National Recovery Administration in a "Notice of Public Hearing on Policy of the National Industrial Recovery Board Relating to Employment Provisions," stated flatly that "geographic and population and other wage differentials, being concomitants of our industrial development, are to be treated as significant realities of the situation."[30]

---

[30]A copy of the notice, dated Jan. 17, 1935, is filed in the Abelson papers. NRA, Bulletin no. 2, "Guiding Principles in Preparing Codes," June 19, 1933, acknowledged the need for geographical wage differentials by stating that minimum wages should be sufficient "to provide a decent standard of

Political pressure from the hinterlands to preserve small business in out-of-town centers would most certainly force concessions that would compromise the principle of uniform labor standards. Some New York manufacturers modified their proposals accordingly. In its original code proposals, the Affiliated Dress Manufacturers' Association of New York City attempted to face realities by prescribing that "all persons engaged in the dress industry elsewhere in the United States shall comply immediately with all and every provision of this code with such appropriate differentials as in the judgment of the administrator shall be deemed fair and equitable." The codes of fair competition for the major industries of the needle trades that received final approval by President Roosevelt accepted the principle of geographical wage differentials in unmistakable terms. The first code of the millinery industry, for example, created four geographical areas, each with a different wage minimum per hour for each job classification:

	Area "A"	Area "B"	Area "C"	Area "D"
Blockers	$1.19	$ .90	$ .80	$ .70
Operators	1.00	.75	.675	.60
Cutters	1.00	.75	.675	.60
Milliners	.55	.475	.45	.45

Such provisions were only the prelude to the continuing fight for wage concessions from the administrators of the code system.[31]

Such concessions to meet this pressure for geographical wage differentials did not force the organized factions of the needle trades to compromise the basic principles on which the protocol movement was founded. Complete uniformity in the terms of employment was not essential to the principle of "legitimate" competition. More often, since 1910, the sponsors of collective bargaining had harped on the necessity for taking labor out of competition by *equalizing labor costs* in the manufacture of their products. Uniform terms of employment gave no assurance of equal labor costs. Identical wage rates per hour for the same operation did not always guarantee identical output, nor did

---

living in the locality where the workers reside." Text of the bulletin was printed in the *New York Herald Tribune* for June 21, 1933.

[31]The text of the original code proposal of the Affiliated Dress Manufacturers' Association is printed in *Women's Wear Daily,* July 24, 1933.

equal piece rates always insure the same quality of production. Labor costs were affected by other considerations than specific wage rates or fixed hours of work.

Those who would write the principles of the protocol movement into codes of fair competition could, therefore, look to the concept of equal labor costs as a criterion for measuring the success of their efforts. Under this concept, geographical differentials in labor standards would be acceptable so long as they did not place New York producers at a competitive disadvantage measured in terms of total labor costs per garment. The critical issue then became one of determining what differentials, if any, would best promote the principle of equal labor cost among all manufacturers within a trade. The Associated Fur Coat and Trimming Manufacturers of New York City struck the keynote of the new approach by stating that the association expected hours and wages to be identical for all fur workers everywhere. But if differentials became necessary, then the association urged "that only such differentials be recommended as will unquestionably and without possible evasion give fair competition to the entire industry as a whole."[32]

While accepting these concessions, manufacturers in other towns and cities were not content to base their claims for wage differentials wholly on comparative labor costs. They found additional reasons for contending that out-of-town producers were less able to meet high labor standards than their New York competitors. At the time the millinery code was under consideration in the summer of 1933, Shirley Tark, executive director of the Midwestern Millinery Association, with headquarters in Chicago,

---

[32]From a "Brief of the Association" to the special fur commission, considering questions of geographical differentials in labor costs. Typewritten copy filed in the Abelson papers. Early in the history of the protocol movement, the fur manufacturing industry had acknowledged the issue of geographical differentials in labor standards through the "most favored employer" clause of the 1914 collective agreement between the Associated Fur Manufacturers and the International Fur Workers' Union:

The Union agrees that in any other agreement with employers it will make in Greater New York, the stipulated conditions of work and wages shall in no way be less than the terms of this agreement. It furthermore pledges, to the limit of its ability and financial resources, *with due regard to local conditions,* to endeavor to obtain these conditions in the entire industry in the country (italics added).

summarized the broader aspects of the case for geographic wage differentials in these terms:

The reason is that New York is a natural market, it gets volume orders, its methods of production are superior, it has a much greater percentage of men workers and these are men who are anxious to work hard, its selling costs are about 5 per cent less than Chicago, it has less inventory loss because it can buy from hand to mouth, its houses need not spend time or money to learn what is new in material and style, it is not required to expend sizable sums annually for express charges, and its product is generally made by machine whereas about 75 per cent of the operations here are by hand.[33]

Equalizing labor costs was far more complicated than setting uniform conditions of employment. At best, this new task could not be accomplished overnight. Bitter arguments over regional differences in labor costs were not resolved with the official adoption of the first industry codes. The differences in wage rates originally approved satisfied no one completely. Minimum wage differentials written into the first codes were too high for some and too low for others. No sooner were they publicized than manufacturers form north, south, east, and west cried out for code revision. Organized labor joined the crusade of the New York manufacturers to save the "legitimate" elements of each industry, while nonunion labor supported the producers of the hinterlands in their demands for more substantial wage differentials to protect their position in the trade.[34]

Delineating areas on which to base wage differentials was a major source of friction. Northern New Jersey millinery manufacturers objected vociferously to being included in Area "A" covering New York City, while their competitors in southern New Jersey, assigned to Area "B," operated under minimum wage rates 20 percent below those of Area "A." New York City coat and suit manufacturers vehemently opposed having Balti-

---

[33]*Women's Wear Daily,* Sept. 19, 1933.

[34]Furriers of twelve southern states gathered at Hotel Peabody and presented a solid front against the "fur aristocracy" of New York. Claiming that the code presented by the Association of Fur Manufacturers of New York would ruin furriers outside of the city, the furriers demanded a wage differential which they held would be fair to all.
    —From a clipping in the Abelson papers, citing the *Press Scimitar,* Memphis, Tenn. (n. d.).

more classified with the western area which enjoyed a substantial code advantage over New York City in minimum wage rates. For sectionalized shops, these Baltimore wage scales were estimated at only 44.6 percent of wage rates in Brooklyn coat and suit shops. In yet another example, the women's coat and suit manufacturers of St. Louis insisted upon a 50 percent wage advantage over New York City, instead of the 15–20 percent favorable wage differential assigned to them in the women's coat and suit code. Everywhere, pleas for code revision were founded on the elemental assumption that relief was necessary to stay in business.[35]

Special Studies of Comparative Wage Rates

In a number of the needle trades, final determination of wage differentials awaited reports of special commissions assigned the task of investigating comparative labor costs and recommending appropriate action. A special fur commission was named to determine whether wage differentials in the first code of the fur manufacturing industry had tended "to promote conditions of fair competition between the various markets and areas of the industry." Similarly, a special commission for the women's coat and suit trade was given the duty of studying "competitive irregularities" among markets including "all petitions and demands filed since the adoption of the coat and suit code by particular localities and markets relative to wages and labor classifications."

Most active of these commissions was the special millinery board sanctioned by executive order of the President in approving the original millinery code of fair competition, December 15,

---

[35]About forty millinery plants in northern New Jersey are reported to have closed in opposition to being classified in Area "A," the same as that for New York. . . . The industry in Massachusetts, which they said was the strongest competitive area to northern New Jersey plants, had been segregated in Area "D" with a rate approximately 40 per cent lower than for New York and northern Jersey. Area "C," embracing the southern and western sections of the country, calls for a minimum 30 per cent lower than Area "A."
—*New York Herald Tribune*, Dec. 30, 1933.

On the women's coat and suit trade, see *Women's Wear Daily*, July 27, 1934, especially the supplement containing the text of the "Report of the Commission for the [women's] Coat and Suit Industry." The fight to have Baltimore's code zone changed from the western area to the eastern area is summarized in the issue of Jan. 30, 1934.

1933. Originally assigned to make exceptions to code standards (see below, p. 629 ff.) this board acquired a variety of other powers under the revised code of November 9, 1934, including the power to investigate the effect of code labor standards "on fair competitive conditions in the areas, markets, or localities and to recommend to the National Industrial Recovery Board amendments or modifications of said Articles on the basis of such findings."[36]

Constituted to represent employers, workers, and the government, these special code agencies, like so many of their counterparts in the long history of collective bargaining, undertook to gather from the field first-hand information that would provide the factual basis for appropriate action. But, whereas all research agencies under the protocol movement had been hampered in their investigations of shops beyond the control of employers' associations and completely stymied in all those shops beyond the range of union control, these code agencies, armed with governmental authority, traveled widely from market to market, inspecting shops, examining books, conducting hearings, and otherwise comparing labor costs under all types of operations and all conditions of employment. A common procedure was to estimate the comparative labor costs of making sample garments that were taken from market to market. After weeks and months of intensive study, these agencies produced the first truly industry-wide surveys of production cost factors in their respective trades.

The special coat and suit commission found, for example, that Baltimore had the lowest labor costs per garment, while New York City had the highest; that indirect labor costs of training and supervising workers in the west were no greater than in the east; that markets outside of New York failed to sustain their claims to higher overhead costs; and that selling costs in New York City were not exceptionally low when compared with selling costs in other parts of the country. On the basis of hearings in thirteen of the largest producing centers, this commission discovered that differences in labor costs were complicated by substantial differ-

---

[36]See the Amended Code of Fair Competition for the Millinery Industry, approved Nov. 9, 1934. The texts of the findings and recommendations of the special millinery board embodied in the board's report of July 21, 1934, and in its supplementary reports of August 15, 1934 and Sept. 20, 1934, were printed in full, along with the Amendments to the Code of Fair Competition for the Millinery Industry, approved Nov. 9, 1934.

ences in labor productivity, which in turn varied widely with the degree of efficiency in operations.[37]

Research studies in the fur industry revealed that, whereas hourly earnings in other cities were 14.1 percent below those of New York City, the total labor costs for manufacturing identical fur garments in other cities were 17.6 percent higher than similar labor costs in New York City. Meanwhile, the special millinery board had discovered so many cost variables between metropolitan areas and the rest of the country that it proposed to continue in operation "with the authority to investigate and recommend relief to individuals or markets or to maintain a balance of fair competition."[38]

While recommendations based on the findings of these special boards led to numerous changes in the codes, perhaps the most obvious result of the studies was the overwhelming evidence that industry-wide standards of fair competition required constant manipulation to meet the shifting variables affecting labor costs

---

[37]The first investigation of wage differentials conducted under the auspices of the NRA disclosed an advantage in labor costs of something over 20 percent for the west over the east. This advantage was estimated at nearly 30 percent for the west over the New York metropolitan area. Alexander Printz and Maxwell Copelof, "Report of Investigation," reproduced in U.S. National Recovery Administration, "Reconvened Hearings on Code," pp. 309–311, as cited in Robinson, *Collective Bargaining and Market Control in the New York Coat and Suit Industry,* p. 107.

[38]These research studies were processed and issued as a part of the National Recovery Administration's extensive collection of "Work Materials." In this series, see no. 5: "Report of the Special Commission on Wage Differentials in the Cap and Cloth Hat Industry"; no. 6: "Report of the Special Commission on Wages and Hours in the Fur Manufacturing Industry"; no. 10; "Report of the Commission for the [women's] Coat and Suit Industry"; and no. 74: E. C. Hutchinson and others, "Administrative and Legal Aspects of Stays, Exemptions, and Exceptions, Code Amendments, Additional Orders of Approval, etc." The report of the women's coat and suit commission was also printed in full as a supplement to *Women's Wear Daily,* July 27, 1934.

Considering New York as 100, the time required to produce a standard article in other cities was 147.4 while the hourly earnings in other cities was only 85.9. The resultant average labor cost in other cities was 117.6, or 17.6% higher than in New York.

—G. C. Gamble, Research and Planning Division, NRA, in letter, dated Oct. 24, 1934, to Paul Abelson, member of the special fur commission investigating comparative labor costs. The letter is filed in the Abelson papers.

and trade practices. The key to success of the code system, therefore, was in the hands of those who administered code provisions, just as the key to success in collective bargaining since 1910 had been in the hands of the impartial machinery. This revelation did not surprise the sponsors of the protocol movement who anticipated the importance of administrative action and, from the outset, sought to gain control over code authorities who would be responsible for interpreting and applying code principles.

The Control of Code Authorities

By authorizing codes of fair competition, the National Industrial Recovery Act presented federal administrators with a task for which they were ill-equipped. Lacking the experiences of the needle trades with collective bargaining, NRA officials had to stumble on the means of achieving their goals. The act itself provided few guideposts of substance or procedure. Beyond general provisions defining the top echelons of administrative authority, the NIRA was completely silent on the institutions and processes for carrying out code objectives. In this setting, nothing was more logical than to confer upon each industry the responsibility for creating administrative agencies that would work out the methods for operating the various code systems.

Collective bargaining had undergone a similar phase of development. In the early years of the protocol movement, the advocates of controlled competition had conferred upon the impartial machinery of each trade full responsibility for developing and operating successful systems of collective bargaining. But the powers originally conferred upon code authorities for the apparel industries even surpassed those commonly exercised by agencies of the impartial machinery under the first collective agreements of the New York market. Only in the light of broad powers that code authorities were presumed to possess could the intensity of the fight for control of these agencies ever be understood.

At the time the code of fair competition for the women's coat and suit industry was approved by the President in the summer of 1933, the powers presumably conferred upon the code authority for that trade were vividly described in the following terms:

In this Authority is vested the widest, most far-reaching powers ever handed down to a governing body since the inception of the collective labor agreements more than a quarter of a century ago. It will become not only the legislative but also the judicial head of the entire cloak industry of the United States. . . .

Every conceivable phase of operations for the coat and suit industry under this code lies in the direction of the Authority. The Authority will determine the modus operandi for the unemployment insurance fund when established for the industry; it will supervise complete distribution and control of the NRA label, which is prescribed for in the code; it has the power of setting up a uniform system of accounting; can recommend the credit system for the industry; evolve the proper trade relations; suggest rules for disposing of distress merchandise and regulate any inequalities that may arise. . . .

Whereas the impartial chairman under former agreements settled all disputes concerning labor, the control vested in the Code Authority is far beyond the imagination of any observer. With a single stroke the code provides the strongest policing weapon yet granted to this industry. The question of trade discounts, returns, memorandum selling, secret rebates, dealings with furriers and hundreds of other minute problems will have the guidance of the trade Authority. . . .

Under the code, the Authority may require reports of statistical information from persons engaged in the coat and suit industry. The keeping of uniform accounts as may be required in order to secure the proper observances and to promote the proper balancing of production, distribution and consumption, the stabilization of the industry and employment. In other words, the Authority has the right to change any system of accounting or method of production prevailing in the industry that may tend to undermine the structure of the industry. . . .

The code provides Authority with the right to recommend to the administrator as to the methods and conditions of trading, the naming and reporting of prices which may be appropriate to avoid discrimination and to prevent and eliminate unfair and destructive prices and practices. . . .

Any inequalities that may arise under the operation of the code that are likely to jeopardize trade stability, production and unemployment can now come before the Authority for proper adjustment. Such changes as may be made will have the same force and effect as any other provision of the code when approved by the trade administrator. . . .

The Authority will receive all applications from firms outside the associations and not under the code for a license to feature the NRA label in their merchandise. They will administer the use of the label and grant the license if they find the applicant complies with the standards set forth in the code. . . .

It has the power to examine all books of accounts of firms operating under the code to ascertain the observance of such, and all employers are obliged to submit their books and records for such examination. It has the power to appoint a director, a staff of accountants and such other employees that may be required for the effective discharge of its functions."[39]

Thus, whoever controlled the code authorities had the power to control the destinies of the code system.

The desire to gain control of the machinery for code administration had undoubtedly inspired the initial rush to organize new trade associations and to draft codes of fair competition. Here again, the existing associations of New York City already bound by collective agreements had the inside track. They lost no time in making provisions for administrative bodies in their proposed codes and in conferring upon these permanent agencies such powers and duties as were necessary to carry out code objectives. Before the term "code authority" was ever adopted, some New York associations had proposed for their industries the creation of NIRA committees on which organized labor, as well as employer groups, were represented. Neither the independent producers nor the organized manufacturers of other areas were given any recognition whatsoever on these industry committees.[40]

The forerunners of these proposed committees that became code authorities were the control commissions, trade councils, and general welfare agencies previously established under collective agreements. Superimposed on the normal machinery of collective bargaining, these institutions had exercised a guiding hand over both legislative and administrative policies of industry-wide concern. After the business crash of 1929, they assumed a renewed importance in the drive to overcome cut-throat competition of the Great Depression.[41]

---

[39] Harry Berlfein in *Women's Wear Daily,* August 15, 1933.

[40] The women's coat and suit code, first to be approved by President Roosevelt for the needle trades, and the fifth in the country, was also the first NRA code in which the term "code authority" was used. In recommending to the President a proposed code for the men's clothing industry, NRA Deputy Administrator Lindsay Rogers stated: "When the codes were submitted to the Administrator, administration by a trade association was contemplated. The device of administration by a Code Authority had not yet evolved." See "Report on the Code of Fair Competition for the Men's Clothing Industry," attached to the government printed copy of the code, approved August 26, 1933, p. 11.

[41] Expressing the need for continuing contacts among the various factions of the dress industry — contacts beyond those inspired by the negotiation of

The first code proposed by the New York employer groups of the women's coat and suit trade, as well as the first code proposed by the local dress and waist industry, called for administrative committees of eight members, two of whom would represent the local jobbers' associations, two the local contractors' association, two the local association of inside manufacturers, and two the International Ladies' Garment Workers' Union. In the women's coat and suit trade, this committee was to become a "planning, fair practice and controlling agency for the industry." Its recommendations when approved by the NRA administrator were to have the same force and effect as any other provision of the code. The committee was to cooperate with the NRA administrator in gaining compliance with code provisions. Thus did the New York associations make clear their intention of reserving to themselves the power to direct this new medium for suppressing "illegitimate" competition.[42]

No one doubted the intention of the organized forces in the New York market to achieve through industry-wide code committees of their own choosing the objectives they had never won through the impartial machinery of collective agreements. Naturally, all moves in this direction aroused manufacturers and workers from other areas not embraced by the charmed circle of New York control. Hastily forming new associations overnight, these

---

labor agreements — Louis Gabbe, president of the Association of Dress Manufacturers (contractors) proposed in 1932 (more than a year before the NRA codes) to establish a permanent medium through which common industry problems could be discussed and resolved:

> The kind of body we shall recommend shall meet at regular intervals — perhaps monthly or bi-monthly. There will be two spokesmen for each organized division — the union and the associations of "inside shop" manufacturers, jobbers and contractors. Every subject of possible concern to the improvement of the industry will come within the scope of this board. . . . The interests of the several branches of the dress trade are so closely intertwined that a board such as we shall formally recommend is not merely advisable it is an absolute necessity.

—*Women's Wear Daily*, Feb. 26, 1932.

[42]See the text of a proposed code of fair competition for the women's coat and suit industry submitted by the Merchants' Ladies' Garment Association (jobbers), the American Cloak and Suit Manufacturers' Association (contractors), and the Industrial Council of Cloak, Suit and Skirt Manufacturers (inside manufacturers) in *ibid.*, July 4, 1933; and the texts of the proposed codes submitted by various associations for the dress industry in the issues of July 20, 24, and 26, 1933.

outside groups called in experts to draft codes that would provide for administrative agencies beyond the control of New York City. Each major industry of the needle trades developed its opposing associations, and each association had its own proposals for constituting code authorities in a manner that would be most favorable to its own interests.

In men's clothing, the battle for control of code authorities was conducted between the Clothing Manufacturers' Association of the United States (unionized manufacturers) and the Industrial Recovery Association of Clothing Manufacturers (nonunionized producers). In the millinery trade, the fight was carried on between the Women's Headwear Group (New York's organized manufacturers bound by collective agreements) and the National Millinery Council (previously unorganized manufacturers largely from other towns and cities). In several trades, jobbers, contractors, and inside manufacturers each waged their own wars between organized groups in the New York market and unorganized groups of similar composition in out-of-town centers. Many of these rival associations supported their claims to control of code authorities by adding the words *National, American,* or *United States* to their titles. They officially opened their doors to all comers throughout the country, although their memberships were predominantly, if not wholly, local or regional.[43]

---

[43]Such, for example, was the case of the National Association of Blouse Manufacturers and the National Skirt Manufacturers' Association, two New York-centered associations that contributed eight of the twelve members of the code authority under the code of fair competition for the blouse and skirt manufacturing industries which became effective on Jan. 1, 1934.

In contrast to the proposed codes of the three major New York dress manufacturers' associations, whose members operated union shops (see texts in *Women's Wear Daily,* July 20 and 24, 1933), was the proposed code of the Metropolitan Dress Manufacturers' Association, whose members operated nonunion shops (see text in the July 26, 1933 issue).

On the origins of the Clothing Manufacturers' Association of the United States and of the Industrial Recovery Association of Clothing Manufacturers, see R. H. Connery, *The Administration of an NRA Code* (1938), pp. 8–12. See also the views of David Drechsler, association counsel, in the *Daily News Record,* June 22, 1934. The fight between these two associations for control of the code authority and the original compromises reached are summarized in Rogers, "Report on the Code of Fair Competition for the Men's Clothing Industry," recommending the code to the President for his approval. The re-

Bases of Representation

The fight over the composition and control of code authorities raised the basic issue of whether to recognize areas and markets in proportion to current production or whether to make allowances for potential development. If the former criterion were accepted, New York City would dominate code authorities; for there were few, if any, needle trade industries in which the New York manufacturers did not play a predominant role, whether measured in terms of output, value of the product, number of producers, or number of workers employed. In 1930, for example, 70 percent of all dresses made in the United States were made in and around New York City where 45,000 workers, mostly women, were engaged in manufacturing dress products worth $634,000,000 a year. And, in 1933, from 80 to 85 percent of all fur wearing apparel was produced in New York City. At that time, 75 percent of all manufacturing units employing labor in this trade belonged to one of three New York associations.[44]

In the early thirties, the women's coat and suit trade had over two thousand active firms in New York City with scarcely more than one hundred in any other town or city. The three local associations of jobbers, contractors, and inside manufacturers that together submitted a code for the industry claimed to represent 75 percent of the total output for the industry. According to its executive director, the Industrial Council (inside manufacturers) alone had 465 members who employed 11,300 workers on their premises, 3,500 more in contracting shops, and 4,000 additional workers in their offices and shipping departments. No other association of inside manufacturers could approach these figures.[45]

---

port is printed in the government pamphlet containing the text of the approved code for the men's clothing industry.

[44]The three fur associations were: the Associated Fur Coat and Trimming Manufacturers, the United Fur Manufacturers' Association, and the New York Fur Trimming Manufacturers' Association. See Brickley, "History of the Code of Fair Competition for the Fur Manufacturing Industry." See also *Women's Wear Daily*, May 5, 1932, for other statistical data on the importance of the New York market in fur manufacturing.

[45]See W. A. Simon, "History of the Code of Fair Competition for the [women's] Coat and Suit Industry" (processed), NRA: Industry Section 3, Division of Business Cooperation (Nov. 11, 1935), U.S. National Archives, Appendix, pp. 24 and 31.

In the millinery trade, the most prominent organization of New York manufactuers — the Women's Headwear Group — claimed that its arch rival, the National Millinery Council, for all the geographic area it presumed to cover, represented no more than a minority of the industry. "The only true representative group of manufacturers of ladies', misses', and children's hats," contended the New Yorkers, "is the Women's Headwear Group, Inc., which has a membership of about 168 members who employ approximately 7,157 workers." To support its position, this New York group produced statistics indicating that the New York metropolitan area accounted for 70 percent of the number of establishments, 70 percent of the number of wage earners, 70 percent of the amount of wages paid, and 70 percent of the value of the product. And "55 percent of all this," they alleged, represented the contribution of the Women's Headwear Group.[46]

So convincing were these statistics that NRA administrators

In his study, "The Migration of Industry: The Shift of Twenty-four Needle Trades from New York State, 1926–1934" (processed), NRA Studies, (March 1936), U.S. National Archives, D. J. Brown presents tables based on the Bureau of the Census, *Census of Manufactures,* which show New York State in a less favorable position and one of declining importance. See particularly, Summary Table III: "Percentage New York State Is of United States for Establishments, Wage Earners, and Value of Products in the Needle Trades, 1927–1933." The figures in this table for the wearing apparel group show that New York State declined between 1927 and 1933 from 62.1% to 57.8% of the number of establishments; from 38% to 31.8% of the number of wage earners; and from 60.5% to 54.8% of the value of the products produced in the United States. Even the most concentrated industry within the needle trade groups covered — that of women's clothing — fell in New York State from 72.4% to 68.5% of the number of establishments; from 58.3% to 50.1% of the number of wage earners; and from 77.9% to 73.2% of the value of the products produced in the United States.

[46]The Women's Headwear Group contended that the Eastern Millinery Association to which the National Millinery Council laid claim was organized exclusively for credit information and that the National Association of Ladies' Hatters, to which the council also laid claim, represented only 30 members and 500 employees, and that many of the association's members also belonged to the Women's Headwear Group, which was characterized as "the only association of the metropolitan area which has a definite written working agreement with the labor union, sanctioned and approved by the American Federation of Labor." *Women's Wear Daily,* August 1, 1933. See also the issue of July 14, 1933 and United Hatters, Cap and Millinery Workers' International Union, Cap and Millinery Department, *Report and Proceedings,* Second Convention (First Regular Convention), Oct. 4–7, 1936, p. 70.

under the first codes to be approved for the needle trades established code authorities whose members were drawn largely from the New York market. Of the ten members on the original women's coat and suit code authority, six represented local New York associations, two the ILGWU, and two the western area. Of the sixteen members on the dress and waist code authority, nine represented New York associations, three the ILGWU, two the eastern area beyond New York City, and two the western area. Fur manufacturing and the millinery trade, along with a score of smaller industries, followed the same general pattern. In each case, New York associations and the unions of their workers already operating under collective labor agreements gained control over the machinery for administering codes of fair competition.[47]

Permitting New York employers' associations and labor unions to dominate the selection of members on code authorities further infuriated out-of-town manufacturers, who saw in New York control of these agencies an attempt by law to impose New York labor standards upon the rest of the country. Within a few weeks after the women's coat and suit code was approved, the Western Area Coat and Suit Council was organized to represent the western area in a determined stand for adequate representation on the code authority. Other out-of-town employer groups throughout the needle trades continued to submit briefs to Washington in support of their claims for representation on the codes. Some asked to have the headquarters of code authorities transferred from New York City to Washington where code administration would be less influenced by the New York environment. Independent producers continued to complain that they had been excluded altogether from code representation.

---

[47]Writing of bases for selecting members of the millinery code authority in his study, "The Millinery Industry," at p. 91, J. C. Worthy stated:

In the first place, there was no really reliable information during the formative period of the Code which might have been used as a basis for a proper allocation of representation. It was anybody's guess how much a given market represented and how many seats should be allocated it. More important, N.R.A. itself did not lay down for many months any definitive standards by which systems of representation might be judged. For instance, it proceeded on the general assumption that code authority members should be elected by trade associations. Not until later was any official concern shown for the unorganized minority.

Some manufacturers refused to cooperate with code authorities until they were adequately represented.

In a number of cases, developments under the codes appear to have borne out the worst fears of out-of-town producers in competition with the New York area. After observing the operations of the women's coat and suit code for seven months, Alexander Printz, leading cloak and suit manufacturer of the Cleveland market, was no longer satisfied with an "expedient New York labor contract" for a code. He objected strenuously to a complete lack of representation on the code authority for manufacturers and workers in certain other markets. "The actual result of the administration by the present Code authority," he stated, "has resulted in injecting the affairs of the Metropolitan New York labor and manufacturing agreement into the Code of Fair Competition for those in the entire industry." He charged that "the Code Authority interprets the Code to promote requirements of the Metropolitan District, but not for the balance of the country."[48]

Likewise in the millinery trade, out-of-town producers raised a united voice against the domination of their code authority by the New York market. Early in June 1934, C. J. Crampton of Dallas, Texas, representing 67 manufacturers in Baltimore, Kansas City, Dallas, Birmingham, Boston, Atlanta, and on the West Coast, advocated a reorganization of the code authority "to make it truly representative of all elements of the industry." Beyond proposing the addition of decentralized subcode agencies, Crampton offered no formula for representation on the millinery code authority, but he insisted on behalf of his group that any dispersion of control away from the organized factions in New York City "would do much to restore the confidence of out-of-town manufacturers."[49]

---

[48]See Simon, "History of the Code of Fair Competition for the [women's] Coat and Suit Industry," pp. 27–28.

For a tirade against "a little clique of New York union organizers and clothing and dress manufacturers" who "now seek to enforce upon the cotton garment industry of the nation the complete domination of that industry by the New York clique," see the speech of Virginia E. Jenckes, congresswoman from Indiana, reported in *Women's Wear Daily*, August 3, 1934.

[49]*Women's Wear Daily*, June 5, 1934.

Subsequent revisions of needle trade codes did, in some cases, provide representation on code authorities for independent manufacturers and more adequate representation for markets beyond the New York metropolitan area. But the employers' associations and labor unions of New York City continued to hold the balance of power on code agencies through their right to select a majority of the members on each code authority. Out-of-town manufacturers were, therefore, compelled to shift the emphasis of their strategy from trying to prevent the extension of New York labor standards throughout each trade demanding special exemptions and concessions from the accepted labor standards imposed by the codes.

Special Concessions and Exemptions

Having taken over the driver's seat on code authorities, the organized forces of the New York market were in a favored position to influence, if not control, the pressures for special allowances, concessions, and exemptions from code operations. During the development of collective bargaining for the needle trades, pleas for special consideration within the realm of law and order had constantly threatened the principle of uniform labor standards. The more nearly complete the coverage of an industry, the greater the danger of internal disruption from pressures for special privileges. Under the codes of fair competition, this problem was greatly magnified by the automatic coverage of all industry firms of whatever size, character, or location. It is not surprising, therefore, that the issue of special concessions and exemptions became the third great subject of controversy under the needle trade codes — along with the issues of wage provisions and the control of code authorities.

There were two means of alleviating the pressures for special consideration. One was to change the codes themselves, creating more refined wage differentials, conceding more generous use of overtime, permitting more variations in hours of work, or granting more numerous exceptions of depressed areas and backward firms from the operation of code provisions. The other procedure was to leave the consideration of special tolerances and exceptions to administrative authorities who would investigate each claim as it arose and then determine the time and conditions under which special concessions, if any, would be granted. Both methods were exemplified in the history of the code of fair competition for the millinery trade.[50]

The green light for special concessions and exemptions from code standards had been flashed by President Roosevelt in his Executive Order 6443 of November 22, 1933, authorizing "such exceptions, exemptions, and modifications as the Administrator for Industrial Recovery may find necessary to avoid undue hardships." Presumably, the chief purpose of this order was to make relief available to those manufacturers who employed aged or handicapped workers incapable of earning the minimum wages set for their jobs. In the case of the millinery trade, the NRA administrators were given the power to appoint a special millinery board, apart from the regular code authority, to handle claims of all firms, areas, and markets seeking concessions from code standards. Once established, this board enjoyed the special privilege of making rules and regulations that, subject to NRA approval, had the effect of code provisions.[51]

---

[50]The formal changes of the codes themselves were classified into *supplemental codes* applicable to particular subdivisions of an industry, *appendices* relating to changes of lesser importance than those of supplemental codes and *amendments* including additions, deletions, or modifications required within the code, its supplements, or appendices. The National Industrial Recovery Act expressly authorized the President, as a condition for approving a code, to "provide such exceptions to and exemptions from the provisions of such code, as the President in his discretion deems necessary to effectuate the policy" of the act.

[51]Executive Order no. 151-1, Dec. 15, 1933, approving the millinery code, contained the following clause:

> A special board shall be appointed by the Administrator for the purpose of determining after notice and hearing whether the scales applying to a particular area, market, or member of the industry should be stayed or modified because of great and unusual hardship to such area, market or member of the industry by reason of the application of such scales thereto.

Although the board's findings were submitted in the form of recommendations to the NRA, these findings were always approved except where fixed policy required otherwise. Worthy, "The Millinery Industry," pp. 100–108. Under the temporary "blanket code" (the President's Re-employment Agreement), approved by the President in July 1933, any provision which because of peculiar circumstances would "create great and unavoidable hardship" could be rendered inoperative as to those directly concerned on request of the industry association to the National Recovery Administration for a stay.

Under the millinery codes, the special millinery board played havoc with industry-wide standards of employment. Nowhere else were so many exceptions made to general standards of conduct established for a trade. As if the creation of four areas each with its own minimum wage scales for different crafts was not enough, the millinery board, subject to confirmation by the NRA administrator, proceeded to make exceptions to existing area wage minimums covering up to 25 percent of the workers employed in each craft. Soon after the original millinery code became effective in December 1933, General Hugh. S. Johnson, NRA administrator, on recommendation of the special millinery board, issued an administrative order granting temporary exceptions from code minimum wage scales to large portions of the millinery industry outside of New York City. By the time the amended millinery code was approved on November 9, 1934, this special board had been officially characterized as an instrument for flexibility in the trade.[52]

Special wage rates below industry standards were applied to workers for lack of training, inexperience, or inefficiency, as well as for old age or physical handicaps. Whole cities were granted tolerances that gave them preferred positions in labor standards. When representatives of Area "D" covering the south and far west insisted that the classified wage scales were too steep, the board recommended an additional 10 percent tolerance for those markets. Some areas were temporarily exempted from the operation of certain code provisions. Some firms were transferred from one area classification to another to give them additional advantages over the standards set for New York City.[53]

Text of the President's Re-employment Agreement is given in Mayers, *A Handbook of NRA*, pp. 335–342, and in *Women's Wear Daily*, July 21, 1933.

[52]See W. A. Harriman, NRA administrative officer, "Report to the President," Nov. 9, 1934, printed with the amendments to the millinery code, p. 11; *Women's Wear Daily*, Feb. 12, 1934. See also, the First Annual Report of the Special Millinery Board, given at pp. 40–47 of the First Annual Report of the Code Authority for the Millinery Industry, Jan. 15, 1935. The report of the special millinery board for Jan. 18, 1935 showed that between Jan. 4, 1934 and Jan. 17, 1935 at least 26 different markets — not to mention individual firms — had petitioned for relief from code standards. Copies of these documents are filed in the Abelson papers.

[53]The amended millinery code of Nov. 9, 1934 contained the following "tolerance clause":

New pressures for special allowances and tolerances kept pace with new evidences of generosity by the special millinery board. An exemption or concession granted one firm, city, or area intensified the demands for special tolerances from other firms, cities, and areas. The amended code of 1934 opened the door to a further breakdown in uniform standards of employment. Thereafter, the board could recommend that a firm be allowed to give substandard wages to 35 percent, instead of 25 percent, of its labor force in each craft or occupation. Other employers who had found 25 percent of their workers slow and incompetent now suddenly discovered that 35 percent of their employees failed to justify the minimum wage scales. Whole cities found reasons for insisting that more than a third of their workers were incapable of earning code wages and that relief was essential to avoid undue hardship.[54]

To alleviate the distress and undue hardship in special and exceptional cases wherein a worker properly belonging to this Industry is threatened with loss of employment or inability to secure employment because he or she is admittedly of very low productive capacity, the Special Millinery Board shall have the power, subject to the disapproval of the National Industrial Recovery Board, to permit the employment of such worker at a wage less than the basic minimum wage of this code established in Section 2 of this Article, provided it is established to the satisfaction of said Board that such a person is admittedly of very low productive capacity because of old age, physical debility, or other subnormal condition.

The Special Millinery Board may, subject to the approval of the National Industrial Recovery Board, provide such rules, regulations and tests as it may deem necessary to establish the fact that such very low productivity is actual and not based on an inequitably measured piece rate or unit of productivity or weekly or hourly rate of payment.

[54]Those in the areas which called for higher wage scales were constantly applying for a shifting to the cheaper areas, and, as part of that plan, where they could not get the shifting to be approved, they sought to have the definitions of the various areas changed so that they would be in the lower-priced labor markets.

In addition, they used to the very limit the 25 per cent tolerance clause — strangely enough, they never had less than 25 per cent handicapped or substandard workers, the limit allowed by the Code, — and were steadily renewing requests for an additional tolerance. Their appeals to the Special Millinery Board, which had jurisdiction of these matters, subject to the approval of the Administrator, very often bordered on the pathetic. ... In most cases their appeals were not in vain. First they received such additional concessions through the Board, and

In other needle trades, code authorities were generally permitted to meet similar pressures for special concessions and exemptions, subject to approval by the NRA administrator. The first code of the fur manufacturing industry permitted temporary stays in the application of wage provisions and otherwise authorized petitions for relief from undue hardship. The men's clothing industry wrestled with a "slow worker" clause which would permit up to 20 percent of the operators to receive less than the minimum wages set for their crafts. The dress and waist industry set up a special exemption committee of its code authority with a detailed procedure for preventing abuses in the operation of the system. Everywhere, provisions for escape from code standards induced a flood of petitions for relief. Each successful venture further stimulated others to move for similar concessions.[55]

Evaluating the Codes

Just as the previously organized factions of the needle trades sponsoring industry codes of fair competition originally focused their attention on equalizing labor costs, so they ultimately measured the success of the codes largely in terms of eliminating

---

later they had the 35 per cent tolerance incorporated into an amended Code.
  —United Hatters, Cap and Millinery Workers' International Union, Cap and Millinery Department, *Report and Proceedings,* Second Convention (First Regular Convention), Oct. 4–7, 1936, p. 65.

"Atlanta, Birmingham, Buffalo, Dallas, Des Moines, Detroit, Los Angeles, Portland, Richmond, Salt Lake City, San Francisco, Seattle, and Sioux City were among those granted 35 percent tolerances." Statement on Exemptions Granted by the Special Millinery Board, August 28, 1914. Copy filed in the Abelson papers. A summary of the functions, organization, and activities of the special millinery board may be found in Worthy, "The Millinery Industry."

[55]Recognizing the difficulties of code administration of small enterprises, especially those that were highly localized in nature or located in small communities, the President issued Executive Order 6710, dated May 15, 1934, exempting employers in towns of under 2,500 population from certain provisions of all codes and agreements. See the testimony of General Hugh S. Johnson, former NRA administrator, before the Senate Committee on Finance. U.S. Senate, 74th Cong., 1st sess., Hearings pursuant to S. Res. 79: *Investigation of the National Recovery Administration* (April 1935), Part 6, p. 246.

competition for cheap labor. What these code supporters sought most from their government-sponsored programs of controlled competition was perhaps best summarized by a participant in the millinery code and a keen student of code activities. Reviewing for the NRA the favorable achievements of the millinery code, J. C. Worthy wrote in 1936 as follows:

> The most significant single accomplishment of the Code was the stabilization of labor costs by means of occupational minima. It was no longer possible for manufacturers to remove from the primary markets in search of cheap labor; it was no longer necessary for legitimate manufacturers to cut wages and work in order to compete with prices set by substandard markets. Labor costs became as stable and as predictable as overhead, and on the whole as uniform as material costs. Wages ceased to be, what they had become during the depression, practically the sole basis of competition.[56]

On the whole, however, the history of the needle trade codes from the passage of the National Industrial Recovery Act on June 16, 1933 to the invalidation of the law by the United States Supreme Court on May 27, 1935 revealed a succession of disappointments for the long-time advocates of industry-wide labor standards. The parties to collective agreements in the New York market who looked with hope to the codes for equalizing the labor costs of production among all competing manufacturers saw their ideals compromised again and again, until the ends achieved by governmental intervention scarcely justified the sacrifice of basic principles which had previously been established through collective bargaining.

During the life of the codes, geographical differentials in labor standards that the New York factions reluctantly conceded as temporary expedients under the codes or that were subsequently introduced by code agencies showed no signs of giving way to more uniform terms of employment. Pressures for stays, tolerances, concessions, exemptions, and allowances increased rather than diminished. Efforts of code authorities to keep down wage

---

[56]Worthy, "The Millinery Industry," p. 112, rephrasing a paragraph from the "Report to the President" that accompanied the government-printed *Amended Code of Fair Competition for the Millinery Industry* (Nov. 9, 1934), p. 13. See also, United Hatters, Cap and Millinery Workers' International Union, Cap and Millinery Department, report of the general executive board in *Report and Proceedings,* Second Convention (First Regular Convention), Oct. 4–7, 1936, pp. 57–68.

differentials were time and again overridden by the authorities in Washington. Political pressures from the hinterlands for differentiating labor costs outweighed political pressures from the New York market for equalizing labor costs. Precedent was on the side of diversity, and governmental officials were reluctant to disturb the status quo lest any disruption of industry swell the ranks of the unemployed.[57]

Although the terms of collective agreements for the apparel industries and the terms of the needle trade codes were essentially alike and in many respects duplicated one another, basic differences soon developed in the way the two systems were applied. These growing distinctions between code administration and contract administration were most evident in areas of special concessions and exemptions to standards set for each trade. While the code administrators permitted generous stays and tolerances over and above geographic wage differentials written into the codes themselves, contract administrators had always held out for rigid controls of any deviations from the terms of collective agreements.

From the days of the first protocols, only the impartial machinery established under collective labor agreements had the power to make concessions, and these exceptions were circumscribed by rigid procedures that minimized the number and character of variations from contract standards. "No employer and no worker or group of workers," stated the 1929 collective agreements of the women's coat and suit trade, "shall have the right to modify or waive any provision of this agreement." And whenever the impartial machinery refused to make exceptions to this rule, it did so without fear that some governmental agency more concerned with alleviating unemployment than with enforcing labor standards would for political reasons override its decisions.[58]

---

[57]The immediate emphasis of the government's recovery program on alleviating unemployment is revealed in H. C. Hoover's "The President's Reemployment Agreement," and in Harry Mulkey's "The So-called Model Code; Its Development and Modification" — two processed Work Materials studies, nos. 82 and 36, respectively, by the National Recovery Administration's Division of Review (March 1936). This emphasis, however deserved, detracted from the main objectives that the organized factions of the needle trades hoped to accomplish through their industry codes.

[58]The firm stand that impartial chairmen under collective agreements have always taken against deviations from contract terms was reflected in an

So long as the administration of needle trade codes was left to New York associations, or to code authorities on which organized groups of the New York market held a controlling hand, there was hope that code intrepretations would follow the precedents and experiences long since accepted through years of collective bargaining. But New York's control over the codes was later dispersed in all directions. Not only were out-of-town organizations and independent firms that had previously been neglected now gaining more and more representation on code agencies, but, what was more important, the NRA administrators in Washington insisted upon having their own chosen representatives sit on code agencies as the eyes and ears of the government. These representatives soon came to wield a strong hand in code policies. With all this, the broad range of legislative and administrative powers originally assumed by code authorities was more and more restricted. Discretion was more limited, powers more clearly defined, decisions more carefully scrutinized, and policy-making functions more frequently exercised from Washington.[59]

The idea that employers' associations and labor unions of New York City operating under the convenient cloak of legalized codes

---

early decision from the Chicago men's clothing market. When a foreman increased piece rates in contravention of the labor agreement and in violation of an arbitration award, Professor H. A. Millis, chairman of the trade board under the collective agreement, ruled that "the action was highly objectionable because it tends to beget discontent, instability in the market, and direct action." These, stated Millis, were the very factors that "the manufacturers, the union, and the impartial machinery have been trying to remove." H. A. Millis, quoted in the Amalgamated Clothing Workers, *The Clothing Workers of Chicago* (1922), p. 207.

In a letter, dated August 1, 1934, to members of the special millinery board established under the NRA code for the millinery industry, Max Zaritsky, president of the United Hatters, Cap and Millinery Workers' International Union, wrote with equal conviction against code deviations but to no avail. "The creation of a group of specially favored employers upon whom you confer unfair competitive advantages as against their competitors and the power of discrimination against a substantial percentage of their workers, is a dangerous precedure," he stated. "It not only defeats the purpose of the N.I.R.A. by sanctioning and perpetuating the unfair competitive practices which it is necessary to uproot if our industry is to be helped, but it also defeats and nullifies the efforts of those who are trying to represent labor constructively and intelligently." Copy filed in the Abelson papers.

[59]See, for example, comments in the *New York Times*, Feb. 18, 1934, and in *Women's Wear Daily*, April 22 and 24, 1934.

would be able to extend the terms of their collective agreements to the four corners of each trade slowly gave way to increasing pressures of interference from out-of-town sources and of dictation from Washington. In some cases, the original code proposals, which, like the first collective agreements, emanated from the New York heart of each industry, had to be compromised before the first codes were ever approved by the President. Further retreats from the high standards of the New York collective agreements were written into the revised codes of fair competition that followed in 1934 and 1935. In short, the adopted needle trade codes of fair competition were too conservative, political pressures supporting the status quo were too great, Washington administrators were too willing to sacrifice principle for expediency.

Enforcing the Codes

The organized forces of the New York market might well have condoned all these retrogressive aspects of code experiences in exchange for the assurance of enforcing the more conservative standards which the code system had set for itself. The evils of geographical wage differentials, of special concessions, and of growing interference from Washington that contributed to the defeat of industry-wide standards might have been overlooked had the National Recovery Administration been able to enforce established code policies uniformly throughout each industry. So great were previous disparities in labor standards between those bound by collective agreements and those who were not that codes of fair competition, for all their shortcomings, represented a forward step toward the goal of uniform labor costs. At least some progress would be made should the limited objectives of the needle trade codes be successfully carried out with the help of the government.

Enforcement of the codes, like the enforcement of collective agreements, was everywhere held to be the paramount problem in establishing a floor under competition. Once the National Industrial Recovery Act had conferred upon government administrators powers that no industry officials had ever enjoyed under collective bargaining, the organized factions of the New York market hastened to utilize these powers to supplement the work of their own impartial machinery operating under collective agreements. For the women's coat and suit trade, at least, the combined efforts of the code authority and the impartial machinery apparently produced some gratifying results. "The year under NRA," announced *Women's Wear Daily* in its first anniversary issue of the National Industrial Recovery Act. "has seen the greatest drive for enforcement and policing of an industry ever witnessed since the first agreements between union and employer were signed. The chisling element was either driven out of the industry or made to meet the standards prescribed."[60]

Nor did the New York manufacturers wish to stop short of more drastic measures within the power of the NRA code systems. Authority to issue and withhold licenses to operate — a power the NIRA would permit only in extreme cases — the New York employers' associations would have their code systems put into operation at once. Both the women's coat and suit trade and the dress and waist industry provided in their proposed codes that all manufacturers outside of New York City who were not already members of an association bound by a collective agreement with the ILGWU be required to obtain an operating license from the industry committee (code authority). Permission to operate under this license would be contingent upon complying with code provisions. Membership in a recognized association would be accepted in lieu of a license, so long as employers kept their association membership in good standing — a requirement that of course embraced compliance with code standards.[61]

---

[60]*Women's Wear Daily*, June 15, 1934. "It was recognized by the Code Authority immediately that unless universal compliance with the code could be secured, no real progress could be made toward carrying out the national recovery program in this industry. . . . The industry itself, for its own protection, recognizes the absolute necessity of obtaining universal compliance with the provisions of the code." M. W. Amberg, director of the millinery code authority, quoted in *ibid.*, April 18, 1934.

In December 1934, the parties to the New York collective agreements of the women's coat and suit trade strengthened their own impartial machinery by establishing a joint "equalization and enforcement board" representing the associations, the ILGWU, and the impartial chairman "to study all problems of the industry such as will tend to bring about greater uniformity and equalization of production costs in the industry and to correct inequality so ascertained in accordance with the terms of the collective agreement." *Ibid.*, Dec. 4, 1934.

[61]See texts of the proposed codes for the women's coat and suit trade and for the dress industry in *ibid.*, July 14, 20, 24, 1933.

After the first needle trade codes were adopted, New York employers' associations and labor unions immediately assumed the role of code agents and proceeded to enforce code provisions with all the techniques and strategies familiar to collective bargaining. Thus, when certain New York firms sought special concessions to match those granted other markets, the unions and employer groups refused to tolerate such deviations from code standards. When certain New York jobbers and inside manufacturers of the women's coat and suit trade sent out their goods to be made up by New Jersey contractors who were operating under a less restrictive state code authority, New York unions and New York associations stopped the practice until New Jersey could be persuaded to rescind its special code and fall in line with federal policy.[62]

In addition, the needle trade unions exerted their own separate pressures upon employers for code enforcement. The millinery workers notified all employers of the industry — independents as well as association members — that infringements of the letter or the spirit of the millinery code would immediately lead to the use of strikes. The ILGWU established a code observance bureau and showed no disposition to wait for slow and cumbersome court proceedings before resorting to direct action against code offenders. Both this union and the fur workers' union were charged with using force and violence to gain compliance with code provisions in the New York market.[63]

For firms beyond the direct control of the parties to collective labor agreements, the enforcement of code provisions was exclusively a problem for federal agents and code authorities — a task which taxed the capacities of all the king's horses and all the king's men. In 1935, the code authority for the millinery industry frankly conceded that it was impossible to set up forces of in-

[62]*Ibid.*, July 27, 1934. "The committee on enforcement reported to the [Code] Authority that they had under inspection the factories of 943 manufacturers and contractors: that they were receiving an average of 518 reports daily, and that the total number of reports to date amounted to 5,052. The committee reported that each of these reports are [*sic*] examined for violations and that 349 were found to contain violations of the millinery code." From an account of enforcement procedures developed during the first five weeks of operation under the code of fair competition for the millinery industry, as given in *ibid.*, Jan. 22, 1934.

[63]*Ibid.*, July 27, 1934; *New York Times*, Sept. 2, 1934; Brickley, "History of the Code of Fair Competition for the Fur Manufacturing Industry."

spection and investigation for the rest of the country that would function as rapidly and effectively as those in New York City. Under the code for cap manufacturing, segments of the industry were so torn by "endless bickerings and wranglings" over comparative labor costs in different markets that a special NRA commission was named to investigate and report its findings. This commission, noted the general executive board of the United Hatters, Cap and Millinery Workers, "confirmed the claim we made all along that, except in name, we had no Code, because the enforcement machinery was wholly and utterly inadequate to accomplish its purpose."[64]

Operating under the terms of the National Industrial Recovery Act, the Federal Trade Commission, the U.S. Department of Justice, and the whole complex machinery of the National Recovery Administration could together offer no adequate substitute for pressures exerted by labor unions and organized employer groups that were already familiar with techniques of enforcing their own labor agreements. For all the delays in operating the machinery of contract administration, governmental agencies of code enforcement were far less able to handle complaints quickly or to render speedy determinations in trades where speed was essential to justice. Battered from pillar to post by the shifting winds of style and season, needle trade industries invariably found that governmental relief came too late to save the victims of code violations.

Far more effective as a weapon of code enforcement was the insignia of the blue eagle displayed in shop windows and the use of code labels attached to garments manufactured under code standards. The authority to issue or withhold labels, first granted under the women's coat and suit code, was subsequently extended to most other needle trade codes but was little used elsewhere. The value of this weapon lay in its application to trade practices as well as to labor standards and in its extension to shops and areas never reached by unions nor bound by collective agreements. Like the previous use of labels under the protocol movement, the presence or absence of an industry code label became far more useful as a symbol for determining when to initiate

---

[64]United Hatters, Cap and Millinery Workers' International Union, Cap and Millinery Department, *Report and Proceedings*, Second Convention (First Regular Convention), Oct. 4–7, 1936, pp. 22–23.

a production or distribution boycott than as a symbol for determining whether consumers should buy or refuse to buy a given product.[65]

In the New York area of the women's coat and suit trade, code label infractions became a violation of collective agreements and so brought down upon the culprit the impartial machinery of collective agreements as well as the separate agencies of code enforcement. Here, the absence of NRA labels attached to the products of the trade became a signal for both types of enforcement agencies to institute production boycotts against non-complying firms. Only those manufacturers entitled to the label could be protected against production boycotts authorized in the code for the retail trade, which stated that "no retailer shall purchase, sell or exchange any merchandise manufactured under a Code of Fair Competition which requires such merchandise to bear an N.R.A. Label, unless such merchandise bears such label." In addition, consumers, above all others, were expected to honor "the little white satin label of the trade with its 'blue eagle' and serial number" carrying "such authority that without it practically no women's coats and suits can be sold today anywhere in the country."[66]

---

[65]Support for code labels among the needle trades was reflected in the formation of the Apparel Codes Label Council, representing nine code authorities (blouse and skirt; coat and suit; dress; garter, suspender, and belt; infants' and children's wear; men's clothing; knitted outerwear; robe and allied products; underwear and negligee products). See NRA Administrative Order no. x-143 (May 15, 1935) entitled "Recognizing the Apparel Codes Label Council and Defining Its Powers and Duties." See also, Administrative Order no. x-135 (Feb. 25, 1935), entitled "Regulations Covering the Use of Labels under Codes of Fair Competition Containing Mandatory Label Provisions."

[66]*New York Times*, editorial, August 12, 1934. Max Meyer, labor arbitrator and chairman of the millinery code authority, saw no other way the codes could be enforced. He contended that the only tangible benefits the codes offered manufacturers came through the operation of label provisions, particularly the prohibitions against use of unlabeled products by the retail trade. *Women's Wear Daily*, Jan. 11, 1935. Use of the NRA label to monopolize production in the hands of selected manufacturers and workers of the women's coat and suit trade is discussed below at pp. 719–721. The women's coat and suit trade went further than did any other industry in working out means of enforcing label requirements — means which included quasi-licensing and provision for registration numbers assigned to each firm. See Robinson, *Collective Bargaining and Market Control in the New York*

Discrepancies in Code Enforcement

Yet the whole array of devices, procedures, and powers at the disposal of the government for code compliance did not prevent shocking disparities in code enforcement, particularly between the New York market and the rest of the country. Original discrepancies in code wage rates and other terms of employment were magnified by inequities in code observance. Predominantly, these differences were most outstanding between firms bound by collective agreements and those that were not. In the one case, the work of governmental agents was supplemented by the contributions of employers' associations and labor unions; in the other, this type of organized support was lacking.

Donald Richberg, general counsel for the NRA, once predicted that the success of the NIRA program would depend upon genuine collective bargaining wherein each organized group of employers and workers would "exercise a corrective influence to prevent abuses of the liberties which are granted to every other group." His predictions were borne out by the vigilance of the organized forces in the New York market toward code enforcement. This vigilance was not limited to wage minimums written into the codes; more important was the provision that wage rates already in effect should in no way be lowered — a clause that automatically incorporated the higher standards of labor agreements into the codes for enforcement purposes. By insisting that codes be enforced on this higher plane, the organized employers and the organized workers of the New York market further aggravated the regional discrepancies in going wage rates.[67]

The result of pressures exerted by parties to collective agree-

Coat and Suit Industry, p. 108. For other pertinent references to studies on the use of insignia and labels as methods of code enforcement, see H. C. Calkin and M. H. Fishbein, "Special List No. 12: Select List of Documents in the Records of the National Recovery Administration." (1954), p. 91, U.S. National Archives. Use of the label under the men's clothing code is treated in Connery, *The Administration of an NRA Code,* p. 82 ff.

[67]The first millinery code contained a clause stating that "the weekly compensation for employment now in excess of the minimum wage herein provided shall not be reduced." This clause, along with special tolerances below the *minimum* occupational wage standards set for each of four areas — tolerances that in some cities were extended to 35% of a firm's labor force — accounts for Max Zaritsky's charge that three large millinery manufacturers had left New York City for Massachusetts where they could operate

ments was that industry codes were generally observed in the previously organized segments of each trade where observance was least needed, and widely circumvented in the previously unorganized markets where minimum labor standards were most essential. One millinery manufacturer from an out-of-town market aptly observed that the codes had made chiselers out of many otherwise honest producers. More serious were the lamentations of a rabbit fur manufacturer that his industry code had provided no escape from a horde of small-time contractors who obtained their labor 30 to 60 percent cheaper under the codes than did the inside manufacturers. "Instead of being relieved by the Code," so he contended, "legitimate Rabbit Manufacturers employing their own workers in their own shops, living up to every rule and regulation of the Code find themselves further handicapped by contractors who are springing up like mushrooms."[68]

Likewise, the inside manufacturers of women's coats and suits were forced to admit that the NRA code had failed to create a "single-standard" industry. Just at the time in the Great Depression that the parties to collective agreements appeared unable to achieve their goals, the inside manufacturers had hailed the NRA with a "wave of hope and enthusiasm that surged over all constructive elements" of the trade. "We reasoned that the power of the government would accomplish what the united strength of the organized groups in the industry had failed to bring about," stated the Industrial Council of Cloak, Suit and Skirt Manufacturers in a letter to the ILGWU, March 1935. But experience under the codes had demonstrated that "protection against ruinous rivalry of irresponsible concerns" had not been forthcoming.[69]

---

under a favorable wage differential of about 50%. Max Zaritsky, president of the United Hatters, Cap and Millinery Workers' International Union, letter dated August 1, 1934, to members of the special millinery board, filed in the Abelson papers.

[68]For the views of a millinery manufacturer, see *Women's Wear Daily*, Jan. 9, 1935. For the lamentations of the rabbit fur manufacturer, see brief submitted at a hearing before the fur manufacturing code authority in New York on July 31, 1934, as quoted in the brief of Pietro Lucchi, president of the International Fur Workers' Union, at a hearing before the National Recovery Administration, March 19, 1935. Copy filed in the Abelson papers.

[69]This letter stated that the employers were conducting negotiations "with the definite understanding that the terms of our collective agreement were

More likely, continued this letter, the women's coat and suit code by giving status to the unorganized firms had served to perpetuate a "two-standard" industry:

> Of course, all Union shops are under the Code also but the term "NRA shop" as now commonly used in the industry refers to the unorganized factories operating under the Code but not under the collective agreements. Prior to the NRA, firms of this kind, which, for obvious reasons, studiously avoided relationship with organized labor and organized employers, were generally classified as sub-standard and were compelled to endure the disfavor which naturally accrued to that status. Competitive advantages gained through pressure upon labor were offset, to some degree, by the disrepute in which such shops were held by the more orderly element in the trade as well as by public opinion. But, under the NRA, those factories have undergone a kind of purification process. It is as if the parasites of yesterday had become the patriots of today.

Although NRA code standards were higher than those to which the unorganized shops had previously been accustomed, greater disparities measured by the standards actually enforced still made those firms "a serious and destructive competitive factor" to the organized elements of the trade.[70]

Union leaders of the millinery industry were equally disillusioned. In the spring of 1935, Max Zaritsky, president of the Cap and Millinery Department, United Hatters, Cap and Millinery Workers, found competition under the codes as vicious as ever. The millinery code authority, so he contended, was helpless to improve the status of the industry nationally; it simply

---

to be made industry-wide in scope through inclusion in the Code of Fair Competition for this trade." The text of the letter is given in *Women's Wear Daily*, March 4, 1935. In his "History of the Code of Fair Competition for the [women's] Coat and Suit Industry" at p. 29, W. A. Simon attributed the successful features of this code's administration to the concentration of the industry in New York City where there existed a high degree of organization among the workers and among the employers.

[70]*Women's Wear Daily*, March 4, 1935. By January 1935, the American Cloak and Suit Manufacturers' Association (contractors) had asked to have the women's coat and suit code amended to put a ban on the assignment and limitation of contractors because the system had not operated to equalize competitive labor costs. *Ibid.*, Jan. 17, 1935.

witnessed the markets fighting each other. By granting to one market certain exemptions that raised a chorus of protests and demands from other markets, the code authority had really aggravated the viciousness of competition in the trade.[71]

Earlier in 1935, Zaritsky had vigorously expressed his opposition to a continuation of special tolerances that had been granted certain out-of-town manufacturers and markets during 1934. "It was hoped," Zaritsky stated, "that the chaotic condition in which the millinery industry was found would be remedied by the equalization of labor costs, which, as the administration has pointed out, was the most vital need of the industry." After noting the contribution that the union had made to this end, Zaritsky concluded. "It is the unanimous opinion of all who have given thought and study to the problems of our industry that unless these labor costs are made equal and kept equal, what little has been achieved during the past year in rehabilitating the industry will be lost and the various factors in it will once more revert to the law of the jungle."[72]

Charges that the codes were inequitably enforced tended to multiply with time. Complaints of code evasions in markets beyond the New York area poured into Washington from many sources. Chicago cloak and suit jobbers were accused of sending work to out-of-town contractors to evade Chicago code rates. The code machinery of the cap manufacturing trade was presumably so helpless to enforce code standards among hundreds of small nonunion shops that the industry became "the property of the least responsible elements in it." Likewise, the executive director of the code authority for the manufacture of men's clothing conceded that intimidation and fear had kept many workers from reporting code infractions while code standards were in some

[71]*Ibid.,* April 11, 1935.

[72]From a 21-page memorandum signed by Max Zaritsky, president, and Alex Rose, vice-president, of the Cap and Millinery Department, United Hatters, Cap and Millinery Workers' International Union. The memorandum was submitted to the special millinery board and a copy directed to Paul Abelson, a member of the board, in a letter, dated Jan. 26, 1935, filed in the Abelson papers. Zaritsky had previously opposed the draft of a revised code for his industry because it perpetuated the evils of special tolerances that imposed unfair competition upon the legitimate elements of the industry. *Women's Wear Daily,* August 3, 1934.

cases being deliberately violated by collusion between workers and employers.[73]

When the millinery code came up for renewal in the spring of 1935 the Eastern Women's Headwear Group, representing some six hundred manufacturers of the New York area and 60 percent of the industry product, opposed code renewal unless the National Recovery Administration could forestall the growth of unfair competition under the code. During the first eighteen months of code operation, the original disparities in wage rates had been magnified by special tolerances, exemptions, and concessions, all of which were further aggravated by inequalities of code enforcement. Charging the Washington authorities with an unequal administration of the law, this New York group termed code violations in such cities as Dallas, Texas, "not only inexcusable but outrageous." The association expressed a willingness to accept a renewal of the code only if the administration in Washington would take immediate steps to remove "competitive injustices foisted upon the industry."[74]

Such charges against code administration had a familiar ring to the sponsors of the protocol movement, who since 1910 had heard similar complaints against the operation of collective bargaining. Of what value was the narrowing of wage differentials in codes of fair competition if code wage scales were not observed uniformly throughout each industry? The cotton textile code —

---

[73]On the Chicago women's coat and suit jobbers, see *ibid.*, June 6, 1934. On the cap manufacturers, see United Hatters, Cap and Millinery Workers' International Union, Cap and Millinery Department, *Report and Proceedings,* Second Convention (First Regular Convention), Oct. 4–7, 1936, p. 22. On the men's clothing code, see the views of G. L. Bell in *Women's Wear Daily,* Jan. 24, 1935.

Not all charges of unequal code enforcement originated in the New York market. In the spring of 1934, Chicago women's coat and suit jobbers told of how they had found it profitable to buy 65% of their finished garments from New York City. "There must be something wrong," observed N. I. Stone, chairman of the women's coat and suit commission investigating comparative labor costs, "where a Chicago jobber finds that instead of having garments made for him by a contractor near Chicago he can make a greater profit by purchasing the garments from a New York jobber." *Ibid.,* June 6, 1934. See the issue of Nov. 8, 1934 for a similar report from Philadelphia dress and waist manufacturers.

[74]*Ibid.,* May 3, 1935, quoting a communication from the Eastern Women's Headwear Group to Max Meyer, chairman of the millinery code authority.

the first code to be approved by the President — had reduced wage differentials in the cotton textile industry between the north and the south from 50 percent to less than 10 percent, but to what avail, if in the absence of collective bargaining, the code standards could not be enforced!

For those who would control competition through collective bargaining, the assets of the code system never showed up where they were most expected. The federal government never became a watchdog to sanction the industry-wide extension of employment standards voluntarily negotiated between the organized factions of labor and management. The National Recovery Administration never developed into an agency for helping the advocates of collective bargaining extend their terms of employment into areas that unions had never penetrated and where collective agreements had never existed. The hope that New York labor standards would be spread by governmental compulsion to the far corners of each trade was never realized. With this futile hope went the false assumption that the government would stand behind the organized forces of the New York market in compelling industry-wide observance of uniform employment standards.

Nor did the acclaimed policy of NRA to help industry govern itself (rather than to impose a government on industry) long survive the pressures from Washington. In some respects, this shifting of control over code administration away from trade associations and labor unions into the hands of government agents adversely affected code enforcement. The objective role that employers' associations working through the impartial machinery of collective agreements had played in gaining compliance with contract terms was subject to severe strain under the codes. With the government bringing charges of noncompliance, many organized employers insisted that their associations defend them, right or wrong. The self-correcting machinery operating within associations under labor agreements lost much of its efficacy under the codes.[75]

---

[75]See Simon, "History of the Code of Fair Competition for the Dress Manufacturing Industry," especially an appendix (pp. 253–280), containing a special report on jobber-contractor relations by special NRA commissioners B. H. Gitchell and A. Feldblum. In this dress industry study, Simon cited the example of the National Dress Manufacturers' Association as one em-

Achievements of the Needle Trade Codes

But the era of the codes did lay the groundwork for more widespread use of collective bargaining. By encouraging the growth of labor unions and employers' associations, the NIRA helped to accomplish the objectives of industry-wide labor standards which had long eluded the sponsors of the protocol movement. Passage of the National Industrial Recovery Act provided the stimulus that hesitant employers had long needed to organize more extensively. "In fact," noted *Women's Wear Daily,* August 25, 1933, "no sooner had the president signed the recovery act than the associations' rosters began to swell.... Firms which have been non-association for years, small and large, now count themselves in the ranks of the organized associations." This increase in the size and number of employer organizations was reflected in the growth and expansion of association-wide labor agreements. Within a year after the NIRA was passed, the general executive board of the ILGWU reported that the union was in contractual relations with sixty-eight different employers' associations in the United States and Canada.[76]

Needle trade unions, likewise, showed a phenomenal rise in memberships. "Labor everywhere is organizing under the incentive of the Recovery Act," exuberantly announced Sidney

---

ployer group that took the position of feeling duty bound to protect its members, not only by ignoring their code violations, but even by helping them to escape the penalties for their code violations. *Ibid.,* appendix, p. 262. See further, pp. 40, 76, and 250 in the body of Simon's study.

[76]ILGWU, *Report and Proceedings,* Twenty-second Convention (May–June 1934), p. 13.

The provisions of the code encouraged the formation of the Clothing Manufacturers Association of the U.S.A. During the years of the NRA, this national association afforded manufacturers in the various markets an opportunity to meet each other personally. The hostile feeling formerly prevalent between the competing centers of clothing production was lessened considerably. Manufacturers now realized that there were many common problems that could be resolved only on a national basis. Whereas previously the clothing industry had been fragmented into many separate markets, the NRA was the catalytic agent that cemented the industry into a national body by means of the CMA.

—Cobrin, *The Men's Clothing Industry: Colonial through Modern Times,* p. 184.

Hillman, president of the Amalgamated Clothing Workers' Union in the summer of 1933. "The shirt industry was almost non-union up to now. In the last eight weeks 20,000 to 30,000 workers have joined the union. This kind of thing is going on everywhere." Even at that time Hillman stated that the workers of the men's clothing industry were already 85 percent organized. Meanwhile, the International Ladies' Garment Workers' Union in less than three years had multiplied its membership eight-fold from a meager 23,876 in 1932 to a booming 198,141 in 1934.[77]

The organized manufacturers who still supported the protocol movement heartily endorsed this transformation. Favorable changes under the dress and waist code, later wrote Mortimer Lanzit, executive director of the National Dress Manufacturers' Association, were not due to the efficiency of code enforcement machinery but to the success of the labor organization in utilizing the Recovery Act to extend its control from 15 percent to over 80 percent of the workers in the dress trade. Similarly, the achievements of the millinery workers' union in gaining a foothold in so many midwestern and southern markets were considered to be a more solid foundation for controlling competition than all the varied wage classifications designated in codes sanctioned by the government.[78]

Aside from the stimulus to the growth of organizations among workers and employers, the era of the codes stressed the importance of collecting, analyzing, and disclosing factual information about each industry — information voluntarily compiled

---

[77]Sidney Hillman in *Christian Science Monitor*, July 11, 1933. The *New York Times* for Oct. 9, 1933 carried an account of David Dubinsky's report to the quarterly meeting of the ILGWU's general executive board in which the union was stated to have increased its membership in six months from 40,000 to 175,000. The impetus that the NIRA gave the ILGWU for successful membership drives is reviewed in ILGWU, *Report and Proceedings*, Twenty-second Convention (May–June 1934), pp. 9–10. See also the membership chart at the front of ILGWU, *Report and Proceedings*, Thirtieth Convention (May 1959).

[78]M. Lanzit, memorandum filed with the NRA, as quoted in *Women's Wear Daily*, Jan. 30, 1935. For growth in the membership of the millinery workers' union, see United Hatters, Cap and Millinery Workers' International Union, *Report and Proceedings*, Second Convention (First Regular Convention), Oct. 4–7, 1936, p. 49. Also see above, p. 497.

and submitted to industry authorities at frequent intervals or else obtainable on demand of administrative agencies through forced inspection of premises and examination of books. For the previously organized segments of each trade, this feature of the codes merely continued existing practices. Utilizing joint or independent research agencies for basic information upon which to negotiate collective agreements had been an established procedure from the inception of the first protocols.[79]

To the previously unorganized segments of each trade, however, the code system introduced the idea of building industry-wide standards of employment upon a solid knowledge of the facts. Special investigations, fact-finding boards, standardized systems of reporting, uniform methods of cost accounting, periodic audits and inspections became a normal phase of business operations. "At least," noted one observer of the women's coat and suit industry on the first anniversary of the NIRA, "the code had enabled the fair-minded and responsible firm to have a definite knowledge of the extent of his competition."[80]

---

[79]Typical were the powers assigned the Bureau of Research established for the women's coat and suit trade during the mid-twenties: "The Bureau shall make such statistical and fact-finding investigations as may be desirable from time to time and build up a body of information about the industry which will enable problems of unemployment, productivity, and wages to be determined intelligently." From the 1927 collective agreement between the American Cloak and Suit Manufacturers' Association and the ILGWU.

[80]*Women's Wear Daily*, June 15, 1934.

> The confidential agency of the Code Authority ... shall have the right ... to require from time to time from members of the industry such reports as it may deem necessary as to wages, hours of labor, costs of production, conditions of employment, number of employees and other matters pertinent to the purpose of this code, and to require members of the industry to submit periodical reports to it in such form and at such times as it may require.
>
> Code of a Fair Competition for the [women's] Coat and Suit Industry, Art. VI, sec. 2 N, as amended.

The 100-page report of a nationwide fact-finding commission for the women's coat and suit trade represented the most successful attempt to survey the problems of an entire industry concerning labor costs, availability of markets, earnings, overhead expenses, complaints, competitive irregularities, working conditions, and the like. "As you know from your own experience, you are sending in transcripts of your payrolls to the Code Au-

In addition, the era of the codes taught the value of self-help in controlling competition for the benefit of the legitimate elements within each trade. Stimulating employers and workers through their own organizations to take the initiative in drafting and enforcing codes of fair competition had been a prime objective of the national recovery program from the outset. "It is not the function of the National Recovery Administration to prescribe what shall be in the codes to be submitted by associations or groups," so NRA *Bulletin* no. 2 of June 19, 1933, had announced. "The initiative in all such matters is expected to come from within the industry itself."

But the failure of these industries, exercising their new prerogatives, to keep within the limitations of the public interest led to a gradual transfer of code responsibilities to governmental agencies operating out of Washington — a development which tended to drive home even more forcibly the lesson of self-help in regulating competition. For the complexities and delays inherent in the system of code administration that was finally devised, coupled with the ignorance of industry conditions and the political maneuverings so often characteristic of governmental officials, soon demonstrated beyond doubt that the federal government was less capable of developing and administering successful codes of fair competition than were the industries themselves.

While the organized factions of each trade welcomed help from the government in carrying out their own programs, they did not want governmental dictation of industry policies. "One of the glaring weaknesses of the NRA," stated Alexander Printz, chairman of the National Coat and Suit Industry Recovery Board, in 1936, "was the fact that federal supervision seemed to be something apart from an industry — or even unfriendly to it — instead

thority," stated N. I. Stone, chairman of the commission, to the San Francisco cloak manufacturers. "So, for the first time in the history of the industry, there is one place where the earnings of every individual in the coat and suit industry anywhere in the United States are reported accurately week by week." As quoted in Robinson, *Collective Bargaining and Market Control in the New York Coat and Suit Industry,* p. 117, citing the NRA Transcript of Hearings Conducted by the Fact Finding Commission in San Francisco, June 13, 1934. The commission's report was printed in a special supplement to *Women's Wear Daily,* July 27, 1934, and in NRA: Division of Review, "Work Materials," no. 10 (March 1936).

of an integral factor of its operation and development." He recommended to the federal coordinator of industry at the time that a new NRA be established along the lines of the NCSIRB. "We sincerely hope," he said, "that any new recovery program will not billet upon the industry a force of officials hastily recruited for the purpose and who regard with ill-disguised suspicion the members of the trade in which they are quartered."[81]

Before the NIRA was invalidated, the Associated Fur Coat and Trimming Manufacturers threatened to withdraw from the fur code authority unless politics was eliminated and unless government administrators learned something of the nature of the industry. As a condition of continued participation, this association demanded that the code authority be "immediately reorganized so that the code may be administered impartially with force, vigor and intelligence and upon all members of the industry alike." In similar vein, the general executive board of the millinery workers' international union conceded that the death of the NIRA had "merely ended the wrangling which had marked the effort to codify the industry from the very first day that the law was passed." By striking down the act, so this board observed, the Supreme Court had "foreclosed any hope that still remained that law and government could be helpful in compelling employers to do what they lacked the foresight and ability to do for themselves." The code system, apparently, had already outlived its usefulness.[82]

Concluding Observations

When a special NRA commission for the women's coat and suit industry, after investigating comparative production costs in

[81]*Women's Wear Daily,* Nov. 13, 1936. "We have had only Government regulation and regimentation by a varied assortment of administrators, who were not, in most cases, at all familiar with the industry as a whole." Central West Garment Association, Des Moines, Iowa, to the Committee on Finance, U.S. Senate, 74th Cong., 1st sess., Hearings, pursuant to S. Res. 79: *Investigation of the National Recovery Administration* (April 1935), Part 6, p. 2730.

[82]For views of the fur manufacturers, see *Women's Wear Daily,* Nov. 6, 1934. For views of the millinery workers' union, see United Hatters, Cap and Millinery Workers' International Union, Cap and Millinery Department, *Report and Proceedings,* Second Convention (First Regular Convention), Oct. 4–7, 1936, p. 24. The NIRA was invalidated in Schechter Poultry Corp. v. U.S., 295 U.S. 495 (May 27, 1935).

thirteen leading markets, reached the conclusion that wage rates and other labor costs were the only variables of any consequence, it revealed the motive that had given direction to the needle trade codes of fair competition. For, if variations in labor standards and labor costs largely accounted for the presence of "illegitimate" competition, then the only logical course was to see that codes of fair competition eliminated these evils. The history of the needle trade codes reveals an overwhelming emphasis given to standardizing terms of employment — issues that largely fell within the scope of collective bargaining — while relatively little attention was devoted to the introduction of "fair trade practices" as a method of regulating competition.

Critical issues that disturbed code administrators for the needle trades were precisely those that had plagued the sponsors of the protocol movement since 1910. Parties to collective agreements who had attempted for so long to extend New York labor standards into the far corners of each trade now sought the same objectives under the codes. Those that opposed the imposition of New York labor agreements upon the rest of the country now opposed the extension of those terms under codes of fair competition. Both under collective bargaining and under the codes, the organized forces of the New York market fought the unorganized forces of other markets on such issues as (1) flat minimum wage rates vs. classified wage minima; (2) industry-wide uniformity vs. geographical differentials in wage rates; (3) centralization of control over administrative machinery by New York City where most of the products were made vs. dispersion of control to reflect potential developments in other parts of the country; and (4) sharp restrictions on concessions and exemptions from established standards vs. generous use of concessions and exemptions to reflect existing differentials in labor costs.

Under the codes, as under collective bargaining, the most vital issue in labor standards was one of enforcement. Here, the overpowering weapon of governmental compulsion available to code administrators had no counterpart under collective bargaining. In the long run, however, this "Big Bertha" of governmental intervention, particularly in the hands of uninformed politicians, was found too unwieldy for timely manipulation required to save the victims of unfair competition in the needle trades. At the end, contract administrators were accomplishing more toward saving the labor standards of the codes than code administrators were accomplishing to save the labor standards of collective agreements or, for that matter, to save the standards of the codes themselves.

Chapter 17

Monopolies and
Fair Trade Practices

WHEREVER attempts to eliminate competition in labor costs approached the goal of one employers' association, one labor union, and one collective agreement for each industry, the charge was sure to be made that the sponsors of the protocol movement were creating monopolies in restraint of trade. These charges became the more impressive where the organized factions of an industry, having gained the power to dictate terms of employment, shut their doors to additional members. Attempts by labor unions and employers' associations to exclude those workers and employers who were incapable of countributing to the stability of their industries invariably aroused suspicions of violating the antitrust laws. At its worst, collective bargaining became a blind to hide collusion between closed labor unions and closed employers' associations for the purpose of raising wages and increasing profits to the mutual benefit of both parties but to the lasting detriment of the public interest.[1]

Such charges were generally based on the assumption that lines

---

[1] "It is the tendency of the Protocol, first to make of the trade a closed corporation; secondly, to eliminate the small manufacturer; thirdly, to force the hands of parties that are not signatories thereto." A newcomer to the trade, quoted by J. Fuchs, "The Viewpoint of the Small Manufacturer," in *Women's Wear*, July 11, 1913. At that time, the newcomer quite inaccurately predicted that once the independents were frozen out, "the friendship between the Association and the unions will spring a leak."

of distinction between the regulation of trade practices and the control of labor standards had been obliterated. Division of markets among employers had gone hand in hand with division of job opportunities among workers. Price-fixing and wage setting were inseparable phases of the same operation. Production controls had accompanied control over hours, wages, and working conditions. Even the lowly immigrant could understand that higher wages and better working conditions were limited by the price of the product and the size of the profits. Particularly where the jobber-contracting system prevailed was the fixing of prices contractors received for their products tied to the fixing of piece rates workers received for their labor. Each factor was directly affected by the other.

An Example in Fur Dressing

Some of the worst elements of monopoly controls through collective bargaining were brought to light in the experiences of the fur dressing industry during the late twenties and early thirties. The typical fur dressing employer of that era joined his association "to improve and stabilize conditions in that industry and to eliminate trade abuses." At the same time, he expressly authorized his organization "to prepare standard agreements to cover contractual relations with employees or others and to cover other conditions common to substantially all members." Armed with this vast range of general powers, his association could strike out in all directions against unwanted competitors. In any such move, whether directed toward minimum labor standards or fair trade practices, the fur workers' union often became a willing collaborator, if not the director of the plot.[2]

At a conference on January 14, 1925, between the Fur Dressers' and Fur Dyers' Association and Locals 2 and 3 of the International Fur Workers' Union, the system of competitive bidding among contractors for skins to be processed was roundly de-

---

[2]An agreement fixing prices for rabbit dressing is reported in *Women's Wear Daily*, March 2, 1927. The text of an agreement on trade practices among members of the Associated Fur Manufacturers appears in the issue of Feb. 24, 1928. A copy of the 1928 agreement between the Fur Dressers' and Fur Dyers' Association and each of its members regulating trade practices in the fur dressing and fur dyeing industry is filed in the Abelson papers.

nounced. Union spokesmen insisted that the employers themselves were to blame for tolerating this type of unwanted competition:

> The Union desires to say that it is not our fault. The bosses say
> "I am sorry; I would like to give you boys work, but what shall I do
> with the other fellow who takes a fox or mink at five cents or ten cents
> cheaper?" The bosses in Brooklyn say they can't compete with other
> localities.
>
> Why can't they get all one price and not cheat the other ones? Why
> should they say "we can't compete with the other localities," when
> they do that? . . .
>
> It is up to the bosses, they should be hand in hand and for one
> price. It is not the fault of the Union. We only want to make a
> decent living.

When an employer representative hastened to explain that the
proposed plan would land employers in jail for violating the antitrust laws, a second union spokesman came to the defense of his
comrade: "He didn't mean, you should go and hit a man on the
head. He meant that you should go and organize and make it a
uniform price for all."[3]

So well, apparently, did the rabbit dressing employers apply
this principle that, in 1928, some 95 percent of them were alleged
to be in collusion to control prices and allocate work. Moreover,
the fur workers' union was charged with supporting the scheme in
order to obtain higher wages. One independent dressing firm
sought an injunction to restrain the Consolidated Rabbit Dressing
Corporation (a convenient vehicle of the organized rabbit dressers) from impeding competition, fixing prices, limiting the plaintiff's freedom of contract, and inducing strikes among the plaintiff's workers as a means of enforcing industry controls. Simultaneously, this corporation came under attack from the American
Rabbit Fur Dealers' and Importers' Association, an association

---

[3]*Minutes,* Conference Representing Fur Dressers' and Fur Dyers' Association as Employers and Locals 2 and 3 of the International Fur Workers'
Union, as Employees (Jan. 14, 1925), pp. 31–32. The concern of the union
with the managerial problems of the trade was enhanced by the fact that
labor costs constituted 80 percent of the total expense of operating the fur
dressing and fur dyeing business. See U.S. v. Fur Dressers' and Fur Dyers'
Association, U.S. District Court, New York, 5 F 2nd 869 (1925) at p. 869.

that had given the corporation exclusive rights to dress rabbit skins. The dealers threatened to terminate their exclusive contract should the dressers again raise prices to meet union demands.[4]

A similar combination of forces to control output and fix prices was organized in 1931 during a strike-lockout over the terms of a new collective agreement between the Associated Employers of Fur Dressers and the International Fur Workers' Union. To strengthen their position, members of the employers' association formed the Co-operative Fur Dressers — a corporation that sought to fill all orders for business during the strike by operating a few plants only. Holding a monopoly position, the Co-operative was able to establish a uniform price for dressing furs — a price that ran about 10 percent higher than the previous competitive level.[5]

This strategy of the organized employers led to a compromise settlement with the union. The association gave up its demand for a 30 percent wage reduction inspired by the depression, and in return the union agreed that the association might concentrate

---

[4]In 1927, the Consolidated Rabbit Dressing Corporation was reported to have negotiated with the American Rabbit Importers' and Dealers' Association a three-year agreement that not only fixed prices for fur dressing but was also expected to produce an exclusive relationship between the two associations. The dealers were to give all their work to this group of dressers, and the dressers' association was to work exclusively for the dealers' association. *Women's Wear Daily,* Jan. 1, 1927.

The files of *Women's Wear Daily* and of *Fur Age Weekly* from 1927 through the early thirties provide the best available sources of information on the monopolistic activities of the fur dressers and dyers. Numerous clippings from these papers for this period are collected in the Abelson papers.

[5]See the files of *Women's Wear Daily* for October and November 1931; and see *Fur Age Weekly,* Nov. 26, 1931. On Dec. 18, 1928, the members of the Associated Employers of Fur Workers (dressers) had entered into an agreement with their association giving it the power, through a committee on the preparation of a new contract, to negotiate a 1929 agreement with the fur workers' union; and, in the absence of such an agreement, to create a "management period" during which this committee would be authorized "to operate all or any number of the plants of the Members, to operate any plant at full or part capacity, to close any plant in all or in part, to operate some plants and to close others, all in its absolute discretion." Profits and losses were to be prorated; and for a violation of the agreement any firm might be assessed up to $5,000 in damages. A copy of this agreement is filed in the Abelson papers.

the work of its thirty-two member firms in ten of its leading shops at least until January 31, 1932. A representative of the employers estimated that the plan "would save the association members $50,000 in use of trucks, delivery, salesmen, overhead and other economies." In addition, he predicted that the concentration measure "would stabilize the trade and arrest the cutthroat competition which had driven a number of fur dressing plants out of business."[6]

The procedures developed in these cases became a pattern for regulating competition in the fur dressing trade. Within the next few years, other groups of unions and associations assumed the power to fix prices, allocate work, and control output. In some cases, monopoly control was established with the help of racketeers operating in the camps of both labor and management. "Lepke" and "Gurrah" (Louis B. Buchalter and Jacob Shapiro), known as the gorilla boys, used forceful devices to monopolize the industry and restrain trade. They were charged with violating the Sherman Antitrust Act and indicted for organizing the Protective Fur Dressers' Corporation "with the avowed purpose of eliminating all competition and fixing prices in the industry."[7]

But combinations and conspiracies for monopoly control over the fur dressing trade were allegedly far more widespread than the limited evidences of open racketeering. In November 1933, the U. S. Department of Justice began antitrust action against five labor organizations and sixty-eight corporations in the trade. Included were members of the Protective Fur Dressers' Corporation and members of the Fur Dressers' Factor Corporation. Both groups were charged with using violence to compel other fur dressers to join their ranks. At the same time, the indictments charged that "beginning in January, 1931, and continuously thereafter the defendants entered into a conspiracy to prevent

---

[6]The quotations are from *Women's Wear Daily,* Nov. 23, 1931. The employers put up a $25,000 bond to insure the return of all the workers to their jobs after January 31, 1932. The files of *Women's Wear Daily* and of *Fur Age Weekly* during the fall and winter of 1931–1932 contain several articles dealing with this problem.

[7]In November 1936, Buchalter and Shapiro were convicted by the courts, fined $10,000 each, and sentenced to serve two years in jail. *New York Times,* Nov. 13, 1936; *Fur Age Weekly,* Nov. 16, 1936.

dealers outside of their group from shipping, selling and delivering skins in New York City."[8]

The leading fur dressing case of conspiring to restrain trade reached the United States Circuit Court of Appeals in 1938. There, the court found that three corporations — Factor, Associated, and Allied — whose members constituted a large majority of employers dressing fur skins in New York and New Jersey, were engaged in a conspiracy permitting members to control and dominate fur dressing throughout the metropolitan area. As usual, the fur workers' union was involved in the scheme. This conspiracy, stated the court, was designed to (a) eliminate competition among fur dressers; (b) fix minimum prices to be charged by dressers in the three associations; (c) pool all orders for dressing and allot them on a quota basis; (d) coerce nonmember dressers into becoming members; (e) employ members of fur workers' unions only; (f) increase the wages of the union members. The specific issue in this case of concern to collective bargaining involved the question of whether the union, to the extent that it cooperated with the three organizations in carrying out their conspiracy, had in effect participated in a restraint of trade.

The union contended that it was not engaged in furthering the *unlawful* ends of the employers but in furthering the *lawful* ends of the union. If the pressure for higher wages caused the employers to enter into an illegal conspiracy, the union was not a party to the action. The court found evidence, however, that the union had urged the dressers to form an association that could raise prices in order to pay better wages. The evidence also showed that, after the "Factor Corporation" was formed, the union participated in furthering a conspiracy by urging recalcitrant employers to join the association. The union had even refused to supply one dresser with labor until he joined the new organization, although the dressing firm was willing to pay the

---

[8]*New York Times,* Nov. 7, 1933. At one stage of development, according to the court testimony of Abe Beckerman, strong-arm henchman of "Lepke" and "Gurrah," independent fur dressing firms were forced through threats, violence, and sheer brutality into joining the Fur Dressers' Factor Corporation, after which prices for dressing furs immediately soared 30 percent over those previously prevailing in the open competitive market. Beckerman's testimony before the U.S. District Court was reported in *Women's Wear Daily,* June 17, 1938. See also an article in the June 15, 1936 issue on several potential methods of controlling prices in the fur dressing trade.

union scale of wages and to sign a standard union contract. On the other hand, the court found no evidence that the union had participated in a reign of terror to get employers into an association. The court concluded that the union was privileged to advise employers to join a lawful association but that it was not privileged to advise joining Factor Corporation, whose purpose was known to be suppression of competition in the fur dressing industry.[9]

Trade Associations and Collective Bargaining

State and federal laws that ensnared the advocates of monopoly controls in the fur dressing industry were a constant threat to other branches of the needle trades. In so far as labor unions and employers' associations operated through collective agreements to restrain trade for their mutual advantages, they were open to charges of illegal conduct under the Sherman Act, the Clayton Act, the Federal Trade Commission Act, as well as under state antitrust laws. Where the parties to collective agreements did not openly and directly violate these statutes, they might still be charged with indirectly supporting unfair methods of competition or indirectly contributing to illegal conspiracies in restraint of trade. For there were no hard and fast lines of demarcation between collective bargaining that lawfully determined the conditions of employment and collective bargaining that unlawfully restrained trade.

Charges that collective bargaining had become a tool for restricting competition and illegally restraining trade were supported by the dual character of employer groups that participated in contract negotiations with labor unions. Many of these employer bargaining groups had previously operated as trade associations established for business and commercial purposes. Under pressure to deal with unions, existing trade groups took on the added function of negotiating labor contracts. Each group hired a labor director with a staff of assistants and conducted its meetings in the double capacity of an employers' association and a trade association.

Comparatively few employer groups in the needle trades were

---

[9]U.S. v. International Fur Workers' Union, U.S. Circuit Court of Appeals, 100 F 2nd 541 (1938).

formed solely for purposes of collective bargaining. Even those that were organized expressly for labor relations soon expanded their activities to include trade relations. Under the power to "foster and promote the industry," the organized manufacturers turned their bargaining agencies into institutions for handling business and commercial problems. Having mastered the art of working together in labor relations, they extended their collaboration into the realm of industrial competition and fair trade practices. Still other associations attributed their origin to the need for machinery to administer the NRA codes during the thirties. Organized to help create and administer codes of fair competition — codes that embraced both labor provisions and fair trade practices — these employer groups, after the death of the codes, continued the broad range of functions to which they had become accustomed under the blue eagle.

Many employer groups began as mixed associations in that they were endowed by their constitutions and by-laws with power both to negotiate labor agreements and to exercise the normal functions of trade groups. Thus, the Cloth Hat and Cap Manufacturers' Association of New York was organized about the close of the first World War "to secure and provide co-operation and united effort in all matters relating to the improvement of conditions in the cap manufacturing industry, including (a) the adjustment of grievances between members; (b) the establishment of trade regulations; (c) the handling of industrial disputes between members and their employees; (d) the establishment of improved conditions in the industry and elimination of unfair or improper practices in the industry; and (e) generally, in all matters tending to the uplift or improvement of the industry, in all its business, social and moral aspects."[10]

---

[10]A printed copy of the constitution, by-laws, and collective agreement of the association is filed in the Abelson papers. The text of the first constitution of the Industrial Council of Cloak, Suit and Skirt Manufacturers appears in *Women's Wear,* July 17, 1924.

The American Cloak and Suit Manufacturers' Association (contractors), formed in 1919 to represent the "legitimate" contractors in the women's coat and suit trade, also spanned the two fields of labor relations and trade controls. Between 1919 and 1929, this association's labor department handled 11,778 reported labor cases; its legal department acted upon 1,039 court cases; its jobbing department adjusted 4,674 complaints against jobbers and collected $1,460,837.61 for its members; its credit department helped to

The Merchants' Ladies' Garment Association

More typical of the active employer groups endowed with mixed trade and labor functions was the dominant association of jobbers in the women's coat and suit trade. Officially established in 1917 "to create stability in the industry and provide a medium through which all disputes may be amicably adjusted and standards for the trade created," the Merchants' Ladies' Garment Association from the outset emphasized its trade functions by aligning with the organized inside manufacturers of the women's cloak and dress industries and with several large associations of retailers to form the Garment Conference Council of wholesalers and retailers — an organization created solely for business purposes, principally for regulating the terms and conditions of sale of manufactured products.[11]

At the same time, the Merchants' Ladies' Garment Association also became a party to another joint committee which included the Associated Woolen and Worsted Manufacturers as well as the Cloak, Suit and Skirt Manufacturers' Protective Association — two associations comprising the major suppliers and the major purchasers, respectively, of raw materials for the manufacture of women's coats and suits. Thus, in the very first year of its existence, the Merchants' Ladies' Garment Association had extended its business and commercial ties over both the suppliers of raw materials and the distributive outlets for its products. These con-

---

minimize bankruptcy losses; and its retail collection department assisted its members in collecting from its customers $69,741.71 which might otherwise have been lost. From a report to the association's tenth convention, April 16, 1929. Copy filed in the Abelson papers.

[11]Within two years of its formation, the Merchants' Ladies' Garment Association grew from 29 members to 140 members to include practically all the important jobbers in the New York women's coat and suit trade. See John Dickinson and Morris Kolchin, *Report of an Investigation* (processed), submitted to Governor Alfred E. Smith's Advisory Commission on the women's coat and suit trade (March 10, 1925), p. 10. See also a typewritten statement entitled, "The Objects and Purposes of This Association," signed by Paul Prager, general secretary of the association, and filed in the Abelson papers.

The Garment Conference Council had been set up in the summer of 1917 under an agreement between four associations of manufacturers and wholesalers of women's garments, on the one hand, and three giant associations of retailers, on the other. *Women's Wear,* Feb. 4 and 24, 1921.

tacts laid the foundation for establishing fair trade practices, quite apart from the subsequent role of the association as a collective bargaining agent.[12]

When this association of jobbers, along with corresponding groups of contractors and inside manufacturers, subsequently came to negotiate collective agreements with the ILGWU, it seldom differentiated its agencies and activities devoted to labor relations from its agencies and activities concerned with business problems. This fusion was inevitable from the very nature of the collective labor agreements. Not only was the usual machinery for labor contract administration sometimes accompanied by special trade agencies on which the union was represented, but the whole structure as well as function of collective bargaining was assumed to embrace the trade interests of employers as well as the labor interests of the organized workers. "The leadership of the Merchants' Ladies' Garment Association," announced Samuel Blumberg, association counsel in 1932, "has always tried in writing its contract with the International Ladies' Garment Workers' Union to take into account the needs and stabilizing requirements of all who participate in the industry."[13]

Further evidences of the wedding between trade and labor functions in this association were disclosed by two public advertisements in the *Women's Wear Daily* for May 2 and 9, 1933, shortly before the National Industrial Recovery Act became law. Under the caption, "Labor Relations and Stabilization in the Cloak and Suit Industry," the Merchants' Ladies' Garment Association publicly explained in the first of these advertisements

---

[12]In July 1925, Maxwell Copelof, president of the Merchants' Ladies' Garment Association, announced plans (1) to analyze "the outstanding problems and practices in our relations with those from whom we buy," including suggestions and proposed agreements "to make those relations more business-like and mutually helpful"; (2) "to prepare a similar analysis and tentative program to deal with our relations with those we sell to." *Women's Wear,* July 10, 1925.

[13]"We are definitely committed to a complete trade organization and for substantial control of both management and labor, recognizing the definite functions of business promotion, distribution and production, and that each is entitled to the proper amount of protection and support in the official performance of its specific program." Samuel Blumberg, as quoted in *Women's Wear Daily,* July 19, 1932.

the purpose and extent of its ties with the International Ladies' Garment Workers' Union:

> Beneath all association activities in the cloak and suit industry lies a single powerful mainspring — the Labor Union. The Merchants' Ladies' Garment Association has recognized this factor and dealt with it helpfully.
>
> The joining of forces with the union in helping to stabilize the industry through enforcement of adequate standards will assure equalized production costs to all fellow merchants.[14]

Then one week later under a second caption, "Trade Regulations and Stabilization in the Cloak and Suit Industry," this association further stated its views:

> The Trade Regulations providing for standard 8% discount in the Cloak and Suit Trade, as well as other Trade Regulations pertaining to transportation charges, communication charges, labels, consignment sales, cancellations, returns, have been approved as helpful stabilizing rules assuring equal terms and conditions to all responsible retailers, and the elimination of one phase of unfair competition which ultimately results in lowering labor standards.

This public announcement was followed by a joint statement of Maxwell Copelof, executive director, and Samuel Blumberg, counsel of the association, stressing the one outstanding problem yet to be resolved at all costs, namely, "the complete unionization of the industry to which all factors must contribute to the limit of their ability."[15]

Few, if any, of the association's trade activities were inherently illegal whether conducted directly or through the medium of collective bargaining — whether exercised alone, through other employer groups, or with the help of labor unions. In most cases, legality hinged upon the purpose or the effect of the particular trade regulation in question. But the parties to collective agreements were obviously suitable agencies for promoting fair or unfair trade practices. They were obviously familiar with the problems of competition which gave rise to combinations and conspiracies in restraint of trade. Less obvious was the role collective

---

[14]*Ibid.*, May 2, 1933. The advertisement was signed by O. J. Rubin, president of the association, and by Maxwell Copelof, executive director.

[15]*Ibid.*, May 9, 1933.

bargaining actually played in trespassing upon the prohibitions of antitrust legislation. Wherever labor agreements endorsed trade practices or trade agreements embraced labor policies, the institutions and processes of collective bargaining were at least subject to contamination by illegal movements to restrain trade.

Bargaining for What Purpose?

Forceful arguments can be adduced to support the view that collective bargaining in the needle trades has always been employer-oriented toward the elimination of "trade" abuses. In so far as the objectives of collective bargaining were officially stated in terms of "uplifting the industry" or "stabilizing the trade" or "stamping out the evils of the trade," the generally assumed motive of improving labor standards for the sake of the workers has no more validity than the less publicized motive of abolishing trade abuses for the sake of the manufacturers. Not only were certain employer-oriented clauses — "maintenance of a high order of discipline and efficiency," "assurance of proper quantity, quality, and cost of production," and "maintenance of good standards of workmanship and conduct" — inserted into contracts at the behest of management, but wage negotiations themselves could be diverted from the "labor" issue of inadequate living standards to the "trade" issue of unwarranted variations in labor costs.[16]

Between 1925 and 1927, New York City's production of men's clothing fell in value by $16,000,000 annually, while Philadelphia's corresponding production rose in value by $30,000,000 annually. "Philadelphia undersells New York because of its over-worked and under-paid labor," stated *Advance,* the official organ of the Amalgamated Clothing Workers. Opposing such competition between New York employers and Philadelphia employers "because in the final count that kind of manufacturers' competition means competition between the clothing workers of Philadelphia and of New York," the union conducted a strike against New York jobbers who sent their suit materials out to be made up by Philadelphia's nonunion contractors, though such a closed-shell union policy could further hamper the sale of New York clothing. More

---

[16]The quoted clauses are from the 1919 collective agreement between the Associated Clothing Manufacturers of Toronto, Canada, and the Amalgamated Clothing Workers of America, printed in the *Daily News Record,* August 26, 1919.

realistically, the union set out to organize the workers of the Philadelphia market to save their own jobs in New York City. "The [organizing] work in Philadelphia is important," announced the head of the union's Eastern Organization Department, "because Philadelphia can make a grave-yard of New York." But who would assume that the union's battle conducted in "foreign" lands to save New York City's labor standards was any less a battle to save the New York market for the manufacturers as well?[17]

Furthermore, the range of powers conferred upon permanent agencies of contract administration under needle trade agreements was seldom if ever limited to fulfilling the objectives of higher wages, shorter hours, and better working conditions. Permitting the impartial machinery to take whatever course would foster and promote the trade gave no sense of direction to contract administrators. Certainly the 1915 collective agreement between the Associated Boys' Clothing Manufacturers of Greater New York and the Amalgamated Clothing Workers' Union never shackled the powers of the joint agencies it created by providing that "any abuses that may exist or arise in the industry, regardless whether same affects either members or non-members of this Association shall be referred to a Committee representing both sides, whose duties shall be to make every effort to eliminate or remedy the same."[18]

---

[17]Facts and quotations are from U.S. District Judge W. H. Kirkpatrick's opinion in Alco-Zander v. Amalgamated Clothing Workers of America, U.S. District Court, E.D. Penn., 35 F. 2nd 203 (1929), at p. 204. "Just as the coal miners' union [in Pennsylvania] died, not because of Pennsylvania, but because of [non-union] West Virginia, so is New York dependent on what will happen not in New York but in Philadelphia. It is in Philadelphia that we must first stop reductions. Fifteen thousand tailors there can break New York." *Ibid.*, quoting a member of the union's general executive board. ACWA's *Advance* assumed that the union had no objections to competition between New York manufacturers and Philadelphia manufacturers so long as that competition was conducted "on the basis of industrial efficiency and managerial and distributive ability," *ibid*.

[18]From a copy of the agreement filed in the Abelson papers. See also the *Daily Trade Record,* August 28, 1915. Under the 1925 collective agreements for the dress industry, the ILGWU and the Association of Dress Manufacturers each contributed five delegates to sit on a Joint Conference Board created "for the purpose of from time to time considering and passing upon general trade problems and to more effectually carry out the purpose and spirit of this agreement." *Women's Wear,* Jan. 19, 1925.

Nor did the 1926 collective agreement between the Hat and Cap Wholesalers' Association of New York City and the Joint Council of New York City representing Locals 1, 2, 3, 17, 23, 30, and 40 of the Cloth Hat, Cap and Millinery Workers' International Union seriously restrict the scope of the bargaining function by providing for a joint committee on welfare "with a view of bettering conditions of the cloth hat and cap industry and the checking and eliminating of trade abuses." Reporting to the sixteenth biennial convention of the international union in May 1927, the union's general executive board listed the creation of this joint committee on welfare as being "among the important gains accomplished by that settlement."[19]

In the fall of 1931, when the newly organized Women's Headwear Group of several hundred millinery manufacturers moved to reinstate collective bargaining with the millinery workers after a lapse of ten years, Jules Weil, president of the association, considered the time ripe "for both groups collectively to co-operate . . . to jointly work towards the stamping out of illegitimate practices and racketeering that has crept into our industry." Both the association and the union appealed for help to Acting Governor H. H. Lehman, who expressed the belief "that increased stability and order could be brought into the industry through the inauguration of collective relations and the joint working out of a constructive program in the interest and protection of all legitimate factors of the industry."[20]

Collective bargaining in the needle trades has been conducted more often on a theme of comparative labor costs — a logical em-

[19]Cloth Hat, Cap and Millinery Workers' International Union, *Report and Proceedings,* Sixteenth Biennial Convention (May 1927), pp. 179, 232. The text of this agreement, effective Sept. 2, 1926, appears as Appendix no. 2, of these *Proceedings,* pp. 230–232; and in *Women's Wear Daily,* Sept. 29, 1926. See also the *Headgear Worker,* April 29, 1927.

[20]*Women's Wear Daily,* Oct. 6, 1931. The early results of this first agreement, March 4, 1932, favored the organized employers as much as the organized workers. "For a period of two weeks, between the signing of the agreement with the Women's Headwear Group and the historic meeting in Cooper Union," stated Max Zaritsky, president of the Cloth Hat, Cap and Millinery Workers' International Union, "our volunteers carried a relentless warfare into the camp of the enemy. Every day scab strongholds were dislodged . . . 30 racketeer shops were captured by the Union Army of Crusaders." Max Zaritsky, "The Millinery Workers Turn the Tide" (pamphlet, 1932), at p. 12. Copy in the Abelson papers.

ployer objective — than on the theme of minimum worker income
— a logical union objective. Recurring demands for wage increases
at the bargaining table have aroused less concern than the spread
of differentials in wage rates among competing producers. A
"most favored employer" clause that guaranteed to all employers
bound by the agreement as favorable labor terms as the union had
conceded to any other employers in the trade was obviously an
employer-oriented provision common to most major labor agreements of the needle trades. But its *union-oriented* counterpart —
a "most favored worker" clause guaranteeing to all union members bound by the agreement as favorable labor terms as the
union had exacted from any other employers in the trade — was
so rare as to be practically nonexistent. Personal favoritism and
rank discrimination that cried out for industrial justice among the
workers were less momentous issues at the bargaining table than
were the problems of how to establish and maintain uniform conditions of employment. Committees on standards have had a more
prominent place in the history of collective bargaining than committees on grievances.[21]

Piece-rate determination has been less a question of how to
prevent inequities in wages and standards of living among workers than it has been a question of how to maintain equality in
labor costs among competing manufacturers. In the millinery
trade, emphasis on comparative labor costs, rather than on general
wage levels, has characterized the history of collective bargaining
since 1915. This emphasis was carried over into the period of the
NRA codes, then returned to the bargaining table thereafter.
"The Association and the Union are desirous of obtaining equali-

---

[21]During the 1919 negotiations of the collective agreement between the
Cloak, Suit and Skirt Manufacturers' Protective Association (party to the
first protocol) and the ILGWU, *Women's Wear* reported that the manufacturers "are unanimous in their views that the underlying basis for the
negotiations now pending is the standardization of the industry, a standardization through the elimination from it of those influences which tend to
make competition for the manufacturers...a competition of cut-throat
slashing by certain unscrupulous offenders of basic business ethics." To accomplish this objective, the manufacturers favored "a unionization of the
entire working force of the industry which may bring about one standard
for all shops both large and small" — an objective that might well lead to
"the elimination of the small submanufacturer who may find himself unable to meet the requirements of the union." *Ibid.*, May 17, 1919.

zation of labor costs as far as possible," runs the major 1936 collective agreement of the millinery trade. "Both parties agree to work out such methods of adjusting piece prices and such standards of piece rates as will effect an equalization of the cost of labor in the industry."[22]

Certainly, the practice of varying labor costs for piece-rate operations on identical parts of different garments with the selling price of the garment smacked more of an employer-oriented attempt to control competition than of a union-oriented attempt at insuring equal justice among workers. Whereas the normal course of competition in the manufacture of wearing apparel began with keeping down costs of production and ended by haggling with buyers over the price of the finished product, some branches of the needle trades followed just the opposite procedure. Here, the stimulus to manufacture began with demands from retailers for garments that could be sold at fixed prices and ended with haggling over the quality of the materials, the kind of workman-

---

[22]From the 1936 collective agreement of the Eastern Women's Headwear Association with the Cap and Millinery Department of the United Hatters, Cap and Millinery Workers' International Union, Locals 24 and 42 of Said Cap and Millinery Department. For the period of the NRA codes, see J. C. Worthy, "The Millinery Industry" (processed), NRA: Division of Review, Industry Studies Section (March 1936). For similar emphasis on equalizing labor costs in the men's clothing trade, see Harry A. Cobrin, *The Men's Clothing Industry: Colonial through Modern Times* (1970), *passim*.

Throughout the history of collective bargaining for the needle trades, the weight of the evidence would seem to indicate that the terms *equal labor costs* and *uniform labor standards* were most often used indiscriminately; yet there is sufficient evidence to warrant the conviction that the leaders on both sides of the bargaining table, if no others, understood the distinction between the terms and acted accordingly. J. H. Cohen, leading spokesman for the organized employers, once sought to clarify the distinction between the worker approach and the employer approach to the problem:

> When we first began to think in these industries of the problem of standardizing [piece-rate] prices, some of the manufacturers had the notion that you could fix exactly the same price of labor for each garment for every factory in the industry. Now, Dr. Stone has pointed out that that cannot be done, because conditions vary in the various shops, and what would be a perfectly fair price for the labor on that garment in shop A would not be fair in shop B.
>
> —*Minutes*, Arbitration Proceedings between the Dress and Waist Manufacturers' Association and the ILGWU (Feb. 14, 1916), vol. 5, pp. 637–638.

ship, and the costs of labor that must go into these garments in order to withstand pressure from competitors who offered more for the same money.

Thus, the management of a large retail outlet, after surveying the consumer market, might conclude that women's blouses could be sold at a profit if they were made available to consumers at standard prices of $3.00 for the cheap grade, $5.00 for the medium grade, and $7.50 for the better grade. Thereupon, the retail management deducted from these standard consumer prices his own mark-ups, sufficient to cover retail operations, and submitted the remaining figure to manufacturers with the simple query: "What is the best you can offer in blouses at these fixed prices?" Such was the origin of the price-range principle that essentially diverted competition in manufacturing from bartering over prices of the finished products to bartering over the quality of the materials and the standards of workmanship as well as the wage rate that should go into making those products.

Where the jobber-contractor system of manufacturing prevailed, the contractor also might be paid a percentage of the wholesale value of the finished product — a percentage that presumably covered his direct labor costs, as well as his overhead and profit, and amounted to roughly one-third of the wholesale price at which the blouse was to be sold. The effect of this procedure was to carry over into the fixed price-range principle the more general practice of establishing such minimum prices to be paid contractors as would "protect producers against unfair competition and the workers against exploitation."[23]

---

[23]*Women's Wear Daily*, Nov. 13, 1930.

The 1950 collective agreement between the National Association of Blouse Manufacturers (jobbers) and the Greater Blouse, Skirt and Neckwear Contractors' Association stated:

> Through the experience of both Associations for more than fifteen (15) years, and based on the consultation and advice of both manufacturers and contractors, it has been found that the blouse industry is set up so that the garments are sold at traditional price ranges. In view of this situation, it is necessary for a manufacturer to have a reasonable predetermined knowledge of the labor costs involved in the construction of his garments. It is likewise necessary for the contractor to have a reasonable predetermined knowledge of the price paid to him in order to pay his labor costs so that he may pay reasonable wages to his employees and comply with wage standards set by governmental agencies

Competition for better quality at fixed prices did not, of course, avert the pressure for lower labor costs. On the contrary, with no variable in the ultimate price of the product, the profits of business had to be derived wholly from operating within fixed price limitations, so that the pressure to reduce labor costs might well have been increased. Seeking relief from this added pressure of producing for a profit within the limits of a fixed price market, the organized workers demanded and received for their labor a certain percentage of the price at which the garments were sold. If in producing a dress to be sold wholesale at $6.75, the labor costs were allocated at 14¢ for the body, 13¢ for the sleeves, 30¢ for the neck, 10¢ for the waistline, and so on, then these standard unit costs would be correspondingly raised in higher priced garments. While this system created inequities among workers in terms of pay for effort expended, it at least forced the employer, restricted by fixed prices and fixed labor costs, to concentrate on the elements of managerial ingenuity that made for success in the business.[24]

---

and the Unions, plus reasonable overhead and a fair and reasonable profit. It is, therefore, agreed by both parties on behalf of their respective members that the following shall be the "floor prices" for the respective price ranges:

$15.75 range	$ 5.25 per dozen	
22.50 "	7.00 " "	
30.00 "	10.00 " "	
36.00 "	11.00 " "	
45.00 "	12.50 " "	

(Some ranges are omitted from the quotation)

[24]*Fortune Magazine,* November 1946, vol. 34, pp. 173 ff. In dress manufacturing, the practice of varying piece rates with the selling price of the garment was perfected through the work of Impartial Chairman Harry Uviller, who established four price-range brackets: (1) dresses selling below $4.75; (2) dresses selling between $4.75 and $6.75; (3) dresses selling between $6.75 and $10.75; and (4) dresses selling above $10.75. A brief account of this system and of subsequent developments brought on by mass production techniques appears in an article by A. H. Raskin in the *New York Times,* Jan. 13, 1960.

In an arbitration award reflecting a common type of chiseling under this method of piece-rate determination, Harry Uviller fined a dress manufacturer $7,200 for settling piece rates on the assumption that garments of a certain style would sell for $1.87 each, and then later selling those garments to the retail trade for $2.25 each. The money went to the union to pay the workers for having been short-changed. Harry Uviller, *Decisions,*

There were other evidences that collective bargaining was an institution for saving the business as well as for saving the jobs. Forbidding employers to sign time contracts with individual workers guaranteeing continuous periods of employment in return for substandard wages helped to save the wage structure of the industry for the union, but these restrictions also helped the manufacturers control overproduction of goods that threatened to become "a menace to the stability of the market." Prohibitions in labor agreements against buying accessories — buttons, laces, artificial flowers, belts, and the like — from nonunion shops certainly helped to strengthen the position of the union in the trade, but these restrictions also helped to suppress unfair business competition that gave some manufacturers an advantage over others. Conversely, what the manufacturers had to offer at the bargaining table frequently might work out to the advantage of the union as well as the employers' association. Reporting on a proposal by the contractors' association to the ILGWU at the negotiations for the 1926 collective labor agreement of the women's coat and suit trade, *Women's Wear,* the leading trade journal, carried the following headlines: "American Association Offers Remedial Program for Cloak and Suit Labor Ills — New Features Include 'Joint Board of Non-Union Control' — Concentration of Production and Distribution among Those Belonging to Organizations — Regulation of Newcomers in Industry."[25]

By offering "its fullest cooperation" to a union seeking agreements with large chain stores and mail-order houses to forbid the

---

Cases no. D-372, 371, 370 (April 2, 1937), vol. 2, pp. 75–77. See also "Labor Costs Based on Selling Prices Torment Dress Trade," *Women's Wear Daily,* July 28, 1927.

[25]*Women Wear,* March 9, 1926. Judicial recognition, if not acceptance, of these dual features of collective bargaining in the needle trades crops up repeatedly in pertinent decisions of the New York courts. "In December, 1933, the two associations, acting for their respective members, entered into a collective agreement designed to establish harmony in the dress manufacturing industry, to provide a basis for equitable and fair business conduct, and to insure payment of wages to labor according to the scale prescribed by the collective bargaining agreement with the trade union, together with the additional reasonable overhead and profit to the contractors." Mr. Justice A. J. Levy, enjoining a contractors' association lockout of further business from a jobbers' association, in National Dress Manufacturers' Association v. United Association of Dress Manufacturers, 151 Misc. 827 (1934), 272 N.Y. Supp. 360.

purchase of unlabeled garments, a powerful group of women's coat and suit manufacturers decidedly bolstered the position of the ILGWU in the trade; but to that extent the employer groups also boosted business for the manufacturers who made labeled products. Likewise, forbidding retailers to do their own jobbing through their own selected contractors helped close one avenue of nonunion production, thereby supporting the union; but at the same time this move helped to keep legitimate manufacturers in the business of supplying retailers with finished products that retailers might otherwise supply for themselves.[26]

Those who defended the general theme of industrial stability were fighting to maintain the status quo. By supporting the "regulatory" clauses of collective agreements, they were seeking to protect business investments, as well as wage rates, from the undermining influence of free competition. In the early years of the protocol movement, it was the inside manufacturers and their organized workers who had most to lose from disturbing the status quo. Later, however, the "legitimate" contractors and their organized workers were equally concerned with protecting the "ins" from the "outs." Indeed, on one occasion during 1939, representatives of two dress contractors' associations, whose members were losing orders and whose workers were losing jobs to newly established inside plants, insisted upon eliminating these new *inside* factories, lest industry standards be endangered by a surplus of unattached contractors. Otherwise, noted Nat Boriskin, executive director of the United Popular Priced Dress Manufacturers' Association, "unemployed [contractor] shops are likely to run wild,

---

[26]The 1932 collective agreement between the Women's Headwear Group and the Cloth Hat, Cap and Millinery Workers' International Union was not only designed to raise labor standards but it was also expected "to eliminate the keen competition that has existed and that has been responsible for excessive price cutting on the part of the manufacturers." *Women's Wear Daily*, April 21, 1932. Six years later, this union signed an agreement with an association of 60 jobbers — the New York Association of Wholesale Distributors of Ladies' and Children's Hats — in which the association was pledged "to cooperate in the effort to stabilize the industry and to refrain from requiring millinery manufacturers to sell merchandise below cost." *Hat Worker*, Jan. 15, 1938. See also a resolution of the National Coat and Suit Industry Recovery Board in *Women's Wear Daily*, May 18, 1939.

and we want to do something to alleviate the situation before they get out of hand."[27]

All restrictions on the freedom of manufacturers to determine the nature of their products, the location of their plants, the sources of their supply, the extent of their production, the methods of their operations, or the character of their markets may have contributed to the observance of negotiated labor agreements; but they also have carried implications of illegally restraining trade. Certainly, the intricate and diversified controls established over the jobber-contracting system — controls that go to the heart of collective bargaining in the needle trades — could as well have been directed to the elimination of undesirable competition among manufacturers as to the enforcement of labor standards. When the 1925 dress industry agreements were being negotiated, the provision that jobbers pay contractors 7 percent above direct production costs was ostensibly included to relieve contractor pressure for chiseling on union labor standards, but this objective was scarcely apparent from the reaction of the organized contractors themselves:

The man who thinks he can put something over on his competitors by accepting less than 7 per cent for overhead and expense will be caught and dealt with most severely, for he is not only killing his own chances of making a profit, but is defeating the whole purpose of the new agreements and injuring everyone else in the dress business.[28]

Wherever falls the weight of the evidence, those who evaluate collective bargaining solely in terms of union demands and union achievements should never forget that Julius H. Cohen, the father of the protocol movement, was a representative of the manufacturer's association and that John A. Dyche, the most active union member at the Brandeis Conferences of 1910, later became a manufacturer. The union-oriented approach to collective bargaining in the needle trades should not overlook the possibility that the ILGWU may at one stage have owed its life to Samuel

---

[27] *Ibid.*, Nov. 1, 1939.

[28] A spokesman at a contractors' meeting to discuss terms of the new agreement with the jobbers, as quoted in *ibid.*, Jan. 23, 1925. Texts of the contractor-union, jobber-contractor, and jobber-union agreements were printed in the issues of Jan. 19, 30, and 31, 1925, respectively.

Klein, executive director of the Industrial Council of Cloak, Suit and Skirt Manufacturers — an association of inside manufacturers that succeeded the original employer group signing the first Protocol of Peace. Klein remained a vigilant advocate of strong unionism in the darkest years of labor union history.

Those who see in the history of needle trade bargaining a one-way street forever strewn with the wreckage of manufacturing firms that could not meet union demands should study the role of employers' associations. While labor unions may virtually hold the keys to independent shops, they have seldom exerted such powers over members of employer groups. The "one-way-street" theory of collective bargaining is hardly consistent with the voluntary action of employers' associations in supporting the principles of the protocol movement. Organized manufacturers compelled to accept one-way dictation at the bargaining table would hardly have shown so much concern for a rigid enforcement of their contracts, nor would they have worked so diligently for the objectives set out in their labor agreements.[29]

Strange Issues at the Bargaining Table

Consider, for example, the demands of the organized employer groups upon the ILGWU during negotiations over the 1932 collective agreement for the women's coat and suit trade. Faced with the Great Depression which had further aggravated cutthroat

---

[29]When certain members of the Popular Priced Dress Manufacturers' Group — an employers' association bound by a 1936 collective agreement with the Dressmakers' Joint Board, ILGWU — secretly moved their plant from New York City to Archbald, Pa., in violation of their labor contract's runaway shop clause, and the union sought the aid of the courts to force the owners to return to New York City and re-employ their old union workers, New York Supreme Court Justice P. J. McCook was careful to note the reaction of the employers' association and the impartial chairman toward the conduct of the member firm: "There are other members of the association. One of the chief objects of joining was protection against unfair competition. If the plaintiffs' charges are true, it is not natural to suppose that defendants' general popularity in the association would grow by reason of their attitude, nor could its [the association's] officers be expected to register great enthusiasm for the Fishmans individually. At any rate, some of the most important assertions made by the latter as witnesses were flatly contradicted by the association's manager and the impartial chairman." Dubinsky v. Blue Dale Dress Co., 162 Misc. 177 (1936) 182, 292 N.Y. Supp. 898. The case is discussed above at pp. 549–550.

competition, the employers were more anxious to gain union support for solving trade problems than they were concerned with rejecting union demands for better terms of employment. To prevent unfair competition among contractors, the inside manufacturers sought union support for minimum production costs that would include overhead for the contractor as well as wages for the worker. The inside manufacturers also expected the union to drive out all skeleton shops operating under substandard conditions. They persistently demanded that all workers in the trade be organized, and that the union establish more effective controls over independent firms holding separate union contracts. Finally, they called upon the union to stop retailers from destroying the markets of the organized factions by dealing with non-union sources of supply.

Meanwhile, the organized jobbers were pressing the union to purify the memberships of the various employers' groups representing the jobbers, the contractors, and the inside manufacturers. Here again, the employers were primarily concerned with gaining union help for resolving trade issues. The executive committee of the Merchants' Ladies' Garment Association (jobbers) opened its demands upon the union with the following statement:

First and foremost, the status of the various factors in the industry must be definitely defined, so that the contractor, the manufacturer and the wholesaler will be placed in the association in which he properly belongs. The agreements now in force between the employers and the Union, and between the employers and the contractors, make it mandatory upon the employers to confine their production to the members of the contractor's association. Yet, the contractor's association include [sic] within their [sic] membership firms who are manufacturers and wholesalers and who are competing with the members of the Industrial Council and with the members of the Merchants' Ladies' Garment Association. Nothing does more to undermine the standards in our industry than this state of affairs. No firms have any place in the contractor's association unless they are in fact contractors. Accordingly, provision must be made in the proposed collective agreements that will definitely define the status of each factor in the industry and place that person, firm or corporation in the association where he may properly function and where he rightfully belongs.

With Samuel Klein, leading spokesman of the manufacturers, blasting the ILGWU for permitting an inside manufacturer to join the jobbers' association, and with the organized jobbers insisting that the union impose oppressive contract terms on independent jobbers, collective bargaining appeared to call for a new definition of objectives. If these new concepts were a far cry from the normally assumed course of labor negotiations, they were, nevertheless, thoroughly in keeping with the principles of the protocol movement.[30]

Still it should not be assumed that the historic course of collective bargaining would have been diverted from the principles of the protocol movement had the terms of collective agreements been dictated solely by needle trade unions. For not only were the

---

[30]The jobbers' demands were printed in *Women's Wear Daily*, May 25, 1932. For earlier charges by the Industrial Council of Cloak, Suit and Skirt Manufacturers (inside producers) that the ILGWU had permitted inside manufacturers to join the contractors' association, see a decision of R. V. Ingersoll, impartial chairman, reported in ILGWU's *Justice*, Sept. 12, 1930.

The 1937 collective agreement of the Infants' and Children's Coat Association with the Cloakmakers' Joint Board, ILGWU, stated that the provisions for contracting out work only to members of the American Cloak and Suit Manufacturers' Association would no longer be valid "if members of the American Association shall contain inside manufacturers producing garments for the market on their own account substantially in the same manner as the members of the association."

Throughout the history of collective bargaining for the needle trades, attempts to divide jobbers, contractors, and inside manufacturers into separate associations remained more an ideal than an a achievement. Not even the élite inside manufacturers who led the field in style, quality, and reliability remained simon-pure. For example, the Affiliated Dress Manufacturers, organized in 1929 by the inside manufacturers of higher priced dresses exclusively for the purpose of bargaining with the ILGWU and its Dressmakers' Joint Board, could not steer clear of contracting. In his NRA Evidence Study no. 9, "The Dress Manufacturing Industry," W. A. Gill pointed out that 178 of the Affiliated's 250 members employed contractors. Within the women's coat and suit trade, the last stronghold of separation collapsed when the Industrial Council of Cloak, Suit and Skirt Manufacturers (inside producers) and the Merchants' Ladies' Garment Association (jobbers) joined together in 1961 to form the New York Coat and Suit Association. Joseph L. Dubow, named to become the executive director of the new association, explained that the combined group "would be able to present a stronger voice in labor negotiations with the International Ladies' Garment Workers' Union, with which the associations have a collective agreement, and would also be able to present a united front in pressing for compliance with fair trade practices in dealing with retailers and suppliers." *New York Times*, June 29, 1961.

efforts of employers to control competition futile without union cooperation, but the unions themselves did not hesitate to fight on their own accord for the solution of trade problems. During the 1932 negotiations of the women's coat and suit trade, officials of the ILGWU lambasted the inside manufacturers for turning their backs on the limitation of contractors as a means of controlling outside production. Since 1924, the Industrial Council of Cloak, Suit and Skirt Manufacturers had consistently supported the principle of contractor limitation; yet this organization now pretended to concentrate its efforts on obtaining minimum costs of production to solve the competitive evils of contracting out work. Throughout the negotiations, the union itself took the stand that trade issues clearly overshadowed any immediate concern for wage rates, hours of work, or conditions of employment.

Again, while L. L. Schwartz, president of the Affiliated Dress Manufacturers' Association (inside producers), was hailing the new 1930 dress industry agreements for marking "the first step in what we trust will be an intensive and sustained effort to bring about stability in our trade," David Dubinsky, president of the ILGWU, was praising the new agreements for going a long way toward eliminating "illegitimate competition, bootleg prices, kickbacks," and other alleged evils of the trade. In similar vein, Julius Hochman, general manager of the Dressmakers' Joint Board, noted that these agreements would "eliminate overproduction in the industry" as well as "eliminate the overpopulation of contractors and workers in the dress trade." Neither union official, apparently, had any direct comments for public consumption on the immediate labor issues of wages, hours, and working conditions.[31]

---

[31] L. L. Schwartz quoted in *Women's Wear Daily*, Feb. 11, 1930; David Dubinsky and Julius Hochman, Feb. 13, 1930.

The 1961–1962 master contract between the Eastern Women's Headwear Association and the United Hatters, Cap and Millinery Workers urged "concerted action on the part of management and labor for the purpose of promoting the sale and use of millinery ... and for stabilizing and improving conditions in the industry." The agreement created a millinery promotion fund and established a national millinery planning board "comprised of representatives of the various unionized millinery markets and representatives of the Union throughout the country." Among its many functions, the board was to direct the uses of the millinery promotion fund, "to study, research and advise on the trends in the millinery industry; to investigate

Employer Control of Trade Practices

After the First World War, business relations between individual employers and between their respective associations were subject to unusual periods of conflict as well as cooperation. On one occasion, the organized contractors of the women's coat and suit trade went to war against the organized jobbers from whom they received work. Finding themselves "threatened with complete ruination by the most burdensome overcharges and most tyrannical treatment and absolute disregard for the costs that enter into the production of garments," contractors belonging to the American Cloak and Suit Manufacturers' Association declared a "strike" against three jobbers of the Merchants' Ladies' Garment Association for refusing to sign an agreement regulating trade practices. The contractors' association had proposed such an agreement to the jobbers on the assumption that law and order between employer groups, like law and order in labor-management relations, were essential to the prosperity of the trade. A letter accompanying the proposal contained the following observation:

Many jobbers who realize that the industry depends upon the welfare of the producers have expressed the desire for standards or laws governing the relationship of jobbers and producers which will tend towards harmony and efficiency. . . . We are enclosing a copy of our standards which will help find the illegitimate jobber, as well as eliminate unfair, inequitable and unjust practices and which will tend to create a stable, healthy and efficient industry.[32]

tariffs and millinery importations and recommend legislation to deal with such imports, and any other matters which will be beneficial to the industry, the employees and the employers." To forestall any trouble with the antitrust laws, the agreement stated that "the Board shall not engage in any price fixing, production controls or allocation of markets."

[32] *Women's Wear Daily,* Sept. 26–27, 1922. That year the jobbing department of the American Cloak and Suit Manufacturers' Association (contractors) reported 657 complaints of contractors against jobbers and 47 complaints of jobbers against contractors, covering the year 1921. These complaints fell into 24 different classifications, including garments not made to order, withholding payments, late deliveries, deductions without reason, failure to complete order, cancellation of orders, overcharges, shortages, fire, theft, lost in transit, disagreement over price of cloth, returned garments, and failure to deliver. *The Cloak and Suit Manufacturer* (an association publication), June 1922.

When the three jobbers refused to cooperate, the organized contractors declined to accept further orders from them, nor would the contractors finish materials or deliver products still in their hands. To strengthen its position in the dispute, the contractors' association established picket lines around the three stockhouses. "With all the thoroughness of a union," reported *Women's Wear*, Sept. 26, 1922, "the cloak and suit sub-manufacturers of this market have effected a stoppage of work at three representative stockhouses."[33]

About the same time, some nine hundred organized contractors of the men's clothing trade representing the combined membership of the coat contractors' association, the vest contractors' association, and the pants contractors' association threatened to close down their industry if necessary to keep up the prices they received for their work. Industrial warfare featuring "strikes" and "lockouts" between organized groups of jobbers and organized groups of contractors were not uncommon in the needle trades, and at least one agreement between these factions expressly authorized the use of these weapons to enforce trade agreements.[34]

At least such episodes reflected a growing demand for standards of business conduct to accompany the rise of the jobber-contracting system. Particularly did the growing demands for limiting and assigning contractors require a peaceful solution for the protec-

---

[33]Earlier, the eight hundred members of the American Cloak and Suit Manufacturers' Association had agreed among themselves to establish their own committee on immediate action, with power to call stoppages of contractors against jobbers who did not recognize the standards of fair dealings set by the contractors' association. *Women's Wear*, Sept. 21, 1922. For a code of trade practices proposed by the Merchants' Ladies' Garment Association (jobbers), see the July 21, 1924 issue.

[34]*Daily News Record*, June 1, 1922. For an earlier episode involving warfare between contractors and jobbers in the manufacture of men's clothing, see *ibid.*, June 19, 28, 31 and August 1, 23, 1916. Later episodes of like character are reported in the issues of Dec. 12 and 14, 1922.

The trade agreement of Dec. 2, 1933 between the National Dress Manufacturers' Association (jobbers) and the United Association of Dress Manufacturers (contractors) authorized members of the jobbers' association to "lockout" noncomplying contractors by refusing to send them any more work; and authorized members of the contractors' association to "strike" noncomplying jobbers by refusing to accept any more work from them. See A. Feldblum, impartial chairman of the dress industry, *Decisions*, Case no. B-1124 (Oct. 29, 1935).

tion of employers and workers alike. By the mid-twenties, this issue had become so important that Governor Alfred E. Smith's Advisory Commission, named to find a basis for settling a dispute over the terms of a new labor agreement for the women's coat and suit trade, devoted most of its time attempting to evolve a satisfactory system of relationships between and among jobbers, contractors, and inside manufacturers of the trade.

Equally as important was the need for working out satisfactory business relationships between the manufacturing interests and their suppliers, on the one hand, or between the manufacturing interests and their retail outlets, on the other. Short of vertical integration under the same management, this problem called for alliances, regulations, and procedures directed toward promoting mutually profitable relationships and capable of resolving conflicts over such issues as insurance rates, express charges, shortages, rebates, late deliveries, discount rates, advertising allowances, selling on consignment, and return of merchandise — conflicts that threatened to undermine legitimate competition and endanger the life of the trade. In 1924, for example, the retailers and wholesalers of the dress industry established a Joint Committee on Trade Relations consisting of four representatives of retailers, four representatives of wholesalers, and a ninth person representing the public. "The body has for its purpose," noted *Women's Wear,* February 2, 1924, "the elimination of trade disputes and of friction between buyer and seller and the promotion of high standards of business ethics."[35]

---

[35]An earlier movement with similar objectives was reported by *Women's Wear,* Feb. 25, 1916, under the caption: "Shirt Manufacturers Seek Cooperation with Textile Men on One End and Retailers on the Other in the Shirt Industry."

During the twenties, a number of vertically related branches of the fur industry in a move to establish trade practice controls set up an advisory committee of the fur industry, whose jurisdiction embraced trappers, dealers, dressers, dyers, manufacturers, and retail merchants. Troubled by the growing evils of excessive discounts, unjustifiable returns, and the pressure of volume buyers, all of these groups through their interassociation committees were able to coordinate their trade practice controls. In 1930, a trade relations bureau representing the dressers, dyers, manufacturers, and merchants was established to see "that trade abuses be eliminated, conditions stabilized and improved, and the industry be established on a sound basis." *Women's Wear,* Nov. 6, 27, 29, 1920; *Women's Wear Daily,* Feb. 24, 1928; Jan. 16 and April 24, 1929; Jan. 30, 1930; *Fur Age Weekly,* Jan. 17, 1927.

This move for cooperation among suppliers, producers, and distributors threatened the inside manufacturers, who had sponsored the protocol movement, with a type of integration that might bypass them altogether. The rise of outside contracting, along with the growth of mass selling through large-scale distributive outlets, had opened the door for retailers to become their own jobbers, supplying their own ideas, selecting their own materials, and having them made up directly through their own contractors. Such a possibility had been foreseen early in the history of the protocol movement. "Retailers could co-operate to take a controlling interest in factories which make reputable but unbranded goods at a minimum cost," observed a writer for *Women's Wear,* January 5, 1916. "The co-operative retailer could agree to handle the output and push the sales in their respective stores, thereby making a handsome profit over and above the ordinary retail profit."[36]

The need for supplying a convenient and peaceful means of resolving complex business problems arising from the nature of production and distribution no doubt had much to do with the expanded use of commercial arbitration as a substitute for court litigation during the twenties. The outstanding leader in this movement was Julius Henry Cohen. In his historical study,

---

[36]If I am shrewd enough to get eight of my friends in a shop to make garments at such a price that Mr. Fishman [an inside manufacturer] cannot possibly make them in his shop and then I sell those garments to Mr. Fishman, it is not very long before I find out to whom Mr. Fishman sells those garments and then I go to that man and sell them to him. . . . If this thing keeps up, the decent manufacturer of popular-priced goods is going to go out of existence in this industry.

—J. H. Cohen, counsel for the manufacturers' associations, in *Minutes,* Board of Arbitrators . . . [women's coat and suit trade] (August 4, 1913), p. 426.

In their initial state of development the chain stores used to get their caps from the manufacturers. Later, however, when they multiplied in numbers and became the biggest buyers of caps, they introduced the practice of jobbing. They started to buy their goods directly from the mills, and also their trimmings, farming out their work to contractors. . . . These practices of chain stores tend to sharpen the cutthroat competition and to demoralize the trade even more.

—Cloth Hat, Cap and Millinery Workers' International Union, Report of the General Executive Board, in *Report and Proceedings,* Seventeenth Biennial Convention (May 1929), p. 8.

Commercial Arbitration and the Law, published in 1918, Cohen observed at the outset that "what business men want is a speedy determination of the facts and a prompt determination of their rights under the facts as found." Cohen's activity in this field contributed to the passage of the New York Arbitration Act of 1920 — the first of its kind in the United States — and this statute in turn hastened the passage of the U. S. Arbitration Act, February 12, 1925.[37]

Union Support for Trade Controls

Wherever members of employers' associations entered into trade agreements among themselves creating peaceful means of resolving their commercial disputes, all unfair business practices that might arise would presumably be controlled without the need for labor union participation. At least that was the assumption on which a number of trade councils were set up during the twenties. Shortly after the First World War, for example, the organized manufacturers of the women's coat and suit trade created a trade council to arbitrate disputes between the organized jobbers and the organized contractors; but this council did not provide for participation by the International Ladies' Garment Workers' Union. Nor did the contractors' board, a similar agency in the men's clothing trade of the early twenties, implicate the Amalgamated Clothing Workers of America. In 1925, the organized jobbers of the dress industry negotiated a trade agreement with the organized contractors covering the usual subjects of trade relations: discount rates, changes in orders, delivery dates, charges for insurance, payment schedules, and the like. But the ILGWU was allowed no part in the administration and enforcement of this agreement.[38]

---

[37]Citation at p. 2. See also, Cohen, *Commercial Arbitration — Its Scope and Limitations* (pamphlet, 1923); and Cohen and Kenneth Dayton, *Handbook and Guide to Commercial Arbitration under the New York and U.S. Arbitration Statutes* (1932), New York Public Library. The pertinent statutes can be found in chap. 275, Laws of New York State, 1920, and in 43 U.S. Statutes at Large 886 (Feb. 12, 1925); U.S. Code (1926), vol. 44, Part 1, p. 167.

[38] On the origin of the trade council in the women's coat and suit trade, see the address of B. Spinrad, chairman, board of directors, at the second annual banquet of the American Cloak and Suit Manufacturers' Association, reported in *American Garment News* (an organ of the association), Dec. 2, 1920, vol. I, pp. 53–54; a mimeographed statement of Samuel Klein, execu-

These early precedents for employer enforcement of trade regulations through administrative agencies of employer design were in keeping with the antiunion "American Way" philosophies of management during the twenties. By the end of the decade, however, the organized manufacturers were forsaking their policies of self-help for the more fruitful rewards that came from union participation in trade controls. Thus, after violations of the 1925 jobber-contractor dress industry agreement had become so prevalent as to nullify the agreement's value, the jobbers and contractors early in 1930 negotiated a second agreement that for administrative purposes utilized the impartial machinery established by the collective labor agreements. Only by bringing the enforcement of trade regulations within the province of administrative agencies on which the union was represented did success appear to be assured. "For the first time in its history," announced Jed Sylbert, president of the Association of Dress Manufacturers in 1930, "the dress industry has a definite code of ethics for dealings between contractors and jobbers with machinery for the enforcement of that code."[39]

tive director of the Industrial Council of Cloak, Suit and Skirt Manufacturers, filed in the Abelson papers; and G. W. Alger, impartial chairman of the women's coat and suit trade, *Decisions,* Case no. 769, under the heading "Minimum Costs of Production Cases, Schedules for Fall of 1932."

For the men's clothing industry, see the text of the 1921 collective agreement between the Clothing Manufacturers' Association of New York and the ACWA in *Daily News Record,* June 3, 1921, and the first decision handed down by W. M. Leiserson, chairman of the board of arbitrators under this agreement. This decision laid down rules governing jobber-contractor relations and set up machinery for handling disputes between jobbers or inside manufacturers and contractors in the men's clothing industry. *Ibid.,* June 29, 1921.

[39]*New York Times,* Feb. 15, 1930. The text of the 1925 agreement between the Wholesale Dress Manufacturers' Association (jobbers) and the Association of Dress Manufacturers (contractors) was printed in *Women's Wear,* Jan. 30, 1925. The issue of Jan. 19, 1925 contained the text of the new collective agreement between the Association of Dress Manufacturers and the ILGWU, while the issue of Jan. 31, 1925 contained the text of the collective agreement between the Wholesale Dress Manufacturers' Association and the ILGWU. Excerpts from the 1930 and 1932 agreements between the organized dress jobbers and the organized dress contractors appear in *Women's Wear Daily,* Feb. 26, 1930 and Feb. 29, 1932. The text of the 1930 collective agreement between the Association of Dress Manufacturers and the ILGWU was printed in the Feb. 18, 1930 issue.

Likewise when representatives from the various branches of the fur industry met in January 1930 to set up a trade relations bureau for "consolidation of interests and concerted co-operation" among dressers, dyers, manufacturers, and dealers, they invited Morris Kaufman, president of the International Fur Workers' Union, and Matthew Woll, vice-president of the American Federation of Labor, to attend and participate in the discussions. Both union leaders expressed their approval of the proceedings and offered their "hearty and sincere support." At a second industrial conference of the fur trade held in May of that year, Matthew Woll told a gathering of some two hundred fur dressers, dyers, raw skin handlers, manufacturers, and retailers that the time had come for more effective action.[40]

Charging the processors, producers, and distributors with creating standards that no one observed, Vice-President Woll stressed the need for better organization among employers of the fur trades to insure a fair return for everyone. He lamented the lack of control over the price structure and pointed to the need for the stabilization of prices as well as the stabilization of labor costs — the former to be accomplished through the latter. He noted one bright spot upon the industrial horizon: a tendency for governmental leaders to recognize that unlimited and unrestrained competition is not the life of trade. And he cited the photoengraving industry as an example of a trade where proper organization "has insured every one a proper return by going even so far as to establish a set of uniform selling prices for photo-engraving."[41]

Union Help for Minimum Production Costs

Union participation in solving trade problems was most sharply focused on attempts to put a floor under production costs for contractors and a ceiling over discount rates for retailers. The proposition that jobbers or inside manufacturers must pay contractors enough to meet their total costs of production, including over-

---

[40]*Ibid.,* Jan. 30, May 20, 1930.

[41]*Ibid.,* May 20, 1930. Price-fixing by the New York photoengravers was condemned by the New York Supreme Court for violating the state antitrust law in Photo-Engravers' Board of Trade of New York v. Addison, 145 Misc. 479 (1932), 260 N.Y. Supp. 332. Earlier, the Federal Trade Commission had reached similar conclusions in another photoengraving case: 12 F.T.C. Docket 29 (1928), summarized in F.T.C. *Annual Report* (1928), pp. 56–57.

head, was not only a union goal supported by employers to take labor costs out of competition, it was also an employer goal supported by unions to help stabilize chaotic conditions within a trade. Contractors of the needle trades were generally subject to cross-fire from the demands of their workers for higher wages and from the demands of their jobbers for lower prices. Trapped in a two-way squeeze which threatened them with extinction, such contractors might either seek to impose lower wages upon their workers — an approach that could be buttressed with threats of temporary lockouts or permanent loss of employment; or they might demand higher prices from their jobbers — an approach that could be supported with threats of direct action which would tie up production at critical periods.

In the September 1922 strike by the organized contractors against the organized jobbers, cited above, the contractors' association at first urged the independent contractors to join their ranks in a concerted effort to save the legitimate contractors from "complete ruination." But it was not until the organized contractors of the women's coat and suit trade had enlisted the help of the ILGWU, in conducting a series of individual shop strikes against coat and suit jobbers during the winter of 1927–1928, that the contractors were able to sign agreements forcing jobbers to accept the principle of minimum production costs. Although these contracts obligated jobbers to pay for garments produced by contractors "a price sufficient to cover the cost of production including the overhead on union conditions and labor standards," they were made with individual jobbers and fell short of a general agreement covering the organized factions of the trade.[42]

Just such a general agreement was consummated in 1929 between the American Cloak and Suit Manufacturers' Association (contractors) and the Merchants' Ladies' Garment Association (jobbers). This contract called for a joint trade council representing the two employer groups — a council that would "endeavor to arrive at a practical program governing the relations of the members of both associations, including a scientific cost of production" and one that would "endeavor to solve the existing difficulties between the members of both associations." Under this plan,

---

[42]The 1922 episode is reported in *Women's Wear,* Sept. 27, 1922; the 1927–1928 developments in *Women's Wear Daily,* Feb. 14, 1928.

the determination of allowances for wage scales and overhead sufficient "to maintain a shop" logically fell upon joint agencies assigned to handle trade problems.[43]

Delay in implementing this provision on minimum costs led the contractors' association at the instigation of the impartial chairman again to fall back upon its own scheme for setting minimum prices on goods to be made up by its members. Through a resolution of September 26, 1929, this association required all orders for the production of garments to be registered with the association before they became valid. Within twenty-four hours after receiving an order, the contractor had to appear in person at the office of the association with a copy of the order and a sample of the garment to be made. The object of this procedure was revealed in the provision that "registration of orders shall be carried through on the basis of minimum cost of production." Members violating the registration procedure were subjected to heavy fines or to expulsion from the association, or both.[44]

Subsequently, at the request of the organized jobbers and in-

---

[43]An earlier agreement between these two associations had provided for a joint trade council "to establish an equitable basis governing the business relations of the sub-manufacturers and the stockhouses to arrive at a practical program governing the relations of the sub-manufacturers and the stockhouses, including a scientific cost of production to solve the existing difficulties between the sub-manufacturers and the stockhouses." *Ibid.,* March 16, 1927; see also issues of March 28 and August 26, 1927.

Under the 1929 agreement between these two associations, disagreements between jobbers and contractors over minimum production costs were to be settled by the impartial chairman functioning under the labor agreements. See the first decision of this character in R. V. Ingersoll, impartial chairman, *Decisions,* Case no. 478 (1930), reported in *Women's Wear Daily,* August 1, 1930.

[44]"Our examiners who scrutinize samples of the garments specified in orders and who analyze the prices set, before the requisitions are registered, have been forced to reject a good number of orders in the two weeks in which the registration system has been in operation.

—Harry Uviller, general manager, American Cloak and Suit Manufacturers' Association, *ibid.,* Oct. 15, 1929.

For a summary of developments in the movement to determine "scientific" production costs that would "help to maintain labor standards and minimize unfair and destructive competition," see a lengthy letter, dated Dec. 3, 1929, from Impartial Chairman R. V. Ingersoll to the managers of the two associations. Copy filed in the Abelson papers. On this subject, see also *Women's Wear Daily,* August 1, 1930 and April 21, 1931.

side manufacturers, the impartial chairman for the industry held hearings on the operation of the contractors' registration system as a method for guaranteeing minimum costs of production. After exhaustive reports from all three business factions of the trade, the impartial chairman in April 1930 ordered the system discontinued and directed the organized jobbers, contractors, and inside manufacturers to devise a joint scheme that would offer greater prospects of enforcement. "Resting upon a policy established by only one organization and without broader authority," wrote Impartial Chairman R. V. Ingersoll of the unilateral registration plan, "evasion is easy to accomplish and difficult to correct."[45]

Failure of the organized employer groups to accomplish their objectives led to the transformation of the "trade" council into a "trade and labor" council. The initiative for this move had come in the spring of 1932 from the inside manufacturers through their demands upon the ILGWU for changes in the collective agreement. These manufacturers confessed that previous employer efforts at establishing and enforcing minimum costs of production for contractors had been fruitless. "Speaking from this costly experience," so they wrote the union, "we assert that these minima are virtually meaningless if the union is not a party to the procedure."[46]

As finally constituted under the 1932 collective labor agreements of the women's coat and suit trade, the trade council included representatives of the ILGWU as well as representatives from the employer groups. Like its predecessor, this council was expected to set a minimum price on what contractors received for making garments — a price that would be adequate to meet labor costs under the collective agreement, as well as adequate to cover overhead costs and provide a reasonable profit for the contractor. The impartial chairman named under the collective labor agreement was made a council member with final authority to resolve all differences and enforce all rulings.[47]

---

[45]The text of R. V. Ingersoll's decision is printed in *ibid.*, April 21, 1930.
[46]*Ibid.*, May 25 and 26, 1932.
[47]A summary of the new terms in the 1932 collective agreement between the Industrial Council of Cloak, Suit and Skirt Manufacturers and the Cloakmakers' Joint Board, ILGWU, is printed in *ibid.*, July 25, 1932. See also G. W. Alger, impartial chairman of the women's coat and suit trade, *Decisions,* Case nos. 596, 769, and 835 (1931–1932).

Drawing the trade council into the orbits of the collective bargaining machinery created a new and more effective means of enforcing "trade" regulations. At the time the new agreement was consummated, Samuel Klein, speaking for the Industrial Council of Cloak, Suit and Skirt Manufacturers (inside producers), reviewed the need for the union's help in controlling minimum production costs: "Our request that the union participate in the fixing of minimum prices for outside production was based on the desire to assure full enforcement of those prices. Under the old contract, the union had not been a party to the determining and enforcing of such charges, with the result that they prevailed 'in principle' only." With equal frankness, Klein then proposed a joint study by jobbers, contractors, inside manufacturers, and the ILGWU under the direction of the impartial chairman to ascertain how minimum costs of production which insured contractors adequate allowances for labor and overhead might also be extended to guarantee inside manufacturers a profitable existence.[48]

Control over Discount Rates

Nowhere was the fusion of trade and labor functions more evident than in attempts to control retail discount rates for the

For similar difficulties in the enforcement of minimum costs of production in the headwear industry during the mid-twenties, see the Cloth Hat, Cap and Millinery Workers' International Union, *Report and Proceedings,* Sixteenth Biennial Convention (May 1927), p. 176. See also proposals on the regulation of minimum production costs in the dress industry, *Women's Wear Daily,* July 19, 1932; and the terms of the 1933 dress industry agreement between the National Dress Manufacturers' Association and the Dressmakers' Joint Board, ILGWU, bearing on the subject.

[48]*Women's Wear Daily,* July 25, 1932, Klein later discovered that union participation in settling and enforcing minimum prices for contracting work did not prevent widespread violations of these price schedules, *ibid.,* March 14, 1933. A similar pessimistic note was expressed by the general executive board of the ILGWU in the union's *Report and Proceedings,* Twenty-Second Convention (May–June 1934), pp. 19–25.

The provisions of collective agreements requiring jobbers to pay their contractors a price for making garments sufficiently high to meet the contractor's overhead as well as his labor costs were held to be legal by Mr. Justice Edward Weinfeld in Greenstein v. National Skirt and Sportswear Association, U.S. District Court, S.D. New York 178 F. Supp. 681 (1959) on the ground that such provisions were necessary to guarantee that contractors would, in fact, pay their laborers the negotiated union wage scales.

women's coat and suit trade. During the twenties, the rise of chain stores, cooperative buying groups, and huge department stores had brought heavy pressure upon jobbers and manufacturers for extra discounts on volume buying. At first, these various employer groups relied upon their own devices to enforce maximum discount rates among their respective members. Ten years after the Garment Conference Council had in 1917 agreed upon standard discount rates for the trade, the Industrial Council of Cloak, Suit and Skirt Manufacturers created a bureau of business standards to enforce these regulations upon its members. In the first year of its existence, this bureau handled 272 complaints of trade violations from 106 member firms. Then, after the crash of 1929, this association of inside manufacturers joined with the Merchants' Ladies' Garment Association (jobbers) and the American Cloak and Suit Manufacturers' Association (contractors) in creating a central bureau of trade practices which was to administer discount regulations for the trade.[49]

When these joint efforts among employer groups manufacturing women's coats and suits failed to stem the tide of demands from giant retailer outlets for higher discount rates than those prescribed for the trade, the organized producers turned for assistance to the ILGWU and the instrumentalities of collective bargaining. They sought to bring the retailers within the scope of the bargaining structure. This move was a logical sequel to the transformation of the mid-twenties which had brought the organized jobbers and the organized contractors into partnership with the inside manufacturers and the ILGWU for joint control of the industry. Once accepted as legitimate factors in the manufacturing process, these contractors and jobbers had negotiated agreements among themselves as well as with the ILGWU. These agreements became part of the collective bargaining system worked out for the industry. Under their terms, the permanent umpire already selected to head the impartial machinery for the labor contracts

---

[49]*Women's Wear Daily*, March 27, 1928; Feb. 19, 1929; July 21 and August 25, 1931. The employer groups participating in the bureau worked out a scale of penalties to be imposed upon their respective members who exceeded the maximum discount rates. No fine was to be less than $250 or more than $5,000 for the first offense, nor less than $500 or more than $10,000 for the second offense. *Ibid.*, July 27, 1931; August 24 and 25, 1931.

was also named as the highest authority for resolving disputes on jobber–contractor–inside manufacturer relationships.[50]

This extension of the impartial machinery under the collective agreements of the mid-twenties had been introduced on the premise that control of jobber–contractor–inside manufacturer relationships would help to preserve labor standards in the trade. Hence no attempt was made to differentiate between the role of the permanent umpire as a "commercial" arbitrator and the role of the permanent umpire as a "labor" arbitrator. He had but one job, he received but one salary, he wore but one robe of authority. He was the impartial chairman for the industry. The scope of his jurisdiction was first set forth in the 1924 collective agreements under which, on recommendation of Governor Smith's Advisory Commission, the office of impartial chairman was established with power to handle controversies between and among employer groups, as well as between those groups and the ILGWU.[51]

Under this expanded sphere of collaboration among manufacturing groups of the women's coat and suit trade, the arbitrator's new powers over trade functions were clearly set forth in the 1929 collective agreement between the organized jobbers (Merchants' Ladies' Garment Association) and the organized contractors (American Cloak and Suit Manufacturers' Association):

It is agreed that should any question arise between the associations in behalf of their members or between the associations themselves regarding any matter or thing arising out of or in connection with the provisions of this agreement, including a breach thereof, or in connection with the business dealings of the members of one association with

---

[50]For a summary of the part played by the union in these developments, see Louis Lorwin (Louis Levine), *The Women's Garment Worker* (1924), pp. 418–421. See also Dickinson and Kolchin, *Report of an Investigation*, pp. 160–162.

[51]For highlights of the 1924 agreement between the Merchants' Ladies' Garment Association (jobbers) and the American Cloak and Suit Manufacturers' Association (contractors), see *Women's Wear*, August 24, 1924. In one of his early decisions rendered under this agreement, R. V. Ingersoll, the first double-barreled impartial chairman of the women's coat and suit trade, acting in his commercial capacity, directed a jobber to pay for twelve extra garments that his contractor had sent to him. The jobber had retained the garments for ten days without rejecting them, whereas the agreement had limited the time that garments could be retained without rejection to only seven days. R. V. Ingersoll, *Decisions*, Case no. 18 (September–December 1924).

the members of the other, including the changing, modifying, or re-adjusting of their business relations, the order blank under which the members will function, whatever the same may be, such difficulty or dispute necessitating a change or modification looking toward the stabilization of the industry and the elevation of its standards, will be referred to the impartial chairman in this industry for his deter-mination and decision, and such decision, when made, will be final, binding and conclusive upon the parties hereto.

The stage had already been set, therefore, when added pressures from powerful buying groups brought on the movement in the late twenties and early thirties for a further expansion of col-lective bargaining which would subject manufacturer-retailer re-lationships to the final and binding authority of an impartial chairman.[52]

Refusing to await the formalization of procedures that would include retailers within the expanding sphere of collective bar-gaining — in contradistinction to the mid-twenties' practice of first admitting the organized contractors into the realm of law and order — the various manufacturing groups of the women's coat and suit trade turned, in 1931, to their impartial chairman for im-mediate relief. In a report on the "Rigid Enforcement of Trade Practices" prepared for Impartial Chairman G. W. Alger during the summer of that year, the Central Bureau of Trade Practices pointed out that the employers could not submit to retailer de-mands for larger discounts without turning to labor for the re-

---

[52]Extracts from the provisions of this 1929 agreement are given in *Women's Wear Daily*, August 1, 1930. In their 1933 agreement, these two associations expressly stated that the procedure outlined for settling their own disputes "shall also apply to all disputes between the Merchants' Association and the Industrial Council of Cloak, Suit and Skirt Manufacturers, Inc., [inside pro-ducers] and the American Association and the Union and between the asso-ciations themselves, and the Impartial Chairman shall serve in that capacity with respect to the determination of all such disputes."

The practice of extending the jurisdiction of arbitrators under labor agreements to controversies between two or more employer groups had an earlier origin in the men's clothing industry. See the 1915 collective agree-ment between the American Clothing Manufacturers' Association and the Amalgamated Clothing Workers of America and some of the early decisions of W. M. Leiserson, one of the first arbitrators in the men's clothing trade. By the early twenties, the office of impartial chairman, with supplemental machinery for settling disputes, was well established in all the principal markets of the men's clothing trade. ACWA's *Advance*, Feb. 11, 1921.

quired savings. Since the collective labor agreements did not expire until June 1932, submission to the demands of retailers would inevitably disrupt the established labor standards for the trade. If retailers pinched jobbers, jobbers would pinch contractors, and if jobbers pinched contractors, contractors would pinch workers, and if contractors pinched workers, the little pig of equal labor costs would not get home at night. "We have tried to show in this communication," so the report concluded, "that the upholding of uniform discounts is indispensable to the fostering of the basic soundness of our industry."[53]

The organized producers obviously wanted their impartial chairman to investigate the conduct of retailers for evidences of undue discount pressures, as well as to examine the books of organized jobbers, contractors, and inside manufacturers for evidences of discount rate infractions. They fully expected him to take appropriate action in the name of enforcing the labor agreements of their industry. Thus, at their request, the impartial chairman on one occasion notified a well-known firm of a retail clothing chain that it had been charged by certain sources of supply in the coat and suit industry with "attempting to depress labor standards by demanding severe price concessions from the organized manufacturers." The firm responded by threatening to get its clothing supply from other sources.[54]

Soon the industry's impartial chairman was himself decrying the fact that "unlimited competition in our trade comes today from forces mainly out of our control in the battlefield of business — retail and chain store pressure for still lower prices, extra discounts, unreasonable short-time deliveries with demands for specials which are almost gifts for basement bargains." Addressing the ILGWU convention in May 1932, G. W. Alger proclaimed that "these forces of unbridled competition are enemies of all branches of the industry" and stressed the need "to coordinate in-

---

[53]*Women's Wear Daily*, July 21, 1931. See also the issue for July 27, 1931. In an earlier effort to gain the voluntary cooperation of retailers, the Industrial Council of Cloak, Suit and Skirt Manufacturers had met in the fall of 1929 with the newly formed Association of Resident Buyers to organize a permanent conference committee that would undertake to eliminate trade evils, enhance marketing efficiency, and resolve all common problems. *Ibid.*, Nov. 26, 1929.

[54]*Ibid.*, August 20, 1931.

dustrial control so that the rapacity of buyers and the heartlessness of their assaults upon a fair price structure can be met." Looking to the effect of these forces on labor standards, he added, "I see no earthly reason why the lives of 27,000 workers should be thrown in to make a bargain hunters' holiday."[55]

Though not oblivious to the legal barriers that might ultimately doom collective bargaining for violations of the antitrust laws, Impartial Chairman G. W. Alger nevertheless strongly advocated joint labor-management controls over the buying policies of distributive outlets. "If against this disruptive force," he continued, "there can be further perfected an organization of workers, employers and wholesalers to define and maintain minimum labor costs and prices which must at least reflect those costs, I am not afraid of going to jail for enforcing them." Following an important decision of the U. S. Supreme Court in 1933, Mr. Alger felt even more secure from legal restraints, so long as the regulation of trade functions contributed to the protection of labor standards. "I have yet to see, nor do I anticipate," so he observed at that time, "a decision of the courts holding that reasonable protection of the rights to live is a conspiracy in restraint of trade."[56]

The Cloak and Suit Control Commission

At least the "oppressed" factions in the manufacture of women's coats and suits — unions, contractors, jobbers, and inside manufacturers — could hope for relief from their tormentors (the retail buying syndicates) through the activities of a special institution created to meet just such emergencies. In their 1929 collective agreement, the Industrial Council of Cloak, Suit and Skirt Manufacturers (inside producers) and the ILGWU, together with its Cloakmakers' Joint Board, had made provision for a control commission with the composition and powers set forth in the following clause:

For the purpose of eliminating sub-standard and sweat shop conditions a Commission composed of the Impartial Chairman in the

---

[55]ILGWU, *Report and Proceedings,* Twenty-first Convention (May 1932), pp. 94–95. Also quoted in *Women's Wear Daily,* March 14, 1933.

[56]For the U.S. Supreme Court decision, see Appalachian Coals, Inc. v. U.S., 288 U.S. 344 (1933). Alger's observations on the case were reported in *Women's Wear Daily,* March 14, 1933. A fuller treatment of the case may be found below at pp. 791–792.

Industry and of an equal number of representatives of the parties hereto and of all other organizations that are subject to the machinery herein established and of three prominent citizens of the City of New York not connected with the Industry who shall be designated by the Governor of the State of New York shall be organized and charged with the duty of analyzing and investigating the many problems affecting this industry including the problem of production and the abatement of the production of garments under sub-standard or sweat shop conditions in the Industry. From time to time it shall make public its findings and recommendations regarding all matters engaging its attention.

"The powers of the commission set up by the agreements are limitless," proudly announced Samuel Klein, executive director for the inside manufacturers.[57]

Acting under the broad sweep of its powers, the Cloak and Suit Control Commission plunged into the problem of gaining retailer cooperation in stabilizing the women's coat and suit trade. Spurred on by the initiative of Governor Roosevelt and Lieutenant Governor Lehman, the members of this commission, including the union representatives, found themselves time and again assembled in Albany or in New York City with representatives from the retail trade and with other spokesmen for the manufacturing interests to seek out solutions for retailer practices that had allegedly undermined the stability of legitimate manufacturing and, hence, of the labor standards set for the trade. "The cloak industry today has a splendid scheme of organization — the kind I hope will be introduced in other industries," stated Lieutenant Governor Lehman before such a conference on Dec. 12, 1929. "It has a strong union and strong employers' organizations; a commission for control, an impartial machinery for the settlement of disputes."

"There is every reason for retailers to help, for sound trade practices mean good merchandise from good sources," Lehman continued. "Harmful practices mean irresponsible manufacturers

---

[57]In *Women's Wear Daily*, July 16, 1929. In reporting on the agreement to organize a joint control commission, the *New York Times,* July 11, 1929, noted that the scope of the commission's powers would extend to chain stores and buying syndicates. The 1930 collective agreement of the Association of Dress Manufacturers with the ILGWU and the Dressmakers' Joint Board in the dress industry provided for a similar commission. The text of this agreement is printed in *Women's Wear Daily*, Feb. 18, 1930.

and poor garments." Mr. Lehman then proposed another meeting between the commission, the trade representatives, and the retailers. Meanwhile, he suggested that a committee be named to meet with Impartial Chairman R. V. Ingersoll, with the chairman of the commission, G. W. Alger, and with others to discuss ways and means for aiding the trade. "Much can still be done in increasing the stabilization of the industry," Lehman insisted.[58]

At the same conference Benjamin Schlesinger, who had resumed the presidency of the ILGWU, fell in line with the proposition advanced by other speakers that production stabilization was impossible without selling stabilization. He did not hesitate to reveal the power that his union could exert against retailers who insisted upon excessive concessions in any form. "Unless you gentlemen do something," so Schlesinger told the delegates, "we will not be able to go far. It would pay us to strike against retailers and chain stores, and we propose to do so, against those favoring the 'sweatshop.' "[59]

---

[58]As quoted in *ibid.,* Dec. 13, 1929. Lehman had openly favored close collaboration between unions, employers' associations, and retailers to prevent unjustified discount rates and other concessions forced upon the trade by volume buying. *Ibid.,* July 31, 1929. Governor Roosevelt, in his invitation to the joint conference of December 12 called "for the purpose of discussing methods of cooperation for the stabilization of the coat and suit industry," had specifically included, among others, the National Retail Dry Goods Association and the Garment Retailers of America, as well as the ILGWU, and the entire personnel of the Cloak and Suit Control Commission. *Ibid.,* Nov. 27, 1929.

[59]*Ibid.,* Dec. 13, 1929. Earlier that fall, the ILGWU had threatened just such a strike to support a retail chain that had accepted union standards. "Union Will Aid Penny on Prices — ILGWU Offers Assurance to Chain Organization that Substandard Competitors Will Not Undersell It," runs a front-page headline in *ibid.,* Sept. 9, 1929. The article stated:

Assurance that non-union producers of coats and suits, with whom the J. C. Penny Co. will refuse to deal, will not be able to undersell the firm by offering their services to other chains or firms indifferent to union production and union standards, were [*sic*] given by the International Ladies' Garment Workers' Union through David Dubinsky, acting president.... Strikes will be called against such producers, it was said, the union intending to conduct a relentless campaign for the stabilization of the industry and the elimination of all sources of illegitimate competition.

At that time, Samuel Klein, executive director of the Industrial Council of Cloak, Suit and Skirt Manufacturers (inside producers), lauded the union

Directed by its able chairman, G. W. Alger, who also became the impartial chairman under the industry's collective labor agreement, the Cloak and Suit Control Commission met on its own volition in 1930 with the executive heads of department stores, chain stores, and buying syndicates to consider problems of excessive discounts. Further meetings were held in 1931 and 1932 to find ways and means of eliminating the drastic price pressures forced on the manufacturers by large-scale buying. Meanwhile, the accountants assigned to the office of the impartial chairman, now acting under the auspices of the commission, examined the books of association members and disclosed numerous infractions of established discount rates. Pleading with retailers to help abolish sweatshops by patronizing union producers, Mr. Alger in September 1932 hinted at "drastic" publicity against those stores seeking to "disorganize" the trade. At the same time, he threatened to organize a group of "retail associates" pledged to cooperate with the commission in maintaining decent living standards.[60]

Giving force to these threats were union representatives on the Control Commission who had joined with spokesmen from management in making clear to retailers that assaults upon maximum discount rates and upon other trade regulations were tantamount

---

for turning to retailers to help end substandard competition. Equally gratified was Harry Uviller, general manager of the American Cloak and Suit Manufacturers' Association (contractors), who foresaw that the union's effort would have a "good effect upon the industry" by aiding the industry's Coat and Suit Control Commission to eliminate substandard and sweatshop production. *Ibid.*, p. 24.

[60]*Ibid.*, April 21, July 21, 1931; Sept. 6, 8, 1932.

At the 1932 labor contract negotiations for the women's coat and suit trade, the jobbers' association had recommended "the inclusion of a provision that the Union, together with the impartial chairman and/or the Commission, will take definite action against any retail firms or buying oragnizations that persist in patronizing non-union resources, thus giving preference to elements that are undermining this industry." But the collective agreements as finally adopted merely authorized the commission "to investigate the practices of retail stores and chain organizations in inducing and fostering non-union and sub-standard production." *Ibid.*, May 25, 1932. A brief account of the early work of the Control Commission is given in ILGWU, *Report and Proceedings,* Twentieth Convention (December 1929) pp. 76–80. More extensive information may be found in the files of *Women's Wear Daily,* beginning in July 1929.

to "an attack upon the very existence of New York's greatest industry." Aside from its contributions to the commission, the ILGWU planned its own series of conferences with large metropolitan retail outlets to suppress demands for excessive discounts. Through these conferences, the ILGWU sought to convince retailers that extra discounts obtained by large-scale buying would, in the words of Lieutenant Governor Lehman, drive the "competent, enterprising, good manufacturers and merchants" out of business and leave the retailers at the mercy of unreliable producers. Price pressures from retailers, so the union contended, was already driving some jobbers to nonunion sources of production and forcing the organized factions of the industry into exclusive jobber-contractor deals as a means of saving their own skins.[61]

Competition and the Law

The process of fusing trade and labor functions under the banner of collective bargaining was founded on legal as well as economic considerations. In so far as labor unions pursuing their legitimate objectives were exempt from the operation of state and federal antitrust laws, while employers' associations were not, the control of trade practices that were illegal when undertaken by employer groups might pass the test of legality when clothed in the wraps of labor agreements. For there was always hope that regulation of business competition might be held indispensable to the control of labor standards and, hence, incidental to the legitimate objectives of bargaining for better terms of employment.

---

[61]See *Women's Wear Daily,* July 31, Dec. 30, 1932; July 19, 1929. A favorable report on the ILGWU's early success in enlisting the cooperation of department stores, mail-order houses, and chain stores is given in ILGWU, *Report and Proceedings,* Twentieth Convention (December 1929), pp. 57–59.

Writing in the *New York Times* of July 21, 1929 Louis Stark, labor reporter, contended that the problem of chain store purchases and group buying had driven jobbers to sources of nonunion production and had led the organized factions of the industry to conclude the arrangement in the 1929 collective labor agreement whereby the jobbers would have their goods made only by the organized contractors who were members of the American Cloak and Suit Manufacturers' Association. For a similar view, see William Bloom, "The Garment Strike Settlement, a Novel Industrial Phenomenon" in *Labor Age,* October 1929. See also *Women's Wear Daily,* July 27, 31, and Nov. 27, 1929.

There was always the possibility that labor unions working with employers' associations through the medium of collective bargaining might immunize employers from the operation of the antitrust laws and so permit both parties to accomplish through joint action what neither could successfully manage alone.

The role labor unions could play in helping employers to achieve monopolistic objectives was clearly exemplified by the experiences of the textile refinishing industry during the early thirties. For years, the manufacturers of men's clothing had followed the custom of sending large bolts of cloth purchased from woolen mills to refinishing firms to be examined, sponged, shrunk, and refinished before being returned to be made into suits. In time, this comparatively simple service industry developed many trade abuses. Manufacturers would insist that refinishers submit false certifications of cloth shortages or fabric defects in attempts to reduce the manufacturers' debts to their suppliers. Spongers would clip the ends of woolen bolts, privately sell the cloth, and pocket the proceeds. Severe competition within the trade drove wages and working conditions down to such sweatshop standards that satisfactory service could no longer be rendered at a profit.

At this stage, a committee of the refinishing employers in 1932 joined a committee of their organized workers in a move to establish an employers' association — the Textile Finishers' Association. Soon this employer group represented 80 percent of the refinishing business in New York City. A fixed scale of prices to be charged clothing manufacturers for various services in the refinishing process was then drawn up, and standard methods of conducting business were adopted. With workers and employers cooperating to enforce these standards, fraud, improper shortages, thefts, rebates, and other evils, including sweatshop conditions of employment, were for the most part eliminated.

Now the Donnelly Act (Section 340 of the General Business Law of New York State) made illegal and void every agreement whereby competition in the manufacture, transportation, marketing, or sale of goods and commodities in the state was restrained or prevented. Soon the organized employers and the union of their workers in the textile refinishing trade were charged with monopolizing business and brought before the courts to justify their conduct. The New York Supreme Court was called upon to decide whether this form of collusion between an employers' association and a labor union violated the state's antitrust law. But the court was not compelled to base its decision on the merits of the case, for it held that the New York antimonopoly law applied to the manufacture, production, and sale of articles and products but not to services such as the refinishing trade was performing. Nevertheless, the Court, citing Appalachian Coals v. U. S., 288 U. S. 344 (1933), argued strongly for the legality of the agreement.[62]

Labor Exemptions from the State Antitrust Laws

Once the Donnelly Act was amended in 1933 to exempt labor unions pursuing their legitimate objectives from the operation of the New York State antitrust law, the state courts were often asked to define the limits of these exemptions. In all such cases, these state courts generally undertook to distinguish between activities in the name of collective bargaining that were designed "to further the ends of labor" and activities in the name of collective bargaining that were intended "to advance the monopolistic aims of employer groups in their efforts to stifle competition."[63]

Here, the state courts sought to determine what agreements controlling competition fell within the legitimate objectives of bona fide labor unions and what agreements controlling competition illegally restrained trade. All labor union activities "having some reasonable connection with wages, hours, health, safety, and the right of collective bargaining" were presumably immune from attack. "The exemption under the Donnelly Act," once stated Judge Jonah J. Goldstein in the New York City Court of General Sessions, "extends not only to the labor unions but also to all

---

[62]"We are of the opinion that this very recent decision in the Appalachian Coal Case, in its application of the rule of reason to an honest effort to improve the conditions of industry, holding that the agreement there is entirely legal and proper, affords strong support to the agreement here under consideration." New York Clothing Manufacturers' Exchange v. Textile Finishers' Association, 238 App. Div. 444 (1933), 265 N.Y. Supp. 105 at p. 113. The Appalachian Coals case is discussed below at pp. 791–792.

[63]The quoted phrases are from Justice Edward R. Koch's opinion in Falciglia v. Gallagher, New York Supreme Court, 164 Misc. 838 (1937), 299 N.Y. Supp. 890 at 895.

those in contractual relations with such unions where the purpose is patently in furtherance of legitimate union purposes."[64]

All those activities and practices of organized labor that "gave sanction to the transformation of labor unions from media for the advance of the welfare of the working classes to convenient instruments to be used in circumventing the [antitrust] law," were clearly illegal. On one occasion, a group of employers seeking monopoly control over the distribution of their products formed themselves into "Distributors' Division, Local no. 20377" of the labor union that represented the workers of their trade. In passing on the legality of this procedure, Mr. Justice Ferdinand Pecora of the New York Supreme Court held that "the Distributors Division is not a *bona fide* union of laborers or workingmen, but merely an aggregation that has taken on the guise and nomenclature of a union in order to obtain an immunity to carry on its activities as an illegal combination to restrain trade and create a monopoly."[65]

[64]The phrase "having some reasonable connection with..." is from Justice Julius Miller's opinion in Bernstein v. Madison Baking Co., New York Supreme Court, 186 Misc. 474 (1942), 38 N.Y.S. 2nd 811 at p. 813. Justice Goldstein's statement is from People v. Gassman, Court of General Sessions, New York City, 182 Misc. 878 (1943); 45 N.Y.S. 2nd 709 at p. 711.

[65]People v. Distributors Division, Smoked Fish Workers' Union Local 20377, 169 Misc. 255 (1938); 7 N.Y.S. 2nd 185 at pp. 186–187. For other cases bearing on this problem, see: Brescia Construction Co. v. Stone Masons' Contractors' Association, New York Supreme Court, 195 App. Div. 647 (1921), 187 N.Y. Supp. 77; De Neri v. Gene Louis, New York Supreme Court, 174 Misc. 1000 (1940), 21 N.Y.S. 2nd 993; Dunkel v. McDonald, New York Supreme Court, 272 App. Div. 267 (1947), 70 N.Y.S. 2nd 653; Enterprise Window Cleaning Co. v. Slowuta, New York Supreme Court, 273 App. Div. 662 (1948), 79 N.Y.S. 2nd 91; Manhattan Storage and Warehouse Co. v. Movers' and Warehousemen's Association of Greater New York, New York Supreme Court, 262 App. Div. 332 (1941), 28 N.Y.S. 2nd 594; Photo-Engravers Board of Trade v. Addison, New York Supreme Court, 145 Misc. 479 (1932), 260 N.Y. Supp. 332; Pleaters, Stitchers and Embroiderers Association v. Jaffe Pleating Co., Municipal Court of New York, 176 Misc. 411 (1941), 27 N.Y.S. 2nd 615; Smethurst v. International Brotherhood of Electrical Workers, Local 786, New York Supreme Court, 272 App. Div. 948 (1947), 72 N.Y.S. 2nd 42 and 73 N.Y.S. 2nd 27; U.S. v. Fur Dressers' and Fur Dyers' Association, U.S. District Court, S.D. New York, 5 F 2nd 869 (1925); Veteran and Affiliated Package Stores Association, 12 New York State Labor Relations Board 164 (1949); Weitzberg v. Dubinsky, New York Supreme Court, 173 Misc. 350 (1940), 18 N.Y.S. 2nd 97; Report of the Special Master, U.S. District Court,

These guideposts established from cases in other industries did not always help to distinguish legal conduct from illegal conduct in the needle trades where elements of controlling competition in labor costs were hopelessly fused with elements of controlling competition in business practices. How, for example, would these guideposts help to determine the legality of accessory clauses in dress industry agreements forbidding dress manufacturers to buy buttons, belts, laces, artificial flowers, and the like from accessory shops not in contractual relations with a designated local of the ILGWU? Even assuming a legitimate purpose of protecting the position of the union in the trade — as against an illegitimate purpose of protecting one group of manufacturers from competition by another — how would these guideposts affect the legality of union enforcement procedures that required all accessory shops seeking union contracts to belong to a particular employers' association?[66]

As a rule, direct efforts to establish minimum wages in labor contracts raised no furor over legality, but setting minimum costs of production for contractors including allowances for overhead took on the aspects of an illegal restraint of trade, even though such a procedure were the only effective means of enforcing minimum wage levels in the contractor shops. Establishing rates of pay for piece work raised no qualms of legality; but constructing a floor under prices at which the products could be sold, or imposing a ceiling over the costs of material to be used in the manufacture of those products, confused measures for guaranteeing piece rates (a legitimate objective) with measures for restricting business competition (an illegitimate objective).[67]

S.D. New York, in Allen Bradley case, 41 F. Supp. 727 (1941) at p. 731. (See plaintiff's abstract of evidence in Allen Bradley case, vol. II, pp. 549–570.)

[66]See the covered button case discussed above at p. 536. In Minkoff v. Jaunty Junior, 36 N.Y.S. 2nd 507 (1942), the New York Supreme Court held that the promotional clause in the master contract between the Popular Priced Dress Manufacturers' Group and the Dressmakers' Joint Board, ILGWU, had some reasonable relation to wages, hours, and employment conditions and, therefore, fell within the valid scope of collective bargaining.

[67]When Impartial Chairman G. W. Alger decided that a coat and suit jobber had failed to meet minimum production costs for garments made up by his contractors, Alger ordered the deficit to be paid but he was careful to point out that the purpose of minimum production costs for garments made by contractors was "to assist in maintaining the wage scales fixed by

No one raised a question if a collective labor agreement between an employers' association and a labor union contained a "most favored employer" clause obligating the union to concede no more favorable terms to other employers; or else obligating the union automatically to grant association members any more favorable concessions that the union subsequently granted to other employers. But legal questions were likely to be raised if an association of jobbers in negotiating a business agreement with an association of contractors obtained similar concessions by which the organized contractors guaranteed to offer no more favorable business concessions to other jobbers unless those concessions were automatically made available to the association jobbers.[68]

In the absence of specific laws to the contrary, no one doubted the power of an employers' association to grant union members a monopoly on employment opportunities under a labor contract. But if a jobbers' association gave to members of a contractors' association a monopoly on outside production, or if the members of a contractors' association agreed to work only for members of a

---

the contracts by making sure that the garments as made would be made at a price at least sufficiently high to enable those wage scales to be paid." G. W. Alger, *Decisions,* Case no. 781 (1932).

Within a week after the U.S. Supreme Court in U.S. v. Trenton Potteries Co., 273 U.S. 382 (1927) had extended the range of antitrust prohibitions on price-fixing agreements, the U.S. Department of Justice initiated proceedings in the U.S. District Court against the National Hat Frame Association, the Hat Frame Manufacturers' Protective Association, their officers, directors, and members, alleging that the agreement among the manufacturers not to sell their products below cost infringed the Sherman Act. *Women's Wear Daily,* Feb. 24, 1927.

[68]But see the 1965 Pennington case discussed below at pp. 868–882 on the legality of most favored employer clauses in collective labor agreements. An example of a most favored employer clause in a jobber-contractor agreement appears in the 1925 contract between the Wholesale Dress Manufacturers' Association (jobbers) and the Association of Dress Manufacturers (contractors): "The Association of Dress Manufacturers agrees to make every possible effort, subsequent to the signing of this agreement, to enter into individual agreements with any and all independent jobbing houses who are in contractual relations with the International Ladies' Garment Workers' Union, and upon terms not more favorable to said jobbers than contained herein." The text of this agreement is printed in *Women's Wear,* Jan. 30, 1925. In the 1930 agreement between these two associations, each extended most favored employer privileges to the other. *Ibid.,* Feb. 24, 1930.

particular jobbers' association — all with a view to controlling "illegitimate" competition — such transactions smacked of a restraint of trade. Yet one type of transaction may have been as essential to the enforcement of labor standards as the other.

A strike among organized contractors to maintain prices they received for the garments they made under a trade agreement with the organized jobbers was directly analogous to a strike among the organized workers to maintain wages they received under a labor agreement with their organized employers. Yet the former — involving a matter of trade relations — carried implications of collusion to restrain trade in violation of the antitrust laws, while the latter — involving a matter of labor relations — clearly fell within the labor exemptions from antitrust legislation. The use of direct action by the Associated Fur Manufacturers in 1926 to gain compliance by the fur workers' union with the restrictive no-strike clause in a collective labor agreement aroused no fears of impinging upon the antitrust laws. But the use of direct action by the Association of Dress Manufacturers (contractors) in 1924 against the Wholesale Dress Manufacturers' Association (jobbers) to gain compliance with the restrictive business clauses of a jobber-contractor agreement might at least have stimulated an investigation by defenders of antitrust legislation. Yet one type of direct action may have been as essential to the enforcement of the industry's labor standards as the other.[69]

Certainly the Ladies' Hat Manufacturers' Protective Association was treading on thin legal ice when it sought to prevent independent firms from making spring hats before the preceding December 1 — the date on which spring fashions were released from Paris. By taking advantage of cheap, nonunion sweatshop labor in the off-season, months before association members could begin production of their Paris fashion lines, the "unscrupulous

---

[69]*Ibid.*, July 22, 1924. For an account of a major strike by the United Association of Dress Manufacturers (contractors) against the National Dress Manufacturers' Association (jobbers) for alleged violations of their 1933 collective agreement — a strike that involved 2,200 shops and 45,000 workers — see *ibid.*, April 16–20, 23, 25–27, 1934. Among the 16 demands made upon the organized jobbers, the organized contractors insisted upon higher allowances from the organized jobbers for overhead and profits. For an earlier strike by 300 dress contractors who were holding out for an increase in the prices they received from the jobbers for the garments they made, see *New York Times,* July 15, 1932.

manufacturers," in a move to "put one over" on their competitors, had been able to flood the spring market with cheap hats at "ridiculously low prices." But the legal case for the organized manufacturers would have been strengthened had the same proposal been incorporated into a collective labor agreement at the instigation of a labor union that was seeking thereby to strengthen its own position and to maintain decent work standards in the trade.[70]

Some regulations for the movement of garments between jobbers and contractors of the women's coat and suit trade, especially those rules imposed by collective agreements between trucking associations and the ILGWU, were on their face designed to help preserve labor standards set for the industry. But other regulations for the shipping of garments, especially those rules imposed by collective agreements between trucking associations and groups of contractors, jobbers, or inside manufacturers — agreements which granted exclusive rights of cartage to certain truckers and fixed the prices to be charged — had the apparent effect, if not the intention, of creating monopolistic controls. Even the supplemental rules promulgated by impartial chairmen and enforced, along with the agreements themselves, by the impartial machinery of the trade, bore the two-faced character of stabilizing business conduct and prompting uniform compliance with the terms of employment.[71]

Some regulations of outside contracting were clearly within the scope of collective bargaining over terms of employment; other regulations took on the character of business controls in restraint of trade. The more elaborate schemes to set up exclusive interlocking relationships among the organized workers, jobbers, contractors, and inside manufacturers fell within the category of doubtful legality. Certain features of these schemes, as developed in the dress industry and in the women's coat and suit trade during the thirties, not only reduced "excessive" competition but tended to destroy "effective" competition. These features were

---

[70]This episode is reported in *Women's Wear*, March 17, 1916.

[71]See particularly the decisions of Impartial Chairman G. W. Alger rendered on Sept. 19 and Oct. 9, 1933; and the decisions of Impartial Chairman S. A. Rosenblatt, rendered on Dec. 19, 1940 and Jan. 31, 1941. These decisions are filed with the collection of decisions by Impartial Chairman J. J. Walker in the Abelson papers.

challenged before the state and federal courts as illegal conspiracies in restraint of trade.[72]

A Victory for Controlled Competition

The advocates of controlled competition won a notable victory in the New York State Supreme Court during the late thirties. The case involved the legality of interlocking agreements among jobbers, contractors, inside manufacturers, and the organized workers of the dress industry to control outside contracting. Under the plan, the organized jobbers and inside manufacturers were permitted to send outside work only to assigned members of the contractors' association, in return for which the contractors' association agreed that its members would take work only from these organized groups. All employers who were bound by these reciprocal arrangements agreed to hire only members of the ILGWU, in return for which members of the ILGWU assigned to the dress industry were obligated to work only for the parties to these agreements. On its face, the plan formed a part of the regular 1936–1939 collective labor agreements to stabilize hours of work, rates of pay, and working conditions for the dress and waist industry.

In 1938, a contractor assigned to certain jobbers who later quit the business was refused registration for work with other associa-

---

[72]It seemed particularly appropriate that judges in dealing with legal issues of monopoly and competition arising from various needle trade activities should so often draw upon a basic principle of interpretation stated by Mr. Justice Louis D. Brandeis in an opinion written for the U.S. Supreme Court to which he had been appointed in 1916:

> But the legality of an agreement or regulation cannot be determined by so simple a test as whether it restrains competition. Every agreement concerning trade, every regulation of trade, restrains. To bind, to restrain, is of their very essence. The true test of legality is whether the restraint imposed is such as merely regulates and thereby promotes competition or whether it is such as may suppress and even destroy competition.

> —Chicago Board of Trade v. United States, 246 U.S. 231 (1918) at p. 238, quoted, among others, by U.S. District Judge E. H. Brewster in William Filene's Sons Co. v. Fashion Originators' Guild, U.S. District Court, D. Mass., 14 F. Supp. 353 (1936) at p. 358, and by U.S. District Judge William Bondy in United States v. Fur Dressers' and Fur Dyers' Association, U.S. District Court, S.D. New York, 5 F. 2nd 869 (1925) at p. 872.

tion jobbers. Denied access to a source of livelihood, this contractor challenged the whole system of limiting and assigned contractors to certain jobbers as a violation of the New York State antitrust laws. But Justice A. J. Levy of the New York Supreme Court sustained the questionable provisions of these agreements on the grounds that they were a part of a general plan to realize the "legitimate" objectives of a bona fide labor union and, hence, were exempt from the operation of the state's antitrust laws. During the course of his opinion, he explained the court's position as follows:

Obviously, in an industry comprised of small units of employers effective collective agreements can be obtained only if the trade union deals with the employers through an association. This method of dealing has the advantage of avoiding a multiplicity of negotiations at every step and enabling a better enforcement of, and respect for, the very collective agreement not only by the union, but through the discipline which the association exercises upon its individual members. ... The collective agreements under consideration are tripartite affairs involving employers, sub-employers or contractors, and employees — members of labor unions. They involve necessarily not only relations between the employers and sub-employers on the one hand and the labor unions on the other, but they also define relations between the employers and the sub-employers, and the definition of the status of one toward the other inevitably affects the provisions for the protection of the interests of union labor. It is therefore almost unavoidable that the portion of the collective agreement which deals merely with the relations between employers and sub-employers is an integral part of the contract involving a bonafide labor union. As such, on its face, it must be presumed to be exempt from the prohibitions of Section 340 of the General Business Law. ...

The stated purpose of eliminating sub-standard conditions in the dress industry, to aid in its stabilization, and to enforce the terms and conditions of the collective agreement, are all consistently carried out by the specific provisions suitable to those ends. They are not foreign to the usual provisions of collective labor agreements, but on the contrary seem, even when superficially read, designed to promote better conditions. Lack of stability among the contractors and the jobbers means industrial unrest, possible unemployment, glut in one part of the industry and famine in the other. In these days of depression, there is a predominating desire to promote an equitable distribution of work where there is insufficient for all. The inevitable result of the assailed provisions is the introduction of a share-the-work plan which is bound to be advantageous to the workers in the industry.[73]

Concluding Observations

Experiences with collective bargaining in the needle trades indicate that lines of demarcation between labor relations and trade relations cannot be accurately drawn. Under the protocol movement, the two concepts were woven into a common fabric for the good of the industry. Trade practices and labor standards became the warp and woof of labor-management collaboration for mutually acceptable objectives. Either the warp of trade relations supported the woof of labor relations, or else the woof of labor relations supported the warp of trade relations. In the first case, trade practices, by reason of their contribution to the maintenance of labor standards, might be immunized from the operation of the antitrust laws. In the other case, collective bargaining that embraced trade controls, although designed to create and enforce labor standards, might, nevertheless, be contaminated by the operation of the antitrust laws.

Unfortunately for the needle trades, legal issues were not always resolved on the basis of economic considerations. Nor did the law always speak with a single voice. The legality of questionable conduct was most likely to be a product of individual interpretation. Judges, lawyers, and administrators often differed in their views. Until these differences were resolved by the highest

---

[73]Sainer v. Affiliated Dress Manufacturers, New York Supreme Court, 168 Misc. 319 (1938), 5 N.Y.S. 2nd 855 at pp. 859–860, 861. Equally strong judicial support for several other features of the collective bargaining system in the needle trades can be found in the opinion of Justice W. P. Burr in Maisel v. Sigman, New York Supreme Court, 123 Misc. 714 (1924), 205 N.Y. Supp. 807; in the opinion of Justice Bernard Shientag in Abeles v. Friedman, New York Supreme Court, 171 Misc. 1042 (1939), 14 N.Y.S. 2nd 252; and in the opinion of Justice Edward Weinfeld in Greenstein v. National Skirt and Sportswear Association, U.S. District Court, S.D. New York, 178 F. Supp. 681 (1959). Other supporting judicial opinions include those of Justice Salvatore Cotillo in American Cloak and Suit Manufacturers' Association v. Brooklyn Ladies' Garment Manufacturers' Association, 143 Misc. 319 (1931), 255 N.Y. Supp. 614; Justice Edgar Merrell in New York Clothing Manufacturers' Exchange v. Textile Finishers' Association, 238 App. Div. 444 (1933), 265 N.Y. Supp. 105; and Justice A. J. Levy in National Dress Manufacturers' Association v. United Association of Dress Manufacturers, 151 Misc. 827 (1934), 272 N.Y. Supp. 360.

tribunals, those most affected by interpretations often followed their own judgments. Further complications arose from the dual character of the federal system. What was legal or illegal under national law may have differed from what was legal or illegal under state law, even though the terms of state and federal statutes were essentially alike. Since most activities of the needle trades fell within the scope of federal jurisdiction, the decisions of federal agencies and the judgments of federal courts were likely to be controlling.

Chapter 18

Trade Regulations
under the Codes

Had the legality of trade regulations under the banner of collective bargaining been previously resolved in the federal courts, the validity of trade practice programs under the NRA codes might have turned more upon economic considerations than upon fine distinctions of the law. But in the absence of legal guideposts, which a thorough airing of labor-management practices under the protocol system might have provided, the whole movement to control competition in trade practices under the codes was the more deeply affected by unpredictable interpretations of the law. Not only did each separate type of trade restriction need to pass the test of legality, but decisions on legal issues were rendered with insufficient background knowledge of experiences under collective bargaining on which the needle trade codes had been founded.

Self-Government in the Needle Trades

Fortunately, perhaps, for the sponsors of the protocol movement, the development of collective bargaining in the needle trades had been singularly immune from interference by federal agents assigned to carry out federal laws. So quietly and unobtrusively did the advocates of controlled competition in labor costs go about the business of organizing their forces, creating their alliances, developing their principles, constructing their machinery, and resolving their problems that the eyes of the law were seldom focused on what transpired behind the scenes. The negotiation and administration of labor agreements remained strictly a "family" affair. Neither the organized workers nor their employers wanted the long arm of the federal government dabbling into their methods of operation.[1]

This is not to assume that whatever transpired behind the scenes was necessarily surreptitious or illegal. More likely, the immunity of collective bargaining from the political forces of society reflected an extraordinary capacity for industrial self-government. Through the years, this capacity had been marked by the give and take of face-to-face negotiations and by a profound respect for authority. Both traits were undoubtedly inherited from Jewish experiences in the ghettos of eastern Europe where, to minimize external controls, community problems had to be resolved by the community itself. This strange mixture of egalitarianism and respect for authority — complete equality in debate yet profound respect for imposed decisions where debate did not suffice — was transplanted to America by the Jewish influence in the needle trades. These traits were fostered by Jewish leaders of both labor and management; they were encouraged by Kehillah, the Jewish industrial community of New York City; and they found full fruition in collective bargaining, where uninhibited negotiations at the conference table reflected one trait just as respect for the awards of arbitrators reflected the other.

Largely as a result of these influences, collective bargaining in the needle trades had always been remarkably self-contained. Some means short of legal compulsion was always available to accomplish the objectives of industrial self-government. No law was required to guarantee free negotiations at the bargaining table. Voluntary inducement was more effective. No agents of government need play the role of mediators and conciliators in the bargaining process. Scores of individuals and private groups freely offered their services. No public administrators were required to apply and interpret the law. Agencies of the impartial machinery

---

[1]Among scores of general investigations by the Federal Trade Commission made at the request of the President, the Congress, the Attorney General, government agencies, or on motion of the Federal Trade Commission itself, pursuant to the Federal Trade Commission Act during the period from 1915 to 1961, only the 1939 investigation into "Millinery Distribution Methods" falls within the needle trades. 47th **Annual Report of the Federal Trade Commission** (June 1961).

performed these functions. No civil courts were necessary to see that the law of the contract was strictly enforced. Labor unions and employers' associations operating under the impartial chairman for the trade could accomplish this objective. Sufficient unto the goals of law and order in industry were voluntary efforts at resolving disputes and subservience to the will of an arbitrator, the highest symbol of authority.

Particularly outstanding was the capacity of the needle trades for devising machinery to guarantee compliance with the terms of collective agreements. In the area of contract administration, where most collective bargaining systems break down, the organized forces of the needle trade industries through trial and error had developed an effective means of holding employers and workers to their commitments. Even the strike — that drastic weapon of industrial warfare — was harnessed and redirected to the goal of enforcing collective agreements. And there is evidence that the parties to labor contracts had come to respect their own voluntary machinery of enforcement over that of governmental agencies assigned to enforce state labor law. Why else would so many collective labor agreements require employers to meet all the standards of safety and sanitation prescribed by the laws of the state?

This capacity for self-development, coupled with a deep-seated fear of governmental controls, accounts for the relatively small number of occasions on which the parties to collective bargaining systems have broken the barriers of their own institutions to seek relief from civil authorities. By the same token, the failure of victimized participants to seek help from the government had created among governmental agencies a sense of false security toward the observance of laws regulating trade. Moreover, so long as industrial giants beyond the needle trades engaged in restrictive practices that aroused public attention and demanded action, neither the Federal Trade Commission nor the U. S. Department of Justice was likely to pry into the questionable effects of collective bargaining on the growth of monopolies in the needle trades.

An Introduction to Trade Controls

Undoubtedly the National Industrial Recovery Act provided additional growing room for perfecting the system of controlled competition that had originally been sponsored by the founders of the protocol movement in 1910. Whatever legal doubts may have hampered the development of trade regulations in the name of collective bargaining need not apply to a code system which openly invited trade practice controls. At the very time that the parties to collective agreements were developing their elaborate schemes for controlling jobber–contractor–inside manufacturer relationships, agents of the federal government who might have stepped forward in the name of the law suddenly found themselves stymied by new legislation that looked to the revival of business prosperity through collusion to restrain trade.

With few qualms of legal conscience, therefore, the organized manufacturers of the needle trades proceeded to prepare codes, or code revisions, that would prohibit, restrict, or control trade practices, quite apart from their efforts at equalizing labor costs. Provisions covering a wide variety of trade functions affecting business competition were sooner or later written into the needle trade codes. The usual prohibitions against deceptive advertising, commercial bribery, defamation of competitors, espionage, coercion — prohibitions that had long been the stock in trade of governmental controls under the Federal Trade Commission Act — were widely adopted.

More stringent controls over delivery charges, advertising allowances, cancellation of orders, selling on consignment, price discrimination, and other terms of sale followed a pattern common to codes outside the needle trades. For the manufacturers of wearing apparel and accessories, the most important of all fair trade practices were those that undertook to prohibit secret rebates, to regulate discount rates, and to limit the return of merchandise. Yet, in the absence of additional concessions granted by the National Industrial Recovery Act, at least some of these restrictions might have failed to pass legal inspection by the Federal Trade Commission or the U. S. Department of Justice.[2]

---

[2]Opinions varied on the relative emphasis to be given labor standards and trade practices, the two major functions of the code system. Some employers with eyes focused on trade practice controls had to buy labor standards to gain their primary objectives. Some unions with eyes fixed on labor standards had to accept employer versions of trade controls to win support for their primary objectives. These differences were reflected in some proposals for moving code authorities into the offices of the impartial machinery to help enforce collective agreements and in contrasting proposals for moving

Jobber-Contractor Relations and the Codes

Directing first attention to business problems against a background of collective bargaining was like reversing heads and tails on the penny of labor-management collaboration. Whereas, for example, the control of jobber–contractor–inside manufacturer relations had previously been assumed in the name of maintaining labor standards, this issue could now be approached directly as a trade problem governing the relations of different business groups to one another. "The Code Authority shall create, within ten (10) days of the effective date of this Code a special committee to study the problem of jobber-contractor relationships," stated the code of fair competition for the infants' and children's wear industry, approved March 27, 1934. "Said committee shall make recommendations to the administrator regarding the establishment as a part of this Code, of such rules and regulations as will tend to stabilize the relationships between jobbers and contractors."

Some employers would use the codes, just as they used collective bargaining, to forbid all outside contracting; others would limit outside production to designated contractors assigned to given jobbers or inside manufacturers. Some trade associations would require a minimum size for all contracting shops; others would prescribe detailed rules and regulations under which outside production would be tolerated. Some employer groups would establish jobber responsibility for code observance by their contractors; others would insist that a floor be established under prices paid contractors for their work; and practically all organized producers were ready to make use of the new facilities to help enforce restrictions on contracting out work.

In so far as the codes introduced controls over jobber–contractor–inside manufacturer relationships, the code authority would be responsible for registering contractors, limiting their number, and designating their assignments. It would prescribe uniform records and accounts, require periodic reports, and determine minimum costs of production. It would investigate all complaints of code infractions, as well as inspect premises and examine books on its own authority. It would bring alleged transgressors to

the impartial machinery of collective agreements into the offices of code authorities to help enforce code regulations.

justice and impose appropriate penalties. All the while, behind the code authorities would stand the power of the federal government to provide assurances that efforts at controlling this system of outside production could be enforced.

All these possibilities hastened the culmination of the movement for limitation and assignment of contractors that had been floundering for lack of means to guarantee industry-wide support. So long as some manufacturers and jobbers were restricted to certain contractors while others were not, so long as some contractors were free to deal with all jobbers while others were not, these far-reaching schemes to regulate the jobber-contracting system continued to meet employer resistance. Only the union held out consistently for the application of restrictive measures that all other organized factions of industry supported in principle.[3]

Even in the women's coat and suit trade, where the pressure for limitation of contractors was greatest, associations of jobbers, contractors, and inside manufacturers were reluctant to apply principles of limitation which had been endorsed by the Governor's Advisory Commission in the mid-twenties. Some restrictions on the number of contractors or submanufacturers that might be employed for particular purposes were introduced into the 1924 and the 1926–1927 collective agreements for the women's coat and suit trade. Under the stimulus provided by the Governor's commission, steps were also taken at that time looking toward the adoption of a more general system of limitation.[4]

Not until the 1932 collective agreements, however, was sub-

---

[3]In July 1932, David Dubinsky, newly chosen president of the ILGWU, urged the organized employer groups that had long supported the principles of controlled competition to accept limitation of contractors at a time when limitation "would bring about standardization of costs in contracting shops and would eliminate the confusion and demoralization which now prevails in the shops."

But Samuel Blumberg, legal counsel of the Merchants' Ladies' Garment Association, speaking for the organized jobbers of the women's coat and suit trade, could not reconcile the request of the ILGWU for limitation of contractors with the fact that the industry was still not substantially unionized. So long as a vast volume of business is being let out to shops that are not in contractual relations with the union, limitation will be impractical, he said. *Women's Wear Daily*, July 1, 13, 1932.

[4]For example, the 1926 collective agreement between the Industrial Council of Cloak, Suit and Skirt Manufacturers and the ILGWU recognized the limitation of contractors in principle, but left the realization of this prin-

stantial progress ever made toward limitation of contractors for the women's coat and suit trade. Under these agreements, each jobber or manufacturer was limited to not more than twice the number of contractors that he might need in the course of a season. At the same time, no contractor was permitted to work for more than two jobbers or inside manufacturers. To that extent, at least, competition among contractors for work or among jobbers and manufacturers for the cheapest bidding contractor was partially limited. Even this concession from cautious employers came only with assurances that the union would succeed in organizing the industry. And when the union allegedly failed to meet this obligation, the organized jobbers and contractors sought immediate release from clauses restricting free access to one another.[5]

Code Enforcement of Jobber-Contractor Controls

Only after the machinery of government-sponsored codes came to the support of industry-sponsored plans did the employer groups of the women's coat and suit trade consent to a more complete system for controlling jobber-contractor relationships. This change of heart was an expression of faith in the power of the federal government to extend code regulations throughout the trade and in the ability of code administrators to enforce whatever regulations were adopted for the industry. Subsequently, action in the realm of jobber-contractor controls was to be based on a code of fair competition, approved August 4, 1933, for the women's coat and suit trade and on five collective agreements adopted in August and September 1933 between and among the organized forces of the industry in New York City.[6]

---

ciple to the future, contingent on restrictions to be imposed on jobbers in general. ILGWU, *Justice,* Nov. 19, 1926.

[5]See above, pp. 510–512.

[6]The five collective agreements were those between the inside manufacturers (Industrial Council of Cloak, Suit and Skirt Manufacturers) and the ILGWU, August 19, 1933; the jobbers (Merchants' Ladies' Garment Association) and the ILGWU, August 23, 1933; the contractors (American Cloak and Suit Manufacturers' Association) and the ILGWU, Sept. 19, 1933; the inside manufacturers and the contractors, August 21, 1933; the jobbers and the contractors, Sept. 20, 1933. The texts of these five agreements may be conveniently found in Hearings before the Committee on Finance, U.S. Senate, 74th Cong., 1st sess., pursuant to S. Res. 79: *Investigation of the Na-*

The pertinent clauses in these five agreements, and in the code of fair competition for the trade, embraced the ultimate goals of those who had long sought to control jobber-contractor relationships. Each jobber or inside manufacturer could designate no more than the number of contractors actually needed to fill his orders. In turn, each designated contractor could work only for the jobbers or inside manufacturers to whom he was assigned. No contractor could be designated who was not a member of the American Cloak and Suit Manufacturers' Association, and no assigned contractor could work for a jobber who was not a member of the Merchants' Ladies' Garment Association or for an inside manufacturer who did not belong to the Industrial Council of Cloak, Suit and Skirt Manufacturers. Moreover, the only acceptable jobbers, contractors, or inside manufacturers were those who employed union workers and who were under agreement with the ILGWU.[7]

---

tional Recovery Administration (April 1935), Part 6, pp. 2549–2579. The ILGWU, *Reports and Proceedings,* of union conventions during the thirties gave summary accounts of developments in the movement to control contracting.

The need for an additional means of enforcement beyond the impartial machinery of collective agreements was strikingly revealed in the detailed charges submitted by the United Association of Dress Manufacturers (contractors) against the National Dress Manufacturers' Association (jobbers) in April 1934. These charges alleged that members of the jobbers' association had violated almost every provision of their voluntary agreement governing their relationships with the contractors, and that the machinery for adjusting disputes between jobbers and contractors had collapsed. *Women's Wear Daily,* April 18, 1934.

[7]Whether any or all of these provisions were to be found in the collective labor agreements of the women's coat and suit trade or only in the code for that industry was of no concern, for the code specifically embraced the labor agreements — at least those between the associations and the ILGWU — and the labor agreements specifically embraced the code, each with the same force and effect as if written into the documents themselves. Moreover, code authorities used the same procedures and imposed the same type of penalties for infractions of jobber-contractor rules as did the impartial machinery under collective agreements. G. W. Alger was impartial chairman under the collective agreements and also the director of the code authority. F. Nathan Wolf, a former accountant for the ILGWU, was secretary of the code authority and a power behind the scene. Compare the terms of the 1933 labor agreements on jobber-contractor relations with the corresponding terms of the women's coat and suit code approved August 4, 1933; and see *Women's*

What remained was to carry out this objective by supplementing the efforts of the impartial machinery with the most effective use of the code machinery. With the code authority for the women's coat and suit trade dominated by the organized factions in New York City (eight of the nine members represented the New York Associations and the ILGWU), the road was opened for a coordination of effort that gave every promise of success. And if the reports of special NRA agents and investigators assigned to study the operation of the women's coat and suit code are to be taken seriously, the organized factions of the trade did attain a substantial measure of success within the first fifteen months of code administration.[8]

Wherever employers' associations were unable to control their members or whenever the ILGWU was unable to control the workers, the code authority could impose the necessary sanctions or assess additional penalties. Thus, in May 1934, a dress manufacturer was directed to pay over to the code authority for the dress manufacturing industry the sum of $3,425 for violating code provisions governing jobber-contractor relationships. The chief weapon of enforcement, however, was the power to grant, withhold, or withdraw the NRA label. No manufactured products could pass into the hands of retail outlets bound by the retail code unless an appropriate label was attached. Possession of the label was, therefore, a prerequisite to business operations and, hence, to employment. Workers were driven into unions and employers into associations in order to obtain the labels for the products of their handiwork. And to make matters worse, those seeking membership in their respective organizations were in some cases denied admittance. These restrictions on operations were the source of many charges of monopolistic controls.[9]

Reporting on the operation of the women's coat and suit code in the New York region for the period from July 26 to August 15, 1934, Allison Smith, special NRA agent, submitted evidence that

---

Wear Daily, May 10, 1934, for similarities in enforcement. For the operation of jobber-contractor relations under the dress industry code, see the Nov. 1, 1933 issue.

[8] In the revised code of August 20, 1934, nine of the fourteen members of the code authority represented the three New York Associations and the ILGWU.

[9] *Women's Wear Daily,* May 10, 1934.

the three New York employers' associations were engaged in a "monopolistic curtailment of operations" tending to augment rather than abate the problem of unemployment. "Preliminary investigation," so Smith reported, ". . . tends to show that this code authority is entirely dominated by the union and Mr. Nathan Wolf. That labels are being withheld from many jobbers and contractors without definitely establishing violations of the code. That labels are used in place of stink bombs to force men into associations and to unionize them." Special Agent Smith thus sumed up his report: "It is beyond a question of doubt that the National Coat and Suit Code Authority works exclusively for the benefit of the above associations and not for the industry as a whole."[10]

The findings of the Smith report were strongly endorsed two months later by a similar report of Special NRA Agent J. C. Howard covering the administration of the women's coat and suit code in the New York, New Jersey, Connecticut area for the period from August 15, to October 15, 1934. After citing clauses from the code and the labor agreements that opened the door to monopolistic practices, Howard, like his predecessor, gave numerous examples of complaints against the operation of the system and then drew the following conclusions:

The code authority is enforcing not the code, but a series of interlocking contracts entered into by the manufacturers, jobbers, and contractors' associations and the union with the following results:

The code authority has denied to manufacturers and jobbers the right to choose their own contractors and the right of contractors to choose their jobbers and manufacturers.

---

[10]Smith supported his charge of curtailment of production by citing a statement from Samuel Klein, executive director of the Industrial Council of Cloak, Suit and Skirt Manufacturers, published in the *New York American* on July 3, 1934, and by citing the minutes of the hearings before the industry's fact-finding commission on June 27 and 28, 1934, at which time allegedly damaging statements were made by Harry Uviller, manager of the American Cloak and Suit Manufacturers' Association, Samuel Klein, executive director of the Industrial Council, Harry Dubow, manager of the Merchants' Ladies' Garment Association, and Isidore Nagler, manager of the Cloakmakers' Joint Board of the ILGWU. The report of Allison Smith is extensively quoted in *Investigation of the National Recovery Administration*, Part 6, pp. 2523–2524, 2526. The report of the NRA fact-finding commission for the women's coat and suit trade was published in a special supplement to *Women's Wear Daily*, July 27, 1934.

The code authority has withheld the issuance of labels to coerce manufacturers, jobbers, and contractors to enter into contracts. Manufacturers, jobbers, and contractors in some instances have been put out of business.

Manufacturers, jobbers, and contractors not members of these associations and not employing union labor have been coerced by the code authority and the union into joining these associations, and employees likewise have been coerced into joining the union.[11]

Monopolies and Production Costs

Along with the question of limiting and assigning contractors under the needle trade codes there arose the key issue of whether to guarantee contractors minimum costs of production — costs that would include a reasonable allowance for overhead as well as all expenses for labor. This issue, like the issue of contractor limitation itself, had a labor face and a trade face. Insuring minimum costs of production would help to enforce labor standards, and so the issue rightfully belonged in the realm of labor problems. At the same time, guaranteeing minimum production costs for contractors would put a floor under business competition and

---

[11]Much of the Howard report, dated Oct. 25, 1934, is quoted in *Investigation of the National Recovery Administration*, Part 6, pp. 2536–2549.

Howard described conditions under the women's coat and suit code in terms that might have applied with equal validity to conditions under collective agreements before the codes:

> The principle of the united front against outsiders is therefore openly recognized. Interlocking provisions in collective agreements between related elements of industry require exchanges of preferential treatment by each group of the members of the other signatory groups. In this manner, manufacturers and jobbers agree to deal only with contractors employing union labor, contractors agree to accept work only from manufacturers or jobbers who are in contractual relationships with the union, and the union agrees that its members shall be permitted to work only for those concerns who are recognized members in good standing of the various employers' associations. The common objective of all elements is to extend the bound of organization as far as possible, so that a minimum of competitive disadvantages will be experienced by those who are operating under the collective agreements.

Highlights of these charges against the women's coat and suit code authority were reviewed in Sherman Trowbridge, *Some Aspects of the Women's Apparel Industry*, NRA: Division of Review, Industry Studies Section (March 1936), pp. 110–116.

so belonged in the realm of trade practices. In either case, the NRA codes offered a new channel for industry-wide extension and enforcement.

Previously, clauses in collective agreements accepting the principle of minimum costs had been largely nullified through inadequate coverage or failures of compliance. But the heyday of relief for all who suffered from excessive price competition between the covered and uncovered establishments was not long in coming. The organized factions of the women's coat and suit trade received a shot in the arm when the code of fair competition for the trade provided that "all firms engaged in the coat and suit industry who cause their garments thus to be made by contractors or sub-manufacturers . . . shall adhere to the payment of rates for such production in an amount sufficient to enable the contractor or sub-manufacturer to pay the employees the wages and earnings provided for in this code together with an allowance for the contractors' overhead."

Just four days after this code of fair competition was approved on August 4, 1933, Harry Uviller, executive director of the American Cloak and Suit Manufacturers' Association (contractors), explained how the new system of guaranteed production costs would operate:

Jobbers and manufacturers must register the exact number of contractors in accordance with their volume of business done last year. Work must be divided equally and contractors must be paid enough to meet the prescribed standards for workers in addition to their overhead. Rules to govern limitations will be laid down by the Coat and Suit Authority. . . . Prices and classifications of garments will be designated by a bureau. Contractors cannot be disengaged or discharged except for cause after a hearing. Overhead will be determined by a percentage of the labor cost, with the lowest overhead percentage set at 33-1/3 percent of labor costs.

Spanning the broader areas of trade as well as labor controls, this form of price regulation permitted the advocates of "fair" competition to move from the less productive fields of labor functions into the greener pastures of direct trade controls now presumably shielded by the canopy of the National Industrial Recovery Act from the penetrating rays of the antitrust sun.[12]

---

[12]*Women's Wear Daily*, August 8, 1933. See also the statement of Maxwell Copelof, executive director, Merchants' Ladies' Garment Association (job-

While the National Industrial Recovery Act exempted approved codes of fair competition from the restrictions of federal antitrust laws, the act did impose limits upon the extent to which such codes would be permitted to restrain trade. Before approving industry codes, the President had to be convinced "that such code or codes are not designed to promote monopolies or to eliminate or oppress small enterprises and will not operate to discriminate against them." He had to be sure that trade associations and employer groups sponsoring such codes "impose no inequitable restrictions on admission to membership therein and are truly representative of such trades or industries or subdivisions thereof." In addition, the act flatly stated that "such code or codes shall not permit monopolies or monopolistic practices."[13]

These general prohibitions opened the way for endless interpretations of numerous trade activities that in some way limited the scope of free competition. What constitued legal or illegal restraint of trade under the codes was determined in the first instance by NRA officials from the President of the United States, who finally approved code provisions down to the separate code authorities and their representatives who implemented and applied code terms. The range of issues varied from means of curtailing production, manipulating prices, and allocating markets, on the one hand, to methods of conducting research, promoting sales, and increasing efficiency, on the other. Between the obviously harmless activities at one extreme and the patently illegal practices at the other, these officials had to pass judgment on more than a thousand different forms of trade regulations.

In the early months of the codes, government officials generally took the position that all but the most obvious monopolistic

---

bers), quoted at p. 23 of W. A. Simon, "History of the Code of Fair Competition for the [women's] Coat and Suit Industry" (processed), NRA: Industry Section 3, Division of Business Cooperation (Nov. 11, 1935), U.S. National Archives.

[13]The act also expressly declared that nothing in Title I on industrial recovery should be construed to impair the powers of the Federal Trade Commission under the Federal Trade Commission Act. In conformance with this policy, some of the NRA codes expressly stated that "No provision of the Code shall be so applied as to permit monopolies or monopolistic practices, or to eliminate, oppress, or discriminate against small enterprises." See, for example, Art. X of the Code of Fair Competition for the Millinery Industry, approved Dec. 15, 1933.

practices fell within the exemptions of the National Industrial Recovery Act. Herein, they were following the initiative of the organized manufacturers who rushed to take advantage of their assumed freedom from the shackles of antitrust restraints. Since the purpose of the act was to encourage industries to work out their own salvation, governmental authorities with some misgivings went along with a number of proposals that clearly bordered on the monopolistic. In the drastic attempt to move upward from the "dead low" of the Great Depression, the announced policy of Congress "to provide for the general welfare by promoting the organization of industry for the purpose of co-operative action among trade groups" was allowed to transcend any "provisos" that retained elements of the antitrust laws.

Manipulating Price Controls

Whatever their concern for uniform labor costs, needle trade manufacturers did not neglect the possibilities of more direct action toward regulating the prices at which their products were sold. The number and variety of trade practices recognized under more than five hundred codes of fair competition reveal the extent to which manufacturers throughout American industry focussed their attention on forms of manipulating the price structure. Price controls were generally considered the key to the rehabilitation of American industry. Restrictions on price cutting below costs of production was the most common type of price control but by no means the only one. Limitations on production with assignment of production quotas, methods of allocating markets, plans for filing price lists in advance of price changes, agreements for open bidding and direct price-fixing, as well as prohibitions on selling below costs, were prominent among the many schemes for price controls.

From an investigation of the first two hundred and fifty completed codes, George Terborgh in his study on *Price Control Devices in NRA Codes,* concluded that the "provisos" of the National Industrial Recovery Act retaining elements of the antitrust laws "have not deterred the NRA from approving codes containing a variety of arrangements for the control of prices and production, some of which appear to be definitely contrary to the antitrust laws as heretofore interpreted by the courts." He classified the forms of price controls into four main types: (1) the fixing of minimum prices under the codes; (2) prohibition against selling below individual cost of production; (3) open price arrangements; and (4) limitation of production or productive capacity.

A later analysis of five hundred codes showed that 79 percent of the codes with trade practice provisions regulated minimum prices, 72 percent called for uniform methods of cost accounting, 59 percent contained open price provisions, while 43 percent contained specific discount limitations and terms of credit.[14]

Many code proposals coming from apparel manufacturers called for price controls directed at selling below costs. The New York dress industry would give its code authority the power to lay down rules on prices and price reporting in order to stabilize the trade. The fur trimming manufacturers would establish a reasonable selling price to insure a fair return on costs of production. The Women's Headwear Group of the millinery industry would forbid willfully destructive price cutting. Generally, code authorities in the needle trades were expected to create and administer uniform systems of cost accounting, prepare standard cost formulae, and otherwise plan for establishing minimum prices below which needle trade products could not be sold.[15]

---

[14]George Terborgh, *Price Control Devices in NRA Codes* (1934), pp. 1, 3. The later analysis is from Brookings Institution, *The National Recovery Administration: An Analysis and Appraisal* (1935), p. 570. See also, *ibid.*, chap. 23, pp. 578–622 on "The Transfer of Power over Prices." In the Brookings' study, forms of price manipulations are classified into (1) limitations on cash discounts and quantity discounts; (2) uniformity in prices and excessive price increases, both arising from open price agreements; (3) excessive surcharges and uniform surcharges; (4) liberal interpretations of costs below which no goods could be sold; and (5) limitations on the manufacture and distribution of second quality goods.

Several of the processed "Work Materials" studies prepared by the NRA's Division of Review and dated March 1936 dealt with the price control issue. See no. 48, E. A. Mag and G. J. Feldman, "Legal Aspects of Price Control"; no. 56, Saul Nelson, "Minimum Price Regulations under Codes of Fair Competition"; and no. 54, S. P. Kaidanovsky, "Trade Practice Conference Rules of the Federal Trade Commission (1919–1936): a Classification for Comparison with the Trade Practice Provisions of the NRA Codes."

[15]It shall be unfair competition for any manufacturer in the Clothing Industry, either directly or indirectly, to sell its manufactured product at a price below its cost as determined without any subterfuge in accordance with sound accounting practice. Cost shall include the cost of piece goods consumed, trimmings, cutting, and making; and a percentage on the selling price to cover all overhead.

"Upon a fair and reasonable price 'floor,' there can be built a structure of wholesome competition," belatedly asserted Samuel Klein, executive director of the Industrial Council of Cloak, Suit and Skirt manufacturers, before the National Industrial Recovery Board, January 9, 1935, "a structure that will be safeguarded against crashing down upon those dependent upon the industry for a livelihood." Klein was urging a practical means of "legitimate cost protection" within the antitrust exemptions of the National Industrial Recovery Act. The needle trades, he insisted, had not inspired the enactment of antitrust legislation nor was there danger of "consumer-mulching" trusts in the manufacture of garments where thousands of firms were competing for products of limited value.[16]

The women's coat and suit manufacturers, so Klein asserted, were seeking a means of escape from the power of chain stores and buying syndicates to determine prices. Any successful pressure on a manufacturer to sell below cost had a snowballing effect. "The sale of a few hundred coats at a price considerably lower than that justified by legitimate costs," he stated, "will automatically establish a below-cost quotation for tens of thousands of garments in that category." Klein wanted approval for a method of cost finding to be formulated and made available to members of

---

—Code of Fair Competition for the Men's Clothing Industry, approved August 26, 1933.

No member of the Industry shall sell or service any fur articles at a price less than his own individual cost as computed by the uniform cost system provided in Article VI, Section 6 (k) of this Code . . . [exceptions cited].

—Code of Fair Competition for the Fur Manufacturing Industry approved May 19, 1934.

Not until the code authority of the full fashioned hosiery industry had ruled that selling hosiery of a certain quality and quantity below $5.75 raised a presumption of selling below cost did the industry find any effective means of preventing sales below cost. *Women's Wear Daily,* April 24, 1934. In their proposed codes of fair competition, the employer groups of the fur trimming industry (see *ibid.,* July 26, 1933) and of the women's blouse industry (see *ibid.,* July 21, 1933) clearly indicated their desire to prohibit sales below cost defined to include overhead and reasonable profit.

[16]Corwin D. Edwards, in his "NRA Trade Practice Experience," one of the unpublished staff studies prepared under the Division of Industrial Economics, National Recovery Administration, pointed out that the stabilization of labor cost was in some industries regarded as the heart of price control.

his industry for use as a guide, but not to be used in any way "to bring about arbitrary uniformity of costs or prices." He recommended that the National Industrial Recovery Board differentiate between cases in which price stabilization was fundamental to industry security and those cases in which "protection of legitimate costs is not required."[17]

Shifting Stands on Price Controls

But the worm of federal policy on price controls had already turned when Samuel Klein made his belated plea for "official assistance in stabilizing our trade." The very first memorandum of the National Recovery Administration in the summer of 1933 had assumed that provisions against selling below costs would be acceptable. The model code drafted in Washington to guide code makers expressly authorized the submission of appropriate provisions regulating sales below cost. And, for a time, NRA officials gave trade associations the benefit of a doubt in approving code provisions on price controls that were of questionable legality.[18]

Very soon, however, the government began to pedal backward from its more advanced position on tolerating forms of price controls. NRA officials, concerned lest trade associations by creating monopolies and suppressing small business might swell the ranks of the unemployed, began to insist upon extensive modifications of trade practices before approving codes, and on occasion even withdrew approval for trade practices previously granted. Fear that the organized manufacturers were abusing their new freedoms inspired the movement to transfer power under the codes

---

[17]"A fortunate purchase — a piece of good fortune attributable to the misfortune of the seller — becomes public property in the trade in an astonishingly short time. The great chains and syndicates, the privately and cooperatively owned resident offices promptly circulate to their members' stores their latest successes in determining values." Statement of Samuel Klein at the National Industrial Recovery Board Hearings on Price Fixing, Jan. 9, 1935. Here cited from the appendix, pp. 29, 30, to Simon, "History of the Code of Fair Competition for the [women's] Coat and Suit Industry."

[18]See studies of the model code from references given in "Special List No. 12 — Select List of Documents in the Records of the NRA," compiled by H. C. Calkin and M. H. Fishbein; especially a study by Harry Mulkey, "The So-called Model Code, Its Development and Modification" (processed), Work Materials no. 36, NRA: Division of Review, Organization Section Studies (March 1936).

from trade associations to code authorities more directly subject to government controls.

Extended hearings on price controls in the early months of 1934 revealed widespread evidences of trade practices that "resulted in raising prices to an unjustified level in the interest of the customer and for the permanent welfare of the industry." From more than a thousand pages of testimony in January 1934, Senator Gerald P. Nye found "startling" disclosures of price-fixing by trade associations, of larger firms dominating small enterprises, of intimidations against noncooperating firms, and of a rapid rise in consumer prices. These findings were confirmed by the National Recovery Review Board named by the President in March 1934 to report on whether the codes fostered monopolies and suppressed small businesses.[19]

While these disclosures were in progress, the National Recovery Administration issued an office memorandum on February 3, 1934, stating that henceforth restrictions on selling below costs would be tolerated only after the code authority for an industry found that destructive price cutting had created an emergency threatening the enforcement of code provisions. This backtracking move was followed by office memo 228, dated June 7, 1934, declaring that price-fixing was contrary to public policy, although it conceded that price floors might still be approved to prevent destructive price cutting. Few such approvals were ever forthcoming.[20]

---

[19]Senator Nye's position was summarized in *The National Recovery Administration: An Analysis and Appraisal*, p. 707. For summaries of the National Recovery Review Board reports — both the Clarence Darrow majority report and the J. F. Sinclair minority report — together with extensive criticisms of these reports, see the *New York Times*, May 21, 1934, and the *New York Herald Tribune* of the same date. The text of the final Darrow Report appears in the *New York Times*, July 2, 1934. For more details, see *Investigation of the National Recovery Administration*, Part 6. For views of the needle trades on the course of price controls under the codes, see the files of *Women's Wear Daily*, beginning with the issue of Jan. 9, 1934. Two good summary articles on monopolies and price-fixing under the codes are: W. P. Mangold, "Six Months of the NRA," *New Republic*, March 21, 1934, vol. 78, pp. 150–152; and W. A. Orton, "Should the Codes Survive," *Current History*, August 1934, vol. 40, pp. 528–535.

[20]Saul Nelson, "Minimum Price Regulation under Codes of Fair Competition" (processed), NRA: Division of Review, Trade Practice Studies Section (March 1936), pp. 26–30. This change of governmental policy on price con-

The new policy against price-fixing received further attention from the National Industrial Recovery Board in the winter of 1934–1935. During the fall of 1934, the board had received an accumulation of evidence tending to show that code provisions for mandatory costing systems and permanent schedules of prices had not promoted the public interest. While recognizing "the value of permissive cost systems, emergency price provisions, and the dangers to the economic structure of destructive price cutting," this board confirmed its opposition to price-fixing "in the form of permanent schedules of minimum prices, with or without mandatory costing systems for the purpose of establishing minimum prices." Accordingly, the board announced public hearings on price-fixing to begin January 9, 1935. It was at these hearings that Samuel Klein on behalf of the women's coat and suit trade had come to the defense of standard cost finding methods to be made available for members of his industry — methods that would fall short of "arbitrary uniformity of costs or prices."[21]

---

trols also produced a shift of power from industrial associations to code authorities:

> A sharp cleavage between code authorities and trade associations to prevent any abuse of industrial self-government by the latter is planned by the National Recovery Administration.... Dominance of an industry by an association instead of an authority is felt to be dangerous and, consequently, the NRA is anxious that the code boards become the ruling power in each industry rather than the association.
>
> Briefly, the reasons are these: Authorities have a fairer representation of medium and small sized plants than have the executive boards of trade associations, most of which are dominated by the large units; the authority is the designated representative of the government, a position which, it is felt, could not be safely entrusted to the "old order" association....
>
> The NRA's main object is to remove the association as a controlling factor in an industry and to vest the code authorities with full supervision. It recognizes that associations have in the past done excellent work in the matter of research, standardization, promotion, development of new products, etc., and is anxious that this work be continued. But as far as trade practices are concerned, the Recovery Administration wants them handled entirely by the code authority.
>
> —*New York Times,* Feb. 18, 1934.

[21]National Recovery Administration, Release no. 9292 (Dec. 17, 1934). In another mimeographed release, entitled "Notice of Public Hearings on Policy of the National Industrial Recovery Board Relating to Price Fixing" and dated Dec. 22, 1934, the National Industrial Recovery Board reiterated its

Some Questionable Trade Practices

Samuel Klein's conservative position at the board's hearings more or less reflected the general stand of the apparel industries toward trade practices under the codes. Bypassing the more radical schemes for limiting production, fixing prices, and allocating markets, employer groups of the apparel industries concentrated their attention on preserving and enforcing standards of business conduct they had long since worked out among themselves. More than a year after receiving its first code, the women's coat and suit trade finally incorporated into its revised code a comprehensive list of trade practices that included many items formulated by trade associations of the industry as far back as 1917.

But the apparel trades could neither rely on their preoccupation with comparative wage rates nor cite their reluctance toward directly manipulating the price structure to gain immunity from charges of monopolistic practices under the "provisos" of the National Industrial Recovery Act. Quite aside from the more dubious controls over jobber–contractor–inside manufacturer relationships that had been worked out under collective bargaining and perfected under the codes, the usual trade regulations for standardizing conditions of sale might well bear evidence of suppressing small-time business enterprises. Moreover, attempts under the codes to regulate discount rates that had been a subject of concern to the women's garment trades since 1917 could easily take on the attributes of monopolistic practices in restraint of trade.

Such potentials of monopolistic controls merely followed the pattern of other industries. The operation of codes in general, so the Consumers' Advisory Board of the NRA reported to the National Industrial Recovery Board in January 1935, had permitted special interests to introduce code provisions that tended to eliminate active price competition. Although the codes were presumed to establish a floor under wages, prices, and business standards, with freedom to compete above those standards, the Consumers' Advisory Board found "that the present codes have

---

stand but recognized "that minimum prices may be proper for the normal operations of certain types of industries, but, in such cases government supervision and control would naturally tend to be increased."

gone far beyond these simple minima." The board that spoke for the consumers thus summarized its findings:

Prohibitions against sales below "cost" with industry itself determining "cost," basing price systems, minimum mark-ups, maximum trade-insurance, resale price maintenance, limitations on discounts and guarantees, minimum prices — such restrictive code provisions have little to do with the establishment of basic standards for labor, quality standards for the consumer or simple honesty for the trade. They may be used, directly or indirectly, to control prices and profits. Their aim is not to regulate competition but to eliminate it.[22]

Whatever their purpose or legality, all these practices tended to suppress the small business man who had been a special object of government attention in the recovery program. Although the apparel trades were a massive conglomeration of small enterprises, the concern of the National Industrial Recovery Act for small business found little support among the organized manufacturers of wearing apparel or among the unions of their workers. "Small business" was a relative term, and to the unions and associations of the needle trades the term was synonymous with illegitimate competition. During the summer of 1933, the ILGWU had objected to the first NRA code proposed by the three major associations of the women's coat and suit trade on the ground that the proposal had tolerated an excessive number of manufacturing units — upwards of two thousand separate establishments in the New York area alone.[23]

The support of manufacturers and labor unions for needle trade codes of fair competition had been inspired, in part, by the hope that only producers of substantial means would be tolerated in each trade. Nowhere beyond the apparel industries had con-

---

[22]Consumers' Advisory Board, memorandum to the National Industrial Recovery Board, quoted in the *New York Times*, Jan. 7, 1935.

[23]In a pamphlet opposing a proposed code of fair competition submitted by the women's coat and suit manufacturers, Morris Hillquit, counsel for the ILGWU, lamented the decline of the inside manufacturers' association from 440 members employing 25,730 workers in 1916 to only 180 members employing 5,000 workers in 1932. He stressed the high mortality rate among contractors and submanufacturers, one-third of whom, he said, went out of business each year. He objected to the idea of an industry code that made no provision for remedying this situation. From a copy of a pamphlet filed in the ILGWU newspaper scrapbook, ILGWU research library.

certed attempts to eliminate small-scale producers (mostly independent contractors) been carried on so systematically for so long a time. The additional freedoms which the National Industrial Recovery Act had bestowed upon business combinations otherwise operating in restraint of trade produced no new methods of suppressing small business that employers' associations and labor unions of the needle trades had not already tried and found wanting under the protocol system.[24]

Intertrade Relations

Another potential source of monopolistic practices arose from the complexities of interindustry competition. By producing garments normally made in other trades, or else by offering alternatives in style and fashion to lure away customers of other industries, a garment manufacturer could extend the range of his competition far beyond his own trade. Thus, manufacturers of women's coats and suits were capable of operating in competition with manufacturers of women's dresses and with manufacturers of women's blouses and skirts. Likewise, manufacturers of fur garments were able to compete with producers of fur-lined or fur-trimmed garments and both groups faced competition from manufacturers of garments made wholly of cloth. For the most part, however, the charges of "illegitimate" competition that accompanied these intertrade complexities arose from differences in labor standards or in accepted rules of business conduct.

Manufacturers temporarily shifting their operations to the products of other industries were usually seeking the additional profit to be derived from producing under lower labor costs and less rigid trade practices than had been established for the product industry. Technically, the transition was simple enough, for so great was the reliance on hand labor that the skills and the machinery required by most of the needle trades were largely interchangeable. Women's coats and suits could always be made by firms normally manufacturing men's clothing, and vice versa. Ladies' dresses could readily be produced by manufacturers of undergarments, and vice versa. Children's apparel was not so specialized as to preclude its production by manufacturers of women's coats and suits, men's clothing, ladies' dresses, or by accessory in-

---

[24]See above, pp. 115–124.

dustries, like the headwear trades. Wherever trade and labor standards differed from one industry to another, the temptation for interindustry raiding created strong disruptive influences as objectionable to the organized manufacturers as to the unions of their workers.[25]

Long before experiences with the NRA codes had publicized the problems of competition between industries of the needle trades, parties to collective agreements seeking to stabilize their trades were harassed by this process of jumping industry barriers. In the absence of multiple-industry associations or multiple-industry trade agreements, the burden of controlling this evil had fallen largely upon multiple-industry unions. By encompassing a number of related trades, the international unions of garment workers, clothing workers, fur workers, and headwear workers were each in a strategic position to see that law and order ruled over large segments of intertrade relations. Moreover, in this particular area of potential conflict, needle trade unions were more inclined to cooperate among themselves than to permit jurisdictional wars over industry boundaries. They tended to uphold industry trade practices and standards of employment against those who would seek to produce industry products under the lower standards of another trade. Through collective bargaining, employers' associations were able to endorse and support union activities in these areas of control without arousing the ire of the antitrust officials.[26]

---

[25]Aspects of this problem were reported from time to time in *Women's Wear Daily*. See, for example, the issues of April 3 and June 9, 1930.

[26]In March 1930 Samuel Klein, executive director of the Industrial Council of Cloak, Suit and Skirt Manufacturers, charged the ILGWU with violating the "most favored employer" clause of the women's coat and suit industry agreements in that the union permitted manufacturers of the dress industry operating under dress industry agreements to make evening wraps, velvety coats, silk coats, and white cloth coats in direct competition with the coat and suit trade and at substantially lower costs which derived from lower wage rates and the option of piece work existing in the dress trade. *Ibid.*, March 12, 1930. For Klein's later charges on behalf of the inside manufacturers' association, the union's reply, and Klein's rebuttal, see *ibid.*, June 17, July 31, and August 6, 1930. See also ILGWU's *Justice*, Sept. 12, 1930.

For an earlier example of the power the ILGWU could exert to prevent a member of the Cloak, Suit and Skirt Manufacturers' Protective Association from transferring his membership to the Dress and Waist Manufacturers' Association in order to gain the advantage of lower labor costs, see the Booth

Intercode Relations

The top administrators of the NRA code system tended to magnify these intertrade problems by approving separate codes for different industries, which were carved out with too little concern for conflicting or overlapping jurisdictions. Thus the code of the blouse and skirt industry sat astride the code for the dress industry and the code for the women's coat and suit trade. The code for the cotton garment industry invaded the realm of dressmaking, cloakmaking, the manufacture of undergarments, raincoats – even the production of men's pants. The millinery code overlapped the knitted outerwear code as well as the code for infants' and children's wear. In more than one trade, custom manufacturers operated under different codes from those of wholesale manufacturers, although both groups produced the same type of products.[27]

Throughout this vast complex of code systems, no two codes were identical either in their labor standards or in their trade practices. The most disturbing differences between codes were those in wage rates. Operating under lower wage scales, dressmaking firms and retail shops could manufacture women's coats and suits unhampered by the higher standards of the wholesale women's coat and suit code. Manufacturers bound by the millinery code found that the products of their industry could be produced more cheaply under the lower labor costs of the knitted outerwear code or the code for infants' and children's wear. Fur manufacturers operating under the retail trade code maintained a competitive advantage in wage rates over those operating under

---

case, discussed at length in *Minutes,* Arbitration Proceedings between the Dress and Waist Manufacturers' Association and the ILGWU (May 17, 1914), vol. 2, pp. 75–195.

[27]There never was and never can be any reason for a separate code for custom milliners. Manufacturers operating under our own [Millinery] Code are now forced to compete with manufacturers making hats of a similar nature where the workmanship is identical but where such so-called "custom milliners" can operate under lower wages and more hours — just another case of creating unfair competition for our manufacturers.

    —Eastern Women's Headwear Association to Max Meyer, chairman of the millinery code authority, letter quoted in *Women's Wear Daily,* May 3, 1935.

the fur manufacturing code. Men's pants could be made more cheaply under the cotton garment code than under the men's clothing code.[28]

Not only did overlapping codes differ in their content; they also differed in the degree to which their terms were enforced. Part of the disparity in labor costs among competing headwear manufacturers was attributed to the fact that the infants' and children's wear code was more loosely enforced than the millinery code. Those manufacturers who transferred from a code authority that enforced compliance with code terms to a code authority that was lax in code enforcement obviously obtained an unfair advantage over their competitors, even if code terms were identical. And what was true of disparities in labor costs was equally true of disparities in trade practices. Women's coat and suit jobbers complained that in some cities their competitors operated under the wholesale drygoods code so that they would not be compelled to follow the trade practice provisions of the coat and suit code.[29]

By controlling competition within each industry, the code system had intensified competition between trades. Code administrators were now faced with the necessity for regulating intertrade competition that had led to code raiding and code jumping. The first step in this direction was to confer upon code authorities power to recommend measures for the coordination of code activities wherever an industry was affected by codes of other industries. The usual procedure was to have code authorities name trade practice committees to meet with similar trade practice committees from other code authorities to formulate rules on intercode relations for approval by the national code administrator. In some cases, temporary committees were named to investigate

---

[28]See, for example, the "Report of the NRA Commission for the [women's] Coat and Suit Industry to the NRA Code Administrator," printed in *ibid.*, special supplement, July 27, 1934. In his NRA study, "The Men's Clothing Industry" (processed), NRA: Division of Review, Industry Studies Section (March 1936), J. W. Hathcock deals at length with jurisdictional conflicts between the men's clothing code and the codes of eight or ten other industries. See particularly, Appendix C: "Production of Men's Clothing under the Cotton Garment Code: the Overlap Problem," pp. 316–473.

[29]*Women's Wear Daily*, May 3, 1935. See also the Feb. 6, 1935 Report of the Fair Trade Practice Bureau established under the women's coat and suit code, quoted in the appendix, pp. 115–118, to Simon, "History of the Code of Fair Competition for the [women's] Coat and Suit Industry."

and report on intercode relations; in other cases, a permanent intercode agency was established to help iron out conflicts and disputes arising between related groups covered by different codes.[30]

Many other proposals were advanced to relieve the inequities of interindustry competition under the codes. Some would limit the production of industry products to those bound by industry codes. Mortimer Lanzit, executive director of the National Dress Manufacturers' Association, proposed a separate division of the National Recovery Administration that would devote its attention exclusively to intercode raiding. Others would let the code follow the product and not the firm. A special commission of the women's coat and suit trade recommended that outside firms making garments ordinarily produced by the coat and suit industry pay the wage scales of the coat and suit code. The more practical minded would fashion a separate remedy to meet each particular need. The cotton garment industry code was amended to provide for a special intercode committee to equalize competition in the manufacture of men's single pants. The committee reduced the wage rates for manufacturing this product under the men's clothing code, while raising the rates for this operation under the cotton garment code.[31]

Still other proposed reforms were directed toward consolidating related codes into a few broad industry groupings that would create basic minimums in trade and labor standards, with the prospect of adding further improvements through collective bargaining. These recommendations varied from the abolition of certain codes — absorbing the blouse and skirt code into the dress and the coat and suit codes, for example — to the consolidation of all needle trade codes into a single master code for this entire group of industries. In the fall of 1934, two members of the Cloak and Suit Code Authority submitted specific recommendations for a single apparel code to be headed by a permanent industrial commission that would supplant "the multitudinous emergency code authorities now existent in the apparel trades." Such a step, they

[30]See "Trade Practices Affecting Relationships between Members under Different Codes," NRA: Office Order no. 66 (Feb. 2, 1934).

[31]See the Report of the NRA Commission for the [women's] Coat and Suit Industry to the NRA administrator. The text of this report is printed in a special supplement to *Women's Wear Daily*, July 27, 1934.

argued, would tend to eliminate much of the unfair competition generated by the code system.[32]

Less extreme proposals were advanced to consolidate more closely related groups of industries within the needle trades. Thus, the various branches of the fur processing, fur manufacturing, and fur distributive industries might well be brought under a single code. The National Recovery Administration itself considered the possibility of simplifying wage scales and trade practices by consolidating or merging closely related codes. In the summer of 1934, some 682 codes were placed in 22 major classifications under four basic groups of enterprises: production of basic materials; fabrication into finished products; services (like transportation or amusement); and distribution, wholesale and retail. The ultimate plan called for ten major divisions to be accompanied by code mergers that would reduce the total number of codes to only 250. Needless to say, all these proposed concentrations of power to curtail "unfair" competition further aroused the suspicions of those assigned to enforce antitrust legislation.[33]

Enforcing Trade Practices

The cooperation required to control competition between industry groups stimulated the growth of vertical combinations essential to the enforcement of trade practices. Just as effective con-

---

[32]Under the present codes complex wage scales and abstruse classifications of crafts obtain for some trades and not for others, creating new conditions of unfair competition as vicious as the old. Further, the complexity of some of the codes makes uniform and fair enforcement impossible. Arbitrary and trivial distinctions are currently the basis for differentiating trades and commodities with the consequence that some concerns fall under a variety of codes, while others cannot be classified for purposes of determining under what code authorities jurisdiction they fall. Some concerns are saddled with intolerably minute wage regulations while others continue to pay pre-NRA wages for pre-NRA hours of work.

—From the "Text of Recommendation for a Single Apparel Code" in *ibid.*, Nov. 5, 1934; Alexander Printz of Cleveland and Milton G. Rosenfeld of St. Louis submitted the recommendations.

[33]*New York Times*, August 28, 1934; *Women's Wear Daily*, July 26, 1933, May 31 and Nov. 16, 1934. On the general problem of overlapping codes, see H. P. Hutchinson, "Problem of Administration in the Overlapping of Code Definitions of Industries and Trades, Multiple Code Coverage..." (processed), NRA: Division of Review, Work Materials no. 39, Organization

trol of labor standards called for support from suppliers and distributors, so the effective control of trade practices depended upon the support of vertically related industries. Most of the fair trade practices belatedly incorporated into the women's coat and suit code were concerned with problems of distribution. None of these practices could be enforced without the help of distributors and retailers. The control of discount rates, the use of code labels, the regulation of style piracy, limitations on the return of merchandise — all these key issues called for cooperation among suppliers, producers, distributors, retailers, and consumers, if established trade practices were to be scrupulously observed.[34]

Successful cooperation in gaining compliance with fair trade practices was a product of bringing pressure for code observances from both ends of every business deal. Buyers as well as sellers had to support the enforcement of discount rates. Senders as well as receivers had to favor restrictions on the return of merchandise. Distributors as well as manufacturers had to stand behind the NRA label as a symbol of fair trade practices. Since the national code of the retail trade forbade any member of the trade to purchase, sell, or exchange unlabeled garments manufactured under a code requiring use of the label, refusal to handle unlabeled goods was the code counterpart of refusal to handle nonunion goods under collective bargaining. If supported by all factions from suppliers of raw materials to consumers of finished products, this medium of itself would guarantee the enforcement of trade practice standards.[35]

Studies Section (March 1936), Appendix no. 2. Part A of this study consists of a proposal for the regrouping of codes.

[34]See Simon, "History of the Code of Fair Competition for the [women's] Coat and Suit Industry," appendix, pp. 115–118, for the Report of the Fair Trade Practice Bureau dated Feb. 6, 1935; and also his, "History of the Code of Fair Competition for the Dress Manufacturing Industry" (processed), NRA Studies (Sept. 23, 1935), at p. 47 for Henry Creange, "Safeguarding Industry against Pilfering of Ideas."

[35]For an account of organizing a national council on trade relations to act as an impartial body for the correction of trade practice abuses between producers and distributors under the provisions of the National Industrial Recovery Act, see the *New York Times,* June 19, 1933. This organization that included industrialists, bankers, wholesalers, retailers, and their respective associations was to function as a division of the American Arbitration Association and was to proceed on the premise that "the successful operation of the new law must depend in a very large measure on the maintenance of

Meanwhile, the New York associations of manufacturers operating under the needle trade codes continued to enforce fair trade practices upon their own members. They heard complaints, conducted investigations, tried suspects, and punished the guilty — just as they had done under voluntary agreements before the codes. Now they were ably assisted by code authorities and trade practice inspectors who often operated with more vigilance. Code authorities also extended their control over independent firms that had signed compliance agreements. Reports of compliance activities bear out the contention that the enforcement of trade practices in the New York area ranked among the greater achievements of the code system.[36]

Evidences that trade practice standards were profitably enforced came from the reports of code authorities. Within months after the trade practice amendments of March 26, 1934 had been added to the original millinery code, approved December 15, 1933, the enforcement of a standard 7½ percent code discount rate had saved the industry $2,500,000 over the pre-code variable discount rate that had averaged 9½ percent. Under the code of fair competition for the dress industry, the trade practice complaint committee spent most of its time enforcing the code provisions on unjustifiable returns. In 1933 and 1934, this committee's efforts led to substantial savings for dress manufacturers from more than

---

fair relations between producers and distributors." Specific rules governing buyers and sellers were to be introduced under an intertrade code to be adopted jointly by associations of producers and associations of distributors, and machinery was to be devised to enforce these measures. "The Council proposes to provide the necessary agency for the self-regulation of producers and distributors in their mutual relations under such intertrade codes," stated the *New York Times*.

[36]Enforcement was gratifyingly effective. Not only did the sanction of the Blue Eagle label prove a powerful charm against the dispersed elements of the trade, but the Code Authority's hand was immeasurably strengthened by the ready-to-hand information-gathering system of the impartial chairman's Accounting Department and the Labor Bureau. It was a mere extension of the procedure of these New York agencies to embrace the entire country under the aegis of the Code. Figuratively speaking, the "well-trained" employers of the metropolis served somewhat as decoys in capturing the "wild" employers in the nation at large.

—D. E. Robinson, *Collective Bargaining and Market Control in the New York Coat and Suit Industry* (1949), p. 210.

$24,000,000 worth of returned merchandise received each year.[37]

At best, these cooperative efforts to enforce fair trade practices failed to uproot many chiselers (mostly small-time contractors) who profited from undermining code standards — just as they had profited from undermining the standards of collective labor agreements. Still working beneath the floors of legitimate competition, these operators justified their resort to secret rebates, cancellation of orders, return of merchandise, excessive discounts, and selling below costs on the assumption that they could not otherwise survive. Exposing these underground deals was no easier for code administrators than it had been for the impartial machinery of collective agreements. While hundreds were detected violating the codes, thousands still operated beyond the pale of the law to harass the advocates of controlled competition.[38]

Nor were vertically related industries always cooperative in helping to enforce fair trade practices. Each group of suppliers, distributors, and retailers, like each group of manufacturers, had its own quota of illegitimate competitors who would not accept the standard of business conduct established for the trade. Some retailers, for example, preferred to design their own products, buy their own materials, select their own contractors, and sell their own finished goods directly to consumers. This practice was ex-

---

[37]For the millinery industry, see the first annual report of Max Meyer, chairman and director of the millinery code authority, Jan. 15, 1935, *Women's Wear Daily*, April 18, 1934; and J. C. Worthy, "The Millinery Industry" (processed), NRA: Division of Review, Industry Studies Section (March 1936), pp. 82–85. For the dress industry, see Simon, "History of the Code of Fair Competition for the Dress Manufacturing Industry," p. 38a.

On Oct. 1, 1934, the code authority for the women's undergarment and negligee industry established a bureau of returns that in the first four months examined 4,192 returned garments, 2,231 of which it sent back to the manufacturers with the notation "claim justified" and 1,961 of which it sent back to the retailers with the notation "claim unjustified." *Bulletin of the Undergarment and Negligee Code Authority*, February 1935.

[38]At the time the first code of fair competition was adopted for the dress manufacturing industry, the dress contractors apparently took the position that the union stood a better chance than the government of controlling the industry. While agreements between contractors and jobbers to fix prices had often been little more than scraps of paper, the union had held the key to effective controls. "They seem to think," observed one writer, "that a strong union is what the trade needs most of all." C. W. Call in *Women's Wear Daily*, August 15, 1933.

pressly prohibited under some codes of the needle trades. Nor would these rebellious factions submit to established procedures for determining trade violations. Those who refused to arbitrate trade issues under code procedures could be reached only by legal prosecutions, which were far too slow and costly to be effective. Only because trade associations, labor unions, and the impartial machinery of collective bargaining came to the support of code authorities were fair trade practice provisions so well observed.[39]

The Law and Public Policy

Aside from unscrupulous elements operating on the outer fringes of each industry, those failing to endorse and observe trade regulations under the codes may have been prompted by doubts of legality or they may have been motivated by questions of public policy. The initial enthusiasm of those who made the first moves to rehabilitate industry through codes of fair competition was seldom restrained by questions of legality or doubts of wisdom. But when the full consequences of the new program became more apparent, many who had once offered their uninhibited support now paused to question the wisdom or doubt the legality of what was transpiring.

The fears of those who paused to think appeared to revolve about the growing belief that there could be no point of permanent suspension between a completely free economy and one dominated by monopolistic controls. The idea of "fair competition" delicately poised between the evils of too much freedom to compete, on the one hand, and the dangers of too little freedom to compete, on the other, was losing its force in the light of experiences under the codes. General Hugh Johnson, NRA administrator, had defined the problem as one of "protections against the ruinous effects of destructive competition on the one hand and against excessive prices and discouraged efficiencies on the other."

---

[39]"A manufacturer or a contractor shall not make garments from fabrics, trimmings, and/or other materials owned or supplied by a retail distributor or agent, representative, or corporate subsidiary or affiliate of such retail distributor." Code of Fair Competition for the Men's Clothing Industry, approved August 26, 1933. This rule was carried over into the trade practice provisions (cut, make, and trim clause) of the postcode National Coat and Suit Industry Recovery Board. See Robinson, *Collective Bargaining and Market Control in the New York Coat and Suit Industry,* pp. 111–112.

More and more students of this problem were coming to believe that once the stream of *free* competition was obstructed by codes of *fair* competition, no concern for the public interest could stop the beavers of monopolistic controls from damming the current altogether.[40]

Lack of concern for the public interest had disturbed the advocates of controlled competition in the needle trades from the inception of the protocol movement. There is no evidence, however, that these sponsors of labor-management collaboration had ever deliberately intended to violate state or federal antimonopoly laws. On the contrary, protection of the public interest which prompted passage of antitrust legislation had always tempered the objectives of those who sought through collective bargaining to establish the reign of law and order in industry. Beyond the use of negotiation, mediation, and arbitration to resolve differences between the "bosses" and the "people" for the benefit of those immediately concerned, there evolved a broader concept of arriving at settlements that would promote the general welfare of the trade. And beyond the industry-oriented approach to collective bargaining lay the further presumption that parties to collective agreements, however united in their desires, must not neglect the public interest.[41]

Having a respect for the public welfare was another outgrowth

---

[40]General Hugh Johnson is quoted in the *New York Times,* Feb. 18, 1934. See also, Johnson's 12-point program to correct weaknesses in the code system, summarized in the *New York Herald Tribune,* Feb. 28, 1934.

> The question then is how the NRA is going to prevent business men from limiting all competition, from allocating production, and establishing monopoly or quasi-monopoly prices. This is a very serious problem, and it would be trifling with realities to dismiss it on the theory that the Sherman act is still more or less in force or that General Johnson's organization can keep an eye on several hundred trade associations and prevent them from combining in restraint of trade.
>
> —From a syndicated article by Walter Lippmann, "The NRA Reexamined," undated clipping filed in the Abelson papers.

Another discussion of the issue appears in W. P. Mangold, "Six Months of the NRA," *New Republic,* March 21, 1934, vol. 78, pp. 150–152.

[41]"In view of their primary responsibility to the consuming public, workers and owners are jointly and severally responsible for the cost and the quality of the service rendered." 1921 collective agreement between the Cleveland Garment Manufacturers' Association and the ILGWU. The text of this agreement is printed in *Women's Wear,* Dec. 24, 1921.

of the Jewish heritage that helped to shape so many institutions of collective bargaining. Following the pattern set by the Jewish communities in eastern Europe, Kehillah, the Jewish organization of business men in New York City, became a symbol of public opinion. Its interests transcended the work of its committee on industrial relations. Kehillah was not only industry-minded, it was public-minded — the voice of the Jewish Community. It operated on the assumption that whatever contributed to the peace and welfare of industry also contributed to the good of the community. Its task was to save industry from unscrupulous exploiters, on the one hand, and from industrial agitators, on the other.[42]

The interests of Kehillah were not unlike those of other third parties who shared so conspicuously in the early development of collective bargaining for the needle trades. Public-spirited citizens who once dominated the negotiation and administration of labor agreements never let the participants forget the public interest. In the early years of the protocol movement, repeated use of public representatives on conference committees and boards of arbitration arose more from the desire to have the public represented than from the need for an impartial umpire. Not only did

---

[42]On behalf of the Jewish Community (Kehillah) and particularly on behalf of its Committee on Industrial Relations, I desire to state that we are ready to lend our moral support and disinterested service to the end that the institutions which you are endeavoring to build up in the fur industry will redound to the welfare of all concerned, and to peace and good-will of the community.
—From a 1914 letter of J. L. Magnes, chairman of Kehillah, to the Associated Fur Manufacturers and the International Fur Workers' Union, in *Minutes* of the fur industry conference committee.

The Kehillah, as you probably know, was organized for the purpose of creating a public opinion among the Jewish residents of this city and especially among those who, recently arriving from Europe, had not yet become sufficiently assimilated with the American people to have been able to grasp the spirit of our institutions. Investigation by Kehillah shows that in industrial matters in particular the workers were being exploited on the one hand by a certain unscrupulous element among the employers and on the other hand by political and industrial agitators.
—Adolph Engel, president, Associated Fur Manufacturers, reporting to association members on achievements in 1914.

Copies of the contents of both these letters are available in the Abelson papers.

labor unions and employers' associations want to enlist public support for checking chaotic conditions in their trades, but arbitrators themselves assumed a responsibility for representing the public as well as the parties.

The arbitrator's initial concern for the public interest was further magnified by the development of market-wide and industry-wide bargaining. When the organized factions of the men's clothing trade approached this goal of industry-wide standards shortly after the First World War, those who feared collusion between labor and management to raise wages and boost profits relied heavily upon third parties to protect the public interest. Industry arbitrators who had led the way in the development of market-wide labor standards for the trade were assumed to be "farsighted, impartial, and of high standing" – men who would prevent the contracting parties from fashioning an industrial empire that would "enrich themselves at the expense of the people who must buy clothes."[43]

Nevertheless, for all their high sense of public duty, industrial arbitrators, in so far as they made a profession of their skills at keeping the peace, had to find ways of satisfying both disputing parties in order to save their jobs. "Full and free private negotiation — that is to say, collective bargaining under a neutral chairman — is all right as far as it goes; but it is open to a serious objection," reflected W. Z. Ripley in 1922. As a representative of the federal government, Ripley had been responsible for keeping the peace in the men's clothing industry during the First World War; and after the war he had helped to develop the institutions of collective bargaining for that trade. Drawing on his own experiences and observations, Ripley continued:

Perhaps it little behooves me, having been instrumental in the creation of this machinery, to criticise it; and yet I apprehend con-

---

[43]*New York Evening Post,* Feb. 18, 1920; see also, *Daily News Record,* Dec. 31, 1920. "In taking into account the interest of the public," concluded the board of arbitration for the Chicago men's clothing market on Dec. 22, 1919, in a decision concerning a wage increase during the life of the collective agreement, "it [the board] is bound to consider both the economic and the public or social value of continuous production and a peaceful and orderly method of conducting industry." The text of this decision is printed in ACWA, *Report and Proceedings,* Fourth Biennial Convention (May 1920), pp. 132–136. The quotation cited is at page 135.

stantly the danger to the public welfare flowing from such a plan. It threatens to leave the public entirely out of account. The workers demand an increase. All the employers are in the arrangement. The increase is granted, and all the employers alike add the increase "and then some" to the price charged for the product.

Without the constant presence of some truly public representative, no chairman, however conscientious, if he be intent upon preserving peace within that industry and if he be employed for that purpose by the industry, can quite be trusted to give due weight to the interest of the inarticulate and unorganized consumer.

Ripley conceded that the dangers in such a system of "purely private adjustment" were serious only where a collective agreement covered an entire trade, an objective toward which the men's clothing industry had just been working.[44]

Few participants in the bargaining process for the needle trades showed more respect for the public interest than did Julius Henry Cohen, father of the protocol movement and legal counsel for several employers' associations. Cohen's concern for the public welfare was reflected in his persistent desire to bypass "petty litigations" for the "root problems" of each trade. It was reflected in the prominent role he would assign public representatives in the composition of all agencies devoted to the objectives of controlled competition. "It seems to me," he once wrote, "that, if, under the jurisdiction of Congress over interstate commerce, we could create a national industrial board, constituted of leading trade unionists, employers and public men and women, we should find a method for applying intelligently and constantly to trade agreements the force of public opinion...."[45]

Certainly the contributions of state and local officials to the development of collective bargaining were never tinged with the thought of endangering the public interest. The mayors of New York City and the governors of New York State, together with the various committees and commissions they created, assumed their responsibilities in the name of the public and directed their efforts accordingly. In the words of Mayor J. P. Mitchel's council of conciliation created in 1915 to save the original Protocol of Peace, such agencies owed no obligation to either party but owed the

---

[44] W. Z. Ripley, "Loading the Olive Branch," in the *Survey Graphic*, Sept. 1, 1922, p. 645.

[45] J. H. Cohen, *Law and Order in Industry* (1916), p. 226.

community a duty to prevent strife and create a better base for future relations.

At times, these agents and agencies of political government urged bold steps for building stability into the needle trades. During the mid-twenties, Governor Smith's Advisory Commission on the women's coat and suit trade was prepared to go farther in limiting and assigning contractors and in establishing minimum costs of production for work done by contractors than the industry was willing to accept at that time. Neither this stand nor Lieutenant Governor Lehman's advocacy of strong labor unions and strong employers' associations to stabilize discount rates against retailer pressures or, for that matter, Governor Roosevelt's conferences with inside manufacturers, jobbers, contractors, workers, and retailers "to foster economic stability" were open invitations to violate the laws of the land. While the public interest demanded action pitched somewhere between unrestrained chaos and official regimentation, such action had to be kept within the confines of the law.[46]

The Law and the Codes

This voluntary work of third parties in protecting the public interest also helps to explain why the latent evils of the protocol movement never came to light until the era of the codes. Even then, the pattern of collusive conduct under the codes that first aroused public concern for a competitive economy came from other industries than the needle trades. In the apparel industries, as elsewhere, fair trade practice slogans could be used to hide questionable forms of price controls. Regulating conditions of sale could be directed to destroying competition in the manufacture and distribution of goods. Bans on sales below cost could be so constructed as to permit few variables in the price structure.

In time, most of the apparel trades sought to take advantage

---

[46]See above, pp. 695–697. When, in the summer of 1932, Acting Governor Lehman was called upon to mediate a dispute over new contract terms in the women's coat and suit trade, he dispatched a telegram to the parties which read in part as follows: "Neither public opinion nor the public interest will sanction any but the most helpful and understanding attitude on the part of all groups in the industry.... I am confidently counting on your full cooperation in my efforts to prevent industrial strife at this time." *Women's Wear Daily,* July 18, 1932.

of their new freedoms. Under the code of the millinery industry, for example, the system of uniform cost accounting devised for the trade took into consideration three elements of costs: (1) *merchandise* (total costs of materials used in the manufacture of a hat); (2) *direct labor* (costs of blocking, operating, cutting, trimming, rounding, steaming, and fitting); and (3) *overhead expenses* (factory expenses, office expenses, administrative expenses, and selling expenses). The sum of all these elements represented the gross cost of a hat below which the product was not to be sold. Along with these elements of a cost-finding system, the Women's Headwear Group had originally sought to add an additional 10 percent for profit. Even barring the 10 percent for profit, however, a liberal estimate of costs assigned to the various factors in production would doubtless approach the actual selling price of the product.[47]

In these moves by industry groups to establish codes that would benefit industry groups, consumers were presumably shielded from the dangers of monopoly power by an NRA advisory board set up for their protection. Consumers also were given the right to attend public hearings on proposed codes, and their interest in code administration was protected by the presence of government representatives on code authorities. Yet, none of these devices could altogether thwart the wolf of monopolistic controls hiding beneath the cloak of fair trade practices. Legal authorities assigned to enforce antimonopoly laws manned their guns and assembled their munitions for a final showdown. Between those business practices that were obviously legal and those that were obviously illegal, they concentrated on the doubtful cases where legality hinged on the particular use made of each questionable trade practice.[48]

---

[47]*Ibid.*, Jan. 24, 1934; see also, "Standard Principles of Cost Finding for the Hat Manufacturing Industry," prepared and published by the Code Authority of the Hat Manufacturing Industry, March 25, 1935. Copy filed in the Abelson papers.

[48]For legal precedents, see the unpublished NRA materials filed in the U.S. National Archives, particularly the appendix to Part II of "Legal Studies — Legal Aspects of Code Practice Provisions," Exhibits I to S inclusive, especially Exhibit K; and C. D. Edwards, "NRA Trade Practice Experiences," one of the staff studies prepared under the Division of Industrial Economics. Edwards stated that the object of the NRA was to check price demoralization by creating an escape from the automatic warping of

Thus uniform accounting systems might be legal when used to calculate costs of operation for business purposes but illegal when used as a cover for price-fixing. Price cutting might be legal when employed in the normal course of business operations, but illegal when designed to eliminate weaker competitors. Conversely, prohibitions against price cutting might be legal if the effect was to save weaker competitors from bankruptcy, but illegal if the effect was to interfere with the normal course of business. Some restraints on selling below costs might, because of their purpose or effect, meet the standards of legality set by the courts, while other restraints would not. Moreover, such legal precedents as may have been established before the NRA codes were not necessarily controlling under the additional freedoms granted industry to control competition by the National Industrial Recovery Act.[49]

Long before adequate lines of distinction between the legal and the illegal could be drawn, however, the United States Supreme Court invalidated the National Industrial Recovery Act. Decisions on the legality of trade practices that might have provided guideposts for future conduct were not forthcoming. Whether the primary concern of the apparel industries with comparative labor costs would have affected the legality of trade regulations remained unanswered. What constituted "reasonable" overhead or "destructive" price cutting or "sound" principles of cost finding was never resolved. Between "legitimate cost protection" to insure industrial stability and "monopolistic price-fixing" to maximize profits lay a shadowy area of dubious legality through which the courts were never permitted to pick their way.[50]

---

price levels that arose from the destructive character of one-sided competition.

[49]In my opinion one of our greatest difficulties between N.R.A. and the Federal Trade Commission is the uncertainty as to whether anything done under authority of an approved code can nevertheless be construed as violation of the antitrust acts.

The antitrust laws prohibit combinations and conspiracies in restraint of trade. There is not a code in the whole category that is not in some sense a combination in restraint of trade. The aim of the antitrust acts is to prohibit monopoly. N.I.R.A. also prohibits monopoly.

—General Hugh Johnson, NRA administrator, as quoted in *New York Herald Tribune*, Feb. 21, 1935.

[50]In Schechter Poultry Corp. v. U.S., 295 U.S. 495 (1935), the U.S. Supreme Court declared unconstitutional Title I of the National Industrial Recovery

Concluding Observations

This general foray into the realm of business controls under the NRA codes exposed the course of development that the regulation of competition might normally be expected to take. Barring some compelling restraint, the additional liberties granted business men to operate in the name of fair trade practices could be expected to culminate in some form of price controls. Experiences under the codes would seem to indicate that once the idea of controlled competition had been accepted, all signs would sooner or later point to price-fixing at the end of the trail.

While bearing no official relationship to the past history of the protocol movement, code experiences with business controls nevertheless aroused a certain amount of curiosity toward similar experiences under collective bargaining. For if, in attempting to regulate fair trade practices under the codes, business firms had run so quickly off the deep end of price-fixing to the detriment of the public interest, why had not the protocol system with similar objectives long since run off the deep end of collusion to restrain trade? And if, through the collusion of business firms, the NRA codes appeared destined to ride roughshod over the public interest — even in the face of NIRA "provisos" that forbade monopolies — then why should similar predictions not await the future of collective bargaining, especially when labor exemptions from the antitrust laws give the parties still more freedom that might be used to override the public interest?

The answer to the first of these questions lay buried in the heritage and traits of the Jewish people who ran the show. Prior to the NRA codes, a profound respect for the decisions of industrial arbitrators, more so than nebulous fears of the law, had kept the institutions of collective bargaining from drifting into forms of regulating output, allocating markets, and fixing prices. It remained to be seen, however, whether industrial arbitrators, after the codes, might still be able to control the questionable conduct of employer groups that had come to enjoy the privileges of restraining trade through their own action. With an NRA

Act of June 16, 1933, principally on two counts: (1) the act exceeded the powers delegated to the national government to regulate interstate commerce; (2) the act exceeded the power of Congress to delegate its legislative functions.

precedent for self-help, employer groups might hesitate to follow the leadership of third parties who defended the public interest in collective bargaining, even though such leadership was soon to be buttressed by the decisions of an aroused legal giant hovering ominously over the proceedings!

Admittedly, the NRA codes had given the needle trades an opportunity to expand and perfect their own system for controlling trade relations, as well as an opportunity to expand and perfect their own system for controlling labor standards. Instead of embarking on radical schemes to fix prices, limit production, and allocate markets under the codes, the apparel industries had for the most part been content to operate along their previously established courses: they made use of the codes (1) to regulate contracting and to guarantee contractors minimum costs of production; (2) to develop uniform systems of cost finding which would permit valid comparisons of production costs; (3) to control discount rates which would check the price-fixing power of buying syndicates; and (4) otherwise to standardize the conditions of sale, particularly the return of merchandise that had so often sapped the profits of business. Even the old competitive problem of industry-jumping under collective agreements to profit from lower labor costs had its counterpart in code-jumping for the same purpose — an evil that received extended attention from code authorities.

While the economics of trade relations under the codes created no sharp breaks with the past, the law of trade relations took on a new importance. Additional freedom from antitrust restraints written into the National Industrial Recovery Act stimulated a new interest in combinations and conspiracies to restrain trade and increased, rather than diminished, the amount of litigation that arose over separating legal from illegal practices. Unfortunately, decisions bearing on the legality of trade regulations more often turned on general considerations applicable to all industries than upon special considerations applicable to the needle trades.

The code system succeeded in publicizing the legal issues behind long-accepted procedures and long-established practices of collective bargaining. Some knowledge of the legal issues raised by fair trade practice programs under codes of fair competition, therefore, provided a background for similar questions yet to be resolved on the more general subject of competition and collective bargaining. Soon, voluntary control of competition by the "legitimate" elements of industrial society was to become hopelessly confused by the necessity for complying with legal restraints. Henceforth, the entire course of collective bargaining was to be influenced more by the thought of keeping within the law than by new ideas for improving existing institutions and methods of operation.

Chapter 19

Trade Practices

beyond the Codes

THE sudden death of the National Industrial Recovery Act on May 27, 1935 created more confusion among the organized factions of the needle trades than the introduction of the law had generated two years earlier. With a background of collective bargaining that closely approximated the goals of the NRA, industries of the apparel trades had slipped into the code system with a minimum of disturbance to the status quo. During the two years of the codes, however, the organized employers of these industries had come to exercise privileges they were loathe to give up. Particularly had these manufacturers of wearing apparel capitalized on their freedom from antitrust restraints by supplementing their labor agreements with more direct forms of trade regulations. Having eaten the once forbidden fruit on which other trades were thriving, these manufacturers acquired more faith in their own ability to control competition. Some would spurn the unions and strike out alone for the promised land of law and order.

Self-Help through Associations

Following the death of the NRA, the organized fur manufacturers of the New York market made known their intention to continue the trade practice provisions that had previously been incorporated into their industry code of fair competition. At a

meeting on June 6, 1935, just ten days after the National Industrial Recovery Act was invalidated, members of the Associated
Fur Coat and Trimming Manufacturers resolved

(a) that the fair trade practice regulations, as contained in the code
of fair competition for the fur manufacturing industry be and the
same hereby are continued;

(b) that each of such provisions be and the same hereby is adopted
as and for the standards of fair trade practice of the members of the
association;

(c) that all of said provisions shall be incorporated into and become
part of the rules and by-laws of the Associated Fur Coat and Trimming Manufacturers, Inc., and binding upon the members on and
after the date of the adoption of this resolution.

Four days later in a "Notice to the Trade," spread in bold headlines over a full page of *Fur Age Weekly,* the association restated
its new policy and publicly announced its determination tó enforce the code provisions "with greater vigor than heretofore." It
threatened that "all violators or anyone inducing our members to
violate same will be drastically dealt with."[1]

The association proceeded to implement this program by creating a trade practice bureau with a staff of accountants to investigate the books of its members, a complaints division to handle
alleged infractions of rules, and an advisory service to guide members principally in the handling of returned merchandise. This
bureau curbed attempts of buyers to make unfair demands on
manufacturers and stressed "the inestimable value of buying on
standard terms and discounts, placing all on an equitable basis."
In 1938, its staff of accountants made 1,315 audits and its complaints division handled 172 cases of returned merchandise. With
the help of this bureau, the association could give "positive assurance" that any violators reported "will, after due trial, be immediately subject to fine, suspension or expulsion from the Association."[2]

This pattern of self-help was closely followed by other organized employer groups of the needle trades. In the women's
coat and suit trade, for example, the Industrial Council of Cloak,
Suit and Skirt Manufacturers had only to reactivate its Bureau of

---

[1]*Women's Wear Daily,* June 6, 1935; *Fur Age Weekly,* June 10, 1935.
[2]*Women's Wear Daily,* July 14, 1938; *Fur Age Weekly,* Feb. 6, 1939.

Business Standards that in 1930 had processed 565 trade complaints, some 354 of which related to the issue of "unjust returns" of merchandise. Similarly, the Popular Priced Dress Manufacturers' Group, having written its former code into its bylaws, set up a special dress returns control bureau to administer cases of alleged unfair returns of merchandise.[3]

The breakdown of trade practice controls that followed the death of the codes magnified the need for creating voluntary organizations of self-help. In the millinery industry, for example, trade relations had gone from bad to worse. "Discounts increased, sometimes to as high as 12 percent," wrote J. C. Worthy, reviewing the aftermath of the millinery code. "The volume of cancellations and returns became greater and greater, pressure began to be exerted to force shipments on consignment and unwarranted allowances for advertising." Part of this post-code breakdown in the needle trades could be attributed to the newer firms that had yet to learn the rules of the road. Speaking for the National Dress Manufacturers' Association in 1935, M. Lanzit, executive director, stressed the need for training newly organized union firms that had never heard of industrial discipline.[4]

Experience under the codes had demonstrated the need for larger business organizations of broader scope to replace smaller groups of more specialized interests, if effective controls were to be assured. Where a fusion of specialized groups was impossible, a federation of specialized groups might at least represent some progress toward success. During the depths of the depression, Her-

---

[3] *Women's Wear Daily,* Feb. 17, 1931, Feb. 5, 1937; *New York Times,* Feb. 5, 1937.

[4] J. C. Worthy, "The Millinery Industry" (processed), NRA: Division of Review, Industry Studies Section (March 1936), p. 116. M. Lanzit in *Women's Wear Daily,* Nov. 12, 1935.

During the mid-thirties, candidates for membership in the Contractors' Division of the Eastern Women's Headwear Association had to pledge themselves not only to obey the bylaws of the association, the rules of the Millinery Stabilization Commission, and the terms of the collective labor agreements, but these candidates also had to agree to charge their customers no less than the cost of labor plus 30% for overhead and administration. All prospective members had to agree to furnish their association each week with a schedule of the prices they charged their customers and the labor costs in manufacturing their products. Refunds, rebates, or allowances of any nature to customers were forbidden. A copy of an application for membership in this association is filed in the Abelson papers.

man Sheidlinger, president, Associated Fur Coat and Trimming Manufacturers, had found the discordant groups of the fur trades like a house divided against itself. "I suggested a year ago," so he told the members of his association in 1933, "and I repeat again tonight that the fur industry needs regimentation of all its diversified forces into one coherent body — a Trade League or Council of Associations to function for the entire Trade leaving intact the autonomy of each Trade Association."[5]

After the codes were invalidated, M. Lanzit directed a movement to create a single dress association (instead of three separate organizations for jobbers, contractors, and inside manufacturers) to wage a common war on illegitimate trade practices. He favored a central fair trade practice bureau to enforce uniform sales contracts and to offset the drastic pressures of buying syndicates. With staggering losses from cancellation of orders, discriminatory discounts, preferential treatment, price discrimination, and returned merchandise running up to $30,000,000 in value annually, Lanzit, speaking for the National Dress Manufacturers' Association, offered "all constructive factors in the community a medium for participating in industry-wide stabilization measures both with regard to labor and fair trade practices."[6]

There was also evidence that employer organization for trade practice controls required vertical expansion as well as horizontal growth. Certainly, the organized manufacturers should have known from experiences under the codes that employer groups of whatever scope would be more effective if they embraced all phases of the production process. By vertical expansion to include associated agencies from suppliers of raw materials to consumers of finished products, new pressures could be exerted on the enforcement of trade regulations. Retailer organizations were in a particularly strategic position either to wreck trade practice controls or else to hold manufacturers to their accepted obligations. For, if retailers and retailer groups would adhere to the business standards adopted by the organized manufacturers regulating

---

[5]*Fur Age Weekly*, Jan. 10, 1933. Even broader in scope was the Apparel Industries Inter-Association Committee representing twelve associations in the needle trades. The committee was set up in 1949 to draft basic trade practice provisions for all the apparel industries. *Women's Wear Daily*, June 2, 1949.

[6]*Ibid.*, Nov. 12, 1935.

terms of sale, and if they would then refuse to deal with producers who evaded those standards, they alone could exert a force strong enough to guarantee the success of trade practice programs.[7]

While manufacturing groups could fine and expel their own members for breaking trade practice rules, they exerted no such power over retailers. Urging department stores, retail chains, and buying syndicates to desist from asking manufacturers to violate established terms of sale was at best an innocuous procedure that seldom produced the desired results. But there was always some hope that code experiences had aroused retailers to see the need for cooperating to control competition. "We call upon all retailers, distributors, and all members of the Fur Manufacturing Industry," so the Associated Fur Coat and Trimming Manufacturers had publicly announced in their notice to the trade, soon after the death of the codes, "to join with us and help us in all our endeavors to continue and maintain Fair Trade Practices in this Fur Industry."[8]

More aggressive were the efforts of the Affiliated Dress Manufacturers (inside producers) in the summer of 1935. Having resolved to continue the trade practice regulations of the code era, this association sent out to its members for distribution to their buying customers a list of trade regulations accompanied by assurances that buyers failing to comply with the standards would be disciplined. Association members were asked to report all retailers seeking preferential treatment in discount rates or in other terms of sale. "The industry, especially the responsible element in it, must continue to do business on a safe, sound, and ethical basis," announced a spokesman for the association. "The trade regulations adopted by the Affiliated Dress Manufacturers, Inc., are merely a continuation of the Code Provisions which were recognized by the retailers as fair and reasonable and to which their representatives have given assent."[9]

Government Support for Employer Self-Help

Unfortunately, the hope that needle trade manufacturers, aroused by the accomplishments of the NRA codes, could devise

---

[7]*Ibid.*, Nov. 12, 1935; Sept. 29, Oct. 13, 1936.

[8]*Fur Age Weekly*, June 10, 1935. For earlier efforts in the women's coat and suit trade to enlist the help of retailers, see above, pp. 693–695.

[9]*Women's Wear Daily*, July 23, 1935.

institutions of self-help that would enforce trade practice regulations through industry-wide cooperation was soon dissipated.
Early in the post-code era, Alexander Printz, prominent cloak and
suit manufacturer of the Cleveland market and a leading ex-
ponent of voluntary cooperation, had asserted that "in many respects the governing of the industry by the business men themselves, free of control by 'theoreticians' and the like, is infinitely
more efficient."[10]

Three years later, however, Printz reported that he had found
it more difficult "to organize diversified and often clashing interests on a purely co-operative basis than under the supervision
of the government." In 1938, he conceded that "the choice does
not narrow down to one between complete absence of governmental supervision on the one hand and the NRA attempt to regulate business on the other." Without excluding the government
altogether, and yet without conceding to government the dominant role it had played under the codes, Printz insisted there was
"ample room for something in between."[11]

Many post-NRA advocates of self-help through employers' associations — particularly those who thumbed their noses at union
participation — looked from the outset to the government for support in their efforts to control trade practices. Although the U. S.
Supreme Court had overthrown the National Industrial Recovery
Act, both the executive department and the Congress could be expected to seek a substitute that would accomplish NRA objectives.
With the help of the government, the essence of the code system
might still be retained under different laws and different supervision. New York industry, so Mortimer Lanzit, executive director
of the National Dress Manufacturers' Association, observed in
December 1935, was still operating at a great disadvantage from
low-cost, out-of-town competition. Rather than remedy the situation through stronger controls by labor unions, Lanzit at that
time urged the government directly to assist industry in maintaining fair trade practices.[12]

Had the National Industrial Recovery Act been allowed to die
a natural death on June 16, 1935, the organized manufacturers of
the needle trades might have won their objectives through new

---

[10]*New York Herald Tribune*, Nov. 3, 1935.
[11]*Women's Wear Daily*, Jan. 25, 1938.
[12]*Ibid.*, Dec. 10, 1935.

laws and regulations. Months before the act expired, agencies of the Congress and the executive, as well as of industry and labor, had considered new legislation which would retain the essentials of the code system with revisions and modifications based upon experiences under the NIRA. Prominent in the discussions was the concept that industry should retain the initiative in devising its own schemes for industrial self-government. While both labor issues and trade issues came up for consideration, a trend that had originated under the codes to separate the two functions, administratively as well as in rule making, played directly into the hands of the organized manufacturers who preferred self-help on trade controls through their own associations.

Early in December 1934, for example, the National Association of Manufacturers had proposed fair trade practice rules to supersede the expiration of the National Industrial Recovery Act on June 16, 1935. These plans called for legislation that would permit the truly representative majority of an industry or market group to draft a code for approval by the administration. Such a code, in addition to provisions on wages, hours, and collective bargaining, would contain trade regulations prohibiting unfair competitive practices destructive of industry welfare. Once approved by the administration, this code, at the request of a majority within the trade, would become binding upon all minority firms. In the absence of such majority requests, minority groups might seek codes of their own that would be valid until superseded by a majority code for the trade.[13]

The views of the needle trades themselves on what should follow the expiration of the NIRA were authoritatively expressed

---

[13]*New York Times,* Dec. 7, 1934. For other proposed reforms to follow the expiration of the National Industrial Recovery Act in 1935, see (1) views of Donald Richberg, general counsel for the NRA, *ibid.,* Nov. 22, 1934; (2) report of a joint conference for business recovery on the subject of legislation to supersede the NRA, *ibid.,* Dec. 20, 1934; (3) a report on the conferees working under President F. D. Roosevelt to draft new legislation for self-government in industry, *ibid.,* Feb. 7, 1935; (4) Donald Richberg, "Seventeen Recommendations on the New NRA," *Women's Wear Daily,* March 8, 1935; (5) President Roosevelt's message to Congress urging a two-year extension of the NIRA, *New York Herald Tribune,* Feb. 21, 1935. Hugh Johnson, chief NRA code administrator, gave his own ideas for reform of the NIRA and reviewed those of others in his *The Blue Eagle from Egg to Earth* (1935), pp. 377–408.

through an apparel industries committee for the renewal of NRA. Purporting to speak for nearly 20,000 manufacturing units and 600,000 workers who together contributed $2,000,000,000 to the national wealth each year, this group sought a reversion to the original objectives they had presumed to underlie the National Industrial Recovery Act – objectives they conceived to be founded on the protocol movement and the shortcomings of collective bargaining. In a letter dated April 5, 1935 to Senator Pat Harrison, they stated their conclusions in part as follows:

> The fact is that if the regulation of fair competition is better than a brutal competitive anarchy, respectable powers of control must be placed in some suitable agency. We would rather have those powers vested in our own representative code authorities than in some distant officialdom, remote from an understanding of our peculiar problems and unresponsive to our true needs.[14]

Once the U. S. Supreme Court had invalidated the codes (contrary to most pertinent decisions in the lower courts), questions of constitutionality seriously impaired the freedom of those planning a continuation of the code system. The necessity for keeping within the law induced Congress on June 14, 1935 to pass Senate Joint Resolution 113, extending to April 1, 1936 Title I of the National Industrial Recovery Act under modifications that would encourage industry to adopt voluntary codes patterned after the NRA system. This move was followed in August by the Guffey Coal Act which set a precedent for separate industry legislation, including price controls, to be administered by special industry commissions. Soon, the textile industry submitted to Congress a request for a national textile act with a national textile commission empowered to fix minimum wages and maximum hours

[14]Hearings before the Committee on Finance, U.S. Senate, 74th Cong. 1st sess., pursuant to S. Res. 79: *Investigation of the National Recovery Administration* (April 1935), Part 6, p. 2830. By a vote of 1,495 to 419, the U.S. Chamber of Commerce overwhelmingly favored new legislation to continue the principles of the National Industrial Recovery Act. "The most diverse elements in our industrial life," stated Donald Richberg, general counsel for the NRA, "have all agreed, and within the last few months, or even within the last few weeks, upon the absolute necessity of an extension of the N.R.A. .... The American Federation of Labor has gone on record completely and unanimously in favor of the absolute necessity of an extension of the N.R.A." Testimony before the Committee on Finance, U.S. Senate, April 1935. *Ibid.*, Part 1, p. 127.

and to establish and maintain fair trade practices. Had the Guffey Coal Act not been invalidated in 1936, several of the needle trades would undoubtedly have requested and received similar legislation.[15]

Meanwhile, President Roosevelt was paving the way for industry groups to take advantage of their revived opportunities. On June 15, 1935, he issued executive orders setting up machinery for continuing a modified NRA and appointed directors for the newly created administrative divisions. Later, in September 1935, he issued further orders for implementing the skeletonized NRA and followed these with detailed rules of procedure for adopting new voluntary agreements to supersede the codes. Under these provisions, governmental supervision of labor standards reached through voluntary negotiations between labor unions and employer groups would be left to an NRA administrator, while governmental controls over voluntary trade practice agreements were transferred to the Federal Trade Commission. At the same time, the President moved hopefully toward more forceful legislation modeled upon the original National Industrial Recovery Act, should the program for voluntary agreements under Senate Joint Resolution 113 prove unsuccessful.[16]

Associations of manufacturers in the apparel trades looked forward to enlisting the help of the Federal Trade Commission in their efforts to establish industry-wide trade practice controls. Sus-

---

[15]See the Guffey-Snyder Coal Act (August 30, 1935), chap. 834, 49 Stat. 991, invalidated in Carter v. Carter Coal Co., 298 U.S. 238 (1936), and the Guffey-Vinson Act on Bituminous Coal, chap. 127, 50 Stat. 72 (1936). On the textile industry, see the Ellenbogen bill discussed below at p. 765. See also Senate Joint Resolution 113, approved June 14, 1935, extending Title I (the title dealing with the codes) of the National Industrial Recovery Act, as amended, to April 1936.

> As extended, the Recovery Act retains none of the original code-making and enforcement provisions which were held illegal by the Supreme Court, but it does leave a presumptive authority for the President to approve voluntary agreements of employers which do not violate the antitrust laws. Suspension of the antitrust laws as provided in the original act is restricted in the resolution adopted today to agreements on collective bargaining with labor, and to child labor, wages, hours and unfair trade practices as defined by existing law.
> —*New York Times,* June 15, 1935.

[16]*Ibid.,* June 17, August 25, Sept. 26 and 27, Oct. 1, 1935.

pending the application of the antitrust laws to voluntary trade practice agreements that were approved and enforced by the Federal Trade Commission — observed Louis H. Solomon, counsel for many employer groups — was an effective means of extending throughout an industry the trade regulations of an association. By declaring certain abuses of legitimate business conduct to be unfair trade practices, the Commission, explained Solomon, gave the terms of an agreement the force of law, thereby providing a legal means of industry-wide enforcement through cease and desist orders.

Attorney Solomon was sponsoring a minor NRA plan for a fair trade practice agreement on behalf of the locally organized fur dressers and dyers — a plan that would become obligatory upon the entire industry when approved by the Federal Trade Commission. While trade regulations common to NRA code provisions on unfair advertising, misbranding goods, defaming a competitor or condemning his product were included, the plan was principally directed to establishing through a board of accountants minimum costs of production below which furs could not be dressed or dyed. The heart of the proposal was stated in the following provisions:

It shall be deemed unfair practice for any dresser or dyer to process furs below cost. Cost herein employed is intended to comprehend, besides material and labor costs, all sales and administrative expenses and all other gross costs within the meaning of good accounting practices.

It shall be unfair practice for any dresser or dyer to give, or his customers to receive any secret rebates, allowances and deductions in any form whatever reducing the price for processing the skins below cost.[17]

---

[17]*Women's Wear Daily*, Jan. 15, 1937. The adoption of this proposal may have been thwarted by a decision of the New York Supreme Court that year in the construction industry: Falciglia v. Gallagher, 164 Misc. 838 (1937), 299 N.Y. Supp. 890. Under a collective agreement between the Greater New York Employing Plasterers' Association and the Operating Plasterers' and Cement Finishers' International Association, Local no. 60, all contractor bids for plastering work were subject to review by an administrative committee of the parties authorized to see that all bids contained certain provisions guaranteeing sufficient income to the contractor to pay union wages to the men employed on the job. The court held that the effect of the agreement

Failures of the Federal Trade Commission

Unhappily for the organized manufacturers of the needle trades, all such carefully worked out schemes for creating enforceable standards of business conduct suffered from one overpowering handicap: they were still subject to the antitrust laws. The chief function of the Federal Trade Commission was to maintain competition, not to destroy it. While the Commission would go along with the more innocuous clauses of voluntary trade agreements — those provisions on deceptive labels, defamation of competitors, enticing away employees, stealing competitors' secrets, inducing breach of contract, and other clauses designed to save business competitors from degenerating into liars and thieves — it would not accept the more critical provisions of voluntary trade practice agreements that adversely affected standards of competition it was obligated to defend.[18]

Terms of discount, selling on consignment, advertising subsidies, return of merchandise, secret rebates and allowances, price discriminations, selling below costs — these were the critical issues affecting business competition that the organized manufacturers wished to regulate through voluntary trade agreements. These were the key areas in which conditions had gone from bad to worse after the death of the codes. Yet, these were precisely the areas in which the Federal Trade Commission would not confirm the limitations the manufacturers sought to impose. Or, if the

---

was to give the committee monopoly power to dictate what plasterers got the plastering jobs.

[18] The [Millinery] Code as approved Dec. 15, 1933, contained little more than the standard trade practice provisions recommended by the Federal Trade Commission. In the usual phraseology these provisions prohibited inaccurate advertising, false billing, inaccurate labeling, inaccurate references to competitors, threats of law suits, secret rebates, commercial bribery, and interference with another's contracts. None of these provisions had any great significance for the industry. They were written into the Code at the suggestion of NRA, but were too general to be of much assistance in dealing with the industry's problems. Its difficulties arose from much more vexing circumstances than occasional lapses from ordinary commercial morality.

—Worthy, "The Millinery Industry," p. 82.

proposals to control such issues were confirmed, the Commission hedged its approval with numerous conditions and restrictive provisos that seriously impaired, where they did not destroy, the objectives the manufacturers had in mind.[19]

Thus, in approving fair trade practice rules for the popular priced dress manufacturing industry, the Federal Trade Commission early in 1938 went along with the manufacturers in declaring that defamation of competitors, false and deceptive statements, or willfully inducing breach of contract between competitors and their customers were unfair methods of competition. But the Commission would outlaw discriminatory rebates, refunds, discounts, credits, and other price differentials only "where the effect thereof may be substantially to lessen competition or tend to create a monopoly in any line of commerce or to injure, destroy or prevent competition with any person who either grants or knowingly receives the benefit of such discrimination."

Likewise, the Federal Trade Commission would declare the shipping of dresses on consignment to be an unfair trade practice only if conducted "for the purpose and with the effect of artificially clogging trade outlets and unduly restricting competitors' use of said trade outlets in getting their goods to consumers through regular channels of distribution." It would prohibit selling below costs only if done "with the intent and with the effect of injuring a competitor, and where the effect may be substantially to lessen competition or tend to create a monopoly or unreasonably restrain trade." Furthermore, in a general statement of policy, the Commission announced that these rules "are not to be used, directly or indirectly, as part of or in connection with any combination or agreement to fix prices, or for the suppression of competition, or otherwise to unreasonably restrain trade." In all

---

[19] See, for example, the charges of the Federal Trade Commission (text in *Women's Wear Daily*, May 3, 1939) that the dress returns control bureau set up by the Popular Priced Dress Manufacturers' Group was a conspiracy in restraint of trade in that it limited the freedom of association members to sell, or of retailers to buy, unless both sellers and buyers conformed to the rules of the bureau. "We certainly do not believe in fixing prices," observed Charles Ballon, legal counsel for the association, "but on the other hand, it seems impossible to operate a wholesale dress business if there are to be returns up to 15 and 20 percent of shipments, which happens when there is no attempt to curtail unwarranted returns." *Ibid.*

these respects, it was of course merely carrying out its mandate under the Federal Trade Commission Act of 1914.[20]

Hopelessly confused by the legal entanglements of these conditions and provisos, the organized manufacturers could not look with assurance to the Federal Trade Commission for the goals they sought to achieve. They could not rely upon hair-splitting interpretations drawn by government agents more concerned with fine distinctions of the law than with the realities of the situation. Whatever the law might or might not contribute, such rules as the Commission would endorse offered no adequate substitute for the more stringent regulations that a thoroughly organized industry, if left to its own devices, would impose upon itself in the name of legitimate competition.

Because the Federal Trade Commission refused to approve key provisions governing discount rates and the return of merchandise that had been proposed in a program for trade practice controls submitted in 1936 by a special millinery stabilization agency in New York City, the Eastern Women's Headwear Association, whose 250 members represented 50 to 60 percent of the national millinery output, took its own steps in 1938 to draft a plan for standardizing discounts and for imposing stringent controls over the return of merchandise. "United action is vital to correct the conditions under which the trade has labored," announced M.E. Lopin, counsel for the association, "and the plan to be presented will stress direct action by the manufacturers themselves on returns, standardizing discounts at 2 per cent, elimination of free labels and advertising allowances, and the elimination of secret rebates." This move was followed by an industry-wide attempt to implement a fair trade practice program through the creation of a national council of millinery manufacturers, said to be the first national body ever formed in the millinery industry.[21]

If only the Federal Trade Commission, or some other govern-

---

[20]The rules for the popular priced dress manufacturing industry approved by the Federal Trade Commission are quoted in full in *ibid.*, Jan. 3, 1938. For another example, see the fair trade practice rules proposed by the Federal Trade Commission and open to suggestions by the fur manufacturers, in *ibid.*, March 15, 1938. The rules finally adopted by the Commission for the fur manufacturing industry were printed in the June 17, 1938 issue.

[21]*Ibid.*, July 8, 1936; *New York Times,* June 4, 1937. United Hatters, Cap and Millinery Workers' International Union, *Report and Proceedings,* Third Convention (May 1939), pp. 130–134.

mental agency, were authorized to put "teeth" into voluntary trade agreements endorsed by a substantial segment of manufacturers, and then to impose those more forceful terms upon the rest of the industry, the legitimate elements within each trade might survive the murderous competition of the unscrupulous factions. Several proposals to increase the power of legitimate manufacturers to write their own fair trade practice terms that would receive industry-wide coverage by law were advanced during and after the codes. Some would modify the antitrust laws; others would create new governmental agencies, perhaps combining the functions of the code authorities with those of the Federal Trade Commission.[22]

So long as the antitrust laws remained unchanged, however, federal authorities could not be expected to approve key trade restraints which had flourished under special exemptions of the National Industrial Recovery Act. Nor could the Federal Trade Commission be counted upon to approve trade practices that had grown up under the protocol movement since 1910, if those practices were separated from the union through the desire of

[22]Although favoring voluntary initiative by each industry in formulating trade practice terms, practically all proposals to supersede the NRA codes called for some form of governmental compulsion. Donald Richberg, general counsel, NRA, looked to the creation of a "super-board" which would combine certain functions of NRA code authorities with those of the Federal Trade Commission. *New York Herald Tribune*, Nov. 22, 1934. The legal and legislative committee of the National Coat and Suit Industry Recovery Board proposed "legislation that would empower national trade bodies comprising an overwhelming majority of firms in their field to bring the 'non-cooperating minority' under the prescribed standards of the majority." *Ibid.*, May 18, 1939. See also, the provisions of the Ellenbogen bill introduced into the U.S. House of Representatives by Congressman Henry Ellenbogen of Pennsylvania on April 14, 1936. This bill to regulate the textile industry, if enacted, would, in the view of Peter Van Horn, president of the National Federation of Textiles, weed out the "fierce and demoralizing competition" of the small mills that chiseled on wages and hours, by creating a commission with government backing to enforce voluntary agreements on fair trade practices, as well as on labor standards set for the industry. See H.R.12285, 74th Cong. 2nd sess. Ellenbogen had introduced a somewhat different bill on Jan. 28, 1936 (H.R.11770). The chief features of the two bills are compared in *Women's Wear Daily*, April 15, 1936. Peter Van Horn's views supporting the second bill are summarized in *ibid.*, April 24, 1936. See also *ibid.*, May 7, 1937. The text of the revised bill was printed in *Daily News Record*, May 7, 1937.

the employers to go their way alone. The inroads that labor-management collaboration had made upon free competition through the years would most certainly be viewed in a different light, once these developments were shorn of their labor relations context. Particularly would the long-established controls over jobber–contractor–inside manufacturer relationships be likely to wither if directly exposed to the penetrating rays of the antitrust sun.

Re-embracing the Unions

Aside from the more rigid controls that federal law would most likely impose upon attempts by employers' associations to solve their own problems, there was another reason for re-embracing labor unions and the protocol system of collective bargaining. Even more important than a front for the law was the indispensable role that labor unions could play in carrying out trade reform programs. The era of the codes had done nothing to resolve the vital problem of enforcement which had plagued the advocates of controlled competition since 1910. Had the federal government adopted a hands-off policy toward employer attempts at trade controls, there would still have been no assurance that the organized manufacturers acting alone could have successfully carried out trade regulations of their own design.

In the absence of union support, lack of cohesion among employers would doubtless have doomed to failure most post-code movements for business controls in the needle trades. While the NRA codes had stimulated growth in the number and membership of employers' associations, most small-time manufacturers were still reluctant to organize for business purposes. When forced into associations, they were no more willing to meet their commitments than when forced to sign labor agreements. In general, the smaller the firm the less likely the owner was to abide by his promises. Only labor unions could readily force independent operators to support plans for stabilizing their industries.[23]

Not even the National Coat and Suit Industry Recovery Board, the most important joint agency set up in the post-code era to continue the work of the codes, could count upon employers to

---

[23]*Women's Wear Daily* for July 15, 1936 reports one case of an agreement among fur dressers to adhere to a fixed price scale. But within three days every employer signing this agreement was allegedly violating its terms.

provide the necessary cooperation for carrying out the board's decisions. "I am convinced as the weeks go by," so Dr. A. L. H. Rubin, central regional director of the Recovery Board, wrote on September 27, 1935, "that we can expect from only a few manufacturers . . . any general help. . . . If this DAMNED INDUSTRY won't do anything to help itself, *then it becomes necessary for us to lean more and more on the Union.*" [24]

Lacking unity among manufacturers, the National Coat and Suit Industry Recovery Board at least hoped for assistance from retailers and consumers. Under the caption, "Industrial Self Government in the Coat and Suit Field," the Recovery Board took over a full page of *Women's Wear Daily* for May 26, 1936, to advertise its program. The board offered a consumers' protection label "to enable retailer and consumer to identify coats and suits produced by responsible firms under decent working conditions." And it expressed deep appreciation "to the ethical and fair minded retailers who have indicated their desire to deal with conscientious manufacturers in a stabilized market." Two days later, the Industrial Council of Cloak, Suit and Skirt Manufacturers also contributed a full-page advertisement stressing "the importance of fair trade practices as a medium of stabilizing the industry and of protecting ethical and conscientious retailers as well as producers." [25]

The type of support that such requests for cooperation from the business factions of a vertically integrated industry might have inspired was once brought to light by a case involving the distribution of millinery products. Sometime after the NRA codes were invalidated, Gimbels' department store offered its customers certain women's hats of imported velour at $3.99, each. Immediately, several other retail outlets, unable to compete with Gimbels' offerings, canceled their orders with millinery suppliers. Thereupon, these suppliers refused to sell Gimbels any more hats. Meanwhile, at least one importer, assuming that Gimbels had acquired the hats at distress prices, joined the chorus of "let me kick him too" by refusing to furnish Gimbels' suppliers with

[24]From FTC exhibit 874B in the Matter of National Coat and Suit Industry Recovery Board, Docket no. 4596, as quoted in D. E. Robinson, *Collective Bargaining and Market Control in the New York Coat and Suit Industry* (1949), p. 179.

[25]*Women's Wear Daily,* May 26 and 28, 1936.

any more imported products. Although investigation revealed that Gimbels had paid the full price of $36.00 a dozen for the hats and was using them as a sale leader, the Gimbels' store owners, under heavy pressure from the industry, agreed henceforth to follow a "constructive policy" that would guarantee the store access to a constant source of supply.[26]

But the hope that such cooperation among business men would force compliance with trade regulations without union help seldom got beyond the realm of wishful thinking. The fact was that attempts to exclude labor unions from participating in the solution of trade problems had better been left to die with the NRA. For only unions could exert the necessary pressures against suppliers, distributors, and retailers to guarantee cooperation in programs of reform. Only unions could provide an effective means of enforcing business controls that would save the legitimate manufacturers from their ruthless competitors. Only the unions could supply a shield that would protect the organized manufacturers from legal sniping by governmental officials armed with the guns of the antitrust laws.

Still another episode from the millinery trade helped to disclose the folly of rejecting union support. Even before the NRA was invalidated, Max Zaritsky, president of the millinery workers' union, had urged the millinery manufacturers to organize on a national scale to suppress vicious competition between markets. Within a few days after the codes were struck down, he had directed a letter to all millinery trade associations recommending that a national millinery congress be convened "in which the representatives of all the millinery manufacturers' associations throughout the nation, and of all other factors that contribute, or can contribute, to the solution of our problems may unite in framing a plan of self government for the industry."[27]

---

[26]For efforts of the millinery manufacturers to enlist the cooperation of chain stores, buying syndicates, and other organized groups of retailers in creating and enforcing fair trade practices, see *ibid.*, May 13 and 27, 1937; *New York Times,* July 23, 1937; and *New York Herald Tribune,* July 23, 1937. See also Millinery Stabilization Commission, "Confidential Information to Members of the Advisory Committee Only," mimeo. letter (no date), copy filed in the Abelson papers.

[27]United Hatters, Cap and Millinery Workers' International Union, Cap and Millinery Department, *Report and Proceedings,* Second Convention (First Regular Convention), Oct. 4–7, 1936, p. 69. See also *Women's Wear*

With the help of leading manufacturers from the New York, Chicago, Cleveland, and New Jersey markets, Zaritsky evolved his plan for an industry-wide association. In addition to manufacturers' delegates, this national organization would have one member representing labor, two representing the supply houses, and two representing the distributors. But only representatives of the manufacturers would have voting rights; all others would act in an advisory capacity. The association would adopt an industry code of fair competition which would contain maximum hours and minimum wages as well as fair trade practices. A label would identify products made under approved standards. Local associations would have charge of code compliance, which would be assured through the cooperation of labor, the supply houses, and the distributors.[28]

But when some forty delegates from millinery associations representing all parts of the country met in Chicago during June 1935 to set up a national association for the millinery industry, they hastily dropped the pilot of the ship. Although Zaritsky had engineered the movement, no representative of the union was invited. Nor were jobbers, buying syndicates, or importers represented. Espousing the cause of self-help through their own associations, these delegates representing the manufacturers preferred to go their way alone. The folly of this decision was soon reflected in the death of the movement for lack of united support from other segments of the trade.[29]

The Post-NRA Machinery of Stabilization

Re-embracing labor unions for more effective trade controls raised anew the continuing issue of whether labor-management plans for regulating business competition should be implemented through the normal patterns of collective bargaining or whether

Daily, April 11, 1935, under the caption "Zaritsky Advocates National Body to Meet Industry Ills."

[28]For the text of Zaritsky's plan, see *ibid.,* June 10, 1935.

[29]United Hatters, Cap and Millinery Workers' International Union, Cap and Millinery Department, *Report and Proceedings,* Second Convention (First Regular Convention), Oct. 4–7, 1936, p. 69. Later, the general executive board of the union reported that on this occasion "the manufacturers returned to their respective cities ready to resume their cutthroat competition." *Ibid.,* Third Convention (May 1939), p. 132. See also *Women's Wear Daily,* June 24 and July 18, 1935.

such plans called for different institutions and procedures particularly designed to help stabilize the trade. Should the organized forces of each industry — those that still supported the principles of the protocol movement — rely upon the usual machinery of contract administration for executing trade policies of industry-wide concern or should they devise more specialized agencies for the joint control of competitive practices?

This problem was as old as the protocol movement itself. Collective bargaining had been founded on the concept of promoting industry welfare for the mutual advantage of the "bosses" and the "people." The permanent impartial machinery created for this objective sometimes embraced special agencies for industry-wide problems and sometimes operated through normal channels without regard to the nature of the issues. Under the National Industrial Recovery Act, code authorities administered both trade provisions and labor provisions of industry codes of fair competition, but tended to separate the administration of the two functions. At the same time, the impartial machinery continued to operate under collective agreements that embraced both trade and labor issues. Precedent already existed for a wide variety of mixed policies and such variations were to continue after the codes.

After the death of the NIRA, the National Coat and Suit Industry Recovery Board of the women's coat and suit trade came nearest to perpetuating the institutions of the codes. In the summer of 1935, delegates of the ILGWU and spokesmen of employers' associations that were represented on the industry's code authority first took steps to set up this board as a nonprofit association "to establish and maintain fair and equitable standards of labor in the Coat and Suit Industry and to establish and maintain standards of fair commercial practices with a view to promoting the common welfare of the industry and the public good." In time the NCSIRB came to embrace twenty manufacturers' associations whose members produced 92 percent of all women's coats and suits made in the United States. In general, the board carried on the functions previously assigned to the code authority of the women's coat and suit trade.[30]

With its separately designated trade and labor functions, the

---

[30]*Ibid.,* May 26 and Dec. 29, 1936.

Recovery Board was to be governed by a national executive board of nineteen members, seven of whom represented New York associations, seven of whom represented employer groups from other areas, and five of whom represented the ILGWU. Four regional boards, six compliance committees (including one on hours and wages and one on fair trade practices), an executive secretary with several administrative bureaus, and a staff of accountants, statisticians, and investigators comprised the machinery for carrying out the purposes of the organization. Altogether, in structure, function, and method of operation, the Recovery Board followed closely the patterns of the industry code.[31]

The corresponding agency of the millinery industry was less inclusive. Aspiring to follow the example of the women's coat and suit trade in continuing code regulations, the New York City factions of the millinery trade failed to win support from out-of-town centers and had to limit their stabilization program to the New York market. In a supplement to the collective labor agreement negotiated during the winter of 1935–1936, representatives of the Eastern Women's Headwear Association and of the millinery workers' unions created a millinery stabilization commission of three public members "to formulate fair trade practices and to govern the relationship of the members of the Industry towards each other and towards other factors in the industry." Subsequently in July 1937, seven employers' associations, together with the United Hatters, Cap and Millinery Workers' International Union and the Joint Board of Millinery Workers' Unions (Locals 24 and 42) became signatories to a code of commercial regulations drafted for the trade.[32]

Aside from research, fact-finding, and reporting on comparative labor costs the Millinery Stabilization Commission, unlike its counterpart in the women's coat and suit trade, left conditions of employment to the normal machinery of the labor agreements and concentrated on formulating and enforcing fair trade prac-

---

[31]The fair trade practice functions of this board were illustrated by the adoption in late August 1937 of a uniform order blank requiring uniform conditions of sale on such items as discount rates, return privileges, memorandum selling, cancellation of orders, secret rebates, and transportation and telephone charges. *Ibid.,* Sept. 1, 1937. For action controlling the return of goods, see *ibid.,* August 31, 1937.

[32]*Ibid.,* July 23, 1937. *Millinery Research,* May 24, 1937, vol. 1, no. 1.

tices. The trade practice agreements, together with the regulations imposed by the commission, covered the salient features of the old millinery code program. Discounts were limited, rebates prohibited, price discriminations barred, selling below costs forbidden, and the "return racket" sharply curtailed. The commission sought to unite suppliers, manufacturers, distributors, and retailers in a joint effort to carry out the fair trade practice program.[33]

The power of the Millinery Stabilization Commission to enforce these provisions was exerted principally through the use of a consumers' protection label, possession of which virtually constituted a license to operate. The "Agreement and Certificate of Compliance and Label Membership" entered into between the commission and each participating manufacturer specified that "the right of the license to the Label Member to the services and benefits of the Commission and to use the Consumers' Protection Label adopted by the Commission shall continue only if, and so long as, the Label Member shall comply with the By-Laws, Trade Practice Provisions, Rules and Regulations of the Commission." Both the millinery workers' union and the Eastern Women's Headwear Association appointed advisory committees to help the commission enforce trade practice regulations.[34]

[33]In 1938 Nathaniel Spector, vice-president of the United Hatters, Cap and Millinery Workers' International Union, proposed the creation of an "Industrial Congress" of 100 members representing manufacturers, jobbers, importers, supply houses, and buying syndicates to act in an advisory capacity to the Millinery Stabilization Commission. "The real problem confronting the millinery industry," he argued, "is not employer-employee relations. The industry needs vision — intelligent industrial planning." *Ibid.,* Jan. 18, 1938, vol. 3, no. 8.

[34]A copy of the label agreement is filed in the Abelson papers. The power of the millinery workers' union to extend MSC controls over independent firms with whom the union held contracts was exemplified in the following clause from the Jan. 31, 1936 Supplementary Agreement between the Eastern Women's Headwear Association and the United Hatters, Cap and Millinery Workers' International Union:

> The Union agrees that in any contracts it may enter into with independent manufacturers, it will be provided that such independent manufacturers shall be required to subscribe to the supervision of the said Millinery Stabilization Commission and to the use of the Consumers' Protection Label. The Union hereby agrees to submit to the Commission a list of all independent firms with whom it has contractual relations, and to notify the Commission of any changes or additions thereto as they occur.

After the codes, special stabilization committees became a common feature of collective agreements in the needle trades. Unlike the millinery industry that operated through a special agency set apart for regulating trade practices, the men's hat industry combined its machinery for trade regulations with its agencies for administering labor provisions. The 1937 collective agreement between the Allied Hat Manufacturers and the United Hatters, Cap and Millinery Workers' International Union and its Locals 7 and 8 provided for a "Board of Trade for the Men's Hat Industry" composed of three members representing the association and three members representing the union, together with an impartial chairman. This board was empowered not only "to adjust all matters in dispute that may arise between the Association and the Union concerning the application of the provisions of this agreement" but also "to confer and advise with respect to all matters affecting the status of the industry as a whole." It examined records, prepared reports, and submitted recommendations "in order to stabilize the Men's Hat Industry, establish greater uniformity of labor costs, reduce the disparity in price caused by unfair labor practices, and to eradicate the evils which have handicapped the growth and progress of the industry in this area."

The stabilization board of the skirt industry was a product of negotiations between the National Skirt Manufacturers' Association and the Cloakmakers' Joint Board and Local 23, ILGWU. The men's shirt industry had its special stabilization agency created by negotiations between the shirt manufacturers and the Amalgamated Clothing Workers. The manufacturers of women's low quality coats and suits had their popular priced coat and suit stabilization committee and the upper end of the trade its board of stability and control. The latter, created by the 1940 major collective agreement for the industry, was invested with the general power "to see that the provisions of the agreements were faithfully

---

For a newspaper account of the work of the Millinery Stabilization Commission, see the files of the *Women's Wear Daily* for the first six months of 1937, especially the issues of Jan. 12, May 12 and 13, 1937. An excellent summary account of the Millinery Stabilization Commission appeared in an article by P. F. Brissenden and J. M. Keating, "Union-Management Co-operation in Millinery Manufacturing in the New York Area," *Industrial and Labor Relations Review*, October 1948, vol. 2, pp. 3–32.

observed and uniformly enforced." In addition, the board was specifically authorized, among others things, to

(1) check all data and reports that association members and truck owners were required to file under collective agreements of the garment trucking industry;

(2) investigate sources of nonunion production in New York and neighboring states and adopt a program to eliminate unfair competition from these nonunion sources;

(3) ascertain the sources where garments covered by the industry agreements are being manufactured by the use of inferior standards;

(4) discover the wholesalers or retailers who purchase garments from substandard sources and adopt valid programs that would prevent those purchasers from

(a) creating unfair competition between manufacturers, jobbers, contractors, and submanufacturers in contractual relations with the union and other producers who manufacture under substandard and nonunion conditions;

(b) inducing the breach of agreements between manufacturers, jobbers, contractors, and submanufacturers and the union;

(c) undermining or causing deterioration of the labor standards and conditions of work prevailing throughout the industry.[35]

One common feature of most stabilization programs was the inclusion of vertical controls that extended from suppliers of raw materials to consumers of finished products. At times, these connections had to be established through the use of economic force. Thus to hasten cooperation among manufacturers, distributors, contractors, yarn houses, and retailers of the knitted outerwear trade, the newly organized Associated Knitwear Contractors called a "stoppage" in 1940 against their jobbers for refusing to deal collectively with the contractors' association. The machinery on which the industry finally hung its vertical integration program was designated the Knitted Outerwear Industrial Board. It was a product of negotiations between the United Knitwear Manu-

---

[35]The 1940 collective agreement of the Industrial Council of Cloak, Suit and Skirt Manufacturers with the ILGWU and its Cloakmakers' Joint Board was in the nature of amendments to the 1937 collective agreement between the parties. For information on the "Stabilization Plan" launched in 1939 by the ACWA for the men's clothing industry, see Twentieth Century Fund, *How Collective Bargaining Works* (1945), pp. 436–443; Harry A. Colbrin, *The Men's Clothing Industry: Colonial through Modern Times* (1970), pp. 194–199.

facturers' League and the ILGWU, Local 155. The formation of this board, so H. R. Lhowe, counsel for the league, alleged, had been prompted by the confusion and lack of cooperation among the different elements in the trade. He made it clear that the board would take up the matter of controlling relations between contractors and manufacturers as well as the scientific determination of piece rates. Labor, he conceded, must get a fair share of the fruits of industry, but first there must be fruits![36]

Union Help for Trade Practice Programs

No organized groups of the post-code era were more concerned with the "fruits of industry" than the needle trade unions themselves. The very strength of these unions, in contrast to the weakness of the manufacturers, ultimately shifted the focus of their efforts from raising labor standards to insuring business profits. In so far as trade practice controls enhanced the fruits of industry, these controls had the support of all needle trade unions. Whether the organized manufacturers accepted cooperation from union sources or preferred to go their way alone, union leaders repeatedly urged employer groups to adopt some effective means of regulating competition in the manufacture, distribution, and sale of needle trade products.

Just as the first association of manufacturers sponsoring the protocol movement in 1910 encouraged the growth of labor unions to equalize labor costs, so the forces of organized labor in the post-code era favored the growth of employer combinations to standardize business practices. Such union support for restrictive rules of business conduct, no less than employer support for union standards of employment, can be understood only in the light of self-interest. Immediately after 1910, employers' associations, although strong enough to dictate terms of employment, nevertheless encouraged cooperation from unions to protect legitimate business from unscrupulous competitors who thrived on lower

---

[36]*Women's Wear Daily,* August 26, 1940. Many of these provisions for post-NRA machinery of stabilization were never implemented — a pattern of development common to many specialized agencies of industry-wide concern created since the beginning of the protocol movement. More important than the particular structure or function of these agencies was the fact that all of them were a product of labor-management negotiations and fell within the orbits of the collective bargaining systems.

labor costs. Immediately after 1935, labor unions, although strong enough to dictate terms of employment, nevertheless encouraged cooperation among employers to suppress illegitimate trade practices, lest a squeeze on profits destroy the source of higher wages and thus kill the goose that laid the golden egg.

Why, queried a writer for the *Jewish Morning Journal,* May 31, 1939, should the ILGWU waste its energies and exhaust its resources in helping employers of the women's coat and suit industry establish and enforce fair trade practices through the National Coat and Suit Industry Recovery Board? Why should the union care whether manufacturers accept returns of merchandise or offer discounts to their customers? Why should union agents not confine their efforts directly to gaining higher wages and better working conditions for their members? To the questions he had posed, the writer offered a plausible answer:

One must not forget that the union in the cloak industry is now the strongest factor; it can obtain whatever it wants provided there is the wherewithal from which to take it. To win demands is not enough. One must be able also to obtain it [*sic*] in practice, and one cannot of course obtain more than there is to be gotten, certainly not continually. The cloak industry consists largely of small enterprises. Large capital has long ago drifted elsewhere. Moreover, there is a scarcity of business which intensifies the fierce competition which has always existed in the industry. If the drift to hopeless demoralization is not checked, which is essentially the task of the Recovery Board, the entire foundation of the cloak industry will sink into the mire as a result of which the workers will for the most part suffer. Taking all of this into consideration, one is forced to the conclusion that the cloakmaker union must be very much concerned regarding the general situation of the industry.[37]

After the codes, needle trade unions made no effort to hide their support for trade practice programs. On the contrary, they openly publicized their contributions and proudly took credit for these ventures in regulated competition. Although the Millinery Stabilization Commission was composed of public members only and its functions officially confined to trade practice programs, there was never any doubt that the millinery workers'

---

[37]William Post, "Jewish Industry in which NRA Principle Still Governs," in the *Jewish Morning Journal,* May 31, 1939. Translation filed in the Abelson papers.

union was an equal partner to the scheme. Not only was this union represented on an advisory committee to help the commission with its work, but the joint character of the enterprise was apparent from the 1936 supplementary agreement between the union and the Eastern Women's Headwear Association by which the commission was created. The opening paragraph of this agreement stated:

A close study of the Millinery Industry since the National Recovery Act was declared unconstitutional reveals the fact that the Millinery Industry is now in a state of chaos due to the lack of planning and to the breaking down of the trade practice provisions in its former code, so that neither the employer nor their workers have any assurance of security either in the obtaining of business or in the obtaining of employment. A co-ordinating agency should be set up with the cooperation of both employers and workers which should supply the necessary information concerning the management and the conduct of the Industry and should devote itself to the consideration of plans and policies for the rehabilitation of the Industry so that the present aimless and planless tendencies of the Industry may be curbed and the evils from which it is suffering checked.[38]

Meanwhile, the ILGWU was playing a still more prominent role in the work of the National Coat and Suit Industry Recovery Board. A pamphlet issued by the educational department of this union proudly affirmed that the stabilization agency of the women's coat and suit trade had been established "through the initiative of the International and with the assistance of the employers' associations!" Addressing the ILGWU convention in 1937, President David Dubinsky contended that "our workers and our organization are largely responsible for the success of this Recovery Board." Vice-president Isidore Nagler was more emphatic in glorifying the union for "assuming a major role in the conduct not merely of union affairs, but of the entire national industry itself."

---

[38]The collective agreement and the supplementary agreement were negotiated and executed by the parties simultaneously. Together they constituted the entire agreement of the parties. Without one, the other would not have been made.

—M. E. Lopin, counsel, Eastern Women's Headwear Association, "Re: Millinery Stabilization Commission" (March 10, 1936); typewritten copy filed in the Abelson papers.

Our Union has been a vital force in the conduct of the Board since its inception. While all elements lend their co-operation and assistance, the Union is the predominant factor in making the Board workable. All agree that as a voluntary agency it could not exist without the Union, that its successes spring from our power. We are its backbone in its stated purpose of promoting the welfare of the industry and of maintaining high labor standards.[39]

Employer groups participating in jointly negotiated labor-management plans for the control of trade practices never disputed these union allegations. On the contrary, spokesmen for the manufacturers gladly conceded the indispensable role unions exerted in the formulation and enforcement of these rules. "The part that labor has played in the industry, through the channels of the Recovery Board," so Alexander Printz, prominent Cleveland manufacturer and a leader in the movement to control competition, told the ILGWU convention in 1937, ". . . has been one that, well, we just couldn't have got along without." He particularly praised Isidore Nagler for having done "everything to help us in our fair trade practices."[40]

When the evil of style piracy threatened the inside dress manufacturers, who survived competition largely on the originality of their styles, Julius Hochman, general manager of the Dressmakers' Joint Board, proposed a system of design registration that would protect owners of original creations for at least six months. Hochman would enforce his plan by having the union refuse to settle piece rates on any style of garment not properly registered. In the collective agreement of the ILGWU with the Associated Garment Industries of St. Louis that year, the union agreed to see that its members did not work for employers who, by reason of having violated the trade practice provisions on style piracy, were no longer in good standing with their association.[41]

In yet another area, the needle trade unions extended a helping hand to the regulation of business competition. These unions

---

[39]ILGWU, "Structure and Functioning of the ILGWU" (pamphlet, n.d.), p. 39; ILGWU, *Report and Proceedings,* Twenty-third Convention (May 1937), pp. 11 and 165 of the *Proceedings.*

[40]"He [Nagler] has gone with us to retail establishments, he has gone with us to the Federal Trade Commission in Washington, he has gone with us to chain stores, he has gone all over." Alexander Printz, *ibid.,* pp. 170–171.

[41]*Women's Wear Daily,* Oct. 18 and 19, 1937.

were as much concerned with controlling overproduction as with regulating minimum prices. Whatever the influence of the codes toward restricting production, manufacturers expected labor unions to help extend these advantages into the post-code era. "The attempt to stabilize the [millinery] industry through the Millinery Code at the beginning of 1934 had at least one good result," observed H. A. Baum, president of the Millinery Manufacturers of New Jersey in 1938, "it drastically curtailed overproduction to a point where manufacturers once again had the courage to figure their merchandise on a profitable basis." Convinced that "only immediate and decisive action by all constructive elements of the millinery industry can stop it from drifting to ruin," Baum called for a national convention of millinery manufacturers and labor representatives from all parts of the country to rehabilitate the industry on a national scale.[42]

Likewise, efforts to stabilize the dress manufacturing industry by limiting production under the codes had been extended into the post-code period. During the codes, the United Association of Dress Manufacturers (contractors), fearing overproduction from the excess of productive machinery, had proposed to a special commission representing jointly the code authority and the impartial machinery under collective agreements, that "jobbers shall not be allowed to open factories and inside manufacturers employing contractors shall not increase the productive capacity of their plants during the life of the collective agreements." After the death of the codes, David Dubinsky, president of the ILGWU, and Julius Hochman, general manager, Dressmakers' Joint Board, contended that the whole post-code system for limitation of contractors in the dress trade had been devised in part to prevent the overproduction and overexpansion of the industry. They charged the dress manufacturers with adding 20,000 workers to the trade at the very time that the industry had already become a buyers' market. "If the manufacturers had any aggressiveness," Hoch-

---

[42]*Ibid.,* May 6, 1938. Control of overproduction had been an objective behind the proposed code of fair competition submitted in 1933 by the American Fur Merchants' Association. This proposal called for a league of associations representing all branches of the fur industry that would be able through cooperative action to avoid the "overextension" of the industry "resulting in insolvencies, forced sales of distressed merchandise and other attendant evils." Text of this proposed code appears in *ibid.,* July 27, 1933.

man argued, "they could make it [the industry] a sellers' market for the first time in years."[43]

Fears of overproduction had long haunted the women's coat and suit trade. While operating under the NIRA, Samuel Klein, executive director of the Industrial Council of Cloak, Suit and Skirt Manufacturers, had moved to have his industry utilize its code authority to curtail production. Like spokesmen for the silk, woolen, rayon, and cotton trades, Klein called for industry-wide cessations of operations to prevent a piling up of surplus stock. After the codes, Klein turned to the union for help, but found it indifferent toward establishing production controls. He sponsored plans to have his association of inside manufacturers meet with the organized jobbers and the ILGWU in a general conference to consider ways and means of curtailing overproduction in the trade.[44]

How the Millinery Union Enforced Trade Controls

In helping apparel manufacturers with their business problems, needle trade unions covered a wide range of operations. Under a two-column caption, "Hat Union to Enforce Mfrs.' Sales at Profit," *Women's Wear Daily* for September 2, 1937 carried an account of the millinery workers' union on a rampage to control business competition. "With the millinery workers' union holding the whip," runs this account, "the Millinery Stabilization Commission moved forward today in what they describe as a

---

[43]The proposals of the United Association are quoted in *ibid.,* May 15, 1934; the views of David Dubinsky and Julius Hochman are recorded in the Jan. 24, 1936 issue.

Efforts to restrict the number of newcomers to the trade — a motive of collective bargaining from the beginnings of the protocol movement — were also reflected in the following regulatory clause of the 1939 dress industry agreements:

> It is the desire of the parties hereto that new firms coming into the dress industry adjust themselves and conform to the industrial stability which the terms of their agreement intend to achieve. To that end the association [named] will in good faith advise applicants for membership that they will avail themselves as far as possible and practicable of the production units already in existence in the dress industry.
>
> —As quoted in ILGWU, *Report and Proceedings,* Twenty-fourth Convention (May–June 1940), p. 57.

[44]*New York American,* July 3, 1924; *Women's Wear Daily,* Feb. 4, 1936.

broad campaign to level competition in the industry and bring the trade, by force if necessary, out of the sphere of selling its merchandise below cost."[45]

Leader in this aggressive scheme was Nathaniel Spector, chairman of the New York Joint Board of the millinery workers' union. On numerous occasions, Spector had roundly scored the "murderous competition" that had forced 55 percent of all ladies' hats on the market at less than 65 cents each. Professing concern for "the legitimate manufacturers' problem as well as the strict union problem," Spector urged the greatest speed in the effective regulation of discount rates and the return of merchandise. "It is high time this union took a hand in bringing stability into this industry," Spector declared. "You manufacturers no longer have to fear out-of-town competition. We have taken care of that situation, and that goes for the Dallas market, Massachusetts and firms upstate. We are now prepared to step into this market and remove the unsettled condition."[46]

Spector had taken his stand in defense of new trade practice regulations signed by representatives of the manufacturers' associations and of the Millinery Workers' Joint Board and promulgated by the Millinery Stabilizaton Commission in July 1937. To implement the rules against selling merchandise below costs, the union had backed a proposed agreement binding firms to the terms of a uniform cost accounting system which enumerated every item of cost in the maunfacture of low-priced millinery. Under this system, manufacturers would be required to inform the Millinery Stabilization Commission exactly what was paid for hat bodies, hat linings, ribbons, and the like; and if these figures of cost did not jibe with the uniform cost chart of the commission, the producer would be called upon to explain the discrepancies.

Behind such support from organized workers for standards of

---

[45]For an earlier article under the caption, "Union Takes Hand in Curbing Market's Non-Profitable Output," see *ibid.,* June 3, 1936.

[46]*Ibid.,* May 13, 1937. Denouncing sales below cost, Max Zaritsky, president of the United Hatters, Cap and Millinery Workers' International Union, commented on the new 1938 millinery agreement as follows: "It seems again the task of the union to preserve the industry and save it from its irresponsible elements. Competition may be the life of business but cut-throat competition is its death." *Hat Worker,* Feb. 15, 1938.

business conduct lay the overwhelming conviction that needle trade unions held the keys to the enforcement of trade practice rules. Only when a producer failed to comply with the business regulations set for his trade was the full power of a union to police an industry revealed. Even those employers who brushed aside all fears of disciplinary action by their own associations and who held in contempt all threats of expulsion from the organized factions of their trade, still rued the day their business operations might be disrupted by union strikes, picket lines, and production boycotts. Those who would otherwise ignore the established rules of business competition still bowed to the law of economic pressure cast in the name of legitimate union activity.[47]

Not until after the death of the NRA codes, did the millinery workers' union step up its campaign of direct action to enforce trade practice regulations. Encouraged by their own employers to uphold legitimate business standards, the leadership of this union became more and more aggressive and determined, if not ruthless. "Members of the industry charged with violating trade practices," stated a brochure of the organized millinery workers, "will be summoned before a Board, presided over by a member of the [Millinery Stabilization] Commission. If found violating the new trade practices, the member accused will be penalized by either a fine, or by a withdrawal of the Consumers' Protection Label, or both. Let no manufacturer labor under any delusion. The suspension of the label is equal to the withdrawal of a license."[48]

What the millinery workers' union had in mind was clearly demonstrated in the case of the Rosenblum Hat Company — a firm that had failed to use the label of the Millinery Stabilization Commission. In this case, the union ordered the workers of the firm to cease work until labels were attached to all goods produced. Once the strike had begun, the workers refused to return to their jobs until the company promised to pay them for time

---

[47]"Officials representing 800 employers and 20,000 workers in the millinery industry of Greater New York and New Jersey signed before Mayor F. H. LaGuardia yesterday the code of fair trade regulations drawn up by the Millinery Stabilization Commission, Inc., to end 'chiseling' by manufacturers and retailers and to permit the employees' union to police the industry and punish violations by penalties and by strike action." *New York Herald Tribune,* July 23, 1937.

[48]From a union brochure entitled, "Little NRA in Effect in Millinery Industry" (n.d.). The contents were also printed in *Women's Wear Daily,* July 27, 1937.

lost while striking to enforce trade practice regulations. Commenting on the union's cooperation, O. W. Pearson, executive secretary of the Millinery Stabilization Commission, stated bluntly: "With this stoppage the union once more publicly demonstrates it will do all in its power to make it possible for the commission to perform its functions, enabling it to carry out the work of rehabilitating the millinery industry, and that other stoppages will be called if necessary." [49]

Obviously, the millinery workers' union was as quick to strike in defense of trade practice rules as in defense of labor standards. During the fall of 1937, the union's attempt to police the industry culminated in a major strike involving 2,500 workers in some 300 shops whose owners had "disregarded the labor agreement and pursued business practices contrary to the provisions of the Millinery Stabilization Commission." Nathaniel Spector, manager of the union joint board, insisted that the workers remain off the job not only until wage provisions were enforced but until the employers' scale of minimum sale prices for their products met with the commission's rulings. In all such cases, the millinery workers stood squarely behind their leadership. "Our union is firmly convinced," stated an earlier brochure of the union joint board, "that the trade practices promulgated by the Commission are for the best interests of all concerned. We are pledged to do our full share in helping to enforce these trade practices."[50]

Having exerted the necessary pressure to keep manufacturers in line, the millinery workers' union set out, hammer and tongs, to win support from retailers for trade regulations governing conditions of sale. The chief enemy of voluntary cooperation among retailers was the buying syndicate that never relaxed pressure for price reductions, even though some manufacturers could no longer meet union wage scales if forced to reduce their prices. The demoralizing influence of this concentrated buying pressure for lower prices aroused Max Zaritsky, president of the millinery workers' international union, to assert that "we intend to force the issue of co-operation and co-ordination in the millinery industry."[51]

In a meeting of the Millinery Stabilization Commission at

---

[49]*Ibid.*, Sept. 3, 1936.

[50]*New York Times,* Sept. 21, 1937; *Hat Worker,* Jan. 15, 1938; D. B. Robinson, *Spotlight on a Union* (1948), pp. 251–252.

[51]*Millinery Research,* Oct. 12, 1937.

which the millinery workers were represented, eight proposals were drafted for submission to buyers as a means of regulating trade abuses. These proposals included the requirements that buyers purchase only those goods bearing the MSC label; that uniform conditions of sale be developed, including the regulalation of the return evil, the formulation of standard discount rates, and a prohibition on advertising allowances. Sales below cost in violation of the Robinson-Patman Act were to be prohibited and all contracting by syndicates and large retailers was to cease. At this meeting Nathaniel Spector, chairman of the Millinery Workers' Joint Board, warned the commission that the union would not continue to tolerate existing conditions in the industry but would take drastic action unless the alleged evils of the trade were rectified.[52]

Thereafter, the millinery workers' union provided many evidences of its power to enforce retailer compliance with the label requirements of the Millinery Stabilization Commission. In 1939, for example, the union and the New York Association of Wholesale Distributors of Ladies' Hats agreed that no member firm would buy hats without an attached label guaranteeing that the product had been manufactured under fair trade practices as well as fair labor standards. That year the union named an advisory committee to discipline jobbers who bought nonlabeled hats from runaway shops. Following along the same lines, a joint conference board of union locals in the men's hat trade took steps to centralize control over all picketing activities against retail shops not observing label requirements.[53]

How the ILGWU Enforced Trade Controls

As the union of the women's coat and suit trade, the ILGWU was equally vigilant in helping manufacturers to gain compliance

[52]*Women's Wear Daily*, May 13, 1937. An advertisement in the issue of July 19, 1937 listed the trade practice provisions that must be met in order to qualify for the consumers' protective label of the Millinery Stabilization Commission. Text of the trade regulations adopted for the millinery industry was printed in the issue of July 16, 1937; see also the issue of July 26, 1937.

[53]For a revealing account of how and why the millinery workers' union undertook to enforce fair trade practices among manufacturers and other business groups, see the report of the union's general executive board to the 1939 convention of the United Hatters, Cap and Millinery Workers' International Union, in *Report and Proceedings*, Third Convention (May 1939),

with fair trade practices. This union's activity was particularly evident in seeking the cooperation of retailers. As early as August 13, 1935, retailers of the industry had endorsed the program of the National Coat and Suit Industry Recovery Board to stabilize the trade and had pledged cooperation in the use of the consumers' protection label. Subsequently, the board forced retailers to live by their pledge by threatening union strikes against suppliers furnishing retailers with nonlabeled goods made in violation of the board's rules.[54]

On occasion, this union's support for the program of the National Coat and Suit Industry Recovery Board amounted to a defense of price controls. Such an instance arose when the popular priced branch of the industry, following a 10 percent across-the-board wage increase granted the workers in the summer of 1937, moved to raise wholesale prices for certain grades of garments from $6.75 to $7.75 and from $10.75 to $11.75. Before complying with these price changes, the organized manufacturers wanted assurances from the union that all competitors in the trade would raise prices to the new levels without increasing the quality of their products.

At the time, F. Nathan Wolf, executive secretary of the National Coat and Suit Industry Recovery Board, led the campaign to raise wholesale prices. Telegrams were sent out warning manufacturers that the sale of fur-trimmed garments for less than $11.75 "will be regarded as a threat against the upholding of the labor standards and will be dealt with as such." In other telegrams, Wolf reminded producers "that use of materials costing more than $1.10 per yard in $6.75 merchandise is regarded as destructive to stability of this division of the industry." Nathan Ohrbach of Ohrbach's department store was ruffled by these developments. "You cannot put manufacturers into a vice and have them prosper," Ohrbach insisted. "The idea of standardizing prices throughout an industry is not sensible."[55]

pp. 63–83; and a lengthy article by I. H. Goldberg on "Gains and Problems of Local 24 Reviewed," in the *Hat Worker*, Jan. 15, 1938.

[54]On August 13, 1935, *Women's Wear Daily* reported that "approval and wholehearted endorsement of the National Coat and Suit Recovery Board program by retailers from all sections of the country are being received daily by Alexander Printz, chairman of the Recovery Board."

[55]The telegrams from the Federal Trade Commission's Docket no. 4596 (National Coat and Suit Industry Recovery Board), Exhibits 888 and 903,

Actively supporting this move to raise prices was Isidore Nagler, manager of the Cloakmakers' Joint Board and a leading figure on the fair trade practice committee of the industry's Recovery Board. Since Nagler was official union spokesman in all bargaining relationships with the organized coat and suit manufacturers, his views could not be taken lightly. To wheel retail outlets into line with trade practice policies of the producers, Nagler wrote the president of the National Association of Apparel Chains on July 29, 1937, in part, as follows:

It may seem somewhat unusual to you for the leader of the labor organization of an industry to communicate with retailers on a matter of buyer-seller relationship. The fact is, however, that the union in the coat and suit industry is firmly of the opinion that the welfare of the employers is of direct and immediate concern to the workers.... I am certain that the firms comprising your organization would not care to accept the responsibility for pursuing policies inimical to labor.[56]

The weight of such gentle hints was often decisive. When large department stores insisted on special discounts for volume buying, or sought to return seasonal garments, or conducted sales at "below-cost" prices, the National Coat and Suit Industry Recovery Board sometimes issued special bulletins on "Non-Collaborating Retailers." On one occasion, when Ohrbach's department store advertised that "in many instances, due to heavy purchasing, combined with our penny profits policy, you (the consumer) pay less than normal wholesale cost," agents of the Recovery Board conducted 94 visits and examined 22 sets of books to see whether firms supplying Ohrbach's had violated discount regulations. Wherever such investigations led to denying firms use of

---

are given as quoted in Robinson, *Collective Bargaining and Market Control in the New York Coat and Suit Industry*, p. 196. Nathan Ohrbach's outburst against price restrictions was quoted in *Women's Wear Daily*, Sept. 1, 1937.

[56]Isidore Nagler, from the Federal Trade Commission's Docket no. 4596 (National Coat and Suit Industry Recovery Board), Exhibit 894, as cited in Robinson, *Collective Bargaining and Market Control in the New York Coat and Suit Industry*, p. 197. For further evidence of organized labor's contributions toward alleviating the evils of depressed selling prices in the women's coat and suit industry, see the report of Bertram Reinitz to the National Coat and Suit Industry Recovery Board in *Women's Wear Daily*, Sept. 1, 1937.

the coat and suit label, the union supplied the pressure for compliance by refusing to handle unlabeled garments.[57]

During the summer of 1936, a special grievance committee composed of the executive directors from several employers' associations supporting the National Coat and Suit Industry Recovery Board was organized to conduct hearings against six firms charged with violating discount and antirebate regulations. Isidore Nagler, manager of the Joint Board of Cloakmakers' Unions, was invited to serve as advisory member of the committee. Under the caption, "Labor Takes a Hand in Upholding Trade Rules," *Women's Wear Daily* for July 18, 1936 gave an account of the decisive role the union was expected to play in the proceedings. "The value of union collaboration in 'putting teeth' into the findings of the Grievance Committee is obvious," runs this account. "Failure to liquidate the penalties recommended by this committee and imposed by the respective association of which the violator is a member would warrant expulsion, automatically placing the firm outside the pale of relationship with the union." The consequences of such banishment were generally understood.[58]

An Equilibrium of Bargaining Power in Trade Relations

In a broader sense, labor unions of the needle trades set their sights on helping manufacturers of wearing apparel to grow in

---

[57]One of the bulletins on "Non-Collaborating Retailers" is filed in the Abelson papers, as is a copy of the National Recovery Board's "Report on Activities to Date in Connection with Ohrbach's Discount Survey."

[58]Faced with unfair competition of retailers who bought skins and had their fur garments made to order, the wholesale fur manufacturers called upon the fur workers' union to help them out of their troubles. "The practice of cloak houses and retailers supplying the manufacturers with skins to make up garments and trimmings is a great evil," runs the terms of the 1938 labor agreement in the fur manufacturing industry, "and should be combatted by the united efforts of the Association and the Union." The parties to this agreement created a joint bureau of general enforcement, primarily to gain compliance with trade practice regulations. From the terms of settlement of the 31-week fur strike, embodied in the collective agreement between the International Fur Workers' Union and the Associated Fur Coat and Trimming Manufacturers, May 25, 1938. See also the annual report for the year 1938 presented by the administrative staff of the Associated Fur Coat and Trimming Manufacturers to the association's annual meeting. A copy of this report is filed in the Abelson papers.

stature with corresponding developments among suppliers of raw materials, on the one hand, and among buyers of needle trade products, on the other. Since the mid-twenties, the organized workers of the apparel industries had become increasingly aware of the inequality in bargaining power that existed between their employers and other business groups. By the late thirties — and even more so thereafter – a handful of textile firms controlled the bulk of raw materials from which women's garments were manufactured. The pressure that these industrial giants exerted upon thousands of small-scale manufacturers who bargained separately for textile goods obviously increased the pressure on those manufacturers for greater economies elsewhere.

Unhappily for the manufacturers, the superior bargaining power of suppliers that raised the costs of raw materials could not be offset through higher prices charged to the distributive outlets of needle trade products. For the retail buyers themselves were also profiting from the increased bargaining strength of large-scale organization. Beginning with the twenties, the rapid development of chain stores, buying syndicates, mail-order houses, and large department stores soon concentrated the bulk of the wholesale market in relatively few hands. These massive outlets were no less effective than large supply houses in taking advantage of their superior bargaining power. Crushed between two arrays of industrial giants, the hapless manufacturers could look for additional savings only to lower overhead, greater efficiencies, or reduced labor costs. What the manufacturers lost through dealing with large-scale suppliers and purchasers, they too often sought to recover by chiseling on labor contracts with their workers.[59]

"In all its relations in the market," noted J. C. Worthy, a care-

---

[59]See the testimony of Lazare Teper, research director, ILGWU, in *Study of Monopoly Power,* Hearings before the Subcommittee on Study of Monopoly Power of the Committee on the Judiciary, House of Representatives, 81st Cong., 1st sess. (July 22, 1949), Serial no. 14, Part 1, pp. 299–326, especially pp. 305–310 on "Concentration of Economic Power — Textiles," and pp. 311–320 on "Concentration of Economic Power — Retailing."

In defending controls over the jobber-contractor system for the California women's sportswear trade against attacks by the Federal Trade Commission, the ILGWU made effective use of the "Giant Textile — Giant Retailer" theme. See M. P. Glushien, attorney for the ILGWU, Brief in support of Initial Decision of Hearing Examiner in the Matter of the California Sportswear and Dress Association, Inc. *et al.,* FTC Docket no. 6325 (n.d.), pp. 19–21. The case is discussed below at pp. 840–848.

ful student of the millinery industry during the thirties, "the industry must deal with large scale enterprise — large at least as compared to millinery. Raw material must be purchased from a handful of houses and about 60 percent of the finished product reaches the ultimate consumer through half a dozen buying syndicates. Between these upper and nether millstones 1350 manufacturers fight desperately for their economic existence." This realistic analysis of the manufacturers' plight was a far cry from the laws of equal opportunity that a free enterprise system was presumed to foster. "Theoretically," reported the general executive board, United Hatters, Cap and Millinery Workers, to the union's 1939 convention, "there is an equality of bargaining power as between the chains or syndicates and the manufacturers."

But that equality of bargaining power, or the freedom of contract, as the courts have called it, is as useful to the millinery manufacturer, who needs these orders in order to survive, as is to the worker his freedom to make an individual contract with his employer. In fact, there is no equality and no freedom. Instead, there is duress — not the kind of duress which is sufficient in law to void a contract — but economic duress, which is as effective and as disastrous as the type of duress which the law prohibits.[60]

The manufacturers in other industries of the needle trades suffered from the same type of inequality in bargaining position. When the Associated Fur Manufacturers in 1928 sought a standard fair trade agreement to regulate terms of sale with the Fur Retailers of America, the organized retailers yelled loud and long that the manufacturers were pursuing the wrong horn of their dilemma. Looking across the manufacturers' valley of small enterprises to the towering peaks of concentrated power held by the organized suppliers, the retailers' association insisted that the manufacturers should attack the organized dealers who had set the price of raw materials too high for the fur manufacturers to prosper.[61]

---

[60]United Hatters, Cap and Millinery Workers' International Union, *Report and Proceedings,* Third Convention (May 1939), p. 68. The union's views on buying syndicates were also expressed in *ibid.,* Second Convention (First Regular Convention), Oct. 4–7, 1936, pp. 54–56. J. C. Worthy's views are from his study, "The Millinery Industry," p. ix.

[61]*Women's Wear Daily,* March 7, 1928. In a letter, dated April 27, 1935, to the Honorable J. J. Cochran, U.S. Representative from Missouri, B. H.

Wherever this disparity in bargaining strength increased the pressures to undermine labor standards, needle trade unions had a personal stake in coming to the rescue of their beleaguered employers. Either they could seek to reduce the bargaining strength of suppliers and purchasers with whom their employers dealt or they could help to increase the bargaining strength of manufacturers for dealing with suppliers and purchasers. The first alternative led union agents to the committee rooms and antechambers of U. S. congressmen in support of more favorable legislation against giant corporations, domestic and foreign. The second alternative produced a number of union efforts to help the manufacturers increase their bargaining power.

Three years after the abortive attempt of the millinery workers in 1935 to help the manufacturers organize on a national scale (see above, pp. 768–769), many of these producers from all parts of the country met again in Chicago during the summer of 1938 to make a determined attack on the major problems of their industry. This time they not only welcomed delegates from the union but invited union leaders to express their views. Max Zaritsky, president of the United Hatters, Cap and Millinery Workers, gave the keynote address in which he harped on the weaknesses in the manufacturers' set-up and pointed to the "outside forces which are able to take advantage of that weakness for their own enrichment and advancement."[62]

The nature of those "outside forces" that threatened the prosperity of the industry was clarified the following year at the

---

Lerner, executive director of the National Association of Blouse Manufacturers, commended the congressman on his resolution to investigate the activities of the American Retail Federation and explained: "The manufacturers in our industries have viewed with growing apprehension, the adverse effect that a huge organization of this type may have upon the morale of the wholesale markets as a result of their combined strength and potential ability to demand certain concessions not ordinarily obtained by the industrial retailer." From the text of the letter printed in a bulletin of the National Association of Blouse Manufacturers. A copy of the bulletin is filed in the Abelson papers. See also, *Women's Wear Daily*, April 24–27, 1935. Earlier, manufacturers of both the dress industry and the women's coat and suit trade had supported bills before the New York legislature regulating resident buyers by naming the conditions necessary to obtain a license to operate. *Ibid.*, March 21 and 24, 1935.

[62]United Hatters, Cap and Millinery Workers' International Union, *Report and Proceedings,* Third Convention (May 1939), p. 133.

union's national convention. In its formal report on May 20, 1939, the union's general executive board supported a national "association of associations" that would help to raise the manufacturers to a level of equality in bargaining power with suppliers of raw materials and with purchasers of millinery products. In support of its stand, the board quoted from an exhaustive survey of the millinery industry by the Women's Bureau of the U. S. Department of Labor:

The economic equilibrium between millinery manufacturer, materials supply house, and millinery purchaser can be attained and maintained by hard, intelligent effort and mutual confidence within the manufacturing branch itself. The strength of the manufacturing branch will be built up to equal that of the branches that service it and that it services, however, only when control is gained over the destroying forces *within* the industry. Such control requires effective cooperation and systematic effort of employer and employee. Not only is a strong union of employees, such as exists, necessary to accomplish this end, but a strong association of employers is necessary in order that both may work together through a voluntary representative organization to promote their common interest in the welfare of the industry."[63]

Just such an analysis had also been drawn from the manufacture of women's coats and suits before the NRA codes ever sanctioned industry organizations to regulate trade. During the movement of the late twenties and early thirties to bring retailers within the orbits of the collective bargaining system, Impartial Chairman G. W. Alger had urged manufacturers and workers alike to organize more effectively against the concentrated power of buying groups. "We have plenty of unity of buyers dealing together to get the uttermost farthing on bankruptcy prices," he stated before the ILGWU convention in 1932, "and no unity of sellers to enforce living prices for merchandise sold."[64]

---

[63]*Ibid.,* p. 131, citing U.S. Department of Labor, Women's Bureau, *Conditions in the Millinery Industry in the United States* (1939), Bulletin no. 169, p. 11.

[64]ILGWU, *Report and Proceedings,* Twenty-first Convention (May 1932), p. 95. In 1929, when certain large retailers demanded of women's coat and suit manufacturers an extra 2 percent discount for office expenses, Impartial Chairman R. V. Ingersoll called for strong resistance, observing that "unfair

Within a year, Mr. Alger was to receive strong judicial support for his stand from the coal mining industry in the case of 137 Appalachian coal mine operators who, to offset the dictatorial powers of large buying interests, had created a central selling agency, Appalachian Coals, Inc., through which all coal for the market was to be graded and sold at the highest price obtainable. Against charges that this plan violated the antitrust laws, Chief Justice Hughes, speaking for the U. S. Supreme Court, reviewed the deplorable conditions peculiar to coal mining in the area and found no proof that voluntary cooperative efforts to correct abuses and help stabilize a depressed industry through a joint selling agency unreasonably restrained trade or that it was detrimental to the public interest. Commenting on the case, Impartial Chairman Alger found striking analogies between the plight of these small coal mining firms and the plight of women's coat and suit manufacturers, and from these analogies he drew the following conclusion:

There would seem, then, to be no reason why the cloak and suit industry should be one [in] which buying is concentrated in the hands of buyers' representatives, and sellers, wholly disorganized, are separately competing against one another in producing merchandise without profit and at an enormous cost of living standards to its workers.[65]

By throwing their weight around, needle trade unions might well contribute to an equality in bargaining power among trade

exactions on their part can be met only by concerted action through well-organized associations." He heartily approved the 50 percent increase within the preceding week of memberships in both the Industrial Council of Cloak, Suit and Skirt Manufacturers (inside producers) and in the Merchants' Ladies' Garment Association (jobbers). *Women's Wear Daily*, July 22, 1929.

See also, the report of D. N. Mosessohn, executive chairman, Associated Dress Industries, to the association's membership in February 1929, urging that aggressive tactics by retailers be matched by more general organization within the wholesale market. He would have the Associated Dress Industries join hands with the Associated Women's Apparel Industries, the sister organization of the women's coat and suit trade, to present a united front against excessive retailer discounts. *Ibid.*, Feb. 19, 1929.

[65]Alger's views on the case were reported in *Women's Wear Daily*, March 14, 1933. "When industry is grievously hurt, when producing concerns fail, when unemployment mounts and communities dependent upon profitable production are prostrated, the wells of commerce go dry." Chief Justice Charles E. Hughes in Appalachian Coals, Inc., v. U.S., 288 U.S. 344 (1933), at p. 372, reversing the decision of the U.S. District Court reported at 1 Fed. Supp. 339 (1932).

groups – just as those unions had contributed to an equality in bargaining power between the "bosses" and the "people." Within the manufacturing process itself, where business stability hinged as much upon orderly relations among jobbers, contractors, and inside manufacturers as upon orderly relations between employer groups and the labor force, needle trade unions were always in a position to bolster the cause of the weaker party. Of course, as was often charged, those unions by joining one business faction of a trade to suppress another for the benefit of the workers might gain immediate objectives at the sacrifice of the best long-term interests of the trade. In any case, building the house of industry upon the solid rock of equality in bargaining power was a goal more easily stated than achieved.

Concluding Observations

Whatever influences the history of collective bargaining in the needle trades may have exerted upon provisions for industry codes of fair competition under Title I of the National Industrial Recovery Act, neither these influences nor the specific guarantee in the act of labor's right to organize and bargain collectively through representatives of their own choosing ever became dominant factors in the over-all history of the codes. Beyond the range of the protocol movement, whose advocates looked through rose-colored glasses upon this new gimmick for industry-wide control of labor standards, the participants in code making and code administration of other industries seldom thought of the codes as more than business aids that liberalized opportunities for joint action among manufacturers on trade policies otherwise falling within the shadow of the Sherman Antitrust Act or the Federal Trade Commission Act. This overriding concept throughout American industry gradually permeated the needle trades and perverted the thinking of many employers who might otherwise never have lost sight of the potential contributions that labor unions could offer in the realm of trade practices.

Encouraged by action of President Roosevelt and the U. S. Congress supporting voluntary codes to follow the NIRA, and hopeful that federal authorities would soft-peddle antitrust restrictions which had previously hampered business efforts to regulate key trade practices, groups of needle trade manufacturers hastened to continue the benefits of trade controls derived from the codes. Imbued from code experiences with a new confidence in their ability to handle their own affairs, these manufacturing groups spurned the help of labor unions on matters of business controls and set out upon the hazardous seas of trade regulations paddling their own canoe. Acting alone, however, they could not steer safely between the antitrust rocks of legal prosecution and the nonenforcement shoals of ineffective regulations. Fortunately, the rebuffed needle trade unions had too much at stake to sit idly by while their inept employers were swamped through their own stupidity. Manning the trusted lifeboats of guaranteed trade practice enforcement and heavily equipped with immunities from the antitrust laws, these unions not only assumed leadership in rescue efforts but obviously saved the business lives of many employers during the stormy post-code years of the later thirties. Not surprisingly, the employers, who soon called for help, extended to their rescuers unprecedented freedom in directing trade controls – concessions that not only were essential to immediate relief, but that also presaged a new era of controlling competition. This era was destined to become less dependent upon collective bargaining, soon to be hedged by new outcroppings of legal barriers, than upon one-way union dictation.

Chapter 20

Labor Practices

beyond the Codes

HOWEVER essential union support may have been for the successful regulation of trade practices, employer groups soon came to re-embrace labor unions still more dearly for their contributions toward equalizing labor costs. Government surveys into the effect of code termination upon labor standards revealed a general reduction in minimum wages and a widespread extension in hours of work, with a corresponding loss in other favorable terms of employment. Chiefly because the collapse of labor standards was less severe in the organized segments of the needle trades than in the unorganized firms, the growing disparities in labor costs again threatened the system of law and order established through years of collective bargaining.[1]

---

[1] Writing in the *New York Times,* July 10, 1935, Louis Stark, labor reporter, disclosed wholesale reductions in labor standards after the NRA codes were invalidated. Wages in the manufacture of neckties, for example, were alleged to have fallen from 25 percent to as much as 75 percent, while hours of work throughout the men's clothing trade were estimated to have jumped upward from 40 hours a week to 48 or 50 hours a week.

The W. P. Roberts' Commission, a fact-finding board named by President Roosevelt to study the effect of the death of the NRA codes, found less drastic violations of NRA code standards in the post-code period than did Daniel C. Roper, secretary of the Department of Commerce. *Women's Wear Daily,* March 18, 1936. See also *New York Times,* July 12, 1935.

In his study of the millinery industry, J. C. Worthy noted a growing disparity in wages and hours of work between the organized shops and the un-

Resurgence of Old Issues

Focusing nationwide attention on the control of trade practices under the codes had distorted the perspective of numerous apparel manufacturers still devoted to the protocol principles of controlled competition. Many firms tended to glorify the god of fair trade practices at the expense of uniform labor costs. Yet nothing in the code era had changed the principal source of excessive competition that plagued the needle trades. Diversity in labor costs through inability to create and maintain industry-wide standards of employment was still the chief roadblock on the highway of controlled competition. While some never lost sight of this obstacle, many who had been falsely indoctrinated under the codes required a new sense of direction.

Even before the codes were invalidated, many leaders of needle trade associations were so obsessed with the thought of devising their own control systems that they tended to foresake the basic principles on which stabilization of labor costs had been founded. During the negotiation of the 1935 collective labor agreement for the women's coat and suit trade, some of the organized employer groups opposed limitation and assignment of contractors, minimum costs of production for contractors (included allowances for overhead), jobber responsibility for wage payment of contractors, and a centralized procedure for piece-rate determination. Only the persistence of union leadership held the manufacturers of women's coats and suits on the course that had been charted by the founders of the protocol movement.[2]

Soon, however, the tools of self-help that the needle trade manufacturers would use to determine their own labor standards began to lose their luster. When representatives of the organized manufacturers in the hosiery industry met in general conference during the spring of 1936 to consider ways and means of regulating competition in the absence of the NRA codes, they turned their attention to diversities in labor costs — the greatest of all

---

organized shops. In the nonunion shops, men worked as long as 60 hours a week, while occupational minima for wages were largely abandoned. J. C. Worthy, "The Millinery Industry," (processed), NRA: Division of Review, Industry Studies Section (March 1936), pp. 116–117.

[2] See Harry Haskel, *A Leader of the Garment Workers: the Biography of Isidore Nagler* (1950), pp. 192–196; and *Women's Wear Daily*, April 9, 1935.

obstacles to "legitimate" competition. Some saw no hope in the ability of the industry to govern itself and so called for a dictator to control all standards of production. One promising suggestion came from John M. Botts, senior partner in Harrington and Waring, who reluctantly advocated that the manufacturers turn over their labor affairs to the hosiery workers' union. Botts admitted that he had "about as much desire for organization from outside as 'the devil had for holy water' but it seemed the only way to obtain uniform hours and wages."[3]

Post-NRA plans to equalize labor costs through union help in standardizing conditions of employment followed patterns that had long been familiar. If these programs contained nothing new, they at least generated less dissension among those responsible for their execution. By the later thirties, much of the doubt, confusion, and uncertainty that had characterized the history of collective bargaining since 1910 had been swept away. For those who once saw as through a glass darkly, the chief issues in labor policy now stood out in bold relief. Years of experience had fused the minds of labor and managment to the common need for joint action in standardizing labor costs. Needle trade unions could restore the true perspective of the protocol movement by leading the forces of law and order back into a concerted attack upon variable labor standards.[4]

Pointing up the resurgence of old issues was the following resolution of the Eastern Women's Headwear Association adopted in May 1936:

WHEREAS, there is a collective agreement existing in the millinery industry subscribed to by the Union, representing labor, and the

---

[3]*Ibid.*, April 24, 1936.

[4]For example, the much debated principle that jobbers and inside manufacturers become responsible for union wage standards in the shops of their contractors was accepted by mutual consent in the 1939 collective agreement between the National Skirt and Sportswear Association and Local 23, ILGWU, wherein the parties "acknowledge that a member of the Association who supplies work to contractors . . . is directly concerned with the payment of the wages of the workers employed by his contractors . . . and . . . to the extent of any work performed on such garments, a member of the Association and his contractors . . . are not neutrals . . . but are jointly engaged in an integrated production effort." As quoted with approval by U.S. District Court Judge Edward Weinfeld, in Greenstein v. National Skirt and Sportswear Association, 178 F. Supp. 681 (1959) at p. 688.

EASTERN WOMEN'S HEADWEAR ASSOCIATION, INC., representing the manufacturers, and

WHEREAS, the said collective agreement definitely promises and undertakes the equalization of all labor costs and standards as a vital step necessary to the stabilization of the industry, and

WHEREAS, much of the chaos in the industry is largely traceable to the confusion of prices paid for the same or similar operations in the same price ranges, and to some extent, the absence of an official settlement of labor prices, rates and standards,

THEREFORE, BE IT RESOLVED, that the EASTERN WOMEN'S HEADWEAR ASSOCIATION, INC., recommend and urge the immediate investigation of all existing labor costs, prices, rates and standards in the industry for the purpose of intelligently determining such standards that may be fixed as fair and equitable to the entire industry with uniformity, and

BE IT FURTHER RESOLVED that the Millinery Stabilization Commission be instructed forthwith to proceed on an exhaustive survey of the entire market, designed to disclose the labor prices, rates and standards prevailing in every hat manufacturing plant in Greater New York, and that such findings be submitted and used as a basis in fixing the proposed uniform standards.[5]

To Organize the Unorganized!

Basic to the revived movement for equalizing labor costs were the intensified efforts to organize the unorganized workers. Over the years nonunion competition, more so than competition from independent firms with union shops, had wrecked all plans for equalizing labor costs. Neither the giant strides in union membership experienced under the codes nor legal encouragement for union organization from the National Labor Relations Act of 1935 had succeeded in weeding out competition from nonunion shops, particularly those in the hinterlands immediately beyond the New York metropolitan district. So great was this source of unfair competition in the late thirties that the Industrial Council of Cloak, Suit and Skirt Manufacturers, standard-bearer of the protocol movement, recommended to the ILGWU "a discussion with the union on the firms that seem to be union in name but

---

[5] A copy of the resolution is filed in the Abelson papers.

We don't care how high the scale may be, provided it is equal for all and that there are no special "agreements" for cap makers' shops or New Jersey Manufacturers.

—Ephraim Bros. Hat Co. to the Millinery Stabilization Commission, letter, dated June 1, 1937, filed in the Abelson papers.

not in standards and a series of monthly conferences with the union relative to non-union production."[6]

For a time at least, the trucking interests — those firms responsible for transporting goods from jobbers to contractors and back again — became a potent force in helping to organize the unorganized. In an award for the women's coat and suit industry, dated September 19, 1933, Impartial Chairman G. W. Alger had approved a garment trucking monopoly for transporting the goods of this trade to be granted to members of the New York and Brooklyn Cloak and Suit Trucking Association and to members of the Garment Center Truck Owner's Association. In return for this monopoly, the members of the two associations were to employ only drivers and helpers who were members of Local 102, ILGWU, and — what is more important — they were "not to handle any trucking for any person, firm or corporation engaged in the coat and suit industry, directly or indirectly, and irrespective of locality unless and until such person, firm or corporation is in contractual relations with the International Ladies' Garment Workers' Union to maintain union standards."[7]

Through the inability of nonunion firms to receive materials or to move their finished products, overpowering pressure would presumably be brought to bear upon nonunion sources of production. After the codes were invalidated, ILGWU Truckers' Local 102 undertook to enforce the principles of Alger's award by entering into agreements with packing houses to prohibit receipt of coat or dress packages not made by union labor. Delivery of coats and dresses out of town, noted *Women's Wear Daily* for August 19, 1937, was thrown into confusion when Local

---

[6] *Women's Wear Daily*, March 16, 1939.

[7] The terms quoted in this award were subsequently written into agreements between local trucking associations and the organized factions of both the dress industry and the women's coat and suit trade. Under these agreements, truck owners were also to register with the union all the manufacturers, jobbers, and contractors with whom they did business and were to prepare for the union daily reports of the deliveries they had made. Truck owners could not accept new accounts until notified by the union that the account had been registered as provided in the general agreement, nor could they be so financially or otherwise interested in carrier firms not under the collective agreements as to defeat the purpose of the restrictions. See *ibid.*, March 7, 1939. A copy of the Alger award cited above is filed with the awards of J. J. Walker, impartial chairman of the women's coat and suit trade, in the Abelson papers.

102 began to enforce this boycott on handling nonunion goods.[8]

Meanwhile the International Fur Workers' Union had not relied wholly upon the law nor had this union awaited encouragement from other sources to increase its membership. True to its long established policy of direct action, the New York Furriers' Joint Council set out by forceful means to resolve the problems of competition from the nonunion, out-of-town, runaway shops. "One of the outstanding achievements we can record," stated the *Furriers' Bulletin,* organ of the Furriers' Joint Council, for April 1936, "is the determined drive against the out-of-town shops, conducted under the supervision of the Organization Department." The *Bulletin* reported individual successes and the methods employed, including a rigid prohibition against permitting any union furrier to work in an out-of-town shop. Then it summarized the achievements of the council in suppressing runaway shops:

> As a result of our persistent work, we have already closed up or brought back to New York more than a dozen out-of-town shops. . . . Other shops were closed and some shops were partly closed. Every remaining shop was fully investigated and connections were established in it. We can state with pride that the backbone of the out-of-town movement was broken and we are well on the way to cleaning up the whole situation.[9]

Organization through Consumer Pressure

In the post-code movement to organize the unorganized, needle trade unions developed a new technique that was to become more and more valuable over the years. Few union leaders of the thirties could have foreseen that the most effective weapon for attacks upon the nonunion shop would ultimately be found in the reaction of public customers at retail stores. Especially after the Taft-Hartley and the Landrum-Griffin Acts had restricted the

---

[8]In his promulgation and supplemental promulgation of rules on trucking restrictions for the women's coat and suit trade, Impartial Chairman J. J. Walker in 1941 again endorsed the principle of monopoly controls and continued in effect the previous awards and promulgations of Impartial Chairmen G. W. Alger and S. A. Rosenblatt. J. J. Walker, *Decisions,* Dec. 9, 1940 and Jan. 31, 1941. In addition to stimulating the growth of unionized shops, these trucking agreements obviously helped to enforce other provisions of the jobber–contractor–inside manufacturer–union relationships under collective agreements of the industry. See above, pp. 349–351.

[9]*Furriers' Bulletin,* April 1936.

use of strikes in organizing campaigns did union leaders shift the scene of battle from manufacturing concerns to retail outlets. Innocent customers, far removed from the immediate employers of nonunion labor, became the primary object of union attention.

The symbol that gave this change of tactics an element of respectability — as well as a front for legality — was the union label. Under this insignia, the organized workers of the needle trades had already won many "fair trade practice" battles for their employers, along with the many "labor standard" battles they had won for themselves. In defense of uniform labor costs — a stated goal of employers' associations as well as of labor unions — the union label was now to become a means of herding retail customers, willy-nilly, into becoming the tools of union victory. If this new highway to success in the growth of union membership was more roundabout, the rewards were no less gratifying than had always come from storming the gates of nonunion plants or shutting off manufacturers from their sources of supply or closing the outlets for their products. So long as these new union techniques minimized disparities in labor costs, who among the legitimate manufacturers supporting the protocol movement would raise a cry of protest?

In the millinery trade, for example, department stores offering nonlabeled Easter hats were picketed by human "bunnies" distributing "don't buy" leaflets to customers at the door. Fearing consumer resistance, store owners hastened to insist upon union-labeled hats from their suppliers. Suppliers of nonunion products with their markets cut off, then demanded union-labeled hats from their producers. Manufacturers in turn had to insist upon an organized labor force that could provide the label essential to the distribution of their goods. This indirect drive for union organization through pressure on the consumer generally received support from other locally organized segments of the labor force. Even the plumbers, the miners, the truckers, and the railroad workers could be induced to support the cause of unionism reflected by a picket line at a retail outlet.[10]

A more recent example of this new technique grew out of an attempt by Local 125 of the millinery workers' union to gain recognition as bargaining agent for some eight hundred millinery

---

[10]The content of this paragraph is based on personal interviews in the early sixties with Gerald Coleman, research director, United Hatters, Cap and Millinery Workers' International Union.

workers employed by the Texas-Miller Company, a firm manufacturing women's hats in Dallas, Texas. Fearing the adverse economic effects on the union of attempting direct pressure against the employer, Local 125 turned to its own international, the United Hatters, Cap and Millinery Workers, for help. A summary of what transpired during the summer, fall, winter, and spring of 1963–1964 was reported in the *New York Times,* June 8, 1964, as follows:

The international opened a nationwide campaign among retailers, organized labor and consumers. Mr. Rose [union president] said the drive sought to explain why hat buyers should demand union-labeled headwear and refuse to purchase hats made without a union contract by Texas-Miller.

In the course of the campaign, however, Texas-Miller filed for a National Labor Relations Board representation election. The election was conducted in March, and the union lost 235 to 278.

Union charges that the company had sought unfairly to influence the workers' decision resulted in the board's setting aside the election on May 14.

In the meantime, the union-label drive apparently was having considerable effect on the business of Texas-Miller, Mr. Rose said. I. Benjamin Parrill, president of the company, acknowledged that the boycott had begun to bother some of the company's important customers.

At any rate, Mr. Rose said, the company called his office and sought to resume negotiations. At first, he said, the talks were provisional and based on the assumption that the workers in Texas would restate their desire for representation by the union.

Last week Mr. Parrill addressed workers at the Corsicana plant, and emphasized the need for the union label for the success of his company's hats. He also stressed the need for union-management unity and harmony.

The union began signing up workers again and by Saturday had 550 of the 800 back in the union. On Friday Mr. Rose and Mr. Parrill met in New York and completed negotiations for a new agreement which was announced yesterday. The four-year pact provides for wage increases of 32-1/2 cents an hour for "front shop" workers and 44 cents for "back shop" workers in addition to other benefits.[11]

---

[11]This case, of course, raised some interesting legal problems. For, if the company at first violated the law in trying to keep the union out, it later may have violated the law in trying to get the union in.

During the post-code era, the slogan "Organize the Unorganized" was applied to manufacturers as well as to workers. "No well rounded campaign of stabilization can be assured of success if close to 50 percent of the industry is felt uncovered . . ." warned the general executive board of the United Hatters, Cap and Millinery Workers, reporting to the union's national convention, May 20, 1939. "First there must be a more or less all inclusive organization of all the manufacturers in all of the markets. For manufacturers cannot be expected to be bound by any decisions that are made or by any reforms that are introduced unless they are parties to the making of those decisions, and participate in the discussions that determine their wisdom or feasibility."[12]

More than ever before, employer groups participating in stabilization programs expected needle trade unions to drive rebellious manufacturers into associations or else out of their trades. Where unions did not impose more onerous terms on independent employers who refused to join an association, those unions must at least extend the labor standards negotiated with employers' associations to all independent firms operating under separate union contracts. Even better was the prospect that unions might refuse altogether to deal with nonassociation firms that were denied use of the consumers' protection label. Moreover, the monopolies granted trucking associations of the women's coat and suit trade to transfer goods between jobbers and contractors in return for help in strengthening the union were also used to halt the flow of goods to and from contractors who did not belong to the American Cloak and Suit Manufacturers' Association.[13]

Another recent example of an appeal to consumers — this one by the organized workers of the blouse manufacturing industry — was based on the use of free shopping bags as an advertising medium:

> The shopping bag has been turned into a strike weapon by the members of the International Ladies' Garment Workers' Union. The message "Judy Bond, Inc., On Strike — Don't Buy Judy Bond Blouses" is printed in large letters on the brightly colored bags. Union volunteers offer them to shoppers outside the entrances to retail stores that sell blouses manufactured by Judy Bond, Inc.
> —*New York Times*, May 17, 1964.

[12] United Hatters, Cap and Millinery Workers' International Union, *Report and Proceedings*, Third Convention (May 1939), p. 130.

[13] On the use of trucking monopolies, see Hearings before the Committee on Finance, U.S. Senate, 74th Cong. 1st sess., pursuant to S. Res. 79: *Investi-*

Union Help in Equalizing Labor Costs

Within the organized segments of the apparel industries, labor unions of the post-code era assumed even greater powers in creating and enforcing uniform terms of employment. This revived activity arose in part from the specter of legal restraints overshadowing employer efforts at standardizing labor costs. Not even the declared motive of protecting labor standards through minimum production costs could guarantee immunity from federal agents aroused to the possibility of antitrust infractions. If the parties to collective agreements did not already foresee that for reasons of legality the union must carry the ball, they at least laid the groundwork for this ultimate transformation.

The dress industry offered a good example of attempts to revitalize collective bargaining for the sake of uniform labor costs. Until the ILGWU assumed the leadership in organizing the manufacturers in 1930, the industry had floundered on the sheer perversity of employers to organize for an aggressive attack upon the evils of their trade. Even during the era of the codes, when cooperation was the watchword of the new freedom from legal restraints, the organized manufacturers and the dressmakers' union could not agree upon a method for standardizing piece rates or upon a full-scale plan for the limitation and assignment of contractors. After the codes, however, attempts at standardizing piece rates through a centralized procedure for piece-rate determination — a problem that had baffled the dress industry from the early years of the protocol movement — finally culminated in the adoption of a unit system for assessing the labor costs of each operation in the manufacture of women's dresses.[14]

---

gation of the National Recovery Administration (April 1935), Part 6, pp. 2525–2528.

[14]The old shop-by-shop procedure for determining piece rates, which continued to exist in the post-code era, was described by the *New York Times* for Feb. 9, 1936 to embrace the following steps — a sequence not unlike that which existed under the first protocols: (1) with an order from a retailer, the jobber makes up a sample garment and sends it out to a contractor for a bid; (2) the contractor meets with the price committee of his organized workers to agree on the labor costs for the garment; (3) the contractor after adding his other costs and profit, then barters with the jobber over the total

"To eliminate still further any elements of doubt and speculation in the settlement of prices," explained Julius Hochman, manager of the Dressmakers' Joint Board, ILGWU, in 1936, "we have devised the Unit System . . . a method of calculating the exact time it would take a worker to make a given dress."

In order to do this the dress is split into component parts. In spite of constant changes in styles, certain parts are common to all dresses at all times. These fundamental parts are called a body. The time necessary to make the various possible body combinations has been studied. Another element in each dress, no matter the style, is the sleeve design. Some dresses have long sleeves, some have short sleeves, some have sleeves that are wide and open; some sleeves have cuffs, some are finished with piping or shirring. The time necessary to make all the various types of sleeves has been determined. The same is true of other "features" on a dress. There may be pointed seams, scalloped yokes, pleats and ruffles. There may be trimmings, such as bows, sashes, straps.

All these parts have been separately studied and their time determined, and listed in a schedule. To find out how long it takes to make a dress under the Unit System, all that is necessary to do is to consult the schedule for the body time and for each additional item. The time is then totaled up and we arrive at the time it would take to make that dress.

The method is called the "Unit System" because the time measuring elements are split up into the smallest possible practical units to get exact results. A unit of time is one-tenth of a minute. Thus there are ten units to a minute and 600 to an hour. If the system shows that a dress is made up of parts scheduling 360 time-units, it means that this dress would take 36 minutes to make.

The next step in the system is to translate the units into terms of money. The wage clauses of the agreement, which fix the value of time for the worker, then establish the piece rate for the dress. Thus workers in all shops everywhere will receive the same rates for the same amount of labor.[15]

---

price to be paid for making the garment; (4) the jobber then repeats this procedure with other contractors until he finds the lowest bidder to whom he offers the work. Earlier efforts to eliminate or control this shop-by-shop bargaining are recounted above, pp. 90–97.

[15] Julius Hochman, *Why This Strike* (pamphlet, 1935). Text of this pamphlet also appears as an appendix to Emil Schlesinger, *The Outside System*

Equally important was the need for devising centralized procedures that would guarantee uniform application of the principles underlying the unit system for piece-rate determination. For example, having the labor costs of a particular dress fixed on the premises of the jobber, with the help of all interested contractors and representatives from the union, would eliminate separate negotiations between the jobber and each contractor, as well as separate negotiations between each contractor and his workers. Then by further centralizing the procedure to include representatives from all organized groups in the manufacturing process — jobbers, contractors, inside producers, and the labor union — the piece rates for any given dress could be measured against a standard set for similar work throughout the industry or market area of keenest competition. Should the organized factions of the industry fail to reach agreement, appeals could be taken to the impartial chairman whose decisions were final and binding.

Lest the impartial chairman be overwhelmed by the number and technical character of such appeals, provision was often made for specialized assistance to lighten his load and bolster his competence. Under the 1935 collective agreements of the women's coat and suit trade, for example, the organized factions of the industry established a highly centralized professional Labor Bureau to assist with piece-rate determinations by establishing standards and supervising their application. Whenever an employer and a committee of his workers disagreed over the piece rate for a particular garment in a given shop, they might be joined by a representative of the bureau, as well as by representatives of the ILGWU and of the employers' association (jobbers, contractors, or inside manufacturers). Failure to reach a satisfactory settlement through these joint negotiations might result in an appeal to the bureau for an official determination of the issue. Only then, if at all, could an appeal be taken to the impartial chairman of the industry.[16]

---

of Production in the Women's Garment Industry in the New York Market (1951), pp. 93–106. For the development of the unit system, see *Women's Wear Daily,* Jan. 11 and August 9, 1934; August 14 and 20, 1935; April 1, 1936.

[16]The Labor Bureau heretofore established shall continue as it now functions, and the classification of standard types and grades of gar-

The greatest progress toward standardizing labor costs that collective bargaining had to offer in the post-code era probably came from attempts to introduce more effective systems for limiting and assigning contractors. Here, the women's coat and suit trade, unlike the dress industry, could draw upon its experiences with limitation and assignment under the industry's code of fair competition. Yet, neither these code experiences nor the experiences under later collective agreements had successfully resolved the issue of how to dispose of an excess number of contractors not absorbed into the new system. Nor had any effective method been devised to prohibit the entry of new contractors into the trade. This inability to bury the dead or to forestall the arrival of new-born firms prompted Sol Schott, president of the American Cloak and Suit Manufacturers' Association (contractors) to conclude that the industry's system of limitation and assignment had not prevented "industrial orphans" from operating

---

ments which it has heretofore adopted shall continue in full force and effect, except as they may from time to time be modified by consent of the Union and all parties in contractual relations with it in the cloak and suit industry. The time consumed by the workers of average skill in the inside and outside shops in the various labor operations involved in making such garments shall form the basis for the piece rates provided herein.

In the adjustment and settlement of piece rates, the member of the Council [inside manufacturers] and/or his representatives, the representatives of the workers of his inside shop and of the shops of his contractors and sub-manufacturers, a representative of the Union and a representative of the Labor Bureau shall participate.

—From the 1948–1951 collective agreement of the Industrial Council of Cloak, Suit and Skirt Manufacturers with the ILGWU and the Cloakmakers' Joint Board.

For analogous procedures worked out under the 1935 collective agreement between the organized jobbers, the organized contractors, and the ILGWU of the dress industry, see *Women's Wear Daily*, August 14, 1935. Where disputes over piece rates in the millinery trade were appealed to the impartial chairman, the 1938 agreement between the Eastern Women's Headwear Association and the United Hatters, Cap and Millinery Workers' International Union provided: "The impartial chairman shall in all such cases be aided by one expert designated by the Association and one expert designated by the Union; and it is the intention of the parties hereto that the experts designated as aids to the Impartial Chairman in the settlement of price disputes are to form a permanent part of the adjustment machinery of this agreement for price settlements.

"under conditions that could not be met by the legitimate producers."[17]

Meanwhile, the organized forces of the dress industry were facing a similar dilemma. Unable to agree upon a system of contractor limitation under the codes, representatives of the National Dress Manufacturers' Association (jobbers), the United Association of Dress Manufacturers (contractors), and the Dressmakers' Joint Board, ILGWU, again took up the issue in the winter of 1935–1936, only to discover that they, too, were confronted with the problem of how to dispose of surplus contractors. During negotiations for a new collective agreement, Julius Hochman, general manager of the Dressmakers' Joint Board, noted that 85,000 of the 105,000 workers in the local trade were hired by contractors; and with 18,000 machines idle even in the midst of the busy season, only a drastic reduction of contractors could halt cutthroat competition in the trade. Yet the fewer the number of contractors admitted into the proposed system of limitation and assignment, the greater was the number of contractors remaining outside the system. Mortimer Lanzit, executive director of the National Dress Manufacturers' Association (jobbers), immediately foresaw "that if a method of closer jobber-contractor relationship should cause from 400 to 600 contractors to be without jobbers, these would undoubtedly constitute a threat against the orderly processes of the outside system of production."[18]

---

[17]*Women's Wear Daily*, Nov. 28, 1939. The operation of the system did, however, produce a shift of workers to the inside shops and to that extent hastened to restore industrial stability essential to effective controls over labor costs:

> The introduction of contractor limitation and designation in 1933 and the affirmation, with material improvements, of this principle of control in industry in the agreement of 1935, have definitely checked some former trends in the cloak and suit industry which threatened it with disintegration and chaos. Whereas in 1933 the number of workers employed in the inside shops was only a little over 4,000, today we have about 14,000 workers employed in the inside factories.
>
> —Report of the ILGWU's general executive board in the union's *Report and Proceedings*, Twenty-third Convention (May 1937), p. 24.

[18]Hochman in *Women's Wear Daily*, Jan. 28, 1936; Lanzit in the issue of Jan. 8, 1936. See also, Hochman's *Why This Strike*. In so far as contractors who were denied participation in the scheme for limitation were forced to leave the industry, Lanzit's fears were, of course, unfounded. But even

Such was the plight of the dress industry leading to the most elaborate provisions on contractor limitation and assignment found anywhere in the needle trades. Still the special machinery set up under the 1936–1939 collective agreements to administer the system fell short of its task. In August 1937, officials of the United Association of Dress Maunfacturers (contractors) complained bitterly of work leakages from jobbers to substandard contractors beyond the membership of the contractors' association. Seeking to overcome this competition, more and more association members, faced with losing their business, renounced their contractual right to at least 35 percent of total labor costs for overhead. Neither the employers' associations nor the unions affected by this breakdown of standards could thwart the apparent determination of these contractors to cut their own throats. At that stage, the best the contractors' association could offer its members was a compromise proposal that would "push up" rapidly sinking percentages for overhead until all members would receive at least 30 (instead of 35) percent above labor costs. No contractor would thereafter be permitted to bargain for less![19]

---

though a thousand contractors — as one estimate had it — were driven from the trade, the evidence indicated that a sufficient number of unassigned contractors would still be around to create destructive competition. In August 1938, for example, Harry Uviller, impartial chairman for the dress industry, reported that between July 27, 1936 and June 30, 1938 only 4,802 of the 7,241 applications for contractor registrations were acted upon favorably. *Women's Wear Daily*, August 26, 1938 and March 14, 1940.

Similarly, in January 1940, Nat Boriskin, president and executive director of the United Popular Dress Manufacturers' Association (contractors), produced figures to show that the number of employed contractors in the low priced dress field had fallen from 1,250 in 1935 to 675 in 1940, while the number of unattached contractors had increased from 60 or 75 in 1935 to approximately 250 in 1940. *Ibid.*, Jan. 8, 1940. Compare the dress contractor registration figures given in ILGWU, *Report and Proceedings*, Twenty-fourth Convention (May-June 1940), p. 56.

[19]*Women's Wear Daily*, August 27, 1937. See also the rules that the National Dress Manufacturers' Association (jobbers) imposed upon its members to support the provisions of the 1936–1939 dress industry agreements on limiting and assigning contractors. *Ibid.*, March 3, 1936. The files of *Women's Wear Daily* from 1935 into the early forties contain much information on this problem. See, for example, the issues of March 28, Nov. 28, and Dec. 8, 1939.

The Problem of Overlapping Industries

Still another opportunity for union leadership in equalizing labor costs within each industry arose from the continuing need for solving problems of overlapping jurisdictions between trades. Industry-hopping for the sake of lower labor costs — a practice that had assumed major proportions under the NIRA — remained a problem after the codes. Mannish style suits for women could still be made more cheaply in men's clothing shops where labor costs were lower than in the corresponding shops of the women's coat and suit trade. Permitting the manufacturers of one industry with lower wage scales to make the products of another industry with higher wage scales was an alleged form of "illegitimate" competition that brought new demands upon the union for action in the post-code era.[20]

Especially had the organized manufacturers of the women's coat and suit trade, an industry with relatively high labor standards, suffered from raids by the dress industry, the cotton garment industry, the rainwear industry, and the men's clothing trade. In December 1935, representatives from the organized coat and suit jobbers, contractors, inside manufacturers, and children's coat and suit firms met and named a committee to study the competitive evils of overlapping. At that time Samuel Klein, executive director of the inside manufacturers' association, estimated that the volume of coat and suit business had been cut in half over the preceding five years and that much of the shrinkage had come from coat and suit production by other trades. He proposed that the union be urged in negotiating its next collective agreement with the dress industry to impose a ban on the manufacture of women's coats and suits by dress shops.[21]

Soon thereafter, the committee on overlapping of the National Coat and Suit Industry Recovery Board was able to report some progress in solving this problem; for Samuel Klein, chairman of this committee, stated in March 1936 that cooperation from the ILGWU had sharply reduced the extent of overlapping that had caused the coat and suit industry to suffer at the hands of the dress industry and of the men's clothing industry. In May 1936,

[20]See above, pp. 732–737.
[21]*Women's Wear Daily,* Dec. 20, 23, 27, and 30, 1935 and Jan. 6, 1936.

the Cloakmakers' Joint Board established an overlapping department of its own, and the union's committee on jurisdiction
recommended that a similar department be established by the
international with power to render decisions based on the principle that "wherever cloaks are produced they shall be produced
under the system and conditions operating in the cloak industry."[22]

Late in 1936, the Dressmakers' Joint Board and the Cloakmakers' Joint Board reached an agreement to promote the transfer of dress shop owners manufacturing women's coats and suits
from the dress manufacturers' association to the corresponding
cloak manufacturers' association, where those shops would be
subject to the labor standards of the women's coat and suit trade
and controlled by the Cloakmakers' Joint Board. Likewise, in
response to agitation led by Samuel Klein for the manufacturers
and by Isidore Nagler for the ILGWU, against having women's
garments made up in men's tailoring shops organized by the
ACWA, the two unions reached an agreement authorizing the
transfer of workers from the ACWA to the ILGWU whenever
men's clothing shops turned to making women's coats and suits.[23]

---

[22]At the 1937 ILGWU convention, a resolution for a union overlapping
department under the jurisdiction of the international was adopted, and
the union's general executive board was instructed to take up with the
Amalgamated Clothing Workers the question of encroachment by the ACWA
upon ILGWU's jurisdiction over the production of women's coats and suits.
ILGWU, *Report and Proceedings,* Twenty-third Convention (May 1937),
pp. 383–385. See also *Women's Wear Daily,* May 14, 1937; and Haskel, *A
Leader of the Garment Workers: the Biography of Isidore Nagler,* pp. 201–
203.

> Some children's dress shops under Local 91 jurisdiction produced
> infants' and children's snow suits as well as "brother and sister coats."
> ... Various men's clothing factories under contract with the Amalga-
> mated Clothing Workers' Union were manufacturing mannish type
> women's suits which had come into vogue and could be made quite
> cheaply under their lower standards of section work involving sub-
> division of operations and the use of more specialized machinery than
> under the tailoring system predominant in the cloak trade.
> —*Ibid.,* p. 201.

[23]"We absolutely demand that the men's and boys' clothing industry discontinue manufacturing women's coats and suits," warned Isidore Nagler, vice-
president, ILGWU, in stating his union's position before Impartial Chairman Henry Moskowitz. *Women's Wear Daily,* April 24, 1936. See also, issue of

Trends toward Industry-wide Labor Standards

Still another reason for a revived interest in labor costs was the growing fear that New York City would fall victim to the "foreign" competition of other markets. Whatever advantages these competing markets held over New York City were largely derived from lower labor costs. Only by creating and enforcing uniform labor standards on a national scale could the foundation be laid for equal labor costs throughout an industry. This basic principle that had been a tenet of collective bargaining since the Brandeis Conferences of 1910 became more vital than ever before, once the death of the codes had shattered all hopes of governmental support for industry-wide standards.

In sentiments long familiar to the supporters of the protocol movement, one writer foresaw a possible exodus of garment firms from New York City that would make the mid-town garment center "look like a series of Grant's tombs." To meet the growing specter of this competitive evil in the making of blouses, the 1935 collective agreement between the National Association of Blouse Manufacturers and the ILGWU, Local 25, provided as follows:

The parties agree to cooperate in stabilizing the industry and in maintaining the present position of New York as a market for this industry, and therefore they agree that the members of the Association in opening new shops or in engaging new contractors will make fair and reasonable efforts in good faith to give preference and employment to the workers in New York City and to the contractors located in New York City. The parties will establish a Joint Committee of four, two of whom are to be designated by the Association and two by the Union, which is authorized to adopt regulations to enable the parties to carry out their intentions as embodied in this clause. The

Jan. 10, 1936. For information on the agreements, see issues of Dec. 22, 1936 and May 14, 1937; and ILGWU, *Report and Proceedings,* Twenty-third Convention (May 1937), pp. 20–22.

Under the antioverlapping provisions of collective agreements for the dress industry, Impartial Chairman Harry Uviller on one occasion directed a member of the National Dress Manufacturers' Association, who was engaged in manufacturing women's coats and suits, to transfer his membership to an employers' association dealing with the Cloakmakers' Joint Board, ILGWU, or else to make independent agreements with that union. Harry Uviller, *Decisions,* Case no. D-483 (Apr. 30, 1937), vol. 2, pp. 105–106.

violation of such adopted regulations shall be deemed a violation of this agreement and shall be adjusted as any other dispute under this agreement.

In the dress trade, Mortimer Lanzit, executive director of the National Dress Manufacturers' Association, would meet this problem through intermarket cooperation. He proposed in 1940 that a national board be formed of ILGWU representatives and industry representatives from all dress markets for the purpose of "making all manufacturing centers truly competitive."[24]

Substantial progress toward the ultimate goal of national employers' associations with industry-wide labor agreements was actually achieved in the men's clothing trade where manufacturing was most widely distributed. In 1936–1937, the Amalgamated Clothing Workers set an example of what could be done to preserve fair competition among competing markets. After failing in the post-World War I period to create a national employers' association on which to hang the institutions of collective bargaining (see above, pp. 554–556), Sidney Hillman, able and determined leader of this union, continued throughout the twenties and early thirties to strive for industry-wide labor standards that would put all workers and all competing manufacturers on an even keel.

Hillman's objective had presumably been achieved in 1933 through the provisions of the men's clothing code. During the code period, Hillman's highly centralized union, covering more than 80 percent of the workers in the trade, was considered more successful than code authorities in promoting a rigid enforcement of code standards. Fewer than 3.5 percent of the workers were estimated to have received less than the code minimum pay scales. After the codes were invalidated, Hillman and his union set out to protect the gains they had achieved. Their first step in the direction of preserving industry-wide standards was to organize the remaining 15 or 20 percent of the workers in the trade. At the union's eleventh biennial convention meeting in Cleveland during May 1936, the ACWA executive board directed that a

[24]*New York Herald Tribune,* Dec. 5, 1939; *Women's Wear Daily,* August 16, 1940. For other efforts to check the exodus of needle trade manufacturers from New York City during this period, see the *New York Times,* Dec. 17, 1939 and *Women's Wear Daily,* Dec. 20, 1939.

general organizing drive be initiated throughout the country and particularly in the south.[25]

Meanwhile, the ACWA was laying plans for a national collective agreement to be negotiated with representatives of manufacturing groups from the various clothing markets. Open support for this move came from the president of the New York Clothing Manufacturers' Exchange who favored "joint market action," but certain Chicago manufacturers were hesitant lest too little account be taken of variations in the trade. Nevertheless, in January 1937, manufacturing representatives of the Chicago, Buffalo, Rochester, Boston, New York, Philadelphia, and Indianapolis markets met at Rochester and approved in principle a joint determination of wage issues.[26]

Beginning on February 1, 1937, negotiations were conducted in New York City between a committee of clothing manufacturers from the various markets and representatives of the Amalgamated Clothing Workers; and two weeks later the first industry-wide agreement of the men's clothing trade was concluded. This three-year contract covering 85 percent of the industry gave to 135,000 workers in the trade a 12 percent across-the-board wage increase. The agreement covered but a single issue, it maintained existing wage differentials, and was never printed; yet it paved the way for other industry-wide agreements subsequently to be negotiated between the ACWA and the Clothing Manufacturers' Association of the United States.[27]

This association of manufacturers had first been organized on a nationwide scale in 1933 to help prepare and administer a code of fair competition which would satisfy the organized factions of the men's clothing trade. Representing the firms whose workers were unionized, the Clothing Manufacturers' Association of the United States with the help of the Amalgamated Clothing Workers of America submitted a code proposal that became the basis of the code later adopted in Washington for the industry. The association and the union then worked hand in hand to supervise

---

[25]*Daily News Record,* May 29, 1936.

[26]*Ibid.,* Jan. 18, 1937.

[27]*Ibid.,* Feb. 15, 1937; *New York Times,* Feb. 14, 1937; *New York Post,* Feb. 19, 1937. For a collection of newspaper clippings and magazine articles covering the period, see ACWA Research Library, "Redbook of Clippings." See also, Harry A. Cobrin, *The Men's Clothing Industry: Colonial through Modern Times* (1970), pp. 235–243.

and enforce the code during its lifetime. "Their successful co-operation in this program," subsequently explained Jacob S. Potofsky, president of the ACWA, "set the pattern for collective bargaining on a national scale."[28]

Enforcement Failures in the Post-code Years

Largely because of enforcement troubles, few of these efforts to equalize labor costs after the death of the codes were successful. The labor unions were overburdened with responsibilities while the employers' associations contributed too little to a common cause. Such progress as was made in organizing the unorganized and in extending uniform labor standards to new shops during any one season might be dissipated in the following season through the added competitive pressures of business recessions, or through some let-up in vigilance required to maintain the status quo. Just as in the early protocol years, labor unions and employers' associations again attacked each other for fiddling with petty grievances and for taking partisan stands where objectivity was essential. "Planned as a dignified Supreme Court for the dress industry," wrote Julius Hochman, general mana-ger, Dressmakers' Joint Board, in 1935, "our tribunal [the office of impartial chairman] became a sort of petty criminal court daily delving into cases of plain thievery."[29]

---

[28]The quotation by J. S. Potofsky is from a typewritten statement presumably prepared for an encyclopedia of labor, and filed in the ACWA Research Library.

Although the Clothing Manufacturers' Association of the United States apparently did not participate as an association in the first unwritten na-tional collective agreement with the ACWA in 1937, it did later become a party with the ACWA to written national agreements covering a limited number of issues. National standards created by these agreements superseded conflicting local standards without completely supplanting the market-wide agreements.

The effect of the union's stabilization program on preserving the New York market of the men's clothing trade in the years immediately following the death of the codes became evident before the end of the decade. The *New York Times* for Dec. 17, 1939 reported that the exodus of men's clothing manufacturers from New York City had been checked, and that local pro-duction of men's clothing had actually risen 25 percent since the ACWA in-troduced its stabilization program.

[29]Hochman, *Why This Strike* at p. 6. "Did the National Association (job-bers) co-operate with the Union in disciplining their members?" Hochman continued. "On the contrary the jobber leaders used all their skill and time

In moments of despair, the organized manufacturers of the needle trades were likely to make labor unions the scapegoat of their troubles, not because these unions had interfered too much with managerial prerogatives but because the unions had accomplished too little in stabilizing their industries. At a public negotiating conference (said to be the first "gold-fish bowl" negotiations in the local needle trades), J. E. Helfer, executive secretary of the Eastern Women's Headwear Association, charged the millinery workers with wage inequities that had created "the great movement for migrating out of town;" and he called upon the union "to shoulder responsibility for recreating New York as a market for profitable production." He demanded "wider responsibility on labor's part to uphold the industry's stability and remove the chaos and confusion that has existed since the demise of the NIRA."[30]

The fur manufacturers were equally dejected. While conceding the value of collective bargaining as an institution for regulating competition, the Associated Fur Coat and Trimming Manufacturers deplored the inequities that the fur workers' union had allowed to develop. Not only had this union permitted fur articles to be manufactured by the women's coat and suit trade on far more advantageous terms, but it had allowed outside contracting, denied to association members, to be "freely practiced by independents, retailers and cloak manufacturers." Charging the union with responsibility for disparities in labor costs, the association concluded that "the Union has utterly failed to suppress, unionize or impose the same labor conditions as are imposed upon our members, upon the direct competitors of members of our Association, as there exist many large producing

---

in defending members caught redhanded falsifying their books, switching price ranges, under-paying their workers and violating the agreement through every subterfuge and evasion." *Ibid.*

[30]*Women's Wear Daily*, Nov. 14, 1935. Two weeks earlier more than 1,000 millinery manufacturers had agreed to participate in a lockout, or protest strike, against the "unfair attitude of labor and the unscrupulous buyer" reflected in special concessions to out-of-town interests. "This inequality in wages brought about by the union's policy of making special deals," noted J. E. Helfer, "is not only contrary to the terms and spirit of the collective agreement, but is so oppressive on the manufacturers that it must be stopped." *Ibid.*, Nov. 1, 1935. See also *New York Herald Tribune*, Nov. 5, 1935.

factors in other jurisdictions as well as in the local market that are not regulated by the Union."[31]

Even more bitter against the union were the manufacturers of the dress industry. At a conference of dress association officials in 1939 to survey the dilemma of the organized dress manufacturers in New York City, evidence was submitted to show that a minimum wage of $26 a week established for the local trade was almost twice the minimum wage of $14 a week paid for similar work in other areas. These disparities brought down upon the dressmakers' unions a tirade of epithets from spokesmen for the several associations represented. Harry Sterngold, chairman of the board of directors for the Popular Priced Dress Manufacturers' Group, charged the ILGWU with bringing "chaos" into the industry. Mortimer Lanzit, executive director of the National Dress Manufacturers' Association, found a growing "lunatic fringe" of small-unit, underfinanced, out-of-town shops taking over more and more production while the union was "asleep at the post." Louis Rubin, executive chairman of the Popular Priced Dress Manufacturers' Association, declared that "we now have peace with the union, but it is the peace of a cemetery!"[32]

Through all these vicissitudes of the post-code era, Samuel Klein, executive director of the inside manufacturers' association for the women's coat and suit industry and the best informed man of his trade, stood at the forefront of those still advocating reliance on unions for the objectives of the protocol movement. Yet Klein himself often despaired of controlling competition through labor unions. In a series of statements at the end of the decade, Klein again harped upon the failures of collective bargaining. The piece-rate structure was still an "anarchy of rates." Week-work standards were still undermined by secret wage concessions accepted in return for guaranteed employment. The fourteen operator rule to eliminate small shops was often disregarded. Control by the international or by the joint board over local union agents was diminishing. More and more firms were enjoying special privileges or the fruits of collusive deals. Growing in number were the nonunion shops and those that were union in name only. Meanwhile, the power of employers' associations to

---

[31]From a copy of the association's report, dated Jan. 5, 1938, filed in the Abelson papers.

[32]*Women's Wear Daily*, Dec. 4, 1939.

enforce standards was waning. "The retreat from the coveted goal of uniformity," lamented Klein, on February 28, 1939, "is degenerating into a rout."[33]

Yet Klein still held out for strong labor unions and employer group bargaining as the most promising sources of future protection from illegitimate competition. In his "Report on the Labor Situation in the Coat and Suit Industry," submitted to his association, February 28, 1939, Klein recommended a series of measures to clean up disparities in labor costs. He proposed that piece-rate negotiations be centralized and that the Labor Bureau attached to the office of impartial chairman be authorized to establish and enforce piece rates. He would also have this bureau investigate inequalities in rates between piece-work firms and week-work firms to the end that labor costs be standardized throughout the trade.[34]

Klein further recommended that the power of local and regional union leaders to grant employers special favors be curtailed; that the advantages currently accruing to nominally unionized firms be terminated; and that the union and the association jointly undertake to organize the nonunion firms. Klein's urgent pleas soon found expression in the Board of Stability and Control (see above, pp. 773–774) created under the 1940 collective labor agreements to attack substandard and nonunion production. Shortly after this joint agency had begun its work, Klein was proclaiming its achievements as "a matter of truly historic significance to the industry and to all those dependent upon it for a livelihood."[35]

Concluding Observations

Once the fallacies of employer shortcuts to "legitimate" competition through their own programs for trade practice controls had been exposed, the organized manufacturers of the needle trades fell back upon the possibility of further developments in

---

[33]For more details, see the pertinent issues of *Women's Wear Daily* for the years 1938 through 1940, especially the issue of March 1, 1939, containing the text of Klein's annual labor report to his association, the Industrial Council of Cloak, Suit and Skirt Manufacturers.

[34]*Ibid.*, March 1, 1939.

[35]Klein's endorsement of the work of the Board of Stability and Control is found in *ibid.*, Feb. 15, 1941.

labor policies. The factors that contributed to the elimination of competition in labor costs under the original Protocol of Peace after 1910 applied with equal validity twenty-five years later to competition beyond the codes. The renewed cries to organize the unorganized, among the manufacturers as well as the workers — the new attacks upon contracting and the small-time operator — the strong appeals for centralized procedures to standardize labor costs both under the piece-rate system and under the week-work system of wage payments — the continuing need for protecting New York City industries from illegitimate competitors of the hinterlands, including the owners of runaway shops — the prime necessity of striving for industry-wide standards as the only long-range goal likely to succeed in taking labor costs out of competition as a factor in production — all these major issues of the first decades under the protocol movement remained the chief issues in labor policies beyond the codes.

In the post-code era, some of these measures to eliminate disparities in labor costs were pursued more successfully than others. In some cases, old ideas for strengthening these efforts were further developed; in other cases, new aids to success were introduced for the first time. Among these more effective procedures and devices of the later thirties were: (1) efforts to perfect the unit system of production as a means of standardizing labor costs; (2) efforts to establish centralized controls over the piece-rate system; (3) use of the trucking system between jobbers or inside manufacturers and contractors to ferret out sources of nonunion production or violations of rules governing the limitation and assignment of contractors; (4) new methods and machinery to control industry-hopping, which had become a medium for illegitimate competition in labor costs; (5) further efforts to introduce industry-wide bargaining; (6) the use of consumer power aroused indirectly, if not unwantingly, through union picketing of retail outlets to strengthen drives for union membership. Yet, the combined efforts in all these directions by the parties to collective agreements failed to satisfy the organized manufacturers who blamed the labor unions for all failures and shortcomings in labor practices beyond the codes.

Chapter 21

Collective Bargaining

before the Bar

T HE ramifications of labor-management plans for industrial stabilization which were developed in the later thirties set the stage for the legal days of reckoning that were sure to follow in the forties and fifties and sixties. Until the forties, most litigation over the legality of controls established through the medium of collective bargaining had arisen in the state courts. After the death of the codes, those contractors who were excluded from assignments to jobbers repeatedly approached the state courts for relief from the organized factions of their trades. Following the 1936 collective agreements of the women's dress industry, for example, it was alleged that in establishing a system for limiting and assigning contractors, the organized groups of the trade had "acquired absolute control over limitation of production, sale and manufacture of dresses in said dress industry."[1]

Sooner or later, the federal executive and the federal courts could be expected to decide whether these controls imposed by industry violated federal statutes regulating unfair competition and restraint of trade. Or these federal authorities might question whether attempts by the state governments to limit controls imposed by industry did, in fact, impinge upon some constitutional

[1]*Women's Wear Daily,* March 14, 1940. Numerous New York State court decisions affecting the limitations that New York antitrust legislation has imposed on the sphere of collective bargaining are cited above in chap. 16. Cited above at pp. 701–709.

right of the parties affected. In reaching such decisions, the judicial and administrative agencies of the national government might agree to follow the state courts by hinging the legality of self-imposed industrial controls on whether the fair trade practices were fashioned to support labor standards or on whether labor standards were designed to enforce fair trade practices. Since most critical issues of collective bargaining had a "trade" face as well as a "labor" face, the fusion of trade and labor functions at the bargaining table opened the door for a wide range of interpretations that gave each federal administrator and each federal judge considerable freedom in charting his own course.[2]

Legal Machinery for Enforcing Trade Controls

Upon the Federal Trade Commission and upon the U. S. Department of Justice (Antitrust Division) fell the initial responsibility of investigating and handling charges against the parties to collective agreements for employing unfair methods of competition or for engaging in combinations and conspiracies to restrain trade. Both these administrative agencies were expected to preserve the free enterprise system from monopolistic tendencies and unfair trade restraints. Both exercised jurisdiction over industries falling within the commerce power of the federal government. But neither was quite prepared to cope with the peculiar combination of legal, economic, and labor issues that characterized the history of collective bargaining for the needle trades.

The judicial procedures that accompanied criminal litigation in the federal courts for alleged violations of the antitrust laws followed the usual patterns of criminal cases. The assistant attorney general in charge of the Antitrust Division and his staff investigated alleged antitrust violations, directed grand jury proceedings, prepared for and conducted the trial of those charged with offenses, prosecuted appeals in the courts, and took the necessary steps to enforce the final judgments. The Antitrust Division might also seek injunctive relief aimed at restoring competitive conditions to the system of free enterprise. Or the injured parties, under the Sherman Act, could institute civil suits for damages

---

[2] For an excellent introduction to the legal complexities that collective bargaining presented under federal legislation, see Archibald Cox, "Labor and the Antitrust Laws — A Preliminary Analysis," *University of Pennsylvania Law Review,* November 1955, pp. 253–284.

with the possibility of recovering up to three times the losses sustained from violations of the law. In any case, the penalties that could be imposed for violating the law or for disobeying an order of the court were supposedly adequate to offset any advantage which might accrue from infractions of the statutes and to act as a deterrent against future offenses.

The Federal Trade Commission, on the other hand, was a quasi-legislative and quasi-judicial body that handled trade practices on a continuing basis. Its function was to prevent rather than punish infractions of the law. The purpose of the Federal Trade Commission Act, once stated U. S. Supreme Court Justice William Douglas, was "to stop in their incipiency acts and practices which, when full blown, would violate those [Sherman and Clayton] Acts . . . as well as to condemn as 'unfair methods of competition' existing violations of them." Through advice, consultation, and guidance, the Commission sought to gain voluntary compliance with antitrust laws and trade practice regulations.[3]

The Commission's division of trade practice conferences — its nearest approach to collective bargaining — allowed each industry to take part in proposing rules which would specify in detail the practices deemed to be permissible under the law. When finally adopted by the Commission, these rules helped to clarify the issue of what could or could not legally be done. By encouraging cooperation and providing authoritative interpretations in advance, the Commission hoped to inspire a joint attack by government and industry upon unfair trade practices.

Where attempts at informal guidance and voluntary cooperation did not suffice, however, the Federal Trade Commission could institute formal proceedings similar to court action against firms charged with violating the statutes. These proceedings included the filing of complaints and of answers to complaints, the presentation of briefs and replies to briefs, the issuance of supplemental statements and the submission of documentary evi-

---

[3]The quotation is from the Federal Trade Commission v. Motion Picture Advertising Service Co. 344 U.S. 392 (1953) at pp. 394–395. "It was, in fact, one of the hopes of those who sponsored the Federal Trade Commission Act that its effect might be prophylactic and that through it attempts to bring about complete monopolization of an industry might be stopped in their incipiency." Mr. Justice Hugo Black in Fashion Originators' Guild v. Federal Trade Commission, 312 U.S. 457 (1941) at p. 466, citing Federal Trade Commission v. Raladam Co., 283 U.S. 643 (1931) at p. 647.

dence, as well as the testimony of witnesses. Every case, therefore, was certain to provide a storehouse of background information on the problems of the industry. If the charges were sustained, the Commission issued "cease and desist" orders requiring the discontinuance of the forbidden practices. A compliance division then took over the responsibility of seeing that the order was obeyed. Failure to comply might lead to contempt proceedings before a federal court or to civil action for the imposition of fines up to $5,000 for each offense.

Those against whom cease and desist orders were issued might seek an appeal to the courts over the decision of the Federal Trade Commission. In such cases, the United States Circuit Court of Appeals could review, affirm, modify, or set aside the order of the Commission. Further review by the United States Supreme Court was possible on a writ of certiorari. Whether charges of violating federal antitrust laws originated in the U. S. Department of Justice or were handled by the Federal Trade Commission, those charges might ultimately be brought for final solution to the highest court in the land. Viewed in the context of legal principles laid down by New York state courts, the United States Supreme Court might then be called upon to decide whether the institutions and processes of collective bargaining were lawfully employed to carry out the legitimate ends of labor unions, or whether they served to hide the unlawful means and illegal ends of business combinations.[4]

Employer Conspiracies to Restrain Trade

Federal authorities did not hesitate to question the legality of certain post-NRA stabilization plans, regardless of whether such schemes formed a part of collective bargaining systems. By twice

---

[4]The overlapping jurisdiction of the Federal Trade Commission with that of the Antitrust Division, U.S. Department of Justice, springs from a section of the Sherman Antitrust Act of July 2, 1890 (26 Stat. 209) stating:

> Every contract, combination in the form of a trust or otherwise, or conspiracy, in restraint of trade or commerce among the several States, or with foreign nations, is hereby declared to be illegal;

and from a comparable section of the Federal Trade Commission Act of Sept. 26, 1914 (38 Stat. 717) stating:

> Unfair methods of competition in commerce, and unfair or deceptive acts or practices in commerce, are hereby declared unlawful.

This overlapping jurisdiction was accepted by the U.S. Supreme Court in Federal Trade Commission v. Cement Institute, 333 U.S. 683 (1948).

striking down certain activities of the truck owners' associations serving the New York garment center, the U. S. Department of Justice and the federal courts gave notice that there were limits beyond which organization for mutual protection would not be tolerated in the needle trades. On December 28, 1944, the government filed criminal charges against six truck owners' associations and five officials, alleging a conspiracy to monopolize and restrain trade in the delivery of dresses and of women's and children's coats and suits. All the defendants pleaded nolo contendere and were fined a total of $58,000. Six months later, the U. S. attorney general filed two civil complaints in the federal courts charging six truck owners' associations, twenty-three corporations, and eighty-nine individuals with conspiracies in violation of the Sherman Antitrust Act.[5]

None of these moves brought lasting reforms, however, for in 1951 the government sought injunctions to prevent four of these trucking associations serving the dress industry from continuing their illegal practices. And, in a companion suit, two trucking associations serving the metropolitan women's coat and suit trade were charged with similar conspiracies. In all of these cases, the defendants were alleged to have divided territories, allocated customers, fixed rates for garment deliveries, and excluded from the trade independent carriers who refused to join their association. Shippers were compelled to use assigned carriers when other methods of transportation might have been cheaper. If these court actions did not affect the legality of vital contributions the trucking associations made to the enforcement of collective labor agreements, they at least gave warning that other restraints on trade serving the ends of collective bargaining might not be immune from the laws of the land.[6]

The hand of the law moved nearer to the objectives of the protocol movement when the highest court in the land twice struck down elaborate schemes by manufacturers of wearing apparel to prevent style piracy. Because the copying of fabric and fashion designs threatened the "legitimate" inside producers who managed to survive competition by the originality and appeal of their products, the issue of style piracy had long been a major concern of both labor unions and employers' associations. Two of the

---

[5]*New York Times,* June 15, 1945.

[6]*Ibid.,* May 1, 1951.

plans to meet this evil reached the Supreme Court of the United States for review in 1941. In each case, the Circuit Court of Appeals had previously affirmed decrees of the Federal Trade Commission ordering the participants in these schemes to "cease and desist" from certain practices found to constitute unfair methods of competition tending toward monopoly.[7]

The leading case, *Fashion Originators' Guild* v. *Federal Trade Commission,* involved an association of 176 manufacurers of women's better dresses; a number of affiliated textile manufacturers, converters, dyers, and printers; and some 12,000 cooperating retailers — all of whom participated in a scheme to prevent the production and sale of fabrics and garments made by copying original creations. In order to eliminate "unfair" competition based on style piracy, the guild forbade manufacturers to sell their garments to any retailer who also bought and sold copies of those garments. At the same time, the affiliated textile manufacturers, converters, dyers, and printers were forbidden to deal with manufacturers who made garments from pirated fabric designs or who sold their products to noncomplying retailers. Heavy fines were imposed upon all guild members violating these regulations.[8]

Not to be overlooked were other features of the program sponsored by the guild. Manufacturers were forbidden to take part in retail advertising, and retailers were forbidden to hold special sales except on days named for that purpose. Manufacurers were prohibited from selling at retail or from selling to those who conducted their business in hotels, homes, and apartment houses. Retailers could not participate with dress manufacturers in fashion shows unless the merchandise used was actually purchased and delivered. All members were required to observe the discount regulations that the guild established for the trade.

Rejecting the argument that "the practices of FOGA were reasonable and necessary to protect the manufacturer, laborer,

---

[7]In 1937, the Associated Garment Industries of St. Louis and the ILGWU negotiated a collective agreement containing a piracy design clause in which the union agreed that none of its members would work for any firm that lost its good standing in the association by reason of violating provisions on style piracy. *Women's Wear Daily,* Oct. 18, 1937.

[8]Fashion Originators' Guild v. Federal Trade Commission, 312 US 457 (1941).

retailer, and consumer against the devasting evils growing from the pirating of original designs," the U. S. Supreme Court by unanimous decision sustained the Federal Trade Commission and the U. S. Circuit Court of Appeals in holding that the activities of the guild "substantially lessened, hindered, and suppressed" competition and tended "to create in themselves a monopoly." The program of the guild was found to contravene the Sherman Antitrust Act in that it (1) narrowed the outlets to which garment manufacturers and textile manufacturers might sell; (2) narrowed the sources from which retailers might buy; (3) subjected all noncomplying retailers to boycott; and (4) suppressed competition from the sale of products of copied designs.[9]

The U. S. Supreme Court reached similar conclusions in the case of *Millinery Creators' Guild* v. *Federal Trade Commission* decided on the same day. Here, the designers and manufacturers of women's hats introduced a plan modeled after that of the Fashion Originators' Guild to protect their products from style piracy. The court found the same type of illegal restraints on outlets for sale of products, on sources of supply, and on competition among retailers. While both plans would obviously benefit the workers as well as their employers, no evidence was submitted that either scheme was a result of collective bargaining or of labor union participation.[10]

---

[9]In addition, the work of the guild was held to contravene paragraph 3 of the Clayton Act which makes it unlawful to sell goods on the understanding that the purchaser will not deal in goods of a competitor where the effect of this arrangement "may be to substantially lessen competition or tend to create a monopoly in any line of commerce." *Ibid.*, pp. 464–465, 467. The case before the U.S. Circuit Court of Appeals is reported at 114 F. 2d 80 (1940).

Contrast the original complaint of the Federal Trade Commission charging the Fashion Originators' Guild with monopoly (text in *Women's Wear Daily*, April 30, 1936) with the Masters' Report (*ibid.*, Nov. 10, 1936) prepared for the U.S. District Court in the case of Wm. Filene's Sons v. Fashion Originators' Guild, 14 F. Supp. 353 (1936) and in the U.S. Circuit Court of Appeals, 90 F 2nd 556 (1937), all of which upheld the guild's plan for style protection in the dress industry against charges of monopoly and restraint of trade.

[10]Millinery Creators' Guild v. Federal Trade Commission, 312 U.S. 469 (1941), affirming the decision of Circuit Judge C. E. Clark in the U.S. Circuit Court of Appeals reported in 109 F. 2nd 175 (1940).

In his study, "The Millinery Industry" (processed), NRA: Division of

The Legality of Joint Stabilization Plans

These federal decisions from the needle trades reaffirmed the position of the state courts that employer groups when acting alone to restrain trade would most likely run afoul of the antitrust laws; but they did not determine the legality of joint labor-management efforts at regulating business conduct. Yet, sooner or later, collective labor agreements that affected trade practices as well as labor practices were sure to come up for clarification at the federal level. Particularly were special stabilization agreements likely to arouse the suspicions of federal agencies responsible for the administration of the federal antitrust laws. The legal issues raised by these stabilization plans were brought into focus during the forties and fifties in a series of cases handled by the Federal Trade Commission.

Numerous complaints that the stabilization programs were violating federal laws arose from the inception of these post-code movements. Within months after the National Coat and Suit Industry Recovery Board was established in 1935, more than a hundred complaints against the board had been filed with the Federal Trade Commission. Likewise, within months of its formation, the Millinery Stabilization Commission was under investigation by the Federal Trade Commission for allegedly restraining trade. Yet, for a time at least, the organized factions of the needle trades appeared little disturbed by these federal clouds of legal doubt cropping up on the horizon.[11]

Defending a proposed agreement to compel the sale of women's hats above costs — a plan to be enforced, if necessary, by union strikes against noncomplying firms — J. E. Helfer, executive director of the Eastern Women's Headwear Association and a member of the Millinery Stabilization Commission, assured the manufacturers in 1936 that they had nothing to fear from the provisions of antitrust laws. "The government," he said, "will not

Review, Industry Studies Section (March 1936) at pp. 32–42 and 86–88, J. C. Worthy deals at length with the problems of controlling style piracy in the millinery trade. See also E. R. A. Seligman, "The Millinery Industry: A Survey" (processed), pp. 19–23. Copy filed in the Abelson papers.

[11]D. E. Robinson, *Collective Bargaining and Market Control in the New York Coat and Suit Industry* (1949), p. 171, citing *Recovery Board Bulletin* of April 1936; *Women's Wear Daily,* June 18, 1936.

legislate anyone out of business because the manufacturer is attempting to stabilize an industry." But, alas, within a few years, this false sense of security generated under the codes was to be shattered by the approaching storm of legal entanglements.[12]

On September 26, 1941, the Federal Trade Commission filed separate complaints against the National Coat and Suit Industry Recovery Board and the Millinery Stabilization Commission alleging in each case numerous violations of the Federal Trade Commission Act and of the antitrust laws. Two years later, a related complaint was filed against the National Association of Blouse Manufacturers, the Blouse and Waist Makers' Union, and others.

Then some ten years after the first charges were filed, the Federal Trade Commission on its own motion quietly dismissed all three complaints on the ground that economic conditions in the early fifties "differed materially" from economic conditions in the early forties, and that the public interest would better be served by dropping these stale complaints. During the intervening years, however, the parties to needle trade agreements, and particularly those parties who created the agencies under attack, were overcome with fear lest their empires of controlled competition not withstand the new onslaughts of the law.[13]

Faced with doubts and uncertainties, soon to be enhanced by still other charges of conspiracy to restrain trade, labor unions and employers' associations committed the decade of the forties to caution and indecision. Those who had previously expressed their views so openly now conversed in subdued tones or couched their

---

[12]*Ibid.*, Sept. 2, 1936. Under its bylaws, the Millinery Stabilization Commission was empowered "to promulgate reasonable rules, regulations and trade-practice provisions, *not in restraint of trade,* which shall be binding on every member of the corporation" (italics added). Operating under this statement of policy, P. F. Brissenden, an original member of the commission, and J. M. Keating, its legal counsel, felt assured that the application of legal theories would be tempered by the realities of industrial life. "It can be said with confidence," so they wrote in 1948, "that the union and the manufacturers' associations in this industry have some basis for the expectation that their joint enterprise will survive the legal test." *Industrial and Labor Relations Review,* October 1948, vol. 2, pp. 19, 24.

[13]The official records in these cases may be found in Federal Trade Commission, Docket no. 4596 (women's coats and suits); Docket no. 4597 (millinery industry); and Docket no. 5068 (blouse industry).

remarks in carefully guarded language. Collective agreements were rewritten with more attention to the legal implications of proposed means and stated objectives. Joint agencies like the Board of Stability and Control in the women's coat and suit trade, suddenly became "hush-hush" where they were not abandoned altogether. Deleted from the constitution of the National Coat and Suit Industry Recovery Board were the clauses that required contractors to be paid enough to meet union wage scales, plus an additional 33-1/3 percent of the wage bill for overhead. Every official enumeration of charges by the government, every supporting brief of government counsel, every sustaining report of a trial examiner struck fear into the hearts of all those who had for so long defended the principles of the protocol movement.[14]

Well might the parties to collective agreements have been concerned. Conviction upon such charges as the Federal Trade Commission leveled against the National Coat and Suit Industry Recovery Board would have struck at the heart of collective bargaining as practiced in the needle trades. For the Recovery Board was an integral part of the collective bargaining system of the women's coat and suit trade. Conversely, the collective labor agreements were an integral part of the plan projected by the Recovery Board for controlling competition in labor costs and business practices.

Like the code authority after which it was patterned, the Recovery Board was closely interlocked with the impartial machinery of the collective labor agreements for the purpose of enforcing both trade and labor regulations. The Recovery Board shared the same offices with the impartial chairman under the labor agreement and used the same staff of accountants and investigators. Violations of rules governing fair trade practices imposed by the National Coat and Suit Industry Recovery Board automatically became violations of the collective labor agreements for the trade. Thus the full weight of the impartial machinery that had been developed for the administration and enforcement of labor agreements was brought to bear upon the offenders of

[14]The stabilization board for the blouse industry, created in 1936 by joint action of the National Association of Blouse Manufacturers and the ILGWU, ceased to function two years later, undoubtedly in anticipation of the legal complications soon to follow. See *Women's Wear Daily*, Dec. 31, 1943.

established trade practices. Indeed, all parties to collective labor agreements automatically became members of the Recovery Board and were bound by its constitution, bylaws, rules, and regulations.[15]

The Recovery Board enforced its decisions through the use of a consumers' protection label which was administered with the help of the parties to collective labor agreements for the trade. Like the NRA blue eagle insignia that stood for compliance with the codes, this consumers' protection label, when attached to finished garments, stood for compliance with the rules and regulations of the Recovery Board. Having the right to use the Recovery Board's consumers' protection label was as much a condition of "good standing" for employers under the collective agreements, as it was a condition of "good standing" within the Recovery Board itself. Under the post-code labor agreements, union members were instructed not to produce garments that failed to meet the conditions required to obtain the Recovery Board's consumers' protection label.[16]

At the same time, the Recovery Board became an agency for extending and enforcing the labor standards of collective agreements. In an official statement of policy, the board set forth the

---

[15]The collective labor agreements for the women's coat and suit trade in the forties contained the following clause:

> For the purpose of eliminating sub-standard and sweatshop conditions in and to aid in the stabilization of the coat and suit industry throughout the United States, the parties hereto shall become parties to the National Coat and Suit Industry Recovery Board, and they hereby agree for themselves and their members that they will be subject to and be bound by the Constitution, By-Laws, rules and regulations of the said Board.
>
> —From the 1943–1948 collective agreement of the Industrial Council of Cloak, Suit and Skirt Manufacturers with the ILGWU.

[16]In the fall of 1936, the National Coat and Suit Industry Recovery Board had enlisted the cooperation of women's clubs and consumer organizations with a total membership of 16,000,000 persons in recognizing the consumers' protection label as "an insignia of the successful efforts of conscientious manufacturers to uphold enlightened standards." *Women's Wear Daily*, Dec. 29, 1936. See also the exhaustive report of Samuel Klein, executive director of the New York inside manufacturers' association and chairman of the fair trade practice committee of the Recovery Board, covering all phases of the women's coat and suit industry in the post-code era. *Ibid.*, Jan. 13, 1937.

obligations of its members toward the collective labor agreements in their respective areas:

The Recovery Board lends such assistance as it is called upon to render in the various markets and regions in connection with labor-employer relationship. It aids in effectuating the respective labor agreements, its investigating facilities being extensively utilized in this connection.

The constitution of the Board stipulates that the labor standards of the collective agreement in an area shall apply to all members in that center. This gives the "Consumers' Protection Label" authentic meaning as the insignia of wholesome labor conditions. In the New York market, the Recovery Board cooperates in the conduct of the Labor Bureau through which piece rate settlements are faciliated.[17]

That the Federal Trade Commission would attack the fair trade practices of the National Coat and Suit Industry Recovery Board was to be expected. With no apparent concern for legal issues, the Recovery Board had taken over the fair trade practice regulations handed down from the indutsry's NRA code of fair competition. That code, as amended, had contained the usual restrictions on advertising allowances, cancellation of orders, selling on consignment, delivery charges, secret rebates, terms of discount, and the return of merchandise. The board was particularly concerned with the problem of standardizing discount rates and regulating the return of merchandise. These two subjects, like most other fair trade regulations, could easily lend themselves to charges of illegal conduct under the laws designed to maintain a competitive economy.

Far more important for the future of controlled competition, however, were the FTC complaints that went to the very heart of collective bargaining. An amendment to the constitution of the Recovery Board had extended regulations on the contracting system found in the New York jobber-contractor agreements to all other manufacturers subscribing to the board and its policies. The Federal Trade Commission attacked the basic concept of limiting and assigning contractors — an issue that had been vital to collective bargaining since the mid-twenties. Other Commis-

---

[17]"The National Coat and Suit Industry Recovery Board" (pamphlet), p. 7, as quoted in Robinson, *Collective Bargaining and Market Control in the New York Coat and Suit Industry*, p. 150.

sion complaints against the Recovery Board questioned the
legality of attempts to eliminate small-time producers, or to
monopolize "the opportunity to secure skilled labor," or to fix
prices through relating standard discount rates to traditionally
observed price lines. Even the control of overlapping between
industries to prevent the undermining of standard labor costs
became a subject of complaint.

Particularly alarming to the advocates of collective bargaining
was the concentration of FTC attacks upon the legality of enforcement methods employed by the Recovery Board. Along with
the basic concept of controlling competition, the development of
successful measures for enforcing contract terms had been the
chief contribution of the protocol movement to the history of
collective bargaining. Yet, the means used to carry out policies of
the National Coat and Suit Industry Recovery Board were precisely those familiar to collective bargaining since the inception
of the first protocol in 1910. Coercion or the threat of coercion
had always been used where necessary to enforce contract terms
or to carry out decisions of the impartial machinery. This ultimate sanction had also been a constant threat to all workers and
employers who failed to support new proposals of the organized
groups for regulating competition within a trade.

Since 1910, the powers assigned to special joint labor-management agencies of industry-wide concern, including those granted
stabilization boards of the post-code era, were often stated in the
unprovocative terms of exploration, reporting, fact-finding, analysis, and recommendation. But behind these innocuous means
for arriving at useful facts and helpful suggestions lay a hidden
power to carry proposed reforms into execution. For the power
of strikes, lockouts, and boycotts had often transformed voluntary
discretion into compulsory action. Such was obviously the case
of the National Coat and Suit Industry Recovery Board and its
consumers' protection label. Charging the Recovery Board and its
agencies with coercive activities, the Federal Trade Commission
attacked the practice of the union "in agreement with other respondents, of not permitting its workers to work on any garment
in the process of manufacture unless such garment was to bear,
and did bear, when completed, one of the above-mentioned
labels."

This effective type of production boycott was extended to the unlabeled garments of independent firms under separate contracts with the union — firms that could obtain labels only by signing certificates of compliance and membership issued by the Recovery Board. The pressures thus exerted on outside firms to join the board led the Federal Trade Commission to charge that "the respondents have sought to compel every coat and suit manufacturer in the country to become a member of respondent Recovery Board and to continue himself in good standing with such Board." The importance of these charges hinged less on the immediate effects of their validity than on the implications they carried for similar powers that labor unions and employers' associations had always exerted in the name of collective bargaining.[18]

Boston Employers Seek Union Cover

Long before the Federal Trade Commission had dismissed the complaints against the National Coat and Suit Industry Recovery Board, the sponsors of controlled competition were aroused to the potential dangers of legal restraints from yet another source. The U. S. Department of Justice (Antitrust Division) had charged an association of Boston contractors engaged in the manufacture of women's sportswear with combining to coerce jobbers of the Boston area into giving out work exclusively to contractors be-

---

[18]*Women's Wear Daily* carried accounts of concerted efforts to refute FTC charges. See particularly, the testimony and cross-examination of David Dubinsky, president of the ILGWU, in the issue of May 8, 1946, and in the *New York Times* of the same date.

No manufacturer is limited in the number of garments which he may manufacture or sell. The more they manufacture the better for the workers, because the larger their earnings. All employers in the industry are entirely free to compete with each other for the market on the basis of the attractiveness of their styles, the quality of their product, the efficiency of their factory organizations and all other legitimate grounds. The provisions for contractor designation were intended to have and have had the effect of stabilizing the labor standards in the industry and maintaining the wages, hours and other conditions of employment, preventing kickbacks and other unlawful practices, decreasing the number of liquidations and bankruptcies and eliminating the incidental social and economic waste.

—Wendell L. Willkie, representing the ILGWU, statement to the Federal Trade Commission, December 1941, as quoted in ILGWU, *Report and Proceedings,* Thirtieth Convention (May 1959), p. 32.

longing to the Women's Sportswear Manufacturers' Association. One objective of the organized contractors was to assist jobbers in getting only as many contractors as their work "may equitably require." Each jobber, in turn, was to divide his work "as equally and as equitably as possible among the association contractors engaged by him."

In August 1944, the contractors' association prepared for job-ber signature a written agreement embodying the features of this plan. The preamble to this agreement stressed the need for (a) creating harmony and promoting the welfare of the sportswear manufacturing industry; (b) establishing a basis for equitable and fair business conduct and dealings; (c) minimizing all industrial conflicts, disputes, and difficulties; and (d) removing the present abuses and evils which constitute the causes of disputes between jobbers and contractors. Although these statements of policy closely parallel those in collective labor agreements, no direct reference was anywhere made to labor unions despite an ac-knowledged purpose of the agreement to maintain a minimum standard of prices charged jobbers for stitching work — a condi-tion long considered essential for the preservation of labor stan-dards in contractor shops.[19]

To force the acceptance of their proposed agreement, the con-tractor's association informed the jobbers, who were members of the Wholesale Garment Association, that failure to sign would lead to a cessation of work on all unfinished materials still in the hands of the contractors. When this threat was applied to the goods of three jobbers, the jobbers' association sought and ob-tained from the state court a restraining order preventing the contractors from using coercion to gain acceptance for their plan. Still, there was no evidence that the ILGWU had exercised a voice in drafting the proposed agreement or in calling the stop-pages that precipitated the request for an injunction.

Once their plans had been thwarted by a court injunction, the organized contractors devised a new strategy to gain their objectives. In view of the legal problems they had encountered

---

[19]The only reference to labor unions in the draft of the agreement came indirectly through the clause on the payment of health and welfare funds that the contractors wished to shift from themselves to the jobbers. The facts are here summarized from the transcript of record in United States v. Women's Sportswear Manufacturers' Association, 336 U.S. 460 (1949).

when acting directly on their own behalf, they chose to have their association run for the cover of labor unions. This sudden change of policy can best be comprehended from the terms of the preamble and the opening paragraph of the revised agreement that the contractors' association prepared for jobber signature on October 17, 1944:

WHEREAS the members of the Association are engaged in furnishing labor for the manufacture of garments for the Jobber in the Boston area; and

WHEREAS the Association, Contractor, and Jobber are each in contractual relationship with the International Ladies' Garment Workers' Union, hereinafter called "I.L.G.W.U.," and have agreed with said I.L.G.W.U. to maintain certain labor standards, to pay certain standards of wages, and to assume certain obligations to the members of said I.L.G.W.U.; and

WHEREAS the parties hereto, in furtherance of their several obligations to said I.L.GW.U., desire to establish a basis of equitable and fair business conduct and dealing; to assist each other in the development of the Boston market; to minimize, as far as possible, all industrial disputes, conflicts, and difficulties; and to remove present abuses and evils which constitute causes of dispute and differences between Contractor and Jobber, and provide for a specific, inexpensive, and efficient means of settlement and determination of all such disputes,

NOW, THEREFORE, . . . it is agreed as follows:

(1) The Jobber, having already agreed with said I.L.G.W.U. to employ only contractors who are in contractual relationship with said I.L.G.W.U., agree [sic] to give all his work to members of the Association who are in good standing with said I.L.G.W.U., so long as members of the Association are available for performance of his work, and are comparable as to price and quality of work with other Contractors who are in contractual relationship with said I.L.G.W.U. and are not members of the Association.

Here, the contractors' association was clearly making a conscious effort to show that the parties were acting "in furtherance of their several obligations to the said I.L.G.W.U." But when the ensuing legal dispute over this issue finally reached the U. S. Supreme Court four years later, the learned justices were not impressed by this attempt to change the character of the agreement. "Benefits to organized labor," observed Mr. Justice Robert Jackson, on behalf of the Court, "cannot be utilized as a cat's-paw to pull employers' chestnuts out of the antitrust fires." Reversing a federal district court decision that had found the association's activities not only outside the sphere of interstate commerce but also unaccompanied by any intention to monopolize supply, control prices, or discriminate between would-be purchasers, Mr. Justice Jackson held that "in the light of its origin and the circumstances of the industry, it seems clear that the intent and effect of the agreement is substantially to restrict competition and to control prices and markets." [20]

The Road to Union Dictation

Although the union in the Boston Women's Sportswear case had kept its own skirts free of the law, the implications of the Supreme Court's decision, when coupled with startling legal developments on other fronts, thoroughly confounded those who would control competition through collective bargaining. At the time the organized Boston contractors had rushed for union cover by recasting their objectives in the mold of fulfilling their union obligations, the prevailing status of the law was presumed to grant labor unions and employers' associations certain freedoms from antitrust restraints when acting jointly in furtherance of labor objectives through the medium of collective bargaining. The advocates of the protocol system had apparently assumed that the very presence of a labor union as a party to collective agreements presupposed the existence of a legitimate labor objective which immunized the terms of the agreement from the operation of the antitrust laws.

The devious route by which this presumption had been reached covers the legislative history of labor exemptions from the antitrust laws, as well as a host of fine-spun interpretations growing out of those exemptions. Suffice it to say that in the eyes of those who still adhered to the principles of the protocol movement, the law of collective bargaining soon took a turn for the worse. For in 1945, the year after the Boston contractors sought union cover, the U. S. Supreme Court in an epoch-making opinion arrived at the conclusion that the presence of a labor organization as a party to a joint union–employer group scheme

---

[20] U.S. v. Women's Sportswear Manufacturers' Association, 336 U.S. 460 (1949) at pp. 463–464. The case in the federal district court is reported in 75 F. Supp. 112 (1947).

for controlling competition in no sense affected the legality or illegality of the operation. If the scheme was illegal when conducted by a group of employers acting alone, it remained illegal irrespective of union participation.

The occasion for this pronouncement which threatened to doom the protocol system of collective bargaining was the Allen Bradley case. Beginning with the early thirties, New York City manufacturers of electrical equipment and New York City contractors who bought electrical equipment and installed it at local construction sites had entered into city-wide agreements with Local 3, International Brotherhood of Electrical Workers, whereby these manufacturers would sell their products only to New York City contractors who operated under closed shop labor agreements with Local 3; and the contractors would buy only from New York City manufacturers who operated under closed shop labor agreements with Local 3. The enforcement of these agreements effectively eliminated out-of-town, as well as nonunion, competition to the mutual advantage of local manufacturers, local contractors, and local electrical workers. Wages rose and profits soared. The parties were indicted for violating the federal antitrust laws and after almost a decade of litigation in the lower courts, the case reached the U. S. Supreme Court for a decision in 1945.[21]

"Quite obviously," observed Mr. Justice Hugo Black, in his opinion for the Supreme Court, "this combination of business men has violated both Sections (1) and (2) of the Sherman Act, unless its conduct is immunized by the participation of the

---

[21]Allen Bradley Co. v. Local Union no. 3, IBEW, 325 U.S. 797 (1945). "The combination among the three groups, union, contractors, and manufacturers, became highly successful from the standpoint of all of them. The business of New York City manufacturers had a phenomenal growth, thereby multiplying the jobs available for the Local's members. Wages went up, hours were shortened, and the New York electrical equipment prices soared, to the decided financial profit of local contractors and manufacturers." *Ibid.* at p. 800.

Between October 1937 and November 1940, Special Master John K. Clark, to whom U.S. District Judge Vincent Leibell referred the case with directions "to hear and determine all issues of law and fact therein," conducted 200 hearings that filled 31 volumes with 25,000 pages of typewritten testimony. In addition, 1,700 exhibits were submitted. See particularly the lower court decisions at 41 F. Supp. 727 (1941) and 145 F. 2nd 215 (1944).

union. . . . Our problem in this case is therefore a very narrow one — do labor unions violate the Sherman Act when, in order to further their own interests as wage earners, they aid and abet business men to do the precise things which that Act prohibited? Having pinpointed the question, the Court then provided the answer:

> We think Congress never intended that unions could, consistently with the Sherman Act, aid non-labor groups to create business monopolies and to control the marketing of goods and services. . . .
>
> But "the purpose of mutual help" [under Section 6 of the Clayton Act] can hardly be thought to cover activities for the purpose of "employer-help" in controlling markets and prices. . . .
>
> Since union members can without violating the Sherman Act strike to enforce a union boycott of goods, it is said they may settle the strike by getting their employers to agree to refuse to buy the goods. Employers and the union did here make bargaining agreements in which the employers agreed not to buy goods manufactured by companies which did not employ members of Local No. 3. We may assume that such an agreement standing alone would not have violated the Sherman Act. But it did not stand alone. It was but one element in a far larger program in which contractors and manufacturers united with one another to monopolize all the business in New York City, to bar all other business men from that area, and to charge the public prices above a competitive level. . . .
>
> Finding no purpose of Congress to immunize labor unions who aid and abet manufacturers and traders in violating the Sherman Act, we hold that the district court correctly concluded that the respondents had violated the Act.[22]

When coupled with the subsequent U. S. Supreme Court decision in the Boston Women's Sportswear case, the tests of legality established by the New York Allen Bradley case raised questions that shook the very foundations of the protocol system. Since 1910, collective bargaining in the needle trades had fused trade and labor functions indiscriminately. Between negotiating the most common terms and conditions of employment, on the one hand, and creating a complete business monopoly of product prices and market controls, on the other, the brew of collective bargaining had been concocted from varying proportions of trade

---

[22]Allen Bradley Co. v. Local Union no. 3, IBEW, 325 U.S. 797 (1945) at pp. 800–801, 808–810.

and labor ingredients carefully mixed to satisfy the immediate needs of the producers. No two brews were alike but, once made, the ingredients were inseparable. Who could say whether any given activity of collective bargaining — like the regulation of the jobber-contractor system — was conducted to promote business ends or to achieve labor objectives? And if for business ends, who would predict whether such activities, apart from collective bargaining, could meet the tests of legality?

Those alarmed at judical decisions threatening to engulf the protocol system of collective bargaining were at least consoled by the possibility of an alternative method for regulating competition. In the Allen Bradley case, Mr. Justice Black, while vigorously condemning the collusive activities of Local 3 with groups of manufacturers and contractors, openly stated that the same ends could have been accomplished by the union acting alone. The Court also strongly implied that separate union agreements with individual employers to buy only those products manufactured by members of Local 3 would have been legal. "Our holding means," concluded Mr. Justice Black, "that the same labor union activities may or may not be in violation of the Sherman Act, dependent upon whether the union acts alone or in combination with business groups." [23]

But if the union, acting alone, or through agreements with individual employers, could take steps leading to so complete and objectionable a monopoly as existed in the Allen Bradley case, then surely the union, acting alone, could continue to enforce the more conservative standards of "legitimate" competition sponsored by the founders and defenders of the protocol movement. To be sure, the one-way use of union power to dictate employer conduct in the realm of trade controls — like an earlier

---

[23]*Ibid.*, p. 810. In a separate opinion, Mr. Justice Owen Roberts took sharp issue with this viewpoint in Mr. Justice Black's opinion, *ibid.*, pp. 813–820. "The course of decision in this court," so Roberts concluded, "has now created a situation in which, by concerted action, unions may set up a wall around a municipality of millions of inhabitants against importation of any goods if the union is careful to make separate contracts with each employer, and if union and employers are able to convince the court that, while all employers have such agreements, each acted independently in making them, — this notwithstanding the avowed purpose to exclude goods not made in that city by the members of the union." *Ibid.*, p. 819.

one-way use of employer power to dictate labor standards — ran counter to the generally accepted division of primary interests between labor and management. Moreover, permitting union dictation of trade policies — a practice forbidden by law to employer groups — smacked of radical labor philosophies that had repeatedly hampered the rise and development of the protocol movement.

Certainly, these observations appear to have been borne out by the aftermath of the Allen Bradley case. Capitalizing on the new gateway to union dictation so graciously left open by the U. S. Supreme Court, Local 3 of the International Brotherhood of Electrical Workers proceeded on its own authority to take such steps as were necessary to continue the exclusive arrangements with contractors and manufacturers that effectively barred all out-of-town competition. This form of one-way union dictation still permitted wages to be raised, profits to be increased, and prices to be boosted. Even had the organized employers objected to this type of union dictation, Local 3 with exclusive control of the skilled labor force and the backing of other unions in the construction trades, could likely have enforced its will. While this system had its merits. as well as its demerits, it was not collective bargaining as developed and practiced under the protocol movement.[24]

The California Women's Sportswear Case

The new approach to controlled competition necessitated by changing concepts of the antitrust laws called for a sharp break with past practice under the protocol movement. Whether this break could be made within the old shell of collective bargaining depended largely upon the ingenuity of legal talent assigned to reconciling past experiences with the latest interpretations of the U. S. Supreme Court. It would have been less difficult to reconcile the objectives set forth in the Brandeis Conferences of 1910 with the new views of governmental agencies on restraint of trade, had the institutions of collective bargaining never been developed before the 1950's. Then the unsuspecting precedents

[24]Only when pressure mounted from out-of-town IBEW locals, whose members, like their employers, suffered from the New York City monopoly held by Local 3, did the International Brotherhood of Electrical Workers take steps to break the Local 3 monopoly.

that were to prove so damaging to the cause of regulated competition might have been avoided. Certainly a movement in its infancy was more likely to survive legal attack especially where its chosen means and stated objectives were tempered from the outset to meet the varying winds of the law. And it was on this distinction between the new and the old that the next legal attack on the institutions of collective bargaining was to be repelled.

In April 4, 1955, the Federal Trade Commission filed a complaint against the California Sportswear and Dress Association, the Associated Sportswear Manufacturers of Los Angeles, the California Apparel Contractors' Association, the ILGWU, Joint Committees of the ILGWU, and the International Brotherhood of Teamsters — a complaint which appeared to attack most of the traditional methods for controlling jobber-contractor relationships through collective bargaining. The three associations were charged with entering into collective agreements and understandings with the unions to adhere to certain practices that restrained competition and restricted trade in offering sportswear for sale. Through these collective agreements, the parties allegedly

(1) required members of the manufacturers' association to deal only with members of the contractors' association and to employ only those contractors in contractors' association individually assigned to them;

(2) required members of the contractors' association to work only for those manufacturers and jobbers to whom they were assigned;

(3) authorized the union to approve changes in contractors and to approve the source of additional contractors not obtained from the contractors' association;

(4) forbade subcontracting in the shops of manufacturers and jobbers;

(5) fixed a procedure for determining prices to be paid members of the contractors' association for work assigned them in order to eliminate individual bargaining on the prices paid for particular garments;

(6) forbade any member of the three associations to acquire additional plants without giving notice to the union, or to acquire any plants outside of Los Angeles during the life of the agreement without a promise not to increase the production of such plants during the life of the agreement;

(7) forbade members of the three associations to acquire an interest in firms manufacturing sportswear within the union's jurisdiction un-

less the firm immediately enter into contractual relations with the unions;

(8) forbade members of the three associations to cause to be manufactured or purchased any accessories except from such persons as have a contract with the union.[25]

To support these charges, the Federal Trade Commission called for testimony from a number of witnesses who were alleged victims of illegal conduct under the collective agreements. A manufacturer testified that he was fined $10,000 by the impartial chairman for using nonunion contractors, and that he was told to observe the collective agreement or close down his shop. A jobber admitted doing business with a nonunion accessory firm in order to compete with other jobbers who employed nonunion contractors at a competitive advantage of 15 percent to 25 percent in labor costs. Nevertheless, the jobber was directed to cease and desist from dealing with his nonunion accessory shop. A contractor testified to having won a contract to finish certain garments at a price acceptable to the manufacturer, but the manufacturer, upon learning that the contractor operated a nonunion shop, refused to carry out the agreement.

The case for the Federal Trade Commission particularly stressed provisions of the collective agreements to fix prices paid contractors for their work. These clauses called for arriving at a price sufficient to meet reasonable overhead and profits for the contractors as well as a price adequate to guarantee the payment of established wage scales for the workers. This little foray into price-fixing, so it was contended, ran counter to decisions of the U. S. Supreme Court striking down efforts to tamper with the price structure, even in the absence of power to control the market. To the extent that price-fixing groups raised, lowered, or stabilized prices, so the Supreme Court had declared, they would be directly interfering with the free play of market forces.[26]

The most important precedent supporting the charges of the Federal Trade Commission had been provided by the Allen Bradley case. In the manufacture of California sportswear, as in the manufacture and installation of New York electrical equipment, the union, so it was alleged, had extended its lawful sphere

[25]Federal Trade Commission, in the Matter of the California Sportswear and Dress Association, *et al.* (1955), Docket no. 6325.

[26]U.S. v. Socony-Vacuum Oil Co., 310 U.S. 150 (1940) at pp. 220–221.

of bargaining for higher wages, shorter hours, and better working conditions into the unlawful sphere of aiding and abetting business groups to accomplish what was otherwise illegal. Here, stated the complaint, the union was not lawfully carrying out legitimate labor objectives but joining with trade associations in practices contrary to the antitrust laws.

At least by the time of the California [women's] Sportswear case, those who would control competition through collective bargaining had no reason to be caught unawares by the nature of the complaints or by the strength of the legal precedents. Following the Allen Bradley decision and the Boston Women's Sportswear case, both employer groups and labor unions throughout the needle trades had foreseen with some trepidation an inevitable showdown that would strike at the heart of the protocol movement. To save their cherished method for controlling competition, the parties to collective agreements had anticipated the need to modify the structures and procedures of collective bargaining. Their problem was to make formal concessions to the law without disturbing the basic character or the binding nature of the controls established.

Fortunately for the future of controlled competition in the needle trades, the circumstances surrounding the California [women's] Sportswear case permitted the critical issues of trade restraints to be cast in a light favorable to the collective agreements. The late development of collective bargaining in the area, the extent of nonunion competition, the apparently hostile attitudes of employers, the relative unimportance of the Los Angeles market, the position of the parties in the trade — all these factors were capable of contributing to the defense of collective bargaining against attacks by the Federal Trade Commission. Moreover, the terms of the collective agreements themselves had been drafted, consciously or unconsciously, to help overcome possible charges of violating the antitrust laws. In addition, the procedures adopted by the parties had, intentionally or unintentionally, played up the labor objectives while minimizing the business aspects of the collective agreements.

The Defense by the ILGWU

To offset charges of restraining trade, the ILGWU sought, first and foremost, to bring the facts of the case within the accepted ruling that labor unions when acting alone in the interests of the workers were immune from the antitrust laws. Although collective bargaining presupposes free and equal participation by the contracting parties in the negotiation and administration of collective agreements, the ILGWU attempted to show that in the Los Angeles market the key clauses in these particular agreements were spawned, hatched, and nurtured by the union over the bitter opposition of employer groups who were parties to the contracts. The impetus for all the contract provisions at issue in this case, contended the union, "came solely and exclusively from the union and . . . were vigorously opposed by the employer groups."[27]

The union argued that lack of cooperation by employers in the schemes under attack was evidenced by the absence of any separate agreements among and between the three employers' associations representing the jobbers, the contractors, and the inside manufacturers. Nor was there any evidence that these three associations consulted with one another about the terms of the separate agreements that each group signed with the union. Moreover, the attempt of the union to introduce each particular provision in question called forth hostile reactions from all the employer groups. "Thus in pressing for its contractor designation program," noted the union in its brief, "the [union] Joint Council was faced with not only the opposition of the jobbers and [inside] manufacturers but of the contractors as well."[28]

Looking back upon the history of collective bargaining, the advocates for the union contended that the movement to control the jobber-contractor system in the women's garment trades had always been union-oriented, union-directed, and union-enforced upon reluctantly subscribing employers. In the Los Angeles market, the union had been compelled to call a strike in 1942 before the employers would concede to the provisions on contracting. Again at the 1953 negotiations which lasted for eight months, the union insisted upon the designation of contractors against the opposition of all three employers' associations. Even the union demand for separate overhead allowances to contractors in determining minimum costs of production that contractors

---

[27]M. P. Glushien, attorney for the ILGWU, Brief in support of Initial Decision of Hearing Examiner, California Sportswear case, p. 3, quoting decision of hearing examiner.

[28]*Ibid.*, pp. 42, 53.

must receive for their work was opposed by all three employers' associations. Likewise, the prohibition on subcontracting within shops was opposed by each of the employer groups, as were the provisions to control runaway shops.

Just as the union alone pushed through these questionable provisions at negotiating conferences, so the union alone applied and enforced these clauses during the life of the collective agreements. At least, such is the conclusion to be drawn from the union's 144-page printed brief which nowhere acknowledges the continuing existence of joint union-association agencies or makes more than passing reference to the role of the impartial machinery in contract administration. Thus, in so far as piece-rate determination was centralized above the shop level — a matter of historic concern in the movement to equalize labor costs — the union's joint council, not the impartial machinery, provided the centralizing influence through the presence of an official union representative at shop negotiations.

Likewise, the joint council of local unions — not some joint union-employer group agency — approved the particular contractors selected by each jobber or inside manufacturer, as well as limited the total number of contractors that each jobber or inside manufacturer might acquire. Then, too, the office of the union joint council — not the office of impartial chairman — received applications from jobbers and inside manufacturers to alter or cancel their contractor designations. Again, it was with the union joint council — not with some agency of the impartial machinery — that employers had to file notice before acquiring an interest in additional plants. And, of course, no one questioned the leadership of the union in suppressing runaway shops. Altogether, from the union's brief, the negotiation and administration of key clauses in collective agreements for the Los Angeles market appeared to be the product of one-way union dictation.[29]

This position of the union was further buttressed by the absence of employer group participation in defense of the charges levied by the Federal Trade Commission. With the single exception of a brief filed by the contractors' association, the three

---

[29]As interpreted by the ILGWU brief, these features of the California collective agreements would appear to have been inspired by the aftermath of the Allen Bradley case (see above, pp. 836–840) .

employer groups washed their hands of all participation in the proceedings. The ILGWU alone had to carry the burden of defense. That defense, in support of one-way union dictation completely devoid of employer collusion, led the union's counsel to draw the following conclusion:

There is not a word of proof — and this deficiency is absolutely fundamental — that these provisions were sought or are desired by the employers; that in any respects they serve the ends of the employers as businessmen; that the employers are engaged in any independent combination or conspiracy of their own to further their interests as businessmen; or that the union is aiding and abetting the employers to carry out such a separate and independent businessmen's conspiracy. Only if this were established might the case perhaps fall within the narrow confines of the *Allen Bradley* doctrine.[30]

The second line of defense that the ILGWU erected against attacks of the Federal Trade Commission was an attempt to show that legitimate labor objectives alone inspired the movement for collective bargaining in the Los Angeles market for the manufacture of women's sportswear. Here, there was no fusion of trade and labor functions. "Nor is there any effort in either the Complaint or the proof to refute the manifest fact that these provisions are designed solely to protect the jobs, wages and decent working conditions of employees, including an equitable distribution of employment opportunities among them."[31]

Provisions for control of the jobber-contractor system, so the ILGWU contended, were the "union security" clauses of collective agreements in the needle trades. To allow garments to be made up in nonunion shops would make of collective bargaining with jobbers and manufacturers an empty shell. To enforce labor standards in outside shops was to preserve the labor standards of inside establishments. To permit the discharge of a contractor in the middle of a season was to throw workers out of employment at the critical period of earning a livelihood. To prevent runaway shops was to protect the work standards and job opportunities of the union membership. To fix minimum prices on payments made to contractors, including an allowance for overhead,

---

[30]Glushien. . . , Brief, p. 74.
[31]*Ibid.,* p. 5.

was to insure that contractors would meet the established wages set for the trade.

To hold jobbers and inside manufacturers responsible for the determination of piece rates, and for the payment of wages in outside contractor shops, was to equalize earnings and work opportunities among employees in all production units. To limit jobbers and inside manufacturers to the number of contractors they actually need, and then to require a division of work between inside and outside shops, was to promote the principle of regularized employment as well as to support the principle of group seniority and share-the-work plans as applied in the needle trades. All these features, concluded the ILGWU, were simon-pure labor objectives, free of employer motivations that the Federal Trade Commission would use to taint the legality of collective bargaining.

The union's third line of defense was an attempt to refute the alleged monopolistic tendencies of the collective agreements. In terms of establishing industry-wide controls, these operations in the Los Angeles market were insignificant. "The unionized portion of the Los Angeles sportswear industry constitutes only 1.5% of the national sportswear volume; and that portion produced by Los Angeles union contractors — the heart of the complaint in this proceeding — amounts to barely three-tenths of one percent (0.3%) of the nation's sportswear output." Nor were the local negotiations subject to national controls. Neither the ILGWU nor the International Brotherhood of Teamsters participated as parent bodies in the bargaining sessions or signed the local agreements. The local employer groups, likewise, acted entirely on their own authority.[32]

Within the Los Angeles market, contended the union, the alleged patterns of exclusive controls did not, in fact, exist. Neither the collective agreements nor the practices of the two associations (jobbers and inside manufacturers) required association members to restrict dealings to members of the contractors' associations. Except for the requirement that outside shops be unionized, jobbers and inside manufacturers were free to select contractors from whatever source. Some jobbers and inside man-

---

[32]*Ibid.,* p. 10.

ufacturers employed contractors who were not only nonassociation but also nonunion. Conversely, union contractors were, in practice, permitted to work for nonunion jobbers. At best, provisions for the designation of contractors were followed only in their general outlines. "There is no evidence in the record whatsoever," concluded the ILGWU in its stand on exclusive controls, "that the provisions limit the output of garments, deprive any entrepreneur of the right to enter the field, control prices, allocate markets, allocate customers, or discriminate among them, or in any other way tend to restrain trade or create a monopoly."[33]

Altogether, these arguments of the union favorably impressed the hearing examiner whose findings corresponded closely with the stand taken by the ILGWU. He found that limiting jobbers and inside manufacturers to the use of certain contractors and restricting their freedom to purchase accessories from whatever source fell within the matrix of employer-employee relations and were historic union goals. The record, so the hearing examiner concluded, "established that the jobber-contractor provisions of the collective agreements represent the culmination of a struggle on the part of the Union, to protect the labor standards of employees in the garment industry, which goes back over forty years." When his decision was confirmed by the Federal Trade Commission and the case was dismissed, the advocates of fair competition once more breathed a sigh of relief.[34]

Concluding Observations

For more than thirty years prior to the early forties, the history of collective bargaining in the needle trades had been characterized by "open covenants, openly arrived at." Self-sustaining efforts at controlling the excesses of competition in labor costs and in trade practices had brought peace and stability to the needle trades. At least to the leaders of the protocol movement, these goals were so obviously in the public interest and so clearly to the advantage of the "bosses" and the "people" that the participants in this evolving drama could not believe their noble experiments would some day be plastered with vicious charges of illegal

---

[33]*Ibid.*, p. 72.

[34]The official records of this case may be found in Federal Trade Commission, in the Matter of the California Sportswear and Dress Association, *et al.* (1955) Docket no. 6325.

conspiracies to restrain trade. The voluminous minutes of negotiating sessions, the verbatim transcripts of labor-management conferences, the mimeographed proceedings of arbitration tribunals,
the permanent records of personal correspondence, as well as the
ease with which newspaper reporters could extract candid opinions
from those in positions of authority, all attest to the open-book approach that would seem to preclude any intention of becoming
entangled with the law.

But the first thirty years of the protocol movement, which had
produced a veritable gold mine of information for researchers
and historians, were to be followed by a second thirty years in
which "the realities of the situation" were often camouflaged with
false fronts of illusory purposes and deceitful means. The combined talents of labor, management, and public-minded neutrals
so badly needed to meet the changing conditions of industrial
society had to be directed toward the necessity of conforming
with the law. Worst of all, the U. S. Supreme Court in the Allen
Bradley case had invited labor unions to reinstate their one-way
system of union dictation that, in the needle trades, had long since
been superseded by the protocol system of labor-management
cooperation. Sooner or later, a direct clash between economics
and the law appeared inevitable; and the prospects of such a
showdown were not long in coming.

Chapter 22

Collective Bargaining

at the Crossroads

THOSE who exulted in the victory of the California [women's] Sportswear case as a triumph for the principles of the protocol movement were soon to face a greater crisis that bade fair to wreck the established system of collective bargaining in the needle trades. For, on March 11, 1959, a federal grand jury returned an indictment against the National Association of Blouse Manufacturers, the Greater Blouse, Skirt and Neckwear Contractors' Association, the Slate Belt Apparel Contractors' Association, the Blouse and Waistmakers' Union, Local 25, ILGWU, and others, charging that for the preceding ten years the defendants and their conspirators had engaged in combinations and conspiracies to restrain trade through agreements

the substantial terms of which have been and are to: fix the prices the members of National would be required to pay to the members of Greater and Slate Belt for blouse contracting work; allocate the blouse contracting work of members of National among the members of Greater and Slate Belt; require members of National to use members of Greater and Slate Belt exclusively to do blouse contracting work; establish a policing and enforcing system to prevent violations of the conspiracy; impose penalties or damages for violations of the conspiracy; and require manufacturers and jobbers of ladies' blouses who were not members of National either to join National or to conform to the aforesaid terms of the conspiracy.[1]

---

[1]U.S. v. Greater Blouse, Skirt and Neckwear Contractors' Association; National Association of Blouse Manufacturers; Slate Belt Apparel Contractors'

The operation of this conspiracy, concluded the indictment, hampered jobbers and inside manufacturers in choosing their own contractors and in distributing work among them. Furthermore, by eliminating competition among members of the two contractors' associations, the conspiracy forced the organized jobbers and inside manufacturers into paying higher prices to their contractors for work. Finally, independent jobbers and independent manufacturers were brought into the conspiracy or compelled to abide by its terms, while independent contractors were deprived of an opportunity to work for the organized factions of the trade. Based on this indictment, the U. S. Department of Justice (Antitrust Division) brought a criminal action against the defendants in the federal district court for the southern district of New York.

Background of the New York Blouse Industry Case

Although these charges against the blouse industry of New York City and the surrounding hinterlands were strikingly similar to those filed by the Federal Trade Commission against the women's sportswear industry of Los Angeles, California, the circumstances under which collective agreements were negotiated and administered in the two areas appeared to differ widely. In the California case, the movement to control competition through collective bargaining had escaped the censure of the Federal Trade Commission chiefly because the union's presentation of the facts, largely uncontroverted, fit the case into the law and the precedents for exempting organized labor from the operation of antitrust laws.

But fitting the blouse industry of the New York City area into the same law and precedents was a far more difficult assignment. In the first place, no one familiar with the history of the protocol movement in the needle trades of New York City would set out to prove that the institutions and processes of collective bargaining were a product of one-way union dictation. The brief with which the ILGWU won its case in California belied the whole concept of collaboration between labor unions and employers' associations to make war on the unorganized elements of industrial

Association; Blouse and Waistmakers' Union, Local 25, ILGWU, *et al.*, U.S. District Court, Southern District of New York (grand jury indictment, dated March 11, 1959), Criminal Action no. CR 153/181.

society — a concept that took shape in the Brandeis Conferences of 1910 and found expression in permanent joint agencies of contract administration devoted to promoting the welfare of the industry.

Organized employer opposition to collective bargaining in the women's sportswear industry of Los Angeles can be reconciled with principles of the protocol movement only by evidence of insufficient strength among unions and employer groups to achieve the goals of controlled competition. In Los Angeles, more than 85 percent of women's sportswear products were made in nonunion shops. At least 270 of the 300 Los Angeles sportswear jobbers and manufacturers operated nonunion shops. Only 20 percent of the union production — or 3 percent of the sportswear made in Los Angeles — was made by contractor shops in which the workers were organized. Faced with such an overwhelming horde of unorganized competitors, in the antiunion climate of Los Angeles, no organized group of manufacturers may have wished to team up with a labor organization in playing Horatio at the Bridge.[2]

By contrast, the organized factions of the blouse industry in the New York area dominated the trade. The extent of this control was set forth in the indictment:

Approximately fifty percent, or $175,000,000, of the blouses sold at wholesale in the United States in 1957 were produced in the four-state area of New York, New Jersey, Pennsylvania and Connecticut by contractors located in those states for jobbers and manufacturers principally located in New York City.

New York City, the center of this four-state area, is, by far, the principal marketing area for the sale of blouses to retailers located throughout the United States. Jobbers and manufacturers located in the New York City market sold approximately three fourths of the blouses sold at wholesale in the United States in 1957.

Virtually all of the contractors located in the four-state area are members of Greater or Slate Belt. Greater has approximately three hundred blouse contractor members, who manufacture principally "medium to better priced" and "high priced" blouses. Slate Belt con-

---

[2]The figures and percentages are from M. P. Glushien, attorney for the ILGWU, Brief in support of *Initial Decision of Hearing Examiner*, California [women's] Sportswear case, FTC Docket no. 6325, p. 10.

sists of approximately one hundred blouse contractors, who manufacture chiefly "popular priced" blouses.

All of the contractors belonging to Greater or Slate Belt have been operated as union establishments by virtue of contractual relations with the ILGWU, or one or more of its locals, chiefly Local 25. In addition, Local 25 maintains contractual relations with National, which is the only association of blouse jobbers and manufacturers doing business in the New York City metropolitan area. National represents the majority of jobbers and manufacturers doing business in this area.

Unlike the more recent entrance of collective bargaining into the women's sportswear industry of Los Angeles, the practice of negotiating and administering collective agreements for the blouse industry of New York City was as old as the protocols. The second of the original protocols had been negotiated in 1913 between the dress and waist manufacturers and Local 25, ILGWU. The National Association of Blouse Manufacturers, an organization of blouse jobbers and inside producers, goes back to the early thirties. Local 25, ILGWU, had maintained contractual relations with this association and with the Greater Blouse, Skirt and Neckwear Contractors' Association since the mid-thirties.

Historically set in the midst of other apparel trades adhering to the principles of the protocol movement, the blouse industry would most likely have followed the same objectives and employed the same means as did other local needle trades for controlling competition. In the light of labor-management collaboration through collective bargaining since 1910, it would have been nonsense to contend in the New York Blouse Industry case — as the ILGWU contended in the California [women's] Sportswear case — that clauses of collective agreements regulating the jobber-contracting system were the very ones "which the employers as businessmen bitterly resisted and which they would certainly like to be rid of if they could." [3]

On the contrary, there was no evidence that the organized forces of the blouse industry — employers as well as workers — had shown any less desire to regulate competition than had the organized factions in other industries of the needle trades. There was no evidence that the blouse industry had been less successful than other needle trades in approaching the goal of one associa-

---

[3]*Ibid.,* p. 75.

tion, one union, and one collective agreement. Nor was there evidence that the various parties to collective agreements in the blouse industry had worked less diligently to perfect a system of exclusive dealings between and among organizations of jobbers, contractors, inside manufacturers, and workers or in policing their industry to enforce these controls, once they had been established. Finally, there was no evidence that the organized groups of the blouse industry had shown any more concern than had the organized groups of other needle trades for keeping within the restrictions of the antitrust laws.

These conclusions appear to be supported by the terms of the 1935 collective agreements for the blouse industry of New York City. That year, the collective agreement of the National Association of Blouse Manufacturers with Local 25, ILGWU, obligated the parties to maintain the position of New York City in the trade. Whenever association members opened new shops or engaged new contractors they were bound to make a fair and reasonable effort to give preference in employment to New York City workers and a preference in letting out work to New York City contractors. A joint labor-management committee was set up to adopt proper regulations to carry out this provision, and violations of these prescribed rules were to be tantamount to violations of the collective agreement itself.

Like the jobbers and inside manufacturers, the organized contractors also negotiated separate agreements in 1935 with Local 25, ILGWU. In addition, the National Association of Blouse Manufacturers and the Greater Blouse, Skirt and Neckwear Contractors' Association entered into an agreement with each other under the terms of which members of "National" agreed to employ only those contractors who were members of "Greater" and members of "Greater" agreed to work only for members of "National." The prices that jobbers paid contractors for making blouses were "to be at all times substantially not more or less, on a fair and reasonable basis, than the actual requirements in each case." The agreement also stated that "in order to preserve equitable business dealings, to further promote fair competition in the industry and to guard against settlements that are either excessive or insufficient," these prices would upon written notice by either party be adjusted between any particular jobber and contractor "by the assistance of a representative of NATIONAL and a representative of GREATER."[4]

Through this centralized procedure for price-fixing between jobbers and contractors, the prices paid for making blouses could be standardized — just as piece rates for workers were standardized by a centralized procedure of piece-rate determination. In addition, the agreement between the two associations contained the usual clauses, common to NRA codes of the needle trades in the thirties, regulating the return of goods, deliveries, insurance, defaults in payment, consignments, and the like. Disputes over the application or interpretation of this agreement were to be handled in the first instance by representatives of the two associations, and if not settled within three days, they were to be referred to a joint committee on which each association was equally represented.

For the enforcement of their contract, the two associations relied upon a controlled use of strikes and boycotts — just as they had accepted a controlled use of strikes and boycotts to enforce their contracts with the ILGWU. "NATIONAL and GREATER agree," runs the 1935 contract between the parties, "that their respective members will not deal with any manufacturer, jobber, or contractor, who, having been determined liable by a majority of such joint committee, has defaulted in the payment of an agreed price to the contractor, unless or until such manufacturer, jobber or contractor shall have totally reimbursed the contractor." Contractors were expressly authorized to conduct strikes against members of National who did not obey the decisions of the joint committee — a procedure that shut off jobber access to contractors and virtually ran the noncomplying firms out of business.

---

[4]A copy of the 1935 collective agreement between the National Association of Blouse Manufacturers and the Greater Blouse, Skirt and Neckwear Contractors' Association is filed in the Abelson papers. The 1935 collective agreement between "National" and Local 25, ILGWU, stated that "Every member of the Association whose garments are not made in his inside shop shall pay to the manufacturer or contractor at least an amount sufficient to enable the manufacturer to pay the workers the wages and earnings provided for in the agreement and in addition a reasonable amount to the contractor to cover his overhead." From a copy of the 1935 agreement filed in the Abelson papers.

For all this questionable conduct, the organized groups of the blouse industry openly disclaimed any intention to violate the antitrust laws. The 1935 agreement between the jobbers (National) and the contractors (Greater) expressly stated that "Greater agrees, on behalf of its members that they will not join together for the purpose of collusively fixing or raising prices of blouses, etc. being manufactured hereunder." But these disclaimers did not stay the Federal Trade Commission from filing a complaint on October 23, 1943 against the National Association of Blouse Manufacturers, the Greater Blouse, Skirt and Neckwear Contractors' Association, the Blouse and Waistmakers' Union (Local 25, ILGWU), and others, charging the parties with entering into agreements, understandings, combinations, and conspiracies to restrain trade in the manufacture and distribution of blouses.

The FTC complaint then proceeded to list specific charges reminiscent of activities under the NRA codes: (1) uniform standards of fair commercial practices had tended to fix prices, limit discounts, regulate returns, and otherwise regiment conditions of sale; (2) restrictions on jobber–manufacturer–contractor relations had monopolized the manufacture and distribution of blouses in the hands of the organized groups; (3) intricate administrative machinery, including a stabilization board, had enforced restrictive rules and regulations through the inspection of books and the imposition of penalties — all to the prejudice of the public and in disregard of the law. The general effect of these infringements, concluded the allegations of the Federal Trade Commission in 1943, was

to unreasonably lessen, suppress and restrain competition in the sale of said merchandise, and to deprive wholesalers. jobbers, selling agents, resident buyers, retailers and the purchasing public of the advantage of prices, terms and conditions of sale, service and other considerations which they would receive and enjoy under conditions of normal and unobstructed and free and fair competition in said trade and industry.

Stoutly denying these allegations, the organized forces of the blouse industry contended that the commercial practices under attack were an outgrowth of customs and usages of the trade that had developed over a number of years. In no case, argued the respondents, did these usages and customs amount to a fixing of price levels that were manipulated from time to time to suit the interests of the contracting parties. Nor were the investigations of disputes between manufacturers and retailers more than voluntary efforts to reconcile differences, devoid of compulsion or the use of sanctions.[5]

The New York Blouse Industry Case

While a knowledge of the industry's prior clashes with the Federal Trade Commission helped to understand the issues in the 1959 grand jury indictment obtained by the U. S. Department of Justice (Antitrust Division), this background information did not explain the failure of the organized factions to repair their legal fences before a second assault by the government. At least, the employer groups and labor union of the blouse industry might have been expected to rephrase their objectives and reconstitute their methods of operation more in keeping with the developments of the law during the forties. Yet, most of the charges in the 1959 indictment against the blouse industry could have been deduced from the very terms of the 1950, 1953, and 1956 collective agreements between and among the employer groups, and from similar terms in corresponding agreements between the employer groups and the ILGWU.

Unlike the more carefully drawn clauses of the Los Angeles agreements which abound with provisos, loopholes in phraseology, and broad statements of policy capable of varied interpretations — features that had helped the ILGWU to defend collective bargaining against the charges of the Federal Trade Commission — the more recent agreements of the blouse industry in New York City drove home in no uncertain terms the charges with which the U. S. Department of Justice would damn the whole jobber–contractor–inside manufacturer–union relationship as a violation of the law. In its 1959 indictment, the federal grand jury looked directly to the 1956 agreement between the National Association of Blouse Manufacturers and the Greater Blouse,

---

[5]A summary of the FTC charges was reported in *Women's Wear Daily,* Oct. 28, 1943 and in the *New York Times,* Oct. 28, 1943. For a summary of the industry's defense, see *Women's Wear Daily,* Dec. 31, 1943. The official records of the case are found in Federal Trade Commission's Docket no. 5068. As previously noted (see above, p. 828), this case, along with two others involving the needle trades, dragged along for years until finally dismissed.

Skirt and Neckwear Contractors' Association for evidence of "an effective system of price fixing, allocation of the blouse contracting work of National's members among the members of Greater and Slate Belt, and a requirement that members of National give their blouse contracting work exclusively to members of Greater and Slate Belt." Similarly, so this indictment stated, the agreements between these employer groups and Local 25, ILGWU, also had provided "among other things, for allocation of the blouse contracting work of National's members among the members of Greater and Slate Belt."

Furthermore, the agreements themselves outlined the machinery and procedures through which employer groups and the ILGWU could take action on behalf of their respective members to enforce the restrictive clauses that constituted the gist of the government's complaint. Sitting at the pinnacle of the grievance machinery with power to render final and binding decisions on trade questions as well as labor questions was an impartial chairman whose jurisdiction extended not only to "questions of interpretation or application of any clause of this agreement" but also to "any acts, conduct or relations between the parties or their respective members, directly or indirectly." The agreements expressly provided that failure to carry out decisions of bipartisan agencies or of the impartial chairman could, under New York State's arbitration laws, lead to support from civil authorities, as though the "mandatory direction, prohibitions or orders" of the impartial machinery were a judgment entered in a civil court of competent jurisdiction. Or else such failure might, as a last resort, unleash upon the noncomplying culprit all the drastic weapons of industrial warfare: boycotts, strikes, pickets, and lockouts. All these potentialities were expressly authorized in the agreements themselves, and few doubted but that their use would serve to make industry controls effective.[6]

Despite this fearful build-up of contract clauses that could be used to justify prosecution and conviction, the final disposition of the New York Blouse Industry case was destined to be anticlimactic. But the sudden turn of events that ultimately helped to provide another respite for collective bargaining in the needle

---

[6]The quotations are from the 1956 collective agreement between the National Association of Blouse Manufacturers and the Greater Blouse, Skirt and Neckwear Contractors' Association.

trades did not come until five years after the original indictment. Meanwhile, pressures continued to mount for the final day of reckoning on which the prime objective of the protocol movement for industry-controlled competition would clash with established public policies for the preservation of free competition. In the preparation for this showdown, nothing was taken for granted. Interested factions enlisted the help of some of the strongest law firms in New York City. So far as the parties could foresee, there could be no further escape from a final determination of the legal issues surrounding the objectives and methods of the protocol movement.

This time, those who were to fight the legal battles on behalf of the ILGWU and the collaborating employers had no apparent intention of evading a direct clash over the fundamental issues. Lawyers for the union disclosed their plan of action when they requested permission of the government to submit a deposition from Herbert H. Lehman, whose ill health was expected to preclude his appearance in court. To rest the defense of collective bargaining as practiced in the needle trades on the shoulders of Mr. Lehman could obviously have but one meaning, namely that the ILGWU — and presumably the employers who worked hand in hand with the union — would undertake to prove from the broad sweep of historical development that the protocol movement had brought order out of chaos and cooperation out of conflict — worthy ends which could be cited to justify a presumption of legality.[7]

Who, better than Herbert H. Lehman, could show how these achievements had operated to the mutual advantage of the workers and employers alike? Mr. Lehman had early developed a life-long interest in needle trade problems and a keen insight into the types of measures that would be required for relief. In the spring of 1914, he was named to the original committee on industrial relations of Kehillah (the Jewish Community) and contributed his time and money to help that organization resolve industrial disputes. From the outset, he understood the principles

---

[7]Long lists of direct interrogatories and cross interrogatories to be submitted to Mr. Lehman may be found in Folder no. 2 of the documents filed in the blouse industry case. All documents connected with the case are available in the U.S. Court House, Room 507, Foley Square, New York City, under file numbers 62 Civ. 377, and Criminal 153/181.

of the protocol movement and what that movement was designed to accomplish. Lehman was cast in the mold of "industrial statesmen" who from the days of Brandeis, Holt, and Hillquit had volunteered their services for the cause of industrial peace and stability. Organized groups from all factions of the needle trades — jobbers, contractors, inside manufacturers, and labor unions — brought their problems to his doorstep and leaned heavily upon him for direction and advice.

Far more important for the blouse industry case, however, was the bridge that Mr. Lehman could erect to span the alleged chasm between self-imposed industrial controls represented by the protocol movement and the protection of the public interest reflected in the antitrust laws. From the mid-twenties when he was named by Governor Alfred E. Smith to an advisory commission on the women's coat and suit trade, on through his long and illustrious public career as Lieutenant Governor and Governor of New York State and as U. S. Senator, Mr. Lehman, perforce, saw the human problems of the industrial world through the eyes of a public servant dedicated to the promotion and protection of the public interest.

While holding public office, Lehman had sponsored and repeatedly supported some of the more advanced proposals for self-imposed industrial controls that would put a floor beneath "legitimate" competition. On three separate occasions, in 1932, 1935, and 1940, Mr. Lehman had been called upon to mediate disputes for the women's coat and suit trade over the adoption or retention of the system for limiting and assigning contractors. In each case, he had recommended the basic elements of the system that was now under attack. Who, therefore, better than Lehman, could throw light upon the issue of whether half a century of collective bargaining in the needle trades should bear the reputable caption, *From Conflict to Cooperation,* or whether the history of this development should more aptly be labeled, *From Conflict to Collusion!* [8]

---

[8] See the affidavit of J. H. Topkis of the law firm of Paul, Weiss, Rifkind, Wharton and Garrison, engaged to represent the ILGWU in the case. The documents compiled in this case contain a number of excerpts from the *New York Times* and the *Women's Wear Daily* showing Mr. Lehman's part in settling the disputes of 1932, 1935, and 1940. *Women's Wear Daily* for the summer months of 1932, 1935, and 1940 carried an extended account of

But the hopes of those supporting the principles of the protocol movement were dashed when it developed that Mr. Lehman's illness would not permit the taking of depositions at his bedside. Momentarily, lawyers assigned to prepare a defense for standardizing labor costs and controlling jobber–contractor–inside manufacturer–union relations through collective bargaining were at their wit's end. Yet, somehow, they had to find a legal justification for stabilizing the blouse industry against the disruptive influences of unconscionable employers and unorganized workers.

Still operating on the premise that the New York Blouse Industry case would be determined on the merits of the fundamental issues, the law firm of Paul, Weiss, Rifkind, Wharton and Garrison, representing the ILGWU, turned to another distinguished citizen of New York, ex-federal judge Simon H. Rifkind, for a defense of collective bargaining. Mr. Rifkind's approach to the problem, like that proposed for Mr. Lehman, was to be as broad as the history of the protocol movement itself. His method was to seek the substitution of a civil action for the pending criminal case. At a hearing before federal district court judge, Edward Weinfeld, on February 6, 1962, Mr. Rifkind suggested an exploration of some means for accommodating his client's views on collective bargaining with the government's views on the antitrust laws.

"You have got to find some method whereby this business can go on," so Mr. Rifkind stated. "This will affect not only blouses, but skirts, coats, suits, and the whole needle trades industry. It will all be governed by very similar systems." With all the earnestness he could command, Mr. Rifkind pleaded with the judge "to put the indictment aside for the time being and to make an earnest effort to come up with a constructive solution in the matter which involves so many business enterprises and so many people who work for a living." Only through "the discovery of a solution to the practical problems of the needle trade industry" could the life of New York's largest business be preserved. But when Mr. Rifkind's plea went for naught, the darkest hour of decision for the future of the needle trades appeared to be at hand.[9]

---

these developments. For Mr. Lehman's contributions, see particularly the issues of July 18 and 25, 1932; June 28, July 2 and 3, 1935; July 10 and 12, 1940.

[9] The quotations are from documents filed with the case.

Then relief suddenly came from an unexpected source: the government itself. For reasons that do not appear obvious from the facts, the Antitrust Division of the U. S. Department of Justice suddenly decided that all the available evidence compiled over a period of five years was not sufficient to win its antitrust case against the union; and that, in view of these circumstances, prosecution of the employers alone would be unfair. Against a shadowy background, with overtones of political interference from Washington, the government thereupon moved to discontinue the case.[10]

Dissension within the Ranks

With this refusal by the government to prosecute the case on grounds of insufficient evidence, the organized factions of the blouse industry were expected to drape themselves about the shoulders of their benefactors in universal acclaim for the godsend that had saved themselves and their institutions from the perils of the law. But to the utter astonishment of almost everyone connected with the case, such a unanimous gesture of gratitude was never forthcoming. The unity of purpose presumed to exist between and among the organized jobbers, inside manufacturers, contractors, and the union of the blouse industry appeared to lack reality. Stretching the canopy of collective agreements over wider and wider areas of production had thinned to the breaking point the effective controls governing competition in the manufacture of women's blouses. The industrial realm of law and order, like Napoleon's invasion of Russia, had apparently been overextended until those on the perimeter were falling prey to the advocates of subversion.

The necessity for extending uniform labor costs and restrictive business practices throughout areas of expanding competitive pressures had always been the nightmare of the protocol movement. Growing diversities in methods of production and super-

---

[10]In a brilliant piece of reporting, J. A. Livingston, financial editor of the *Philadelphia Evening Bulletin,* assembled from his own field investigations convincing evidence that political manipulations culminating in action from the White House had been responsible for the government's sudden change of policy. See Livingston's three articles in the issues of April 7, 8, and 9, 1964.

vision, in the skill and reliability of the labor force, in accessibility to markets and raw materials, in the moral fiber and business integrity of employers had multiplied problems of control, especially where these diversities were extended over wide geographic areas. Attempts in the thirties to meet these diversities by law had been the Waterloo of industrial codes of fair competition under the National Industrial Recovery Act. Now, the voltary attempts of jobbers, contractors, inside manufacturers, and the labor union of the blouse industry to meet these diversities through collective bargaining appeared doomed to defeat from dissension within the ranks.

So long as the manufacture of women's blouses was largely confined to metropolitan New York, the organized factions of the industry could man the dykes of controlled competition with some assurance of locating the smallest leaks in time to prevent disaster. But when blouse makers in considerable numbers (mostly contractors working for New York jobbers) began to operate in the hinterlands of New Jersey and Pennsylvania, patrolling the dykes became more difficult. Once new manufacturing processes were superimposed on geographic dispersion of the blouse industry, added pressures for release from restrictive jobber–contractor–inside manufacturer–union relationships threatened to break down the entire structure of collective bargaining.

At the time of the pending Blouse Industry case, the chief trouble maker within the organized factions of the trade was the Slate Belt Apparel Contractors' Association of Pennsylvania — an organization whose independent strength proved to be the greatest weakness of the protocol system. Here was an association of 160 contractors doing a $45,000,000 volume of business each year, and providing needed employment for 10,000 union members (mostly women) in the slate belt region of eastern Pennsylvania. But the major source of the association's strength lay not in its size but in the ability of its members to transform blouse manufacturing processes from small-shop handicraft operations into those of mass-production, assembly-line techniques. Directing this technological transition was a former union official, Robert Mickus, now manager of the slate belt employers' association. To Robert Mickus came an inquiring newspaper editor seeking on-the-scene impressions of technological developments:

Mickus will readily take you around well-lighted airy plants in the tiny towns of Roseto, Bath, Bangor and Pen Argyl, Pa.

"See those machines," he'll say, "Reese buttonholers — $900 a piece. And those — chain pinkers without bobbins — $600 and those — safety stitchers — $630. And you better add another $130 for motors and stands."

The editor could plainly see that the age of technology was invading the last major stronghold of the small shop in American industry.[11]

These out-of-town contractors were now creating another paradox in the history of collective bargaining for the needle trades. While their predecessors had moved by night and chiseled by day — carrying their offices in their hats, beating down the price of labor, and undercutting the business standards of their competitors — these new contractors of the slate belt district were a breed of a different color: they maintained large establishments with expensive equipment; their plants were permanent fixtures on the landscape; and through the savings of assembly-line techniques, they were not only able but willing to meet the best of wage scales and fringe benefits for the sake of an efficient labor force.

Here, a basic principle of the protocol movement that the labor standards of New York City be extended to all outlying areas of competition, was suddenly thrown into reverse. Out-of-town contractors, once the scourge of the industry, could now set the pace in economies of operation for the "bosses" and in benefits of employment for the "people." Moreover, New York City offered few prospects of meeting these advantages of operation available to the hinterlands. Space was too scarce, taxes were too high, traffic was too congested, even if permission were obtained for the demolition of lofts and tenements that would need to be replaced. Mounting pressures to move outside were threatening another basic tenet of the protocol system — namely, that the control and direction of each needle trade industry, if not the bulk of its production, must be kept within the confines of metropolitan New York.[12]

Such were the economic and political forces leading the Slate

[11]Livingston in *ibid.*, April 9, 1964.

[12]For attempts by the city government to sustain and revitalize the garment trades in New York City, see the *New York Times*, July 5, 1967.

Belt Apparel Contractors' Association to reject the government's generous motion to throw out of court a criminal case in which the association itself was a defendant. "You want the government to prosecute your client and prove guilt beyond a reasonable doubt?" queried the astonished federal judge, Edward Weinfeld, of the association's counsel, J. W. Castles, 3rd (Weinfeld's federal district court in Manhattan had the power to accept or reject the government's motion to nol-pros the case). It was fairer to say that what Attorney Castles wanted for his clients was not conviction for violating the antitrust laws but relief from the bondage of New York City. His slate belt contractors feared the prospects of conviction and punishment for antitrust infractions with less intensity than they desired to escape from the shackles of New York controls over the blouse industry.

So, when the government moved to stay prosecution, a great legal battle ensued to convince Judge Weinfeld that the grand jury indictment contained evidences of misconduct far too convincing to be dismissed on motion of the government without a trial. Through his slate belt clients, who were themselves parties to the vast complex of controls they now wished to be rid of, Attorney J. W. Castles, 3rd, had access to the inside story of potential impingements upon antitrust legislation. But he scarcely needed to go beyond the disclosures already made by the government's able battery of lawyers assigned to the case over the preceding five years. Indeed, Castle's own affidavit on behalf of his clients did little more than restate and summarize a few of the more serious charges filed in the grand jury indictment of March 11, 1959, in the government's supplemental Bill of Particulars, dated December 15, 1959, and in the government's Further Bill of Particulars, filed on May 18, 1960.

Thus, in his affidavit supporting presecution on behalf of the Slate Belt Apparel Contractors' Association, Attorney J. W. Castles, 3rd, reviewed the indictment's account of developments, noting

that in 1949 Greater [New York contractors], National [New York jobbers] and Local 25 [ILGWU] formed a plan to stabilize the blouse industry; that Slate Belt became affiliated in 1949 with Greater so as to be bound by all agreements made by Greater; that in 1950 Greater and National entered into an agreement which would (i) fix the price to be paid contractors; (ii) allocate blouse contracting work of members of National among the members of Greater and Slate Belt; (iii) require members of National to give their blouse contracting work exclusively to members of Greater and Slate Belt; and (iv) establish an enforcement system to carry out the agreement.

Still taking his cue from the indictment itself, Castles recounted how Slate Belt had broken out of these restrictive arrangements in 1953 to gain a separate union contract, only to be forced back into the system two years later "upon the refusal of the Northeast Department of the ILGWU to renew Slate Belt's independent agreement with the Pennsylvania locals, and upon the intervention of one Harry Strasser who it is alleged 'was instrumental in arranging Slate Belt's reaffiliation with Greater.' "[13]

Turning to the government's voluminous Bill of Particulars that provided additional details on allegations in the grand jury indictment, Attorney J. W. Castles, 3rd, cited items 15, 16, 17, and 18 that together designated by name, date, and other details literally hundreds of instances showing the impact of the conspiracy on the parties to the agreement. "Inspection of these items in the Government's Bill of Particulars," noted Castles, "will reveal far more effectively and conclusively than any summary the extensive and detailed nature of the evidence in the Government's possession to prove that

(1) members of National had in fact been deprived of working with contractors of their own choosing (item 15); (2) members of National

---

[13]Little of value can be added to the essential principles of the Blouse Industry case by playing up the role of certain questionable characters who may at times have managed to horn in on the manipulation of industry controls for their own advantage (Harry Strasser had been a business partner of Albert Anastasia, executioner for Murder, Inc.). These sinister influences appear to crop up from time to time in all branches of the needle trades, regardless of the bargaining system, and in spite of concerted efforts by unions and employer groups to weed them out. More direct evidences of underworld connections were revealed in the disputes growing out of the 1958 dress negotiations during which an association of dress contractors in northeastern Pennsylvania refused to sign a master labor agreement negotiated in New York City for a seven-state area. At that time, ILGWU President David Dubinsky pledged that his union would continue to fight the racketeering element in Pennsylvania, as well as in New York City, where he conceded that racketeers controlled 10% of the industry. For references to a running account of this dress industry dispute, see the *New York Times Index* for 1958 and for 1959.

had in fact not been able to distribute their work among contractors in the manner desired (item 16); (3) jobbers not members of National had been made to abide by the terms of the conspiracy (item 17); and (4) contractors not members of Greater or Slate Belt were deprived of an opportunity to work for members of National (item 18)."[14]

The more convincing the evidence that the counsel for the Slate Belt Association compiled in support of having the New York Blouse Industry case go to trial, the more deeply he buried his own Pennsylvania clients in the hope that suffering death from the antitrust laws today would bring a resurrection of freedom from New York controls tomorrow. But the federal judge, who had the power to reject the government's motion to dismiss the case, would not be moved. Whatever the merits of the arguments for prosecution, the practical difficulties of requiring the U. S. Department of Justice to continue a case that it had insisted could not be won were overpowering.

Thus was the legality of collective bargaining as practiced in the needle trades once more left unresolved. The parties to the self-imposed system of controlled competition, featuring equal labor costs and restrictions on jobber–contractor–inside manufacturer–union relations, were once more left without legal guidance. Even their anticipated season of relief from the pressures of impending prosecution offered no more than a lull between the storms. For scarcely had the roar of the New York Blouse Industry case subsided than the towering thunderheads of new legal disturbances appeared on the horizon. Although spawned completely outside the apparel industries, these new disturbances soon gained a momentum that threatened completely to engulf the historic system of collective bargaining in the needle trades.

---

[14]The quotations are from the affidavit of J. W. Castles, 3rd, submitted Jan. 16, 1964, to the U.S. District Court, Southern District of New York in Criminal Action no. 153/181 (the New York Blouse Industry case), pp. 4–5, 7. Further to strengthen the evidence supporting a trial based on the grand jury indictment, counsel for the Slate Belt Apparel Contractors' Association sought and obtained separate affidavits from R. A. Bicks, Lawrence Gochberg, and R. S. Daniels, all of whom, as former attorneys in the Department of Justice, had previously worked on the case. All three were convinced that the facts fully supported the allegations in the indictment, and all three fully expected that the government would prosecute the case to a successful conclusion.

United Mine Workers v. Pennington

The most startling of these new developments arose in the bituminous coal industry. Under the 1950 National Bituminous Coal Wage Agreement (as subsequently amended) — an agreement negotiated between the Bituminous Coal Operators' Association and the United Mine Workers' Union — whatever wages, hours, and working conditions were negotiated for the miners, and whatever royalties the operators agreed to pay into the union's Welfare Retirement Fund, the union would try to exact from other associations and from independent coal operators with whom it negotiated separate agreements. As a result, all coal operators holding union contracts — whether independent or association members, large or small, and wherever located — would be paying the same wage scales, offering the same conditions, and meeting the same fringe benefits. With essential labor costs standardized for all operators, industry pressures to overcome competition by chiseling on the terms of employment would be relieved.[15]

James M. Pennington, one of the defendants in this case, was a partner in the Phillips Bros. Coal Company, a small independent firm that failed to meet the royalty assessments under its union contract. When sued by the union for back payments, the

---

[15]The objective of this Contract is to provide the maximum possible continuity and stability of employment under the conditions set forth herein. The parties hereto agree that bituminous coal mines shall be so operated as not to debase or lower the standards of wages, hours, safety requirements and other conditions of work, established by this contract. The parties recognizing their obligation each as to the other to exercise all possible efforts and means to attain these objectives further agree as follows:

A. During the period of this Contract, the United Mine Workers of America will not enter into, be a party to, nor will it permit any agreement or understanding covering any wages, hours or other conditions of work applicable to employees covered by this Contract on any basis other than those specified in this Contract or any applicable District Contract.

—From the protective wage (most favored employer) clause that became an amendment, dated December 1, 1958, to the 1950 collective agreement negotiated between the Bituminous Coal Operators' Association and the United Mine Workers of America.

firm challenged the whole collective bargaining system as a violation of the Sherman Antitrust Act on the following allegations:

(1) To meet the problem of overproduction, the union and the coal operators' association had agreed to weed out small competitors by forcing them to accept the same labor terms imposed upon the larger companies. The achievement of this goal was hastened by the jointly approved mechanization of the coal industry — a development under the master contract that reduced employment but increased productivity, thus permitting the mechanized firms to pay higher wages and higher royalties, still further beyond the reach of small unmechanized firms whose only alternative under union pressure was to go out of business.

(2) To exclude the production and sale of nonunion coal, the union and the large companies agreed upon a series of steps that included refusal to lease coal lands to nonunion operators, and a refusal to buy or sell nonunion coal.

(3) Further to suppress small-scale nonunion operators, the union and the large companies sought to destroy the business of those firms supplying coal to the Tennessee Valley Authority, both by insisting that the government establish high minimum wage scales under the Walsh-Healey Act and by undercutting small operators making "spot market" sales excluded from the Walsh-Healey Act.[16]

From verdicts against the union in the lower federal courts, the case came up to the U. S. Supreme Court for review. The essential question before the Court was whether on the facts of the case the United Mine Workers' Union was exempt from liability under the Sherman Antitrust Act. The answer to this question appeared to turn principally on whether the union could lawfully negotiate with a group of employers certain wage scales and fringe benefits that, by the terms of the resulting agreement, the union was obligated to try to extend to other employers

---

[16]Summarized from an article on the case by D. E. Feller and J. D. Anker, "Analysis of Impact of Supreme Court's Antitrust Holdings," Bureau of National Affairs, *Labor Relations Reference Manual* (1965), vol. 59, pp. 104–110.

A major part of Phillips' case, however, was that the union entered into a conspiracy with the large operators to impose the agreed-upon wage and royalty scales upon the smaller, nonunion operators, regardless of their ability to pay and regardless of whether or not the union represented the employees of these companies, all for the purpose of eliminating them from the industry, limiting production and preempting the market for the large, unionized operators.

with whom it negotiated separate contracts. More particularly, did the presence of such a "most favored employer" clause in the multiemployer labor agreement extend the activities of the union into the realm of aiding employers to create business monopolies affecting prices and produce markets, contrary to the antitrust laws? Or was such a provision, although negotiated with an employer group, primarily directed to helping the union carry out its legitimate objective of controlling wages, hours, and working conditions in the labor market — a matter exempt from the operation of the antitrust laws?[17]

This issue hit directly at one of the two most cherished concepts in the history of collective bargaining for the needle trades. The first basic concept, covered by the New York Blouse Industry case, had revolved primarily around the fundamental issue of controlling jobber–contractor–inside manufacturer–union relationships as a means of protecting labor standards for the workers and of preventing disparities in labor costs for the employers. In like manner, the UMW-Pennington case hit with equal force at the second basic principle — namely, that the provisions of negotiated labor agreements must be standardized throughout areas of competitive pressures until the range of uniform employment terms for the workers, or of uniform labor costs for the employers, be made coterminous with the outermost bounds of each industry.

In both cases, the need for control was premised on the assumption that nothing short of these two steps would offer adequate protection against ruthless competitors — workers and employers, alike — who gained their advantage largely through savings from sweatshop operations. And, in both cases, the courts were expected to pass judgment on whether the purpose and effect of these controls established through collective bargaining were contrary to public policy expressed by the antitrust laws, or whether these controls were in keeping with public policy ex-

---

—Mr. Justice Byron White, majority opinion in United Mine Workers of America v. James M. Pennington, 381 U.S. 657 (1965) at p. 664.

[17]From an award of damages against the union by the U.S. District Court for the Eastern District of Tennessee, the United Mine Workers took an appeal to the U.S. Court of Appeals, 6th Circuit, which affirmed the lower court's decision, 325 F 2nd 804 (1963), after which certiorari was granted for review by the U.S. Supreme Court.

pressed by union exemptions from antitrust legislation. Whatever the merits of the legal arguments, pro and con, one conclusion stands out from the long history of collective bargaining in the needle trades: the protocol movement could not have survived had the law denied to the participants in the bargaining process either form of activity now subject to legal attack.

Certainly the principle of putting a floor under terms of employment that would be uniformly applicable to all competing firms of an industry had been a cornerstone of collective bargaining in the needle trades since the Brandeis Conferences of 1910. Success in taking labor costs out of competition had been the chief factor in gaining higher wages, shorter hours, and better working conditions over the years. Conversely, failure to do so had been the greatest roadblock to higher standards of living for union members. Industry-wide organization of the workers as a prerequisite to uniform standards of employment has continued to be the keystone of union policy in the needle trades. "Don't forget," observed a women's garment manufacturer in the spring of 1966, "that they [the ILGWU leaders] have had to reconcile the fact that, much as they wanted to see union rates go up, they could not push them up too much above the non-union plants or we would be put at an even greater cost-price disadvantage. After all, the normal union rate is between $1.90 and $2.00 an hour. This makes for a low-paying industry."[18]

The Majority Opinion: Mr. Justice White

That is why representatives of labor unions and employers' associations guiding the destinies of collective bargaining in the needle trades viewed with alarm the findings of the U. S. Supreme Court in the UMW-Pennington case, holding that the most effective and widely used procedures for creating and maintaining industry-wide standards of employment (short of governmental intervention exemplified by the NRA codes) had run afoul of the antitrust laws. Writing for a majority of the Court, Mr. Justice Byron White prepared an opinion that condemned most favored employer clauses in multiemployer agreements obligating the union to seek similar terms from other employers with whom it negotiated separate contracts. "We think a union forfeits its exemption from the antitrust laws," stated the majority opinion,

[18]As quoted in the *New York Times,* March 27, 1966.

"when it is clearly shown that it has agreed with one set of employers to impose a certain wage scale on other bargaining units."[19]

Mr. Justice White several times restated this basic conclusion:

There is nothing in the [government's] labor policy indicating that the union and the employers in one bargaining unit are free to bargain about the wages, hours and working conditions of other bargaining units or to attempt to settle these matters for the entire industry. On the contrary, the duty to bargain unit by unit leads to a quite different conclusion. The union's obligation to its members would seem best served if the union retained the ability to respond to each bargaining situation as the individual circumstances might warrant, without being strait-jacketed by some prior agreement with the favored employers. . . .

The policy of the antitrust laws is clearly set against employer-union agreements seeking to prescribe labor standards outside the bargaining unit. One could hardly contend, for example, that one group of employers could lawfully demand that the union impose on other employers wages that were significantly higher than those paid by the requesting employers, or a system of computing that, because of differences in methods of production, would be more costly to one set of employers than to another. . . .

From the viewpoint of antitrust policy, moreover, all such agreements between a group of employers and a union that the union will seek specified labor standards outside the bargaining unit suffer from a more basic defect, without regard to predatory intention or effect in the particular case. For the salient characteristic of such agreements is that the union surrenders its freedom of action with respect to its bargaining policy. Prior to the agreement the union might seek uniform standards in its own self-interest but would be required to assess in each case the probable costs and gains of a strike or other collective action to that end and thus might conclude that the objective of uniform standards should temporarily give way. After the

[19]The Court's attack on the movement for industry-wide standards was apparently broad enough to encompass any evidence that one or more employers in negotiating an agreement with the union had encouraged or supported, directly or indirectly, that union in its efforts to extend the negotiated labor standards to other firms, even in the absence of written inducements to do so. A labor agreement with a leading firm that was presumed to set a pattern for negotiating contract terms with other competing firms was no less an evidence of restraining trade than a multiemployer contract with a most favored employer clause. See the dissenting opinion of Mr. Justice Arthur Goldberg in UMW v. Pennington, 381 U.S. 657, and Amalgamated Meat Cutters v. Jewel Tea Co., 381 U.S. 676 (1965) at p. 722.

agreement the union's interest would be bound in each case to that of the favored employer group. It is just such restraints upon the freedom of economic units to act according to their own choice and discretion that run counter to antitrust policy.[20]

The Minority Opinion: Mr. Justice Goldberg

Against these grave threats to industry-wide standards posed by the majority opinion, the defenders of collective bargaining in the needle trades found a worthy champion in Mr. Justice Arthur Goldberg, whose dissenting opinion, like an earlier dissenting opinion of Mr. Justice Louis Brandeis in the Duplex-Deering case, appeared more probable than the majority ruling to become a landmark in the evolution of the law. From his wealth of intimate experiences with collective bargaining, this spokesman for the minority in the UMW-Pennington case directed his legal attack on the majority opinion against the alleged flaw of assuming that the courts and juries under antitrust legislation — rather than Congress through its national labor policy — should determine what limitations, if any, to impose on union policies within the accepted realm of union activities.[21]

To point up the consequences of having judges and juries, rather than Congress, set limits on the scope of collective bar-

---

[20]United Mine Workers of America v. James M. Pennington, 381 U.S. 657 (1965) at pp. 665–666, 668. In a concurring opinion, Mr. Justice William Douglas, with whom Mr. Justice Hugo Black and Mr. Justice Tom Clark agreed, stressed the illegal objectives rather than the illegal means employed:

> Congress can design an oligopoly for our society, if it chooses. But business alone cannot do so as long as the antitrust laws are enforced. Nor should business and labor working hand-in-hand be allowed to make that basic change in the design of our so-called free enterprise system. If the allegations in this case are to be believed, organized labor joined hands with organized business to drive marginal operators out of existence.... According to those allegations, high wage and welfare terms of employment were imposed on the small, marginal companies by the union and the major companies with the knowledge and intent that the small ones would be driven out of business.
>
> The only architect of our economic system is Congress. We are right in adhering to its philosophy of the free enterprise system as expressed in the antitrust laws and as enforced by Allen Bradley Co. v. Union, supra, until the Congress delegates to big business and big labor the power to remold our economy in the manner charged here.
>
> —*Ibid.* at pp. 674–675.

[21]Duplex Printing Press Co. v. Deering, 254 U.S. 443 (1920) at pp. 479–488.

gaining over mandatory subjects, Mr. Justice Goldberg cited the case of *Alco-Zander Co. v. Amalgamated Clothing Workers:*

That case involved a situation where the unionized garment industry in New York was being undersold by the lower-priced, nonunion
garment industry of Philadelphia. The union, fearing for the future
of the jobs of its members employed in the unionized New York industry, started an organizing drive in Philadelphia. A federal district
court enjoined, as a violation of the antitrust laws, the union's organizational campaign which consisted of primary strikes and peaceful
picketing. The court declared that "the primary purpose of the campaign for the unionization of the Philadelphia market was the protection of the unionized markets in other states," and that "the object
of the strikes was to put an end to all production in Philadelphia
under nonunion conditions and only to permit it to be resumed if
and when the manufacturers were willing to operate upon a union
basis and under union wage scales." It is clear, therefore, that the
court enjoined the union's activities as antitrust violations because it
believed that this purpose and object was socially and economically
undesirable.[22]

From the voluminous congressional legislation favorable to
organized labor, Mr. Justice Goldberg gathered evidence to support his position that Congress intended to prevent just such
judicial interference with the purposes and objectives of collective bargaining as the majority opinion would impose in the
UMW-Pennington case. Retracing the legislative history and
judicial interpretations of organized labor's exemptions from the
federal antitrust laws, Mr. Justice Goldberg concluded:

In my view, this history shows a consistent congressional purpose
to limit severely judicial intervention into collective bargaining under
cover of the wide umbrella of the antitrust laws, and, rather, to deal
with what Congress deemed to be specific abuses on the part of labor
unions by specific proscriptions in the labor statutes. I believe that
the court should respect this history of congressional purpose and
should reaffirm the court's holdings in *Apex* and *Hutcheson* which,

---

[22]Mr. Justice Goldberg's dissenting opinion in UMW v. Pennington, 381
U.S. 657 (1965), and Amalgamated Meat Cutters v. Jewel Tea Co., 381 U.S.
676 (1965) at p. 717, citing Alco-Zander Co. v. Amalgamated Clothing Workers of America, U.S. District Court, Eastern District of Penn., 35 F. 2nd
203 (1929) at p. 205.

unlike earlier decisions, gave effect to, rather than frustrated, the congressional design.[23]

Control through Congress or the Courts

Had Mr. Justice Goldberg and his minority colleagues convinced other members of the Court that restrictions on union activities falling within the scope of mandatory subjects of bargaining should be imposed by Congress and enforced through special administrative agencies set up to carry out national labor policy, such a legal victory could not have allayed the fears of the needle trades. Mr. Justice White, himself, in his majority opinion, had conceded the validity of multiemployer or association-wide bargaining free of influence on other bargaining units; and he had supported the right of a labor union to seek the same terms of employment from one employer as from another, so long as the union was not motivated by employer pressures from other bargaining units. Would a majority opinion to leave restrictions on bargaining to Congress and the executive have insured greater protection from governmental interference with historic procedures for attaining industry-wide labor standards or uniform labor costs?[24]

Based on the number of congressional investigations into multi-employer bargaining and the many proposals for restricting that type of negotiating procedure, the organized forces of the needle trades had no assurance that the modest sop to the legality of employer-group contracts offered by the U. S. Supreme Court in the UMW-Pennington case would be any less favorable than the legal concessions that could be extracted from the political

---

[23]*Ibid.*, p. 709. Mr. Justice Goldberg cited examples of union abuses under the labor statutes that had produced specific congressional remedies — such as the restrictions on secondary boycotts and on hot cargo agreements. *Ibid.*, pp. 707–708. He differentiated the Allen Bradley case from the UMW-Pennington case on the ground that Allen Bradley involved two elements not present in UMW-Pennington: "(1) union participation in price fixing and market allocation with the only union interest being the indirect prospect that these anticompetitive devices might increase employers' profits that might trickle down to the employees, (2) accomplished by the union's joining a combination or conspiracy of the employers." *Ibid.*, p. 707. The Allen Bradley case is reviewed above at pp. 836–840.

[24] We think it beyond question that a union may conclude a wage agreement with the multi-employer bargaining unit without violating the antitrust laws and that it may as a matter of its own policy, and not

branches of the government. Nor could the needle trade advocates of industry-wide work standards find any solace in having
the National Labor Relations Board, rather than the courts, interpret the National Labor Relations Act, as amended, particularly the clauses on the duty to bargain. In his dissenting opinion,
Mr. Justice Goldberg had noted that the UMW-Pennington case
"bristles with potential unfair labor practices." Authority to
charge the parties to collective agreements in the soft coal mining
industry with unfair labor practices gave the National Labor Relations Board a lever with which to pry the foundations from
under the established bargaining procedures that had been vital
to the survival of the protocol movement in the needle trades.[25]

Already the NLRB had ruled in 1963 that the protective wage
clause of the National Bituminous Coal Wage Agreement, forbidding signatory coal operators from handling, using, selling,
transporting, or dealing in coal that was mined under terms less
favorable to the workers than those specified in the national
agreement, violated Section 8 (e) of the National Labor Relations
Act, as amended. And in the garment industry itself, the NLRB
had ruled in 1959 that the Bernhard-Altmann Texas Corporation
and the ILGWU, by entering into a labor agreement covering
the firm's production and shipping employees, when less than a
majority of the workers in the bargaining unit belonged to the
union, had violated Sections 8 (a) 2 and 1, and Section 8 (b) 1 A of
the National Labor Relations Act, as amended.[26]

The statutory duty to bargain, as interpreted by the Na-

---

by agreement with all or part of the employers of that unit, seek the
same wages from other employers.
    —Mr. Justice White, majority opinion in the UMW-Pennington
        case, 381 U.S. 657 (1965) at p. 664.

[25] See the dissenting opinion of Mr. Justice Goldberg in UMW v. Pennington, 381 U.S. 657 (1965), and in Amalgamated Meat Cutters v. Jewel Tea Co.,
381 U.S. 676 (1965) at p. 709, n. 13.

[26] For the Bituminous Coal case, see 144 NLRB 228 (August 27, 1963); see
also 148 NLRB 249 (August 7, 1964). In March 1966, an NLRB trial examiner
ruled that a clause imposing a penalty of 80¢ a ton on all coal purchased by
unionized operators from nonunion operators violated the hot cargo provision, Section 8 (e), of the Taft-Hartley Act, as amended. The clause had been
inserted into the 1964 collective agreement between the Bituminous Coal
Operators' Association and the United Mine Workers' Union as a substitute
for the protective wage clause that had previously been invalidated on the
same grounds. Bureau of National Affairs, *Daily Labor Report,* March 22,
1966. For the Women's Garment case, see 122 NLRB 1289 (Feb. 6, 1959),

tional Labor Relations Board, was even more likely to ensnare the advocates of industry-wide standards. If the General Electric Company violated the statutory duty to bargain when it submitted to the International Union of Electrical Workers a thoroughly studied, all-inclusive, carefully prepared initial bargaining offer from which, barring proof of mistakes, the company refused to waver, then why should not the National Labor Relations Board also charge any union with refusal to bargain that submits for separate negotiations with an independent firm the identical terms of a master contract previously negotiated with an employers' association, especially when the union insists that those terms be met? For what purpose, therefore, would the needle trades flee the judicial tentacles of the antitrust laws to be impaled on the administrative barbs of the National Labor Relations Board?[27]

Goldberg's Defense of Industry-wide Standards

For these reasons, support for the needle trade movement toward industry-wide standards received its greatest boost not from Mr. Justice Goldberg's brilliant interpretation of the law but from his rudimentary defense of the necessity for eliminating competition in wages, hours, and working conditions. Few unions understood better than did the United Mine Workers that the goals of organized labor were limited by the range of differentials in competitive labor costs. The pressure for higher standards of living had to be aimed at the lowest ranking firms on the totem pole of wage scales — the employers that held the key positions. "It is no secret," stated Mr. Justice Goldberg, "that the United Mine Workers acting to further what it considers to be the best interests of its members, espouses a philosophy of achieving uniform high wages, fringe benefits, and good working conditions."

As the *quid pro quo* for this, the Union is willing to accept the burdens and consequences of automation. Further, it acts upon the view that the existence of marginal operators who cannot afford these high wages, fringe benefits, and good working conditions does not serve the best interests of the working miner but, on the contrary,

---

sustained by the U.S. Supreme Court in ILGWU v. NLRB 366 U.S. 731 (1961).

[27]For the GE decision, see 150 NLRB 192 (1964).

depresses wage standards and perpetuates undesirable conditions. This has been the articulated policy of the Union since 1933.[28]

In the history of soft coal mining, employer group bargaining — the first step in the movement for industry-wide standards — goes back to the turn of the century. But, for the first fifty years, there were too many competing employer groups operating in too many different coal fields scattered over too many states. With labor costs constituting a major factor in total costs of production, contract negotiations brought industrial warfare, growing out of employer resistance to wage differentials in competing coal fields. "From 1930 until the formation of the Bituminous Coal Operators' Association and the negotiation of a uniform wage agreement between the Association and the union in 1950," stated Mr. Justice Goldberg, "bargaining in the coal industry was highlighted by bitter and protracted negotiations. Costly strikes were a recurring phenomenon and government seizure of the mines was characteristic of most of the period. . . . Since this change in 1950, collective bargaining has been, to a marked degree, stabilized in the industry. There have been no governmental seizures or nation-wide strikes."[29]

Nor were experiences with multiemployer bargaining in coal mining an unusual phenomenon. "Today," stated Mr. Justice Goldberg, "between 80% and 100% of the workers under union agreement are covered by multi-employer contracts in such im-

---

[28] Mr. Justice Goldberg, dissenting opinion in UMW v. Pennington, 381 U.S. 657 (1965), and Amalgamated Meat Cutters v. Jewel Tea Co., 381 U.S. 676 (1965) at p. 698.

[29]*Ibid.*, pp. 730–731. "Since 1950, the negotiation of collective-bargaining contracts for the [soft coal] industry has commenced with the negotiation of an agreement with the Bituminous Coal Operators' Association, herein called BCOA, representing the northern Appalachian group. The terms of the BCOA agreement are then presented to the Southern Coal Producers' Association, the Midwest operators' associations, and individual operators, who apparently adopt the BCOA agreement. This procedure has resulted in a uniform agreement under which 74 to 79 percent of bituminous coal in the United States has been produced since 1950." R. O. Lewis, W. A. Boyle, and John Owens as agents for the United Mine Workers of America and as members of the Joint Industry Contract Committee established by the National Bituminous Coal Wage Agreement of 1950 and E. G. Fox, C. W. Davis, H. K. Beebe as agents for the Coal Operators signatory to the National Bituminous Coal Wage Agreement of 1950 and as members of the Joint Industry Contract Committee established by that agreement, 144 NLRB 228 (1963) at pp. 230–231.

portant industries as men's and women's clothing, coal mining, building construction, hotel, longshoring, maritime, trucking, and warehousing. Between 60% and 80% of unionized workers are under multi-employer pacts in baking, book and job printing, canning and preserving, textile dyeing and finishing, glass and glassware, malt liquor, pottery and retail trades. . . . Furthermore, in some other major industries relatively uniform terms of employment are obtained through the negotiation of a contract with one leading employer and the subsequent acceptance of that contract's key provisions, with only minor modifications by the other employers in the industry."[30]

Further to strengthen the defense of industry-wide standards, Mr. Justice Goldberg brought to his support examples of state and federal labor legislation that, at least, established floors under competition for labor even if it failed to bring about industry-

---

[30]Mr. Justice Goldberg, dissenting opinion in UMW v. Pennington, 381 U.S. 657 (1965), and Amalgamated Meat Cutters v. Jewel Tea Co., 381 U.S. 676 (1965) at p. 713, n. 20, citing L. G. Reynolds, *Labor Economics and Labor Relations* (3rd ed., 1959), p. 170; and N. W. Chamberlain, *Collective Bargaining* (1951), pp. 259–263.

All movements for industry-wide standards, whether made through industry-wide bargaining, or through multiemployer agreements with most favored employer clauses, must recognize the necessity for some variations in the terms of employment. Concessions to meet local conditions or special circumstances are as essential to industrial organizations as to political governments. The need for some degree of federalism exists in the most monolithic societies, industrial or political. Sponsors of the protocol movement were never blind to the diversities that underlay their most closely knit groups, or else their collective agreements would have reflected going wage rates rather than minimum standards for the trade. Convincing evidence of attention to diversities was revealed in the movement for industry-wide standards among the manufacturers of men's and boys' clothing shortly after the First World War. At that time, manufacturers of the Chicago market were concerned lest too little attention be given to their own differences:

> The clothing industry in this market is made up of various kinds of manufacturing units. First of all the nature of the problem varies according to size of the several houses; the problem of the ready-made house is not uniformly the problem of the tailor-to-the-trade or the cut-trim-make houses; the problems of children's houses and specialty houses are not the same problems as the problems of men's houses. Any effective cooperation must proceed from a recognition of the differences that exist in the market.

> —From the Chicago men's clothing manufacturers' demands on the Amalgamated Clothing Workers, as quoted in *Daily News Record,* Feb. 15, 1921.

wide standards of employment. A public desire to abolish substandard sweatshop conditions of labor had inspired minimum
wage laws and limitations on maximum hours of work. This purpose lay beneath the NRA codes of fair competition drafted to
fight the depression of the thirties. The National Labor Relations [Wagner] Act of 1935 had attributed industrial distresses
to an inequality in bargaining power that had depressed wages
and prevented "the stabilization of competitive wage rates and
working conditions within and between industries."

The need for putting a floor under competition for labor had
in part motivated Congress to pass the Davis-Bacon Act, the
Walsh-Healey Act, and the Fair Labor Standards Act. "Congress,"
continued Mr. Justice Goldberg, "has also recognized that some
labor organizations seek, as in Pennington, through industry-
wide bargaining, to eliminate differences in labor standards
among employers. This was common knowledge in 1935 when
the Wagner Act was passed. The aims and practices of unions
engaging in industry-wide bargaining were well known in 1947
at the time of the Taft-Hartley revision. Then and on subsequent
occasions Congress refused to enact bills to restrict or prohibit
industry-wide bargaining."[31]

Finally, Mr. Justice Goldberg produced evidence that the U. S.
Supreme Court itself had on occasion gone along with his views
and those of Congress. "Indeed," he stated, "this Court to implement congressional policy sanctioning multi-employer bargaining, permitted employers to resort, under certain circumstances,

---

[31]Mr. Justice Goldberg, dissenting opinion in UMW v. Pennington, 381
U.S. 657 (1965), and Amalgamated Meat Cutters v. Jewel Tea Co., 381 U.S.
676 (1965) at 711–712.

Since the days of the First World War, the policy of the federal government
has been to prevent wage rates in firms over which it has any control from
dropping below the minimum standards already prevailing in the industry for
the localities concerned. In practice, these standards have been taken from the
unionized segments of the specified industry in the designated locality. See
report of the War Labor Conference Board: "Principles and Policies to
Govern Relations between Workers and Employers in War Industries for
the Duration of the War" (March 1918), in *National War Labor Board,* U.S.
Department of Labor, BLS Bulletin 287 (December 1921), p. 33; Davis-Bacon
Act, 46 Stat. 1494 (1931), 40 U.S.C. Par. 276a; Walsh-Healey Act, 49 Stat. 2036
(1936), 41 U.S.C. Par. 35 ff.; Fair Labor Standards Act, 52 Stat. 1060 (1938),
29 U.S.C. Pars. 201–219. (Citations are to the 1958 edition of the United
States Code.)

to lockouts to protect the integrity of the multi-employer bargaining unit." Even more fundamental were the views of the Court in *Apex Hosiery Co.* v. *Leader,* holding that a union sit-down strike as an organizational tool did not violate the antitrust laws: "Since, in order to render a labor combination effective it must eliminate the competition from non-union made goods," stated Mr. Justice Harlan Stone in that case ". . . an elimination of price competition based on differences in labor standards is the objective of any national labor organization."[32]

Thus, with the Court's own precedents would the dissent in the UMW-Pennington case fight the majority attempt to fragmentize collective bargaining until the objectives of organized labor were beyond achievement. Even more fatal to collective bargaining was the Court's assumption in this case that the union could accomplish its objectives unilaterally without implicating employers through joint agreements that might bring down upon the heads of both parties all the weight of antitrust legislation. "The plain fact is," noted Mr. Justice Goldberg, "that it makes no sense to turn antitrust liability of employers and unions concerning subjects of mandatory bargaining on whether the union acted 'unilaterally' or in 'agreement' with employers."

A union can never achieve substantial benefits for its members through unilateral action; I should have thought that the unsuccessful history of the Industrial Workers of the World, which eschewed collective bargaining and espoused a philosophy of winning benefits by unilateral action, proved this beyond question. . . . The history of labor relations in this country shows, as Congress has recognized, that progress and stability for both employers and employees can be achieved only through collective bargaining agreements involving mutual rights and responsibilities. . . .

[32]Mr. Justice Goldberg, dissenting opinion in UMW v. Pennington, 381 U.S. 657 (1965), and Amalgamated Meat Cutters v. Jewel Tea Co., 381 U.S. 676 (1965) at p. 713. Mr. Justice Stone is quoted in Apex Hosiery Co. v. Leader 310 U.S. 469 (1940) at p. 503.
On association-wide lockouts to protect the integrity of multiemployer bargaining units, see National Labor Relations Board v. Truck Drivers' Union no. 449 (the Buffalo Linen Supply Case), 353 U.S. 87 (1947); and National Labor Relations Board v. John Brown (the Carlsbad Retail Food Store case), 380 U.S. 278 (1965). Further ramifications on the use of the lockout to support employer bargaining positions are discussed in Frederic Freilicher, "The Supportive Lockout," *Syracuse Law Review,* Spring 1968, vol. 19, pp. 599–617.

Where there is an "agreement" to seek uniform wages in an industry, in what item is competition restrained? The answer to this question can only be that competition is restrained in employee wage standards. That is, the union has agreed to restrain the free competitive market for labor by refusing to provide labor to other employers below the uniform rate.... The very purpose and effect of a labor union is to limit the power of an employer to use competition among workingmen to drive down wage rates and enforce substandard conditions of employment. If competition between workingmen to see who will work for the lowest wage is the ideal, all labor unions should be eliminated.[33]

Lessons from the Needle Trades

Just as the needle trades have been looking to the soft coal industry for guidelines of legal conduct under the antitrust laws, so may other industries look to the needle trades for the foundations of self-help in the realm of labor-management relations. So long as experiences with collective bargaining indicate that outside interference is a poor substitute for self-help, the protocol movement has something to offer industrial societies everywhere. Within the framework of their own industries, the needle trades have had a long and continuous history of seeking out the roads to industrial peace and stability. Their efforts at evolving institutions and procedures adapted to their needs have always been self-contained.

One key to the success of these developments has consisted of prolonged, resourceful, and determined efforts to guarantee the sanctity of contracts. The early contributions of the needle trades to the enforcement of labor agreements set the highwater mark of self-contained attempts to gain compliance with contractual obligations. Within the framework of each industry, employers' associations and labor unions were dedicated to keeping their respective members in line. Impartial machinery was erected to hold the "bosses" and the "people" strictly accountable for their conduct. Unfortunately, these means for insuring observance of contracts — and especially for controlling wildcat strikes — have suffered a gradual retrogression since the First World War. Cur-

---

[33]Mr. Justice Goldberg, dissenting opinion in UMW v. Pennington, 381 U.S. 657 (1965), and Amalgamated Meat Cutters v. Jewel Tea Co., 381 U.S. 676 (1965) at pp. 721–723.

rent evidences of a growing disrespect for the obligations of contracts would, however, appear to justify a reexamination of needle trade experiences under the protocol movement.

In the second place, experiences of the needle trades strongly support the assumption that collective bargaining cannot prosper short of offering benefits to both parties at the bargaining table. Here, the secret formula of success in the needle trades lies in concentrating on problems of mutual concern to both the workers and their employers. From the Brandeis Conferences of 1910, the goals of collective action have always been hitched to the lodestar of industry welfare. The need for resolving industry-wide problems has united the "bosses" and the "people" into concerted efforts at overcoming their common enemies. Through their labor unions and employers' associations, the organized factions of each industry have made war on the unorganized elements who thrive on undercutting "legitimate" labor standards and on undermining "legitimate" trade practices.

In the third place, the movement for industry-wide standards that would abolish unfair discrepancies in labor costs and prevent chiseling on accepted rules of business conduct has in recent years brought the needle trades face to face with the law. Collaboration between labor unions and employers' associations to maintain a floor under "legitimate" competition has obliterated lines of distinction between "labor" problems and "trade" problems — a distinction that has long served the courts in passing on the legality of joint action through collective bargaining. But the contributions to industrial peace and industrial stability that the needle trades have made over the years, in the face of well-nigh insuperable odds, should weigh heavily with those who formulate, interpret, and apply public policy. At least the law should be flexible enough to accommodate different experiments designed to promote the welfare of the trade. Only with the clearest evidences of impingement on the public interest should the merits of industrial stability and industrial peace be overthrown by legal decisions that would substitute one-way union dictation or outside governmental control for the established institutions of collective bargaining.

Moreover, public policy and the law must be tempered to accommodate recent turbulent changes in the economics of the needle trades. The coming of large-scale enterprise in the manufacture of dresses reflected by such giant corporations as Jonathan Logan ($100 million in dress sales annually) or Bobbie Brooks ($75 million), and the introduction of new technological processes exemplified by the work of the slate belt association in Pennsylvania, have already threatened to out-date certain features of the protocol system originally designed to meet unlicensed competition from small shops with handicraft methods of production. But the principles of the protocol movement may yet be applied on a more imposing scale. Already, the ILGWU has readjusted its bargaining machinery to negotiate corporation-wide contracts with these new industrial giants. Already, these large firms that have little to fear from the small fry, may be looking to a super association of industrial giants for multiemployer bargaining with the ILGWU on an industry-wide scale, lest failure to standardize labor costs and commercial trade practices bring ruthless competition among the giants themselves. The analogies between the needle trades and other industries would then become more obvious.[34]

Case of the New York Milk Distributors

Recently, the lessons of the needle trades have been applied to the business of processing and distributing milk and milk products in the greater New York area. Under the November 1965 collective agreement between the Greater New York Milk Dealers' Labor Committee and three locals of the teamsters' union, provision was made for the first permanent impartial chairman ever assigned to the trade. Behind this major innovation lies a history of hard times that had adversely affected workers and employers, alike. A survey of 27 large, medium, and small dairies handling 54.4 percent of milk sold in the New York metropolitan area during 1964 had revealed a 36 percent decline in profits over the preceding year, or a reduction in unit profits to only .00146 cents a quart. With many cost factors closely regulated by governmental agencies, with a strong union always seeking higher wages and more fringe benefits, and without the protection of fair trade regulations, such as existed in twenty other states, New York

---

[34]*New York Times,* March 18, 1966; *Philadelphia Evening Bulletin,* April 9, 1964.

milk distributors faced the necessity of further reducing costs in order to survive. Four companies had operated at a loss during 1964 and the prospects for 1965 were even darker.[35]

Locals of the teamsters' union representing the workers were likewise victimized by new money-saving gimmicks that had reduced employment and increased resistance to union demands. Substituting for home deliveries were new milk stores, vending machines, milk depots in settlement houses, and supermarkets that had led to shrinking job opportunities for union members and had threatened union work standards achieved through years of hard bargaining. Neither unions nor employers could survive price cutting so intense that milk had to be sold below cost. In desperation, union members resorted to strikes and picket lines against the latest variation in methods of milk distribution, the "cut price, cash and carry milk store."[36]

For obvious reasons, the teamsters' union became as concerned with methods of milk distribution as the employers were concerned with indirect means of reducing labor costs. By the terms of their previous agreements, the union and the employer bargaining group had already prohibited milk sales from trucks and from milk depots except in settlement houses. A union proposal to levy a royalty on each quart of milk sold and delivered "by any means that the union identify as being other than conventional" was turned down by an arbitration board in 1964, but the arbitrators planted the seeds of "protocolism" which were to mature at the 1965 negotiations:

Upon finding that a distributive practice or a policy of pricing at unreasonably low levels is undermining and destroying established methods of distribution and with it the job security and contract

---

[35]Findings of the survey by Ernst and Ernst, certified public accountants, as reported in Metropolitan Dairy Institute, *Digest*, November 1965, vol. 8, no. 9, p. 1.

[36]On one occasion, when such picketing was extended to a milk processing firm that supplied these cut-rate stores with milk, the teamsters' union was charged with secondary boycott picketing in violation of the National Labor Relations Act, as amended. But a judge of the federal district court refused to enjoin the picketing, explaining that the processor's interest in the distributive plan and the "general industry-wide effect of alleged irregular 'store' operations combine to make the dispute common" to both companies. 54 LRRM 2287 48 LC 18458 Par.

standards the Unions have achieved, the Board should be authorized to seek to devise that form of relief which best protects the legitimate concerns of the Unions without impairing the public interest or unduly infringing upon management's prerogatives. Furthermore, the Board should take into account, in specific cases, the extent to which relief should be withheld because competing companies not under contract with the Unions are engaging in such practices. Obviously, it would serve no purpose to restrain certain Employers if others would then be free to continue the same predatory and destructive practices.[37]

With these words of advice, the board of arbitration in its official award directed the parties to incorporate into their 1963–1965 collective agreement the following "distributive practices" clause:

(a) If any of the Unions, upon investigation, determines in a specific case that milk or dairy products are being distributed in a manner or at a price which unfairly impairs other forms of distribution to the prejudice of the wages, working conditions and job security of its members, it shall have the right forthwith to bring such complaint before the Board of Arbitration appointed pursuant to the stipulation of the parties to administer these provisions.

(b) If any of the Employers, in the process of introducing new or different methods of distributing milk or milk products, shall encounter actions by the Unions in violation of the contract in opposition to any such innovation, regardless of reasonable new rates of compensation and conditions of employment which might be involved therein, it shall have similar recourse to said Board of Arbitration.

The board of arbitration was then empowered "to take such action or issue such orders, including injunctive relief, authorization to resort to self help, or any other remedy, which in its opinion it shall deem necessary and advisable in the circumstances" to protect job security and consumer interest in methods of milk distribution.[38]

So the stage was set for crowning this new realm of law and order with an impartial chairman whose special duties were thus defined in the 1965 agreement:

---

[37]From the Opinion of the Board of Arbitration in the Matter of the Arbitration between Milk Industry and Milk Drivers Local 584, 602, and 607, Affiliated with the International Brotherhood of Teamsters Re: Company Stores and Other Outlets (May 4, 1964), p. 15.

[38]*Ibid.*, pp. 15–16.

(16b) Without limiting or changing the foregoing [arbitration provisions in the previous contract], the Chairman shall exercise jurisdiction over the parties where practices or acts of Employers adversely affect the legal interests and rights of the employees or Unions under this agreement and where acts or practices of the Unions adversely affect the legal interests and rights of Employers under this agreement. In any such matter the Chairman shall have the power to proceed upon his own initiative or upon the filing with him of a complaint or grievance by any party to any agreement containing a counterpart of this provision.

To foreclose possible involvements with the law, the 1965 agreement also established guidelines that would presumably absolve the industry and its impartial chairman of any intent to violate the law, and that would at the same time renounce all activities leading to that end:

(16c) In all matters arising under subparagraph (b) hereof, the Chairman shall be guided by and limited to a consideration of the subject matter authorized to the Federal Trade Commission, without regard as to whether such matter relates to interstate commerce, and shall, to the extent permitted by law, endeavor to protect and promote open, free and fair competition and to prevent unfair methods of competition and unfair or destructive acts and practices.

"You are embarking on a novel and constructive experiment," happily announced the newly chosen impartial chairman, Theodore W. Kheel, to representatives of the milk companies and the teamsters' union, shortly after the 1965 negotiations had been concluded. But what may have appeared a novelty to line operators in milk distribution could scarcely have been a novelty to the lawyers and technicians who, in working out the pertinent clauses of the new agreement, had only to draw from half a century of needle trade experiences that were in evidence all around them. Indeed, to those versed in the needle trade ways of meeting "illegitimate" competition, the only novelty in the milk case consisted in a reversion to needle trade practices that were most common in the early years of the protocol movement.

Like the manufacturers of the needle trades, employers of the milk industry had been stung by efforts on their own behalf to regulate competition — efforts that contravened the Federal Trade Commission Act or the antitrust laws; see *U. S.* v. *Borden* 308 U. S. 188 (1939). Like the labor unions of the needle trades, the cooperatives of the milk industry had been stung by legal precedents that allegedly thwarted congressional efforts to exempt cooperatives from the antitrust laws; see *Maryland and Virginia Milk Processing Association* v. *United States*, 362 U. S. 458 (1960). In both industries, the employers had hoped by collaborating with exempt agencies to purify dubious employer conduct and thus to free employers from antitrust prosecutions. But, in both cases, they had succeeded only in contaminating the agency with which they dealt, as well as themselves. What was left for the milk industry was a revision to the early needle trade practice of endowing an impartial chairman under a collective labor agreement with broad powers to formulate and execute such policies as were needed to promote the good of the industry.

How this new system for controlling competition could be expected to operate was soon demonstrated. Charging Sunnydale Farms with selling milk below cost at the sacrifice of union jobs, union commissions, and employer payments into union welfare and pension funds, three locals of the teamsters' union, in April 1966, sought relief from their impartial chairman under the terms of their 1965 milk industry agreement. By the authority granted to him in this contract, Impartial Chairman T. W. Kheel gave the union the right to renegotiate those clauses of the contract relating to commissions and jobs, as well as those clauses relating to union pension and welfare funds. At the same time, he gave the union, for the period of renegotiation, a weapon of effective action by suspending the contract provisions banning strikes and lockouts. While conceding that employers had a right to set the prices for their products, Mr. Kheel held, nevertheless, that when price wars — particularly those involving sales below costs — adversely affect union members, those members could seek relief under the terms of their contract.[39]

---

[39]In the Matter of the Arbitration between Milk Drivers' Local 584, International Brotherhood of Teamsters and Sunnydale Farms, Inc., *et al.* (April 20, 1966). In this award, Impartial Chairman T. W. Kheel reviewed the developments under the 1963 agreement with copious extracts from the 1964 arbitration award, restated at length the substance of the union's complaints (without a corresponding review of the employers' position), and then authorized a remedy that could not help but have a far-reaching effect upon the institutions of collective bargaining, as well as upon the determination of public policy toward restraint of trade. A brief summary of the case appeared in the *New York Times*, April 24, 1966.

Concluding Observations

If competition is the life of free enterprise, then the regulation of competition may well succeed in maximizing this goal of American industry, just as regulating freedom of speech is capable of increasing the total extent of free speech in political society. But adherence to the concept of regulated competition does not resolve the issue of how these restrictions should be imposed or to what lengths they should be carried. Assuming that the good of society demands restricted competition in work standards and in trade practices, lawmakers have encouraged the growth of labor unions and have supported the institutions of collective bargaining, while insisting that the employers observe minimum standards of business conduct. Meanwhile, voluntary controls over competition in labor standards and in trade practices have been the central theme of collective bargaining in the needle trades since 1910. Gradually expanding markets and ever widening areas of competition have magnified destructive differentials in wage rates and in trade practices and have brought intensified demands for industry-wide standards.

In so far as the achievement of union goals has called for the regulation of business conduct, collective bargaining in the needle trades has embraced controls over processes of production and distribution. For their own self-interest, labor unions have helped the organized employers to suppress those business competitors who would flout the established rules of business conduct — just as the organized manufacturers, for their own self-interest, have helped their organized employees to control the unorganized workers who would seek to undermine uniform labor standards established for their trades. Collective bargaining has thus permitted the organized "bosses" and the organized "people" to lift their sights above their petty differences to the major problems of competition that face their industries and threaten their common sources of livelihood. Admittedly, their joint efforts to promote industry welfare have brought a substantial measure of peace and stability to their trades.

In so doing, however, the organized segments of labor and management may have opened a rift between their own self-imposed controls for the good of their industries and established public policies adopted by civil governments for the protection of free competition. While voluntary controls have the merit of support from those who create them and are more likely to be adapted to the needs of an industry, they may lack an unbiased perspective in creating norms of conduct that would protect the outside minority, the consumer, and the general public. Through collective bargaining, these self-imposed controls may open the door to excessive "cahooting" between negotiating teams seeking more and more for themselves at public expense. Ostensibly directed toward eliminating inequities in business standards, as well as labor standards, the sponsors of collective bargaining in the needle trades may have created new inequities between the "ins" and the "outs" until society suffers more from the evils of labor-management collusion than from the dangers of industrial conflict.

Whether a workable compromise between direct governmental restraints and self-imposed controls over competition for jobs and for business can be found remains to be seen. The public search for such a compromise long ago led to the enactment of the Federal Trade Commission Act of 1914 and later inspired the passage of Title I, National Industrial Recovery Act, as well as of subsequent state and federal statutes on labor-management relations. It may be prophetic that, of all these acts, the one offering the most comprehensive system of governmental controls was the first to be forgotten. "I venture the assertion," once predicted Donald Richberg, general counsel of the National Recovery Administration, addressing the Associated Grocery Manufacturers of America on developments likely to follow the NRA codes, "that under present conditions no law and no process of codification can establish successfully more than elementary standards of fair competition or do more than provide the basis for the gradual improvement in conditions under which business men must compete with each other and employers and employees struggle for advantage in reaping separately the benefits of their common efforts."[40]

Beyond the minimum standards that Donald Richberg would concede to governmental controls, a further compromise between subjecting the whole realm of labor-management relations to government dictation, or leaving the parties completely free to

---

[40]*New York Times,* Nov. 22, 1934.

work out their own salvation at the bargaining table, might be achieved by extending to the organized segments of each industry the power of initiative, subject to governmental review. Once manufacturers' associations and labor unions representing a substantial portion of an industry had formulated basic standards of employment and of business conduct, those standards might be subject to modification by a government agency, either at the behest of adversely affected interests within the trade or else on behalf of protecting the public welfare. The resulting agreement might then be approved for industry-wide application by authority of law. Such was precisely the program Julius H. Cohen, father of the protocol movement, advocated long before the codes. Indeed, such was essentially the system of collective bargaining that has prevailed in the needle trades since 1910, with impartial chairmen, permanent umpires, or boards of arbitration for each industry playing the role of civil governments. So long as the possibility of applying such a program to American industry still exists, a study of competition and collective bargaining in the needle trades should continue to be rewarding.

Index

(Where entries appear six or more times in a chapter, the chapter is cited rather than the pages.)